TOM CHEEK

2013 FORD C. FRICK AWARD WINNER FOR BROADCASTING EXCELLENCE

Tom Cheek, who called the first 4,306 regular-season and 41 postseason games in Toronto Blue Jays history has been selected as the 2013 recipient of the Ford C. Frick Award, presented annually for excellence in broadcasting by the National Baseball Hall of Fame and Museum.

Cheek, who passed away on Oct. 9, 2005, will be honoured as part of Hall of Fame Weekend 2013 July 26-29 in Cooperstown, N.Y.

"Tom Cheek was the voice of summer for generations of baseball fans in Canada and beyond," said Hall of Fame President Jeff Idelson. "He helped a nation understand the elements of the game and swoon for the summer excitement that the expansion franchise brought a hockey-crazed nation starting in the late 1970s. He then authored the vocal narrative of a team that evolved into one of the most consistent clubs of the 1980s and 1990s. We are thrilled to celebrate Tom's legacy with baseball broadcasting's highest honour."

Born June 13, 1939 – Cheek was raised in a Navy family and joined the armed forces himself in 1957, serving in the Air Force until discharged in 1960. Cheek's father, also named Tom, was a World War II hero who served as a fighter pilot in the Battle of Midway in 1942.

After continuing his education at SUNY Plattsburgh and the Cambridge School of Broadcasting in Boston, Cheek worked as a disc jockey in Plattsburgh, N.Y., and as sports director for a group of three stations in Burlington, Vt., calling University of Vermont sports for several years.

In 1974, Cheek began work as a backup announcer on Montreal Expos broadcasts. Then in 1976 at the age of 37, he landed the job as the radio voice of the expansion Blue Jays. Paired first with Hall of Fame pitcher Early Wynn and later with Jerry Howarth starting in 1981, Cheek's rich baritone voice and his passionate-yet-lighthearted approach to his job dazzled fans eager to embrace Toronto's new role as an American League outpost.

His call of Joe Carter's World Series-winning home run in Game 6 of the 1993 Fall Classic – ***"Touch 'em all Joe! You'll never hit a bigger home run in your life."*** – quickly became embedded in the sports conscious of Blue Jays fans around the globe.

Cheek called every regular season and postseason Blue Jays game from the franchise's birth on April 7, 1977 through June 2, 2004. The next day, Cheek took the first of two days off to attend the funeral of his father. But upon his return, Cheek sensed he was not right physically when he was unable to retain information he had read only minutes earlier. On June 13, 2004 – his 65th birthday – Cheek underwent surgery to remove a brain tumor, but some of the tumor was unreachable. A little more than a year later, Cheek passed away on Oct. 9, 2005.

TORONTO BLUE JAYS BASEBALL CLUB

1 BLUE JAYS WAY, SUITE 3200, ROGERS CENTRE
TORONTO, ONTARIO M5V 1J1
(416) 341-1000

www.bluejays.com

THE 2013 TORONTO BLUE JAYS MEDIA GUIDE

Data for the 2013 Toronto Blue Jays Media Guide was gathered through February 15, 2013.

Produced by: Toronto Blue Jays Communications Department
Jay Stenhouse, Mal Romanin, Sue Mallabon, Erik Grosman

Stats provided by: Major League Baseball Information System, Elias Sports Bureau, Stats Inc.

Creative Services: Caledon Data Management, Eden, Ontario
John Pasternak, Dan Diamond and Jennifer Adams

Cover Design: Toronto Blue Jays

Photo Credits: Jim Goins, Fred Thornhill, Chuck Kotchman, Sun Media

2013
OFFICIAL GUIDE

CONTENTS

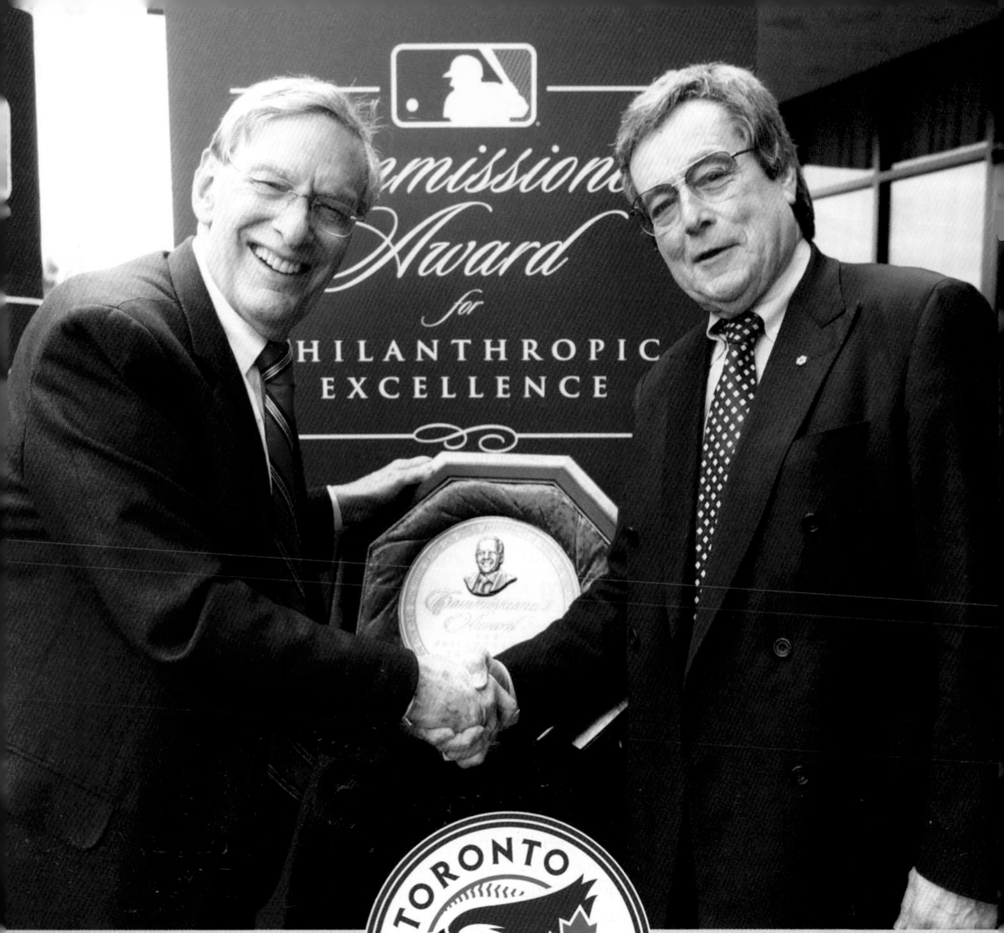

Toronto Blue Jays Receive
2012 Commissioner's Award for Philanthropic Excellence

2012 RECIPIENT OF THE COMMISSIONER'S AWARD FOR PHILANTHROPIC EXCELLENCE

Toronto Blue Jays Baseball Academy Recognized for Making a Difference in the Lives of Youth throughout Canada

Major League Baseball and Baseball Commissioner Allan H. (Bud) Selig named the Toronto Blue Jays as the 2012 recipient of the Commissioner's Award for Philanthropic Excellence, which was created in 2010 to annually recognize an extraordinary charitable and philanthropic effort of an MLB Club. The Blue Jays are being honored for the "Toronto Blue Jays Baseball Academy," a series of initiatives to help support youth across Canada and provide them with opportunities on and off the field of play. The Jays Care Foundation, the official charity of the Toronto Blue Jays, will receive a $10,000 grant from Major League Baseball as part of this recognition.

"The Toronto Blue Jays Baseball Academy program embodies the franchise's significant investment in the young people of Canada," Commissioner Selig said. "The determination of the Blue Jays to provide thousands of children with the tools to succeed in baseball and in life has made a remarkable difference in not just Toronto but in many other communities as well, and Canadians should take great pride in their country's Major League Baseball team. I commend the Blue Jays and all of our Clubs for embracing the game's essential social responsibilities and making a positive impact in their respective communities year after year."

"We are honoured to receive the Commissioner's Award for Philanthropic Excellence," said Paul Beeston, President and CEO, Toronto Blue Jays. "We made an organizational decision several years ago to reach out to communities not just in Toronto but all across the country, as we recognized our responsibilities as Canada's only Major League team. The support we have received from all provinces has been overwhelming and it was imperative that our programs reflected that passion. The creation of the Toronto Blue Jays Baseball Academy, combined with the tremendous efforts of the Jays Care Foundation, has had a significant impact on the youth of the nation. We are very proud of this recognition and it speaks volumes to the efforts of many in our organization and our key partners, including Boys and Girls Clubs of Canada, Baseball Canada and Little League Canada. Together we have truly made a positive impact in our communities across Canada."

BLUE JAYS BASEBALL ACADEMY

BLUE JAYS HONDA SUPER CAMPS

The Blue Jays Baseball Academy will host 17 Blue Jays Honda Super Camps in 2013. The three-day baseball camps take place in 10 Canadian provinces, and are open to participants ages 9-16. The camps teach the baseball fundamentals of hitting, fielding, pitching and base running. Instructors include: Roberto Alomar, Duane Ward, Jesse Barfield, Homer Bush and Devon White. The camps run from 9 a.m. to 1 p.m. at a cost of $230. Registration will be available on www.bluejays.com/camps and is limited to the first 150 registrants. In addition, working with local Boys & Girls Clubs, the Toronto Blue Jays, through Jays Care Foundation, will donate registration fees for a select number of players in each of the camps to help remove barriers to participation. The Toronto Chapter of the Baseball Writers of America Association (BBWAA) will also donate registration fees for a select number of children. Blue Jays Honda Super Camps are conducted in partnership with Baseball Canada and Little League Canada.

BLUE JAYS HONDA INSTRUCTIONAL CLINICS

The Blue Jays Baseball Academy will host 40 Blue Jays Honda Instructional Clinics in 2013. These one-day baseball clinics take place across Ontario and are open to players ages 8-14 of all abilities. Blue Jays Baseball Academy instructors focus on teaching baseball players the fundamentals of baseball. Each participant will receive a Blue Jays hat, t-shirt and a Baseball Academy program. The cost for the clinic is $40 and half of the revenue is donated back to the host association. More than $60,000 was donated to Ontario-based organizations in 2012. To sign up for a Blue Jays Honda Instructional Clinic, visit www.bluejays.com/clinics

BLUE JAYS NATIONAL COACHES CLINIC

The Blue Jays Baseball Academy will be hosting its annual National Coaches Clinic in January 2014. Coaches from across Canada are encouraged to attend the weekend-long clinic, and learn how to apply the concepts of pitching, catching, hitting, and fielding in practice. Baseball Canada will provide professional development credit for each of the modules the coaches attend, and host four NCCP Instructor Beginner Context modules, including: base running, infielding, outfielding and hitting. At a cost of $150 per participant, the Coaches Clinic will offer participants specialized insight into body mechanics, drills and game strategies.

TOURNAMENT 12

The Toronto Blue Jays are excited to host a national, amateur tournament, Tournament 12, at Rogers Centre from September 20-24, 2013. The goal of the tournament is to showcase the best college-eligible amateur baseball players in the country to professional scouts from all teams and educational institutions across North America. The tournament will feature 12 teams from across Canada, including: three from Ontario; two from British Columbia, Quebec and Alberta, respectively; one team representing the Maritimes; and one team representing Manitoba and Saskatchewan. The final squad will be a Blue Jays Scout Team comprised of players from coast to coast. Legendary Blue Jays Hall of Famer, Roberto Alomar, will act as the Honourary Tournament Commissioner.

ROOKIE LEAGUE

Jays Care Foundation, in partnership with Toronto Community Housing (TCH) and Boys and Girls Clubs of Canada (BGCC), offers a safe, fun, active and engaging baseball program for children, ages 6-12, living in under-resourced communities. Rookie League is a cost-free program that uses the game of baseball as a foundation to teach children the importance of team work, cooperation and self-esteem. Toronto Blue Jays serve as Honourary Captains for each of the Rookie League divisions and all program sites are provided with shirts, hats, equipment and baseball coaching to facilitate programming. Last year, Rookie League impacted over 4,400 children and youth across Canada.

In 2013, Rookie League will be celebrating its 25th season in Toronto, with the goal of providing 1,000 children from 45 TCH neighbourhoods with baseball programming and supporting employment and development for 90 youth. The seven-week summer program will continue to break down community barriers by bringing underserved neighbourhoods together to play.

Across Canada, the program will expand from 36 communities and aim to serve 4,000 children and youth in 41 BGC neighbourhoods across all 10 provinces and one territory.

For more information and to apply, please visit bluejays.com/jayscare.

JAYS CARE FOUNDATION

Since 1992, Jays Care Foundation has created opportunities for children and youth in need by providing access to programs that promote regular physical activity, encourage the pursuit of higher education and develop fundamental life skills. In addition, the Foundation has made possible the building of safe youth spaces for recreational programming, inspiring engagement through the sport of baseball. As the charitable arm of Canada's only MLB team, Jays Care is making a Major League effort to invest in Canadian children and communities from coast to coast.

JAYS CARE COMMUNITY CLUBHOUSE

The Jays Care Community Clubhouse is a fully-renovated luxury suite that accommodates up to 35 special guests for a fun, unforgettable experience at every Blue Jays home game. This interactive space for kids is equipped with Blue Jays memorabilia donated by team members, a PlayStation Move system for interactive games, a laptop computer featuring educational websites and an amazing view from third base! Guests are treated to ballpark fare, healthy snacks, a meet-and-greet with Ace, a special video-board welcome and, occasionally, even a special visit from one of the Blue Jays players. From Sick Kids to baseball teams, campers to youth mentors, the Jays Care Community Clubhouse hosted more than 60 different community and charitable organizations with more than 2,800 children and families cheering on their Toronto Blue Jays in 2012. For more information on booking opportunities in the Jays Care Community Clubhouse, please visit bluejays.com/jayscare.

FIELD OF DREAMS

Jays Care Foundation Field of Dreams grants build safe spaces for children and youth in need across Canada with the goal of providing opportunities in sport and education, and growing the game of baseball.

Since 2000, Jays Care has invested more than $3.5 million in 35 Field of Dreams projects across the country. Some of the projects include a major field lighting project at Stan Wadlow Park in East York, the recreation room in the new Ronald McDonald House Toronto, a Community Clubhouse at Camp Oochigeas' Toronto location, and the development of a new clubhouse for the Langley Boys and Girls Club.

In 2012, Jays Care disbursed more than $900,000 in Field of Dreams funding to seven charitable and community groups from coast to coast and opened eight youth spaces that are impacting more than 7,600 kids.

GRAND SLAM GRANTS

Grand Slam Grants are awarded to charitable and community groups across Ontario that offer children and youth programming with a focus on physical activity, education and life-skill development. In 2012, Jays Care Foundation disbursed more than $470,000 in Grand Slam Grants funding to 12 charitable and community groups that are impacting more than 2,200 children and youth. For more information and to apply, please visit bluejays.com/jayscare.

HOME RUN SCHOLARS

This four-year partnership with Pathways to Education provides 100 students with mentoring, tutoring, and financial support in an effort to reduce the high school dropout rate in Toronto's priority neighbourhoods of Lawrence Heights and Rexdale. To date, 92 students have successfully graduated

from high school and 70 students have pursued post-secondary education. For many of them, they are the first in their families to go to college or university. Jays Care Foundation's $450,000 partnership with Pathways realized a 76 per cent decrease in students deemed academically "at risk."

FUNDRAISING EVENTS & EXPERIENCES

THE CURVE BALL

This much-anticipated fundraising event featuring the entire Blue Jays team will be held on May 13th on the field at Rogers Centre. To purchase a table or inquire about sponsorship opportunities, please call Lauren Abesdris at 416.341.1690.

18TH ANNUAL CHARITY GOLF CLASSIC

Seventy-five foursomes, including your Toronto Blue Jays, compete in a fantastic day on the links on July 8th at the Club at Bond Head. To purchase a foursome or inquire about sponsorship opportunities, please call Lauren Abesdris at 416.341.1690.

SPORTSNET CHARITY BROADCAST AUCTION

Live on your SPORTSNET channel across Canada, Jays Care Foundation will host its Charity Broadcast Auction on May 1st during the Blue Jays vs. Boston Red Sox game. Fans can call in to bid on exclusives Blue Jays experiences and memorabilia or purchase a fan pack. All of the proceeds from this event support Jays Care programs and outreach initiatives. For more information on the auction, please visit www.bluejays.com/broadcastauction

CHARITY HOME RUN DERBY (TORONTO & VANCOUVER)

Ever dreamed of hitting your own Major League home run? Teams of four will swing for the fences competing for the championship title! The 4th Annual Toronto Home Run Derby will take place on Wednesday, June 19th at Rogers Centre. The 2nd Annual Vancouver Home Run Derby is scheduled for Wednesday, June 26th in partnership with the Vancouver Canadians at Nat Bailey Stadium. In order to qualify, teams of four must fundraise a minimum of $15,000. To register your team in Toronto or Vancouver, please call Lauren Abesdris at 416.341.1690.

50/50 DRAWS

Jays Care Foundation 50/50 draws presented by Ericsson are held at every Blue Jays home game and offer fans the opportunity to win a prize totalling almost $10,000! Look for the SUPER SIZE Jackpots at select games on the 2013 schedule with a prize valued at almost $30,000. More than $377,000 was awarded to lucky winners in 2012!

VIDEO BOARD GREETINGS

Fans can reserve a BIRTHDAY or ANNIVERSARY message or SPECIAL WELCOME greetings to be displayed on the Video Board during their selected Blue Jays home game by making a $100 donation to Jays Care Foundation. Celebrate your special occasion and support Jays Care! For more information or to book your greeting, call 416.341.1020.

BOARD OF DIRECTORS

Melinda Rogers, Chairman of the Board
Stu Hutcheson, Vice Chair, Secretary & Treasurer

DIRECTORS:

Paul Beeston	James Dodds	Dan Nowlan
Ron Carinci	Amoryn Engel	John Macintyre
Ian Charlton	Jamie Haggarty	Peter Sisam
Peter Dawe	Keith Pelley	

STAFF

Danielle Bedasse, Executive Director (mat leave 2013)
Rob Drynan, Executive Director (interim 2013)
Shari Ralph-Topolie, Manager, Finance & Administration (mat leave 2013)
Brendan Mohammed, Manager, Programs & Outreach
Lauren Abesdris, Manager, Fundraising & Development
Troy Beharry, Coordinator, Grants & In-stadium Programs
Todd Erskine, Coordinator, Rookie League & Baseball Programs
Rachel McKee, Coordinator, Communications
Heather Ryan, Coordinator, Fundraising
Taryn Linder, Administrative Assistant

PITCH IN FOR JAYS CARE

Donate online at www.bluejays.com/supportjayscare

Jays Care Foundation
1 Blue Jays Way, Suite 3200
Toronto, ON M5V 1J1
Phone: 416-341-1456
Fax: 416-341-1146

Email: jayscarefoundation@bluejays.com
Web: www.bluejays.com/jayscare
Twitter: @jayscare

Charitable Registration #: 89084 7189 RR0001

TORONTO BLUE JAYS
BASEBALL CLUB & ROGERS CENTRE

EXECUTIVE OFFICE

Vice Chairman, Rogers Communications Inc .... Phil Lind
President, Rogers Media .... Keith Pelley
President and CEO, Toronto Blue Jays & Rogers Centre .... Paul Beeston
Senior Vice President, Baseball Operations and General Manager .... Alex Anthopoulos
Senior Vice President, Business Operations .... Stephen R. Brooks
Vice President, Special Projects .... Howard Starkman
Special Assistant to the Organization .... Roberto Alomar
Executive Assistant to the President and CEO .... Sue Cannell

BASEBALL

Senior Vice President, Baseball Operations and General Manager .... Alex Anthopoulos
Vice President, Baseball Operations and Assistant General Manager .... Tony LaCava
Assistant General Manager .... Jay Sartori
Assistant General Manager .... Andrew Tinnish
Special Assistant to the General Manager .... Dana Brown
Consultant .... George Bell
Consultant .... Cito Gaston
Consultant .... Paul Quantrill
Administrator, Baseball Operations .... Heather Connolly
Baseball Information Analyst .... Joe Sheehan
Executive Assistant to the General Manager .... Anna Coppola
Director, Team Employee Assistance Program .... Ray Karesky
Director, Team Safety .... Ron Sandelli
Director, Team Travel and Clubhouse Operations .... Mike Shaw
Head Trainer .... George Poulis
Assistant Trainer .... Mike Frostad
Equipment Manager .... Jeff Ross
Clubhouse Manager .... Kevin Malloy
Visiting Clubhouse Manager .... Len Frejlich
Strength and Conditioning Coordinator .... Bryan King
Coordinator, Advance Scouting and Video ... Ryan Mittleman
Video Operations .... Robert Baumander
Team Employee Assistance Program .... Brian Shaw
Medical Advisor .... Dr. Bernie Gosevitz
Consulting Physician .... Dr. Ron Taylor
Consulting Team Physician .... Dr. Irv Feferman
Consulting Team Physician .... Dr. Noah Forman
Consulting Massage Therapist .... Todd Earl
Consulting Neurologist .... Dr. Jonathan Gladstone
Consulting Orthopedic Surgeon .... Dr. Allan Gross
Consulting Orthopedic Surgeon .... Dr. Steven Mirabello
Consulting Orthopedic Surgeon .... Dr. Jason Smith
Consulting Orthopedic Surgeon .... Dr. John Theodoropoulos
Consulting Podiatrist .... Dr. Glenn Copeland
Consulting Internal Medicine Physician ..... Dr. James Fischer
Consulting Chiropractor .... Dr. Pat Graham
Consulting Chiropractor .... Dr. Mark Scappaticci
Consulting Chiropractor .... Dr. Mike Prebeg

BLUE JAYS.COM

Marketing Producer .... John Matthew IV

BUILDING SERVICES

Vice President, Building Services .... Kelly Keyes
Executive Assistant .... Roger Le Blanc
Director, Capital Projects .... Jennifer Angiolella
Manager, Technical Production and Broadcast Services .... Mike Christiansen
Engineer, Technical Production and Broadcast Services .... Steph Gagnon
Coordinator, Capital Projects and Videoboard Production .... Kylie Kruk
Head Groundskeeper .... Tom Farrell

BUSINESS AFFAIRS

Vice President, Business Affairs and Legal Counsel .... Matthew Shuber
Executive Assistant, Business Affairs (Mat Leave) .... Liza Daniel
Executive Assistant, Business Affairs .... Suey Lau

COMMUNICATIONS

Vice President, Communications .... Jay Stenhouse
Manager, Baseball Information .... Mal Romanin
Coordinator, Baseball Information .... Erik Grosman
Coordinator, Communications .... Sue Mallabon

CONVERSIONS AND SHOW SERVICES

Director, Conversions and Show Services ..... Frank Grespan
Manager, Conversions .... Scot Murdoch
Event Set-up Technician .... Hernan Rosa
Field Technician .... Jake Grady
Field Technician .... Theo Kournetas
Field Technician .... Tyler Letofski
Field Technician .... Dave Matkowski
Field Technician .... Tony Mucha
Field Technician .... Jason Nicol
Field Technician .... Craig Noakes
Field Technician .... Craig Spencer
Field Technician .... Rob Stiles
Show Services Coordinator .... Medlyn Parchment Sr.
Show Services Technician .... Tracy Trotman

CORPORATE PARTNERSHIPS

Vice President, Corporate Partnerships .... Mark Ditmars
Director, Corporate Partnerships and Business Development .... John Griffin
Director, Corporate Partnerships and Business Development .... David O'Reilly
Director, Corporate Partnerships and Business Development .... Rob Swann
Director, Marketing Services .... Natalie Agro
Director, Marketing Services .... Krista Semotiuk
Senior Manager, Corporate Partnerships and Business Development .... Mark Palmer
Senior Manager, Marketing Services .... Honsing Leung
Manager, Marketing Services .... Manpreet Pandha
Executive Assistant .... Darla McKeen
Senior Coordinator, Marketing Services .... Owen Welsh

ENGINEERING

Manager, Engineering .... Dave McCormick
Engineering Assistant .... Michael Stasiuk
Senior Building Operator .... Abel Cruz
Senior Building Operator .... KC Pang
Senior Building Operator .... Russell Shapland
Senior Building Operator .... Romeo Panlilio
Maintenance Technician .... Juan Carlos Medrano
Maintenance Technician .... Tyrone Porras
Roof Technician .... Lee Brennan
Electrician .... Paul Zuschlag

EVENTS

Vice President, Building Services .... Kelly Keyes
Executive Assistant, Events .... Lori Parker
Senior Director, Event Production .... Joe Novak
Director, Events .... Lesley Lovell
Manager, Event Planning .... Cara Henry
Manager, Event Planning .... Rebecca Leighton
Coordinator, Events .... Laura Attwell
Coordinator, Public Relations/Event Marketing . Steph Porter
Coordinator, Technical Production .... Carol Balfour

FACILITY SERVICES

Director, Facility Services .... Wayne Sills
Manager, Facility Services .... Virginia Douglas
Facility Services, Service Technician ....Billy Robertson
Facility Services Technician .... Jonathan Cornwall
Facility Services Technician.................... Rui Da Silva Cedros
Facility Services Technician............................Louis Leandro
Facility Services Technician...........................Shawn MacKay
Facility Services Technician.......................... Bruce Standing
Facility Services Technician.............................Laureta Veiga
Painter...Robert Price

FINANCE AND ADMINISTRATION

Senior Vice President,
Business Operations ....Stephen R.Brooks
Executive Assistant...Donna Kuzoff
Senior Director, Controller...............................Lynda Kolody
Director, Payroll and Benefits.......................Brenda Dimmer
Director, Risk Management .... Suzanne Joncas
Senior Manager, Assistant Controller .... Ciaran Keegan
Financial Business Manager (RC)........Leslie Galant-Gardiner
Financial Business Manager (TBJ).................. Tanya Proctor
Manager, Revenue Reporting & Analysis.......Craig Whitmore
Manager, Stadium Payroll............................ Sharon Dykstra
Manager, Ticket Receipts and Vault Services..Joseph Roach
Financial Analyst .... Mike Asadoorian
Financial Analyst .... Emerita Flores
Financial Analyst ....Melissa Paterson
Payroll and Finance Analyst .... Tony Phung
Payroll Analyst ....Joyce Chan

FLORIDA OPERATIONS

Director and General Manager, Florida Operations
....Shelby Nelson
Assistant General Manager...................... Janette Donoghue
Accounting Manager .... Gayle Gentry
Manager, Community Relations,
Group and Retail Sales .... Kathi Beckman
Manager, Sales.. Mike Liberatore
Supervisor, Ticket Sales & Operations .... Jonathan Valdez
Administrative Assistant/ Receptionist ....Michelle Smith
Stadium Operations Supervisor .... Leon Harrell
Stadium Operations Supervisor ....Zac Phelps
Head Superintendent, Sports Turf ....Patrick Skunda

HEALTH AND SAFETY

Health and Safety Specialist ....Ailen Taitt-Kinsey
Health and Safety Co-Chair, Management...........Tom Farrell
Health and Safety Co-Chair, Worker..............Billy Robertson

HUMAN RESOURCES

Director, Human Resources.......................... Paulette Soper
Senior Manager, Human Resources .... Fiona Nugent
Advisor, Human Resources .... Reena Patel

INFORMATION TECHNOLOGY

Director, Information Technology .... Mike Maybee
Manager, Information Technology...............Anthony Miranda
Voice/Data Network Operations Specialist..... Donny Catinari
IT Support Analyst...Yvan Duval
IT Support Analyst...Richard Solis
IT Support Coordinator............................ Katrina LeCavalier

JAYS CARE FOUNDATION

Executive Director (Mat Leave) ....Danielle Bedasse
Executive Director (Interim) ....Rob Drynan
Manager, Finance and Administration
(Mat Leave)...Shari Ralph-Topolie
Manager, Fundraising and Development......Lauren Abesdris
Manager, Programs and Outreach....... Brendan Mohammed
Administrative Assistant ....Taryn Linder
Coordinator, Communications........................Rachel McKee
Coordinator, Fundraising ....Heather Ryan
Coordinator, Grants and In-Stadium Programs
.... Troy Beharry
Coordinator, Rookie League and Baseball Programs
....Todd Erskine

MARKETING AND COMMUNITY RELATIONS

Vice President, Marketing and
Merchandising .... Anthony Partipilo
Executive Assistant, Marketing ....Maria Cresswell
Director, Game Entertainment and
Promotions ....Marnie Starkman
Manager, Community Marketing and
Player Relations .... Holly Gentemann
Manager, Direct Marketing ....Jenny Koschanow
Manager, Direct Marketing (Mat Leave)........ Sherry Thurston
Manager, Promotions and Fan Activation ..... Michelle Seniuk
Manager, Social Marketing .... Rob Jack
Manager, Special Events ....Kristy-Leigh Boone
Manager, Stadium Entertainment................... Daniel Joseph
Sr. Graphic Designer ....Dave Rodgers
Sr. Motion Graphics Designer ....Ryan Stone
Motion Graphics Designer .... Andrew Gyorgyfi
Graphic Designer...Corey McDonald
Coordinator, Amateur Baseball ...........................T.J. Burton
Coordinator, Special Events..........................Steve Whidden
Ambassador, Amateur Baseball......................... Jim Fanning
Ambassador, Amateur Baseball......................Sean McCann

OFFICE SERVICES

Office Services Coordinator ....Piero Aceto
Office Services Coordinator ....Sam Platsis
Receptionist ....Mary Anne Sturley
Gate 9 Security/Information .... Pete Gaskin

PARKING OPERATIONS

Manager, Parking ....Michelle Gustar
Supervisor, Parking .... Shiraz Salih
Part Time Team Leader .... John Rait
Disabled Parking Services ....Ken Chapman
Parking Attendant..........................Meconnen Gebremaryam
Parking Attendant......................................Yoseph Sinework
Parking Attendant............................. Tesfaldet Weldeamlak
Valet Driver .... Faisal Abubaker
Valet Driver ....Tesfaye Desta
Valet Driver ....Tesfaie Gebre
Valet Driver ....Jamal Hassen
Valet Driver ....Bala Viswanathan

SECURITY

Manager, Security Operations ....Robert Hamilton
Supervisor, Security Operations................Ben Cumberbatch
Control Room Guard ....Bojan Fogl
Control Room Guard ....Althea Hussey
Control Room Guard .... Jennifer Jollimore
Control Room Guard .... Laura Morden
Security Guard ....Juri Batraks
Security Guard .... Desmond Buchanan
Security Guard ....Ryan Cobham
Security Guard .... Anish Dutta
Security Guard ....Randall Harris
Security Guard .... Kyle Rutherford
Security Guard .... Matthew Wilson
Gate 3 Reception .... John Mays

STADIUM OPERATIONS

Vice President, Stadium Operations and
Security... Mario Coutinho
Executive Assistant, Stadium Operations
and Security..June Sym
Director, Guest Experience..............................Carmen Day
Manager, Event Services .... Julie Minott
Manager, Game Operations.......................Karyn Gottschalk
Supervisor, Guest Experience .... Matt Black
Coordinator, Guest Experience ....Maureen Kinghorn
Coordinator, Guest Experience......................... Lisa Simons
Administrative Assistant................................. Marion Farrell

TBJ MERCHANDISING

Vice President, Marketing and Merchandising .... Anthony Partipilo
Director, Purchasing and Jays Shop Direct .... Helen Maunder
Director, Stadium Merchandising .... Michael Andrejek
Manager, Jays Shop Gate 5 Rogers Centre .... Teresa Michalski
Manager, Jays Shop Sears Yonge and Dundas .... Veronica Zavala
Manager, Stadium Events .... Arto Emas
Manager, Warehouse Distribution .... Darryl De Franco
Assistant Manager, Jays Shop Gate 5 Rogers Centre .... Viya Sagarakis
Assistant Manager, Jays Shop Gate 5 Rogers Centre .... John Walters
Sales Supervisor .... Stephanie Thomas
Sales Supervisor .... Sara Webb
Merchandise Buyer .... Diana Goucher
Coordinator, Jays Shop Direct .... Connie Hum
Customer Service Representative, Jays Shop Direct .... Ryan Fisher
Customer Service Representative, Jays Shop Direct .... Jennifer McMahon
Administrative Assistant .... Brittany Casals
Warehouse Assistant .... Matthew An
Warehouse Assistant .... David Costa
Warehouse Assistant .... Andrew Franchi
Team Leader, Rogers Centre Tours .... Robert Murphey

TICKET OPERATIONS

Director, Ticket Operations .... Justin Hay
Director, Ticket Services .... Sheila Stella
Manager, Box Office .... Christina Dodge
Manager, Ticket Operations .... Scott Hext
Coordinator, Ticket Operations .... Eric Cowell
Coordinator, Ticket Services .... Sonia Privato
Sales Analyst, Ticket Operations .... Richard Overend

TICKET SALES AND SERVICE

Vice President, Ticket Sales and Service .... Jason Diplock
Executive Assistant .... Stacey Jackson
Director, Luxury Suite Sales and Service .... Mike Hook
Director, Ticket Sales .... Franc Rota
Manager, Group Sales .... Ryan Gustavel
Manager, Season Ticket Services .... Erik Bobson
Manager, Ticket Sales .... John Santana
Account Manager, Group Sales .... Andrew Haley
Account Manager, Group Sales .... Paul Rabeau
Account Manager, Luxury Suite Sales and Service .... Chris Schmidt
Account Executive, Group Sales .... Andy Topolie
Account Executive, Group Sales .... Jon Westover
Account Executive, Luxury Suite Sales and Service .... Al McNinch
Account Executive, Luxury Suite Sales and Service .... Sara Mickle
Account Executive, Luxury Suite Sales and Service .... Jeremy Zulauf
Account Executive, Season Ticket Services .... Jonathan Bagnell
Account Executive, Season Ticket Services .... Kris Erickson
Account Executive, Season Ticket Services .... Adam Hagerman
Account Executive, Ticket Sales .... Josh Fromstein
Account Executive, Ticket Sales .... Jeff Gale
Account Executive, Ticket Sales .... Alex Husarewych
Account Executive, Ticket Sales .... Glenn Jackson
Account Executive, Ticket Sales .... Trevor Johnson
Account Executive, Ticket Sales .... Mike Skrobacky
Account Executive, Ticket Sales .... Ryan Stevenson
Account Executive, Ticket Sales .... Christian Taylor
Coordinator, Luxury Suite Sales and Service .... Adele Biggs

NAME THE TEAM CONTEST

The Blue Jays were named in a contest conducted in June and July of 1976. Over 30,000 individual entries were received, suggesting over 4,000 names for the new American League club. From the list of names submitted, specially-appointed panels of judges selected ten names to submit to the Board of Directors. The Directors chose the name "Blue Jays" from that list and announced their decision on August 12th, at which time the team officially became the Toronto Blue Jays Baseball Club.

A total of 154 people submitted the name "Blue Jays" and a drawing was held to select a grand prize winner from those who submitted the name. Dr. William Mills of Etobicoke, Ontario, won a pair of season tickets for 1977 and an all-expenses paid trip for himself and his family to watch the Blue Jays at spring training in Dunedin, Florida. Nine runners-up also won season tickets.

"GET YOUR TICKETS HERE"

Phone Hours of Operation
Single Game:
Monday to Saturday: 9:30 am - 10:00 pm
Sundays & Stat. Holidays: 9:00 am - 8:00 pm
Season Tickets, Packs & Groups:
Monday to Friday: 9:00 am - 8:00 pm
Game day weekends (regular season): 9:00 am - 5:00 pm

Box Office Hours of Operation (Regular Season):
Monday to Friday: 8:00 am - 8:00 pm
Saturday & Sunday: 10:00 am - 6:00 pm
Ordering Online: Find the Perfect seat 24/7 online at www.bluejays.com

CLUB OFFICERS

PHIL LIND
VICE CHAIRMAN, ROGERS COMMUNICATIONS

Phil Lind is Vice Chairman of Rogers Communications Inc. a diversified Canadian communications company with three operating divisions: Rogers Wireless, Rogers Cable and Rogers Media... Joined Rogers in 1969 when the company owned two radio stations and had 15,000 cable customers...Worked closely with company founder and President and CEO Ted Rogers for 40 years...Instrumental in the expansion of Rogers Communications over the years leading efforts to acquire Canadian Cablesystems, Premier Cablevision, Maclean Hunter Ltd...Headed the company's successful expansion to the United States in the 80's...A sports enthusiast, he spearheaded the creation of sports service Rogers Sportsnet and secured sports programming rights including the NFL Sunday Ticket for Rogers cable customers...Key proponent of the group which brought Buffalo Bills games to Rogers Centre...Has received many honours and in 2002 was appointed to the Order of Canada and received in the same year an honorary Doctor of Laws degree from the University of British Columbia... In 2012 he was inducted into the U.S. Cable Hall of Fame, the 3rd Canadian to be so honoured... Serves as a director of many organizations including Brookfield Asset Management Inc. Rogers Communications Inc. and the Art Gallery of Ontario.

KEITH PELLEY
PRESIDENT, ROGERS MEDIA INC.

Was appointed President, Rogers Media in September 2010 and is responsible for leading the overall operations of the company's diverse portfolio, including Television, Radio, Publishing, Digital Media, The Shopping Channel, the Toronto Blue Jays, and Rogers Centre... Under his leadership, Rogers Media operates as a fully integrated media company, delivering world-class content and leveraging synergies and opportunities across all divisions... A passionate sports advocate, Pelley has more than 25 years of experience in the sports and broadcasting industries... Prior to joining Rogers Media, Pelley was Executive Vice-President of Strategic Planning at CTVglobemedia and President of Canada's Olympic Broadcast Media Consortium, where he led Rogers' and CTV's unprecedented coverage of the Vancouver 2010 Olympic Winter Games... Under his vision and guidance, the Consortium delivered the Top 5 most-watched events in Canadian television history, with 99 per cent of the Canadian population experiencing the 2010 Winter Games through one of the Consortium's media platforms... Was President and CEO of the Toronto Argonauts Football Club (2003 to 2007), where under his guidance, the club rose in popularity with average home-game attendance more than tripling in just four years... In his first full year with the club, helped guide the Argos to the 2004 Grey Cup title... Began his career in 1986 at TSN, where he worked for 16 years in various roles of increasing responsibility... Started as an Editorial Assistant in the newsroom and worked his way up to Senior News Producer and Event Producer for CFL, curling, tennis and baseball... Left TSN in 1994 to produce NFL football for FOX, but returned to TSN as Senior Vice-President of Programming & Production in 1997... Was appointed President in 2001, where he remained until 2003 before joining the Argonauts... Devotes much of his time to numerous charitable organizations and serves on the Board of Directors of Own the Podium, Jays Care Foundation and the Holland Bloorview Kids Rehabilitation Hospital Foundation... Is a member of the Special Olympics Ontario Hall of Fame and received the Ryerson Alumni Achievement Award in 2011.

PAUL BEESTON
PRESIDENT & CEO, TORONTO BLUE JAYS & ROGERS CENTRE

October 27, 2009 appointed President and Chief Executive Officer of the Toronto Blue Jays Baseball Club and Rogers Centre for a three year term... Held the position of Interim President and Chief Executive of the Toronto Blue Jays and Rogers Centre from October 2008 to October 2009... Was the first employee of the Toronto Blue Jays - May 10, 1976... Became Vice-President of Business Operations in 1977, Executive Vice-President, Business in 1984, President and Chief Operating officer in 1989 and Chief Executive Officer in 1991... From 1997 until 2002 he served as President and Chief Operating Officer of Major League Baseball... Earned a Bachelor of Arts in Economics and Political Science from the University of Western Ontario in 1967 and was awarded an honorary Doctor of Laws degree from the University in 1994 and, in 2001, an honorary Doctor of Social Sciences from Niagara University in Niagara Falls, New York... He began his professional career with the accounting firm, Coopers & Lybrand in 1968, obtained his Chartered Accountant designation in 1971, and remained with the firm until 1976... 1988 was named a Fellow of the Institute of Chartered Accountants...1994 earned the distinction of Canadian Baseball Man of the Year...1998 appointed as a Member of the Order of Canada...2002 was inducted in to the Canadian Baseball Hall of Fame and the Canada's Sports Hall of Fame in 2006... Sits on the Board of Directors of Loblaw Companies Limited, President's Choice Bank, Gluskin Sheff & Associates Inc. and the Centre for Addiction and Mental Health Foundation... Additionally, he is a member of the Board of Trustees of the National Baseball Hall of Fame in Cooperstown, New York.

ALEX ANTHOPOULOS
SENIOR VICE PRESIDENT, BASEBALL OPERATIONS & GENERAL MANAGER

Entering his fourth season as Senior Vice President, Baseball Operations & General Manager… Born May 25, 1977 in Montreal, Quebec... Raised and schooled in the city, attending Lower Canada College and Marianopolis College... Majored in economics at McMaster University in Hamilton, Ontario... Moved into the baseball world in 2000, accepting an internship in the Montreal Expos Media Relations department... His work there led to a job offer with the club as an Assistant in International Scouting the following year... Named as a Coordinator of Scouting Operations in 2002… The Expos expanded his duties in 2003 adding the title of Scouting Supervisor for Canada... Joined the Blue Jays organization shortly after the completion of the 2003 regular season, being named as a Scouting Coordinator... Named Assistant to the General Manager following the 2005 season... Promoted to the position of Vice President, Baseball Operations & Assistant General Manager on January 8, 2006...On October 3, 2009 accepted the position of Senior Vice President, Baseball Operations & General Manager… Of Greek descent, he has lent his services to the Greek National baseball team around the 2003 European Championships before serving as an advance scout for Greece in the 2004 Summer Olympiad in Athens.

STEPHEN BROOKS
SENIOR VICE PRESIDENT, BUSINESS OPERATIONS

Promoted to his current role of Senior Vice President, Business Operations in January 2011 from his previous role as Vice President, Finance and Administration... Assumed the role of Vice-President, Finance and Administration in March 2009 having spent the previous five years with the Rogers group of companies as Director, External Reporting, Rogers Communications Inc. and more recently as Corporate Controller, Rogers Media Inc… Prior to joining Rogers in 2004, was a senior manager in the Technology, Media and Telecommunications practice of Deloitte and Touche LLP in New York, New York where his four year tenure focused almost exclusively on publicly-traded companies in the telecommunications industry… Prior to joining the New York practice in 2000, was with Deloitte and Touche LLP in Vancouver, BC where he began his career in 1994… Is a member of the Board of Directors of the Canadian Mental Health Association, York Region currently serving as the Board's President… A Chartered Accountant and Certified Public Accountant (Illinois)… A graduate of the University of British Columbia and the British Columbia Institute of Technology... He and his wife reside in Toronto and have one child.

ROBERTO ALOMAR
SPECIAL ASSISTANT TO THE ORGANIZATION

A 12-time All-Star and 10-time Gold Glove winning second baseman... Was elected to the Hall of Fame in a ceremony on July 24, 2010... Received the 3rd highest vote total in history at 90% majority... Is the only player in Blue Jay history to have their number retired (#12)... Over his 17-year career, batted .300 with a .371 on-base percentage and .443 slugging percentage with the San Diego Padres, Toronto Blue Jays, Baltimore Orioles, Cleveland Indians, New York Mets, Chicago White Sox and Arizona Diamondbacks... The switch hitter totaled 2,724 hits, 1,508 runs, 504 doubles, 80 triples, 210 home runs, 474 stolen bases and 1,134 RBI... A member of the World Series Championship clubs in 1992 and 1993. Alomar was a key contributor, as his performance in the 1992 AL Championship Series earned him MVP honours...The 1998 MVP of the All-Star game in Denver, Colorado, became just the 20th second basemen to enter the Hall of Fame... Also became the first Toronto Blue Jay player to enter the Hall with a Blue Jays cap.

GEORGE BELL
CONSULTANT

Played in 12 seasons for the Toronto Blue Jays (1981, 1983–1990), Chicago Cubs (1991) and Chicago White Sox (1992–1993)… Ranks 3rd in club history in total bases (2201), RBI (740) and extra base hits (471)… Best season came in 1987, finishing with a .308 average, 47 HR and 134 RBI, being awarded the American League MVP… On April 4, 1988, Bell became the first player in Major League history to hit three home runs on an opening day… On May 28, 1989, hit a walk-off home run in a 7–5 victory over the Chicago White Sox in the final Major League game played at Exhibition Stadium… Is one of nine men enshrined on the Blue Jays Level of Excellence.

CITO GASTON
CONSULTANT

Clarence Edwin Gaston... Born March 17, 1944 in San Antonio, Texas... Along with Pat Hentgen was the first to be named a Club Ambassador... Is one of nine men on the Level of Excellence... Led the Blue Jays to two World Series Championships, two American League Championships, four American League East titles and a franchise record in games managed with 1764 and wins with 913 over 12 seasons... Received honorary Doctorate of Law from the University of Toronto on June 10, 1994... Named "The Sporting News" Sportsman of the Year in 1993 along with Blue Jays Executive Vice-President and General Manager, Pat Gillick... Named Baseball Man of the Year in Canada in 1989 by the Toronto-Montreal BBWAA... Managed the American League All-Star Game in 1993 and 1994 and was an All-Star Coach in 1991... Joined the Toronto Blue Jays coaching staff on November 4, 1981... Appointed interim manager on May 15, 1989... Named to the permanent post on May 31, 1989... Held the position of Blue Jays manager until September 24, 1997... Was hired as manager for a second time on June 20, 2008... Would remain in the role through the end of the 2010 season... Hired as Blue Jays hitting coach for the 2000 and 2001 seasons... Originally signed by the Milwaukee Brewers after an all-star career at Holy Cross High School in Corpus Christi, Texas... Had an 11-year career with three separate clubs (ATL-1967,1975-78, SD-1969-74, PIT-1978)... In 1,026 games, batted .256 with 91 home runs and 387 RBI... Best season was 1970, batting .318 with 29 home runs and 93 RBI and was named Padres MVP... Appeared in the 1970 All-Star Game, going 0-2... During his years as manager Cito gave much of his time to charity events throughout Toronto.

PAUL QUANTRILL
CONSULTANT

Played 14 seasons in the major leagues appearing in 841 games with Boston, Philadelphia, Toronto, Los Angeles Dodgers, New York Yankees, San Diego and Florida posting a 3.83 ERA... Led the elague in appearances in each of 2001, 2002 & 2003... Was selected to the All-Star game in 2001 and holds the New York Yankees record for appearances with 86 in 2004... Spent six seasons in a Blue Jays uniform from 1996-2001, posting a 3.67... Inducted in the Canadian Baseball Hall of Fame on June 19, 2010.

BUSINESS OPERATIONS

MARIO COUTINHO
VICE PRESIDENT, STADIUM OPERATIONS & SECURITY

Named to his current position in October 2005, overseeing the management of all event staff and security operations at Rogers Centre, including Blue Jays home games... Also handles risk management issues on behalf of Rogers Centre ... Began his career with the Blue Jays Baseball Club working part-time in 1983 in game day operations... Employment on a full-time basis came in 1989 as the Club's Manager of Game Operations... In the ensuing years he held a variety of positions in stadium operations, taking over as the department's Director in 1999... Has played a key role in the staging of two World Series and the 1991 All-Star Game in Toronto, leading to his appointment to Major League Baseball's Senior Advisory Committee for Security and Stadium Operations in 2000... Continues to sit as Co-chair for this eight-person committee... In addition to his duties with the Blue Jays, also served as the Manager of Stadium Operations for the CFL's Toronto Argonauts between 1994 and 1997... Coordinated the event staff and security for the NFL's America Bowl games held in 1995 and 1997... Served on the committee and hosted the 1999 Youth Employment Task Force for the City of Toronto Currently serves on the planning committee for the Toronto Police Emergency Management Symposium (since 2008) . Born on the island of Sao Miguel in the Azores on March 24, 1962... Moved to Toronto as an infant... Graduated from the University of Toronto with a Bachelor of Science degree in 1985, after having undertaken his secondary schooling at Toronto's De La Salle College... Currently living in Markham, Ontario with his wife and son.

JASON DIPLOCK
VICE PRESIDENT, TICKET SALES AND SERVICE

Was named Vice President of Ticket Sales and Service in July of 2008...Held the position of Vice President of Florida Operations for the Toronto Blue Jays and General Manager of the Dunedin Blue Jays in September 2006 and held that post until moving into his current role... Jason has been with the Blue Jays since 1999 starting as an Account Manager renewing season tickets... In 2001, he was promoted to the position of Assistant Manager of Ticket Sales overseeing several sales areas including Consumer Sales and Premier Client Services... He was again promoted in December of 2003 to the position of Director of Ticket Sales... In that role Jason was responsible for Group Development, Consumer Sales, Direct Mail & Collateral and Premier Client Services... Before joining the Blue Jays' organization, Jason held the position of Director of Sales and Marketing for the Brampton Battalion Hockey Club of the Canadian Hockey League from 1997 to 1999... He currently resides in Oakville with his wife and two children.

MARK DITMARS
VICE-PRESIDENT CORPORATE PARTNERSHIPS

Joined the Toronto Blue Jays organization in July of 2011... A graduate of the University of Windsor... Spent 20 years with Labatt Breweries of Canada in various Sales and Marketing roles, including Director of Marketing, Bud Light Brand Manager and Budweiser Brand... Managed developing marketing strategies for many sports properties including the NFL, Formula 1 and Nascar... Was Vice President Sales for EMI Music Canada responsible for Sales Revenue of many artists, including Katy Perry, Coldplay and The Beatles through retail channels such as Walmart and iTunes... Is a certified amateur coach through the Ontario Baseball Association, coaching in the AAA Mississauga Majors and Twins organizations... Played football at both Wilfred Laurier and University of Windsor.

KELLY KEYES
VICE PRESIDENT, BUILDING SERVICES

2013 will mark Kelly's 24th year with the organization... Appointed to her current position in 2004, the eight Stadium Departments that presently report directly to Kelly are Capital Projects, Conversions, Engineering, Events, Event Production, Facility Services, Video Board Production and Toronto Blue Jays' "World's Fastest Grounds Crew"... Born November 18, 1968 ... Kelly was raised, educated and currently resides in the city of Toronto.

ANTHONY PARTIPILO
VICE PRESIDENT, MARKETING & MERCHANDISING

Responsible for leading the Marketing and Merchandising efforts of the Toronto Blue Jays and Rogers Centre... After several years as Vice-President Marketing for a major consumer electronics retailer, he joined the Blue Jays organization in February 2004 as the Managing Director of TBJ Merchandising where his responsibilities included operating and growing merchandising and retailing operations for the Toronto Blue Jays... He rebranded all retail operations as "Jays Shop™", launched www.jaysshop.ca, opened the 1,800 sq.ft. Jays Shop at Sears, Yonge & Dundas, and the built the largest team shop in Canada at over 8,000 sq.ft. inside Rogers Centre... The club's merchandise sales have grown over 400% and now rank as one of the highest per capita in Major League Baseball... In November 2009 was promoted to Vice-President Marketing and Merchandising... Was born and currently lives in Toronto, an avid runner, lover of all things sports and politics and proud father of three daughters... Previously served as a Board Member for the Sunshine Foundation for Kids, and as a committee Vice-Chair at the Canadian Marketing Association (CMA).

MATTHEW SHUBER
VICE PRESIDENT, BUSINESS AFFAIRS AND LEGAL COUNSEL

Originally joined the Blue Jays in 2003, in the role of business and legal advisor... Was promoted to his current position as Vice President in March, 2011... Responsibilities now include the oversight and management of certain key relationships and business matters relating to Major League Baseball and the Blue Jays' intellectual property, as well as providing ongoing strategic, business and legal advice and direction on a myriad of different organizational imperatives (including ticketing, merchandising, corporate partnerships, marketing, and broadcasting) ... Attended Schulich School of Business MBA program in 2003 on Dean's Entrance Scholarship, completing core courses... Called to the Ontario Bar in 1999... Prior to entering the business world, was in legal practice as criminal defence counsel at the Toronto firm of Cooper, Sandler and West (Austin Cooper, Q.C., Mark Sandler and Peter West)... In 1996, worked with Harry Radomski at Goodmans, LLP on commercial litigation, patents and National Hockey League-related matters... Received law degree from Osgoode Law School in Toronto in 1997, and was the recipient of six separate academic awards, including the award for highest standing in Commercial Law, Taxation Law and Business Associations and the award for standing second in Year II of the law school program... Bachelor of Arts from the University of Toronto, graduating with high distinction in 1994... Attended the Toronto French School and is fluent in French... Member of the Board of Directors of the Jewish Camp Council of Toronto since 2005, currently holding the position of Vice President... Avid photographer and traveller... Occasional musician and sportsman... Married with one son.

HOWARD STARKMAN
VICE PRESIDENT, SPECIAL PROJECTS

The Blue Jays have been Howie's life... Will complete 37 full years with the Blue Jays in 2013 and his 47th year in the pro sports industry... Started with the club, as Director, Public Relations, in July 1976 as one of the first employees hired... Title changed to Vice-President, Media Relations in 1999... Became Vice-President, Special Projects in 2002... Began his career in the sports business with summer employment at Maple Leaf Gardens (Toronto) in the summer of 1964... After attending University of Western Ontario and University of Toronto he began full time with Maple Leaf Gardens in 1967 in the ticket department... Moved on to the Gardens promotion and group sales department in 1968... In 1969 with Jim Gregory taking over as General Manager of the NHL Toronto Maple Leafs became the Director of Administration and Publicity for the hockey team... Hired by Peter Bavasi for the Blue Jays... During his 37 years with the Blue Jays has been active in a wide a range of areas on behalf of the Blue Jays organization including overseeing the team's publicity, media relations, broadcasting, team travel and print publications including the production of 26 media guides... His career includes highlights such as 'Name The Team Contest", first Blue Jays regular season game April 7, 1977 at Exhibition Stadium, American League Championship Series in 1985, 1989, 1991, 1992, 1993, the opening of SkyDome in June 1989, the 1991 All-Star Game and, of course, the 1992 and 1993 World Series...Oversaw the 2009 World Baseball Classic at Rogers Centre on behalf of Blue Jays/Rogers Centre... As VP Special Projects is involved in planning, scheduling, broadcasting, and program publishing... Received the prestigious Robert O. Fishel Award in the 1995 for excellence in the field of Public Relations... Received the President's Award from Sports Media Canada in 2012 recognizing his body of work over his career in the sports field... Served as PR director on the 1998 Major League All-Star squad tour of Japan... Has worked as a Major League Baseball public relations official for 15 World Series and ten All-Star Games... In 2006 was Major League Baseball Public Relations liaison with Team Canada at the World Baseball Classic... As well, worked for the NHL for six Stanley Cup Finals... Two-time winner of The Toronto Chapter of BBWAA 'Good Guy Award'... Member of SABR... Member of the BAT Awareness Committee... Vice-Chairman of the Toronto Entertainment BIA board... Was named the Sports Media Canada Presidents Award... Born February 23, 1945 in Toronto... Married with two children, making his home in Mississauga.

JAY STENHOUSE
VICE PRESIDENT, COMMUNICATIONS

The 2013 season will mark his 29th in the organization... Started with the organization in 1985 assisting with game day operations as runner and then as quartermaster... In that role often was assigned to assist the Public Relations department... Joined the Blue Jays in a full-time capacity in 1992 being named the Coordinator, Statistical Information within the Public Relations Department... In 1996 was promoted to Assistant Director, Public Relations and took on a greater role in the production of the media guide and traveling with the team...In October 2002 was promoted to take the lead role in the department as Director, Communications...Was then named Vice-President, Communications in October 2005 with the responsibility of overseeing media communications for both the Toronto Blue Jays and Rogers Centre...During his tenure with the club has assisted Major League Baseball at numerous All-Star Games and Post Season series...Attended the MLB Executive Development Program...Born and raised in Weston, Ontario, he now makes his home in Etobicoke with his wife and two children... Obtained a Bachelor of Arts degree in economics from Toronto's York University in 1991 after graduating from Weston Collegiate Institute in 1987... A former junior hockey player, he continues to be active in local hockey.

BASEBALL OPERATIONS

TONY LACAVA
VICE PRESIDENT, BASEBALL OPERATIONS AND ASSISTANT GENERAL MANAGER

Born May 21, 1961 in Pittsburgh, Pennsylvania... Graduated from Central Catholic in 1979 where he played baseball... Obtained an Associates Degree from Gulf Coast Community College before transferring to the University of Pittsburgh... Left Pitt after two years to sign with the Pittsburgh Pirates as a non-drafted free agent... Spent two seasons in the club's minor league system as an infielder with Bradenton and Greenwood in 1983 and Macon in 1984... Joined the Anaheim Angels organization as an Associate Scout in 1989... Promoted to full-time duties as an Area Scout in 1991... Promoted again to the position of Regional Crosschecker in 1996, serving through 1999... Joined the Atlanta Braves as the National Scouting Supervisor in 2000... Named as the Director, Player Development for the Montreal Expos in September of that year overseeing the club's minor league field personnel and the farm teams... Spent the 2002 season with the Cleveland Indians as the National Crosschecker... Joined the Blue Jays organization on October 15, 2002 as Assistant to the General Manager... Was named Assistant General Manager, Player Personnel in October of 2007 and was named to his current position in spring of 2011... Married with three children... Resides in Oakmont, Pennsylvania.

DANA BROWN
SPECIAL ASSISTANT TO THE GENERAL MANAGER

In his fourth season as Special Assistant to the General Manager after eight seasons as Director of Scouting for the Nationals/Expos organization... Prior to that he worked with the Pittsburgh Pirates for eight years as area scouting supervisor and East Coast scouting coordinator... With a major influence during his time with the Nationals/Expos organziation, his selections as Director of Scouting included Ryan Zimmerman (2005, first round), Stephen Strasburg (2009, first round), Drew Storen (2009, first round), Jordan Zimmermann (2007, second round), Danny Espinosa (2008, third round), Ian Desmond (2004, third round) and John Lannan (2005, 11th round)... Also drafted All-Star Chad Cordero (2003, first round), Aaron Crow (2008, first rounder who did not sign) and Bill Bray (2004, first round), who was an essential cog in the Nationals' acquisition of Austin Kearns, Felipe Lopez and Ryan Wagner from Cincinnati in an eight-player trade in July 2006... His 2007 draft class was later rated as the "best in baseball" by industry-expert Baseball America - selections included Ross Detwiler (first round), Jordan Zimmermann (second round) and Derek Norris (fourth round)... A graduate of Seton Hall University, Brown played with Pirate teammates Craig Biggio, Mo Vaughn and John Valentin in 1987 prior to being drafted by Philadelphia in 1989 as an outfielder. On February 21, 2008, Brown was inducted into SHU's Athletic Hall of Fame... In January of 2012 was inducted into the New Jersey Sports-Writer's Hall of Fame... He played three pro seasons in the Phillies' chain before enjoying a two-year stint as a minor-league coach... Began his scouting career in 1994... Resides in Franklin Park, NJ with his wife and two children.

JAY SARTORI
ASSISTANT GENERAL MANAGER

Named to his current position on September 13, 2010 coming over from the Washington Nationals where he was Director, Baseball Operations for one season... Prior to his appointment in Washington worked with Major League Baseball's Labor Relations Department in the role of Manager of Salary and Contract Administration... While working for the Commissioner's Office, he provided advice and interpretations on the Basic Agreement and Major League Rules to all 30 clubs, conducted research and analysis for industry-wide meetings and initiatives, served as a key administartor for both Salary Arbitration Support Program and Rule 4 Draft Support Program, managed enhancements to MLB's IT systems and functioned as the primary contact for Club personnel regarding Major League contract terms... Sartori was also a key member of the MLB Collective Bargaining team that successfully negotiated a second consecutive CBA without a work stoppage in 2006... Jay was born and raised in Lynnfield, MA and currently resides in Toronto, Ontario... Prior to joining the Commissioner's Office, Sartori worked in the investment banking industry for Robertson Stephens and Pacific Growth Equities... Sartori graduated with a Finance and MIS degree from Boston College in 2001.

ANDREW TINNISH
ASSISTANT GENERAL MANAGER

Born April 28, 1976 in Hamilton, Ontario... Grew up in Nepean, Ontario where he played minor baseball for East Nepean... Played baseball for Niagara University (NCAA) in 1997... Graduated from Brock University with a degree in Sports Management... Played for the Brock Badgers baseball club from 1995-1999... Was awarded the honour of Brock University Male Athlete of the Year for the 1999-2000 school year, as well as being named team MVP in the 1996, 1998 and 1999 seasons... Went on to pitch for the Quebec Capitales of the Northern League in the summer of 1999, appearing in 22 games, compiled a 3-1 record covering 38.2 innings... First joined the Blue Jays in April 2001 as an Intern in Baseball Operations... Moved into a full-time position in January 2002 as an Assistant in the Baseball Operations department... During July/August of 2002 acted as Hitting Coach for Team Canada at the FISU World University Games in Italy... Was named an Area Scout for the Blue Jays, covering North Florida and Alabama, before being promoted to Scouting Coordinator in August 2003... Elevated to the position of Assistant Scouting Director on September 2006, a role he performed until his promotion to Director, Amateur Scouting on October 9, 2009 where he oversaw the direction of the Amateur Scouts in preparation for each season's Amateur draft...Named as Assistnat General Manager on June 21, 2012.

MIKE SHAW
DIRECTOR, TEAM TRAVEL AND CLUBHOUSE OPERATIONS

Born October 30, 1968 in Halifax, Nova Scotia... Raised in Montreal, Quebec... Played baseball through the junior ranks in the Montreal Lac St. Louis League... Graduated from Montreal's Marymount Academy in 1986, capturing a provincial physical education award in his final year... Attended Dawson College, earning a Diploma in Social Sciences in 1989... Graduated with an Honours Bachelor of Commerce in Sports Administration from Sudbury's Laurentian University in 1995... Joined the Blue Jays organization in 1996 taking on a part-time position in the Club's ticket office... Joined the PR staff as an assistant in 1997, before being appointed as the Manager, Baseball Information in 1999... Appointed to Manager of Team Travel in November 2004, overseeing the team's transportation and accommodations in Spring Training and throughout the regular season... Was promoted to Director of Team Travel and Clubhouse Operations in January, 2011... Married with two children... Resides in Oakville.

HEATHER CONNOLLY
ADMINISTRATOR, BASEBALL OPERATIONS

Completed 26 years with the Blue Jays Organization…Named to her current position in January 2010, working alongside senior management in baseball operations…Prepares and maintains all Major League paperwork including contracts for players, coaches, scouts and support staff, immigration documents, employment visas, and hiring paperwork…Serves as an active liaison with the Commissioner's Office, the Department of Immigration and Human Resources Canada in this regard…Also plays an important role in the preparation and maintenance of the financial budget for baseball operations…Originally joined the Club in February 1984, working as an Administrative Assistant in Ticket Sales & Service…Moved from the box office in December 1988, being named as Executive Assistant, Baseball Operations & Player Personnel…In November 2004 named Executive Baseball Assistant, Major League Operations…Served in this capacity until being named to her current role…Born on November 4, 1961 in Toronto…Raised and educated in the city at Richview Collegiate Institute and Humber College…Has one grown son and one grandson.

RON SANDELLI
DIRECTOR, TEAM SAFETY

A highly recognized 30-year veteran of the Toronto Police, he has overseen team security for the Toronto Blue Jays Baseball Club since November 2001... Born July 5, 1944 in Toronto... Raised and educated in the city at York Memorial Collegiate and the University of Toronto... Entered Police College in 1965, being named as a Constable in July of that year... Climbed steadily through the investigational ranks of the Toronto Police, being named as a Detective in the "Fraud Squad" in 1974... Entered the city's Intelligence Unit in 1977 as a Detective rising to the post of Unit Commander of Police Intelligence Services... Spent ten years in the CFSEU (Combined Forces Special Enforcement Unit), the first unit of its kind in Canada specializing in the investigation and apprehension of suspects involved with organized crime... Became recognized as an expert authority in the field of organized crime, being called to testify in cases around the globe... Retired from active police duty in 1995... Prior to his retirement, served as the Resident Agent for the Blue Jays between the 1993 and 1995 seasons... Shortly afterwards began working privately in security for a subsidiary of Magna International... An avid baseball fan and player, he led the Toronto Police Fast Pitch Team to three gold medal wins and one silver medal at the bi-annual World Police Games during the 1980's, including a championship victory over the LAPD in the inaugural competition... Served as a player/manager earning the nickname "Coach", a moniker that has stuck with him since... A resident of Aurora, he is married with two children and four grandchildren.

BEHIND THE SCENES

GEORGE POULIS
HEAD TRAINER

George, 48, begins his 11th year as the head athletic trainer with the Blue Jays' Major League Club after serving as the assistant athletic trainer for three years... Prior to the Blue Jays, he was an athletic trainer in the San Diego Padres' Minor League system for 10 years. Poulis got his first experience with professional sports in 1986 as an athletic training intern for the NFL's Cleveland Browns Football Club... A Cleveland native, Poulis earned his undergraduate degree from Baldwin-Wallace College in Berea, Ohio, and earned his master's degree from the University of Alabama... He worked his way up through the Padres' Minor League system with stops in Waterloo, Iowa (Class A); Wichita, Kan.; Memphis, Tenn.; Mobile, Ala. (Class AA); and Las Vegas, NV (Class AAA)... At the conclusion of the 1998 Minor League season, Poulis assisted the San Diego Padres' Athletic Training Staff during the 1998 playoffs and World Series... During the off-season, Poulis and his wife live in Florida with their three daughters.

MIKE FROSTAD
ASSISTANT TRAINER

Enters his 18th season in the Toronto Blue Jays organization and his second as Assistant Trainer, holding the position during the 2010 season as well... A Calgary native, he earned his undergraduate degree from the University of Calgary and is certified by the NATA... Worked his way up through the Blue Jays system, working in St. Catharines, Ontario (Short-A), Medicine Hat (Rookie), Hagerstown (A) and Dunedin (A)... Has spent seven of the last eight years as the Minor League Medical Coordinator for the Blue Jays... In 2004 and 2005 won the Athletic Trainer of the Year award for the Florida State League... Was also the recipient of the Minor League Athletic Trainer of the Year Award in 2005... Spent the 2010 season with the Blue Jays major league club... Resides in Florida during the off-season.

BRYAN KING
STRENGTH & CONDITIONING COORDINATOR

Named to his position as the Blue Jays Major League Strength & Conditioning Coach in January 2009, and is now in his fifth season...Graduated from the University of Oklahoma in 2003 while lettering in baseball as an outfielder...Signed with the Seattle Mariners in January of 2002, spending one year with the Mariners organization... In 2003 played with the Springfield Ducks of the Central Independent League...Starting in 2004, worked with the Cleveland Indians for two years as a minor league strength coach...Oversaw the off-season workouts of all-star pitcher C.C. Sabathia in 2005...Spent the 2006 season with the Texas Rangers AAA affiliate (Oklahoma City) before being hired as the Toronto Blue Jays Minor League Strength and Conditioning Coordinator in 2007, where he spent two seasons, prior to his appointment as Major League Strength & Conditioning Coach... Is certified as a Certified Strength and Conditioning Specialist in addition to a Registered Strength and Conditioning Coach under the NSCA.

TODD EARL
MASSAGE THERAPIST

Returns for his third season with the Toronto Blue Jays... A long-time resident of the Tampa Bay, Florida area, Todd spent several years with the Tampa Bay Buccaneers, before joining the staff of the Blue Jays... Is a 2005 graduate of Suncoast School of Massage, and resides in Riverview, Florida... Enjoys hiking, going to the movies, and yoga... Has one daughter who is currently on active duty with the United States Navy.

JEFF ROSS
EQUIPMENT MANAGER

One of the few remaining charter employees... Joined the Club prior to its inception and has served in his current capacity as Equipment Manager since 1981... Ran the visiting clubhouse at Exhibition Stadium during the Blue Jays first four seasons of operation... Responsibilities include maintenance of all uniforms and equipment as well as overseeing the transport of such items during the regular season... Graduated from Darcy McGee High School in Montreal... Attended Dawson College and worked part-time for the Montreal Expos as a member of their grounds crew and in the clubhouses... Enjoys golf and fishing... Married... Montreal native now makes his home in Palm Harbor, Florida.

KEVIN MALLOY
CLUBHOUSE MANAGER

Originally joining the Blue Jays in 1982, he has served as the team's Clubhouse Manager since 1996... Graduated from Seneca College in 1987 where he studied Marketing and Administration... Has worked for the Toronto Blue Jays since 1982 when he began as a seasonal assistant in the Blue Jays Clubhouse... Responsible for co-coordinating the clubhouse responsibilities with Equipment Manager, Jeff Ross and overseeing and directing the seasonal clubhouse assistants... Married with two children... Enjoys ice hockey, downhill skiing and golf... Resides in Pickering, Ontario.

LEN FREJLICH
VISITING CLUBHOUSE MANAGER

Stands as one of the few remaining charter employees... Joined the Club prior to its inception and has served as the Visiting Clubhouse Manager since 1996... Began working with the club in the ticket office, serving as Assistant Director, Tickets in the club's inaugural season... Joined the operations department for the 1986 season as the Assistant Director... Responsible for hosting all visiting clubs and the care of their equipment and uniforms... Attended Michael Power Collegiate in Toronto before graduating from Wilfred Laurier University where he studied Business Administration... Married with one child... Enjoys horse racing, ice hockey and golf.

ALEX ANDREOPOULOS
BULLPEN CATCHER

Alekos (Alex) Andreopoulos… Married with one child… Born and raised in Toronto, Ontario… Named to his current position in 2003… Attended Seton Hall from 1992-95, the catcher earned conference all-star honours in each of his seasons… Named as the Big East Conference Rookie of the Year and included on Baseball America's Freshman All American team in 1992… Selected in the 17th round by Milwaukee in 1995, he spent eight seasons in the minors in the Brewers, Indians, Expos and Cardinals organizations… Batted .288 with 37 home runs and 268 RBI in 525 career minor league games.

JESUS FIGUEROA
BATTING PRACTICE PITCHER

Jesus Maria Figueroa… Has held his current position as Batting Practice Pitcher since the 1989 season… Born on February 20, 1957 the Santa Domingo, Dominican Republic native was originally signed by the New York Yankees in 1974 spent eight seasons in the minors and one in the Majors… In 1980 appeared in 115 games for the Chicago Cubs, batting .253 with one home run and 11 RBI… Started 29 games with 25 coming in CF… His lone home run came off Pirates RHP Eddie Solomon.

RYAN MITTLEMAN
COORDINATOR, ADVANCE SCOUTING AND VIDEO

Joined the organization in 2005 as Manager of Baseball Information in the communications department... Moved into the scouting department in 2006 and spent the next five seasons as the Coordinator of Amatuer Scouting... Became Assistant Scouting Director in 2011 before spending 2012 as a Pro Scout... Is in his first season as Coordinator of Advance Scouting and Video... Born in Providence Rhode Island, however has resided in Toronto since 1985... Excelled in hockey playing on the US under 17 and 18 teams... Won silver medals with both squads, leading the under 17 club in goals... Attended Boston College University playing Division-1 hockey for the Eagles from 1995-97.

ROBERT BAUMANDER
VIDEO OPERATIONS

Joined the organization in 1980 working with the Grounds Crew… In 1981 moved into Video Production, while studying Film and TV Production at Humber College… Has now been the Video Coordinator for both the Major League team and minor league affiliates for more than 20 years… Born in North York, Ontario, he enjoys photography, woodworking and bird watching in the off-season.

MANAGER AND COACHES

JOHN GIBBONS

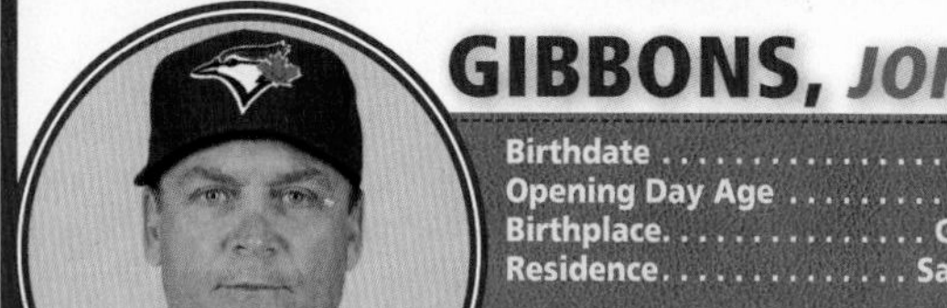

GIBBONS, *JOHN*

Birthdate .... **June 8, 1962**
Opening Day Age **50**
Birthplace .... **Great Falls, MT**
Residence .... **San Antonio, TX**

5
MANAGER

APPOINTED:

Named as the Manager for the Toronto Blue Jays for the second time on November 20, 2012...Was appointed on October 4, 2004 in his first stint as manager.

PERSONAL:

John Michael Gibbons... Married with three children... Graduated from MacArthur High School in San Antonio, TX where he was an All-District and All-City selection... Spent parts of three seasons as a catcher with the Mets.

PROFESSIONAL CAREER:

- Was a first round selection by the New York Mets in the 1980 draft.
- Named as the lone catcher on the post-season All-Star Team in 1983 for Jackson in the Texas League... Shared the Doubleday Award with Herm Winningham as the club's Most Valuable Player.
- Made his ML debut on April 11, 1984 vs Atlanta going 0-5 with an RBI in a 6-1 victory... First ML hit was a single against the Expos Bryn Smith in the Mets home opener on April 17.
- Selected to appear in the International League All-Star Game and was named to the year end All-Star team in 1987.
- Appeared in eight games for the Mets in 1986 hitting .474 with a home run and an RBI... Hit safely in each of the five games he started for the Mets... As a starter was 9-18... On September 20 vs the Phillies collected a career high four hits and belted his only ML home run against Mike Jackson, a solo shot in a 9-5 win.
- Hit two grand slams to become the Tidewater in 1987 franchise leader in slams with five.
- Joined the Dodgers organization on April 1, 1988 being traded for IF Craig Shipley.
- Joined the Texas Rangers organization as a free agent in 1989 and spent the entire season with Oklahoma of the American Association (AAA).
- In 1990 Joined the Phillies organization and spent the season with Scranton of the International League (AAA).

COACHING CAREER:

- Spent first four seasons in Mets organization as a roving minor league instructor and coach at Capito City (A).
- Made his managerial debut in 1995 and led Kingsport to the Appalachian League Championship (A)... Was named the Appalachian League Manager of the Year after posting a 48-18 record in the regular season...Captured his second championship in as many years as he led St. Lucie to a Florida State League (A) Championship in 1996...Was the Eastern League Manager of the Year in 1988 at Birmingham and winner of the Casey Stengal Award as the Mets organizational Manager-of-the-Year...Spent three seasons leading the Norfolk Tides of the International League (AAA)... Led the Tides to a first place finish in 2001 after posting an 85-57 record.
- Named Bullpen Catcher for the Toronto Blue Jays on January 1, 2002... Promoted to First Base Coach on June 3, 2002.
- Managed three games as interim manager in place of Carlos Tosca during the 2003 season winning all three games....Was named interim manager of the Blue Jays on August 8, 2004 as Carlos Tosca was relieved of his duties... Appointed as the ninth full-time manager in Blue Jays history on October 4, 2004.
- Remained in the role as manager until June 20, 2008 finsihing with a 305-305 record, highlighted by an 87-75 record in and second place finish in 2006.
- Spent three seasons as the Kansas City Royals Bench Coach from 2009-2011
- Managed the San Antonio Missions (AA) of the Texas League in the San Diego Padres organization, finishing with a 60-80 record.

JOHN GIBBONS

Year Club & League	AVG	G	AB	R	H	2B	3B	HR	RBI	BB	SO	SB
Minor Totals	.254	1178	3837	498	974	166	21	107	514	482	894	30
MAJOR TOTALS	.220	18	50	5	11	4	0	1	2	6	16	0

MANAGERIAL/COACHING CAREER

1991-93	Instructor, Minor League (Mets)
1994	Coach, Columbia, South Atlantic League (Mets)
1995	Manager, Kingsport, Appalachian League (Mets)
1996-97	Manager, St. Lucie, Florida State League (Mets)
1998	Manager, Binghamton, Eastern League (Mets)
1999-01	Manager, Norfolk, International League (Mets)
2002	Bullpen Catcher/First Base Coach, Toronto Blue Jays
2003	First Base Coach, Toronto Blue Jays
2004	First Base Coach/Interim Manager, Toronto Blue Jays
2005-08	Manager, Toronto Blue Jays
2009-11	Bench Coach, Kansas City Royals
2012	Manager, San Antonio, Texas League (Padres)
2013-	Manager, Toronto Blue Jays

RECORD AS MANAGER

Year	Club & League	W-L	PCT	Finish
1995	Kingsport (Appy)	48-18	.727	1st in div, won championship
1996	St. Lucie (FSL)	71-62	.534	3rd (1st half), 1st (2nd half), won championship
1997	St. Lucie (FSL)	54-81	.400	4th (1st half), 6th (2nd half)
1998	Binghamton (East)	82-60	.577	2nd, lost in semis
1999	Norfolk (Int)	77-63	.550	3rd in div
2000	Norfolk (Int)	65-79	.451	3rd in div
2001	Norfolk (Int)	85-57	.599	1st in div, lost in semis
2003	TORONTO (AL)	3-0	1.000	(interim)
2004	TORONTO (AL)	20-30	.400	
2005	TORONTO (AL)	80-82	.494	3rd in div
2006	TORONTO (AL)	87-75	.537	2nd in div
2007	TORONTO (AL)	83-79	.512	3rd in div
2008	TORONTO (AL)	35-39	.473	5th in div
2012	San Antonio (Tex)	60-80	.429	4th in div
Minor Totals		542-500	.520	
MAJOR TOTALS		305-305	.500	(3-0 as interim manager)

POST SEASON PLAY

Year	Club & League	W-L	PCT	Finish
1995	Kingsport (Appy)	2-1	.667	(Won Championship)
1996	St. Lucie (FSL)	5-1	.833	(Won Championship)
1998	Binghamton (East)	1-3	.250	(Lost in semi-finals)
2001	Norfolk (Int)	2-3	.400	(Lost in semi-finals)
TOTALS		10-8	.556	

AGE WHEN MANAGERS TOOK OVER THEIR FIRST GAME

MANAGER	FIRST GAME	AGE	MANAGER	FIRST GAME	AGE
Bobby Mattick	April 9, 1980	64	Carlos Tosca	June 3, 2002	48
Cito Gaston	June 20, 2008	63	John Farrell	April 1, 2011	48
Jim Fregosi	April 6, 1999	57	Cito Gaston	May 15, 1989	45
Mel Queen	September 24, 1997	55	Jimy Williams	April 8, 1986	42
Buck Martinez	April 1, 2001	52	Bobby Cox	April 6, 1982	40
Roy Hartsfield	April 7, 1977	51	John Gibbons**	August 8, 2004	40
Tim Johnson	April 1, 1998	48			

** denotes active manager

BLUE JAYS MANAGERS

	G	W	L	PCT	YEARS
Gaston, Cito	1764	913	851	.518	1989-1997, 2008–2010
Cox, Bobby	647	355	292	.549	1982-1985
Gibbons, John**	610	305	305	.500	2004-2008
Williams, Jimy	522	281	241	.538	1986-1989
Hartsfield, Roy	484	166	318	.343	1977-1979
Tosca, Carlos	382	191	191	.500	2002-2004
Fregosi, Jim	324	167	157	.515	1999-2000
Farrell, John	324	154	170	.475	2011-2012
Mattick, Bobby	268	104	164	.388	1980-1981
Martinez, Buck	215	100	115	.465	2001-2002
Johnson, Tim	162	88	74	.543	1998
Queen, Mel	5	4	1	.800	1997

** denotes active manager

Don Wakamatsu served as Interim Manager from Aug. 26-Sept. 4, 2011 (3-8) in the absence of Manager John Farrell (pneumonia) & on Sept. 26 (0-1) due to personal reasons

Brian Butterfield served as Interim Manager from July 10-11, 2009 (1-1) in the absence of Cito Gaston (family funeral)

John Gibbons served as Interim Manager from May 2-3, 2003 (2-0) in the absence of Manager Carlos Tosca (Daughter's graduation) and in the absence of Manager Carlos Tosca (suspension) on Sept. 5, 2003 (1-0)

Cookie Rojas served as Interim Manager from May 24-26, 2001 (1-2) in the absence of Manager Buck Martinez (family funeral)

Gene Tenace served as Interim Manager from May 27-29, 1994 (2-1) in the absence of Manager Cito Gaston (suspension)

Gene Tenace served as Interim Manager from Aug. 21-Sept. 26, 1991 (19-14) in the absence of Manager Cito Gaston (ruptured disk in lower back)

Harry Warner served as Interim Manager from May 20-29, 1978 (3-9) in the absence of Manager Roy Hartsfield (Wife's illness)

Records are for regular season games only

HALE, *DEMARLO*

Birthdate . . . . July 16, 1961
Opening Day Age 51
Birthplace. . . . . .Chicago, IL
Residence. . . . . Orlando, FL

16

BENCH COACH

APPOINTED:

Named as Bench Coach on November 26, 2012.

PERSONAL:

Played four seasons at Southern University in Baton Rouge, LA after graduating from Chicago Vocational High School in 1979... Played baseball and basketball in high school.

PROFESSIONAL CAREER:

- Was selected by the Red Sox in the 17th round of the June 1983 draft and played fiver minor league seasons as a 1B/OF in the Boston (1983-86) and Oakland (1988) organizations.
- Batted .267 with 26 home runs, 206 RBI and 67 steals in 482 games.

COACHING CAREER:

- Has posted a 615-633 minor league record as manager over nine seasons.
- Joined the Red Sox in 1992 as a coach with New Britain after four years instructing at Bucky Dent's Baseball School.
- Managed in the Red Sox system for seven seasons from 1993-99, seeing his clubs reach the post-season three times.
- Was honoured by the Red Sox with the inaugural Edward F. Kenney Player Development Award in 1994.
- Named Midwest League Manager of the Year in 1995 and chosen to manage the AA All-Star games in 1997 and 1999 and was a coach on the US Team at 1999 Futures Game.
- His 1999 AA Trenton squad posted a 92-50 record being selected Minor League Team of the Year by Baseball America... Also earned Manager of the Year honours as well.
- Managed in the Rangers system for two seasons from 2000-01 finishing second in the PCL East Division in both seasons.
- Was promoted to the Major League staff in 2002 and remained in the role of Firstbase/Outfield Coach for Texas through 2005.
- Served six seasons with the Red Sox, four as Third Base Coach (2006-09) and two as Bench Coach (2010-11).
- Was the Baltimore Orioles Third Base Coach in 2012 when the club reached the post-season for the first time since 1997.
- Joins the Blue Jays as Bench Coach in 2013.

PLAYING CAREER

Year Club & League	AVG	G	AB	R	H	2B	3B	HR	RBI	BB	SO	SB
Minor Totals	.267	548	1911	286	510	77	12	28	234	172	268	79

COACHING CAREER

1992	Coach, New Britain, Eastern League (Red Sox)
1993	Manager, Fort Lauderdale, Florida State League (Red Sox)
1994	Manager, Sarasota, Florida State League (Red Sox)
1995	Manager, Michigan, Midwest League (Red Sox)
1996	Manager, Sarasota, Florida State League (Red Sox)
1997-99	Manager, Trenton, Eastern League (Red Sox)
2000-01	Manager, Oklahaoma, Pacific Coast League (Rangers)
2002-05	First Base Coach, Texas Rangers
2006-09	Bench Coach, Boston Red Sox
2010-11	Third Base Coach, Boston Red Sox
2012	Third Base Coach, Baltimore Orioles
2013-	Bench Coach, Toronto Blue Jays

RECORD AS MANAGER

Year	Club & League	W-L	PCT.
1993	Fort Lauderdale (FSL)	46-85	.351
1994	Sarasota (FSL)	69-64	.519
1995	Michigan (Midwest)	75-63	.543
1996	Sarasota (FSL)	68-69	.493
1997	Trenton (Eastern)	71-70	.504
1998	Trenton (Eastern)	71-70	.504
1999	Trenton (Eastern)	92-50	.648
2000	Oklahoma (PCL)	69-74	.483
2001	Oklahoma (PCL)	74-69	.518
CAREER TOTALS		615-633	.508

HENTGEN, PAT

Birthdate . . . . November 13, 1968
Opening Day Age 44
Birthplace. . . . . Detroit, MI
Residence. . . . . Shelby Township, MI

41

BULLPEN COACH

APPOINTED:

Appointed to the position of Bullpen Coach by Manager John Gibbons on December 10, 2012... Had previously been Toronto's Bullpen Coach in 2011... Served as a Club Ambassador from 2007-2010 and the 2012 season.

PERSONAL:

Patrick George Hentgen... Married with three children... Graduated in 1986 from Fraser High School where he played varsity baseball for three years and varsity football for two years... Drafted in the 5th round of the 1986 June draft by the Toronto Blue Jays.

PROFESSIONAL CAREER:

- In 14 seasons, appeared in 344 games posting a 131-112 record and an ERA of 4.32... Spent 10 seasons in a Blue Jays uniform... Made 183 consecutive starts from April 17, 1993-August 24, 1998... Holds the Blue Jays record for wins on the road with Roy Halladay at 12... Appeared in the post season on two occasions (1993-Toronto/2000 St. Louis)... Started one World Series game in 1993 at PHI, picking up the win with six innings of one run ball... Was selected as an All-Star on three occasions (1993, 1994 & 1997)... Tossed 40 consecutive scoreless innings from April 29-May 25, 1997.
- In 1996 won the AL Cy Young Award, posting a 20-10 with a 3.22 ERA and 177 strikeouts, becoming the first Blue Jay to win the award... Is one of only five Blue Jays to win 20+ games in a season, along with Jack Morris, Roger Clemens, David Wells and Roy Halladay.
- Spent one season in St. Louis and three in Baltimore before returning to the Blue Jays for his final season in 2004... Among all-time leaders in club history, ranks 4th in winning pct. (.557), complete games (31), 5th in wins (107) and innings pitched (1636).

COACHING CAREER:

- Began his coaching career as a Bullpen Coach with the Blue Jays in 2011.
- Returns to the role in 2013 after a one year absence.

PLAYING RECORD

Year Club & League	W-L	ERA	G	GS	CG	ShO	SV	IP	H	R	ER	BB	SO
Minor Totals	43-47	3.20	174	164	4	2	1	908.0	759	389	323	397	773
TORONTO TOTALS	107-85	4.28	270	238	31	9	0	1636.0	1677	850	778	599	1028
MAJOR TOTALS	131-112	4.32	344	306	34	10	1	2075.1	2111	1076	996	775	1290

MANAGERIAL/COACHING CAREER

2011 Bullpen Coach, Toronto Blue Jays
2013- Bullpen Coach, Toronto Blue Jays

Blue Jays bullpen coach, Pat Hentgen at the amateur clinic in Toronto on January 5, 2013

BIOGRAPHIES LAST SEASON HISTORY RECORDS OPPONENTS PLAYER DEV. MEDIA & MISC.

MOTTOLA, *CHAD*

Birthdate .... October 15, 1971
Opening Day Age 41
Birthplace................. Augusta, GA
Residence.................. Orlando, FL

39

HITTING COACH

APPOINTED:

Named to the position of Hitting Coach on November 26, 2012.

PERSONAL:

Charles Edward Mottola... Attended St. Thomas Aquinas High School in Fort Lauderdale, Florida where in his senior year hit .624 with 24 home runs... Was an All-American selection in his senior year at the University of Central Florida.

PROFESSIONAL CAREER:

- Selected by the Cincinnati Reds in the first round (5th overall) in the 1992 draft.
- Appeared in 59 games over five seasons for Cincinnati, Florida, Baltimore and Toronto batting .200 with four home runs and 12 RBI.
- Played 16 seasosn in the minor leagues hitting .280 with 249 home runs and 1034 RBI, including a career best 33 home runs and 102 RBI in 2000 with Syracuse earning Blue Jays Minor League Player of the Year honours

COACHING CAREER:

- Joined the coaching ranks assisiting with the Blue Jays Extended Spring Training program at the end of the 2007 season.
- Remained as Hitting Coach with the Gulf Coast squad through 2008.
- Spent one season as a Roving Minor League Hitting Coach in 2009 before moving to Las Vegas (AAA) where he would spend the next three seasons at Hitting Coach.
- Was added to the Blue Jays Major League coaching staff following the AAA season at Las Vegas as the hitting coach in 2011-2012... In 2013 makes his Major League coaching debut, becoming the Club's hitting coach.

PLAYING RECORD

Year Club & League	AVG	G	AB	R	H	2B	3B	HR	RBI	BB	SO	SB
Minor Totals	.280	1800	6645	1002	1859	358	43	249	1034	557	1282	183
MAJOR TOTALS	.200	59	125	17	25	6	0	4	12	10	28	2

COACHING CAREER

2007-08	Hitting Coach, Gulf Coast, Gulf Coast League (Blue Jays)
2009	Roving Minor League Coach (Blue Jays)
2010-12	Hitting Coach, Las Vegas, Pacific Coast League (Blue Jays)
2013	Hitting Coach, Toronto Blue Jays

TWICE THE POWER:

After Edwin Encarnacion hit a club leading 42 home runs in 2012 it marked just the 4th time in club history that Toronto has had two different players reach the 40-HR plateau in back-to-back seasons...Jose Bautista hit a MLB leading 43-HR in 2011.

	Season	Players
1.	1999	Shawn Green (42)/Carlos Delgado (44)
	2000	Carlos Delgado (41)/Tony Batista (41)
2.	1998	Jose Canseco (46)
	1999	Shawn Green (42)/Carlos Delgado (44)
3.	1986	Jesse Barfield (40)
	1987	George Bell (47)
4.	2011	Jose Bautista (43)
	2012	Edwin Encarnacion (42)

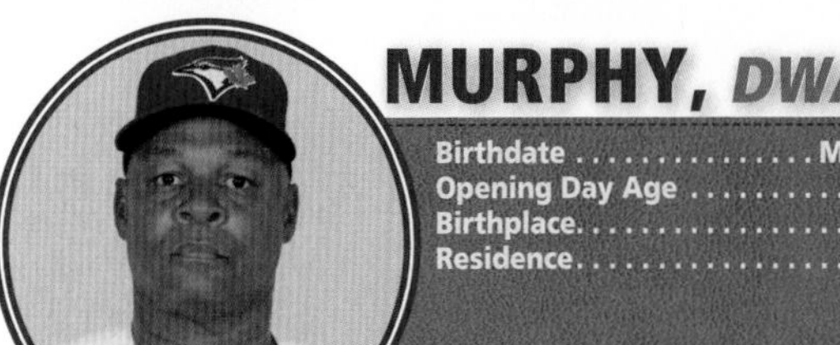

MURPHY, *DWAYNE*

Birthdate . . . . March 18, 1955
Opening Day Age 58
Birthplace. . . . . Merced, CA
Residence. . . . . Chandler, AZ

25

FIRST BASE COACH

APPOINTED:

Named as First Base Coach for the Toronto Blue Jays on June 20, 2008... Appointed Hitting Coach for the 2010 season... Returns to role of First Base Coach in 2013.

PERSONAL:

Dwayne Keith Murphy... Married with three children... Starred in both baseball and football at Antelope Valley High School in California... Earned a scholarship for football at Arizona State University, but turned it down to begin his baseball career... Graduated from high school in 1973... Following his playing career, coached high school football for four seasons (1991, 1993-1995) before beginning his baseball coaching career.

PRO CAREER:

- Drafted in the 15th round of the 1973 Free Agent Draft by the Oakland Athletics... Made his professional debut that summer with Lewiston... As a Major Leaguer, batted .246 with 166 home runs and 609 RBI in 1360 games.
- Made his Major League debut with the A's in on April 8, 1978 against the Angels, and spent his first full season in the majors in 1979.
- Won the first of his **six consecutive Rawlings Gold Glove Awards** as an outfielder in 1980... Led the AL with 507 putouts, making just five errors, none over the last 79 games during that season, while setting a career high with 157 hits batting .274 on the season.
- Named as a Sporting News All-Star in 1981 after leading the AL with 15 game-winning RBI and ranking second in the league with 73 walks.
- During the 1984 season, smacked a career high 33 home runs, tying for third in the AL... Led all AL outfielders with 14 assists... Finished up his Major League career with one-year stops in Detroit (1988), and Philadelphia (1989), before concluding his playing days with a season for the Yakult Swallows in Japan .

COACHING CAREER:

- Joined the Arizona Diamondbacks organization... Made his coaching debut, managing Phoenix in the Arizona Rookie League... Was on the coaching staff of the High Desert Mavericks of the California League in 1997 when they captured the league championship that season.
- In the Diamondbacks' first season, was appointed as the team's First Base & Outfield Coach at the Major League level... Spent three seasons in that capacity... Named as Arizona's hitting coach in 2001, serving three seasons in that role, including Arizona's 2001 World Series Championship season.
- Joined the Blue Jays organization on January 1, 2005 being named as the coach for the Class AAA Syracuse SkyChiefs of the International League for the 2005 and 2006 campaigns... In his fifth season in the Blue Jays organization was named Roving Hitting Instructor.
- Began season as Roving Hitting Instructor and was appointed as First Base Coach for the Toronto Blue Jays on June 20, 2008... Named to the role of Hitting Coach for the 2010 season, seeing the club hit a record 257 home runs.
- Served in capacity of Hitting Coach from 2010-2012.
- Returns to the role of First Base Coach in 2013.

PLAYING CAREER

Year Club & League	AVG	G	AB	R	H	2B	3B	HR	RBI	BB	SO	SB
Minor Totals	.253	613	1954	274	495	75	23	35	204	392	372	144
MAJOR TOTALS	.246	1360	4347	648	1069	139	20	166	609	747	953	100

MANAGERIAL/COACHING CAREER

1996	Manager, Phoenix, Arizona (Diamondbacks)
1997	Coach, High Desert, California (Diamondbacks)
1998-00	First Base & Outfield Coach, Arizona Diamondbacks
2001-03	Hitting Coach, Arizona Diamondbacks
2005-06	Coach, Syracuse, International (Blue Jays)
2007-08	Roving Hitting Instructor (Blue Jays)
2008-09	First Base Coach, Toronto Blue Jays
2010-12	Hitting Coach, Toronto Blue Jays
2013-	First Base Coach, Toronto Blue Jays

RECORD AS MANAGER

Year	Club & League	W-L	PCT	Finish
1996	Phoenix (Arizona)	20-36	.357	6th
CAREER TOTALS		20-36	.357	

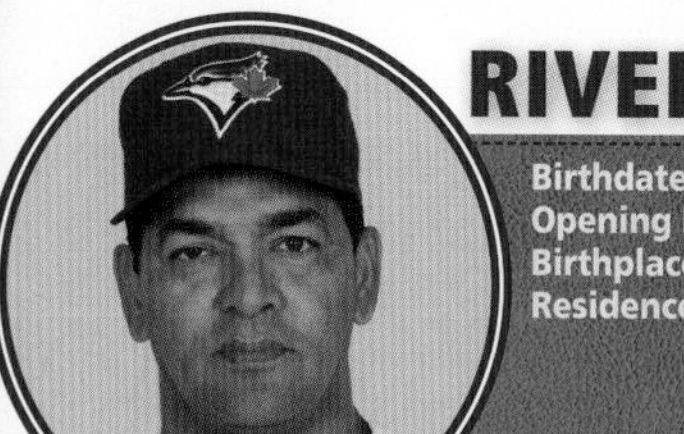

RIVERA, *LUIS*

Birthdate . . . . .January 3, 1964
Opening Day Age 49
Birthplace. . . . . .Cidra, Puerto Rico
Residence. . . . . Caguas, Puerto Rico

63

THIRD BASE COACH

APPOINTED:

Named Coaching Assistant of the Toronto Blue Jays on November 10, 2010...Named Third Base Coach on November 26, 2012.

PERSONAL:

Luis Antonio Rivera... Graduated from Luis Munoz Iglesias in Puerto Rico inn 1981... Played Little League in Guaynabo, Puerto Rico... Signed by the Montreal Expos on Sept. 22, 1981.

PROFESSIONAL CAREER:

- Played parts of 11 seasons and 781 games in the Major Leagues from 1986-98 with Montreal, Boston, New York-NL, Houston & Kansas City... Recorded his finest big league season in 1992 with the Red Sox when he hit .258 (107-414) with 22-2B, 3-3B, 8HR & 40RBI in 129 games... He compiled a Major League career average of .233 (516-2215), with 28HR & 209RBI in 781 games... Played professionally for 18 seasons from 1981-98.

COACHING & MANAGING CAREER:

- Spent six seasons from 2000-05 coaching and managing in the Cleveland Indians Player Development system... Managed the Kinston (A) Indians to a record of 76-64 (.543) in 2005, guiding the club to the finals of the Carolina League Championship Series... Managed Lake County (A) Captains in 2003-04, winning South Atlantic League Manager of the Year honours in 2003 after the Captains compiled a minor league-best record of 97-43 (.693)... In his three seasons as Manager at Kinston and Lake County his teams posted a record of 246-173 (.587) leading his teams to the playoffs in two of the three years... Was also a coach at Kinston for three seasons from 2000-02.
- Joined the Blue Jays organization after four seasons as the Cleveland Indians Infield and First Base Coach after being named to the post on November 3, 2005.
- Managed in his first season with the New Hampshire Fisher Cats (AA) leading them to their first post-season birth since 2004 finishing 2nd in the Eastern Division...Lost in the first round of the playoffs to Trenton 3-0.
- Made his debut as a Blue Jays Coach in 2011 as a Coaching Assistant and spent two seasons in that capacity.
- Takes over as Third Base Coach for the 2013 season.

PLAYING RECORD

Year Club & League	AVG	G	AB	R	H	2B	3B	HR	RBI	BB	SO	SB
Minor Totals	.245	1070	3765	499	924	185	26	57	420	336	617	105
MAJOR TOTALS	.233	781	2215	249	516	114	12	28	209	171	443	20

COACHING & MANAGERIAL CAREER

2000-02	Coach, Kinston, Carolina League (Indians)
2003-04	Manager, Lake County, South Atlantic League (Indians)
2005	Manager, Kinston, Carolina League (Indians)
2006-09	Infield and First Base Coach (Indians)
2010	Manager, New Hampshire, Eastern League (Blue Jays)
2011-12	Coaching Assistant, Toronto Blue Jays
2013	Third Base Coach Toronto Blue Jays

RECORD AS MANAGER

Year	Club & League	W-L	PCT.	Position
2003	Lake County (SAL)	97-43	.693	1st (Lost in finals)
2004	Lake County (SAL)	73-66	.525	3rd
2005	Kinston (Car)	76-64	.543	2nd (Lost in finals)
2010	New Hampshire (East)	79-62	.560	1st (Lost in semis)
CAREER TOTALS		325-235	.580	

WALKER, *PETE*

Birthdate ....April 8 1969
Opening Day Age 43
Birthplace................ Beverly, MA
Residence.............. Quaker Hill, CT

40

PITCHING COACH

APPOINTED:

Named as Bullpen Coach on November 7, 2011...On November 26, 2012 took over the position of Picthing Coach.

PERSONAL:

Peter Brian Walker... Married with three children... Earned letters in baseball and basketball at East Lyme (CT) High School... Graduated in 1987... Went to the University of Connecticut from 1988-1990 and helped the Huskies capture the Big East Championship in 1990

PROFESSIONAL CAREER:

- Selected in the 7th round by the New York Mets in 1990.
- Played eight seasons in the Major Leagues, the last four with the Toronto Blue Jays.
- 124 of his 144 games, and all 31 starts came as a Blue Jay, posting a career 20-14 record with a 4.48 ERA.
- In his best season made 20 of his 31 career starts in 2002 with Toronto, posting a 10-5 record with 4.33 ERA.

COACHING CAREER:

- Began his coaching career with the Blue Jays organization in 2009, working with the clubs' rehabbing pitchers.
- Was named the Pitching Coach at New Hampshire for 2011 and led a squad that won the Eastern League Championship.
- Made his debut at the Major League level in 2012 as the Blue Jays Bullpen Coach.
- Assumes the role of Pitching Coach in 2013.

PLAYING CAREER

Year Club & League	W-L	ERA	G	IP	H	R	ER	BB	SO
Minor Totals	67-65	3.77	399	1004.0	982	500	421	385	745
TORONTO TOTALS	19-14	4.32	124	308.2	320	160	148	121	179
MAJOR TOTALS	20-14	4.48	144	339.1	362	181	169	133	191

MANAGERIAL/COACHING CAREER

2009-10	Rehab Pitching Coach (Blue Jays)
2011	Pitching Coach, New Hampshire, Eastern League (Blue Jays)
2012	Bullpen Coach, Toronto Blue Jays
2013	Pitching Coach, Toronto Blue Jays

FIRST TRIP LUCKY

The Toronto Blue Jays became the 10th franchise in history to win the World Championship in its 1st trip to the fall classic. The Florida Marlins became the 11th franchise to accomplish the feat in 1997, Arizona Diamondbacks the 12th in 2001 and the Anaheim Angels in 2002.

1903	Boston Red Sox
1905	New York Giants
1906	Chicago White Sox
1914	Boston Braves
1919	Cincinnati Reds
1920	Cleveland Indians
1924	Washington Senators
1926	St. Louis Cardinals
1969	New York Mets
1992	**Toronto Blue Jays**
1997	Florida Marlins
2001	Arizona Diamondbacks
2002	Anaheim Angels

Blue Jays hitting coach, Chad Mottola at the amateur clinic in Toronto on January 5, 2013

New Toronto Bench Coach, DeMarlo Hale at the amateur clinic in Toronto

2013 TORONTO BLUE JAYS

JOSE BAUTISTA

2013 TORONTO BLUE JAYS 40-MAN ROSTER

MANAGER: John Gibbons (5)

COACHES: DeMarlo Hale (16) Bench, Pat Hentgen (41) Bullpen, Chad Mottola (39) Hitting, Dwayne Murphy (25) 1B, Luis Rivera (63) 3B, Pete Walker (40) Pitching

TRAINERS: George Poulis, Mike Frostad **MANAGER, TEAM TRAVEL: Mike Shaw**

STRENGTH AND CONDITIONING COACH: Bryan King **VICE PRESIDENT, COMMUNICATIONS: Jay Stenhouse**

NO.	PITCHERS (21)	B	T	HT.	WT.	BORN	BIRTHPLACE	RESIDENCE	2012 CLUB	W-L	ERA	G	GS	CG	SV	IP	H	R	ER	BB	SO	ML SER
56	BUEHRLE, Mark	L	L	6-2	195	03-23-79	St. Charles, MO	Lemont, IL	MIAMI (NL)	13-13	3.74	31	31	1	0	202.1	197	88	84	40	125	12.078
27	CECIL, Brett	R	L	6-1	216	07-02-86	Dunkirk, MD	Clearwater, FL	New Hampshire (East)	3-2	3.38	9	9	0	0	42.2	44	18	16	14	34	
									Las Vegas (PCL)	1-2	2.50	6	6	0	0	39.2	36	11	11	7	33	
									TORONTO (AL)	2-4	5.72	21	9	0	0	61.1	70	40	39	23	51	2.152
46	CRAWFORD, Evan	R	L	6-2	190	09-02-86	Prattville, AB	Auburn, AL	New Hampshire (East)	0-0	0.00	3	0	0	0	4.0	3	1	0	2	5	
									Las Vegas (PCL)	1-4	6.83	26	0	0	0	27.2	38	22	21	12	20	
									TORONTO (AL)	0-0	6.75	10	0	0	0	8.0	10	6	6	4	5	0.041
50	DELABAR, Steve	R	R	6-5	220	07-17-83	Fort Knox, KY	Elizabethtown, KY	Tacoma (PCL)	0-1	3.75	9	0	0	1	12.0	11	10	5	12	12	
									SEATTLE (AL)	2-1	4.17	34	0	0	0	36.2	23	17	17	11	46	
									TORONTO (AL)	2-2	3.38	27	0	0	0	29.1	23	12	11	15	46	1.015
43	DICKEY, R.A.	R	R	6-2	216	10-29-74	Nashville, TN	Nashville, TN	NEW YORK (NL)	20-6	2.73	34	33	5	0	233.2	192	78	71	54	230	7.007
4	DRABEK, Kyle	R	R	6-1	228	12-08-87	Victoria, TX	The Woodlands, TX	TORONTO (AL)	4-7	4.67	13	13	0	0	71.1	67	41	37	47	47	1.119
48	HAPP, J.A.	L	L	6-6	194	10-19-82	Peru, IL	Chicago, IL	HOUSTON (NL)	7-9	4.83	18	18	0	0	104.1	112	58	56	39	98	
									TORONTO (AL)	3-2	4.69	10	6	0	0	40.1	35	21	21	17	46	4.047
36	HUTCHISON, Drew	L	R	6-2	195	08-22-90	Lakeland, FL	Lakeland, FL	New Hampshire (East)	2-1	2.16	3	3	0	0	16.2	16	4	4	3	12	
									TORONTO (AL)	5-3	4.60	11	11	0	0	58.2	59	31	30	20	49	0.167
44	JANSSEN, Casey	R	R	6-3	205	09-17-81	Orange, CA	Manhattan Beach, CA	TORONTO (AL)	1-1	2.54	62	0	0	22	63.2	44	18	18	11	67	6.063
33	JEFFRESS, Jeremy	R	R	6-0	190	09-21-87	South Boston, VA	South Boston, VA	NW Arkansas (TL)	0-0	0.00	1	0	0	1	1.1	0	0	0	1	3	
									Omaha (PCL)	5-4	4.97	37	0	0	2	58.0	52	34	32	25	61	
									KANSAS CITY (AL)	0-0	6.75	13	0	0	0	13.1	19	14	10	13	13	0.145
64	JENKINS, CHAD	R	R	6-3	226	12-22-87	Chattanooga, TN	Canton, GA	New Hampshire (East)	5-9	4.96	20	20	0	0	114.1	145	67	63	31	57	
									TORONTO (AL)	1-3	4.50	13	3	0	0	32.0	32	16	16	11	16	0.060
55	JOHNSON, Josh	L	R	6-7	225	01-31-84	Minneapolis, MN	Miami, FL	MIAMI (NL)	8-14	3.81	31	31	0	0	191.1	180	84	81	65	165	7.026
49	LINCOLN, Brad	L	R	6-0	223	05-25-85	Lake Jackson, TX	Pearland, TX	Indianapolis (Int)	1-0	2.25	2	2	0	0	12.0	10	3	3	0	9	
									PITTSBURGH (NL)	4-2	2.73	28	5	0	1	59.1	51	19	18	14	60	
									TORONTO (AL)	1-0	5.65	24	0	0	0	28.2	29	18	18	10	28	1.143
62	LOUP, Aaron	L	L	6-0	208	12-19-87	Raceland, LA	Hahnville, LA	New Hampshire (East)	0-3	2.78	37	0	0	3	45.1	46	19	14	14	43	
									TORONTO (AL)	0-2	2.64	33	0	0	0	30.2	26	10	9	2	21	0.083
29	McGOWAN, Dustin	R	R	6-3	229	03-24-82	Savannah, GA	Tallahassee, FL	TORONTO (AL)	Did not pitch												6.113
23	MORROW, Brandon	R	R	6-3	197	07-26-84	Santa Rosa, CA	Scottsdale, AZ	Dunedin (FSL)	0-0	1.50	2	2	0	0	6.0	8	2	1	3	6	
									New Hampshire (East)	1-0	2.51	3	3	0	0	14.1	10	4	4	3	12	
									TORONTO (AL)	10-7	2.96	21	21	3	0	124.2	98	45	41	41	108	5.091
38	OLIVER, Darren	R	L	6-3	249	10-06-70	Kansas City, MO	Southlake, TX	TORONTO (AL)	3-4	2.06	62	0	0	2	56.2	43	13	13	15	52	17.127
47	PEREZ, Luis	L	L	6-0	210	01-20-85	Guayubin Monte Cr., DR	Guayubin Monte Cr., DR	TORONTO (AL)	2-2	3.43	35	0	0	0	42.0	38	16	16	16	39	1.119
32	ROGERS, Esmil	R	R	6-3	205	08-14-85	Santo Domingo, DR	San Pedro de Marc., DR	COLORADO (NL)	0-2	8.06	23	0	0	0	25.2	36	23	23	18	29	
									CLEVELAND (AL)	3-1	3.06	44	0	0	0	53.0	47	19	18	12	54	2.135
24	ROMERO, Ricky	R	L	6-0	225	11-06-84	Los Angeles, CA	Downey, CA	TORONTO (AL)	9-14	5.77	32	32	1	0	181.0	198	122	116	105	124	4.000
21	SANTOS, Sergio	R	R	6-3	240	07-04-83	Los Angeles, CA	Yorba Linda, CA	TORONTO (AL)	0-1	9.00	6	0	0	2	5.0	6	5	5	4	4	3.000

NO.	CATCHERS (4)	B	T	HT.	WT.	BORN	BIRTHPLACE	RESIDENCE	2012 CLUB	AVG.	G	AB	R	H	2B	3B	HR	RBI	BB	SO	SB	ML SER
9	ARENCIBIA, J.P.	R	R	6-0	199	01-05-86	Miami, FL	Miami, FL	Dunedin (FSL)	.200	1	5	0	1	1	0	0	0	1	0	0	
									TORONTO (AL)	.233	102	347	45	81	16	0	18	56	18	108	1	2.059
22	BLANCO, Henry	R	R	5-11	224	08-29-71	Caracas, VZ	Miranda, VZ	ARIZONA (NL)	.188	21	64	6	12	3	0	1	7	3	18	1	14.136
6	JIMENEZ, A.J.	R	R	6-0	201	05-01-90	San Juan, PR	Bayamon, PR	New Hampshire (East)	.257	27	105	14	27	4	1	2	10	5	14	2	0.000
30	THOLE, Josh	L	R	6-1	190	10-28-86	Breese, IL	Glendale, AZ	Buffalo (Int)	.200	2	5	0	1	0	0	0	0	0	0	0	
									NEW YORK (NL)	.234	104	321	24	75	15	0	1	21	27	50	0	2.142

NO.	INFIELDERS (9)	B	T	HT.	WT.	BORN	BIRTHPLACE	RESIDENCE	2012 CLUB	AVG.	G	AB	R	H	2B	3B	HR	RBI	BB	SO	SB	ML SER
1	BONIFACIO, Emilio	S	R	5-10	195	04-23-85	Santo Domingo, DR	Santo Domingo, DR	Jupiter (FSL)	.167	9	30	6	5	1	0	0	4	6	9	3	
									MIAMI (NL)	.258	64	244	30	63	3	4	1	11	25	52	30	4.066
30	COOPER, David	L	L	6-0	201	02-12-87	Stockton, CA	Stockton, CA	Las Vegas (PCL)	.314	68	261	45	82	27	1	10	52	37	34	0	
									TORONTO (AL)	.300	45	140	16	42	11	0	4	11	4	22	0	0.136
35	DeROSA, Mark	R	R	6-1	205	02-26-75	Passaic, NJ	Suwanee, GA	Potomac (Car)	.091	4	11	1	1	0	0	0	2	0	3	0	
									WASHINGTON (NL)	.188	48	85	13	16	5	0	0	6	14	18	1	12.061
10	ENCARNACION, Edwin	R	R	6-2	228	01-07-83	La Romana, DR	La Romana, DR	TORONTO (AL)	.280	151	542	93	152	24	0	42	110	84	94	13	7.085
2	GOINS, Ryan	L	R	5-10	170	02-13-88	Round Rock, TX	Round Rock, TX	New Hampshire (East)	.289	136	546	66	158	33	4	7	61	47	78	15	0.000
3	IZTURIS, Maicer	S	R	5-8	155	09-12-80	Berquisimeto, VZ	Berquisimeto, VZ	LOS ANGELES (AL)	.256	100	289	35	74	11	0	2	20	25	38	17	8.038
13	LAWRIE, Brett	R	R	6-0	223	01-18-90	Langley, BC	Peoria, AZ	Blue Jays (GCL)	.000	1	1	0	0	0	0	0	0	0	0	0	
									Dunedin (FSL)	.000	1	3	0	0	0	0	0	0	0	1	0	
									TORONTO (AL)	.273	125	494	73	135	26	3	11	48	33	86	13	1.055
26	LIND, Adam	L	L	6-2	222	07-17-83	Muncie, IN	Palm Harbor, FL	New Hampshire (East)	.545	3	11	2	6	0	0	1	1	2	4	0	
									Las Vegas (PCL)	.392	32	125	24	49	10	0	8	29	15	26	1	
									TORONTO (AL)	.255	93	321	28	82	14	2	11	45	29	61	0	5.058
7	REYES, Jose	S	R	6-0	160	06-11-83	Santiago, DR	Santiago, DR	MIAMI (NL)	.287	160	642	86	184	37	12	11	57	63	56	40	9.111

NO.	OUTFIELDERS (6)	B	T	HT.	WT.	BORN	BIRTHPLACE	RESIDENCE	2012 CLUB	AVG.	G	AB	R	H	2B	3B	HR	RBI	BB	SO	SB	ML SER
19	BAUTISTA, Jose	R	R	6-0	192	10-19-80	Santo Domingo, DR	Santo Domingo, DR	Blue Jays (GCL)	.000	1	3	0	0	0	0	0	0	1	1	0	
									New Hampshire (East)	.500	1	4	2	2	0	0	2	5	1	1	0	
									TORONTO (AL)	.241	92	332	64	80	14	0	27	65	59	63	5	7.165
53	CABRERA, Melky	S	L	6-0	168	08-11-84	Bajos de Haina, DR	Bajos de Haina, DR	SAN FRANCISCO (NL)	.346	113	459	84	159	25	10	11	60	36	63	13	6.148
11	DAVIS, Rajai	R	R	5-9	195	10-19-80	Norwich, CT	East Lyme, CT	TORONTO (AL)	.257	142	447	64	115	24	3	8	43	29	102	46	5.167
8	GOSE, Anthony	L	L	6-1	195	08-10-90	Bellflower, CA	Bellflower, CA	Las Vegas (PCL)	.286	102	420	87	120	21	10	5	43	49	101	34	
									TORONTO (AL)	.223	56	166	25	37	7	3	1	11	17	59	15	0.079
28	RASMUS, Colby	L	L	6-2	190	08-11-86	Columbus, GA	Phenix City, AL	TORONTO (AL)	.223	151	565	75	126	21	5	23	75	47	149	4	4.000
14	SIERRA, Moises	R	R	6-0	229	09-24-88	Santo Domingo, DR	Santo Domingo, DR	Las Vegas (PCL)	.289	100	377	62	109	16	1	17	63	39	86	7	
									TORONTO (AL)	.224	49	147	14	33	4	0	6	15	8	44	1	0.065

NON-ROSTER PLAYERS

NO.	PITCHERS (12)	B	T	HT.	WT.	BORN	BIRTHPLACE	RESIDENCE	2012 CLUB	W-L	ERA	G	GS	CG	SV	IP	H	R	ER	BB	SO	ML SER
60	BECK, Chad	R	R	6-4	250	01-17-85	Jasper, TX	Woodville, TX	Las Vegas (PCL)	2-0	1.31	43	0	0	18	48.0	39	7	7	13	24	
									TORONTO (AL)	0-0	6.32	14	0	0	0	15.2	21	12	11	5	9	0.072
54	BUSH, David	R	R	6-2	209	11-09-79	Pittsburgh, PA	Bridgton, ME	Lehigh Valley (Int)	4-3	3.16	11	11	1	0	62.2	69	27	22	8	37	6.150
52	GERMANO, Justin	R	R	6-3	200	08-06-82	Pasadena, CA	San Marcos, CA	Pawtucket (Int)	9-4	2.40	17	16	1	0	105.0	82	33	28	13	72	
									BOSTON (AL)	0-0	0.00	1	0	0	0	5.2	5	0	0	2	7	
									CHICAGO (NL)	2-10	6.75	13	12	0	0	64.0	81	52	48	19	45	2.130
51	HINSHAW, Alex	L	L	6-4	173	10-31-82	Pomona, CA	Beaverton, OR	Tucson (PCL)	0-0	3.72	14	0	0	0	19.1	14	8	8	10	18	
									SAN DIEGO (NL)	1-1	4.50	31	0	7	0	28.0	23	14	14	20	36	
									CHICAGO (NL)	0-0	135.00	2	0	0	0	0.1	4	5	5	1	0	1.109
75	HOTTOVY, Tommy	L	L	6-1	195	07-09-81	Kansas City, MO	Kansas City, MO	Omaha (PCL)	2-2	2.52	41	0	0	7	50.0	42	18	14	16	61	
									KANSAS CITY (AL)	0-0	2.89	9	0	0	0	9.1	11	3	3	5	6	0.062

NO.	PITCHERS – cont'd	B	T	HT.	WT.	BORN	BIRTHPLACE	RESIDENCE	2012 CLUB	W-L	ERA	G	GS	CG	SV	IP	H	R	ER	BB	SO	ML SER
71	NOLIN, Sean	L	L	6-4	230	12-26-89	Seaford, NY	Seaford, NY	Dunedin (FSL)	9-0	2.19	17	15	0	0	86.1	72	26	21	21	90	
									New Hampshire (East)	1-0	1.20	3	3	0	0	15.0	9	3	2	6	18	0.000
34	ORTIZ, Ramon	R	R	6-0	174	05-23-73	Cotui, DR	Cotui, DR	Scranton/WB (Int)	13-6	3.45	27	27	1	0	169.1	167	75	65	37	104	8.115
57	PEREZ, Juan	R	L	6-0	170	09-03-78	Villa Rivas, DR	San Fran. de Macoris, DR	Nashville (PCL)	4-2	3.60	38	0	0	0	40.0	32	17	16	20	54	
									MILWAUKEE (NL)	0-1	5.14	10	0	0	0	7.0	6	4	4	8	10	0.160
74	STILSON, John	R	R	6-3	207	07-28-90	Texarkana, TX	Texarkana, TX	Dunedin (FSL)	3-0	2.82	13	13	0	0	54.1	56	22	17	19	47	
									New Hampshire (East)	2-4	5.04	17	9	0	1	50.0	54	33	28	23	44	0.000
77	STOREY, Mickey	R	R	6-1	185	03-16-86	Fort Lauderdale, FL	West Palm Beach, FL	Oklahoma City (PCL)	7-4	3.05	38	2	0	2	65.0	62	24	22	14	72	
									HOUSTON (NL)	0-1	3.86	26	0	0	0	30.1	27	14	13	10	34	0.062
66	THOMPSON, Richard	R	R	6-1	210	07-01-84	Hornsby, NSW, Australia	Hot Springs, AK	Sacramento (PCL)	4-2	3.34	46	0	0	3	62.0	46	24	23	23	58	
									LOS ANGELES (AL)	0-1	15.53	2	0	0	0	2.1	5	4	4	1	3	
									OAKLAND (AL)	0-0	0.00	1	0	0	0	0.2	1	0	0	0	0	2.071
45	VARGAS, Claudio	R	R	6-4	235	06-19-78	Valverde Mao, DR	Santiago, DR	Nashville (PCL)	7-1	3.69	20	20	0	0	109.2	48	45	11	32	84	
									Laguna (Mex)	0-1	4.22	11	0	0	5	10.2	11	5	5	2	9	6.093
37	WAGNER, Neil	R	R	6-0	215	01-01-84	Minneapolis, MN	Edan Prairie, MN	Sacramento (PCL)	1-1	5.49	15	0	0	1	19.2	20	13	12	6	24	
									Tucson (PCL)	3-1	5.44	31	0	0	0	43.0	57	30	26	17	32	0.034

NO.	CATCHERS (3)	B	T	HT.	WT.	BORN	BIRTHPLACE	RESIDENCE	2012 CLUB	AVG.	G	AB	R	H	2B	3B	HR	RBI	BB	SO	SB	ML SER
76	MURPHY, Jack	S	R	6-4	235	04-06-88	Sarasota, FL	Sarasota, FL	Dunedin (FSL)	.223	86	278	31	62	13	1	10	51	35	67	0	
									New Hampshire (East)	.333	8	24	5	8	1	0	2	4	3	7	0	0.000
15	NICKEAS, Mike	R	R	6-0	205	02-13-83	Vancouver, BC	Sandy Springs, GA	Buffalo (Int)	.364	22	66	10	24	6	0	1	6	6	9	0	
									NEW YORK (NL)	.174	47	109	8	19	3	0	1	13	8	27	0	1.081
69	OCHINKO, Sean	R	R	5-10	205	10-21-87	Parkland, FL	Baton Rouge, LA	Dunedin (FSL)	.306	28	108	21	33	12	0	1	13	10	16	0	
									New Hampshire (East)	.264	59	216	26	57	11	1	8	29	8	40	0	0.000

NO.	INFIELDERS (8)	B	T	HT.	WT.	BORN	BIRTHPLACE	RESIDENCE	2012 CLUB	AVG.	G	AB	R	H	2B	3B	HR	RBI	BB	SO	SB	ML SER
58	JIMENEZ, Luis	L	L	6-3	275	05-07-82	Bobare, Edo. Lara, VZ	Barquisimeto, VZ	Tacoma (PCL)	3.10	125	471	64	146	32	2	20	81	64	97	3	
									SEATTLE (AL)	0.59	7	17	0	1	0	0	1	0	1	4	0	0.030
70	LAROCHE, Andy	R	R	6-0	205	09-13-83	Fort Scott, KC	Steamboat Springs, CO	Columbus (Int)	2.34	46	145	18	34	1	0	5	16	20	28	0	
									Pawtucket (Int)	2.64	50	182	23	48	3	0	7	25	18	24	1	3.096
72	LOEWEN, Adam	L	L	6-6	245	04-09-84	Vancouver, BC	Surrey, BC	St. Lucie (FSL)	.286	4	14	2	4	1	0	0	1	3	2	0	
									Buffalo (Int)	.227	59	207	32	47	10	0	8	26	30	55	4	2.135
18	McCOY, Mike	R	R	5-9	171	04-02-81	San Diego, CA	San Diego, CA	Las Vegas (PCL)	.263	85	278	46	73	13	1	3	31	58	51	21	
									TORONTO (AL)	.173	32	52	10	9	1	0	1	7	4	6	2	2.010
59	NEGRYCH, Jim	L	R	5-10	180	03-02-85	Buffalo, NY	Lancaster, NY	Harrisburg (East)	.600	3	5	0	3	2	0	0	3	3	0	0	
									Syracuse (Int)	.264	91	276	31	73	9	1	8	39	40	41	2	0.000
68	SCHIMPF, Ryan	L	R	5-9	181	04-11-88	Covington, LA	Covington, LA	Dunedin (FSL)	.266	96	361	59	96	29	3	14	61	48	89	4	
									New Hampshire (East)	.279	33	111	21	31	8	0	8	15	23	32	3	0.000
67	VELEZ, Eugenio	S	R	6-1	171	05-16-82	San Padro de Mac., DR	San Padro de Mac., DR	Memphis (PCL)	.280	136	457	70	128	34	5	11	58	51	99	37	2.111
73	ZAWADZKI, Lance	S	R	5-11	185	05-26-85	Framingham, MA	San Antonio, TX	Gwinnett (Int)	.231	48	147	12	34	5	1	3	17	7	31	3	
									Albuquerque (PCL)	.000	5	13	1	0	0	0	0	0	1	4	0	
									Memphis (PCL)	.281	8	32	2	9	1	1	0	3	1	6	1	0.040

NO.	OUTFIELDERS (2)	B	T	HT.	WT.	BORN	BIRTHPLACE	RESIDENCE	2012 CLUB	AVG.	G	AB	R	H	2B	3B	HR	RBI	BB	SO	SB	ML SER
17	LANGERHANS, Ryan	L	L	6-3	195	02-20-80	San Antonio, TX	Leander, TX	Salt Lake (PCL)	.250	96	336	59	84	21	6	11	54	63	113	6	
									LOS ANGELES (AL)	.000	2	1	0	0	0	0	0	0	0	1	0	5.136
20	NANITA, Ricardo	L	L	6-1	195	06-12-81	Santo Domingo, DR	Santo Domingo, DR	Las Vegas (PCL)	.306	92	333	49	102	17	0	12	62	23	39	3	0.000

2013 TORONTO BLUE JAYS ROSTER

BY POSITION, NUMERICAL & ALPHABETICAL AS OF FEBRUARY 5, 2013

BY POSITION

PITCHERS - 21 (+13 NR)

60 BECK, Chad (NR)
56 BUEHRLE, Mark
54 BUSH, David (NR)
27 CECIL, Brett
46 CRAWFORD, Evan
50 DELABAR, Steve
43 DICKEY, R.A.
4 DRABEK, Kyle
52 GERMANO, Justin: RHP (NR)
48 HAPP, J.A.
51 HINSHAW, Alex (NR)
75 HOTTOVY, Tommy (NR)
36 HUTCHISON, Drew
44 JANSSEN, Casey
33 JEFFRESS, Jeremy
64 JENKINS, Chad
55 JOHNSON, Josh
49 LINCOLN, Brad
62 LOUP, Aaron
29 McGOWAN, Dustin
23 MORROW, Brandon
71 NOLIN, Sean (NR)
38 OLIVER, Darren
34 ORTIZ, Ramon (NR)
57 PEREZ, Juan (NR)
47 PEREZ, Luis
32 ROGERS, Esmil
24 ROMERO, Ricky
21 SANTOS, Sergio
74 STILSON, John (NR)
77 STOREY, Mickey (NR)
66 THOMPSON, Richard (NR)
45 VARGAS, Claudio (NR)
37 WAGNER, Neil (NR)

CATCHERS - 4 (+3 NR)

9 ARENCIBIA, J.P.
22 BLANCO, Henry
6 JIMENEZ, A.J.
76 MURPHY, Jack (NR)
15 NICKEAS, Mike (NR)
69 OCHINKO, Sean (NR)
30 THOLE, Josh

INFIELDERS - 9 (+8 NR)

1 BONIFACIO, Emilio
31 COOPER, David
35 DeROSA, Mark
10 ENCARNACION, Edwin
2 GOINS, Ryan
3 IZTURIS, Maicer
58 JIMENEZ, Luis (NR)
70 LaROCHE, Andy (NR)
13 LAWRIE, Brett
26 LIND, Adam
72 LOEWEN, Adam (NR)
18 McCOY, Mike (NR)
59 NEGRYCH, Jim (NR)
7 REYES, Jose
68 SCHIMPF, Ryan (NR)
67 VELEZ, Eugenio (NR)
73 ZAWADZKI, Lance (NR)

OUTFIELDERS - 6 (+2 NR)

19 BAUTISTA, Jose
53 CABRERA, Melky
11 DAVIS Rajai
8 GOSE, Anthony
17 LANGERHANS, Ryan (NR)
20 NANITA, Ricardo (NR)
28 RASMUS, Colby
14 SIERRA, Moises

MANAGER

5 GIBBONS, John

COACHES

16 HALE, DeMarlo: Bench
41 HENTGEN, Pat: Bullpen
39 MOTTOLA, Chad: Hitting
25 MURPHY, Dwayne: 1B
63 RIVERA, Luis: 3B
40 WALKER, Pete: Pitching

BULLPEN CATCHER - BP PITCHER

61 ANDREOPOULOS, Alex
65 FIGUEROA, Jesus

NUMERICAL

1 BONIFACIO, Emilio: IF
2 GOINS, Ryan: IF
3 IZTURIS, Maicer: IF
4 DRABEK, Kyle: RHP
5 GIBBONS, John: MGR
6 JIMENEZ, A.J.: C
7 REYES, Jose: IF
8 GOSE, Anthony: OF
9 ARENCIBIA, J.P.: C
10 ENCARNACION, Edwin: IF
11 DAVIS Rajai: OF
12 RETIRED
13 LAWRIE, Brett: IF
14 SIERRA, Moises: OF
15 NICKEAS, Mike: C (NR)
16 HALE, DeMarlo: Bench
17 LANGERHANS, Ryan: OF (NR)
18 McCOY, Mike: IF (NR)
19 BAUTISTA, Jose: OF
20 NANITA, Ricardo: OF (NR)
21 SANTOS, Sergio: RHP
22 BLANCO, Henry: C
23 MORROW, Brandon: RHP
24 ROMERO, Ricky: LHP
25 MURPHY, Dwayne: 1B
26 LIND, Adam: IF
27 CECIL, Brett: LHP
28 RASMUS, Colby: OF
29 McGOWAN, Dustin: RHP
30 THOLE, Josh: C
31 COOPER, David: IF
32 ROGERS, Esmil: RHP
33 JEFFRESS, Jeremy: RHP
34 ORTIZ, Ramon: RHP (NR)
35 DeROSA, Mark: INF
36 HUTCHISON, Drew: RHP
37 WAGNER, Neil: RHP (NR)
38 OLIVER, Darren, LHP
39 MOTTOLA, Chad: Hitting
40 WALKER, Pete: Pitching
41 HENTGEN, Pat: Bullpen
42 RETIRED
43 DICKEY, R.A.: RHP
44 JANSSEN, Casey: RHP
45 VARGAS, Claudio: RHP (NR)
46 CRAWFORD, Evan: LHP
47 PEREZ, Luis: LHP
48 HAPP, J.A.: LHP
49 LINCOLN, Brad: RHP
50 DELABAR, Steve: RHP
51 HINSHAW, Alex: LHP (NR)
52 GERMANO, Justin: RHP (NR)
53 CABRERA, Melky: OF
54 BUSH, David: RHP (NR)
55 JOHNSON, Josh: RHP
56 BUEHRLE, Mark: LHP
57 PEREZ, Juan: LHP (NR)
58 JIMENEZ, Luis: 1B/DH (NR)
59 NEGRYCH, Jim: IF (NR)
60 BECK, Chad: RHP (NR)
61 ANDREOPOULOS, Alex
62 LOUP, Aaron, LHP
63 RIVERA, Luis: 3B
64 JENKINS, Chad: RHP
65 FIGUEROA, Jesus
66 THOMPSON, Richard: RHP (NR)
67 VELEZ, Eugenio: IF (NR)
68 SCHIMPF, Ryan: IF (NR)
69 OCHINKO, Sean: C (NR)
70 LaROCHE, Andy: IF (NR)
71 NOLIN, Sean: LHP (NR)
72 LOEWEN, Adam: IF (NR)
73 ZAWADZKI, Lance: IF (NR)
74 STILSON, John: RHP (NR)
75 HOTTOVY, Tommy: LHP (NR)
76 MURPHY, Jack: C (NR)
77 STOREY, Mickey: RHP (NR)

ALPHABETICAL

9 ARENCIBIA, J.P.: C
19 BAUTISTA, Jose: OF
60 BECK, Chad: RHP (NR)
22 BLANCO, Henry: C
1 BONIFACIO, Emilio: IF
56 BUEHRLE, Mark: LHP
54 BUSH, David: RHP (NR)
53 CABRERA, Melky: OF
27 CECIL, Brett: LHP
31 COOPER, David: IF
46 CRAWFORD, Evan: LHP
11 DAVIS Rajai: OF
50 DELABAR, Steve: RHP
35 DeROSA, Mark: INF
43 DICKEY, R.A.: RHP
4 DRABEK, Kyle: RHP
10 ENCARNACION, Edwin: IF
52 GERMANO, Justin: RHP (NR)
2 GOINS, Ryan: IF
8 GOSE, Anthony: OF
48 HAPP, J.A.: LHP
51 HINSHAW, Alex: LHP (NR)
75 HOTTOVY, Tommy: LHP (NR)
36 HUTCHISON, Drew: RHP
3 IZTURIS, Maicer: IF
44 JANSSEN, Casey: RHP
33 JEFFRESS, Jeremy: RHP
64 JENKINS, Chad: RHP
6 JIMENEZ, A.J.: C
58 JIMENEZ, Luis: 1B/DH (NR)
55 JOHNSON, Josh: RHP
17 LANGERHANS, Ryan: OF (NR)
70 LaROCHE, Andy: IF (NR)
13 LAWRIE, Brett: IF
49 LINCOLN, Brad: RHP
26 LIND, Adam: IF
72 LOEWEN, Adam: IF (NR)
62 LOUP, Aaron, LHP
18 McCOY, Mike: IF (NR)
29 McGOWAN, Dustin: RHP
23 MORROW, Brandon: RHP
76 MURPHY, Jack: C (NR)
20 NANITA, Ricardo: OF (NR)
59 NEGRYCH, Jim: IF (NR)
15 NICKEAS, Mike: C (NR)
71 NOLIN, Sean: LHP (NR)
69 OCHINKO, Sean: C (NR)
38 OLIVER, Darren: LHP
34 ORTIZ, Ramon: RHP (NR)
57 PEREZ, Juan: LHP (NR)
47 PEREZ, Luis: LHP
28 RASMUS, Colby: OF
7 REYES, Jose: IF
32 ROGERS, Esmil: RHP
24 ROMERO, Ricky: LHP
21 SANTOS, Sergio: RHP
68 SCHIMPF, Ryan: IF (NR)
14 SIERRA, Moises: OF
74 STILSON, John: RHP (NR)
77 STOREY, Mickey: RHP (NR)
30 THOLE, Josh: C
66 THOMPSON, Richard: RHP (NR)
45 VARGAS, Claudio: RHP (NR)
67 VELEZ, Eugenio: IF (NR)
37 WAGNER, Neil: RHP (NR)
73 ZAWADZKI, Lance: IF (NR)

(NR) Non Roster Invitee
(DL) 15 - Day Disabled List

HOW THE 2013 BLUE JAYS WERE BUILT (40-MAN ROSTER)

TRADES (19)

Jose Bautista – from the Pittsburgh Pirates in exchange for a player to be named later (C Robinzon Diaz) on Aug. 25, 2008

Emilio Bonifacio – from the Miami Marlins along with RHP Josh Johnson, LHP Mark Buehrle, SS Jose Reyes, C John Buck and cash considerations in exchange for SS Yunel Escobar, SS Adeiny Hechavarria, RHP Henderson Alvarez, C Jeff Mathis, LHP Justin Nicolino, RHP Anthony Desclafani and OF Jake Marisnick on Nov. 19, 2012

Mark Buehrle – from the Miami Marlins along with RHP Josh Johnson, SS Jose Reyes, IF Emilio Bonifacio, C John Buck and cash considerations in exchange for SS Yunel Escobar, SS Adeiny Hechavarria, RHP Henderson Alvarez, C Jeff Mathis, LHP Justin Nicolino, RHP Anthony Desclafani and OF Jake Marisnick on Nov. 19, 2012

Rajai Davis – from the Oakland A's in exchange for RHP Trystan Magnuson and RHP Daniel Farquhar on Nov. 17, 2010

Steve Delabar – from the Seattle Mariners in exchange for OF Eric Thames on July 30, 2012

R.A. Dickey – from the New York Mets along with C Josh Thole and C Mike Nickeas in exchange for C John Buck, C Travis d'Arnaud, RHP Noah Syndergaard and OF Wuilmer Beccera on Dec. 17, 2012

Kyle Drabek – from the Philadelphia Phillies along with OF Michael Taylor & C Travis d'Arnaud in exchange for RHP Roy Halladay & cash considerations on Dec. 16, 2009

Anthony Gose – from the Houston Astros in exchange for IF Brett Wallace on July 29, 2010

J.A. Happ – from the Houston Astros along with RHP Brandon Lyon and J.A. Happ in exchange for OF Ben Francisco, RHP Francisco Cordero, RHP Asher Wojciechowski, RHP Joe Musgrove, LHP David Rollins, C Carlos Perez and a player to be named later (RHP Kevin Comer) on July 20, 2012

Jeremy Jeffress – from the Kansas City Royals in exchange for cash considerations on Nov. 8, 2012

Josh Johnson – from the Miami Marlins along with LHP Mark Buehrle, SS Jose Reyes, IF Emilio Bonifacio, C John Buck and cash considerations in exchange for SS Yunel Escobar, SS Adeiny Hechavarria, RHP Henderson Alvarez, C Jeff Mathis, LHP Justin Nicolino, RHP Anthony Desclafani and OF Jake Marisnick on Nov. 19, 2012

Brett Lawrie – from the Milwaukee Brewers in exchange for RHP Shaun Marcum Dec. 6, 2010

Brad Lincoln – from the Pittsburgh Pirates in exchange for OF Travis Snider on July 30, 2012

Brandon Morrow – from the Seattle Mariners in exchange for RHP Brandon League & OF Johermyn Chavez on Dec. 23, 2009

Colby Rasmus – from the St. Louis Cardinals along with LHP Trever Miller, LHP Brian Tallet and RHP P.J. Walters in exchange for RHP Octavio Dotel, LHP Marc Rzepczynski, OF Corey Patterson and RHP Edwin Jackson July 27, 2011

Jose Reyes – from the Miami Marlins along with LHP Mark Buehrle, RHP Josh Johnson, IF Emilio Bonifacio, C John Buck and cash considerations in exchange for SS Yunel Escobar, SS Adeiny Hechavarria, RHP Henderson Alvarez, C Jeff Mathis, LHP Justin Nicolino, RHP Anthony Desclafani and OF Jake Marisnick on Nov. 19, 2012

Esmil Rogers – from the Cleveland Indians in exchange for C/IF Yan Gomes and IF Mike Aviles on Nov. 3, 2012

Sergio Santos – from the Chicago White Sox in exchange for RHP Nestor Molina on Dec. 6, 2011

Josh Thole – from the New York Mets along with RHP R.A. Dickey and C Mike Nickeas in exchange for C John Buck, C Travis d'Arnaud, RHP Noah Syndergaard and OF Wuilmer Beccera on Dec. 17, 2012

FREE AGENTS (6)

Henry Blanco – signed on Jan. 11, 2013

Melky Cabrera – signed on Nov. 19, 2012

Mark DeRosa – signed on Jan. 22, 2013

Edwin Encarnacion – signed on Dec. 16, 2010

Maicer Izturis – signed on Nov. 8, 2012

Darren Oliver – signed on Jan. 9, 2012

FIRST-YEAR PLAYER DRAFT (13)

J.P. Arencibia – 1st round (21 overall) in 2007

Brett Cecil – 1st round (supplemental, 38 overall) in 2007

David Cooper – 1st round (17 overall) in 2008

Evan Crawford – 8th round in 2008

Ryan Goins – 4th round in 2009

Drew Hutchison – 15th round in 2009

Casey Janssen – 4th round in 2004

Chad Jenkins – 1st round (20 overall) in 2009

A.J. Jimenez – 9th round in 2008

Adam Lind – 3rd round in 2004

Aaron Loup – 9th round in 2009

Dustin McGowan – 1st round (supplemental, 33 overall) in 2000

Ricky Romero – 1st round (6 overall) in 2005

NON-DRAFTED FREE AGENTS (2)

Luis Perez – signed on July 30, 2003

Moises Sierra – signed on Dec. 20, 2005

BIRTHDAYS (40-Man Roster/Manager/Coaches)

JANUARY

3 – Luis Rivera - Coach (49)
5 – J.P. Arencibia (27)
7 – Edwin Encarnacion (30)
18 – Brett Lawrie (23)
20 – Luis Perez (28)
31 – Josh Johnson (29)

FEBRUARY

12 – David Cooper (26)
13 – Ryan Goins (25)
26 – Mark DeRosa (38)

MARCH

18 – Dwayne Murphy - Coach (58)
23 – Mark Buehrle (34)
24 – Dustin McGowan (31)

APRIL

8 – Pete Walker - Coach (44)
23 – Emilio Bonifacio (28)

MAY

1 – A.J. Jimenez (23)
25 – Brad Lincoln (28)

JUNE

8 – John Gibbons - MGR (51)
11 – Jose Reyes (30)

JULY

2 – Brett Cecil (27)
4 – Sergio Santos (30)
16 – DeMarlo Hale - Coach (52)
17 – Steve Delabar (30)
17 – Adam Lind (30)
26 – Brandon Morrow (29)

AUGUST

10 – Anthony Gose (23)
11 – Colby Rasmus (27)
11 – Melky Cabrera (29)
14 – Esmil Rogers (28)
22 – Drew Hutchison (23)
29 – Henry Blanco (42)

SEPTEMBER

2 – Evan Crawford (27)
12 – Maicer Izturis (33)
17 – Casey Janssen (31)
21 – Jeremy Jeffress (26)
24 – Moises Sierra (24)

OCTOBER

6 – Darren Oliver (42)
15 – Chad Mottola - Coach (42)
19 – Rajai Davis (33)
19 – J.A. Happ (31)
19 – Jose Bautista (33)
89 – Josh Thole (27)
29 – R.A. Dickey (39)

NOVEMBER

6 – Ricky Romero (29)
13 – Pat Hentgen - Coach (45)

DECEMBER

8 – Kyle Drabek (26)
19 – Aaron Loup (26)
22 – Chad Jenkins (26)

ARENCIBIA, *J.P.*

Birthdate . . . . January 5, 1986
Opening Day Age 27
Birthplace. . . . . Miami, FL
Residence. . . . . Nashville, TN
Bats/Throws . . . . R/R
Height/Weight 6-0/199
Contract Status . . . . signed thru 2013
M.L. Service 2.059

9

CATCHER

PERSONAL:

Jonathan Paul Arencibia... Single... Hit .330 over his college career at University of Tennessee, cementing himself prominently in the school's record books... Ranks 3rd in UT history in total bases (381), 4th in RBIs (165), tied for 5th in home runs (33), tied for 6th in doubles (48), 7th in hits (230) and 9th in at-bats (690)... Tied Alex Rodriguez's Westminster Christian High career record for home runs with 17 in 2004... Participated in the Blue Jays Winter Tour in 2011, 2012 and 2013.

LAST SEASON:

- Finished with 18 home runs in his 2nd full season and now has 42 as a catcher ranking 4th on the all-time Blue Jays list for catchers.
- Was placed on the disabled list on July 26 after being hit on the right hand by a foul ball vs. OAK on the 25th...Suffered a non-displaced fracture and did not return until Sept. 7.
- Batted .242 with 16 home runs and 50 RBI in 81 games prior to the injury and .197 with two home runs and six RBI in 21 games following...In his final 10 games did bat .379 with two home runs and six RBI.
- Finished T-3rd among AL catchers with 52 RBI and 5th with 17 home runs.
- Hit a game-winning home run on Opening Day at CLE in the 16th inning...Was the second year in a row he has homered on Opening Day and the 3rd year in a row he has homered in his first game...Only Jack Hannahan currently has a longer streak at four years.
- Had his best month in May posting a .278 average with eight home runs and 19 RBI... The eight home runs tied for the most by a TOR catcher in any month (Ernie Whitt hit 8-HR in Sept/1987).
- In 17 July games batted .321 with six home runs and 13 RBI.
- Became the first Blue Jays catcher to win AL Player-of-the-Week honours (May 14-20) batting .360 with four home runs and 10 RBI.
- Sept. 24 at BAL hit his 2nd career grand slam off Jake Arrieta...May 18 vs. NYM had two home runs and a career high six RBI...Had three multi-home run games and now has six in his career.
- With runners in scoring position batted .295 with eight home runs and 44 RBI in just 78 at-bats.
- Threw out 18.5 pct of potential base stealers and had a catchers ERA of 4.76.

J.P. ARENCIBIA

Bold – career high

Year	Club & League	AVG	G	AB	R	H	2B	3B	HR	RBI	SH-SF	HP	BB-IBB	SO	SB-CS	SLG	OBP	OPS
2007	Auburn (NYP)	.254	63	228	31	58	17	1	3	25	0-2	5	14-1	56	0-0	.377	.309	.686
2008	Dunedin (FSL)	.315	59	248	38	78	22	0	13	62	0-2	1	11-2	46	0-0	.560	.344	.904
	New Hampshire (East)	.282	67	262	32	74	14	0	14	43	0-4	2	7-0	55	0-0	.496	.302	.798
2009	Las Vegas (PCL)	.236	116	466	67	110	32	1	21	75	0-2	6	26-0	114	0-1	.444	.284	.728
2010	Las Vegas (PCL)	.301	104	412	76	124	36	1	32	85	0-6	3	38-1	85	0-0	.626	.359	.986
	TORONTO (AL)	.143	11	35	3	5	1	0	2	4	0-0	0	2-0	11	0-0	.343	.189	.532
2011	TORONTO (AL)	.219	**129**	443	**47**	**97**	**20**	**4**	**23**	**78**	0-3	4	**36**-3	**133**	**1**-1	.438	.282	.720
2012	Dunedin (FSL)	.200	1	5	0	1	1	0	0	0	0-0	0	1-0	0	0-0	.400	.333	.733
	TORONTO (AL)	.233	102	347	45	81	16	0	18	56	1-3	3	18-1	108	**1**-0	.435	.275	.710
Minor Totals		.275	410	1621	244	445	122	3	83	290	0-16	17	97-4	366	0-1	.507	.319	.826
MAJOR TOTALS		.222	242	825	95	183	37	4	43	138	1-6	7	56-4	252	2-1	.433	.275	.708

HOME RUN BREAKDOWN

			ONE GAME									
Total	H	A	2	3	4	GS	LO	XN	IP	PH	RHP	LHP
43	24	19	6	0	0	2	0	1	0	0	28	15

ALL-TIME SINGLE SEASON CLUB LEADERS AMONG BLUE JAY CATCHERS

HOME RUNS

1.	**J.P. Arencibia**	**23**	**2011**
2.	John Buck	20	2010
3.	Darrin Fletcher	19	2000
	Ernie Whitt	19	1987
	Ernie Whitt	19	1985

RBI

1.	Darrin Fletcher	80	1999
2.	**J.P. Arencibia**	**75**	**2011**
3.	Ernie Whitt	72	1987
4.	Rod Barajas	69	2009
5.	Ernie Whitt	69	1988

EXTRA BASE HITS

1.	**J.P. Arencibia**	**47**	**2011**
2.	John Buck	44	2010
	Darrin Fletcher	44	1999
	Ernie Whitt	44	1987
5.	Ernie Whitt	42	1985

TRANSACTIONS

- Selected by the Toronto Blue Jays in the 1st round (21st overall) of the 2007 First Year Player Draft
- On disabled list (fractured right hand) from July 26-September 7, 2012; included rehabilitation assignment at Dunedin (A), Sept. 2

GAME HIGHS

ML Debut	Aug. 7, 2010 vs. TB	**RBI**	6 - May 18, 2012 vs. NYM
Runs	3 - 2x, last May 18, 2012 vs. NYM	**Stolen Bases**	1 - 2x, last April 22, 2012 at KC
Hits	4 - Aug. 7, 2010 vs. TB	**Last ML Home Run**	Sept. 27, 2012 vs. NYY
Doubles	2 - 2x, last July 14, 2012 vs. CLE	**Longest Hitting Streak**	6G - 2x, last Sept. 24-28, 2012
Home Runs	2 - 6x, last July 5, 2012 vs. KC	**Longest Hitless Streak**	22AB - June 30-July 7, 2011

MILESTONES

Category		Date	Opponent	Pitcher	Notes
Hit	1	Aug. 7, 2010	Tampa Bay	Shields	HR-1st pitch of 1st ML-at bat
Home Run	1	Aug. 7, 2010	Tampa Bay	Shields	2R-1st pitch of 1st ML-at bat
Multi-Homer Game (6)					
	6	July 5, 2012	Kansas City	Hochevar, Collins	2R, 1R
Grand Slam (2)	1	June 3, 2011	at Baltimore	Britton	5th inning
	2	Sept. 24, 2012	at Baltimore	Arrieta	7th inning
Extra-Inning HR(1)					
	1	April 5, 2012	at Cleveland	Asencio	3R, 16th inning
RBI	1	Aug. 7, 2010	Tampa Bay	Shields	2R-HR (1st pitch of career)
Stolen Base	1	Aug. 29, 2011	Tampa Bay	Gomes C-Jaso	2nd base

CAREER FIELDING

POSITION	PCT	G	PO	A	E	TC	DP
C	.994	224	1492	132	10	1634	5

PROFESSIONAL CAREER:

2007:

- Led Auburn in doubles with 17 in his first professional season.
- Won a championship with the Doubledays.

2008:

- Named as a Mid-season All-Star with Dunedin (A)... Was the starting catcher in the all-star game, went 2-for-3.
- Named Florida State League Player of the Week in back to back weeks from May 19-25 and May 26-June 1.
- Named organizational Player of the Month in May.
- Promoted to New Hampshire (AA) on June 16.
- Named to the Arizona Fall League All-Prospect team.

2009:

- Spent the entire season at Las Vegas (AAA).
- His 21 home runs ranked 2nd on the club.
- Caught 104 games, throwing out 25% of base stealers (27-for-107).

2010:

- Spent the majority of the season with Las Vegas (AAA), leading the minors in home runs for much of the season prior to being promoted to Toronto on Aug. 5.
- Made his **Major League debut** on Aug. 7 vs. TB... Became the first player in the modern era to record four hits, including two home runs in his Major League debut, finishing the day 4-5 with one double, two home runs and three RBI... Hit the first pitch he saw at the Major League level for a home run off James Shields.
- Was named the Pacific Coast League (AAA) Most Valuable Player...
- Named a mid-season and post-season All-Star in AAA after batting .301 with 32 home runs and 85 RBI... The 32 home runs were T-3rd for most by a Blue Jays minor leaguer in team history...
- Selected as the R. Howard Webster winner at Las Vegas (AAA).
- Was selected to participate in the PCL Home Run Derby during All-Star festivities.
- Earned Player of the Week honours June 28-July 4.

MOST HOME RUNS BY A TORONTO CATCHER – ALL TIME

(CLUB HISTORY) (SINGLE SEASON)

Ernie Whitt	1977-1989	127
Darrin Fletcher	1998-2002	59
Pat Borders	1988-1999	51
J.P. Arencibia	**2010-current**	**42**
Gregg Zaun	2004-2008	40

2011:

- In his first full season in the Major Leagues appeared in 129 games, including 122 as catcher.
- Among AL catchers ranked 1st in home runs (23), T-1st in triples (4), 2nd in RBI (75), T-2nd in extra base hits (47) and 3rd in total bases (190).
- Among AL rookies ranked 2nd in home runs (23), 2nd in walks (36), T-2nd in RBI (78), 3rd in extra base hits (47), 3rd in total bases (194), and T-5th in triples (4).
- His 23 home runs as a catcher are the most home runs by any Blue Jays catcher in team history...Hit his 21st HR on Sept. 7 vs. BOS to pass John Buck for the all-time club mark.
- Fell one home run shy of the all-time Blue Jays rookie mark of 24 by Eric Hinske in 2002.
- The 23 home runs were T-3rd most by a rookie catcher in Major League history behind Mike Piazza (35-1993), Matt Nokes (28-1987) and tied with Giovanni Soto (23-2008).
- Among Blue Jays catchers set marks for home runs, extra base hits, T-1st in triples and fell five RBI short of Darrin Fletcher's 80 in 1999.
- Became just the 6th player in Club history to record a multi-home run game on Opening Day, joining Doug Ault (1977), John Mayberry (1980), George Bell (1988), Shannon Stewart (2000) and Tony Batista (2000)... The two Opening Day homers marked his 2nd career multi-homer day (ML debut) and set a career high for RBI with five.
- Became the first rookie to have a multi-homer day on Opening Day since Gary Gaetti with MIN in 1982 and the first Blue Jay rookie to hit a home run on Opening Day since Carlos Delgado in 1994.
- Became the first player to start his career with multiple home run games in consecutive seasons in Major League history and the first to do so in consecutive seasons since Joe Torre did so for the Braves in 1965-66.

MOST HOME RUNS BY MLB CATCHERS (2011-2012)

Brian McCann (ATL)	43
Matt Wieters (BAL)	43
J.P. Arencibia (TOR)	**40**
Russell Martin (NYY)	39
Jarrod Saltalamacchia (BOS)	39

HR BY ROOKIE CATCHERS

(SINGLE SEASON)

	Player	Year	HR
1.	Mike Piazza, LAD	1993	35
2.	Matt Nokes, DET	1987	28
3.	**J.P. Arencibia, TOR**	**2011**	**23**
	Geovany Soto, CHC	2008	23
5.	Rudy York, DET	1937	22
	Carlton Fisk, BOS	1972	22

FIRST MAJOR LEAGUE HIT AS A HOME RUN

There have been eight Blue Jays to have hit a home run for their first Major League hit... They are as follows:

J.P. Arencibia	— Aug. 7, 2010 vs. TB
Ryan Roberts	— Aug. 3, 2006 at NYY
Mark Hendrickson (pitcher)	— June 21, 2003 at MON
Junior Felix	— May 4, 1989 vs. CAL
Kelly Gruber	— Sept. 25, 1984 at BOS
Tony Johnson	— May 24, 1982 vs. BAL
Steve Staggs	— July 1, 1977 vs. TEX
Al Woods	— Apr. 7, 1977 vs. CWS

BLUE JAYS HOME RUNS, FIRST MAJOR LEAGUE APPEARANCE

When **AL WOODS** batted for Steve Bowling in the 5th inning on Apr. 7, 1977 he became the 11th player in Major League history to hit a home run as a pinch hitter in his first at bat.

JUNIOR FELIX on May 4, 1989 became the 11th major leaguer to homer on his first major league pitch vs California's Kirk McCaskill (solo).

J.P. ARENCIBIA on Aug. 7, 2010 became the 3rd Blue Jay to homer in his first ML appearance and 2nd to do so on the first pitch, off Tampa Bay's James Shields (2R). Became only the 5th player in ML history to hit 2-HR in his first ML game and first catcher to do so.

BAUTISTA, *JOSE*

Birthdate .... **October 19, 1980**
Opening Day Age **32**
Birthplace .... **Santo Domingo, DR**
Residence .... **Santo Domingo, DR**
Bats/Throws .... **R/R**
Height/Weight **6-0/192**
Contract Status .... **signed thru 2015**
M.L. Service **7.165**

19

OUTFIELDER

PERSONAL:

Jose Antonio Bautista... Single... Has two children... Attended Chipola (FL) Community College... Attended De La Salle High School in Santo Domingo... Favourite athlete growing up was NBA Hall of Famer, Michael Jordan...Has been featured as the cover athlete for the Canadian edition of MLB 12: The Show and MLB 13: The Show...Participated in the Toronto/Winnipeg portion of the Blue Jays 2013 Winter Tour.

LAST SEASON:

- Was sidelined on July 16 at NYY after damaging a tendon in his left wrist while completing a swing during his AB in the 8th inning...Returned to the lineup Aug. 24, but was removed on Aug. 25 with recurring soreness...Had season ending surgery on Sept. 4.
- At the time of his injury ranked 2nd in BB (58), T-2nd in HR (27) and T-3rd in RBI (65) in the AL.
- Earned Honda Player-of-the-Month honours for the club in May and June...Posted a .257 average with nine home runs and 22 RBI in May...Also recorded a team high 20 runs scored along with four doubles and 13 walks...In June batted .271 with 14 home runs and 30 RBI... The 14 home runs set a Blue Jays record for home runs in a single month, surpassing the 12 hit by Carlos Delgado (Aug. 1999), Jose Cruz (Aug., 2001) and Bautista twice (May and Aug., 2010)...Led all Major Leaguers in home runs, (14) RBI (30), walks (22) and slugging (.750) for the month of June.
- With his 27 home runs now has 140 as a Blue Jay, passing Ed Sprague (113), Kelly Gruber (114), Shawn Green (119), Jose Cruz Jr. (122), Fred McGriff (125) and Ernie Whitt (131) in 2012, and ranks 7th on the Blue Jays all-time list.
- Homered on Opening Day in the Blue Jays 7-4 16-inning win at CLE on April 5...Was the second consecutive season he has homered on Opening Day.
- Took part in the All-Star game for the 2nd straight season, 3rd overall (2010-2012)...Ranked 3rd in voting among OF at 4,971,155...Is the 3rd Blue Jay to be voted in as a starter in back to back seasons (Alomar, Carter being the others)... Started in RF, batted 4th (0-1, BB, K)...Represented the AL in the 2012 State Farm Home Run Derby...Lost in the finals to Prince Fielder...Marked the 2nd straight year that he took part in the HR Derby.
- Had two multi-home run games and now has 17 in his career, with all but two coming as a Blue Jay.
- Despite missing time in 2012, still leads all Major Leaguers in home runs with 124 since 2010, 12 ahead of Miguel Cabrera.

JOSE BAUTISTA

Bold – career high; Red – league high

Year	Club & League	AVG	G	AB	R	H	2B	3B	HR	RBI	SH-SF	HP	BB-IBB	SO	SB-CS	SLG	OBP	OPS
2001	Williamsport (NYP)	.286	62	220	43	63	10	3	5	30	0-0	6	21-0	41	8-1	.427	.364	.791
2002	Hickory (SAL)	.301	129	438	72	132	26	3	14	57	5-2	8	67-3	104	3-2	.470	.402	.872
2003	Lynchburg (Caro)	.242	51	165	28	40	14	2	4	20	0-0	3	27-0	48	1-5	.424	.359	.783
	Pirates (Gulf)	.348	7	23	5	8	1	0	1	3	0-1	0	4-1	7	0-0	.522	.429	.951
2004	BALTIMORE (AL)	.273	16	11	3	3	0	0	0	0	0-0	0	1-0	3	0-0	.273	.333	.606
	TAMPA BAY (AL)	.167	12	12	1	2	0	0	0	1	0-0	0	3-0	7	0-1	.167	.333	.500
	KANSAS CITY (AL)	.200	13	25	1	5	1	0	0	1	0-0	0	1-0	12	0-0	.240	.231	.471
	PITTSBURGH (NL)	.200	23	40	1	8	2	0	0	0	1-0	0	2-0	18	0-0	.250	.238	.488
2005	Altoona (East)	.283	117	445	63	126	27	1	23	90	2-2	10	48-2	101	7-3	.503	.364	.867
	Indianapolis (Int)	.255	13	51	6	13	3	0	1	4	0-0	0	4-0	10	1-1	.373	.309	.682
	PITTSBURGH (NL)	.143	11	28	3	4	1	0	0	1	0-0	0	3-0	7	1-0	.179	.226	.405
2006	Indianapolis (Int)	.277	29	101	12	28	9	0	2	9	0-2	2	14-1	19	2-1	.426	.370	.796
	PITTSBURGH (NL)	.235	117	400	58	94	20	**3**	16	51	3-4	16	46-2	110	2-4	.420	.335	.755
2007	Pirates (Gulf)	.375	2	8	1	3	2	0	0	1	0-0	0	0-0	1	0-0	.625	.375	1.000
	PITTSBURGH (NL)	.254	142	532	75	135	**36**	2	15	63	4-6	4	68-1	101	6-3	.414	.339	.753
2008	Indianapolis (Int)	.300	5	20	6	6	2	0	2	8	0-0	0	3-0	6	1-0	.700	.391	1.091
	PITTSBURGH (NL)	.242	107	314	38	76	15	0	12	44	6-3	2	38-4	77	1-1	.404	.325	.729
	TORONTO (AL)	.214	21	56	7	12	2	0	3	10	2-1	0	2-1	14	0-0	.411	.237	.648
2009	TORONTO (AL)	.235	113	336	54	79	13	**3**	13	40	6-2	4	56-1	85	4-0	.408	.349	.757
2010	TORONTO (AL)	.260	**161**	569	**109**	148	35	**3**	**54**	**124**	0-4	10	100-2	**116**	**9**-2	.617	.378	.995
2011	TORONTO (AL)	.302	149	513	105	**155**	24	2	**43**	103	0-4	6	**132-24**	111	**9**-5	**.608**	.447	**1.056**
2012	Blue Jays (Gulf)	.000	1	3	0	0	0	0	0	0	0-0	0	1-0	1	0-0	.000	.250	.250
	New Hampshire (East)	.500	1	4	2	2	0	0	2	5	0-0	0	1-0	1	0-0	2.000	.600	2.600
	TORONTO (AL)	.241	92	332	64	80	14	0	27	65	0-4	4	59-2	63	5-2	.527	.358	.886
Minor Totals		.285	417	1478	238	421	94	9	52	227	7-7	29	190-7	339	23-13	.470	.376	.846
TORONTO TOTALS		.262	536	1806	339	474	88	8	140	342	8-15	24	349-30	389	27-9	.553	.386	.939
AL TOTALS		.261	577	1854	344	484	89	8	140	344	8-15	24	354-30	411	27-10	.544	.384	.928
NL TOTALS		.241	400	1314	175	317	74	5	43	159	14-13	22	157-7	313	10-8	.403	.329	.732
MAJOR TOTALS		.253	977	3168	519	801	163	13	183	503	22-28	46	511-37	724	37-18	.486	.362	.848

ALL-STAR GAME RECORD

Year	Club and League	AVG	G	AB	R	H	2B	3B	HR	RBI	SH-SF	HP	BB-IBB	SO	SB-CS
2010	AL at LAA	.000	1	1	0	0	0	0	0	0	0-0	0	0-0	0	0-0
2011	AL at ARI	.500	1	2	0	1	0	0	0	0	0-0	0	0-0	0	0-0
2012	AL at KC	.000	1	1	0	0	0	0	0	0	0-0	0	1-0	1	0-0
ALL-STAR TOTALS		.250	3	4	0	1	0	0	0	0	0-0	0	1-0	1	0-0

WORLD BASEBALL CLASSIC

Year	Club and League	AVG	G	AB	R	H	2B	3B	HR	RBI	SH-SF	HP	BB-IBB	SO	SB-CS
2009	Dominican Republic	.333	3	3	1	1	0	0	0	0	0-0	0	0-0	1	0-0

HOME RUN BREAKDOWN

Total	H	A	ONE GAME 2	ONE GAME 3	ONE GAME 4	GS	LO	XN	IP	PH	RHP	LHP
183	93	90	16	1	0	4	4	2	1	0	133	50

TRANSACTIONS

- Selected by the Pittsburgh Pirates in the 20th round of the 2000 First Year Player Draft
- Selected by the Baltimore Orioles in the Rule 5 Draft on December 15, 2003
- Claimed on waivers by the Tampa Bay Rays on June 3, 2004
- Traded to the Kansas City Royals in exchange for cash considerations on June 28, 2004
- Traded to the New York Mets in exchange for C Justin Huber on July 30, 2004
- Traded to the Pittsburgh Pirates along with IF Ty Wigginton and RHP Matt Peterson in exchange for RHP Kris Benson and IF Jeff Keppinger on July 20, 2004
- Traded to the Toronto Blue Jays in exchange for a player to be named later on August 21, 2008. C Robinzon Diaz was the player to be named later in a deal completed on August 25, 2008
- On disabled list (left wrist inflammation) from July 17-August 24, 2012; included rehabilitation assignment at Gulf Coast Blue Jays (rookie) August 20 and New Hampshire (AA) August 23
- On disabled list (left wrist inflammation) from August 26-remainder of season, 2012

GAME HIGHS

ML Debut	April 4, 2004 vs. BOS	**RBI**	5 - 6x, last Sept. 30, 2010 at MIN
Runs	4 - April 22, 2011 vs. TB	**Stolen Bases**	2 - Sept. 7, 2011 vs. BOS
Hits	4 - 4x, last July 27, 2010 vs. BAL	**Last ML Home Run**	July 2, 2012 vs. KC
Doubles	3 - April 23, 2010 at TB	**Longest Hitting Streak**	12G - April 10-25, 2007
Home Runs	3 - May 15, 2011 at MIN	**Longest Hitless Streak**	27AB - July 30-Aug. 30, 2008

MLB BATTING LEADERS (2010–2012)

HOME RUNS

1.	**Jose Bautista**	**124**
2.	Miguel Cabrera	112
3.	Albert Pujols	109
4.	Curtis Granderson	108
5.	Prince Fielder	100
	Josh Hamilton	100

OPS

1.	Miguel Cabrera	1.025
2.	Joey Votto	.998
3.	**Jose Bautista**	**.992**
4.	Josh Hamilton	.952
5.	David Ortiz	.950

WALKS

1.	Prince Fielder	306
2.	Joey Votto	295
3.	**Jose Bautista**	**291**
4.	Carlos Pena	275
5.	Ben Zobrist	266

OBP

1.	Joey Votto	.434
2.	Miguel Cabrera	.420
3.	Prince Fielder	.412
4.	**Jose Bautista**	**.408**
5.	Joe Maurer	.401

SLG

1.	Miguel Cabrera	.604
2.	**Jose Bautista**	**.593**
3.	Josh Hamilton	.583
4.	Joey Votto	.564
5.	Ryan Braun	.563

CAREER FIELDING

POSITION	PCT	G	PO	A	E	TC	DP
1B	1.000	13	63	2	0	65	2
2B	1.000	5	11	15	0	26	5
3B	.959	383	239	755	43	1037	54
OF	.981	531	911	57	19	987	17

MILESTONES

Category		Date	Opponent	Pitcher	Notes
Hit	1	April 7, 2004	Boston	Mendoza	PH-single
Home Run	1	May 13, 2006	Florida	Olsen	2R
	100	August 26, 2010	at Detroit	Scherzer	1R
Multi-Homer Game (17)					
	16	June 19, 2012	at Milwaukee	Thornburg, Axford	1R, 1R
3-Homer Game (1)					
	1	May 15, 2011	at Minnesota	Duensing, Slowey (2)	1R, 1R, 2R
Grand Slams (4)					
	1	June 11, 2006	at San Francisco	Worrell	8th inning
	2	Sept. 19, 2006	at Los Angeles (NL)	Dessens	6th inning
	3	July 30, 2010	Cleveland	Masterson	4th inning
	4	Sept. 30, 2010	at Minnesota	Neshek	3rd inning
Leadoff HR (4)	1	June 15, 2006	at St. Louis	Mulder	—
	2	June 12, 2007	Texas	Millwood	—
	3	June 17, 2007	Chicago (NL)	Vazquez	—
	4	Sept. 29, 2009	at Boston	Buchholz	---
Extra Inning HR (2)					
	1	May 14, 2011	at Minnesota	Hoey	2R, 11th inning
	2	July 9, 2011	at Cleveland	Perez	1R, 10th inning
Inside the Park (1)					
	1	July 7, 2010	Minnesota	Slowey	2R, 5th inning
RBI	1	June 24, 2004	at Toronto	Adams	Groundout
Stolen Base	1	Sept. 26, 2005	at Los Angeles (NL)	Carrara C-Navarro	2nd base

FEWEST GAMES TO 100 CAREER HR AS A BLUE JAY

Jose Bautista	**379**
Fred McGriff	473
Joe Carter	475

PLAYERS TO WIN BACK-TO-BACK MLB HOME RUN TITLES, SINCE 1920

Babe Ruth	1918-1929 (7x)
Jimmie Foxx	1932-1933
Ted Williams	1941-1942
Ralph Kiner	1947-1952 (5x)
Johnny Mize	1947-1948
Harmon Killebrew	1963-1964
Mike Schmidt	1974-1981 (3x)
Cecil Fielder	1990-1991
Juan Gonzalez	1992-1993
Mark McGwire	1996-1999 (3x)
Alex Rodriguez	2002-2003
Jose Bautista	**2010-2011**

PROFESSIONAL CAREER:

2004:

- Made his **Major League debut** on April 4 vs. BOS as a pinch-hitter.
- Singled off Boston's Ramiro Mendoza as a pinch hitter in first Major League plate appearance on April 7 at Camden Yards.
- Was designated for assignment on May 25 and was claimed off waivers by Tampa Bay on June 3...Was designated for assignment on June 25... Was acquired by Kansas City on June 28 for cash considerations...Was then acquired by the New York Mets on July 30 in exchange for minor league C Justin Huber... Was later acquired that day by the Pittsburgh Pirates...

2005:

- Was named Pittsburgh's Minor League Player of the Year as he led all farmhands in RBI (94) and ranked 3rd in home runs behind Brad Eldred (28) and Josh Bonifay (25).
- Was selected to play in the MLB Future's Game... Walked and singled in his two plate appearances with the World Team.

2006:

- Was recalled by Pittsburgh on May 7.
- Took Florida's Scott Olsen deep for his first career home run on May 13.
- Took San Francisco's Tim Worrell deep for his first career grand slam on June 11.

2007:

- Suffered a lacerated left hand while sliding into 3rd base at ATL on July 14 and was placed on 15-day DL on July 15... Had stitches removed from hand on July 25.
- Enjoyed his first career two-homer game on Aug. 25 at HOU.

2008:

- Traded to the Toronto Blue Jays in exchange for C Robinzon Diaz on Aug. 21.
- Snapped a career high 27 at bat hitless streak (July 30-Aug. 30) with a RBI single off Brian Bruney in the 7th inning.
- Hit his 1st HR as a Blue Jay on Sept. 2 vs. MIN (2R off Perkins).

2009:

- Homered in four consecutive games from Sept. 28-Oct. 2 and hit five over the seasons final seven games.
- Led all Toronto outfielders in assists with 11, ranking 4th in the AL... He did so in only 70 starts, less than half of those above him on the leaderboard... In fact his 0.15 assists per nine innings was the highest in the majors of any player with 70 or more starts, and represents the 4th highest mark in Blue Jays history (Bailor 0.21-1980)... Posted two assists on July 25 vs. TB, marking the 1st time a Blue Jay outfielder had done so since 2004, and only the 10th time in club history.

2010:

- Led the Majors in home runs (54), extra base hits (92), and T-1st in total bases (351)...Among the AL ranked 2nd in walks (100), 3rd in RBI (125), SLG (.617) and OPS (.995).
- Became only the 4th player (5th time) in MLB history to record at least 35-2B, 50-HR, 100-BB in the same season... Is only the 16th player in history to hit 54 or more home runs.
- Was named to the Sporting News All-Star Team as an outfielder, was named a Silver Slugger in the AL as an outfielder and also was selected as the Hank Aaron Award winner as the most outstanding offensive performer in the AL.
- Earned a selection to the All-Star game in Anaheim, going 0-1.
- Was the only player this season to win AL Player of the Month awards twice (July/August) and was the only player to win Player of the Week awards three times.
- Led the AL in home runs in four separate months becoming the first to do so since Ken Griffey Jr. in 1997.
- Set a Blue Jays record with his 54 home runs, surpassing the 47 by George Bell in 1987 (min 300 AB, previous season).
- His increase in home runs (41) year-over-year set a new MLB record, passing Davey Johnson who increased his total by 38 in 1973... Led the league in home runs by 15 (Konerko -39), representing the 2nd largest gap since 1940 (Mantle-52, Wertz-32 in 1956).
- Had nine multi-homer games, five more than anyone else in the league... The nine multi-homer games are tied for the club record with George Bell (1987).
- His 33 home runs at home was the most since Alex Rodriguez hit 34 in 2000.
- Recorded an inside-the-park home run on July 7 vs. MIN.
- His 124 RBI are the most for a Blue Jay since Carlos Delgado had 145 in 2003.
- Finished T-2nd in OF assists (12), however did so in only 113 games, leading to a league best 0.11 assists per nine innings.

ALL-TIME SINGLE SEASON CLUB LEADERS (TOP 5) – BATTING DEPARTMENTS

***LED LEAGUE**

HOME RUNS

1.	**Jose Bautista**	**54***	**2010**
2.	George Bell	47	1987
3.	Jose Canseco	46	1998
4.	Carlos Delgado	44	1999
4.	**Jose Bautista**	**43***	**2011**

WALKS

1.	**Jose Bautista**	**132***	**2011**
2.	Carlos Delgado	123	2000
3.	Fred McGriff	119	1989
4.	John Olerud	114	1993
5.	Carlos Delgado	111	2001

SLG % (450 PA)

	Player	SLG	Year
1.	Carlos Delgado	.664	2000
2.	**Jose Bautista**	**.617**	**2010**
3.	**Jose Bautista**	**.608***	**2011**
4.	George Bell	.605	1987
5.	John Olerud	.599	1993

OBP % (450 PA)

	Player	OBP	Year
1.	John Olerud	.473	1993
2.	Carlos Delgado	.470	2000
3.	**Jose Bautista**	**.447**	**2011**
4.	Tony Fernandez	.427	1999
5.	Carlos Delgado	.426	2003

2011:

- Led the Major Leagues in home runs (43), walks (132), slugging percentage (.608) and OPS (1.056)... Became the first player to lead the Majors in the above categories since Barry Bonds in 2001, and the first AL player since Ted Williams in 1942.
- Marked the second consecutive season he led the Majors in home runs being the first to do so since Mark McGwire who did it in four straight seasons from 1996-99.
- Became just the 5th player in Major League history to record at least 40 home runs, 130 walks, and nine stolen bases in a single season... Finished just .0003 points behind for the AL lead behind Cabrera in on base percentage.
- Earned his second consecutive Hank Aaron Award, recongnizing the league's top hitter... Became just the 3rd player to capture this award in consecutive seasons (Alex Rodriguez, 2001-2003 and Barry Bonds, 2001-2002) and was the 6th recipient to win this award on multiple occasions (Alex Rodriguez-4, Barry Bonds-3, Manny Ramirez-2, Derek Jeter-2 and Albert Pujols-2).
- Was named AL Player of the Month for both April and May, earning the honour in four of the last five months dating back to last season.
- Batted .366 in April with nine home runs and 28 walks... The 28 walks set a new Club record for that month, surpassing the 26 by Carlos Delgado in 2001... In fact it was the 3rd highest total for walks for any month in Club history, two behind the 30 Fred McGriff had in both August & September of 1989.
- In May batted .360 with 11 home runs and 23 RBI... His 11 home runs in May led the AL... It was the 5th straight month he led the AL in HR... Last player to do that was Jimmie Foxx (June, 1933 – April, 1934).
- Was named Co-Player of the Week ending July 3, batting .391 with three doubles, four home runs and eight RBI.
- Received a ML record 7,454,753 votes & became the 10th Blue Jay to be voted to start the All-Star Game... Started in RF and went 1-2 in the game.
- Enjoyed his first career 3-HR game on May 15 at MIN... It marked the 18th time in Club history (14th player) that a Jay has gone deep at least three times in the same game.
- Became the 2nd Blue Jay since Carlos Delgado in 1999-2000 and first player since David Ortiz in 2004-06 to have consecutive 40+ home run seasons.
- Set a Blue Jays record with 31 home runs at the All-Star break breaking the mark of 29 by George Bell in 1987.
- July 9 at CLE hit his 100th & 101st HR as a Jay in 379 games, becoming the quickest to 100-HR in Club history (previous best: Fred McGriff in 473 games).
- His Major League leading 132 walks marks the most since Barry Bonds had 132 in 2007 and is the most by any AL player since Jason Giambi had 137 in 2000... Led the AL with 24 intentional walks... Started the season in RF, then moved to 3B where he would make 25 consecutive starts before finishing the season in RF.
- Reached base safely in 136 of his 149 games... Had separate streaks of reaching base safely in 23 and 24 games.
- April 22-24 vs. TB had a stretch of reaching base safely in 11 consecutive plate appearances... Tied Tony Fernandez (1999) for 2nd on that Club list.

Jose Bautista signing autographs at the Toronto Blue Jays Winter Tour stop in Winnipeg, Manitoba

BECK, *CHAD*

Birthdate	January 17, 1985
Opening Day Age	28
Birthplace	Jasper, TX
Residence	Woodville, TX
Bats/Throws	R/R
Height/Weight	6-4/250
Contract Status	signed thru 2013
M.L. Service	0.072

60

PITCHER

NON-ROSTER

PERSONAL:

Chad Lee Beck... Selected by the Diamondbacks in the 14th round of the 2006 First-Year Player Draft... Attended Louisana-Lafayette College.

LAST SEASON:

- Was recalled from Las Vegas (AAA) of the Pacific Coast League on five separate occasions...Appeared in 14 games out of the bullpen.
- Pitched more than one inning in just two out of 14 outings...Did record a career high 3.2 innings on June 11 vs. WAS.
- Left-handed batters hit .310, while right-handed hitters .324.
- In 43 games with Las Vegas posted a record of 2-0 with a 1.31 ERA...Led the squad with 18 saves, going 18-19 in save situations...Was a career high in saves and career low ERA.
- Named to the Pacific Coast League roster in the 2012 AAA All-Star Game.

CHAD BECK

Bold – career high

Year	Club & League	W-L	ERA	G	GS	CG	ShO	SV	IP	H	R	ER	HR	HB	BB-IBB	SO	WP	BK	OBA
2006	Yakima (NOR)	1-5	6.25	16	2	0	0	0	40.1	47	37	28	8	2	18-0	45	3	1	.296
2007	South Bend (Mid)	1-2	4.33	31	0	0	0	1	52.0	53	27	25	5	3	20-1	48	5	0	.264
2008	South Bend (Mid)	2-0	2.04	7	0	0	0	0	17.2	13	7	4	0	0	3-0	19	2	1	.186
	Visalia (CAL)	6-5	3.98	25	15	0	0	1	95.0	86	45	42	8	5	25-0	89	10	0	.239
2009	Dunedin (FSL)	0-0	4.35	9	0	0	0	0	10.1	12	9	5	1	1	6-1	14	2	0	.279
	Lansing (Mid)	6-8	5.94	20	20	1	0	0	110.2	135	78	73	10	9	29-0	85	7	1	.297
2010	Dunedin (FSL)	3-6	3.72	41	11	0	0	0	101.2	97	44	42	5	1	31-0	79	6	0	.244
2011	Dunedin (FSL)	0-0	1.69	1	1	0	0	0	5.1	4	1	1	1	1	1-0	7	0	0	.222
	New Hampshire (East)	7-4	3.69	22	14	0	0	0	95.0	92	41	39	7	3	28-0	70	2	0	.258
	Las Vegas (PCL)	2-4	6.70	8	8	0	0	0	41.2	61	36	31	7	2	26-0	23	3	0	.341
	TORONTO (AL)	0-0	0.00	3	0	0	0	0	2.1	1	0	0	0	0	0-0	3	0	0	.125
2012	Las Vegas (PCL)	2-0	1.31	43	0	0	0	18	48.0	39	7	7	2	1	13-1	24	2	0	.218
	TORONTO (AL)	0-0	6.32	**14**	0	0	0	0	**15.2**	21	12	11	**2**	0	**5**-0	**9**	1	1	.318
Minor Totals		30-34	4.33	223	71	1	0	20	617.2	639	332	297	54	28	200-3	503	42	3	.264
MAJOR TOTALS		0-0	5.50	17	0	0	0	0	18.0	22	12	11	2	0	5-0	12	1	1	.297

TRANSACTIONS

- Selected by the Arizona Diamondbacks in the 14th round of the 2006 First Year Player Draft
- Traded to the Toronto Blue Jays in exchange for IF David Eckstein on August 31, 2008
- Claimed off waivers by the Pittsburgh Pirates on October 25, 2012
- Claimed off waivers by the Toronto Blue Jays on January 4, 2013
- Claimed off waivers by the Pittsburgh Pirates on October 25, 2012
- Claimed off waivers by the Toronto Blue Jays on January 4, 2013

GAME HIGHS

ML Debut	Sept. 13, 2011 at BOS
Innings Pitched:	
Starter	None
Reliever	3.2 - June 11, 2012 vs. WSH
Walks:	
Starter	None
Reliever	2 - 2x, last Sept. 21, 2012 at TB
Strikeouts:	
Starter	None
Reliever	3 - June 11, 2012 vs. WSH
Hits Allowed	4 - Sept. 4, 2012 vs. BAL
Runs Allowed	3 - June 11, 2012 vs. WSH

ER Allowed	2 - 4x, last Sept. 26, 2012 at BAL
HR Allowed	1 - 2x, last Sept. 26, 2012 at BAL
Low Hit CG	None
Last Win	None
Last Save	None
Last CG	None
Last ShO	None
Last Start	None
Last Relief App.	Oct. 1, 2012 vs. MIN
Longest Win Streak	None
Longest Losing Streak	None
Scoreless Innings Streak	2.1 - 2x, last June 11-July 24, 2012

CAREER FIELDING

POSITION	PCT	G	PO	A	E	TC	DP
P	.750	17	1	2	1	4	0

PROFESSIONAL CAREER:

2006:

- Made his professional debut with Yakima of the Nortwest League (Short-A)... Started two of 16 games.

2007:

- Spent the full season at South Bend in the Midwest League (Low-A), pitching exclusively out of the bullpen.

2008:

- Began the season with South Bend before being promoted to Visalia (High-A) where he spent the majority of the season.
- Made 15 starts at Visalia, limiting opponents to a .239 average.

2009:

- Acquired by the Blue Jays after the 2008 season, made his debut at Dunedin (High-A).

2010:

- Spent all 2010 with Dunedin, splitting time between the rotation and bullpen... Was third on the club with 41 appearances.

2011:

- Made three appearances with the Blue Jays and split the rest of the season between Dunedin (A), New Hampshire (AA) and Las Vegas (AAA).
- Made his **ML Debut** Sept. 13 at BOS and threw just one pitch to retire Dustin Pedroia, the only hitter he faced.
- His 142.0IP in the minors was a career high besting his previous high of 121.0IP in 2009.
- Made five appearances in the Arizona Fall League, without allowing a run in 8.0 innings.

SHUTOUTS

Year by Year	W	L
1977	3	15
1978	5	19
1979	7	15
1980	9	12
1981	4	20
1982	13	9
1983	8	8
1984	10	4
1985	9	4
1986	12	6
1987	8	10
1988	17	3
1989	12	7
1990	9	10
1991	16	9
1992	14	10
1993	11	1
1994	4	4
1995	8	10
1996	7	9
1997	16	11
1998	11	4
1999	9	8
2000	4	7
2001	10	9
2002	6	6
2003	6	5
2004	11	12
2005	8	14
2006	6	6
2007	9	4
2008	13	12
2009	10	5
2010	11	8
2011	10	8
2012	11	9
Total	**337**	**313**

Club by Club	W	L
Baltimore	31	39
Boston	21	38
Chicago (A)	28	14
Cleveland	19	20
Detroit	22	15
Kansas City	28	16
Los Angeles (A)	26	20
Minnesota	26	16
New York (A)	22	26
Oakland	26	21
Seattle	27	10
Tampa Bay	11	13
Texas	18	21
Atlanta	1	6
Chicago (N)	0	1
Cincinnati	2	0
Colorado	2	1
Miami	0	2
Houston	0	1
Los Angeles	2	0
Montreal/Washington	5	3
New York (N)	1	3
Philadelphia	1	2
Pittsburgh	0	1
San Diego	1	0
San Francisco	1	0
St. Louis	2	2
Total	**337**	**313**

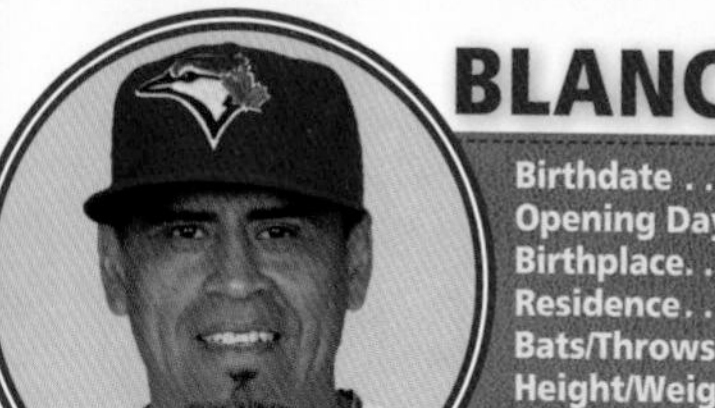

BLANCO, *HENRY*

Birthdate . . . . **August 29, 1971**
Opening Day Age **41**
Birthplace . . . . **Caracus, VZ**
Residence . . . . **Miranda, VZ**
Bats/Throws . . . . **R/R**
Height/Weight **5-11/220**
Contract Status . . . . **signed thru 2013**
M.L. Service **14.136**

22

CATCHER

PERSONAL:

Henry Ramon Blanco...Attended Antonio Jose de Sucre High School...Participates in the Garth Brooks Teammates for Kids Foundation... Co-founded in 1999 by Garth Brooks, the foundation exists to develop and implement innovative concepts that generate funds for the benefit of children's charities.

LAST SEASON:

- Played 21 games for Arizona in his 15th Major League season...Started 18 of his 21 games behind the plate.
- Threw out three of six potential base stealers.
- Recorded three of his 12 hits in one contest on May 22 vs. LAD, going 3-4 with a double
- Had his season end prematurely, suffering a torn ligament in his left thumb in early August.

HENRY BLANCO

Bold – career high

Year	Club and League	AVG	G	AB	R	H	2B	3B	HR	RBI	SH-SF	HP	BB-IBB	SO	SB-CS	SLG	OBP	OPS
1990	Dodgers (GCL)	.219	60	178	23	39	8	0	1	19	0-4	1	26-0	41	7-2	.281	.316	.597
1991	Vero Beach (FSL)	.143	5	7	0	1	0	0	0	0	0-0	0	2-0	0	0-0	.143	.333	.476
	Great Falls (Pio)	.255	62	216	35	55	7	1	5	28	2-3	1	27-0	39	3-6	.366	.336	.702
1992	Bakersfield (CAL)	.234	124	401	42	94	21	2	5	52	10-9	9	51-3	91	10-6	.334	.328	.662
1993	San Antonio (TEX)	.195	117	374	33	73	19	1	10	42	2-1	4	29-0	80	3-3	.332	.260	.592
1994	San Antonio (TEX)	.230	132	405	36	93	23	2	6	38	5-3	2	53-2	67	6-6	.341	.320	.661
1995	San Antonio (TEX)	.255	88	302	37	77	18	4	12	48	0-0	4	29-2	52	1-1	.460	.328	.788
	Albuquerque (PCL)	.227	29	97	11	22	4	1	2	13	1-2	0	10-1	23	0-0	.351	.294	.645
1996	San Antonio (TEX)	.267	92	307	39	82	14	1	5	40	3-5	0	28-2	38	2-3	.368	.324	.692
	Albuquerque (PCL)	.167	2	6	1	1	0	0	0	0	0-0	0	0-0	3	0-0	.167	.167	.334
1997	Albuquerque (PCL)	.313	91	294	38	92	20	1	6	47	1-3	1	37-2	63	7-4	.449	.388	.837
	LOS ANGELES (NL)	.400	3	5	1	2	0	0	1	1	0-0	0	0-0	1	0-0	1.000	.400	1.400
1998	San Bernardino (CAL)	.316	7	19	5	6	1	0	2	3	0-0	0	4-0	6	1-0	.684	.435	1.119
	Albuquerque (PCL)	.269	48	134	19	36	11	0	4	23	0-2	0	22-1	27	2-0	.440	.367	.807
1999	Colorado Springs (PCL)	.333	15	57	8	19	4	0	3	12	1-1	0	1-0	12	0-1	.561	.339	.900
	COLORADO (NL)	.232	88	263	30	61	12	**3**	6	28	3-2	1	34-1	38	1-1	.369	.320	.689
2000	Indianapolis (Int)	.333	1	3	1	1	1	0	0	0	0-0	0	1-0	0	0-0	.667	.500	1.167
	MILWAUKEE (NL)	.236	93	284	29	**67**	**24**	0	7	31	0-4	0	**36**-6	60	0-3	.394	.318	.712
2001	MILWAUKEE (NL)	.210	104	314	33	66	18	**3**	6	31	5-2	2	34-6	**72**	**3**-1	.344	.290	.634
2002	ATLANTA (NL)	.204	81	221	17	45	9	1	6	22	2-5	1	20-5	51	0-2	.335	.267	.602
2003	ATLANTA (NL)	.199	55	151	11	30	8	0	1	13	3-1	1	10-2	21	0-0	.272	.252	.524
2004	MINNESOTA (AL)	.206	**114**	315	**36**	65	19	1	**10**	**37**	11-3	3	21-0	56	0-3	.368	.260	.628
2005	CHICAGO (NL)	.242	54	161	16	39	6	0	6	25	4-2	0	11-1	24	0-0	.391	.287	.678
2006	CHICAGO (NL)	.266	74	241	23	64	15	2	6	**37**	4-2	0	14-1	38	0-0	.419	.304	.723
2007	Peoria (Mid)	.316	8	19	3	6	1	0	1	5	0-1	1	3-1	3	0-0	.526	.417	.943
	Iowa (PCL)	.200	3	10	2	2	0	0	0	1	0-0	0	0-0	3	0-0	.200	.200	.400
	CHICAGO (NL)	.167	22	54	3	9	3	0	0	4	1-1	0	2-0	12	0-0	.222	.193	.415
2008	CHICAGO (NL)	.292	58	120	15	35	3	0	3	12	2-0	0	6-1	22	0-0	.392	.325	.717
2009	SAN DIEGO (NL)	.235	67	204	21	48	12	0	6	16	1-1	0	26-2	50	0-0	.382	.320	.702
2010	NEW YORK (NL)	.215	50	130	10	28	5	0	2	8	0-3	0	11-2	26	1-0	.300	.271	.571
2011	ARIZONA (NL)	.250	37	100	12	25	3	1	8	12	0-0	0	12-1	21	0-1	.540	.330	.870
2012	ARIZONA (NL)	.188	21	64	6	12	3	0	1	7	0-0	0	3-0	18	1-0	.281	.224	.505
Minor Totals		.247	884	2829	333	699	152	13	62	371	25-34	23	323-14	548	42-32	.376	.326	.701
NL TOTALS		.230	807	2312	227	531	121	10	59	247	25-23	5	219-28	454	6-8	.367	.295	.662
MAJOR TOTALS		.227	921	2627	263	596	140	11	69	284	36-26	8	240-28	510	6-11	.367	.291	.658

DIVISION SERIES RECORD

Year	Club and League	AVG	G	AB	R	H	2B	3B	HR	RBI	SH-SF	HP	BB-IBB	SO	SB-CS
2002	ATLANTA (NL)	.167	2	6	0	1	0	0	0	0	0-0	0	0-0	2	0-0
2004	MINNESOTA (AL)	.250	4	8	1	2	0	0	1	2	1-1	0	0-0	2	0-1
2011	ARIZONA (NL)	.000	1	1	0	0	0	0	0	0	0-0	0	0-0	0	0-0
DIVISION SERIES TOTALS		.200	7	15	1	3	0	0	1	2	1-1	0	0-0	4	0-1

HOME RUN BREAKDOWN

			ONE GAME									
Total	H	A	2	3	4	GS	LO	XN	IP	PH	RHP	LHP
69	36	33	4	0	0	1	0	3	0	0	40	29

TRANSACTIONS

- Signed by the Los Angeles Dodgers on November 12, 1989
- On disabled list (stomach ulcer) from June 16-25, 1993
- On disabled list (strained right groin muscle) from June 27-July 8, 1995
- On disabled list (sore right shoulder) from April 5-May 10, 1997
- On disabled list (right shoulder surgery and right hand fracture) from March 22-July 29, 1998
- Signed by the Colorado Rockies on December 18, 1998
- Traded to the Milwaukee Brewers along with RHP Jamie Wright in exchnage for IF Jeff Cirillo and LHP Scott Karl as part of a nine player, four team trade on December 13, 1999
- On disabled list (right index finger laciration) from April 15-May 2, 2000
- Traded to the Atlanta Braves in exchnage for C Paul Bako and RHP Jose Cabrera on March 20, 2002
- On disabled list (strained left oblique) from August 12-27, 2002
- Signed by the Minnesota Twins on December 18, 2003
- Signed by the Chicago Cubs on December 8, 2004
- On disabled list (cervical herniated disc) from May 31-August 20, 2007
- Signed by the San Diego Padres on January 21, 2009
- On disabled list (strained right hamstring) from July 5-28, 2009
- Signed by the New York Mets on December 4, 2009
- Signed by the Arizona Diamondbacks on December 17, 2010
- On disabled list (torn ligament in left thumb) from August 6-remainder of season
- Signed by the Toronto Blue Jays on January 11, 2013

GAME HIGHS

ML Debut	July 25, 1997 vs. PHI	**RBI**	4 - 3x, last Sept. 26, 2006 vs. MIL
Runs	4 - Sept. 27, 2001 at ARI	**Stolen Bases**	1 - 6x, last April 19, 2012 vs. ATL
Hits	4 - 3x, last Sept. 26, 2006 vs. MIL	**Last ML Home Run**	July 19, 2012 at CIN
Doubles	2 - 9x, last May 30, 2010 at MIL	**Longest Hitting Streak**	9G - May 30-June 21, 2006
Home Runs	2 - 4x, last May 16, 2011 vs. SD	**Longest Hitless Streak**	24AB - 2x, last May 10-27, 2001

CAREER FIELDING

POSITION	PCT	G	PO	A	E	TC	DP
C	.994	867	5328	458	35	5821	74
1B	1.000	10	50	4	0	54	3
3B	--	2	0	0	0	0	0
OF	--	1	0	0	0	0	0

MILESTONES

Category		Date	Opponent	Pitcher	Notes
Hit	1	July 25, 1997	Philadelphia	Park	PH single, 1st ML AB
Home Run	1	Sept. 28, 1997	at Colorado	Thomson	1R
Multi-Homer Game (4)					
	1	July 22, 1999	at Los Angeles (NL)	Masoaka, Mills	2R, 1R
	2	April 10, 2004	at Detroit	Johnson, Patterson	2R, 1R
	3	April 11, 2009	San Francisco	Sanchez (2)	1R, 1R
	4	May 16, 2011	San Diego	Richard (2)	1R, 1R
Grand Slam (1)	1	May 12, 2000	at Pittsburgh	Schmidt	2nd inning
Walkoff HR (1)	1	May 8, 2010	New York (NL)	Mota	11th inning, 1R
Extra-Inning HR (3)					
	1	Aug. 5, 2000	at Los Angeles (NL)	Fetters	10th inning
	2	May 2, 2002	at Milwaukee	DeJean	10th inning
	3	May 8, 2010	New York (NL)	Mota	11th inning
RBI	1	Sept. 28, 1997	at Colorado	Thomson	HR, 1R
Stolen Base	1	Sept. 15, 1999	New York (NL)	Hershiser C-Piazza	2nd base

PROFESSIONAL CAREER:

1997:

- Recalled from AAA on July 25 making his **Major League debut** that night vs the Phillies... Had a pinch-single off Scott Ruffcorn for his first Major League hit in his first plate appearance.
- Returned to Los Angeles Sept. 2 when rosters expanded... Belted his first Major League homer off John Thomson September 28 at Coors Field.
- Shoulder was arthroscopically repaired on October 3 by Dr. Frank Jobe.

1999:

- Signed as a free agent with Colorado prior to the 1999 season and saw his most extensive time in the Majors... Appeared in 88 games for the Rockies... Had a .992 fielding percentage, committing just 5 errors in 625 total chances.
- On July 22, he hit a pair of homers against his former team in a 12-11 Colorado win for his first career two homer game.

2000:

- Went to Milwaukee as part of a six-player, three-team trade in December 1999, moving to his third club in as many years.
- Established career marks in hits, doubles, walks... Surpassed the 20-doubles mark for the first time in his Major League career, hitting 24 two-base hits and 7 homers.
- Threw out 38 of 66 (57.6 percent) runners attempting to steal.
- Was on the disabled list April 15-May 2 with a laceration on his right index finger.
- On May 12, he hit his first career grand slam off Pittsburgh's Jason Schmidt.

2001:

- Saw action in 104 games with the Brewers, including his first career Opening Day start on April 2 at LAD.
- Scored a career high four runs on Sept. 27 at ARZ

2002:

- Appeared in 81 games with the Braves and hit .204 with six home runs and 22 RBI.
- Was traded by the Brewers to the Braves on March 20 for RHP Jose Cabrera and C Paul Bako
- Appeared in two NLDS games vs. the Giants, going 1-6.

2003:

- Hit .199 with one home run and 13 RBI with a .996 fielding pct. in 55 games in his final season with the Braves.

2004:

- Established career-highs in home runs (10), runs scored (36) and games (114) in his lone season with the Twins.
- Started a career-high 95 games at catcher…threw out 25 of 56 (44.6 percent) attempted base stealers.
- Posted his first career 4-hit game on April 14 at CLE.
- Went 2-for-8 (.250) in 4 ALDS games (3 starts) vs. Yankees… Hit a solo home run in Game 4 (off Javier Vazquez).

2005:

- Played 54 games in his first season with the Cubs…threw out 19 of 39 (48.7 percent) would-be base stealers.
- Tied a career-high with 4 hits on July 24 at St.L.

2006:

- Tied his career high with 37 RBI (also 2004) in his second season with the Cubs and batted .266 (64-for-241).
- Had a career-high 9-game hitting streak from May 30-June 21 (.500, 16-for-32).
- Matched his career-high with 4 RBI twice (June 19 at CLE and Sept. 26 vs. MIL)… Also tied his career high with four hits on Sept. 26 vs. Brewers.
- Made his first-ever start (second appearance) at first base on Sept. 3 vs. Giants (also Sept. 28, 1997 at COL)

2007:

- Appeared in just 22 games (13 starts) with the Cubs due to a cervical herniated disc and hit .167 (9-for-54).
- On the disabled list from May 31-Aug. 20 with a cervical herniated disk… Made 11 rehab appearances with Single-A Peoria and Triple-A Iowa.

2008:

- Hit a career-best .292 (35-for-120) with three home runs and 12 RBI in his final season with the Cubs.
- Appeared in 58 games (28 starts) as catcher…threw out 9 of 21 (42.9 percent) would-be base stealers.

2009:

- Hit .235 (48-for-204) in 67 games in his only season with the Padres.
- Played in 60 games (58 starts) as catcher and one at third base…threw out 14 of 41 (34.1 percent) of attempted base stealers.
- On the disabled list from July 5-28 with a strained right hamstring.

2010:

- Batted .215 (28-for-130) with two homers and eight RBI in 50 games with the Mets…threw out 11 of 22 of attempted base stealers (50.0 percent).
- His stolen base on April 24 vs. Braves was his first since July 28, 2001, a span of 567 games.
- Hit his first walk-off home run of his career in the 11th inning on May 8 vs. SF (off Guillermo Mota).
- Placed on the bereavement list from May 10-15.

2011:

- Appeared in 37 games in his first season with the D-backs and hit .250 (25-for-100) with eight homers and 12 RBI.
- His eight home runs were the most since 10 in 2004.
- Combined with teammate Miguel Montero to lead the Majors in caught-stealing percentage (37.1), a club record and 12th-best mark in the National League since 1998.
- Threw out 8-of-21 (38.1%) would-be base stealers, second-best in baseball (min. 30 games)… Also ranked 10th with a .995 fielding percentage (1 E in 192 TC)... Recorded his fourth-career 2-homer game on May 16 vs. SD, his first since April 11, 2009 vs. SF.
- Played in 47 games with Margarita of the Venezuelan Winter League.
- Appeared in 1 game in the NLDS vs. Brewers, going 0-1.

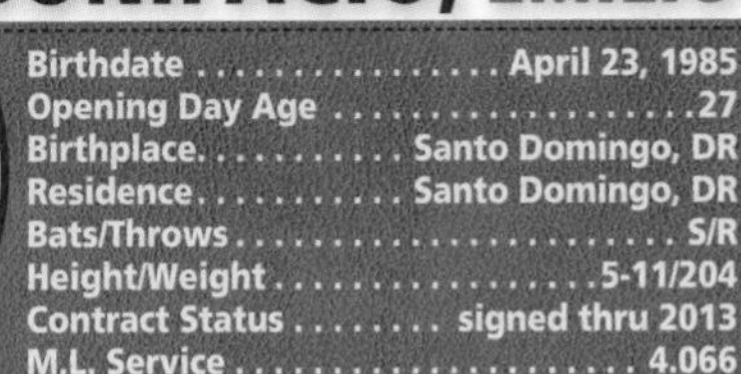

1

INFIELDER

PERSONAL:

Emilio Jose Bonifacio Rosario... Attended Loyola High School In Santa Domingo, Dominican Republic... Married with one child.

LAST SEASON:

- Missed considerable time due to injury, appearing in just 64 games... Placed on 15-day disabled list on May 19, missing 46 games after undergoing surgery to repair a sprained left thumb... After returning from DL on July 13, was placed on again from Aug. 4-19 after re-injuring left thumb... Appeared in three games before missing remainder of season after suffering a right knee sprain on Aug. 22.
- Despite limited action, stole 30 bases (33 attempts), tying him for 9th in National League... Stolen base percentage of 90.9 (30-33) was tied with Tony Campana for second in NL, behind Everth Cabrera (91.7), who led league with 44 steals (48 attempts).
- Began season by stealing 20 straight bases without being caught, establishing a Marlins record for most consecutive stolen bases to begin a season... Additionally, from Sept. 27, 2011 to May 18, 2012, had stolen 21 consecutive bases without being caught.
- Had 28 singles to start season before recording first extra-base hit, a double, on May 9 at Houston... Marked longest streak of singles to open a season in Marlins history.
- Tied Marlins record with two triples on May 13 vs. Mets, doing so in consecutive at-bats in seventh and ninth innings... Became just fourth Marlin to triple twice in a game.
- Went 2-3 with his lone home run of season on July 23 vs. Atlanta.
- Recorded six games with two steals, first doing so on April 7 at CIN... Followed suit on April 17 vs. CHC, April 19 vs. CHC, May 3 at SF, May 11 vs. NYM and July 20 at PIT.
- Appeared in 51 games in center field (50 starts) and 15 games at second base (14 starts).

EMILIO BONIFACIO

Bold – career high

Year	Club and League	AVG	G	AB	R	H	2B	3B	HR	RBI	SH-SF	HP	BB-IBB	SO	SB-CS	SLG	OBP	OPS
2002	DSL (DSL)	.300	68	227	60	68	9	5	1	15	2-0	0	51-1	55	51-12	.396	.428	.824
2003	Missoula (Pio)	.199	54	146	20	29	1	1	0	16	4-1	3	18-0	43	15-3	.219	.298	.517
2004	South Bend Silver (Mid)	.260	120	411	59	107	9	6	1	37	9-2	3	25-3	122	40-10	.319	.306	.625
2005	South Bend Silver (Mid)	.270	127	522	81	141	14	7	1	44	7-4	2	56-0	90	55-17	.330	.341	.671
2006	Lancaster (CAL)	.321	130	546	117	175	35	7	7	50	8-4	6	44-0	104	61-14	.449	.375	.824
2007	Mobile (Sou)	.285	132	551	84	157	21	5	2	40	4-1	2	38-1	105	41-13	.352	.333	.685
	ARIZONA (NL)	.217	11	23	2	5	1	0	0	2	0-0	0	4-0	3	0-1	.261	.333	.594
2008	Tucson (PCL)	.302	85	367	49	111	18	5	1	29	6-2	0	27-0	64	17-8	.387	.348	.735
	Columbus (Int)	.452	8	31	9	14	2	0	0	3	0-1	0	4-0	4	4-2	.516	.500	1.016
	ARIZONA (NL)	.167	8	12	3	2	1	0	0	2	0-0	0	0-0	5	1-0	.250	.167	.417
	WASHINGTON (NL)	.248	41	157	26	39	5	5	0	12	0-3	0	14-0	41	6-4	.344	.305	.649
2009	FLORIDA (NL)	.252	127	461	72	116	11	6	1	27	8-4	2	34-0	95	21-9	.308	.303	.611
2010	New Orleans (PCL)	.274	40	164	19	45	8	3	0	11	2-0	0	16-0	33	8-4	.360	.339	.699
	FLORIDA (NL)	.261	73	180	30	47	6	3	0	10	1-3	0	17-0	42	12-0	.328	.320	.648
2011	FLORIDA (NL)	.296	**152**	565	**78**	**167**	**26**	**7**	**5**	**36**	11-5	1	**59**-1	**129**	**40**-11	.393	.360	.753
2012	Jupiter (FSL)	.167	9	30	6	5	1	0	0	4	0-0	0	6-0	9	3-1	.200	.306	.506
	MIAMI (NL)	.258	64	244	30	63	3	4	1	11	4-0	1	25-1	52	30-3	.316	.330	.646
Minor Totals		.284	773	2995	504	852	118	39	13	249	42-15	16	285-5	629	295-84	.363	.348	.711
MAJOR TOTALS		.267	476	1642	241	439	53	25	7	100	24-15	4	153-2	367	110-28	.343	.329	.671

HOME RUN BREAKDOWN

Total	H	A	ONE GAME 2	3	4	GS	LO	XN	IP	PH	RHP	LHP
7	3	4	0	0	0	0	1	0	1	0	5	2

TRANSACTIONS

- Signed by the Arizona Diamondbacks on December 27, 2001
- Traded to the Washington Nationals in exchange for RHP Jon Rauch on July 22, 2008
- Traded to the Florida Marlins along with RHP P.J. Dean and IF Jake Smolinski in exchange for LHP Scott Olsen and OF Josh Willingham on November 11, 2008
- Traded to the Toronto Blue Jays along with RHP Josh Johnson, LHP Mark Buehrle, SS Jose Reyes, C John Buck and cash considerations in exchange for RHP Henderson Alvarez, SS Yunel Escobar, SS Adeiny Hechavarria, C Jeff Mathis, LHP Justin Nicolino, RHP Anthony Desclafani and OF Jake Marisnick on November 19, 2012

GAME HIGHS

ML Debut	Sept. 2, 2007 vs. COL	**RBI**	3 - 4x, last Sept. 1, 2011 at NYM
Runs	4 - April 6, 2009 vs. WSH	**Stolen Bases**	3 - 2x, last July 10, 2011 vs. HOU
Hits	4 - 2x, last July 4, 2009 vs. PIT	**Last ML Home Run**	July 23, 2012 vs. ATL
Doubles	2 - 3x, last June 10, 2011 vs. ARI	**Longest Hitting Streak**	26G - June 28-July 28, 2011
Home Runs	1 - 7x, last July 23, 2012 vs. ATL	**Longest Hitless Streak**	23AB - Aug. 7-13, 2008

CAREER FIELDING

POSITION	PCT	G	PO	A	E	TC	DP
2B	.960	75	119	171	12	302	46
3B	.942	128	68	208	17	293	22
SS	.964	96	120	197	12	329	40
OF	.990	160	295	8	3	306	0

MILESTONES

Category		Date	Opponent	Pitcher	Notes
Hit	1	Sept. 10, 2007	at San Francisco	Lincecum	RBI single
Home Run	1	April 6, 2009	Washington	Tavarez	inside the park (2R)
Lead-off HR (1)	1	Sept. 25, 2011	at Milwaukee	Narveson	--
Inside the Park (1)					
	1	April 6, 2009	Washington	Tavarez	2R
RBI	1	Sept. 10, 2007	at San Francisco	Lincecum	single
Stolen Base	1	July 4, 2008	San Diego	Bell C-Hundley	3rd base
	100	May 16, 2012	at Atlanta	Minor C-McCann	2nd base

PROFESSIONAL CAREER:

2007:

- Recalled from Mobile (AA) on Sept. 1 vs. Colorado and made his **Major League debut** on Sept. 2 as a pinch runner against the Rockies.
- Made his first start on Sept. 10 at San Francisco, picking up his first Major League hit and RBI with a single in the fifth inning.

2008:

- Traded to Washington, July 22 for RHP Jon Rauch.
- Recalled by Nationals, Aug. 1 and finished the season with a .248 average (39x157), five doubles, five triples and 12 RBI in 41 games.

2009:

- Was his first full season at the Major League level.
- Ranked sixth in the Majors in infield hits with 34.
- Tied with Nyjer Morgan for third in MLB with 14 bunt hits.
- Hit inside-the-park home run on Opening Day (off J. Tavarez), and became the first player since July 7, 2001 (Cesar Izturis) with an inside-the-park home run as his first career homer... Was the first inside-the-park home run on Opening Day since Carl Yastrzemski on April 10, 1968.

2010:

- Was recalled on June 7 and finished the season hitting .266 in his final 69 games.
- Made 37 starts after his recall; 14 in center field, eight at shortstop, five in left field, four in right field, four at third base and two at second base.

2011:

- Had a 26-game hitting streak from June 28 to July 28, third-longest hit streak of season in National League and Majors.
- Earned Jeff Conine "Mr. Marlin" Award from South Florida chapter of the BBWAA, awarded to player who embodies playing the game right.
- Finished season ranking third among NL leadoff hitters (min. 50 games) in batting average (.310), trailing only Jose Reyes (.336) and Starlin Castro (.327).
- Had second-highest on-base percentage (.376) among NL leadoff hitters (min. 50 games), trailing only Reyes (.383).
- Tied for second in NL in stolen bases, with Matt Kemp, Cameron Maybin and Drew Stubbs.
- Set new career high in steals with 40... Stolen base percentage of 78.4 (40-for-51) was third-highest in Club history for a base runner with at least 40 attempts, trailing Chuck Carr in 1994 (80.0, 32-for-40) and Hanley Ramirez in 2007 (78.5, 51-for-65).
- Named NL Player of the Month in July after leading league (sixth in Majors) with a .380 (38x100) average... Led NL in bunt hits (16) and infield hits (45).
- Tied franchise record by appearing at three different positions on April 2 and July 22, both times vs. Mets.

BUEHRLE, *MARK*

Birthdate . . . . March 20, 1979
Opening Day Age 34
Birthplace. . . . . St. Charles, MO
Residence. . . . . Lemont, IL
Bats/Throws . . . . L/L
Height/Weight 6-2/244
Contract Status . . . . signed thru 2015
M.L. Service 12.078

56

PITCHER

PERSONAL:

Mark Alan Buehrle (Burr-lee)... Married with two children... Has been very active in spreading awareness of pet adoption... Appeared on the Late Show with David Letterman on July 27, 2009, reading 'The Top 10 Things That Went Through Mark Buehrle's Mind During His Perfect Game'... Made two appearances on the "Oprah Winfrey Show" following the White Sox' World Series Championship in 2005... Graduated from Jefferson Junior College (MO) and was selected as a NJCAA Third-Team All-America... Attended and graduated from Francis Howell North High School in St. Charles, Mo.

BUEHRLE AMONG MLB

LEADERS SINCE 2001

Category	Rank	No.
Pickoffs	1st	85
GIDP	1st	291
IP	1st	2627.2
Quality Starts	1st	247
Games Started	1st	393
Wins	3rd	170
Complete Games	4th	28

LAST SEASON:

- Finished season with 202.1 innings pitched over 31 starts, giving him 10 wins, 30 starts and 200.0 innings pitched for the 12th straight season, extending longest active streak in the Majors... Became just second pitcher ever to record a streak of 12 or more seasons with more than 200.0 innings pitched and fewer than 61 walks, joining Cy Young, who did so in 13 straight seasons from 1897-1907... He and CC Sabathia are the only active pitchers with at least 10 wins each season since 2001.
- Threw 28th complete game of career on May 5 at San Diego... Allowed one run on five hits with two walks and three strikeouts... Marked start of undefeated month, finishing May with a 4-0 record and a 3.19 ERA (36.2 IP/13 ER), while holding opponents to a .235 average.
- Issued just 40 walks (three intentional), fifth-fewest among NL starters (min. 30 starts), and seventh in Majors... Finished behind Cliff Lee (28 in 30 GS), Joe Blanton (34 in 30 GS), Bronson Arroyo (35 in 32 GS) and Kyle Lohse (38 in 33 GS) in NL... His 40 walks were fewest allowed in a season in which he made at least 30 starts (also, 2005).
- Recorded a season-high eight strikeouts on July 5 at MIL and Sept. 28 vs. PHI... Marked his most in a game since an eight strikeout performance on July 9, 2011 at MIN... His 125 strikeouts were most in a campaign since fanning 140 in 2008, and was sixth-highest single-season total in his career... Had streak of four consecutive games with at least seven strikeouts from June 24-July 14, which was a career-best run... Entering season, had never gone more than two consecutive starts with seven+ strikeouts... Recorded 1,500th strikeout on Sept. 8 at WAS, hitting mark with second strikeout of afternoon... Is one of 25 active pitchers with 1,500-or-more strikeouts.
- Secured 12th consecutive season with 10-plus wins on August 15 against PHI... Is tied with CC Sabathia for the longest active streak of 10-plus win seasons... Is 41st pitcher ever to have a streak reach at least 12 seasons, and seventh with a run that began after 1970, joining Greg Maddux (20, all-time record; 1988-2007), Mike Mussina (17; 1992-2008), Nolan Ryan (16; 1971-86), Tom Glavine (14; 1989-2002), Javier Vazquez (12; 2000-11) and Sabathia (2001-present).
- Was 11-3 with a 2.43 ERA when pitching at least 7.0 innings, doing so 16 times... Held opponents to a .222 average in those games, and recorded 80 strikeouts to 15 walks (one intentional)... Was 2-10 with a 5.57 ERA in 15 starts when not completing 7.0 innings, with a .304 opponents average and 45 strikeouts to 25 walks (two intentional).
- Took an 8-8 record with a 3.25 ERA into All-Star break (17 starts), marking his lowest ERA heading into the Midsummer Classic since turning in a 3.03 in 2007... Went 5-5, 4.36 in 14 second-half starts.
- Did not make an error in 60 total chances, and has committed just two errors since start of 2008 season (273 TC/.993).

MARK BUEHRLE

Bold – career high

Year Club & League	W-L	ERA	G	GS	CG	ShO	SV	IP	H	R	ER	HR	HB	BB-IBB	SO	WP	BK	OBA
1999 Burlington (Mid)	7-4	4.10	20	14	1	1	3	98.2	105	49	45	8	5	16-1	91	3	6	.271
2000 Birmingham (Sou)	8-4	2.28	16	16	1	1	0	118.2	95	37	30	8	10	17-0	68	1	0	.222
CHICAGO (AL)	4-1	4.21	28	3	0	0	0	51.1	55	27	24	5	3	19-1	37	0	0	.272
2001 CHICAGO (AL)	16-8	3.29	32	32	4	**2**	0	221.1	188	89	81	24	8	48-2	126	1	5	.230
2002 CHICAGO (AL)	**19**-12	3.58	34	34	**5**	**2**	0	239.0	236	102	95	25	3	**61**-7	134	6	1	.260
2003 CHICAGO (AL)	14-**14**	4.14	**35**	**35**	2	0	0	230.1	250	124	106	22	5	**61**-2	119	1	0	.278
2004 CHICAGO (AL)	16-10	3.89	**35**	**35**	4	1	0	**245.1**	257	119	106	33	8	51-2	**165**	0	0	.271
2005 CHICAGO (AL)	16-8	3.12	33	33	3	1	0	236.2	240	99	82	20	4	40-4	149	2	2	.262
2006 CHICAGO (AL)	12-13	4.99	32	32	1	0	0	204.0	247	124	113	**36**	6	48-5	98	0	1	.305
2007 CHICAGO (AL)	10-9	3.63	30	30	3	1	0	201.0	208	86	81	22	5	45-5	115	1	0	.269
2008 CHICAGO (AL)	15-12	3.79	34	34	1	0	0	218.2	240	106	92	22	5	52-4	140	4	0	.281
2009 CHICAGO (AL)	13-10	3.84	33	33	1	1	0	213.1	222	97	91	27	5	45-3	105	2	1	.275
2010 CHICAGO (AL)	13-13	4.28	33	33	3	0	0	210.1	246	105	100	17	1	49-1	99	3	5	.295
2011 CHICAGO (AL)	13-9	3.59	31	31	0	0	0	205.1	221	93	82	21	2	45-3	109	1	0	.277
2012 MIAMI (NL)	13-13	3.74	31	31	1	0	0	202.1	197	88	84	26	4	40-3	125	2	0	.258
Minor Totals	15-8	3.11	36	30	2	2	3	217.1	200	86	75	16	15	33-1	159	4	6	.245
AL TOTALS	161-119	3.83	390	365	27	8	0	2476.2	2610	1171	1053	274	55	564-39	1396	21	15	.273
MAJOR TOTALS	174-132	3.82	421	396	28	8	0	2679.0	2807	1259	1137	300	59	604-42	1521	23	15	.272

ALL-STAR GAME RECORD

Year Club & League	W-L	ERA	G	GS	CG	ShO	SV	IP	H	R	ER	HR	HB	BB-IBB	SO	WP	BK
2002 CWS at MIL	0-0	0.00	1	0	0	0	0	0.1	2	0	0	0	0	0-0	1	0	0
2005 CWS at DET	1-0	0.00	1	1	0	0	0	2.0	3	0	0	0	0	0-0	3	0	0
2006 CWS at PIT								Did Not Play									
2009 CWS at STL	0-0	0.00	1	0	0	0	0	1.0	0	0	0	0	0	0-0	0	0	0
ALL-STAR TOTALS	1-0	0.00	3	1	0	0	0	3.1	5	0	0	0	0	0-0	4	0	0

DIVISION SERIES RECORD

Year Club & League	W-L	ERA	G	GS	CG	ShO	SV	IP	H	R	ER	HR	HB	BB-IBB	SO	WP	BK
2000 CHICAGO (AL)	0-0	0.00	1	0	0	0	0	0.1	2	0	0	0	0	0-0	1	0	0
2005 CHICAGO (AL)	1-0	5.14	1	1	0	0	0	7.0	8	4	4	0	0	1-0	2	0	0
2008 CHICAGO (AL)	0-1	6.43	1	1	0	0	0	7.0	10	5	5	1	0	0-0	3	0	0
DIVISION SERIES TOTALS	1-1	5.65	3	2	0	0	0	14.1	20	9	9	1	0	1-0	6	0	0

LEAGUE CHAMPIONSHIP SERIES RECORD

Year Club & League	W-L	ERA	G	GS	CG	ShO	SV	IP	H	R	ER	HR	HB	BB-IBB	SO	WP	BK
2005 CHICAGO (AL)	1-0	1.00	1	1	1	0	0	9.0	5	1	1	1	1	0-0	4	0	0

WORLD SERIES RECORD

Year Club & League	W-L	ERA	G	GS	CG	ShO	SV	IP	H	R	ER	HR	HB	BB-IBB	SO	WP	BK
2005 CHICAGO (AL)	0-0	4.91	2	1	0	0	1	7.1	7	4	4	1	0	0-0	6	0	0

TRANSACTIONS

- Selected by the Chicago White Sox in the 38th round of the 1998 First Year Player Draft
- Signed by the Miami Marlins on December 20, 2011
- Traded to the Toronto Blue Jays along with RHP Josh Johnson, SS Jose Reyes, IF/OF Emilio Bonifacio, C John Buck and cash considerations in exchange for RHP Henderson Alvarez, SS Yunel Escobar, SS Adeiny Hechavarria, C Jeff Mathis, LHP Justin Nicolino, RHP Anthony Desclafani and OF Jake Marisnick on November 19, 2012

GAME HIGHS

ML Debut	July 16, 2000 vs. MIL
Innings Pitched:	
Starter	9.0 - 23x, last May 5, 2012 at SD
Reliever	4.2 - Aug. 24, 2000 vs. BAL
Walks:	
Starter	6 - May 11, 2003 at SEA
Reliever	3 - 2x, last Aug. 24, 2000 vs. BAL
Strikeouts:	
Starter	12 - April 16, 2005 vs. SEA
Reliever	5 - Aug. 24, 2000 vs. BAL
Hits Allowed	15 - Sept. 15, 2011 at KC
Runs Allowed	11 - July 2, 2006 at CHC
ER Allowed	10 - July 2, 2006 at CHC
HR Allowed	4 - Sept. 20, 2004 vs. MIN
Low Hit CG	0 - 2x, last July 23, 2009 vs. TB
Last Win	Sept. 15, 2012 vs. CIN
Last Save	None
Last CG	May 5, 2012 at SD
Last ShO	July 23, 2009 vs. TB
Last Start	Sept. 28, 2012 vs. PHI
Last Relief App.	Oct. 1, 2000 vs. KC
Longest Win Streak	9G - April 16-June 28, 2005
Longest Losing Streak	9G - April 20-June 11, 2003
Scoreless Innings Streak	25.0 - June 5-22, 2005

CAREER FIELDING

POSITION	PCT	G	PO	A	E	TC	DP
P	.976	421	147	515	16	678	46

MILESTONES

Category		Date	Opponent	Notes
Start	1	July 19, 2000	at Minnesota	won - 7.0 IP, 6H, 2ER, BB, 5K
	100	Sept. 3, 2003	Boston	no decision - 6.2 IP, 8H, 2ER, BB, 3K, HR
	200	Sept. 2, 2006	at Kansas City	won - 6.0 IP, 9H, 3ER, BB, 3K
	300	Sept. 23, 2009	Minnesota	loss - 3.1 IP, 8H, 4ER, BB
Win	1	July 19, 2000	at Minnesota	1st career start - 7.0 IP, 6H, 2ER, BB, 5K
	100	June 10, 2007	Houston	8.0 IP, 6H, ER, BB, 4K, HR
ShO (8)	8	July 23, 2009	Tampa Bay	perfect game - 9.0 IP, 6K
10+ Strikeout Games (1)				
	1	April 16, 2005	Seattle	12 strikeouts
No-Hitter (2)	1	April 18, 2007	Texas	9.0 IP, BB, 8K
	2	July 23, 2009	Tampa Bay	perfect game - 9.0 IP, 6K
Perfect Game (1)				
	1	July 23, 2009	Tampa Bay	9.0 IP, 6K
Strikeout	500	June 29, 2004	Minnesota	Cuddyer
	1000	June 29, 2008	Chicago (NL)	Lee
	1500	Sept. 8, 2012	Washington	LaRoche

PROFESSIONAL CAREER:

2000:

- Made 28 appearances with three starts as a rookie... Became the White Sox primary setup man for second half of season... Made first career start on July 19, 2000 vs. Minnesota, earning the win.

2001:

- Went 16-8 with a 3.29 ERA in his first full Major League season… Became the first Sox pitcher to win 16 games since Alex Fernandez (16-10) in 1996 and the first lefty since Floyd Bannister (16-11) in 1987… Ranked among the AL leaders in runners per 9.0 IP (2nd, 9.9), ERA (4th), opponents average (4th, .230), shutouts (T4th, two), complete games (T5th, 4) and IP (10th, 221.1) … 3.29 ERA topped all AL southpaws… Also ranked among the AL leaders in on-base percentage (2nd, .279), hits per 9.0 IP (3rd, 7.64), strikeout-to-walk ratio (8th, 2.63) and slugging percentage (10th, .377).
- Two shutouts were the most by a Sox pitcher since Fernandez in 1995 and most by a lefty since Jerry Reuss in 1988... Was 15-5 with a 2.79 ERA (53 ER/171.0 IP) over his final 24 starts … Led the AL in ERA (2.99) as late as 9/8 before finishing fourth.
- Threw 24.2 consecutive scoreless innings from May 26-June 7, the most by a Sox pitcher since Tommy John went 25.0 IP from June 13-25/67… 2.08 ERA in June was second in the AL.
- Recorded back-to-back complete game wins on Aug. 3 vs. TB and Aug. 8 at ANA… Tossed a one-hit shutout on Aug. 3 vs. TB.
- Recorded his first career shutout on 5/26 at Detroit… Made his first Opening Day roster.

2002:

- Ranked among the AL leaders in IP (2nd, 239.0), games started (T2nd, 34), complete games (T2nd, 5), shutouts (T2nd, 2), wins (T4th, 19) and quality starts (T5th, 23).
- 19 wins tied for second among AL lefties… 239.0 IP were the most by a Sox pitcher since Alex Fernandez threw 258.0 in 1996… Five complete games were the most by a Sox pitcher since Fernandez (six in 1996)… Also ranked among the AL leaders in pickoffs (T1st, 8), batters faced (3rd, 984), hits allowed (4th, 236), pitches thrown (4th, 3,501), GIDP (T6th, 24), losses (T8th, 12) and pitches per start (10th, 102.97)… 12 home wins ranked second in baseball behind Arizona's Randy Johnson (14).
- Made first All-Star appearance on July 9 at MIL, allowing one run on two hits over 2.0 IP.
- Starts lasted an average of 2:41, including eight played in less than 2:30.
- Was a member of the Major League All-Star Team that played in Japan in November… Made one start before leaving with a bruised left shoulder sustained when hit by a line drive off the bat of Hideki Matsui.

PITCHERS WITH MULTIPLE NO-HITTERS

Pitcher	No.
Nolan Ryan	7
Sandy Koufax	4
Larry Corcoran	3
Bob Feller	3
Cy Young	3
Mark Buehrle	**2**
Jim Bunning	2
Steve Busby	2
Carl Erskine	2
Bob Forsch	2
Pud Galvin	2
Roy Halladay*	2
Ken Holtzman	2
Randy Johnson	2
Addie Joss	2
Dutch Leonard	2
Jim Maloney	2
Christy Mathewson	2
Hideo Nomo	2
Allie Reynolds	2
Frank Smith	2
Warren Spahn	2
Bill Stoneman	2
Virgil Trucks	2
Johnny Vander Meer	2
Justin Verlander	2
Ed Walsh	2
Don Wilson	2

including Game 1 of 2010 NLDS

MOST STARTS BY ACTIVE PITCHERS WITH NO DL STINTS

Pitcher	Starts
Livan Hernandez	474
Mark Buehrle	**396**
Derek Lowe	377
Bronson Arroyo	323
Matt Cain	235

BIOGRAPHIES LAST SEASON HISTORY RECORDS OPPONENTS PLAYER DEV. MEDIA & MISC.

2003:

- Made career-high 35 starts (matched in 2004)… Threw at least 220.0 IP with 100 strikeouts for the third straight season.
- Ranked among the AL leaders in starts (T2nd), quality starts (3rd, 24), IP (5th) and double play grounders (T5th, 24)… Also ranked among the AL leaders in hits allowed (2nd, 250), runs allowed (4th, 124) and losses (T7th, 14).
- Compiled a seven-game winning streak from June 16-July 29 (2.88 ERA).
- Did not allow a steal until Sept. 3 vs. Boston (Johnny Damon)… His starts lasted an average of 2:33, including three that were played in less than 2:00 (all vs. Oakland's Mark Mulder), six in 2:07 or less and 14 in less than 2:25… Game on May 6 at OAK lasted 1:49, the fastest in the Major Leagues in 2003 and the Sox fastest since May 23/84 at KC (also 1:49)… Earned his 50th career win on Aug. 23 vs. TEX.

PITCHERS WITH MULTIPLE NO-HITTERS AND RAWLINGS GOLD GLOVE AWARDS

Mark Buehrle is the only pitcher in baseball history to have thrown multiple no-hitters and earn more than one Rawlings Gold Glove Award. Buehrle (2009) and Bob Gibson (1971) are the only two pitchers to throw a no-hitter in the same season they captured baseball's top fielding award.

2004:

- Became the first White Sox pitcher to lead the AL in IP since Wilbur Wood threw 359.1 IP in 1973.
- Became first Sox pitcher to make 35 starts in back-to-back seasons since Jim Kaat and Wilbur Wood in 1974-75… His 165 strikeouts were the fifth-highest total by a Sox lefty since 1975, trailing Floyd Bannister (198 in 1985 and 193 in 1983), Wilson Alvarez (181 in 1996) and Britt Burns (172 in 1985).
- His five complete games tied Mike Sirotka (1998) and Greg Hibbard (1991) for the most by a Sox lefty since 1990… Ranked among the AL leaders in complete games (T1st), starts (T1st), quality starts (3rd, 23), shutouts (T4th, 1), fewest walks per 9.0 IP (5th, 1.87), wins (T6th, 16), strikeout-to-walk ratio (7th, 3.24), ERA (8th, 3.89) and strikeouts (9th).
- Picked off 10 runners, most in the AL… Induced 33 double play grounders, third in the AL… Received 6.64 runs of support per 9.0 IP, sixth-most in the AL.
- Starts lasted an average of 2:33, quickest in the AL, and 11 were played in less than 2:20.
- Made his third straight Opening Day start on April 5 at KC (ND, 2 ER/6.2 IP).
- Was named AL Pitcher of the Month for May (first career monthly honour) after going 4-0 with a 1.58 ERA (7 ER/40.0 IP).
- Faced the minimum 27 batters in a two-hit shutout on July 21 at CLE, the first Sox pitcher to accomplish that feat since LaMarr Hoyt on May 2/84 vs. NYY).

2005:

- Finished fifth in the AL Cy Young voting, receiving five third-place votes.
- Recorded at least 14 wins, 200.0 IP, 30 starts and 100 strikeouts for the fifth straight season... Became the first Sox pitcher since Wilbur Wood (1971-75) to record at least 10 wins, 100 strikeouts and 200.0 IP in five consecutive seasons... Led the AL in IP and ranked among the leaders ERA (3rd), wins (T5th), complete games (T4th, 3), runners per 9.0 IP (5th, 10.80), shutouts (T5th, 1), walks per 9.0 IP (6th, 1.52), strikeout-to-walk ratio (7th, 3.73), opponents slugging percentage (7th, .380) and starts (T8th, 33).
- Became the first White Sox pitcher since Wood in 1972-73 to lead the AL in IP in back-to-back seasons... Also ranked among the AL leaders in opponents grounded into double plays (2nd, 29) and pickoffs (T2nd, 5)... His 149 strikeouts were the second-highest total of his career (165 in 2004).
- Was named to his second career AL All-Star Team (also 2002), becoming the 6th pitcher in White Sox history to earn the win at the Midsummer Classic... His win was the first by a Sox pitcher who started the All-Star Game.
- Made 20 quality starts, including 10 in a row from May 8-June 28.
- Was named AL Pitcher of the Month for June after going 3-0 with a 0.96 ERA (4 ER/37.2 IP) and 31 strikeouts... It was his second career monthly honor (May 2004).
- His starts lasted an average of 2:40.
- Threw at least 6.0 IP in 49 consecutive starts from May 11, 2004-July 26, 2005, the longest streak in the Major Leagues since Steve Carlton went 69 straight with Philadelphia from 1979-82... Streak came to an end on 8/1 in Baltimore when he was ejected by home plate umpire Brian Gorman after hitting B.J. Surhoff with a pitch.
- Compiled a career-high, nine-game winning streak from April 16-June 28 (2.34 ERA, 28 ER/107.2 IP)... Streak spanned 14 starts and was the longest by a Sox pitcher since Wilson Alvarez tied the club record with 15 straight wins from 1993-94.
- His 10-1 start was the best by a Sox starting pitcher since James Baldwin also won 10 of his first 11 decisions in 2000.
- Made 4th consecutive Opening Day start on April 4 vs. CLE, the longest streak by a Sox pitcher since Jack McDowell also made four straight from 1991-94 and longest by a Sox lefty since Wood made five in a row from 1972-76.
- His career-high scoreless streak of 25.0 consecutive IP ended on June 22 vs. KC.
- May 11/97 vs. OAK game lasted 1:39, the fastest in the Major Leagues since Sept. 30/84 when Atlanta beat San Diego at home, also in 1:39.

MLB PICK-OFF LEADERS

SINCE 1974

Pitcher	Pickoffs
Andy Pettitte	102
Kenny Rogers	94
Mark Langston	91
Mark Buehrle	**89**
Randy Johnson	81

2006:

- Suffered his first losing record (12-13) in six full Major League seasons.
- Became the first pitcher in White Sox history to make 30 or more starts in six consecutive seasons... Also became one of seven pitchers (eight times) in franchise history to record 10 or more victories in at least six consecutive seasons and the first since Joel Horlen (1963-69).
- Joined Livan Hernandez (2000-06), Freddy Garcia (2001-06) and Barry Zito (2001-06) as the only active pitchers to throw 200.0 IP in each of the last six seasons.
- His 204.0 IP and 98 strikeouts both were career lows (221.1 IP in 2001 and 119 strikeouts in 2003)... Also became the first Sox pitcher since Greg Hibbard in 1990 to throw more than 200.0 IP and strike out less than 100 batters.
- Ranked among the American League leaders in hits allowed (T1st, 247), home runs allowed (T2nd, 36), runs allowed (4th, 124), earned runs allowed (6th, 113) and losses (T6th).
- Led the AL with 10 pickoffs and tied for 10th by inducing 21 double plays.
- Sox turned two triple plays while he was on the mound: May 14 at Minnesota and Sept. 18 vs. Detroit, both on infield pop ups with runners moving... Became the first pitcher since Washington's Bruce Howard in 1968 to be on the mound for two triple plays in one season.
- His 11.48 ERA in July was the highest in the Major Leagues and surpassed his previous career monthly high of 7.16 (May 2003) by more than four runs.
- Averaged 2.12 walks per 9.0 IP (48 BB), the 12th-lowest average in the AL, and 4.3 strikeouts per 9.0 IP, down from his 5.4 career average entering the season... Issued just 22 walks in his last 19 starts (114.1 IP).
- Posted a 9.56 ERA (34 ER/32.0 IP) in the first inning, with opponents hitting .395 (58-147)... Allowed a first-inning run in each of his final seven starts, giving up 10 runs total on 19 hits in that span... Minus the first inning, his season ERA would have been 4.13 (79 ER/172.0 IP), and opponents would have batted .285 (189-662).
- Threw a career-low 51 pitches in a loss on July 15 at NYY... Allowed a career-high 11 runs (10 earned) on 13 hits over 5.0 IP on 7/2 at the CHC.
- Made his 5th straight Opening Day start, the longest streak by a Sox pitcher since Wilbur Wood from 1972-76.

2007:

- Recorded 10 wins, 30 starts and 200.0 IP for the 7th consecutive season, joining Livan Hernandez (2000-current) as the only pitchers in baseball to accomplish that feat (Javier Vazquez fell 2.0 IP short in 2004 of joining that elite group)... Is the only pitcher in White Sox history to make 30 starts and throw 200.0 IP in seven straight seasons and is one of seven to record 10 or more victories in at least seven consecutive seasons (first since Joe Horlen, 1963-69).
- Ranked among the AL leaders in complete games (T3rd, 3), shutouts (T4th, 1) and ERA (10th, 3.63)... Lowered his ERA from 4.99 in 2006 to 3.63 in 2007, the sixth-largest improvement in the major leagues.
- Issued just 2.01 walks per 9.0 IP (45 BB), the eighth-best figure in the AL.
- His 10 wins, 30 starts and 201.0 IP all were career lows...
- Allowed 22 home runs in 201.0 IP, down from a career-high 36 in 204.0 IP in 2006.
- Made 20 quality starts, tied for the 12th highest total in the AL.
- Averaged 5.1 strikeouts per 9.0 IP, up from 4.3 in 2006... Averaged 6.7 IP and 103.4 pitches per start.
- Picked off five runners, tied for the most in the AL... Induced 20 double-play grounders, tied for 13th-most in the league...
- **Threw the 16th no-hitter in White Sox history on April 18 vs. Texas**, the first since Wilson Alvarez on Aug. 11/ 91 at BAL and first at home since Joe Horlen on Sept. 10/67 vs. DET... It was the first no-hitter in the major leagues since Florida's Anibal Sanchez on Sept. 6/06 vs. ARZ and first in the AL since Boston's Derek Lowe on April 27/02 vs. TB... Retired the first 13 hitters before issuing a one-out walk to Sammy Sosa in the fifth inning, who he then picked off first base ... It marked the second time in his career in which he faced the minimum 27 batters... The game was the first in major-league history (more than 180,000 games) to feature a no-hitter (Buehrle), grand slam (Jermaine Dye) and multihomer effort (Jim Thome)... Game lasted 2:03, the fastest no-hitter since 1988 when Cincinnati's Tom Browning threw a perfect game against the LAD in 1:51... Including next start vs. KC retired 39 consecutive batters.
- May 31, 2010, allowed solo home runs to Aaron Hill in the second and Frank Thomas in the eighth but otherwise retired every batter (24 of 26 total) ... retired 16 straight hitters between homers... Game lasted 1:50, his sixth career start played in less than 2:00... Jays became the first team in major-league history to win a game without a baserunner.
- Earned his 100th career victory on 6/10 vs. Houston, allowing one run on six hits over 8.0 IP... Became the 5th pitcher in history to record each of his first 100 career wins with the Sox, joining Red Faber, Joe Horlen, Ted Lyons and Ed Walsh.
- Gave up a career high tying 14 hits on July 23 vs. Detroit.
- Made his season debut on 4/5 vs. Cleveland but left after just 1.1 IP when he was hit in the left forearm by a line drive off the bat of Ryan Garko ... start was the shortest of his career.

BUEHRLE'S STARTS UNDER 2:00

Date	Opp.	Dec.	ER/IP	Time
4/30/03	vs. Oak.	L	4 ER/6.0IP	1:54
5/6/03	at Oak.	L	2 ER/7.1 IP	1:49
8/8/03	vs. Oak.	W	2 ER/9.0 IP	1:53
4/4/05	vs. Cle.	W	0 ER/8.0 IP	1:51
4/16/05	vs. Sea.	W	1 ER/9.0 IP	1:39
5/31/07	at Tor.	L	2 ER/8.0 IP	1:50
7/17/10	at Min.	L	3 ER/8.0 IP	1:52
10/2/10	vs. Cle.	W	2 ER/6.0 IP	1:46

BIOGRAPHIES LAST SEASON HISTORY RECORDS OPPONENTS PLAYER DEV. MEDIA & MISC.

2008:

- Registered 10 wins, 30 starts and 200.0 IP for the 8th consecutive season, the only pitcher in baseball to accomplish that feat.
- Won 15 or more games for the 5th time in his career.
- Ranked among American League leaders in quality starts (1st, 24) and opponents GIDP (1st, 34), starts (T1st, 34), pickoffs (T3rd, 7), IP (5th, 218.2), wins (10th, 15) and walks per 9.0 IP (11th, 2.14).
- Allowed one or no earned runs in 13 of his last 26 starts.
- Recorded 60.8 percent of his outs on ground balls, the 8th highest total in the AL.
- Starts lasted an average of 2:38 after his 2007 starts were played in 2:39.
- Pitched on three days rest for the third time and second time in three starts, threw 111 pitches, tied for his second-highest total of the season.
- Made his sixth career Opening Day start on March 31 at CLE, 2nd most in franchise history behind Billy Pierce (seven)... Allowed seven runs on seven hits over 1.2 IP, the second-shortest start of his career.

2009:

- **Threw the 18th perfect game in Major League history on July 23 vs. Tampa Bay and set a Major League record by retiring 45 consecutive batters over three starts from July 18-28** (see notes on following page).
- Won his first American League Rawlings Gold Glove Award, becoming the first White Sox player to garner the honour since Robin Ventura in 1998... Joined Jim Kaat (1974-75) as the only Sox pitchers to capture the top fielding award.
- Recorded 10 wins, 30 starts and 200.0 IP for the 9th consecutive season, the longest active streak in the Major Leagues... Became the second pitcher in Sox history to record 10 or more victories in at least nine consecutive seasons, joining Doc White (1903-13).
- Made 30-plus starts for the 9th straight season, extending his White Sox franchise record.
- Was named to his fourth AL All-Star Team, the second-highest total by a White Sox pitcher behind Billy Pierce (seven)...Ranked among the AL leaders in pickoffs (1st, eight), starts (T4th, 33) and IP (8th, 213.1).
- Was 2-7 with a 4.78 ERA (42 ER/79.0 IP) in 13 starts after his perfect game on July 23 vs. Tampa Bay... Induced 28 double play grounders, 2nd most in the AL, after leading the league in 2008 with 34.
- Made his 7th career Opening Day start on April 7 vs. KC, tying Billy Pierce (1951-52, '54, '56-59) for the most in White Sox history.
- Was the first Sox pitcher to start the season 5-0 since Jose Contreras in 2006 (9-0) and first lefty since Wilson Alvarez in 1994 (8-0).
- Hit his first career home run on June 14 at MIL, a solo shot off Jeff Suppan... Homer was the first by a Sox pitcher since Jon Garland on June 18/06 at CIN.
- Induced six double play grounders on Aug. 7 vs. CLE (all by Buehrle), setting a franchise record and tying the AL record (14th time)... Became the first pitcher to induce six GIDP's since Kansas City's Dick Drago May 6, 1972 at BAL... Also reached the 2,000.0 IP-plateau in that start.

MOST CONSECUTIVE BATTERS RETIRED IN MAJOR LEAGUE HISTORY

Pitcher, Club	No.	Dates
Mark Buehrle, CWS	**45**	**7/18-28/09**
Bobby Jenks, CWS	41	7/17-8/12/07
Jim Barr, SF	41	8/23-29/72
Tom Browning, CIN	40	9/11-21/88
Randy Johnson, ARI	39	5/12-23/04

MLB PERFECT GAMES

Pitcher, Club	Date	Opp.
Felix Hernandez, SEA	8/15/2012	vs. TB
Philip Humber, CWS	4/21/2012	at SEA
Roy Halladay, PHI	5/29/2010	at FLA
Dallas Braden, OAK	5/9/2010	vs. TB
Mark Buehrle, CWS	**7/23/2009**	**vs. TB**
Randy Johnson, ARI	5/18/2004	at ATL
David Cone, NYY	7/18/1999	vs. MON
David Wells, NYY	5/17/1998	vs. MIN
Kenny Rogers, TEX	7/28/1994	vs. CAL
Dennis Martinez, MON	7/28/1991	vs. LAD
Tom Browning, CIN	9/16/1988	vs. LAD
Mike Witt, CAL	9/30/1984	vs. TEX
Len Barker, CLE	5/15/1981	vs. TOR
Catfish Hunter, OAK	5/8/1968	vs. MIN
Sandy Koufax, LAD	9/9/1965	vs. CHC
Jim Bunning, PHI	6/21/1964	vs. NYM
Don Larsen, NYY*	10/8/1956	vs. BKN
Charlie Robertson, SOX	4/30/1922	vs. DET
Addie Joss, CLE	10/2/1908	vs. CWS
Cy Young, BOS	5/5/1904	vs. PHI
Monte Ward, PROV	6/17/1880	vs. BUF
Lee Richmond, WOR	6/12/1880	vs. CLE

**Game 5 of 1956 World Series*

2010:

- Recorded 10 wins, 30 starts and 200.0 IP for the 10th consecutive season, extending both his own franchise record and also the longest active streak in the Major Leagues.
- Won his second straight American League Rawlings Gold Glove Award, becoming the first White Sox player to garner the honour in back-to-back seasons since Robin Ventura in 1991-93... Also won mlb.com's GIBBY (Greatness in Baseball Yearly) Play of the Year for his assist between his legs on Opening Day vs. CLE.
- Ranked among AL Leaders in starts (T4th), walks per 9.0 IP (6th, 2.1) and complete games (T8th, 3)... Also led the Major Leagues with 11 pickoffs... His 99 strikeouts were the second-fewest of his career (98 in 2006).
- Was charged with a major-league high five balks, matching his total from the previous eight seasons combined... Threw 2.1 scoreless IP on May 26 at Cleveland before being ejected by first-base umpire Joe West for disputing two balk calls... Became the first Sox pitcher called for two balks in one game since Scott Radinsky on June 8/93 vs. DET... Ejection was the second of his career (also Aug. 1/05 at BAL)... Was called for two balks for the second time of the season on 9/10 vs. Kansas City, again with West on the umpiring crew.
- Made his eighth career Opening Day start on April 5 vs. CLE, breaking a tie with Billy Pierce for the most in franchise history.
- Registered back-to-back complete games on July 17-23 for the third time in his career... Went the distance for the 25th time in his career in a losing effort on July 17 at MIN... Game lasted just 1:52, his eighth career start played in under 2:00.

2011:

- Recorded at least 10 wins, 30 starts and 200.0 IP for 11th consecutive season to mark longest active streak in Majors... Streak is also a White Sox' club record.
- Only pitcher to throw a minimum of 200.0 innings in each of last 11 seasons, and streak of 11 straight campaigns with 10-or-more wins is tied with CC Sabathia for longest current run in baseball.
- Recorded at least 6.0 IP in 27 of 31 starts, including 22 quality starts.
- For first time in career, went an entire season without recording at least one complete game.
- Earned his third consecutive Rawlings Gold Glove Award after committing just one error in 56 total chances (.982).
- Became first pitcher in White Sox' history to win three Gold Glove Awards and first player in Club history to record three consecutive Gold Gloves since current manager Robin Ventura from 1991-93.
- Made his 9th career Opening Day start, April 1 at CLE a White Sox' record and remains tied with Roy Halladay and Livan Hernandez for most Opening Day starts among active pitchers.
- Earned Major League record 24th career Interleague victory on May 21 vs. Dodgers, breaking tie with Jamie Moyer.
- Went 18 consecutive starts with three runs or less from April 27-August 11, tying a White Sox' record.

LHP Mark Buehrle at spring training meeting the media for the first time

BUSH, *DAVE*

Birthdate	November 9, 1979
Opening Day Age	33
Birthplace	Pittsburgh, PA
Residence	Bridgton, ME
Bats/Throws	R/R
Height/Weight	6-2/204
Contract Status	signed thru 2013
M.L. Service	6.150

PITCHER
NON-ROSTER

PERSONAL:

David Thomas Bush... Married with three children... 1998 graduate of Conestoga High School (PA) where he was named Central League MVP as a junior and senior... 2002 graduate of Wake Forest University where he earned degrees in both psychology and sociology... Named First Team All-American and First Team All-ACC in 2002... Named Preseason ACC Pitcher of the Year and Top Senior Pro Prospect by Baseball America... Hobbies: Reading, woodworking, hiking and camping.

LAST SEASON:

- Spent the first half of the season with Lehigh Valley (AAA) in the Phillies organization.
- Walked only eight in 62.2 innings at the AAA level with Lehigh Valley.
- Was scheduled to be Lehigh Valley's Opening Day starter however was suspended for an incident during a spring contest on March 28 vs Pittsburgh.
- Opted out of his contract on June 5 and signed with Sky Wyverns of the Korean Baseball Organization.
- Went 4-3 with a 4.43 ERA in 17 games for Sky Wyverns.

DAVE BUSH

Bold – career high

Year	Club & League	W-L	ERA	G	GS	CG	ShO	SV	IP	H	R	ER	HR	HB	BB-IBB	SO	WP	BK	OBA
2002	Auburn (NYP)	1-1	2.82	18	0	0	0	10	22.1	13	9	7	1	2	7-2	39	0	0	.159
	Dunedin (FSL)	0-1	2.03	7	0	0	0	0	13.1	10	3	3	1	1	2-0	9	1	1	.222
2003	Dunedin (FSL)	7-3	2.81	14	14	0	0	0	77.0	64	29	24	6	7	9-0	75	4	0	.223
	New Haven (East)	7-3	2.78	14	14	1	0	0	81.0	73	26	25	4	4	19-1	73	2	0	.239
2004	Syracuse (Int)	6-6	4.06	16	16	2	1	0	99.2	108	52	45	7	6	20-1	88	4	1	.278
	TORONTO (AL)	5-4	3.69	16	16	1	1	0	97.2	95	47	40	11	6	25-2	64	3	0	.255
2005	Syracuse (Int)	2-2	4.42	9	9	0	0	0	55.0	65	28	27	6	2	9-0	40	1	0	.298
	TORONTO (AL)	5-11	4.49	25	24	2	0	0	136.1	142	73	68	20	13	29-3	75	2	0	.269
2006	MILWAUKEE (NL)	**12**-11	4.41	**34**	**32**	**3**	**2**	0	**210.0**	201	111	103	26	18	38-2	**166**	6	0	.252
2007	MILWAUKEE (NL)	**12**-10	5.12	33	31	0	0	0	186.1	217	110	106	27	11	44-1	134	3	0	.290
2008	Nashville (PCL)	0-0	1.50	1	1	0	0	0	6.0	3	3	1	1	0	2-0	7	0	0	.136
	MILWAUKEE (NL)	9-10	4.18	31	29	0	0	0	185.0	163	92	86	**29**	10	48-3	109	2	1	.234
2009	Wisconsin Timber (Mid)	0-0	0.00	2	2	0	0	0	7.2	4	1	0	0	0	1-0	9	0	0	.148
	Huntsville (Sou)	0-2	9.95	2	2	0	0	0	6.1	7	7	7	0	1	5-0	4	0	0	.318
	MILWAUKEE (NL)	5-9	6.38	22	21	0	0	0	114.1	131	84	81	19	15	37-2	89	2	0	.294
2010	MILWAUKEE (NL)	8-**13**	4.54	32	31	0	0	0	174.1	198	108	88	28	4	**65**-6	107	1	1	.286
2011	Iowa (PCL)	1-2	6.14	5	5	0	0	0	22.0	28	15	15	3	4	9-0	12	0	0	.318
	Lehigh Valley (Int)	1-2	3.91	4	4	0	0	0	23.0	20	10	10	3	2	6-0	16	0	0	.233
	TEXAS (AL)	0-1	5.79	17	3	0	0	0	37.1	47	27	24	6	3	9-2	23	2	0	.309
2012	Lehigh Valley (Int)	4-3	3.16	11	11	1	1	0	62.2	69	27	22	5	3	8-0	37	1	0	.274
Minor Totals		29-25	3.52	103	78	4	2	10	476.0	464	210	186	37	32	97-4	409	13	2	.255
TORONTO TOTALS		10-15	4.15	41	40	3	1	0	234.0	237	120	108	31	19	54-5	139	5	0	.263
AL TOTALS		10-16	4.38	58	43	3	1	0	271.1	284	147	132	37	22	63-7	162	7	0	.270
NL TOTALS		46-53	4.80	152	144	3	2	0	870.0	910	505	464	129	58	232-14	605	14	2	.269
MAJOR TOTALS		56-69	4.70	210	187	6	3	0	1141.1	1194	652	596	166	80	295-21	767	21	2	.269

DIVISION SERIES RECORD

Year	Club & League	W-L	ERA	G	GS	CG	ShO	SV	IP	H	R	ER	HR	HB	BB-IBB	SO	WP	BK
2008	MILWAUKEE (NL)	1-0	1.69	1	1	0	0	0	5.1	5	1	1	0	0	0-0	3	0	0

TRANSACTIONS

- Selected by the Toronto Blue Jays in the 2nd round of the 2002 First Year Player Draft
- Traded to the Milwaukee Brewers along with OF Gabe Gross and a player to be named later (LHP Zach Jackson) in exchange for 1B Lyle Overbay and a player to be named later (RHP Ty Taubenheim) on December 7, 2005
- On disabled list (micro tear of right triceps) from June 23-August 26, 2009; included rehabilitation assignment at Wisconsin (A) and Huntsville (A) from July 10-August 27
- Signed by the Texas Rangers on January 30, 2011
- Signed by the Chicago Cubs on July 14, 2011
- Signed by the Philadelphia Phillies on August 15, 2011
- Signed by the Toronto Blue Jays on December 20, 2012

CAREER FIELDING

POSITION	PCT	G	PO	A	E	TC	DP
P	.981	210	94	118	4	216	10

GAME HIGHS

ML Debut	July 2, 2004 at MON	**Runs Allowed**	10 - July 20, 2010 at PIT
Innings Pitched:		**ER Allowed**	8 - 3x, last Sept. 2, 2009 at STL
Starter	9.0 - 4x, last Sept. 10, 2006 vs. HOU	**HR Allowed**	4 - 2x, last Aug. 11, 2010 vs. ARI
Reliever	4.2 - June 11, 2011 at MIN	**Low Hit CG**	2 - Oct. 1, 2004 vs. NYY
Walks:		**Last Win**	Sept. 29, 2010 at NYM
Starter	5 - 2x, last June 30, 2010 vs. HOU	**Last Save**	None
Reliever	2 - June 27, 2007 vs. HOU	**Last CG**	Sept. 10, 2006 vs. HOU
Strikeouts:		**Last ShO**	Sept. 10, 2006 vs. HOU
Starter	13 - July 10, 2008 vs. COL	**Last Start**	June 2, 2011 at CLE
Reliever	5 - June 11, 2011 at MIN	**Last Relief App.**	June 30, 2011 at HOU
Hits Allowed	11 - 2x, last Sept. 2, 2009 at STL	**Longest Win Streak**	4G - Aug. 5-29, 2008
		Longest Losing Streak	7G - May 24-Sept. 7, 2009
		Scoreless Innings Streak	17.0 - July 8-25, 2004

MILESTONES

Category		Date	Opponent	Notes
Start	1	July 2, 2004	at Montreal	loss - 5.2 IP, 4H, ER, BB, 4K
	100	Sept. 12, 2007	at Pittsburgh	no decision - 4.0, 5H, 4ER, 2BB, 2K
Win	1	July 25, 2004	Tampa Bay	as a starter - 7.1 IP, 8H, ER, BB, 2K, HR
ShO (3)	1	Oct. 1, 2004	New York (AL)	9.0 IP, 2H, 3BB, 11K
	2	April 22, 2006	Cincinnati	9.0 IP, 4H, 2BB, 9K
	3	Sept. 10, 2006	Houston	9.0 IP, 5H, 10K
10+ Strikeout Games (4)				
	1	Oct. 1, 2004	New York (AL)	11 strikeouts
	2	Sept. 10, 2006	Houston	10 strikeouts
	3	July 10, 2008	Colorado	13 strikeouts
	4	Sept. 12, 2009	at Arizona	11 strikeouts
Strikeout	500	July 10, 2008	Colorado	Vizcaino

PROFESSIONAL CAREER:

2004:

- Had his contract selected by Toronto on July 2 and made his **ML debut** that night in a start vs MTL in Puerto Rico (L, 5.2 IP, 4 H, ER)... Remained in TOR's starting rotation for the remainder of the season
- Went 4-0, 2.77 ERA (16 ER, 52.0 IP) in eight starts at SkyDome... Team was 5-3 in his starts.
- Took a no-hitter into the 8th inning until Damian Miller's one-out single, July 20 at OAK (ND, 8.0 IP, H, 3 BB, 6 SO).
- Recorded his 1st ML win, July 25 vs TB.
- Threw a 2-hit SHO with 11 SO, the first of his ML career, Oct. 1 vs NYY

2005:

- Began the season with Toronto making 10 starts before being optioned to Syracuse (AAA) after going winless... Was recalled on July 21 and went 5-6 with a 4.23 ERA in his final 15 agmes (14 starts)
- Took the loss in both of his CG, May 18 at MIN and Aug. 13 at BAL
- Was named Toronto's 7th-best prospect according to Baseball America after the season

2006:

- Spent his first full season with MIL where he set career highs in nearly every category... Led MIL's staff with a career-high 12 wins... Set career highs in CG (3) and SHO (2), both of which were tied for the most on the team (Chris Capuano)... Ranked 2nd on the staff in IP (210.0), SO (166) and quality starts (18), also career highs.
- Pitched 6.0 or more innings in 25 of his 32 starts (78%), including each of his first nine starts of the year.
- Threw a 4-hit SHO with nine strikeouts, April 22 vs CIN and a 5-hit SHO with 10 SO, Sept. 10 vs HOU... Struck out a season-best 10 batters, 9/10 vs HOU

2007:

- Matched his career high with 12 wins for MIL... Led the staff in SO (134)... Finished T-1st in wins (12) and 2nd in both starts (31) and IP (186.1)... Tied Jeff Suppan for the team lead in quality starts (15).
- Pitched 6.0 or more innings in 22 of his 31 starts (71%).
- Recorded the win in both of his relief appearances, June 27 vs HOU and July 31 vs NYM.

2008:

- Finished 2nd on MIL staff in IP (185.0) and 3rd in starts (29)... Had the 2nd-most quality starts on the staff (16)... Held opponents to .234 AVG (163-698).
- Went 7-3, 3.23 ERA (41 ER, 114.1 IP) over last 18 games (17 GS) of the season.
- June 19 vs. TOR had 7.0 hitless innings before Lyle Overbay's leadoff triple in the 8th ended his no-hit bid.
- Recorded career-high 13 SO, July 10 vs COL; became the 1st pitcher in franchise history with at least 13 SO and 0 BB in a game.
- Earned MIL's only victory of the postseason in Game 3 of the NLDS, Oct. 4 vs PHI at Miller Park (5.1 IP, ER, 0 BB, 3 SO).

2009:

- Due to injury, made only 21 starts for MIL, his fewest since 2004 (16).
- Pitched 7.1 hitless innings on April 25 at PHI before a pinch HR by Matt Stairs ended his no-hit bid.
- On the 15-day DL (micro tear of the right triceps muscle), June 23-Aug. 26; suffered the injury when he was struck by a line drive by Hanley Ramirez on June 4 at FLA

2010:

- Tied for 2nd on the staff in starts (31), ranked 3rd in innings (174.1), tied for 4th in wins (8), and 5th in strikeouts (107)... Was 2nd in quality starts (18), matching career best (2006)... Led Milwaukee in losses (career high 13)... Received lowest run support of any Brewers starter at 4.49 runs per game.
- Recorded just one win in his 1st 13 starts (1-5) before victory on June 15 at LAA... Posted consecutive wins only once all season, June 15-25.
- Allowed 37 ER in 22.2 IP in a total of six starts ... compiled a 3.03 ERA (51 ER/151.1 IP) in his other 25 starts.
- Permitted 20 unearned runs, most for any major league pitcher in the past three seasons (2008-10).
- Issued three or fewer earned runs 23 times but five or more on seven occasions.
- Tied the Major League record (3rd time) by allowing four consecutive homers (Adam LaRoche, Miguel Montero, Mark Reynolds, Stephen Drew) in the 4th inning on August 11 vs. Arizona.
- Did not have a complete game for the 4th straight year... Had gone 115 starts since his last CG, a 5-hit SHO on Sept. 10, 2006 vs. HOU... Was the 5th longest streak among active pitchers behind: 127-Scott Olsen; 121-Scott Kazmir; 117-Rodrigo Lopez; and 116-Jorge De La Rosa.

2011:

- Split the season between three organizations: TEX, CHI and PHI.
- Was a non-roster invitee to spring training with TEX and made the Opening Day roster... Shuttled between the rotation and the bullpen; went 0-0, 4.09 ERA (5 ER, 11.0 IP) in three starts... Pitched at least 2.0 innings in 6 of his 14 relief appearances.
- Designated for assignment on July 1 and was released on July 6.
- Signed by CHC on July 14 and assigned to Iowa (AAA)... Released on Aug. 10.
- Signed with the Phillies on Aug. 15 and was assigned to Lehigh Valley (AAA).

Hanging out with ACE in the Jays Care Community Clubhouse, a fully-renovated luxury suite at Rogers Centre

CABRERA, *MELKY*

Birthdate .... August 11, 1984
Opening Day Age 28
Birthplace........... Bajos De Haina, DR
Residence........... Bajos De Haina, DR
Bats/Throws .... S/L
Height/Weight 6-0/168
Contract Status .... signed thru 2014
M.L. Service 6.148

OUTFIELDER

PERSONAL:

Melky Astacio Cabrera... Has three children... Took part in Yankees' hurricane relief donation of $35,000 in cash and food to Dominican Republic in October of 2007... Honoured with Munson Award for his excellence and philanthropic work in community at 28th Annual Thurman Munson Dinner on Feb. 5, 2008.

LAST SEASON:

- Opened up the season with an eight-game hitting streak.
- On Aug. 15 it was announced by Major League Baseball that he was suspended 50 games for testing positive for testosterone, a performance-enhancing substance...Was eligible to return for the post-season, but was not added to the Giants roster.
- At the time of his suspension led the Majors with 159 hits and 52 multi-hit games while batting .346 -- the second-highest average in the National League... Was leading the league in runs with 84.
- Was named Most Valuable Player in the All-Star Game played in Kansas City, going 2-for-3 with a two-run home run.
- Recorded a career high 10 triples (T-5th in NL).
- Batted .429 in May with three homers, five triples, seven doubles and 17 RBI.
- Established a San Francisco era record for the most hits in the month of May with 51... Surpassed Willie Mays, who had 49 in May of 1958... Tied Randy Winn (Sept. '05), a SF-era record with 51 hits in a single calendar month.
- His 39 multi-hit games were a new Giants franchise record prior to the All-Star break.

MELKY CABRERA

Bold – career high

Year	Club and League	AVG	G	AB	R	H	2B	3B	HR	RBI	SH-SF	HP	BB-IBB	SO	SB-CS	SLG	OBP	OPS
2002	DSL Yankees (DSL)	.335	60	218	37	73	19	3	3	29	0-3	3	18-3	23	7-2	.491	.388	.879
2003	Staten Island (NYP)	.283	67	279	34	79	10	2	2	31	4-1	4	23-1	36	13-5	.355	.345	.700
2004	Battle Creek (Mid)	.333	42	171	35	57	16	3	0	16	0-2	0	15-0	23	7-2	.462	.383	.845
	Tampa (FSL)	.288	85	333	48	96	20	3	8	51	0-3	5	23-1	59	3-1	.438	.341	.779
2005	Columbus (Int)	.248	26	101	15	25	3	0	3	17	2-0	0	9-0	15	2-0	.366	.309	.675
	Trenton (East)	.275	106	426	57	117	22	3	10	60	1-5	4	28-2	72	11-2	.411	.322	.733
	NEW YORK (AL)	.211	6	19	1	4	0	0	0	0	0-0	0	0-0	2	0-0	.211	.211	.422
2006	Columbus (Int)	.385	31	122	19	47	6	2	4	24	0-2	1	10-0	9	3-1	.566	.430	.996
	NEW YORK (AL)	.280	130	460	75	129	26	2	7	50	5-1	2	**56**-3	59	12-5	.391	.360	.751
2007	NEW YORK (AL)	.273	150	545	66	149	24	8	8	73	10-9	5	43-0	68	13-5	.391	.327	.718
2008	Scranton-W. Barre (Int)	.333	15	57	8	19	2	0	0	5	0-1	0	8-0	9	1-3	.368	.409	.777
	NEW YORK (AL)	.249	129	414	42	103	12	1	8	37	4-3	3	29-5	58	9-2	.341	.301	.642
2009	NEW YORK (AL)	.274	154	485	66	133	28	1	13	68	4-4	4	43-4	59	10-2	.416	.336	.752
2010	ATLANTA (NL)	.255	147	458	50	117	27	3	4	42	5-3	1	42-11	64	7-1	.354	.317	.671
2011	KANSAS CITY (AL)	.305	**155**	658	**102**	**201**	**44**	5	**18**	**87**	7-5	1	35-3	**94**	**20**-10	.470	.339	.809
2012	SAN FRANCISCO (NL)	.346	113	459	84	159	25	**10**	11	60	1-5	0	36-4	63	13-5	.516	.390	.906
Minor Totals		.301	432	1707	253	513	98	16	30	233	7-17	17	134-7	246	47-16	.429	.354	.784
AL TOTALS		.279	724	2581	352	719	134	17	54	315	30-22	15	206-15	340	64-24	.406	.333	.739
NL TOTALS		.301	260	917	134	276	52	13	15	102	6-8	1	78-15	127	20-6	.435	.354	.789
MAJOR TOTALS		.284	984	3498	486	995	186	30	69	417	36-30	16	284-30	467	84-30	.414	.338	.752

ALL-STAR GAME RECORD

Year	Club and League	AVG	G	AB	R	H	2B	3B	HR	RBI	SH-SF	HP	BB-IBB	SO	SB-CS
2012	NL at KC	.667	1	3	2	2	0	0	1	2	0-0	0	0-0	0	0-0

DIVISION SERIES RECORD

Year	Club and League	AVG	G	AB	R	H	2B	3B	HR	RBI	SH-SF	HP	BB-IBB	SO	SB-CS
2006	NEW YORK (AL)	.000	2	3	0	0	0	0	0	0	0-0	0	0-0	0	0-0
2007	NEW YORK (AL)	.188	4	16	2	3	0	0	1	2	0-0	0	0-0	1	0-0
2009	NEW YORK (AL)	.167	3	12	1	2	0	0	0	0	0-0	0	0-0	5	0-0
2010	SAN FRANCISCO (NL)	.000	3	8	1	0	0	0	0	1	0-0	0	0-0	1	0-0
DIVISION SERIES TOTALS		.128	12	39	4	5	0	0	1	3	0-0	0	0-0	7	0-0

LEAGUE CHAMPIONSHIP SERIES RECORD

Year	Club and League	AVG	G	AB	R	H	2B	3B	HR	RBI	SH-SF	HP	BB-IBB	SO	SB-CS
2009	NEW YORK (AL)	.391	6	23	3	9	2	0	0	4	0-0	0	3-0	6	0-0

WORLD SERIES RECORD

Year	Club and League	AVG	G	AB	R	H	2B	3B	HR	RBI	SH-SF	HP	BB-IBB	SO	SB-CS
2009	NEW YORK (AL)	.154	4	13	1	2	0	0	0	0	0-0	0	0-0	3	0-0

HOME RUN BREAKDOWN

Total	H	A	ONE GAME 2	3	4	GS	LO	XN	IP	PH	RHP	LHP
69	29	40	2	0	0	2	0	3	0	0	44	25

TRANSACTIONS

- Signed by the New York Yankees on November 13, 2001
- Traded to the Atlanta Braves along with LHP Mike Dunn and RHP Arodys Vizcaino in exchange for RHP Javier Vasquez and LHP Boone Logan on December 22, 2009
- Signed by the Kansas City Royals on December 16, 2010
- Traded to the San Francisco Giants in exchnage for LHP Jonathan Sanchez and LHP Ryan Verdugo on November 7, 2011
- Signed by the Toronto Blue Jays on November 19, 2012

GAME HIGHS

ML Debut	July 7, 2005 vs. CLE	**RBI**	5 - 4x, last Aug. 10, 2011 at TB
Runs	4 - July 3, 2011 at COL	**Stolen Bases**	2 - 3x, last May 27, 2012 at MIA
Hits	4 - 9x, last May 27, 2012 at MIA	**Last ML Home Run**	Aug. 4, 2012 at COL
Doubles	2 - 13x, last May 24, 2012 at MIA	**Longest Hitting Streak**	18G - July 25-Aug. 13, 2007
Home Runs	2 - 2x, last July 3, 2011at COL	**Longest Hitless Streak**	19AB - June 27-July 1, 2008

CAREER FIELDING

POSITION	PCT	G	PO	A	E	TC	DP
OF	.988	960	1965	66	24	2055	16

MILESTONES

Category		Date	Opponent	Pitcher	Notes
Hit	1	July 7, 2005	Cleveland	Millwood	single
Home Run	1	June 15, 2006	Cleveland	Lee	1R
Multi-Homer Game (2)					
	1	April 22, 2009	Oakland	Anderson, Giese	1R, 2R
	2	July 3, 2011	at Colorado	Hammel	1R, 3R
Grand Slam (2)	1	July 5, 2006	at Cleveland	Byrd	4th inning
	2	July 29, 2011	at Cleveland	Carrasco	4th inning
Walk-off HR (2)	1	July 18, 2006	Seattle	Mateo	1R, 11th inning
	2	April 22, 2009	Oakland	Giese	2R, 14th inning
Extra-Inning HR (3)					
	1	July 18, 2006	Seattle	Mateo	1R, 11th inning
	2	April 22, 2009	Oakland	Giese	2R, 14th inning
	3	May 27, 2011	at Texas	Bush	1R, 14th inning
RBI	1	May 9, 2006	Boston	Beckett	single
Stolen Base	1	May 20, 2006	at New York (NL)	Martinez C-Castro	2nd base

PROFESSIONAL CAREER:

2005:

- Appeared in six games with NYY, batting .211 (4-for-19) with 1 run.
- Had his contract purchased from Columbus on July 7 and made his Major League debut that night, starting in center field vs. Cleveland... Went 1-for-4 and collected 1st Major League hit (single off Kevin Millwood in 5th inning).

2006:

- Tied for 2nd in AL with 12 outfield assists... Led all American League rookies with 75 runs, 12 stolen bases, 56 walks, 12 outfield assists and a .360 on-base percentage; ranked second with 26 doubles, third with 129 hits, fourth with 50 runs batted in, 31 multi-hit games, 180 total bases and 35 extra-base hits, and fifth with a .280 batting average.
- Began season with AAA Columbus and was recalled May 9... Started in right field that night vs. Boston and was 2-3 with his 1st Major League RBI.
- Established his single-game career high with four hits May 30 win at Detroit.
- Hit his 1st career Major League home run June 15 vs. Cleveland... Began his Major League career with 130 homerless at-
- bats... According to Elias, it was longest such streak by Yankees player to start career since Bobby Meacham went 281 at-bats without homer from 1983-84.
- Hit 1st career grand slam and collected career-high 5 RBI on July 5 at Cleveland... Became youngest Yankees player, at 21 years old, to hit walk-off home run since Mickey Mantle on April 23, 1953 vs. Boston (also at age 21).
- Reached base safely in 20 straight games (via hit, walk or HP) from June 25-July 18... Marked longest such streak by Yankees rookie since Derek Jeter reached base safely in 23 straight games in 1996.
- Went 0-for-3 in two Division Series games vs. Detroit.

2007:

- Started 101 of Yankees' final 111 games of season in CF with team going 72-39 (.649)... During that stretch, hit .290 (119-for-411) with 21 2Bs, 7 3Bs, 6 HRs, 58 RBI and 10 stolen bases.
- Tied for 3rd in AL with 16 outfield assists, tied for 4th with nine sacrifice flies, tied for 5th with 10 sacrifice hits and tied for 6th with eight 3Bs.
- Led all Major League center fielders with 14 assists.
- Had a career-high 18-game hitting streak, July 25-Aug. 13, batting .400 (30-for-75).
- Hit game-winning walk-off single in 10th inning and tied career high with five RBI on Sept. 22 vs. Toronto.
- In four division series games vs. Cleveland, was 3-for-16 with 2 RBI... Hit solo home run off Fausto Carmona in Game 2 loss, accounting for lone Yankees run in game.

2008:

- Hit 1st career Opening Day home run, solo shot off Roy Halladay, snapping stretch of 163 at-bats without homer (since Aug. 12, 2007)... Marked 92nd Opening Day home run in Yankees history and he became 57th different Yankee to homer on Opening Day.
- Served two-game suspension (reduced from 3 games) for his involvement in spring training altercation on March 12 at Tampa Bay.
- Was optioned to Triple-A Scranton/Wilkes-Barre on Aug. 15... Was recalled from Scranton/WB on Sept. 5, but did not appear in game with NYY until Sept. 13, when he appeared as an 8th-inning defensive replacement in CF in Game 2 vs. TB.
- Batted .462 (6-for-13) in 12 Sept. games (3 starts) following his recall.

2009:

- Set career highs in doubles (28) and home runs (13) in 154 games with NYY.
- Batted .277 (91-for-328) with eight home runs as a right-handed batter and .268 (42-for-157) with five longballs as a left-handed batter.
- Recorded three outfield assists and his 38 career OF assists, are T-4th in the Majors over the last four seasons (2006-09)... His 14 assists as a center fielder over the same span are second-most in MLB behind TB's B.J. Upton (16).
- Became just the 11th player in Yankees history to hit for the cycle on Aug. 2 at CWS... The four hits matched his career high...Tied his career-high with four hits Aug. 21 at BOS... Recorded four straight multi-hit games for the first time in his career from Aug. 31-Sept. 3... Tied his season high with four RBI on Sept. 13 vs. BAL.
- On July 17 vs. DET, recorded two outfield assists for the third time in his career and first since July 15/07 at TB.
- Was named the Major League Baseball Clutch Performer of the Month Presented by Pepsi Award winner for May... In 24 games, he batted .321 (27-for-84) with nine runs, six doubles, one home run and 11 RBI.
- Recorded walk-off hits on May 15 vs. MIN and May 23 vs. PHI.
- Missed four games with a bruised right shoulder, May 27-31.
- Hit solo-home run in the second inning and a two-run, walk-off homer in the 14th on April 22 vs. OAK, marking his first career multi-HR game and second career walk-off home run (July 18/06 vs. SEA)... Hit solo-home run on April 17 vs. CLE and a two-run homer April 18 vs. CLE, marking just the second time in his career he homered in consecutive games (also 8/9-10/06 at CWS).
- Hit .167 (2-for-12) in three games vs. MIN in LDS... Posted three multi-hit games in six contests vs. LAA in LCS, batting .391 (9-for-23) with two doubles, four RBI and six walks... In Game 4, had three hits and a team-high four RBI... Was 2-for-13 (.154) in four games in World Series vs. PHI.

2010:

- Was acquired by Braves along with LHP Mike Dunn and RHP Arrodys Vizcaino from New York-AL in exchange for RHP Javier Vazquez and LHP Boone Logan on Dec. 22, 2009.
- Spent first full season in the National League with Atlanta... Got off to slow start, batting just .195 (15-for-77) in April before hitting combined .288 (68-for-236) from May through July.
- Made 115 starts, all in outfield... Played 48 games in center field, 46 in left and 21 in right.
- Went hitless in 8 at-bats in 3 games against San Francisco during NL Division Series.

2011:

- Was acquired by San Francisco from Kansas City in November of 2010... Completed his 1st and only season with Royals setting career highs in nearly every offensive category, including batting average (.305), runs (102), hits (201), doubles (44), home runs (18), RBI (87) and stolen bases (20).
- Ranked 9th in American League in batting average and finished 4th in AL in hits, 7th in total bases (309) and tied for 8th in doubles and runs scored... Finished 2nd in Majors to Yankees' Curtis Granderson with 85 RBI from number 2 spot in batting order.
- Became just 6th Royals player (7th time) to reach 200+ hits in season and 1st since 2000 (Johnny Damon, 214; Mike Sweeney, 206).
- Posted 61 multi-hit games, tied for 2nd in Major Leagues and 4th-best single-season total in club history... Tied for 6th in Majors with 13 outfield assists... Recorded his 2nd career 2-HR game on July 3 at Colorado, hitting solo HR in 1st inning and 3-run shot in 3rd... Also set career-high with 4 runs scored and matched careerbest with 5 RBI... Also drove in five runs on Aug. 10 at Tampa Bay (4th time in his career).

CECIL, *BRETT*

Birthdate . . . . July 2, 1986
Opening Day Age 26
Birthplace . . . . Dunkirk, MD
Residence . . . . Clearwater, FL
Bats/Throws . . . . R/L
Height/Weight 6-1/216
Contract Status . . . . signed thru 2013
M.L. Service 2.152

PITCHER

PERSONAL:

Brett Aarion Cecil... Married with one child... Resides in Dunkirk, Maryland... Brett was the Blue Jays 1st round pick (supplemental), 38th overall, in the 2007 First-Year Player Draft... Son of Duane and Linda Cecil... Attended University of Maryland, majored in criminal justice... Was a closer on the Terrapins squad when drafted... Participated in the Blue Jays Winter Tour in 2012 and 2013.

LAST SEASON:

- Made 21 appearances, including nine starts... Was recalled from New Hampshire (AA) on June 28 and made all nine starts before being optioned to Las Vegas (AAA) on Aug. 3... Returned to the club Sept. 3 and spent the balance of the season in the bullpen.
- As a starter went 2-4 with a 5.72 ERA...Out of the bullpen was 0-0 with a 5.73 ERA.
- Allowed three runs or less in six of his eight starts...In those six posted a 3.53 ERA.
- Limited left-handed hitters ro a .214 average and now has held them to a .232 mark in his career... Right-handed hitters hit .319 with a .934 OPS.
- Allowed 11 home runs in 61.1 innings and has now has given up a 1.61 HR/9 over the last two seasons... Prior to that allowed just 1.18 HR/9 in his first two seasons.
- Began the season with New Hampshire making nine starts going 3-2 with a 3.38 ERA... Held Eastern League hitters to a .267 average... Made six starts for Las Vegas gong 1-2 with a 2.50 ERA... Did not allow more than three runs in any of his AAA starts.

BRETT CECIL

Bold – career high

Year	Club & League	W-L	ERA	G	GS	CG	ShO	SV	IP	H	R	ER	HR	HB	BB-IBB	SO	WP	BK	OBA
2007	Auburn (NYP)	1-0	1.27	14	13	0	0	0	49.2	36	10	7	1	3	11-0	56	0	0	.197
2008	Dunedin (FSL)	0-0	1.74	4	4	0	0	0	10.1	6	2	2	1	0	2-0	11	0	0	.167
	New Hampshire (East)	6-2	2.55	18	18	0	0	0	77.2	66	24	22	4	5	23-0	87	2	0	.227
	Syracuse (Int)	2-3	4.11	6	6	0	0	0	30.2	28	17	14	1	0	16-0	31	2	0	.237
2009	Las Vegas (PCL)	1-5	5.69	9	9	1	0	0	49.0	53	37	31	2	3	19-0	32	1	0	.273
	TORONTO (AL)	7-4	5.30	18	17	0	0	0	93.1	116	59	55	17	5	38-0	69	0	0	.308
2010	Las Vegas (PCL)	2-0	2.45	2	2	0	0	0	11.0	13	4	3	0	0	2-0	11	1	0	.302
	TORONTO (AL)	**15**-7	4.22	**28**	**28**	0	0	0	**172.2**	175	87	81	18	1	**54**-2	**117**	7	1	.264
2011	Las Vegas (PCL)	8-2	5.26	12	12	2	1	0	78.2	89	51	46	15	0	24-0	63	1	0	.283
	TORONTO (AL)	4-**11**	4.73	20	20	**2**	**1**	0	123.2	122	68	65	**22**	6	42-1	87	1	0	.256
2012	New Hampshire (East)	3-2	3.38	9	9	0	0	0	42.2	44	18	16	2	2	14-0	34	1	0	.267
	Las Vegas (PCL)	1-2	2.50	6	6	0	0	0	39.2	36	11	11	1	1	7-0	33	2	0	.248
	TORONTO (AL)	2-4	5.72	21	9	0	0	0	61.1	70	40	39	11	3	23-0	51	0	0	.294
Minor Totals		24-16	3.51	80	79	3	1	0	389.1	371	174	152	27	14	118-0	358	10	0	.249
MAJOR TOTALS		28-26	4.79	87	74	2	1	0	451.0	483	254	240	68	15	157-3	324	8	1	.275

TRANSACTIONS

- Selected by the Toronto Blue Jays in the 1st round (supplemental – 38th overall) of the 2007 First Year Player Draft

GAME HIGHS

ML Debut	May 5, 2009 vs. CLE
Innings Pitched:	
Starter	9.0 - July 24, 2011 at TEX
Reliever	2.0 - 3x, last Sept. 28, 2012 vs. NYY
Walks:	
Starter	6 - July 2, 2010 at NYY
Reliever	2 - Sept. 3, 2012 vs. BAL
Strikeouts:	
Starter	10 - May 3, 2010 at CLE
Reliever	2 - Sept. 28, 2012 vs. NYY
Hits Allowed	11 - 2x, last Sept. 24, 2010 vs. BAL
Runs Allowed	8 - 3x, last June 18, 2012 vs. LAA
ER Allowed	8 - 3x, last June 18, 2012 vs. LAA
HR Allowed	5 - May 20, 2009 at BOS
Low Hit CG	4 - July 24, 2011 at TEX
Last Win	July 3, 2012 vs. KC
Last Save	None
Last CG	July 24, 2011 at TEX
Last ShO	July 24, 2011 at TEX
Last Start	Aug. 3, 2012 at OAK
Last Relief App.	Oct. 1, 2012 vs. MIN
Longest Win Streak	5G - May 19-June 10, 2010
Longest Losing Streak	7G - Aug. 9-Sept. 25, 2011
Scoreless Innings Streak	18.2 - July 10-26, 2009

FIELDING

Year	PCT	G	PO	A	E	TC	DP
P	.931	87	6	48	4	58	3

MILESTONES

Category		Date	Opponent	Notes
Start	1	May 5, 2009	Cleveland	ND, 6.0 IP, 6H, ER, 6K
Win	1	May 10, 2009	at Oakland	8.0 IP, 5H, 2BB, 6K
10+ Strikeout Games (1)				
	1	May 3, 2010	at Cleveland	10 strikeouts

PROFESSIONAL CAREER:

2009:

- Made his **Major League debut** on May 5 vs. CLE... Received a no-decision (6.0IP, 6H, ER, 6K) in a 10-6 win... Became the first American League pitcher to strike out six or more batters without a walk in his Major League debut since Robinson Checo of the Red Sox did it in 1997 against the Yankees.
- Was the first player from the 2007 draft for the Blue Jays to reach the Majors.
- Had a career high scoreless innings streak of 18.2 from July 10-26.

2010:

- Led the club with 15 victories, despite beginning the year at Las Vegas (AAA).
- Made 15 starts vs. AL East opponents, producing an 11-2 record with a 3.47 ERA... The 11 wins were 2nd to only Jon Lester (12-2) by any pitcher vs. the East... Included a 4-0 mark vs. NYY and a 3-1 record vs. TB, both playoff clubs.
- On May 7 at CLE, took a perfect game into the 7th inning, losing it with a one-out walk and the no-hitter three batters later... Won 5-1 finishing with eight innings of one-hit ball.

2011:

- Was optioned to Las Vegas (AAA) on April 21... Made 12 starts for the 51s, going 8-2 with a 5.26 ERA.
- Won seven consecutive starts for Las Vegas and added two complete games, including one shutout.
- Was recalled to Toronto on June 20.
- Recorded his 2nd complete game and first career shutout, a four-hit, 3-0 win at TEX on July 24.
- Held left-handed hitters to a .186 average, and only five extra-base hits (none of which were home runs).

LHP Brett Cecil signing autographs at the Toronto Blue Jays Winter Tour stop in Winnipeg, Manitoba

COOPER, *DAVID*

Birthdate	February 12, 1987
Opening Day Age	26
Birthplace	Stockton, CA
Residence	Stockton, CA
Bats/Throws	L/L
Height/Weight	6-0/201
Contract Status	signed thru 2013
M.L. Service	0.136

31

INFIELDER

PERSONAL:

David Fletcher Cooper... Was a Louisville Slugger third-team All-American, batting .359 with a team leading 19 home runs & 55 RBI in 56 games at Cal-State Fullerton in his junior season... Was a semifinalist for the Dick Howser Trophy, USA Baseball's Golden Spikes Award & the Wallace Award... Was a member of the 2006 College World Series All-Tournament team... Flirted with a College World Series record with seven consecutive hits, tying Terry Francona (1980) & fell one hit short of the record held by Dave Magadan (1983) & Barry Bonds (1984)... Led all players at the 2006 College World Series with a .533 average (8-for-15) including five RBI... Transferred to University of California for his final two collegiate seasons.

LAST SEASON:

- In his second season appeared in 45 games with Toronto, making 35 starts, including 26 at 1B and nine at DH.
- After his first recall batted .364 in his first 12 contests with three doubles and two home runs...Following that batted .143 over his next 12 before being optioned to Las Vegas... Was recalled again on July 30 and proceded to hit .307 with eight doubles and two home runs in 21 contests before being disabled with upper back soreness on August 26... Did not play after that date.
- Finished August batting .329 with 10 of his 23 hits going for extra bases (8-2B/2HR)... His 10 XBH ranked 7th in the AL for the month of August at the time of his injury.
- Posted two three-hit contests and now has four career... Had a career high three RBI at CWS on June 5... Once again vs. CWS collected a walk-off single in the 11th inning in 3-2 victory.
- Handles left-handed pitching well, batting .294 and over his two seasons in the majors has hit .292 vs. lefties... From the 7th inning on, batted .391 with four doubles and three home runs.
- With Las Vegas, played in 68 contests, batting .314 with 27 doubbles, 10 home runs and 52 RBI... Finsihed 7th in RBI on the club despite appearing in only 68 games...Hit .329 vs. lefties and .309 vs. righties.

DAVID COOPER

Bold – career high

Year	Club & League	AVG	G	AB	R	H	2B	3B	HR	RBI	SH-SF	HP	BB-IBB	SO	SB-CS	SLG	OBP	OPS
2008	Auburn (NYP)	.341	21	85	10	29	10	1	2	21	0-0	0	10-2	16	0-1	.553	.411	.964
	Lansing (Mid)	.354	24	96	15	34	10	0	2	17	0-0	0	10-0	14	0-0	.521	.415	.936
	Dunedin (FSL)	.304	24	92	10	28	9	0	1	13	0-0	0	10-1	16	0-0	.435	.373	.808
2009	New Hampshire (East)	.258	128	473	62	122	32	0	10	66	0-4	2	59-3	92	0-0	.389	.340	.729
2010	New Hampshire (East)	.257	132	498	59	128	30	1	20	78	0-2	1	52-1	74	0-0	.442	.327	.769
2011	Las Vegas (PCL)	.364	120	467	77	170	51	1	9	96	0-9	2	67-6	43	1-3	.535	.439	.974
	TORONTO (AL)	.211	27	71	9	15	7	0	2	**12**	0-2	1	**7**-0	14	0-0	.394	.284	.678
2012	Las Vegas (AAA)	.314	68	261	45	82	27	1	10	52	0-5	1	37-4	34	0-1	.540	.395	.935
	TORONTO (AL)	.300	**45**	140	**16**	**42**	**11**	0	**4**	11	0-0	1	4-0	**22**	0-1	.464	.324	.788
Minor Totals		.301	517	1972	278	593	169	4	54	343	0-20	6	245-17	289	1-5	.473	.376	.849
MAJOR TOTALS		.270	72	211	25	57	18	0	6	23	0-2	2	11-0	36	0-1	.441	.310	.750

HOME RUN BREAKDOWN

			ONE GAME									
Total	H	A	2	3	4	GS	LO	XN	IP	PH	RHP	LHP
6	3	3	0	0	0	0	0	0	0	0	6	0

TRANSACTIONS

- Selected by the Toronto Blue Jays in the 1st round (17 overall) of the 2008 First Year Player Draft
- On disabled list (upper back soreness) from August 26-remainder of season, 2012

GAME HIGHS

ML Debut	April 29, 2011 at NYY	**RBI**	3 - June 5, 2012 at CWS
Runs	1 - 25x, last Aug. 21, 2012 at DET	**Stolen Bases**	None
Hits	3 - 4x, last Aug. 21, 2012 at DET	**Last ML Home Run**	Aug. 8, 2012 at TB
Doubles	2 - 3x, last Aug. 21, 2012 at DET	**Longest Hitting Streak**	5G - Aug. 1-5, 2012
Home Runs	1 - 6x, last Aug. 8, 2012 at TB	**Longest Hitless Streak**	18AB - June 7-15, 2012

CAREER FIELDING

POSITION	PCT	G	PO	A	E	TC	DP
1B	.986	44	316	32	5	353	31

MILESTONES

Category		Date	Opponent	Pitcher	Notes
Hit	1	May 1, 2011	at New York (AL)	Nova	Single
Home Run	1	May 10, 2011	Boston	Bard	1R
RBI	1	April 30, 2011	at New York (AL)	Burnett	Sac Fly

PROFESSIONAL CAREER:

2008:

- Played on three different Clubs (Auburn-A, Lansing-A & Dunedin-A) in his first professional season... Combined to hit .333 (91-273) with five home runs & 51 RBI in 69 games between all three levels.

2009:

- Led the Fisher Cats with 32 doubles, a figure which ranked T-6th in the Eastern League.

2010:

- Doubled his previous career high in home runs, hitting 20, all coming from May through the end of the season.
- Hit a grand slam and added five RBI on May 25.
- With runners in scoring position/2 outs batted .313 with a .967 OPS.

2011:

- Had his contract selected on April 29 and made his **Major League debut** that same day at NYY.
- Did not record a hit until his 3rd game on May 1 at NYY a single off Ivan Nova in the 2nd inning.
- Appeared in 13 games with TOR prior to being optioned to Las Vegas (AAA) on May 16...Batted just .121 (4-33) during that time.
- Hit a go-ahead pinch-hit home run off Daniel Bard in the 8th inning on May 10 vs. BOS for his first career home run... Also added a walk-off sacrifice fly in the 10th inning of that same game.
- Returned to the club on Sept. 7 for the remainder of the season... Posted a .289 average with six doubles, one home run and seven RBI over that stretch of 14 games.
- Led the Pacific Coast League in average with a .364 mark, doubles with 51 and OBP at .439... The doubles ranked 2nd and the RBI's was T-10th in all of the minor leagues.
- Was named to the Pacific Coast League Mid-season and Post-season All-Star squads.
- With the 51s, batted .392 and posted a OPS of 1.016 vs. LHP.

LONGEST HITTING STREAKS

(15 GAMES OR MORE)

28 games	**Shawn Green, 1999**
26 games	John Olerud, 1993
26 games	Shannon Stewart, 1999
22 games	George Bell, 1989
22 games	Carlos Delgado, 2000
21 games	Damaso Garcia, 1983
21 games	Lloyd Moseby, 1983
21 games	Dave Martinez, 2000
20 games	Damaso Garcia, 1982
20 games	Vernon Wells, 2003
20 games	Mike Bordick, 2003
20 games	Reed Johnson, 2003
19 games	Alfredo Griffin, 1980
19 games	Roberto Alomar, 1995
19 games	Carlos Delgado, 1998
19 games	Jose Cruz Jr., 2001
18 games	Damaso Garcia, 1986
18 games	Tony Fernandez, 1987
18 games	Jose Cruz Jr., 1998
17 games	John Mayberry, 1980
17 games	Damaso Garcia, 1982
17 games	George Bell, 1987
17 games	Dave Winfield, 1992
17 games	Tony Batista, 1999
17 games	Vernon Wells, 2004
17 games	Bengie Molina, 2006
16 games	Dave McKay, 1978
16 games	Jesse Barfield, 1985
16 games	Damaso Garcia, 1985
16 games	Tony Fernandez, 1989
16 games	Roberto Alomar, 1992
16 games	Joe Carter, 1992
16 games	Ed Sprague, 1995
16 games	Carlos Delgado, 1997
16 games	Shannon Stewart, 1999
16 games	Shannon Stewart, 2001
16 games	Eric Hinske, 2004
15 games	Roy Howell, 1977
15 games	George Bell, 1986
15 games	Kelly Gruber, 1989
15 games	Tony Fernandez, 1990
15 games	Kelly Gruber, 1990
15 games	Roberto Alomar, 1991
15 games	Joe Carter, 1994
15 games	Alex Gonzalez, 2000
15 games	Lyle Overbay, 2006
15 games	Frank Thomas, 2007
15 games	Aaron Hill, 2007
15 games	Lyle Overbay, 2009

CRAWFORD, *EVAN*

Birthdate . . . . September 2, 1986
Opening Day Age 26
Birthplace. . . . . .Prattville, AL
Residence. . . . . Auburn, AL
Bats/Throws . . . . R/L
Height/Weight 6-2/190
Contract Status . . . . signed thru 2013
M.L. Service 0.041

46
PITCHER

PERSONAL:

Evan Shane Crawford... Attended Auburn University and Prattville High School in Alabama, where he led his team to an Alabama state-record with 47 wins and a state 6A runner-up... Threw two no-hitters, was the team's best hitter his senior year, and Perfect Game USA ranked him #88 out of the top 100 HS players, and was the 8th best left-handed pitcher.

LAST SEASON:

- Made his Major League debut on April 15 vs. BAL, tossing a scoreless inning.
- Made nine appearances overall in three separate stints with club.
- Did not allow a run in his first four outings totalling four innings... Allowed six earned over his final four innings.
- Began the season with New Hampshire (AA), making just three appearances before being promoted to Toronto... Spent most of the season with Las Vegas (AAA) making 26 appearances out of the bullpen... PCL batters hit .328, while allowing 21 earned runs in 27.2 innings.
- Was placed on the disabled list Aug. 14 and did not pitch for the balance of the season.

EVAN CRAWFORD

Bold – career high

Year	Club & League	W-L	ERA	G	GS	CG	ShO	SV	IP	H	R	ER	HR	HB	BB-IBB	SO	WP	BK	OBA
2008	Auburn (NYP)	0-2	3.03	13	5	0	0	0	29.2	21	13	10	0	4	16-0	23	4	0	.193
2009	Auburn (NYP)	1-5	4.06	14	14	1	0	0	57.2	60	35	26	1	3	31-1	38	3	0	.269
2010	Lansing (Mid)	3-2	4.01	16	7	0	0	0	49.1	51	24	22	2	3	20-0	39	4	1	.273
	Dunedin (FSL)	1-2	2.04	23	0	0	0	3	35.1	31	11	8	0	2	14-1	33	3	0	.237
2011	New Hampshire (East)	3-5	3.35	45	0	0	0	2	51.0	50	23	19	3	1	21-1	62	1	0	.260
2012	New Hampshire (East)	0-0	0.00	3	0	0	0	0	4.0	3	1	0	0	0	2-0	5	0	0	.200
	Las Vegas (PCL)	1-4	6.83	26	0	0	0	0	27.2	38	22	21	2	0	12-0	20	5	0	.328
	TORONTO (AL)	0-0	6.75	10	0	0	0	0	8.0	10	6	6	3	1	4-1	5	0	1	.333
Minor Totals		9-20	3.75	140	26	1	0	5	254.2	254	129	106	8	13	116-3	220	20	1	.261

TRANSACTIONS

- Selected by the Toronto Blue Jays in the 8th round of the 2008 First Year Player Draft

GAME HIGHS

ML Debut	April 15, 2012 vs. BAL
Innings Pitched:	
Starter	None
Reliever	2.0 - May 22, 2012 at TB
Walks:	
Starter	None
Reliever	3 - April 19, 2012 vs. TB
Strikeouts:	
Starter	None
Reliever	3 - May 14, 2012 vs. TB
Hits Allowed	5 - May 22, 2012 at TB
Runs Allowed	2 - 3x, last May 22, 2012 at TB
ER Allowed	2 - 3x, last May 22, 2012 at TB
HR Allowed	2 - April 30, 2012 vs. TEX
Low Hit CG	None
Last Win	None
Last Save	None
Last CG	None
Last ShO	None
Last Start	None
Last Relief App.	July 29, 2012 vs. DET
Longest Win Streak	None
Longest Losing Streak	None
Scoreless Innings Streak	4.0 - April 15-29, 2012

CAREER FIELDING

POSITION	PCT	G	PO	A	E	TC	DP
P	1.000	10	0	1	0	1	0

PROFESSIONAL CAREER:

2008:

- Made his professional debut for Auburn on June 19, tossing 2.2 scoreless innings.

2009:

- Spent his second full season with Short-season A Auburn... Pitched exclusively as a starter, recording his first complete game.

2010:

- Began his season with Lansing (Low-A) splitting time between the rotation and bullpen.
- Recorded a 4.50 ERA as a starter and a 2.93 ERA in the bullpen.
- Was promoted to Dunedin (High-A), where he spent the balance of the season making 23 relief appearances... From July onwards (21 outings) recorded a 1.08 ERA for Dunedin.

2011:

- Moved to AA for the first time in his career, spending the entire season at New Hampshire... Pitched exclusively out of the bullpen making 45 appearances.
- His 45 games led all Fisher Cats pitchers, and his 10.9 strikeouts per nine innings led all Fisher Cat relievers.
- Made 11 relief appearances in the Arizona Fall League... Posted a 0-1 record with a 3.18 ERA with one save.

LONGEST RAIN DELAYS

AT EXHIBITION STADIUM

- 3:34 delay to start game vs. CLE, Aug. 2, 1987 (W 11-5)... Game started at 5:09 pm and ended at 7:55 pm (time of game-2:46)
- 3:18 delay to start game vs. BOS, Sept. 26, 1985 (L 4-1)... Game started at 1:53 pm and ended at 1:02 am (time of game-2:09)
- 3:16 delay in bottom of 5th inning vs. BOS, June 22, 1985 (L 5-3)... Game started at 1:39 pm and ended at 7:47 pm (time of game-2:25)
- 3:01 delay vs. BOS, June 17, 1984 (W 5-3)... 1:33 delay to start game and 1:28 delay at start of bottom of the 5th inning... Game started at 3:08 pm and ended 7:47 pm (time of game-2:48)

AT ROGERS STADIUM

- 0:26 delay on July 26, 2003 vs. the Chicago White Sox
- 0:14 delay on August 10, 1991 vs. the Boston Red Sox

LONGEST RAIN DELAYS ON THE ROAD

- 3:47 delay in the 5th inning at CLE, Apr. 10, 2009 (W 13-7)... Game started at 4:08 pm and ended at 11:20 pm (time of game-3:25)
- 3:05 delay to start game at CIN, June 8, 2003 (W 5-0)... Game started at 1:15 pm and ended at 3:37 pm
- 2:21 delay to start game at CLE, July 31, 1996 (L 4-2)... Game started at 7:39 and ended at 10:57

LATEST ENDING GAMES

- 1:25 am at BAL, June 19, 1998 (time of game-5:49), L 7-4 in 15 innings
- 1:06 am at BOS, May 3, 1996 (time of game-3:20), L 8-7...Suspended game after 6 innings, resumed next day.
- 1:05 am vs. NYY, Apr. 19, 2001 (at SkyDome, time of game-5:57), L 6-5 in 17 innings
- 1:02 am vs. BOS, Sept. 26, 1985 vs. BOS (time of game-2:09), L 4-1...3:18 delay to start game.
- 1:02 am at BAL, Aug. 3, 1984 (time of game-2:45), W 5-2...2:07 rain delay in top of 4th inning.

SUSPENDED GAMES

The Blue Jays have played four suspended games in their history.

1) Aug. 28, 1980 vs. MIN (L 7-5 in 15 innings)...Game was suspended after 14 innings due to 5 pm Canadian National Exhibition curfew.
2) Sept. 17, 1980 at NYY (L 8-7 in 13 innings)...Game was completed the next day after the contest had been halted the night before with the Jays batting in the 10th inning.
3) May 3, 1996 at BOS (L 8-7)...Play was stopped at 1:06 am after 6 innings due to 1:00 am curfew...The game was completed the next day.
4) July 23, 2008 at BAL (W 5-1)...Contest was suspended in the 6th inning due to rain with the Jays leading by a score of 2-1...The game was continued the next day on July 24.

DAVIS, *RAJAI*

Birthdate .... October 19, 1980
Opening Day Age 32
Birthplace .... Norwich, CT
Residence .... East Lyme, CT
Bats/Throws .... R/R
Height/Weight 5-9/195
Contract Status .... signed thru 2013
M.L. Service 5.167

11

OUTFIELDER

PERSONAL:

Rajai Lavae Davis... Married... Graduated from New London (CT) High School in 1999, playing baseball, basketball and football... Attended University of Connecticut at Avery Point (Groton, CT).

MOST STOLEN BASES AMONG THE MAJORS SINCE 2009

1.	Michael Bourn	216
2.	**Rajai Davis**	**171**
3.	Juan Pierre	162
4.	B.J. Upton	151
5.	Ichiro Suzuki	137

LAST SEASON:

- Played 142 games, his most since playing 143 games in 2010....Started 117 games, 96 in LF, 14 in RF, 5 in CF and 2 at DH.
- Set a career high with eight home runs... Had first career multi-home run game on May 18 vs. NYM.
- Led the club with 46 stolen bases and was 2nd in the AL to Mike Trout with 49... Was his 3rd season with 40+ steals... Had 10 games with multiple stolen bases and now has 38 in his career... Tied a career high with three steals on July 8 at CWS... Is the 6th different Blue Jay to steal 45+ in a season, the most since Shannon Stewart stole 51 in 1998.
- Recorded a hit in seven consecutive plate appearances from Sept. 28-29, one shy of the club mark held by Rance Mulliniks, Paul Molitor, Tony Fernandez and Adam Lind... Matched a career high with four hits (7th time) on Sept. 28 vs. NYY.
- Batted .285 vs. left-handed hitters and .243 vs. right-handed hitters... With runners in scoring position batted .317.
- Made a career high eight errors, four more than his previous high.

RAJAI DAVIS

Bold – career high

Year	Club & League	AVG	G	AB	R	H	2B	3B	HR	RBI	SH-SF	HP	BB-IBB	SO	SB-CS	SLG	OBP	OPS
2001	Williamsport (NYP)	.083	6	12	1	1	0	0	0	0	0-0	0	2-0	4	0-1	.083	.214	.297
	Pirates (GCL)	.262	26	84	19	22	1	0	0	4	3-1	1	13-0	26	11-3	.274	.364	.638
2002	Pirates (GCL)	.384	58	224	38	86	16	5	4	35	0-3	3	20-0	25	24-6	.554	.436	.990
	Williamsport (NYP)	.000	1	4	0	0	0	0	0	0	0-0	0	0-0	1	0-0	.000	.000	.000
	Hickory (SAL)	.429	6	14	4	6	0	0	0	3	1-0	1	6-0	2	2-2	.429	.619	1.048
2003	Hickory (SAL)	.305	125	478	84	146	21	7	6	54	8-2	6	55-0	65	40-13	.416	.383	.799
2004	Lynchburg (Caro)	.314	127	509	91	160	27	7	5	38	4-0	2	59-2	60	57-15	.424	.388	.812
2005	Altoona (East)	.281	123	499	82	140	22	5	4	34	6-1	12	43-2	76	45-9	.369	.351	.720
2006	Indianapolis (Int)	.283	100	385	53	109	17	1	2	21	2-0	3	27-0	59	45-13	.348	.335	.683
	PITTSBURGH (NL)	.143	20	14	1	2	1	0	0	0	1-0	0	2-0	3	1-3	.214	.250	.464
2007	Indianapolis (Int)	.318	53	211	31	67	12	4	4	30	2-2	3	21-0	25	27-9	.469	.384	.853
	PITTSBURGH (NL)	.271	24	48	6	13	2	1	0	2	1-1	0	7-0	3	5-2	.354	.357	.711
	SAN FRANCISCO (NL)	.282	51	142	26	40	9	1	1	7	2-0	4	14-1	25	17-4	.380	.363	.743
2008	SAN FRANCISCO (NL)	.056	12	18	2	1	0	0	0	0	0-0	0	1-0	6	4-0	.056	.105	.161
	OAKLAND (AL)	.260	101	196	28	51	5	4	3	19	2-1	1	7-0	34	25-6	.372	.288	.660
2009	OAKLAND (AL)	.305	125	390	65	119	27	5	3	48	2-4	7	**29**-0	70	41-12	.423	.360	.783
2010	OAKLAND (AL)	.284	**143**	525	**66**	**149**	**28**	3	5	**52**	1-5	4	26-0	78	**50**-11	.377	.320	.697
2011	Dunedin (FSL)	.400	2	5	1	2	0	0	1	1	0-0	0	0-0	1	0-0	1.000	.400	1.400
	New Hampshire (East)	.300	4	10	1	3	1	0	0	0	0-0	2	2-0	2	0-2	.400	.500	.900
	TORONTO (AL)	.238	95	320	44	76	21	**6**	1	29	1-1	1	15-0	63	34-11	.350	.273	.623
2012	TORONTO (AL)	.257	142	447	64	115	24	3	**8**	43	1-4	6	**29**-3	**102**	46-13	.378	.309	.687
Minor Totals		.305	631	2435	405	742	117	29	26	220	26-9	33	248-4	346	251-73	.409	.375	.784
TORONTO TOTALS		.249	237	767	108	191	45	9	9	72	2-5	7	44-3	165	80-24	.366	.294	.660
AL TOTALS		.272	606	1878	267	510	105	21	20	191	7-15	19	106-3	347	196-53	.382	.315	.696
NL TOTALS		.252	107	222	35	56	12	2	1	9	4-1	4	24-1	37	27-9	.338	.335	.672
MAJOR TOTALS		.270	713	2100	302	566	117	23	21	200	11-16	23	130-4	384	223-62	.377	.317	.694

HOME RUN BREAKDOWN

				ONE GAME								
Total	H	A	2	3	4	GS	LO	XN	IP	PH	RHP	LHP
21	12	9	1	0	0	2	1	0	0	0	12	9

TRANSACTIONS

- Selected by the Pittsburgh Pirates in the 38th round of the 2001 First Year Player Draft
- On disabled list (sore right wrist) July 14-23, 2006
- Traded to the San Francisco Giants along with a player to be named later (RHP Stephen Macfarland) in exchange for RHP Matt Morris on July 31, 2007
- Claimed on waivers by the Oakland Athletics on April 23, 2008
- Traded to the Toronto Blue Jays in exchange for RHP Trystan Magnuson and RHP Daniel Farquhar on November 17, 2010
- On disabled list (aggravated right ankle strain) from April 12-28; included rehabilitation assignment at New Hampshire (AA) from April 22-28
- On disabled list (torn left hamstring) from August 15-remainder of the season, 2011; included rehabilitation assignment at Dunedin (A) from September 3-5

GAME HIGHS

ML Debut	Aug. 14, 2006 vs. MIL	**RBI**	5 - 2x, last Aug. 12, 2012 vs. NYY
Runs	4 - Aug. 10, 2007 vs. PIT	**Stolen Bases**	3 - 5x, last July 8, 2012 at CWS
Hits	4 - 7x, last Sept. 28, 2012 vs. NYY	**Last ML Home Run**	Sept. 29, 2012 vs. NYY
Doubles	2 - 7x, last Aug. 12, 2012 vs. NYY	**Longest Hitting Streak**	14G - Sept. 13-26, 2009
Home Runs	2 - May 18, 2012 vs. NYM	**Longest Hitless Streak**	26AB - July 4-16, 2012

CAREER FIELDING

POSITION	PCT	G	PO	A	E	TC	DP
2B	-	1	0	0	0	0	0
OF	.985	637	1254	30	19	1303	6

MILESTONES

Category		Date	Opponent	Pitcher	Notes
Hit	1	Aug. 29, 2006	Chicago (NL)	Zambrano	Pinch hit double
Home Run	1	Aug. 17, 2007	at Florida	Olsen	2R
Grand Slam (2)	1	Sept. 5, 2008	at Baltimore	Bierd	8th inning
	2	July 7, 2010	Los Angeles (AL)	Kazmir	3rd inning
Leadoff HR (1)	1	July 30, 2012	at Seattle	Iwakuma	--
RBI	1	June 22, 2007	at Los Angles (AL)	Saunders	Single
Stolen Base	1	Aug. 16, 2006	Milwaukee	Helling C-Rivera	2nd base
	100	April 17, 2010	Baltimore	Guthrie C-Wieters	2nd base
	200	July 8, 2012	at Chicago (AL)	Santiago C-Pierzynski	2nd base

PROFESSIONAL CAREER:

2006:

- Was recalled by Pittsburgh on Aug. 14 and went 0 for 1 in **Major League debut** that night against Milwaukee (flied out as a pinch hitter).

2007:

- Was called up to Pittsburgh in June and traded to San Francisco at the end of July... Was acquired by the Giants at the July 31 trade deadline with a player to be named later (RHP Stephen Macfarland) in exchange for RHP Matt Morris.
- Hit safely in 27 of his 33 starts with the Giants (31 in center field, one in left field, one in right field)... After joining the Giants Aug. 1, his 17 stolen bases were the sixth highest total in the National League... Hit his first career home run Aug. 17 at Florida, a two-run shot off Scott Olsen.

2012 MLB STOLEN BASE LEADERS

1.	Mike Trout, LAA	49
2.	**Rajai Davis, TOR**	**46**
3.	Everth Cabrera, SD	44
4.	Michael Bourn, ATL	42
5.	Ben Revere, MIN	40
	Jose Reyes, MIA	40

2008:

- Was claimed by the A's off waivers from San Francisco on April 23 and went on to steal a team leading 25 bases with Oakland... His 29 steals in 226 plate appearances tied for fourth most in the Major Leagues since 1900 among players with 250 or fewer plate appearances... They were the most since Rex Hudler had 29 steals in 229 plate appearances with Montreal in 1988... Had 207 plate appearances with Oakland and only three players in Athletics history had more steals with 250 or fewer plate appearances.
- Made his Major League second base debut on June 18 at Arizona in the 8th inning but did not have any chances... Was his first appearance in the infield since playing two games at second base for Single-A.

2009:

- Overall, he ranked 5th in the AL with a 41 stolen bases... Became the 9th player (24th time) in Oakland history steal 40 bases in a season... Was the first to do it since Rickey Henderson had 66 in 1998... Led the A's in stolen bases for the second consecutive season and also topped the club with five triples.
- Hit .325 after the All-Star Break and tied for the Major League lead with 30 stolen bases
- Started a team-leading 93 games in center field and also had four starts in right field... Had eight assists, which ranked third among AL center fielders, but also committed four errors, which tied for third most.

2010:

- Set career highs in games played (143), runs (66), hits (149), doubles (28), home runs (5), RBI (52) and stolen bases (50)...
- Ranked 3rd in the majors in stolen bases... Became the 5th Athletic to have two seasons of 40+ steals and finished 8th in A's history with 116 steals.
- T-3rd in four hit games in the AL with four and T-8th in infield hits with 29... Collected four multi-hit games in the A's first five games, joining Mark Kotsay as the only other A's player to accomplish the feat.
- Had an 11-game hit streak from June 3-19, and posted a career high 0-19 streak from June 19-29.

2011:

- Appeared in 95 games prior to being placed on the disabled list on Aug. 15.
- His .238 average was a career low.
- Stole 34 bases despite starting only 82 games (LF-4, CF-71, RF-7)... The 34 steals led the club and ranked T-7th in the AL... On July 19 vs. SEA, stole three bases despite entering the game in the 9th inning as a pinch runner.
- Aug. 14 tore his left hamstring running out a ground ball and was placed on the 15-day disabled list... Did not appear in game after that and was transferred to the 60-day disabled list on Sept. 7.

DELABAR, *STEVE*

Birthdate	July 17, 1983
Opening Day Age	29
Birthplace	Fort Knox, KY
Residence	Elizabethtown, KY
Bats/Throws	R/R
Height/Weight	6-4/232
Contract Status	signed thru 2013
M.L. Service	1.015

PITCHER

PERSONAL:

Steven Edward Delabar... Attended Central Hardin High School in Elizabethtown, KY... Attended Volunteer State (TN) Junior College... Was a substitute teacher in Kentucky prior to signing with Seattle Mariners in April of 2011... Originally selected by San Diego in the 29th round of the 2003 June draft… Signed May 5, 2004 by Padres scout Billy Merkel.

LAST SEASON:

- In 61 games between Seattle and Toronto posted a 4-3 record with a 3.82 ERA.
- Was acquired by the Blue Jays on July 31 from Seattle for OF Eric Thames.
- Overall held opponents to a .193 average... With Seattle, opponents batted .177 and struck out 11.3 batters per nine and with Toronto, held opponents to a .213 average while fanning 14.1 per nine.
- Worked 2.0+ innings in nine games... In those outings had a 0.50 ERA with 32 strikeouts in 18 innings (18.0IP, 4H, 1ER, 8BB, 32K)... In fact allowed hits in just two of the nine games.
- Was much better when rested... In 24 games with two or more days rest posted a 1.72 ERA (31.1IP/6ER)... When pitching on back-to-back days or with just one days rest, posted a 5.71 ERA in 37 games (34.2IP/22ER).
- Was dominant at home holding opponents to a .155 average, posting a 4-1 record with a 2.25 ERA... On the road opponents batted .211 while going 0-2 with a 5.70 ERA.
- Recorded a strikeout per nine total of 12.55 on the season... That total was the highest in the AL for any picther with a minimum of 60 innings...On Aug. 13 struck out six without allowing a hit in two innings... Became the first pitcher in Major League history to record four strikeouts in one frame during extra innings... Also became the first pitcher in franchise history to strike out four batters in one inning.

STEVE DELABAR

Bold – career high

Year	Club & League	W-L	ERA	G	GS	CG	ShO	SV	IP	H	R	ER	HR	HB	BB-IBB	SO	WP	BK	OBA
2005	Eugene (NOR)	4-6	4.76	16	16	0	0	0	75.2	84	45	40	7	15	18-0	59	4	0	.279
2006	Fort Wayne (Mid)	8-9	3.41	27	27	1	0	0	145.0	129	66	55	8	7	65-0	118	12	1	.242
2007	Lake Elsinore (CAL)	2-6	5.59	20	0	0	0	0	29.0	26	21	18	5	2	16-1	33	3	1	.236
	Fort Wayne (Mid)	2-5	5.96	21	12	0	0	0	68.0	63	49	45	8	13	46-0	48	6	0	.248
2008	Fort Wayne (Mid)	2-1	5.27	11	0	0	0	0	13.2	17	8	8	0	1	5-1	12	0	0	.321
	Florence (FRN)	0-0	2.84	4	0	0	0	0	6.1	6	2	2	1	2	2-0	7	4	0	.261
	Brockton (CAN)	3-3	3.01	11	11	0	0	0	68.2	67	25	23	5	1	16-1	43	5	1	.264
2009								Did Not Play											
2010								Did Not Play											
2011	High Desert (CAL)	1-1	4.38	7	0	0	0	3	12.1	12	6	6	0	2	8-0	20	3	0	.245
	Jackson (Sou)	1-3	2.05	23	0	0	0	12	30.2	23	10	7	0	1	26-3	30	0	0	.209
	Tacoma (PCL)	1-1	0.69	10	0	0	0	0	13.0	11	1	1	0	2	6-1	18	2	0	.224
	SEATTLE (AL)	1-1	2.57	6	0	0	0	0	7.0	5	2	2	1	1	4-1	7	0	0	.217
2012	Tacoma (PCL)	0-1	3.75	9	0	0	0	1	12.0	11	10	5	0	1	12-0	12	1	1	.239
	SEATTLE (AL)	**2-1**	4.17	**34**	0	0	0	0	**36.2**	23	17	17	**9**	5	**11**-1	**46**	3	0	.177
	TORONTO (AL)	**2-2**	3.38	**27**	0	0	0	0	**29.1**	23	12	11	**3**	0	**15**-0	**46**	3	0	.213
Minor Totals		31-44	3.96	188	78	1	0	16	563.0	535	301	248	39	55	256-7	473	43	5	.250
MAJOR TOTALS		5-4	3.70	67	0	0	0	0	73.0	51	31	30	13	6	30-2	99	6	0	.195

TRANSACTIONS

- Selected by the San Diego Padres in the 29th round of the 2003 First Year Player Draft
- Signed by the Seattle Mariners on April 20, 2011
- Traded to the Toronto Blue Jays in exchange for OF Eric Thames on July 31, 2012

GAME HIGHS

ML Debut	Sept. 11, 2011 vs. KC
Innings Pitched:	
Starter	None
Reliever	2.0 - 9x, last Sept. 12, 2012 vs. SEA
Walks:	
Starter	None
Reliever	2 - 3x, last Aug. 17, 2012 vs. TEX
Strikeouts:	
Starter	None
Reliever	6 - Aug. 13, 2012 vs. CWS
Hits Allowed	4 - Aug. 10, 2012 vs. NYY
Runs Allowed	3 - 3x, last Aug. 10, 2012 vs. NYY

ER Allowed	3 - 3x, last Aug. 10, 2012 vs. NYY
HR Allowed	2 - April 11, 2012 at TEX
Low Hit CG	None
Last Win	Sept. 5, 2012 vs. BAL
Last Save	None
Last CG	None
Last ShO	None
Last Start	None
Last Relief App.	Oct. 2, 2012 vs. MIN
Longest Win Streak	3G - July 2-Sept. 5, 2012
Longest Losing Streak	2G - Sept. 15-19, 2012
Scoreless Innings Streak	6.0 - June 14-July 4, 2012

CAREER FIELDING

POSITION	PCT	G	PO	A	E	TC	DP
P	1.000	67	5	3	0	8	0

MILESTONES

Category		Date	Opponent	Notes
Win	1	Sept. 14, 2011	New York (AL)	as a reliever - 1.0 IP

PROFESSIONAL CAREER:

2005:

- Tied for Northwest League lead in games started (16).

2006:

- Ranked 4th among Padres minor leaguers in strikeouts (118) and 6th in ERA (3.41).

2007:

- Split the season between Fort Wayne and High-A Lake Elsinore in the California League.
- Pitched exclusively out of the bullpen for Lake Elsinore (2-6, 5.59).

2008:

- Made 11 relief appearances with Fort Wayne (2-1, 5.27) before being released by the Padres on May 23.
- On the disabled list April 23-May 16 with a sprained left ankle.
- Played for two independent league teams, Florence (Frontier League) and Brocton (CanAm League).

2009:

- Appeared in 12 games (3 GS) for Brockton in the CanAm League... Went 3-3 with a 3.76 ERA (11 ER, 26.1 IP).
- Suffered a broken right elbow and was released on June 30.

2010:

- Did not play professional baseball recovering from a broken right elbow that required a metal plate and nine screws.

2011:

- Made **ML debut** Sept. 11 vs. Kansas City, striking out Alex Gordon and Melky Cabrera.
- Earned first ML win Sept. 14 vs. New York (AL) in Seattle with a scoreless 12th inning.
- Signed by the Mariners as a minor league free agent on April 20, 2011.
- Had not pitched above the Single-A level prior to this season.

MOST STRIKEOUTS BY AL RELIEVER – 2012

1.	Tim Collins, KC	93
2.	**Steve Delabar, SEA-TOR**	**92**
3.	Greg Holland, KC	91
4.	Wade Davis, TB	87
	Tom Wilhelmsen, SEA	87

MOST WINS IN RELIEF IN ONE SEASON

(MINIMUM OF 8)

Mark Eichhorn	14	1986	Duane Ward	9	1988
Jeff Musselman	12	1987	Billy Koch	9	2000
Paul Quantrill	11	2001	Dale Murray	8	1982
Dennis Lamp	11	1985	Joey McLaughlin	8	1982
Mark Eichhorn	10	1987	Roy Lee Jackson	8	1982
Mike Timlin	10	1991	Roy Lee Jackson	8	1983
Tom Henke	9	1986	Tom Henke	8	1989

DEROSA, *MARK*

Birthdate	February 26, 1975
Opening Day Age	38
Birthplace	Passaic, NJ
Residence	Suwanee, GA
Bats/Throws	R/R
Height/Weight	6-1/215
Contract Status	signed thru 2013
M.L. Service	12.061

35

INFIELDER

PERSONAL:

Mark Thomas DeRosa... Played college baseball and football at University of Pennsylvania, spurning athletic scholarship offers from Rutgers, Seton Hall and William & Mary... Played 3 seasons of baseball, during which Penn went 75-50 (.600) and captured a pair out outright Ivy League/Lou Gehrig Division titles and shared another in '96 with Princeton... Tallied 102 career RBI and is member of Penn's Baseball Hall of Fame... Was the Quakers' starting quarterback in '94 and '95... Quakers went 16-3 in those 2 seasons, including a perfect 9-0 (7-0 Ivy) mark in '94... In 2 seasons as Penn's quarterback, threw for 3885 yards (4th on Penn's all-time career list) and 29 touchdowns... As a senior in 1995, threw for 2053 yards (7th on Penn's all-time list) and 16 TD's... Threw for a single-game career-best 360 yards on Nov. 19, 1994 against Cornell... Graduated from and played baseball and football at Bergen Catholic (NJ) High.

LAST SEASON:

- Closed the season on a strong note, batting .316 (6-for-19) in September.
- Posted 14 walks in 101 plate appearances.
- Missed 75 games during the campaign due to a pair of stints on the disabled list (left oblique, April 28-June 24; left abdomen, Aug. 5-31).

MARK DEROSA

Bold – career high

Year	Club and League	AVG	G	AB	R	H	2B	3B	HR	RBI	SH-SF	HP	BB-IBB	SO	SB-CS	SLG	OBP	OPS
1996	Eugene (Nor)	.259	70	255	43	66	13	1	2	28	0-2	5	38-1	48	3-4	.341	.363	.704
1997	Durham (Caro)	.269	92	346	51	93	11	3	8	37	2-4	10	25-2	73	6-8	.387	.332	.719
1998	Greenville (Sou)	.267	125	461	67	123	26	2	8	49	5-2	5	60-2	57	7-13	.384	.356	.740
	ATLANTA (NL)	.333	5	3	2	1	0	0	0	0	0-0	0	0-0	1	0-0	.333	.333	.666
1999	Richmond (Int)	.272	105	364	41	99	16	2	1	40	3-4	5	21-1	49	7-6	.335	.317	.652
	ATLANTA (NL)	.000	7	8	0	0	0	0	0	0	0-0	0	0-0	2	0-0	.000	.000	.000
2000	Richmond (Int)	.292	101	370	62	108	22	3	3	35	6-4	3	38-0	36	13-4	.392	.359	.751
	ATLANTA (NL)	.308	22	13	9	4	1	0	0	3	0-0	0	2-0	1	0-0	.385	.400	.785
2001	Richmond (Int)	.296	49	186	31	55	18	0	2	17	1-4	1	17-0	22	7-3	.425	.351	.776
	ATLANTA (NL)	.287	66	164	27	47	8	0	3	20	1-2	5	12-6	19	2-1	.390	.350	.740
2002	Myrtle Beach (Caro)	.000	2	7	0	0	0	0	0	0	0-0	0	1-0	1	0-0	.000	.125	.125
	Richmond (Int)	.255	16	55	9	14	3	0	0	6	0-0	2	5-0	2	2-0	.309	.339	.648
	ATLANTA (NL)	.297	72	212	24	63	9	2	5	23	2-3	3	12-3	24	2-3	.429	.339	.768
2003	ATLANTA (NL)	.263	103	266	40	70	14	0	6	22	0-1	5	16-0	49	1-0	.383	.316	.699
2004	ATLANTA (NL)	.239	118	309	33	74	16	0	3	31	4-6	3	23-3	53	1-3	.320	.293	.613
2005	TEXAS (AL)	.243	66	148	26	36	5	0	8	20	0-0	2	16-0	35	1-0	.439	.325	.764
2006	Oklahoma (PCL)	.500	3	12	2	6	1	0	0	0	0-0	0	0-0	1	0-0	.583	.500	1.083
	TEXAS (AL)	.296	136	520	78	**154**	**40**	2	13	74	0-2	6	44-1	102	4-4	.456	.357	.813
2007	CHICAGO (NL)	.293	**149**	502	64	147	28	**3**	10	72	3-4	7	58-2	93	1-2	.420	.371	.791
2008	CHICAGO (NL)	.285	**149**	505	**103**	144	30	**3**	21	**87**	2-8	9	**69**-0	**106**	**6**-0	.481	.376	.857
2009	CLEVELAND (AL)	.270	71	278	47	75	13	0	**13**	50	1-3	3	29-1	63	1-1	.457	.342	.799
	ST. LOUIS (NL)	.228	68	237	31	54	10	1	**10**	28	1-2	4	18-0	58	2-1	.405	.291	.696
2010	San Jose (CAL)	.000	1	4	0	0	0	0	0	0	0-0	0	1-0	1	0-0	.000	.200	.200
	Fresno (PCL)	.364	3	11	1	4	1	0	0	1	0-0	0	1-0	2	0-0	.455	.417	.872
	SAN FRANCISCO (NL)	.194	26	93	9	18	3	0	1	10	0-0	2	9-0	16	0-2	.258	.279	.537
2011	San Jose (CAL)	.400	2	5	2	2	1	0	0	0	0-0	0	1-0	1	0-0	.600	.500	1.100
	Fresno (PCL)	.310	11	42	6	13	1	0	0	3	1-0	0	0-0	8	0-0	.333	.310	.643
	SAN FRANCISCO (NL)	.279	47	86	9	24	2	0	0	12	0-1	2	8-0	18	1-1	.302	.351	.653
2012	Potomac (Caro)	.091	4	11	1	1	0	0	0	2	0-0	0	4-0	3	0-0	.091	.333	.424
	WASHINGTON (NL)	.188	48	85	13	16	5	0	0	6	1-1	0	14-0	18	1-0	.247	.300	.547
Minor Totals		.274	584	2129	316	584	113	11	24	218	18-20	31	212-6	304	45-38	.372	.346	.717
AL TOTALS		.280	273	946	151	265	58	2	34	144	1-5	11	89-2	200	6-5	.453	.347	.801
NL TOTALS		.267	880	2483	364	662	126	9	59	314	14-28	40	241-14	458	17-13	.396	.338	.734
MAJOR TOTALS		.270	1153	3429	515	927	184	11	93	458	15-33	51	330-16	658	23-18	.412	.340	.752

DIVISION SERIES RECORD

Year	Club and League	AVG	G	AB	R	H	2B	3B	HR	RBI	SH-SF	HP	BB-IBB	SO	SB-CS
2001	ATLANTA (NL)	1.000	1	1	0	1	0	0	0	0	0-0	0	0-0	0	0-0
2002	ATLANTA (NL)	.429	4	7	2	3	1	1	0	3	0-0	0	1-0	1	0-0
2003	ATLANTA (NL)	.429	4	7	1	3	2	0	0	2	0-0	0	1-0	2	0-0
2007	CHICAGO (NL)	.333	3	9	2	3	0	0	0	0	0-0	1	2-0	2	0-0
2008	CHICAGO (NL)	.333	3	12	2	4	2	0	1	4	0-0	0	0-0	1	0-0
2009	ST. LOUIS (NL)	.385	3	13	1	5	1	0	0	1	0-0	0	0-0	2	0-0
DIVISION SERIES TOTALS		.388	18	49	8	19	6	1	1	10	0-0	1	4-0	8	0-0

LEAGUE CHAMPIONSHIP SERIES RECORD

Year	Club and League	AVG	G	AB	R	H	2B	3B	HR	RBI	SH-SF	HP	BB-IBB	SO	SB-CS
2001	ATLANTA (NL)	.000	4	4	0	0	0	0	0	0	0-0	0	0-0	0	0-0

WORLD BASEBALL CLASSIC RECORD

Year	Club and League	AVG	G	AB	R	H	2B	3B	HR	RBI	SH-SF	HP	BB-IBB	SO	SB-CS
2009	UNITED STATES	.316	6	19	3	6	1	1	1	9	0-0	1	1-0	3	0-0

HOME RUN BREAKDOWN

			ONE GAME									
Total	H	A	2	3	4	GS	LO	XN	IP	PH	RHP	LHP
93	48	45	4	0	0	5	0	2	0	2	57	36

TRANSACTIONS

- Selected by the Atlanta Braves in the 7th round of the 1996 First Year Player Draft
- On disabled list (strained ligaments in right ankle) from May 18-July 16, 2002
- Signed by the Texas Rangers on January 21, 2005
- On disabled list (sprained left foot) from April 19-29, 2006
- Signed by the Chicago Cubs on November 14, 2006
- Traded to the Cleveland Indians in exchange for RHP Jeff Stevens, RHP Chris Archer and LHP John Gaub on December 31, 2008
- Traded to the St. Louis Cardinals in exchnage for RHP Chris Perez and RHP Jess Todd on July 1, 2009
- On disabled list (sprained left wrist) from July 7-17, 2009
- Signed by the San Francisco Giants on January 1, 2010
- On disabled list (sore left wrist) from May 17-remainder of season, 2010
- On disabled list (wrist cartilage inflammation) from April 28-May 10, 2011
- On disabled list (strained left wrist) from May 19-August 4, 2011
- Signed by the Washington Nationals on December 28, 2011
- On disabled list (strained left oblique) from April 29-June 25, 2012
- On disabled list (left abdominal strain) from August 6-September 1, 2012
- Signed by the Toronto Blue Jays on January 22, 2013

GAME HIGHS

ML Debut	Sept. 2, 1998 vs. HOU	**RBI**	6 - 4x, last April 18, 2009 at NYY
Runs	4 - 2x, last April 28, 2009 vs. BOS	**Stolen Bases**	2 - Sept. 12, 2009 vs. ATL
Hits	5 - 2x, last Sept. 17, 2007 vs. CIN	**Last ML Home Run**	April 5, 2010 at HOU
Doubles	2 - 9x, last Aug. 5, 2008 vs. HOU	**Longest Hitting Streak**	11G - 2x, last May 9-20, 2008
Home Runs	2 - 4x, last Sept. 21, 2009 at HOU	**Longest Hitless Streak**	26AB - April 20-Aug. 10, 2011

CAREER FIELDING

POSITION	PCT	G	PO	A	E	TC	DP
1B	.987	36	142	5	2	149	21
2B	.980	314	507	697	24	1228	151
3B	.955	338	172	557	34	763	46
SS	.972	140	151	304	13	468	67
OF	.955	249	416	9	2	427	1

BLUE JAYS WHO LED LEAGUE IN FIELDING PERCENTAGE

YEAR	PLAYER	POSITION	PERCENTAGE
1984	Rance Mulliniks	3B	.968
1985	Rance Mulliniks	3B	.971
1986	Rance Mulliniks	3B	.975
	Tony Fernandez	SS	.983
1988	Fred McGriff	1B	1.000
1989	Tony Fernandez	SS	.992
1990	Manuel Lee	2B	.993
1991	Devon White	CF	.998
1995	Roberto Alomar	2B	.994

YEAR	PLAYER	POSITION	PERCENTAGE
1997	Alex Gonzalez	SS	.986
2004	Vernon Wells	CF	.997
	Eric Hinske	3B	.978
2005	Vernon Wells	CF	1.000
2009	Lyle Overbay	1B	.998
2010	Vernon Wells	CF	1.000

16 Blue Jays pitchers have led or tied for league lead in fielding (35 or more chances).

MILESTONES

Category		Date	Opponent	Pitcher	Notes
Game	1000	Aug. 22, 2009	at San Diego	--	as 3B
Hit	1	Sept. 20, 1998	at Arizona	Nunez	PH-single
Home Run	1	July 21, 2001	Montreal	Lloyd	walk-off (1R), 10th inning
Multi-Homer Game (4)					
	1	Aug. 9, 2006	at Oakland	Zito, Halsey	3R, 3R
	2	June 30, 2008	at San Francisco	Zito, Sadler	2R, GS
	3	July 21, 2009	at Houston	Rodriguez, Wright	1R, 1R
	4	Sept. 21, 2009	at Houston	Rodriguez, Paronto	1R, 1R
Grand Slam HR (5)					
	1	Aug. 4, 2006	at Los Angeles (AL)	Lackey	5th inning
	2	June 3, 2007	Atlanta	Cormier	1st inning
	3	June 30, 2008	at San Francisco	Sadler	8th inning
	4	Aug. 6, 2008	Houston	Backe	3rd inning
	5	June 9, 2009	Kansas City	Wright	7th inning
Pinch-hit HR (2)					
	1	May 1, 2003	at Houston	Wagner	2R, 9th inning
	2	Sept. 17, 2005	Seattle	Guadardo	1R, 9th inning
Walk-off HR (2)	1	July 21, 2001	Montreal	Lloyd	1st ML HR
	2	May 3, 2006	Baltimore	Halama	1R, 12th inning
Extra-inning HR (2)					
	1	July 21, 2001	Montreal	Lloyd	10th inning, 1st ML HR
	2	May 3, 2006	Baltimore	Halama	1R, 12th inning
RBI	1	May 14, 2000	at Philadelphia	Miller	PH - 3R double
Stolen Base	1	June 17, 2001	Boston	Castillo C-Mirabelli	2nd base

PROFESSIONAL CAREER:

1998:

- Made his Major League debut on Sept. 2 vs. HOU... Notched his first MLB hit, a pinch hit single off Vladimir Nunez, on Sept. 20 at ARI.

1999:

- Spent majority of season with Richmond, hitting .272 en route to a .317 on-base percentage

2000:

- Hit .308 in 22 games with Atlanta.
- With Richmond, batted .292 with 22 doubles.

2001:

- Was recalled on June 1 by Atlanta and batted .287 in 66 games with the Braves, holding down the shortstop position between an injury to Rafael Furcal and the acquisition of Rey Sanchez.
- On July 21 vs, MON, hit first career homer, a game-ending solo shot in the 10th inning off Graeme Lloyd.

2002:

- Started season at Triple-A with Richmond.
- Most of season was spent with Atlanta and hit .297, but a severe right ankle injury, sustained while rounding first base on May 17 at COL rendered a nearly two month stint on the DL.

2003:

- Eclipsed the 100-game plateau for the first time for the Braves in first complete big league campaign.

2004:

- His season ended prematurely upon tearing the ACL in right knee on Sept. 25 vs. FLA.
- Had surgery performed a week later and successfully rehabbed in the off-season.

2005:

- Signed with the Texas Rangers as a minor-league free agent... Appeared in 66 games, his fewest since 2001, however hit eight home runs in just 148 at-bats... Made 41 starts, starting 21 games in right field, eight at second base, seven at shortstop, four at third base and one as designated hitter.
- Penn alum started seven games alongside Chris Young (Princeton)... Became just the 2nd Ivy League duo to start for the same team in the last 50 years.

2006:

- Set career highs in almost every category including 136 games and 520 at-bats... Also set career highs with 78 runs scored, 40 doubles, 13 home runs and 74 RBI.
- Spent the last two days under .300 for the first time since April 30.
- His 74 RBI were more than the 73 he totaled in his last 3 seasons (2003-05) with Atlanta and Texas.
- Was named Rangers' Player of the Month for August after finishing the month with a batting average of .327 with five home runs and a team best 25 RBI.
- Was named AL Player of the Week for week ending Aug. 13, batting .433 (13-30) with two doubles, four home runs and 15 RBI
- Started games at six different position and was one of just nine big leaguers in '06 to start games at all four infield positions.

2007:

- Returned to the NL and hit .293 with 10 home runs and 72 RBI for the NL Central champion Cubs
- Appeared at six different positions in career-high 149 games... Played 93 games at 2nd base (88 starts), 37 games at 3rd base (31 starts), one game at shortstop, 22 games in right field (13 starts), one start in left field and nine games at 1st base (5 starts)
- Batted .317 (44-for-139) with RISP, including .328 (19-for-58) clip with RISP and 2 outs in an inning.
- Hit his 2nd career grand slam June 3 vs. Atlanta... Recorded his 500th career major league hit with a 7th inning single June 13 vs. Seattle... Had career-high five hits Aug. 16 and Sept. 17, both vs. Cincinnati.
- Batted .333 (3-for-9) with 2 runs scored in 3 starts in NLDS against Arizona.

2008:

- Set personal bests with 21 home runs, 87 RBI, 103 runs, 69 walks and a .376 OBP in 149 games for the Cubs.
- Finished tied for 11th in the National League in runs and 16th in on-base %... Hit .310 off left-handed pitching (.398OB/.497SLG/.894OPS) and .322 with runners in scoring position, which ranked 6th in the entire National League.
- Played at least 20 games at four different positions, appearing at six different spots on the season...Played 95 games at second base (80 starts), 22 at third base (10 starts), 38 in right field (32 starts), 27 in left field (21 starts), one at first base and one at shortstop.
- Among players who appeared in at least 90 games at second base, finished T-3rd in home runs (21), 4th in RBI (87) and 3rd in on-base % (.376).
- Invited to participate in the 2009 WBC for TEAM USA.
- Was just the second Cub since 1956 to collect an extra-base hit in eight consecutive games when he turned the trick Aug. 21-28... The eight consecutive games with an extra-base hit was part of a 10-game hitting streak, August 19-28 (16-38, .421 with an .895 slugging percentage)... Homered in four straight games, Aug. 21-24, the first Cub to do so since Fred McGriff accomplished the feat September 20-23, 2001.

2009:

- Was invited to participate in 2009 WBC for Team USA and batted .316 (6-for-19) with HR and team-leading 9 RBI in 6 games.
- Started year with Cleveland after being acquired from Cubs on Dec. 31 for pair of minor league pitchers.
- Was acquired by St. Louis in trade from Cleveland in exchange for right-handed pitchers Chris Perez and Jesse Todd on June 27.
- Went on disabled list with left wrist sprain July 1 and missed 13 games before being activated July 17.

2010:

- Underwent surgery Oct. 26, 2009 to repair torn tendon sheath in his left wrist, an injury he sustained soon after joining St. Louis in trade from Cleveland on July 1
- Was limited to just 26 games in his 1st season with San Francisco after having season cut short due to season-ending surgery in July on his left wrist.
- Became just the 3rd Giant since 2002 to homer in his debut with team, hitting solo shot in 8th inning off LHP Tim Byrdak on April 5 at Houston

2011:

- Had endured two separate DL stints that were necessitated by inflammation in left wrist (missed 13 games) and a left wrist strain (69).
- Hit .400 (14-for-35) with 8 RBI in final 16 contests of the season.

AT THE ALL STAR BREAK

(TOP 5)

AVERAGE

Year	Player	AVG
1993	J. Olerud	.395
1999	T. Fernandez	.372
2006	C. Delgado	.363
1994	P. Molitor	.342
2000	S. Stewart	.339

RUNS

Year	Player	R
2003	C. Delgado	76
2003	V. Wells	75
2000	C. Delgado	74
2011	J. Bautista	73
2000	R. Mondesi	73

HITS

Year	Player	H
2003	V. Wells	121
1993	J. Olerud	120
1986	T. Fernandez	118
2001	S. Stewart	118
2000	C. Delgado	116
1994	P. Molitor	116

HOME RUNS

Year	Player	HR
2011	J. Bautista	31
1987	G. Bell	29
2000	C. Delgado	28
2003	C. Delgado	28
2012	J. Bautista	27

RBI

Year	Player	RBI
2003	C. Delgado	97
2003	V. Wells	84
1994	J. Carter	80
2000	C. Delgado	80
1999	C. Delgado	77

STOLEN BASES

Year	Player	SB
1997	O. Nixon	37
1999	S. Stewart	29
1993	R. Alomar	28
1984	D. Garcia	27
1991	R. Alomar	27

ERA

Year	Player	ERA
1997	R. Clemens	1.69
1985	D. Stieb	1.87
1992	J. Guzman	2.11
1991	J. Key	2.23
2005	R. Halladay	2.41

WINS

Year	Player	W
2000	D. Wells	15
1997	R. Clemens	13
2003	R. Halladay	13
2005	R. Halladay	12
2006	R. Halladay	12

SAVES

Year	Player	SV
2006	B. Ryan	24
1998	R. Myers	22
1993	D. Ward	22
2000	B. Koch	20
2010	K. Gregg	20

STRIKEOUTS

Year	Player	SO
1997	R. Clemens	140
2008	A. Burnett	126
1992	J. Guzman	122
2008	R. Halladay	121
1998	R. Clemens	120

DICKEY, *R.A.*

Birthdate	October 29, 1974
Opening Day Age	38
Birthplace	Nashville, TN
Residence	Nashville, TN
Bats/Throws	R/R
Height/Weight	6-4/213
Contract Status	signed thru 2015
M.L. Service	7.007

43

PITCHER

PERSONAL:

Robert Allen (R.A.) Dickey... Is a 1993 graduate of Montgomery Bell Academy (TN) High School... Named an All-American in baseball his senior year... Attended the University of Tennessee (Knoxville) where he holds the school record for career wins (38)... Went 38-10 with a 3.40 ERA in his career for the Volunteers... Majored in English... Member of the bronze medal winning U.S. Olympic team at the 1996 Summer Games in Atlanta.... Helped form a non-profit organization called Honoring Thy Father Mission, aimed at reaching out to school, athletic and church youth groups as well as performing missionary work in Latin American countries... Active in the Fellowship of Christian Athletes... Was the recipient of the "Ya Gotta Have Heart" Award at the BBWAA Dinner on January 25, 2011... Received the "Tennessee Male Athlete of the Year" Award on February 11, 2011 in Nashville, TN... Was inducted into the Tennessee Baseball Hall of Fame on January 18, 2012... Climbed Mount Kilimanjaro in January, 2012 with Mets bullpen catcher Dave Racaniello and former teammate and current Cleveland Indians pitcher Kevin Slowey... Raised over $100,000 during the climb for Bombay Teen Challenge, an organization dedicated to rescuing young women from forced prostitution... Honored at the Thurman Munson Dinner on January 31, 2012 with a "Thurman Award."... His autobiography "Wherever I Wind Up, My Quest for Truth, Authenticity and the Perfect Knuckleball" was released in March, 2012... Is featured in a documentary film titled "Knuckleball".

LAST SEASON:

- Selected by the BBWAA as the 2012 Cy Young Award Winner becoming the first knuckleballer to win the award.
- Became the Mets first 20-game winner since Frank Viola, who won 20 games in 1990, and sixth in team history... Joined Tom Seaver, Jerry Koosman, Dwight Gooden, David Cone and Viola.
- Set career-bests in wins (20), innings pitched (233.2), ERA (2.73), complete games (five), shutouts (three), and WHIP (1.05).
- Named to the 2012 National League All-Star team, the first such honour of his career... Pitched 1.0 inning, allowing no runs.
- Ranked in the top two in all three NL triple crown categories (wins, ERA, strikeouts)...Tied for second in the Major Leagues with 20 wins... Struck out 230 in 233.2 innings, which ranked third in the Majors and first in the NL... Was fourth in the Majors and second in the NL with a 2.73 ERA... Finished fourth in the NL with a 1.05 WHIP... Finished first in the NL with 22 starts of pitching at least 7.0 innings... Recorded 27 quality starts, to lead the Majors... His strikeout to walk ratio of 4.26 ranked fourth in the Majors and third in the NL... Limited opposing righthanded batters to a .218 (102-468) batting average, good for seventh in the NL... Had 15 starts in which he struck out eight or more, tying him for second in the Majors.
- Was the National League Pitcher of the Month for June... It was his first career Pitcher of the Month honour... Began the month with 37.0 consecutive innings without surrendering an earned run... The streak dated from June 2 vs. St. L to June 24 vs. NYY... Went 5-0 in six starts, leading the Majors for the month in ERA (0.93), innings pitched (48.1) and strikeouts (55)...His five wins are also tied for the most in the majors.
- Struck out an NL-leading 230 batters... Struck out double-digits seven times, the most in the NL... Set his career-high total in strikeouts three different times this season... Recorded 12 and 13 strikeouts in back-to-back starts at TB on June 13 and again vs. BAL on June 18, respectively, setting a new career-high each time... First set his career-high by striking out 11 at PIT on May 22... Matched his career-high with 13 strikeouts in his start vs. PIT on Sept. 27.
- Became the 10th pitcher since 1900 to record consecutive one-hitters (June 13 at TB and June 18 vs. BAL)... Became the first pitcher in modern baseball history (since 1900) to register back-to-back complete game one-hitters with 10 strikeouts or more in both starts... Became the first pitcher to throw consecutive one-hitters since Toronto's Dave Stieb in 1988... Stieb one-hit CLE on the road on Sept. 24 and then allowed one hit vs. BAL on Sept. 30… The last National Leaguer to do so was Jim Tobin for the 1944 Boston Braves, who tossed a one-hitter on April 23 vs. PHI and a no-hitter on April 27 vs. Brooklyn... His June 24 start vs. the Yankees ended three streaks: 44.2 innings pitched without allowing an earned run, 52.2 innings pitched without allowing a home run, and 105 at-bats without allowing an extra-base hit…The start also snapped his 11-game quality start streak... Hurled five straight starts where he did not allow an earned run and notched eight or more strikeouts from May 22-June 18, the longest such streak in Major League history... The previous mark was four by Gaylord Perry (1967), Ray Culp (1968) and Pedro Martinez (2002).
- Since 2010, has posted a 2.95 ERA (202 earned runs/616.2 innings)... Among pitchers with at least 500.0 innings since 2010, his 2.95 ERA ranks fifth best in the NL.
- Pitched at least 7.0 innings and allowed one run or less 15 times... The total was the most in the National League and two behind Felix Hernandez (Seattle) for the Major League lead with 17.
- Went 13-1 in day games...The 13 daytime victories were the most wins in the Majors since Rick Reuschel went 15-5 in 1977 for the Chicago Cubs.

R.A. DICKEY

Bold – career high

Year	Club & League	W-L	ERA	G	GS	CG	ShO	SV	IP	H	R	ER	HR	HB	BB-IBB	SO	WP	BK	OBA
1997	Charlotte (FSL)	1-4	6.94	8	6	0	0	0	35.0	51	32	27	8	0	12-1	32	5	3	.340
1998	Charlotte (FSL)	1-5	3.30	57	0	0	0	38	60.0	58	31	22	9	0	22-3	53	3	2	.249
1999	Tulsa (TEX)	6-7	4.55	35	11	0	0	10	95.0	105	60	48	13	2	40-1	59	9	0	.283
	Oklahoma (PCL)	2-2	4.37	6	2	0	0	0	22.2	23	12	11	1	1	7-1	17	2	0	.261
2000	Oklahoma (PCL)	8-9	4.49	30	23	2	0	1	158.1	167	83	79	13	7	65-1	85	5	2	.281
2001	Oklahoma (PCL)	11-7	3.75	24	24	3	0	0	163.0	164	77	68	14	7	45-1	120	3	0	.262
	TEXAS (AL)	0-1	6.75	4	0	0	0	0	12.0	13	9	9	3	0	7-1	4	1	0	.283
2002	Oklahoma (PCL)	8-7	4.09	37	19	1	0	0	154.0	176	81	70	8	4	47-5	109	5	0	.295
2003	Oklahoma (PCL)	1-1	1.20	3	2	0	0	0	15.0	14	3	2	1	0	3-0	4	0	0	.259
	TEXAS (AL)	9-8	5.09	**38**	13	1	1	**1**	116.2	135	68	66	16	5	38-5	94	5	2	.292
2004	Frisco (TEX)	1-1	1.98	4	4	0	0	0	13.2	16	5	3	0	0	1-0	9	0	0	.286
	TEXAS (AL)	6-7	5.61	25	15	0	0	**1**	104.1	136	77	65	17	4	33-1	57	5	1	.311
2005	Oklahoma City (PCL)	10-6	5.99	19	17	1	0	0	121.2	152	88	81	12	8	39-0	81	9	2	.308
	TEXAS (AL)	1-2	6.67	9	4	0	0	0	29.2	29	23	22	4	2	17-0	15	2	0	.254
2006	TEXAS (AL)	0-1	18.90	1	1	0	0	0	3.1	8	7	7	6	0	1-0	1	0	0	.471
	Oklahoma City (PCL)	9-8	4.92	22	19	3	1	1	131.2	134	80	72	17	11	46-0	61	6	2	.272
2007	Nashville (PCL)	13-6	3.72	31	22	3	0	0	169.1	159	80	70	18	7	60-0	119	12	0	.252
2008	Tacoma (PCL)	2-5	3.44	7	7	0	0	0	49.2	58	25	19	2	3	8-0	30	2	0	.297
	SEATTLE (AL)	5-8	5.21	32	14	0	0	0	112.1	124	65	65	15	2	51-4	58	11	1	.284
2009	MINNESOTA (AL)	1-1	4.62	35	1	0	0	0	64.1	74	34	33	8	4	30-1	42	4	0	.290
	Rochester Red (Int)	2-1	5.13	5	5	1	1	0	33.1	39	20	19	1	0	9-1	18	4	0	.289
2010	Buffalo (Int)	4-2	2.23	8	8	2	1	0	60.2	55	21	15	3	3	8-0	37	4	1	.239
	NEW YORK (NL)	11-9	2.84	27	26	2	1	0	174.1	165	62	55	13	4	42-3	104	11	0	.251
2011	NEW YORK (NL)	8-**13**	3.28	33	32	1	0	0	208.2	202	85	76	18	9	**54**-2	134	9	1	.256
2012	NEW YORK (NL)	**20**-6	2.73	34	**33**	**5**	**3**	0	**233.2**	192	78	71	**24**	9	**54**-2	**230**	4	1	.226
Minor Totals		79-71	4.25	296	169	16	3	50	1283.0	1371	698	606	120	53	412-14	834	69	12	.277
AL TOTALS		22-48	5.43	144	48	1	1	2	444.2	519	283	267	69	17	177-12	271	28	4	.293
NL TOTALS		39-28	2.95	94	91	8	4	0	616.2	559	225	202	55	22	150-7	468	24	2	.244
MAJOR TOTALS		61-56	3.99	238	139	9	5	2	1059.1	1078	508	469	124	39	327-19	739	52	6	.265

ALL-STAR GAME RECORD

Year	Club & League	W-L	ERA	G	GS	CG	ShO	SV	IP	H	R	ER	HR	HB	BB-IBB	SO	WP	BK
2012	NL at KC	0-0	0.00	1	0	0	0	0	1.0	1	0	0	0	0	0-0	1	0	0

TRANSACTIONS

- Selected by the Texas Rangers in the 1st round (18th overall) of the 1996 First Year Player Draft
- On disabled list (strained right rhomboid ligament) from June 26-July 19, 2004
- On disabled list (upper back strain) from July 30-August 23, 2004
- On disabled list (right triceps inflammation) from April 13-May 25, 2005
- Signed by the Milwaukee Brewers on January 12, 2007
- Signed by the Minnesota Twins on November 30, 2007
- Selected by the Seattle Mariners in the Rule 5 Draft on December 6, 2007
- Returned to the Minnesota Twins on March 29, 2008
- Traded to the Seattle Mariners for C Jair Fernandez on March 29, 2008
- Signed by the Minnesota Twins on December 25, 2008
- Signed by the New York Mets on January 5, 2010
- Traded to the Toronto Blue Jays along C Josh Thole and C Mike Nickeas in exchange for C John Buck, C Travis d'Arnaud, RHP Noah Syndergaard and OF William Beccera on December 17, 2012

GAME HIGHS

ML Debut	April 22, 2001 vs. OAK
Innings Pitched:	
Starter	9.0 - 8x, last Aug. 31, 2012 at MIA
Reliever	5.2 - June 3, 2008 vs. LAA
Walks:	
Starter	6 - Sept. 17, 2011 at ATL
Reliever	4 - May 7, 2001 vs. CWS
Strikeouts:	
Starter	13 - 2x, last Sept. 27, 2012 vs. PIT
Reliever	6 - June 3, 2008 vs. LAA
Hits Allowed	11 - 3x, last July 5, 2012 vs. PHI
Runs Allowed	9 - 2x, last June 13, 2004 vs. STL
ER Allowed	9 - 2x, last June 13, 2004 vs. STL
HR Allowed	6 - April 6, 2006 vs. DET
Low Hit CG	1 - 3x, last June 18, 2012 vs. BAL
Last Win	Sept. 27, 2012 vs. PIT
Last Save	Sept. 30, 2004 vs. ANA
Last CG	Aug. 31, 2012 at MIA
Last ShO	Aug. 31, 2012 at MIA
Last Start	Oct. 2, 2012 at MIA
Last Relief App.	July 21, 2012 vs. LAD
Longest Win Streak	11G - April 25-July 21, 2012
Longest Losing Streak	5G - 2x, last April 8-May 14, 2011
Scoreless Innings Streak	32.2 - May 22-June 13, 2012

CAREER FIELDING

POSITION	PCT	G	PO	A	E	TC	DP
P	.969	238	62	223	9	294	18

MILESTONES

Category		Date	Opponent	Notes
Start	1	July 11, 2003	Kansas City	loss - 5.0IP, 6H, 4ER, BB, K, HR
	100	Aug. 21, 2011	Milwaukee	no decision - 7.0 IP, 6H, 2ER, 4K, HR
Win	1	April 24, 2003	Boston	as a reliever - 3.0 IP, 2H, ER, 2BB, 2K
ShO (5)	1	Aug. 20, 2003	at Detroit	9.0 IP, 6H, BB, 7K
	2	Aug. 13, 2010	Philadelphia	9.0 IP, H, BB, 7K
	3	June 2, 2012	St. Louis	9.0 IP, 7H, 9K
	4	June 18, 2012	Baltimore	9.0 IP, H, 2BB, 13K
	5	Aug. 31, 2012	at Miami	9.0 IP, 5H, 3BB, 7K
10+ Strikeout Games (8)				
	8	Sept. 27, 2012	Pittsburgh	13 strikeouts
Strikeout	500	Sept. 12, 2011	Washington	Marrero

PROFESSIONAL CAREER:

2001:

- Purchased by the Rangers on April 19... Pitched one scoreless inning in **Major League debut** on April 22 versus OAK, then allowed 9 runs in 11 innings in his last three games... Lost to CWS on May 7.
- Optioned to Oklahoma for rest of season on May 8.

2002:

- Spent the entire season at Oklahoma (AAA) of the Pacific Coast League.
- Led the club in innings pitched and strikeouts, was tied for first in wins and tied for second in starts.

2003:

- Appeared in 38 games for the Rangers and went 9-8, 5.09 with one save.
- Went 5-5, 5.25 (43 ER/73.2 IP) in 13 starts and 4-3, 4.81 (23 ER/43 IP) in 25 relief appearances... Finished second on the staff in strikeouts (94), was third in innings (116.2), and tied for third in wins (9), the latter matching the second most by an AL rookie.
- His .529 winning percentage was tops among AL rookies with 100 or more innings pitched... Ranked third among AL rookies in strikeouts (94) and pitched fifth most innings (116.2).
- As a reliever, allowed a run in 14 of 25 games... Permitted nine of 23 inherited runners to score, including just one in three bases loaded situations.
- Recorded first big league victory in relief on April 24 vs. Boston.
- Went 1-1 at the plate with single in first big league at-bat, June 7 vs. Montreal in San Juan.
- Pitched a 6-hit complete game shutout on August 20 at Detroit... First CG shutout by a Texas pitcher since Kenny Rogers, April 19, 2002 at Seattle, a span of 272 games between CG shutouts... The first CG shutout by a Texas rookie since Rick Helling, May 6, 1994 vs. Minnesota and the 12th CG shutout ever for a Texas rookie, the second in the last 15 seasons... Was his first professional CG shutout and was one of four CG shutout by an AL rookie in 2003.
- Recorded first major league save two days earlier on Aug. 18 at Detroit... Was the shortest span for a pitcher with first Major League CG shutout and save in Major League history... Previous shortest span had been by Jackie Brown, also with the Rangers: save on July 26, 1973 vs. CAL and CG shutout on July 29, 1973 (game one) at OAK.
- Went 4-1 in August to set a club record for rookie wins in a month (tied by Colby Lewis in September).

2004:

- Made 25 appearances for Texas, including career high 15 starts, and spent 2 stints on the disabled list... Ranked T-3rd on staff with 5 quality starts, T-4th in starts and 2nd with 4 pickoffs.
- Made Opening Day roster as Rangers' 4th starter... Made season debut in home opener on April 9, earning win by allowing 3 unearned runs in 7.0 innings.
- Was on the disabled list from June 25-July 18 and July 30-Aug. 22, both times with a strained right rhomboid muscle in his back.
- Earned 2nd career save on Sept. 30 vs. ANA.

NL PITCHING LEADERS – 2012

ERA		W		CG	
Clayton Kershaw, LAD	2.53	Gio Gonzalez, WSH	21	**R.A. Dickey, NYM**	**5**
R.A Dickey, NYM	**2.73**	**R.A. Dickey, NYM**	**20**	Ricky Nolasco, MIA	3
Johnny Cueto, CIN	2.78	Johnny Cueto, CIN	19	Adam Wainwright, STL	3

ShO		IP		SO	
R.A. Dickey, NYM	**3**	**R.A. Dickey, NYM**	**233.2**	**R.A. Dickey, NYM**	**230**
6 players tied	2	Clayton Kershaw, LAD	227.2	Clayton Kershaw, LAD	229
		Matt Cain, SF	219.1	Cole Hamels, PHI	216

2005:

- Went 1-2 with a 6.67 ERA in nine games/four starts over two stints with Texas in 2005.
- Made Opening Day roster for second consecutive season... Was 0-1, 8.10 (6 ER/6.2 IP) in five relief appearances in first stint from April 5-13... Took loss in home opener, on April 11 vs. LAA, allowing a solo homer to Orlando Cabrera to lead off the 10th inning.
- Left game on April 12 vs. LAA due to injury... Placed on the 15-day disabled list on April 13 with right triceps inflammation... Activated from the disabled list and optioned to Oklahoma on May 25...
- Was recalled on Sept. 12 and went 1-1, 6.26 (16 ER/23.0 IP) in four starts in 2nd Major League stint of 2005... Made first start of the season on Sept. 13 vs. Baltimore, allowing three runs in 7.0 innings to take no decision... Was first quality start since June 2, 2004 at CLE.
- Earned lone ML win of the season on Sept. 18 vs. Seattle, despite allowing six runs in 5.2 innings.
- Made 5 of his 9 appearances against LAA... Used knuckleball as his primary pitch during his 2nd stint with the club... Began throwing the knuckler with Oklahoma in July... Worked on the pitch with Rangers Hall of Famer Charlie Hough during a road trip to Anaheim in Sept.

2006:

- Took the loss in his only start with the Rangers on April 6th vs. Detroit, allowing eight hits and seven runs in 3.1 innings pitched, while tying a modern major league record by giving up six home runs.
- Optioned to Oklahoma (AAA) of the Pacific Coast League on April 7th... Was designated for assignment on April 23rd... Was outrighted to Oklahoma on April 26th.
- Made four trips to the disabled list during the season with a sore right shoulder.

2007:

- Spent the entire season with Nashville (AAA) of the Pacific Coast League, leading the league with 13 wins.
- Named Pacific Coast League Pitcher of the Year.

2012 NL CY YOUNG AWARD

R.A. Dickey, NYM	**209 votes**
Clayton Kershaw, LAD	96 votes
Gio Gonzalez, WSH	93 votes
Johnny Cueto, CIN	75 votes
Craig Kimbrel, ATL	41 votes

TOUGH TO HANDLE

In 2012, R.A. Dickey became the 1st knuckleball pitcher to win the Cy Young Award since it was first presented in 1956...Dickey is the 6th knuckleballer to finish in the top 10 in Cy Young voting, joining Bob Purkey, Phil Niekro, Joe Niekro, Wilbur Wood and Tim Wakefield...Listed below are knuckleball pitchers and where they placed in Cy Young voting.

Year	Pitcher, Team	Place
1962	Bob Purkey, Reds	3
1969	Phil Niekro, Braves	2
1971	Wilbur Wood, White Sox	3
1972	Wilbur Wood, White Sox	2
1973	Wilbur Wood, White Sox	5
1974	Phil Niekro, Braves	3
1978	Phil Niekro, Braves	6
1979	Joe Niekro, Astros	2
1979	Phil Niekro, Braves	6
1980	Joe Niekro, Astros	4
1982	Phil Niekro, Braves	5
1995	Tim Wakefield, Red Sox	3
2012	**R.A. Dickey, Mets**	**1**

2008:

- Started the season at Triple-A Tacoma (SEA)... Recalled by SEA on April 14 and pitched 1.0 scoreless inning of relief that night vs. KC, marking his first game in the Majors in over two years (April 6, 2006).
- Made two relief appearances for the Mariners and was sent back to Tacoma... Started five games and was recalled to Seattle.
- Tossed 14.0 consecutive scoreless innings upon his return... Earned his first win of the season on June 9 at Toronto, pitching 2.0 scoreless inning of relief, first win since September 18, 2005 vs. Seattle... Tossed 7.0 shutout innings June 24 at NYM, picking up his second career hit (single).
- Tied an MLB record, throwing four wild pitches in the fifth inning of a game August 17 at Minnesota (fifth MLB pitcher with four).
- Went 2-0, 2.00 (36.0 IP, 8 ER) with a .205 batting-average-against in 18 relief appearances with the Mariners and did not allow a run in 13 of those 18 relief appearances.

2009:

- Made the Twins' Opening Day roster and made his first and only start on April 10th at Chicago (AL)... Earned the win with 5.0 innings of three-run ball.
- Moved to the bullpen and made 34 more appearances...Recorded nine consecutive scoreless outings (12.2 innings), June 3rd-June 28th.
- Went at least 4.0 innings in three straight appearances from May 18th through May 30th.
- Optioned to Rochester (AAA) of the International League on August 7th... Was designated for assignment on August 29th...

2010:

- Set then career highs in wins, starts, innings, strikeouts, and complete games in his first season with the Mets.
- Finished seventh in the National League in ERA, fourth with a 1.99 home ERA (18 earned runs/81.1 innings) and third with a night ERA of 2.53 (33 earned runs/117.1 innings).
- His walk per nine inning rate of 2.2 was the best of his career and the third-best mark in the NL... Finished the season with five starts where he did not walk a batter, after entering the season with only three starts for his career with no base on balls.
- Allowed just three runs and limited opponents to a .156 (14-90) batting average, with three extra-base hits and 22 strikeouts in the first inning... The .156 batting average was the best mark in the major leagues among qualifying pitchers.
- Threw a one-hitter, the 35th in franchise history, to beat the Phillies, 1-0, on August 13th at Citi Field... Was the second complete-game effort of Dickey's career and the only hit he allowed was a line-drive single by pitcher Cole Hamels... He struck out seven, one off his season-high, and walked one... Also paired with Johan Santana, who had thrown a shutout in his start the night before, to become the first Mets pitchers to post consecutive complete-game shutouts since Pedro Astacio and Jeff D'Amico tossed back-to-back two hitters on May 14 and May 15, 2002 at Los Angeles...The last pitcher to throw a complete-game one-hitter in a 1-0 victory with the only hit by the pitcher was Sandy Koufax on May 23, 1960.
- Set a Mets record and led all Major League pitchers by handling 61 total chances without an error...Broke Tom Glavine's club record set in 2005, when the lefthander had 55 total errorless chances.
- Finished with four, two-hit games, the most multiple-hit games in one year by a Mets pitcher since Mike Hampton had five in 2000 to tie the club record set by Dwight Gooden in 1985.
- Started the season with Buffalo (AAA) of the International League, where he threw a near perfect game...Set a Buffalo modern-day record when he retired 27 straight hitters on April 29 vs. Durham...Fernando Perez singled on an 0-2 pitch to start the game before Dickey set down the next 27 hitters in order.
- Had his contract selected from Buffalo (AAA) of the International League on May 19.
- Became the first pitcher in Mets history to go 6-0 in his first seven starts on June 23 vs. Detroit.
- Went at least 7.0 innings in 13 turns after having just 11 starts of that length previously.
- His start on July 29 came on three-days rest... Became just the second pitcher over the past four seasons to start a game on short rest (no more than three days between starts) and throw more than 8.0 shutout innings... The other was Johan Santana who accomplished the feat in a 2-0 shutout win for the Mets against the Marlins on the next to last day of the 2008 season.

2011:

- Set career-highs in innings pitched, starts, and strikeouts.
- Finished the season with 12 straight quality starts dating back to July 25, the longest such streak of his career... Tied for the longest in the NL (Javier Vazquez and Tim Hudson) and tied for the second longest in the Majors in 2011 (Jered Weaver, 15)... The 12-game run also ties Vazquez for the longest active streak in the Majors... Finished with 22 quality starts to lead the team.
- Recorded a career-high 10 strikeouts vs. PIT on May 31... Pitched at least 7.0 innings in 16 of his 32 starts. ... Also pitched into the eighth inning in three straight starts from May 31-June 11, the first time in his career in which he accomplished that feat.
- Compiled a 1.82 ERA in September (seven earned runs/34.2 innings), which ranked eighth in the Majors among pitchers with at least five September starts...
- Committed just his second error as a Met in a start on August 10.
- Made the second Home Opening Day start of his career and first with the Mets on April 8 vs. WAS... Suffered the loss, working 5.0 innings and allowing three runs... Started the Texas Rangers' home opener in 2004 vs. Anaheim...
- Made his 100th Major League start on August 21 against the Brewers at Citi Field... Since 1947, the only pitcher who was older at the time of his 100th career start than Dickey (36 years, 296 days) was Masato Yoshii (age 36 years, 356 days on April 11, 2002) with Montreal... Other than Yoshii, the last pitcher to make his 100th big league start at such an advanced age was Ed Heusser in 1946 (age 37 years, 103 days) with Cincinnati.

2012 NL Cy Young Award winner, R.A. Dickey, being introduced to Toronto at a press conference held at Rogers Centre on January 7, 2013

DRABEK, *KYLE*

Birthdate............December 8, 1987
Opening Day Age....................25
Birthplace................Victoria, TX
Residence..........The Woodlands, TX
Bats/Throws.......................R/R
Height/Weight................6-1/228
Contract Status........signed thru 2013
M.L. Service....................1.119

4

PITCHER

PERSONAL:

Kyle Jordan Drabek... Is the son of former Major League Cy Young Award winner Doug Drabek... Graduate of Woodlands High School... While there he was an Aflac, USA Today, and Louisville Slugger high-school All-American at pitcher and shortstop... Was paired up on a Houston summer team with current Cincinnati Reds outfielder Jay Bruce... While in high school was named 2005 and 2006 Texas 5-A player of the year... During the 2006 spring season, the Highlanders won the Texas 5-A State Championship... During his high-school career, compiled a record of 30-1 on the mound while belting 27 home runs... In the 2006 Texas regional semifinal, he set the Woodlands High School record for most strikeouts in a game by a pitcher (19), recording a no-hitter... Was 10-0 in his senior year (10 starts) while posting an ERA of 1.18 in 65.0 IP, allowed 34 hits, walked 23 and struck out 112.

LAST SEASON:

- Made just 13 starts after having his season end prematurely on June 13 vs. WAS with an elbow injury...Had a second Tommy John surgery on June 19.
- Team was 5-8 in his starts...Allowed two or less runs in eight of his 13 starts.
- Saw his opponent's average drop from .321 in 2011 to .250...His GB/FB ratio inproved from 1.35 to 1.88 and his 12 GDP's was 8th in the AL at the time of his injury and still ranked 3rd on the club in 2012.
- Walked four or more in eight of his 15 starts including a career high six on April 20 at KC and May 21 at TB...Ended the season with a 5.93 walks per nine total which was 2nd highest in the AL (min 70.0 IP).
- Picked up the win on May 21 at TB becoming the 1st AL starter to walk at least six batters, throw at least three wild pitches & still earn the win since Juan Guzman (TOR) on July 15, 1994 vs. TEX (6-IP, 6-BB, 3-WP).
- Pitched well at Rogers Centre, posting a 3-3 record with a 2.70 ERA while holding opponents to a .215 average...On the road was 1-4 with a 6.75 ERA and a .286 opponent's average.
- Recorded a career high 7.1 innings on April 15 vs. BAL, just the 4th time he has tossed at least 7.0 innings in his career... Allowed a career high nine runs on May 27 at TEX.

KYLE DRABEK

Bold – career high

Year	Club & League	W-L	ERA	G	GS	CG	ShO	SV	IP	H	R	ER	HR	HB	BB-IBB	SO	WP	BK	OBA
2006	Phillies (Gulf)	1-3	7.71	6	6	0	0	0	23.1	33	24	20	2	2	11-0	14	0	1	.333
2007	Lakewood (SAL)	5-1	4.33	11	10	0	0	0	54.0	50	29	26	9	2	23-0	46	1	0	.239
2008	Phillies (Gulf)	0-1	2.25	4	4	0	0	0	12.0	6	3	3	0	1	6-0	6	2	0	.150
	Williamsprt (NYP)	1-2	2.21	4	4	0	0	0	20.1	11	6	5	1	1	6-0	10	3	0	.159
2009	Clearwater (FSL)	4-1	2.48	10	9	1	1	0	61.2	49	19	17	0	2	19-0	74	2	1	.218
	Reading (East)	8-2	3.64	15	14	0	0	0	96.1	92	40	39	9	1	31-2	76	2	3	.252
2010	New Hampshire (East)	14-9	2.94	27	27	1	1	0	162.0	126	67	53	12	4	68-0	132	5	2	.215
	TORONTO (AL)	0-3	4.76	3	3	0	0	0	17.0	18	9	9	2	0	5-0	12	2	0	.295
2011	Las Vegas (PCL)	5-4	7.44	15	15	1	0	0	75.0	111	70	62	12	2	41-0	45	9	2	.355
	TORONTO (AL)	**4**-5	6.06	**18**	**14**	0	0	0	**78.2**	87	54	53	**10**	1	**55**-0	**51**	11	0	.289
2012	TORONTO (AL)	**4-7**	4.67	13	13	0	0	0	71.1	67	41	37	**10**	1	47-0	47	7	0	.250
Minor Totals		38-23	4.01	92	89	3	2	0	504.2	478	258	225	45	15	205-2	403	24	9	.251
MAJOR TOTALS		8-15	5.34	34	30	0	0	0	167.0	172	104	99	22	2	107-0	110	20	0	.273

TRANSACTIONS

- Selected by the Philadelphia Phillies in the 1st round (18th overall) in the 2006 First Year Player Draft
- Traded to the Toronto Blue Jays along with OF Michael Taylor and C Travis d'Arnaud in exchange for RHP Roy Halladay and cash considerations on December 16, 2009
- On disabled list (torn right elbow ligament) from June 15-remainder of season, 2012

GAME HIGHS

ML Debut	Sept. 15, 2010 at BAL
Innings Pitched:	
Starter	7.1 - April 15, 2012
Reliever	2.0 - 2x, last Sept. 20, 2011 vs. LAA
Walks:	
Starter	6 - 3x, last May 21, 2012 at TB
Reliever	1 - 3x, last Sept. 26, 2011 at CWS
Strikeouts:	
Starter	8 - April 30, 2012 vs. TEX
Reliever	3 - Sept. 17, 2011 vs. NYY
Hits Allowed	9 - 2x, last June 7, 2011 at KC
Runs Allowed	9 - May 27, 2012 at TEX
ER Allowed	9 - May 27, 2012
HR Allowed	3 - June 12, 2011 vs. BOS
Low Hit CG	None
Last Win	May 21, 2012 at TB
Last Save	None
Last CG	None
Last ShO	None
Last Start	June 13, 2012 vs. WSH
Last Relief App.	Sept. 26, 2011 at CWS
Longest Win Streak	2G - 3x, last May 16-21, 2012
Longest Losing Streak	4G - April 25-May 11, 2012
Scoreless Innings Streak	8.2 - May 16-22, 2011

CAREER FIELDING

POSITION	PCT	G	PO	A	E	TC	DP
P	.909	34	12	28	4	44	4

MILESTONES

Category		Date	Opponent	Notes
Start	1	Sept. 15, 2010	at Baltimore	ND, 6.0 IP, 9H, 3ER, 3BB, 5K
Win	1	April 2, 2011	Minnesota	As a starter - 7.0 IP, 3H, ER, 3BB, 7K

PROFESSIONAL CAREER:

2006:

- Made his 1st pro start, July 15 vs Tigers (L, 1.0 IP, 4 H, 3 R, 3 ER, 1 BB, 1 SO).
- Selected as a 2006 First Team All-American by Baseball America in June.
- Rated the 2nd–best prospect in the Phillies minor league system by Baseball America.

2007:

- Named to the South Atlantic League All-Star team.
- Had season-ending ligament replacement surgery ("Tommy John") on his right elbow, July 25 (Dr. David Altchek).

2008:

- Began season on disabled list recovering from "Tommy John" surgery.
- Participated in Florida Instructional League.

2009:

- Was promoted to Reading (AA) in the Eastern League.
- Received the Paul Owens Award recognizing him as the top pitcher in the Phillies system.
- On Dec. 16 was traded to the Toronto Blue Jays along with OF Michael Taylor and C Travis d'Arnaud in exchange for RHP Roy Halladay and cash considerations.
- Was ranked by Baseball America as the Blue Jays #1 prospect.

2010:

- Spent the majority of the season with New Hampshire (AA) of the Eastern League before being promoted to Toronto on Sept. 15.
- Made his **ML debut** on Sept. 15 at BAL, recorded a qualiy start, tossing six innings, allowing three runs in a 4-1 loss.
- Made his first start vs. the Orioles just as his father did on June 15, 1986... Fanned Ty Wigginton in the first inning for his first Major League strikeout.
- Was named Eastern League Pitcher of the Year in 2010 after recording a 14-9 record with a 2.94 ERA in 27 starts for New Hampshire (AA)... Led the Eastern League with his 14 victories, while finishing 3rd in ERA (2.94), IP (162) and strikeouts (132).
- On July 4 pitched a no-hitter in a game vs. New Britain walking two and striking out three, becoming the first Fisher Cat to throw a nine inning **no-hitter** in club history... The performance earned him Eastern League Pitcher of the Week honours.
- Was named to the Eastern League Mid and Post Season All-Star squads.
- Took the ball in game #1 of the Eastern League East Division Finals, going six innings, however took the loss 2-0 in their first playoff game in six seasons.
- Rated as the #3 prospect by Baseball America in the Eastern League.

2011:

- Picked up his first Major League win in his first start on April 2 vs. MIN as he allowed just one run and one hit over seven innings, walked three, struck out seven and pitched 5.1 hitless innings to start the game.
- Pitched just 0.2 innings June 1 vs. CLE which was the shortest start of his career and the shortest start by a Blue Jay since May 30, 2007 at NYY when Jesse Litsch also went 0.2 innings.
- After his recall on Sept. 7 spent the remainder of the season in the bullpen... Made his 1st career relief appearance on Sept. 9, pitched a scoreless inning of relief.

ENCARNACION, *EDWIN*

Birthdate . . . . .January 7, 1983
Opening Day Age .30
Birthplace. . . . . La Romana, DR
Residence . . . . La Romana, DR
Bats/Throws . . . . R/R
Height/Weight 6-2/228
Contract Status . . . . signed thru 2015
M.L. Service 7.085

10
INFIELDER

PERSONAL:

Edwin Elpidio Encarnacion... Has one child... Attended Manuel Toro High School in Caguas, Puerto Rico... In three consecutive seasons participated in Major League Baseball's All-Star Futures Game (2003-05).

LAST SEASON:

- Set career highs in most offensive categories, including home runs (42), RBI (110), walks (84) and stolen bases (13).
- Among AL hitters ranked 1st in HR/AB (12.90), 3rd in OPS (.941), T-3rd in RBI (110), 4th in HR (42), 5th in SLG (.557), OBP (.384), 7th in BB (84) and T-10th in XBH (66).
- One of six players in the Major Leagues to have hit 40+ HR in 2012... Was one of eight players to have reached the 40 HR mark dating back to 2010... 21 of his 42 home runs have come with two strikes which led the Majors, with 10 of his 42 homers coming on a 1-2 pitch... Had at least five home runs in each month, the first Blue Jay to do so since Aaron Hill in 2009.
- Earned Honda Player of the Month honours for the club in April, August and September... Posted a .322 average with eight home runs and 22 RBI in April, .270 with seven home runs and 18 RBI in August and also had seven home runs and 20 RBI in September.
- Had a four-game home run streak April 27-30... Became one of three players (Delgado/Carter) to have two streaks of four or more consecutive games with a home run in their Blue Jays career.
- April 28 vs. SEA hit his 4th career grand slam... July 14 vs. CLE added his 8th multi-HR game of his career.
- Batted .305 with 23 home runs and 91 RBI with runners on base and with runners in scoring position, batted .311 with nine home runs and 61 RBI... In close and late situations batted .310 with four home runs and 10 RBI.
- Started 82 games at DH, 66 at 1B, 2 in LF and one at 3B.

EDWIN ENCARNACION

Bold – career high

Year	Club & League	AVG	G	AB	R	H	2B	3B	HR	RBI	SH-SF	HP	BB-IBB	SO	SB-CS	SLG	OBP	OPS
2000	Rangers (Gulf)	.311	51	177	31	55	6	3	0	36	3-3	1	21-1	27	3-1	.379	.381	.760
2001	Savannah (SAL)	.306	45	170	23	52	9	2	4	25	1-2	2	12-0	34	3-3	.453	.355	.808
	Dayton (Mid)	.162	9	37	2	6	2	0	1	6	0-0	0	1-0	5	0-1	.297	.184	.481
	Billings (Pio)	.261	52	211	27	55	8	2	5	26	0-2	0	15-0	29	8-1	.389	.307	.696
2002	Dayton (Mid)	.282	136	518	80	146	32	4	17	73	0-6	7	40-2	108	25-7	.458	.338	.796
2003	Chattanooga (SOU)	.272	67	254	40	69	13	1	5	36	0-5	3	22-0	44	8-3	.390	.331	.721
	Potomac (CARO)	.321	58	215	40	69	15	1	6	29	1-3	1	24-1	32	7-1	.484	.387	.871
2004	Chattanooga (SOU)	.281	120	469	73	132	35	1	13	76	1-3	0	53-3	79	17-3	.443	.352	.795
2005	Louisville (Int)	.314	78	290	44	91	23	0	15	54	0-3	4	33-1	53	7-2	.548	.388	.936
	CINCINNATI (NL)	.232	69	211	25	49	16	0	9	31	0-0	3	20-2	60	3-0	.436	.308	.744
2006	Louisville (Int)	.306	10	36	6	11	3	0	1	1	0-0	0	2-0	11	0-0	.472	.342	.814
	CINCINNATI (NL)	.276	117	406	60	112	**33**	1	15	72	0-3	13	41-3	78	6-3	.473	.359	.832
2007	Louisville (Int)	.413	11	46	12	19	3	0	3	7	0-0	0	1-0	4	1-0	.674	.426	1.100
	CINCINNATI (NL)	.289	139	502	66	145	25	1	16	76	0-1	14	39-4	86	8-1	.438	.356	.794
2008	CINCINNATI (NL)	.251	146	506	75	127	29	1	26	68	0-5	10	61-1	**102**	1-0	.466	.340	.806
2009	Louisville (Int)	.270	11	37	5	10	1	0	2	8	0-0	0	8-0	6	0-0	.459	.400	.859
	CINCINNATI (NL)	.209	43	139	10	29	6	**1**	5	16	0-0	2	24-0	38	1-1	.374	.333	.707
	TORONTO (AL)	.240	42	154	25	37	5	**1**	8	23	0-3	3	13-0	29	1-0	.442	.306	.748
2010	Dunedin (FSL)	.100	3	10	2	1	0	0	1	1	0-0	1	2-0	3	0-0	.400	.308	.708
	Las Vegas (PCL)	.438	7	32	9	14	2	0	3	13	0-0	1	2-0	2	0-0	.781	.486	1.267
	TORONTO (AL)	.244	96	332	47	81	16	0	21	51	0-4	2	29-1	60	1-0	.482	.305	.787
2011	TORONTO (AL)	.272	134	481	70	131	36	0	17	55	0-3	3	43-2	77	8-2	.453	.334	.787
2012	TORONTO (AL)	.280	**151**	542	**93**	**152**	24	0	**42**	**110**	0-7	11	**84**-12	94	**13**-3	.557	.384	.941
Minor Totals		.292	658	2502	394	730	152	14	76	391	6-27	20	236-8	437	79-22	.455	.354	.809
TORONTO TOTALS		.266	423	1509	235	401	81	1	88	239	0-17	19	169-15	260	23-5	.496	.344	.839
NL TOTALS		.262	514	1764	236	462	109	4	71	263	0-9	42	185-10	364	19-5	.449	.345	.794
MAJOR TOTALS		.264	937	3273	471	863	190	5	159	502	0-26	61	354-25	624	42-10	.471	.344	.815

HOME RUN BREAKDOWN

Total	H	A	ONE GAME 2	3	4	GS	LO	XN	IP	PH	RHP	LHP
159	84	75	7	1	0	4	0	2	1	1	111	48

TRANSACTIONS

- Selected by the Texas Rangers in the 9th round of the 2000 First Year Player Draft
- Traded to the Cincinnati Reds along with OF Ruben Mateo in exchange for RHP Rob Bell on June 15, 2001
- On disabled list (sprained left ankle) from June 9-July 5, 2006; included a rehabilitation assignment at Louisville (AAA) from June 27-July 5
- Traded to the Toronto Blue Jays along with RHP Josh Roenicke and RHP Zachary Stewart in exchange for 3B Scott Rolen on July 31, 2009
- On disabled list (strained left hamstring) from August 24-September 5, 2009
- On disabled list (strained right shoulder) from April 15-May 17, 2010; included rehabilitation assignment at Dunedin (A) from May 14-16
- On disabled list (left wrist sprain) from August 28-September 13, 2010
- Claimed on waivers by the Oakland Athletics on November 12, 2010
- Signed by the Toronto Blue Jays on December 16, 2010
- On disabled list (sprained left wrist) from August 28-September 13, 2010

GAME HIGHS

ML Debut	June 24, 2005 at CLE	**RBI**	5 - 3x, last April 28, 2012 vs. SEA
Runs	4 - 2x, last July 20, 2011 vs. SEA	**Stolen Bases**	2 - 5x, last Aug. 4, 2012 at OAK
Hits	4 - 5x, last Aug. 31, 2011 at BAL	**Last ML Home Run**	Sept. 26, 2012 at BAL
Doubles	3 - July 20, 2010 at KC	**Longest Hitting Streak**	14G - April 10-24, 2008
Home Runs	3 - May 21, 2010 at ARI	**Longest Hitless Streak**	22AB - 2x, last May 3-9, 2012

CAREER FIELDING

POSITION	PCT	G	PO	A	E	TC	DP
1B	.992	95	803	41	7	851	78
3B	.934	664	479	1104	112	1695	103
OF	1.000	3	3	0	0	3	0

MILESTONES

Category		Date	Opponent	Pitcher	Notes
Hit	1	July 1, 2005	Houston	Pettitte	Pinch hit double
Home Run	1	July 29, 2005	at San Diego	Breslow	1R
	100	Oct. 3, 2010	at Minnesota	Blackburn	1R
Multi-Homer Game (8)					
	8	July 14, 2012	Cleveland	Jimenez, Accardo	2R, 1R
3-Homer Game (1)					
	1	May 21, 2010	at Arizona	Haren (2), Gutierrez	1R, 1R, 1R
Extra Inning HR (2)					
	1	April 20, 2008	Milwaukee	Gagne	1R, 10th inning
	2	Sept. 22, 2011	Los Angeles (AL)	Richards	1R, 12th inning
Grand Slam (4)	1	Apr. 11, 2006	at Chicago (NL)	Ohman	6th inning
	2	Aug. 29, 2008	San Francisco	Zito	3rd inning
	3	April 13, 2009	Milwaukee	Gallardo	3rd inning
	4	April 28, 2012	Seattle	Iwakuma	8th inning
Pinch Hit HR (1)	1	May 5, 2007	Colorado	Cook	2R
Inside The Park	1	Aug. 31, 2007	at St. Louis	Reyes	1R
Walkoff HR (2)	1	April 2, 2008	Arizona	Lyon	3R, 9th inning
	2	Sept. 22, 2011	Los Angeles (AL)	Richards	1R, 12th inning
RBI	1	July 29, 2005	at San Diego	Lawrence	Double
Stolen Base	1	July 26, 2005	at Los Angeles (NL)	Perez C-Phillips	2nd base

PROFESSIONAL CAREER:

2005:

- Prior to the season was named by USA Today Sports Weekly as the best hitter in the organization and by Baseball America as the minor leagues' fifth-best prospect at third base... Following the season was rated by BA as the sixth-best overall prospect in the International League...
- In his first season at Class AAA was the organization's Minor League Hitter of the Year, an International League mid-season and post-season All-Star, a Baseball America Class AAA All-Star and a member of the XM Satellite Radio All-Star Futures Game world roster... At the Triple-A All-Star Game in Sacramento, an 11-2 loss to the Pacific Coast League All-Stars, he homered to earn International League Player of the Game honours.
- On June 24 at CLE made his **Major League debut** in a start at 3B (0-4, 2K).

2006:

- Led the club with 33 doubles and 109 starts at 3B.
- At 26 years, 86 days old was the youngest player to start at 3B for the Reds on Opening Day since Dan Driessen in 1974 (22 years, 249 days). From June 9-July 5 missed 25 G while on the 15-day disabled list with a sprained left ankle.
- On Apr. 11 at CHI hit his first career grand slam (off Will Ohman)... Produced his first two career two-homer games five days apart (Aug. 11 at Phi, Aug. 16 at StL).

2007:

- Ranked among the National League leaders in hitting with RISP (3rd), hitting on the road (9th) and HBP (14, T-4th).
- On May 5 vs Colorado hit his first career pinch-hit HR (off Aaron Cook)... On Aug. 31 at STL hit an inside-the-park HR (off Anthony Reyes), the first of his career and the first in the 2-year history of new Busch Stadium.

2008:

- Ranked 2nd on the club in home runs (26) behind Adam Dunn's 32... Produced his third career 2-homer game (April 20 vs MIL), a grand slam (Aug. 29 vs SF, off Barry Zito) and a walkoff HR (April 2 vs ARZ).
- Produced the first of the Reds' 11 walkoff victories, in the bottom of the ninth of the 6-5 win on April 2 vs ARZ hit a 3-run HR off Brandon Lyon... On Aug. 29 vs SF had a grand slam and 5 RBI.
- From June 24-28 missed 5 games with low back spasms... On Sept. 17 was scratched with a mild sprain of his left wrist and missed 5 games... Suffered that injury on a checked swing vs Randy Johnson on Sept. 13 at ARZ.
- Was ejected twice, by HP umpire Eric Cooper on May 22 at SD for arguing balls and strikes and by 3B umpire Chad Fairchild on July 1 vs PIT for arguing a play at third base... Were the first ejections of his career.

2009:

- Suffered a broken wrist at the end of April that sidelined him for two month.
- Was traded to the Toronto Blue Jays on July 31 along with RHP Josh Roenicke and RHP Zach Stewart in exchange for 3B Scott Rolen... Made his Blue Jays debut on Aug. 1 at OAK, going 1-4.

2010:

- Played in 96 games this season for the Blue Jays starting 95 times at 3B and once as the DH.
- Hit 20+ home runs for the second time in his career and the first time since hitting a career high 26 in 2008... Hit a home run in four consecutive games (five total) in the last series of the season at MIN.
- Was optioned to Las Vegas (AAA) June 20 and then outrighted June 21... Had his contract selected from Las Vegas on July 2.
- Was placed on the disabled list Aug. 28 with a sprained left wrist...Returned to action on Sept. 13... Hit three home runs in a game for the first time in his career May 21 at ARI which was his 5th multi-homer game in his career.

AL OFFENSIVE LEADERS – 2012

HOME RUNS	
Miguel Cabrera, DET	44
Curtis Granderson, NYY	43
Josh Hamilton, TEX	43
Edwin Encarnacion, TOR	**42**
Adam Dunn, CWS	41

RBI	
Miguel Cabrera, DET	139
Josh Hamilton, TEX	128
Edwin Encarnacion, TOR	**110**
Josh Willingham, MIN	110
Prince Fielder, DET	108

OBP	
Joe Maurer, MIN	.416
Prince Fielder, DET	.412
Mike Trout, LAA	.399
Miguel Cabrera, DET	.393
Edwin Encarnacion, TOR	**.384**

SLG	
Miguel Cabrera, DET	.606
Josh Hamilton, TEX	.577
Mike Trout, LAA	.564
Adrian Beltre, TEX	.561
Edwin Encarnacion, TOR	**.557**

OPS	
Miguel Cabrera, DET	.999
Mike Trout, LAA	.963
Edwin Encarnacion, TOR	**.941**
Prince Fielder, TB	.940
Josh Hamilton, TEX	.930

BIOGRAPHIES LAST SEASON HISTORY RECORDS OPPONENTS PLAYER DEV. MEDIA & MISC.

2011:

- Played 36 games at third base, 25 games at first base and the balance as a pinch hitter or designated hitter.
- When appearing at first or the designated hitter position batted .298 with 24 doubles, 14 home runs and 47 RBI... When appearing at third base his offense dipped to .213 with12 doubles, three home runs and eight RBI.
- Recorded 36 doubles which was the highest total on the club, ranking 14th in the AL... Had the highest number of doubles in the AL for anyone with under 500 at-bats.
- In the first half batted .255 with six home runs and 19 RBI... In the second half improved to .291 with 11 home runs and 29 RBI... Walked only nine times in the first half producing a .283 OBP, as opposed to drawing 34 walks in the second half, producing a .382 OBP.
- Missed time in April due to left wrist soreness and spent time on the bereavement list.
- Made six of his 12 errors in April and did not hit his first home run of the season until May 29 vs. CWS... Had a season high 13-game hit streak from July 31-Aug. 14, and hit in 21 of 23 games from July 24-Aug. 19... Had a stretch of reaching base safely in eight consecutive plate appearances from Aug. 7-10... Sept. 7 vs. BOS recorded five RBI matching his career high (2nd time).
- Recorded a walk-off home run on Sept. 22 vs. LAA, his 2nd career... Played in the Dominican Winter League posting a .133 average (2-15) with one home run and four RBI.

BLUE JAYS AMERICAN LEAGUE LEADERS

BATTING LEADERS

Year	Category	Player	Totals
1980	Triples	Alfredo Griffin	15
1986	Home Runs	Jesse Barfield	40
1987	RBI	George Bell	134
	Total Bases	George Bell	369
1989	Home Runs	Fred McGriff	36
	Hitting Streak	George Bell	22
1990	Triples	Tony Fernandez	17
1993	Average	John Olerud	.363
	Hits	Paul Molitor	211
	Doubles	John Olerud	54
	OBP	John Olerud	.473
	Hitting Streak	John Olerud	26
1995	Hit by Pitch	Ed Sprague	15
1999	Total Bases	Shawn Green	361
	Doubles	Shawn Green	45
	Hitting Streak	Shawn Green	28
	Extra Base Hits	Shawn Green	87
2000	Doubles	Carlos Delgado	57
	Total Bases	Carlos Delgado	378
	Extra Base Hits	Carlos Delgado	99
	Hit by Pitch	Carlos Delgado	15
2003	RBI	Carlos Delgado	145
	Hits	Vernon Wells	215
	Doubles	Vernon Wells	49
	Total Bases	Vernon Wells	373
	Extra Base Hits	Vernon Wells	87
2005	Hit by Pitch	Shea Hillenbrand	22
2006	Hit by Pitch	Reed Johnson	21
2009	At Bats	Aaron Hill	682
	Plate App.	Aaron Hill	734
2010	Home Runs	Jose Bautista	54
	Extra Base Hits	Jose Bautista	92
	Total Bases	Jose Bautista	351
2011	Home Runs	Jose Bautista	43
	Walks	Jose Bautista	132
	Intentional Walks	Jose Bautista	24
	SLG	Jose Bautista	.608

PITCHING LEADERS

Year	Category	Player	Totals
1982	Games Started	Jim Clancy	40
	Complete Games	Dave Stieb	19
	Shutouts	Dave Stieb	5
	Innings Pitched	Dave Stieb	288.1
1984	Winning Percentage	Doyle Alexander	.739
	Innings Pitched	Dave Stieb	267.0
1985	ERA	Dave Stieb	2.48
1987	Winning Percentage	John Cerutti	.733
	ERA	Jimmy Key	2.76
	Games	Mark Eichhorn	89
	Games Finished	Tom Henke	62
1991	Games	Duane Ward	81
1993	Winning Percentage	Juan Guzman	.824
	Games Finished	Duane Ward	70
1996	ERA	Juan Guzman	2.93
	Complete Games	Pat Hentgen	10
	Innings Pitched	Pat Hentgen	265.2
1997	ERA	Roger Clemens	2.05
	Wins	Roger Clemens	21
	Complete Games	Pat Hentgen	9
		Roger Clemens	9
	Innings Pitched	Pat Hentgen	264.0
		Roger Clemens	264.0
	Strikeouts	Roger Clemens	292
	Shutouts	Pat Hentgen	3
		Roger Clemens	3
1998	ERA	Roger Clemens	2.65
	Wins	Roger Clemens	20
	Strikeouts	Roger Clemens	271
1999	Complete Games	David Wells	7
	Innings Pitched	David Wells	231.2
2000	Wins	David Wells	20
	Complete Games	David Wells	9
2001	Games	Paul Quantrill	80
2002	Innings Pitched	Roy Halladay	239.1
2003	Wins	Roy Halladay	22
	Games	Trever Miller	79
	Games Started	Roy Halladay	36
	Complete Games	Roy Halladay	9
	Innings Pitched	Roy Halladay	266.0
2005	Complete Games	Ray Halladay	5
2007	Games	Scott Downs	81
	Complete Games	Roy Halladay	7
2008	Complete Games	Roy Halladay	9
	Innings Pitched	Roy Halladay	246.0
	Strikeouts	Strikeouts	231
2009	Shutouts	Roy Halladay	4
	Complete Games	Roy Halladay	9

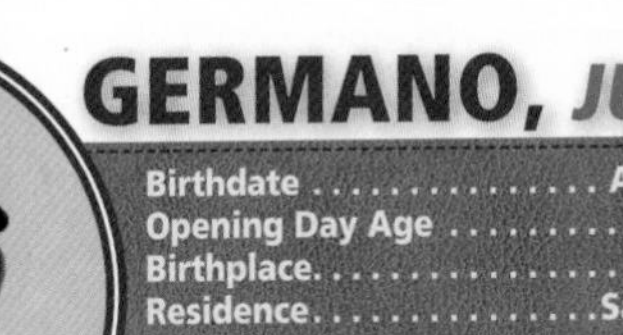

GERMANO, JUSTIN

- Birthdate: August 6, 1982
- Opening Day Age: 30
- Birthplace: Pasadena, CA
- Residence: San Marcos, CA
- Bats/Throws: R/R
- Height/Weight: 6-2/210
- Contract Status: signed thru 2013
- M.L. Service: 2.130

PITCHER
NON-ROSTER

PERSONAL:

Justin Willima Germano... Graduated from Claremont (CA) High School... Married with one child... Broke Mark McGwire's Claremont, California Little League record for most home runs in a season.

LAST SEASON:

- Allowed two or fewer runs in three of his first four starts for the Cubs, going 2-1 with a 4.03 ERA (10 ER/22.1 IP) from July 30-Aug. 15.
- Surrendered two or fewer walks in all but one of his Major League starts
- Recorded his first win as a Cub, July 30 vs. the Pirates... Was his first Major League start since a 6-5 loss to the White Sox, Oct. 3, 2010, with CLE.
- Began the year with Triple-A Pawtucket in Boston's system... Had a 1.69 ERA (8 ER/42.2 IP) and was 4-1 in six June games (five starts) before his promotion.
- Promoted to the Red Sox, July 4, and threw 5.2 shutout innings of relief, July 7 vs. the Yankees.
- Designated for assignment on July 13 and later traded to the Chicago Cubs on July 19.

JUSTIN GERMANO

Bold – career high

Year	Club & League	W-L	ERA	G	GS	CG	ShO	SV	IP	H	R	ER	HR	HB	BB-IBB	SO	WP	BK	OBA
2000	AZL (Ariz)	5-5	4.59	17	8	0	0	1	66.2	65	36	34	4	3	9-0	67	5	1	.249
2001	Fort Wayne (Mid)	2-6	4.98	13	13	0	0	0	65.0	80	47	36	7	7	16-1	55	6	0	.302
	Eugene (NOR)	6-5	3.49	13	13	2	0	0	80.0	77	35	31	5	5	11-0	74	1	0	.246
2002	Fort Wayne (Mid)	12-5	3.18	24	24	1	0	0	155.2	166	63	55	14	4	19-2	119	4	2	.269
	Lake Elsinore (CAL)	2-0	0.95	3	3	0	0	0	19.0	12	3	2	1	1	5-0	18	1	0	.174
2003	Lake Elsinore (CAL)	9-5	4.23	19	19	1	0	0	110.2	127	61	52	4	9	25-1	78	2	0	.287
	Mobile Bay (Sou)	2-5	4.34	9	9	1	0	0	58.0	60	34	28	6	5	13-3	44	0	0	.268
2004	Mobile Bay (Sou)	2-1	2.51	5	5	0	0	0	32.1	31	11	9	3	1	7-0	20	0	0	.258
	Portland (PCL)	9-5	3.38	20	20	2	2	0	122.2	113	48	46	12	5	25-0	98	3	0	.249
	SAN DIEGO (NL)	1-2	8.86	7	5	0	0	0	21.1	31	24	21	2	0	14-0	16	0	0	.341
2005	Portland (PCL)	7-6	3.70	19	19	1	1	0	112.0	111	56	46	13	5	32-1	100	2	0	.259
	Louisville (Int)	3-2	4.01	8	8	0	0	0	49.1	62	27	22	7	5	5-0	38	2	0	.313
2006	Louisville (Int)	8-6	3.69	19	18	0	0	0	117.0	124	53	48	11	9	22-0	67	1	2	.279
	CINCINNATI (NL)	0-1	5.40	2	1	0	0	0	6.2	8	4	4	1	1	3-1	8	0	0	.296
	Scranton-W. Barre (Int)	2-0	2.82	6	6	0	0	0	38.1	40	13	12	2	1	2-0	25	0	0	.265
2007	Portland (PCL)	4-0	1.69	5	5	0	0	0	32.0	23	7	6	0	1	3-1	20	1	0	.197
	SAN DIEGO (NL)	**7**-**10**	4.46	**26**	**23**	0	0	0	**133.1**	133	72	66	**14**	8	**40**-3	**78**	1	0	.259
2008	SAN DIEGO (NL)	0-3	5.98	12	6	0	0	0	43.2	54	31	29	8	1	13-2	17	4	0	.305
	Portland (PCL)	2-9	5.51	17	16	1	0	0	98.0	119	67	60	12	2	25-1	67	3	0	.300
2009		Did Not Play																	
2010	Akron (East)	2-1	2.79	7	1	0	0	0	19.1	17	6	6	0	0	4-1	16	0	0	.239
	Columbus (Int)	3-2	3.38	17	6	1	1	1	53.1	49	23	20	8	1	10-1	37	2	0	.241
	CLEVELAND (AL)	0-3	3.31	23	1	0	0	0	35.1	27	15	13	6	6	8-1	29	0	0	.206
2011	CLEVELAND (AL)	0-1	5.68	9	0	0	0	0	12.2	15	8	8	1	2	5-0	5	0	0	.288
	Columbus (Int)	1-2	4.22	16	6	1	1	3	49.0	50	23	23	5	3	4-1	39	0	1	.272
2012	Pawtucket Red (Int)	9-4	2.40	17	16	1	0	0	105.0	82	33	28	15	5	13-0	72	1	0	.211
	BOSTON (AL)	0-0	0.00	1	0	0	0	0	5.2	5	0	0	0	0	2-0	7	1	0	.227
	CHICAGO (NL)	2-**10**	6.75	13	12	0	0	0	64.0	81	52	48	7	7	19-2	45	4	0	.309
Minor Totals		90-69	3.67	254	215	12	5	5	1383.1	1408	646	564	129	72	250-13	1054	34	6	.263
AL TOTALS		0-4	3.52	33	1	0	0	0	53.2	47	23	21	7	8	15-1	41	1	0	.229
NL TOTALS		10-26	5.62	60	47	0	0	0	269.0	307	183	168	32	17	89-8	164	9	0	.287
MAJOR TOTALS		10-30	5.27	93	48	0	0	0	322.2	354	206	189	39	25	104-9	205	10	0	.277

TRANSACTIONS

- Selected by the San Diego Padres in the 13th round of the 2000 First Year Player Draft
- Traded to the Cincinnati Reds along with RHP Travis Chick in exchange for IF Joe Randa on July 23, 2005
- Traded to the Philadelphia Phillies in exchnage for LHP Rheal Cormier on July 31, 2006
- Claimed off waivers by the San Diego Padres on March 19, 2007
- Signed by the Cleveland Indians on March 24, 2010
- Signed by the Boston Red Sox on January 9, 2012
- Traded to the Chicago Cubs in exchnage for cash considerations on July 19, 2012
- Signed by the Toronto Blue Jays on November 9, 2012

BIOGRAPHIES | LAST SEASON | HISTORY | RECORDS | OPPONENTS | PLAYER DEV. | MEDIA & MISC.

GAME HIGHS

ML Debut	May 22, 2004 at PHI	**Runs Allowed**	10 - April 21, 2008 at HOU
Innings Pitched:		**ER Allowed**	10 - April 21, 2008 at HOU
Starter	7.0 - April 16, 2008 vs. COL	**HR Allowed**	3 - May 2, 2008 at FLA
Reliever	5.2 - July 7, 2012 vs. NYY	**Low Hit CG**	None
Walks:		**Last Win**	Aug. 15, 2012 vs. HOU
Starter	5 - 2x, last Sept. 18, 2012 vs. CIN	**Last Save**	None
Reliever	2 - Sept. 22, 2007 vs. COL	**Last CG**	None
Strikeouts:		**Last ShO**	None
Starter	8 - 2x, last Sept. 11, 2012 at HOU	**Last Start**	Sept. 29, 2012 at ARI
Reliever	7 - July 7, 2012 vs. NYY	**Last Relief App.**	July 21, 2012 at STL
Hits Allowed	10 - 5x, last Sept. 29, 2012 at ARI	**Longest Win Streak**	5G - May 13-June 14, 2007
		Longest Losing Streak	8G - Aug. 20-Sept. 29, 2012
		Scoreless Innings Streak	11.1 - Aug. 8-27, 2010

CAREER FIELDING

POSITION	PCT	G	PO	A	E	TC	DP
P	1.000	93	28	53	0	81	4

MILESTONES

Category		Date	Opponent	Notes
Start	1	May 22, 2004	at Philadelphia	ML debut - 5.0 IP, 5H, 4ER, HR, 4BB, 5K
Win	1	May 22, 2004	at Philadelphia	ML debut, as a starter, 5.0 IP, 5H, 4ER, HR, 4BB, 5K

PROFESSIONAL CAREER:

2004:

- Recalled by the Padres on May 18 and started three games with a 6.59 ERA (10 ER/13.2 IP) before being optioned back to Portland June 6.
- Earned the win with four runs allowed over a 5.0-inning start in his ML debut on May 22 at PHI.
- Recalled again on Sept. 6 and pitched in four more games (two starts) for the Padres.

2006:

- Had two stints with the Reds… Recalled to the Majors on May 30 and threw a scoreless inning of relief that day at CHC... Optioned back to AAA on June 5 but returned for a July 29 start at MIL in which he allowed 4 runs in 5.2 innings for the loss but fanned a career-high 8 batters.

2007:

- Received an average of just 3.65 runs of support per 9.0 innings (54 RS/133.1 IP), the 4th-lowest run support average in the National League (min. 120.0 IP)…The Padres scored just 12 total runs while he was in the game in his 10 losses.
- Went 5-0 with a 2.36 ERA (11 ER/42.0 IP) in his first seven starts with San Diego after his contract was purchased from Triple-A Portland on May 7.
- Allowed three earned runs or less in a career-high six straight starts from Aug. 5-Sept. 2, posting a 3.44 ERA (13 ER/34.0 IP) in that time.
- Made three relief appearances over the final two weeks of the season.

2008:

- Joined the bullpen on May 9 and made six relief appearances from May 9-21, posting a 4.66 ERA (5 ER/9.2 IP) in that role… Held opponents scoreless in his first four relief appearances (5.1 IP).

2009:

- Spent the season with the Fukuoka SoftBank Hawks of the NBP's Pacific League, his only season in Japan.
- Went 5-4 with a 4.38 ERA (37 ER/76.0 IP) in 14 games, including 13 starts…Walked just 10 batters and struck out 42.

2010:

- Spent the last 2 months of the season with Cleveland and made 22 relief appearances and one start for the Tribe... Promoted to the Majors on July 30 and posted a 2.16 ERA (8 ER/33.1 IP) and .169 opponent avg. (20-for-118) in relief with Cleveland.
- Allowed the first batter to reach in just 2 of his 22 Major League outings (single, walk) and posted a .156 clip (5-for-32) against leadoff batters overall with the Indians.
- 17 of his 22 relief appearances with Cleveland were scoreless… Did not allow an earned run in his 1st 11 outings with the club from July 30-Aug. 27 (16.2 IP), the longest such streak of his career.
- Posted a .1372 opponent AVG (7-for-51) over his last nine relief appearances of the year from Sept. 5-29, the 2nd-best mark in the AL in that time (min. 50 BF) after BOS's Jon Lester (.1368).
- Took the loss in his only start of the season, Oct. 3 at CWS in Cleveland's final game… Was his 1st ML start since May 2, 2008 while with SD.

2011:

- Split the season between the Indians organization and Korea.
- Made the Indians Opening Day roster after entering Spring Training as a non-roster invitee… Pitched in nine games for the Tribe in relief, including six scoreless appearances.
- Went five straight appearances without a run allowed from April 8-28 (6.0 IP).
- Designated for assignment on May 19 and outrighted to AAA Columbus on May 24…Remained with the Clippers until his Aug. 5 release.
- Tossed the 1st 9.0-inning perfect game in Clippers history on July 26 at Syracuse, the only no-hitter at the AAA level in 2011…Threw 95 pitches (69 strikes) in the 3-0 win…Was named International League Pitcher of the Week for 7/25-31.
- Finished year with Samsung of the Korean Baseball Organization and went 5-1 with a 2.78 ERA (14 ER/45.1 IP).

GOINS, *RYAN*

Birthdate . . . . .February 13, 1988
Opening Day Age 25
Birthplace. . . . . .Round Rock, TX
Residence. . . . . .Round Rock, TX
Bats/Throws . . . . L/R
Height/Weight 5-10/170
Contract Status . . . . signed thru 2013
M.L. Service 0.000

2

INFIELDER

PERSONAL:

Ryan M. Goins... Attended Dallas Baptist College, playing as a position player and pitcher... His dad and uncle both played in the minor leagues.

LAST SEASON:

- Spent the season with New Hampshire (AA)
- Led the Eastern League with 158 hits and his 33 doubles and a .289 average were team highs... Had four hits on three seperate occasions.
- Posted a .338 average with runners in scoring position on his way to registering career highs in most offensive categories.
- Batted .366 over the first four innings of a contest and .215 from the 5th inning on.
- Named a Post-Season Eastern League All-Star.
- Played in the Arizona Fall league for Salt River, posting a .133 average with one double and five RBI in 13 games.

RYAN GOINS

Bold – career high

Year	Club & League	AVG	G	AB	R	H	2B	3B	HR	RBI	SH-SF	HP	BB-IBB	SO	SB-CS	SLG	OBP	OPS
2009	Blue Jays (GCL)	.111	3	9	1	1	0	0	0	0	0-0	0	0-0	2	0-0	.111	.111	.222
	Auburn (NYP)	.297	24	101	15	30	5	1	0	8	1-0	0	8-0	23	2-2	.366	.349	.715
	Lansing (Mid)	.198	19	81	6	16	4	0	0	9	0-1	0	7-0	23	1-2	.247	.258	.505
2010	Lansing (Mid)	.308	77	295	49	91	19	2	3	35	4-3	1	35-0	60	6-7	.417	.380	.797
	Dunedin (FSL)	.205	47	166	8	34	9	0	0	18	3-2	0	11-0	33	1-1	.259	.251	.510
2011	Blue Jays (GCL)	.000	1	3	0	0	0	0	0	0	0-0	0	0-0	1	0-0	.000	.000	.000
	Dunedin (FSL)	.286	101	353	50	101	24	5	3	52	10-3	0	32-0	67	2-2	.408	.343	.751
2012	New Hampshire (East)	.289	136	546	66	158	33	4	7	61	19-6	0	47-3	78	15-9	.403	.342	.745
Minor Totals		.277	408	1554	195	431	94	12	13	183	37-15	1	140-3	287	27-23	.378	.335	.713

TRANSACTIONS

- Selected by the Toronto Blue Jays in the 4th round of the 2009 First Year Player Draft

PROFESSIONAL CAREER:

2009:

- Made his professional debut splitting time between Rookie, Short season-A and Low-A.

2010:

- Began the season at Lansing (Low-A), prior to finishing his season in Dunedin (High-A).
- Recorded his first professional home run on opening day, in his first at-bat of the season.
- Batted .300+ in each month except April with Lansing.

2011:

- Spent the season wih Dunedin of the Flordia State League (A).
- Recorded 31 multi-hit games, with all but three being two-hit contests.

2010 HOME RUN FACTS

- Led the Majors with a Club record 257-HR
- Hit 46 more HR than the next best team-BOS with 211...Largest gap in the Majors since 1968
- The 257-HR ranked T-3rd most in MLB history for a single season
- The 56-HR hit in Sept./Oct. was T-1st all time in MLB history for that particular month (CIN hit 56 in 1999)
- Hit a Club record 146-HR at home which ranks as the 3rd most by any Club in the Majors since 1952
- Matched a Club record (2nd time & 1st since 2000) with seven players recording at least 20+ HR in a season
- Were the 1st Club in MLB history to have 20+ HR from each defensive position (including DH)
- Hit 257-HR & allowed 150-HR making for a differential of 107 which represented the 2nd best mark in MLB history (1927 Yankees were +116).

GOSE, *ANTHONY*

Birthdate .... August 10, 1990
Opening Day Age 23
Birthplace .... Paramount, CA
Residence .... Bellflower, CA
Bats/Throws .... L/L
Height/Weight 6-1/195
Contract Status .... signed thru 2013
M.L. Service 0.079

8

OUTFIELDER

PERSONAL:

Anthony Robert Gose... Attended Bellflower High School in California... While in school earned 2008 Rawlings 1st team All-American honours... That same year was named California All-Region 1st team... Was signed and scouted by Tim Kissner with the Phillies... Participated in the 2013 Winter Tour

LAST SEASON:

- Appeared in 56 games in his rookie season in two separate stints with the parent club.
- Made his Major League debut on July 17 at NYY, going 1-2, with his first hit coming on a bunt single.
- Stole 15 bases in 56 games...The 15 steals are T-3rd among Blue Jay rookies, behind Alfredo Griffin (23 in 153G) and Junior Felix (18 in 110G)...The 15 steals are the most since Alex Rios stole 15 in 2004 (111G).
- Sept. 8 at BOS hit his first Major League home run with 3-run shot off Andrew Bailey...Also recorded 5RBI in the contest becoming the first Blue Jay rookie to do so since JP Arencibia on April 1, 2011.
- Hit in five straight games from Sept. 24-28, going 5-16.
- Oct. 1, produced a walk-off single in the bottom of the 10th for a 6-5 win vs. MIN.
- Started 21 games in RF, 15 in CF and 13 in LF...Had two outfield assists, both coming in LF.
- Appeared in 102 games for Las Vegas (AAA) batting .286 with 21 doubles, 10 triples, five home runs, 43 RBI and 34 stolen bases...Batted .313 vs. right-handed pitchers and .176 vs. left-handed hitters.
- Named to the SiriusXM All-Star Futures Game...Singled and walked in his two plate appearances.

ANTHONY GOSE

Bold – career high

Year	Club & League	AVG	G	AB	R	H	2B	3B	HR	RBI	SH-SF	HP	BB-IBB	SO	SB-CS	SLG	OBP	OPS
2008	Phillies (GCL)	.256	11	39	4	10	2	1	0	3	0-0	1	1-0	12	3-1	.359	.293	.652
2009	Lakewood (SAL)	.259	131	510	72	132	24	9	2	52	9-3	15	35-2	110	76-20	.353	.323	.676
2010	Clearwater (FSL)	.263	103	418	67	110	17	11	4	21	5-0	6	32-4	103	36-27	.385	.325	.710
	Dunedin (FSL)	.255	27	94	21	24	3	2	3	6	2-1	3	13-0	29	9-5	.426	.360	.786
2011	New Hampshire (East)	.253	137	509	87	129	20	7	16	59	2-1	13	62-0	154	70-15	.415	.349	.764
2012	Las Vegas (PCL)	.286	102	420	87	120	21	10	5	43	4-1	5	49-1	101	34-12	.419	.366	.785
	TORONTO (AL)	.223	56	166	25	37	7	3	1	11	4-0	2	17-0	59	15-3	.319	.303	.622
Minor Totals		.264	511	1990	338	525	87	40	30	184	22-6	43	192-7	509	228-80	.393	.341	.734

HOME RUN BREAKDOWN

			ONE GAME									
Total	H	A	2	3	4	GS	LO	XN	IP	PH	RHP	LHP
1	0	1	0	0	0	0	0	0	0	0	1	0

TRANSACTIONS

- Selected by the Philadelphia Phillies in the 2nd round of the 2008 First Year Player Draft
- Traded to the Houston Astros along with IF Jonathan Villar and LHP J.A. Happ in exchange for RHP Roy Oswalt on July 29, 2010
- Traded to the Toronto Blue Jays in exchange for 1B Brett Wallace on July 29, 2010

GAME HIGHS

ML Debut	July 17, 2012 at NYY	**RBI**	5 - Sept. 8, 2012 at BOS
Runs	2 - 3x, last Sept. 27, 2012 vs. NYY	**Stolen Bases**	2 - 2x, last Sept. 7, 2012 at BOS
Hits	2 - 7x, last Sept. 23, 2012 at TB	**Last ML Home Run**	Sept. 8, 2012 at BOS
Doubles	1 - 7x, last Sept. 28, 2012 vs. NYY	**Longest Hitting Streak**	5G - Sept. 24-28, 2012
Home Runs	1 - Sept. 8, 2012 at BOS	**Longest Hitless Streak**	13AB - Aug. 18-Sept. 5, 2012

CAREER FIELDING

POSITION	PCT	G	PO	A	E	TC	DP
OF	.991	54	106	2	1	109	2

MILESTONES

Category		Date	Opponent	Pitcher	Notes
Hit	1	July 17, 2012	at NewYork (AL)	Rapada	single
Home Run	1	Sept. 8, 2012	at Boston	Bailey	3R
RBI	1	July 27, 2012	Detroit	Porcello	1R, single
Stolen Base	1	July 27, 2012	Detroit	Porcell C-Avila	2nd base

PROFESSIONAL CAREER:

2008:

- Began pro career with the Gulf Coast Phillies... Hit safely in nine of 11 games.

2009:

- Spent season with Lakewood (A)... Led all minor league players in stolen bases (76)... Led South Atlantic League in at-bats (510) and was 4th in triples (9)... Named to SAL Mid-Season All-Star team.

2010:

- Began the season with Clearwater (A) in the Phillies organization before being acquired by Houston and then sent to the Blue Jays on July 29 in exchange for 1B Brett Wallace.
- Overall, appeared in 130 games, batting .262 with 20 doubles, 13 triples, seven home runs and 45 stolen bases.
- Finished the season ranking 1st in the Florida State League in stolen bases (45), T-1st in triples (13), 2nd in runs (88), 7th in hits (134) and T-9th in total bases (201).

2011:

- Played the entire season at New Hampshire, his first season at the AA level and first full season in the Blue Jays organization... Was named to the Eastern League Post Season All-Star team and was selected by Eastern League Manager's as the fastest Baserunner in a Baseball America poll.
- Posted 70 stolen bases to lead the Eastern League... The 70 steals also ranked 2nd in all of minor league baseball and was the 5th highest total in Blue Jays minor league history... Was caught only 15 times for a 82.4% success rate.
- Added 16 home runs after having nine in his first three professional seasons, while registering 43 extra base hits... His 62 walks, .415 slugging percentage and .763 OPS are also career highs.
- Defensively, committed just three errors while adding 14 assists in 137 games.

LEADING OFF

The most leadoff home runs in one season:

Six Times: Devon White (1991)

Five Times: Devon White (1992), Devon White (1993)

Four Times: Devon White (1994), Shannon Stewart (2000), Jose Cruz Jr. (2001), Frank Menechino (2004), Alex Rios (2006, 2007), Fred Lewis (2010)

FEWEST GAMES TO 500 RBI AS A BLUE JAY

Joe Carter	663 games
Carlos Delgado	714 games
George Bell	809 games
Vernon Wells	813 games
Jesse Barfield	977 games

FEWEST GAMES TO 1,000 HITS IN BLUE JAY HISTORY

Shannon Stewart	819 games
Damaso Garcia	867 games
Vernon Wells	890 games
Tony Fernandez	894 games
George Bell	922 games
Joe Carter	982 games

HAPP, *J.A.*

48

PITCHER

Birthdate	October 19, 1982
Opening Day Age	30
Birthplace	Peru, IL
Residence	Chicago, IL
Bats/Throws	L/L
Height/Weight	6-6/194
Contract Status	signed thru 2013
M.L. Service	4.047

PERSONAL:

James Anthony (J.A.) Happ... Name pronounced Jay... Graduate of St. Bede High School in Chicago... Earned team MVP in his senior season and was named Bureau County Athlete of the Year... Was a four year letter winner in baseball and basketball... Averaged 22 points in his senior year in basketball and is all-time leading scorer in St. Bede history... Attended Northwestern for three seasons... Became forst Wildcat in history to be named All-Big-Ten in three straight seasons... Led the Big-Ten in ERA (2.68) and strikeouts (106) in his senior season.

LAST SEASON:

- Combined to go 10-11 with a 4.79 ERA in 28 games, including 24 starts between Houston and Toronto... Won 10 or more games for the second time in his career... In his 28 starts, team was 13-15 and 3-3 as a Blue Jay... Posted 14 quality starts
- Was acquired by Toronto from Houston on July 20 in a 10-player deal.
- Made four relief appearances for the Blue Jays after being acquired, posting a 5.14 ERA, despite holding opponents to a .200 average... As a starter with Toronto made six starts going 3-2 with a 4.59 ERA, holding the opposition to a .244 average.
- With Toronto struck out 46 batters in 40.1 innings for a 10.3 strikeout per nine total, becoming one of two Blue Jays pitchers to post a strikeout per nine total of more than 10 (min 40IP) along with Jason Frasor (10.92).
- Performs much better after the All-Star break, going 4-2 with a 4.05 ERA as opposed to 6-9 with a 5.14 ERA prior to the break... In his career is now 19-14 with a 3.80 ERA prior to the break and 16-21 with a 4.55 ERA after.
- Posted a career high with 144 strikeouts... On Aug. 17 vs. TEX recorded six consecutive strikeouts... The mark tied a Blue Jays record done twice previously by Ted Lilly in 2004 and Mark Rzepczynski in 2010... Posted 10 strikeouts on May 27 at LAD, matching a career high...In his final start with Toronto fanned nine Orioles on Sept. 3.
- Had his season end prematurely with a right foot fracture and had surgery following his Sept. 3 start.

J.A. HAPP

Bold – career high

Year	Club & League	W-L	ERA	G	GS	CG	ShO	SV	IP	H	R	ER	HR	HB	BB-IBB	SO	WP	BK	OBA
2004	Batavia (NYP)	1-2	2.02	11	11	0	0	0	35.2	22	8	8	1	3	18-0	37	0	0	.185
2005	Lakewood (SAL)	4-4	2.36	14	12	0	0	0	72.1	57	26	19	3	5	26-0	70	4	1	.213
	Reading (East)	1-0	1.50	1	1	0	0	0	6.0	3	1	1	0	0	2-0	8	1	0	.150
2006	Clearwater (FSL)	3-7	2.81	13	13	0	0	0	80.0	63	35	25	9	2	19-0	77	1	2	.216
	Reading (East)	6-2	2.65	12	12	0	0	0	74.2	58	27	22	2	3	29-0	81	0	0	.214
	Scranton-Wilkes (Int)	1-0	1.50	1	1	0	0	0	6.0	3	1	1	1	1	1-0	4	0	0	.136
2007	PHILADELPHIA (NL)	0-1	11.25	1	1	0	0	0	4.0	7	5	5	3	0	2-0	5	0	0	.368
	Ottawa (Int)	4-6	5.02	24	24	0	0	0	118.1	118	74	66	12	0	62-1	117	2	1	.265
2008	Lehigh Valley (Int)	8-7	3.60	24	23	0	0	0	135.0	116	58	54	14	1	48-0	151	4	0	.234
	PHILADELPHIA (NL)	1-0	3.69	8	4	0	0	0	31.2	28	13	13	3	1	14-1	26	1	0	.233
2009	PHILADELPHIA (NL)	**12**-4	2.93	**35**	23	**3**	**2**	0	**166.0**	149	55	54	20	5	56-2	119	2	0	.244
2010	Clearwater (FSL)	0-1	6.00	1	1	0	0	0	3.0	3	2	2	0	0	0-0	2	1	0	.231
	Reading (East)	1-0	8.03	3	3	0	0	0	12.1	18	11	11	3	1	4-0	10	1	0	.333
	Lehigh Valley (Int)	0-1	4.84	5	4	0	0	0	22.1	26	12	12	3	0	15-0	22	0	0	.295
	PHILADELPHIA (NL)	1-0	1.76	3	3	0	0	0	15.1	13	4	3	1	0	12-0	9	1	0	.232
	HOUSTON (NL)	5-4	3.75	13	13	1	1	0	72.0	60	33	30	7	1	35-1	61	3	0	.230
2011	Oklahoma City (PCL)	1-0	1.50	3	3	0	0	0	18.0	11	5	3	0	0	9-0	16	0	0	.177
	HOUSTON (NL)	6-**15**	5.35	28	**28**	0	0	0	156.1	157	103	93	**21**	2	**83**-5	134	3	2	.265
2012	HOUSTON (NL)	7-9	4.83	18	18	0	0	0	104.1	112	58	56	17	1	39-0	**98**	5	0	.275
	TORONTO (AL)	3-2	4.69	10	6	0	0	0	40.1	35	21	21	2	1	17-1	**46**	2	0	.236
Minor Totals		30-30	3.45	112	108	0	0	0	583.2	498	260	224	48	16	233-1	595	14	4	.232
NL TOTALS		32-33	4.16	106	90	4	3	0	549.2	526	271	254	72	10	241-9	452	15	2	.255
MAJOR TOTALS		35-35	4.19	116	96	4	3	0	590.0	561	292	275	74	11	258-10	498	17	2	.253

DIVISION SERIES RECORD

Year	Club & League	W-L	ERA	G	GS	CG	ShO	SV	IP	H	R	ER	HR	HB	BB-IBB	SO	WP	BK
2009	PHILADELPHIA (NL)	0-0	9.00	2	1	0	0	0	3.0	6	3	3	0	0	2-0	4	0	0

LEAGUE CHAMPIONSHIP SERIES RECORD

Year	Club & League	W-L	ERA	G	GS	CG	ShO	SV	IP	H	R	ER	HR	HB	BB-IBB	SO	WP	BK
2008	PHILADELPHIA (NL)	0-0	3.00	1	0	0	0	0	3.0	4	1	1	0	0	2-0	2	0	0
2009	PHILADELPHIA (NL)	0-0	0.00	3	0	0	0	0	0.2	0	0	0	0	0	3-0	0	0	0
LEAGUE TOTALS		0-0	2.45	4	0	0	0	0	3.2	4	1	1	0	0	5-0	2	0	0

TRANSACTIONS

- Selected by the Philadelphia Phillies in the 3rd round of 2004 First Year Player Draft
- Traded to the Houston Astros along with IF Jonathan Villar and OF Anthony Gose in exchange for RHP Roy Oswalt on July 29, 2010
- Traded to the Toronto Blue Jays along with RHP David Carpenter and RHP Brandon Lyon in exchange for a player to be named later, RHP Asher Wojciechowski, C Carlos Perez, LHP David Rollins, RHP Joseph Musgrove, RHP Francisco Cordero and OF Ben Francisco on July 20, 2012. The Blue Jays sent RHP Kevin Comer to the Astros to complete the trade on August 16, 2012
- On disabeld list (fractured right foot) from September 7-remainder of season, 2012

GAME HIGHS

ML Debut	June 30, 2007 vs. NYM	**ER Allowed**	8 - June 13, 2012 at SF
Innings Pitched:		**HR Allowed**	3 - 3x, last July 16, 2012 vs. MIL
Starter	9.0 - 3x, last Aug. 30, 2010 vs. STL	**Low Hit CG**	2 - Aug. 30, 2010 vs. STL
Reliever	3.2 - May 7, 2009 at NYM	**Last Win**	Aug. 29, 2012 at NYY
Walks:		**Last Save**	None
Starter	7 - July 7, 2011 at FLA	**Last CG**	Aug. 30, 2010 vs. STL
Reliever	3 - April 23, 2009 vs. MIL	**Last ShO**	Aug. 30, 2010 vs. STL
Strikeouts:		**Last Start**	Sept. 3, 2012 vs. BAL
Starter	10 - 2x, last May 27, 2012 at LAD	**Last Relief App.**	Aug. 2, 2012 at OAK
Reliever	5 - Sept. 9, 2008 vs. FLA	**Longest Win Streak**	7G - April 27-July 19, 2009
Hits Allowed	11 - June 13, 2012 at SF	**Longest Losing Streak**	7G - May 19-July, 7, 2011
Runs Allowed	8 - 2x, last June 13, 2012 at SF	**Scoreless Innings Streak**	16.0 - July 29-Aug. 11, 2009

CAREER FIELDING

POSITION	PCT	G	PO	A	E	TC	DP
P	1.000	116	23	67	0	90	0

MILESTONES

Category		Date	Opponent	Notes
Start	1	June 30, 2007	New York (NL)	ML debut - loss, 4.0 IP, 7H, 5ER, 3HR, 2BB, 5K
Win	1	Sept. 17, 2008	at Atlanta	as a starter - 6.0 IP, 3H, BB, 2K
ShO (3)	1	June 27 ,2009	at Toronto	9.0 IP, 5H, 4K
	2	Aug. 5, 2009	Colorado	9.0 IP, 4H, 2BB, 10K
	3	Aug. 30, 2010	St. Louis	9.0 IP, 2H, BB, 4K
10+ Strikeout Games (2)				
	1	Aug. 5, 2009	Colorado	10 strikeouts
	2	May 27, 2012	at Los Angeles (NL)	10 strikeouts

PROFESSIONAL CAREER:

2007:

- Went to spring training with the Phillies as a non-roster invitee... Spent most of the season with Ottawa (AAA).
- Had his contract purchased on June 30 and made his **ML debut** that day in a start vs NYM (L, 4.0 IP, 7 H, 5 R, 5 ER, 2 BB, 5 SO)... Was optioned back to Ottawa following the game.

2008:

- Winner of the Paul Owens Award as the best pitcher in the Phillies minor league system... Began the season with Lehigh Valley (AAA) and had 3 stints with the Phillies.
- Recalled on July 4 and made two starts (0-0, 3.27 ERA) before being optioned back to Lehigh Valley on July 10... Recalled again on July 29 and made one relief appearance (2.0 IP, 4 H, 4 R, 4 ER, 2 BB, SO) before being optioned back to Lehigh Valley on Aug. 8...Had his final recall on Sept. 1 and made two starts, both against ATL (1-0, 1.42 ERA, .178 opp avg).
- Earned his 1st ML win, Sept. 17 at ATL (6.0 IP, 3 H, BB, 2 SO)... Pitched at least 6.0 innings in 3 of his 4 ML starts ... Went 1-0, 2.28 ERA in his four starts; 0-0, 7.88 ERA in four relief appearances.
- Was hitless for the season: 0-for-10 in the minor leagues, 0-for-7 in the majors.

2009:

- Finished 2nd in the BBWAA's NL Rookie of the Year voting, garnering 94 points (10 first-place votes, 11 second-place votes and 11 third-place votes); was the only player named on every one of the 32 ballots cast by the BBWAA... Won the Players Choice Award for NL Outstanding Rookie, voted by MLB players and presented by the MLBPA, and was named NL Rookie of the Year by The Sporting News.
- Led all NL rookies in innings (166.0), SO (119), winning pct. (.750), CG (3) and SHO (2), tied for the lead in wins (12), ranked 2nd in ERA (2.93) and finished 3rd in starts (23) and opponents avg (.244)... Named to the Topps Rookie All-Star team...
- Became the 1st Phillies rookie with 12 wins in a season since 1959 (Jim Owens . 12-12) and 4th in the last 40 years to pitch 2 SHO in same season (Tom Underwood - 1975, Pat Combs - 1990 and Tyler Green - 1995).
- Had the 8th-best ERA among all NL pitchers and T-2nd in winning %... Tied for the team lead in wins and CG and had the best ERA.
- Began the season in the bullpen...Went 2-0, 2.49 ERA through 12 relief appearances before being moved into the rotation on May 23 at NYY.
- Started the season 7-0 before taking his 1st loss, July 24 vs STL (6.0 IP, 10 H, 5 ER, 6 SO)... Pitched his first two career SHO: June 27 at TOR (9.0 IP, 5 H, 4 SO) and Aug. 5 vs COL (9.0 IP, 4 H, 2 BB, 10 SO).
- Missed two starts due to a right intercostal muscle (oblique) strain suffered in batting practice, Sept. 5 at HOU... Went 7-2 with an NL-best 1.99 ERA in 18 road games (13 starts)...Held opposing hitters to a .158 avg (21-133) with RISP and .077 (1-13) with the bases loaded... Held left-handed hitters to a .216 avg (32-148).
- Went 10-4, 2.99 ERA in 23 starts; the Phillies went 14-9 (.609) in his starts.
- Collected his 1st ML hit, July 2 at ATL (Javier Vazquez)... Got his 1st ML RBI, Sept. 24 at MIL.
- Made his 1st career postseason start in Game 3 of the NLDS, 10/11 at COL (ND)...Had a 2.70 ERA (1 ER, 3.1 IP) in 6 postseason relief appearances.

2010:

- Made 13 starts for Houston, posting a 5-4 record and a 3.75 ERA (30ER/72IP), after being acquired by the club from Philadelphia, along with OF Anthony Gose and SS Jonathan Villar, in exchange for RHP Roy Oswalt on July 29.
- Left-handed hitters hit .179 (12-67) against him this season, the 12th-lowest opponent batting average against lefties among all NL pitchers (min. 50 AB).
- His two-hit, complete-game shutout on Aug. 30 vs. STL marked the first time an Astros LHP hurled a complete game allowing two hits-or-less since Bob Knepper had a one-hit, 1-0 shutout over ATL in the Astrodome on Sept. 21, 1988.
- His win on Aug. 25 at PHI gave him victories against both clubs he's pitched for this season, becoming the 4th pitcher to accomplish this since 2005.
- Following his second start of the season, went on the DL on April 16 with a strained left forearm... Began a rehab assignment on June 8 and made five rehab starts for Clearwater (A), Reading (AA) and Lehigh Valley (AAA) before being reinstated from the 15-day DL on July 6... Optioned to Lehigh Valley that day and made three more starts before recalled by the Phillies on July 25.

2011:

- Set career highs in starts and strikeouts (134) after beginning the season as the Astros fourth starter.
- Spent most of the season with the Astros but missed three turns in the rotation after being optioned to Triple A OKC from Aug. 6-24.

PITCHERS AT THE PLATE

In 1997 with the introduction of INTER-LEAGUE PLAY, Blue Jays pitchers took their turn hitting. **WOODY WILLIAMS** became the first Blue Jays pitcher to come to bat and also had the first hit, a single, in his second at bat off Curt Schilling on June 13, 1997.

On June 21 at Montreal, **MARK HENDRICKSON** became the first Blue Jay to homer in interleague play (1R off KIM).

Regular Season	AVG	AB	R	H	2B	3B	HR	RBI	SH-SF	HP	BB	SO	SB	SLG	OBP
1977-96	.000	1	0	0	0	0	0	0	0-0	0	0	0	0	.000	.000
1997	.118	17	1	2	1	0	0	0	0-0	0	2	5	0	.176	.211
1998	.100	20	0	2	0	0	0	0	2-0	0	1	4	0	.100	.143
1999	.053	19	0	1	0	0	0	0	2-0	0	1	10	0	.053	.100
2000	.071	28	0	2	0	0	0	0	0-0	0	1	14	0	.071	.103
2001	.188	16	0	3	1	1	0	1	5-0	0	0	6	0	.375	.188
2002	.100	20	1	2	0	0	0	0	2-0	0	0	5	0	.100	.100
2003	.214	28	5	6	1	0	1	3	0-0	0	0	8	0	.357	.214
2004	.000	20	0	0	0	0	0	0	3-0	0	0	10	0	.000	.000
2005	.000	18	1	0	0	0	0	0	1-0	0	0	7	0	.000	.000
2006	.105	19	1	2	0	0	0	0	0-0	0	0	8	0	.105	.105
2007	.211	19	0	4	0	0	0	1	0-0	0	1	7	0	.211	.250
2008	.000	16	0	0	0	0	0	0	3-0	0	0	5	0	.000	.000
2009	.000	20	0	0	0	0	0	0	2-0	0	0	13	0	.000	.000
2010	.111	18	1	2	1	0	0	1	1-0	0	1	10	0	.167	.158
2011	.091	22	1	2	0	0	0	2	0-0	0	1	10	0	.091	.130
2012	.150	20	2	3	0	0	0	0	1-0	0	0	8	0	.150	.150
Totals	**.093**	**321**	**13**	**31**	**4**	**1**	**1**	**8**	**22-0**	**0**	**8**	**130**	**0**	**.125**	**.119**

HINSHAW, *ALEX*

Birthdate .... October 31, 1982
Opening Day Age 30
Birthplace................. Pomona, CA
Residence............... Beaverton, OR
Bats/Throws .... L/L
Height/Weight 6-2/175
Contract Status .... signed thru 2013
M.L. Service 1.109

51
PITCHER
NON-ROSTER

BIOGRAPHIES | LAST SEASON | HISTORY | RECORDS | OPPONENTS | PLAYER DEV. | MEDIA & MISC.

PERSONAL:

Alexander Omar Hinshaw... Attended Claremont High School in California and attended Chaffey College and San Diego State University... Married... His uncle (mother's brother), Gul Ahmed Sherzada, was previously Afghanistan's ambassador to Spain... Credits his love of baseball to his grandmother, who would watch baseball with him while his parents worked... Learned to throw from grandmother, who was the only lefty in his family... Was selected three times in the First-Year Player Draft before signing with the Giants in 2005: 2000 - San Francisco Giants (28th round), 2002 - San Francisco Giants (29th round), 2003 - Florida Marlins (25th round, 2005 - San Francisco Giants (15th round).

LAST SEASON:

- Began the season with Tucson (AAA) in the Padres sytem making 14 appearances.
- Was recalled to San Diego on May 8 and made 31 appearnces out of the bullpen... Held Lefties to a .196 average and .217 overall... Seven of 31 outings were one inning or less and 22 of 31 were scoreless... Fanned 36 in 28 innings however walked 20.
- Was designated for assignment on Aug. 14 and claimed by the Cubs on Aug. 19
- Appeared in two games with the Cubs, the final outing allwoing five runs without retiring any of the five batters faced, including three home runs.

ALEX HINSHAW

Bold – career high

Year	Club & League	W-L	ERA	G	GS	CG	ShO	SV	IP	H	R	ER	HR	HB	BB-IBB	SO	WP	BK	OBA
2005	Salem-Keizer (NOR)	0-1	3.68	25	0	0	0	0	22.0	17	9	9	1	3	18-1	33	2	0	.227
2006	San Jose (CAL)	6-3	4.26	30	10	0	0	0	69.2	58	48	33	6	10	60-1	78	6	0	.227
2007	Connecticut (East)	3-1	1.96	17	5	0	0	0	41.1	22	13	9	2	2	19-0	50	2	0	.155
2008	Fresno (PCL)	0-0	0.57	13	0	0	0	7	15.2	5	1	1	0	0	4-0	21	0	0	.098
	SAN FRANCISCO (NL)	**2**-1	3.40	**48**	0	0	0	0	**39.2**	31	16	15	5	3	**29**-4	**47**	5	0	.220
2009	Fresno (PCL)	1-2	3.96	46	0	0	0	1	52.1	42	25	23	3	3	32-0	72	3	0	.212
	SAN FRANCISCO (NL)	0-0	12.00	9	0	0	0	0	6.0	10	8	8	2	0	7-0	2	1	0	.385
2010	Fresno (PCL)	2-4	4.82	50	0	0	0	0	56.0	47	35	30	3	7	40-1	65	7	1	.225
2011	Fresno (PCL)	0-0	9.00	13	0	0	0	0	10.0	15	10	10	0	0	11-2	11	1	1	.366
	Richmond Flying (East)	2-0	3.60	32	0	0	0	1	35.0	24	15	14	1	5	28-0	47	7	1	.190
2012	Tucson (PCL)	0-0	3.72	14	0	0	0	0	19.1	14	8	8	0	2	10-0	18	1	0	.206
	SAN DIEGO (NL)	1-1	4.50	31	0	0	0	0	28.0	23	14	14	**5**	2	20-2	36	1	0	.217
	CHICAGO (NL)	0-0	135.00	2	0	0	0	0	0.1	4	5	5	**3**	0	1-0	0	0	0	.800
Minor Totals		14-11	3.84	240	15	0	0	9	321.1	244	164	137	16	32	222-5	395	29	3	.209
MAJOR TOTALS		3-2	5.11	90	0	0	0	0	74.0	68	43	42	15	5	57-6	85	7	0	.245

TRANSACTIONS

- Selected by the San Francisco Giants in the 15th round of the 2005 First Year Player Draft amateur draft
- Signed by the San Diego Padres on December 1, 2011
- Claimed off waivers by the Chicago Cubs on August 19, 2012
- Signed by the Toronto Blue Jays on November 21, 2012

GAME HIGHS

ML Debut	May 15, 2008 vs. HOU	**Runs Allowed**	5 - Aug. 27, 2012 vs. MIL
Innings Pitched:		**ER Allowed**	5 - Aug. 27, 2012 vs. MIL
Starter	None	**HR Allowed**	3 - Aug. 27, 2012 vs. MIL
Reliever	2.0 - 3x, last July 28, 2012 at MIA	**Low Hit CG**	None
Walks:		**Last Win**	July 14, 2012 at LAD
Starter	None	**Last Save**	None
Reliever	2 - 12x, last July 30, 2012 at CIN	**Last CG**	None
Strikeouts:		**Last ShO**	None
Starter	None	**Last Start**	None
Reliever	4 - May 17, 2012 vs. LAD	**Last Relief App.**	Aug. 27, 2012 vs. MIL
Hits Allowed	5 - May 17, 2012 vs. LAD	**Longest Win Streak**	1G - 3x, last July 14, 2012
		Longest Losing Streak	1G - 2x, last May 28, 2012
		Scoreless Innings Streak	6.0 - June 26-July 9, 2008

CAREER FIELDING

POSITION	PCT	G	PO	A	E	TC	DP
P	.917	90	3	8	1	12	0

MILESTONES

Category		Date	Opponent	Notes
Win	1	June 1, 2008	San Diego	as reliever - 1.0 IP, 2H, 2ER, HR, 2K

PROFESSIONAL CAREER:

2008:

- Began the season with Triple-A Fresno before making his Major League debut with the Giants.
- Contract was selected from Fresno on May 15 and made his **Major League debut** the same day vs. HOU.
- Tallied his first win June 1 vs. SD.
- Ranked 11th among NL relievers with 10.66 strikeouts per 9.0 IP... Also recorded a .220 opponents average (31-for-141), which ranked eighth among left-handed NL relievers.
- Prior to joining the Giants, served as Fresno's closer...converted seven of eight save opportunities in 13 appearances before being called up.

2009:

- Made his first Opening Day roster, beginning the season with the Giants.
- Made seven appearances in the Major Leagues before being optioned to Triple-A Fresno.
- Spent the majority of the year in Triple-A, making two more big league appearances toward the end of the season... Optioned back to Triple-A on April 21 and was recalled Aug. 28.

2010:

- Played for Triple-A Fresno the entire season, making 50 relief appearances.
- Ranked second on his team in relief appearances... Limited left-handed hitters to a .179 average (14-for-78), allowing only three extra-base hits... Averaged 10.4 strikeouts per 9.0 IP.

2011:

- Split the campaign between AA Richmond and AAA Fresno, making a combined 45 relief appearances.
- Went 2-0 with a 4.80 ERA (24 ER/45.0 IP) between his two minor league stops... Averaged 11.6 strikeouts per 9.0 innings with 58 on the year.

DOUBLEHEADER

The Blue Jays have played 102 doubleheaders in franchise history and have a 20-39-43... The Blue Jays last played back-to-back doubleheaders on July 28 & 29, 1997 in Milwaukee and lost all four games... Toronto has played 10 back-to-back twin bills and are 2-6-2 including four straight doubleheaders over six days in 1978 from June 11 - 16... Have played eight split gate doubleheaders (split DH do not count as doubleheaders)... In 1980 the Blue Jays posted their best doubleheader record at 5-1-4, while in 1978 they lost a franchise high eight, winning three and splitting six.

DOUBLEHEADER SHUTOUTS

Did you know that the Blue Jays have never shut out opponents in both ends of a doubleheader... Conversely, the Blue Jays have been shut out in both ends of a doubleheader twice, losing 8-0 and 6-0 to Boston at Toronto on September 5, 1977 and 15-0 and 2-0 to New York at Toronto on September 25, 1977.

DOUBLEHEADER VS. EACH CLUB

		DH	
TORONTO vs	W	L	S
Baltimore	2	8	3
Boston	1	2	6
Chicago (A)	3	1	6
Cleveland	5	3	10
Detroit	2	1	2
Kansas City	0	3	0
Los Angeles (A)	1	0	1
Milwaukee	1	9	2
Minnesota	1	3	1
New York (A)	1	5	4
Oakland	1	2	3
Seattle	1	1	1
Tampa Bay	0	0	0
Texas	1	1	4
TOTALS	**20**	**39**	**43**

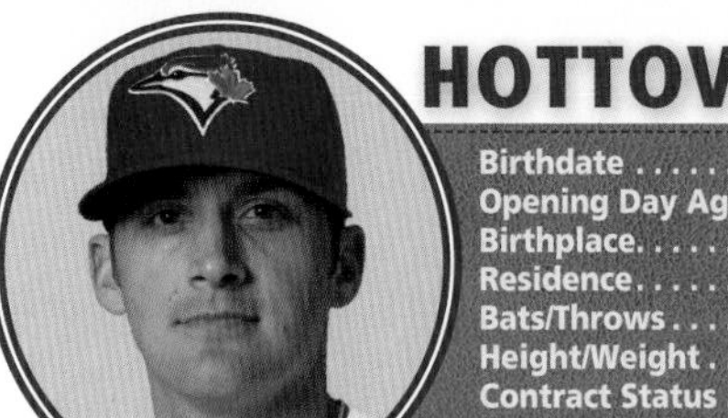

HOTTOVY, *TOMMY*

Birthdate .... July 9, 1981
Opening Day Age 31
Birthplace.............. Kansas City, MO
Residence.............. Kansas City, MO
Bats/Throws .... L/L
Height/Weight 6-1/205
Contract Status .... signed thru 2013
M.L. Service 0.062

75
PITCHER
NON-ROSTER

PERSONAL:

Thomas L. Hottovy... Resides in Kansas City, Mo... Married with one child... Graduated from Park Hill South High School in Riverside, Mo... Graduated first in his class, was the KC Star's Male Scholar-Athlete of the Year and also was chosen as Missouri's High School Heisman Award winner... Graduated from and played baseball at Wichita State University... Was 9-3 with a 2.25 ERA as a senior and was named First Team All-Missouri Valley Conference.

LAST SEASON:

- Spent most of the season with Omaha of the Pacific Coast League (AAA)... Collected seven saves second most on the club and recorded lowest ERA on staff (min 50 IP)...Posted a 3.81 K/BB ratio, also the best on staff.
- Made nine appearances for the Royals making his debut on April 25 at CLE.
- Was recalled on four separate occasions throughout the season.
- Allowed runs in just three of nine appearances...Tossed 2.0 innings in three outings.

TOMMY HOTTOVY

Bold – career high

Year	Club & League	W-L	ERA	G	GS	CG	ShO	SV	IP	H	R	ER	HR	HB	BB-IBB	SO	WP	BK	OBA
2004	Lowell (NYP)	0-1	0.89	14	14	0	0	0	30.1	24	5	3	0	3	4-0	39	2	0	.211
2005	Wilmington (Caro)	3-12	5.45	25	23	0	0	0	104.0	116	74	63	18	7	37-2	82	8	0	.282
2006	Wilmington (Caro)	8-6	2.80	21	21	2	0	0	122.0	109	49	38	3	5	35-0	91	6	0	.237
	Portland (East)	2-4	4.17	7	7	0	0	0	41.0	28	20	19	1	3	15-2	31	2	0	.190
2007	Portland (East)	4-10	5.61	24	23	0	0	0	120.1	144	78	75	17	3	49-0	69	6	1	.304
2008	Portland (East)	1-0	5.00	2	2	0	0	0	9.0	9	7	5	2	1	2-0	4	0	0	.250
2009	Lowell (NYP)	1-0	2.25	5	0	0	0	0	8.0	4	2	2	1	0	3-0	12	0	0	.148
	Portland (East)	0-2	3.46	16	0	0	0	0	26.0	26	12	10	2	2	10-0	29	3	0	.263
2010	Portland (East)	3-2	5.22	15	0	0	0	0	39.2	49	25	23	6	0	20-1	34	5	1	.302
	Pawtucket (Int)	0-1	4.54	26	0	0	0	0	35.2	37	19	18	5	4	23-2	22	5	0	.264
2011	Portland Sea (East)	0-0	1.93	8	0	0	0	1	18.2	12	4	4	0	0	4-0	18	0	0	.185
	BOSTON (AL)	0-0	6.75	8	0	0	0	0	4.0	4	3	3	0	1	3-0	2	0	0	.267
	Pawtucket (Int)	2-0	2.75	24	0	0	0	1	36.0	23	13	11	8	1	9-0	29	0	0	.181
2012	Omaha (PCL)	2-2	2.52	41	0	0	0	7	50.0	42	18	14	6	4	16-0	61	0	0	.221
	KANSAS CITY (AL)	0-0	2.89	**9**	0	0	0	0	**9.1**	11	3	3	**2**	1	**5**-0	**6**	0	0	.306
Minor Totals		26-40	4.00	228	90	2	0	9	640.2	623	326	285	69	33	227-7	521	37	2	.254
MAJOR TOTALS		0-0	4.05	17	0	0	0	0	13.1	15	6	6	2	2	8-0	8	0	0	.294

TRANSACTIONS

- Selected by the Boston Red Sox in the 4th round of the 2004 First Year Player Draft
- Signed by the Kansas City Royals on November 15, 2011
- Traded to the Texas Rangers for cash considerations on November 8, 2012
- Claimed off waivers by the Toronto Blue Jays on January 10, 2013

GAME HIGHS

ML Debut	June 3, 2011 vs. OAK
Innings Pitched:	
Starter	None
Reliever	2.0 - 3x, last Sept. 29, 2012 at CLE
Walks:	
Starter	None
Reliever	2 - 2x, last June 30, 2012 at MIN
Strikeouts:	
Starter	None
Reliever	2 - 2x, last May 6, 2012 vs. NYY
Hits Allowed	2 - 6x, last Sept. 29, 2012 at CLE
Runs Allowed	2 - June 14, 2011 at TB
ER Allowed	2 - June 14, 2011 at TB
HR Allowed	1 - 2x, last June 30, 2012 at MIN
Low Hit CG	None
Last Win	None
Last Save	None
Last CG	None
Last ShO	None
Last Start	None
Last Relief App.	Sept. 29, 2012 at CLE
Longest Win Streak	None
Longest Losing Streak	None
Scoreless Innings Streak	2.2 - Sept. 23-Oct. 1, 2012

CAREER FIELDING

POSITION	PCT	G	PO	A	E	TC	DP
P	1.000	17	1	1	0	2	0

BIOGRAPHIES LAST SEASON HISTORY RECORDS OPPONENTS PLAYER DEV. MEDIA & MISC.

PROFESSIONAL CAREER:

2006:

- Led the Carolina League (A) with two complete games and ranked 3rd with a 2.80 ERA.

2007:

- Worked 120.1 innings in 24 games (23 starts) with Portland of the Eastern League (AA).

2008:

- Limited to two starts before being sidelined...Underwent Tommy John surgery and missed remainder of season.

2009:

- Upon his return from Tommy John surgery, was converted to a full-time reliever.

2010:

- Spent time with both Portland of the Eastern League (AA) and Pawtucket of the International League (AAA).

2011:

- Spent time at three different levels in the Boston organization, opening the campaign with Portland (AA), followed by a promotion to Pawtucket (AAA), eventually making his Major League debut for the Red Sox.
- Had his contract selected on June 3 and made his big league debut that night vs. OAK, retiring the only batter he faced, David DeJesus, on a groundout.
- Named the first-ever Lou Gorman Award winner, presented to a Red Sox minor leaguer who has demonstrated dedication and perseverance in overcoming obstacles while working his way to the Major Leagues.
- Following the season, made 12 relief appearances for Aguilas in the Dominican Winter League and posted a 3.52 ERA with one save, striking out 9 and walking two in 7.2 innings.

HOME POSTPONEMENTS

1. April 22, 1977, vs. Boston (Friday—Day)
2. April 23, 1977, vs. Boston (Saturday—Day)
3. September 24, 1977, vs. New York (Saturday—Day)
4. September 30, 1977, vs. Cleveland (Friday—Night)
5. October 1, 1977, vs. Cleveland (Saturday—Day)
6. April 20, 1978, vs. New York (Thursday—Day)
7. May 8, 1978, vs. Oakland (Monday—Night)
8. May 14, 1978, vs. Seattle (Sunday—Day)
9. June 12, 1978, vs. Minnesota (Monday—Night)
10. May 25, 1979, vs. Boston (Friday—Night)
11. April 14, 1980, vs. Milwaukee (Monday—Opening Day)
12. April 28, 1980, vs. Kansas City (Monday—Night)
13. May 13, 1980, vs. Seattle (Tuesday—Night)
14. June 19, 1980, vs. Chicago (Thursday—Night)
15. May 5, 1981, vs. Cleveland (Tuesday—Night)—Fog
16. August 30, 1981, vs. Kansas City (Sunday—Day)
17. September 21, 1981, vs. Oakland (Monday—Night)
18. June 5, 1982, vs. Cleveland (Satuday—Day)
19. June 25, 1982, vs. Minnesota (Friday—Night)
20. September 14, 1982, vs. Oakland (Tuesday—Night)
21. April 30, 1983, vs. Chicago (Saturday—Day)
22. May 29, 1983, vs. Boston (Sunday—2nd g—DH)
23. July 4, 1983, vs. Seattle (Monday—Night)
24. April 30, 1984, vs. Texas (Monday—Night) (Winds)
25. April 16, 1986, vs. Baltimore (Wednesday—Day)
26. September 10, 1986, vs. New York (Wednesday—Night)
27. October 4, 1986, vs. Milwaukee (Saturday—Day)
28. April 15, 1988, vs. Minnesota (Friday—Night) (Cold)
29. May 17, 1989, vs. California (Sunday—Day)
30. April 12, 2001, vs. Kansas City (Thursday—Night) — unsafe roof

HUTCHISON, *DREW*

Birthdate .... August 22, 1990
Opening Day Age 21
Birthplace................. Lakeland, FL
Residence................. Lakeland, FL
Bats/Throws .... L/R
Height/Weight 6-2/195
Contract Status .... signed thru 2013
M.L. Service 0.167

36
PITCHER

PERSONAL:

Andrew S. Hutchison... Attended Lakeland Senior High School in Florida, where he earned all-county first team high school honours and third team all-state honours... Mother played golf and softball at Florida Southern University.

LAST SEASON:

- Became the 8th youngest pitcher to ever start a game for the Blue Jays on April 21 at KC, Jeff Byrd (20 years-221 days), Phil Huffman (20-294), Henderson Alvarez (21-114), Roy Halladay (21-129), Mike Darr (21-167), Jerry Garvin (21-171), Jim Clancy (21-220), Drew Hutchison (21-243)... Picked up the win becoming the first Blue Jays pitcher to win his debut since Ricky Romero on April 9, 2009.
- Is one home win short of tying Jesse Carlson (2008) and Jeff Musselman (1987) for most consecutive home decisions won to start a career at four.
- Left his last start after just 0.2 innings and nine pitches vs. PHI on June 15 with right elbow soreness..Was the 3rd starter in four starts to leave due to injury (Morrow-oblique, Drabek-elbow)...Had Tommy John surgery in August.
- Recorded four quality starts in his last six (excluding his final start), posting a 4-2 record with a 3.47 ERA... In the four wins allowed just three total earned runs in 26 innings.
- Held opponents to a .257 average...The first time through the order batters hit just .188... In five home starts posted a 3-0 record with a 2.36 ERA... Was 2-3 with a 6.47 ERA on the road.
- Suffered his first Major League loss and allowed Albert Pujols' first AL home run on May 6 at LAA... Fanned nine on May 28 vs. BAL and tossed seven innings twice (May 28 vs. BAL, June 3 vs. BOS).
- Team was 7-4 in his starts and walked one or less in six of them.

DREW HUTCHISON

Bold – career high

Year	Club & League	W-L	ERA	G	GS	CG	ShO	SV	IP	H	R	ER	HR	HB	BB-IBB	SO	WP	BK	OBA
2010	Auburn (NYP)	1-1	3.00	10	10	0	0	0	45.0	34	18	15	1	4	12-0	44	3	0	.201
	Lansing (Mid)	1-2	1.52	5	5	0	0	0	23.2	17	7	4	1	2	7-0	19	0	1	.191
2011	Lansing (Mid)	6-2	2.63	14	14	0	0	0	72.0	68	29	21	1	3	19-0	84	2	0	.245
	Dunedin (FSL)	5-3	2.74	11	10	0	0	0	62.1	42	20	19	3	4	14-1	66	1	0	.194
	New Hampshire (East)	3-0	1.20	3	3	0	0	0	15.0	10	2	2	0	2	2-0	21	3	0	.192
2012	New Hampshire (East)	2-1	2.16	3	3	0	0	0	16.2	16	4	4	1	0	3-0	12	0	0	.262
	TORONTO (AL)	5-3	4.60	11	11	0	0	0	58.2	59	31	30	8	5	20-0	49	1	0	.257
Minor Totals		18-9	2.49	46	45	0	0	0	234.2	187	80	65	7	15	57-1	246	9	1	.216

TRANSACTIONS

- Selected by the Toronto Blue Jays in the 15th round of the 2009 First Year Player Draft
- On disabled list (right UCL sprain) from June 16-remainder of season, 2012

GAME HIGHS

ML Debut	April 21, 2012 at KC	**ER Allowed**	6 - May 22, 2012 at TB
Innings Pitched:		**HR Allowed**	2- 3x, last June 9, 2012 at ATL
Starter	7.0 - 2x, last June 3, 2012 vs. BAL	**Low Hit CG**	None
Reliever	None	**Last Win**	June 3, 2012 vs. BOS
Walks:		**Last Save**	None
Starter	4 - 2x, last May 17, 2012 vs. NYY	**Last CG**	None
Reliever	None	**Last ShO**	None
Strikeouts:		**Last Start**	June 15, 2012 vs. PHI
Starter	9 - May 28, 2012 vs. BAL	**Last Relief App.**	None
Reliever	None	**Longest Win Streak**	2G - 2x, last May 28-June 3, 2012
Hits Allowed	8 - 2x, last May 6, 2012 at LAA	**Longest Losing Streak**	1G - 3x, last June 9, 2012
Runs Allowed	6 - 2x, last May 22, 2012 at TB	**Scoreless Innings Streak**	11.2 - May 28-June 3, 2012

CAREER FIELDING

POSITION	PCT	G	PO	A	E	TC	DP
P	1.000	11	2	7	0	9	0

MILESTONES

Category		Date	Opponent	Notes
Start	1	April 21, 2012	at Kansas City	W, 5.1, 8H, 5ER, 2HR, 3BB, 4K
Win	1	April 21, 2012	at Kansas City	as a starter - 5.1, 8H, 5ER, 2HR, 3BB, 4K

PROFESSIONAL CAREER:

2010:

- Made his professional debut at Auburn (Short Season-A).
- Picked up his first win on July 10, tossing five innings of 2-run ball.
- Held NY-Penn League hitters to a .201 average.
- Was promoted to Lansing (Low-A) for the balance of the season.
- Made five starts for the Lugnuts, allowing zero or one run in four of five starts.
- Midwest League hitters batted just .191.
- Overall combined to go 2-3 with a 2.49 ERA in 15 starts.

2011:

- Spent time at three different levels, starting in Lansing (Low-A), moving to Dunedin (High-A) and finishing in New Hampshire (AA), combining to go 14-5 with a 2.53 ERA in 28 games (27 starts).
- Was the Pitcher of the Week from June13-19 for the Midwest League.
- Was promoted to Dunedin (A) after his June 19 start and made 11 appearances, 10 starts.
- In his 10 starts with Dunedin posted a 5-2 record with a 1.86 ERA, including a 1.57 ERA in his last four starts.
- Made his final three starts of the year at New Hampshire (AA)... Won all three starts, allowing runs in only one of his starts.
- Was named Eastern League Pitcher of the Week from Aug. 29-Sept. 5.

BLUE JAYS PITCHERS WHOSE ML DEBUT CAME AS A STARTER

Jerry Garvin - April 10, 1977 vs Chicago: W 3-1 (8.0IP, 6H, ER, 4BB, 2K)

Jeff Byrd - June 20, 1977 vs Cleveland: ND in a 8-5 loss (5.0IP, 5H, 3ER, 5BB, 4K)

Jim Clancy - July 26, 1977 vs Texas: L 14-0 (2.0IP, 5H, 5ER, 3BB, 1K)

Mike Darr - September 6, 1977 vs Boston: L 11-2 (1.1IP, 3H, 5ER, 1HR, 4BB, 1K, 1HB)

Phil Huffman-April 10, 1979 at Chicago: W 10-2 (6.0IP, 7H, ER, 3K)

Dave Stieb - June 29, 1979 at Baltimore: L 6-1 (6.0IP, 6H, 5ER, 2BB, 5K, 2HR)

Butch Edge - August 13, 1979 at Oakland: W 4-2 (6.2IP, 6H, ER, 2BB, 5K)

Luis Leal - May 25, 1980 vs New York: W 9-6 (7.2IP, 12H, 3ER, 4BB)

Mark Eichorn-August 30, 1982 vs. Baltimore: L 6-3 (4.2IP, 6H, 5ER, 3BB, 5K)

Matt Williams-August 2, 1983 vs. New York: W 13-6 (5.0IP, 5H, 5ER, 4BB, 3K, 3HR)

David Wells-June 30, 1987 vs. New York: L 4-0 (4.0IP, 9H, 4ER, 2BB, 4K)

Alex Sanchez - May 23, 1989 vs Minnesota: ND in a 2-1 win (6.0IP, 5H, ER, 5BB, 1K)

Mauro Gozzo - August 8, 1989 vs Texas: W 7-0 (8.0IP, 3H, 3BB, 4K)

Denis Boucher-April 12, 1991 vs. Milwaukee: ND in a 5-4 win (5.1IP, 5H, 3ER, BB, K, 2HR)

Juan Guzman - June 7, 1991 at Baltimore: L 5-3 (4.2IP, 6H, 4ER, 3BB, 4K)

Scott Brow - April 28, 1993 vs Kansas City: L 5-3 (6.0IP, 5H, 4ER, 2BB, 2K)

Giovanni Carrara - July 29, 1995 vs Oakland: W 18-11 (5.0IP, 7H, 5ER, 5BB, 2K)

Jeff Ware - September 2, 1995 at Chicago: L 10-4 (1.1IP, 7H, 6ER, 3BB, 1K)

Chris Carpenter - May 12, 1997 at Minnesota: L 12-2 (3.0IP, 8H, 5ER, 3BB, 5K)

Roy Halladay - September 20, 1998 at Tampa Bay: ND in a 7-5 win (5.0IP, 8H, 2ER, 1HR, 2BB, 5K)

Pasqual Coco - July 17, 2000 vs New York Mets: ND in a 7-5 loss (4.0IP, 5H, 4ER, 1HR, 5BB, 2K)

Brandon Lyon - August 4, 2001 vs Baltimore: W 2-1 (7.1IP, 4H, ER, 1BB, 5K)

Mike Smith - April 26, 2002 at Anaheim: L 4-0 (4.0IP, 7H, 4ER, 2BB, 1K)

David Bush - July 2, 2004 at Montreal: L 2-0 (5.2IP, 4H, ER, 1BB, 4K)

Gustavo Chacin - September 20, 2004 at New York: W 6-3 (7.0IP, 4H, 3ER, 3BB, 2K)

Dustin McGowan - July 30, 2005 vs Texas: ND in a 3-2 loss (5.0IP, 2H, ER, 3BB, 6U)

Casey Janssen - April 27, 2006 vs. Baltimore: ND in a 7-5 loss (4.0IP, 3H, 2ER, 3BB)

Ty Taubenheim - May 20, 2006 at Colorado: L 5-1 (5.0IP, 5H, 3ER, 2HB, 3BB, 3K)

Jesse Litsch - May 15, 2007 vs. Baltimore: W 2-1 (8.2IP, 4H, ER, 3BB, K)

David Purcey - April 18, 2008 vs. Detroit: ND in a 8-4 loss (4.1IP, 2H, ER, 7BB, 3K)

Scott Richmond - July 30, 2008 vs. Tampa Bay: L 3-2 (5.1IP, 7H, 3ER, 4K)

Ricky Romero - April 9, 2009 vs. Detroit: W 6-2 (6.0IP, 7H, 2ER, 2BB, 5K)

Robert Ray - May 2, 2009 vs. Baltimore: ND in a 5-4 win (5.2IP, 4H, 3ER, 4BB, 2K)

Brett Cecil - May 5, 2009 vs. Cleveland: ND in a 10-6 win (6.0IP, 6H, ER, 6K)

Brad Mills - June 18, 2009 at Philadelphia: ND in a 8-7 win (3.2IP, 6H, 4ER, 4BB, 2K)

Mark Rzepczynski - July 7, 2009 at Tampa Bay: ND in a 3-1 loss (6.0IP, 2H, ER, 4BB, 7K)

Kyle Drabek - September 15, 2010 at Baltimore: L 3-1 (6.0IP, 9H, 3ER, 3BB, 5K)

Zach Stewart - June 16, 2011 at Baltimore: ND in a 4-3 loss (7.0IP, 7H, 2ER, HR, BB, 4K)

Henderson Alvarez -August 10, 2011 vs. Oakland: ND in a 8-4 win (5.2IP, 8H, 3ER, HR, BB, 4K)

Drew Hutchison - April 21, 2012 at Kansas City: W 9-5 (5.1IP, 8H, 5ER, 3BB, 4K, 2HR)

IZTURIS, *MAICER*

Birthdate . . . . September 12, 1980
Opening Day Age 32
Birthplace. . . Barquisimeto Estado Lara, VZ
Residence. . . Barquisimeto Estado Lara, VZ
Bats/Throws . . . . S/R
Height/Weight 5-8/170
Contract Status . . . . signed thru 2015
M.L. Service 8.038

3
INFIELDER

PERSONAL:

Maicer Eduardo Izturis (My-sair iss-TUR-iss)... Half-brother of Cesar Izturis... Took part in numerous community events and youth baseball clinics.

LAST SEASON:

- Played in at least 100 games in back-to-back seasons for just the second time in his career.
- Batted .291 over his final 54 games including a .310 clip from July 29 on.
- Swiped a career-high 17 bases, including a steal of home on Sept. 12, his final stolen base of the season.
- Was 17-for-19 in stolen bases attempts on the year.
- Hit first home run on July 15, 1st since July 29, 2011 at Detroit (90 G)... Ended longest homerless drought of career.
- Hit .277 (72-260) this year as a starter but went 2-22 as a pinch-hitter.

MAICER IZTURIS

Bold – career high

Year	Club and League	AVG	G	AB	R	H	2B	3B	HR	RBI	SH-SF	HP	BB-IBB	SO	SB-CS	SLG	OBP	OPS
1998	Burlington (Appy)	.290	55	217	33	63	8	2	2	33	2-0	0	17-0	32	16-6	.373	.342	.715
1999	Columbus (SAL)	.300	57	220	46	66	5	3	4	23	1-3	1	20-0	28	14-2	.405	.357	.762
2000	Columbus (SAL)	.276	10	29	4	8	1	0	0	1	0-0	0	3-0	3	0-0	.310	.344	.654
2001	Kinston (Caro)	.240	114	433	47	104	16	6	1	39	10-4	8	31-1	81	32-9	.312	.300	.612
2002	Kinston (Caro)	.262	58	233	28	61	13	1	1	30	3-1	1	24-0	26	24-6	.339	.332	.671
	Akron (East)	.277	67	253	34	70	12	7	0	32	5-3	3	17-0	28	8-4	.379	.326	.705
2003	Akron (East)	.280	53	218	31	61	11	5	1	20	6-2	1	24-1	23	14-6	.390	.351	.741
	Buffalo (Int)	.262	85	301	43	79	16	4	2	29	9-2	1	24-0	28	14-6	.362	.317	.679
2004	Edmonton (PCL)	.338	99	376	65	127	19	2	3	36	4-2	4	57-1	30	14-12	.423	.428	.851
	MONTREAL (NL)	.206	32	107	10	22	5	2	1	4	2-0	2	10-1	20	4-0	.318	.286	.604
2005	Salt Lake (PCL)	.452	10	31	10	14	4	0	0	2	1-0	0	7-0	4	4-2	.581	.553	1.134
	LOS ANGELES (AL)	.246	77	191	18	47	8	**4**	1	15	1-1	0	17-2	21	9-3	.346	.306	.652
2006	Salt Lake (PCL)	.306	9	36	5	11	5	1	0	5	0-2	0	5-0	5	1-0	.500	.372	.872
	LOS ANGELES (AL)	.293	104	352	64	103	21	3	5	44	5-1	3	**38**-1	35	14-6	.412	.365	.777
2007	Salt Lake (PCL)	.353	5	17	3	6	1	0	0	0	0-0	0	3-1	2	0-2	.412	.450	.862
	R. Cucamonga (CAL)	.318	7	22	5	7	1	0	0	3	0-1	0	6-0	3	0-0	.364	.448	.812
	LOS ANGELES (AL)	.289	102	336	47	97	17	2	6	51	1-4	0	33-2	39	7-1	.405	.349	.754
2008	R. Cucamonga (CAL)	.500	1	2	0	1	0	0	0	0	0-0	0	0-0	1	0-0	.500	.500	1.000
	LOS ANGELES (AL)	.269	79	290	44	78	14	2	3	37	2-2	1	26-0	27	11-2	.362	.329	.691
2009	LOS ANGELES (AL)	.300	114	387	**74**	116	22	3	**8**	**65**	3-7	5	35-2	41	13-5	.434	.359	.793
2010	Salt Lake (PCL)	.286	2	7	1	2	0	0	0	1	0-0	0	0-0	0	0-1	.286	.286	.572
	LOS ANGELES (AL)	.250	61	212	27	53	13	1	3	27	1-2	2	21-0	27	7-3	.363	.321	.684
2011	LOS ANGELES (AL)	.276	**122**	449	51	**124**	**35**	0	5	38	0-4	8	33-3	**65**	9-6	.388	.334	.722
2012	LOS ANGELES (AL)	.256	100	289	35	74	11	0	2	20	3-0	2	25-0	38	**17**-2	.315	.320	.635
Minor Totals		.284	632	2395	355	680	112	31	14	254	41-20	19	238-4	294	141-56	.374	.351	.725
AL TOTALS		.276	759	2506	360	692	141	15	33	297	16-21	21	228-10	293	87-28	.384	.339	.723
MAJOR TOTALS		.273	791	2613	370	714	146	17	34	301	18-21	23	238-11	313	91-28	.381	.337	.718

DIVISION SERIES RECORD

Year	Club and League	AVG	G	AB	R	H	2B	3B	HR	RBI	SH-SF	HP	BB-IBB	SO	SB-CS
2007	LOS ANGELES (AL)	.333	3	12	1	4	2	0	0	0	0-0	0	0-0	2	2-0
2009	LOS ANGELES (AL)	.143	2	7	1	1	0	0	0	1	0-0	0	0-0	2	1-0
DIVISION SERIES TOTALS		.263	5	19	2	5	2	0	0	1	0-0	0	0-0	4	3-0

LEAGUE CHAMPIONSHIP SERIES RECORD

Year	Club and League	AVG	G	AB	R	H	2B	3B	HR	RBI	SH-SF	HP	BB-IBB	SO	SB-CS
2005	LOS ANGELES (AL)	--	1	0	0	0	0	0	0	0	0-0	0	0-0	0	0-0
2009	LOS ANGELES (AL)	.100	4	10	1	1	1	0	0	1	0-1	0	1-1	1	0-0
LEAGUE SERIES TOTALS		.100	5	10	1	1	1	0	0	1	0-1	0	1-1	1	0-0

HOME RUN BREAKDOWN

			ONE GAME										
Total	H	A	2	3	4	GS	LO	XN	IP	PH	RHP	LHP
34	11	23	0	0	0	1	3	0	0	0	28	6

TRANSACTIONS

- Signed by the Cleveland Indians on April 1, 1998
- Traded to the Montreal Expos along with OF Ryan Church in exchange for LHP Scott Stewart on January 5, 2004
- Traded to the Los Angeles Angels of Anaheim along with OF Juan Rivera in exchnage for OF Jose Guillen on November 19, 2004
- On disabled list (sprained MCL in left knee) from April 26-June 17, 2005
- On disabled list (strained left hamstring) from April 24-June 8, 2006
- On disabled list (tightness in right hamstring) from May 3-14, 2007
- On disabled list (right hamstring irritation) from May 22-July 1, 2007
- On disabled list (torn ulnar collateral ligament of left thumb) from August 14-remainder of season, 2008
- On disabled list (right shoulder inflammation) from May 6-24, 2010
- On disabled list (strained left forearm) from June 16-July 18, 2010
- On disabled list (right shoulder inflammation) from August 20-September 26, 2010
- Signed by the Toronto Blue Jays on November 8, 2012

GAME HIGHS

ML Debut	Aug. 27, 2004 vs. SD	**RBI**	4 - 4x, last Aug. 7, 2009 vs. TEX
Runs	4 - Aug. 21, 2007 vs. NYY	**Stolen Bases**	2 - 4x, last July 23, 2012 vs. KC
Hits	4 - 3x, last June 12, 2009 vs. SD	**Last ML Home Run**	July 30, 2012 at TEX
Doubles	2 - 11x, last Sept. 10, 2011 vs. NYY	**Longest Hitting Streak**	13G - 2x, last May 31-June 14, 2008
Home Runs	1 - 34x, last July 30, 2012 at TEX	**Longest Hitless Streak**	16AB - April 20-30, 2011

CAREER FIELDING

POSITION	PCT	G	PO	A	E	TC	DP
2B	.990	246	381	647	10	1038	149
3B	.947	290	142	451	33	626	41
SS	.972	194	255	464	21	740	96
OF	1.000	2	1	1	0	2	1

MILESTONES

Category		Date	Opponent	Pitcher	Notes
Hit	1	Aug. 27, 2004	San Diego	Tankersley	single in 1st ML AB
Home Run	1	Aug. 31, 2004	Chicago (NL)	Prior	1R
Grand Slam (1)	1	Aug. 10, 2007	Minnesota	Baker	6th inning
Leadoff HR (3)	1	June 6, 2008	at Oakland	Blanton	--
	2	June 7, 2008	at Oakland	Smith	--
	3	July 29, 2011	at Detroit	Porcello	--
RBI	1	Aug. 29, 2004	San Diego	Wells	groundout
Stolen Base	1	Sept. 7, 2004	at Chicago (NL)	Wuertz	2nd base
				C-Barrett	

PROFESSIONAL CAREER:

2004:

- Started seventh professional season with AAA Edmonton… Ranked second among Expos minor leaguers in batting... Also ranked second in PCL in on-base percentage (.428)… Named by Baseball America as one of Minor League Baseball's 12 breakout players… Had contract selected by Montreal, Aug. 27 and made **Major League debut** the same day… Singled in first plate appearance (Dennis Tankersley)… First MLB HR came off Mark Prior, Aug. 31 vs. Cubs.

2005:

- Played key utility role in first season with Angels, making starts at third base (26), shortstop (21) and second base (1)... Batted .349 (15/43) with RISP.
- Committed three errors Sept. 20 vs. Tex., first Angel with three in a game since Gary DiSarcina (8-21-99).
- Made 18 starts at shortstop during O. Cabrera injury (June 20-July 10).
- Collected a double in six-straight games, June 29-July 4.
- Appeared in same ML game with half-brother Cesar for first time, June 25 vs. LAD.
- Missed 46 games due to a sprained MCL of left knee (April 27-June 18)… Suffered injury during early BP, April 26 at NYY… Also missed first eight games in Sept. with deep bruise in right quadriceps.
- Named Angels outstanding rookie in Spring Training…Hit .344 (22/64) with 16 RBI and team-leading 18 runs scored.
- Made first Opening Day roster.

2006:

- Spent most of first half on disabled list (April 24-June 8) with a strained left hamstring.
- Switch-hitter batted .307 (82/267) from the left side as opposed to .247 (21/85) from the right side…Made starts at third base (78), shortstop (4) and second base (3)…Batted in leadoff spot in 18 of last 19 starts…Batted .319 (66/207) in #2 spot…Collected two hits in inning (6th), July 4 at Seattle – did it again, July 26 at Tampa Bay – 2nd inn.

2007:

- Had two trips to disabled list with right hamstring injuries (missed 38 games).
- One of Angels top performers down the stretch as he hit safely in 24 of last 31 games batting .354 (40/113)... Led Angels batting .406 (39/96) with RISP… Hit .351 at home (59/168) compared to .226 (38/168) on road.
- 2-run home run in 8th inning, Aug. 11 vs. Minnesota marked his fourth HR in span of 11 games…Hit first career grand slam in 6th inning, Aug. 10 vs. Minnesota (Scott Baker).

2008:

- Was Opening Day shortstop, however had season-ending surgery in mid-August... Diagnosed with a torn ulnar collateral ligament in his left thumb and underwent surgery Aug. 19... Originally suffered injury diving for a ball Aug. 1 at NYY and re-aggravated the injury diving for a ball on Aug. 13 vs. SEA... Placed on 15-day DL Aug. 15 (retro to Aug. 14)... Missed 61 games on two DL stints... Also on DL May 1-13 with a strained lower back.
- Hit safely in 32 of last 40 games (.321; 52-162) and ended campaign batting .269 (78-290) with 44 runs, 14 doubles, two triples, three home runs and 37 RBI in 79 games...
- Committed just four errors in 75 infield starts... Made starts at shortstop (50), second base (20), and third base (5)...
- Batted in third spot 14 times (Angels were 11-3)... Made 18 starts in leadoff spot... Collected game winning RBI with pinch-hit single in 11th inning July 10 at Texas... Marked first pinch-hit appearance of season and first PH-RBI of career... Collected game-winning walkoff RBI single June 1 vs. Toronto (off B.J. Ryan)... Tied career-high with four hits May 31 vs. Toronto (2nd time).
- Had 13-game hit streak (May 31 - June 14) to match career-high (2005)... Collected third home run of season June 7 at Oakland... Marked second straight game leading off with HR, third Angel in club history to accomplish feat (Rex Hudler, May 20-21, 1996 & Brian Downing, April 14-15, 1987) and first to do so from both sides of the plate in franchise annals.

2009:

- Established career-highs in every major offensive category - batting average (.300), runs (74), hits (116), HR (8) and RBI (65).
- Was Angels' top hitter in June batting .338 (22-65)... Hit .380 (19/50) batting right-handed and .288 (97-337) batted from the left side.
- Committed just four errors in 101 combined games at second base (68), third base (5) and shortstop (28).
- Hit in every spot in lineup this season with exception of #4 & #5 slots... Batted .302 (32-106) with RISP and is a career .327(136-416) hitter with RISP.
- Did not have a stint on the DL for first time as an Angel.

2010:

- Limited to 61 games on three D.L. stints (strained left forearm & right shoulder inflammation twice)...Placed on DL Aug. 22 for third time of season (right shoulder inflammation) and ninth time in career.
- Hit .298 (17-57) with RISP in 2010 and is a career .323 (153-473) hitter with RISP for his career... Batted in every slot except for 9th in 2010.
- Committed just two errors in 57 combined games at SS, 3B & 2B... Has committed just five errors in last 129 combined games at second base and shortstop.
- Homered in consecutive games, May 31 & June 1 (3rd time in career to homer in consecutive games).

2011:

- Spent seventh season with Angels and established career highs in several categories including games (122),
- hits (124) and doubles (35)... 35 doubles led team.
- Was Halos' primary leadoff batter making 89 starts atop lineup, hitting .283 in the spot.
- Led Halos batting .319 (76/238) on road (T5th in AL).
- Broke up Justin Verlander's no-hitter with RBI single with two outs in 8th, July 31 at Detroit (lone hit on day for Angels).

SWITCH-HITTERS (39)

Name	Pos.	Name	Pos.
Roberto Alomar	IF	Lee Mazzilli	OF/DH
Alan Ashby	C	Dave McKay	IF
Bobby Brown	OF	Brian McRae	OF
Domingo Cedeno	IF	Otis Nixon	OF
Dave Collins	OF	Ray Olmedo	IF
Felipe Crespo	IF	Tomas Perez	IF
Jose Cruz Jr.	OF	Geno Petralli	C/IF
Junior Felix	OF	Tony Phillips	OF
Tony Fernandez	IF	David Segui	IF/DH
Luis Figueroa	IF	Ruben Sierra	OF
Alfredo Griffin	IF	Brian Simmons	OF
John Hattig	IF	Omar Vizquel	IF
Dave Hollins	DH	Turner Ward	OF
Orlando Hudson	IF	Mitch Webster	OF
Cesar Izturis	IF	Devon White	OF
Bobby Kielty	OF	Mark Whiten	OF
Chris Latham	OF	Ted Wilborn	OF
Manny Lee	IF	Mookie Wilson	OF
Nelson Liriano	IF	Gregg Zaun	C
Felipe Lopez	IF		

JANSSEN, *CASEY*

Birthdate .... **September 17, 1981**
Opening Day Age **31**
Birthplace .... **Orange, CA**
Residence ....**Manhattan Beach, CA**
Bats/Throws .... **R/R**
Height/Weight **6-3/205**
Contract Status .... **signed thru 2013**
M.L. Service **6.063**

44
PITCHER

PERSONAL:

Robert Casey Janssen... Attended UCLA where he was 1st Team All-PAC 10 as a pitcher... Spent time as a DH and at first base at UCLA to take advantage of his hitting abilities... Majored in Sociology... Hit a home run in his first college at-bat... Off-season home is in Huntington Beach, California... Enjoys watching college football.

LAST SEASON:

- In his 7th season in the Majors, was his first season as the team closer, assuming the role on May 9... Posted a career high in strikeouts (67) and had a career low opponents average (.195).
- His .195 opponents average ranked 7th in the AL for pitchers with aminimum of 60 IP... His .172 average vs. left-handed hitters ranked 6th in the AL with a minimum of 100 at-bats.
- Converted 22 of 25 save opportunities and 22 of 24 after assuming closers role... After May 9 converted 15 consecutive saves and each of his last six... In his 22 saves did not allow a single run while issuing just two walks and 10 hits... Also faced the minimum batters in 13 of the 22.
- On the road allowed only six runs for a 1.86 ERA and a .186 opponents average... During the day allowed just two runs for a 0.86 ERA.
- Posted a 5.02 ERA vs. AL East opponents and a 0.51 vs. the rest of AL and NL.

CASEY JANSSEN

Bold – career high

Year	Club & League	W-L	ERA	G	GS	CG	ShO	SV	IP	H	R	ER	HR	HB	BB-IBB	SO	WP	BK	OBA
2004	Auburn (NYP)	3-1	3.48	10	10	0	0	0	51.2	47	21	20	2	2	10-0	45	2	0	.240
2005	Lansing (Mid)	4-0	1.37	7	7	0	0	0	46.0	27	8	7	0	1	4-0	38	1	0	.174
	Dunedin (FSL)	6-1	2.26	10	10	0	0	0	59.2	46	16	15	2	2	12-0	51	1	0	.216
	New Hampshire (East)	3-3	2.93	9	9	0	0	0	43.0	49	20	14	3	2	4-0	47	2	0	.288
2006	Syracuse (Int)	1-5	4.85	9	9	0	0	0	42.2	47	23	23	3	2	8-0	32	2	0	.287
	TORONTO (AL)	**6**-**10**	5.07	19	**17**	0	0	0	**94.0**	103	58	53	**12**	7	**21**-3	44	3	2	.275
2007	TORONTO (AL)	2-3	2.35	**70**	0	0	0	6	72.2	67	22	19	4	3	20-2	39	4	0	.247
2008	TORONTO (AL)						Injured – Did Not Play												
2009	Blue Jays (Gulf)	0-0	9.00	1	0	0	0	0	1.0	2	1	1	0	0	0-0	0	0	0	.400
	Dunedin (FSL)	0-0	0.69	4	3	0	0	0	13.0	6	1	1	0	0	2-0	10	0	0	.136
	New Hampshire (East)	1-0	2.40	6	1	0	0	0	15.0	12	6	4	0	0	5-0	12	1	1	.218
	Las Vegas (PCL)	0-0	5.40	7	0	0	0	0	6.2	4	4	4	0	0	1-0	7	0	0	.167
	TORONTO (AL)	2-4	5.85	21	5	0	0	1	40.0	59	29	26	5	2	14-1	24	1	0	.341
2010	TORONTO (AL)	5-2	3.67	56	0	0	0	0	68.2	74	29	28	8	4	**21**-1	63	4	0	.272
2011	Las Vegas (PCL)	0-0	0.00	1	0	0	0	0	2.0	1	0	0	0	0	0-0	3	0	0	.143
	TORONTO (AL)	**6**-0	2.26	55	0	0	0	2	55.2	47	14	14	2	2	14-1	53	2	0	.228
2012	TORONTO (AL)	1-1	2.54	62	0	0	0	**22**	63.2	44	18	18	7	3	11-1	**67**	2	1	.195
Minor Totals		18-10	2.87	64	49	0	0	0	280.2	241	100	89	10	9	46-0	245	9	1	.233
MAJOR TOTALS		22-20	3.60	283	22	0	0	31	394.2	394	170	158	38	21	101-9	290	15	3	.259

TRANSACTIONS

- Selected by the Toronto Blue Jays in the 4th round of the June 2004 First Year Player Draft
- On disabled list (right elbow contusion) from July 17-26, 2005
- On disabled list (labrum tear in right shoulder) for entire 2008 season
- On disabled list (right shoulder strain) from April 5-30, 2009; included rehabilitation assignment at Dunedin (A), April 27
- On disabled list (right shoulder strain) from June 17-August 13, 2009; included rehabilitation assignment at Gulf Coast Blue Jays (rookie) from July 13; July 17-23 at New Hampshire (AA) and Las Vegas (AAA) from July 26-August 12

GAME HIGHS

ML Debut	April 27, 2006 vs. BAL	**ER Allowed**	7 - June 17, 2006 at FLA
Innings Pitched:		**HR Allowed**	3 - July 5, 2006 at TEX
Starter	8.0 - May 17, 2006 at LAA	**Low Hit CG**	None
Reliever	3.0 - 3x, last Aug. 21, 2011 at OAK	**Last Win**	April 7, 2012 at CLE
Walks:		**Last Save**	Oct. 2, 2012 vs. MIN
Starter	4 - June 17, 2006 at FLA	**Last CG**	None
Reliever	3 - 2x, last May 7, 2011 vs. DET	**Last ShO**	None
Strikeouts:		**Last Start**	June 13, 2009 vs. FLA
Starter	6 - June 8, 2009 at TEX	**Last Relief App.**	Oct. 2, 2012 vs. MIN
Reliever	5 - Aug. 21, 2011 at OAK	**Longest Win Streak**	6G - May 21-Sept. 19, 2011
Hits Allowed	11 - 2x, last May 29, 2009 vs. BOS	**Longest Losing Streak**	4G - July 5-24, 2006
Runs Allowed	7 - June 17, 2006 at FLA	**Scoreless Innings Streak**	16.2 - July 26-Aug. 30, 2011

CAREER FIELDING

POSITION	PCT	G	PO	A	E	TC	DP
P	.945	283	41	45	5	91	1

MILESTONES

Category		Date	Opponent	Notes
Start	1	April 27, 2006	Baltimore	L, 4.0 IP, 3H, 2ER, 2HB, 3BB
Win	1	May 7, 2006	Los Angeles (AL)	7.1 IP, H, BB, 3K
Save	1	April 8, 2007	at Tampa Bay	2.0 IP, K

PROFESSIONAL CAREER:

2005:

- Selected as the Midwest League Pitcher of the Week after a pair of starts in which he allowed just five hits and no earned runs.
- Finished April 4-0 with a 1.53 ERA earning the nod as the Blue Jays Organizational Pitcher of the Month.
- Selected to participate in the Midwest League All-Star Game, but was promoted to Dunedin where he posted a 6-1 record with a 2.01 ERA in 10 starts.
- Named as a Blue Jays Minor League Star of the Month in June while with Dunedin.

2006:

- Made his **Major League debut** on April 27 vs. BAL, allowing 2 ER over 4.0 IP (loss).
- Recorded his 1st Major League win May 7 at LAA, allowing just one hit through 7.1 innings.
- Led all rookie starters allowing only 2.01 walks per nine innings... T-10th in wins by a rookie with six, 7th in starts (17), 8th in innings pitched (94), and 10th in batting avg. allowed (.275).

2007:

- Appeared in 70 games, to rank 2nd on the team and T-11th in the AL.
- Led all Blue Jays relievers with 72.2 IP and finished 2nd on the club with six saves... His 2.35 ERA was 3rd on the club, while his 24 holds were T-1st.
- April 8 at TB, worked 2.0 scoreless innings for his 1st career save... May 14 vs. BAL earned his 1st win of the season & 1st career as a reliever.

2008:

- Underwent surgery on March 18 to repair a tear in his labrum... Did not pitch in 2008.

2009:

- Began the season on the disabled rehabbing his shoulder... Was activated on April 30.
- May 29 collected his first win as a starter since June 30, 2006.
- Picked up his first save, Aug. 21 vs. LAA and first since Sept. 24, 2007.
- May 23 made his first appearance in the Majors since Sept. 24, 2007 and his first start since July 24, 2006 after missing the entire 2008 season.

2010:

- Recorded the win in three of the Jays first six games of the season becoming only the sixth pitcher in ML history to do so and first since Jose Melendez with SD in 1992.
- Won back to back games April 8 at TEX and April 9 at BAL becoming the first Blue Jays pitcher since Jesse Carlson Sept. 2 and 3, 2008.
- His five wins tied for the Club lead by a reliever (Scott Downs).

2011:

- At 6-0 became only the third Blue Jays pitcher and first since Dennis Lamp (11-0) and Tom Filer (7-0) in 1985 to win at-least six games in a season without a loss... Became the first Blue Jays pitcher to start a season at least 6-0 since John Frascatore in 1999 (went 7-0).
- His six wins were tied for the Club lead by a reliever with Shawn Camp and was T-3rd in the AL... Was 3rd on the Club with seven holds.
- Had a stretch of 16.2 scoreless innings pitched from July 26-Aug. 30 which was the longest by any Blue Jays pitcher and a new career high.
- Posted a record of 4-0 with a one save and a 1.61 ERA (28.0IP/5ER) in 27 games after the All-Star Break.
- Was optioned to Las Vegas (AAA) on April 8 and appeared in one game with the 51's pitching two scoreless innings... Was recalled on April 12 and spent the remainder of the season with the Blue Jays.

JEFFRESS, *JEREMY*

Birthdate	September 21, 1987
Opening Day Age	25
Birthplace	South Boston, VA
Residence	South Boston, VA
Bats/Throws	R/R
Height/Weight	6-0/194
Contract Status	signed thru 2013
M.L. Service	0.145

33

PITCHER

PERSONAL:

Jeremy Ross Jeffress... Participated in 2011 Royals FanFest... Graduated from Halifax County (Va.) High school, where he also played basketball... Named Baseball America's eighth-best high school prospect prior to his senior season at Halifax.

LAST SEASON:

- Spent most of his season with Omaha (AAA), but also made 13 relief appearances for the Royals.
- Allowed just one earned run over his first 11 outings (10.1 IP) despite 10 hits and nine walks, however allowed nine earned runs over his final two appearances (3.0 IP) on nine hits and four walks.
- Allowed runs in just three of 13 outings.
- Aug. 13 vs. OAK, fanned three in his one inning of work.
- With Omaha fanned 61 batters and allowed only 52 hits in 58 innings.

JEREMY JEFFRESS

Bold – career high

Year	Club & League	W-L	ERA	G	GS	CG	ShO	SV	IP	H	R	ER	HR	HB	BB-IBB	SO	WP	BK	OBA
2006	AZL (Ariz)	2-5	5.88	13	4	0	0	0	33.2	30	26	22	0	6	25-0	37	13	0	.227
2007	West Virginia (SAL)	9-5	3.13	18	18	0	0	0	86.1	62	43	30	8	7	44-0	95	13	5	.201
2008	Brevard County (FSL)	4-6	4.08	15	14	1	1	0	79.1	65	39	36	5	5	41-0	102	5	1	.226
	Huntsville (Sou)	2-1	5.52	4	4	0	0	0	14.2	17	9	9	2	2	11-0	13	0	1	.298
2009	Huntsville (Sou)	1-3	7.57	8	8	0	0	0	27.1	26	29	23	1	1	33-0	34	3	0	.255
	Brevard County (FSL)	2-1	2.18	6	5	1	0	0	33.0	16	13	8	2	3	22-0	36	5	0	.145
2010	Wisconsin (Mid)	0-0	0.00	5	0	0	0	0	8.0	0	0	0	0	1	3-0	14	0	0	.000
	Brevard County (FSL)	0-0	5.40	8	0	0	0	1	10.0	10	8	6	0	0	7-0	14	5	0	.244
	Huntsville (Sou)	1-1	1.26	11	0	0	0	3	14.1	8	3	2	0	1	2-0	15	1	0	.160
	MILWAUKEE (NL)	**1**-0	2.70	10	0	0	0	0	10.0	8	4	3	0	0	6-1	8	1	0	.229
2011	Omaha Storm (PCL)	2-3	7.13	16	3	0	0	3	24.0	27	20	19	5	1	18-1	24	4	0	.293
	Northwest Arkansas (TEX)	1-3	4.26	9	8	0	0	0	31.2	32	17	15	2	2	22-0	20	7	0	.271
	KANSAS CITY (AL)	**1-1**	4.70	**14**	0	0	0	**1**	**15.1**	12	8	8	**1**	0	11-0	**13**	1	0	.222
2012	Omaha Storm (PCL)	5-4	4.97	37	0	0	0	2	58.0	52	34	32	4	0	25-2	61	4	0	.246
	Northwest Arkansas (TEX)	0-0	0.00	1	0	0	0	1	1.1	0	0	0	0	0	1-0	3	0	0	.000
	KANSAS CITY (AL)	0-0	6.75	13	0	0	0	0	13.1	19	14	10	0	0	**13**-0	**13**	1	0	.317
Minor Totals		29-32	4.31	151	64	2	1	10	421.2	345	241	202	29	29	254-3	468	60	7	.225
AL TOTALS		1-1	5.65	27	0	0	0	1	28.2	31	22	18	1	0	24-0	26	2	0	.272
MAJOR TOTALS		2-1	4.89	37	0	0	0	1	38.2	39	26	21	1	0	30-1	34	3	0	.262

TRANSACTIONS

- Selected by the Milwaukee Brewers in the 1st round (16th overall) of the 2006 First Year Player Draft
- Traded to the Kansas City Royals along with OF Lorenzo Cain, SS Alcides Escobar and RHP Jake Odorizzi in exchange for SS Yuniesky Betancourt, RHP Zack Greinke and cash considerations on December 19, 2010
- Traded to the Toronto Blue Jays in exchange for cash considerations on November 8, 2012

GAME HIGHS

ML Debut	Sept. 1, 2010 at CIN
Innings Pitched:	
Starter	None
Reliever	2.0 - 5x, last Sept. 5, 2012 vs. TEX
Walks:	
Starter	None
Reliever	3 - 3x, last Sept. 23, 2012 vs. CLE
Strikeouts:	
Starter	None
Reliever	3 - Aug. 16, 2012 vs. OAK
Hits Allowed	6 - Sept. 30, 2012 at CLE
Runs Allowed	6 - Sept. 23, 2012 vs. CLE
ER Allowed	6 - Sept. 23, 2012 vs. CLE
HR Allowed	1 - April 3, 2011 vs. LAA
Low Hit CG	None
Last Win	April 5, 2011 vs. CWS
Last Save	April 13, 2011 at MIN
Last CG	None
Last ShO	None
Last Start	None
Last Relief App.	Sept. 30, 2012 at CLE
Longest Win Streak	1G - 2x, last April 5, 2011
Longest Losing Streak	1G - May 18, 2011
Scoreless Innings Streak	8.0 - Sept. 8-26, 2010

CAREER FIELDING

POSITION	PCT	G	PO	A	E	TC	DP
P	.917	37	4	7	1	12	0

MILESTONES

Category		Date	Opponent	Notes
Win	1	Sept. 24, 2010	Florida	as reliever - 2.0 IP, H, 2BB, 2K
Save	1	April 13, 2011	at Minnesota	2.0 IP, H, K

PROFESSIONAL CAREER:

2006:

- Following his first professional season in 2006 with the Arizona Brewers, named by Baseball America as the second-best prospect in the Arizona League.

2007:

- Suspended 50 games on August 30, 2007 for violating the MiLB Drug Treatment and Prevention Program.

2008:

- Named Brewers Minor League Pitcher of the Year, striking 155 in 94 innings.

2009:

- Suspended 100 games on June 29, 2009 for violating the Minor League Drug Treatment and Prevention Program.

2010:

- Was recalled by MIL on Sept. 1, 2010 and made his **Major League debut** that night, tossing a scoreless inning of relief at CIN.
- Appeared in 10 games, tossing an inning in eight...Allowed runs in just two outings.
- Selected to pitch in the 2010 AFL's Rising Stars Game and struck out a pair in a scoreless frame.

2011:

- Began the season in the Royals bullpen before being optioned to the minors on May 19 and then pitching at both Omaha and NW Arkansas the rest of the way.
- Following the campaign, pitched for the Surprise Saguaros in the Arizona Fall League... Struck out 15 with 8 walks in 11.0 innings in relief... Struck out the side in a scoreless inning in the Rising Stars Game.

PITCHERS, TOP DUOS BY WINS

38-2008	Roy Halladay (20) — A.J. Burnett (18)
37-1992	Jack Morris (21) — Juan Guzman (16)
36-1997	Roger Clemens (21) — Pat Hentgen (15)
35-2003	Roy Halladay (22) — Kelvim Escobar (13)
33-1982	Dave Stieb (17) — Jim Clancy (16)
33-1984	Doyle Alexander (17) — Dave Stieb (16)
33-1993	Pat Hentgen (19) — Juan Guzman (14)
33-1996	Pat Hentgen (20) — Erik Hanson (13)
32-1983	Dave Stieb (17) — Jim Clancy (15)
32-1987	Jimmy Key (17) — Jim Clancy (15)
32-1998	Roger Clemens (20) — Chris Carpenter (12) — Pat Hentgen (12)
31-1985	Doyle Alexander (17) — Jimmy Key (14) — Dave Stieb (14)
31-1990	Dave Stieb (18) — Jimmy Key (13) — Todd Stottlemyre (13)
31-1991	Jimmy Key (16) — Todd Stottlemyre (15) — David Wells (15)
31-1999	David Wells (17) — Kelvim Escobar (14)
31-2006	Roy Halladay (16) — Ted Lilly (15)
30-1989	Dave Stieb (17) — Jimmy Key (13)
30-2000	David Wells (20) — Chris Carpenter (10) — Frank Castillo (10) — Kelvim Escobar (10)
30-2009	Roy Halladay (17) — Ricky Romero (13)

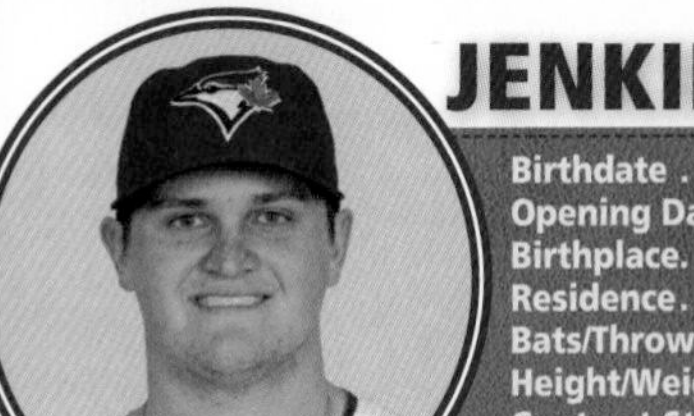

JENKINS, *CHAD*

Birthdate . . . . December 22, 1987
Opening Day Age 25
Birthplace. . . . . Chattanooga, TN
Residence. . . . . Canton, GA
Bats/Throws . . . . R/R
Height/Weight 6-3/226
Contract Status . . . . signed thru 2013
M.L. Service 0.060

PITCHER

PERSONAL:

Stephen Chad Jenkins... Attended Kennesaw State University... Graduated from Cherokee High School in Georigia where he was named Cherokee County Player-of-the Year... In 2009 was named both Atlantic Sun Conference Player of the Year and Atlantic Sun Conference All-Star SP going 8–1 with a 2.54 ERA, along with a 9.6 Ks/9in and a 1.03 WHIP that season.

LAST SEASON:

- In his first season in the Majors made 13 appearances, including three starts... Did not allow a run through his first five appearances covering seven innings… Allowed only two hits in those contests.
- Made10 appearances out of the bullpen prior to concluding the season in the rotation... In those 10 outings, posted a 0-1 record with a 4.91 ERA...In his three starts was 1-2 with a 3.95 ERA... Held opponents to a .229 average as a starter.
- Picked up his first Major League win in his last start on Oct. 2 vs. MIN... Allowed two earned runs over five innings in a 4-3 victory.
- In his Major League debut as a starter held the Rays to one run (Upton-HR) on two hits in five innings... Took the loss in a 3-0 defeat.
- In his 10 relief appearances pitched more than one inning in five of the 10 games, including a team high five innings of relief on Sept. 2 vs. TB.
- Overall opponents hit .260 with a .749 OPS... Left-handed batters were .283 with an .832 OPS... Right-handed batters were .238 with a .669 OPS.
- Made 20 starts for New Hampshire (AA) posting a 5-9 record with a 4.96 ERA… In his last three starts in AA, recorded a 1-0 record with a 2.21 ERA… Overall batters posted a .310 average in his 20 starts.

CHAD JENKINS

Bold – career high

Year	Club & League	W-L	ERA	G	GS	CG	ShO	SV	IP	H	R	ER	HR	HB	BB-IBB	SO	WP	BK	OBA
2010	Lansing (Mid)	5-4	3.63	13	13	1	0	0	79.1	87	35	32	5	1	13-0	64	3	0	.277
	Dunedin (FSL)	2-6	4.33	13	13	1	0	0	62.1	73	37	30	6	0	18-1	42	1	0	.281
2011	Dunedin (FSL)	4-5	3.07	11	11	0	0	0	67.1	71	33	23	3	0	14-1	44	2	0	.267
	New Hampshire (East)	5-7	4.13	16	16	1	0	0	100.1	93	48	46	8	2	27-0	74	9	0	.247
2012	New Hampshire (East)	5-9	4.96	20	20	0	0	0	114.1	145	67	63	17	5	31-0	57	5	0	.310
	TORONTO (AL)	1-3	4.50	13	3	0	0	0	32.0	32	16	16	5	1	11-1	16	0	0	.260
Minor Totals		21-31	4.12	73	73	3	0	0	423.2	469	220	194	39	8	103-2	281	20	0	.279

TRANSACTIONS

- Selected by the Toronto Blue Jays in the 1st round (20th overall) in the June 2009 First Year Player Draft

GAME HIGHS

ML Debut	Aug. 7, 2012 at TB	**ER Allowed**	4 - Aug. 25, 2012 at BAL
Innings Pitched:		**HR Allowed**	1 - 5x, last Oct. 2, 2012 vs. MIN
Starter	5.0 - 2x, last Oct. 2, 2012 vs. MIN	**Low Hit CG**	None
Reliever	5.0 - Sept. 2, 2012 vs. TB	**Last Win**	Oct. 2, 2012 vs. MIN
Walks:		**Last Save**	None
Starter	3 - Sept. 28, 2012 vs. NYY	**Last CG**	None
Reliever	2 - Aug. 25, 2012 at BAL	**Last ShO**	None
		Last Start	Oct. 2, 2012 vs. MIN
Strikeouts:		**Last Relief App.**	Sept. 14, 2012 vs. BOS
Starter	4 - Sept. 23, 2012 at TB	**Longest Win Streak**	1G - Oct. 2, 2012
Reliever	3 - Sept. 2, 2012 vs. TB	**Longest Losing Streak**	3G - Aug. 23-Sept. 28, 2012
Hits Allowed	7 - Sept. 2, 2012 vs. TB	**Scoreless Innings Streak**	7.0 - Aug. 7-18
Runs Allowed	4 - Aug. 25, 2012 at BAL		

CAREER FIELDING

POSITION	PCT	G	PO	A	E	TC	DP
P	.889	13	5	3	1	9	0

MILESTONES

Category		Date	Opponent	Notes
Start	1	Sept. 23, 2012	at Tampa Bay	loss - 5.0 IP, 2H, ER, HR, BB, 4K
Win	1	Oct. 2, 2012	Minnesota	as a starter - 5.0 IP, 5H, 2ER, HR, BB, 2K

PROFESSIONAL CAREER:

2010:

- In his first professional season, began at Lansing (Low-A) before being promoted to Dunedin (High-A) at the end of June for the balance of the season.
- Selected as a Midwest League All-Star.

2011:

- Began the season with Dunedin (High-A) before a promotion to New Hampshire (AA), where he would finish the season.
- Was promoted to New Hampshire (AA) in time for his June 11 start... Made 16 starts for the Fisher Cats, holding Eastern League opponents to a .247 average.

BLUE JAYS FIRST CHOICE IN JUNE DRAFT

Year	Player	Year	Player
1977	Tom Goffena-SS, #25	1995	Roy Halladay-RHP, #17
1978	Lloyd Moseby-OF, #2	1996	Billy Koch-RHP, #4
1979	Jay Schroeder-C, #3	1997	Vernon Wells-OF, #5
1980	Garry Harris-SS, #2	1998	Felipe Lopez-SS, #8
1981	Matt Williams-RHP, #5	1999	Alexis Rios-OF, #19
1982	Augie Schmidt-SS, #2	2000	Miguel Negron-OF, #18
1983	Matt Stark-C, #9	2001	Gabe Gross-OF, #15
1984	Dane Johnson-RHP, #46	2002	Russ Adams-SS, #14
1985	Greg David-OF, #25	2003	Aaron Hill-SS, #13
1986	Earl Sanders-RHP, #25	2004	David Purcey-LHP, #16
1987	Alex Sanchez-RHP, #17	2005	Ricky Romero-LHP, #6
1988	Ed Sprague-3B, #25	2006	Travis Snider-OF, #14
1989	Eddie Zosky-SS, #19	2007	Kevin Ahrens-INF, #16
1990	Steve Karsay-RHP, #22	2008	David Cooper-IB, #17
1991	Shawn Green-OF, #16	2009	Chad Jenkins-RHP, #20
1992	Shannon Stewart-OF, #19	2010	Deck McGuire-RHP, #11
1993	Chris Carpenter-RHP, #15	2011	Tyler Beede-RHP, #21
1994	Kevin Witt-INF, #28	2012	DJ Davis-OF, #17

JIMENEZ, A.J.

Birthdate .... May 1, 1990
Opening Day Age 22
Birthplace. .... San Juan, PR
Residence. .... Bayamon, PR
Bats/Throws .... R/R
Height/Weight 6-0/175
Contract Status .... signed thru 2013
M.L. Service 0.000

CATCHER

PERSONAL:

Antonio "A.J." Jimenez... Attended Academia Discipulos de Cristo High School (Bayamon, Puerto Rico)... Was a roommate of fellow Jays prospect Dickie Thon when playing together in Puerto Rico... Was an outfielder before being converted into a catcher... Caught RHP Stephen Strasburg of the Washington Nationals in the Arizona Fall League in 2009.

LAST SEASON:

- Caught 27 games for the Fisher Cats before having his season end prematurely... Had Tommy John surgery in late May.
- Opened the season with a season high three hit effort and ended with six multi-hit games.
- Threw out 55% of potential base stealers (12-22) and has now recorded a 48.8% total over the last three seasons (120-246).

A.J. JIMENEZ

Bold – career high

Year	Club & League	AVG	G	AB	R	H	2B	3B	HR	RBI	SH-SF	HP	BB-IBB	SO	SB-CS	SLG	OBP	OPS
2008	BlueJays (GCL)	.191	19	47	5	9	2	0	0	5	1-0	1	3-0	16	5-2	.234	.255	.489
2009	Lansing (Mid)	.263	80	278	30	73	15	1	3	31	5-3	1	7-0	72	5-2	.356	.280	.636
2010	Lansing (Mid)	.305	70	262	35	80	22	0	4	54	1-8	3	18-1	56	17-4	.435	.347	.782
	Dunedin (FSL)	.111	2	9	1	1	0	0	1	1	0-0	0	0-0	5	0-0	.444	.111	.555
2011	Dunedin (FSL)	.303	102	379	49	115	29	1	4	52	8-4	3	28-0	60	11-2	.417	.353	.770
2012	New Hampshire (East)	.257	27	105	14	27	4	1	2	10	1-1	1	5-0	14	2-3	.371	.295	.666
Minor Totals		.282	300	1080	134	305	72	3	14	153	16-16	9	61-1	223	40-13	.394	.322	.715

TRANSACTIONS

- Selected by the Toronto Blue Jays in the 9th round of the 2008 First Year Player Draft

PROFESSIONAL CAREER:

2008:

- Made his professional debut in June with the Gulf Coast Blue Jays.

2009:

- In his first full season, caught 72 games at Lansing (A).
- Hit his first professional home run on July 3.

2010:

- Was one of five catchers in the Blue Jays system to earn All-Star selections, along with Carlos Perez, Travis d'Arnaud, Brian Jeroloman and J.P. Arencibia.
- With runners on base batted .352 (43-122), and saw that rise to .376 with runners in scoring position (32-85).
- In 11 at-bats with the base loaded, collected seven hits, including two doubles and a grand slam on June 10, a career high six RBI day.
- Saw his first action in High-A for Dunedin, appearing in two games in September.

2011:

- Received the R. Howard Webster Award for Dunedin as the team MVP.
- Led the club with a .303 average and was 2nd on the club with 115 hits and 29 doubles.
- Earned the distinction as the best defensive catcher in the Florida State League as voted by FSL Managers in a Baseball America poll.
- Was named to the Florida State League Mid Season and Post Season All-Satr squads.
- Made only six errors in 98 games, while throwing out 44% of potential base stealers (38-86).
- Played in the Puerto Rican Winter League, posting a .189 average with one home run and eight RBI.

MOST HR BY BLUE JAYS' TOP DUO, ALL-TIME (TOP 5)

Year	HR	Players
1999	86	Carlos Delgado 44, Shawn Green 42
2010	85	Jose Bautista 54, Vernon Wells 31
1998	84	Jose Canseco 46, Carlos Delgado 38
2000	82	Carlos Delgado 41, Tony Batista 41
2003	75	Carlos Delgado 42, Vernon Wells 33
1987	75	George Bell 47, Jesse Barfield 28

JIMINEZ, *LUIS*

Birthdate . . . . **May 7, 1982**
Opening Day Age **30**
Birthplace. . . . . **Bobare, Edo. Lara, VZ**
Residence. . . . **Barquisimeto, Edo. Lara, VZ**
Bats/Throws . . . . **L/L**
Height/Weight **6-3/280**
Contract Status . . . . **signed thru 2013**
M.L. Service **0.030**

INFIELDER
NON-ROSTER

PERSONAL:

Luis Antonio Camacaro Jimenez (hee-MEN-ez)... Originally signed with Oakland as a non-drafted free agent on Jan. 18, 1999.

LAST SEASON:

- Saw action in 1,016 minor league games before making his Major League debut Sept. 4 vs. Boston... Appeared in 7 games with the Mariners... Made 4 starts at DH.
- Collected his first hit vs. OAK on Sept. 7, a single off A.J. Griffin in the 4th inning... Marked his only hit in 17 at-bats.
- Named the Tacoma Rainiers Offensive Player of the Year hitting .310 with 64 runs, 32 doubles, 2 triples, 20 HR, 81 RBI, 64 BB, .514 SLG, .907 OPS in 125 games.
- Hit .364 (36-99) with 19 runs scored, 9 doubles, 1 triple, 7 home runs and 23 RBI over 28 games in August... During the month, he led the PCL in on-base percentage (.462) and OPS (1.148), while ranking 2nd in slugging (.687) and total bases (68), T-2nd in extra-base hits (17), 5th in average (.364), T-5th in RBI (23) and home runs (7) and T-9th in hits (35).
- Reached base safely in 28 consecutive games, April 29-June 1, batting .382 with 22 runs scored, 8 doubles, 5 home runs and 24 RBI; was tied for the 10th-longest streak in the PCL this season.
- Named a Pacific Coast League Mid-Season All-Star after hitting .318 with 40 runs, 19 doubles, 1 triple, 13 home runs, 52 RBI, .942 OPS.
- Participated in the Triple-A Home Run Derby... Hit 11 home runs, including 6 in the 2nd round (most by any player in a round).

LUIS JIMENEZ

Bold – career high

Year	Club and League	AVG	G	AB	R	H	2B	3B	HR	RBI	SH-SF	HP	BB-IBB	SO	SB-CS	SLG	OBP	OPS
1999	Athletics (DSL)	.212	34	104	9	22	2	2	0	11	0-2	1	13-0	25	1-1	.269	.300	.569
2000	Athletics (DSL)	.285	59	214	45	61	7	4	5	37	1-0	2	39-2	45	3-4	.425	.400	.825
2001	AZL (Ariz)	.214	24	70	8	15	1	1	0	12	0-4	0	8-0	23	2-0	.257	.280	.537
2002	Bluefield (Appy)	.375	51	176	40	66	13	1	8	42	0-1	1	33-1	33	9-1	.597	.474	1.071
2003	Aberdeen (NYP)	.244	53	168	17	41	9	0	1	21	2-0	1	26-0	40	7-4	.315	.349	.664
2004	Columbus (SAL)	.288	110	392	62	113	24	1	20	75	1-3	3	51-2	104	6-2	.508	.372	.880
2005	New Britain Rock (East)	.278	116	431	61	120	29	1	16	69	0-0	2	45-2	104	3-2	.462	.349	.811
2006	Portland Sea (East)	.276	115	395	74	109	22	2	17	70	0-6	5	58-4	90	9-2	.471	.371	.842
2007	Pawtucket Red (Int)	.148	25	81	4	12	2	0	1	7	0-1	0	9-0	21	1-0	.210	.231	.441
	Bowie (East)	.328	90	320	57	105	18	0	22	79	0-5	0	41-6	71	1-1	.591	.399	.990
2008	Harrisburg (East)	.260	77	246	35	64	8	0	14	42	0-1	0	35-6	44	3-0	.463	.351	.814
	Columbus (Int)	.330	33	91	9	30	4	0	1	10	1-1	0	12-3	22	0-1	.407	.404	.811
2009	Nippon Ham (CNT)	.231	39	121	13	28	5	0	5	14	0-0	1	5-0	35	0-0	.397	.268	.665
2010								Did Not Play										
2011	Jackson (Sou)	.317	30	101	17	32	3	1	4	18	0-1	0	18-2	17	2-0	.485	.417	.902
	Tacoma (PCL)	.285	74	284	51	81	12	1	12	57	0-3	1	39-2	55	2-1	.461	.370	.831
2012	Tacoma (PCL)	.310	125	471	64	146	32	2	20	81	0-0	1	64-2	97	3-0	.514	.394	.908
	SEATTLE (AL)	.059	7	17	0	1	0	0	0	0	0-0	0	1-0	4	0-0	.059	.111	.170
Minor Totals		.287	1016	3544	553	1017	186	16	141	631	5-28	17	491-32	791	52-19	.468	.374	.842

TRANSACTIONS

- Signed by the Oakland Athletics on January 18, 1999
- Signed by the Baltimore Orioles on October 29, 2001
- Selected by the Los Angeles Dodgers in the Rule 5 Draft on December 15, 2003
- Signed by the Minnesota Twins on December 17, 2004
- Signed by the Boston Red Sox on February 1, 2006
- Signed by the Baltimore Orioles on May 15, 2007
- Signed by the Washington Nationals on November 17, 2007
- Signed by the Seattle Mariners on January 6, 2011
- Signed by the Toronto Blue Jays on December 11, 2012

GAME HIGHS

ML Debut	Sept. 4, 2012 vs. BOS	**RBI**	None
Runs	None	**Stolen Bases**	None
Hits	1 - Sept. 7, 2012 vs. OAK	**Last ML Home Run**	None
Doubles	None	**Longest Hitting Streak**	1G - Sept. 7, 2012
Home Runs	None	**Longest Hitless Streak**	15AB - Sept. 7-23, 2012

BIOGRAPHIES | LAST SEASON | HISTORY | RECORDS | OPPONENTS | PLAYER DEV. | MEDIA & MISC.

MILESTONES

Category		Date	Opponent	Pitcher	Notes
Hit	1	Sept. 7, 2012	Oakland	Griffin	single

PROFESSIONAL CAREER:

2002:

- Signed with Baltimore as a minor league free agent on Oct. 29, 2001… Paced Appalachian League with .375 batting average and .597 slugging percentage…named Appalachian League All-Star.

2004:

- Selected by Los Angeles (NL) in the minor league portion of the Rule 5 draft on Dec. 14, 2003… Hit 20 home runs for Columbus (A) in the South Atlantic League.

2005:

- Signed with Minnesota as a minor league free agent on Dec. 17, 2004… In only season in Twins chain, hit .306 with 15 homers against opposing right-handed pitchers.

2006:

- Tailed 22 doubles, team-best 17 homers, 70 RBI and a career-high 58 walks for AA Portland of the Eastern League… Played for Lara in the Venezuelan Winter League (.306, 4 HR, 24 RBI).

2007:

- Hit 23 home runs at two levels in Boston organization… 22 homers with Bowie ranked 5th in the Eastern League… Played for Lara in the Venezuelan Winter League (.273, 2 HR, 8 RBI).

2008:

- Signed with Washington as a minor league free agent on Nov. 28, 2007… Split season between Harrisburg and Columbus… Played for Lara in the Venezuelan Winter League (.329, 6 HR, 31 RBI).

2009:

- Appeared in 39 games with the Nippon Ham Fighters in the Japan Pacific League… Played for Lara in the Venezuelan Winter League (.326, 9 HR, 43 RBI).

2010:

- Played for Lara in the Venezuelan Winter League… Led the league in home runs (12) and walks (57), while also ranking among the league leaders in RBI (40, 2nd), on-base percentage (.475, 2nd) runs scored (36, 4th) and total bases (102, T4th)… Did not play during the regular minor league season.

2011:

- Combined to bat .294 (113-385) with 16 home runs and 75 RBI in 104 games with AA Jackson (30 G) and AAA Tacoma (74 G).
- Opened the season on the Jackson disabled list with a right groin strain (April 7-20).
- Batted .317 (32x101) with four homers and 18 RBI in 30 games with the Generals… Promoted to Tacoma May 12-July 30.
- Played for Lara in the Venezuelan Winter League… Led the VWL in games played (63), T3rd in home runs (10), 5th in total bases (108) and 9th in batting average (.300)…won the DWL All-Star Game home run derby.

ALL-TIME LONGEST HOMERLESS STRETCHES

ORGANIZED BY AT BATS

ALFREDO GRIFFIN

DATES OF HOME RUNS	PITCHER	SPAN OF DROUGHT
July 30, 1980 vs. Oakland	Langford	255 Games, 956 At Bats
July 26, 1982 at Boston	Eckersly	

BOB BAILOR

DATES OF HOME RUNS	PITCHER	SPAN OF DROUGHT
May 7, 1978 at Seattle	Pole	228 Games, 845 At Bats
Aug. 22, 1979 at Seattle	Honeycutt	

OTIS NIXON

DATES OF HOME RUNS	PITCHER	SPAN OF DROUGHT
Apr. 16, 1996 vs. Detroit	Gohr	205 Games, 806 At Bats
Aug. 1, 1997 at Detroit	Moehler	

MANNY LEE

DATES OF HOME RUNS	PITCHER	SPAN OF DROUGHT
June 17, 1990 at New York	Lapointe	245 Games, 804 At Bats
May 6, 1992 at Seattle	Acker	

GARTH IORG

DATES OF HOME RUNS	PITCHER	SPAN OF DROUGHT
Aug. 2, 1980 vs. California	Laroche	240 Games, 771 At Bats
Sept. 28, 1982 vs. Minnesota	Viola	

JOHNSON, *JOSH*

- **Birthdate** .... January 31, 1984
- **Opening Day Age** 29
- **Birthplace** .... Minneapolis, MN
- **Residence** .... Las Vegas, NV
- **Bats/Throws** .... L/R
- **Height/Weight** 6-7/251
- **Contract Status** .... signed thru 2013
- **M.L. Service** 7.026

55

PITCHER

PERSONAL:

Joshua Michael Johnson... Is married with two children... Graduated from Jenks High School (OK) in 2002... Named to All-State team as a senior... Also played basketball.

LAST SEASON:

- Returned from injury-shortened 2011 to make 31 starts and pitch 191.1 innings, both of which were second-highest totals in career (33 starts and 209.0 IP in 2009).
- Did not record his first win of season until May 15 against PIT... In seven starts prior, had gone 0-3 with a 5.87 ERA (38.1 IP/25 ER), and opponents were batting .329... Over a nine-start span beginning with first win, went 5-2 with a 2.45 ERA (58.2/16), and held opponents to a .242 average.
- Won 50th career game on May 20 at CLE, and lowered career ERA to 3.10 in the process... Only active starting pitchers at time who had a lower ERA when winning 50th game were Clayton Kershaw (2.83), Tim Lincecum (2.91) and Barry Zito (3.04).
- Had best month of season in June, despite settling for a 2-2 record... Owned a 1.87 ERA (33.2/7) in five starts, which was 5th-lowest mark in National League for month, behind R.A. Dickey (0.93), Zack Greinke (1.70), Johnny Cueto (1.72) and Kyle Lohse (1.80)... Opponents batting average (.205) was tied with Matt Cain for fifth-lowest in NL in June, behind Dickey (.131), Johan Santana (.180), Lohse (.185) and Greinke (.203).
- Closed out season with 1-3 record in Sept., despite a 2.91 ERA (34.0IP/11ER) in five starts... Allowed three or fewer runs in each start and limited opponents to five-or-fewer hits.
- Miami scored just 2.92 runs per 9.0 innings of support, marking the lowest run support average in Majors (min. 30 starts)... Also marked lowest in franchise history for a pitcher who made at least 30 starts, breaking Anibal Sanchez's record of 3.16 in 2011.
- Allowed just 14 home runs, which tied Aaron Harang (31 GS), Felix Hernandez (33 GS) and Edinson Volquez (31 GS) for the third-fewest in the Majors among pitchers with at least 30 starts, behind Gio Gonzalez (nine in 32 GS) and Lucas Harrell (13 in 32 GS).
- Finished first-half of season with a 5-5 record and a 4.06 ERA (102.0/46) in 17 starts, with 85 strikeouts to 34 walks (four intentional)... For his career, is 33-18, 2.71(518.2/156) in 87 first-half appearances (80 starts)... Went 3-9 with a 3.53 ERA (89.1/35) in 14 starts in second-half, notching 80 strikeouts to 31 walks (three intentional)... Overall, is 23-19, 3.73 (398.0/165) in 67 career appearances (64 starts) following All-Star break.

JOSH JOHNSON

Bold – career high

Year	Club & League	W-L	ERA	G	GS	CG	ShO	SV	IP	H	R	ER	HR	HB	BB-IBB	SO	WP	BK	OBA
2002	Marlins (GCL)	2-0	0.60	4	3	0	0	0	15.0	8	3	1	0	2	3-0	11	0	0	.154
	Jamestown (NYP)	0-2	12.38	2	2	0	0	0	8.0	15	15	11	0	1	7-0	5	0	0	.385
2003	Greensboro (SAL)	4-7	3.61	17	17	0	0	0	82.1	69	44	33	5	9	29-0	59	2	0	.223
2004	Jupiter (FSL)	5-12	3.38	23	22	1	0	0	114.1	124	63	43	4	3	47-1	103	12	0	.285
2005	Carolina (Sou)	12-4	3.87	26	26	1	0	0	139.2	139	67	60	4	4	50-4	113	7	1	.261
	FLORIDA (NL)	0-0	3.65	4	1	0	0	0	12.1	11	5	5	0	1	10-0	10	0	0	.256
2006	FLORIDA (NL)	12-7	3.10	31	24	0	0	0	157.0	136	63	54	**14**	4	**68**-6	133	3	1	.236
2007	Carolina (Sou)	0-0	1.74	2	2	0	0	0	10.1	8	2	2	0	0	5-0	9	0	0	.216
	Jupiter (FSL)	0-0	0.79	3	3	0	0	0	11.1	9	2	1	0	0	0-0	13	1	0	.220
	FLORIDA (NL)	0-3	7.47	4	4	0	0	0	15.2	26	17	13	1	0	12-3	14	1	0	.388
2008	Greensboro (SAL)	0-1	3.60	1	1	0	0	0	5.0	8	2	2	0	0	0-0	7	0	0	.364
	Jupiter (FSL)	0-0	5.06	1	1	0	0	0	5.1	6	3	3	1	0	2-0	2	0	0	.273
	Carolina (Sou)	1-1	3.32	3	3	0	0	0	19.0	22	9	7	0	0	3-1	14	0	0	.289
	FLORIDA (NL)	7-1	3.61	14	14	1	0	0	87.1	91	36	35	7	1	27-1	77	4	0	.275
2009	FLORIDA (NL)	**15**-5	3.23	**33**	**33**	**2**	0	0	**209.0**	184	77	75	**14**	6	58-6	**191**	10	0	.237
2010	FLORIDA (NL)	11-6	2.30	28	28	1	0	0	183.2	155	51	47	7	5	48-2	186	4	0	.229
2011	FLORIDA (NL)	3-1	1.64	9	9	0	0	0	60.1	39	13	11	2	1	20-2	56	2	1	.185
2012	MIAMI (NL)	8-**14**	3.81	31	31	0	0	0	191.1	180	84	81	**14**	4	65-7	165	5	0	.252
Minor Totals		24-27	3.58	82	80	2	0	0	410.1	408	210	163	14	19	146-6	336	22	1	.261
MAJOR TOTALS		56-37	3.15	154	144	4	0	0	916.2	822	346	321	59	22	308-27	832	29	2	.242

TRANSACTIONS

- Selected by the Florida Marlins in the 4th round of the 2002 First Year Player Draft
- On disabled list (ulnar nerve irritation in right arm) from March 23-June 18, 2007
- On disabled list (right forearm stiffness) from July 5-remainder of season, 2007
- On disabled list (recovery from Tommy John) from March 21-July 10, 2008
- On disabled list (right shoulder inflammation) from May 21-remainder of season, 2011
- Traded to the Toronto Blue Jays along with IF Emilio Bonifacio, C John Buck, LHP Mark Buehrle, SS Jose Reyes and cash considerations in exchange for RHP Anthony DeSclafani, OF Jake Marisnick, LHP Justin Nicolino, RHP Henderson Alvarez, SS Yunel Escobar, SS Adeiny Hechavarria and C Jeff Mathis on November 19, 2012

GAME HIGHS

ML Debut	Sept. 10, 2005 at PHI	**Runs Allowed**	8 - June 18, 2007 at CWS
Innings Pitched:		**ER Allowed**	7 - June 23, 2007 vs. MIN
Starter	9.0 - 4x, last April 26, 2010 vs. SD	**HR Allowed**	3 - July 2, 2006 vs. BOS
Reliever	4.0 - Sept. 24, 2005 at ATL	**Low Hit CG**	3 - April 26, 2010 vs. SD
Walks:		**Last Win**	Sept. 6, 2012 vs. MIL
Starter	6 - 2x, last July 29, 2012 vs. SD	**Last Save**	None
Reliever	3 - Sept. 16, 2005 vs. PHI	**Last CG**	April 26, 2010 vs. SD
Strikeouts:		**Last ShO**	None
Starter	10 - May 3, 2010 at CLE	**Last Start**	Sept. 26, 2012 at ATL
Reliever	3 - April 3, 2006 at HOU	**Last Relief App.**	April 28, 2006 vs. COL
Hits Allowed	12 - 2x, last Sept. 4, 2010 vs. ATL	**Longest Win Streak**	6G - Sept. 13, 2008-May 14, 2009
		Longest Losing Streak	4G - 2x, last Aug. 9-25, 2012
		Scoreless Innings Streak	20.0 - May 13-29, 2010

CAREER FIELDING

POSITION	PCT	G	PO	A	E	TC	DP
P	.977	154	85	129	5	219	11

MILESTONES

Category		Date	Opponent	Notes
Start	1	Sept. 30, 2005	Atlanta	no decision - 5.1 IP, 4H, 2ER, 4BB, 7K
Win	1	April 18, 2006	at Cincinnati	as a reliever - 3.0 IP, 2BB
10+ strikeout games (6)				
	6	Sept. 4, 2010	Atlanta	12 strikeouts

PROFESSIONAL CAREER:

2005:

- Made ML debut in relief on September 10, 2005 at Philadelphia.

2006:

- Began season in bullpen, going 1-2 with a 3.86 ERA in seven appearances before breaking into rotation full-time on May 4... Went 11-5 with a 3.03 ERA in 24 starts.
- Was one of four Marlins' rookies to win 10 games, becoming first quartet of rookie 10-game winners in ML history (Scott Olsen, 12; Ricky Nolasco, 11; Anibal Sanchez, 10)... Earned first ML win on April 18 at Cincinnati, with 3.0 scoreless innings of relief in a 12-6 victory.
- Named NL Rookie of the Month twice in 2006... In May, went 3-1 with a 1.96 ERA in six starts; in June (co-winner, along with former teammate Dan Uggla), went 3-1 with a 1.78 ERA in four starts.
- Was leading NL in ERA at end of July (2.52), the first rookie to lead NL in ERA at end of July since Mark Gardner with Montreal in 1990, and just third NL rookie ever to enter August leading league in ERA (also Lou Fette, Boston in 1937).

2007:

- Made four Major League starts in 2007 before having season-ending Tommy John surgery on August 3.

2008:

- Began season on DL recovering from Tommy John surgery; procedure was performed on August 3, 2007, by Dr. James Andrews.
- Started rehab assignment on June 14, less than one year after surgery, posting a 1-2 record and 3.68 ERA (29.1IP/12ER) in five rehab starts prior to being activated from 60-day DL on July 10; made first start of 2008 on July 10 at Los Angeles-NL
- Tossed first career complete game on August 27 at Turner Field.

ERA LEADERS FROM 2010-2012 – MLB

Clayton Kersshaw, LAD	2.56
Jered Weaver, LAA	2.73
Justin Verlander, DET	2.79
Josh Johnson, MIA	**2.87**
Cliff Lee, PHI	2.89

2009:

- His .750 winning percentage in was highest in Marlins history among pitchers with at least 10 wins in one season.
- Earned NL Player of the Week honours on April 14 after going 2-0 with a 0.57 ERA and one complete game in first two starts. Was first POW honour of career.
- Named to NL All-Star team, marking first All-Star selection (did not play).
- Posted a .818 winning percentage through first 20 starts (9-2) to set a Club record... Previous high was .733 by Dontrelle Willis in 2003 and Carl Pavano in 2004 (both 11–4).
- Earned win on August 10 at Philadelphia to improve career record to 30-13; at the time, only four other active pitchers reached 30 career wins with as few as 13 losses: Tim Hudson (30-8), Roy Oswalt (30-9), Tim Lincecum (30-11) and Jon Lester (30-12).
- Hit third home run of season on August 4 at Washington, tying Club record for home runs by a pitcher, also done by Dontrelle Willis (2006) and Alex Fernandez (1999).

2010:

- Recorded lowest ERA (2.30) in National League in 2010, and led Club in strikeouts, was second in innings pitched, third in starts and fourth in wins.
- Missed final three weeks of season with a strained muscle in his back, but was not placed on DL.
- Led NL in home ERA (1.57) and held opponents to 10th-lowest average against (.229).
- Named to second consecutive NL All-Star team after posting lowest first-half ERA in Club history (1.70)... Went 2.0 innings in Midsummer Classic, allowing no hits while striking out two.
- His 23 earned runs allowed were fewest among Marlins' starters with 15-or-more first-half starts in Club history.
- In 13 starts after May 8, went 7-2 with a 0.79 ERA (91.1/8), and did not allow more than two runs in any start during span... Held opponents to zero or one run 12 times during stretch... Was first pitcher since Greg Maddux in 1995 to go 13 consecutive starts without allowing more than two runs.
- Earned NL Pitcher of the Month honours in June after going 3-1 with a 1.18 ERA (38.0IP/5ER) in five starts... Issued just six walks compared to 38 strikeouts.
- Held opponents to a .203 average against in first half, lowest among Marlins' starters in franchise history... Previous mark was .205, by Al Leiter in 1996.
- On April 26 vs. San Diego, struck out 12 batters in a complete-game win while going 3-4 with three RBI as a batter... Only three other pitchers had at least three hits and three-or-more RBI at plate while striking out at least 12 opposing batters in same game: Dazzy Vance did it for 1925 Brooklyn Dodgers, as did J.R. Richard for 1976 Astros and Steve Carlton for 1977 Phillies (Elias Sports Bureau).
- Owned a 1.62 ERA over first 19 starts, becoming only sixth pitcher in division era (since 1969) to have an ERA that low in first 19 starts of a season: Vida Blue in 1971 (1.37), Gaylord Perry in 1974 (1.45), Greg Maddux in 1998 (1.54), Pedro Martinez in 2000 (1.42) and Roger Clemens in 2005, with a mark of 1.47 (Elias Sports Bureau).
- After allowing one run in 8.0 innings on June 20 vs. TB, became third pitcher over last 100 seasons to have eight straight starts of at least 6.0 IP and allow no more than one run... Other two were Bob Gibson in 1968 (11 in a row) and J.R. Richard in 1979 (8).

2011:

- Made just nine starts in 2011 due to right shoulder inflammation.
- Since 1913, when earned runs were first officially compiled, posted fourth-lowest ERA (0.88; 41.0 IP/4 ER) in Major League history through end of April (min. 40.0 IP)... Was preceded by Fernando Valenzuela (0.20 ERA; 45.0/1) in 1981 and 1985 (0.21 ERA; 42.0/1), and Juan Marichal (0.86 ERA; 42.0/4) in 1965.

MOST WINS vs LOSSES BY A PITCHER

(10 OR MORE)

+15	Jack Morris	1992	21-6	+11	Doyle Alexander	1984	17-6
	Roy Halladay	2003	22-7		Dennis Lamp	1985	11-0
+14	Roger Clemens	1997	21-7		Juan Guzman	1992	16-5
	Roger Clemens	1998	20-6		Juan Guzman	1993	14-3
+12	Dave Stieb	1990	18-6		Roy Halladay	2006	16-5
	David Wells	2000	20-8	+10	Pat Hentgen	1993	19-9
	Roy Halladay	2002	19-7		Pat Hentgen	1996	20-10

LANGERHANS, *RYAN*

Birthdate . . . . .February 20, 1980
Opening Day Age 33
Birthplace. . . . . San Antonio, TX
Residence. . . . . .Leander, TX
Bats/Throws . . . . L/L
Height/Weight 6-3/220
Contract Status . . . . signed thru 2013
M.L. Service 5.136

17

OUTFIELDER

NON-ROSTER

PERSONAL:

Ryan David Langerhans (LAN-ger-hans)... Married with one child... Is a 1998 graduate of Round Rock (TX) High… Played for father, John, who was inducted to the Texas High School Baseball Coaches Hall of Fame in Feb. 2007… Father, a 1B, reached Double-A level in Cleveland organization in the 1970's… Earned Class 5A All-State honours by the Texas High School Baseball Coaches Association as a junior in '97 (others on the 5A squad: Josh Beckett, Vernon Wells)… Went 11-1 with a 1.45 ERA and batted .427 with 36 RBI… Led Round Rock High to 5A State Championship… Earned Honorable Mention accolades on the 1998 USA Today All-USA baseball team.

LAST SEASON:

- Appeared in two games for the Angels last season, striking out in his only at-bat.
- In 96 games for Salt Lake of the PCL (AAA), recorded 38 extra-base hits including 11 home runs... Walked 63 times in just 336 at-bats.
- Spent a month on the disabled list (May 22-June 23) with a seperated shoulder.

RYAN LANGERHANS

Bold – career high

Year	Club and League	AVG	G	AB	R	H	2B	3B	HR	RBI	SH-SF	HP	BB-IBB	SO	SB-CS	SLG	OBP	OPS
1998	GCL (GCL)	.277	43	148	15	41	10	4	2	19	0-1	0	19-1	38	2-5	.439	.357	.796
1999	Macon (SAL)	.268	121	448	66	120	30	1	9	49	2-2	7	52-2	99	19-11	.400	.352	.752
2000	Myrtle Beach (Caro)	.212	116	392	55	83	14	7	6	37	4-0	9	32-1	104	25-11	.329	.286	.615
2001	Myrtle Beach (Caro)	.287	125	450	66	129	30	3	7	48	2-0	8	55-3	104	22-13	.413	.374	.787
2002	Greenville (Sou)	.251	109	391	57	98	23	2	9	62	4-5	6	68-3	83	10-5	.389	.366	.755
	ATLANTA (NL)	.000	1	1	0	0	0	0	0	0	0-0	0	0-0	0	0-0	.000	.000	.000
2003	Greenville (Sou)	.253	94	336	42	85	23	2	6	38	2-0	3	46-3	85	10-10	.387	.348	.735
	Richmond (Int)	.280	38	132	13	37	10	2	4	11	1-1	1	11-1	29	2-1	.477	.338	.815
	ATLANTA (NL)	.267	16	15	2	4	0	0	0	0	0-0	0	0-0	6	0-0	.267	.267	.534
2004	Richmond (Int)	.298	135	456	103	136	34	3	20	72	4-2	6	70-3	113	5-9	.518	.397	.915
2005	ATLANTA (NL)	.267	128	326	48	87	22	3	8	42	2-3	5	37-3	75	0-2	.426	.348	.774
2006	ATLANTA (NL)	.241	131	315	46	76	16	3	7	28	0-1	3	50-8	91	1-2	.378	.350	.728
2007	ATLANTA (NL)	.068	20	44	3	3	1	0	0	1	0-1	1	6-1	16	0-1	.091	.192	.283
	OAKLAND (AL)	.000	2	4	0	0	0	0	0	0	0-0	0	1-0	2	0-0	.000	.200	.200
	Columbus (Int)	.275	14	51	11	14	3	0	1	2	2-0	0	6-0	15	1-0	.392	.351	.743
	WASHINGTON (NL)	.198	103	162	24	32	6	2	6	22	1-1	1	22-1	63	3-0	.370	.296	.666
2008	Columbus (Int)	.310	62	213	40	66	16	2	3	31	1-2	1	40-4	57	12-3	.446	.418	.864
	WASHINGTON (NL)	.234	73	111	17	26	5	2	3	12	2-0	1	25-1	31	2-0	.396	.380	.776
2009	Syracuse (Int)	.278	64	205	34	57	16	0	9	40	2-3	2	30-2	50	7-6	.488	.371	.859
	SEATTLE (AL)	.218	38	101	12	22	6	1	3	10	3-3	1	14-1	28	0-1	.386	.311	.697
2010	Tacoma (PCL)	.282	12	39	8	11	5	0	0	3	2-0	0	7-0	11	3-1	.410	.391	.801
	SEATTLE (AL)	.196	60	107	16	21	2	1	3	4	1-0	0	24-1	51	4-1	.318	.344	.662
2011	Tacoma (PCL)	.313	57	214	46	67	10	0	16	37	0-2	2	37-1	63	3-6	.584	.416	1.000
	Reno (PCL)	.308	38	130	23	40	10	2	6	23	0-1	1	39-2	31	8-1	.554	.468	1.022
	SEATTLE (AL)	.173	19	52	6	9	0	0	3	6	1-0	0	11-0	22	0-1	.346	.317	.663
2012	Salt Lake (PCL)	.250	96	336	59	84	21	6	11	54	0-1	1	63-2	113	6-6	.446	.369	.815
	LOS ANGELES (AL)	.000	2	1	0	0	0	0	0	0	1-0	0	0-0	1	0-0	.000	.000	.000
Minor Totals		.271	1124	3941	638	1068	255	34	109	526	26-20	47	575-28	995	135-88	.436	.369	.805
AL TOTALS		.196	121	265	34	52	8	2	9	20	6-3	1	50-2	104	4-3	.343	.323	.666
NL TOTALS		.234	472	974	140	228	50	10	24	105	11-5	11	140-14	282	6-5	.380	.335	.715
MAJOR TOTALS		.226	593	1239	174	280	58	12	33	125	11-9	12	190-16	386	10-8	.372	.332	.704

DIVISION SERIES RECORD

Year	Club and League	AVG	G	AB	R	H	2B	3B	HR	RBI	SH-SF	HP	BB-IBB	SO	SB-CS
2005	ATLANTA	.333	4	12	1	4	1	0	0	0	0-0	1	3-1	3	1-0

HOME RUN BREAKDOWN

			ONE GAME									
Total	H	A	2	3	4	GS	LO	XN	IP	PH	RHP	LHP
33	13	20	2	0	0	1	0	4	0	4	24	9

TRANSACTIONS

- Selected by the Atlanta Braves in the 3rd round of the 1998 First Year Player Draft
- Traded to the Oakland Athletics as part of a conditional deal on April 29, 2007
- Traded to the Washington Nationals in exchange for OF Chris Snelling on May 2, 2007
- Traded to the Seattle Mariners in exchange for IF/OF Mike Morse on June 28, 2009
- Traded to the Arizona Diamondbacks in exchange for cash considerations on July 29, 2011
- Signed by the Los Angeles Angels of Anaheim on December 23, 2011
- Signed by the Toronto Blue Jays on December 18, 2012

GAME HIGHS

ML Debut	April 28, 2002 vs. HOU	**RBI**	6 - May 8, 2005 vs. HOU
Runs	3 - 2x, last July 2, 2006 vs. BAL	**Stolen Bases**	1 - 10x, last July 18, 2010 at LAA
Hits	3 - 7x, last Aug. 6, 2010 vs. KC	**Last ML Home Run**	April 12, 2011 vs. TOR
Doubles	2 - 4x, last July 3, 2009 at BOS	**Longest Hitting Streak**	7G - April 3-10, 2006
Home Runs	2 - 2x, last May 11, 2005 at COL	**Longest Hitless Streak**	29AB - April 11-28, 2007

CAREER FIELDING

POSITION	PCT	G	PO	A	E	TC	DP
1B	1.000	8	36	2	0	38	5
OF	.994	478	787	15	5	807	2

MILESTONES

Category		Date	Opponent	Pitcher	Notes
Hit	1	Sept. 5, 2003	Pittsburgh	Meadows	single
Home Run	1	April 18, 2005	at Houston	Wheeler	1R
Multi-Homer Game (2)					
	1	May 8, 2005	Houston	Astacio, Duckworth	2R, 2R
	2	May 11, 2005	at Colorado	Acevedo, Tsao	1R, 1R
Grand Slam (1)	1	May 27, 2007	at St. Louis	Flores	8th inning
Pinch Hit HR (4)	1	Aug. 25, 2006	Washington	Rivera	2R, 9th inning
	2	Aug. 12, 2008	New York (NL)	Santana	1R, 7th inning
	3	Sept. 6, 2008	at Atlanta	Gonzalez	1R, 10th inning
	4	June 15, 2010	at St. Louis	Franklin	1R, 9th inning
Extra-Inning HR (4)					
	1	April 18, 2005	at Houston	Wheeler	1st career HR, 12th inning
	2	Sept. 6, 2008	at Atlanta	Gonzalez	1R, 10th inning
	3	Aug. 7, 2009	Tampa Bay	Howell	2R, 11th inning
	4	Aug. 25, 2009	Oakland	Breslow	2R, 10th inning
Walk-off HR (2)	1	Aug. 7, 2009	Tampa Bay	Howell	2R, 11th inning
	2	Aug. 25, 2009	Oakland	Breslow	2R, 10th inning
RBI	1	April 18, 2005	at Houston	Wheeler	HR, 1st career, 1R
Stolen Base	1	Aug. 3, 2006	at Pittsburgh	Chacon C-Cota	2nd base

PROFESSIONAL CAREER:

2002:

- Made his Major League debut on April 28, 2002 vs. HOU.
- On DL May 23-June 17 due to surgery to repair a torn meniscus in his left knee.
- Named Greenville's Player of the Year after finishing 1st on club in RBI (62), runs (57), and walks (68).

2003:

- Split the season with Greenville (94 games), Richmond (38 games) and Atlanta (16 games)... Was a starting CF in the Southern League All-Star Game.
- Recalled by Atlanta on Sept. 2... Made first MLB start in nightcap of Sept. 5 twinbill vs. Pittsburgh... Recorded first big league hit (RBI single off Brian Meadows).
- Recipient of Bill Lucas Award, given annually to minor leaguer that best represents the Braves on and off the field.

2004:

- Won the Hank Aaron Award as Atlanta's top minor league offensive performer... Received the Tommie Aaron Memorial Award as Richmond's MVP... Ranked 2nd in the IL in runs, 7th in extra-base hits and 8th in doubles.

2005:

- Ranked 3rd among NL rookies in doubles, 4th in extra-base hits (33) and 5th in OBP (.348)... Started in LF in 3 of 4 games in Atlanta's NLDS loss to Houston.
- Hit first career homer, a 12th-inning solo shot off Dan Wheeler on April 18 at Houston.

2006:

- Committed just one error in 199 chances in the outfield... Hit a solo home run on Opening Day (April 3 at LAD) to account for decisive run in 11-10 win... Hit first career pinch-hit homer off Saul Rivera, Aug. 25 vs. Washington.

2007:

- After playing first nine pro seasons in the Atlanta organization, was traded twice in a week—first to Oakland and then to Washington… Hit first career grand slam off Randy Flores on May 27 at St. Louis with the Nationals.
- Played in only two games with Oakland before being acquired by Washington 3 days after joining the A's.

2008:

- Split the season between the Nationals and Columbus (AAA).
- Recorded 100th career RBI Sept. 5 at Atlanta.

2009:

- Acquired from the Washington Nationals on June 28 in minor league trade for INF/OF Mike Morse.
- Selected from AAA Tacoma June 30... Appeared in 38 games with the Mariners, including 30 starts (LF- 26, CF-3, RF-1).
- Hit first career walk-off home run, a 2-run shot in the bottom of the 11th inning on Aug. 7 vs. TB (off J. Howell).
- Hit 2nd walk-off 2-run home run of the season in bottom of the 10th inning on Aug. 25 vs. OAK (off C. Breslow).
- Did not play from Sept. 18-Oct. 3, after injuring neck on diving play Sept. 17 vs. CWS.

2010:

- Recorded a .344 OBP; 2nd on the club (Ichiro, .394).
- Made Opening Day roster but was designated for assignment April 8 (4th day of season).
- Outrighted to Tacoma (AAA) April 12... Was later selected from Tacoma and rejoined Mariners May 3.
- Following the season had surgery (performed by Mariners Medical Director Dr. Edward Khalfayan) to remove loose bodies from left elbow.

2011:

- Split time between Tacoma of the Pacific Coast League (AAA) and Reno (AAA).
- Was traded to the Arizona Diamondbacks in exhange for cash considerations on July 29.
- Posted a 1.022 OPS in 38 games with Reno in the Diamondbacks organization.

HOME RUN TRIVIA

PLAYER WHO HOMERED IN THEIR FINAL MAJOR LEAGUE AT BAT

WILLIE AIKENS, April 27, 1985. He came to bat for last time, pinch-hitting at Texas in the ninth inning. Batting for Tony Fernandez against Tommy Boggs, Aikens crashed a dramatic game-tying, two-run homer and Toronto went on to win 9-8. Three days later, Aikens was "designated for assignment" winding up in the minor leagues.

DESIGNATED HITTER

As a designated hitter, **BRAD FULLMER** hit 32 home runs in 2000 to surpass the club mark of 25 home runs by a DH set in 1998 by **JOSE CANSECO**. Prior to 1998 the most home runs hit by a Blue Jays DH was 23 set by **DAVE WINFIELD** in 1992.

TWO IN ONE INNING, BATTER

JOE CARTER is the only Blue Jay to hit two home runs in one inning. He had his two on October 3, 1993 at Baltimore in the 2nd inning.

SWITCH HITTING HOME RUNS IN ONE GAME, BATTER

ROBERTO ALOMAR hit home runs from the both sides of the plate in the same game twice. He accomplished the feat, both at Rogers Centre. May 10, 1991 vs Chicago White Sox and May 3, 1995 vs Chicago White Sox. **DEVON WHITE** did so once with Toronto at Minnesota on June 1, 1992. **JOSE CRUZ Jr.** did it August 24, 1997 at Kansas City. The last Jay to do so was **GREGG ZAUN** on September 13, 2006 at Seattle.

40 HOME RUN SEASONS

In 1999 **CARLOS DELGADO** with 44 home runs and **SHAWN GREEN** with 42 home runs, became the first Blue Jays tandem to each hit 40 or more home runs in the same season. In 2000, the Blue Jays again had two players, **CARLOS DELGADO** and **TONY BATISTA** each hit 41, hit 40 plus homers in a season. Overall the Blue Jays have had eight players, done 11 times, hit 40 or more home runs in a season: **JOSE BAUTISTA** hit a Club record 54 in 2010 & became just the 2nd Jay to collect 40+ HR in back to back seasons, 1st since **CARLOS DELGADO** (1999-2000). **CARLOS DELGADO** is the only Blue Jay player to hit 40 or more home runs in a season three times (1999, 2000, 2003).

HOME RUNS BY THE FIRST TWO BATTERS OF GAME

DEVON WHITE and **ROBERTO ALOMAR** on August 18, 1991 at Detroit accomplished this feat for the first time in Blue Jays history. The second time occured on June 14, 2006 vs. Baltimore when **ALEX RIOS** and **FRANK CATALANOTTO** did so.

HOME RUN IN FIRST MAJOR LEAGUE AT BAT

AL WOODS as a pinch-hitter, on April 7, 1977 vs the Chicago White Sox at Exhibition Stadium in Toronto's first game ever.

JUNIOR FELIX, May 4, 1989 vs the California Angels at Exhibition Stadium.

J.P. ARENCIBIA, August 7, 2010 vs the Tampa Bay Rays at Rogers Centre.

HOMERING AT HOME

In 2010, the Toronto Blue Jays set a Club record with 146 home runs hit at home. Surpassed the previous best in 2000 when Toronto homered 134 home runs at home. **JOSE BAUTISTA** homered in the 6th inning on September 24, 2010 vs. BAL for #135 at home to break the previous record.

MOST PLAYERS WITH 30 OR MORE HOME RUNS

The 2000 Blue Jays had four players hit 30 or more home runs, which tied the ML record. It was just the second time the feat had been accomplished in the AL as the Anaheim Angels also had four players hit 30 plus homers earlier in the 2000 season.

20 HOME RUNS AT THE ALL-STAR BREAK

The 2000 Blue Jays became the first team in ML history to have four players hit 20 or more home runs at the All-Star Break. **CARLOS DELGADO** hit 28, **TONY BATISTA** hit 24, **RAUL MONDESI** hit 22 and **JOSE CRUZ Jr.** hit 20.

LAROCHE, *ANDY*

Birthdate .... Septmber 13, 1983
Opening Day Age 29
Birthplace .... Fort Scott, KC
Residence .... Steamboat Springs, CO
Bats/Throws .... R/R
Height/Weight 6-0/205
Contract Status .... signed thru 2013
M.L. Service 3.096

70
INFIELDER
NON-ROSTER

PERSONAL:

Andrew Christian Laroche... Is a 2001 graduate of Fort Scott (KS) High School... Attended Grayson County Community College and was slated to attend Rice University before signing with the Dodgers... Played with his older brother, Adam, for the Pirates in 2008-09, becoming the eighth set of brothers to play as teammates for the Bucs and the first since Eddie and Johnny O'Brien in 1958... His father, Dave, appeared in 647 games over 14 seasons from 1970-83 and pitched for the Indians from 1975-77, leading the club in appearances and saves in both 1975 and 1976... Captured a gold medal while playing for Team USA in the IBAF World Cup in Taiwan following the 2007 season... Invited children with down syndrome to PNC Park for a VIP treatment during the 2009 season; guests got one-on-one time with Andy, watched batting practice from the Pirates dugout, met Andy's teammates and received autographs and memorabilia.

LAST SEASON:

- Split time between Columbus (AAA) and Pawtucket (AAA) of the International League.
- Began the season in the Cleveland Indians organization, appearing in 46 games with Columbus (AAA), posting a .234 batting average with a .338 OBP.
- Spent time on the disabled list twice while with Columbus, April 11-20 and from June 16-25, both times with a left shoulder strain.
- Was released by Cleveland on June 26... Signed a minor league contract with the Boston Red Sox two days later.
- Was assigned to Pawtucket of the International League (AAA) where he hit .264 with a .800 OPS.
- Recorded 22-XBH in 50 games with Pawtucket.

ANDY LAROCHE

Bold – career high

Year	Club and League	AVG	G	AB	R	H	2B	3B	HR	RBI	SH-SF	HP	BB-IBB	SO	SB-CS	SLG	OBP	OPS
2003	Ogden (Pio)	.211	6	19	1	4	1	0	0	5	0-1	0	1-0	4	0-0	.263	.238	.501
2004	Columbus (SAL)	.283	65	244	52	69	20	0	13	42	2-2	8	29-1	30	12-5	.525	.375	.900
	Vero Beach (FSL)	.237	62	219	26	52	13	0	10	34	2-3	2	17-0	42	2-3	.434	.295	.729
2005	Vero Beach (FSL)	.333	63	249	54	83	14	1	21	51	0-2	1	19-3	38	6-1	.651	.380	1.031
	Jacksonville (Sou)	.273	64	227	41	62	12	0	9	43	0-2	3	32-2	54	2-2	.445	.367	.812
2006	Jacksonville (Sou)	.309	62	230	42	71	13	0	9	46	0-2	4	41-1	32	6-3	.483	.419	.902
	Las Vegas (PCL)	.322	55	202	35	65	14	1	10	35	0-1	2	25-0	32	3-2	.550	.400	.950
2007	Las Vegas (PCL)	.309	73	265	55	82	18	1	18	48	0-4	3	39-0	42	2-2	.589	.399	.988
	LOS ANGELES (NL)	.226	35	93	16	21	5	0	1	10	0-1	1	20-5	24	2-1	.312	.365	.677
2008	Jacksonville (Sou)	.318	6	22	5	7	1	0	0	1	0-0	0	3-0	6	1-0	.364	.400	.764
	Las Vegas (PCL)	.293	39	123	35	36	3	0	5	28	0-4	2	37-1	14	2-1	.439	.452	.891
	LOS ANGELES (NL)	.203	27	59	6	12	1	0	2	6	0-0	0	10-0	7	0-0	.322	.319	.641
	PITTSBURGH (NL)	.152	49	164	11	25	4	0	3	12	2-1	2	14-1	30	2-0	.232	.227	.459
2009	PITTSBURGH (NL)	.258	**150**	524	**64**	**135**	**29**	**5**	**12**	**64**	6-2	8	**50**-1	**84**	**3**-1	.401	.330	.731
2010	PITTSBURGH (NL)	.206	102	247	26	51	8	0	4	16	2-1	2	19-0	43	1-1	.287	.268	.555
2011	Sacramento River (PCL)	.254	54	197	24	50	12	0	4	27	0-2	6	19-0	24	3-2	.376	.335	.711
	OAKLAND (AL)	.247	40	93	10	23	6	1	0	5	1-0	2	8-1	19	0-0	.333	.320	.653
2012	Columbus (Int)	.234	46	145	18	34	5	0	5	16	0-0	1	20-0	28	0-0	.372	.331	.703
	Pawtucket (Int)	.264	50	182	23	48	15	0	7	25	0-1	3	18-3	24	1-1	.462	.338	.800
Minor Totals		.285	645	2324	411	663	141	3	111	401	4-24	35	300-11	370	40-22	.492	.372	.864
NL TOTALS		.224	363	1087	123	244	47	5	22	108	10-5	13	113-7	188	8-3	.338	.304	.641
MAJOR TOTALS		.226	403	1180	133	267	53	6	22	113	11-5	15	121-8	207	8-3	.337	.305	.642

HOME RUN BREAKDOWN

			ONE GAME									
Total	H	A	2	3	4	GS	LO	XN	IP	PH	RHP	LHP
22	10	12	1	0	0	0	0	0	0	1	15	7

TRANSACTIONS

- Selected by the Los Angeles Dodgers in the 39th round of the 2003 First Year Player Draft
- On disabled list (right thumb surgery) from March 21-May 3, 2008; included rehabilitation assignment at Jacksonville (AA) from April 23-28 and at Las Vegas (AAA) from April 29-May 2
- Traded to the Pittsburgh Pirates in a three team trade in which the Pirates sent OF Jason Bay to the Boston Red Sox, the Red Sox sent OF Manny Ramirez to the Los Angeles Dodgers and IF/OF Craig Hansen and OF Brandon Moss to the Pirates and the Dodgers sent RHP Bryan Morris to the Pirates on July 31, 2008
- Signed by the Oakland Athletics on January 24, 2011
- Signed by the Cleveland Indians on December 21, 2011
- Signed by the Boston Red Sox on June 28, 2012
- Signed by the Toronto Blue Jays on January 30, 2013

GAME HIGHS

ML Debut	May 6, 2007 at ATL	**RBI**	6 - Sept. 28, 2009 vs. LAD
Runs	4 - Sept. 28, 2009 vs. LAD	**Stolen Bases**	1 - 8x, last June 10, 2010 at WAS
Hits	5 - Sept. 28, 2009 vs. LAD	**Last ML Home Run**	Sept. 24, 2010 vs. HOU
Doubles	2 - 4x, last Sept. 28, 2009 at CHC	**Longest Hitting Streak**	11G - 2x, last May 15-26, 2009
Home Runs	2 - Sept. 28, 2009 vs. LAD	**Longest Hitless Streak**	28AB - May 12-20, 2011

CAREER FIELDING

POSITION	PCT	G	PO	A	E	TC	DP
1B	1.000	4	39	3	0	42	3
2B	.978	17	22	22	1	45	6
3B	.953	316	187	651	41	879	74
OF	--	1	0	0	0	0	0

MILESTONES

Category		Date	Opponent	Pitcher	Notes
Hit	1	May 6, 2007	Atlanta	Davies	double
Home Run	1	Sept. 20, 2007	at Colorado	Herges	1R
Multi-Homer Game (1)	1	Sept. 28, 2009	Los Angeles (NL)	Kuroda, McDonald	1R, 2R
Pinch Hit HR (1)	1	Sept. 24, 2010	Houston	Myers	1R, 6th inning
RBI	1	May 7, 2007	at Florida	Nolasco	sac fly
Stolen Base	1	May 7, 2007	at Florida	Nolasco C-Olivo	2nd base

PROFESSIONAL CAREER:

2007:

- Entered the season rated as the Dodgers' top prospect by Baseball America and reached the big leagues for the first time in his five-year professional career.
- Recalled from Triple-A Las Vegas on May 6.
- Collected his first Major League hit in his **Major League debut** on May 6 in just his second at-bat, cracking a ground-rule double off Atlanta's Kyle Davies.
- Drew one walk every 5.75 plate appearances, the third-best mark in the NL and fifth best in the Majors behind Barry Bonds (3.61), Jack Cust (4.83), Pat Burrell (5.25), and Jim Thome (5.64) (min. 100 plate appearances).
- Slugged his first Major League home run on Sept. 20 at Colorado off Matt Herges.
- Was named as the Topps Pacific Coast League Player of the Month in July when he batted .411 with 12 homers and 28 RBI for the 51s.

2008:

- Was rated as Los Angeles' second-best prospect by Baseball America entering the season.
- Began season on 15-day disabled list recovering from right thumb surgery performed on March 10 by Dr. Steve Shin in Los Angeles... Suffered a tear of the ulnar collateral ligament in his thumb while attempting to catch a pickoff throw from catcher Danny Ardoin in the March 7 spring training game vs. St. Louis.
- Was recalled from his rehab assignment, reinstated from the disabled list and optioned back to Las Vegas on May 3.
- Was acquired by Pittsburgh on July 31 and started 45 of the final 54 games at third base.

2009:

- Ranked third among NL third basemen in fielding pct. (.968) behind San Diego's Kevin Kouzmanoff (.990) and Los Angeles' Casey Blake (.973)... Ranked second in assists (321) behind Washington's Ryan Zimmerman (325)... Also ranked second in double plays turned (34) behind Philadelphia's Pedro Feliz (35) and third in total chances (432) behind Zimmerman (459) and Feliz (437).
- Led Pirates in games played, hits, doubles and RBI.
- Had a career day, going 5-for-5 with two home runs, six RBI and four runs scored on Sept. 28 vs. Los Angeles.

2010:

- Compiled his best batting average in April when he hit .333.
- Made a total of 52 starts at third base, four at second base and two at first base.

2011:

- Opened the season on the Oakland A's Major League roster.
- Was designated for assignment on June 5 and outrighted to Triple-A Sacramento on June 8, spending the rest of the season with the River Cats.

LAWRIE, *BRETT*

Birthdate	January 18, 1990
Opening Day Age	23
Birthplace	Langley, BC
Residence	Peoria, AZ
Bats/Throws	R/R
Height/Weight	6-0/223
Contract Status	signed thru 2013
M.L. Service	1.055

13

INFIELDER

PERSONAL:

Brett Russell Lawrie... Single... Brother of former University of Washington softball pitcher, Danielle Lawrie... A product of the Langley Blaze of the British Columbia Premier League... Is the highest Canadian position player selected in the entry draft (16th overall)... Was a member of the Canadian Junior National Team at the 2008 World Junior Baseball Championship where he led the tournament with a .469 average, three home runs and 16 RBI... Was also selected to play for Canada at the 2008 Summer Olympics... Represented Canada once again during the 2009 World Baseball Classic at Rogers Centre.

LAST SEASON:

- In his first full season as a Blue Jay appeared in 125 games... Made 123 starts at 3B and one a DH... Played four innings at SS on May 27 at TEX.
- Recorded 40 XBH (26-2B, 3-3B, 11HR) and .729 OPS.
- Hit .319 vs. left-handed pitchers with a .813 OPS... The .319 average was the highest on the club and ranked 13th in the AL...Was more effective at Rogers Centre, posting a .302 average and a .811 OPS as opposed to .248/.656 on the road... Hlt .600 (3-5) with the bases load, including one double and eight RBI... From the 7th inning or later, posted a .293 average and now has a .299 career average in those situations as opposed to .268 average from innings 1-6.
- Through June recorded a .279 average with eight home runs and a .778 OPS... After that batted just .244 with three home runs and a .654 OPS.
- July 18 at NYY fell into the camera bay attempting a catch and suffered a leg contusion keeping him out of the lineup for two days... Suffered a right oblique strain on Aug. 3 at OAK and did not return until Sept. 7 at BOS... May 15 vs. TB had an altercation with an umpire (threw helmut that hit umpire) that resulted in a four game suspension.
- On May 1 vs. TEX hit a walk-off home run in the 9th inning to give the club an 8-7 victory.
- Had eight, three-hit games and now has 10 in his career... Posted a nine game hitting streak from June 10-19 matching his career high.
- On April 22, stole home on the front end of a double steal with C J.P. Arencibia in the 8th inning... It marked just the 16th time in franchise history that a Blue Jays player has stolen home and the 14th time as part of a double steal.

BRETT LAWRIE

Bold – career high

Year	Club & League	AVG	G	AB	R	H	2B	3B	HR	RBI	SH-SF	HP	BB-IBB	SO	SB-CS	SLG	OBP	OPS
2009	Wisconsin (Mid)	.274	105	372	48	102	18	5	13	65	0-6	4	41-1	70	19-11	.454	.348	.802
	Huntsville (Sou)	.269	13	52	6	14	0	1	0	0	0-0	1	0-0	14	0-2	.308	.283	.591
2010	Huntsville (Sou)	.285	135	554	90	158	36	16	8	63	2-1	5	47-3	118	30-13	.451	.346	.797
2011	Dunedin (FSL)	.125	4	8	0	1	0	0	0	1	0-0	3	0-0	1	0-0	.125	.364	.489
	Las Vegas (PCL)	.353	69	292	64	103	24	6	18	61	4-1	6	26-0	53	13-2	.661	.415	1.076
	TORONTO (AL)	.293	43	150	26	44	8	**4**	9	25	2-0	3	16-1	31	7-1	.580	.373	.953
2012	Blue Jays (Gulf)	.000	1	1	0	0	0	0	0	0	0-0	0	0-0	0	0-0	.000	.000	.000
	Dunedin (FSL)	.000	1	3	0	0	0	0	0	0	0-0	0	0-0	1	0-0	.000	.000	.000
	TORONTO (AL)	.273	**125**	494	**73**	**135**	**26**	3	**11**	**48**	2-2	5	**33**-0	**86**	**13**-8	.405	.324	.729
Minor Totals		.295	328	1282	208	378	78	28	39	190	6-8	19	114-4	257	62-28	.491	.359	.850
MAJOR TOTALS		.278	168	644	99	179	34	7	20	73	4-2	8	49-1	117	20-9	.446	.336	.781

WORLD BASEBALL CLASSIC

Year	Club and League	AVG	G	AB	R	H	2B	3B	HR	RBI	SH-SF	HP	BB-IBB	SO	SB-CS
2009	Canada	-	1	0	0	0	0	0	0	0	0-0	0	0-0	0	0-0

HOME RUN BREAKDOWN

			ONE GAME									
Total	H	A	2	3	4	GS	LO	XN	IP	PH	RHP	LHP
20	12	8	0	0	0	1	2	1	0	0	16	4

TRANSACTIONS

- Selected by the Milwaukee Brewers in the 1st round (16th overall) in the 2008 First Year Player Draft
- Traded to the Toronto Blue Jays in exchange for RHP Shaun Marcum on December 6, 2010
- On disabled list (fractured right middle finger) September 21-remainder of season, 2011
- On disabeld list (strained right oblique) from August 9-September 6, 2012; included rehabilitation assignment at Gulf Coast Blue Jays (Rookie) from August 18-19 and Dunedin (A) September 5

GAME HIGHS

ML Debut	Aug. 5, 2011 at BAL	**RBI**	4 - Aug. 10, 2011 vs. OAK
Runs	4 - June 22, 2012 at MIA	**Stolen Bases**	2 - Aug. 29, 2011 vs. TB
Hits	3 - 10x, last Sept. 30, 2012 vs. NYY	**Last ML Home Run**	Sept. 30, 2012 vs. NYY
Doubles	2 - June 15, 2012 vs. PHI	**Longest Hitting Streak**	9G - 2x, last April 21-29, 2012
Home Runs	1 - 20x, last Sept. 30, 2012 vs. NYY	**Longest Hitless Streak**	17AB - June 6-10, 2012

CAREER FIELDING

POSITION	PCT	G	PO	A	E	TC	DP
3B	.957	166	122	393	23	538	33
SS	1.000	1	1	0	0	1	0

MILESTONES

Category		Date	Opponent	Pitcher	Notes
Hit	1	Aug. 5, 2011	at Baltimore	Hunter	ML debut, RBI single
Home Run	1	Aug. 7, 2011	at Baltimore	Simon	1R
Grand Slam (1)	1	Aug. 10, 2011	Oakland	Breslow	6th inning
Walk-off HR (2)	1	Sept. 5, 2011	Boston	Wheeler	1R, 11th inning
	2	May 1, 2012	Texas	Adams	1R, 9th inning
Leadoff HR (2)	1	June 18, 2012	at Milwaukee	Wolf	--
	2	July 22, 2012	at Boston	Lester	--
Extra Inning HR (1)					
	1	Sept. 5, 2011	Boston	Wheeler	1R, 11th inning
RBI	1	Aug. 5, 2011	at Baltimore	Hunter	1B, 1st career PA
Stolen Base	1	Aug. 14, 2011	Los Angeles (AL)	Walden C-Wilson	3rd base

PROFESSIONAL CAREER:

2009:

- Hit his first home run on April 10, his second professional game.
- Was selected to play for the World Team at the 2009 MLB All-Star Futures Game at Busch Stadium in St. Louis.
- Was promoted to the Double-A Huntsville Stars in mid-August.

2010:

- Led the Southern League in hits (158), triples (16), runs (90) and extra base hits (60), despite being the second youngest regular in the league.
- Earned a Post-Season All-Star selection and on June 23 was selected to the 2010 Futures Games, his second selection, where he led off for the World Team, going 0-3.

2011:

- Had his contract purchased by Toronto on August 5th and appeared in 43 games in his rookie season.
- Began the season in Las Vegas (AAA) with the 51s.
- Led all Blue Jays minor leaguers in extra base hits at the time of his promotion and led the PCL with a .661 SLG and 1.076 OPS.
- Was named the #1 prospect by Baseball America in the Pacific Coast League following the 2011 season.
- Earned Player-of-the-Week honours for his efforts from May 16-22.
- Aug. 5 at BAL made his **ML debut**, becoming the 15th Canadian to play for the Blue Jays.
- Went 2-4 with an RBI, collecting his first hit with a single off Tommy Hunter in his first at-bat.
- Hit his first home run on Aug. 7 at BAL off Alfredo Simon.
- On Aug. 10 vs. OAK hit his first career grand slam, becoming the 2nd Canadian born player to do so as a Blue Jay along with Matt Stairs... Is the youngest player to hit a grand slam for the Blue Jays since Junior Felix on June 2, 1989.

WALK-OFF HOME RUNS

The Toronto Blue Jays have recorded 61 total walk-off home runs in franchise history. On June 15, 2003 vs. the Chicago Cubs, OF Reed Johnson hit a leadoff home run and ended the game in the 10th inning with a walk-off home run. Johnson became just the 4th player in ML history to accomplish that feat. The most walk-off home runs hit in a single season by Toronto is six accomplished in 2011. Cecil Fielder is the only Blue Jay to hit a pinch hit walk-off home run accomplished back on September 4, 1987 vs. SEA (10th inning-solo HR). George Bell (Sept. 4, 1988 vs. Tex-9th inn) and Gregg Zaun (Sept. 6, 2008 vs. TB-13th inn) are the only two Jays to end a game on a walk-off grand slam.

- Posted six home runs in August, the 2nd most from a Toronto rookie in their first full month in the Majors... Only Carlos Delgado with eight in April of 1994 had more.
- Sept. 5 vs. BOS added his first career walk-off, with a home run in the 11th inning, breaking a 0-0 tie.
- Was on disabled list from June 1 through July 18 in Las Vegas after suffering a broken left hand from an HBP.
- Was disabled for the second time on Sept. 21 with a fractured right middle finger and did not appear in a game for the balance of the season... At the time of being disabled led all rookies in the Major Leagues in triples (4), slugging (.580), OPS (.953) and was T-1st in home runs (9) and extra base hits (21) since his debut on Aug. 5.
- Joined only four other active players to have hit at least nine home runs with 25 RBI in their first 35 career games (A. Pujols – 12/39, C. Davis – 11/26, A. Dunn – 11/31, J. Francoeur – 10/30).

CANADIAN BASEBALL HALL OF FAME AND MUSEUM

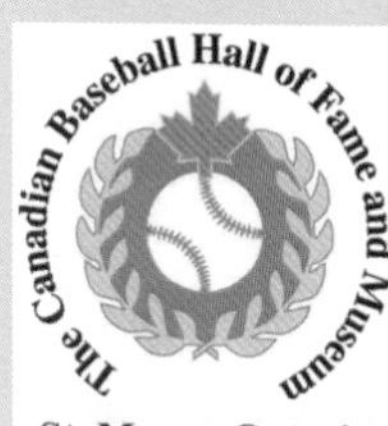

P.O. Box 1838
386 Church St. S. (Museum)
140 Queen St. E. (Office)
St. Marys, ON N4X 1C2
Web site: www.baseballhalloffame.ca
E-mail: baseball@baseballhalloffame.ca
Phone: (519) 284-1838 **Fax:** (519) 284-1234

Hours: May (weekends only)
Sat: 10:30 am-4:00 pm
Sun: 12:00 pm-4:00 pm

June to October
Daily: 10:30 am-4:00 pm
Sun: 12:00 am-4:00 pm

DIRECTOR OF OPERATIONS:

Scott Crawford
Board Chair

Margaret King

MUSEUM OPENS FOR 2013, MAY 4

TORONTO BLUE JAYS CLINIC IN MAY

2013 CELEBRITY BALL GAME

Thursday, June 27

2013 CELEBRITY GOLF TOURNAMENT

Friday, June 28

2013 HALL OF FAME INDUCTION CEREMONY

Saturday, June 29

2013 KIDS ON DECK

Week-long children baseball camps, July 6-12

TORONTO BLUE JAYS' HALL-OF-FAMERS

1985 - Ron Taylor
1986 - Bobby Prentice
1997 - Pat Gillick
1999 - Bobby Mattick
2000 - Jim Fanning
2001 - Dave McKay
2002 - Paul Beeston, Cito Gaston & Don McDougall
2003 - Joe Carter
2004 - N.E. (Peter) Hardy
2005 - Dave Stieb
2008 - Tony Fernandez & Peter Widdrington
2009 - Ernie Whitt
2010 - Roberto Alomar & Paul Quantrill
2011 - Tom Henke
2012 - George Bell, Rob Ducey & Tom Cheek

NOTABLE BLUE JAYS ARTIFACTS AT THE HALL:

1977 - Photo from 1st pitch in Blue Jays history
1992 & 1993 - World Series Rings
1993 - Joe Carter's helmet from World Series home run...SkyDome's homeplate from World Series...World Series MVP trophy from Paul Molitor
2007 - Matt Stairs game used bat
2009 - Scott Richmond signed hat
2010 - Shawn Hill's shoes
2011 - Brett Lawrie game used bat... Mark Teahen's cleats
Roger Clemens Jersey
Pitching rubber and seats from Exhibition Stadium
Tom Cheek microphone
Dave Stieb's Jersey and spikes
Dave McKay's glove
Several items from the Labatt's Blue Jays archives
Paul Quantrill game used glove and jersey
2012 - Brett Lawrie game used bat

LINCOLN, *BRAD*

Birthdate . . . . May 25, 1985
Opening Day Age 28
Birthplace. . . . . Lake Jackson, TX
Residence. . . . . Pearland, TX
Bats/Throws . . . . L/R
Height/Weight 6-0/223
Contract Status . . . . signed thru 2013
M.L. Service 1.143

49
PITCHER

PERSONAL:

Brad Eric Lincoln... Is a 2003 graduate of Brazoswood High School in Clute, TX, where he lettered in baseball... Was also a quarterback on the football team... Named to All-County, All-State and All-District teams in baseball his senior year... Was named to the All-Greater Houston Area team in 2003... Finished collegiate career with 293 strikeouts, ranking third in Houston's career list... Captured Conference USA Pitcher-of-the-Year honours as a junior in 2006 and was named to the All-Conference USA First-Team as both a pitcher and designated hitter... Was the winner of the Brooks Wallace Award, given to college baseball's top player, and the 20th annual Dick Howser trophy as the 2006 College Baseball Player-of-the-Year... Was a semi-finalist for the Roger Clemens Award (College Baseball's Pitcher-of-the-Year).

LAST SEASON:

- Was acquired at the trade deadline on July 31 in a deal with Pittsburgh in exchange for Travis Snider.
- Combined to go 5-2 with one save and a 3.68 ERA in 52 outings (five starts), between Pittsburgh and Toronto... Struck out 88 batters in 88.0 innings.
- Out of the bullpen with the Pirates allowed just two earned runs in 35.2 innings for a 0.50 ERA in 23 games... NL hitters batted just .176 when he pitched in relief... As a starter was 2-2 with a 6.08 ERA.
- Was used exclusively as a reliever in Toronto in his 24 appearances... Did not allow a run in his first four outings with Toronto, then allowed eight earned in his next four outings... Allowed runs in just six of his 24 appearances with the Blue Jays... Of the six, five were multiple run outings including six he allowed in 0.2 innings on Sept. 22 at TB.
- Allowed 14 home runs in 88.0 innings and six in 28.2 with Toronto.

BRAD LINCOLN

Bold – career high

Year	Club & League	W-L	ERA	G	GS	CG	ShO	SV	IP	H	R	ER	HR	HB	BB-IBB	SO	WP	BK	OBA
2006	Pirates (Gulf)	0-0	0.00	2	2	0	0	0	7.2	6	1	0	0	0	1-0	9	0	0	.222
	Hickory (SAL)	1-2	6.75	4	4	0	0	0	16.0	25	15	12	2	1	6-0	10	1	0	.368
2007		Injured - Did Not Play																	
2008	Hickory (SAL)	5-5	4.65	11	11	0	0	0	62.0	72	34	32	8	2	6-0	46	1	2	.288
	Lynchburg (Caro)	1-5	4.75	8	8	1	0	0	41.2	42	24	22	5	1	11-0	29	0	0	.259
2009	Altoona (East)	1-5	2.28	13	13	1	1	0	75.0	63	22	19	4	2	18-0	65	3	0	.228
	Indianapolis (Int)	6-2	4.70	12	12	0	0	0	61.1	72	37	32	7	1	10-1	42	2	1	.300
2010	Indianapolis (Int)	7-5	4.12	17	17	0	0	0	94.0	83	47	43	9	7	24-0	84	4	0	.235
	PITTSBURGH (NL)	1-**4**	6.66	11	**9**	0	0	0	52.2	66	42	39	9	5	15-0	25	1	0	.310
2011	Indianapolis (Int)	7-8	4.19	19	19	0	0	0	111.2	115	55	52	6	9	21-0	94	3	0	.270
	PITTSBURGH (NL)	2-3	4.72	12	8	0	0	0	47.2	54	27	25	4	2	16-4	29	0	0	.286
2012	Indianapolis (Int)	1-0	2.25	2	2	0	0	0	12.0	10	3	3	0	2	0-0	9	0	0	.227
	PITTSBURGH (NL)	**4**-2	2.73	**28**	5	0	0	**1**	**59.1**	51	19	18	**8**	1	**14**-1	**60**	0	0	.274
	TORONTO (AL)	**1**-0	5.65	**24**	0	0	0	0	**28.2**	29	18	18	**6**	0	**10**-1	**28**	1	0	.264
Minor Totals		29-32	4.02	88	88	2	1	0	481.1	488	238	215	41	25	97-1	388	14	3	.264
NL TOTALS		7-9	4.62	51	22	0	0	1	159.2	171	88	82	21	8	45-5	114	1	0	.274
MAJOR TOTALS		3-7	5.74	23	17	0	0	0	100.1	120	69	64	13	7	31-4	54	1	0	.299

TRANSACTIONS

- Selected by the Pittsburgh Pirates in the 1st round (4th overall) of the 2006 First Year Player Draft
- Traded to the Toronto Blue Jays in exchange for OF Travis Snider on July 30, 2012

GAME HIGHS

ML Debut	June 9, 2010 at WSH
Innings Pitched:	
Starter	7.0 - June 30, 2010 at CHC
Reliever	3.1 - Aug. 3, 2012 at OAK
Walks:	
Starter	4 - Sept. 24, 2011 vs. CIN
Reliever	3 - April 18, 2012 at ARI
Strikeouts:	
Starter	7 - June 23, 2012 vs. DET
Reliever	4 - 4x, last Oct. 1, 2012 vs. MIN
Hits Allowed	9 - 2x, last June 12, 2012 at BAL
Runs Allowed	7- July 20, 2010 vs. MIL
ER Allowed	7 - July 20, 2010 vs. MIL
HR Allowed	2 - 6x, last Sept. 22, 2012 at TB
Low Hit CG	None
Last Win	Sept. 8, 2012 at BOS
Last Save	July 21, 2012 vs. MIA
Last CG	None
Last ShO	None
Last Start	June 23, 2012 vs. DET
Last Relief App.	Oct. 1, 2012 vs. MIN
Longest Win Streak	3G - April 18-May 14, 2012
Longest Losing Streak	3G - Sept. 1-18, 2011
Scoreless Innings Streak	13.1 - July 13-Aug. 12, 2012

CAREER FIELDING

POSITION	PCT	G	PO	A	E	TC	DP
P	1.000	75	23	28	0	51	2

MILESTONES

Category		Date	Opponent	Notes
Start	1	June 9, 2010	at Washington	no decision - 6.0 IP, 7H, 5ER, HR, 2BB, 3K
Win	1	June 30, 2010	at Chicago (NL)	as a starter - 7.0 IP, 4H, BB, 6K
Save	1	July 21, 2012	Miami	1.1 IP, H, 3K

PROFESSIONAL CAREER:

2006:

- Made professional debut on July 8 vs. GCL Red Sox and tossed 3.2 scoreless innings.
- Was promoted to Hickory on July 17.

2007:

- Missed entire season after undergoing reconstructive surgery to repair ligament damage in right elbow on April 3 (surgery performed by Dr. James Andrews in Birmingham, AL).

2008:

- Was promoted to Lynchburg on July 16... His only victory with the Hillcats came in a 5.0-inning, rain-shortened game vs. Wilmington on July 23 - his first professional complete game.

2009:

- Ranked third among Pittsburgh farmhands with 107 strikeouts and second in ERA.
- Represented the United States at the MLB Futures Game in St. Louis.
- Played for Gold-Medal winning Team USA in the World Cup tournament in Europe from Sept. 2-27 and went 3-0 with a 2.70 ERA.
- Was the winning pitcher in Championship Game against Cuba on Sept. 27.

2010:

- Began season with Indianapolis (AAA).
- Was recalled by Pittsburgh on June 9 and received a no-decision in his **Major League debut** that night in Washington.
- Pitched a career-high 7.0 innings and struck out a career-high six batters while winning first big league game (2-0) on June 30 at Chicago (NL).
- Was optioned back to Indianapolis on July 26.
- Was recalled by Pittsburgh on Sept. 7.
- Made first professional relief appearance on Sept. 22 vs. STL and gave up three runs (two earned) in 1.0 inning.

2011:

- Pitched a career-high 159.1 innings between Triple-A and the Major Leagues.
- Was recalled by Pittsburgh to start game two of a doubleheader at Washington on July 2.
- Was optioned back to AAA on July 3.
- Was recalled by Pittsburgh on Aug. 6 and remained in the big leagues... Made four relief appearances before joining starting rotation on Aug. 22.

PERFECT STARTS TO A SEASON

Following is a list of Blue Jays pitchers starting the season perfectly (minimum 5-0)

YEAR	PITCHER	RECORD	NOTES	YEAR	PITCHER	RECORD	NOTES
1997	Roger Clemens	11-0	starter	1992	Juan Guzman	6-0	starter
1985	Dennis Lamp	11-0	reliever	2012	Carlos Villanueva	6-0	start/rel.
1985	Tom Filer	7-0	starter	1977	Jerry Garvin	5-0	starter
1999	John Frascatore	7-0	reliever	1992	Pat Hentgen	5-0	reliever
2011	Casey Janssen	6-0	reliever	1993	Juan Guzman	5-0	starter
1984	Luis Leal	6-0	starter	2001	Paul Quantril	5-0	reliever
1988	Duane Ward	6-0	reliever	2009	Jason Frasor	5-0	reliever

LIND, *ADAM*

Birthdate . . . . July 17, 1983
Opening Day Age 30
Birthplace. . . . . Muncie, IN
Residence. . . . . Palm Harbor, FL
Bats/Throws . . . . L/L
Height/Weight 6-2/222
Contract Status . . . . signed thru 2013
M.L. Service 5.058

26

INFIELDER

PERSONAL:

Adam Alan Lind... Married with one child... Attended Highland High School in Indiana... Signed by Joel Grampietro... Attended University of South Alabama... In 2003, was named as a Freshman 2nd team All-American first baseman... In 2004 he was named a Sun Belt Conference All-Star outfielder.

LAST SEASON:

- Played in 93 games, the first time he has not reached the 100 game plateau since appearing in 88 in 2008... Started 57 games at 1B and 28 at DH.
- Was optioned to Las Vegas (AAA) on May 31 after batting .140 in May... Through April/May was hitting .186 with three home runs and 11 RBI.
- In Las Vegas, batted .392 with 10 doubles, eight home runs and 29 RBI in just 32 games earning a recall to Toronto on June 25.
- After recall posted a .288 average with five home runs and 16 RBI in 24 games before suffering a mid-back strain that would keep him out until August 27... Upon his return batted .301 with 13 XBH and 18 RBI in 35 contests... In fact over his final 22 contests posted a .347 average and a .946 OPS.
- Batted .202 vs. left-handed pitching and now has posted a .186 mark vs, lefties since 2010... Prior to that had posted a .257 average vs. lefties in his career.
- Preferred the home turf batting .270 with a .782 OPS as oppossed to .241/.674 on the road.
- Oct. 1 vs, MIN went 4-4 with a double and two RBI marking the 4th time in his career he has posted four hits without recording an out.
- In now five home runs shy of Jose Cruz Jr. for 10th on the all-time club list.

ADAM LIND

Bold – career high

Year	Club & League	AVG	G	AB	R	H	2B	3B	HR	RBI	SH-SF	HP	BB-IBB	SO	SB-CS	SLG	OBP	OPS
2004	Auburn (NYP)	.312	70	266	43	83	23	0	7	50	1-2	2	24-0	36	1-0	.477	.371	.848
2005	Dunedin (FSL)	.313	126	495	80	155	42	4	12	84	0-6	4	49-7	77	2-1	.487	.375	.862
2006	New Hampshire (East)	.310	91	348	43	108	24	0	19	71	0-3	2	25-0	87	2-1	.543	.357	.900
	Syracuse (Int)	.394	34	109	20	43	7	0	5	18	0-3	2	23-0	18	1-0	.596	.496	1.092
	TORONTO (AL)	.367	18	60	8	22	8	0	2	8	0-0	0	5-0	12	0-0	.600	.415	1.015
2007	Syracuse (Int)	.299	46	174	20	52	8	2	6	28	0-1	1	14-3	42	0-0	.471	.353	.824
	TORONTO (AL)	.238	89	290	34	69	14	0	11	46	2-2	1	16-0	65	1-2	.400	.278	.678
2008	Syracuse (Int)	.328	51	189	24	62	17	2	6	50	0-2	3	19-2	36	1-1	.534	.394	.928
	TORONTO (AL)	.282	88	326	48	92	16	**4**	9	40	1-4	2	16-3	59	**2**-0	.439	.316	.755
2009	TORONTO (AL)	.305	**151**	587	**93**	**179**	**46**	0	**35**	**114**	0-4	5	**58**-7	**110**	1-1	.562	.370	.932
2010	TORONTO (AL)	.237	150	569	57	135	32	3	23	72	0-3	3	38-3	144	0-0	.425	.287	.712
2011	Dunedin (FSL)	.600	3	10	2	6	3	0	0	4	0-0	0	2-0	1	0-0	.900	.667	1.567
	TORONTO (AL)	.251	125	499	56	125	16	0	26	87	0-8	3	32-4	107	1-1	.439	.295	.734
2012	New Hampshire (East)	.545	3	11	2	6	0	0	1	1	0-0	0	2-1	4	0-0	.818	.615	1.434
	Las Vegas (PCL)	.392	32	125	24	49	10	0	8	29	0-3	0	15-0	26	1-0	.664	.448	1.112
	TORONTO (AL)	.255	93	321	28	82	14	2	11	45	0-3	0	29-1	61	0-0	.414	.314	.729
Minor Totals		.327	456	1727	258	564	134	8	64	335	1-20	14	173-13	327	8-3	.525	.388	.913
MAJOR TOTALS		.265	714	2652	324	704	146	9	117	412	3-24	14	194-18	558	5-4	.460	.316	776

HOME RUN BREAKDOWN

			ONE GAME									
Total	**H**	**A**	**2**	**3**	**4**	**GS**	**LO**	**XN**	**IP**	**PH**	**RHP**	**LHP**
117	59	58	7	1	0	3	0	2	0	2	99	18

TRANSACTIONS:

- Selected by the Toronto Blue Jays in the 3rd round of the June 2004 First Year Player Draft
- On disabled list (sore lower back) May 17-June 3, 2011; included rehabilitation assignment at Dunedin (A) June 1-3
- On disabled list (mid-back strain) from July 30-August 25, 2012; included rehabilitation assignment at New Hampshire (AA) August 23-25

GAME HIGHS

ML Debut	Sept. 2, 2006 at BOS	**Stolen Bases**	1 – 5x, last April 15, 2011 at BOS
Runs	3 – 6x, last April 26, 2011 at TEX	**Last ML Home Run**	Sept. 28, 2012 vs. NYY
Hits	5 - June 4, 2009 vs. LAA	**Longest Hitting Streak**	14G - July 1-21, 2010
Doubles	3 – 2x, last June 4, 2009 vs. LAA	**Longest Hitless Streak**	22AB - July 27-Aug. 3, 2011
Home Runs	3 - Sept. 29, 2009 at BOS		
RBI	8 - Aug. 31, 2009 at TEX		

CAREER FIELDING

POSITION	PCT	G	PO	A	E	TC	DP
1B	.995	181	1567	110	9	1686	159
OF	.997	224	356	8	1	365	1

MILESTONES

Category		Date	Opponent	Pitcher	Notes
Hit	1	Sept. 2, 2006	at Boston	Dinardo	Double
Home Run	1	Sept. 10, 2006	at Los Angeles (AL)	Ja. Weaver	2R
	100	Aug. 13, 2011	Los Angeles (AL)	Weaver	Grand Slam
Multi-Homer Game (8)					
	8	June 29, 2012	Los Angeles (AL)	Santana, Takahashi	3R, 1R
3-Homer Game (1)					
	1	Sept. 29, 2009	at Boston	Buchholz (2), Saito	2R, 1R, 1R
Grand Slam (3)	1	Aug. 31, 2009	at Texas	Holland	4th inning
	2	June 8, 2011	at Kansas City	Adcock	6th inning
	3	Aug. 13, 2011	Los Angeles (AL)	Weaver	5th inning
Pinch Hit HR (2)	1	May 27, 2007	at Minnesota	Silva	1R
	2	May 21, 2010	at Arizona	Gutierrez	1R
Walk-off (3)	1	Sept. 26, 2009	Seattle	Kelley	1R, 10th inning
	2	Sept. 12, 2010	Tampa Bay	Soriano	2R, 9th inning
	3	June 14, 2011	Baltimore	Uehara	1R, 11th inning
Extra Inning HR (2)					
	1	Sept. 26, 2009	Seattle	Kelley	1R, 10th inning
	2	June 14, 2011	Baltimore	Uehara	1R, 11th inning
RBI	1	Sept. 9, 2006	at Los Angeles (AL)	Escobar	Double
Stolen Base	1	May 6, 2007	at Texas	Loe C-Stewart	2nd base

PROFESSIONAL CAREER:

2004:

- Named as a R. Howard Webster Award winner as Auburn's MVP.
- Named to the post-season New York-Penn League All-Star Team.

2005:

- Became the 20th player in the organization's history to win two or more Webster Awards, capturing his second team MVP award in as many seasons.
- Selected to the year-end Florida State League All-Star team after ranking first in the league with 42 doubles and 58 extra base hits, second with a .313 batting average and 155 hits and fourth with 84 RBI and 80 runs scored.
- Selected to participate in the Florida State League All-Star Game, but struck out in his only plate appearance.

2006:

- Had his contract purchased on Sept. 1, making his **Major League debut** on Sept. 2 at BOS.
- Recorded his first Major League hit on Sept. 2 at BOS, a double off of Lenny Dinardo.
- Hit his 1st Major League HR Sept 10th at LAA off Jared Weaver in his 14th career at-bat.
- Was named the R. Howard Webster Award winner for New Hampshire (AA)... Became just the 3rd player in the history of the organization to win three or more Webster Awards (Carlos Delgado and Luis Lopez being the others).
- Named Eastern League MVP (AA), ranking 1st in HR (19), and RBI (71)... Ranked 2nd in avg. (.310).

2007:

- His 11 HR were the most by a Jay rookie since 2002 when Eric Hinske slammed a Club record 25 & Josh Phelps added 15.
- Among AL rookies, ranked 4th in home runs and 3rd with five outfield assists.

RBI RECORDS BY POSITION (SEASON)

POSITION	PLAYER	RBI	YEAR
1B	Carlos Delgado	137	2000
2B	Aaron Hill	107	2009
3B	Tony Batista	114	2000
SS	Tony Batista	79	1999
LF	George Bell	126	1987
CF	Vernon Wells	117	2003
RF	Shawn Green	123	1999
C	Darrin Fletcher	80	1999
DH	Brad Fullmer	104	2000

2008:

- Began the season with the Syracuse Chiefs (AAA) and batted .365 (23-63) with three home runs & 16 RBI in 21 games prior to being recalled by Toronto on April 26.
- Among AL leaders in July, ranked 4th in batting average (.379), T-4th in doubles (10), 9th in SLG (.644) & T-9th in hits (33).

2009:

- Set career highs in virtually all offensive categories, including leading the club in batting average (.305), RBI (114) & slugging (.562).
- Was awarded the AL Silver Slugger as a Designated Hitter, representative of the best offensive player at his position.
- Received the Edgar Martinez Award, as the top Designated Hitter.
- Ranked 5th in the AL in total bases (330), 5th in doubles (46), 2nd in extra-base hits (81), 3rd in RBI (114) & 5th in home runs (35).
- His 100+ RBI season was the most from a left-handed hitter for Toronto since Carlos Delgado posted 145 in 2003.
- On opening day April 6 vs. DET finished the contest with a then career high six RBI (most by a Jay since Reed Johnson had six-July 1, 2005 at BOS)… The 6-RBI are the most by a Blue Jay in Opening Day history… The four hits matched the Club record (4th time) for the most hits by a Jay on Opening Day.
- Was first Blue Jays player to hit three home runs in the teams first five games since Carlos Delgado (five in 2001)… His 12 RBI are the most in Blue Jays history after seven games, since Joe Carter had 12 in 1994.
- Sept. 29 at BOS, hit home runs in three consecutive at-bats marking the 1st time a Blue Jay has hit three home runs in a game since Frank Thomas did so against the same Red Sox in 2007…
- Sept. 26 vs. SEA, hit the 1st walk-off home run of his career… In fact, became only the 2nd player in Blue Jays history to hit two lead-changing home runs in the 8th inning or later in a game (Roberto Alomar – 1991).
- Had a career best eight-RBI contest, Aug. 31 at TEX… The eight RBI are the 2nd highest single game total in club history (Roy Howell-9).
- Adam Lind (114 RBI) & Aaron Hill (108 RBI) became just the 2nd pair in Blue Jays history to record at least 35-HR, 35-2B & 100-RBI in the same season… Also, the 221 combined RBI between the two are the most by a Blue Jay duo since 2003 when Delgado (145) & Wells (117) combined for 262.

2010:

- His 23rd and final home run of the season came on the Club's final game, where he appeared as a left fielder... It gave the Blue Jays 20+ home runs from all eight fielding positions plus DH in the batting order, the only team in Major League history to accomplish the feat.
- Hit a walk-off home run Sept. 12 vs. TB which was the 2nd walk-off home run of his career (previous: Sept. 26/09 vs. SEA).

2011:

- Hit 20+ home runs for the 3rd consecutive season, despite playing in just 125 games, which was his lowest total since playing in just 88 games in 2008..
- Played in 109 games at 1st base this season after only playing there eight times prior to this season and was 4th in the AL in fielding percentage at .996, making just four errors.
- His home run off Carl Pavano vs. MIN on opening day was his 3rd straight in opening day contests, going 9-12, with 3HR and 10RBI over the three contests.
- Was voted Honda Player of the Month for June by the Toronto Chapter of the BBWAA... Hit .311 (28-90) with nine home runs and 22 RBI... Finished the month T-2nd in the AL in HR (9), 6th in RBI (22) & 7th in SLG (.644).
- Homered in a career high four straight games from June 14-17, marking the 11th time in Club history and only the 10th different player to do so.
- Was placed on the 15-day DL for the first time in his career on May 17 (retro May 8) with lower back stiffness.

"BIG" RBI GAMES

(6 OR MORE)

RBI	PLAYER	DATE	OPPONENT	RBI	PLAYER	DATE	OPPONENT
9	Roy Howell	Sept. 10, 1977	NYY (A)	6	Ernie Whitt	Sept. 12, 1987	NYY (H)
8	Adam Lind	Aug. 31, 2009	TEX (A)	6	Ernie Whitt	Sept. 27, 1988	Bal (A)
7	John Mayberry	June 26, 1978	BAL (H)	6	Kelly Gruber	April 16, 1989	KC (H)
7	Otto Velez	May 4, 1980	CLE (H) G1	6	George Bell	June 8, 1990	Mil (A)
7	George Bell	May 9, 1987	TEX (A)	6	Charlie O'Brien	May 14, 1997	Det (A)
7	Josh Phelps	July 7, 2004	SEA (H)	6	Carlos Delgado	June 7, 2000	Atl (A)
7	Lyle Overbay	Aug. 20, 2010	BOS (A)	6	Raul Mondesi	May 4, 2001	Sea (A)
6	Roy Howell	July 3, 1979	DET (A)	6	Raul Mondesi	June 29, 2001	Bos (H)
6	Barry Bonnell	May 3, 1980	CLE (H)	6	Jose Cruz Jr.	June 25, 2002	TB (A)
6	Lloyd Moseby	Aug. 19, 1981	KC (A)	6	Carlos Delgado	Sept. 25, 2003	TB (H)
6	Damaso Garcia	May 10, 1985	SEA (H)	6	Reed Johnson	July 1, 2005	BOS (A)
6	Jesse Barfield	May 18, 1986	CLE (H)	6	Adam Lind	April 6, 2009	Det (H)
6	George Bell	June 11, 1987	BAL (A)	6	J.P. Arencibia	May 18, 2012	NYM (H)

LOEWEN, *ADAM*

Birthdate	April 9, 1984
Opening Day Age	28
Birthplace	Vancouver, BC
Residence	Surrey, BC
Bats/Throws	L/L
Height/Weight	6-6/235
Contract Status	signed thru 2013
M.L. Service	2.135

72

INFIELDER

NON-ROSTER

PERSONAL:

Adam Alexander Loewen... Single... Was only the 4th Canadian ever taken in the 1st round of the draft and the highest selection (4th overall) since Canadians were made eligible for the Major League Draft in 1985... Graduated from Fraser Valley Christian High School, which did not have a baseball team... Played for Team Canada's national junior team for three years and he was ranked the No. 4 high school prospect in the draft by Baseball America... With Team Canada in 2000, beat eventual World Junior League champion Korea and was named Team Canada MVP despite being the youngest member of the team... In 2001, he tossed a no-hitter against the Pittsburgh Pirates' Dominican Summer League team, striking out 16, and overall allowed only three hits with 33 strikeouts in 16.0 innings for Team Canada... Led Surrey to the Little League World Series at Williamsport in 1996... Had signed a letter of intent to play for Arizona State University before being drafted... Attended Chipola Junior College in Marianna, FL, where he went 6-1 with a 1.83 ERA in 12 pitching appearances... Also played first base when not pitching and batted .353 with a home run and 38 RBI in 45 games.

LAST SEASON:

- Spent the season with Buffalo of the International League (AAA) in the Mets system.
- Appeared in just 59 games, however posted 10 doubles and eight home runs.
- Played 12 games before being sidelined with a stress fracture of the second metatarsal in his right foot... Hit .270 with three home runs in his first 12 games and .218 with five home runs in 47 games after returning from injury.
- Marked his fourth season as a position player.

ADAM LOEWEN

Bold – career high

Year	Club & League	W-L	ERA	G	GS	CG	ShO	SV	IP	H	R	ER	HR	HB	BB-IBB	SO	WP	BK	OBA
2003	Aberdeen (NYP)	0-2	2.70	7	7	0	0	0	23.1	13	7	7	0	4	9-0	25	2	0	.167
2004	Delmarva (SAL)	4-5	4.11	20	19	1	0	0	85.1	77	47	39	3	4	58-0	82	8	4	.250
	Frederick (Caro)	0-2	6.75	2	2	1	0	0	8.0	7	6	6	2	0	9-0	3	0	0	.259
2005	Frederick (Caro)	10-8	4.12	28	27	1	0	0	142.0	130	77	65	8	14	86-0	146	15	1	.245
2006	Bowie (East)	4-2	2.72	9	8	0	0	0	49.2	46	17	15	3	2	26-0	55	6	2	.250
	Ottawa (Int)	2-0	1.27	3	3	0	0	0	21.1	10	3	3	0	0	3-0	21	1	0	.143
	BALTIMORE (AL)	**6-6**	5.37	**22**	**19**	0	0	0	**112.1**	111	72	67	8	8	**62**-0	**98**	3	1	.259
2007	BALTIMORE (AL)	2-0	3.56	6	6	0	0	0	30.1	27	14	12	1	3	26-0	22	1	1	.239
2008	Frederick (Caro)	0-0	0.00	3	1	0	0	0	3.0	1	0	0	0	0	0-0	5	0	0	.100
	Bowie (East)	1-0	1.35	6	0	0	0	0	6.2	7	3	1	1	2	2-0	6	0	0	.280
	BALTIMORE (AL)	0-2	8.02	7	4	0	0	0	21.1	25	19	19	5	0	18-0	14	2	0	.305
Minor Totals		21-19	3.61	78	67	3	0	0	339.1	291	160	136	17	26	193-0	343	32	7	.236
MAJOR TOTALS		8-8	5.38	35	29	0	0	0	164.0	163	105	98	14	11	106-0	134	6	2	.261

Bold – career high

Year	Club & League	AVG	G	AB	R	H	2B	3B	HR	RBI	SH-SF	HP	BB-IBB	SO	SB-CS	SLG	OBP	OPS
2009	Dunedin (FSL)	.236	103	335	47	79	22	3	4	31	0-2	4	50-0	114	5-2	.355	.340	.695
2010	New Hampshire (East)	.246	129	459	70	113	31	3	13	70	1-2	9	66-1	142	17-6	.412	.351	.763
2011	Las Vegas (PCL)	.306	134	520	83	159	46	4	17	85	1-3	0	61-2	136	11-7	.508	.377	.884
	TORONTO (AL)	.188	14	32	4	6	1	0	1	4	0-0	2	3-0	13	0-0	.297	.313	.610
2012	St. Lucie (FSL)	.286	4	14	2	4	1	0	0	1	0-0	0	3-0	2	0-0	.357	.412	.769
	Buffalo (Int)	.227	59	207	32	47	10	0	8	26	0-0	1	30-1	55	4-1	.391	.328	.719
Minor Totals		.262	429	1535	234	402	110	10	42	213	2-7	14	210-4	449	37-16	.429	.354	.783

WORLD BASEBALL CLASSIC

Year	Club & League	W-L	ERA	G	GS	CG	ShO	SV	IP	H	R	ER	HR	HB	BB-IBB	SO	WP	BK
2006	Canada	1-0	0.00	1	1	0	0	0	3.2	3	0	0	0	0	3-0	0	0	0

HOME RUN BREAKDOWN

			ONE GAME									
Total	H	A	2	3	4	GS	LO	XN	IP	PH	RHP	LHP
1	1	0	0	0	0	0	0	0	0	0	1	0

TRANSACTIONS

- Selected by the Baltimore Orioles in the 1st round (4th overall) of the 2002 First Year Player Draft
- On disabled list (stress fracture of left elbow) May 2-remainder of season, 2007
- On disabled list (stress fracture of left elbow) April 25-June 30, 2008; included rehabilitation assignment with Frederick (AA) June 10-15 and with Bowie (AAA) June 18-28
- On disabled list (stress fracture of left elbow) July 8-remainder of season, 2008
- Signed by the Toronto Blue Jays on October 24, 2008
- Signed by the New York Mets on November 12, 2011
- Signed by the Toronto Blue Jays on January 14, 2013

GAME HIGHS

ML Debut	May 23, 2006 at SEA	**ER Allowed**	6 - Aug. 11, 2006 at BOS
Innings Pitched:		**HR Allowed**	2 – 2x, last April 5, 2008 vs. SEA
Starter	8.0 - Aug. 22, 2006 vs. MIN	**Low Hit CG**	None
Reliever	4.1 - May 27, 2006 at LAA	**Last Win**	April 21, 2007 vs. TOR
Walks:		**Last Save**	None
Starter	7 - April 21, 2007 vs. TOR	**Last CG**	None
Reliever	2 - 3x, last July 6, 2008 vs. TEX	**Last ShO**	None
Strikeouts:		**Last Start**	April 24, 2008 at SEA
Starter	8 - 2x, last Sept. 24, 2006 vs. MIN	**Last Relief App.**	July 6, 2008 vs. TEX
Reliever	6 - May 27, 2006 at LAA	**Longest Win Streak**	3G – Aug. 16-Sept. 2, 2006
Hits Allowed	11 – June 8, 2006 vs. TOR	**Longest Losing Streak**	2G - 2x, last April 16-Aug. 3, 2008
Runs Allowed	7 – June 13, 2006 at TOR	**Scoreless Innings Streak**	10.0 - April 6-16, 2007

GAME HIGHS

ML Debut	May 23, 2006 at SEA	**RBI**	2 - Sept. 14, 2011 at BOS
Runs	1 - 4x, last Sept. 21, 2011 vs. LAA	**Stolen Bases**	None
Hits	2 - 2x, last Sept. 14, 2011 at BOS	**Last ML Home Run**	Sept. 11, 2011 vs. BAL
Doubles	1 - Sept. 26, 2011 at CWS	**Longest Hitting Streak**	2G - Sept. 7-11, 2011
Home Runs	1 - Sept. 11, 2011 vs. BAL	**Longest Hitless Streak**	15AB - Sept. 17-26, 2011

CAREER FIELDING

POSITION	PCT	G	PO	A	E	TC	DP
P	1.000	35	5	22	0	27	0
OF	.864	8	19	0	3	22	0

MILESTONES

Category		Date	Opponent	Pitcher	Notes
Hit	1	Sept. 7, 2011	Boston	Bard	single
Home Run	1	Sept. 11, 2011	Baltimore	Hunter	1R
RBI	1	Sept. 11, 2011	Baltimore	Hunter	HR (1R)

PROFESSIONAL CAREER:

2003:

- Orioles No. 1 pick in 2002 draft agreed to terms on May 27, 2003, shortly before the midnight deadline to sign players selected in the previous year's draft... Was signed to a 5-year Major League contract.
- Rated by Baseball America as the Orioles' No. 1 prospect.

2004:

- Left his start on May 13 vs. Charleston-SC after 3.0 innings with a muscle strain in his left rib cage... Was sidelined for four weeks.
- Went to Orioles' fall instructional league camp but was diagnosed with a slightly torn left labrum... Rehabbed through the fall and did not require surgery.

2005:

- Was 2nd on Frederick and tied for 4th in Carolina League (A) with 146 strikeouts... Led Orioles farmhands and the Carolina League and was 2nd among all minor leaguers with 86 walks allowed.
- Made two starts in the Carolina League playoffs, going 0-1 and allowing five earned runs in 10.0 IP.
- Pitched for Peoria in the Arizona Fall League... Went 2-1 with a 1.67 ERA in seven games.

2006:

- Was recalled from Bowie on May 23 and made his **Major League debut** that night at Seattle.
- Did not allow a home run from July 21 to Sept. 19, a string of 216 batters in between... It was the longest homerless streak by a Major League pitcher at the time, according to the Elias Sports Bureau.
- Following his relief outing on July 21, returned to the starting rotation for the remainder of the season, winning six of his last 13 starts.
- Won his first Major League game on July 26 at KC, allowing one run in 5.0 IP in the Orioles' 4-3 victory.
- Pitched for Canada in the World Baseball Classic and earned the win over the United States on March 8, pitching 3.2 scoreless innings.

2007:

- Made six starts in his 2nd season with the O's but did not pitch after May 1 due to an elbow injury.
- Left his May 1 start at DET after 5.0 innings and was placed on the disabled list on May 4, retro to May 2, with a stress fracture in his left elbow... Underwent surgery to have a screw inserted into the elbow on June 14.

2008:

- Started four games for the O's and appeared in three other contests before suffering a season ending re-injury of a stress fracture in his left elbow that he suffered in 2007.
- Was placed on the disabled list on April 25 with left elbow soreness after his fourth & final start.
- Activated from the disabled list on June 30 & joined the Orioles bullpen before being shut down & placed on the disabled list again on July 8 with a re-injury of the stress fracture that sidelined him in 2007.
- Was given his unconditional release by the Orioles on Oct. 20, 2008.
- Signed with the Toronto Blue Jays on Oct. 24, 2008 & will began making the transformation to position player after suffering recurring stress fractures in his pitching elbow the last two seasons.

2009:

- Played the full season at Dunedin (A) in the Florida State League, in his first year as a position player.
- His 50 walks led the club and his .340 OBP ranked 2nd.
- Commited only four errors, with just three coming in the outfield for a .977 fielding percentage.

2010:

- Played the entire year with New Hampshire (AA) of the Eastern League.
- Had two, two home run games: May 4 vs. New Britain and June 2 at Reading.

2011:

- Returned to the Major Leagues for the first time since July 6, 2008 and his first time as a position player.
- His contract was selected by Toronto on September 7...Started in rightfield that night vs. Boston...Went 1-3 with a single against Daniel Bard.
- Hit his first Major League home run, a solo shot, on September 11 vs. Baltimore (off Tommy Hunter).
- Spent the majority of the year with Las Vegas (AAA) of the Pacific Coast League.
- Was 6th in all of the minor leagues in doubles... Ranked 2nd in the PCL to teammate David Cooper in that category.

TIP O'NEILL AWARD

The James (Tip) O'Neill award is given to a Canadian baseball player that is judged to have excelled in individual achievement and team contribution while adhering to the highest of the game of baseball. Tip O'Neill, a Canadian, batted .492 in 1887 which is the highest single season batting average ever recorded. The award is presented annually by the Canadian Baseball Hall of Fame & Museum.

Here is a list of the previous recipients of the Tip O'Neill award:

2012 – Joey Votto
2011 – Joey Votto/John Axford
2010 – Joey Votto
2009 – Jason Bay
2008 – Justin Morneau
2007 – Russell Martin
2006 – Justin Morneau
2005 – Jason Bay
2004 – Jason Bay
2003 – Éric Gagné
2002 – Éric Gagné & Larry Walker
2001 – Corey Koskie & Larry Walker
2000 – Ryan Dempster
1999 – Jeff Zimmerman
1998 – Larry Walker
1997 – Larry Walker
1996 – Jason Dickson
1995 – Larry Walker
1994 – Larry Walker
1993 – Rob Butler
1992 – Larry Walker
1991 – Daniel Brabant
1990 – Larry Walker
1989 – Steve Wilson
1988 – Kevin Reimer
1987 – Larry Walker
1986 – Rob Ducey
1985 – Dave Shipanoff
1984 – Terry Puhl

O' CANADA

The Blue Jays have posted an overall record of 11-23 in games which occur on Canada Day (July 1)...Are 9-14 at home (2-7 at Exhibition Stadium/7-7 at Rogers Centre) and are 2-9 on the road...Toronto did not play a game on Canada Day in 1981 and 1993.

Are 1-0 vs. LAA, 1-1 vs. PHI, 1-1 vs. CLE, 2-0 vs. TB, 1-4 vs. SEA, 1-4 vs. BOS, 0-1 vs. DET, 1-5 vs. BAL, 0-1 vs. KC, 1-1 vs. TEX, 2-1 vs. OAK, 0-2 vs. NYY, 1-0 vs. NYM & 0-1 vs. MON on Canada Day.

LOUP, *AARON*

Birthdate .... December 19, 1987
Opening Day Age 25
Birthplace. .... Raceland, LA
Residence. .... Hahnville, LA
Bats/Throws .... L/L
Height/Weight 6-0/208
Contract Status .... signed thru 2013
M.L. Service 0.083

62
PITCHER

PERSONAL:

Aaron Christopher Loup... Attended Tulane University, majored in digital design... Attended Hahnville High School in Louisiana... Was a two-time first-team All-District 6-5A and all-metro... Participated in the Blue Jays Winter Tour in 2013.

LAST SEASON:

- Made 33 appearances in his first Major League season.
- Held opponents to a .232 average, including .207 mark and only two XBH (2-2B) vs. left-handed hitters.
- Made his Major League debut on July14 vs. CLE, tossing two perfect innings.
- 10 of his 33 outings were for more than one inning... In those contests posted a 0.96 ERA (18.2IP/2ER).
- Allowed runs in five of his first nine outings and then allowed a run in just one of his final 24 outings... In 14 day games did not give up a run totalling 14.2 innings... Allowed just five hits in those day game outings.
- When used on back-to-back days or with one day rest posted a 2.40 ERA in 20 games... Had a 3.77 ERA vs. the AL East and 1.65 vs. all other clubs.
- Began the season with New Hampshire (AA) until his recall to Toronto on July 13... Made 37 relief appearances for the Fisher Cats... Posted a 0-3 record with three saves and a 2.78 ERA... Has 11 outings of two or more innings... With runners in scoring position at AA limited hitters to a .218 average.

AARON LOUP

Bold – career high

Year	Club & League	W-L	ERA	G	GS	CG	ShO	SV	IP	H	R	ER	HR	HB	BB-IBB	SO	WP	BK	OBA
2009	Blue Jays (Gulf)	2-1	3.86	13	0	0	0	3	16.1	17	9	7	0	3	3-0	19	1	0	.274
2010	Lansing (Mid)	3-2	4.54	35	5	0	0	2	73.1	79	37	37	4	5	22-1	73	3	0	.283
2011	Dunedin (FSL)	4-3	4.66	48	0	0	0	5	65.2	67	38	34	6	6	27-2	56	6	1	.269
2012	New Hampshire (East)	0-3	2.78	37	0	0	0	3	45.1	46	19	14	4	5	14-1	43	3	1	.263
	TORONTO (AL)	0-2	2.64	33	0	0	0	0	30.2	26	10	9	0	0	2-0	21	1	1	.232
Minor Totals		9-9	4.13	133	5	0	0	13	200.2	209	103	92	14	19	66-4	191	13	3	.273

TRANSACTIONS

- Selected by the Toronto Blue Jays in the 9th round of the 2009 First Year Player Draft

GAME HIGHS

ML Debut	July 14, 2012 vs. CLE
Innings Pitched:	
Starter	None
Reliever	2.1 - July 22, 2012 at BOS
Walks:	
Starter	None
Reliever	1 - 2x, last Sept. 15, 2012 vs. BOS
Strikeouts:	
Starter	None
Reliever	3 - 2x, last Sept. 1, 2012 vs. TB
Hits Allowed	5 - Sept. 4, 2012 vs. BAL
Runs Allowed	4 - Sept. 4, 2012 vs. BAL
ER Allowed	4 - Sept. 4, 2012 vs. BAL
HR Allowed	None
Low Hit CG	None
Last Win	None
Last Save	None
Last CG	None
Last ShO	None
Last Start	None
Last Relief App.	Oct. 2, 2012 vs. MIN
Longest Win Streak	None
Longest Losing Streak	2G - July 16-Aug. 3, 2012
Scoreless Innings Streak	10.1 - Aug. 5-Sept. 1, 2012

CAREER FIELDING

POSITION	PCT	G	PO	A	E	TC	DP
P	1.000	33	2	7	0	9	0

PROFESSIONAL CAREER:

2009:

- Made his professional debut as a member of the Gulf Coast Blue Jays on July 21...Allowed 5ER over 0.1 IP in that contest and allowed only 2ER in his other 12 outings over 16IP..

2010:

- Made his first career start on April 30 vs. Fort Wayne (no decision)
- Made five starts over 35 appearances with the Lugnuts

2011:

- Played the entire season with the Dunedin Blue Jays (A)
- Made 48 appearances, all in relief, posting a 4.66 ERA (34ER/65.2 IP)
- Posted a career high five saves

McCOY, *MIKE*

Birthdate	April 2, 1981
Opening Day Age	32
Birthplace	San Diego, CA
Residence	San Diego, CA
Bats/Throws	R/R
Height/Weight	5-9/179
Contract Status	signed thru 2013
M.L. Service	2.010

18

INFIELDER

NON-ROSTER

PERSONAL:

Michael "Mike" Howard McCoy... Married with two children... Attended Grossmont High School in El Cajon, California before playing for the University of San Diego... As a junior led the Toreros in doubles (16) and stolen bases (26), helping USD capture the 2002 West Coast Conference title.

LAST SEASON:

- Made 12 starts, three at 2B, four at 3B, three in CF and one in LF in his third season in the organization... Was recalled twice, once on May 29 then again on August 11.
- Hit his 3rd career home run off Matt Harrison, August 19 vs. TEX.
- Collected three hits in his first eight at-bats, then was 6-44 through the balance of the season.
- With Las Vegas (AAA) appeared in 85 games, batting .263 with 13 doubles, one triple, three home runs, 31 RBI and 21 stolen bases... Had time at second base, shortstop, thrid base, left field and centre field... Posted a .306 average following the PCL All-Star break...Had a .460 on base percentage when leading off an inning.

MIKE McCOY

Bold – career high

Year	Club & League	AVG	G	AB	R	H	2B	3B	HR	RBI	SH-SF	HP	BB-IBB	SO	SB-CS	SLG	OBP	OPS
2002	Johnson Cty (Appy)	.312	50	154	46	48	9	1	4	22	2-1	3	42-0	23	18-7	.461	.465	.926
2003	Peoria (Mid)	.252	131	464	67	117	16	5	5	46	10-3	16	51-0	77	24-10	.341	.345	.686
2004	Peoria (Mid)	.216	55	194	26	42	8	3	2	17	8-2	3	24-1	35	9-3	.320	.309	.629
	Palm Beach (FSL)	.301	61	176	34	53	12	1	2	23	2-1	5	31-2	32	7-4	.415	.418	.833
	Tennessee (Sou)	.000	3	6	0	0	0	0	0	0	0-0	0	0-0	3	0-0	.000	.000	.000
2005	Palm Beach (FSL)	.270	86	282	47	76	13	2	1	27	8-3	3	36-1	56	18-3	.340	.355	.695
	Springfield (TEX)	.143	5	14	1	2	0	0	0	1	0-1	1	0-0	5	0-0	.143	.188	.331
2006	Springfield (TEX)	.249	129	474	64	118	14	2	3	37	16-0	7	62-0	98	30-9	.306	.344	.650
2007	Springfield (TEX)	.221	24	68	5	15	3	1	0	10	2-1	0	14-1	14	1-3	.294	.349	.643
	Memphis (PCL)	.247	90	239	31	59	8	0	3	16	11-0	1	45-0	43	12-4	.318	.368	.686
2008	Norfolk (Int)	.276	53	152	25	42	6	1	2	16	4-1	0	19-0	27	6-3	.368	.355	.723
	Frederick (Caro)	.600	1	5	1	3	0	0	0	1	0-0	0	0-0	1	0-1	.600	.600	1.200
	Colorado Springs (PCL)	.343	39	140	32	48	7	2	4	27	1-6	0	15-0	20	7-1	.507	.391	.898
2009	Colorado Springs (PCL)	.307	132	462	102	142	27	5	2	52	16-11	3	80-1	70	40-6	.400	.405	.805
	COLORADO (NL)	.000	12	5	1	0	0	0	0	0	1-0	0	0-0	2	2-0	.000	.000	.000
2010	Las Vegas (PCL)	.310	53	213	48	66	14	1	6	26	6-2	1	37-0	31	17-2	.469	.411	.881
	TORONTO (AL)	.195	46	82	9	16	4	0	0	3	0-0	0	8-0	20	5-1	.244	.267	.511
2011	Las Vegas (PCL)	.311	38	148	33	46	6	0	2	20	4-0	1	33-0	23	14-5	.392	.440	.831
	TORONTO (AL)	.198	**80**	197	**26**	**39**	**8**	0	**2**	**10**	5-0	1	**25**-1	**41**	**12**-2	.269	.291	.561
2012	Las Vegas (PCL)	.263	85	278	46	73	13	1	3	31	7-5	1	58-0	51	21-10	.349	.386	.735
	TORONTO (AL)	.173	32	52	10	9	1	0	1	7	0-0	0	4-0	6	2-1	.250	.232	.482
Minor Totals		.274	1035	3469	608	950	156	25	39	372	97-37	45	547-6	609	224-71	.367	.376	.743
TORONTO TOTALS		.193	158	331	45	64	13	0	3	20	5-0	1	37-1	67	19-4	.260	.276	.536
MAJOR TOTALS		.190	170	336	46	64	13	0	3	20	6-0	1	37-1	69	21-4	.256	.273	.529

HOME RUN BREAKDOWN

Total	H	A	ONE GAME 2	3	4	GS	LO	XN	IP	PH	RHP	LHP
3	1	2	0	0	0	0	0	0	0	0	2	1

TRANSACTIONS

- Selected by the St. Louis Cardinals in the 34th round of the 2002 First Year Player Draft
- Traded to the Baltimore Orioles in exchange for cash considerations on March 22, 2008
- Traded to the Colorado Rockies in exchange for IF Juan Castro on July 19, 2008
- Claimed off waivers by the Toronto Blue Jays on November 9, 2009

GAME HIGHS

ML Debut	Sept. 9, 2009 vs. CIN	**RBI**	3 - Sept. 17, 2011 vs. NYY
Runs	3 - Sept. 11, 2011 vs. BAL	**Stolen Bases**	2 - 3x, last Sept. 26, 2011 at CWS
Hits	3 - 3x, last Sept. 20, 2011 vs. LAA	**Last ML Home Run**	Aug. 19, 2012 vs. TEX
Doubles	2 - 2x, last July 21, 2011 vs. SEA	**Longest Hitting Streak**	5G - Sept. 1-5, 2011
Home Runs	1 - 3x, last Aug. 19, 2012 vs. TEX	**Longest Hitless Streak**	18AB - April 20-June 8, 2010

CAREER FIELDING

POSITION	PCT	G	PO	A	E	TC	DP
P	--	1	0	0	0	0	0
2B	.991	34	32	75	1	108	13
3B	1.000	26	8	24	0	32	1
SS	.964	34	48	86	5	139	15
OF	.987	45	74	3	1	78	0

MILESTONES

Category		Date	Opponent	Pitcher	Notes
Hit	1	April 8, 2010	at Texas	Wilson	Single
Home Run	1	April 30, 2011	at New York (AL)	Burnett	1R
RBI	1	April 8, 2010	at Texas	Feliz	RBI single
Stolen Base	1	Sept. 24, 2009	San Diego	Richard C-Hundley	3rd base

PROFESSIONAL CAREER:

2002:

- Was named to the Appalachian League All-Star team as a middle infielder.
- Ranked 4th in the league with 42 walks and a .465 on-base percentage.

2003:

- Spent the entire season with Peoria (A) as one of the club's primary middle infielders.

2004:

- Split the season between three stops in the Cardinals system... Began the season with Peoria for the 2nd straight year before being transfered to Palm Beach.

2005:

- Spent the majority of the season at Palm Beach (A) before being transfered to Springfield at the end of the season.

2006:

- Had a career best 30 stolen bases, which were the 2nd most in the Cardinals minor league system, and 3rd most in the Texas League.

2007:

- Split the season between Springfield (AA) and Memphis (AAA) in the St. Louis system.

2008:

- Spent the majority of the season with Norfolk, although he played one game for Frederick (A) in July, before being released and signed by Colorado.
- After signing with Colorado Springs, he became the club's primary 2nd baseman for the remainder of the season.

2009:

- Appeared in 12 games for the Rockies after his first promotion to the Major Leagues on Sept. 8.
- On Sept. 9 was inserted as a defensive replacement in the top of the 9th inning vs. CIN, making his **Major League debut**.
- Fanned vs. Kip Wells on Sept. 10 in his first Major League at-bat.
- Batted .307 for the Sky Sox, leading the club with a .405 on base percentage, 2nd in stolen bases with 40 and T-2nd with 27 doubles.
- Appeared at every position on the diamond except first base and catcher (60-SS, 38-3B, 24-CF, 10-RF, 7-LF, 6-2B, 1-P).
- May 14 vs. Iowa was called upon to pitch an inning... Retired all three batters he faced.

2010:

- Made his first opening day lineup, staying with the club until June 16.
- Was recalled by the Blue Jays on July 22 and again on Aug. 28... Played 46 games in total with the Blue Jays, making 20 starts (seven at 2B, five at SS, six in LF, two in RF).
- Was one of two Blue Jays to make a start at four different positions on the field that season (McDonald).
- Recorded 1st ML hit April 8 at TEX off C.J. Wilson to leadoff the game.

2011:

- Appeared in a career high 80 games, splitting time between Las Vegas (AAA) and Toronto.
- In total was optioned and recalled six times for a total seven different stints with the Blue Jays this season.
- Appeared at every spot on the diamond except for C, LF and 1B (2B-10, SS-26, 3B-16, CF-16, RF-5, P-1).
- Made the majority of his starts at shortstop, starting there on 21 occasions in 52 total starts... Made only five errors all season with four coming as a shortstop.
- On June 11 vs. BOS, recorded his first outing in the Major Leagues as a pitcher... Closed out the 16-4 loss with a 1-2-3 ninth, the only one recorded by Toronto hurlers that day... Recorded outs on Carl Crawford, Marco Scutaro and JD Drew.
- It marked his 4th professional outing as a pitcher (three minor league)... Has allowed only one run in 6.2 innings for a 1.35 ERA.
- April 30 vs. NYY hit his first career home run off AJ Burnett.
- June 9 at KC walked a career high four times, which was the most by a Blue Jay since Alex Rios accomplished the feat on May 19, 2007 at PHI... The four walks tied a club record, done 14 times by 10 different players.

McGOWAN, *DUSTIN*

29

PITCHER

Birthdate	March 24, 1982
Opening Day Age	31
Birthplace	Savannah, GA
Residence	Tallahassee, FL
Bats/Throws	R/R
Height/Weight	6-3/232
Contract Status	signed thru 2014
M.L. Service	5.113

PERSONAL:

Dustin Michael McGowan... Married with one child... Was drafted out of Long County High School in Ludowici, GA... Named as the team MVP in both baseball and basketball... All Region in basketball... All State in baseball... Played Little League, Junior and Senior League... Enjoys fishing, hunting and golf.

LAST SEASON:

- On March 26 signed a two year contract extension with the Blue Jays.
- Spent the enitre 2012 season on the disabled list... Has spent the enitre year on the disabled list in three of his last four seasons.
- Was placed on the 15-day disabled list on April 3 with plantar fasciitis of his right foot... Was later transferred to the 60-day disabled list on May 25 after recurring soreness in his throwing shoulder.

DUSTIN MCGOWAN

Bold – career high

Year	Club & League	W-L	ERA	G	GS	CG	ShO	SV	IP	H	R	ER	HR	HB	BB-IBB	SO	WP	BK	OBA
2000	Medicine Hat (Pio)	0-3	6.48	8	8	0	0	0	25.0	26	21	18	2	3	25-0	19	8	0	.274
2001	Auburn (NYP)	3-6	3.76	15	14	0	0	0	67.0	57	33	28	1	4	49-0	80	16	0	.234
2002	Charleston-WV (SAL)	11-10	4.19	28	28	1	0	0	148.1	143	77	69	10	5	59-0	163	12	0	.251
2003	Dunedin (FSL)	5-6	2.85	14	14	1	1	0	75.2	62	29	24	1	4	25-0	66	9	0	.223
	New Haven (East)	7-0	3.17	14	14	1	0	0	76.2	78	28	27	1	4	19-0	72	5	1	.261
2004	New Hampshire (East)	2-0	4.06	6	6	0	0	0	31.0	24	14	14	4	0	15-0	29	2	0	.209
2005	Dunedin (FSL)	0-1	4.29	5	5	0	0	0	21.0	21	12	10	2	2	5-0	20	0	0	.256
	New Hampshire (East)	0-2	3.34	6	6	0	0	0	35.0	35	16	13	6	1	10-0	33	1	0	.269
	TORONTO (AL)	1-3	6.35	13	7	0	0	0	45.1	49	34	32	7	7	17-0	34	7	0	.277
2006	Syracuse (Int)	3-5	4.39	23	13	0	0	1	84.0	77	45	41	7	3	39-0	86	10	0	.240
	TORONTO (AL)	1-2	7.24	16	3	0	0	0	27.1	35	27	22	2	2	25-2	22	3	1	.304
2007	Syracuse (Int)	0-2	1.64	5	5	0	0	0	22.0	16	6	4	0	0	9-0	29	2	0	.208
	TORONTO (AL)	**12-10**	4.08	**27**	27	2	1	0	**169.2**	146	80	77	14	2	**61**-3	**144**	13	0	.230
2008	TORONTO (AL)	6-7	4.37	19	19	1	0	0	111.1	115	60	54	9	5	38-1	85	5	0	.273
2009	TORONTO (AL)								Injured - Did Not Play										
2010	TORONTO (AL)								Injured - Did Not Play										
2011	Dunedin (FSL)	0-2	2.87	7	7	0	0	0	15.2	13	5	5	0	0	7-0	17	0	0	.228
	New Hampshire (East)	0-2	2.75	5	5	0	0	0	19.2	18	7	6	2	0	7-0	18	0	0	.247
	TORONTO (AL)	0-2	6.43	5	4	0	0	0	21.0	20	15	15	4	1	13-0	20	3	0	.247
2012	TORONTO (AL)								Injured - Did Not Play										
Minor Totals		32-39	3.75	136	125	3	1	1	621.0	570	293	259	36	26	269-0	632	65	2	.243
MAJOR TOTALS		20-24	4.80	80	60	3	1	0	374.2	365	216	200	36	17	154-6	305	31	1	.255

TRANSACTIONS

- Selected by the Toronto Blue Jays in the 1st round (supplemental - 33rd overall) in the 2000 First Year Player Draft
- On disabled list (right elbow soreness) May 13-September 20, 2004
- On disabled list (right shoulder soreness) July 9-remainder of season, 2008
- On disabled list (torn right labrum) for the entire 2009 season
- On disabled list (right shoulder strain) for the entire 2010 season
- On disabled list (recovery from right shoulder suregry) March 12-September 4, 2011; included rehabilitation assignment at Dunedin (A) July 2-26 and at New Hampshire (AA) July 27-September 3
- On disabled list (plantar fasciitis of right foot) for entire season, 2012

GAME HIGHS

ML Debut	July 30, 2005 vs. TEX
Innings Pitched:	
Starter	9.0 – 3x, last June 10, 2008 vs. SEA
Reliever	4.0 - Sept. 6, 2011 vs. BOS
Walks:	
Starter	7 - April 24, 2008 at TB
Reliever	4 - Aug. 5, 2006 vs. CWS
Strikeouts:	
Starter	12 - Sept. 7, 2007 at TB
Reliever	5 - Sept. 6, 2011 vs. BOS
Hits Allowed	10 - April 14, 2008 at BAL

Runs Allowed	12 - Aug. 21, 2005 at DET
ER Allowed	10 - Aug. 21, 2005 at DET
HR Allowed	3 – 2x, last June 17, 2008 at MIL
Low Hit CG	1 - June 24, 2007 vs. COL
Last Win	June 22, 2008 at PIT
Last Save	None
Last CG	June 10, 2008 vs. SEA
Last ShO	June 24, 2007 vs. COL
Last Start	Sept. 26, 2011 at CWS
Last Relief App.	Sept. 6, 2011 vs. BOS
Longest Win Streak	3G - 2x, last July 19- Aug. 5, 2007
Longest Losing Streak	3G - Aug. 21-Sept. 1, 2005
Scoreless Innings Streak	16.0 - July 19-30, 2007

BIOGRAPHIES LAST SEASON HISTORY RECORDS OPPONENTS PLAYER DEV. MEDIA & MISC.

CAREER FIELDING

POSITION	PCT	G	PO	A	E	TC	DP
P	.910	80	35	46	8	89	6

MILESTONES

Category		Date	Opponent	Notes
Start	1	July 30, 2005	Texas	ND, 5.0 IP, 2H, ER, 3BB, 6K
Win	1	Aug. 9, 2005	Detroit	6.1 IP, 8H, 4ER, BB, 4K
10+ Strikeout Games (1)				
	1	Sept. 7, 2007	at Tampa Bay	12 strikeouts
SHO	1	June 24, 2007	Colorado	Took a no-hitter to the 9th (Baker leadoff 1B)—H, BB, 7K.

PROFESSIONAL CAREER:

2004:

- Had his season cut short due to a pre-existing injury to his right elbow... Was placed on the disabled list May 13 and missed the remainder of the season.
- Underwent reconstructive elbow surgery on May 13, otherwise known as "Tommy John" surgery... The operation was performed by Dr. James Andrews in Birmingham, Alabama.

2005:

- Was recalled by the Blue Jays from Class AA, New Hampshire Fisher Cats on July 30th.
- Made his **Major League debut** on July 30 vs. TEX... Received a no decision in a 3-2 loss... 5.0IP, 2H, ER, 3BB, 6K... The six strikeouts were then the most ever by a Blue Jays starter in his ML Debut.
- August 9 vs. DET registered his first ML win.
- Became the 4th first round (or supplemental 1st round) pick in team history to debut as a starter and the first to do so since Roy Halladay on September 20, 1998 at TB... The other two Blue Jays 1st round picks to debut as a starter are Alex Sanchez and Chris Carpenter.

2006:

- Made three separate stints with the Blue Jays this season.
- Earned his 1st career victory in relief on May 30 at BOS.

2007:

- On June 24 vs. COL became the 6th different pitcher (9th time) in Blue Jay history to carry a no-hitter into the 9th inning... Allowed a single to begin the 9th inning to Jeff Baker... The one-hitter marked the 17th one-hitter in Club history (14th by an individual).
- Recorded a career high 15.1 consecutive scoreless innings from July 19-30.
- Voted by the BBWAA as Clubs' pitcher of the month for July, compiling a record of 3-1 with a 2.78 ERA (10ER/32.1IP) in five starts.
- Had a career 12 strikeouts on Sept. 7 at TB.

2008:

- Had season ending debridement (fraying of the labrum) surgery on his right shoulder July 31.
- At the time of his last start in July, ranked 6th in the AL in home ERA.
- Tossed his 3rd complete game of his career, June 10 vs. SEA.

2009:

- Did not pitch... Recovering from debridement (fraying of the labrum) surgery on his right shoulder, July 31, 2008.

2010:

- Did not pitch... Had surgery on his right shoulder to repair a torn rotator cuff on June 22, performed by Dr. James Andrews.
- Was transferred from the 15-Day to the 60-Day disabled list April 15 where he remained for the remainder of the season.

2011:

- Returned to the Major Leagues for the first time since July 8, 2008, making five appearances, including four starts.
- Appeared in a Major League game on Sept. 6 vs. BOS for the first time since starting July 8, 2008 vs. BAL... In his first appearance on Sept. 6, tossed four innings, allowing three runs to the Red Sox.
- His final four outings were all starts... Posted a 0-2 record with a 6.35 ERA in those starts.
- Made 12 rehab starts, splitting time between Dunedin (A) and New Hampshire (AA)... Those appearances were the first of any kind since 2008.

MORROW, *BRANDON*

Birthdate . . . . July 26, 1984
Opening Day Age 29
Birthplace. . . . . Santa Rosa, CA
Residence. . . . . Scottsdale, AZ
Bats/Throws . . . . R/R
Height/Weight 6-3/197
Contract Status . . . . signed thru 2014
M.L. Service 5.091

23

PITCHER

PERSONAL:

Brandon John Morrow (MORE-owe)... Married... Graduated from Rancho Cotate High School in June, 2002... Earned first-team all-league, first-team All-Redwood Empire, first-team All-North Coast Section and second-team All-State honours... Competed for the California All-Stars at the 2002 Sunbelt Classic in McAlester, Oklahoma... Attended the University of California at Berkeley... One of 10 semifinalists for the Roger Clemens Award as the nation's top collegiate pitcher... Named first-team All-Pac-10, going 7-4 with a 2.05 ERA (2nd in Pac-10)... Had 97 strikeouts (4th in Pac-10) in 96.7 innings (9th in Pac-10)... Was named National Pitcher of the Week after 6.1 innings, no hits, no runs, one walk and a career-high 12 strikeouts at UC Irvine Feb. 3... Also named a Cape Cod League All-Star in the summer 2005 for the Yarmouth-Dennis Red Sox... Named a third-team preseason All-American and the fifth-best professional prospect out of the Cape Cod League by Baseball America.

LAST SEASON:

- Was one of only four AL pitchers to post an ERA below 3.00 with a minimum of 120 IP (Price, Verlander, Weaver)... Won 10 or more games for the third consecutive season.
- Was removed from his start on June 11 with an oblique strain and was kept out until Aug. 25... Was 7-4 with a 3.01 ERA in 13 starts prior to being hurt and 3-3 with a 2.87 ERA in eight starts after.
- In the 10 games he won was dominant, allowing just seven earned runs in 92.2 IP for 0.68 ERA... Held opponents to a .168 average in those contests.
- Posted three shutouts ranking 2nd in the AL (Hernandez-5) despite making only 21 starts... The three shutouts were the most by a Blue Jay since Roy Halladay had four in 2009... Tied Jared Weaver for the AL lead with a .214 opponents average (min 120 IP)... Has a 23.2 scoreless innings streak from April 23-May 9 which was the longest for any AL starter in 2012.
- Was more dominant as the game progressed with hitters batting .240 the first time through the order and .201 after that... Since 2007 has posted a .231 opponent's average which ranks 4th in the AL (min 2400 AB).
- Tossed a season high 119 picthes on June 6 recording his 3rd shutout... Had his shortest start of his career lasting just 0.2 IP, giving up 6 ER in a 14-3 loss... Made five starts during the day, going 3-0 with a 0.26 ERA, allowing just one run in 34 innings.
- Held left-handed hitters to a .188 average.

BRANDON MORROW

Bold – career high

Year	Club & League	W-L	ERA	G	GS	CG	ShO	SV	IP	H	R	ER	HR	HB	BB-IBB	SO	WP	BK	OBA
2006	Mariners (ARIZ)	0-2	2.77	7	4	0	0	0	13.0	10	4	4	0	0	9-0	13	3	0	.227
	Inland Empire (CAL)	0-0	0.00	1	1	0	0	0	3.0	0	0	0	0	0	0-0	4	0	0	.000
2007	SEATTLE (AL)	3-4	4.12	**60**	0	0	0	0	63.1	56	29	29	3	1	50-5	66	4	0	.243
2008	West Tenn (SOU)	0-0	0.00	6	0	0	0	0	7.1	3	1	0	0	0	6-0	8	2	0	.125
	Tacoma (PCL)	1-2	5.01	6	5	0	0	0	23.1	17	13	13	2	0	11-0	26	3	0	.200
	SEATTLE (AL)	3-4	3.34	45	5	0	0	**10**	64.2	40	26	24	10	0	34-1	75	5	0	.174
2009	Tacoma (PCL)	5-3	3.60	10	10	1	1	0	55.0	50	24	22	2	1	23-0	40	6	0	.242
	SEATTLE (AL)	2-4	4.39	26	10	0	0	6	69.2	66	38	34	10	0	44-1	63	3	0	.248
2010	TORONTO (AL)	10-7	4.49	26	26	1	1	0	146.1	136	76	73	11	9	66-0	178	8	0	.248
2011	Dunedin (FSL)	0-2	7.71	3	3	0	0	0	9.1	13	9	8	0	0	6-0	11	3	0	.310
	TORONTO (AL)	**11-11**	4.72	30	**30**	0	0	0	**179.1**	162	103	94	**21**	12	**69**-1	**203**	12	1	.237
2012	Dunedin (FSL)	0-0	1.50	2	2	0	0	0	6.0	8	2	1	0	0	3-0	6	0	0	.348
	New Hampshire (East)	1-0	2.51	3	3	0	0	0	14.1	10	4	4	2	0	3-0	12	1	0	.200
	TORONTO (AL)	10-7	2.96	21	21	**3**	**3**	0	124.2	98	45	41	12	2	41-0	108	3	0	.214
Minor Totals		7-9	3.56	38	28	1	1	0	131.1	111	57	52	6	1	61-0	120	18	0	.229
TORONTO TOTALS		31-25	4.16	77	77	4	4	0	450.1	396	224	208	44	23	176-1	489	23	1	.235
MAJOR TOTALS		39-37	4.10	208	92	4	4	16	648.0	558	317	295	67	24	304-8	693	35	1	.231

TRANSACTIONS

- Selected by the Seattle Mariners in the 1st round (5th overall) of the 2006 First Year Player Draft
- On disabled list (right tricep tendinitis) April 24-May 9, 2009
- Traded to the Toronto Blue Jays in exchange for RHP Brandon League and OF Johermyn Chavez on December 23, 2009
- On disabled list (right forearm inflammation) March 31-April 20, 2011; included rehabilitation assignment at Dunedin (A) April 7-19
- On disabled list (strained left oblique) from June 13-August 25, 2012; included rehabilitation assignment at Dunedin (A) July 29 and New Hampshire (AA) from August 8-24

GAME HIGHS

ML Debut	April 3, 2007 vs. OAK	**ER Allowed**	9 - June 11, 2011 vs. BOS
Innings Pitched:		**HR Allowed**	3 - 5x, last April 18, 2012 vs. TB
Starter	9.0 - 4x, last June 6, 2012 at CWS	**Low Hit CG**	1 - Aug. 8, 2010 vs. TB
Reliever	3.1 - April 23, 2007 at TEX	**Last Win**	Oct. 3, 2012 vs. MIN
Walks:		**Last Save**	May 10, 2009 at MIN
Starter	6 - 3x, last May 10, 2010 at BOS	**Last CG**	June 6, 2012 at CWS
Reliever	4 - June 11, 2007 at CLE	**Last ShO**	June 6, 2012 at CWS
Strikeouts:		**Last Start**	Oct. 3, 2012 vs. MIN
Starter	17 - Aug. 8, 2010 vs. TB	**Last Relief App.**	June 9, 2009 at BAL
Reliever	4 - May 12, 2008 at TEX	**Longest Win Streak**	5G - 2x, last June 18-Jul. 20, 2011
Hits Allowed	11 - 2x, last Sept. 11, 2012 vs. SEA	**Longest Losing Streak**	4G - 3x, last Aug. 23-Sept. 13, 2011
Runs Allowed	9 - June 11, 2011 vs. BOS	**Scoreless Innings Streak**	24.1 - April 23-May 9, 2012

CAREER FIELDING

POSITION	PCT	G	PO	A	E	TC	DP
P	.944	208	23	44	4	71	3

MILESTONES

Category		Date	Opponent	Notes
Start	1	Sept. 5, 2008	New York (AL)	W, 7.2 IP, H, ER, 3BB, 8K
Win	1	April 23, 2007	at Texas	Relief - 3.1 IP, H, ER, 2BB, 2K
Save	1	June 11, 2008	at Toronto	1.0 IP, 2K
ShO (4)	1	Aug. 8, 2010	Tampa Bay	9.0 IP, H, 2BB, 17K
	2	May 3, 2012	at Los Angeles (AL)	9.0 IP, 3H, 8K
	3	May 19, 2012	New York (NL)	9.0 IP, 3H, BB, 8K
	4	June 6, 2012	at Chicago (AL)	9.0 IP, 2H, 2BB, 5K
10+ Strikeout Games (8)				
	1	Aug. 8, 2010	Tampa Bay	17 strikeouts
	2	Aug. 23, 2010	New York (AL)	12 strikeouts
	3	April 23, 2011	Tampa Bay	10 strikeouts
	4	June 29, 2011	Pittsburgh	10 strikeouts
	5	July 31, 2011	Texas	11 strikeouts
	6	Aug. 17, 2011	at Seattle	12 strikeouts
	7	May 9, 2012	at Oakland	10 strikeouts
	8	Oct. 3, 2012	Minnesota	11 strikeouts
Strikeout	500	July 26, 2011	Baltimore	Reimold

PROFESSIONAL CAREER:

2006:

- Began pro career with Peoria, appearing in seven games, four starts.

2007:

- Made **Major League debut** April 3 vs. Oakland with 1.0 scoreless IP… Became the 3rd player from the 2006 draft class to pitch in the Majors (Andrew Miller, DET; Joe Smith, NYM).
- Among AL rookie relievers, ranked 2nd in strikeouts (66), 3rd in appearances (60) and 4th in ERA (4.12).
- Earned first ML win April 23 at Texas, allowing one hit in career-high 3.1 IP… Recorded 18.2 consecutive scoreless innings April 20-June 8… Also recorded scoreless streak of 17.0 IP over 15 outings July 17-Aug. 24 (23 strikeouts/7 walks).

2008:

- Relief ERA of 1.47 ranked 2nd-lowest in club history (min. 30.0 IP), trailing only J.J. Putz (1.38 in 2007).
- Made first Major League start in 101st career appearance, Sept. 5 vs. New York… Allowed one hit, one run and struck out nine in 7.2 innings.
- No-hit the Yankees through 7.2 innings, becoming the first player in more than 40 years to take a no-hitter that far into a game in his first career start… Boston's Billy Rohr went 8.2 innings without allowing a hit on Opening Day in 1967 at Yankee Stadium (4/14/67)… Joined Juan Marichal (1960), Rudy May (1965) and Steve Woodward (1997) as the only players since 1900 to pitch at least 7.2 innings, allow one hit and strike out at least eight in their first ML start.
- Recorded a then career high 17.2 consecutive scoreless innings during stretch, the longest streak by a Mariners pitcher in 2008.
- Missed five games (back spasms) June 20-24 (at ATL & at NYM).
- Optioned to Tacoma (AAA) on Aug. 5 to begin transition to become a starting pitcher.

2009:

- Placed on 15-day disabled list with biceps tendintis in right arm, April 24-May 9.
- Optioned to Tacoma July 11 and recalled back to Seattle on Sept. 9.

200 STRIKEOUT SEASONS BY A BLUE JAY, ALL TIME

Roger Clemens, 1997	292
Roger Clemens, 1998	271
A.J. Burnett, 2008	231
Roy Halladay, 2009	208
Roy Halladay, 2008	206
Roy Halladay, 2003	204
Brandon Morrow, 2011	**203**

2010:

- At the time of his final start, ranked 5th in the AL in strikeouts and led the league with a 10.95 strikeouts per nine inning total.
- Aug. 8 vs. TB carried a no-hitter into the 9th inning with two outs before giving up a single to Evan Longoria... Became the 6th pitcher (9th time) in franchise history to lose a no-hit bid in the 9th (previous: Dustin McGowan on June 24, 2007 vs. COL)... Was the 1st pitcher to record 17 strikeouts in a game since Johan Santana with MIN on Aug. 19, 2007 vs. TEX (17-SO)... Became just the 4th pitcher since 1954 to record at least 17 strikeouts when tossing a CG-1 hitter... The 17 strikeouts ranks 2nd on the all-time Club list in a single game one shy of Roger Clemens' 18 on Aug. 25, 1998 vs. KC.
- Followed the 17-K game with his 2nd highest career total (12) vs. NYY, Aug. 23.
- Was voted by the Toronto chapter of the BBWAA as the Blue Jays Player-of-the-Month for June, registering a 1.91 ERA in five starts.

2011:

- Posted career highs in wins (11), starts (30), innings pitched (179.1) and strikeouts (203).
- Did not make his first start until April 23... Was shut down after his March 18 spring start with forearm tightness, returning after three rehab starts for Dunedin.
- Was one of seven AL hurlers to post 200+ strikeouts (203)... Led the league with 10.19 strikeouts per nine innings, more than a full strikeout higher than second place finisher Michael Pineda (9.11).
- Posted four games of 10+ strikeouts, including a season high 12 on Aug. 17 at SEA.
- Had a team season high of 18 scoreless innings Sept. 18-28.
- Won five straight decisions from June 18-July 20.

STRIKEOUTS PER 9 INNINGS (2010-2012), MLB LEADERS

1.	**Brandon Morrow, TOR**	**9.77**
2.	Tim Lincecum, SF	9.38
3.	Clayton Kershaw, LAD	9.32
4.	Yovani Gallardo, MIL	9.22
5.	Max Scherzer, DET	9.17

TOP 5 STRIKEOUT PER 9 INNINGS SEASON, CLUB HISTORY

Roger Clemens, 1998	10.39
Brandon Morrow, 2011	**10.19**
Roger Clemens, 1997	9.95
A.J. Burnett, 2007	9.56
A.J. Burnett, 2008	9.39

NEAR NO-HITTERS SPOILED IN THE 9TH INNING

Pitcher	Date	Opposition	Outs	Final	Details
Jim Clancy	Sept. 28/82 (G#1)	Minnesota (H)	0	3-0 win	Bush single
Dave Stieb	Aug. 24/85	Chicago (A)	0	6-3 win	Law home run
Dave Stieb	Sept. 24/88	Cleveland (A)	2	1-0 win	Franco single
Dave Stieb	Sept. 30/88	Baltimore (H)	2	4-0 win	Traber single
Dave Stieb	Aug. 4/89	New York (H)	2	2-1 win	Kelly double, Sax single
David Cone	June 17/95	Texas (H)	1	4-3 win	Gil single
Roy Halladay	Sept. 27/98	Detroit (H)	2	2-1 win	Higginson home run
Dustin McGowan	June 24/07	Colorado (H)	0	5-0 win	Baker single
Brandon Morrow	Aug. 8/10	Tampa Bay (H)	2	1-0 win	Longoria single

MURPHY, *JACK*

Birthdate . . . . April 6, 1988
Opening Day Age 24
Birthplace. . . . . .Sarasota, FL
Residence. . . . . .Sarasota, FL
Bats/Throws . . . . S/R
Height/Weight 6-4/235
Contract Status . . . . signed thru 2013
M.L. Service 0.000

76

CATCHER
NON-ROSTER

PERSONAL:

John "Jack" Murphy... Attended Bartow High School in Sarasota... Attended Princeton and holds the top career fielding percentage of any Princeton Tiger... Attended Princeton along with Blue Jays farmhand Daniel Barnes.

LAST SEASON:

- Spent the majority of the season at Dunedin (A) appearing in 86 games for the Blue Jays... 84 games came as a catcher, with one as a 1B and one at DH.
- Hit .251 vs. RH pitchers and .172 vs. LH pitchers with Dunedin.
- Appeared in eight games with New Hampshire (AA) in July, posting a double and two home runs... Hit .438 vs. righties and .125 vs lefties with the Fisher Cats.
- Overall threw out 38.2% of potential base stealers (29-76).

JACK MURPHY

Bold – career high

Year	Club and League	AVG	G	AB	R	H	2B	3B	HR	RBI	SH-SF	HP	BB-IBB	SO	SB-CS	SLG	OBP	OPS
2009	Auburn (NYP)	.279	19	61	7	17	3	0	2	8	0-0	0	11-0	8	0-0	.426	.389	.815
	BlueJays (GCL)	.261	28	88	12	23	8	0	1	14	0-0	0	11-1	17	1-1	.386	.343	.729
2010	Lansing (Mid)	.000	2	2	0	0	0	0	0	1	0-1	0	1-0	0	0-0	.000	.250	.250
	Auburn (NYP)	.224	35	116	8	26	9	0	3	12	0-0	1	8-0	29	0-0	.379	.280	.659
2011	New Hampshire (East)	.167	3	6	0	1	0	0	0	0	0-0	0	2-0	2	0-0	.167	.375	.542
	Lansing (Mid)	.222	50	162	14	36	11	0	3	24	0-1	1	21-0	43	0-2	.346	.314	.660
2012	New Hampshire (East)	.333	8	24	5	8	1	0	2	4	0-1	0	3-0	7	0-0	.625	.393	1.018
	Dunedin (FSL)	.223	86	278	31	62	13	1	10	51	2-5	3	35-2	67	0-0	.385	.312	.697
Minor Totals		.235	231	737	77	173	45	1	21	114	2-8	5	92-3	173	1-3	.384	.321	.705

TRANSACTIONS

- Selected by the Toronto Blue Jays in the 31st round of the 2009 First Year Player Draft

PROFESSIONAL CAREER:

2009:

- Split time between the Gulf Coast club and Auburn in his first professional season... Had 14 extra-base hits in 47 contests.

2010:

- Spent the majority of the season at short-season Auburn, while adding two games at Lansing (A) in the Midwest League... Tossed out 46% of would be bast stealers... Had 12 extra-base hits in 37 contests.

2011:

- Played 50 games with Lansing and three at New Hampshire (AA)... Posted 11 doubles and had three home runs for the 3rd consecutive season... Played one game at 1B for the first time in his career.

REACHING BASE 300 TIMES

JOHN OLERUD and **CARLOS DELGADO** are the only Blue Jays to have reached base 300 times during a season (hits, walks and hit by pitch)... **OLERUD** reached base 321 times during the 1993 season when he notched 200 hits, 114 base on balls and seven hit by pitch... **DELGADO** reached base 334 times in the 2000 season collecting 196 hits, 123 base on balls and 15 hit by pitch... In 2003 **DELGADO** reached base 300 times, collecting 172 hits, 109 base on balls and 19 hit by pitch.

BLUE JAYS TEAMMATES WITH 30+ HR, 30+ 2B & 100+ RBI (ONE SEASON)

Year	Player 1	HR	2B	RBI	Player 2	HR	2B	RBI
2009	Adam Lind	35	46	114	Aaron Hill	36	37	108
2003	Carlos Delgado	42	38	145	Vernon Wells	33	49	117
2000	Carlos Delgado	41	57	137	Tony Batista	41	32	114
1999	Carlos Delgado	44	39	134	Shawn Green	42	45	123
1998	Carlos Delgado	38	43	115	Shawn Green	35	33	100
1996	Joe Carter	30	35	107	Ed Sprague	36	35	101
1986	Jesse Barfield	40	35	108	George Bell	31	38	108

NANITA, *RICARDO*

Birthdate . . . . June 12, 1981
Opening Day Age 31
Birthplace. . . . . Santo Domingo, DR
Residence. . . . . Santo Domingo, DR
Bats/Throws . . . . L/L
Height/Weight 6-1/195
Contract Status . . . . signed thru 2013
M.L. Service 0.000

OUTFIELDER
NON-ROSTER

PERSONAL:

Ricardo Michael Nanita... Attended Florida International University after transferring from Chipola Junior College... Led FIU in nearly every offensive category... Was named second team All-Sun Belt... Left Chipola as the all-time single season leader in average (.394) and doubles (34)... Graduated from San Juan Bautista High School in the Dominican Republic.

LAST SEASON:

- In his 10th professional season and first exclusively in Las Vegas, recorded 17 doubles and 12 home runs in 93 games... His .306 average marked the third striaght year posting an average over .300.
- Aug. 18 had a double and a career high three home runs vs. Sacramento... Hit .322 vs. RH pitchers...Had nine home runs in Aug.
- Appeared at 1B, LF, RF and DH during the season.
- Hit .308 with one home run and 12 RBI in games in the Dominican Winter League for Toros del Este.

RICARDO NANITA

Bold – career high

Year	Club & League	AVG	G	AB	R	H	2B	3B	HR	RBI	SH-SF	HP	BB-IBB	SO	SB-CS	SLG	OBP	OPS
2003	Great Falls White (Pio)	.384	47	185	38	71	7	4	5	37	1-3	6	17-2	28	11-6	.546	.445	.991
2004	Kannapolis (SAL)	.316	61	225	32	71	12	2	1	31	0-2	3	26-0	32	5-4	.400	.391	.791
	Winston-Salem (Caro)	.241	55	187	21	45	8	1	2	28	6-4	3	23-2	46	7-4	.326	.327	.653
2005	Winston-Salem (Caro)	.292	120	415	73	121	36	2	9	54	8-4	10	61-2	53	14-11	.453	.392	.845
2006	Birmingham (Sou)	.286	106	364	48	104	14	3	8	42	10-5	2	51-6	56	11-6	.407	.372	.779
2007	Birmingham (Sou)	.260	123	427	45	111	21	0	5	42	4-6	5	33-3	53	10-8	.344	.316	.660
2008	Birmingham (Sou)	.286	111	412	52	118	22	2	9	51	8-2	5	37-0	56	14-9	.415	.351	.766
2009	Nationals (GCL)	.286	9	28	7	8	1	0	1	7	0-2	0	4-0	6	1-0	.429	.353	.782
	Harrisburg (East)	.294	41	126	17	37	10	1	5	19	3-1	0	9-2	18	1-2	.508	.338	.846
2010	New Hampshire (East)	.238	6	21	2	5	3	0	0	3	0-1	0	0-0	3	0-0	.381	.227	.608
2011	New Hampshire (East)	.299	58	201	25	60	11	1	3	23	0-2	3	11-0	24	9-0	.408	.341	.749
	Las Vegas (PCL)	.363	51	193	38	70	13	0	8	33	1-2	1	18-1	22	6-4	.554	.416	.970
2012	Las Vegas (PCL)	.306	93	333	49	102	17	0	12	62	1-5	4	23-2	39	3-3	.465	.353	.818
Minor Totals		.296	881	3117	447	923	175	16	68	432	42-39	42	313-20	436	92-57	.428	.364	.792

TRANSACTIONS

- Selected by the Chicago White Sox in the 14th round of the 2003 First Year Player Draft
- Selected in the Rule 5 Draft by the Washington Nationals on December 11, 2008
- Signed by the Toronto Blue Jays on August 24, 2010

PROFESSIONAL CAREER:

2003:

- Was cited by Baseball America as making the Best Pro Debut and Best Late Round Pick by the White Sox in the 2003 draft class.
- Led the Pioneer League in average (.384) and finsihed 2nd in on base percentage (.445).
- Named to the Minor League Rookie All-Star team.
- Named to the PL Post Season All-Star team.
- Compiled a PL record 30-game hitting streak.

2004:

- Combined to hit .282 with 59 RBI between Winston-Salem and Kannapolis.

2005:

- Established career highs in runs (73), hits (121), home runs (nine) and RBI (54).

2006:

- Was cited by Baseball America as having the Best Strike Zone Discipline in the White Sox system.
- Selected to the Southern League Mid and Post Season All-Star squads.

2007:

- Spent his second full season with Birmingham (AA)... Ranked 2nd on the team in hits.

2008:

- Was with Birmingham (AA) for a 3rd consecutive season.

2009:

- Joined the Nationals organization for 2009 spending most fo the season at Harrisburg (AA).

2010:

- Signed by the Blue Jays late in 2010 and appeared in six games at New Hampshire (AA) after playing the majority of the season in Mexico.

2011:

- Began his season in New Hampshire (AA) before being promoted to Las Vegas (AAA).
- Added two multi-home run games among his eight home runs with the 51s.
- Played in the Dominican Winter League, posting a .299 average with seven doubles, six home runs and 20 RBI in 35 games.

TRIPLE PLAYS

BY TORONTO (4)

APRIL - 22/78 vs. Chicago White Sox - With Jim Clancy pitching in the Chicago second, after Bobby Bonds homered Lamar Johnson doubled and stayed at second on an infield hit by Ron Blomberg. Junior Moore followed with an attempted bunt that was lined to Clancy who threw to John Mayberry at first to double Blomberg. Mayberry then fired the ball to Luis Gomez at second and Johnson was tripled up before he could return to the bag. Final Score-Toronto 4 Chicago 2.

SEPTEMBER - 7/79 at Cleveland Indians - With Phil Huffman pitching in Cleveland's eighth and the bases loaded, Ted Cox grounded to third baseman, Roy Howell, who stepped on the bag forcing Mike Hargrove, threw to second baseman, Luis Gomez, who erased Rick Manning and then relayed to first baseman, John Mayberry to nip Cox. Final Score -Cleveland 9 Toronto 8.

SEPTEMBER - 21/79 vs. New York Yankees - With Tom Underwood pitching in New York's seventh, Chris Chambliss and Roy Staiger were at first and second on consecutive singles. Damaso Garcia, the batter, lined sharply to second baseman Dave McKay, who threw to Craig Kusick at first to double Staiger. Kusick relayed to shortstop Alfredo Griffin at second base to catch Chambliss off base for the third out. Final Score-Toronto 3 New York 2.

APRIL - 20/12 at Kansas City Royals - With Kyle Drabek pitching in the bottom of the Royal's 3rd inning, Alex Gordon and Yunesky Betancourt were on first and second on a double and a walk. Eric Hosmer, the batter, lined sharply to to first baseman Adam Lind, who then touched first base for out #2 and then threw to Yunel Escobar at shortstop who touched 2nd base for the 3rd out. Final Score - Toronto 4 Kansas City 3

BY OPPOSITION (6)

SEPTEMBER - 9/78 vs. Baltimore - With Scott McGregor pitching in the Blue Jays' sixth Doug Ault and Dave McKay hit consecutive singles to put Toronto runners on first and second. Rick Cerone followed with a hard grounder to Doug DeCinces who stepped on third for the first out and then threw to Rick Dauer at second for a forceout. Dauer then fired the ball to first baseman Eddie Murray, beating Cerone to the bag. Final Score-Baltimore 4 Toronto 0.

SEPTEMBER - 10/91 vs. Seattle - With Brian Holman pitching for Seattle in the Blue Jays' fifth. Devon White and Roberto Alomar led off with consecutive singles to put men on first and second. Joe Carter stepped up to the plate and hit a grounder to third where Edgar Martinez threw to Harold Reynolds at second for the first out, Reynolds then relayed a throw to first to get Carter. Then, Mariner first baseman, Tino Martinez threw home where Seattle catcher David Valle put the tag on Devon White for the third out. Final Score-Seattle 5 Toronto 4.

JULY - 13/95 at Seattle-With Jeff Nelson pitching for Seattle in the Blue Jays' ninth inning, Shawn Green led off with a single and moved to second on a hit by Alex Gonzalez. Sandy Martinez, the next batter, then attempted to bunt. Seattle pitcher Jeff Nelson let the ball drop in front of him and threw to second where shortstop Luis Sojo tagged out Green, stepped on second to force Gonzalez, and then threw to first (to second baseman Joey Cora covering) to get Martinez. Final Score-Toronto 4 Seattle 1.

JULY - 28/97 (2nd game) at Milwaukee-With Joel Adamson pitching for Milwaukee in the Blue Jays' fourth inning, Ed Sprague led off with a single to left field. Benito Santiago singled to center and advanced Sprague to second. Alex Gonzalez hit a ground ball to third baseman Jeff Wills who touched third to force Sprague and then threw to Mark Loretta at second to force Santiago. Loretta then made the relay to first to Dave Nilsson to get Gonzalez. Final score-Toronto 3 at Milwaukee 9.

SEPTEMBER - 13/02 vs. Tampa Bay-With Dewon Brazelton pitching for Tampa Bay in the Blue Jays' fifth inning, Chris Woodward led off with a single to left-center field. Dave Berg was then hit by a pitch. Ken Huckaby lined out to Andy Sheets at second base who threw to shortstop Chris Gomez who tagged Chris Woodward for the put-out. Gomez threw to first baseman Aubrey Huff which doubled-up Dave Berg at first, for the third out. Final score-Toronto 5 Tampa Bay 2.

MAY 12/08 (2nd game) at Cleveland - With Cliff Lee pitching for Cleveland in the Blue Jays' fifth inning, Kevin Mench led off with a single, Marco Scutaro the singled to centre. Lyle Overbay then lined into an unassisted triple play with second baseman Asdrubal Cabrera making all three outs.

NEGRYCH, *JIM*

Birthdate . . . . March 2, 1985
Opening Day Age 28
Birthplace. . . . . Buffalo, NY
Residence. . . . . Lancaster, NY
Bats/Throws . . . . X/X
Height/Weight 5-9/185
Contract Status . . . . signed thru 2013
M.L. Service 0.000

INFIELDER
NON-ROSTER

PERSONAL:

Jim William Negrych... Was a two-time All-American at the University of Pittsburgh... Attended St. Francis High School in Athol Springs, NY where was named two-time All-Western New York.

LAST SEASON:

- In his 7th professional season spent the majority of the season with Syracuse of the International League (AAA).... Appeared in 91 games with Syracuse and three with Harrisburg (AA).
- Combined to hit .270 with 20 extra-base hits, including eight home runs... Walked 43 times in 333 at-bats... Posted four hits on June 30 vs. Norfolk and posted 17 multi-hit games.
- Played 54 games at 2B, however also appeared at 1B, 3B, LF and DH... Made just four errors.
- Hit .287 prior to the break and .229 after the break... Hit .309 vs. lefties and .253 vs. righties.

JIM NEGRYCH

Bold – career high

Year	Club and League	AVG	G	AB	R	H	2B	3B	HR	RBI	SH-SF	HP	BB-IBB	SO	SB-CS	SLG	OBP	OPS
2006	Williamsport (NYP)	.267	42	146	12	39	7	2	2	17	1-4	2	13-1	19	1-1	.384	.327	.711
2007	Hickory (SAL)	.282	86	340	57	96	14	4	2	48	3-2	4	27-0	48	4-1	.365	.340	.705
2008	Lynchburg (Caro)	.370	104	386	77	143	36	1	5	62	0-6	4	55-4	55	7-6	.508	.448	.956
	Altoona (East)	.310	25	87	10	27	5	0	0	10	3-0	1	11-1	14	5-1	.368	.394	.762
2009	Altoona (East)	.272	93	323	51	88	18	1	3	30	6-1	3	45-3	37	8-1	.362	.366	.728
2010	Indianapolis (Int)	.295	48	166	26	49	7	2	3	19	3-1	0	21-1	34	8-2	.416	.372	.788
	Altoona (East)	.274	75	230	33	63	11	3	1	35	1-1	3	31-2	45	2-5	.361	.366	.727
2011	Jacksonville (Sou)	.304	121	398	60	121	22	1	5	46	7-7	1	45-1	52	11-7	.402	.370	.772
2012	Harrisburg (East)	.600	3	5	0	3	2	0	0	3	0-1	0	3-0	0	0-1	1.000	.667	1.667
	Syracuse (Int)	.264	91	276	31	73	9	1	8	39	5-2	1	40-0	41	2-4	.391	.357	.748
Minor Totals		.298	688	2357	357	702	131	15	29	309	29-25	19	291-13	345	48-29	.403	.376	.779

TRANSACTIONS

- Selected by the Pittsburgh Pirates in the 6th round of the 2006 First Year Player Draft
- Traded to the Miami Marlins in exchange for C Carlos Paulino on March 30, 2011
- Signed by the Washington Nationals on April 13, 2012
- Signed by the Toronto Blue Jays on November 20, 2012

PROFESSIONAL CAREER:

2008:

- Was the Pirates Minor League Player of the Year while playing for the Lynchburg Hillcats... Was a Carolina League Mid-Season All-Star and a Carolina League Post-Season All-Star... Hit .359 over three levels with 47 extra-base hits.

2009:

- Had his season end prematurely on July 29 when colliding with SS... Developed a hemotoma in his abdomen from collison and needed emergency surgery

2010:

- Was named an Milb.com Organizational All-Star in the Pirates system posting a combined .283 average with 18 doubles, five triples, four home runs and 54 RBI for Altoona (AA) and Indianapolis (AAA).

2011:

- Traded to the Florida Marlins for catcher Carlos Paulino and spent season with Jacksonville (AA)... Was the second time in his career to post an average above .300.

CONSECUTIVE GAMES WITH AT LEAST 1 RBI

(MINIMUM 7 GAMES)

PLAYER	GAMES	RBI	DATES
Willie Upshaw	8	15	September 11-20, 1983
Carlos Delgado	8	11	April 16-23, 2000
Carlos Delgado	8	17	June 4-12, 2003
Matt Stairs	8	13	Aug. 28-Sept. 8, 2007
Roberto Alomar	7	10	April 19-25, 1992
Devon White	7	9	May 9-15, 1995
Carlos Delgado	7	16	June 4-11, 2000
Jose Cruz Jr.	7	13	Sept. 29-Oct. 5 (G2), 2001
Jose Bautista	7	13	Sept. 25-Oct 2, 2009

NICKEAS, *MIKE*

Birthdate .... February 13, 1983
Opening Day Age 30
Birthplace................ Vancouver, BC
Residence............ Sandy Springs, GA
Bats/Throws .... R/R
Height/Weight 6-0/213
Contract Status .... signed thru 2013
M.L. Service 1.081

CATCHER
NON-ROSTER

PERSONAL:

Michael James (Mike) Nickeas... Graduated from Westlake (CA) High School in 2001... Won four letters and made the honour roll all four years in high school... Led his high school team to the Mamonte League Championship in 2000 and 2001... Spent the summer of 2001 with the USA Junior Pan-Am Team that captured the silver medal at the Junior Pan-Am Championship in Camaguey, Cuba... Named to the All-Tournament team... Attended Georgia Tech, was a management major... Was the team captain in 2004... Named second-team pre-season All-American by Baseball America... In 2003, he spent the summer months with the USA Baseball National Team, helping Team USA capture the silver medal at the Pan-American Games in the Dominican Republic... His father, Mark, a native of Southport, England, was an accomplished soccer player... His father played professionally for Liverpool, the Plymouth Argyle and Chester in the English Football League... Also played in the North American Soccer League with the Vancouver Whitecaps... Has American (mother), British (father) and Canadian Citizenship (birth).

LAST SEASON:

- Made his second consecutive Opening Day roster... Had two separate stints with the Mets... Optioned to Buffalo (AAA) of the International League on July 26 before returning on Sept. 1.
- Hit his first career grand slam, and the Mets' first since 2011, on May 26 vs. San Diego (Thayer)... Set a career best with four RBI.
- Struck out a career-worst three times on May 15 vs. MIL.
- Hit .333 (8-24) with runners in scoring position... Went 8-62 (.129) at home.
- Finished with a 4.07 catcher's ERA (137 earned runs/303.0 innings) and threw out 25 percent of potential base stealers (6-24).

MIKE NICKEAS

Bold – career high

Year	Club and League	AVG	G	AB	R	H	2B	3B	HR	RBI	SH-SF	HP	BB-IBB	SO	SB-CS	SLG	OBP	OPS
2004	Spokane (NOR)	.288	62	233	42	67	18	0	10	55	2-1	4	33-0	53	2-0	.494	.384	.878
2005	AZL (Ariz)	.286	6	21	2	6	1	0	1	6	0-0	1	3-0	4	0-0	.476	.400	.876
	Frisco (TEX)	.202	68	242	22	49	7	1	5	24	2-3	1	20-0	43	1-1	.302	.263	.565
2006	Bakersfield (CAL)	.297	17	64	6	19	4	0	0	6	0-1	5	6-0	17	0-0	.359	.395	.754
	Frisco (TEX)	.248	39	113	15	28	7	0	2	15	3-4	6	21-0	22	1-1	.363	.382	.745
	Binghamton (East)	.167	4	12	1	2	0	0	0	3	0-1	1	1-0	4	0-0	.167	.267	.434
2007	St. Lucie (FSL)	.208	26	77	6	16	7	0	0	4	0-0	4	17-1	20	0-0	.299	.378	.677
	Binghamton (East)	.217	65	212	26	46	10	0	1	15	2-3	2	18-0	37	2-3	.278	.281	.559
2008	Binghamton (East)	.196	17	51	2	10	1	0	1	4	0-1	0	7-1	7	0-0	.275	.288	.563
	New Orleans (PCL)	.215	54	163	16	35	9	0	2	17	2-4	1	14-1	42	0-1	.307	.275	.582
2009	Buffalo (Int)	.000	2	6	0	0	0	0	0	0	0-0	0	1-0	3	0-0	.000	.143	.143
	Binghamton (East)	.182	18	55	3	10	1	0	0	7	2-1	0	9-0	9	0-0	.200	.292	.492
2010	Binghamton (East)	.283	82	265	27	75	15	0	5	33	0-0	4	49-0	43	1-1	.396	.403	.799
	Buffalo (Int)	.214	7	28	1	6	1	0	0	0	0-0	0	1-0	7	0-0	.250	.241	.491
	NEW YORK (NL)	.200	5	10	0	2	0	0	0	0	0-0	0	0-0	5	0-0	.200	.200	.400
2011	Buffalo (Int)	.214	60	168	15	36	9	0	2	15	3-3	2	16-1	27	0-0	.304	.286	.590
	NEW YORK (NL)	.189	21	53	4	10	1	0	**1**	6	2-0	0	4-0	11	0-1	.264	.246	.510
2012	Buffalo (Int)	.364	22	66	10	24	6	0	1	6	1-2	0	6-1	9	0-0	.500	.405	.905
	NEW YORK (NL)	.174	**47**	109	**8**	**19**	**3**	0	**1**	**13**	2-1	2	**8**-0	**27**	0-0	.229	.242	.471
Minor Totals		.242	549	1776	194	429	96	1	30	210	17-24	31	222-5	347	7-7	.347	.332	.680
MAJOR TOTALS		.180	73	172	12	31	4	0	2	19	4-1	2	12-0	43	0-1	.238	.241	.479

HOME RUN BREAKDOWN

			ONE GAME									
Total	H	A	2	3	4	GS	LO	XN	IP	PH	RHP	LHP
2	2	0	0	0	0	1	0	0	0	0	1	1

TRANSACTIONS

- Selected by the Texas Rangers in the 5th round of the 2004 First Year Player Draft
- Traded to the New York Mets in exchange for OF Victor Diaz on August 30, 2006
- Signed by the New York Mets on November 7, 2012
- Traded to the Toronto Blue Jays along with RHP R.A. Dickey and C Josh Thole in exchange for RHP Noah Syndergaard, C Travis d'Arnaud, OF Wuilmer Becerra and C John Buck on December 17, 2012

GAME HIGHS

ML Debut	Sept. 4, 2010 at CHC	**RBI**	4 - May 26, 2012 vs. SD
Runs	1 - 12x, last Sept. 17, 2012 vs. PHI	**Stolen Bases**	None
Hits	2 - 4x, last June 25, 2012 at CHC	**Last ML Home Run**	May 26, 2012 vs. SD
Doubles	1 - 4x, last June 25, 2012 at CHC	**Longest Hitting Streak**	5G - June 13-28, 2012
Home Runs	1 - 2x, last May 26, 2012 vs. SD	**Longest Hitless Streak**	17AB - May 12-21, 2012

CAREER FIELDING

POSITION	PCT	G	PO	A	E	TC	DP
C	.993	69	412	27	3	442	3

MILESTONES

Category		Date	Opponent	Pitcher	Notes
Hit	1	Sept. 29, 2010	Milwaukee	Gallardo	single
Home Run	1	April 21, 2011	at Houston	Happ	1R
Grand Slam (1)	1	May 26, 2012	San Diego	Thayer	8th inning
RBI	1	April 14, 2011	Colorado	De La Rosa	double - 2RBI

PROFESSIONAL CAREER:

2004:

- Named the Best Defensive Catcher in the Rangers organization by Baseball America... Was also rated among the publcation's Top 20 Prospects in the AL.

2005:

- Split the year between Frisco (AA) of the Texas League and the Arizona (R) League Rangers.
- Suffered a broken finger in the second game of a doubleheader, May 29 vs. Springfield...Was placed on the disabled list on May 30.

2006:

- Played in 60 games for three different teams: Bakersfield (A) of the California League; Frisco (AA) of the Texas League and Binghamton (AA) of the Eastern League.
- Acquired from the Rangers on August 30.

2008:

- Split the season between Binghamton (AA) of the Eastern League and New Orleans (AAA) of the Pacific Coast League.
- Missed time to a left oblique muscle strain.

2009:

- Season was cut short due to injuries... Underwent surgery on July 28 to remove a bone spur.
- Played in only 20 games combined between Buffalo (AAA) of the International League and Binghamton (AA) of the Eastern League.
- Went on the disabled list two times during the year... First with a left oblique muscle strain and then with a right elbow strain.

2010:

- Contract was selected from Buffalo (AAA) of the International League on September 2... Made his **Major League debut,** starting at CHC on September 4 after appearing in 467 minor league games... Was 0-2 in his debut.
- Appeared in five games for New York, three starts... Went 2-4 and picked up his first big league hit (a second-inning single against Yovani Gallardo) in the first game of a doubleheader vs. MIL on Sept. 29... Also started against MIL on Sept. 30.
- Spent the majority of the season with Binghamton (AA) of the Eastern League... Was on Buffalo (AAA) the International League's roster on Opening Day but was transferred to Binghamton after one game.
- Named to the EL's mid-season All-Star Game.
- Placed on the disabled list on May 24 with a right hamstring strain...Activated on May 2... Moved from Binghamton to Buffalo on August 25.
- Ranked third in the EL with a .355 (27-76) catchers caught-stealing percentage.

2011:

- Had three separate stints with the Mets.
- Made his first Opening Day roster and appeared in eight games before being optioned to Buffalo (AAA) of the International League on April 29.
- Returned to the Mets on July 28... Made one start on August 2 and went 0-3 before the Mets optioned him to Buffalo (AAA) on August 5.
- Recalled for the third and final time on August 24... Appeared in 12 games and went 5-30 (.167) with three RBI.
- Drove in the first two runs of his Major League career with a second-inning double to the wall in left on April 14 vs. COL (Game Two)... The double was also his first Major League extra-base hit.
- Hit his first career home run on April 21 vs. HOU (off J.A. Happp).
- Threw out four of 13 runners (31 percent) attempting to steal... Pitchers had a 2.94 ERA (47 earned runs/143.2 innings) when he caught.
- In 60 games with Buffalo, he hit .214 (36-168) with two home runs and 15 RBI.
- Threw out 39 percent (12-31) of runners attempting to steal at Buffalo.

NOLIN, *SEAN*

Birthdate ....December 26, 1989
Opening Day Age 23
Birthplace..................Seaford, NY
Residence..................Seaford, NY
Bats/Throws......................L/L
Height/Weight..................6-5/235
Contract Status........ signed thru 2013
M.L. Service.................... 0.000

71

PITCHER
NON-ROSTER

PERSONAL:

Sean Patrick Nolan... Attended San Jacinto College North in Houston, Texas.

LAST SEASON:

- Spent the majority of the season with Dunedin of the Florida State League (A)... Was promoted to New Hampshire where he would complete his season with three starts for the Fisher Cats.
- In 20 games, 18 starts was a combined 10-0 with a 2.04 ERA... Allowed just 81 hits in 101.1 innings, while walking 27 and fanning 108.
- Led Dunedin in wins and strikeouts, while posting the lowest ERA (min 60IP).
- Was the only pitcher in the Florida State League to win as many as nine games without a loss.
- Allowed three or more runs in only four of his starts... At New Hampshire did not allow more than one run in any of his three starts.

SEAN NOLIN

Bold – career high

Year	Club & League	W-L	ERA	G	GS	CG	ShO	SV	IP	H	R	ER	HR	HB	BB-IBB	SO	WP	BK	OBA
2010	BlueJays (GCL)	0-0	0.00	1	1	0	0	0	2.0	1	0	0	0	0	1-0	4	0	0	.167
	Auburn (NYP)	0-2	6.05	6	6	0	0	0	19.1	25	13	13	0	2	9-0	22	2	0	.312
2011	Lansing (Mid)	4-4	3.49	25	21	0	0	1	108.1	102	56	42	9	4	31-0	113	4	1	.253
2012	Dunedin (FSL)	9-0	2.19	17	15	0	0	0	86.1	72	26	21	7	4	21-0	90	0	0	.226
	New Hampshire (East)	1-0	1.20	3	3	0	0	0	15.0	9	3	2	0	1	6-0	18	0	0	.170
Minor Totals		14-6	3.04	52	46	0	0	1	231.0	209	98	78	16	11	68-0	247	6	1	.243

TRANSACTIONS

- Selected by the Toronto Blue Jays in the 6th round of the 2010 First Year Player Draft

PROFESSIONAL CAREER:

2010:

- Made his professional debut, spending time at two levels, making one start with the Rookie League club and six at Auburn (short-season)... Combined to go 0-2 with a 5.48 ERA.

2011:

- Spent the entire season at Lansing (A-) making the second most starts on the club... Made 21 starts and four relief appearances... Picked up his first professional save.

MINOR LEAGUE PLAYER OF THE YEAR

The following is a list of Toronto minor league players that have been named Minor League Player of the Year:

PLAYER/POSITION	YEAR	PUBLICATION	CLUB	STATS
Carlos Delgado/C	1992	USA Today Baseball Wkly	Dunedin (A)	30HR, 100RBI, .324BA
Derek Bell/OF	1991	Baseball America	Syracuse (AAA)	13HR, 93RBI, .346BA

OCHINKO, *SEAN*

Birthdate	October 21, 1987
Opening Day Age	25
Birthplace	Parkland, FL
Residence	Baton Rouge, LA
Bats/Throws	R/R
Height/Weight	5-11/205
Contract Status	signed thru 2013
M.L. Service	0.000

CATCHER
NON-ROSTER

PERSONAL:

Sean Peter Ochinko... Attended LSU... Named to 2009 NCAA Regional All-Tournament Team... Named to Baseball America's Top 300 High School Players of 2006... Attended Stoneman Douglas High School in Parkland, Florida and was a 2006 Puma Pre-season All-American... Led team to three district championships and a regional semifinal appearance in 2005.

LAST SEASON:

- Returned to Dunedin for a second season however was promoted to New Hampshire after 28 games, completing his season with the Fisher Cats.
- Hit .306 with Dunedin, including 12 doubles prior to his promotion with a .342 vs. lefties.
- Recorded 20 extra-base hits in New Hampshire in 59 contests...Hit .321 vs. lefties... Appeared at catcher in the majority of games, although also saw time at first base and DH.... With the Fisher Cats hit .307 before the break and .216 after.

SEAN OCHINKO

Bold – career high

Year	Club and League	AVG	G	AB	R	H	2B	3B	HR	RBI	SH-SF	HP	BB-IBB	SO	SB-CS	SLG	OBP	OPS
2009	Auburn (NYP)	.324	52	188	40	61	20	0	6	32	0-1	2	16-2	26	1-0	.527	.382	.909
2010	Lansing (Mid)	.311	109	412	57	128	37	0	8	65	0-6	5	30-0	58	1-0	.459	.360	.819
2011	Dunedin (FSL)	.261	121	459	65	120	35	1	16	79	0-3	7	37-0	77	1-2	.447	.324	.771
2012	Dunedin (FSL)	.306	28	108	21	33	12	0	1	13	0-0	1	10-0	16	0-0	.444	.370	.814
	New Hampshire (East)	.264	59	216	26	57	11	1	8	29	1-1	5	8-1	40	0-0	.435	.304	.739
Minor Totals		.289	369	1383	209	399	115	2	39	218	1-11	20	101-3	217	3-2	.459	.343	.802

TRANSACTIONS

- Selected by the Toronto Blue Jays in the 11th round of the 2009 First Year Player Draft

PROFESSIONAL CAREER:

2009:

- Made his professional debut with Auburn (short-season), leading the club in average, OBP and SLG

2010:

- Spent his first full season with Lansing (A-) of the Midwest League... Led the Lugnuts in doubles and average

2011:

- Moved up to the Florida State League with Dunedin (A+)... Posted a team leading 52 extra-base hits, including 35 doubles.... Finished 3rd in the league in doubles.

20 OR MORE HITS

HITS	DATE	OPPONENT	BLUE JAYS-OPP. SCORE
25	Aug. 9, 1999	at Texas	19-4
24	June 26, 1978	Baltimore	24-10
22	June 24, 2008	Cincinnati	14-1
22	Aug. 17, 2008	at Boston	15-14
22	Sept. 29, 1985	at Milwaukee	13-5
22	Sept. 22, 1999	at Boston	14-9
22	May 16, 2003	at Kansas City	18-1
21	June 26, 1983	at Seattle	19-7
21	Sept. 14, 1987	Baltimore	18-3
21	June 8, 1992	at New York	16-3
21	Sept. 4, 1992	Minnesota	16-5
21	July 19, 1993	at Chicago	15-7
21	Aug. 24, 1997	at Kansas City (13 Inn)	11-8
21	Aug. 19, 1998	at Seattle	16-2
21	Apr. 24, 2009	at Chicago	14-0
20	July 9, 1985	at Seattle (13 Inn)	9-4
20	May 14, 1987	at Minnesota	16-4
20	April 11, 1988	New York	17-9
20	June 22, 1992	at Texas	16-7
20	Aug. 13, 2000	at Minnesota	13-3
20	Aug. 6, 2002	Seattle	14-12
20	June 23, 2003	vs Baltimore	13-4
20	July 1, 2004	at Tampa Bay	14-0
20	Aug. 8, 2005	Detroit (12 Inn)	8-9
20	Aug. 7, 2010	Tampa Bay	17-11
20	Aug. 20, 2010	at Boston	16-2
20	July 14, 2011	New York	16-7
20	Aug. 31, 2011	at Baltimore	13-0

BIOGRAPHIES LAST SEASON HISTORY RECORDS OPPONENTS PLAYER DEV. MEDIA & MISC.

OLIVER, *DARREN*

Birthdate . . . . .October 6, 1970
Opening Day Age 42
Birthplace. . . . . Kansas City, MO
Residence. . . . . Southlake, TX
Bats/Throws . . . . R/L
Height/Weight 6-3/249
Contract Status . . . . signed thru 2013
M.L. Service 17.127

38

PITCHER

PERSONAL:

Darren Christopher Oliver… Married with two children… Is the son of Bob Oliver, former Major League infielder with the Pittsburgh Pirates, Kansas City Royals, California Angels, Baltimore Orioles and New York Yankees from 1965- 1975… Hobby: fishing… Lettered three times in baseball and twice in basketball at Rio Linda (CA) High School (graduated 1988)… Earned all-city and all-league honours in senior year.

LAST SEASON:

- In his 19th Major League season and first in Toronto posted the lowest ERA of his career at 2.06.
- His ERA was T-3rd lowest in the AL for pitchers with a minimum of 50 innings and also led the club.
- Held opponent's to a .214 average, including a .196 mark vs. right-handed hitters... Ranked 16th in the AL vs. right-handed hitters (min 100AB)...Allowed batters to hit .320 when leading off an inning, however limited opponents to a .179 mark following that... Allowed only two hits in eight Interleague contests.
- Passed the 700 game and 1200 strikeout plateau, finishing the year with 716 games played and 1219 strikeouts... Appeared in more than 60 games for a fourth straight season and five of the last six... Only Matt Thronton has done so in each of the last six seasons as a Major League lefty.
- From May through July appeared in 34 games, posting a 2-1 record with one save and a 1.16 ERA... Had three separate streaks of nine, 10 and 11 games throughout the season without allowing a run and gave up an earned run in only 10 of his 62 outings... Allowed more than one run in only two contests.
- Posted his 6th and 7th career saves on July 15 vs. CLE and August 4 at OAK.
- Tossed 2.1 innings on May 26 at TEX, his most since going 2.1 at SEA on Aug. 4, 2010.

OLDEST & YOUNGEST BLUE JAYS

OLDEST BLUE JAYS

Player	D.O.B	Last Game	Age at last Game
Phil Niekro	4/01/39	Aug. 29, 1987	48 yrs, 4 mths, 28 days
Omar Vizquel	4/24/67	Oct. 3, 2012	45 yrs, 6 mths, 21 days
Dave Stieb	7/22/57	Sept. 25, 1998	41 yrs, 2 mths, 3 days
Dave Winfield	10/03/51	Oct. 24, 1992	41 yrs, 0 mths, 21 days
Darren Oliver	10/06/70	Oct. 2, 2012	41 yrs, 0 mths, 4 days
Matt Stairs	2/27/68	Aug. 27, 2008	40 yrs, 5 mths, 29 days
Dave Parker	6/09/51	Oct. 2, 1991	40 yrs, 3 mths, 23 days
Dan Plesac	2/04/42	May 22, 2002	40 yrs, 3 mths, 18 days
Frank Thomas	5/27/68	April 18, 2008	40 yrs, 1 mth, 9 days

YOUNGEST BLUE JAYS

Player	D.O.B	1st Game	Age at 1st Game
Brian Milner	11/17/59	June 23, 1978	18 yrs, 7 mths, 6 days
Fred Manrique	11/5/61	August 23, 1981	19 yrs, 9 mths, 18 days
Manny Lee	6/17/65	April 10, 1985	19 yrs, 9 mths, 24 days
Travis Snider	2/2/88	August 29, 2008	20 yrs, 6 mths, 27 days

DARREN OLIVER

Bold – career high

Year	Club & League	W-L	ERA	G	GS	CG	ShO	SV	IP	H	R	ER	HR	HB	BB-IBB	SO	WP	BK	OBA
1988	Rangers (GCL)	5-1	2.15	12	9	0	0	0	54.1	39	16	13	0	2	18-0	59	3	2	.203
1989	Gastonia (SAL)	8-7	3.16	24	23	2	1	0	122.1	86	54	43	4	5	82-1	108	15	2	.199
1990	Rangers (GCL)	0-0	0.00	3	3	0	0	0	6.0	1	1	0	0	1	1-0	7	1	0	.053
	Gastonia (SAL)	0-0	13.50	1	1	0	0	0	2.0	1	3	3	0	0	4-0	2	0	1	.143
1991	Charlotte (FSL)	0-1	4.50	2	2	0	0	0	8.0	6	4	4	1	0	3-0	12	1	0	.200
1992	Charlotte (FSL)	1-0	0.72	8	2	1	1	2	25.0	11	2	2	0	2	10-2	33	3	0	.133
	Tulsa (TEX)	0-1	3.14	3	3	0	0	0	14.1	15	9	5	1	0	4-0	14	0	0	.246
1993	Tulsa (TEX)	7-5	1.96	46	0	0	0	6	73.1	51	18	16	1	9	41-0	77	9	0	.197
	TEXAS (AL)	0-0	2.70	2	0	0	0	0	3.1	2	1	1	1	0	1-0	4	0	0	.154
1994	Oklahoma (PCL)	0-0	0.00	6	0	0	0	1	7.1	1	0	0	0	1	3-2	6	0	0	.045
	TEXAS (AL)	4-0	3.42	43	0	0	0	**2**	50.0	40	24	19	4	6	35-4	50	2	2	.223
1995	TEXAS (AL)	4-2	4.22	17	7	0	0	0	49.0	47	25	23	3	1	32-1	39	4	0	.257
1996	Charlotte (FSL)	0-1	3.00	2	1	0	0	0	12.0	8	4	4	1	2	3-0	9	0	0	.190
	TEXAS (AL)	**14**-6	4.66	30	30	1	**1**	0	173.2	190	97	90	20	10	76-3	112	5	1	.279
1997	TEXAS (AL)	13-**12**	4.20	32	**32**	**3**	**1**	0	**201.1**	213	111	94	**29**	11	**82**-3	104	7	0	.271
1998	Oklahoma (PCL)	0-0	0.00	1	1	0	0	0	5.0	2	0	0	0	0	1-0	1	0	0	.118
	TEXAS (AL)	6-7	6.53	19	19	2	0	0	103.1	140	84	75	11	10	43-1	58	6	1	.325
	ST. LOUIS (NL)	4-4	4.26	10	10	0	0	0	57.0	64	31	27	7	0	23-1	29	1	3	.283
1999	ST. LOUIS (NL)	9-9	4.26	30	30	2	**1**	0	196.1	197	96	93	16	11	74-4	**119**	6	2	.265
2000	Tulsa (TEX)	0-1	11.57	1	1	0	0	0	4.2	10	7	6	0	0	2-0	5	1	0	.417
	Oklahoma (PCL)	2-1	1.97	7	7	1	1	0	32.0	22	11	7	2	1	14-0	28	0	0	.196
	TEXAS (AL)	2-9	7.42	21	21	0	0	0	108.0	151	95	89	16	4	42-3	49	4	1	.339
2001	Oklahoma (PCL)	0-0	0.00	1	1	0	0	0	3.0	3	0	0	0	0	0-0	3	0	0	.250
	Tulsa (TEX)	0-1	5.40	1	1	0	0	0	5.0	4	3	3	1	1	2-0	5	0	0	.235
	TEXAS (AL)	11-11	6.02	28	28	1	0	0	154.0	189	109	103	23	6	65-0	104	8	2	.306
2002	Memphis (PCL)	0-2	7.88	5	5	0	0	0	16.0	17	16	14	1	0	17-0	9	2	0	.298
	BOSTON (AL)	4-5	4.66	14	9	1	**1**	0	58.0	70	30	30	7	6	27-0	32	1	0	.317
2003	COLORADO (NL)	13-11	5.04	33	**32**	1	0	0	180.1	201	108	101	21	8	61-3	88	0	0	.284
2004	FLORIDA (NL)	2-3	6.44	18	8	0	0	0	58.2	75	44	42	13	1	17-1	33	1	0	.319
	HOUSTON (NL)	1-0	3.86	9	2	0	0	0	14.0	12	6	6	1	0	4-0	13	0	0	.240
2005	Tucson (PCL)	1-0	6.38	4	4	0	0	0	18.1	33	14	13	3	1	3-0	8	0	0	.393
	Iowa (PCL)	0-3	13.50	3	3	0	0	0	13.1	28	20	20	3	0	5-0	10	0	0	.444
2006	NEW YORK (NL)	4-1	3.44	45	0	0	0	0	81.0	70	33	31	13	3	21-2	60	1	0	.231
2007	LOS ANGELES (AL)	3-1	3.78	61	0	0	0	0	64.1	58	31	27	5	1	23-2	51	1	1	.239
2008	LOS ANGELES (AL)	7-1	2.88	54	0	0	0	0	72.0	67	24	23	5	4	16-2	48	3	0	.254
2009	LOS ANGELES (AL)	5-1	2.71	63	1	0	0	0	73.0	61	22	22	5	5	22-8	65	7	0	.237
2010	TEXAS (AL)	1-2	2.48	**64**	0	0	0	1	61.2	53	20	17	4	2	15-4	65	0	0	.242
2011	TEXAS (AL)	5-5	2.29	61	0	0	0	**2**	51.0	47	17	13	3	1	11-1	44	0	1	.236
2012	TORONTO (AL)	3-4	2.06	62	0	0	0	**2**	56.2	43	13	13	3	4	15-0	52	3	0	.214
Minor Totals		24-24	3.26	130	67	4	3	9	422.0	338	182	153	18	25	213-5	396	35	5	.220
AL TOTALS		82-66	4.50	571	147	8	3	7	1279.1	1371	703	639	139	71	505-33	877	51	9	.277
NL TOTALS		33-28	4.60	145	82	3	1	0	587.1	619	318	300	71	23	200-11	342	9	5	.273
MAJOR TOTALS		115-94	4.53	716	229	11	4	7	1866.2	1990	1021	939	210	94	705-44	1219	60	14	.276

DIVISION SERIES RECORD

Year	Club & League	W-L	ERA	G	GS	CG	ShO	SV	IP	H	R	ER	HR	HB	BB-IBB	SO	WP	BK
1996	TEXAS (AL)	0-1	3.38	1	1	0	0	0	8.0	6	3	3	1	1	2-0	3	0	0
2006	NEW YORK (NL)	0-0	20.25	1	0	0	0	0	1.1	3	3	3	1	0	0-0	0	0	0
2007	LOS ANGELES (AL)	0-0	27.00	1	0	0	0	0	0.2	2	2	2	0	0	0-0	0	0	0
2008	LOS ANGELES (AL)	0-0	0.00	2	0	0	0	0	1.1	0	0	0	0	0	1-0	1	0	0
2009	LOS ANGELES (AL)	1-0	0.00	3	0	0	0	0	2.1	1	0	0	0	0	0-0	2	0	0
2010	TEXAS (AL)	0-1	4.15	3	0	0	0	0	4.1	3	2	2	0	0	1-0	5	0	0
2011	TEXAS (AL)	0-0	6.75	2	0	0	0	0	1.1	3	1	1	0	0	0-0	1	0	0
DIVISION SERIES TOTALS		1-2	5.12	13	1	0	0	0	19.1	18	11	11	2	1	4-0	12	0	0

LEAGUE CHAMPIONSHIP SERIES RECORD

Year	Club & League	W-L	ERA	G	GS	CG	ShO	SV	IP	H	R	ER	HR	HB	BB-IBB	SO	WP	BK
2006	NEW YORK (NL)	0-0	0.00	1	0	0	0	0	6.0	3	0	0	0	0	1-0	3	1	0
2009	LOS ANGELES (AL)	0-0	4.26	5	0	0	0	0	6.1	6	3	3	0	0	4-2	6	0	0
2010	TEXAS (AL)	0-0	7.71	3	0	0	0	1	2.1	1	2	2	0	0	3-0	1	0	0
2011	TEXAS (AL)	0-0	0.00	3	0	0	0	0	2.2	0	0	0	0	0	0-0	2	0	0
LEAGUE TOTALS		0-0	2.60	12	0	0	0	1	17.1	10	5	5	0	0	8-2	12	1	0

WORLD SERIES RECORD

Year	Club & League	W-L	ERA	G	GS	CG	ShO	SV	IP	H	R	ER	HR	HB	BB-IBB	SO	WP	BK
2010	TEXAS (AL)	0-0	3.38	2	0	0	0	0	2.2	3	1	1	0	0	0-0	4	0	0
2011	TEXAS (AL)	1-0	11.57	3	0	0	0	0	2.1	3	3	3	1	0	0-0	3	0	0
WORLD SERIES TOTALS		1-0	7.20	5	0	0	0	0	5.0	6	4	4	1	0	0-0	7	0	0

TRANSACTIONS

- Selected by the Texas Rangers in the 3rd round of the 1988 First Year Player Draft
- On disabled list (partial tear of rotator cuff) June 27-remainder of season, 1995
- On disabled list (strained left shoulder) June 11-26, 1998
- Traded to the St. Louis Cardinals along with INF Fernando Tatis and INF Mark Little in exchange for INF Royce Clayton and RHP Todd Stottlemyre on July 31, 1988
- Signed by the Texas Rangers on January 27, 2000
- On disabled list (left shoulder tendinitis) June 21-July 20, 2000
- On disabled list (left shoulder tendinitis) August 1-September 1, 2000
- Traded to the Boston Red Sox in exchange for OF Carl Everett on December 13, 2001
- On disabled list (bruised and lacerated hand) May 8-June 6, 2001
- Signed by the St. Louis Cardinals on July 19, 2002
- Signed by the Colorado Rockies on January 24, 2003
- Signed by the Florida Marlins on January 29, 2004
- Traded to the Houston Astros in exchange for future considerations on July 22, 2004
- On disabled list (tightness in left shoulder) August 6-September 6, 2004
- Signed by the Arizona Diamondbacks on April 16, 2005
- Signed by the Chicago Cubs on May 7, 2005
- Signed by the New York Mets on December 16, 2005
- Signed by the Los Angeles Angels of Anaheim on December 11, 2006
- On disabled list (strained left triceps muscle) April 19-May 2, 2009
- Signed by the Texas Rangers on December 22, 2009
- Signed by the Toronto Blue Jays on January 9, 2012

GAME HIGHS

ML Debut	Sept. 1, 1993 at BOS
Innings Pitched:	
Starter	9.0 - 8x, last April 30, 2002 vs. BAL
Reliever	5.0 - July 7, 2006 vs. FLA
Walks:	
Starter	7 - Sept. 2, 2001 at KC
Reliever	4 - May 24, 1995 at CWS
Strikeouts:	
Starter	11 - Aug. 3, 1999 vs. SD
Reliever	6 - May 6, 2006 vs. ATL
Hits Allowed	12 - April 10, 2001 at ANA
Runs Allowed	9 - 2x, last Aug. 9, 2003 vs. PIT
ER Allowed	8 - 3x, last April 27, 2004 at COL
HR Allowed	5 - April 7, 2004 at COL
Low Hit CG	3 - July 21, 2001 at TB
Last Win	Aug. 27, 2012 at NYY
Last Save	Aug. 4, 2012 at OAK
Last CG	Aug. 31, 2003 at LAD
Last ShO	April 30, 2002 vs. BAL
Last Start	April 18, 2009 at MIN
Last Relief App.	Oct. 2, 2012 vs. MIN
Longest Win Streak	6G - May 6-Sept. 24, 2008
Longest Losing Streak	6G - June 16-Sept. 30, 2000
Scoreless Innings Streak	17.0 - June 21-July 29, 1994

CAREER FIELDING

POSITION	PCT	G	PO	A	E	TC	DP
P	.972	716	71	272	10	353	17

MILESTONES

Category		Date	Opponent	Notes
Start	1	May 19, 1995	Milwaukee	L, 3.1 IP, 3H, ER, 2BB, K
	100	April 16, 1999	at Houston	W, 5.3 IP, 9H, 3ER, HR, 2BB, 2K
	200	June 19, 2003	San Diego	W, 6.2 IP, 5H, 3ER, 4BB, 2K
Win	1	July 1, 1994	Detroit	As a reliever - 0.1 IP
	50	July 23, 1999	at Colorado	As a starter - 7.0 IP, 8H, 2ER, HR, 3BB, K
	100	Sept. 19, 2008	at Texas	As a reliever - 2.1 IP, 3H, 2ER, 2K
Save	1	June 8, 1994	New York (AL)	1.0 IP
ShO (4)	1	June 8, 1996	Toronto	9.0 IP, 5H, 4K
	2	July 16, 1997	Texas	9.0 IP, 8H, ER, 4K
	3	Aug. 3, 1999	St. Louis	9.0 IP, 4H, 2BB, 11K
	4	April 30, 2002	Baltimore	9.0 IP, 8H, 4K
10+ Strikeout Games (3)				
	1	June 9, 1995	Chicago (AL)	10 strikeouts
	2	June 5, 1998	San Diego	10 strikeouts
	3	Aug. 3, 1999	San Diego	11 strikeouts
Strikeout	500	Sept. 18, 1999	Houston	Tony Eusabio
	1000	May 8, 2009	Kansas City	David Dejesus

PROFESSIONAL CAREER:

1993:

- Made **Major League debut** on Sept. 1 in Boston, walking only batter faced (intentional BB to Mike Greenwell).
- Underwent arthroscopic surgery on Nov. 23 to remove loose bodies from back of left elbow.

1994:

- Led AL rookies in games (43) and ERA (3.42 – min. 35 G).
- Earned first ML victory on July 1 vs. Detroit with first save on June 8 against New York-AL.
- Had 17.0-inning scoreless streak, June 21-July 29, the longest scoreless inning streak by Texas reliever since 1984.
- Underwent surgery on Oct. 25 to remove bone chips from left elbow

1995:

- Began the season in middle relief while recovering from off-season elbow surgery.
- Lost first Major League start, 1-0 on May 19 vs. Milwaukee with first victory in that role coming on June 4 vs. Minnesota.
- Left June 26 start at Oakland after 1.0 inning with pain in left shoulder… Was diagnosed with partial tear of left rotator cuff and was placed on 15-day disabled list… Dr. Frank Jobe performed surgery on shoulder, Aug. 25 in Inglewood, CA.

1996:

- Won a pro career-high 14 games for AL West Division champs… Ranked 4th in AL in winning percentage (.700), 2nd-best mark in Rangers history at the time.
- Did not lose consecutive decisions all season.

1997:

- Was the Rangers Pitcher of the Year.
- Led club in victories (13), and T1st in starts (32) and complete games (3) and was 2nd in innings (201.1).
- Started first regular season interleague game in ML history, dropping a 4-3 decision, June 12 vs. San Francisco.
- Was Rangers July Player of the Month (3-1, 3.82).

1998:

- Had back-to-back complete games, May 3 at Boston and May 9 vs. Cleveland.
- On 15-day disabled list, June 11-26 after straining a muscle in left shoulder while swinging a bat, June 10 at Colorado.
- Acquired by the Cardinals on July 31, earning first NL victory in 2nd start, Aug. 9 vs. Chicago-NL.

1999:

- Recorded 50th career win, July 23 at Colorado.
- Fanned career high 11 in 4-hit CG SHO, Aug. 3 vs. San Diego.

2000:

- In first year back with Rangers, placed 3rd on the staff in starts (21) and innings (108.0).
- Had two stints on DL due to tendinitis in left shoulder, June 21-July 20 and Aug. 1-Sept. 1.

2001:

- Ranked 2nd on the Texas staff in wins (11) and was 3rd in starts (28), innings (154.0), and strikeouts (104).
- Placed on 15-day disabled list, May 8, due to laceration on left thumb… Activated from DL, June 6.

2002:

- Began season in Boston's rotation.
- Pitched an 8-hit CG SHO, April 30 vs. Baltimore… Was his first CG SHO since Aug. 3, 1999 vs. San Diego and first by Red Sox left-hander since Frank Viola, April 18, 1993.
- Was designated for assignment on June 25, and released on July 2.
- Signed minor league contract with St. Louis on July 19.

2003:

- Led Colorado with 13 wins, one shy of career high and at time, 2nd-most by LHP pitcher in Rockies history.
- Connected for first pro home run, July 10 vs. San Francisco off Brian Powell.

2004:

- Opened the season in the Marlins rotation but was 2-2, 7.94 in eight starts before going to the bullpen at end of May.
- Was traded to the Astros on July 22.
- Left Aug. 5 start vs. Atlanta after 1.0 inning due to tightness in left shoulder… Was placed on 15-day DL on Aug. 10, and missed 28 contests before activation on Sept. 6.

2005:

- Was released from Colorado minor league contract on March 31.
- Signed by Arizona on April 16 and was then released on May 3.
- Signed by Chicago-NL on May 7.
- Retired as an active player on May 21 and did not play the rest of the season.

2006:

- Signed with New York-NL as a minor league free agent and earned spot in Mets' bullpen in spring training.
- Ranked 6th among NL relievers and 11th in the majors with 81.0 innings pitched and also finished 6th in NL allowing 10.44 base runners per 9 innings.
- Was 1-0 with a 0.69 ERA (1 ER/13.0 IP) in six games in July to earn Mets Pitcher of the Month honours.

2007:

- Ranked 2nd on the staff in games finished (20) and 3rd in appearances (61) in first season with the Angels.

2008:

- Ranked T3rd in the AL in relief wins (7).
- Led staff in relief innings (72.0) and ranked 4th in appearances (54).
- Blown save on June 8 at Oakland was just 2nd of ML career and first since July 4, 1994 vs. Detroit… Snapped a string of 176 relief appearances without a blown save, 3rd-longest streak in majors since 1956... Recorded 100th career ML victory, Sept. 19 at Texas.

2009:

- Had the lowest ERA on the Angels' staff (40.0 or more IP) and placed 3rd with 63 appearances… Also topped club with 20 holds, T-9th in the AL, and 69.0 relief innings.
- Placed on 15-day DL on April 23 (retroactive to April 19) with a strained left triceps muscle… Activated on May 3.

2010:

- Was 2nd on the club in relief strikeouts (65), while placing 3rd in innings (61.2), holds (14) and appearances (career high 64), the latter being the most games ever for a Rangers pitcher, 39 years of age or older.
- Ranked 9th among AL relievers (50.0+ IP) with a 2.48 ERA, the lowest mark of his career, and was T-11th in the league in relief strikeouts.
- Issued runs in 15 of 64 games and retired 42 first batters permitted just 9 of 41 inherited runners to score, a 22.0% success rate that ranked as 9th-best in the AL... Compiled 1.10 WHIP, lowest mark of his career, while his 9.4 strikeouts-per-9 was also a career best.

2011:

- Led the Rangers in relief wins (5) and holds (16), and placing second in appearances (61).
- Earned his two saves in consecutive outings, April 23 vs. Kansas City and April 27 against Toronto… Save against the Royals came at the age of 40 years, 199 days, the oldest Ranger to ever record a save… That record lasted for one day before Arthur Rhodes' save on April 24 vs. KC came at 41 years, 182 days of age.
- Did not issue a home run in final 48 games and 39.2 IP after Hideki Matsui's walk-off blast on May 2 at Oakland… Issued the first walk-off homer of ML career in 599th appearance to Brandon Inge on April 13 at Detroit… Was the longest such streak to begin career since Kyle Farnsworth permitted his first walkoff homer in his 617th ML game on April 19, 2009.
- Made 600th career appearance, April 16 at New York (AL), recording lone out on a caught stealing.

BLUE JAYS AND ARBITRATION

Baseball arbitration was born out of the Basic Agreement settlement of 1972, though it was not actually put into place until before the 1974 season and was not used in 1976 and 1977.

The following are the list of Blue Jays who have gone to arbitration:

YEAR	PLAYER	OFFERED	ASKED	CLUB W/L
1980	Dave Lemanczyk-RHP	$130,000	$ 165,000	WON
	Roy Howell-3B	$110,000	$ 133,000	LOST
1982	Dave Stieb-RHP	$250,000	$ 325,000	WON
1983	Damaso Garcia-2B	$300,000	$ 400,000	LOST
	Roy Lee Jackson-RHP	$155,000	$ 225,000	WON
1988	Tom Henke-RHP	$725,000	$1,025,000	WON
1991	Roberto Alomar-2B	$825,000	$1,250,000	LOST
1997	Bill Risley-RHP	$380,000	$ 550,000	WON

ORTIZ, *RAMON*

Birthdate . . . . May 23, 1973
Opening Day Age 39
Birthplace. . . . . Cotui, DR
Residence. . . . . Cotui, DR
Bats/Throws . . . . R/R
Height/Weight 6-0/174
Contract Status . . . . signed thru 2013
M.L. Service 8.115

34
PITCHER
NON-ROSTER

PERSONAL:

Diogenes Ramon Ortiz... Graduated from 8th Intermedian High School in the Dominican Republic... Is an experienced barber and owns a barbershop in his hometown of Cotui in the Dominican Republic... Was honoured by the Santa Ana City Council in 2001 for his efforts in the Santa Ana Police Department's holiday celebration that benefitted 10,000 people.

LAST SEASON:

- Released by the San Francisco Giants on March 26 and signed by the Yankees to a minor league contract on April 4.
- Spent the season with Scranton-Wilkes Barre of the International League (AAA).
- Led the club in wins (13), IP (169.1) and ERA (3.45) in his 27 starts.
- Was his first full season in the minor leagues since 1998.

RAMON ORTIZ

Bold – career high

Year	Club & League	W-L	ERA	G	GS	CG	ShO	SV	IP	H	R	ER	HR	HB	BB-IBB	SO	WP	BK	OBA
1996	AZL (Ariz)	5-4	2.12	16	8	2	2	1	68.0	55	28	16	5	2	27-0	78	5	2	.216
	Boise (NOR)	1-1	3.66	3	3	0	0	0	19.2	21	10	8	3	1	6-0	18	0	1	.263
1997	Cedar Rapids (Mid)	11-10	3.58	27	27	8	4	0	181.0	156	78	72	22	7	53-0	225	14	5	.230
1998	Midland (TEX)	2-1	5.55	7	7	0	0	0	47.0	50	31	29	10	1	16-0	53	3	1	.275
1999	Erie (East)	9-4	2.82	15	15	2	2	0	102.0	88	38	32	12	2	40-0	86	1	0	.237
	Edmonton (PCL)	5-3	4.05	9	9	0	0	0	53.1	46	26	24	7	2	19-0	64	6	2	.227
	LOS ANGELES (AL)	2-3	6.52	9	9	0	0	0	48.1	50	35	35	7	2	25-0	44	2	2	.265
2000	Lake Elsinore (CAL)	1-0	3.00	1	1	0	0	0	6.0	8	2	2	0	0	2-0	7	0	0	.333
	Edmonton (PCL)	6-6	4.55	15	15	1	0	0	89.0	74	49	45	7	4	37-0	76	7	1	.223
	LOS ANGELES (AL)	8-6	5.09	18	18	2	0	0	111.1	96	69	63	18	2	55-0	73	7	4	.236
2001	LOS ANGELES (AL)	13-11	4.36	32	32	2	0	0	208.2	223	114	101	25	12	**76**-6	135	7	0	.274
2002	LOS ANGELES (AL)	15-9	3.77	32	32	**4**	**1**	0	**217.1**	188	97	91	**40**	5	68-0	**162**	7	3	.230
2003	LOS ANGELES (AL)	**16**-13	5.20	32	32	1	0	0	180.0	209	121	104	28	12	63-0	94	4	0	.287
2004	LOS ANGELES (AL)	5-7	4.43	34	14	0	0	0	128.0	139	64	63	18	4	38-4	82	5	3	.280
2005	Sarasota (FSL)	0-1	9.00	1	1	0	0	0	3.0	7	4	3	1	0	0-0	3	0	0	.412
	CINCINNATI (NL)	9-11	5.36	30	30	1	0	0	171.1	206	110	102	34	7	51-1	96	4	1	.302
2006	WASHINGTON (NL)	11-**16**	5.57	33	**33**	0	0	0	190.2	230	127	118	31	18	64-14	104	4	3	.297
2007	MINNESOTA (AL)	4-4	5.14	**28**	10	0	0	0	91.0	112	54	52	12	5	15-1	44	2	1	.298
	COLORADO (NL)	1-0	7.62	**10**	0	0	0	0	13.0	15	11	11	4	1	7-0	7	0	0	.306
2008	Orix (PAC)	4-7	5.82	17	17	0	0	0	82.0	102	59	53	10	7	20--	32	1	0	.000
2009	Fresno (PCL)	5-6	3.05	35	16	2	1	0	129.2	124	53	44	11	0	34-0	114	2	1	.248
2010	Buffalo (Int)	2-3	3.94	8	8	1	0	0	48.0	43	22	21	1	2	8-0	32	1	1	.239
	Durham (Int)	0-1	6.35	4	4	0	0	0	17.0	23	13	12	2	0	6-0	12	0	0	.315
	LOS ANGELES (NL)	1-2	6.30	16	2	0	0	0	30.0	33	22	21	5	0	16-2	21	1	1	.287
2011	Iowa (PCL)	6-3	4.26	16	16	0	0	0	99.1	115	53	47	12	3	20-0	81	4	1	.292
	CHICAGO (NL)	1-2	4.86	22	2	0	0	0	33.1	31	20	18	6	0	11-2	25	1	0	.244
2012	Scranton W.Barre (Int)	13-6	3.45	27	27	1	0	0	169.1	167	75	65	18	5	37-0	104	2	0	.261
Minor Totals		66-49	3.66	184	157	17	9	1	1032.1	977	482	420	111	29	305-0	953	45	15	.249
AL TOTALS		63-53	4.65	185	147	9	1	0	984.2	1017	554	509	148	42	340-11	634	34	13	.266
NL TOTALS		23-31	5.54	111	67	1	0	0	438.1	515	290	270	80	26	149-19	253	10	5	.295
MAJOR TOTALS		86-84	4.93	296	214	10	1	0	1423.0	1532	844	779	228	68	489-30	887	44	18	.275

DIVISION SERIES RECORD

Year	Club & League	W-L	ERA	G	GS	CG	ShO	SV	IP	H	R	ER	HR	HB	BB-IBB	SO	WP	BK
2002	ANAHEIM (AL)	0-0	20.25	1	1	0	0	0	2.2	3	6	6	0	1	4-0	1	1	0
2004	ANAHEIM (AL)	0-0	4.50	1	0	0	0	0	2.0	2	1	1	0	0	1-1	0	0	0
DIVISION SERIES TOTALS		0-0	13.50	2	1	0	0	0	4.2	5	7	7	0	1	5-1	1	1	0

LEAGUE CHAMPIONSHIP SERIES RECORD

Year	Club & League	W-L	ERA	G	GS	CG	ShO	SV	IP	H	R	ER	HR	HB	BB-IBB	SO	WP	BK
2002	ANAHEIM (AL)	1-0	5.05	1	1	0	0	0	5.1	10	3	3	0	0	1-0	3	0	0

WORLD SERIES RECORD

Year	Club & League	W-L	ERA	G	GS	CG	ShO	SV	IP	H	R	ER	HR	HB	BB-IBB	SO	WP	BK
2002	ANAHEIM (AL)	1-0	7.20	1	1	0	0	0	5.0	5	4	4	2	0	4-1	3	0	0

TRANSACTIONS

- Signed by the California Angels on May 23, 1995
- On disabled list (recovering from torn labrum - right shoulder) from March 25-April 11, 2000
- Traded to the Cincinnati Reds in exchange for RHP Dustin Moseley on December 14, 2004
- On disabled list (strained right groin) from April 9-May 1, 2005
- Signed by the Washington Nationals on December 29, 2005
- Signed by the Minnesota Twins on January 22, 2007
- Traded to the Colorado Rockies in exchange for IF Matt Macri on August 15, 2007
- Signed by the San Francisco Giants on February 10, 2009
- Signed by the Los Angeles Dodgers on February 2, 2010
- Signed by the New York Mets on June 23, 2010
- Signed by the Tampa Bay Rays on August 18, 2010
- Signed by the Chicago Cubs on April 10, 2011
- Signed by the San Francisco Giants on March 26, 2012
- Signed by the New York Yankees on April 4, 2012
- Signed by the Toronto Blue Jays on December 18, 2012

GAME HIGHS

ML Debut	Aug. 19, 1999 at CWS
Innings Pitched:	
Starter	9.0 - 9x, last Sept. 10, 2005 vs. PIT
Reliever	6.0 - June 8, 2007 vs. WSH
Walks:	
Starter	6 - 2x, last Aug. 13, 2000 vs. NYY
Reliever	4 - April 23, 2010 at WSH
Strikeouts:	
Starter	10 - 2x, last May 5, 2002 at TOR
Reliever	6 - May 20, 2004 vs. NYY
Hits Allowed	12 - 2x, last Aug. 25, 2004 vs. KC
Runs Allowed	9 - 2x, last July 14, 2002 at KC
ER Allowed	9 - 2x, last July 14, 2002 at KC
HR Allowed	4 - 3x, last June 17, 2005 vs. ATL
Low Hit CG	Aug. 8, 2000 vs. BOS
Last Win	Sept. 11, 2011 vs. NYM
Last Save	None
Last CG	Sept. 10, 2005 vs. PIT
Last ShO	Aug. 31, 2002 vs. BAL
Last Start	July 10, 2011 at PIT
Last Relief App.	Sept. 28, 2011 at SD
Longest Win Streak	6G - Aug. 14-Sept. 20, 2002
Longest Losing Streak	4G - 2x, last April 22-May 15, 2007
Scoreless Innings Streak	14.2 - June 14-25, 2003

CAREER FIELDING

POSITION	PCT	G	PO	A	E	TC	DP
P	.900	296	84	169	28	281	10

MILESTONES

Category		Date	Opponent	Notes
Start	1	Aug. 19, 1999	at Chicago (AL)	ML debut, won, 8.0 IP, 4H, ER, BB, 3K
	100	May 16, 2003	at Boston	no decision - 6.0 IP, 8H, 4ER, 2BB, 3K, HR
	200	Oct. 1, 2006	New York (NL)	loss - 1.1 IP, 7H, 6ER
Win	1	Aug. 19, 1999	at Chicago (AL)	ML debut, 8.0 IP, 4H, ER, BB, 3K
ShO (1)	1	Aug. 31, 2002	Baltimore	9.0 IP, 5H, 6K
10+ Strikeout Games (2)				
	1	April 5, 2001	at Texas	10 strikeouts
	2	May 5, 2002	at Toronto	10 strikeouts

PROFESSIONAL CAREER:

1999:

- Recalled by Anaheim, Aug. 18, and registered 2-3 record with 6.52 ERA in nine starts... Earned win in **Major League debut**, Aug. 19 at Chicago (9-2)...Allowed one run on four hits and one walk with three strikeouts in eight innings (longest outing of season)...Along with Brian Cooper (Sept. 7 vs. Chicago), became first Angels to win Major League debuts in same season since 1966 (Minnie Rojas - Clyde Wright).

2000:

- Began the season on the 15-day disabled list with a torn labrum in his right shoulder... Tossed a two-hitter,outdueled Pedro Martinez and allowed just two baserunners in a 2-1 victory vs. Boston on August 8.... The two-hitter was the first by an Angels' rookie since Mike Witt did it on April 26, 1981.

2001:

- Spent the entire year with the Angels and led the club in wins, complete games, innings pitched and strikeouts... Recorded a season high 10 strikeouts, April 5 at Texas... Pitched into the seventh inning in 23 of 32 starts.

2002:

- Spent the year with Anaheim and established new career highs in innings (217.1), complete games (four) and strikeouts 162)... Led the Angels in innings and strikeouts... Tied career-high 10 strikeouts, May 5 at Toronto.
- Went 6-0 in his final nine starts to help Anaheim reach the playoffs as the American League Wild Card winners... Earned the win in five straight starts, August 31-September 20.
- Retired the first 16 batters faced en route to his first complete-game shutout, August 31 vs. Baltimore.
- Made one start in each round of the postseason, all of which resulted in Anaheim wins... Earned the win in a 6-3 victory at Minnesota in Game 2 of the ALCS... Recorded the win in a 10-4 victory at San Francisco in Game 3 of the World Series.

2003:

- Established a career-high 16 wins, which tied for the eighth most in the American League... The 16 wins were the most by an Angels righthander since Bert Blyleven won 17 games in 1989.
- Recorded 11 wins prior to the All-Star break, the most by an Anaheim pitcher since Chuck Finley and Mark Langston each recorded 12 in 1991.
- Made 100th career start, May 16 at Boston.
- Earned his 50th career win in a 3-1 victory, July 22 at Tampa Bay.
- Recorded his 500th career strikeout (Corey Koskie) at Minnesota, September 3.

2004:

- Was moved to the bullpen where he spent the majority of the year... Made his first career appearance out of the bullpen on May 12 at New York (AL).
- Made one postseason appearance in relief during the Angels 9-3 loss vs. Boston in Game 1 of the American League Division Series.
- Traded to the Cincinnati Reds in exchange for pitcher RHP Dustin Mosley on December 14.

2005:

- Placed on the 15-day disabled list April 18 with a strained right groin (missed four starts), suffered a similar injury during spring training... Reinstated from the disabled list May 1.
- Left his start early on May 22 vs. Cleveland due to swelling under his left eye after being hit by a comebacker, did not miss a start.

2006:

- Was the only Nationals pitcher that did not miss a start.
- Led the Nationals in quality starts (15), wins (11), starts (33), innings (190.2) and strikeouts (104)... With 33 starts, reached the 30-start plateau for the fifth time in the last six years.
- Took a no-hitter into the ninth inning of an eventual 4-1 win vs. St. Louis on September 4 (Aaron Miles singled to left-center).

2007:

- Pitched six-plus innings in seven of 10 starts...had four quality starts.
- Traded to Colorado in exchange for infielder Matt Macri, August 15.

2008:

- Made 17 starts with Orix of Japan's Pacific League, going 4-7 with a 5.82 ERA in 82.0 IP.

2009:

- Pitched for Licey in the Dominican Winter League and went 3-2 with a 3.68 ERA (15 ER/36.2 IP) in seven starts... Struck out 17 and walked just four batters.

2010:

- Began the season with the Dodgers - making 16 appearances overall (two starts).
- April 5 at PIT made his first appearance in the Majors since the end of the 2007 season.
- Split time between Durham and Buffalo of the International League (AAA)... Combined to post a record of 2-4 with a 4.57 ERA in 12 starts.

2011:

- Promoted July 5 and made his Cubs debut that night, getting the start against Washington at Nationals Park.
- Transitioned to the bullpen to begin the second half.
- With Iowa (AAA), went 5-1 with a 3.74 ERA (22 ER/53.0 IP) in his final eight starts before heading to Chicago.

NO SWEEPS

The 1992 Toronto Blue Jays became only the sixth team in Major League history to complete a season without being swept in a series. Following is a list of the previous five teams:

1904 New York Giants
1905 Philadelphia Athletics
1910 Chicago Cubs
1921 Cleveland Indians
1943 St. Louis Cardinals

PERER, *JUAN*

Birthdate	September 3, 1978
Opening Day Age	34
Birthplace	Villa Rivas, DR
Residence	San Francisco de Macoris, DR
Bats/Throws	R/L
Height/Weight	6-0/170
Contract Status	signed thru 2013
M.L. Service	0.160

57

PITCHER

NON-ROSTER

PERSONAL:

Juan Pablo Perez... Married with three children.

LAST SEASON:

- Appeared in 10 games for the Brewers between May 19-June 17.
- Held opponents to a .231 average, including a .154 mark vs. lefties.
- Pitched one full inning in six of 10 appearances.
- Appeared in 38 games, all in relief for Nashville of the Pacific Coast League (AAA)... Held PCL hitters to a .224 average, including a .215 mark vs. lefties... Fanned 54 in 40 innings... Recorded a 2.81 ground ball-fly ball ratio.

JUAN PEREZ

Bold – career high

Year	Club & League	W-L	ERA	G	GS	CG	ShO	SV	IP	H	R	ER	HR	HB	BB-IBB	SO	WP	BK	OBA
1999	Red Sox (DSL)	6-6	1.94	13	13	1	1	0	69.2	38	29	15	1	2	30-0	107	5	1	.159
2000	Red Sox (GCL)	3-1	2.36	9	5	0	0	1	34.1	24	12	9	2	1	13-0	43	0	0	.192
2001	Augusta (SAL)	8-8	3.58	26	25	0	0	0	125.2	118	69	50	14	3	42-0	113	9	0	.251
2002	Sarasota (FSL)	0-6	3.78	16	14	0	0	0	66.2	71	34	28	4	2	19-0	39	4	0	.274
2003	Sarasota (FSL)	3-4	2.37	33	0	0	0	18	38.0	34	15	10	0	0	12-2	37	4	0	.230
	Portland (East)	3-3	3.82	18	0	0	0	0	30.2	37	19	13	4	0	11-1	24	2	0	.306
2004	Portland (East)	5-1	4.14	46	0	0	0	6	78.1	72	46	36	12	2	37-5	79	7	0	.237
2005	Pawtucket (Int)	4-5	4.50	40	1	0	0	1	62.0	61	31	31	7	5	29-0	74	5	2	.261
2006	Norfolk (Int)	0-1	2.86	43	0	0	0	0	63.0	65	24	20	4	2	34-0	55	4	0	.266
	Indianapolis (Int)	0-0	0.00	4	0	0	0	0	7.0	3	0	0	0	0	3-0	6	0	0	.136
	PITTSBURGH (NL)	0-**1**	8.10	7	0	0	0	0	3.1	5	3	3	1	2	1-0	3	0	0	.385
2007	Indianapolis (Int)	3-2	4.69	40	0	0	0	2	55.2	52	31	29	5	1	25-2	63	7	1	.243
	PITTSBURGH (NL)	0-0	4.38	**17**	0	0	0	0	**12.1**	14	7	6	**2**	0	**8**-0	**10**	1	0	.286
2008	Pirates (GCL)	1-0	0.00	4	0	0	0	0	6.0	2	1	0	0	3	2-0	8	0	0	.091
	Indianapolis (Int)	2-2	3.57	20	0	0	0	1	22.2	17	10	9	3	2	12-0	35	4	0	.207
2009	Gwinnett (Int)	2-4	3.47	47	0	0	0	1	57.0	40	28	22	7	2	36-1	59	7	0	.191
2010	AZL (Ariz)	0-0	0.00	2	0	0	0	0	2.0	0	0	0	0	0	0-0	5	1	0	.000
	Albuquerque (PCL)	4-3	2.96	45	0	0	0	1	45.2	38	19	15	4	2	20-1	53	5	0	.224
2011	Lehigh Valley (Int)	0-5	5.70	36	0	0	0	4	36.1	37	24	23	5	0	25-1	53	4	0	.262
	PHILADELPHIA (NL)	**1**-0	3.60	8	0	0	0	0	5.0	1	2	2	0	0	5-0	8	1	0	.062
2012	Nashville (PCL)	4-2	3.60	38	0	0	0	0	40.0	32	17	16	3	1	20-0	54	6	0	.224
	MILWAUKEE (NL)	0-**1**	5.14	10	0	0	0	0	7.0	6	4	4	**2**	1	**8**-1	**10**	0	0	.231
Minor Totals		48-53	3.49	480	58	1	1	35	840.2	741	409	326	75	28	370-13	907	74	4	.235
MAJOR TOTALS		1-2	4.88	42	0	0	0	0	27.2	26	16	15	5	3	22-1	31	2	0	.250

TRANSACTIONS

- Signed by the Boston Red Sox on September 2, 1998
- Signed by the New York Mets on October 28, 2005
- Claimed off waivers by the Pittsburgh Pirates on August 23, 2006
- Signed by the Atlanta Braves January 22, 2009
- Signed by the Los Angeles Dodgers on December 4, 2009
- Signed by the Philadelphia Phillies on November 19, 2010
- Signed by the Milwaukee Brewers on December 21, 2011
- Signed by the Toronto Blue Jays on December 11, 2012

GAME HIGHS

ML Debut	Sept. 7, 2006 at CHC	**Runs Allowed**	3 - Sept. 1, 2007 at MIL
Innings Pitched:		**ER Allowed**	3 - Sept. 1, 2007 at MIL
Starter	None	**HR Allowed**	2 - Sept. 1, 2007 at MIL
Reliever	2.0 - 2x, last Sept. 27, 2007 vs. ARI	**Low Hit CG**	None
Walks:		**Last Win**	July 8, 2011 vs. ATL
Starter	None	**Last Save**	None
Reliever	4 - April 13, 2007 vs. SF	**Last CG**	None
Strikeouts:		**Last ShO**	None
Starter	None	**Last Start**	None
Reliever	3 - 3x, last May 26, 2012 at ARI	**Last Relief App.**	June 17, 2012 at MIN
Hits Allowed	4 - Sept. 1, 2007 at MIL	**Longest Win Streak**	1G - July 8, 2011 vs. ATL
		Longest Losing Streak	1G - 2x, last May 21, 2012
		Scoreless Innings Streak	4.0 - June 23-July 15, 2011

CAREER FIELDING

POSITION	PCT	G	PO	A	E	TC	DP
P	1.000	42	0	3	0	3	0

MILESTONES

Category		Date	Opponent	Notes
Win	1	July 8, 2011	Atlanta	as reliever - 1.0 IP, 3K

PROFESSIONAL CAREER:

1999:

- Was named Boston's Minor League Pitcher-of-the-Year for the DSL Club after posting a 1.94 ERA in 13 starts with the DSL Red Sox... Led team in ERA, innings pitched and strikeouts.

2003:

- Went 6-7 with a 3.01 ERA in 51 relief appearances between Sarasota (Red Sox' A) and Portland his first season as a reliever... Set minor league career high in games and saves... Led all Boston minor leaguers in saves.

2004:

- Spent full season with Portland (Red Sox' AA)... Was selected to All-Star Futures Game, but did not appear in the contest on July 11.

2005:

- Spent entire season with Pawtucket his first season at the AAA level.

2006:

- Began season with Norfolk (Mets' AAA)... Was claimed off waivers by Pittsburgh on Aug. 23 and finished minor league campaign with AAA Indianapolis.
- Had contract purchased by Pittsburgh on Sept. 6... Retired the only batter he faced (Juan Pierre) in **major league debut** on Sept. 7 at Chicago (NL)... Was scored upon in three straight outings from Sept. 8-24... Served up a home run to Josh Bard and suffered first career loss on Sept. 24 at San Diego... Did not allow a run in final three appearances (2.0ip)... Allowed three of his four inherited runners to score.

2007:

- Was one of just two rookies on Pittsburgh's Opening Day roster (also infielder Don Kelly).
- Made season debut on April 3 at Houston and surrendered a single to lone batter he faced... Allowed one unearned run in 1.1 innings in second appearance on April 6 at Cincinnati... Worked 1.0 inning or less in seven of his eight appearances during first stint with Pirates from April 3-19.
- Was optioned to AAA Indianapolis on April 22... Made four appearances (4.0IP/2ER) before being placed on the disabled list on May 3 with a left calf strain.
- Was recalled by Pittsburgh on Sept. 1 and surrendered four hits (two homers) and three runs while striking out a career-high three batters in 2.0IP that night at Milwaukee... Made four straight scoreless outings (3.1IP) from 9/3-15 and was scored upon twice in his last eight games with the Pirates (7.0IP/3ER)...Was not involved in a save situation while pitching with Pittsburgh and allowed two of his nine inherited runners to score.

2008:

- Spent the first three months of the season at Extended Spring Training at the Pirates' complex in Bradenton, Fla., recovering from left elbow surgery... Was activated off the Indianapolis (AAA) disabled list on July 1.

2009:

- Appeared in 47 games for Triple-A Gwinnett (Braves)... Overall, limited left-handed batters to a .171 (12-for-70) average, while all opponents hit just .191... Limited opponents to a .103 (6-for-58) average with runners in scoring position and did not allow a hit (0-for-5) with the bases loaded.

2010:

- Spent the season with Albuquerque (AAA)... 33 of his 45 appearances were scoreless... Was on the DL with a right oblique strain... Held opponents to a .184 avg (16-87) with runners on base; 0-for-6 with the bases loaded.

2011:

- Signed as a free agent with Milwaukee on Dec. 2 after splitting the season between AAA Lehigh Valley and the Phillies.
- Was 1-0 with a 3.60 ERA in eight games with Philadelphia.

PEREZ, *LUIS*

Birthdate . . . . .January 20, 1985
Opening Day Age 28
Birthplace. . . . .Guayubin, Monte Cristi, DR
Residence. . . . .Guayubin, Monte Cristi, DR
Bats/Throws . . . . L/L
Height/Weight 6-0/210
Contract Status . . . . signed thru 2013
M.L. Service 1.119

47
PITCHER

PERSONAL:

Luis Manuel Gonzalez Perez... Married with one child... Signed with the Toronto Blue Jays as a non-drafted free agent in July of 2003.

LAST SEASON:

- Appeared in 35 games for Toronto in the first half of the season before being disabled with left elbow soreness.
- Did not pitch for the remainder of the season and had Tommy John surgery in late July.
- Appeared in 23 of the clubs first 53 contests... Did not allow a run in his first eight outings totalling 12.2 innings... Included a four inning no-hit performance at CLE on opening in the 7-4, 16-inning win... Streak was snapped when he allowed a grand slam to Michael Saunders in the 10th inning April 27 vs. SEA.
- Through May had posted a 2.45 ERA (25.2IP/7ER)... In June and July recorded a 4.96 ERA (16.1IP/9ER).
- Eight of his 35 appearances were for two or more innings... In those contests posted a 0.52 ERA (17.1IP/1ER).
- Held left-handed hitters to a .194 avearge (12-62) and all hitters to a .244 mark overall... Posted a 2.84 ERA and a .209 opponents average vs. AL East batters.

LUIS PEREZ

Bold – career high

Year	Club & League	W-L	ERA	G	GS	CG	ShO	SV	IP	H	R	ER	HR	HB	BB-IBB	SO	WP	BK	OBA
2005	Toronto (DSL)	2-3	4.96	12	11	0	0	0	52.2	42	37	29	3	6	28-0	68	6	0	.206
2006	Toronto (DSL)	4-0	1.38	14	14	0	0	0	85.0	47	19	13	0	7	23-0	107	7	0	.158
2007	Auburn (NYP)	3-3	3.70	16	16	0	0	0	75.1	73	37	31	1	9	38-0	71	4	1	.252
2008	Lansing (Mid)	5-12	3.60	28	23	0	0	0	137.1	136	68	55	4	16	51-0	137	6	7	.264
2009	New Hampshire (East)	9-11	3.55	28	27	2	0	0	162.1	145	78	64	11	13	67-2	112	6	0	.239
2010	New Hampshire (East)	5-6	4.54	13	12	1	0	0	73.1	67	43	37	6	4	37-0	49	4	1	.246
	Las Vegas (PCL)	5-5	6.13	15	15	1	0	0	86.2	107	66	59	5	12	47-0	56	7	3	.305
2011	Las Vegas (PCL)	2-2	4.60	8	8	0	0	0	45.0	37	23	23	5	3	23-0	43	3	0	.230
	TORONTO (AL)	**3-3**	5.12	**37**	**4**	0	0	0	**65.0**	74	40	37	**9**	5	**27**-1	**54**	4	0	.287
2012	TORONTO (AL)	2-2	3.43	35	0	0	0	0	42.0	38	16	16	3	3	16-0	39	0	0	.244
Minor Totals		35-42	3.90	134	126	4	0	0	717.2	654	371	311	35	70	314-2	643	43	12	.242
MAJOR TOTALS		5-5	4.46	72	4	0	0	0	107.0	112	56	53	12	8	43-1	93	4	0	.271

TRANSACTIONS

- Signed by the Toronto Blue Jays on July 30, 2003
- On disabled list (torn ligament in left elbow) from July 12-remainder of season, 2012

GAME HIGHS

ML Debut	April 16, 2011 at BOS	**ER Allowed**	8 - Sept. 6, 2011 vs. BOS
Innings Pitched:		**HR Allowed**	2 - Sept. 1, 2011 at BAL
Starter	6.0 – Aug. 21, 2011 at OAK	**Low Hit CG**	None
Reliever	4.0 - 3x, last April 5 at CLE	**Last Win**	April 20, 2012 at KC
Walks:		**Last Save**	None
Starter	4 - Aug. 27, 2011 vs. TB	**Last CG**	None
Reliever	3 - 2x, last April 5 at CLE	**Last ShO**	None
Strikeouts:		**Last Start**	Sept. 6, 2011 vs. BOS
Starter	6 - Sept. 1, 2011 at BAL	**Last Relief App.**	July 8, 2012 at CWS
Reliever	4 - 4x, last April 20, 2012 at KC	**Longest Win Streak**	2G - 2x, last April 5-20, 2012
Hits Allowed	10 – Sept. 6, 2011 vs. BOS	**Longest Losing Streak**	2G - 2x, last April 27-June 26, 2012
Runs Allowed	8 - Sept. 6, 2011 vs. BOS	**Scoreless Innings Streak**	13.0 - 2x, last April 5-27, 2012

CAREER FIELDING

POSITION	PCT	G	PO	A	E	TC	DP
P	.800	72	3	9	3	15	1

MILESTONES

Category		Date	Opponent	Notes
Start	1	Aug. 21, 2011	at Oakland	W, 6.0 IP, H, 2BB, 4K
Win	1	May 28, 2011	Chicago (AL)	As a reliever - 3.2 IP, 2H

PROFESSIONAL CAREER:

2005-06:

- Spent 2005 and 2006 in the Dominican Summer League, earning Player-of-the-Year honours in 2006.

2007:

- Picked up his first win June 28, going 8.0 innings, a season high.

2008:

- Led the Lugnuts, in innings pitched (137.1), strikeouts (137), walks (51) and losses (12).
- Was 2-0 with a 1.42 ERA in six June starts, leading to a Midwest League All-Star nod... His month of June earned him Minor League Pitcher of the Month honours for the club.

2009:

- Was tied for the Eastern League lead in starts (27), also finishing 2nd in innings pitched (162.1), 4th in strikeouts (112), 4th in ERA (3.55) and T-9th in wins (9).
- Participated in the 11th annual XM Satellite Radio All-Star Futures Game, representing the World Team.

2010:

- Picked up Eastern League (AA) Pitcher of the Week honours ending April 19.

2011:

- Made his **Major League debut** on April 16 at Fenway Park vs. BOS and pitched 1.1 scoreless innings of relief, allowed one hit and struck out two.
- Had a stretch from May 28-June 12 where he did not allow a run in 12.2 consecutive innings over five appearances.
- The 2.28 G/FB ratio led the Blue Jays and ranked 2nd in the AL (min 60-IP).

CONSECUTIVE WINS IN CONSECUTIVE GAME STARTS

(MINIMUM 6 WINS)

Roy Halladay	11	May 1-June 22, 2003
Roger Clemens	8	April 30-June 6, 1997
Doyle Alexander	7	Aug. 27-Oct. 1, 1983
Pat Hentgen	6	July 6-Aug. 6, 1996
David Wells	6	April 19-May 14, 2000
A.J. Burnett	6	July 3-Aug. 19, 2008

CONSECUTIVE WINNING STREAKS BY PITCHERS

(MINIMUM 9 WINS)

WINS	PITCHER	DATES
15	Roger Clemens	June 3- September 21, 1998
15	Roy Halladay	May 1- July 27, 2003
11	Dennis Lamp	April 26- September 23, 1985
11	Roger Clemens	April 2- June 6, 1997
10	Juan Guzman	June 22- October 1, 1991
9	Dave Stieb	May 1- June 20, 1988
9	Frank Castillo	June 12- September 27, 2000

RASMUS, *COLBY*

Birthdate . . . . August 11, 1986
Opening Day Age 26
Birthplace. . . . . Columbus, GA
Residence. . . . . Phenix City, AL
Bats/Throws . . . . L/L
Height/Weight 6-2/190
Contract Status . . . . signed thru 2013
M.L. Service 4.000

28

OUTFIELDER

PERSONAL:

Married with one child... Graduated from Russell County High School... Helped lead his high school to the National Championship his senior year (2005)... Also pitched in high school and was clocked at 91 mph off the mound... Broke Bo Jackson's Alabama state single-season record with 24 home runs... His Little League team won the U.S. championship at the 1999 Little League World Series -- lost the overall championship 5-0 to Hirakata, Osaka, Japan... Brother Cory (RHP) was the 38th overall pick in the supplemental round of the 2006 draft by the Atlanta Braves... Father Tony was a 10th-round draft pick of the Angels in January 1986 and is the coach of Russell County HS... Colby was named the Cardinals top prospect in 2007, 2008 and 2009 by Baseball America... Participated in the 2013 Winter Tour.

LAST SEASON:

- In his first full season in Toronto played in a career high 151 games... Started 138 game in CF and three at DH.
- Tied his career high with 23 home runs and set a new mark for RBI with 75.
- Among AL centrefielders ranked 5th in RBI (72), HR (22) and 6th in BB (46).
- Posted a .259 average with 17 home runs and 53 RBI prior to the All-Star break... Following the break hit .176 with six home runs and 22 RBI... In his career now has a .266 average and a .818 OPS in the first half of the season and a .209/.615 total in the second half.
- Batted .238 vs. right-handed pitching and .182 vs. left-handed pitching... Was productive with men in scoring position, posting a .276 average with seven home runs and 52 RBI... Enjoyed his best month in June, recording eight home runs and 25 RBI and a .291 average... Were the most home runs in a month since hitting nine in June of 2010...In his career has now hit 23 home runs in June with a .281 average and a .853 OPS... Has not hit more than 12 home runs in any other month.
- On June 5 at CWS collected five hits, representing a career high, coming within a triple of the cycle...Aug. 1-7 posted multiple hits in four consecutive games... June 23 at Miami hit his 3rd career grand slam in the 9th inning of a 7-1 victory... Had two multi-home run games and now has four career... June 19 at MIL hit a game-tying 9th inning home run off John Axford in a 10-9 victory.
- Posted a career high seven outfield assists.

COLBY RASMUS

Bold – career high

Year	Club & League	AVG	G	AB	R	H	2B	3B	HR	RBI	SH-SF	HP	BB-IBB	SO	SB-CS	SLG	OBP	OPS
2005	Johnson City (Appy)	.296	62	216	47	64	16	5	7	27	1-3	3	21-2	73	13-3	.514	.362	.876
2006	Quad Cities (Mid)	.310	78	303	49	94	22	3	11	50	3-3	3	29-2	55	17-5	.512	.373	.885
	Palm Beach (FSL)	.254	53	193	22	49	4	5	5	35	0-2	3	27-3	35	11-3	.404	.351	.755
2007	Springfield (TEX)	.275	128	472	93	130	37	3	29	72	0-2	12	70-0	108	18-3	.551	.381	.932
2008	Memphis (PCL)	.251	90	331	56	83	15	0	11	36	3-3	1	49-3	72	15-3	.396	.346	.742
	Cardinals (GCL)	.556	3	9	1	5	1	0	1	2	0-0	0	3-0	2	0-0	1.000	.667	1.667
	Palm Beach (FSL)	.000	3	9	1	0	0	0	0	0	0-0	1	1-0	3	0-0	.000	.182	.182
2009	ST. LOUIS (NL)	.251	147	474	72	119	22	2	16	52	5-2	3	36-3	95	3-1	.407	.307	.714
2010	ST. LOUIS (NL)	.276	144	464	**85**	**128**	**28**	3	**23**	66	2-4	1	**63**-9	148	**12**-8	.498	.361	.859
2011	ST. LOUIS (NL)	.246	94	338	61	83	14	**6**	11	40	1-2	0	45-2	77	5-2	.420	.332	.753
	TORONTO (AL)	.173	35	133	14	23	10	0	3	13	1-1	0	5-0	39	0-0	.316	.201	.517
2012	TORONTO (AL)	.223	**151**	565	75	126	21	5	**23**	**75**	2-4	7	47-5	**149**	4-3	.400	.289	.689
Minor Totals		.277	417	1533	269	425	95	16	64	222	7-13	23	200-10	348	74-17	.485	.366	.852
TORONTO TOTALS		.213	186	698	89	149	31	5	26	88	3-5	7	52-5	188	4-3	.384	.273	.657
NL TOTALS		.259	385	1276	218	330	64	11	50	158	8-8	4	144-14	320	20-11	.444	.334	.777
MAJOR TOTALS		.243	571	1974	307	479	95	16	76	246	11-13	11	196-19	508	24-14	.422	.313	.735

DIVISION SERIES RECORD

Year	Club & League	AVG	G	AB	R	H	2B	3B	HR	RBI	SH-SF	HP	BB-IBB	SO	SB-CS
2009	ST. LOUIS (NL)	.444	3	9	1	4	3	0	0	1	0-0	0	2-0	1	0-0

HOME RUN BREAKDOWN

				ONE GAME								
Total	H	A	2	3	4	GS	LO	XN	IP	PH	RHP	LHP
76	30	46	4	0	0	3	0	1	0	1	63	13

TRANSACTIONS

- Selected by the St. Louis Cardinals in the 1st round (28th overall) of the June 2005 First Year Player Draft
- Traded to the Toronto Blue Jays along with RHP P.J. Walters, LHP Brian Tallet and LHP Trever Miller in exchange for RHP Edwin Jackson, RHP Octavio Dotel, LHP Marc Rzepczynski and OF Corey Patterson on July 27, 2011
- On disabled list (jammed right wrist) August 26-September 15, 2011; included rehabliltation assignment at New Hampshire (AA) September 10-14

GAME HIGHS

ML Debut	April 7, 2009 vs. PIT	**RBI**	6 - June 2, 2011 vs. SF
Runs	4 - 3x, last June 5, 2012 at CWS	**Stolen Bases**	1 - 24x, last June 28, 2012 vs. LAA
Hits	5 - June 5, 2012 at CWS	**Last ML Home Run**	Sept. 28, 2012 vs. NYY
Doubles	3 - April 15, 2011 at LAD	**Longest Hitting Streak**	10G - June 1-11, 2009
Home Runs	2 - 3x, last June 19, 2012 at MIL	**Longest Hitless Streak**	26AB - Aug. 15-22, 2012

CAREER FIELDING

POSITION	PCT	G	PO	A	E	TC	DP
OF	.981	541	1142	15	23	1180	3

MILESTONES

Category		Date	Opponent	Pitcher	Notes
Hit	1	April 7, 2009	Pittsburgh	Snell	Single
Home Run	1	May 2, 2009	at Washington	Martis	1R
Multi-HR Game (4)					
	1	April 21, 2010	at Arizona	Jackson, Qualls	2R, 1R
	2	Sept. 9, 2010	at Atlanta	Martinez, Kawakami	1R, 1R
	3	April 22, 2012	at Kansas City	Teaford, Herrera	2R, 1R
	4	June 19, 2012	at Milwaukee	Thornburg, Axford	1R, 1R
Walkoff HR (2)	1	July 1, 2009	San Francisco	Howry	1R, 10th inning
	2	Aug. 16, 2009	San Diego	Bell	2R, 9th inning
Pinch Hit HR (1)	1	June 22, 2010	at Toronto	Frasor	2R
Grand Slam (3)	1	Aug. 11, 2010	at Cincinnati	Arroyo	5th inning
	2	June 2, 2011	San Francisco	Mota	7th inning
	3	June 23, 2012	at Miami	Mujica	9th inning
Extra Inning HR (1)					
	1	July 1, 2009	San Francisco	Howry	1R, 10th inning
RBI	1	April 14, 2009	at Arizona	Qualls	Single
Stolen Base	1	April 14, 2009	at Arizona	Scherzer C-Montero	2nd base

PROFESSIONAL CAREER:

2006:

- The Cardinals top prospect climbed to High-A ball in his second professional season en route to being named Cardinals Minor League Player of the Year.
- Led all Cardinals farmhands with 85 RBI and his 28 stolen bases ranked third among STL minor leaguers.
- Selected to play in the Midwest League All-Star Game held in Quad Cities on June 20 where he doubled and had a pair of hits in his start in RF and was the only player on the West side to have two hits.

2007:

- Named the Cardinals Minor League Player of the Year for a second-straight season... Became just the second Cardinal farmhand to win back-to-back Minor League Player of the Year awards since the award's inception in 1995 (John Gall, 2002-03).
- Was named to the First Team Minor League All-Star team as an outfielder and to the Double-A All Star team by Baseball America and was also named to Topps' Double-A All-Star team.
- His 29 homers and 93 runs scored led the Texas League, as did his .551 slugging pct.
- Selected to play in the Texas League All- Star Game where he was the starting centerfielder and singled, walked and scored a run in the game.
- Named to the Texas League Post-Season All-Star Team... Joined teammate C Bryan Anderson at the Futures Game during Major League All-Star break in San Francisco.
- Selected to the Team USA roster that won the gold medal in the 2007 Baseball Federation World Cup in Chinese Taipei... Was one of three players named as the tournament's Best Three Outfielders.
- Named to the TOPPS /Minor League Baseball Double-A All-Star Team... Baseball America named him as the Best Defensive Outfielder in the Texas League, the Most Exciting Player and possessing the Best Outfield arm in the League.

2008:

- Played in just one July game before he was placed on the DL on July 8 with a strained right groin... Briefly came off the DL on July 18 but was returned back to the DL July 23 with a sprained right knee... Was reinstated from the disabled list on Aug. 28 and played in three games for Palm Beach (A).
- Selected to both Futures Game and Team USA Olympic rosters, but did not play due to injury.
- Named by Baseball America as the top prospect in Cardinals system and among all Triple-A players in the PCL.

2009:

- Made his **ML debut** on April 7 vs. PIT, going 2-4 with a walk... Led all rookies in games played (147), finished 2nd in homers (16), 4th in RBI (52), runs (72), hits (119), doubles (22) and multi-hit games (32) and his 40 extra-base hits ranked 5th.
- Was just the sixth Cardinals rookie since 1954 to start 100 or more games in CF, joining Ray Lankford ('91), Bake McBride ('74), Curt Flood ('58), Bill Virdon ('55) and Wally Moon ('54).
- Was the youngest Opening Day player (22 yrs) for the Cardinals since Albert Pujols (21 yrs) in 2001... Hit a pair of walk-off home runs.

2010:

- Set a career high in almost every offensive category in his second full season in the Majors.
- Hit first career grand slam on his 24th birthday (Aug. 11 at CIN) becoming the fifth player (3rd Cardinal) in MLB history to hit his first grand slam on his birthday.
- Hit a 483-foot home run at KC (June 27), the longest by any NL player in 2010.
- Named National League Player of the Week (May 31-June 6), batting .500 with 3 HR & 9 RBI.
- Hit nine home runs in the month of June, tying for second best in the NL.

2011:

- Acquired on July 27 from St. Louis Cardinals along with LHP Brian Tallet, LHP P.J. Walters and LHP Trever Miller in exchange for RHP Edwin Jackson (acquired from CWS), RHP Octavio Dotel, LHP Marc Rzepczynski and OF Corey Patterson.
- Made his Blue Jays debut on July 28 vs. BAL, going 0-5.
- Aug. 6 hit his first home run as a Blue Jay off Chris Tillman of BAL.

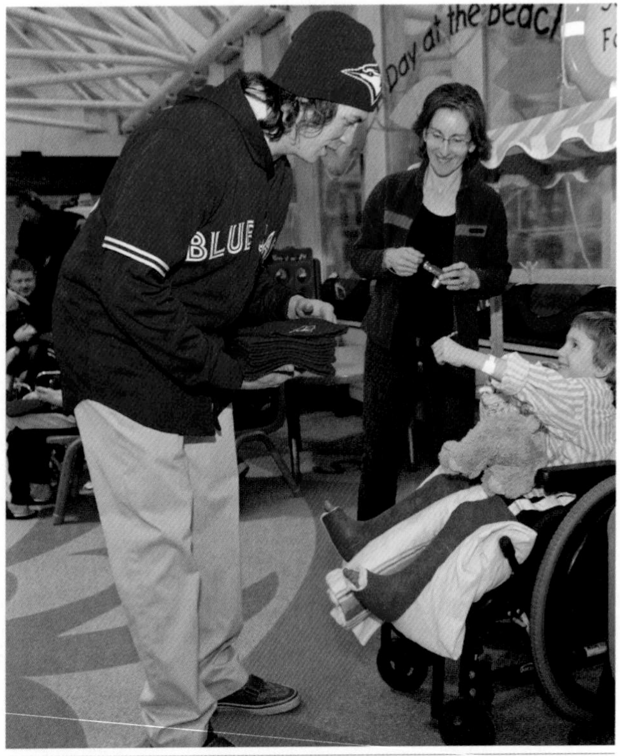

OF Colby Rasmus at a hospital meeting children in Edmonton, Alberta as part of the 2013 Toronto Blue Jays Winter Tour

REYES, *JOSE*

Birthdate	June 11, 1983
Opening Day Age	29
Birthplace	Santiago, DR
Residence	Santiago, DR
Bats/Throws	S/R
Height/Weight	6-0/160
Contract Status	signed thru 2017
M.L. Service	9.111

7

INFIELDER

PERSONAL:

Jose Bernabe Reyes... Attended Liceo Delia Reyes High School in the Dominican Republic... Played for Felix de Leon, since his high school did not have a baseball team... Founded the Santiago RBI program, which is an extension of Major League Baseball's RBI program... Program is designed to help youngsters learn the fundamentals of baseball while gaining an education... As part of the program, Reyes continues to donate money to help rebuild fields in his hometown.

LAST SEASON:

- Had the 5th most hits in the NL in the second half (94) and was tied with Miguel Cabrera and Mike Trout for 9th in the Majors.
- His 26-game hitting streak from July 13-Aug. 8 was the longest of his career and the longest in the Majors... It was the 17th streak of his career to surpass 10 games.
- His hitting streak was the longest by a reigning batting champion since Joe DiMaggio's 56-game streak in 1941, and the first of 25-or-more games by a reigning NL champ since Rogers Hornsby, who had a 33-game streak in 1922.
- He was just the 3rd player since 1933 to record a hit in his teams first 26 games following the All-Star break, joining Hal Trosky in 1936 (26 games) and Albert Pujols in 2003 (29).
- Led the team with 50 multiple-hit games, which ranked 2nd among NL shortstops, behind Starlin Castro (51) and 5th in the Majors behind Derek Jeter (64), Alcides Escobar (53) and Elvis Andrus (51).
- Reached 40 steals for the first time since swiping 56 bags in 2008, and for the fifth time in his career.
- Among Dominican-born players, he is the all-time leader in career triples (111), ahead of Juan Samuel (102), and is 2nd in stolen bases (410) behind Cesar Cedeno (550).
- Batted .667 (8-for-12) in extra innings with three runs scored, a double, three triples, a home run, four RBI and a .765 OBP (five walks, four intentional).
- His 12 hits in extra innings were the most of any player in the Majors in 2012 and among 129 players who had at least 10 extra-inning plate appearances, his average was the highest.
- He was the first player since Ryne Sandberg in 1984 to collect an "extra-inning cycle" in a season and is now 20-33 (.606) in extra innings since the start of 2011.

JOSE REYES

Bold – career high

Year	Club and League	AVG	G	AB	R	H	2B	3B	HR	RBI	SH-SF	HP	BB-IBB	SO	SB-CS	SLG	OBP	OPS
2000	Kingsport (Appy)	.250	49	132	22	33	3	3	0	8	3-1	3	20-0	37	10-4	.318	.359	.677
2001	Capital City (SAL)	.307	108	407	71	125	22	15	5	48	5-3	2	18-0	71	30-10	.472	.337	.809
2002	St. Lucie (FSL)	.288	69	288	58	83	10	11	6	38	4-4	1	30-1	35	31-13	.462	.353	.815
	Binghamton (East)	.287	65	275	46	79	16	8	2	24	2-0	2	16-1	42	27-11	.425	.331	.756
2003	Norfolk (Int)	.269	42	160	28	43	6	4	0	13	4-1	1	15-0	25	26-5	.356	.333	.689
	NEW YORK (NL)	.307	69	274	47	84	12	4	5	32	2-3	0	13-0	36	13-3	.434	.334	.768
2004	St. Lucie (FSL)	.261	6	23	3	6	2	0	0	1	0-0	0	0-0	3	2-0	.348	.261	.609
	Binghamton (East)	.111	4	18	2	2	0	0	0	3	0-1	0	2-0	4	3-1	.111	.190	.301
	NEW YORK (NL)	.255	53	220	33	56	16	2	2	14	4-0	0	5-0	31	19-2	.373	.271	.644
2005	NEW YORK (NL)	.273	**161**	696	99	190	24	**17**	7	58	4-4	2	27-0	78	**60**-15	.386	.300	.686
2006	NEW YORK (NL)	.300	153	647	**122**	194	30	**17**	**19**	**81**	2-0	1	53-6	81	**64**-17	.487	.354	.841
2007	NEW YORK (NL)	.280	160	681	119	191	36	12	12	57	5-1	1	**77**-13	78	**78**-21	.421	.354	.775
2008	NEW YORK (NL)	.297	159	688	113	**204**	**37**	**19**	16	68	5-3	1	66-8	**82**	56-15	.475	.358	.833
2009	NEW YORK (NL)	.279	36	147	18	41	7	2	2	15	0-1	0	18-1	19	11-2	.395	.355	.750
2010	St. Lucie (FSL)	.000	1	4	0	0	0	0	0	1	0-0	0	0-0	0	0-0	.000	.000	.000
	NEW YORK (NL)	.282	133	563	83	159	29	10	11	54	4-3	2	31-4	63	30-10	.428	.321	.749
2011	Brooklyn (NYP)	.333	1	3	1	1	1	0	0	0	0-0	0	0-0	0	0-0	.667	.333	1.000
	Binghamton (East)	.333	3	9	3	3	0	0	1	1	0-0	0	1-0	0	0-0	.667	.400	1.067
	NEW YORK (NL)	.337	126	537	101	181	31	**16**	7	44	2-4	0	43-9	41	39-7	.493	.384	.877
2012	MIAMI (NL)	.287	160	642	86	184	**37**	12	11	57	5-6	0	63-9	56	40-11	.433	.347	.780
Minor Totals		.284	348	1319	234	375	60	41	14	137	18-10	9	102-2	217	129-44	.424	.338	.761
MAJOR TOTALS		.291	1210	5095	821	1484	259	111	92	480	33-25	7	396-50	565	410-103	.440	.342	.782

ALL-STAR GAME RECORD

Year	Club and League	AVG	G	AB	R	H	2B	3B	HR	RBI	SH-SF	HP	BB-IBB	SO	SB-CS
2006	NL at PIT					Did Not Play									
2007	NL at SF	.750	1	4	1	3	1	0	0	0	0-0	0	0-0	0	1-0
2010	NL at LAA					Did Not Play									
2011	NL at ARZ					Did Not Play									
ALL-STAR TOTALS		.750	1	4	1	3	1	0	0	0	0-0	0	0-0	0	1-0

DIVISION SERIES RECORD

Year	Club and League	AVG	G	AB	R	H	2B	3B	HR	RBI	SH-SF	HP	BB-IBB	SO	SB-CS
2006	NEW YORK (NL)	.167	3	12	2	2	0	0	0	3	0-0	0	2-0	2	1-1

CHAMPIONSHIP SERIES RECORD

Year	Club and League	AVG	G	AB	R	H	2B	3B	HR	RBI	SH-SF	HP	BB-IBB	SO	SB-CS
2006	NEW YORK (NL)	.281	7	32	5	9	1	1	1	2	0-0	0	2-0	2	0-0

WORLD BASEBALL CLASSIC

Year	Club and League	AVG	G	AB	R	H	2B	3B	HR	RBI	SH-SF	HP	BB-IBB	SO	SB-CS
2006	Dominican Republic	.167	4	6	1	1	0	0	0	0	0-0	0	1-0	0	2-0
2009	Dominican Republic	.111	3	9	2	1	0	0	0	0	0-0	0	2-0	2	0-0
WBC Totals		.133	7	15	3	2	0	0	0	0	0-0	0	3-0	2	2-0

HOME RUN BREAKDOWN

Total	H	A	2	ONE GAME 3	4	GS	LO	XN	IP	PH	RHP	LHP
92	46	46	6	1	0	2	17	1	1	0	68	24

TRANSACTIONS

- Signed by the New York Mets on August 16, 1999
- On disabled list (left ankle sprain) September 5-remainder of season, 2003
- On disabled list (stress fracture of left fibula) August 13-September 24, 2004
- On disabled list (right calf tendinitis) May 26-remainder of season, 2009
- On disabled list (hyperactive thyroid) March 26-April 10, 2010
- Signed by the Miami Marlins on December 9, 2011
- Traded to the Toronto Blue Jays along with LHP Mark Buehrle, RHP Josh Johsnon, IF/OF Emilio Bonifacio, C John Buck and cash considerations in exchange for IF Yunel Escobar, IF Adeiny Hechavarria, C Jeff Mathis, RHP Henderson Alvarez, OF Jake Marisnick, RHP Justin Nicolino and RHP Anthony Desclafani on November 19, 2012

GAME HIGHS

ML Debut	June 10, 2003 at TEX	**RBI**	5 - June 15, 2003 at ANA
Runs	4 - Aug. 4, 2012 at WAS	**Stolen Bases**	3 - 7x, last Sept. 25, 2008 vs. CHC
Hits	5 - May 5, 2006 vs. ATL	**Last ML Home Run**	Aug. 26, 2012 at LAD
Doubles	3 - 3x, last Aug. 20, 2012 at ARZ	**Longest Hitting Streak**	26G - July 13-Aug. 8, 2012
Home Runs	3 - Aug. 15, 2006 at PHI	**Longest Hitless Streak**	18AB - 2x, last April 15-19, 2010

CAREER FIELDING

POSITION	PCT	G	PO	A	E	TC	DP
2B	.980	43	75	117	4	196	26
SS	.973	1159	1591	3158	131	4880	670

MILESTONES

Category		Date	Opponent	Pitcher	Notes
Game	500	June 15, 2007	at New York (AL)	--	as SS
	1000	June 28, 2011	at Detroit	--	as SS
Hit	1	June 10, 2003	at Texas	Thomson	single (1st ML AB)
	1000	May 25, 2010	Philadelphia	Moyer	single
Home Run	1	June 15, 2003	at Anaheim	Washburn	grand slam
Multi-Homer Game (7)					
	7	Sept. 27, 2011	Cincinnati	Arroyo (2)	1R, 1R
3-Homer Game (1)					
	1	Aug. 15, 2006	at Philadelphia	Wolf (2), Sanches	1R, 1R, 2R
Grand Slam HR (2)					
	1	June 15, 2003	at Anaheim	Washburn	1st ML HR
	2	Aug. 6, 2006	Philadelphia	Mathieson	4th inning
Leadoff HR (17)					
	17	July 20, 2012	at Pittsburgh	Correia	--
Inside the Park (1)					
	1	Sept. 7, 2006	Los Angeles (NL)	Penny	3R, 6th inning
Extra Inning (1)	1	July 3, 2012	at Milwaukee	Hernandez	1R, 10th inning
RBI	1	June 12, 2003	at Texas	Powell	groundout
Stolen Base	1	June 15, 2003	at Anaheim	Washburn C-Molina	2nd base
	100	April 25, 2006	at San Francisco	Wright C-Matheny	2nd base
	200	July 8, 2007	at Houston	Oswalt C-Ausmus	2nd base
	300	May 12, 2009	Atlanta	Bennett C-McCann	2nd base
	400	Sept. 1, 2012	New York (NL)	Ramirez C-Shoppach	2nd base

PROFESSIONAL CAREER:

2001:

- Named the Mets Minor League Player of the Year

2002:

- Named the Mets Minor League Player of the Year
- Selected to the MLB Futures Game and earned MVP honours in that contest
- Named as an Eastern League (A) All-Star
- Named USA Today Minor League Player of the Year

2003:

- Among National League rookies, he was 2nd in batting and stolen bases, 4th in slugging percentage (.434), T5th in triples, 5th in multi-hit games (29).
- Made his **Major League debut**, June 10th at Texas (started at shortstop)... Went 2-4 with a double and two runs... Singled in his first major league at-bat (Thomson).
- His 17-game hitting streak from July 30th-August 18th was the longest by a rookie in the NL.
- Collected the first multiple-home run game of his career on Aug. 28 at ATL (Mike Hampton and Trey Hodges)... Hit a home run from each side of the plate, becoming the first rookie to accomplish that feat since Brian Simmons of the Chicago White Sox on Sept. 26, 1988 at KC... Also became the youngest player in Major League history to accomplish the feat at 20 years and 78 days old.
- Went 3-4 with a grand slam (Washburn), five RBI (tied for the club- and a stolen base), June 15th at Anaheim... Became the youngest player in the majors to hit a grand slam since 19-year-old Tony Conigliaro hit one for the Boston Red Sox in 1964... Picked up his first major league RBI on June 12 at Texas.
- Was placed on the 15-Day disabled list on September 5th (retroactive to September 1st) with a Grade 2 sprain of the left ankle... Injured his ankle sliding into second base on August 31st vs. Philadelphia.

2004:

- Placed on the 15-Day Disabled List on Aug. 13 (retroactive to August 12th) with a stress fracture of the left fibula... Was reinstated on Sept. 24.
- Was placed on the 15-Day Disabled List on March 15th with a strained right hamstring... Was reinstated from the DL on June 19.

2005:

- Led the Majors in triples and at-bats... Led the National League in stolen bases.
- Set the club record with 161 games at shortstop.
- Stole his 60th base of the season, October 1st vs. Colorado, becoming only the second Met to steal 60 or more bases in a single season.
- Became the 3rd active player to have a 20-plus game hitting streak before the age of 23.
- Had at least one stolen base in six straight games (eight total) from July 17th-July 23rd... It was the longest streak in baseball since Baltimore's Luis Matos stole a base in six straight contests in October of 2001.
- Became the 1st NL player to have seven triples in a month since Houston's Craig Reynolds in May, 1981.
- Recorded his 2nd career multi-home run game, April 19 at PHI.

2006:

- Led the Majors with 17 triples and 64 stolen bases.
- Notched his 60th stolen base on September 24 vs. Washington to become the first player in club history to have consecutive seasons with 60 or more swipes... The last National League player to have back-to-back seasons with 60 or more stolen was Marquis Grissom with the Expos in 1991 and 1992... Cleveland's Kenny Lofton was the last Major League player to have consecutive seasons with 60 or more swipes when he did it three years in a row (1992-1994).
- Became the 1st player in Major League history to have 122 runs or more, 194 hits or more, 19 home runs or more and 64 stolen bases or more in a single season.
- Hit his 1st career inside-the-park home run in the 6th inning on Sept. 7 vs. LAD (off Brad Penny).
- Tied a franchise record and became the seventh Met to hit three home runs in a game on August 15th at Philadelphia (off Randy Wolf-2 and Brian Sanches).
- Hit a home run from each side of the plate on Aug. 15 at Philadelphia for the 2nd time in his career.
- Was named the National League's starting shortstop, his first selection, for the All-Star Game in Pittsburgh on July 11th... Did not play due to an injury.
- Was named the National League Player of the Week for the week ending June 25th... Became only the second player in franchise history to win back-to-back National League Player of the Week awards.
- Became the ninth player in Mets history to hit for the cycle, June 21st vs. Cincinnati... Was 4-5 in the contest... Was only the 3rd player in the last 25 years to hit a leadoff home run and hit for the cycle in the same game, June 21 vs. Cincinnati.
- Registered his 1st career five-hit game (5-7), May 5 vs. Atlanta.
- Collected his 13th triple this year on Aug. 1 at FLA, to become the first National League player to have 30 or more triples over a two-season span since Juan Samuel hit 32 for the Phillies spanning 1984 (19) and 1985 (13).
- Received seven stitches in his left pinky finger after cutting his finger sliding into first base in the 6th inning on July 7 vs. Florida.
- Is the 1st National League player to have a three-home run game and hit for the cycle in the same season since the Cubs' Andre Dawson in 1987.
- Was selected the NL's Co-Player of the Week with teammate David Wright for the week ending June 18th.
- Went 5-18 (.277) with five runs scored, four RBI, a home run and a stolen base in four games for Major League Baseball during the All-Star Tour in Japan... Also hit a "sayanara" walkoff home run in the bottom of the 10th inning in Game Five to give Major League Baseball a 5-3 win.
- Cracked a leadoff home run (off Chris Carpenter) in Game Six of the NLCS vs. St. Louis... It was Jose's first career post-season home run.

2007:

- His 78 stolen bases were most in the majors since Marquis Grissom swiped 78 bases with Montreal in 1992... In addition, he is the first Major League infielder to have 78 or more stolen bases in a season since Maury Willis had 94 stolen bases in 1965.
- Became the 1st infielder to register three straight seasons of 60 or more stolen bases since the current modern stolen base rule was put into effect in 1898... Became the 1st Major League player since Kenny Lofton (1992-1994) to compile three consecutive seasons with 60 or more stolen bases.
- Registered his 4th multi-home game of his career, Sept. 25 vs. WAS (Jason Bergmann, Jesus Colome).
- Was elected the starting shortstop for the NL All-Star team, July 11th at San Francisco... Was 3-4 with a double, a run scored and a stolen base in the National League's, 5-4, loss. with three stolen bases on June 15th.
- Became only the 4th player over the last 40 years to have hit a triple from each side of the plate in the same game on two separate occasions... The Yankees' Roy White (1969 and 1970) and Bernie Williams (1998 and 1999), and Dmitri Young for the Reds in 2000 and the Tigers in 2003.

OFFENSIVE LEADERS AMONG MLB SHORTSTOPS

(SINCE 2005)

Runs		Hits		2B	
Derek Jeter	795	Derek Jeter	1496	Jimmy Rollins	273
Jimmy Rollins	793	**Jose Reyes**	**1343**	Derek Jeter	231
Jose Reyes	**738**	Jimmy Rollins	1314	**Jose Reyes**	**231**

3B		XBH		SB	
Jose Reyes	**105**	Jimmy Rollins	482	**Jose Reyes**	**378**
Jimmy Rollins	64	**Jose Reyes**	**421**	Jimmy Rollins	273
Stephen Drew	52	Hanley Ramirez	389	Hanley Ramirez	219

2008:

- Led the National League and was third in the Majors with 204 hits... Finished 2nd in the big leagues in stolen bases and tied for fifth in the National League in runs scored.
- Has 65 triples over the last four years... Since 1950, the only other player with 60 or more triples over a four year period is Lance Johnson who collected 61 from 1993-1996.
- Reached base safely in a franchise record 41 straight games form April 22nd-June 8th... Celebrated his 25th birthday on June 11th and had 257 career stolen bases with 57 triples for his career... The only other player with 250 stolen bases and at least 50 triples befor his 25th birthday was Ty Cobb (344 stolen bases, 89 triples).
- Over the last 75 years, only Stan Musial, Willie Wilson and Carl Crawford have had three straight seasons of 15 or more triples.
- Became the 1st player in Major League history to have 20 or more doubles (23), 10 or more triples (10), 10 or more home runs (10), and 30 or more stolen bases (32) prior to the All-Star Break.

2009:

- Left the game on May 20 at Los Angeles with an injury to his right leg... Placed on the 15-Day Disabled List on May 26th.
- Stole his 300th career base, May 10 vs. Pittsburgh... Is one of only 10 active players with 300 or more stolen bases (Juan Pierre, Omar Vizquel, Johnny Damon, Luis Castillo, Carl Crawford, Bobby Abreu, Ichiro Suzuki, Jimmy Rollins and Derek Jeter)... Also is one of only two active players under the age of 30 with 300 or more stolen bases (Crawford).
- Underwent surgery on Oct. 15 to clean up scar tissue around the accessory hamstring tendon behind his right knee (semi tendinosis)... Dr. Daniel E. Cooper, on the recommendation of Mets Medical Director Dr. David Altchek, performed the surgery at the Carrell Clinic in Dallas, TX... Did not require surgery for the hamstring muscle tear in his right leg which he suffered during his rehabilitation in September.

2010:

- Was diagnosed with a hyperactive thyroid on March 11... Returned to baseball activity on March 23 and appeared in his first minor league spring training game on March 30... Began the season on the 15-Day disabled list on April 5, retroactive to March 26, with his thyroid condition.
- Hit his 75th career triple on April 21 vs. Atlanta in his 804th career game... Among players who debuted in the Majors since 1950, only one reached 75 triples in fewer games than Reyes: Garry Templeton, who collected his 75th triple in his 787th game.
- Collected his 1,000th career hit on May 25 vs. Philadelphia... Became the quickest in franchise history to reach the milestone.
- Missed time from June 30-July 6 with a strained right oblique... Returned to action on July 6 vs. Cincinnati but left the game on July 10 vs. Atlanta with the same injury.
- Was named to the National League All-Star team, but was unable to play due to injury.
- Hit his 80th career triple on August 15 vs. Philadelphia... Was one of only six active players with 80 or more triples (Carl Crawford-105, Johnny Damon-100, Jimmy Rollins-98, Cristian Guzman-89, Juan Pierre-82).

2011:

- Hit .337 and became the 11th different shortstop to win batting crown and 1st since Hanley Ramirez hit .342 in 2009... Other shortstops to win title were Jack Glasscock (1890), Honus Wagner (seven times as shortstop, last 1911), Arky Vaughan (1935) and Dick Groat (1960) in National League and Luke Appling (1936, '43), Lou Boudreau (1944), Alex Rodriguez (1996), Nomar Garciaparra (1999, 2000) and Michael Young (2005) in American League (Elias Sports Bureau).
- Tied for Major League lead in triples with Philadelphia's Shane Victorino.
- Named to NL All-Star team as starting shortstop... Was 3rd starting nod (also 2006 & 2007), but did not participate because of strained left hamstring.
- Became 1st Major Leaguer since 1900 to post three multi-triple games in one season before end of May.
- Played 1,000th ML game on June 28 at Detroit... At time of his 1,000th game, had 98 triples and 360 steals... Only other player with as many triples and steals in first 1,000 games was Ty Cobb, who had 106 triples and 391 stolen bases when he played his 1,000th game in 1912.
- Became third player in last 80 seasons to have 11 triples within team's first 60 games, joining Rod Carew (11, 1977) and Curtis Granderson (12, 2007).
- Finished June with 45 hits, 29 runs, seven triples and 11 stolen bases in 26 games; last Major Leaguer to reach all four of those levels in one calendar month was Ty Cobb in July, 1912.
- Had 42 multi-hit games in team's first 81 games, tying for 9th-most in ML history since 1919; record is 46 (Bill Terry-1930, Joe Medwick-1937).

SS Jose Reyes being introduced to the Toronto media at a press conference held at Rogers Centre on January 17, 2013

ROGERS, *ESMIL*

Birthdate	August 14, 1985
Opening Day Age	27
Birthplace	Santo Domingo, DR
Residence	San Pedro de Macoris, DR
Bats/Throws	R/R
Height/Weight	6-1/190
Contract Status	signed thru 2013
M.L. Service	2.135

32
PITCHER

PERSONAL:

Esmil Antonio Rogers... Played three seasons in the Dominican Summer League as an infielder prior to converting to a pitcher.

LAST SEASON:

- Acquired mid-season by Cleveland from Colorado on June 13.
- Had five holds over the last month of the season (six holds total with Cleveland).
- Did not allow an earned run in 30 of his 44 outings with the Indians, limiting hitters to a .237 (47-198) average against while with the Indians.
- Right-handed hitters batted .220 off him with 30 strikeouts and hitters batted .253 with runners on base.
- Over his last 23 outings from Aug. 8 through the end of the season he recorded an ERA of 3.28 (24.2IP, 22H, 9ER).
- Eight of 28 inherited runners (28.6%) scored with Cleveland, overall on the year recorded a mark of 15 of 43 (35%).
- Went 2-0 with a 2.45 ERA in 11 Sept. games (11.0IP, 6H, 3R/ER) after recording a 2.04 ERA in 13 August games (17.2IP, 20H, 4R/ER).
- Started the year in the Colorado bullpen, opening the season with four scoreless outings (7.1IP, 6H, 0R, 9K) before allowing four runs in 1.1IP on April 21 at MIL... Had four outings with the Rockies where he allowed at least 3ER, including five earned runs on May 5 vs. ATL... Was designated for assignment on June 9 and acquired by Cleveland four days later.
- With Rockies right-handed batters hit .400 off him and he allowed 10ER in seven games in Coors Field (7.0IP, 10H, 10BB)...Averaged 10.2 strikeouts per nine with Colorado... Owns a career ERA of 8.15 in Coors Field (77.1IP, 115H, 70ER, .348avg).

ESMIL ROGERS

Bold - career high

Year	Club & League	W-L	ERA	G	GS	CG	ShO	SV	IP	H	R	ER	HR	HB	BB-IBB	SO	WP	BK	OBA
2006	Casper (Pio)	3-6	6.96	15	15	1	0	0	63.1	78	53	49	8	13	24-1	40	8	1	.306
2007	Asheville (SAL)	7-4	3.75	19	18	1	0	0	117.2	125	60	49	6	7	42-0	90	10	4	.272
2008	Modesto (CAL)	9-7	3.95	25	25	0	0	0	143.2	146	73	63	9	4	45-0	116	6	3	.264
2009	Tulsa (TEX)	8-2	2.48	15	15	0	0	0	94.1	87	30	26	2	6	19-0	83	3	1	.243
	Colorado Springs (PCL)	3-5	7.42	12	11	0	0	0	60.2	77	50	50	9	3	35-2	46	7	3	.317
	COLORADO (NL)	0-0	4.50	1	1	0	0	0	4.0	3	2	2	0	0	2-0	3	0	0	.231
2010	Colorado Springs (PCL)	3-3	5.75	12	11	0	0	0	61.0	62	41	39	6	4	19-0	53	3	2	.261
	COLORADO (NL)	2-3	6.13	28	8	0	0	0	72.0	94	59	49	5	5	26-2	66	5	2	.318
2011	Tulsa (TEX)	0-1	2.25	1	1	0	0	0	4.0	5	3	1	1	0	1-0	2	0	1	.278
	Colorado Springs (PCL)	1-2	6.26	5	5	0	0	0	23.0	36	16	16	3	2	5-0	15	3	0	.364
	COLORADO (NL)	6-6	7.05	18	13	0	0	0	83.0	110	65	65	14	6	47-5	63	5	1	.320
2012	COLORADO (NL)	0-2	8.06	23	0	0	0	0	25.2	36	23	23	2	2	18-2	29	5	0	.324
	CLEVELAND (AL)	3-1	3.06	44	0	0	0	0	53.0	47	19	18	5	3	12-2	54	5	0	.237
Minor Totals		34-30	4.65	104	101	2	0	0	567.2	616	326	293	44	39	190-3	445	40	15	.277
NL TOTALS		8-11	6.77	70	22	0	0	0	184.2	243	149	139	21	13	93-9	161	15	3	.318
MAJOR TOTALS		11-12	5.95	114	22	0	0	0	237.2	290	168	157	26	16	105-11	215	20	3	.301

TRANSACTIONS

- Signed by the Colorado Rockies on July 10, 2003
- Traded to the Cleveland Indians in exchange for cas considerations on June 12, 2012
- Traded to the Toronto Blue Jays in exchange for IF Mike Aviles and C/IF Yan Gomes on November 3, 2012

GAME HIGHS

ML Debut	Sept. 12, 2009 at SD
Innings Pitched:	
Starter	7.1 - April 7, 2011 at PIT
Reliever	5.0 - July 30, 2011 at SD
Walks:	
Starter	7 - Aug. 14, 2011 at STL
Reliever	3 - 4x, last May 13, 2012 at LAD
Strikeouts:	
Starter	7 - 2x, last Aug. 26, 2011 at LAD
Reliever	6 - Sept. 28, 2010 vs. LAD
Hits Allowed	12 - Aug. 20, 2011 vs. LAD
Runs Allowed	9 - Sept. 18, 2011 vs. SF
ER Allowed	9 - Sept. 18, 2011 vs. SF
HR Allowed	4 - Sept. 18, 2011 vs. SF
Low Hit CG	None
Last Win	Sept. 20, 2012 vs. MIN
Last Save	None
Last CG	None
Last ShO	None
Last Start	Sept. 18, 2011 vs. SF
Last Relief App.	Oct. 2, 2012 vs. CWS
Longest Win Streak	5G - 2x, last Aug. 15-Sept. 20, 2008
Longest Losing Streak	5G - Aug. 14-Sept. 18, 2011
Scoreless Innings Streak	14.0 - July 10-Aug. 5, 2005

CAREER FIELDING

POSITION	PCT	G	PO	A	E	TC	DP
P	.946	114	27	26	3	56	4

MILESTONES

Category		Date	Opponent	Notes
Start	1	Sept. 12, 2009	at San Diego	ML debut - no decision, 4.0 IP, 3H, 2ER, 2BB, 3K
Win	1	May 23, 2010	at Kansas City	as reliever - 2.0 IP, 5H, 2ER

PROFESSIONAL CAREER:

2006:

- After spending his first three professional seasons as an infielder, converted to a pitcher in 2006.
- Ranked second in the Pioneer League in games started... Opponents batted .306... Was credited with a complete game in his final start of the season on Sept. 7 at Orem in an 8-4 win... Tossed just 5.0 innings as the games was called early due to power issues.

2007:

- In his second full season as a pitcher, went 7-4 with a 3.75 ERA in 19 games/18 starts.
- Struck out 90 batters and issued 42 walks... 12 of his 18 starts were quality outings... Tossed at least 6.0 frames in 15 starting assignments and allowed three earned runs or less in 13 contests... Held opposing batters at a .272 average against... Tossed his 2nd career complete game on July 22 vs. Charleston, pitching 9.0 innings and allowing three runs on five hits.

2008:

- Set career highs in several categories while spending the entire season with Modesto... Set career bests in starts (25) innings pitched (143.2) and strikeouts (116), while holding opponents to a career low .264 average against... Had 12 quality starts.

2009:

- Made 29 starts for Modesto, the most of any pitcher on the club... His 131 strikeouts and two complete games were second-most on the club... Was twice named the California League Pitcher of the Week... Finished second on the team, and second in the Cal League with 170.1 innings pitched.
- Following the season was named by Baseball America as the 10th-best prospect in Colorado's farm system.

2010:

- Was named to the Opening Day roster for the first time in his career but was optioned to the minors on April 16.
- Made five starts from Aug. 8-31... In his first appearance out of the bullpen after making five starts, struckout his only batter faced on four pitches with bases loaded.
- Earned first MLB win May 23 at KC... Inherited bases loaded, one-out situation and induced double play after allowing base hit to first batter.
- Tossed a career-high 6.1 innings in his start Aug. 20 at ARI... Was issued a no decision in that start but allowed just one run on six hits, one walk and six strikeouts.
- Made the move between Colorado Springs and the big league club five times during the season.
- Drove in his first career RBI on Aug. 8 at PIT when he went 2-for-3 with two doubles and scored a run.

2011:

- Made 13 starts and five relief appearances for the Rockies, his third season in the Major Leagues.
- 13 starts mark his most starts in a single-season... 2011 marked highs in nearly every category... Topped his career marks in wins (6), innings pitched (83.0) and starts (13)... Also tallied career highs in walks (47), losses (6), opponent batting average (.320) and home runs allowed (14).
- Began the season in the starting rotation and made five starts before seeing three relief outings in May and June.
- Was placed on the 15-day disabled list with a right lat muscle strain May 7 and returned July 25... Before returning to the rotation in August, Rogers made three appearances out of the bullpen following his return from the DL... Finished the season as the long reliever out of the Rockies bullpen, making two relief outings in the season's final week.

Taking in a ball game in the Jays Care Community Clubhouse, a fully-renovated luxury suite at Rogers Centre

ROMERO, *RICKY*

Birthdate . . . . November 6, 1984
Opening Day Age 28
Birthplace. . . . . Los Angeles, CA
Residence. . . . . Downey, CA
Bats/Throws . . . . R/L
Height/Weight 6-0/225
Contract Status . . . . signed thru 2015
M.L. Service 4.000

24

PITCHER

PERSONAL:

Ricardo Romero Jr... Single... After spending three years at Garfield High School Romero graduated from Theodore Roosevelt High School in East Los Angeles... In his senior year he was named L.A. City Section Co-Player of the Year and Eastern League co-MVP for baseball, going (12-1) with a 0.53 ERA and 162 strikeouts for the Rough Riders... Upon graduation, attended Cal State Fullerton from 2001 to 2005... The lefty starter helped the Titans capture a National Title in the 2004 College World Series, pitching the team into the semifinals past Miami (FL) and winning game one of the World Series against Texas... Selected to the All-Tournament team for that season and played for the U.S. National Team pitching to a 3-1 record with a 1.57 ERA... In 2005 he led Fullerton in wins (13) and the Titans returned back to the World Series... Particpated in the Toronto Blue Jays Winter Tour - 2011 and 2012.

LAST SEASON:

- Posted 14 losses and a 5.97 ERA which represented career worst totals... Led the team with his 32 starts for the third consecutive season.
- Produced 22 GDP's ranking 11th in the AL...Has posted 105 since the 2009 season, which is the most in the Major Leagues, 12 more than Felix Hernendez.
- Had a 13 game losing streak which represented the longest streak in the Majors... Also tied a Blue Jays record for consecutive losses along with Tom Underwood (1978-79)... During the streak recorded a 7.42 ERA, with a .324 opponent's average and 6.1 walks per nine.
- Issued 105 walks in 181 innings for a 5.2 per nine total... Had walked just 3.5 per nine in his career through 2011.
- Once again this season fared better against righ-handed hitters than left-handed hitters... Posted a .268 average vs. righties and a .310 average vs. lefties...Has now posted a career mark of .240 against righties and .288 vs. lefties.
- Was the Opening Day starter in Cleveland on April 5th for his second consecutive Opening Day assignment.
- Won four consecutive decisions from April 11-May 2 and from May 18-June 22, after that lost 13 straight before winning his final decision on Sept. 24 at BAL.
- Allowed four or more runs in eight consecutive starts and a career high eight runs in back-to-back starts on June 27 and July 2... Club suffered its biggest shutout loss in his July 25 start (16-0), lasting only 1.1 innings and allowing eight earned runs... On Sept. 2 had his shortest start of his career, lasting only 1.0 IP vs. TB, giving up seven earned runs.

RICKY ROMERO

Bold – career high

Year	Club & League	W-L	ERA	G	GS	CG	ShO	SV	IP	H	R	ER	HR	HB	BB-IBB	SO	WP	BK	OBA
2005	Dunedin (FSL)	1-0	3.82	8	8	0	0	0	30.2	36	13	13	2	0	7-0	22	5	1	.283
	Auburn (NYP)	0-0	0.00	1	1	0	0	0	2.0	2	0	0	0	0	1-0	2	1	0	.250
2006	Dunedin (FSL)	2-1	2.47	10	10	1	1	0	58.1	48	17	16	5	1	14-0	61	0	0	.224
	New Hampshire (East)	2-7	5.08	12	12	0	0	0	67.1	65	43	38	7	1	26-0	41	6	0	.256
2007	New Hampshire (East)	3-6	4.89	18	18	1	0	0	88.1	98	57	48	9	4	51-0	80	9	0	.279
	Dunedin (FSL)	0-0	3.86	1	1	0	0	0	4.2	4	2	2	0	0	1-0	2	0	0	.250
2008	New Hampshire (East)	5-5	4.96	21	21	0	0	0	121.2	139	70	67	9	6	55-0	78	11	1	.294
	Syracuse (Int)	3-3	3.38	7	7	1	0	0	42.2	42	17	16	3	2	20-0	38	2	0	.263
2009	Dunedin (FSL)	0-1	13.50	1	1	0	0	0	4.0	6	6	6	2	0	1-0	5	1	0	.333
	New Hampshire (East)	0-0	1.69	1	1	0	0	0	5.1	3	2	1	0	0	5-0	4	0	0	.188
	Las Vegas (PCL)	0-0	7.20	1	1	0	0	0	5.0	8	4	4	0	1	2-0	3	0	0	.381
	TORONTO (AL)	13-9	4.30	29	29	0	0	0	178.0	192	88	85	18	10	79-0	141	6	1	.284
2010	TORONTO (AL)	14-9	3.73	**32**	**32**	3	1	0	210.0	189	98	87	15	8	82-3	174	18	1	.242
2011	TORONTO (AL)	**15**-11	2.92	**32**	**32**	**4**	**2**	0	**225.0**	176	85	73	**26**	14	80-2	**178**	9	1	.216
2012	TORONTO (AL)	9-**14**	5.77	**32**	**32**	1	0	0	181.0	198	122	116	21	10	**105**-1	124	8	0	.282
Minor Totals		16-23	4.42	81	81	3	1	0	430.0	451	231	211	37	15	183-0	336	35	2	.272
MAJOR TOTALS		51-43	4.09	125	125	8	3	0	794.0	755	393	361	80	42	346-6	617	41	3	.254

ALL-STAR GAME RECORD

Year	Club & League	W-L	ERA	G	GS	CG	ShO	SV	IP	H	R	ER	HR	HB	BB-IBB	SO	WP	BK
2011	AL at ARI							Did Not Pitch										

TRANSACTIONS

- Selected by the Toronto Blue Jays in the 1st round (6th overall) of the 2005 First Year Player Draft
- On disabled list (right oblique strain) from April 20-May 15, 2009

GAME HIGHS

ML Debut	April 9, 2009 vs. DET	**Runs Allowed**	9 - 2x, last June 27, 2012 at BOS
Innings Pitched:		**ER Allowed**	8 - 4x, last July 25, 2012 vs. OAK
Starter	9.0 - 6x, last Sept. 19, 2011 vs. LAA	**HR Allowed**	3 - May 26, 2009 at BAL
Reliever	None	**Low Hit CG**	2 - Aug. 3, 2010 at NYY
Walks:		**Last Win**	Sept. 24, 2012 at BAL
Starter	8 - Aug. 21, 2012 at DET	**Last Save**	None
Reliever	None	**Last CG**	July 18, 2012 at NYY (6.0 IP)
Strikeouts:		**Last ShO**	Aug. 18, 2011 at OAK
Starter	12 - 3x, last June 15, 2011 vs. BAL	**Last Start**	Sept. 29, 2012 vs. NYY
Reliever	None	**Last Relief App.**	None
Hits Allowed	12 - July 18, 2012 at NYY	**Longest Win Streak**	6G - July 27-Aug. 29, 2011
		Longest Losing Streak	13G - June 27-Sept. 12, 2012
		Scoreless Innings Streak	24.0 - June 24-July 6, 2009

CAREER FIELDING

POSITION	PCT	G	PO	A	E	TC	DP
P	.959	125	38	147	8	193	7

MILESTONES

Category		Date	Opponent	Notes
Start	1	April 9, 2009	Detroit	W, 6.0 IP, 7H, 2ER, 2BB, 5K
	100	May 8, 2012	at Oakland	no decision - 6.0 IP, 5H, 2ER, 5BB, 7K, HR
Win	1	April 9, 2009	Detroit	6.0 IP, 7H, 2ER, 2BB, 5K
Sho (3)	1	May 15, 2010	Texas	5H, 12K
	2	June 26, 2011	at St. Louis	4H, 5K
	3	Aug. 18, 2011	at Oakland	3H, 6K
10+ Strikeout Games (4)				
	1	April 13, 2010	Chicago (AL)	12 strikeouts
	2	May 15, 2010	Texas	12 strikeouts
	3	April 24, 2011	Tampa Bay	10 strikeouts
	4	June 15, 2011	Baltimore	12 strikeouts
Strikeout	500	April 11, 2012	Boston	McDonald

PROFESSIONAL CAREER:

2009:

- Made 29 starts as a rookie, recording 178 innings and 141 strikeouts to rank 2nd on the club to only Roy Halladay.
- Posted 13 wins to rank 2nd in the AL for rookies… His 16 quality starts were the most from any AL rookie… Also finished 3rd in innings pitched (178), 2nd in strikeouts (141), 4th in ERA (4.30) & 1st with a 2.24 ground/fly ball ratio among rookies.
- His seven wins prior to the All-Star break ranked T-1st on the all-time Blue Jays list for rookies (Chacin-2005, Timlin-1991, Musselman-1987, Garvin-1977).
- Became one of 16 pitchers to earn a victory in their debut as a Blue Jays starter, April 9 vs. DET.
- His 13 wins ranks him T-2nd on the Blue Jays list for wins by a rookie, one behind Mark Eichhorn in 1986… In fact he is tied with Gustavo Chacin for wins by a rookie starter as Eichhorn recorded his wins as a reliever.
- April 9 vs. DET was the first time in Major League history that both starting pitchers, Romero & Rick Porcello of the Tigers were making their **Major League debut** and were both first round picks in the draft (Since MLB draft began in 1965)… Picked up the win over the Tigers by a 6-2 score earning his first victory (6.0 IP, 7H, 2ER, 2BB, 5K).
- From June 24-July 6, covering four starts, posted 24 consecutive scoreless innings… It represented the highest streak by any AL starter in 2009, tied with Zack Greinke & teammate Roy Halladay… In fact his streak matches the 24 Mark Eichhorn recorded as a rookie in 1986.
- Led the Majors, having opponents ground into 30 double plays, aided by leading the AL with a 2.24 GB/FB ratio.
- Was placed on the 15-day disabled list on April 20 with a right oblique strain… Returned for the balance of the season on May 25.

2010:

- Made 32 starts in his sophomore season, leading the club in starts, innings pitched (210), T-1st in quality starts (20) and 2nd in ERA (3.73).
- Was one of only 21 AL pitchers to record 200+ innings, finishing 13th… Needed only 15.4 pitches per inning, which was 8th fewest in the AL… Ranked T-4th in the AL in Opp. GDP with 25 and over the last two seasons ranks 1st in the Majors with 52 Opp. GDP… His GB/FB rate of 2.30 ranked 2nd in the AL.
- Earned his first victory of the season on April 13 vs. CWS (4-2 win)… Had a no-hitter into the 8th, before an Alex Rios home run ended the bid…(8.0IP, H, 2ER, HR, 2BB, 12K).
- Recorded his 1st career shutout, May 15 vs. TEX (6-0)… Became the first Blue Jays hurler to toss a shutout, other than Roy Halladay, since Jesse Litsch in 2008.
- On Aug. 14 signed a five-year contract extention with the Blue Jays.

MOST WINS, ALL-TIME, BY A BLUE JAY LEFT-HANDER

Jimmy Key	116
David Wells	84
Ricky Romero	**51**
John Cerutti	46
Ted Lilly	37

2011:

- Made 32 starts for the second consecutive season... Led the team in starts, wins (15), quality starts (25), innings pitched (225.0) and ERA (2.92), also the second consecutive season he has led the club in starts and innings pitched.
- His 225.0 innings pitched was a career high and he was one of seven AL pitchers to throw 210.0 or more innings in the last two seasons.
- Held opponents to a .193 average in the second half, the lowest figure among AL starters.
- Was named AL Pitcher of the Month for August, going 5-0 with a 2.05 ERA and a Major League low .160 opponents average...Was the first Blue Jay to win the award since Halladay in April of 2007.
- Also named AL Player of the Week ending Aug. 7, becoming the 1st Toronto hurler to win AL Player of the Week since Roy Halladay on May 18, 2009.
- Made his first All-Star squad, however did not pitch in the contest.
- In the AL ranked 4th in GB/FB ratio (1.85), T-4th in Complete Games (4) and Quality Starts (25), 5th in fewest pitches per inning (15.0) and 6th in opponents average (.216).
- Is the first Toronto hurler to record two road shutouts in the same season since David Cone had two in 1995, recording shutouts on June 26 at STL and August 18 at OAK.
- Became the first American League pitcher to drive in two or more runs (1-4, 2RBI) while tossing a shutout on June 26 at STL, since California's Clyde Wright vs. TEX in ANA on Sept. 14, 1972.
- Became just the fourth Blue Jays left-hander to start on Opening Day and first since David Wells in 2000 (Tom Underwood-1979, Jimmy Key 1987-1989, David Wells-2000)... Became the first Blue Jays left-handed pitcher since Jimmy Key in 1989 to win on Opening Day.

LHP Ricky Romero hanging out with children at the Central Toronto YMCA grand opening of youth zone in partnership with Jays Care Foundation – April 27, 2012

SANTOS, *SERGIO*

Birthdate . . . . .July 4, 1983
Opening Day Age 30
Birthplace. . . . . Los Angeles, CA
Residence. . . . . Yorba Linda, CA
Bats/Throws . . . . R/R
Height/Weight 6-3/240
Contract Status . . . . signed thru 2014
M.L. Service 3.000

21
PITCHER

PERSONAL:

Sergio Jose Santos... Married with three children... Graduated in 2002 from Mater Dei High School in Santa Ana, CA... Played baseball and football ... Was a member of the 2001 Junior National Pan Am Silver Medalist Team that played in Camaguey, Cuba.

LAST SEASON:

- Began the season as the closer however appeared in only six games before being disabled with right shoulder inflammation... Did not pitch for the balance of the season.
- Following attempts to strengthen and rehab the shoulder unsucessfully, he underwent shoulder surgery on July 25.
- Blew his first two save opportunties before collecting two in his final two chances.

SERGIO SANTOS

Bold – career high

Year	Club & League	W-L	ERA	G	GS	CG	ShO	SV	IP	H	R	ER	HR	HB	BB-IBB	SO	WP	BK	OBA
2009	Kannapolis (SAL)	0-1	7.36	8	0	0	0	0	7.1	8	6	6	0	0	3-0	10	2	0	.286
	Winston-Salem (Caro)	0-0	5.87	8	0	0	0	0	7.2	9	5	5	2	1	3-0	7	2	0	.290
	Birmingham (Sou)	0-1	10.38	7	0	0	0	0	8.2	15	10	10	0	3	7-0	6	1	0	.375
	Charlotte (Int)	0-1	9.00	3	0	0	0	0	5.0	5	5	5	0	0	7-0	7	1	0	.263
2010	CHICAGO (AL)	2-2	2.96	56	0	0	0	1	51.2	53	18	17	2	3	26-3	56	8	0	.261
2011	CHICAGO (AL)	**4-5**	3.55	**63**	0	0	0	**30**	**63.1**	41	25	25	**6**	3	**29**-5	**92**	5	0	.181
2012	TORONTO (AL)	0-1	9.00	6	0	0	0	2	5.0	6	5	5	1	0	4-0	4	1	0	.316
Minor Totals		0-3	8.16	26	0	0	0	0	28.2	37	26	26	2	4	20-0	30	6	0	.314
MAJOR TOTALS		6-8	3.53	125	0	0	0	33	120.0	100	48	47	9	6	59-8	152	14	0	.223

Bold – career high

Year	Club & League	AVG	G	AB	R	H	2B	3B	HR	RBI	SH-SF	HP	BB-IBB	SO	SB-CS	SLG	OBP	OPS
2002	Missoula (Pio)	.272	54	202	38	55	19	2	9	37	0-3	3	29-0	49	6-3	.520	.367	.887
2003	Lancaster (CAL)	.287	93	341	55	98	13	2	8	49	3-3	4	41-0	64	5-4	.408	.368	.776
	El Paso (TEX)	.255	37	137	13	35	7	1	2	16	1-2	0	8-0	25	0-0	.365	.293	.658
2004	El Paso (TEX)	.282	89	347	53	98	19	5	11	52	1-2	3	24-1	89	3-2	.461	.332	.793
2005	Tucson (PCL)	.239	132	490	55	117	21	3	12	68	0-6	2	34-3	108	2-2	.367	.288	.655
2006	Syracuse (Int)	.214	128	481	48	103	24	1	5	38	2-0	2	24-1	96	1-3	.299	.254	.553
2007	Syracuse (Int)	.191	13	47	4	9	2	0	0	4	1-1	0	1-0	10	2-0	.234	.204	.438
	New Hampshire (East)	.250	113	432	63	108	34	2	20	62	0-2	6	43-1	97	2-0	.477	.325	.802
2008	Syracuse (Int)	.183	26	93	7	17	5	0	0	4	0-0	0	5-0	13	2-1	.237	.224	.461
	Rochester (Int)	.242	86	297	44	72	24	0	5	43	0-5	1	16-0	59	4-1	.374	.279	.653
Minor Totals		.248	771	2867	380	712	168	16	72	373	8-24	21	225-6	610	27-16	.393	.305	.699

TRANSACTIONS

- Selected by the Arizona Diamondbacks in the 1st round (27th overall) of the 2002 First Year Player Draft
- Traded to the Toronto Blue Jays along with INF Troy Glaus in exchange for RHP Miguel Batista and INF Orlando Hudson on December 27, 2005
- Claimed off waivers by the Minnesota Twins on May 16, 2008
- Signed by the Chicago White Sox on January 12, 2009
- Traded to the San Francisco Giants in exchange for future considerations on March 20, 2009
- Traded to the Chicago White Sox in exchnage for future considerations on April 1, 2009
- Traded to the Toronto Blue Jays in exchange for RHP Nestor Molina on December 6, 2011
- On disabled list (right shoulder inflammation) from April 22-remainder of season, 2012

GAME HIGHS

ML Debut	April 8, 2010 vs. CLE	**ER Allowed**	4 – 2x, last June 10, 2011 vs. OAK
Innings Pitched:		**HR Allowed**	2 - Sept. 3, 2011 at DET
Starter	None	**Low Hit CG**	None
Reliever	2.0 - 9x, last May 28, 2011 at TOR	**Last Win**	Sept. 10, 2011 vs. CLE
Walks:		**Last Save**	April 20, 2012 at KC
Starter	None	**Last CG**	None
Reliever	3 - 3x, last April 9, 2012 vs. BOS	**Last ShO**	None
Strikeouts:		**Last Start**	None
Starter	None	**Last Relief App.**	April 20, 2012 at KC
Reliever	3 - 10x, last Sept. 26, 2011 vs. TOR	**Longest Win Streak**	2G - 2x, last May 8-11, 2011
Hits Allowed	5 - May 20, 2011 vs. LAD	**Longest Losing Streak**	3G - May 20-June 10, 2011
Runs Allowed	4 – 2x, last June 10, 2011 vs. OAK	**Scoreless Innings Streak**	20.0 - April 2-May 17, 2011

CAREER FIELDING

POSITION	PCT	G	PO	A	E	TC	DP
P	1.000	125	7	12	0	19	3

MILESTONES

Category		Date	Opponent	Notes
Win	1	Aug. 5, 2010	at Detroit	2.0 IP, H, BB, 2K
Save	1	July 5, 2010	Los Angeles (AL)	1.1 IP, K

PROFESSIONAL CAREER:

2002:

- In his first year of pro ball at Missoula of the Pioneer League (Rookie-Advanced), ranked 3rd among league leaders with a .569 slugging percentage, tied for 3rd with 30 extra-base hits, ranked 4th with 19 doubles and tied for 5th with nine home runs.
- Hit his first pro home run on July 24 at Provo.

2003:

- Rated by Baseball America as the No. 7 prospect in the Diamondbacks organization.
- He tied a California League record with three home runs for Lancaster (A) in a win at High Desert May 23, finishing the contest 3-4 with six RBI... He also became the first player in franchise history to homer three times in a single game.
- Participated in the Arizona Fall League, batting .250 over 26 games for Scottsdale with three home runs, 10 RBI and nine extra-base hits which ranked 3rd on the club.
- He was rated by Baseball America as having the 3rd-best infield arm in the Fall League.

2004:

- On June 9 vs. Wichita, when he connected for a two-run blast and a grand slam, totaling seven RBI, establishing a new career single-game best.
- His season was ended on July 22... He was disabled for the remainder of the season due to a left shoulder subluxation.

2005:

- Smacked a grand slam off Fresno's Matt Cain on May 8, part of a five-RBI day.
- Led PCL shortstops with 26 errors.

2006:

- Spent the 2006 season with Syracuse of the International League, his second at the Triple-A level.
- Started 126 games at shortstop.

2007:

- Spent the majority of the season with the New Hampshire Fisher Cats of the Eastern League (AA).
- Was promoted to Syracuse (AAA) on Sept. 5.
- Was selected to the Eastern League All-Star team...Started at shortstop, finishing the contest going 1-for-1.
- Was the winner of the Home Run Derby at the All-Star gala.
- Was the "Star of the Month" in April with the Fisher Cats.
- Among Fisher Cat leaders, ranked 3rd in runs (63), 3rd in total bases (206), T-2nd in doubles (34), 2nd in home runs (20) and 3rd in RBI (68).
- In 24 games in the Arizona Fall League, batted .319 (30-94) with five home runs and 20 RBI with the Scottsdale Scorpions.

2008:

- Split the season between the Toronto and Minnesota organizations.
- Claimed off waivers by Minnesota on May 14.
- Signed by the White Sox as a free agent on November 27.
- Hit .315 (23-73) with four homers and six RBI in 18 games with Obregon of the Mexican Pacific Winter League.

2009:

- Was used as a pitcher for the first time in his career.
- Combined to go 0-3 with an 8.16 ERA (26 ER/28.2 IP) in 26 relief appearances over four stops in the White Sox farm system.
- Was a non-roster invitee as an outfielder to Chicago's Spring Training.
- Was traded to San Francisco on March 20 in exchange for cash considerations and dealt back to the White Sox for cash on 4/1...
- Placed on the disabled list from July 12-20 with back spasms.
- Struck out a season-high four batters in his debut with the Knights on Aug. 30 at Norfolk.
- Went 1-2 with a 7.11 ERA (10 ER/12.2 IP) and 19 strikeouts in 10 relief appearances with Peoria of the Arizona Fall League.

2010:

- Went 2-2 with a 2.96 ERA (17 ER/51.2 IP), one save and 56 strikeouts in 56 games in his first Major League season.
- Ranked among AL rookie relief leaders in strikeouts per 9.0 IP (1st, 9.75), ERA (2nd), holds (2nd, 14), strikeouts (2nd), appearances (3rd) and IP (5th).
- Posted the second-best strikeout per 9.0 IP ratio among White Sox rookie relievers in club history, trailing only Bobby Jenks in 2005 (11.44).
- His 14 holds were the most by a Chicago rookie reliever since Kelly Wunsch in 2000 (25), and his 56 strikeouts were the most since Neal Cotts in 2004 (57).
- Made his **Major League debut** on April 8 vs. Cleveland with 1.0 scoreless IP... Also registered his first strikeout (Michael Brantley).
- Established a White Sox record with 12 straight scoreless outings to start a Major League career... Also set a club mark with 11.1 scoreless IP.
- Boasted a 0.48 ERA (1 ER/18.2 IP) and 23 strikeouts in his first 20 games.
- Earned his first career save on July 5 vs. the Angels and first win on Aug. 5 at Detroit (0 ER/2.0 IP).
- Entered the season rated by Baseball America as possessing the Best Fastball among Sox farmhands.

2011:

- Among relievers, ranked 2nd in strikeouts (92), 3rd in strikeouts per 9.0 IP (13.14), T-3rd in first batter efficiency (.125), 6th in opponents average (.181) and hits per 9.0 IP (5.8), 8th in saves (30) and save percentage (83.3).
- Established a Major League record with 25 consecutive scoreless appearances (26.2 IP) on the road to begin a season from April 2-Aug. 30, breaking Mariano Rivera's record of 24 set in 2005.
- Did not allow a run in his first 16 games (20.0 IP) to start the season.
- His 92 strikeouts were the most by a Chicago reliever since Octavio Dotel also struck out 92 in 2008 and tied for 8th most all-time in club history, while his .181 (41-226) opponent average was the lowest since 2005.
- Ranked 6th among AL relievers with a 1.47 ERA (5 ER/30.2 IP) on the road.
- Struck out at least one batter in 22 consecutive games from May 1-July 18, the longest streak by a White Sox reliever since at least 1918, surpassing Roberto Hernandez 17-game streak.
- Was the first pitcher in baseball history to walk and strike out three in 1.0 IP and still record the save (No. 30) on Sept. 26 vs. Toronto.

AN EARLY START

Here is a list of the youngest starting pitchers to appear in a game in club history

Age as of 1st start for Blue Jays:

Jeff Byrd	20 yrs, 221 days
Phil Huffman	20 yrs, 294 days
Henderson Alvarez	21 yrs, 114 days
Roy Halladay	21 yrs, 129 days
Mike Darr	21 yrs, 167 days
Jerry Garvin	21 yrs, 171 days
Jim Clancy	21 yrs, 220 days
Drew Hutchison	21 yrs, 243 days

SCHIMPF, *RYAN*

Birthdate . . . . April 11, 1988
Opening Day Age 24
Birthplace. . . . . Covington, LA
Residence. . . . . Covington, LA
Bats/Throws . . . . L/R
Height/Weight 5-9/181
Contract Status . . . . signed thru 2013
M.L. Service 0.000

INFIELDER
NON-ROSTER

PERSONAL:

Ryan Michael Schimpf... Parents are Craig and Pam Schimpf... Has a younger and older brother... Chose to attend LSU because he has been a lifelong Tiger fan and his father attended LSU... Majored in general studies at LSU... Named the MVP of the 2008 Valley League Championship Series -- batted .392 during the summer with three doubles, 11 homers and 27 RBI in 27 games... Participated in the '07 CICL All-Star Game and was named the No. 7 prospect in the league by Baseball America magazine.

LAST SEASON:

- Split time between Dunedin of the Florida State League (A) and New Hampshire (AA) of the Eastern League.
- Began the season with Dunedin, appearing in 96 games while posting an OPS of .832.
- Named a Florida State League mid-season all-star.
- Named MiLB.com organizational all-star.
- Promoted to New Hampshire on July 31.
- In 33 contests with the Fisher Cats, posted an OPS of .980, including eight doubles and eight home runs.
- Hit .309 with eight home runs and 15 RBI in August.

RYAN SCHIMPF

Bold – career high

Year	Club and League	AVG	G	AB	R	H	2B	3B	HR	RBI	SH-SF	HP	BB-IBB	SO	SB-CS	SLG	OBP	OPS
2009	BlueJays (GCL)	.500	2	4	1	2	0	1	0	0	0-0	0	2-0	0	1-0	1.000	.667	1.667
	Auburn (NYP)	.287	34	129	25	37	7	1	3	14	4-2	3	15-0	24	4-1	.426	.369	.795
2010	Lansing (Mid)	.240	92	337	46	81	23	10	6	45	4-5	10	39-0	96	11-7	.421	.332	.753
	Dunedin (FSL)	.221	18	68	10	15	3	1	2	7	1-0	1	4-0	27	3-0	.382	.274	.656
2011	Dunedin (FSL)	.240	57	196	30	47	9	2	10	36	0-3	7	22-0	52	2-0	.459	.333	.792
2012	Dunedin (FSL)	.266	96	361	59	96	29	3	14	61	0-6	4	48-2	89	4-2	.479	.353	.832
	New Hampshire (East)	.279	33	111	21	31	8	0	8	15	1-0	2	23-2	32	3-1	.568	.412	.980
Minor Totals		.256	332	1206	192	309	79	18	43	178	10-16	27	153-4	320	28-11	.459	.349	.807

TRANSACTIONS

- Selected by the Toronto Blue Jays in the 5th round of the 2009 First Year Player Draft

PROFESSIONAL CAREER:

2009:

- In his first professional season, appeared in 36 games, all but two was with the Auburn Doubledays.
- Hit .287 with 11-XBH in those 34 contests with Auburn.

2010:

- Split time between Lansing of the Midwest League (A) and Dunedin of the Florida State League (A).
- Began the season at Lansing where he was named a mid-season all-star.
- Recorded 23-2B, 10-3B and 6-HR in 92 games with the Lugnuts.
- Promoted to Dunedin Blue Jays on Aug. 12.

2011:

- Was placed on the disabled list from April 7-June 9 with patella tendinitis of the right knee.
- Spent the entire season with the Dunedin Blue Jays (A).
- In 57 games posted an OPS of .792 while recording 21-XBH (10-HR).

LONGEST HITLESS STREAKS

(25 OR MORE AT-BATS)

PLAYER	AB	DATE
Ed Sprague	35	May 21-May 31, 1994
Alex Gonzalez	33	August 28-September 8, 1996
Buck Martinez	32	April 29-May 26, 1985
Mike Stanley	30	April 22-May 3, 1998
Carlos Delgado	29	July 9-16, 1998
Tomas Perez	28	September 7-25, 1997
Russ Adams	28	September 11-18, 2005
Tony Batista	27	July 25-August 1, 2000
Troy Glaus	27	July 31-August 11, 2007
George Bell	26	May 8-14, 1986
Kelly Gruber	26	May 2-June 12, 1986
Kelly Gruber	26	August 17-27, 1990
Pat Tabler	26	September 6-October 6, 1991
Vernon Wells	26	September 9-16, 2002
Rajai Davis	26	July 4-16, 2012
Colby Rasmus	26	August 15-22, 2012
Raul Mondesi	25	April 21-29, 2000
Aaron Hill	25	May 30-June 5, 2009

SIERRA, *MOISES*

Birthdate . . . . September 24, 1988
Opening Day Age 25
Birthplace. . . . . Santo Domingo, DR
Residence. . . . . Santo Domingo, DR
Bats/Throws . . . . R/R
Height/Weight 6-0/229
Contract Status . . . . signed thru 2013
M.L. Service 0.065

14

OUTFIELDER

PERSONAL:

Moises Sierra... Was signed by the Blue Jays as a non-drafted free agent on December 20, 2005... Scouted and signed by Hilario Soriano.

LAST SEASON:

- Made his Major League debut on July 31 at SEA and collected a single in his first at-bat off Jason Vargas... Would go on to play in 49 games in his first season in Toronto... Started 40 games, with 35 coming in RF and 5 at DH.
- Had seven multi-hit games, including two, three-hit contests... Hit his first home run on Aug. 13 vs. CWS off Jake Peavy, a solo shot that put the team ahead 2-1 in the 7th inning... Recorded a three RBI contest at NYY on Sept. 20.
- Batted .333 in July, .284 in August, and .157 in Sept./Oct.
- On Aug. 31 ended the game with an OF assist from RF, throwing out Elliott Johnson at home to preserve a 2-1 win.
- Played 100 games for Las Vegas in his first season above AA...Posted a .278 average with 17 home runs and 63 RBI... The home runs and RBI were club highs... Hit .302 vs. lefties... Hit .303 before the break and .222 after... Had four hits on June 2 with a double and home run.

MOISES SIERRA

Bold – career high

Year	Club & League	AVG	G	AB	R	H	2B	3B	HR	RBI	SH-SF	HP	BB-IBB	SO	SB-CS	SLG	OBP	OPS
2006	Blue Jays (DSL)	.253	69	245	35	62	16	1	4	26	0-1	11	24-0	50	17-3	.376	.345	.721
2007	Blue Jays (GCL)	.203	43	143	17	29	5	1	5	15	1-1	4	5-0	39	2-2	.357	.248	.605
2008	Lansing (Mid)	.246	130	451	50	111	16	5	9	39	1-3	8	26-0	114	12-11	.364	.297	.661
2009	Dunedin (FSL)	.286	110	405	56	116	24	2	5	56	1-4	15	34-3	66	10-2	.393	.360	.753
	New Hampshire (East)	.353	8	34	1	12	1	0	1	6	0-1	0	1-0	8	0-1	.471	.361	.832
2010	Blue Jays (GCL)	.265	10	34	4	9	2	0	1	3	0-0	0	4-0	8	0-0	.412	.342	.754
	Dunedin (FSL)	.162	10	37	4	6	1	0	1	5	0-2	0	1-0	11	0-1	.270	.175	.445
2011	New Hampshire (East)	.277	133	495	81	137	19	3	18	67	1-4	12	39-2	93	16-14	.436	.342	.778
2012	Las Vegas (PCL)	.289	100	377	62	109	16	1	17	63	0-2	4	39-2	86	7-6	.472	.360	.832
	TORONTO (AL)	.224	49	147	14	33	4	0	6	15	0-0	2	8-0	44	1-0	.374	.274	.648
Minor Totals		.266	613	2221	310	591	100	13	61	280	4-18	54	173-7	475	64-40	.405	.332	.737

HOME RUN BREAKDOWN

			ONE GAME									
Total	H	A	2	3	4	GS	LO	XN	IP	PH	RHP	LHP
6	3	3	0	0	0	0	0	0	0	0	3	3

TRANSACTIONS

- Signed by the Toronto Blue Jays on December 20, 2005

GAME HIGHS

ML Debut	July 31, 2012 at SEA	**RBI**	3 - Sept. 20, 2012 at NYY
Runs	3 - Sept. 24, 2012 at BAL	**Stolen Bases**	1 - Aug. 9, 2012 at TB
Hits	3 - 2x, last Aug. 12, 2012 vs. NYY	**Last ML Home Run**	Sept. 24, 2012 at BAL
Doubles	1 - 4x, Sept. 22, 2012 at TB	**Longest Hitting Streak**	4G - Aug. 12-16, 2012
Home Runs	1 - 6x, last Sept. 24, 2012 at BAL	**Longest Hitless Streak**	14AB - Aug. 23-27, 2012

CAREER FIELDING

POSITION	PCT	G	PO	A	E	TC	DP
OF	1.000	39	67	3	0	70	0

MILESTONES

Category		Date	Opponent	Pitcher	Notes
Hit	1	July 31, 2012	at Seattle	Vargas	single, 1st ML at bat
Home Run	1	Aug. 13, 2012	Chicago (AL)	Peavy	1R
RBI	1	Aug. 2, 2012	Oakland	Cook	groundout
Stolen Base	1	Aug. 9, 2012	at Tampa Bay	Moore C-Lobaton	2nd base

PROFESSIONAL CAREER:

2006:

- In his first professional season at the age of 17 played 69 games with the Blue Jays Dominican Summer League team hitting .253 with four home runs.
- His first professional home runs came June 13.

2007:

- In his first season in North America only hit .203 in 43 games with the GCL Blue Jays.

2008:

- Spent the entire season with Lansing (A) where he hit .310 in the month of April with two doubles, two triples, two home runs and 11 RBI.

2009:

- Spent the majority of the season with Dunedin (A).
- Named Organizational Player of the Month for June where he batted .384 (33-for-86) with eight extra base hits and 19 RBI in 24 games.
- Named to the Florida State Mid-Season All Star Game.
- Named Florida State League Player of the Week June 8-14 (.423, 5XBH, 9RBI).
- Named R. Howard Webster award winner with Dunedin.
- Was promoted to New Hampshire (AA) on Aug. 30 where he played the last eight games of the season hitting .353 (12-for-34) with a home run and six RBI.

2010:

- Only appeared in 20 games because of two separate stints on the DL.
- Began the season on the disabled list with Dunedin (A) and was sent on a rehab assignment to the GCL Blue Jays until June 25 when he was reinstated… Only played four games before once again being placed on the DL with a right wrist injury.

2011:

- Spent the entire season at New Hampshire of the Eastern League (AA).
- Named to the Eastern League Mid Season All-Star team after posting 14 doubles and 13 home runs with 49 RBI prior to the break.
- In a manager's poll conducted by Baseball America, was named Best Outfield Arm in the Eastern League.
- Played in the Dominican Winter League, posting a .217 average with one home run and 14 RBI.

FIVE HITS OR MORE

There have been 16 different Blue Jays to have recorded at least five hits in a single game in franchise history...The feat has been accomplished 19 times overall with a Club record six hits by Frank Catalanotto on May 1, 2004 at CWS.

Frank Catalanotto	6	May 1, 2004 at CWS (GM 2), 6-for-6
Roy Howell	5	Sept. 10, 1977 at NYY, 5-for-5
Rick Bosetti	5	April 27, 1979 vs. MIL, 5-for-5
Barry Bonnell	5	April 10, 1982 vs. MIL, 5-for-5 (10 inn)
Damaso Garcia	5	June 19, 1982 at OAK, 5-for-5 (12 inn)
George Bell	5	April 6, 1988 vs. KC, 5-for-5
Kelly Gruber	5	June 12, 1989 vs. DET, 5-for-6 (11 inn)
George Bell	5	Sept. 24, 1990 vs. MIL, 5-for-5
Fred McGriff	5	Sept. 1, 1990 at CLE, 5-for-5
John Olerud	5	April 29, 1993 vs. KC, 5-for-5
Paul Molitor	5	Sept. 4, 1995 vs. KC (GM 1), 5-for-5
Carlos Delgado	5	May 7, 1998 at SEA, 5-for-5
Tony Fernandez	5	May 7, 1999 vs. TEX, 5-for-5
Shannon Stewart	5	Sept. 19, 2002 at BAL, 5-for-5
Frank Catalanotto	5	July 9, 2003 vs. BOS, 5-for-5
Alex Rios	5	Aug. 8, 2005 vs. DET, 5-for-5 (12 inn)
Alex Rios	5	Aug. 17, 2008 at BOS, 5-for-6
Adam Lind	5	June 4, 2009 vs. LAA, 5-for-5
Corey Patterson	5	May 28, 2011 vs. CWS, 5-for-7 (14 inn)
Colby Rasmus	5	June 5, 2012 at CWS, 5-for-5

STILSON, *JOHN*

Birthdate	July 28, 1990
Opening Day Age	22
Birthplace	Texarkana, TX
Residence	Texarkana, TX
Bats/Throws	R/R
Height/Weight	6-3/200
Contract Status	signed thru 2013
M.L. Service	0.000

74

PITCHER
NON-ROSTER

PERSONAL:

John Jacob Stilson... Is the son of Tommy and Lorna Stilson of Texarkana... Has a younger sister, Kaci... A wildlife and fisheries major, hopes to one day own his own game ranch... Enjoys hunting, fishing, playing golf and bowling in his spare time... In his first season at Texas A&M, turned in one of the best seasons in school history... Chosen by his teammates to receive the C.E. "Pat" Olsen Outstanding Pitcher Award, given annually to Texas A&M's best pitcher... Broke the school record and was the national leader in earned run average at 0.80.

LAST SEASON:

- In his first professional season, split time between Dunedin of the Flordia State League (A) and New Hampshire of the Eastern League (AA).
- Began the season with Dunedin, posting a record of 3-0 with a 2.82 ERA in 13 games, all starts.
- Fanned 47 batters over 54.1 innings with Dunedin.
- Promoted to New Hampshire on June 16
- His first nine appearances with the Fisher Cats were all as a starter (2-3, 4.85)... His last eight games came out of the pen where he posted an ERA of 5.73 (7ER/11.0 IP).
- Placed on the disabled list (right shoulder impingement) from July 30-Aug. 15.

JOHN STILSON

Bold – career high

Year	Club & League	W-L	ERA	G	GS	CG	ShO	SV	IP	H	R	ER	HR	HB	BB-IBB	SO	WP	BK	OBA
2012	Dunedin (FSL)	3-0	2.82	13	13	0	0	0	54.1	56	22	17	2	1	19-0	47	0	2	.265
	New Hampshire (East)	2-4	5.04	17	9	0	0	1	50.0	54	33	28	6	3	23-0	44	6	0	.277
Minor Totals		5-4	3.88	30	22	0	0	1	104.1	110	55	45	8	4	42-0	91	6	2	.271

TRANSACTIONS

- Selected by the Toronto Blue Jays in the 3rd round of the 2011 First Year Player Draft

PROFESSIONAL CAREER:

2011:

- Was selected by the Toronto Blue Jays in the 3rd round of the First Year Player Draft
- Signed his professional contract on Aug. 13

HOW LONG DID IT TAKE

LONGEST OFFICIAL GAME
HOME 5:57-April 19/01 vs New York (A) (17inn.)
ROAD 5:49-June 19/98 at Baltimore (15 inn.)

SHORTEST OFFICIAL GAME
1:04-Sept. 15/77 vs Baltimore (forfeit, 4.5 inn.)

LONGEST NINE-INNING GAME
HOME 4:15-April 11/88 vs New York
ROAD 4:12-Sept. 15/93 at Detroit;
4:12-April 1/02 at Boston;

SHORTEST NINE-INNING GAME
ROAD 1:39-June 16/77 vs Detroit
HOME 1:33-Sept. 28/82 (1st gm) vs Minnesota

WINNING WHILE GETTING OUT-HIT BY 9 OR MORE

The Blue Jays have won two games in Club history when being out-hit by at least nine:

Oct. 2, 1977 vs. CLE (outhit by 9, won 11-2)

Sept. 24, 2010 vs. BAL (outhit by 11, won 16-5)

STOREY, *MICKEY*

Birthdate	March 16, 1986
Opening Day Age	27
Birthplace	Ft. Lauderdale, FL
Residence	West Palm Beach, FL
Bats/Throws	R/R
Height/Weight	6-1/185
Contract Status	signed thru 2013
M.L. Service	0.062

77

PITCHER

NON-ROSTER

PERSONAL:

Mickey Charles Storey... Graduated from Deerfield Beach High School (Florida)... Attended Florida Atlantic University... Signed by Trevor Schaffer.

LAST SEASON:

- The 26-year old rookie began the season in Triple A OKC's bullpen before making 26 appearances for the Astros.
- After his arrival in Houston on Aug. 3, ranked T-4th in innings pitched and 9th in strikeouts among NL relievers.
- Led the club in percentage of swings that miss (30.1%) by generating 74 misses on 246 total swings.
- Was struck by a line drive on Sept. 12 vs CHC and left the game due to contusions in his right hand and jaw.
- Prior to the injury on Sept. 12, had a 3.00 ERA (8ER/24IP) with 25 strikeouts over 18 appearances.
- Made 38 appearances (two starts) with Triple A OKC, going 7-4 with a 3.05 ERA (22ER/65IP) and 72 strikeouts... Gave up just 14 walks and led the club in wins and ranked 2nd in strikeouts.
- Was named the club's Pitcher of the Month for both June and July.

MICKEY STOREY

Bold – career high

Year	Club & League	W-L	ERA	G	GS	CG	ShO	SV	IP	H	R	ER	HR	HB	BB-IBB	SO	WP	BK	OBA
2008	AZL (Ariz)	2-2	3.27	14	0	0	0	1	22.0	17	8	8	2	1	6-0	23	1	0	.210
2009	Kane County (Mid)	0-0	0.52	13	0	0	0	9	17.1	5	1	1	0	2	1-0	23	0	0	.088
	Sacramento River (PCL)	0-0	0.00	2	0	0	0	0	3.0	0	0	0	0	0	0-0	4	0	0	.000
	Stockton (CAL)	1-1	2.28	22	0	0	0	9	23.2	19	10	6	2	1	6-0	35	1	0	.213
	Midland (TEX)	1-0	0.00	4	0	0	0	0	7.2	3	0	0	0	1	1-0	9	0	0	.120
2010	Sacramento River (PCL)	1-1	5.54	11	0	0	0	1	13.0	15	10	8	3	0	5-0	14	1	1	.278
	Midland (TEX)	5-4	3.30	43	1	0	0	8	71.0	58	31	26	5	3	22-2	63	5	1	.222
2011	Midland (TEX)	3-3	4.03	27	0	0	0	4	38.0	41	17	17	3	3	13-2	31	3	1	.281
	Oklahoma City (PCL)	1-0	3.99	23	0	0	0	2	29.1	35	13	13	3	0	12-0	28	1	0	.297
2012	Oklahoma City (PCL)	7-4	3.05	38	2	0	0	2	65.0	62	24	22	8	3	14-1	72	3	1	.248
	HOUSTON (NL)	0-1	3.86	26	0	0	0	0	30.1	27	14	13	2	1	10-0	34	0	0	.237
Minor Totals		21-15	3.13	197	3	0	0	36	290.0	255	114	101	26	14	80-5	302	15	4	.234

TRANSACTIONS

- Selected by the Oakland Athletics in the 31st round of the 2008 First Year player Draft
- Traded to the Houston Astros in exchange for future considerations on June 30, 2011
- Claimed off waivers by the New York Yankees on November 20, 2012
- Claimed off waivers by the Houston Astros on December 6, 2012
- Claimed off waivers by the Toronto Blue Jays on December 19, 2012

GAME HIGHS

ML Debut Aug. 3, 2012 at ATL

Innings Pitched:
Starter None
Reliever 2.0 - 7x, last Sept. 29, 2012 at MIL

Walks:
Starter None
Reliever 2 - Aug. 19, 2012 vs. ARI

Strikeouts:
Starter None
Reliever 4 - 2x, last Sept. 9, 2012 at CIN
Hits Allowed 4 - Sept. 23, 2012 vs. PIT

Runs Allowed 2 - 2x, last Sept. 19, 2012 at STL
ER Allowed 2 - 2x, last Sept. 19, 2012 at STL
HR Allowed 1 - 2x, last Aug. 25, 2012 at NYM
Low Hit CG None
Last Win None
Last Save None
Last CG None
Last ShO None
Last Start None
Last Relief App. Oct. 3, 2012 at CHC
Longest Win Streak None
Longest Losing Streak 1G - Aug. 7, 2012
Scoreless Innings Streak 4.0 - Sept. 25-Oct. 3, 2012

CAREER FIELDING

POSITION	PCT	G	PO	A	E	TC	DP
P	.750	26	1	2	1	4	0

PROFESSIONAL CAREER:

2008:

- Made his professional debut with the A's rookie league team (Arizona).
- Fanned 23 batters over 22.0 innings in 14 relief appearances.

2009:

- Led Oakland Athletics farmhands with 18 saves.
- Played in the Arizona Fall League

2010:

- Among all Oakland farmhands ranked 6th in saves.
- Played for Bravos de Margarita of the Venezuelan League in the Winter League.

2011:

- Began the season playing in the Texas League (AA) with Midland.
- Posted a 4.03 ERA over 27 games with four saves.
- Worked a total of 38.0 IP issuing just 13 walks and fanned 31 over that span.
- Traded to the Houston Astros in exchange for future considerations on June 30, 2011
- Assigned to Oklahoma City of the Pacific Coast League (AAA).
- With OKC owned a 3.99 ERA in 23 games and collected two saves... Struck out 28 batters over 29.1 IP.

1-0 GAMES BREAKDOWN

The Blue Jays have played 92 games that have resulted in a 1-0 decision.
In those 92 games, the club's record is 50-42.

YEAR	WON	LOST
1977	0	0
1978	0	1
1979	0	3
1980	5	1
1981	0	2
1982	1	1
1983	0	0
1984	2	0
1985	1	0
1986	1	2
1987	0	2
1988	3	0
1989	0	2
1990	3	2
1991	5	1
1992	3	3
1993	1	0
1994	1	1
1995	0	1
1996	3	0
1997	2	1
1998	2	1
1999	1	1
2000	0	1
2010	2	2
2011	2	0
2012	0	1
TOTALS	50	42

VERSUS OPPONENTS

TEAM	WON	LOST
ATLANTA	1	1
BALTIMORE	2	6
BOSTON	4	6
CALIFORNIA/ANAHEIM	2	3
CHICAGO	5	1
CLEVELAND	5	3
COLORADO	0	1
DETROIT	3	2
KANSAS CITY	4	1
LOS ANGELES (NL)	1	0
MILWAUKEE	1	1
MINNESOTA	2	2
MONTREAL	2	0
NEW YORK (AL)	1	3
NEW YORK (NL)	0	1
OAKLAND	8	3
PITTSBURGH	0	1
SEATTLE	4	0
ST. LOUIS	0	1
TAMPA BAY	2	3
TEXAS	3	3
TOTALS	50	42

THOLE, *JOSH*

Birthdate	October 28, 1986
Opening Day Age	26
Birthplace	Breese, IL
Residence	Glendale, AZ
Bats/Throws	L/R
Height/Weight	6-0/214
Contract Status	signed thru 2014
M.L. Service	2.142

30

CATCHER

PERSONAL:

Joshua Michael (Josh) Thole... Graduated from Breese Mater Dei High School (IL) in 2005... Was All-State in baseball and also played football... Enjoys playing golf and fishing.

LAST SEASON:

- Was the team's Opening Day catcher for the second straight season.
- Went to the DL on May 8 with a concussion suffered during a home plate collision with Philadelphia's Ty Wigginton... Activated on June 1.
- Snapped a career worst 0 for 30 with an eighth-inning single on Sept. 1... The skid dated to August 14 and spanned 11 games.
- Reached safely in 18 straight games with a plate appearance to begin the year, the longest streak to start a season by a catcher in team history.
- Batted .379 (11-29) with four runs scored over a career high 10-game hitting streak, April 16-April 27.
- Hit his only home run of the season on April 29 at COL (Moyer).
- Walked a career high-tying three times on June 23 vs. NYY... Had done it once before on April 29, 2011.
- Caught Johan Santana on June 1 vs. St. L in the first no-hitter in Mets history... It was his first game back from the concussion... Only one other catcher caught a no-hitter in his first game back after missing 22 or more games: The Angels' Ellie Rodriguez had a 37-game absence before catching Nolan Ryan's nono on June 1, 1975.
- Finished with a 3.77 catcher's ERA (334 earned runs/798.1 innings), the best mark on the team... Caught 26 of Cy Young winner R.A. Dickey's 33 starts.

JOSH THOLE

Bold – career high

Year	Club and League	AVG	G	AB	R	H	2B	3B	HR	RBI	SH-SF	HP	BB-IBB	SO	SB-CS	SLG	OBP	OPS
2005	Mets (GCL)	.269	35	104	14	28	2	1	1	12	2-0	4	20-0	11	1-1	.337	.406	.743
2006	Kingsport (Appy)	.235	36	98	13	23	4	0	1	12	0-2	3	7-1	25	1-1	.306	.300	.606
2007	Savannah (SAL)	.267	117	389	46	104	17	0	0	36	4-0	4	61-1	57	4-4	.311	.372	.683
2008	St. Lucie (FSL)	.300	111	347	49	104	25	2	5	56	1-5	4	45-2	38	2-1	.427	.382	.809
2009	Binghamton (East)	.328	103	384	48	126	29	2	1	46	1-9	6	42-3	34	8-4	.422	.395	.817
	NEW YORK (NL)	.321	17	53	2	17	2	**1**	0	9	0-2	0	4-0	5	**1**-0	.396	.356	.752
2010	Buffalo (Int)	.267	48	165	20	44	19	1	2	17	1-2	1	22-0	25	0-0	.430	.353	.783
	NEW YORK (NL)	.277	73	202	17	56	7	**1**	**3**	17	0-0	1	24-1	25	**1**-0	.366	.357	.723
2011	NEW YORK (NL)	.268	**114**	340	22	**91**	**17**	0	**3**	**40**	1-3	4	**38**-6	47	0-2	.344	.345	.689
2012	Buffalo (Int)	.200	2	5	0	1	0	0	0	0	0-0	0	0-0	0	0-0	.200	.200	.400
	NEW YORK (NL)	.234	104	321	**24**	75	15	0	1	21	4-1	1	27-6	**50**	0-0	.290	.294	.584
Minor Totals		.288	452	1492	190	430	96	6	10	179	9-18	22	197-7	190	16-11	.381	.375	.756
MAJOR TOTALS		.261	308	916	65	239	41	2	7	87	5-6	6	93-13	127	2-2	.333	.331	.664

HOME RUN BREAKDOWN

			ONE GAME									
Total	H	A	2	3	4	GS	LO	XN	IP	PH	RHP	LHP
7	3	4	0	0	0	0	0	1	0	0	6	1

TRANSACTIONS

- Selected by the New York Mets in the 13th round of the 2005 First Year Player Draft
- Traded to the Toronto Blue Jays along with RHP R.A. Dickey and C Mike Nickeas in exchang for RHP Noah Syndergaard, C Travis d'Arnaud, OF Wuilmer Becerra and C John Buck on November 19, 2012

GAME HIGHS

ML Debut	Sept. 3, 2009 at COL	**RBI**	3 - 4x, last Sept. 16, 2011 at ATL
Runs	3 - Sept. 5, 2010 at CHC	**Stolen Bases**	1 - 2x, last Aug. 3, 2010 at ATL
Hits	4 - 2x, last Aug. 10, 2011 vs. SD	**Last ML Home Run**	April 29, 2012 at COL
Doubles	1 - 41x, last Sept. 22, 2012 vs. MIA	**Longest Hitting Streak**	10G - April 16-27, 2012
Home Runs	1 - 7x, last April 29, 2012 at COL	**Longest Hitless Streak**	30AB - Aug. 15-Sept. 1, 2012

CAREER FIELDING

POSITION	PCT	G	PO	A	E	TC	DP
C	.994	279	1760	126	12	1898	9

MILESTONES

Category		Date	Opponent	Pitcher	Notes
Hit	1	Sept. 3, 2009	at Colorado	Marquis	single in the 1st ML at bat
Home Run	1	July 20, 2010	at Arizona	Enright	1R
Extra-Inning HR (1)					
	1	Oct. 1, 2010	Washington	Clippard	10th inning, 1R
Walk-off HR (1)	1	Oct. 1, 2010	Washington	Clippard	10th inning, 1R
RBI	1	Sept. 8, 2009	Florida	Van Den Hurk	sac fly
Stolen Base	1	Sept. 3, 2009	at Colorado	Marquis C-Iannetta	2nd base

PROFESSIONAL CAREER:

2008:

- Appeared in 75 games behind the plate after spending his first three professional seasons primarily at first base.
- Named to the FSL All-Star team...Went 1-1 in the game at Viera, FL.

2009:

- Recalled from Binghamton (AA) of the Eastern League on September 1st.
- Made his first **Major League debut**, September 3rd at Colorado and went 2-5 with a double... Collected his first big league hit, a single, in his first at-bat against Jason Marquis in the second inning.
- Collected his first career RBI with a sacrifice fly in the fourth inning on September 8th at Florida.
- Went 4-4 with a run scored and an RBI in the day game of a split doubleheader on September 13th at Philadelphia to become the youngest catcher in Mets' history to pick up four hits in a game (22 years, 320 days) and was the youngest, regardless of position, since Jose Reyes had his sixth career four-hit game, September 27, 2005.
- Finished second in the Venezuelan Winter League with a .381 (59-155) batting average... Had 16 doubles, two triples, three home runs and 28 RBI in 44 games with Leones del Caracas.

2010:

- Recalled by the Mets on May 10 but did not appear in a game before being optioned back to Buffalo on May 15.
- Recalled from Buffalo for the second time on June 24 and spent the remainder of the season with the Mets.
- Connected on his first major league home run, July 20 at Arizona... It was a solo shot off of Barry Enright.
- Hit the first walkoff home run of his career to give the Mets a 2-1 win on October 1 vs. Washington... The solo home run came in the 10th inning against Tyler Clippard.
- Threw out five consecutive base stealers from July 9-August 8.

2011:

- Tied his personal-best with four hits on August 10 vs. San Diego.
- Placed on the Paternity Leave List on July 19... Reinstated on July 20.
- Left the game on September 1 in the top of the second inning with a contusion of the left wrist.

JAYS WITH 6+ MULTI-HR GAMES IN ONE SEASON

Player	Season	Multi-HR games
Jose Bautista	2010	9
George Bell	1987	9
Carlos Delgado	1998	6
Carlos Delgado	1999	6
Vernon Wells	2006	6

*In 2010 it marked the first time in Club history that Toronto had as many as six players with a multi-HR game before the start of June.

FIRST TO 100 HOME RUNS

In 2010, the Blue Jays became the first team in the Majors to reach 100 home runs in a season for the second time in franchise history (1990 & 2010).

Year	Game	Date	Opponent
1990	75	June 28	Boston
2010	65	June 14	San Diego

THOMPSON, *RICH*

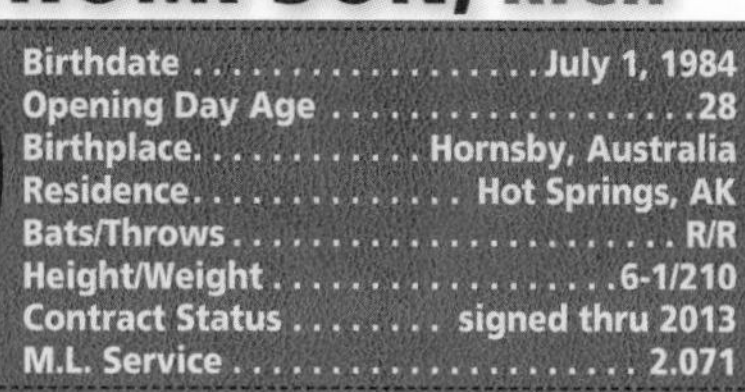

PERSONAL:

Richard Graeme Thompson... Was part of a MLB traveling team sent to Taiwan for a five-game series vs. Chinese Taipei at the 2011 Taiwan All-Star Series in November... Became the first of 31 Australians to play in the Major Leagues to be selected for a traveling All-Star Series... Graduated St. Ives High School (Sydney, AUS)... Is a native of Hornsby, Australia... Third Australian native to appear with Angels (Trent Durrington and Craig Shipley)... Was originally signed by Angels' scout Grant Weir.

LAST SEASON:

- Claimed off waivers by the Oakland A's from the Los Angeles Angels of Anaheim on April 20.
- Was outrighted to Sacramento of the Pacific Coast League (AAA) on April 27.
- Made 46 relief appearances for Sacramento and posted an ERA of 3.34 (23ER/62.0 IP).
- Fanned 58 batters over 62.0 IP while opponents hit just .206 over that span.

RICH THOMPSON

Bold – career high

Year	Club & League	W-L	ERA	G	GS	CG	ShO	SV	IP	H	R	ER	HR	HB	BB-IBB	SO	WP	BK	OBA
2002	AZL (Ariz)	2-0	2.70	15	0	0	0	1	23.1	14	12	7	0	1	9-0	29	1	1	.167
2003	Cedar Rapids (Mid)	1-2	0.24	31	0	0	0	9	37.2	18	5	1	1	0	13-0	54	6	0	.140
	Rancho Cucamonga (CAL)	2-2	4.91	24	0	0	0	8	29.1	28	19	16	4	2	18-1	33	5	0	.246
2004	Rancho Cucamonga (CAL)	3-2	3.94	41	5	0	0	4	77.2	76	36	34	9	3	33-2	71	4	1	.252
2005	Rancho Cucamonga (CAL)	6-8	5.27	42	15	0	0	3	121.1	132	76	71	20	2	53-1	92	12	2	.277
2006	Arkansas (TEX)	3-4	5.13	42	0	0	0	10	66.2	52	39	38	13	4	27-0	60	6	1	.218
	Salt Lake (PCL)	0-1	12.46	4	0	0	0	1	4.1	9	6	6	1	0	4-0	3	0	0	.500
2007	Rancho Cucamonga (CAL)	0-0	0.00	1	0	0	0	0	2.0	1	0	0	0	0	0-0	3	1	0	.125
	Arkansas (TEX)	2-3	2.01	21	3	0	0	0	49.1	34	15	11	5	3	14-1	50	3	1	.193
	Salt Lake (PCL)	3-0	2.19	16	0	0	0	1	24.2	17	7	6	2	3	6-0	32	3	0	.193
	LOS ANGELES (AL)	0-0	10.80	7	0	0	0	0	6.2	10	8	8	4	0	3-0	9	2	0	.345
2008	AZL (Ariz)	0-0	3.00	7	0	0	0	2	9.0	6	3	3	0	0	2-0	13	1	0	.194
	Salt Lake (PCL)	1-0	4.05	10	0	0	0	0	13.1	12	6	6	1	1	9-0	11	1	0	.240
	LOS ANGELES (AL)	0-0	22.50	2	0	0	0	0	2.0	4	5	5	0	0	2-0	1	1	0	.400
2009	Salt Lake (PCL)	3-1	3.12	29	0	0	0	0	43.1	41	19	15	7	2	11-0	51	2	0	.246
	LOS ANGELES (AL)	0-0	5.12	13	0	0	0	0	19.1	27	11	11	**6**	1	7-0	21	5	0	.329
2010	Salt Lake (PCL)	1-1	0.61	19	0	0	0	2	29.2	17	2	2	0	0	10-0	30	1	0	.177
	LOS ANGELES (AL)	**2**-0	1.37	13	0	0	0	0	19.2	12	4	3	2	0	4-0	15	4	0	.171
2011	LOS ANGELES (AL)	1-**3**	3.00	**44**	0	0	0	0	**54.0**	46	18	18	5	0	**20**-0	**56**	1	1	.224
2012	Sacramento River (PCL)	4-2	3.34	46	0	0	0	3	62.0	46	24	23	7	0	23-2	58	5	0	.206
	LOS ANGELES (AL)	0-1	15.43	2	0	0	0	0	2.1	5	4	4	1	0	1-0	3	0	0	.417
	OAKLAND (AL)	0-0	0.00	1	0	0	0	0	0.2	1	0	0	0	0	0-0	0	0	0	.333
Minor Totals		31-26	3.62	348	23	0	0	44	593.2	503	269	239	70	21	232-7	590	51	6	.228
MAJOR TOTALS		3-4	4.21	82	0	0	0	0	104.2	105	50	49	18	1	37-0	105	13	1	.255

TRANSACTIONS

- Signed by the Anaheim Angels on February 13, 2002
- On disabled list (right shoulder inflammation) from August 7-27, 2010
- Claimed off waivers by the Oakland Athletics on April 20, 2012
- Signed by the Toronto Blue Jays on December 11, 2012

GAME HIGHS

ML Debut	Sept. 1, 2007 vs. TEX
Innings Pitched:	
Starter	None
Reliever	3.1 - April 3, 2011 at KC
Walks:	
Starter	None
Reliever	2 - 7x, last Aug. 21, 2011 vs. BAL
Strikeouts:	
Starter	None
Reliever	5 - July 28, 2010 vs. BOS
Hits Allowed	5 - April 12, 2012 at MIN
Runs Allowed	5 - April 4, 2008 vs. TEX
ER Allowed	5 - April 4, 2008 vs. TEX
HR Allowed	2 - 4x, last Aug. 15, 2011 vs. TEX
Low Hit CG	None
Last Win	May 1, 2011 at TB
Last Save	None
Last CG	None
Last ShO	None
Last Start	None
Last Relief App.	April 23, 2012 vs. CWS
Longest Win Streak	2G - Sept. 10-Oct. 1, 2011
Longest Losing Streak	2G - May 15-July 16, 2011
Scoreless Innings Streak	9.1 - Aug. 4-Sept. 25, 2010

CAREER FIELDING

POSITION	PCT	G	PO	A	E	TC	DP
P	.867	82	6	7	2	15	0

MILESTONES

Category		Date	Opponent	Notes
Win	1	Sept. 10, 2010	Seattle	as reliever - 2.0 IP

PROFESSIONAL CAREER:

2007:

- Had contract selected by Angels, Sept. 1... Made **Major League debut** that night vs. Texas (1 IP, 1 H, 2 SO).
- Was MLB Futures Game World Team Selection.

2008:

- Started the season pitching in two games for the Angels (0-0, 22.50) before being optioned to Salt Lake on April 5.
- Was recalled on April 26 and tossed one scoreless inning at Detroit before being optioned back to Salt Lake on April 28.
- Placed on disabled list on May 9 with right shoulder nerve inflammation... Activated off the disabled list on September 1 and recalled on the same day.

2009:

- Made three appearances before being optioned, April 25... Recalled May 27 for his longest stint, making nine appearances before being optioned July 11.
- Was recalled, September 1 and spent remainder of season on big league roster.

2010:

- Saw Major League action for fourth consecutive season, posting a 2-0 record with a 1.37 ERA (19.2 IP - 3 ER) in 13 appearances with Angels.
- Was recalled from triple-A Salt Lake, July 2 after posting a 1-1 record with two saves and a 0.61 ERA (29.2 IP - 2 ER) in 19 appearances and being named to Pacific Coast League 2010 All-Star Team.
- Was placed on disabled list, August 7 and reactivated on August 28, missing 18 games with right shoulder inflammation.

2011:

- Made a career high 44 appearances, posting a 1-3 record, a 3.00 ERA (54.0 IP - 18 ER) with 25 walks, and 56 strikeouts.
- Set career-bests with 56 strikeouts and 54 innings pitched.
- Was part of a MLB traveling team sent to Taiwan for a five-game series vs. Chinese Taipei at the 2011 Taiwan All-Star Series in November... Became the first of 31 Australians to play in the Major Leagues to be selected for a traveling All-Star Series.

CALL IT A DRAW

The Blue Jays have played three tie games in their history. The first one was on May 13, 1984 at Cleveland. With one out in the top of the 8th inning, the rains came and play could not resume with the score tied at 4-4. The game had to be completely replayed as part of a TWDH on August 15. The second occurrence was in Cleveland on August 26, 1986. Play was halted after nine innings due to rain with the scored tied at 6-6. The game was completely replayed as part of an August 27 TWDH. The third time was on April 26, 1998 after six innings. The Blue Jays and White Sox were tied at 5-5 when the rains came and cancelled the game in Chicago. The game was completely replayed on July 15 as part of a TWDH. Though the games were rained out, the statistics from the games were entered into the books.

IN FIRST PLACE

(BEFORE GAMES ON THE 1ST)

MAY 1st	JUNE 1st	JULY 1st	AUG. 1st	SEPT. 1st	OCT. 1st
1981	1983	1983	1985	1985	1987
1985	1985	1985	1991	1989	1989
1992	1991 (T)	1991	1992	1991	1991
2001 (T)	1992	1992	1993	1992	1992
		1993		1993	1993
		2000			

VARGAS, *CLAUDIO*

Birthdate . . . . June 19,1978
Opening Day Age 34
Birthplace. . . . . Valverde Mao, DR
Residence. . . . . Santiago, DR
Bats/Throws . . . . R/R
Height/Weight 6-3/208
Contract Status . . . . signed thru 2013
M.L. Service 6.093

45
PITCHER
NON-ROSTER

PERSONAL:

Claudio Vargas Almonte... Has one child.

LAST SEASON:

- Spent the entire season with Nashville of the Pacific Coast League (AAA) in the Milwaukee Brewers organization.
- Signed with the Brewers as a minor league free agent on May 14.
- Posted a record of 7-1 with a 3.69 ERA in 20 games, all starts.
- Worked 109.2 innings, his heaviest workload since tossing 134.1 innings as a member of the Milwaukee Brewers in 2007.
- Worked at least six innings in 10 of his 20 starts including a season high - 8.0 innings on Aug. 20 vs. Omaha.
- Recorded seven quality starts.

CLAUDIO VARGAS

Bold – career high

Year	Club & League	W-L	ERA	G	GS	CG	ShO	SV	IP	H	R	ER	HR	HB	BB-IBB	SO	WP	BK	OBA
1996	DSL (DSL)	2-3	3.09	15	4	0	0	0	46.2	41	25	16	1	0	26-0	37	4	1	.230
1997	DSL (DSL)	6-2	2.50	13	10	3	1	0	72.0	62	32	20	3	3	31-0	81	5	2	.232
1998	Brevard County (FSL)	0-1	4.66	2	2	0	0	0	9.2	15	5	5	1	0	4-0	9	0	0	.366
	Marlins (Gulf)	0-4	4.08	5	4	0	0	0	28.2	24	15	13	1	3	7-0	27	2	0	.226
1999	Kane County (Mid)	5-5	3.88	19	19	1	0	0	99.2	97	47	43	8	0	41-0	88	2	2	.255
2000	Brevard County (FSL)	10-5	3.28	24	23	0	0	0	145.1	126	64	53	10	7	44-3	143	3	0	.234
	Portland (East)	1-1	3.60	3	2	0	0	0	15.0	16	9	6	1	1	6-0	13	0	0	.276
2001	Portland (East)	8-9	4.19	27	27	0	0	0	159.0	122	77	74	25	11	67-1	151	2	1	.211
2002	Calgary (PCL)	4-11	6.72	17	16	1	0	0	76.1	88	63	57	18	4	35-0	61	3	1	.291
	Harrisburg (East)	2-2	4.64	8	8	0	0	0	33.0	38	17	17	2	3	9-0	34	3	0	.286
2003	Edmonton (PCL)	0-0	2.79	2	2	0	0	0	9.2	7	3	3	1	1	5-2	12	0	0	.189
	Harrisburg (East)	1-0	0.75	2	2	0	0	0	12.0	7	1	1	0	1	3-0	13	0	0	.171
	MONTREAL (NL)	6-8	4.34	23	20	0	0	0	114.0	111	59	55	16	7	41-5	62	2	0	.255
2004	MONTREAL (NL)	5-5	5.25	**45**	14	0	0	0	118.1	120	75	69	26	7	**64**-7	89	8	0	.266
2005	New Orleans (PCL)	2-2	4.18	5	5	0	0	0	28.0	24	13	13	4	0	12-0	35	2	0	.231
	WASHINGTON (NL)	0-3	9.24	4	4	0	0	0	12.2	22	15	13	4	0	7-2	5	0	0	.373
	ARIZONA (NL)	9-6	4.81	21	19	0	0	0	119.2	124	66	64	21	7	40-3	90	6	0	.266
2006	ARIZONA (NL)	**12-10**	4.83	31	**30**	0	0	0	**167.2**	185	101	90	**27**	8	52-2	**123**	9	1	.274
2007	MILWAUKEE (NL)	11-6	5.09	29	23	0	0	**1**	134.1	153	80	76	23	2	54-3	107	4	0	.285
2008	St. Lucie (FSL)	0-0	1.80	1	1	0	0	0	5.0	3	2	1	0	0	0-0	6	0	0	.188
	New Orleans (PCL)	5-2	4.36	8	8	0	0	0	43.1	47	24	21	5	0	13-1	43	1	0	.280
	NEW YORK (NL)	3-2	4.62	11	4	0	0	0	37.0	33	20	19	4	2	11-0	20	1	0	.244
2009	Inland Empire (CAL)	0-1	5.40	3	3	0	0	0	5.0	3	3	3	1	0	1-0	3	0	0	.158
	Albuquerque (PCL)	0-0	3.46	7	0	0	0	1	13.0	15	5	5	3	0	1-0	12	0	0	.288
	LOS ANGELES (NL)	0-0	1.64	8	0	0	0	0	11.0	7	2	2	1	1	4-0	10	0	0	.184
	MILWAUKEE (NL)	1-0	1.78	28	0	0	0	0	30.1	18	6	6	2	1	11-1	20	0	0	.175
2010	Albuquerque (PCL)	2-6	5.89	10	10	0	0	0	47.1	52	34	31	6	0	20-1	45	3	0	.277
	MILWAUKEE (NL)	1-0	7.32	17	0	0	0	0	19.2	28	16	16	3	0	10-0	18	2	0	.337
2011	Colorado Springs (PCL)	2-2	11.08	8	4	0	0	0	26.0	50	34	32	6	1	13-0	19	1	0	.407
2012	Nashville (PCL)	7-1	3.69	20	20	0	0	0	109.2	112	48	45	11	4	32-1	84	6	0	.269
Minor Totals		57-57	4.20	199	170	5	1	1	984.1	949	521	459	107	39	370-9	916	37	7	.253
MAJOR TOTALS		48-40	4.83	217	114	0	0	1	764.2	801	440	410	127	35	294-23	544	32	1	.268

TRANSACTIONS

- Signed by the Florida Marlins on August 25, 1995
- Traded to the Montreal Expos along with OF Cliff Floyd, IF Wilton Guerrero and cash considerations to the Montreal Expos in exchange for a player to be named later (RHP Donald Levinski) , LHP Graeme Lloyd, IF Mike Mordecai, RHP Carl Pavano and RHP Justin Wayne on July 11, 2002
- On disabled list (tendinitis in right shoulder) from August 6-September 15, 2003
- On disabled list (right elbow strain) from March 16-May 11, 2005
- Claimed off waivers by the Arizona Diamondbacks on June 3, 2005
- Traded to the Milwaukee Brewers along with RHP Greg Aquino and C Johnny Estrada in exchnage for LHP Doug Davis, LHP Dana Eveland and OF Dave Krynzel on November 25, 2006
- On disabled list (strained lower back) from August 25-September 9, 2007
- Signed by the New York Mets on April 11, 2008
- Signed by the Los Angeles Dodgers on January 5, 2009
- On disabled list (right elbow tendinitis) from April 6-July 3, 2009
- Traded to the Milwaukee Brewers in exchnage for OF Vinny Rottino on July 31, 2009
- Signed by the Los Angeles Dodgers on June 16, 2010
- Signed by the Colorado Rockies on January 11, 2011
- Signed by the Milwaukee Brewers on May 16, 2012
- Signed by the Toronto Blue Jays on December 11, 2012

GAME HIGHS

ML Debut	April 26, 2003 vs. HOU	**Runs Allowed**	8 - 2x, last May 13, 2006 at STL
Innings Pitched:		**ER Allowed**	8 - 2x, last May 13, 2006 at STL
Starter	8.0 - 3x, last July 27, 2007 at STL	**HR Allowed**	3 - 4x, last June 26, 2007 vs. HOU
Reliever	4.2 - June 2, 2008 at SF	**Low Hit CG**	None
Walks:		**Last Win**	April 18, 2010 at WSH
Starter	7 - Sept. 23, 2005 vs. SD	**Last Save**	June 10, 2007 at TEX
Reliever	5 - Aug. 18, 2004 at SF	**Last CG**	None
		Last ShO	None
Strikeouts:		**Last Start**	May 29, 2008 vs. LAD
Starter	11 - April 18, 2007 vs. PIT	**Last Relief App.**	May 26, 2010 vs. HOU
Reliever	7 - June 26, 2004 at TOR	**Longest Win Streak**	3G - 7x, last May 24-June 11, 2008
Hits Allowed	12 - Aug. 6, 2007 at COL	**Longest Losing Streak**	5G - July 8-Aug. 5, 2003
		Scoreless Innings Streak	17.0 - April 23-May 9, 2007

CAREER FIELDING

POSITION	PCT	G	PO	A	E	TC	DP
P	.956	217	44	86	6	136	7

MILESTONES

Category		Date	Opponent	Notes
Start	1	April 26, 2003	Houston	no decision - 6.0 IP, 2H, ER, HR, 4BB, 7K
	100	June 20, 2007	San Francisco	won - 5.0 IP, 4H, 4ER, 4BB, 3K, HR
Win	1	May 14, 2003	at San Francisco	8.0 IP, 5H, 2ER, HR, 3BB, K
10+ Strikeout Games (1)				
	1	April 18, 2007	Pittsburgh	11 strikeouts
Save	1	June 10, 2007	at Texas	1.0 IP, H

PROFESSIONAL CAREER:

2003:

- Was named Eastern League Player of the Week for the period ending April 20.
- Was recalled by Montreal on April 24... Made his **Major League debut** on April 26 vs. Houston and received no decision.
- Recorded his first career victory in a 6-3 win on May 14 at San Francisco.
- Was named Expos Player of the Month for June as he went 3-1 with a 1.43 ERA in six starts.
- Was placed on the 15-day disabled list on Aug. 8 with tendinitis in the right shoulder.

2004:

- Spent his first full season in the Majors and went 5-5 with a 5.25 ERA in 45 games (14 starts) with Montreal.

2005:

- Began the season on the disabled list for Washington with a right elbow sprain... Was reinstated from the disabled list on May 11 and made his season debut that day at Arizona.
- Was designated for assignment on May 26... Was claimed off waivers by Arizona on June 3.
- Was named Diamondbacks Player of the Month for July as he went 2-1 with a 2.01 ERA in 5 starts.

2006:

- Set career highs in nearly every category, including wins, starts, innings pitched (167.2) and strikeouts (123).
- Was traded to Milwaukee, along with C Johnny Estrada and RHP Greg Aquino, in exchange for LHP Doug Davis, LHP Dana Eveland and OF Dave Krynzel on November 25.

2007:

- Notched his first career save on June 10 at Texas.
- Was placed on the 15-day disabled list from Aug. 28-Sept. 8 with a strained low back... Was reinstated on Sept. 9 and made his final four appearances of the season in relief.

2008:

- Signed a minor league deal with the New York Mets on April 11... His contract was purchased by the Mets on May 13 and he made his first start of the season on May 14 vs. Washington.
- Was designated for assignment by the Mets on June 25.
- Was sharp for Aguilas del Cibao in the Dominican Winter League, going 3-1 with a 4.02 ERA (14 ER/31.1 IP) and 31 strikeouts in six starts this offseason.

2009:

- Began the season on the 60-day disabled list with the Dodgers with right elbow tendinitis (missed 79 games)... Was reinstated from the disabled list on July 3 after rehab stints at Class-A Inland Empire and Triple-A Albuquerque.
- Was traded to Milwaukee on July 31 for C Vinny Rottino.
- Pitched for Aguilas in the Dominican Winter League.

2010:

- Was designated for assignment by the Brewers on May 29... Released by the Brewers on June 4 and cleared waivers, becoming a free agent.
- On June 16 the Los Angeles Dodgers signed him to a Minor League contract... Was later released on Aug. 17.

2011:

- Spent the entire season with Colorado Springs of the Pacific Coast League (AAA).
- Appeared in just eight games (four starts) and allowed 32 earned runs over 26.0 innings of work.
- Was on the disabled list from April 7-May 7 with a right hamstring strain.

FOUR CONSECUTIVE EXTRA INNING GAMES

The Club record for most consecutive extra-inning games is four which occurred from September 16 to 20, 1991... The Blue Jays posted a record of 1-3 over that span... On Sept. 16, L 5-6 in 11 inn at SEA; on Sept. 17, L 4-5 in 11 inn at SEA; on Sept. 18, W 5-3 in 12 inn and on Sept. 20, L 5-6 in 11 inn at OAK.

PLAYERS WITH MOST SEASONS AS A BLUE JAY

(MINIMUM OF 8 SEASONS)

Seasons	Player	Years
15	Dave Stieb	1979-1992; 1998
12	Jim Clancy	1977-1988
12	Tony Fernandez	1983-1990; 1993; 1998-1999; 2001
12	Ernie Whitt	1977-1978; 1980-1989
12	Carlos Delgado	1993-2004
12	Roy Halladay	1998-2009
12	Vernon Wells	1999-2010
11	Rance Mulliniks	1982-1992
10	Lloyd Moseby	1980-1990
10	Duane Ward	1986-1995
10	Pat Hentgen	1991-1999; 2004
10	Shannon Stewart	1995-2003, 2008
9	Jesse Barfield	1981-1989
9	George Bell	1981; 1983-1990
9	Kelly Gruber	1984-1992
9	Garth Iorg	1978; 1980-1987
9	Jimmy Key	1984-1992
8	Jason Frasor	2004-2011
8	Pat Borders	1988-1994; 1999
8	Alex Gonzalez	1994-2001
8	Alfredo Griffin	1979-1984; 1992-1993
8	Juan Guzman	1991-1998
8	Tom Henke	1985-1992
8	Manuel Lee	1985-1992
8	John Olerud	1989-1996
8	Ed Sprague	1991-1998
8	David Wells	1987-1998; 1999-2000
8	Greg Myers	1987; 1989-1992; 2003-2005

VELEZ, *EUGENIO*

Birthdate	May 16, 1982
Opening Day Age	30
Birthplace	San Pedro de Macoris, DR
Residence	San Pedro de Macoris, DR
Bats/Throws	S/R
Height/Weight	6-1/170
Contract Status	signed thru 2013
M.L. Service	2.111

67

INFIELDER

NON-ROSTER

PERSONAL:

Eugenio (Vancomper) Velez... Has one child...Was named after his mother, Pura Eugenia Vancamper... Resides in San Pedro de Macoris, Dominican Republic.

LAST SEASON:

- Spent the season at Memphis of the Pacific Coast League (AAA) in the St, Louis Cardinals organization.
- Posted an .807 OPS in 136 games with Memphis.
- Recorded 50 extra base hits including a career high 34 doubles.

EUGENIO VELEZ

Bold - career high

Year	Club and League	AVG	G	AB	R	H	2B	3B	HR	RBI	SH-SF	HP	BB-IBB	SO	SB-CS	SLG	OBP	OPS
2005	Lansing (Mid)	.285	67	239	25	68	11	3	4	34	0-4	2	9-0	40	7-5	.406	.311	.717
2006	Augusta (SAL)	.315	126	460	90	145	29	20	14	90	1-5	8	34-2	81	64-15	.557	.369	.926
2007	Connecticut (East)	.298	96	376	55	112	17	9	1	25	4-3	2	26-0	66	49-17	.399	.344	.743
	Fresno (PCL)	.278	4	18	5	5	0	0	0	0	0-0	1	2-0	3	5-0	.278	.381	.659
	SAN FRANCISCO (NL)	.273	14	11	5	3	0	2	0	2	0-0	0	2-0	3	4-0	.636	.385	1.021
2008	Fresno (PCL)	.310	42	171	25	53	11	4	5	15	0-0	0	17-0	32	13-9	.509	.372	.881
	SAN FRANCISCO (NL)	.262	**98**	275	32	72	**16**	**7**	1	30	1-1	1	14-2	40	**15**-6	.382	.299	.681
2009	Fresno (PCL)	.297	45	182	30	54	13	3	3	26	0-2	0	13-2	26	16-9	.451	.340	.791
	SAN FRANCISCO (NL)	.267	84	285	**40**	**76**	13	5	**5**	**31**	2-2	2	**16**-1	**55**	11-5	.400	.308	.708
2010	Fresno (PCL)	.302	82	321	50	97	13	5	7	35	6-0	1	24-0	55	31-16	.439	.353	.792
	SAN FRANCISCO (NL)	.164	29	55	7	9	2	0	2	8	5-0	0	6-0	9	0-0	.309	.246	.555
2011	Albuquerque (PCL)	.339	55	218	33	74	15	3	2	31	3-2	1	11-0	36	6-6	.463	.371	.834
	LOS ANGELES (NL)	.000	34	37	5	0	0	0	0	1	0-0	1	2-0	11	1-0	.000	.075	.075
2012	Memphis (PCL)	.280	136	457	70	128	34	5	11	58	2-1	5	51-3	99	37-9	.449	.358	.807
Minor Totals		.301	653	2442	383	736	143	52	47	314	16-17	20	187-7	438	228-86	.460	.354	.814
MAJOR TOTALS		.241	259	663	89	160	31	14	8	72	8-3	4	40-3	118	31-11	.367	.287	.654

HOME RUN BREAKDOWN

Total	H	A	ONE GAME 2	3	4	GS	LO	XN	IP	PH	RHP	LHP
8	4	4	0	0	0	0	2	0	0	0	8	0

TRANSACTIONS

- Signed by the Toronto Blue Jays on August 27, 2001
- Selected by the San Francisco Giants in the 2005 Rule 5 Draft on December 8, 2005
- Signed by the Los Angeles Dodgers on December 13, 2010
- Signed by the St. Louis Cardinals on December 21, 2011
- Signed by the Toronto Blue Jays on December 11, 2012

GAME HIGHS

ML Debut	Sept. 5, 2007 at COL	**RBI**	4 - 2x, last Sept. 14, 2009 vs. COL
Runs	2 - 13x, last Oct. 4, 2009 at SD	**Stolen Bases**	2 - 2x, last Oct. 4, 2009 at SD
Hits	3 - 10x, last April 17, 2010 at LAD	**Last ML Home Run**	April 16, 2010 at LAD
Doubles	2 - 2x, last Sept. 24, 2008 vs. COL	**Longest Hitting Streak**	16G - May 9-Aug. 10, 2009
Home Runs	1 - 8x, last April 16, 2010 at LAD	**Longest Hitless Streak**	37AB - July 4-Sept. 28, 2011

CAREER FIELDING

POSITION	PCT	G	PO	A	E	TC	DP
2B	.963	116	175	193	14	382	38
OF	.950	91	110	3	6	119	0

MILESTONES

Category		Date	Opponent	Pitcher	Notes
Hit	1	Sept. 14, 2007	at San Diego	Young	pinch-hit triple
Home Run	1	Aug. 30, 2008	at Cincinnati	Ramirez	2R
Leadoff HR (2)	1	Sept. 3, 2009	at Philadelphia	Martinez	--
	2	Sept. 18, 2009	at Los Angeles (NL)	Padilla	--
RBI	1	Sept. 30, 2007	at Los Angeles (NL)	Meloan	pinch-hit 2R triple
Stolen Base	1	Sept. 16, 2007	at San Diego	Peavy	2nd base
				C-Bard	

PROFESSIONAL CAREER:

2007:

- Double-A All-Star played for SF's top two minor league outposts, before being recalled by Giants Sept. 4.
- Made his **Major League debut** Sept. 5 in Colorado, grounding out as pinch-hitter.
- Collected 1st big league hit Sept. 14 at San Diego, pinch-3B off Padres' Chris Young... Went 1-for-3 with run and stolen base during 1st ML start (Sept. 20 vs. Reds, at 2B).
- Put together Eastern League All-Star campaign with Connecticut despite missing 1st two months with injured wrist, batting .298 with 17-2B, 9-3B, HR, 25RBI and 49 steals in 96 games.
- Named to Arizona Fall League's Top Prospects Team after solid 17-game stint with Scottsdale Scorpions... Ranked 3rd in league with 14 stolen bases (in 15 attempts), while batting .303 (23-for-76) with 5 2B, 2 3B, 1 HR and 9 RBI.

2008:

- Made 1st Opening Day roster after impressive spring with the Giants.
- Ranked among NL rookies in avg. (7th), 2Bs (7th), hits (10th), 3Bs (1st), stolen bases (1st), slugging pct. (9th - .382) and extra base hits (T8th - 24).
- His 7-3B were most by SF rookie in single season since Gary Maddox also had 7-3B in 1972.
- Making 25 starts before being optioned to triple-A Fresno May 21... Was recalled from triple-A July 8 and hit .310 avg. with HR and 21 RBI after the All-Star break.
- Posted "walk-off" hits in back-to-back games Sept. 9 and 10 (vs. Arizona), becoming 1st Giant to achieve feat in consecutive games since Daryl Spencer Aug. 23-24, 1958.
- Hit 1st career HR Aug. 30 at Cincinnati, 2-run shot in 2nd inning off RHP Ramon Ramirez.

2009:

- Made Opening Day roster for his 2nd-consecutive season.
- Made three separate stints with Giants during season.
- Had career-best 16-game hitting streak from May 19-Aug. 10, during which he batted .420 (29-for-69) with 14 runs, 4 2B, 3 HR and 11 RBI with 11 multi-hit contests.
- His hit streak spanned 84 days... There have been six single-season hit streaks of 20 or more games in bigs that have lasted more than 62 days... Ed Delahanty had longest such streak with 22-game that spanned 113 days from May 11-Aug. 31, 1889.
- Hit his 1st career leadoff home run Sept. 3 at Philadelphia on 1st pitch of game by Pedro Martinez.

2010:

- Began year on Opening Day roster, however was optioned to Triple-A Fresno on three different occasions.
- Landed on the 15-day disabled list on July 24 after suffering head contusion and concussion when he was struck on side of head by line drive off the bat of Pat Burrell while sitting in dugout at Chase Field... Was taken to St. Joe's Medical Hospital in Phoenix where CT scan came back negative and showed no skull fractures... Remained hospitalized overnight, but was released the next day.
- Was activated from DL and optioned to Triple-A on Aug. 11.
- Ranked fifth in the Pacifc Coast League in steals.

2011:

- Began the season on the disabled list after suffering an ankle injury at the end of the Cactus League season.
- Dating back to 2010 was hitless in his last 46 at-bats, which broke the previous Dodgers record of 0-for-45, set in 1909 by Bill Bergen (Brooklyn).
- Set a Major League record for a non-pitcher by going 0-for-37 on the season... The previous record was 0-for-35 in 1937, by Hal Finney of the Pittsburgh Pirates.

WAGNER, *NEIL*

Birthdate .... January 1, 1984
Opening Day Age 29
Birthplace............ Minneapolis, MN
Residence............ Eden Prairie, MN
Bats/Throws .... R/R
Height/Weight 6-0/215
Contract Status .... signed thru 2013
M.L. Service 0.034

37
PITCHER
NON-ROSTER

PERSONAL:

Neil K. Wagner was originally signed by Cleveland scout Les Pajari... Graduated from Eden Prairie HS (MN)... Attended North Dakota State University... Broke NDSU school records for career saves (18), single-season saves (12 in 2004) and single-season appearances (28 in 2004)... Was a two-time North Central Conference Pitcher of the Week in 2004 and was named to first-team All-NCC and all-Central Region that year.

LAST SEASON:

- Spent time with both Sacramento (AAA) and Tuscon (AAA) of the Pacific Coast League.
- Was claimed off waivers by the San Diego Padres from the Oakland Athletics organization on May 28.
- Finished the season with Tuscon, making 31 appearances (all in relief).

NEIL WAGNER

Bold – career high

Year	Club & League	W-L	ERA	G	GS	CG	ShO	SV	IP	H	R	ER	HR	HB	BB-IBB	SO	WP	BK	OBA
2006	Mahoning Valley (NYP)	0-1	1.39	26	0	0	0	17	32.1	16	5	5	1	0	9-0	50	2	0	.143
2007	Lake County (SAL)	1-4	3.68	34	0	0	0	11	44.0	41	21	18	3	3	11-0	49	1	0	.246
	Kinston (Caro)	0-0	3.00	16	0	0	0	0	24.0	17	8	8	2	0	6-0	18	1	0	.198
2008	Kinston (Caro)	3-6	4.50	41	0	0	0	3	62.0	67	34	31	1	1	21-0	81	5	1	.275
	Akron (East)	0-2	3.60	7	0	0	0	0	10.0	10	5	4	1	0	4-0	11	0	0	.256
2009	Akron (East)	1-3	2.95	46	0	0	0	2	61.0	48	24	20	3	1	32-2	69	6	0	.214
2010	Akron (East)	1-1	6.28	13	0	0	0	4	14.1	17	12	10	0	1	7-0	15	0	0	.283
	Midland (TEX)	6-2	3.70	33	0	0	0	1	48.2	55	25	20	1	0	27-4	45	3	0	.282
2011	Midland (TEX)	1-3	3.38	28	0	0	0	4	37.1	31	18	14	0	1	13-2	53	2	0	.225
	Sacramento (PCL)	2-1	3.10	22	0	0	0	2	29.0	27	10	10	2	0	10-0	34	0	0	.241
	OAKLAND (AL)	0-0	7.20	6	0	0	0	0	5.0	6	7	4	1	1	3-0	4	0	0	.300
2012	Sacramento (PCL)	1-1	5.49	15	0	0	0	1	19.2	20	13	12	1	2	6-1	24	4	0	.263
	Tucson (PCL)	3-1	5.44	31	0	0	0	0	43.0	57	30	26	2	0	17-1	32	5	1	.320
Minor Totals		19-25	3.77	312	0	0	0	45	425.1	406	205	178	17	9	163-10	481	29	2	.249

TRANSACTIONS

- Selected by the Cleveland Indians in the 21st round of the 2005 First Year Player Draft
- Traded to the Oakland Athletics in exchnage for a player to be named later on May 11, 2010
- Selected off waivers by the San Diego Padres on May 28, 2012
- Signed by the Toronto Blue Jays on November 15, 2012

GAME HIGHS

ML Debut	Aug. 30, 2011 at CLE
Innings Pitched:	
Starter	None
Reliever	1.0 - 4x, last Sept. 20, 2011 vs. TEX
Walks:	
Starter	None
Reliever	1 - 3x, last Sept. 20, 2011 vs. TEX
Strikeouts:	
Starter	None
Reliever	1 - 4x, last Sept. 9, 2011 at TEX
Hits Allowed	3 - Sept. 9, 2011 at TEX
Runs Allowed	5 - Sept. 9, 2011 at TEX
ER Allowed	2 - 2x, last Sept. 9, 2011 at TEX
HR Allowed	1 - Sept. 9, 2011 at TEX
Low Hit CG	None
Last Win	None
Last Save	None
Last CG	None
Last ShO	None
Last Start	None
Last Relief App.	Sept. 20, 2011 vs. TEX
Longest Win Streak	None
Longest Losing Streak	None
Scoreless Innings Streak	2.0 - Aug. 30-31, 2011

CAREER FIELDING

POSITION	PCT	G	PO	A	E	TC	DP
P	--	6	0	0	0	0	0

PROFESSIONAL CAREER:

_2006:_

- Was named to the Topps/Minor League Baseball Short-A/Rookie All-Star Team after posting a 1.39 ERA and a career-high 17 saves in his professional debut at Mahoning Valley.
- Had the second best strikeout per nine inning ratio among New York-Penn League relievers and ranked third in saves.
- Named to the NYPL Midseason All-Star team.
- Had a 12-game, 17.0-inning scoreless streak from June 26 to Aug. 1.

_2007:_

- Pitched for Lake County and Kinston and was a combined 1-4 with 11 saves and a 3.44 ERA in a career-high 50 relief appearances.
- Pitched for West Oahu in the Hawaiian Winter League and was 0-1 with a 9.68 ERA in 12 relief appearances.

_2008:_

- Struck out a career-high 90 batters in a career-high 72.0 innings, an average of 11.25 strikeouts per nine innings.
- Averaged 11.76 strikeouts per nine innings overall with Kinston, which was second best among Carolina League relievers.
- Was promoted to Akron Aug. 14.
- Was 0-1 with a 5.59 ERA in 13 relief appearances with Surprise in the Arizona Fall League.

_2009:_

- Spent the entire season at Double-A Akron and was 1-3 with two saves and a 2.95 ERA in 46 relief appearances.
- Compiled a 4.50 ERA (4.0IP, 4H, 2ER, BB, 3K) in four postseason appearances.

_2010:_

- Traded to the Oakland organization for cash considerations, May 11.
- Assigned to Double-A Midland and went 6-2 with a save and a 3.70 ERA in 33 relief appearances with the RockHounds.
- Allowed just one home run in 63.0 innings.
- Was on the disabled list from June 2-8 with a sprained left ankle.

_2011:_

- Was selected by the A's on Aug. 30, making his **Major League debut** that night at Cleveland... Struck out the first batter he faced, Carlos Santana.

MILEAGE

During the 2013 season the Toronto Blue Jays will travel 29,172 miles (46,948 km) from the time the Club leaves spring training through the end of the regular season. The Blue Jays will make 38 separate flights.

From	To	Distance Miles	Distance Kilometers
Toronto	Detroit	206	331
Detroit	Kansas City	707	1139
Kansas City	Toronto	1091	1756
Toronto	Baltimore	335	539
Baltimore	New York	311	500
New York	Toronto	343	553
Toronto	Tampa Bay	1098	1767
Tampa Bay	Boston	1161	1870
Boston	Toronto	431	695
Toronto	New York	343	553
New York	Toronto	343	553
Toronto	Atlanta	884	1422
Atlanta	San Diego	1887	3037
San Diego	San Francisco	458	738
San Francisco	Toronto	2412	3881
Toronto	Chicago	436	701
Chicago	Texas	562	904
Texas	Toronto	1396	2246
Toronto	Tampa Bay	1098	1767
Tampa Bay	Boston	1161	1870

From	To	Distance Miles	Distance Kilometers
Boston	Toronto	431	695
Toronto	Cleveland	361	581
Cleveland	Baltimore	1065	1714
Baltimore	Toronto	335	539
Toronto	Oakland	2402	3865
Oakland	Anaheim	83	133
Anaheim	Seattle	762	1226
Seattle	Toronto	2178	3505
Toronto	Tampa Bay	1098	1767
Tampa Bay	New York	1008	1622
New York	Houston	1417	2281
Houston	Toronto	1302	2095
Toronto	Phoenix	2055	3307
Phoenix	Minnesota	1331	2142
Minnesota	Toronto	831	1337
Toronto	Boston	431	695
Boston	Baltimore	1232	1984
Baltimore	Toronto	335	539
TOTAL DISTANCE		**32,729**	**52,672**

ZAWADZKI, *LANCE*

Birthdate . . . . May 26, 1985
Opening Day Age 27
Birthplace . . . . Framingham, MA
Residence . . . . San Antonio, TX
Bats/Throws . . . . S/R
Height/Weight 5-11/185
Contract Status . . . . signed thru 2013
M.L. Service 0.040

73
INFIELDER
NON-ROSTER

PERSONAL:

Lance Frederick Zawadzki... Graduated from St. John's High School in Shrewsbury, MA... While at San Diego State, recorded the first-ever hit at San Diego's PETCO Park, doubling off the wall against the University of Houston on March 11, 2004... Was drafted out of high school by the Expos in the 48th round of the 2003 First-Year Player Draft and again by the Cardinals in the 15th round of the 2006 draft, but did not sign.

LAST SEASON:

- Spent time between three different clubs in 2012... Appeared in five games with Alburquerque of the Pacific Coast League (AAA), 48 games with Gwinnett of the International League (AAA) and eight contests with Memphis of the Pacific Coast League (AAA).
- Began the season in the Los Angeles Dodgers organization at Albequerque (AAA).
- Was placed on the DL on April 27 (strained left hamstring) and activated on May 6.
- Released by the Dodgers and signed with the Atlanta Braves on May 21.
- Was released by the Braves on July 28 and joined his 3rd organization in 2012, this time with the St. Louis Cardinals on Aug. 10, signing a minor league contract.
- Was placed on the disabled list (strained left hamstring) on Aug. 20 though the remainder of the season.

LANCE ZAWADZKI

Bold – career high

Year	Club and League	AVG	G	AB	R	H	2B	3B	HR	RBI	SH-SF	HP	BB-IBB	SO	SB-CS	SLG	OBP	OPS
2007	AZL (Ariz)	.433	10	30	8	13	3	0	1	5	0-0	0	3-0	8	0-0	.633	.485	1.118
	Eugene (NOR)	.267	25	101	13	27	4	1	2	14	0-0	1	10-0	24	1-0	.386	.339	.725
2008	Fort Wayne (Mid)	.273	119	454	66	124	26	5	7	58	1-5	4	54-0	101	28-3	.399	.352	.751
	San Antonio (TEX)	.333	2	3	1	1	0	0	0	0	0-0	0	0-0	2	0-0	.333	.333	.666
2009	Lake Elsinore (CAL)	.276	36	145	19	40	6	2	10	34	0-0	1	18-2	29	3-1	.552	.360	.912
	San Antonio (TEX)	.289	92	346	59	100	19	5	5	43	0-0	2	44-4	74	14-1	.416	.372	.788
2010	Portland (PCL)	.231	61	225	34	52	10	1	1	16	0-1	1	21-0	57	5-5	.298	.298	.596
	San Antonio (TEX)	.216	35	148	21	32	5	1	4	17	0-0	0	13-1	34	7-1	.345	.280	.625
	SAN DIEGO (NL)	.200	20	35	4	7	2	0	0	1	2-0	0	5-2	7	1-0	.257	.300	.557
2011	Omaha Storm (PCL)	.233	91	326	44	76	13	6	8	40	1-0	0	25-2	76	15-3	.383	.288	.671
2012	Albuquerque (PCL)	.000	5	13	1	0	0	0	0	0	1-0	0	1-0	4	0-0	.000	.071	.071
	Gwinnett (Int)	.231	48	147	12	34	5	1	3	17	2-0	1	7-0	31	3-1	.340	.271	.611
	Memphis (PCL)	.281	8	32	2	9	1	1	0	3	0-0	0	1-0	6	1-0	.375	.303	.678
Minor Totals		.258	532	1970	280	508	92	23	41	247	5-6	10	197-9	446	77-15	.390	.328	.718

TRANSACTIONS

- Selected by the San Diego Padres in the 4th round of the 2007 First Year Player Draft
- Claimed off waivers by the Kansas City Royals on November 5, 2010
- Signed by the Los Angeles Dodgers on November 4, 2011
- Signed by the Atlanta Braves on May 21, 2012
- Signed by St. Louis Cardinals on August 10, 2012
- Signed by the Toronto Blue Jays on December 18, 2012

GAME HIGHS

ML Debut	May 2, 2010 vs. MIL	**RBI**	1 - May 31, 2010 vs. NYM
Runs	1 - 4x, last May 30, 2010 vs. WSH	**Stolen Bases**	1 - June 6, 2010 at PHI
Hits	1 - 7x, last June 16, 2010 vs. TOR	**Last ML Home Run**	None
Doubles	1 - 2x, last June 8, 2010 at NYM	**Longest Hitting Streak**	3G - May 13-31, 2010
Home Runs	None	**Longest Hitless Streak**	8AB - May 2-13, 2010

CAREER FIELDING

POSITION	PCT	G	PO	A	E	TC	DP
2B	.931	7	9	18	2	29	2
3B	1.000	1	1	4	0	5	1
SS	1.000	3	2	5	0	7	1

MILESTONES

Category		Date	Opponent	Pitcher	Notes
Hit	1	May 2, 2010	Milwaukee	Wolf	single
RBI	1	May 31, 2010	New York (NL)	Perez	single
Stolen Base	1	June 6, 2010	at Philadelphia	Blanton C-Schneider	2nd base

PROFESSIONAL CAREER:

2007:

- Combined for a .305 batting average (40-for-131) with seven doubles, one triple, three home runs and 19 RBI in 35 games between Rookie-level Peoria and Short-A Eugene.

2008:

- Played the majority of the season at Single-A Fort Wayne, splitting time at shortstop and second base.

2009:

- Split season between Single-A Lake Elsinore and Double-A San Antonio, appearing a combined 128 games.
- After joining San Antonio, hit .371 (39-for-105) over his first 31 games from May 30-June 29.
- Tallied multi-hit games in five consecutive contests June 17-21, including a 6-for-6 performance with one RBI and four runs scored June 20 at Midland... Went 15-for-21 (.714) over the stretch and was named Texas League Player of the Week for June 15-21.

2010:

- Saw his first action at the Major League level, appearing in 20 games for the San Diego Padres.
- Made his **Major League debut** on May 2 vs. Milwaukee, starting at second base.
- Singled in his first big league at bat off Brewers' lefty Randy Wolf.

2011:

- Spent the 2011 campaign with Kansas City's Triple-A Omaha in his first season with the Royals organization.
- Stole 15 bases for his fourth straight season with 12 or more steals.

COMEBACKS

Trailing by three or more runs after eight innings and winning the game

Date	Inning	Opponent	Previous Score	Final Score
April 5, 2012	Bottom 9th	at CLE	L 1-4	W 7-4 (16 inn)
August 12, 2010	Bottom 9th	vs. BOS	L 2-5	W 6-5
June 5, 2007	Bottom 9th	vs. TB	L 6-11	W 12-11
April 27, 2003	Bottom 9th	vs. KC	L 4-9	W 10-9
June 29, 2002	Bottom 10th	vs. MTL	L 1-4	W 5-4
April 14, 2001	Bottom 9th	vs. KC	L 1-4	W 5-4
August 1, 1995	Top 9th	at BAL	L 6-10	W 12-10
May 7, 1992	Top 9th	at SEA	L 3-7	W 8-7
June 4, 1989	Top 12th	at BOS	L 6-10	W 13-11
April 20, 1987	Top 10th	at CLE	L 2-6	W 8-7
July 18, 1978	Top 10th	at SEA	L 6-9	W 13-12

LARGEST LEAD CHANGES

(6 RUNS OR MORE)

DEFICITS OVERCOME IN A VICTORY:

10 runs - June 4, 1989 at BOS (W 13-11, 11 inn.)
7 runs - April 27, 2003 vs KC (W 10-9)
7 runs - June 5, 2007 vs. TB (W 12-11)
6 runs - May 14, 2010 vs. TEX (W 16-10)
6 runs - Sept. 17, 2008 vs BAL (W 8-7)
6 runs - June 1, 2003 vs BOS (W 11-8)
6 runs - Sept. 23, 2000 vs TB (W 7-6)
6 runs - Aug. 23, 2000 vs KC (W 9-8)
6 runs - May 7, 1992 at SEA (W 8-7)
6 runs - April 23, 1990 vs CLE (W 12-9)
6 runs - May 16, 1989 vs CLE (W 7-6)
6 runs - Sept. 4, 1988 vs TEX (W 9-7)
6 runs - July 2, 1983 vs SEA (W 7-6)
6 runs - Aug. 19, 1983 vs BOS (W 8-7)
6 runs - June 3, 1980 vs CAL (W 7-6, 11 inn.)
6 runs - Aug. 1, 1980 vs CAL (W 9-8)

LEADS SURRENDERED IN A LOSS:

8 runs - June 4, 1995 at CLE (L 9-8)
8 runs - Sept. 7, 1979 at CILE (L 9-8)
8 runs - Aug. 21, 2006 vs OAK (L 12-10)
8 runs - July 25, 2009 vs TB (L 10-9 in 12 inn.)
7 runs - Aug. 2, 2002 vs BAL (L 9-8)
7 runs - July 2, 1995 vs BAL (L 9-7)
7 runs - April 15, 1994 at CAL (L 14-13)
7 runs - April 11, 2011 at SEA (L 8-7)
6 runs - Aug. 15, 2004 vs BAL (L 11-7)
6 runs - Aug. 15, 2004 vs BAL (L 11-7)
6 runs - May 7, 2000 vs CLE (L 10-8)
6 runs - Aug. 27, 1993 at SEA (L 7-6)
6 runs - July 22, 1988 vs SEA (L 10-9, 11 inn.)
6 runs - May 17, 1985 at MIN (L 7-6, 11 inn.)
6 runs - July 28, 1982 at BOS (L 9-7)
6 runs - Sept. 24, 1980 at DET (L 9-8, 10 inn.)
6 runs - Aug. 15, 2004 vs BAL (L 11-7)
6 runs - Aug. 1, 2008 at TEX (L 9-8)

2012 SEASON IN REVIEW

EDWIN ENCARNACION

2012 TORONTO BLUE JAYS SEASON IN REVIEW

WHERE WE STACKED UP:

Finished the 2012 season with a record of 73-89 (.451), ranking 4th in the AL East for the 5th consecutive year…Ended up 22.0 games back of the 1st place New York Yankees (95-67)…The 73 victories represents Toronto's lowest win total since the 2004 campaign (67-94)…Offensively among the AL, TOR ranked 7th in runs (716), despite the fact that the Blue Jays were the 1st club to 500 runs earlier in the season…Ranked 5th in HR (198), 11th in AVG (.245) & 9th in OPS (.716)…The Blue Jays pitched to a 4.64 ERA (11th in AL), allowed 784 runs (4th most in AL) & fanned 1142 (11th in AL)…Toronto's starting staff ranked 10th in the AL with a 4.82 ERA & the bullpen posted a 4.33 ERA which ranked 14th in the AL.

ON THE HOMEFRONT:

Finished with a 41-40 record at Rogers Centre, recording their 8th consecutive winning season at home & have gone 361-284 (.560) over that stretch…TOR hit 102 home runs at Rogers Centre which ranked 5th in the AL & were 7th in runs scored with 368…Toronto's pitching staff posted an ERA of 4.50 at home which ranked 12th in the AL.

COME ON IN:

Completed the season with a final attendance of 2,099,663 for an average of 25,922 per game…The total ranked 8th in the AL…Exceeded the 2,000,000 mark in home attendance for the 1st time since 2008 (2,400,416)…In fact, it was a 15.49% increase from last year's total of 1,818,103, representing the largest increase the club has seen since the 1st season of SkyDome/Rogers Centre in 1989…Toronto recorded three sellouts this season: April 9 vs. BOS (48,473), June 17 vs. PHI (45,060) & on Aug. 11 vs. NYY (45,582)…Drew 11 crowds of at least 40,000 during the 2012 season…Last season, the Jays had just five crowds of 40,000.

ON THE ROAD:

Posted a 32-49 record on the road & recorded their 9th consecutive losing season away from Rogers Centre…Finished the first half of the season with a 20-24 record on the road & followed that up with a 12-25 record after the All-Star break…The Jays scored 348 runs on the road (7th in AL), hit 96 home runs (4th in AL) & ranked 11th in average (.242).

2012 GLANCING AT THE JAYS

2012 Record	73-89, 4th, 22.0 GB
2012 Attendance (Total & AVG) – 81 dates	2,099,663/25,922
'11 Season (Hm. Attendance)-81 dates	1,818,103/22,446
Come From Behind Wins	31
Last Shutout by Blue Jays	6-0, Sept. 27 vs. NYY
Last Shutout by Opponent	3-0, Sept. 23 at TB
April '12/'11/'10	12-11/13-14/12-12
May '12/'11/'10	15-13/15-13/12-15
June '12/'11/'10	13-14/12-15/9-17
July '12/'11/'10	11-14/15-11/14-11
August '12/'11/'10	9-19/13-15/15-13
September/October '12/'11/'10	13-18/13-13/16-14
Pre All-Star '12/'11/'10	43-43/45-47/44-45
Post All-Star '12/'11/'10	30-46/36-34/41-32
Under JOHN FARRELL	154-170
'11 Season- 162 games	81-81
Best/Worst- 162 games	96-66 ('87,'92)/53-109 ('79)
Vs. RHS/LHS	52-62/21-27
Blue Jays/Opponents scoring first	45-33/28-56
GMS decided in final AB/Walk-Off	11-15/4-7
1-Run/2-Run Games	15-25/11-11
Franchise Record	2828-2879
Home/Road	41-40/32-49
Day/Night	29-30/44-59
Series Record/Home/Road	17-26-9/10-12-4/7-14-5
Vs. EAST/CENTRAL/WEST/NL	29-43/21-16/14-21/9-9
After 7.0, Ahead/Tied/Trailing	63-4/3-10/7-75
After 8.0, Ahead/Tied/Trailing	64-2/4-9/5-78
Extra-Inning Games/Home/Road	7-6/3-1/4-5

2012 AT ROGERS CENTRE

Blue Jays HR Dome Open/Cld	58/44
Opponents HR Dome Open/Cld	60/42
Open/closed/other	22-24/15-14/4-2
All-time	1023-861
Open	546-486
Closed	416-331
Open/Closed	61-44

HOMESTANDS & ROAD TRIPS:

Homestands	Opponent(s)	Record	YtD
April 9-19	BOS (3), BAL (3), TB (3)	4-5	4-5
April 27- May 2	SEA (3), TEX (3)	4-2	8-7
May 14-20	TB (2), NYY (2), NYM (3)	4-3	12-10
May 28- June 3	BAL (3), BOS (3)	4-2	16-12
June 11-17	WAS (3), PHI (3)	3-3	19-15
June 28- July 5	LAA (4), KC (4)	4-4	23-19
July 13-15	CLE (3)	2-1	25-20
July 24-29	OAK (3), DET (3)	3-3	28-23
Aug. 10-19	NYY (3), CHI (4), TEX (3)	3-7	31-30
Aug. 30-Sept. 5	TB (4), BAL (3)	3-4	34-34
Sept. 11-16	SEA (3), BOS (3)	2-4	36-38
Sept. 27-Oct. 3	NYY (4), MIN (3)	5-2	41-40

Road Trips	Opponent(s)	Record	YtD
April 5-8	CLE (3)	2-1	2-1
April 20-26	KC (4), BAL (3)	4-3	6-4
May 3-13	LAA (4), OAK (2), MIN (4)	5-5	11-9
May 21-27	TB (3), TEX (3)	1-5	12-14
June 5-10	CHI (3), ATL (3)	3-3	15-17
June 18-27	MIL (3), MIA (3), BOS (3)	4-5	19-22
July 6-8	CHI (3)	1-2	20-24
July 16-22	NYY (3), BOS (3)	3-3	23-27
July 30- Aug. 9	SEA (3), OAK (4), TB (3)	2-8	25-35
Aug. 20-29	DET (3), BAL (3), NYY (3)	2-6	27-41
Sept. 7-9	BOS (3)	3-0	30-41
Sept. 18-26	NYY (3), TB (3), BAL (3)	2-8	32-49

CROWDS OF 40,000 OR MORE AT ROGERS CENTRE (RANKED IN ORDER OF ATTENDANCE)

Date	Opponent	Attendance	Result	Record
9-April	Boston	48,473	L 2-4	0-1
11-Aug.	New York Yankees	45,582	L 5-2	4-6
17-June	Philadelphia	45,060	W 6-2	3-4
12-Aug.	New York Yankees	43,924	W 10-7	5-6
2-June	Boston	43,390	L 4-7	0-3
16-June	Philadelphia	42,070	W 6-5	2-4
3-June	Boston	41,925	W 5-1	1-3
20-May	New York Mets	41,867	L 5-6	0-2
28-July	Detroit	41,832	W 5-1	4-4
13-June	Washington	41,677	L 2-6	1-4
10-Aug.	New York Yankees	41,610	L 10-4	4-5

2012 MAJOR LEAGUE STANDINGS

A.L. EAST	WON	LOST	PCT.	GB	LAST 10 GAMES	STREAK	HOME	ROAD	vs EAST	vs CENT	vs WEST	vs N.L.
* NEW YORK	95	67	.586	-	7-3	WON 4	51-30	44-37	41-31	21-16	20-15	13-5
x BALTIMORE	93	69	.574	2.0	6-4	LOST 1	47-34	46-35	43-29	23-15	16-18	11-7
x TAMPA BAY	90	72	.556	5.0	8-2	WON 1	46-35	44-37	41-31	16-18	24-14	9-9
x **TORONTO**	**73**	**89**	**.451**	**22.0**	**7-3**	**WON 3**	**41-40**	**32-49**	**29-43**	**21-16**	**14-21**	**9-9**
x BOSTON	69	93	.426	26.0	1-9	LOST 8	34-47	35-46	26-46	24-16	8-24	11-7

A.L. CENTRAL	WON	LOST	PCT.	GB	LAST 10 GAMES	STREAK	HOME	ROAD	vs EAST	vs CENT	vs WEST	vs N.L.
* DETROIT	88	74	.543	-	8-2	WON 1	50-31	38-43	21-18	43-29	13-20	11-7
x CHICAGO	85	77	.525	3.0	4-6	WON 1	45-36	40-41	19-21	37-35	20-12	9-9
x KANSAS CITY	72	90	.444	16.0	2-8	LOST 1	37-44	35-46	16-21	34-38	14-21	8-10
x CLEVELAND	68	94	.420	20.0	6-4	LOST 1	37-44	31-50	14-22	31-41	15-21	8-10
x MINNESOTA	66	96	.407	22.0	3-7	LOST 5	31-50	35-46	11-23	35-37	11-27	9-9

A.L. WEST	WON	LOST	PCT.	GB	LAST 10 GAMES	STREAK	HOME	ROAD	vs EAST	vs CENT	vs WEST	vs N.L.
* OAKLAND	94	68	.580	-	8-2	WON 6	50-31	44-37	28-18	23-18	33-24	10-8
x TEXAS	93	69	.574	1.0	3-7	LOST 3	50-31	43-38	24-16	28-19	27-30	14-4
x LOS ANGELES	89	73	.549	5.0	6-4	LOST 2	46-35	43-38	22-20	25-20	30-27	12-6
x SEATTLE	75	87	.463	19.0	3-7	WON 2	40-41	35-46	18-28	25-16	24-33	8-10

N.L. EAST	WON	LOST	PCT.	GB	LAST 10 GAMES	STREAK	HOME	ROAD	vs EAST	vs CENT	vs WEST	vs A.L.
* WASHINGTON	98	64	.605	-	6-4	WON 2	50-31	48-33	42-30	29-13	17-13	10-8
y ATLANTA	94	68	.580	4.0	7-3	WON 1	48-33	46-35	46-26	19-19	21-13	8-10
PHILADELPHIA	81	81	.500	17.0	4-6	LOST 2	40-41	41-40	33-39	24-16	19-16	5-10
NEW YORK	74	88	.457	24.0	5-5	WON 1	36-45	38-43	32-40	17-22	17-19	8-7
MIAMI	69	93	.426	29.0	3-7	LOST 1	38-43	31-50	27-45	18-20	19-15	5-13

N.L. CENTRAL	WON	LOST	PCT.	GB	LAST 10 GAMES	STREAK	HOME	ROAD	vs EAST	vs CENT	vs WEST	vs A.L.
* CINCINNATI	97	65	.599	-	5-5	LOST 1	50-31	47-34	19-15	49-30	22-12	7-8
ST. LOUIS	88	74	.543	9.0	7-3	WON 1	50-31	38-43	14-20	45-32	21-15	8-7
MILWAUKEE	83	79	.512	14.0	4-6	LOST 1	49-32	34-47	15-19	45-34	17-17	6-9
PITTSBURGH	79	83	.488	18.0	4-6	LOST 1	45-36	34-47	17-14	39-42	13-19	10-8
CHICAGO	61	101	.377	36.0	2-8	WON 1	38-43	23-58	13-19	31-50	12-22	5-10
HOUSTON	55	107	.340	42.0	5-5	LOST 1	35-46	20-61	12-20	29-50	8-28	6-9

N.L. WEST	WON	LOST	PCT.	GB	LAST 10 GAMES	STREAK	HOME	ROAD	vs EAST	vs CENT	vs WEST	vs A.L.
* SAN FRANCISCO	94	68	.580	-	5-5	LOST 1	48-33	46-35	15-19	27-14	45-27	7-8
LOS ANGELES	86	76	.531	8.0	8-2	WON 1	45-36	41-40	20-12	25-18	35-37	6-9
ARIZONA	81	81	.500	13.0	4-6	LOST 1	41-40	40-41	14-20	20-21	38-34	9-6
SAN DIEGO	76	86	.469	18.0	4-6	WON 1	42-39	34-47	12-20	22-21	34-38	8-7
COLORADO	64	98	.395	30.0	6-4	WON 1	35-46	29-52	15-22	19-19	28-44	2-13

* -CLINCHED DIVISION TITLE
x -ELIMINATED
y -CLINCHED PLAYOFF BERTH

WILD CARD STANDINGS

AMERICAN LEAGUE DIVISION LEADERS

Team	Wins	Losses	Pct.	GB
NEW YORK	95	67	.586	-
DETROIT	88	74	.543	-
OAKLAND	94	68	.580	-

AMERICAN LEAGUE WILD CARD RACE

Team	Wins	Losses	Pct.	GB
z BALTIMORE	93	69	.574	-
z TEXAS	93	69	.574	-
TAMPA BAY	90	72	.556	3.0
LOS ANGELES	89	73	.549	4.0
CHICAGO	85	77	.525	8.0

z -Clinched Wild Card

NATIONAL LEAGUE DIVISION LEADERS

Team	Wins	Losses	Pct.	GB
WASHINGTON	98	64	.605	-
CINCINNATI	97	65	.599	-
SAN FRANCISCO	94	68	.580	-

NATIONAL LEAGUE WILD CARD RACE

Team	Wins	Losses	Pct.	GB
z ATLANTA	94	68	.580	-
z ST. LOUIS	88	74	.543	-
LOS ANGELES	86	76	.531	2.0
MILWAUKEE	83	79	.512	5.0
ARIZONA	81	81	.500	7.0
PHILADELPHIA	81	81	.500	7.0
PITTSBURGH	79	83	.488	9.0

z -Clinched Wild Card

2012 MISCELLANEOUS STATISTICS

	HOME		ROAD		TOTALS	
	W	L	W	L	W	L
VS. BALTIMORE	5	4	2	7	7	11
VS. BOSTON	4	5	7	2	11	7
VS. NEW YORK	5	4	2	7	7	11
VS. TAMPA BAY	3	6	1	8	4	14
TOTALS VS. EAST	**17**	**19**	**12**	**24**	**29**	**43**
VS. CLEVELAND	2	1	2	1	4	2
VS. CHICAGO	1	3	3	3	4	6
VS. DETROIT	2	1	0	3	2	4
VS. KANSAS CITY	2	2	4	0	6	2
VS. MINNESOTA	3	0	2	2	5	2
TOTALS VS. CENTRAL	**10**	**7**	**11**	**9**	**21**	**16**
VS. LOS ANGELES	2	2	2	2	4	4
VS. OAKLAND	1	2	3	3	4	5
VS. SEATTLE	3	3	0	3	3	6
VS. TEXAS	3	3	0	3	3	6
TOTALS VS. WEST	**9**	**10**	**5**	**11**	**14**	**21**
TOTALS VS. A.L.	**36**	**36**	**28**	**44**	**64**	**80**
VS. ATLANTA	0	0	1	2	1	2
VS. MIAMI	0	0	2	1	2	1
VS. MILWAUKEE	0	0	1	2	1	2
VS. WASHINGTON	0	3	0	0	0	3
VS. NEW YORK	2	1	0	0	2	1
VS. PHILADELPHIA	3	0	0	0	3	0
TOTALS VS. N.L.	**5**	**4**	**4**	**5**	**9**	**9**
OVERALL TOTALS	**41**	**40**	**32**	**49**	**73**	**89**

DOUBLEHEADERS
(HOME) WON 0 LOST 0 SPLIT 0
(ROAD) WON 0 LOST 0 SPLIT 1
ATTENDANCE
HOME 2,099,663 (81 DATES) 25,922 AVG
ROAD 2,326,019 (80 DATES) 29,075 AVG

	TOR	OPP.
DOUBLE PLAYS	167	135
TRIPLE PLAYS	1	0
LEFT ON BASE	1026	1101
GRAND SLAM HR	3	8
HOME RUNS - HOME	102	102
HOME RUNS - ROAD	96	102

	HOME		ROAD		TOTALS	
	W	L	W	L	W	L
SHUTOUTS	7	4	4	5	11	9
SHO - INDIVIDUAL	1	0	3	1	4	1
EXTRA INNINGS	3	1	4	5	7	6
ONE-RUN DECISIONS	9	9	6	16	15	25
TWO-RUN DECISIONS	7	5	4	6	11	11
VS. LH STARTERS	11	13	10	14	21	27
VS. RH STARTERS	30	27	22	35	52	62
GRASS FIELDS	0	0	31	41	31	41
ARTIFICIAL FIELDS	41	40	1	8	42	48
DAY GAMES	17	14	12	16	29	30
NIGHT GAMES	24	26	20	33	44	59

	WON	LOST
STARTERS	52	69
RELIEVERS	21	20
STREAKS	4	7

ALL-STARS & AWARD WINNERS:

ALL-STAR GAME:

For the 3rd consecutive season, OF Jose Bautista was named to the American League All-Star team…Was voted in as a starter for the 2nd straight year…Ranked 3rd in voting among OF at 4,971,155…Is the 3rd Jay to be voted in as a starter in back to back seasons (Roberto Alomar & Joe Carter being the others)…Started in RF, batted 4th (0-1, BB, K)…Represented the AL in the 2012 State Farm Home Run Derby…Lost in the finals to Prince Fielder…Marked the 2nd straight year that he took part in the HR Derby.

MLB AWARDS:

AL Player of the Week: J.P. Arencibia (May 14-20) – It marked the 1st time J.P. has earned the weekly honor and it marks the 1st time ever that a Blue Jays catcher…In six games, Arencibia batted .360 (9-for-25) with four home runs, 10 RBI and seven runs scored…Recorded a .920 SLG & 23 total bases while adding two doubles & a walk.

AL Player of the Month: Jose Bautista (June) - Batted .271 (26-for-96) with four doubles, 14 home runs, 30 RBI, 22 walks & 24 runs scored in 27 games during June to capture his 5th career monthly award…Finished tops in homers, RBI and slugging percentage (.750), T-1st in walks & extra-base hits (18)…His 14 homers established a new Club record for the most hit in any single month & it marked the most hit in a calendar month by any player since Colorado's Troy Tulowitzki hit 15 round trippers in September 2010…It also was the most for an A.L. player since New York's Alex Rodriguez hit 14 home runs in April 2007.

BBWAA AWARDS:

HONDA PLAYER OF THE MONTH:

APRIL: Edwin Encarnacion (23G, 8-2B, 8-HR, 21-RBI, .322 AVG, 1.054 OPS)
MAY: Jose Bautista (28G, 4-2B, 9-HR, 22-RBI, .234 AVG, .894 OPS)
JUNE: Jose Bautista (27G, 4-2B, 14-HR, 30-RBI, 22-BB, .271 AVG, 1.158 OPS)
JULY: Carlos Villanueva (4GS, 4-0, 1.93 ERA, 23.1 IP, 15H, 5ER, 9-BB, 23-SO)
AUGUST: Edwin Encarnacion (27G, 3-2B, 7-HR, 18-RBI, .270 AVG, .883 OPS)
SEPTEMBER: Edwin Encarnacion (24G, 7-HR, 20-RBI, 18-BB, .238 AVG, .889 OPS)

TORONTO BLUE JAYS 2012 DAY BY DAY

* Sellout Date & Opp	W/L	Score	Time	Attend.	Record/H/R	Pos.	CAPS=CG r=relief Win/Loss/Save
4/4				OFF DAY			
4/5 @ CLE	W	7-4 (16)	5:14	43,190	1-0/0-0/1-0	1st, 0.5 GA	**Perez-r**/Ascencio
4/6				OFF DAY		T-1st, --GA	
4/7 @ CLE	W	7-4 (12)	3:38	18,842	2-0/0-0/2-0	1st, 1.0 GA	**Janssen-r**/Sipp
4/8 @ CLE	L	3-4	2:51	10,518	2-1/0-0/2-1	3rd, 1.0 GB	Lowe/**Carreno**/Perez
4/9 BOS	L	2-4	3:02	* 48,473	2-2/0-1/2-1	3rd, 1.5 GB	Atchison-R/**Santos-R**/Aceves
4/10 BOS	W	7-3	3:19	26,351	3-2/1-1/2-1	3rd, 0.5 GB	**Drabek**/Bard
4/11 BOS	W	3-1	2:13	25,285	4-2/2-1/2-1	2nd, 0.5 GB	**Romero**/LESTER/**Santos**
4/12				OFF DAY		T-1st, --GA	
4/13 BAL	L	5-7	2:40	21,988	4-3/2-2/2-1	T-1st, --GA	O'Day-R/**Oliver-R**/Johnson
4/14 BAL	L	4-6	2:57	28,355	4-4/2-3/2-1	T-2nd, 1.0 GB	Ayala-R/**Cordero-R**/Johnson
4/15 BAL	W	9-2	2:39	20,252	5-4/3-3/2-1	T-1st, --GA	**Drabek**/Matusz
4/16				OFF DAY		2nd, 0.5 GB	
4/17 TB	W	7-3	3:05	15,331	6-4/4-3/2-1	2nd, 0.5 GB	**Romero**/Niemann
4/18 TB	L	2-12	3:11	15,828	6-5/4-4/2-1	2nd, 0.5 GB	Price/**Morrow**
4/19 TB	L	4-9	3:43	18,976	6-6/4-5/2-1	4th, 1.5 GB	Hellickson/**Alvarez**
4/20 @ KC	W	4-3	3:14	23,065	7-6/4-5/3-1	3rd, 0.5 GB	**Perez-R**/Holland-R/**Santos**
4/21 @ KC	W	9-5	3:03	27,804	8-6/4-5/4-1	2nd, 0.5 GB	**Hutchison**/Teaford-R
4/22 @ KC	W	5-3	3:08	26,891	9-6/4-5/5-1	T-1st, --GA	**Romero**/Duffy/**Cordero**
4/23 @ KC	W	4-1	2:31	13,267	10-6/4-5/6-1	T-1st, --GA	**Morrow**/Chen/**Cordero**
4/24 @ BAL	L	1-2	2:22	11,058	10-7/4-5/6-2	T-1st, --GA	Hunter/**Alvarez**/Strop
4/25 @ BAL	L	0-3	2:24	10,415	10-8/4-5/6-3	T-3rd, 1.0 GB	Hammel/**Drabek**/Strop
4/26 @ BAL	L	2-5	2:51	13,725	10-9/4-5/6-4	4th, 2.0 GB	O'Day-R/**Janssen-R**/Ayala
4/27 SEA	L	5-9 (10)	3:35	24,303	10-10/4-6/6-4	4th, 3.0 GB	Furbush/**Perez**
4/28 SEA	W	7-0	2:45	30,765	11-10/5-6/6-4	4th, 2.0 GB	Morrow/Millwood
4/29 SEA	W	7-2	2:36	22,320	12-10/6-6/6-4	4th, 2.0 GB	**Alvarez**/Vargas
4/30 TEX	L	1-4	2:59	21,945	12-11/6-7/6-4	4th, 3.0 GB	Darvish/**Drabek**/Nathan
5/1 TEX	W	8-7	2:56	18,774	13-11/7-7/6-4	4th, 3.0 GB	**Cordero-R**/Adams-R
5/2 TEX	W	11-5	2:45	25,123	14-11/8-7/6-4	3rd, 3.0 GB	**Romero**/Harrison
5/3 @ LAA	W	5-0	2:11	28,359	15-11/8-7/7-4	3rd, 3.0 GB	**MORROW**/Haren
5/4 @ LAA	W	4-0	2:10	33,160	16-11/8-7/8-4	3rd, 3.0 GB	**ALVAREZ**/Santana
5/5 @ LAA	L	2-6	2:54	39,018	16-12/8-7/8-5	3rd, 3.0 GB	Wilson/**Drabek**
5/6 @ LAA	L	3-4	2:51	37,548	16-13/8-7/8-6	3rd, 3.0 GB	Williams/**Hutchison**/Hawkins
5/7				OFF DAY		3rd, 3.0 GB	
5/8 @ OAK	L	3-7	2:58	10,784	16-14/8-7/8-7	4th, 3.0 GB	Balfour-R/**Cordero-R**
5/9 @ OAK	W	5-2	3:01	14,815	17-14/8-7/9-7	3rd, 3.0 GB	**Morrow**/Ross/**Janssen**
5/10 @ MIN	W	6-2	2:45	31,438	18-14/8-7/10-7	3rd, 2.0 GB	**Alvarez**/Marquis
5/11 @ MIN	L	6-7	3:17	33,387	18-15/8-7/10-8	4th, 3.0 GB	Blackburn/**Drabek**/Capps
5/12 @ MIN	W	2-1	2:50	38,820	19-15/8-7/11-8	4th, 3.0 GB	**Hutchison**/Walters/**Janssen**
5/13 @ MIN	L	3-4	2:59	36,889	19-16/8-7/11-9	4th, 3.0 GB	Diamond/**Romero**/Capps
5/14 TB	L	1-7	3:21	15,289	19-17/8-8/11-9	4th, 3.0 GB	Ramos-R/**Morrow**
5/15 TB	L	3-4	2:36	15,612	19-18/8-9/11-9	4th, 4.0 GB	Price/**Alvarez**/Rodney
5/16 NYY	W	8-1	2:45	28,915	20-18/9-9/11-9	4th, 4.0 GB	**Drabek**/Kuroda
5/17 NYY	W	4-1	2:37	31,266	21-18/10-9/11-9	3rd, 4.0 GB	**Hutchison**/Hughes/**Janssen**
5/18 NYM	W	14-5	2:53	26,712	22-18/11-9/11-9	3rd, 4.0 GB	**Romero**/Niese
5/19 NYM	W	2-0	2:12	34,962	23-18/12-9/11-9	3rd, 4.0 GB	**MORROW**/Hefner-R
5/20 NYM	L	5-6	3:15	41,867	23-19/12-10/11-9	3rd, 4.0 GB	Gee/**Alvarez**/Francisco
5/21 @ TB	W	6-2	3:13	10,844	24-19/12-10/12-9	3rd, 3.0 GB	**Drabek**/Hellickson
5/22 @ TB	L	5-8	3:03	12,307	24-20/12-10/12-10	3rd, 4.0 GB	Davis-R/**Hutchison**/Rodney
5/23 @ TB	L	4-5 (11)	3:57	11,471	24-21/12-10/12-11	3rd, 4.0 GB	McGee-R/**Oliver-R**
5/24				OFF DAY		3rd, 4.0 GB	
5/25 @ TEX	L	3-14	3:17	46,789	24-22/12-10/12-12	4th, 5.0 GB	Holland/**Morrow**
5/26 @ TEX	L	7-8 (13)	4:38	47,430	24-23/12-10/12-13	4th, 5.0 GB	Tateyama-R/**Frasor-R**
5/27 @ TEX	L	6-12	2:48	46,637	24-24/12-10/12-14	4th, 5.0 GB	Darvish/**Drabek**
5/28 BAL	W	6-2	2:48	16,575	25-24/13-10/12-14	4th, 4.0 GB	**Hutchison**/Hunter/**Janssen**
5/29 BAL	W	8-6	3:11	17,352	26-24/14-10/12-14	4th, 3.0 GB	**Romero**/Arrieta
5/30 BAL	W	4-1	2:28	17,754	27-24/15-10/12-14	4th, 2.0 GB	**Morrow**/Hammel/**Janssen**
5/31				OFF DAY		T-4th, 3.0 GB	
6/1 BOS	L	2-7	3:00	29,678	27-25/15-11/12-14	T-4th, 3.0 GB	Buchholz/**Alvarez**
6/2 BOS	L	4-7	3:05	43,390	27-26/15-12/12-14	5th, 3.0 GB	Doubront/**Drabek**/Aceves
6/3 BOS	W	5-1	2:52	41,925	28-26/16-12/12-14	T-4th, 3.0 GB	**Hutchison**/Bard
6/4				OFF DAY		T-4th, 3.0 GB	
6/5 @ CWS	W	9-5	2:44	23,107	29-26/16-12/13-14	4th, 2.0 GB	**Romero**/Humber
6/6 @ CWS	W	4-0	2:50	25,672	30-26/16-12/14-14	4th, 2.0 GB	**MORROW**/Quintana
6/7 @ CWS	L	3-4	2:50	25,743	30-27/16-12/14-15	4th, 2.0 GB	Reed-R/**Cordero-R**
6/8 @ ATL	L	3-4(10)	3:53	42,488	30-28/16-12/14-16	4th, 3.0 GB	Martinez-R/**Cordero-R**
6/9 @ ATL	L	2-5	2:34	32,819	30-29/16-12/14-17	4th, 4.0 GB	Hanson/**Hutchison**/Kimbrel
6/10 @ ATL	W	12-4	3:14	20,222	31-29/16-12/15-17	4th, 4.0 GB	**Villanueva-R**/Henrnadez-R
6/11 WSH	L	3-6	3:03	18,513	31-30/16-13/15-17	4th, 4.5 GB	Jackson/**Morrow**
6/12 WSH	L	2-4	2:52	22,538	31-31/16-14/15-17	4th, 5.5 GB	Wang/**Alvarez**/Clippard
6/13 WSH	L	2-6	2:52	41,677	31-32/16-15/15-17	T-4th, 6.5 GB	Strasburg/**Drabek**
6/14				OFF DAY		T-4th, 6.5 GB	
6/15 PHI	W	3-0	2:47	28,266	32-32/17-15/15-17	4th, 6.5 GB	**Villanueva-R**/Worley/**Janssen**
6/16 PHI	W	6-5 (10)	3:14	42,070	33-32/18-15/15-17	4th, 6.5 GB	**Cordero-R**/Savery-R
6/17 PHI	W	6-2	2:46	* 45,060	34-32/19-15/15-17	4th, 6.5 GB	**Cecil**/Kendrick
6/18 @ MIL	L	6-7	2:52	32,223	34-33/19-15/15-18	4th, 7.5 GB	Loe-R/**Coello-R**/Axford
6/19 @ MIL	W	10-9	3:46	36,334	35-33/19-15/16-18	4th, 6.5 GB	**Oliver-R**/Axford-R
6/20 @ MIL	L	3-8	3:03	33,077	35-34/19-15/16-19	5th, 6.5 GB	Gallardo/**Carreno**
6/21				OFF DAY		5th, 6.5 GB	
6/22 @ MIA	W	12-5	3:02	22,387	36-34/19-15/17-19	5th, 5.5 GB	**Romero**/Sanchez
6/23 @ MIA	W	7-1	2:49	24,448	37-34/19-15/18-19	T-4th, 5.5 GB	**Oliver-R**/Cishek
6/24 @ MIA	L	0-9	2:29	27,888	37-35/19-15/18-20	5th, 6.5 GB	Buehrle/Chavez
6/25 @ BOS	W	9-6	3:01	37,208	38-35/19-15/19-20	T-4th, 6.5 GB	**Alvarez**/Doubront/**Janssen**
6/26 @ BOS	L	1-5	3:02	37,755	38-36/19-15/19-21	5th, 7.5 GB	Miller-R/**Perez-R**
6/27 @ BOS	L	4-10	2:40	37,744	38-37/19-15/19-22	5th, 8.5 GB	Lester/**Romero**
6/28 LAA	L	7-9	3:16	24,668	38-38/19-16/19-22	5th, 8.5 GB	Haren/**Cecil**/Frieri
6/29 LAA	W	7-5	3:12	24,538	39-38/20-16/19-22	5th, 7.5 GB	Cordero-R/**Walden-R**/Janssen
6/30 LAA	W	11-2	2:44	29,287	40-38/21-16/19-22	5th, 7.5 GB	**Alvarez**/Richards
7/1 LAA	L	6-10	3:29	34,853	40-39/21-17/19-22	5th, 8.5 GB	Isringhausen-R/**Cordero-R**
7/2 KC	L	3-11	2:36	17,127	40-40/21-18/19-22	5th, 8.5 GB	Teaford/**Romero**

Date & Opp	W/L	Score	Time	Attend.	Record/H/R	Pos.	CAPS=CG r=relief Win/Loss/Save
7/3 KC	W	6-3	2:30	15,516	41-40/22-18/19-22	5th, 7.5 GB	**Cecil**/Mazzaro/**Janssen**
7/4 KC	W	4-1	2:45	17,831	42-40/23-18/19-22	T-4th, 7.5 GB	**Villanueva**/Mendoza/**Janssen**
7/5 KC	L	6-9	3:16	20,598	42-41/23-19/19-22	5th, 8.0 GB	Hochevar/**Alvarez**/Broxton
7/6 @ CWS	L	2-4	2:31	27,129	42-42/23-19/19-23	5th, 9.0 GB	Peavy/**Laffey**/Reed
7/7 @ CWS	L	0-2	2:25	25,399	42-43/23-19/19-24	5th, 9.5 GB	Floyd/**Romero**/Thornton
7/8 @ CWS	W	11-9	3:48	27,190	43-43/23-19/20-24	T-4th, 9.5 GB	**Frasor-R**/Axelrod/**Janssen**
7/9-12			ALL-STAR BREAK			T-4th, 9.5 GB	
7/13 CLE	L	0-1	2:40	32,308	43-44/23-20/20-24	5th, 10.5 GB	Masterson/**Romero**/Perez
7/14 CLE	W	11-9	3:15	32,517	44-44/24-20/20-24	T-4th, 10.5 GB	**Laffey**/Jimenez/**Janssen**
7/15 CLE	W	3-0	2:42	26,407	45-44/25-20/20-24	T-4th, 9.5 GB	**Villanueva**/Lowe/**Oliver**
7/16 @ NYY	L	3-6	3:04	42,819	45-45/25-20/20-25	5th, 10.5 GB	Robertson-R/**Loup-R**/Soriano
7/17 @ NYY	L	1-6	3:08	44,975	45-46/25-20/20-26	5th, 11.5 GB	Sabathia/**Cecil**/Soriano
7/18 @ NYY	L	0-6 (7)	2:12	45,986	45-47/25-20/20-27	5th, 12.5 GB	KURODA/**Romero**
7/19				OFF-DAY		5th, 12.0 GB	
7/20 @ BOS	W	6-1	3:01	38,093	46-47/25-20/21-27	5th, 11.0 GB	**Laffey**/Beckett
7/21 @ BOS	W	7-3	3:04	38,170	47-47/25-20/22-27	5th, 10.0 GB	**Villanueva**/Cook
7/22 @ BOS	W	15-7	3:28	37,737	48-47/25-20/23-27	4th, 9.0 GB	**Alvarez**/Lester
7/23				OFF-DAY		4th, 9.5 GB	
7/24 OAK	L	2-7	3:00	25,686	48-48/25-21/23-27	T-4th, 9.5 GB	Blackley/**Cecil**
7/25 OAK	L	0-16	3:12	23,948	48-49/25-22/23-27	T-4th, 10.5 GB	Griffin/**Romero**
7/26 OAK	W	10-4	2:38	39,003	49-49/26-22/23-27	4th, 10.0 GB	**Lyon-R**/Milone
7/27 DET	W	8-3	2:52	33,962	50-49/27-22/23-27	4th, 10.0 GB	**Villanueva**/Porcello
7/28 DET	W	5-1	2:34	41,832	51-49/28-22/23-27	4th, 9.0 GB	**Alvarez**/Sanchez
7/29 DET	L	1-4	2:33	35,975	51-50/28-23/23-27	4th, 9.0 GB	Fister/**Cecil**/Valverde
7/30 @ SEA	L	1-4	2:45	22,443	51-51/28-23/23-28	5th, 9.0 GB	Iwakuma/**Romero**/Luetge
7/31 @ SEA	L	2-7	2:54	21,434	51-52/28-23/23-29	5th, 9.0 GB	Vargas/**Laffey**
8/1 @ SEA	L	3-5	2:21	22,537	51-53/28-23/23-30	5th, 10.0 GB	Beavan/**Villanueva**/Wilhelmsen
8/2 @ OAK	L	1-4	2:47	10,823	51-54/28-23/23-31	5th, 10.5 GB	Colon/**Alvarez**/Cook
8/3 @ OAK	L	4-5 (15)	4:47	30,169	51-55/28-23/23-32	5th, 11.5 GB	Blackley-R/**Loup-R**
8/4 @ OAK	W	3-1 (11)	3:37	17,121	52-55/28-23/24-32	5th, 10.5 GB	**Chavez-R**/Blevins/**Oliver**
8/5 @ OAK	W	6-5	2:57	18,308	53-55/28-23/25-32	5th, 10.0 GB	**Laffey**/Milone/**Janssen**
8/6				OFF-DAY		5th, 10.0 GB	
8/7 @ TB	L	1-4	2:35	13,823	53-56/28-23/25-33	5th, 10.0 GB	Shields/**Happ**/Rodney
8/8 @ TB	L	2-3	2:42	13,441	53-57/28-23/25-34	5th, 11.0 GB	Cobb/**Villanueva**/Rodney
8/9 @ TB	L	1-7	2:54	23,462	53-58/28-23/25-35	5th, 12.0 GB	Moore/**Alvarez**
8/10 NYY	L	3-10	3:08	41,610	53-59/28-24/25-35	5th, 13.0 GB	Garcia/**Romero**
8/11 NYY	L	2-5	2:47	* 45,582	53-60/28-25/25-35	5th, 14.0 GB	Nova/**Laffey**
8/12 NYY	W	10-7	2:49	43,924	54-60/29-25/25-35	5th, 13.0 GB	**Happ**/Hughes/**Janssen**
8/13 CWS	W	3-2 (11)	3:05	16,828	55-60/30-25/25-35	5th, 13.0 GB	**Delabar-R**/Jones-R
8/14 CWS	L	2-3	2:31	18,919	55-61/30-26/25-35	5th, 14.0 GB	Quintana/**Alvarez**/Reed
8/15 CWS	L	5-9	2:39	20,119	55-62/30-27/25-35	5th, 15.0 GB	Floyd/**Romero**
8/16 CWS	L	2-7	2:34	19,855	55-63/30-28/25-35	5th, 15.0 GB	Liriano/**Laffey**
8/17 TEX	W	3-2	2:42	26,816	56-63/31-28/25-35	5th, 15.0 GB	**Happ**/Darvish/**Janssen**
8/18 TEX	L	1-2	2:47	30,033	56-64/31-29/25-35	5th, 15.0 GB	Kirkman-R/**Villanueva**/Nathan
8/19 TEX	L	2-11	2:34	35,701	56-65/31-30/25-35	5th, 16.0 GB	Harrison/**Alvarez**
8/20				OFF-DAY		5th, 15.5 GB	
8/21 @ DET	L	3-5	2:56	39,499	56-66/31-30/25-36	5th, 15.5 GB	Scherzer/**Romero**/Valverde
8/22 @ DET	L	2-3	2:47	37,225	56-67/31-30/25-37	5th, 15.5 GB	Sanchez/**Laffey**/Valverde
8/23 @ DET	L	2-3 (11)	3:25	39,910	56-68/31-30/25-38	5th, 16.0 GB	Benoit-R/**Jenkins-R**
8/24 @ BAL	L	4-6	2:52	25,754	56-69/31-30/25-39	5th, 17.0 GB	Britton/**Villanueva**/Johnson
8/25 @ BAL	L	2-8	2:41	25,082	56-70/31-30/25-40	5th, 17.0 GB	S. Johnson/**Morrow**
8/26 @ BAL Postponed Due To Rain (re-scheduled for Sept. 24 as a DH)						5th, 17.5 GB	--
8/27 @ NYY	W	8-7 (11)	3:44	42,962	57-70/31-30/26-40	5th, 16.5 GB	**Oliver-R**/Lowe-R
8/28 @ NYY	L	1-2	2:28	42,472	57-71/31-30/26-40	5th, 17.5 GB	Hughes/**Romero**/Soriano
8/29 @ NYY	W	8-5	3:37	46,010	58-71/31-30/27-40	5th, 16.5 GB	**Happ**/Sabathia/**Janssen**
8/30 TB	W	2-0	2:34	22,711	59-71/32-30/27-40	5th, 16.0 GB	**Villanueva**/Moore/**Janssen**
8/31 TB	W	2-1	2:28	20,158	60-71/33-30/27-40	5th, 15.0 GB	**Morrow**/Hellickson/**Janssen**
9/1 TB	L	4-5	3:14	20,478	60-72/33-31/27-40	5th, 16.0 GB	Davis-R/**Alvarez**/Rodney
9/2 TB	L	4-9	2:58	18,568	60-73/33-32/27-40	5th, 16.0 GB	Price/**Romero**
9/3 BAL	L	0-4	2:51	17,220	60-74/33-33/27-40	5th, 16.0 GB	Saunders/**Happ**
9/4 BAL	L	0-12	2:48	13,556	60-75/33-34/27-41	5th, 16.0 GB	Britton/**Villanueva**
9/5 BAL	W	6-4	2:46	14,458	61-75/34-34/27-40	5th, 16.0 GB	**Delabar-R**/Gonzalez
9/6				OFF-DAY		5th, 15.5 GB	
9/7 @ BOS	W	7-5	3:08	37,156	62-75/34-34/28-40	5th, 15.5 GB	**Alvarez**/Doubront
9/8 @ BOS	W	9-2	2:55	37,107	63-75/34-34/29-40	4th, 14.5 GB	**Lincoln-R**/Matsuzaka
9/9 @ BOS	W	4-3	3:03	37,226	64-75/34-34/30-41	4th, 14.5 GB	**Lyon-R**/Buchholz/Janssen
9/10				OFF-DAY		4th, 14.5 GB	
9/11 SEA	L	3-4	2:48	12,935	64-76/34-35/30-41	4th, 14.5 GB	Ramirez/**Morrow**/Wilhelmsen
9/12 SEA	L	2-3	2:55	13,519	64-77/34-36/30-41	4th, 15.5 GB	Millwood/**Romero**/Wilhelmsen
9/13 SEA	W	8-3	2:39	13,756	65-77/35-36/30-41	4th, 15.5 GB	**Alvarez**/Henrandez
9/14 BOS	L	5-8	3:42	21,888	65-78/35-37/30-41	4th, 15.5 GB	Carpenter-R/**Oliver-R**/Bailey
9/15 BOS	L	2-3	3:09	27,325	65-79/35-38/30-41	5th, 16.5 GB	Breslow-R/**Delabar-R**/Bailey
9/16 BOS	W	5-0	2:42	21,698	66-79/36-38/30-41	4th, 16.5 GB	**Lyon-R**/Lester
9/17				OFF-DAY		4th, 16.5 GB	
9/18 @ NYY Postponed Due To Rain (re-scheduled for Sept. 19 as a DH)						5th, 16.5 GB	
9/19 @ NYY (1)	L	2-4	2:41	39,859	66-80/36-38/30-42	5th, 17.5 GB	Pettitte/**Alvarez**/Soriano
9/19 @ NYY (2)	L	1-2	3:06	39,997	66-81/36-38/30-43	5th, 18.5 GB	Eppley-R/**Delabar-R**/Soriano
9/20 @ NYY	L	7-10	3:41	40,511	66-82/36-38/30-44	5th, 19.5 GB	Hughes/**Laffey**/Robertson
9/21 @ TB	L	1-12	2:56	14,187	66-83/36-38/30-45	5th, 20.5 GB	Shields/**Villanueva**
9/22 @ TB	L	5-11	3:25	15,699	66-84/36-38/30-46	5th, 21.5 GB	Badenhop/**Morrow**
9/23 @ TB	L	0-3	3:00	18,985	66-85/36-38/30-47	5th, 21.5 GB	Hellickson/**Jenkins**/Rodney
9/24 @ BAL (1)	L	1-4	2:43	--	66-86/36-38/30-48	5th, 22.0 GB	Johnson/**Alvarez**/Johnson
9/24 @ BAL (2)	W	9-5	3:15	31,015	67-86/36-38/31-48	5th, 22.0 GB	**Romero**/Chen
9/25 @ BAL	W	4-0	2:44	30,205	68-86/36-38/32-48	5th, 21.0 GB	**Laffey**/Saunders
9/26 @ BAL	L	2-12	2:47	26,513	68-87/36-38/32-49	5th, 22.0 GB	Gonzalez/**Villanueva**
9/27 NYY	W	6-0	2:36	23,060	69-87/37-38/32-49	T-4th, 21.0 GB	**Morrow**/Nova
9/28 NYY	L	4-11	3:43	25,785	69-88/37-39/32-49	T-4th, 22.0 GB	Kuroda/**Jenkins**
9/29 NYY	W	3-2	2:54	36,139	70-88/38-39/32-49	4th, 21.0 GB	**Hill-R**/Pettitte/**Janssen**
9/30 NYY	L	6-9	3:25	31,418	70-89/38-40/32-49	4th, 22.0 GB	Logan-R/**Oliver-R**
10/1 MIN	W	6-5 (10)	3:14	12,359	71-89/39-40/32-49	4th, 22.0 GB	**Lyon-R**/Duensing-R
10/2 MIN	W	4-3	2:33	13,930	72-89/40-40/32-49	4th, 22.0 GB	**Jenkins**/Swarzak/**Janssen**
10/3 MIN	W	2-1	2:21	19,769	73-89/41-40/32-49	4th, 22.0 GB	**Morrow**/Diamond/**Lyon**

TORONTO BLUE JAYS 2012 ATTENDANCE DAY BY DAY

* Sellout

	NUM	M/D	OPP	H/R	D/N	TIME OF GAME	ATTENDANCE	YTD HOME	YTD ROAD	H/R DATE
APRIL	01	04/05	@CLE	R	D	5:14	43,190		43,190	1
		04/06	-Off Day-							
	02	04/07	@CLE	R	D	3:38	18,842		62,032	2
	03	04/08	@CLE	R	D	2:51	10,518		72,550	3
	04	04/09	BOS	H	N	3:02	* 48,473	48,473		1
	05	04/10	BOS	H	N	3:19	26,351	74,824		2
	06	04/11	BOS	H	D	2:13	25,285	100,109		3
		04/12	-Off Day-							
	07	04/13	BAL	H	N	2:40	21,988	122,097		4
	08	04/14	BAL	H	D	2:57	28,355	150,452		5
	09	04/15	BAL	H	D	2:39	20,252	170,704		6
		04/16	-Off Day-							
	10	04/17	TB	H	N	3:05	15,331	186,035		7
	11	04/18	TB	H	N	3:11	15,828	201,863		8
	12	04/19	TB	H	N	3:43	18,976	220,839		9
	13	04/20	@KC	R	N	3:14	23,065		95,615	4
	14	04/21	@KC	R	N	3:03	27,804		123,419	5
	15	04/22	@KC	R	D	3:08	26,891		150,310	6
	16	04/23	@KC	R	N	2:31	13,267		163,577	7
	17	04/24	@BAL	R	N	2:22	11,058		174,635	8
	18	04/25	@BAL	R	N	2:24	10,415		185,050	9
	19	04/26	@BAL	R	N	2:51	13,725		198,775	10
	20	04/27	SEA	H	N	3:35	24,303	245,142		10
	21	04/28	SEA	H	D	2:45	30,765	275,907		11
	22	04/29	SEA	H	D	2:36	22,320	298,227		12
	23	04/30	TEX	H	N	2:59	21,945	320,172		13
MAY	24	05/01	TEX	H	N	2:56	18,774	338,946		14
	25	05/02	TEX	H	D	2:45	25,123	364,069		15
	26	05/03	@LAA	R	N	2:11	28,359		227,134	11
	27	05/04	@LAA	R	N	2:10	33,160		260,294	12
	28	05/05	@LAA	R	N	2:54	39,018		299,312	13
	29	05/06	@LAA	R	D	2:51	37,548		336,860	14
		05/07	-Off Day-							
	30	05/08	@OAK	R	N	2:58	10,784		347,644	15
	31	05/09	@OAK	R	D	3:01	14,815		362,459	16
	32	05/10	@MIN	R	N	2:45	31,438		393,897	17
	33	05/11	@MIN	R	N	3:17	33,387		427,284	18
	34	05/12	@MIN	R	N	2:50	38,820		466,104	19
	35	05/13	@MIN	R	D	2:59	36,889		502,993	20
	36	05/14	TB	H	N	3:21	15,289	379,358		16
	37	05/15	TB	H	N	2:36	15,612	394,970		17
	38	05/16	NYY	H	N	2:45	28,915	423,885		18
	39	05/17	NYY	H	N	2:37	31,266	455,151		19
	40	05/18	NYM	H	N	2:53	26,712	481,863		20
	41	05/19	NYM	H	D	2:12	34,962	516,825		21
	42	05/20	NYM	H	D	3:15	41,867	558,692		22
	43	05/21	@TB	R	N	3:13	10,844		513,837	21
	44	05/22	@TB	R	N	3:03	12,307		526,144	22
	45	05/23	@TB	R	D	3:57	11,471		537,615	23
		05/24	-Off Day-							
	46	05/25	@TEX	R	N	3:17	46,789		584,404	24
	47	05/26	@TEX	R	D	4:38	47,430		631,834	25
	48	05/27	@TEX	R	D	2:48	46,637		678,471	26
	49	05/28	BAL	H	N	2:48	16,575	575,267		23
	50	05/29	BAL	H	N	3:11	17,352	592,619		24
	51	05/30	BAL	H	N	2:28	17,754	610,373		25
		05/31	-Off Day-							
JUNE	52	06/01	BOS	H	N	3:00	29,678	640,051		26
	53	06/02	BOS	H	D	3:05	43,390	683,441		27
	54	06/03	BOS	H	D	2:52	41,925	725,366		28
		06/04	-Off Day-							
	55	06/05	@CWS	R	N	2:44	23,107		701,578	27
	56	06/06	@CWS	R	N	2:50	25,672		727,250	28
	57	06/07	@CWS	R	N	2:50	25,743		752,993	29
	58	06/08	@ATL	R	N	3:53	42,488		795,481	30
	59	06/09	@ATL	R	D	2:34	32,819		828,300	31
	60	06/10	@ATL	R	D	3:14	20,222		848,522	32
	61	06/11	WAS	H	N	3:03	18,513	743,879		29
	62	06/12	WAH	H	N	2:52	22,538	766,417		30
	63	06/13	WAS	H	D	2:52	41,677	808,094		31
		06/14	-Off Day-							
	64	06/15	PHI	H	N	2:47	28,266	836,360		32
	65	06/16	PHI	H	D	3:14	42,070	878,430		33
	66	06/17	PHI	H	D	2:46	* 45,060	923,490		34
	67	06/18	@MIL	R	N	2:52	32,223		880,745	33
	68	06/19	@MIL	R	N	3:46	36,334		917,079	34
	69	06/20	@MIL	R	D	3:03	33,077		950,156	35
		06/21	-Off Day-							
	70	06/22	@MIA	R	N	3:02	22,387		972,543	36
	71	06/23	@MIA	R	D	2:49	24,448		996,991	37
	72	06/24	@MIA	R	D	2:29	27,888		1,024,879	38
	73	06/25	@BOS	R	N	3:01	37,208		1,062,087	39
	74	06/26	@BOS	R	N	3:02	37,755		1,099,842	40
	75	06/27	@BOS	R	D	2:40	37,744		1,137,586	41
	76	06/28	LAA	H	N	3:16	24,668	948,158		35
	77	06/29	LAA	H	N	3:12	24,538	972,696		36
	78	06/30	LAA	H	D	2:44	29,287	1,001,983		37
JULY	79	07/01	LAA	H	D	3:29	34,853	1,036,836		38
	80	07/02	KC	H	N	2:36	17,127	1,053,963		39
	81	07/03	KC	H	N	2:30	15,516	1,069,479		40
	82	07/04	KC	H	N	2:45	17,831	1,087,310		41
	83	07/05	KC	H	N	3:16	20,598	1,107,908		42

	NUM	M/D	OPP	H/R	D/N	TIME OF GAME	ATTENDANCE	YTD HOME	YTD ROAD	H/R DATE
	84	07/06	@CWS	R	N	2:31	27,129		1,164,715	42
	85	07/07	@CWS	R	D	2:25	25,399		1,190,114	43
	86	07/08	@CWS	R	D	3:48	27,190		1,217,304	44
		07/09		All Star Break						
		07/10		All-Star Game @ Kansas City						
		07/11		All Star Break						
		07/12	-Off Day-							
	87	07/13	CLE	H	N	2:40	32,308	1,140,216		43
	88	07/14	CLE	H	D	3:15	32,517	1,172,733		44
	89	07/15	CLE	H	D	2:42	26,407	1,199,140		45
	90	07/16	@NYY	R	N	3:04	42,819		1,260,123	45
	91	07/17	@NYY	R	N	3:08	44,975		1,305,098	46
	92	07/18	@NYY	R	D	2:12	45,986		1,351,084	47
		07/19	-Off Day-							
	93	07/20	@BOS	R	N	3:01	38,093		1,389,177	48
	94	07/21	@BOS	R	N	3:04	38,170		1,427,347	49
	95	07/22	@BOS	R	D	3:28	37,737		1,465,084	50
		07/23	-Off Day-							
	96	07/24	OAK	H	N	3:00	25,686	1,224,826		46
	97	07/25	OAK	H	N	3:12	23,948	1,248,774		47
	98	07/26	OAK	H	D	2:38	39,003	1,287,777		48
	99	07/27	DET	H	N	2:52	33,962	1,321,739		49
	100	07/28	DET	H	D	2:34	41,832	1,363,571		50
	101	07/29	DET	H	D	2:33	35,975	1,399,546		51
	102	07/30	@SEA	R	N	2:45	22,443		1,487,527	51
	103	07/31	@SEA	R	N	2:54	21,434		1,508,961	52
AUG.	104	08/01	@SEA	R	N	2:21	22,537		1,531,498	53
	105	08/02	@OAK	R	N	2:47	10,823		1,542,321	54
	106	08/03	@OAK	R	N	4:47	30,169		1,572,490	55
	107	08/04	@OAK	R	D	3:37	17,121		1,589,611	56
	108	08/05	@OAK	R	D	2:57	18,308		1,607,919	57
		08/06	-Off Day-							
	109	08/07	@TB	R	N	2:35	13,823		1,621,742	58
	110	08/08	@TB	R	N	2:42	13,441		1,635,183	59
	111	08/09	@TB	R	D	2:54	23,462		1,658,645	60
	112	08/10	NYY	H	N	3:08	41,610	1,441,156		52
	113	08/11	NYY	H	D	2:47	* 45,582	1,486,738		53
	114	08/12	NYY	H	D	2:49	43,924	1,530,662		54
	115	08/13	CWS	H	N	3:05	16,828	1,547,490		55
	116	08/14	CWS	H	N	2:31	18,919	1,566,409		56
	117	08/15	CWS	H	N	2:39	20,119	1,586,528		57
	118	08/16	CWS	H	N	2:34	19,855	1,606,383		58
	119	08/17	TEX	H	N	2:42	26,816	1,633,199		59
	120	08/18	TEX	H	D	2:47	30,033	1,663,232		60
	121	08/19	TEX	H	D	2:34	35,701	1,698,933		61
		08/20	-Off Day-							
	122	08/21	@DET	R	N	2:56	39,499		1,698,144	61
	123	08/22	@DET	R	N	2:47	37,225		1,735,369	62
	124	08/23	@DET	R	D	3:25	39,910		1,775,279	63
	125	08/24	@BAL	R	N	2:52	25,754		1,801,033	64
	126	08/25	@BAL	R	N	2:41	25,082		1,826,115	65
		08/26	@BAL	R	D	PPD due to rain - Double Header Sept. 24				
	127	08/27	@NYY	R	N	3:44	42,962		1,869,077	66
	128	08/28	@NYY	R	N	2:28	42,472		1,911,549	67
	129	08/29	@NYY	R	D	3:37	46,010		1,957,559	68
	130	08/30	TB	H	N	2:34	22,711	1,721,644		62
	131	08/31	TB	H	N	2:28	20,158	1,741,802		63
SEPT.	132	09/01	TB	H	D	3:14	20,478	1,762,280		64
	133	09/02	TB	H	D	2:58	18,568	1,780,848		65
	134	09/03	BAL	H	D	2:51	17,220	1,798,068		66
	135	09/04	BAL	H	N	2:48	13,556	1,811,624		67
	136	09/05	BAL	H	N	2:46	14,458	1,826,082		68
		09/06	-Off Day-							
	137	09/07	@BOS	R	N	3:08	37,156		1,994,715	69
	138	09/08	@BOS	R	N	2:55	37,107		2,031,822	70
	139	09/09	@BOS	R	D	3:03	37,226		2,069,048	71
		09/10	-Off Day-							
	140	09/11	SEA	H	N	2:48	12,935	1,839,017		69
	141	09/12	SEA	H	N	2:55	13,519	1,852,536		70
	142	09/13	SEA	H	N	2:39	13,756	1,866,292		71
	143	09/14	BOS	H	N	3:42	21,888	1,888,180		72
	144	09/15	BOS	H	D	3:09	27,325	1,915,505		73
	145	09/16	BOS	H	D	2:42	21,698	1,937,203		74
		09/17	-Off Day-							
		09/18	@NYY	R	N	PPD due to rain - Double Header Sept. 19				
	146	09/19	@NYY	R	D	2:41	39,859		2,108,907	72
	147	09/19	@NYY	R	N	3:06	39,997		2,148,904	73
	148	09/20	@NYY	R	N	3:41	40,511		2,189,415	74
	149	09/21	@TB	R	N	2:56	14,187		2,203,602	75
	150	09/22	@TB	R	N	3:25	15,699		2,219,301	76
	151	09/23	@TB	R	D	3:00	18,985		2,238,286	77
	152	09/24	@BAL	R	D	2:43				
	153	09/24	@BAL	R	N	3:15	31,015		2,269,301	78
	154	09/25	@BAL	R	N	2:44	30,205		2,299,506	79
	155	09/26	@BAL	R	N	2:47	26,513		2,326,019	80
	156	09/27	NYY	H	N	2:36	23,060	1,960,263		75
	157	09/28	NYY	H	N	3:43	25,785	1,986,048		76
	158	09/29	NYY	H	D	2:54	36,139	2,022,187		77
	159	09/30	NYY	H	D	3:25	31,418	2,053,605		78
OCT.	160	10/01	MIN	H	N	3:14	12,359	2,065,964		79
	161	10/02	MIN	H	N	2:33	13,930	2,079,894		80
	162	10/03	MIN	H	N	2:21	19,769	2,099,663		81

2012 PRE ALL-STAR BREAK

BATTING

																								PINCH HIT		
PLAYER	AVG	G	AB	R	H	TB	2B	3B	HR	RBI	SH	SF	HP	BB	IBB	SO	SB	CS	DP	E	SLG	OBP	AB	H	HR	RBI
Arencibia,J	.225	70	249	31	56	106	11	0	13	41	1	2	2	11	1	76	1	0	2	4	.426	.261	3	0	0	0
Bautista,J	.244	86	315	59	77	170	12	0	27	65	0	4	4	55	2	59	4	2	11	2	.540	.360	0	0	0	0
Cooper,D	.292	24	65	8	19	28	3	0	2	6	0	0	1	3	0	9	0	1	1	1	.431	.333	6	3	0	0
Davis,R	.253	71	182	30	46	71	7	3	4	23	1	2	1	15	3	38	23	6	5	5	.390	.310	2	0	0	0
Encarnacion,E	.295	83	308	55	91	174	14	0	23	58	0	3	8	37	3	56	9	2	4	2	.565	.382	0	0	0	0
Escobar,Y	.254	83	331	43	84	111	10	1	5	32	4	4	1	22	0	36	2	1	13	8	.335	.299	1	0	0	0
Francisco,B	.244	23	45	5	11	17	4	1	0	2	0	0	0	3	0	7	0	1	0	0	.378	.292	6	1	0	2
Gomes,Y	.211	17	38	6	8	18	1	0	3	8	0	2	2	2	0	13	0	0	1	0	.474	.273	5	2	1	3
Johnson,K	.246	80	297	39	73	115	8	2	10	37	1	4	1	40	2	93	7	1	5	8	.387	.333	2	0	0	0
Lawrie,B	.291	81	327	51	95	139	16	2	8	33	0	1	5	17	0	52	11	8	6	12	.425	.334	0	0	0	0
Lind,A	.206	47	160	15	33	62	8	0	7	20	0	0	0	18	1	35	0	0	4	4	.388	.287	4	0	0	0
Mathis,J	.247	27	73	14	18	38	5	0	5	8	2	0	0	5	0	27	1	0	1	0	.521	.295	2	0	0	0
McCoy,M	.375	8	8	1	3	3	0	0	0	2	0	0	0	1	0	0	0	0	0	0	.375	.444	1	1	0	0
Rasmus,C	.259	85	320	46	83	158	18	3	17	53	1	1	3	30	4	70	4	2	5	5	.494	.328	1	0	0	0
Romero,R	.200	18	5	1	1	1	0	0	0	0	0	0	0	0	0	2	0	0	0	1	.200	.200	0	0	0	0
Thames,E	.243	46	148	17	36	54	7	1	3	11	0	2	1	9	0	40	0	1	7	1	.365	.288	7	0	0	1
Villanueva,C	.500	24	2	1	1	1	0	0	0	0	0	0	0	0	0	0	0	0	0	0	.500	.500	0	0	0	0
Vizquel,O	.208	33	72	8	15	15	0	0	0	2	1	0	0	5	0	7	2	0	3	1	.208	.260	8	2	0	0
RIGHT	.200		20		4	4	0	0	0	1	0	0	0	2	0	3			1		.200	.273	2	0	0	0
LEFT	.212		52		11	11	0	0	0	1	1	0	0	3	0	4			2		.212	.255	6	2	0	0
TORONTO	**.254**	**86**	**2956**	**430**	**750**	**1281**	**124**	**13**	**127**	**401**	**12**	**25**	**29**	**273**	**16**	**626**	**64**	**25**	**68**	**65**	**.433**	**.320**	**48**	**9**	**1**	**6**
OPPONENT	**.256**	**86**	**2935**	**408**	**751**	**1279**	**179**	**8**	**111**	**386**	**17**	**17**	**34**	**307**	**11**	**601**	**45**	**21**	**77**	**72**	**.436**	**.332**	**47**	**7**	**0**	**1**

PITCHING

PITCHER	R/L	W	L	ERA	G	GS	CG	GF	SHO	SV	IP	H	R	ER	HR	HB	BB	IBB	SO	WP	BK	OPP AVG
Alvarez,H	R	5	7	4.36	17	17	1	0	1	0	107.1	124	58	52	17	3	23	0	36	1	0	.290
Beck,C	R	0	0	3.38	3	0	0	0	0	0	5.1	4	3	2	1	0	2	0	4	1	1	.200
Carpenter,A	R	0	0	6.75	1	0	0	1	0	0	1.1	3	1	1	1	0	0	0	1	0	0	.429
Carreno,J	R	0	2	6.60	6	2	0	1	0	0	15.0	16	11	11	5	0	11	0	9	0	0	.276
Cecil,B	L	2	1	6.75	5	5	0	0	0	0	26.2	31	21	20	6	1	10	0	21	0	0	.295
Chavez,J	R	0	1	7.08	7	2	0	2	0	0	20.1	21	18	16	4	2	7	1	26	0	0	.256
Coello,R	R	0	1	12.79	6	0	0	1	0	0	6.1	10	9	9	2	1	4	0	11	0	0	.357
Cordero,F	R	3	5	6.00	39	0	0	15	0	2	33.0	48	24	22	7	1	14	3	25	4	0	.350
Crawford,E	L	0	0	7.04	9	0	0	2	0	0	7.2	10	6	6	3	1	4	1	5	0	1	.345
Drabek,K	R	4	7	4.67	13	13	0	0	0	0	71.1	67	41	37	10	1	47	0	47	7	0	.250
Dyson,S	R	0	0	0.00	1	0	0	0	0	0	0.1	0	0	0	0	0	1	0	1	0	0	.000
Frasor,J	R	1	1	3.74	39	0	0	7	0	0	33.2	29	14	14	4	0	18	1	42	2	1	.238
Hutchison,D	R	5	3	4.60	11	11	0	0	0	0	58.2	59	31	30	8	5	20	0	49	1	0	.257
Igarashi,R	R	0	0	36.00	2	0	0	0	0	0	1.0	5	4	4	0	0	2	0	2	0	0	.625
Janssen,C	R	1	1	2.36	33	0	0	23	0	12	34.1	25	9	9	4	2	5	1	35	1	1	.202
Laffey,A	L	0	1	2.67	7	3	0	0	0	0	27.0	21	10	8	4	0	5	0	14	0	0	.212
Mathis,J	R	0	0	0.00	1	0	0	1	0	0	1.0	1	0	0	0	0	1	0	0	0	0	.250
Morrow,B	R	7	4	3.01	13	13	3	0	3	0	77.2	54	28	26	7	1	24	0	67	2	0	.194
Oliver,D	L	2	2	1.42	36	0	0	5	0	0	31.2	22	5	5	2	2	7	0	34	1	0	.198
Pauley,D	R	0	0	9.95	5	0	0	3	0	0	6.1	11	7	7	1	2	2	0	2	0	0	.393
Perez,L	L	2	2	3.43	35	0	0	6	0	0	42.0	38	16	16	3	3	16	0	39	0	0	.244
Richmond,S	R	0	0	6.00	3	0	0	2	0	0	3.0	5	2	2	1	0	0	0	2	1	0	.357
Romero,R	L	8	4	5.22	18	18	0	0	0	0	110.1	104	69	64	15	7	58	0	76	2	0	.250
Santos,S	R	0	1	9.00	6	0	0	4	0	2	5.0	6	5	5	1	0	4	0	4	1	0	.316
Villanueva,C	R	3	0	3.05	24	2	0	9	0	0	44.1	37	16	15	5	2	22	4	49	2	0	.226
TORONTO		**43**	**43**	**4.45**	**86**	**86**	**4**	**82**	**6**	**16**	**770.2**	**751**	**408**	**381**	**111**	**34**	**307**	**11**	**601**	**26**	**4**	**.256**
OPPONENTS		**43**	**43**	**4.43**	**86**	**86**	**1**	**85**	**3**	**22**	**770.2**	**750**	**430**	**379**	**127**	**29**	**273**	**16**	**626**	**23**	**3**	**.254**

2012 POST ALL-STAR BREAK

BATTING

																							PINCH HIT			
PLAYER	AVG	G	AB	R	H	TB	2B	3B	HR	RBI	SH	SF	HP	BB	IBB	SO	SB	CS	DP	E	SLG	OBP	AB	H	HR	RBI
Arencibia,J	.255	32	98	14	25	45	5	0	5	15	0	1	1	7	0	32	0	0	2	0	.459	.308	2	0	0	0
Bautista,J	.176	6	17	5	3	5	2	0	0	0	0	0	0	4	0	4	1	0	0	0	.294	.333	0	0	0	0
Cooper,D	.307	21	75	8	23	37	8	0	2	5	0	0	0	1	0	13	0	0	0	0	.493	.316	2	1	0	0
Davis,R	.260	71	265	34	69	98	17	0	4	20	0	2	5	14	0	64	23	7	3	3	.370	.308	1	0	0	0
Encarnacion,E	.261	68	234	38	61	128	10	0	19	52	0	4	3	47	9	38	4	1	2	2	.547	.385	0	0	0	0
Escobar,Y	.251	62	227	15	57	81	12	0	4	19	3	0	3	13	1	34	3	0	8	4	.357	.300	2	1	0	0
Francisco,B	.200	4	5	0	1	2	1	0	0	0	0	0	0	1	0	3	0	0	0	0	.400	.333	0	0	0	0
Gomes,Y	.200	26	60	3	12	18	3	0	1	5	1	1	1	4	0	19	0	0	2	1	.300	.258	3	0	0	0
Gose,A	.223	56	166	25	37	53	7	3	1	11	4	0	2	17	0	59	15	3	1	1	.319	.303	3	0	0	0
Hechavarria,A	.254	41	126	10	32	46	8	0	2	15	5	1	1	4	0	32	0	0	2	3	.365	.280	1	1	0	0
Johnson,K	.195	62	210	22	41	70	11	0	6	18	1	0	4	22	2	66	7	1	3	3	.333	.284	2	1	0	1
Lawrie,B	.240	44	167	22	40	61	10	1	3	15	2	1	0	16	0	34	2	0	3	5	.365	.304	0	0	0	0
Lind,A	.304	46	161	13	49	71	6	2	4	25	0	3	0	11	0	26	0	0	6	1	.441	.343	2	2	0	0
Loup,A	.000	33	1	0	0	0	0	0	0	0	0	0	0	0	0	0	0	0	0	0	.000	.000	0	0	0	0
Mathis,J	.203	43	138	11	28	45	8	0	3	19	4	1	0	4	0	41	0	0	1	2	.326	.224	3	0	0	0
McCoy,M	.136	24	44	9	6	10	1	0	1	5	0	0	0	3	0	6	2	1	1	0	.227	.191	1	0	0	0
Rasmus,C	.176	66	245	29	43	68	3	2	6	22	1	3	4	17	1	79	0	1	2	1	.278	.238	5	1	0	0
Sierra,M	.224	49	147	14	33	55	4	0	6	15	0	0	2	8	0	44	1	0	3	0	.374	.274	6	1	0	2
Snider,T	.250	10	36	6	9	20	2	0	3	8	0	1	0	3	0	14	0	0	0	1	.556	.300	0	0	0	0
Torrealba,Y	.214	10	28	3	6	9	0	0	1	2	0	0	0	2	0	7	0	0	0	0	.321	.267	1	0	0	0
Vizquel,O	.259	27	81	5	21	28	5	1	0	5	0	2	0	2	0	10	1	2	2	2	.346	.271	4	1	0	0
RIGHT	.231		26		6	8	2	0	0	1	0	0	0	0	0	4			0		.308	.231	1	0	0	0
LEFT	.273		55		15	20	3	1	0	4	0	2	0	2	0	6			2		.364	.288	3	1	0	0
TORONTO	**.235**	**76**	**2531**	**286**	**596**	**950**	**123**	**9**	**71**	**276**	**21**	**20**	**26**	**200**	**13**	**625**	**59**	**16**	**41**	**36**	**.375**	**.296**	**38**	**9**	**0**	**3**
OPPONENT	**.266**	**76**	**2582**	**376**	**688**	**1136**	**155**	**7**	**93**	**357**	**18**	**18**	**21**	**267**	**9**	**541**	**42**	**22**	**66**	**36**	**.440**	**.338**	**50**	**9**	**0**	**5**

PITCHING

PITCHER	R/L	W	L	ERA	G	GS	CG	GF	SHO	SV	IP	H	R	ER	HR	HB	BB	IBB	SO	WP	BK	OPP AVG
Alvarez,H	R	4	7	5.51	14	14	0	0	0	0	80.0	92	52	49	12	0	31	2	43	2	1	.290
Beck,C	R	0	0	7.84	11	0	0	2	0	0	10.1	17	9	9	1	0	3	0	5	0	0	.370
Carpenter,A	R	0	0	4.70	5	0	0	3	0	0	7.2	4	4	4	3	0	6	0	8	1	0	.148
Carpenter,D	R	0	0	30.38	3	0	0	1	0	0	2.2	8	10	9	1	1	2	1	4	0	0	.471
Carreno,J	R	0	0	5.14	5	0	0	2	0	0	7.0	6	4	4	2	0	3	0	7	0	0	.240
Cecil,B	L	0	3	4.93	16	4	0	2	0	0	34.2	39	19	19	5	2	13	0	30	0	0	.293
Chavez,J	R	1	0	36.00	2	0	0	0	0	0	1.0	4	4	4	2	0	3	0	1	0	0	.571
Cordero,F	R	0	0	0.00	2	0	0	2	0	0	1.1	0	0	0	0	0	0	0	1	0	0	.000
Crawford,E	L	0	0	0.00	1	0	0	1	0	0	0.1	0	0	0	0	0	0	0	0	0	0	.000
Delabar,S	R	2	2	3.38	27	0	0	1	0	0	29.1	23	12	11	3	0	15	0	46	3	0	.213
Dyson,S	R	0	0	81.00	1	0	0	0	0	0	0.1	4	3	3	0	0	1	0	0	0	0	.800
Frasor,J	R	0	0	5.40	11	0	0	2	0	0	10.0	13	6	6	2	2	4	0	11	3	0	.310
Happ,J	L	3	2	4.69	10	6	0	3	0	0	40.1	35	21	21	2	1	17	1	46	2	0	.236
Hill,S	R	1	0	0.00	1	0	0	0	0	0	3.0	0	0	0	0	0	2	0	0	0	0	.000
Janssen,C	R	0	0	2.76	29	0	0	24	0	10	29.1	19	9	9	3	1	6	0	32	1	0	.186
Jenkins,C	R	1	3	4.50	13	3	0	6	0	0	32.0	32	16	16	5	1	11	1	16	0	0	.260
Korecky,B	R	0	0	18.00	1	0	0	1	0	0	1.0	1	2	2	1	0	1	0	0	0	0	.250
Laffey,A	L	4	5	5.25	15	13	0	1	0	0	73.2	79	46	43	13	5	32	1	34	2	0	.276
Lincoln,B	R	1	0	5.65	24	0	0	4	0	0	28.2	29	18	18	6	0	10	1	28	1	0	.264
Loup,A	L	0	2	2.64	33	0	0	3	0	0	30.2	26	10	9	0	0	2	0	21	1	1	.232
Lyon,B	R	4	0	2.88	30	0	0	10	0	1	25.0	19	8	8	2	1	9	1	28	1	0	.207
Mathis,J	R	0	0	18.00	1	0	0	1	0	0	1.0	3	2	2	0	0	0	0	0	0	0	.500
Morrow,B	R	3	3	2.87	8	8	0	0	0	0	47.0	44	17	15	5	1	17	0	41	1	0	.246
Oliver,D	L	1	2	2.88	26	0	0	6	0	2	25.0	21	8	8	1	2	8	0	18	2	0	.233
Romero,R	L	1	10	6.62	14	14	1	0	0	0	70.2	94	53	52	6	3	47	1	48	6	0	.328
Villanueva,C	R	4	7	4.78	14	14	0	0	0	0	81.0	76	43	43	18	1	24	0	73	4	1	.252
TORONTO		**30**	**46**	**4.87**	**76**	**76**	**1**	**75**	**5**	**13**	**673.0**	**688**	**376**	**364**	**93**	**21**	**267**	**9**	**541**	**30**	**3**	**.266**
OPPONENTS		**46**	**30**	**3.56**	**76**	**76**	**1**	**75**	**6**	**26**	**680.0**	**596**	**286**	**269**	**71**	**26**	**200**	**13**	**625**	**21**	**6**	**.235**

2012 INTERLEAGUE TEAM BATTING/PITCHING

																									PINCH HIT		
PLAYER	AVG	G	AB	R	H	TB	2B	3B	HR	RBI	SH	SF	HP	BB	IBB	SO	SB	CS	DP	E	SLG	OBP	AB	H	HR	RBI
Alvarez,H	.000	3	1	0	0	0	0	0	0	0	0	0	0	0	0	1	0	0	0	0	.000	.000	0	0	0	0
Arencibia,J	.241	15	54	6	13	23	4	0	2	12	0	1	0	2	1	20	0	0	0	1	.426	.263	2	0	0	0
Bautista,J	.286	18	63	16	18	46	1	0	9	18	0	0	1	16	0	11	2	1	1	0	.730	.438	0	0	0	0
Carreno,J	.000	1	1	0	0	0	0	0	0	0	0	0	0	0	0	0	0	0	0	0	.000	.000	0	0	0	0
Cecil,B	.000	2	2	0	0	0	0	0	0	0	0	0	0	0	0	2	0	0	0	0	.000	.000	0	0	0	0
Chavez,J	.000	2	2	0	0	0	0	0	0	0	1	0	0	0	0	2	0	0	0	0	.000	.000	0	0	0	0
Cooper,D	.143	12	21	1	3	3	0	0	0	0	0	0	0	1	0	5	0	0	0	1	.143	.182	6	3	0	0
Davis,R	.316	18	57	6	18	28	2	1	2	9	1	0	0	5	2	19	5	2	0	0	.491	.371	0	0	0	0
Drabek,K	.000	2	2	0	0	0	0	0	0	0	0	0	0	0	0	1	0	0	0	0	.000	.000	0	0	0	0
Encarnacion,E	.261	18	69	14	18	34	4	0	4	7	0	0	2	9	1	17	0	0	1	0	.493	.363	0	0	0	0
Escobar,Y	.234	18	64	8	15	19	1	0	1	6	3	1	0	6	0	6	1	0	1	1	.297	.296	1	0	0	0
Francisco,B	.167	2	6	1	1	1	0	0	0	0	0	0	0	1	0	0	0	0	0	0	.167	.286	0	0	0	0
Gomes,Y	.278	10	18	5	5	12	1	0	2	6	0	1	2	2	0	7	0	0	1	0	.667	.391	3	2	1	3
Hutchison,D	.000	2	2	0	0	0	0	0	0	0	0	0	0	0	0	0	0	0	0	0	.000	.000	0	0	0	0
Johnson,K	.246	18	69	7	17	20	1	1	0	6	0	2	0	4	0	21	2	1	1	0	.290	.280	1	0	0	0
Laffey,A	.000	4	1	0	0	0	0	0	0	0	0	0	0	0	0	0	0	0	0	0	.000	.000	0	0	0	0
Lawrie,B	.300	15	60	15	18	34	5	1	3	8	0	0	2	8	0	8	2	3	0	2	.567	.400	0	0	0	0
Mathis,J	.158	6	19	3	3	4	1	0	0	0	1	0	0	0	0	6	1	0	1	0	.211	.158	0	0	0	0
McCoy,M	.400	6	5	0	2	2	0	0	0	0	0	0	0	1	0	0	0	0	0	0	.400	.500	1	1	0	0
Rasmus,C	.309	17	68	11	21	43	4	0	6	17	0	0	0	6	0	12	0	1	1	1	.632	.365	0	0	0	0
Romero,R	.200	4	5	1	1	1	0	0	0	0	0	0	0	0	0	2	0	0	0	0	.200	.200	0	0	0	0
Thames,E	.250	3	12	2	3	4	1	0	0	2	0	0	0	1	0	5	0	0	0	0	.333	.308	0	0	0	0
Villanueva,C	.500	7	2	1	1	1	0	0	0	0	0	0	0	0	0	0	0	0	0	0	.500	.500	0	0	0	0
Vizquel,O	.308	8	13	1	4	4	0	0	0	0	0	0	0	0	0	1	0	0	0	0	.308	.308	4	1	0	0
RIGHT	.500		4		2	2	0	0	0	0	0	0	0	0	0	1			0		.500	.500	0	0	0	0
LEFT	.222		9		2	2	0	0	0	0	0	0	0	0	0	0			0		.222	.222	4	1	0	0
TORONTO	**.261**	**18**	**616**	**98**	**161**	**279**	**25**	**3**	**29**	**91**	**6**	**5**	**7**	**62**	**4**	**146**	**13**	**8**	**7**	**6**	**.453**	**.333**	**18**	**7**	**1**	**3**
OPPONENTS	**.261**	**18**	**613**	**86**	**160**	**281**	**42**	**2**	**25**	**82**	**4**	**2**	**8**	**66**	**1**	**132**	**12**	**4**	**11**	**8**	**.458**	**.340**	**20**	**3**	**0**	**0**

PITCHER	R/L	W	L	ERA	G	GS	CG	GF	SHO	SV	IP	H	R	ER	HR	HB	BB	IBB	SO	WP	BK	OPP AVG
Alvarez,H	R	0	2	9.00	3	3	0	0	0	0	16.0	29	16	16	3	0	4	0	7	0	0	.397
Beck,C	R	0	0	3.38	3	0	0	0	0	0	5.1	4	3	2	1	0	2	0	4	1	1	.200
Carreno,J	R	0	1	15.00	1	1	0	0	0	0	3.0	5	5	5	3	0	2	0	3	0	0	.385
Cecil,B	L	1	0	2.45	2	2	0	0	0	0	11.0	10	3	3	2	0	4	0	7	0	0	.244
Chavez,J	R	0	1	10.38	2	2	0	0	0	0	8.2	10	10	10	2	2	4	0	10	0	0	.278
Coello,R	R	0	1	18.69	5	0	0	0	0	0	4.1	7	9	9	2	1	4	0	8	0	0	.350
Cordero,F	R	1	1	1.23	9	0	0	6	0	0	7.1	6	2	1	1	0	4	0	6	0	0	.222
Crawford,E	L	0	0	27.00	2	0	0	1	0	0	0.2	0	2	2	0	1	1	0	0	0	0	.000
Delabar,S	R	0	0	0.00	2	0	0	1	0	0	3.0	0	0	0	0	1	2	0	4	1	0	.000
Drabek,K	R	0	1	6.75	2	2	0	0	0	0	9.1	13	7	7	1	0	6	0	1	0	0	.342
Frasor,J	R	0	0	2.45	8	0	0	2	0	0	7.1	7	2	2	1	0	3	0	12	1	0	.241
Hutchison,D	R	0	1	6.43	2	2	0	0	0	0	7.0	7	5	5	2	0	2	0	8	0	0	.259
Igarashi,R	R	0	0	9.00	1	0	0	1	0	0	1.0	1	1	1	0	0	2	0	2	0	0	.250
Janssen,C	R	0	0	0.00	6	0	0	5	0	2	6.0	3	0	0	0	0	0	0	6	0	0	.143
Laffey,A	L	0	0	3.00	4	0	0	0	0	0	9.0	6	3	3	2	0	2	0	4	0	0	.188
Morrow,B	R	1	1	1.00	2	2	1	0	1	0	9.0	4	1	1	0	0	1	0	8	0	0	.133
Oliver,D	L	2	0	0.00	8	0	0	0	0	0	7.0	2	0	0	0	1	3	0	9	0	0	.091
Pauley,D	R	0	1	0.00	4	0	0	3	0	0	3.2	4	1	0	0	0	1	0	1	0	0	.286
Perez,L	L	0	0	4.09	7	0	0	1	0	0	11.0	12	5	5	2	0	4	0	9	0	0	.279
Romero,R	L	2	0	4.70	4	4	0	0	0	0	23.0	25	13	12	3	3	11	0	15	1	0	.281
Villanueva,C	R	2	0	0.00	7	0	0	1	0	0	12.1	9	0	0	0	0	8	1	14	0	0	.205
TORONTO		**9**	**9**	**4.69**	**18**	**18**	**1**	**17**	**1**	**2**	**159.1**	**160**	**86**	**83**	**25**	**8**	**66**	**1**	**132**	**3**	**1**	**.261**
OPPONENTS		**9**	**9**	**5.19**	**18**	**18**	**0**	**18**	**0**	**4**	**159.2**	**161**	**98**	**92**	**29**	**7**	**62**	**4**	**146**	**6**	**2**	**.261**

2012 TRANSACTIONS

Jan. 1	**RHP JASON FRASOR** acquired from the Chicago White Sox in exchange for **RHP MYLES JAYE** and **RHP DANIEL WEBB**
Jan. 9	**LHP DARREN OLIVER** signed as a free agent
Jan. 17	**IF/OF MARK TEAHEN** was given his unconditional release
Jan. 23	**IF OMAR VIZQUEL** signed as a minor league free agent with an invite to Spring Training
Feb. 1	**RHP FRANCISCO CORDERO** signed as a free agent
Feb. 22	**RHP RICK VANDENHURK** signed as a free agent
March 10	**IF BRIAN BOCOCK, C BRIAN JEROLOMAN, OF RICARDO NANITA, C CARLOS PEREZ, RHP SCOTT RICHMOND** and **RHP RYAN TEPERA** returned to minor league camp
March 12	**RHP NELSON FIGUEROA, RHP JIM HOEY** and **IF RYAN GOINS** returned to minor league camp
March 14	**RHP TRYSTAN MAGNUSON, SS ADEINY HECHAVARRIA** and **OF MOISES SIERRA** optioned to minor league camp
March 15	**RHP CHAD BECK** and **RHP DANIEL FARQUHAR** optioned to minor league camp
March 16	**RHP JOEL CARRENO** and **LHP EVAN CRAWFORD** were optioned to minor league camp
March 17	**RHP CHAD JENKINS** returned to minor league camp
March 18	**C A.J. JIMENEZ, RHP JERRY GIL** and **RHP DECK McGUIRE** returned to minor league camp… **1B MIKE McDADE** and **C TRAVIS d'ARNAUD** optioned to minor league camp
March 21	**RHP RICK VANDENHURK** claimed on outright waivers by the Cleveland Indians.
March 24	**RHP DREW CARPENTER, RHP JESSE CHAVEZ, RHP ROBERT COELLO** and **OF ANTHONY GOSE** returned to minor league camp
March 25	**C/IF YAN GOMES, IF JONATHAN DIAZ** and **IF CHRIS WOODWARD** returned to minor league camp… **1B DAVID COOPER** and **OF TRAVIS SNIDER** optioned to minor league camp
March 28	**IF MIKE McCOY** was optioned to minor league camp
March 29	**RHP DREW HUTCHISON** was optioned to minor league camp
April 3	**RHP DUSTIN McGOWAN** placed on 15-day DL (right foot), retro to March 26… **LHP AARON LAFFEY** returned to Las Vegas (AAA), **LHP BRETT CECIL** optioned to New Hampshire (AA), **RHP JOEL CARRENO** recalled from New Hampshire (AA), **IF OMAR VIZQUEL** had contract selected
April 4	**RHP JESSE LITSCH** placed on the 15-day DL (right shoulder), retro to March 26… **IF LUIS VALBUENA** claimed off waivers by the Chicago Cubs
April 9	**RHP JOEL CARRENO** optioned to Las Vegas (AAA)… **LHP AARON LAFFEY** had contract selected from Las Vegas (AAA)
April 13	**RHP SERGIO SANTOS** was placed on the paternity list… **LHP EVAN CRAWFORD** was recalled from New Hampshire (AA)
April 15	**RHP SERGIO SANTOS** returned from paternity list & **LHP AARON LAFFEY** optioned to Las Vegas (AAA)
April 20	**RHP DREW HUTCHISON** had contract selected from New Hampshire (AA) & **LHP EVAN CRAWFORD** optioned to New Hampshire (AA)… **RHP JESSE LITSCH** transferred from the 15-day to the 60-day DL (right shoulder)
April 22	**RHP SERGIO SANTOS** placed on the 15-day DL (right shoulder inflammation)… **LHP EVAN CRAWFORD** recalled from New Hampshire (AA)
May 2	**RHP JOEL CARRENO** recalled from Las Vegas (AAA) & **LHP EVAN CRAWFORD** optioned to Las Vegas (AAA)
May 14	**LHP EVAN CRAWFORD** recalled from Las Vegas (AAA) & **RHP JOEL CARRENO** optioned to New Hampshire (AA)
May 15	**RHP TRYSTAN MAGNUSON** outrighted off of the 40-man roster
May 16	**C/IF YAN GOMES** had contract selected from Las Vegas (AAA) & **1B ADAM LIND** optioned to Las Vegas (AAA)
May 25	**1B DAVID COOPER** recalled from Las Vegas (AAA) & **RHP RYOTA IGARASHI** had contract selected from Las Vegas (AAA)… **LHP EVAN CRAWFORD** optioned to Las Vegas (AAA), **OF BEN FRANCISCO** placed on 15-day DL (left hamstring), retro to May 21 & **RHP DUSTIN McGOWAN** transferred from the 15-day to the 60-day DL
May 27	**RHP JESSE CHAVEZ** had contract selected from Las Vegas (AAA) & **RHP CHAD BECK** recalled from Las Vegas (AAA)… **C/IF YAN GOMES** optioned to Las Vegas (AAA) & **RHP RYOTA IGARASHI** designated for assignment
May 28	**LHP AARON LAFFEY** recalled from Las Vegas (AAA) & **RHP CHAD BECK** optioned to Las Vegas (AAA)
May 29	**IF MIKE McCOY** recalled from Las Vegas (AAA) & **OF ERIC THAMES** optioned to Las Vegas (AAA)… **RHP RYOTA IGARASHI** claimed off waivers by the New York Yankees
May 31	**RHP ROBERT COELLO** had contract selected from Las Vegas (AAA)… **LHP AARON LAFFEY** optioned to Las Vegas (AAA)… **1B ADAM LIND** outrighted to Las Vegas (AAA)
June 2	**RHP CHRIS SCHWINDEN** claimed off waivers from the New York Mets… **RHP DANIEL FARQUHAR** designated for assignment
June 6	**RHP JESSE CHAVEZ** optioned to Las Vegas (AAA) & **C/IF YAN GOMES** recalled from Las Vegas (AAA)… **RHP CHRIS SCHWINDEN** claimed off waivers by the Cleveland Indians
June 7	**RHP ROBERT COELLO** optioned to Las Vegas (AAA) & **RHP CHAD BECK** recalled from Las Vegas (AAA)
June 9	**RHP DANIEL FARQUHAR** claimed on waivers by the Oakland Athletics
June 11	**C/IF YAN GOMES** optioned to Las Vegas (AAA)… **LHP EVAN CRAWFORD** and **LHP AARON LAFFEY** recalled from Las Vegas (AAA)… **RHP CHAD BECK** optioned to Las Vegas (AAA)
June 12	**RHP BRANDON MORROW** placed on 15-day DL (strained left oblique)
June 13	**C/IF YAN GOMES** recalled from Las Vegas (AAA)
June 15	**RHP KYLE DRABEK** placed on 15-day DL (right elbow), retro to June 14… **LHP BRETT CECIL** recalled from Las Vegas (AAA)
June 16	**RHP DREW HUTCHISON** placed on 15-day DL (right elbow)… **RHP ROBERT COELLO** recalled from Las Vegas (AAA)
June 19	**RHP JESSE CHAVEZ** recalled from Las Vegas (AAA) & **LHP EVAN CRAWFORD** optioned to Las Vegas (AAA)

June 20	**RHP DAVID PAULEY** claimed off waivers from the Los Angeles Angels of Anaheim... **RHP JOEL CARRENO** recalled from Las Vegas (AAA) & **C/IF YAN GOMES** optioned to Las Vegas (AAA)
June 21	**RHP DAVID PAULEY** added to the 25-man roster & **RHP JOEL CARRENO** optioned to Las Vegas (AAA)
June 22	**RHP ALAN FARINA** reinstated from the 60-day DL (right elbow) & optioned to Dunedin (A)... **RHP KYLE DRABEK** transferred from the 15-day to the 60-day DL (right elbow)
June 25	**1B ADAM LIND** had contract selected from Las Vegas (AAA) & **OF BEN FRANCISCO** activated from the 15-day DL (left hamstring)... **1B DAVID COOPER** and **IF MIKE McCOY** optioned to Las Vegas (AAA) & **RHP SERGIO SANTOS** transferred from the 15-day to the 60-day DL (right shoulder)
June 26	**RHP SCOTT RICHMOND** had contract selected from Las Vegas (AAA)... **RHP DREW HUTCHISON** transferred from the 15-day to the 60-day DL (right elbow)
July 2	**RHP ALAN FARINA** outrighted to Dunedin (A)
July 3	**RHP DREW CARPENTER** had contract selected from Las Vegas (AAA)... **RHP DAVID PAULEY** designated for assignment
July 5	**RHP SAM DYSON** had contract selected from New Hampshire (AA)... **RHP SCOTT RICHMOND** optioned to Las Vegas (AAA)
July 13	**LHP AARON LOUP** had contract selected from New Hampshire (AA)... **LHP LUIS PEREZ** placed on the 60-day DL (left elbow UCL tear), retro to July 9
July 15	**RHP CHAD BECK** recalled from Las Vegas (AAA) & **RHP JESSE CHAVEZ** optioned to Las Vegas (AAA)
July 17	**OF JOSE BAUTISTA** placed on 15-day DL (left wrist) & **OF ANTHONY GOSE** had contract selected from Las Vegas (AAA)... **RHP BRANDON MORROW** transferred from the 15-day to the 60-day DL (left oblique)
July 19	**C/IF YAN GOMES** recalled from Las Vegas (AAA)... **RHP SAM DYSON** optioned to New Hampshire (AA)
July 20	**LHP J.A. HAPP, RHP BRANDON LYON** and **RHP DAVID CARPENTER** acquired from the Houston Astros in exchange for **OF BEN FRANCISCO, RHP FRANCISCO CORDERO, RHP ASHER WOJCIECHOWSKI, RHP JOE MUSGROVE, LHP DAVID ROLLINS, C CARLOS PEREZ** & a player to be named later... **RHP DAVID CARPENTER** has been optioned to Las Vegas (AAA)... **OF TRAVIS SNIDER** recalled from Las Vegas (AAA)... **RHP ROBERT COELLO** transferred from the 15-day to the 60-day DL
July 21	**RHP JASON FRASOR** placed on the 15-day DL (right forearm tightness), retro to July 17
July 26	**RHP CHAD BECK** optioned to Las Vegas (AAA)... **C J.P. ARENCIBIA** placed on the 15-day DL (right hand)... **RHP JOEL CARRENO** and **LHP EVAN CRAWFORD** recalled from Las Vegas (AAA)
July 30	**1B/DH ADAM LIND** placed on the 15-day DL (mid-back), retro to July 26... **1B DAVID COOPER** recalled from Las Vegas (AAA)
July 31	**RHP BRAD LINCOLN** acquired from the Pittsburgh Pirates in exchange for **OF TRAVIS SNIDER**... **RHP STEVE DELABAR** acquired from the Seattle Mariners in exchange for **OF ERIC THAMES**... **RHP JOEL CARRENO** and **LHP EVAN CRAWFORD** optioned to Las Vegas (AAA)... **OF MOISES SIERRA** recalled from Las Vegas (AAA)
Aug. 4	**LHP BRETT CECIL** optioned to Las Vegas (AAA), **RHP DREW CARPENTER** designated for assignment, **RHP JESSE CHAVEZ** and **SS ADEINY HECHVARRIA** recalled from Las Vegas (AAA)
Aug. 5	**RHP CHAD JENKINS** selected from New Hampshire (AA) & **RHP JESSE CHAVEZ** designated for assignment
Aug. 7	**RHP DREW CARPENTER** elected free agency
Aug. 9	**3B BRETT LAWRIE** placed on the 15-day DL, retro to Aug. 4 with right oblique strain
Aug. 10	**RHP DAVID CARPENTER** recalled from Las Vegas (AAA)... **RHP JUAN ABREAU** claimed off waivers from the Houston Astros & **RHP SCOTT RICHMOND** designated for assignment
Aug. 11	**RHP DAVID CARPENTER** optioned to Las Vegas (AAA) & **IF MIKE McCOY** recalled from Las Vegas (AAA)
Aug. 16	**RHP KEVIN COMER** sent to the Houston Astros as the player to be named later from the 10-player trade completed on July 2
Aug. 20	**C/IF YAN GOMES** optioned to Las Vegas (AAA)
Aug. 21	**C YORVIT TORREALBA** had contract selected from New Hampshire (AA)
Aug. 22	**SS YUNEL ESCOBAR** placed on the paternity list... **RHP CHAD BECK** recalled from Las Vegas (AAA)
Aug. 24	**OF JOSE BAUTISTA** returned from rehab assignment & reinstated from the 15-day DL... **RHP CHAD BECK** optioned to Las Vegas (AAA)... **RHP JESSE CHAVEZ** traded to the Oakland Athletics for cash considerations... **OF ANTHONY GOSE** and **SS ADEINY HECHAVARRIA** optioned to Las Vegas (AAA)
Aug. 25	**RHP BRANDON MORROW** reinstated from the 60-day disabled list & **SS YUNEL ESCOBAR** reinstated from the paternity list
Aug. 26	**OF JOSE BAUTISTA** (left wrist inflammation) & **1B DAVID COOPER** (mid-back strain), retro to Aug. 23, placed on the 15-day DL... **IF ADEINY HECHAVARRIA** was recalled from Las Vegas (AAA) & **1B/DH ADAM LIND** was reinstated from the 15-day DL
Sept. 3	LHP BRETT CECIL recalled from Las Vegas (AAA)... **RHP JASON FRASOR** returned from rehab assignment & reinstated from the 15-day DL (right forearm)
Sept. 4	**RHP CHAD BECK** and **OF ANTHONY GOSE** both recalled from Las Vegas (AAA)
Sept. 7	**LHP J.A. HAPP** placed on the 15-day disabled list (fractured R foot), retro to Sept. 4 ... **C J.P. ARENCIBIA** and **3B BRETT LAWRIE** returned from medical rehab assignments & reinstated from the 15-day DL... **RHP DAVID CARPENTER, RHP JOEL CARRENO** and **C/IF YAN GOMES** all recalled from Las Vegas (AAA)
Sept. 18	**SS YUNEL ESCOBAR** was suspended for three games by the club... The suspension is the result of his decision to display an unacceptable message while participating in a Major League Game
Sept. 21	**SS YUNEL ESCOBAR** was activated from suspended list... **C YORVIT TORREALBA** was traded to the Milwaukee Brewers in exchange for a player to be named later or cash considerations
Sept. 24	**RHP SHAWN HILL** and **RHP BOBBY KORECKY** had contracts selected from Las Vegas (AAA)... **LHP J.A. HAPP** transferred from the 15-day to the 60-day DL
Oct. 4	**LHP AARON LAFFEY, RHP SHAWN HILL** and **RHP BOBBY KORECKY** all outrighted off the 40-man roster
Oct. 9	**RHP ROBERT COELLO** re-instated from the 60-day DL (right shoulder) & outrighted off the 40-man roster
Oct. 10	**RHP JESSE LITSCH** re-instated from the 60-day DL (right shoulder) & elected free agency in lieu of accepting an outright assignment to the minor leagues
Oct. 17	**OF SCOTT COUSINS** claimed off waivers from the Miami Marlins... **RHP CORY WADE** claimed off waivers from the New York Yankees
Oct. 18	**RHP TYSON BRUMMETT** claimed off waivers from the Philadelphia Phillies
Oct. 21	**IF MIKE AVILES** acquired from the Boston Red Sox in exchange for **RHP DAVID CARPENTER**... **MGR JOHN FARRELL** released from his contract
Oct. 22	**C BOBBY WILSON** claimed off waivers from the Los Angeles Angels of Anaheim... **RHP CHAD BECK** designated for assignment
Oct. 23	**RHP DAVID HERNDON** claimed off waivers from the Philadelphia Phillies... **RHP TYSON BRUMMETT** designated for assignment
Oct. 25	**RHP CHAD BECK** claimed off waivers by the Pittsburgh Pirates

BIOGRAPHIES LAST SEASON HISTORY RECORDS OPPONENTS PLAYER DEV. MEDIA & MISC.

Oct. 26 **RHP TYSON BRUMMETT** outrighted to Las Vegas (AAA)

Oct. 31 **LHP SCOTT MAINE** claimed off waivers by the Cleveland Indians… **RHP KYLE DRABEK, LHP J.A. HAPP, RHP DREW HUTCHISON, RHP DUSTIN McGOWAN, LHP LUIS PEREZ** and **RHP SERGIO SANTOS** all reinstated from the 60-day DL… **OF SCOTT COUSINS** and **RHP DAVID HERNDON** were designated for assignment

Nov. 3 **RHP ESMIL ROGERS** acquired from the Cleveland Indians in exchange for **IF MIKE AVILES** and **C/IF YAN GOMES**

Nov. 6 **OF SCOTT COUSINS** claimed off waivers by the Seattle Mariners… **RHP DAVID HERNSON** claimed off waivers by the New York Yankees

Nov. 8 **IF MAICER IZTURIS** signed as a free agent… **RHP JEREMY JEFFRESS** acquired from the Kansas City Royals in exchange for cash considerations

Nov. 9 **RHP JUSTIN GERMANO** signed to a minor league contract with an invite to Major League Spring Training

Nov. 19 **SS JOSE REYES, IF/OF EMILIO BONIFACIO, C JOHN BUCK, RHP JOSH JOHNSON, LHP MARK BUEHRLE** and cash considerations acquired from the Florida Marlins in exchange for **SS YUNEL ESCOBAR, IF ADEINY HECHAVARRIA, C JEFF MATHIS, RHP HENDERSON ALVAREZ, OF JAKE MARISNICK, LHP JUSTIN NICOLINO** and **RHP ANTHONY DESCLAFANI**… **RHP JOEL CARRENO** designated for assignment… **OF MELKY CABRERA** signed as a free agent

Nov. 20 **JOHN GIBBONS** hired as Manager… **IF RYAN GOINS, C A.J. JIMENEZ** had contracts selected to the 40-man roster… **1B MIKE McDADE, IF MIKE McCOY** and **RHP CORY WADE** all designated for assignment

Nov. 21 **OF RICARDO NANITA, IF JIM NEGRYCH, RHP NEIL WAGNER** and **LHP ALEX HINSHAW** all signed to minor league contracts with invites to Major League Spring Training

Nov. 26 **DEMARLO HALE** named as Bench Coach, **CHAD MOTTOLA** named as Hitting Coach, **DWAYNE MURPHY** moves to First Base and Outfield Coach, **LUIS RIVERA** moves to Third Base Coach and **PETE WALKER** named as Pitching Coach.

Nov. 30 **RHP JOEL CARRENO** and **IF MIKE McCOY** cleared waivers and both optioned to Buffalo (AAA)… **RHP CORY WADE** cleared waivers and elected free agency… **1B MIKE McDADE** was claimed off waivers by the Cleveland Indians… **C BOBBY WILSON** was non-tendered

Dec. 3 **C ELI WHITESIDE** claimed off waivers from the New York Yankees

Dec. 10 **PAT HENTGEN** named Bullpen Coach

Dec. 11 **RHP CLAUDIO VARGAS, RHP RICHARD THOMPSON, LHP JUAN PEREZ, IF EUGENIO VELEZ** and **1B/DH LUIS JIMENEZ** signed to minor league contracts with invitations to attend Major League Spring Training

Dec. 12 **C ELI WHITESIDE** claimed off waivers by the Texas Rangers

Dec. 17 **RHP R.A. DICKEY, C JOSH THOLE** and **C MIKE NICKEAS** acquired from the New York Mets in exchange for **RHP NOAH SYNDERGAARD, C TRAVIS d'ARNAUD, C JOHN BUCK** and **OF WUILMER BECCERA**

Dec. 18 **RHP RAMON ORTIZ** and **OF RYAN LANGERHANS** signed to minor league contracts with invites to attend Major League Spring Training

Dec. 19 **RHP DAVE BUSH** signed to minor league contract with invite to Major League Spring Training… **RHP MICKEY STOREY** claimed on waivers from Houston Astros

Dec. 21 **IF RUSS CANZLER** claimed on waivers from the Cleveland Indians… **RHP MICKEY STOREY** outrighted to minors

2013

Jan. 2 **IF RUSS CANZLER** awarded to the Cleveland Indians on waiver claim

Jan. 4 **RHP CHAD BECK** claimed on waivers from the Pittsburgh Pirates

Jan. 10 **RHP TOMMY HOTTOVY** claimed on waivers from the Texas Rangers… **RHP CHAD BECK** designated for assignment

Jan. 11 **RHP TOMMY HOTTOVY** designated for assignment… **C HENRY BLANCO** signed as a free agent

Jan. 12 **1B ADAM LOEWEN** signed to a minor league contract with invite to Major League Spring Training

Jan. 15 **RHP CHAD BECK** outrighted to minors

Jan. 16 **RHP TOMMY HOTTOVY** outrighted to minors

Jan. 22 **IF MARK DeROSA** signed as a free agent… **RHP SAM DYSON** designated for assignment

Jan. 30 **IF ANDY LaROCHE** signed to minor league contract with invite to Major League Spring Training… **RHP SAM DYSON** awarded to Miami on waiver claim

2012 SEASON HIGHS & LOWS

CLUB

MOST RUNS, GAME

15	TORONTO	AT	BOSTON	7/22/12	

MOST RUNS, INNING

8	TORONTO	VS	CLEVELAND	7/14/12	INNING 3

MOST HITS, GAME

18	TORONTO	AT	ATLANTA	6/10/12	
18	TORONTO	AT	BOSTON	7/22/12	

MOST TOTAL BASES, GAME

32	TORONTO	AT	MILWAUKEE	6/19/12	
32	TORONTO	AT	BOSTON	7/22/12	

MOST DOUBLES, GAME

6	TORONTO	VS	CLEVELAND	7/14/12	
6	TORONTO	VS	BALTIMORE	4/15/12	

MOST TRIPLES, GAME

2	TORONTO	VS	DETROIT	7/27/12	

MOST HOME RUNS, GAME

6	TORONTO	AT	MILWAUKEE	6/19/12	

MOST HOME RUNS, DOUBLEHEADER

3	TORONTO	AT	BALTIMORE	9/24/12	

MOST EXTRA BASE HITS, GAME

9	TORONTO	VS	CLEVELAND	7/14/12	

MOST WALKS, GAME

9	TORONTO	AT	CHICAGO	7/08/12	

MOST STRIKEOUTS, GAME

15	TORONTO	AT	SEATTLE	7/30/12	
15	TORONTO	AT	NEW YORK	9/20/12	
16	TORONTO	AT	OAKLAND	8/03/12	15 INNINGS
16	TORONTO	AT	CLEVELAND	4/05/12	16 INNINGS

MOST STOLEN BASES, GAME

4	TORONTO	VS	LOS ANGELES	6/29/12	
4	TORONTO	AT	MINNESOTA	5/13/12	
4	TORONTO	AT	KANSAS CITY	4/22/12	
4	TORONTO	AT	CHICAGO	7/08/12	
4	TORONTO	AT	OAKLAND	8/04/12	11 INNINGS

MOST DOUBLE PLAYS, GAME

4	TORONTO	VS	TAMPA BAY	4/17/12	
4	TORONTO	AT	KANSAS CITY	4/21/12	
4	TORONTO	AT	BALTIMORE	9/24/12	GAME 2
4	TORONTO	AT	BALTIMORE	4/25/12	

MOST ERRORS, GAME

4	TORONTO	VS	TAMPA BAY	5/15/12	

MOST LEFT ON BASE, GAME

13	TORONTO	VS	TAMPA BAY	4/19/12	

MOST INNINGS, GAME

16.0	CLEVELAND	VS	TORONTO	4/05/12	

LONGEST TIME, GAME

3:48	CHICAGO	VS	TORONTO	7/08/12	
5:14	CLEVELAND	VS	TORONTO	4/05/12	16 INNINGS

SHORTEST TIME, GAME

2:10	LOS ANGELES	VS	TORONTO	5/04/12	

HIGHEST ATTENDANCE, GAME

48,473	TORONTO	VS	BOSTON	4/09/12	

LONGEST WINNING STREAK

4	TORONTO	5/16/12	THRU	5/19/12
4	TORONTO	9/05/12	THRU	9/09/12

LONGEST LOSING STREAK

7	TORONTO	8/18/12	THRU	8/25/12
7	TORONTO	9/19/12	THRU	9/24/12

INDIVIDUAL BATTING

LONGEST HITTING STREAK

10	Encarnacion,E		6/25/12	THRU	7/04/12
10	Davis,R		7/26/12	THRU	8/05/12
10	Hechavarria,A		9/16/12	THRU	9/29/12

MOST RUNS, GAME

4	Lawrie,B	AT	MIAMI	6/22/12
4	Rasmus,C	AT	CHICAGO	6/05/12

MOST HITS, GAME

5	Rasmus,C	AT	CHICAGO	6/05/12

MOST TOTAL BASES, GAME

10	Escobar,Y	AT	NEW YORK	8/29/12

MOST DOUBLES, GAME

3	Escobar,Y	AT	NEW YORK	8/29/12

MOST TRIPLES, GAME

1	20 PLAYERS TIED

MOST HOME RUNS, GAME

2	Encarnacion,E	VS	CLEVELAND	7/14/12
2	Arencibia,J	VS	KANSAS CITY	7/05/12
2	Lind,A	VS	LOS ANGELES	6/29/12
2	Rasmus,C	AT	MILWAUKEE	6/19/12
2	Bautista,J	AT	MILWAUKEE	6/19/12
2	Arencibia,J	AT	TEXAS	5/27/12
2	Arencibia,J	VS	NEW YORK	5/18/12
2	Davis,R	VS	NEW YORK	5/18/12
2	Bautista,J	AT	MINNESOTA	5/11/12
2	Rasmus,C	AT	KANSAS CITY	4/21/12

MOST EXTRA BASES, GAME

4	Escobar,Y	AT	NEW YORK	8/29/12

MOST RUNS BATTED IN, GAME

6	Arencibia,J	VS	NEW YORK	5/18/12

MOST STOLEN BASES, GAME

3	Davis,R	AT	CHICAGO	7/08/12

INDIVIDUAL PITCHING

MOST STRIKEOUTS GAME (STARTER)

11	Morrow,B	VS	MINNESOTA	10/03/12

MOST STRIKEOUTS GAME (RELIEVER)

7	Chavez,J	AT	TEXAS	5/27/12
7	Villanueva,C	AT	TEXAS	5/25/12

MOST INNINGS, GAME (STARTER)

9.0	Morrow,B	AT	CHICAGO	6/06/12
9.0	Morrow,B	VS	NEW YORK	5/19/12
9.0	Alvarez,H	AT	LOS ANGELES	5/04/12
9.0	Morrow,B	AT	LOS ANGELES	5/03/12

MOST INNINGS, GAME (RELIEVER)

5.0	Jenkins,C	VS	TAMPA BAY	9/02/12
5.0	Chavez,J	AT	TEXAS	5/27/12

MOST HOME RUNS ALLOWED, GAME

4	Villanueva,C	AT	BALTIMORE	9/26/12

LONGEST WINNING STREAK

6	Villanueva,C		6/10/12	THRU	7/27/12

LONGEST LOSING STREAK

13	Romero,R		6/27/12	THRU	9/12/12

MOST CONSECUTIVE SCORELESS INNINGS

23.2	Morrow,B		4/23/12	THRU	5/09/12

2012 TORONTO FINAL PITCHING STATISTICS

+ = ROOKIE

PITCHER	R/L	W	L	ERA	G	GS	CG	GF	ShO	SV	IP	H	R	ER	HR	HB	BB	IBB	SO	WP	BK	OPP AVG
Alvarez,H	R	9	14	4.85	31	31	1	0	1	0	187.1	216	110	101	29	3	54	2	79	3	1	.290
+Beck,C	R	0	0	6.32	14	0	0	2	0	0	15.2	21	12	11	2	0	5	0	9	1	1	.318
+Carpenter,A	R	0	0	5.00	6	0	0	4	0	0	9.0	7	5	5	4	0	6	0	9	1	0	.206
Carpenter,D	R	0	0	30.38	3	0	0	1	0	0	2.2	8	10	9	1	1	2	1	4	0	0	.471
+Carreno,J	R	0	2	6.14	11	2	0	3	0	0	22.0	22	15	15	7	0	14	0	16	0	0	.265
Cecil,B	L	2	4	5.72	21	9	0	2	0	0	61.1	70	40	39	11	3	23	0	51	0	0	.294
Chavez,J	R	1	1	8.44	9	2	0	2	0	0	21.1	25	22	20	6	2	10	1	27	0	0	.281
+Coello,R	R	0	1	12.79	6	0	0	1	0	0	6.1	10	9	9	2	1	4	0	11	0	0	.357
Cordero,F	R	3	5	5.77	41	0	0	17	0	2	34.1	48	24	22	7	1	14	3	26	4	0	.340
+Crawford,E	L	0	0	6.75	10	0	0	3	0	0	8.0	10	6	6	3	1	4	1	5	0	1	.333
+Delabar,S	R	2	2	3.38	27	0	0	1	0	0	29.1	23	12	11	3	0	15	0	46	3	0	.213
Drabek,K	R	4	7	4.67	13	13	0	0	0	0	71.1	67	41	37	10	1	47	0	47	7	0	.250
+Dyson,S	R	0	0	40.50	2	0	0	0	0	0	0.2	4	3	3	0	0	2	0	1	0	0	.667
Frasor,J	R	1	1	4.12	50	0	0	9	0	0	43.2	42	20	20	6	2	22	1	53	5	1	.256
Happ,J	L	3	2	4.69	10	6	0	3	0	0	40.1	35	21	21	2	1	17	1	46	2	0	.236
Hill,S	R	1	0	0.00	1	0	0	0	0	0	3.0	0	0	0	0	0	2	0	0	0	0	.000
+Hutchison,D	R	5	3	4.60	11	11	0	0	0	0	58.2	59	31	30	8	5	20	0	49	1	0	.257
Igarashi,R	R	0	0	36.00	2	0	0	0	0	0	1.0	5	4	4	0	0	2	0	2	0	0	.625
Janssen,C	R	1	1	2.54	62	0	0	47	0	22	63.2	44	18	18	7	3	11	1	67	2	1	.195
+Jenkins,C	R	1	3	4.50	13	3	0	6	0	0	32.0	32	16	16	5	1	11	1	16	0	0	.260
Korecky,B	R	0	0	18.00	1	0	0	1	0	0	1.0	1	2	2	1	0	1	0	0	0	0	.250
Laffey,A	L	4	6	4.56	22	16	0	1	0	0	100.2	100	56	51	17	5	37	1	48	2	0	.260
Lincoln,B	R	1	0	5.65	24	0	0	4	0	0	28.2	29	18	18	6	0	10	1	28	1	0	.264
+Loup,A	L	0	2	2.64	33	0	0	3	0	0	30.2	26	10	9	0	0	2	0	21	1	1	.232
Lyon,B	R	4	0	2.88	30	0	0	10	0	1	25.0	19	8	8	2	1	9	1	28	1	0	.207
Mathis,J	R	0	0	9.00	2	0	0	2	0	0	2.0	4	2	2	0	0	1	0	0	0	0	.400
Morrow,B	R	10	7	2.96	21	21	3	0	3	0	124.2	98	45	41	12	2	41	0	108	3	0	.214
Oliver,D	L	3	4	2.06	62	0	0	11	0	2	56.2	43	13	13	3	4	15	0	52	3	0	.214
Pauley,D	R	0	0	9.95	5	0	0	3	0	0	6.1	11	7	7	1	2	2	0	2	0	0	.393
Perez,L	L	2	2	3.43	35	0	0	6	0	0	42.0	38	16	16	3	3	16	0	39	0	0	.244
Richmond,S	R	0	0	6.00	3	0	0	2	0	0	3.0	5	2	2	1	0	0	0	2	1	0	.357
Romero,R	L	9	14	5.77	32	32	1	0	0	0	181.0	198	122	116	21	10	105	1	124	8	0	.282
Santos,S	R	0	1	9.00	6	0	0	4	0	2	5.0	6	5	5	1	0	4	0	4	1	0	.316
Villanueva,C	R	7	7	4.16	38	16	0	9	0	0	125.1	113	59	58	23	3	46	4	122	6	1	.242
TORONTO		**73**	**89**	**4.64**	**162**	**162**	**5**	**157**	**11**	**29**	**1443.2**	**1439**	**784**	**745**	**204**	**55**	**574**	**20**	**1142**	**56**	**7**	**.261**
OPPONENTS		**89**	**73**	**4.02**	**162**	**162**	**2**	**160**	**9**	**48**	**1450.2**	**1346**	**716**	**648**	**198**	**55**	**473**	**29**	**1251**	**44**	**9**	**.245**

OVER UNDER

In 2009, the Jays became the first American League Club since the 1918 Chicago White Sox & just the 8th Major League Club, all time, to finish a season at least 10 games below the .500 mark while scoring more runs than they had allowed.

Year	Club	Record	Run Differential
1907	Cincinnati Reds	66-87	526+/519- (7)
1918	Chicago White Sox	57-67	457+/446- (11)
1953	New York Giants	70-84	768+/747- (21)
1972	San Francisco Giants	69-86	662+/649- (13)
1980	St. Louis Cardinals	74-88	738+/710- (28)
1984	Pittsburgh Pirates	75-87	615+/567- (48)
2001	Colorado Rockies	73-89	923+/906- (17)
2009	Toronto Blue Jays	75-87	798+/771- (27)

BIOGRAPHIES LAST SEASON HISTORY RECORDS OPPONENTS PLAYER DEV. MEDIA & MISC.

STARTING PITCHERS

PITCHER	T	W	L	PCT	ERA	G	GS	CG	IP	H	TBF	R	ER	HR	SH	SF	HB	BB	IBB	SO	WP	BK	OPP AVG
Alvarez,H	R	9	14	.391	4.85	31	31	1	187.1	216	807	110	101	29	2	4	3	54	2	79	3	1	.290
Carreno,J	R	0	2	.000	9.00	2	2	0	9.0	11	41	9	9	5	0	0	0	6	0	6	0	0	.314
Cecil,B	L	2	4	.333	5.72	9	9	0	50.1	55	217	33	32	11	2	3	1	19	0	42	0	0	.286
Chavez,J	R	0	1	.000	10.38	2	2	0	8.2	10	42	10	10	2	0	0	2	4	0	10	0	0	.278
Drabek,K	R	4	7	.364	4.67	13	13	0	71.1	67	317	41	37	10	0	1	1	47	0	47	7	0	.250
Happ,J	L	3	2	.600	4.59	6	6	0	33.1	30	140	17	17	2	2	2	1	12	1	39	2	0	.244
Hutchison,D	R	5	3	.625	4.60	11	11	0	58.2	59	257	31	30	8	1	1	5	20	0	49	1	0	.257
Jenkins,C	R	1	2	.333	3.95	3	3	0	13.2	11	54	6	6	2	0	0	1	5	0	8	0	0	.229
Laffey,A	L	4	6	.400	4.81	16	16	0	86.0	90	370	51	46	14	2	0	5	30	1	41	1	0	.270
Morrow,B	R	10	7	.588	2.96	21	21	3	124.2	98	504	45	41	12	1	3	2	41	0	108	3	0	.214
Romero,R	L	9	14	.391	5.77	32	32	1	181.0	198	829	122	116	21	7	4	10	105	1	124	8	0	.282
Villanueva,C	R	5	7	.417	4.50	16	16	0	92.0	87	375	46	46	18	2	4	1	25	0	86	4	1	.254
TOTALS		**52**	**69**	**.430**	**4.82**	**162**	**162**	**5**	**916.0**	**932**	**3953**	**521**	**491**	**134**	**19**	**22**	**32**	**368**	**5**	**639**	**29**	**2**	**.265**

RELIEF PITCHERS

PITCHER	T	W	L	PCT	ERA	APP	GF	SV	IP	H	TBF	R	ER	HR	SH	SF	HB	BB	IBB	SO	WP	BK	OPP AVG
Beck,C	R	0	0	.000	6.32	14	2	0	15.2	21	72	12	11	2	0	1	0	5	0	9	1	1	.318
Carpenter,A	R	0	0	.000	5.00	6	4	0	9.0	7	40	5	5	4	0	0	0	6	0	9	1	0	.206
Carpenter,D	R	0	0	.000	30.38	3	1	0	2.2	8	20	10	9	1	0	0	1	2	1	4	0	0	.471
Carreno,J	R	0	0	.000	4.15	9	3	0	13.0	11	56	6	6	2	0	0	0	8	0	10	0	0	.229
Cecil,B	L	0	0	.000	5.73	12	2	0	11.0	15	53	7	7	0	1	0	2	4	0	9	0	0	.326
Chavez,J	R	1	0	1.000	7.11	7	2	0	12.2	15	60	12	10	4	0	1	0	6	1	17	0	0	.283
Coello,R	R	0	1	.000	12.79	6	1	0	6.1	10	33	9	9	2	0	0	1	4	0	11	0	0	.357
Cordero,F	R	3	5	.375	5.77	41	17	2	34.1	48	160	24	22	7	4	0	1	14	3	26	4	0	.340
Crawford,E	L	0	0	.000	6.75	10	3	0	8.0	10	36	6	6	3	1	0	1	4	1	5	0	1	.333
Delabar,S	R	2	2	.500	3.38	27	1	0	29.1	23	126	12	11	3	1	2	0	15	0	46	3	0	.213
Dyson,S	R	0	0	.000	40.50	2	0	0	0.2	4	8	3	3	0	0	0	0	2	0	1	0	0	.667
Frasor,J	R	1	1	.500	4.12	50	9	0	43.2	42	191	20	20	6	1	2	2	22	1	53	5	1	.256
Happ,J	L	0	0	.000	5.14	4	3	0	7.0	5	30	4	4	0	0	0	0	5	0	7	0	0	.200
Hill,S	R	1	0	1.000	0.00	1	0	0	3.0	0	11	0	0	0	0	0	0	2	0	0	0	0	.000
Igarashi,R	R	0	0	.000	36.00	2	0	0	1.0	5	10	4	4	0	0	0	0	2	0	2	0	0	.625
Janssen,C	R	1	1	.500	2.54	62	47	22	63.2	44	242	18	18	7	1	1	3	11	1	67	2	1	.195
Jenkins,C	R	0	1	.000	4.91	10	6	0	18.1	21	82	10	10	3	1	0	0	6	1	8	0	0	.280
Korecky,B	R	0	0	.000	18.00	1	1	0	1.0	1	5	2	2	1	0	0	0	1	0	0	0	0	.250
Laffey,A	L	0	0	.000	3.07	6	1	0	14.2	10	59	5	5	3	0	0	0	7	0	7	1	0	.192
Lincoln,B	R	1	0	1.000	5.65	24	4	0	28.2	29	123	18	18	6	2	1	0	10	1	28	1	0	.264
Loup,A	L	0	2	.000	2.64	33	3	0	30.2	26	117	10	9	0	2	1	0	2	0	21	1	1	.232
Lyon,B	R	4	0	1.000	2.88	30	10	1	25.0	19	104	8	8	2	1	1	1	9	1	28	1	0	.207
Mathis,J	R	0	0	.000	9.00	2	2	0	2.0	4	11	2	2	0	0	0	0	1	0	0	0	0	.400
Oliver,D	L	3	4	.429	2.06	62	11	2	56.2	43	221	13	13	3	1	0	4	15	0	52	3	0	.214
Pauley,D	R	0	0	.000	9.95	5	3	0	6.1	11	33	7	7	1	0	1	2	2	0	2	0	0	.393
Perez,L	L	2	2	.500	3.43	35	6	0	42.0	38	175	16	16	3	0	0	3	16	0	39	0	0	.244
Richmond,S	R	0	0	.000	6.00	3	2	0	3.0	5	15	2	2	1	0	1	0	0	0	2	1	0	.357
Santos,S	R	0	1	.000	9.00	6	4	2	5.0	6	24	5	5	1	0	1	0	4	0	4	1	0	.316
Villanueva,C	R	2	0	1.000	3.24	22	9	0	33.1	26	146	13	12	5	0	0	2	21	4	36	2	0	.211
TOTALS		**21**	**20**	**.512**	**4.33**	**495**	**157**	**29**	**527.2**	**507**	**2263**	**263**	**254**	**70**	**16**	**13**	**23**	**206**	**15**	**503**	**27**	**5**	**.253**

PITCHING AT HOME

PITCHER	ERA	W	L	G	GS	CG	ShO	SV	IP	AB	H	R	ER	HR	HB	BB	SO	WP	OPP AVG
Alvarez,H	4.82	4	9	16	16	0	0	0	99.0	397	114	56	53	14	3	24	42	2	.287
Beck,C	8.64	0	0	7	0	0	0	0	8.1	38	13	9	8	1	0	3	4	1	.342
Carpenter,A	7.50	0	0	3	0	0	0	0	6.0	24	6	5	5	4	0	3	7	0	.250
Carpenter,D	54.00	0	0	1	0	0	0	0	0.2	5	3	4	4	0	1	1	1	0	.600
Carreno,J	4.50	0	0	3	0	0	0	0	4.0	14	3	2	2	1	0	1	3	0	.214
Cecil,B	5.70	2	3	12	5	0	0	0	36.1	139	38	23	23	7	2	13	35	0	.273
Chavez,J	54.00	0	0	2	0	0	0	0	1.0	8	5	8	6	2	0	2	1	0	.625
Coello,R	2.25	0	0	2	0	0	0	0	4.0	16	5	1	1	0	0	2	6	0	.313
Cordero,F	7.13	3	2	22	0	0	0	0	17.2	78	28	15	14	6	1	7	18	2	.359
Crawford,E	7.20	0	0	8	0	0	0	0	5.0	18	4	4	4	2	1	4	4	0	.222
Delabar,S	4.30	2	1	13	0	0	0	0	14.2	58	13	8	7	1	0	7	22	1	.224
Drabek,K	2.70	3	3	6	6	0	0	0	36.2	135	29	15	11	2	1	16	28	0	.215
Dyson,S	0.00	0	0	1	0	0	0	0	0.1	1	0	0	0	0	0	1	1	0	.000
Frasor,J	3.74	0	0	24	0	0	0	0	21.2	86	25	9	9	1	1	10	25	1	.291
Happ,J	4.71	2	1	5	3	0	0	0	21.0	76	17	11	11	2	1	6	24	1	.224
Hill,S	0.00	1	0	1	0	0	0	0	3.0	9	0	0	0	0	0	2	0	0	.000
Hutchison,D	2.36	3	0	5	5	0	0	0	26.2	99	20	8	7	1	3	11	23	0	.202
Janssen,C	3.12	0	0	35	0	0	0	14	34.2	124	25	12	12	5	0	4	29	1	.202
Jenkins,C	4.50	1	1	9	2	0	0	0	20.0	78	20	10	10	3	0	7	8	0	.256
Korecky,B	18.00	0	0	1	0	0	0	0	1.0	4	1	2	2	1	0	1	0	0	.250
Laffey,A	5.28	1	2	10	7	0	0	0	44.1	174	46	28	26	12	3	17	25	1	.264
Lincoln,B	5.93	0	0	13	0	0	0	0	13.2	56	17	9	9	3	0	3	15	0	.304
Loup,A	3.00	0	0	15	0	0	0	0	15.0	54	14	6	5	0	0	1	9	1	.259
Lyon,B	0.71	3	0	14	0	0	0	1	12.2	44	8	1	1	1	1	4	12	0	.182
Mathis,J	18.00	0	0	1	0	0	0	0	1.0	6	3	2	2	0	0	0	0	0	.500
Morrow,B	3.01	6	4	13	13	1	1	0	77.2	288	65	26	26	8	1	23	70	2	.226
Oliver,D	2.93	0	3	32	0	0	0	1	27.2	100	25	9	9	1	3	10	25	1	.250
Pauley,D	9.00	0	0	2	0	0	0	0	4.0	18	6	4	4	1	1	0	1	0	.333
Perez,L	4.15	0	1	17	0	0	0	0	21.2	79	21	10	10	2	2	7	17	0	.266
Richmond,S	9.00	0	0	2	0	0	0	0	2.0	12	5	2	2	1	0	0	1	1	.417
Romero,R	6.42	5	7	15	15	0	0	0	81.1	323	92	59	58	11	5	40	60	3	.285
Santos,S	11.57	0	1	3	0	0	0	1	2.1	8	3	3	3	0	0	3	3	1	.375
Villanueva,C	3.00	5	2	20	9	0	0	0	69.0	245	54	24	23	9	3	23	68	2	.220
TOTALS	**4.50**	**41**	**40**	**81**	**81**	**1**	**7**	**17**	**734.0**	**2814**	**728**	**385**	**367**	**102**	**33**	**256**	**587**	**21**	**.259**

GAME DELAYS AT ROGERS CENTRE

DATE	TEAM	REASON	DURATION
June 7, 1989	Milwaukee	Rain	6 minutes
August 27, 1990	Milwaukee	Bugs	35 minutes
August 10, 1991	Boston	Rain	14 minutes
July 21, 1994	Texas	Rain	7 minutes
June 18, 1997	Atlanta	Fog	14 minutes
July 26, 2003	Chicago (A)	Rain	26 minutes

PITCHING ON THE ROAD

PITCHER	ERA	W	L	G	GS	CG	ShO	SV	IP	AB	H	R	ER	HR	HB	BB	SO	WP	OPP AVG
Alvarez,H	4.89	5	5	15	15	1	1	0	88.1	347	102	54	48	15	0	30	37	1	.294
Beck,C	3.68	0	0	7	0	0	0	0	7.1	28	8	3	3	1	0	2	5	0	.286
Carpenter,A	0.00	0	0	3	0	0	0	0	3.0	10	1	0	0	0	0	3	2	1	.100
Carpenter,D	22.50	0	0	2	0	0	0	0	2.0	12	5	6	5	1	0	1	3	0	.417
Carreno,J	6.50	0	2	8	2	0	0	0	18.0	69	19	13	13	6	0	13	13	0	.275
Cecil,B	5.76	0	1	9	4	0	0	0	25.0	99	32	17	16	4	1	10	16	0	.323
Chavez,J	6.20	1	1	7	2	0	0	0	20.1	81	20	14	14	4	2	8	26	0	.247
Coello,R	30.86	0	1	4	0	0	0	0	2.1	12	5	8	8	2	1	2	5	0	.417
Cordero,F	4.32	0	3	19	0	0	0	2	16.2	63	20	9	8	1	0	7	8	2	.317
Crawford,E	6.00	0	0	2	0	0	0	0	3.0	12	6	2	2	1	0	0	1	0	.500
Delabar,S	2.45	0	1	14	0	0	0	0	14.2	50	10	4	4	2	0	8	24	2	.200
Drabek,K	6.75	1	4	7	7	0	0	0	34.2	133	38	26	26	8	0	31	19	7	.286
Dyson,S	81.00	0	0	1	0	0	0	0	0.1	5	4	3	3	0	0	1	0	0	.800
Frasor,J	4.50	1	1	26	0	0	0	0	22.0	78	17	11	11	5	1	12	28	4	.218
Happ,J	4.66	1	1	5	3	0	0	0	19.1	72	18	10	10	0	0	11	22	1	.250
Hutchison,D	6.47	2	3	6	6	0	0	0	32.0	131	39	23	23	7	2	9	26	1	.298
Igarashi,R	36.00	0	0	2	0	0	0	0	1.0	8	5	4	4	0	0	2	2	0	.625
Janssen,C	1.86	1	1	27	0	0	0	8	29.0	102	19	6	6	2	3	7	38	1	.186
Jenkins,C	4.50	0	2	4	1	0	0	0	12.0	45	12	6	6	2	1	4	8	0	.267
Laffey,A	3.99	3	4	12	9	0	0	0	56.1	211	54	28	25	5	2	20	23	1	.256
Lincoln,B	5.40	1	0	11	0	0	0	0	15.0	54	12	9	9	3	0	7	13	1	.222
Loup,A	2.30	0	2	18	0	0	0	0	15.2	58	12	4	4	0	0	1	12	0	.207
Lyon,B	5.11	1	0	16	0	0	0	0	12.1	48	11	7	7	1	0	5	16	1	.229
Mathis,J	0.00	0	0	1	0	0	0	0	1.0	4	1	0	0	0	0	1	0	0	.250
Morrow,B	2.87	4	3	8	8	2	2	0	47.0	169	33	19	15	4	1	18	38	1	.195
Oliver,D	1.24	3	1	30	0	0	0	1	29.0	101	18	4	4	2	1	5	27	2	.178
Pauley,D	11.57	0	0	3	0	0	0	0	2.1	10	5	3	3	0	1	2	1	0	.500
Perez,L	2.66	2	1	18	0	0	0	0	20.1	77	17	6	6	1	1	9	22	0	.221
Richmond,S	0.00	0	0	1	0	0	0	0	1.0	2	0	0	0	0	0	0	1	0	.000
Romero,R	5.24	4	7	17	17	1	0	0	99.2	380	106	63	58	10	5	65	64	5	.279
Santos,S	6.75	0	0	3	0	0	0	1	2.2	11	3	2	2	1	0	1	1	0	.273
Villanueva,C	5.59	2	5	18	7	0	0	0	56.1	221	59	35	35	14	0	23	54	4	.267
TOTALS	**4.79**	**32**	**49**	**81**	**81**	**4**	**4**	**12**	**709.2**	**2703**	**711**	**399**	**378**	**102**	**22**	**318**	**555**	**35**	**.263**

1991 ALL-STAR GAME

The 1991 All-Star Game was played at SkyDome (now Rogers Centre) in Toronto on Tuesday, July 9, 1991... It was the first time that the game had been held in Toronto and just the second time that it had been held outside of the United States (Montreal 1982)... Three Blue Jays players were selected to participate in the 63rd All-Star Game: second baseman Roberto Alomar, outfielder Joe Carter and pitcher Jimmy Key as well, manager Cito Gaston was a coach and Tommy Craig was named AL trainer... 52,382 fans came to SkyDome to watch the action unfold in person and millions more watched and listened to the mid-season classic on television and radio... 56 players from both the National and American Leagues came to Toronto to participate... Of those 56 players, 49 saw action as the American League defeated the National League by a 4-2 count... Toronto pitcher Jimmy Key was credited with the win in his second career All-Star Game appearance... Joe Carter was 1-1 with a run scored and Roberto Alomar went 0-4... It was the fourth consecutive win for the American League dating back to 1988.

2012 TORONTO FINAL BATTING STATISTICS

+ = ROOKIE

PLAYER	AVG	G	AB	R	H	TB	2B	3B	HR	RBI	SH	SF	HP	BB	IBB	SO	SB	CS	GIDP	E	SLG	OBP	PINCH HIT AB	PINCH HIT H	PINCH HIT HR	PINCH HIT RBI
Alvarez,H	.000	31	1	0	0	0	0	0	0	0	0	0	0	0	0	1	0	0	0	4	.000	.000	0	0	0	0
Arencibia,J	.233	102	347	45	81	151	16	0	18	56	1	3	3	18	1	108	1	0	4	4	.435	.275	5	0	0	0
Bautista,J	.241	92	332	64	80	175	14	0	27	65	0	4	4	59	2	63	5	2	11	2	.527	.358	0	0	0	0
+Carreno,J	.000	11	1	0	0	0	0	0	0	0	0	0	0	0	0	0	0	0	0	1	.000	.000	0	0	0	0
Cecil,B	.000	21	2	0	0	0	0	0	0	0	0	0	0	0	0	2	0	0	0	1	.000	.000	0	0	0	0
Chavez,J	.000	9	2	0	0	0	0	0	0	0	1	0	0	0	0	2	0	0	0	1	.000	.000	0	0	0	0
+Cooper,D	.300	45	140	16	42	65	11	0	4	11	0	0	1	4	0	22	0	1	1	1	.464	.324	8	4	0	0
Davis,R	.257	142	447	64	115	169	24	3	8	43	1	4	6	29	3	102	46	13	8	8	.378	.309	3	0	0	0
Drabek,K	.000	13	2	0	0	0	0	0	0	0	0	0	0	0	0	1	0	0	0	3	.000	.000	0	0	0	0
Encarnacion,E	.280	151	542	93	152	302	24	0	42	110	0	7	11	84	12	94	13	3	6	4	.557	.384	0	0	0	0
Escobar,Y	.253	145	558	58	141	192	22	1	9	51	7	4	4	35	1	70	5	1	21	12	.344	.300	3	1	0	0
Francisco,B	.240	27	50	5	12	19	5	1	0	2	0	0	0	4	0	10	0	1	0	0	.380	.296	6	1	0	2
+Gomes,Y	.204	43	98	9	20	36	4	0	4	13	1	3	3	6	0	32	0	0	3	1	.367	.264	8	2	1	3
+Gose,A	.223	56	166	25	37	53	7	3	1	11	4	0	2	17	0	59	15	3	1	1	.319	.303	3	0	0	0
+Hechavarria,A	.254	41	126	10	32	46	8	0	2	15	5	1	1	4	0	32	0	0	2	3	.365	.280	1	1	0	0
+Hutchison,D	.000	11	2	0	0	0	0	0	0	0	0	0	0	0	0	0	0	0	0	0	.000	.000	0	0	0	0
Johnson,K	.225	142	507	61	114	185	19	2	16	55	2	4	5	62	4	159	14	2	8	11	.365	.313	4	1	0	1
Laffey,A	.000	22	1	0	0	0	0	0	0	0	0	0	0	0	0	0	0	0	0	0	.000	.000	0	0	0	0
Lawrie,B	.273	125	494	73	135	200	26	3	11	48	2	2	5	33	0	86	13	8	9	17	.405	.324	0	0	0	0
Lind,A	.255	93	321	28	82	133	14	2	11	45	0	3	0	29	1	61	0	0	10	5	.414	.314	6	2	0	0
+Loup,A	.000	33	1	0	0	0	0	0	0	0	0	0	0	0	0	0	0	0	0	0	.000	.000	0	0	0	0
Mathis,J	.218	71	211	25	46	83	13	0	8	27	6	1	0	9	0	68	1	0	2	2	.393	.249	5	0	0	0
McCoy,M	.173	32	52	10	9	13	1	0	1	7	0	0	0	4	0	6	2	1	1	0	.250	.232	2	1	0	0
Rasmus,C	.223	151	565	75	126	226	21	5	23	75	2	4	7	47	5	149	4	3	7	6	.400	.289	6	1	0	0
Romero,R	.200	32	5	1	1	1	0	0	0	0	0	0	0	0	0	2	0	0	0	2	.200	.200	0	0	0	0
+Sierra,M	.224	49	147	14	33	55	4	0	6	15	0	0	2	8	0	44	1	0	3	0	.374	.274	6	1	0	2
Snider,T	.250	10	36	6	9	20	2	0	3	8	0	1	0	3	0	14	0	0	0	1	.556	.300	0	0	0	0
Thames,E	.243	46	148	17	36	54	7	1	3	11	0	2	1	9	0	40	0	1	7	1	.365	.288	7	0	0	1
Torrealba,Y	.214	10	28	3	6	9	0	0	1	2	0	0	0	2	0	7	0	0	0	0	.321	.267	1	0	0	0
Villanueva,C	.500	38	2	1	1	1	0	0	0	0	0	0	0	0	0	0	0	0	0	0	.500	.500	0	0	0	0
Vizquel,O	.235	60	153	13	36	43	5	1	0	7	1	2	0	7	0	17	3	2	5	3	.281	.265	12	3	0	0
TORONTO	**.245**	**162**	**5487**	**716**	**1346**	**2231**	**247**	**22**	**198**	**677**	**33**	**45**	**55**	**473**	**29**	**1251**	**123**	**41**	**109**	**101**	**.407**	**.309**	**86**	**18**	**1**	**9**
OPPONENTS	**.261**	**162**	**5517**	**784**	**1439**	**2415**	**334**	**15**	**204**	**743**	**35**	**35**	**55**	**574**	**20**	**1142**	**87**	**43**	**143**	**108**	**.438**	**.335**	**97**	**16**	**0**	**6**

HOME RUN BREAKDOWN vs EACH CLUB (LAST SEASON)

TORONTO vs	2012 HR F	2012 HR A
Baltimore	21	32
Boston	23	17
Chicago (AL)	13	16
Cleveland	6	9
Detroit	6	4
Kansas City	10	7
Los Angeles (AL)	11	10
Minnesota	7	4
New York (AL)	22	17
Oakland	11	12
Seattle	11	10
Tampa Bay	15	25

TORONTO vs	2012 HR F	2012 HR A
Texas	13	16
Atlanta	4	2
Miami	3	5
Milwaukee	10	6
New York (NL)	6	1
Philadelphia	2	3
Washington	4	8
Totals	**198**	**204**

BATTING AT HOME

BATTER	AVG	G	AB	R	H	2B	3B	HR	RBI	SH	SF	HP	BB	SO	SB	CS	GI DP	E
Arencibia,J	.210	49	162	22	34	9	0	9	25	1	1	2	8	50	0	0	2	2
Bautista,J	.229	45	157	32	36	7	0	11	27	0	2	0	31	31	4	1	5	2
Cooper,D	.288	20	73	7	21	5	0	1	4	0	0	0	2	12	0	1	1	1
Davis,R	.258	72	229	32	59	11	3	5	27	0	2	0	16	58	24	3	3	2
Encarnacion,E	.284	75	250	50	71	9	0	23	57	0	2	8	47	43	5	2	4	1
Escobar,Y	.247	72	275	30	68	10	1	6	32	2	2	3	17	34	2	0	11	3
Francisco,B	.250	17	32	3	8	3	1	0	2	0	0	0	3	7	0	0	0	0
Gomes,Y	.265	22	49	7	13	2	0	3	7	1	2	2	5	15	0	0	3	1
Gose,A	.232	29	82	16	19	3	3	0	3	0	0	2	11	27	11	1	0	1
Hechavarria,A	.237	20	59	7	14	5	0	1	6	4	0	0	0	13	0	0	1	1
Johnson,K	.236	72	258	34	61	14	1	10	34	1	1	1	28	81	9	0	6	5
Lawrie,B	.302	60	232	33	70	13	1	7	27	1	0	4	15	37	6	6	3	8
Lind,A	.270	47	163	16	44	10	1	6	30	0	2	0	15	33	0	0	5	3
Mathis,J	.282	33	110	17	31	9	0	5	17	1	0	0	6	34	0	0	1	1
McCoy,M	.130	12	23	3	3	1	0	1	4	0	0	0	2	3	0	0	0	0
Rasmus,C	.215	73	256	34	55	7	2	8	27	1	3	4	21	65	2	3	1	2
Sierra,M	.184	26	76	5	14	1	0	3	7	0	0	1	5	23	0	0	1	0
Snider,T	.174	6	23	4	4	1	0	2	5	0	0	0	1	8	0	0	0	1
Thames,E	.277	21	65	10	18	5	0	1	4	0	1	1	6	21	0	0	1	0
Torrealba,Y	.125	5	16	0	2	0	0	0	0	0	0	0	1	2	0	0	0	0
Vizquel,O	.246	28	57	6	14	2	1	0	2	1	0	0	4	8	2	0	4	1
PITCHERS	**.000**	**81**	**0**	**0**	**0**	**0**	**0**	**0**	**0**	**0**	**0**	**0**	**0**	**0**	**0**	**0**	**0**	**12**
TOTALS	**.249**	**81**	**2647**	**368**	**659**	**127**	**14**	**102**	**347**	**13**	**18**	**28**	**244**	**605**	**65**	**17**	**52**	**47**

BATTING ON THE ROAD

BATTER	AVG	G	AB	R	H	2B	3B	HR	RBI	SH	SF	HP	BB	SO	SB	CS	GI DP	E
Arencibia,J	.254	53	185	23	47	7	0	9	31	0	2	1	10	58	1	0	2	2
Bautista,J	.251	47	175	32	44	7	0	16	38	0	2	4	28	32	1	1	6	0
Cooper,D	.313	25	67	9	21	6	0	3	7	0	0	1	2	10	0	0	0	0
Davis,R	.257	70	218	32	56	13	0	3	16	1	2	6	13	44	22	10	5	6
Encarnacion,E	.277	76	292	43	81	15	0	19	53	0	5	3	37	51	8	1	2	3
Escobar,Y	.258	73	283	28	73	12	0	3	19	5	2	1	18	36	3	1	10	9
Francisco,B	.222	10	18	2	4	2	0	0	0	0	0	0	1	3	0	1	0	0
Gomes,Y	.143	21	49	2	7	2	0	1	6	0	1	1	1	17	0	0	0	0
Gose,A	.214	27	84	9	18	4	0	1	8	4	0	0	6	32	4	2	1	0
Hechavarria,A	.269	21	67	3	18	3	0	1	9	1	1	1	4	19	0	0	1	2
Johnson,K	.213	70	249	27	53	5	1	6	21	1	3	4	34	78	5	2	2	6
Lawrie,B	.248	65	262	40	65	13	2	4	21	1	2	1	18	49	7	2	6	9
Lind,A	.241	46	158	12	38	4	1	5	15	0	1	0	14	28	0	0	5	2
Mathis,J	.149	38	101	8	15	4	0	3	10	5	1	0	3	34	1	0	1	1
McCoy,M	.207	20	29	7	6	0	0	0	3	0	0	0	2	3	2	1	1	0
Rasmus,C	.230	78	309	41	71	14	3	15	48	1	1	3	26	84	2	0	6	4
Sierra,M	.268	23	71	9	19	3	0	3	8	0	0	1	3	21	1	0	2	0
Snider,T	.385	4	13	2	5	1	0	1	3	0	1	0	2	6	0	0	0	0
Thames,E	.217	25	83	7	18	2	1	2	7	0	1	0	3	19	0	1	6	1
Torrealba,Y	.333	5	12	3	4	0	0	1	2	0	0	0	1	5	0	0	0	0
Vizquel,O	.229	32	96	7	22	3	0	0	5	0	2	0	3	9	1	2	1	2
PITCHERS	**.105**	**81**	**19**	**2**	**2**	**0**	**0**	**0**	**0**	**1**	**0**	**0**	**0**	**8**	**0**	**0**	**0**	**7**
TOTALS	**.242**	**81**	**2840**	**348**	**687**	**120**	**8**	**96**	**330**	**20**	**27**	**27**	**229**	**646**	**58**	**24**	**57**	**54**

2012 vs. RIGHTHANDERS

BATTER	AVG	G	AB	R	H	2B	3B	HR	RBI	SH	SF	HP	BB	SO	SB	CS	GIDP	SLG	OBP
Arencibia,J	.230	93	257	35	59	11	0	12	39	1	2	3	14	80	1	0	3	.412	.275
Bautista,J	.255	90	247	48	63	11	0	22	51	0	4	3	47	50	3	2	6	.567	.375
Cooper,D	.302	42	106	14	32	8	0	4	11	0	0	1	4	16	0	0	1	.491	.333
Davis,R	.243	122	296	34	72	15	2	4	29	1	4	4	17	67	23	11	6	.348	.290
Encarnacion,E	.273	147	406	62	111	16	0	28	79	0	4	9	57	63	6	2	5	.520	.372
Escobar,Y	.251	138	407	44	102	20	0	7	35	6	3	4	21	53	5	1	17	.351	.292
Francisco,B	.176	14	17	2	3	2	0	0	0	0	0	0	2	3	0	0	0	.294	.263
Gomes,Y	.192	31	52	5	10	2	0	1	7	1	2	2	5	19	0	0	0	.288	.279
Gose,A	.207	54	135	21	28	5	2	1	8	0	0	2	17	48	15	3	0	.296	.305
Hechavarria,A	.266	32	79	7	21	6	0	1	11	4	1	1	3	22	0	0	2	.380	.298
Johnson,K	.234	131	368	48	86	16	2	12	41	2	4	4	44	117	12	1	6	.386	.319
Lawrie,B	.256	118	359	49	92	17	3	8	37	2	2	4	25	62	7	5	7	.387	.310
Lind,A	.276	86	232	23	64	13	1	9	34	0	2	0	23	44	0	0	7	.457	.339
Mathis,J	.218	65	147	19	32	10	0	5	22	4	1	0	6	50	1	0	2	.388	.247
McCoy,M	.188	26	32	6	6	0	0	0	4	0	0	0	0	5	2	1	0	.188	.188
Rasmus,C	.238	143	411	64	98	17	3	20	63	1	3	2	35	105	3	1	6	.440	.299
Sierra,M	.187	40	91	9	17	2	0	3	8	0	0	2	4	32	0	0	3	.308	.237
Snider,T	.174	9	23	2	4	1	0	0	1	0	1	0	3	7	0	0	0	.217	.259
Thames,E	.233	43	120	13	28	5	1	3	10	0	2	1	6	34	0	1	7	.367	.271
Torrealba,Y	.174	9	23	3	4	0	0	1	2	0	0	0	2	6	0	0	0	.304	.240
Vizquel,O	.243	54	107	10	26	3	1	0	5	1	2	0	5	10	3	2	4	.290	.272
PITCHERS	**.133**		**15**	**2**	**2**	**0**	**0**	**0**	**0**	**1**	**0**	**0**	**0**	**5**	**0**	**0**	**0**	**.133**	**.133**
TOTALS	**.244**		**3930**	**520**	**960**	**180**	**15**	**141**	**497**	**24**	**37**	**42**	**340**	**898**	**81**	**30**	**82**	**.405**	**.309**

PITCHER	AVG	AB	H	HR	HB	BB	SO
Alvarez,H	.265	340	90	13	2	15	40
Beck,C	.324	37	12	0	0	1	5
Carpenter,A	.200	20	4	2	0	2	6
Carpenter,D	.333	9	3	1	1	1	3
Carreno,J	.295	44	13	5	0	3	9
Cecil,B	.319	182	58	10	0	20	36
Chavez,J	.241	54	13	2	2	6	13
Coello,R	.353	17	6	2	1	1	7
Cordero,F	.329	70	23	5	0	4	13
Crawford,E	.615	13	8	2	1	4	2
Delabar,S	.169	59	10	1	0	10	28
Drabek,K	.307	127	39	7	0	21	25
Dyson,S	.600	5	3	0	0	1	1
Frasor,J	.245	98	24	3	1	7	35
Happ,J	.236	110	26	1	0	15	36
Hill,S	.000	5	0	0	0	1	0
Hutchison,D	.259	108	28	4	3	9	23
Igarashi,R	.667	6	4	0	0	1	1
Janssen,C	.218	110	24	5	2	4	37
Jenkins,C	.238	63	15	2	1	5	7
Korecky,B	.000	2	0	0	0	0	0
Laffey,A	.269	268	72	11	2	29	31
Lincoln,B	.306	62	19	3	0	6	14
Loup,A	.259	54	14	0	0	1	10
Lyon,B	.230	61	14	2	0	3	15
Mathis,J	.400	5	2	0	0	1	0
Morrow,B	.246	207	51	7	1	18	46
Oliver,D	.196	107	21	1	2	6	29
Pauley,D	.313	16	5	0	1	1	1
Perez,L	.277	94	26	2	0	10	16
Richmond,S	.571	7	4	1	0	0	1
Romero,R	.268	474	127	12	3	77	84
Santos,S	.500	8	4	0	0	2	3
Villanueva,C	.246	240	59	8	1	16	65
TOTALS	**.266**	**3082**	**821**	**112**	**24**	**301**	**642**

2012 vs. LEFTHANDERS

BATTER	AVG	G	AB	R	H	2B	3B	HR	RBI	SH	SF	HP	BB	SO	SB	CS	GIDP	SLG	OBP
Arencibia,J	.244	43	90	10	22	5	0	6	17	0	1	0	4	28	0	0	1	.500	.274
Bautista,J	.200	43	85	16	17	3	0	5	14	0	0	1	12	13	2	0	5	.412	.306
Cooper,D	.294	18	34	2	10	3	0	0	0	0	0	0	0	6	0	1	0	.382	.294
Davis,R	.285	70	151	30	43	9	1	4	14	0	0	2	12	35	23	2	2	.437	.345
Encarnacion,E	.301	72	136	31	41	8	0	14	31	0	3	2	27	31	7	1	1	.669	.417
Escobar,Y	.258	70	151	14	39	2	1	2	16	1	1	0	14	17	0	0	4	.325	.319
Francisco,B	.273	16	33	3	9	3	1	0	2	0	0	0	2	7	0	1	0	.424	.314
Gomes,Y	.217	24	46	4	10	2	0	3	6	0	1	1	1	13	0	0	3	.457	.245
Gose,A	.290	18	31	4	9	2	1	0	3	4	0	0	0	11	0	0	1	.419	.290
Hechavarria,A	.234	19	47	3	11	2	0	1	4	1	0	0	1	10	0	0	0	.340	.250
Johnson,K	.201	73	139	13	28	3	0	4	14	0	0	1	18	42	2	1	2	.309	.297
Lawrie,B	.319	59	135	24	43	9	0	3	11	0	0	1	8	24	6	3	2	.452	.361
Lind,A	.202	49	89	5	18	1	1	2	11	0	1	0	6	17	0	0	3	.303	.250
Mathis,J	.219	34	64	6	14	3	0	3	5	2	0	0	3	18	0	0	0	.406	.254
McCoy,M	.150	11	20	4	3	1	0	1	3	0	0	0	4	1	0	0	1	.350	.292
Rasmus,C	.182	80	154	11	28	4	2	3	12	1	1	5	12	44	1	2	1	.292	.262
Sierra,M	.286	25	56	5	16	2	0	3	7	0	0	0	4	12	1	0	0	.482	.333
Snider,T	.385	6	13	4	5	1	0	3	7	0	0	0	0	7	0	0	0	1.154	.385
Thames,E	.286	18	28	4	8	2	0	0	1	0	0	0	3	6	0	0	0	.357	.355
Torrealba,Y	.400	3	5	0	2	0	0	0	0	0	0	0	0	1	0	0	0	.400	.400
Vizquel,O	.217	25	46	3	10	2	0	0	2	0	0	0	2	7	0	0	1	.261	.250
PITCHERS	**.000**		**4**	**0**	**0**	**0**	**0**	**0**	**0**	**0**	**0**	**0**	**0**	**3**	**0**	**0**	**0**	**.000**	**.000**
TOTALS	**.248**		**1557**	**196**	**386**	**67**	**7**	**57**	**180**	**9**	**8**	**13**	**133**	**353**	**42**	**11**	**27**	**.410**	**.311**

PITCHER	AVG	AB	H	HR	HB	BB	SO
Alvarez,H	.312	404	126	16	1	39	39
Beck,C	.310	29	9	2	0	4	4
Carpenter,A	.214	14	3	2	0	4	3
Carpenter,D	.625	8	5	0	0	1	1
Carreno,J	.231	39	9	2	0	11	7
Cecil,B	.214	56	12	1	3	3	15
Chavez,J	.343	35	12	4	0	4	14
Coello,R	.364	11	4	0	0	3	4
Cordero,F	.352	71	25	2	1	10	13
Crawford,E	.118	17	2	1	0	0	3
Delabar,S	.265	49	13	2	0	5	18
Drabek,K	.199	141	28	3	1	26	22
Dyson,S	1.000	1	1	0	0	1	0
Frasor,J	.273	66	18	3	1	15	18
Happ,J	.237	38	9	1	1	2	10
Hill,S	.000	4	0	0	0	1	0
Hutchison,D	.254	122	31	4	2	11	26
Igarashi,R	.500	2	1	0	0	1	1
Janssen,C	.172	116	20	2	1	7	30
Jenkins,C	.283	60	17	3	0	6	9
Korecky,B	.500	2	1	1	0	1	0
Laffey,A	.239	117	28	6	3	8	17
Lincoln,B	.208	48	10	3	0	4	14
Loup,A	.207	58	12	0	0	1	11
Lyon,B	.161	31	5	0	1	6	13
Mathis,J	.400	5	2	0	0	0	0
Morrow,B	.188	250	47	5	1	23	62
Oliver,D	.234	94	22	2	2	9	23
Pauley,D	.500	12	6	1	1	1	1
Perez,L	.194	62	12	1	3	6	23
Richmond,S	.143	7	1	0	0	0	1
Romero,R	.310	229	71	9	7	28	40
Santos,S	.182	11	2	1	0	2	1
Villanueva,C	.239	226	54	15	2	30	57
TOTALS	**.254**	**2435**	**618**	**92**	**31**	**273**	**500**

AMERICAN LEAGUE 2012 SITUATIONAL STATISTICS

AL BATTING VS LHP

	AVG	AB	R	H	2B	3B	HR	RBI	SB	CS	TBB	SO	OBP	SLG
Rangers	.285	1497	---	426	84	7	48	208	22	18	131	308	.347	.446
Angels	.277	1484	---	411	84	6	53	187	20	5	130	282	.337	.449
Red Sox	.271	1677	---	454	89	5	60	226	29	12	126	345	.322	.437
Twins	.266	1730	---	460	73	8	42	219	42	14	163	318	.332	.390
Yankees	.263	1931	---	508	92	6	78	266	21	13	212	414	.339	.438
Royals	.257	1734	---	446	94	9	41	193	34	17	140	328	.313	.393
Tigers	.253	1659	---	419	91	11	41	196	6	8	178	359	.329	.395
Orioles	.252	1482	---	374	65	7	51	173	17	7	136	347	.320	.409
White Sox	.252	1447	---	365	69	5	62	191	21	10	136	323	.320	.435
Blue Jays	**.248**	**1557**	**---**	**386**	**67**	**7**	**57**	**180**	**42**	**11**	**133**	**353**	**.311**	**.410**
Mariners	.244	1945	---	474	83	11	55	200	33	11	144	435	.297	.383
Rays	.238	1592	---	379	80	8	46	196	40	14	176	437	.319	.385
Athletics	.236	1844	---	436	90	13	62	218	28	16	175	485	.306	.400
Indians	.234	1862	---	436	84	8	40	209	38	20	190	381	.312	.352
League Avg.	**.255**	**1803**	**---**	**459**	**88**	**8**	**56**	**220**	**30**	**13**	**166**	**393**	**.320**	**.405**

AL BATTING AT HOME

	AVG	AB	R	H	2B	3B	HR	RBI	SB	CS	TBB	SO	OBP	SLG
Rangers	.285	2772	447	790	164	16	108	425	55	22	240	520	.347	.473
Red Sox	.279	2828	419	788	211	9	88	399	43	14	229	592	.335	.453
Tigers	.278	2696	393	749	136	27	92	375	21	14	253	488	.342	.451
Royals	.278	2767	341	768	156	20	62	322	70	20	202	450	.328	.416
Twins	.274	2735	366	750	137	20	69	354	70	19	273	497	.343	.415
Angels	.272	2646	348	720	141	13	82	336	51	11	193	503	.325	.428
White Sox	.268	2719	417	730	124	15	120	405	57	22	252	580	.336	.458
Yankees	.266	2668	406	709	122	3	138	394	47	11	277	572	.338	.469
Orioles	.258	2726	387	704	143	5	127	365	40	7	242	622	.323	.454
Indians	.249	2749	323	685	141	9	64	304	62	20	271	539	.322	.377
Blue Jays	**.249**	**2647**	**368**	**659**	**127**	**14**	**102**	**347**	**65**	**17**	**244**	**605**	**.317**	**.423**
Athletics	.235	2703	342	635	119	15	92	328	75	21	289	657	.311	.392
Rays	.231	2614	329	603	115	15	82	314	70	21	298	623	.314	.380
Mariners	.220	2598	257	571	106	8	56	239	50	16	248	598	.291	.331
League Avg.	**.260**	**2912**	**395**	**758**	**149**	**14**	**98**	**377**	**59**	**18**	**270**	**603**	**.327**	**.422**

AL BATTING WITH RUNNERS ON

	AVG	AB	R	H	2B	3B	HR	RBI	SB	CS	TBB	SO	OBP	SLG
Tigers	.286	1345	---	384	82	5	35	506	9	2	175	272	.367	.432
Royals	.275	1366	---	376	70	15	19	472	43	5	125	272	.335	.390
Rangers	.275	1363	---	375	70	14	40	547	23	4	183	254	.356	.435
White Sox	.272	1276	---	347	49	11	46	492	7	4	136	283	.341	.436
Red Sox	.271	1338	---	363	77	4	45	513	28	3	152	279	.339	.436
Athletics	.265	1228	---	325	66	10	42	456	51	8	186	325	.359	.437
Angels	.262	1407	---	368	72	7	41	527	32	8	140	300	.325	.410
Blue Jays	**.260**	**1195**	**---**	**311**	**51**	**6**	**43**	**460**	**52**	**13**	**151**	**283**	**.339**	**.421**
Orioles	.256	1174	---	301	64	3	49	446	16	8	131	280	.331	.441
Yankees	.256	1329	---	340	68	3	55	515	27	5	205	290	.352	.436
Twins	.252	1407	---	354	65	7	28	513	37	9	198	290	.341	.367
Rays	.243	1250	---	304	65	9	27	460	34	7	180	340	.336	.374
Indians	.239	1374	---	329	60	5	34	481	32	7	190	288	.330	.365
Mariners	.239	1217	---	291	59	5	31	417	20	4	157	275	.324	.372
League Avg.	**.260**	**1405**	**---**	**366**	**70**	**8**	**41**	**523**	**31**	**6**	**177**	**310**	**.341**	**.409**

AL BATTING, PRE ALL-STAR BREAK

	AVG	AB	R	H	2B	3B	HR	RBI	SB	CS	TBB	SO	OBP	SLG
Rangers	.280	3010	443	844	161	19	103	430	65	26	271	601	.343	.449
Tigers	.269	2927	387	786	160	19	82	368	33	9	259	587	.333	.420
Angels	.268	2917	378	783	136	12	94	360	65	15	233	556	.324	.420
Red Sox	.268	2996	432	803	208	7	99	409	37	15	259	644	.329	.441
Royals	.264	2921	344	771	165	17	68	324	55	22	214	521	.318	.402
Yankees	.262	2893	412	759	152	8	134	396	47	11	302	613	.336	.459
White Sox	.260	2911	409	756	118	18	103	397	58	22	252	656	.323	.419
Indians	.258	2917	385	754	155	15	78	368	59	23	309	539	.333	.402
Twins	.258	2911	354	751	151	14	73	343	66	21	275	566	.325	.395
Blue Jays	**.254**	**2956**	**430**	**750**	**124**	**13**	**127**	**401**	**64**	**25**	**273**	**626**	**.320**	**.433**
Orioles	.240	2890	351	694	133	8	106	330	31	21	237	690	.302	.402
Rays	.232	2833	363	658	120	16	85	345	70	23	308	694	.314	.376
Mariners	.230	2949	337	677	135	13	73	318	57	23	255	681	.291	.358
Athletics	.225	2866	319	645	125	14	83	302	67	20	295	683	.301	.365
League Avg.	**.255**	**2921**	**381**	**745**	**145**	**13**	**93**	**363**	**55**	**19**	**267**	**618**	**.321**	**.409**

AL BATTING VS RHP

	AVG	AB	R	H	2B	3B	HR	RBI	SB	CS	TBB	SO	OBP	SLG
Tigers	.275	3817	---	1048	188	28	122	502	53	15	333	744	.337	.434
Angels	.273	4052	---	1107	189	16	134	545	114	28	319	831	.330	.427
Rangers	.269	4093	---	1100	219	25	152	572	69	26	347	795	.329	.446
Royals	.268	3902	---	1046	201	28	90	450	98	21	264	704	.318	.403
Yankees	.266	3593	---	954	188	7	167	508	72	14	353	762	.336	.461
Indians	.259	3663	---	949	182	16	96	426	72	24	365	706	.330	.396
Twins	.258	3832	---	988	197	22	89	448	93	23	342	751	.322	.390
White Sox	.256	4071	---	1044	159	24	149	535	88	33	325	880	.318	.417
Red Sox	.256	3927	---	1005	250	11	105	469	68	19	302	852	.312	.405
Orioles	.245	4078	---	1001	205	9	163	504	41	22	344	968	.308	.420
Blue Jays	**.244**	**3930**	**---**	**960**	**180**	**15**	**141**	**497**	**81**	**30**	**340**	**898**	**.309**	**.405**
Rays	.240	3806	---	914	170	22	129	469	94	30	395	886	.316	.398
Athletics	.239	3683	---	879	177	19	133	458	94	16	375	902	.312	.405
Mariners	.229	3549	---	811	158	16	94	384	71	24	322	824	.295	.362
League Avg.	**.256**	**4153**	**---**	**1062**	**204**	**19**	**135**	**520**	**85**	**25**	**363**	**884**	**.319**	**.412**

AL BATTING ON THE ROAD

	AVG	AB	R	H	2B	3B	HR	RBI	SB	CS	TBB	SO	OBP	SLG
Angels	.276	2890	419	798	132	9	105	396	83	22	256	610	.337	.437
Yankees	.264	2856	398	753	158	10	107	380	46	16	288	604	.336	.438
Rangers	.261	2818	361	736	139	16	92	355	36	22	238	583	.320	.420
Tigers	.258	2780	333	718	143	12	71	323	38	9	258	615	.327	.395
Royals	.252	2869	335	724	139	17	69	321	62	18	202	582	.305	.385
Indians	.252	2776	344	700	125	15	72	331	48	24	284	548	.325	.386
Rays	.248	2784	368	690	135	15	93	351	64	23	273	700	.319	.407
Twins	.247	2827	335	698	133	10	62	313	65	18	232	572	.307	.367
Mariners	.247	2896	362	714	135	19	93	345	54	19	218	661	.300	.403
White Sox	.243	2799	331	679	104	14	91	321	52	21	209	623	.300	.387
Blue Jays	**.242**	**2840**	**348**	**687**	**120**	**8**	**96**	**330**	**58**	**24**	**229**	**646**	**.302**	**.391**
Red Sox	.242	2776	315	671	128	7	77	296	54	17	199	605	.295	.376
Athletics	.241	2824	371	680	148	17	103	348	47	11	261	730	.310	.415
Orioles	.237	2834	325	671	127	11	87	312	18	22	238	693	.299	.381
League Avg.	**.251**	**3043**	**380**	**763**	**143**	**13**	**93**	**363**	**55**	**20**	**260**	**674**	**.313**	**.398**

AL BATTING WITH BASES LOADED

	AVG	AB	R	H	2B	3B	HR	RBI	SB	CS	TBB	SO	OBP	SLG
Rays	.376	117	---	44	6	0	4	116	0	0	14	24	.418	.530
Red Sox	.343	102	---	35	12	0	3	95	0	0	3	21	.328	.549
Blue Jays	**.317**	**82**	**---**	**26**	**6**	**1**	**3**	**81**	**0**	**1**	**5**	**22**	**.350**	**.524**
Mariners	.316	114	---	36	8	0	2	99	0	0	10	15	.346	.439
Angels	.300	90	---	27	2	2	2	82	0	0	8	20	.324	.433
Rangers	.285	137	---	39	6	4	3	112	0	0	5	22	.299	.453
Royals	.283	99	---	28	3	0	1	69	0	0	2	17	.274	.343
Athletics	.268	123	---	33	9	1	4	94	0	1	6	34	.288	.455
White Sox	.267	120	---	32	3	0	6	91	0	0	5	26	.294	.442
Yankees	.247	154	---	38	8	0	10	132	0	0	15	28	.290	.494
Orioles	.238	101	---	24	3	0	3	59	0	0	6	22	.275	.356
Indians	.227	154	---	35	4	0	3	105	0	0	11	32	.268	.312
Twins	.227	141	---	32	6	0	2	101	0	0	12	29	.269	.312
Tigers	.217	120	---	26	6	0	1	70	0	0	6	22	.243	.292
League Avg.	**.271**	**118**	**---**	**32**	**5**	**0**	**3**	**93**	**0**	**0**	**7**	**23**	**.294**	**.390**

AL BATTING, POST ALL-STAR BREAK

	AVG	AB	R	H	2B	3B	HR	RBI	SB	CS	TBB	SO	OBP	SLG
Angels	.281	2619	389	735	137	10	93	372	69	18	216	557	.340	.447
Yankees	.267	2631	392	703	128	5	111	378	46	16	263	563	.338	.446
Tigers	.267	2549	339	681	119	20	81	330	26	14	252	516	.337	.425
Royals	.266	2715	332	721	130	20	63	319	77	16	190	511	.315	.398
Rangers	.264	2580	365	682	142	13	97	350	26	18	207	502	.323	.442
Twins	.263	2651	347	697	119	16	58	324	69	16	230	503	.324	.386
Orioles	.255	2670	361	681	137	8	108	347	27	8	243	625	.321	.434
Athletics	.252	2661	394	670	142	18	112	374	55	12	255	704	.320	.445
Red Sox	.252	2608	302	656	131	9	66	286	60	16	169	553	.299	.385
White Sox	.250	2607	339	653	110	11	108	329	51	21	209	547	.313	.425
Rays	.248	2565	334	635	130	14	90	320	64	21	263	629	.320	.414
Indians	.242	2608	282	631	111	9	58	267	51	21	246	548	.313	.358
Mariners	.239	2545	282	608	106	14	76	266	47	12	211	578	.301	.381
Blue Jays	**.235**	**2531**	**286**	**596**	**123**	**9**	**71**	**276**	**59**	**16**	**200**	**625**	**.296**	**.375**
League Avg.	**.256**	**2610**	**338**	**667**	**126**	**12**	**85**	**324**	**51**	**16**	**225**	**568**	**.318**	**.411**

AL PINCH HITTERS

	AVG	AB	R	H	2B	3B	HR	RBI	SB	CS	TBB	SO	OBP	SLG
Orioles	.298	57	3	17	3	0	1	6	2	0	1	13	.404	.322
Tigers	.289	76	12	22	4	0	5	16	0	0	5	15	.539	.345
Athletics	.262	65	9	17	1	1	2	15	1	0	7	13	.400	.338
Rays	.257	113	21	29	4	0	1	13	4	0	22	33	.319	.382
White Sox	.242	62	9	15	2	0	2	6	0	0	10	16	.371	.356
Mariners	.227	44	2	10	1	0	1	6	1	0	4	21	.318	.300
Indians	.221	68	5	15	6	0	1	11	1	1	7	22	.353	.303
Yankees	.203	59	4	12	3	0	0	5	0	0	12	17	.254	.338
Rangers	.197	61	8	12	3	0	1	12	0	0	4	14	.295	.242
Blue Jays	**.169**	**59**	**1**	**10**	**2**	**0**	**0**	**5**	**1**	**0**	**4**	**20**	**.203**	**.234**
Twins	.169	83	7	14	5	0	0	5	1	0	8	34	.229	.242
Red Sox	.165	79	15	13	1	0	2	7	0	0	7	18	.253	.239
Royals	.152	33	3	5	1	0	1	3	1	0	3	13	.273	.222
Angels	.145	76	4	11	2	0	2	9	0	0	9	21	.250	.230
TOTALS	**.216**	**935**	**103**	**202**	**38**	**1**	**19**	**119**	**12**	**1**	**103**	**270**	**.320**	**.299**

AL DESIGNATED HITTERS

	AVG	AB	R	H	2B	3B	HR	RBI	SB	CS	TBB	SO	OBP	SLG
Red Sox	.308	588	94	181	42	1	29	102	4	3	83	101	.531	.394
Tigers	.303	595	90	180	41	0	14	103	6	1	49	71	.442	.354
Royals	.294	592	81	174	44	0	17	95	4	1	69	101	.454	.365
Rangers	.287	602	94	173	36	3	26	108	9	3	56	97	.487	.347
Orioles	.282	616	71	174	32	1	16	70	2	2	27	63	.416	.318
Indians	.266	587	82	156	34	2	23	94	2	2	56	149	.448	.337
Blue Jays	**.262**	**576**	**81**	**151**	**30**	**1**	**22**	**76**	**11**	**2**	**62**	**127**	**.432**	**.339**
Rays	.260	620	83	161	34	7	18	77	18	6	51	104	.424	.320
Yankees	.252	568	74	143	21	1	30	85	4	4	68	130	.451	.337
White Sox	.247	559	58	138	28	0	21	83	2	3	87	168	.410	.357
Twins	.245	564	68	138	26	0	26	96	5	0	70	135	.429	.331
Athletics	.244	578	69	141	27	0	18	91	4	0	61	118	.384	.313
Angels	.237	573	68	136	25	3	14	70	19	7	87	126	.365	.337
Mariners	.226	558	48	126	29	2	9	57	4	3	69	180	.333	.317
TOTALS	**.266**	**8176**	**1061**	**2172**	**449**	**21**	**283**	**1207**	**94**	**37**	**895**	**1670**	**.430**	**.341**

ATTENDANCE AT THE BREAK

YEAR	W-L	PCT.	POS.	GBL	HOME ATTENDANCE
1977	34-58	.370	7th	–19.0	1,020,152
1978	32-53	.376	7th	–26.0	804,890
1979	29-64	.312	7th	–31.5	785,030
1980	33-43	.434	7th	–17.0	675,556
1981*	16-42	.276	7th	–19.0	426,795
1982	37-47	.440	7th	–11.5	637,057
1983	43-33	.566	1st	+1.0	786,503
1984	50-34	.595	2nd	–7.0	1,247,799
1985	53-35	.602	1st	+2.5	1,123,502
1986	47-43	.522	5th	–10.5	1,442,158
1987	51-36	.586	2nd	–3.0	1,413,455
1988	42-46	.477	6th	–11.5	1,473,480
1989	42-45	.483	T4th	–7.0	1,559,163
1990	47-38	.553	2nd	–0.5	2,288,900
1991	49-34	.590	1st	+5.5	2,090,001
1992	53-34	.609	1st	+4.0	2,416,036
1993	49-40	.551	1st	+0.5	2,340,240
1994	38-48	.442	5th	–12.5	2,116,873
1995*	27-40	.403	5th	–11.5	1,295,643
1996	38-49	.437	3rd	–15.0	1,289,964
1997	40-43	.482	T3rd	–14.0	1,547,513
1998	46-42	.523	3rd	–18.5	1,319,694
1999	47-43	.522	3rd	–7.0	1,181,546
2000	48-41	.539	2nd	0.0	816,825
2001	42-46	.477	3rd	–11.0	1,041,822
2002	34-52	.395	4th	–20.5	766,790
2003	49-46	.516	3rd	–9.0	1,087,864
2004	39-49	.443	4th	–17.0	913,198
2005	44-44	.500	4th	–5.5	910,866
2006	49-39	.557	3rd	–4.5	1,186,106
2007	43-44	.494	T2nd	–10.0	1,194,984
2008	47-48	.495	4th	–9.0	1,293,270
2009	44-46	.489	4th	–11.0	982,117
2010	44-45	.494	4th	-12.5	783,773
2011	44-45	.494	4th	-12.5	913,846
2012	43-43	.500	T4th	-9.5	1,107,908

* Strike Season

AL STARTERS PITCHING

	ERA	W	L	Sv	SvOp	GS	CG	IP	H	R	ER	HR	TBB	IBB	SO
Rays	3.34	70	51	0	0	162	7	993.2	879	415	369	99	320	14	900
Tigers	3.76	63	51	0	0	162	9	972.0	981	458	406	104	263	11	885
Athletics	3.80	64	54	0	0	162	1	958.0	972	434	404	102	253	13	667
Mariners	3.93	55	62	0	0	162	8	1002.2	975	466	438	122	263	7	718
Angels	4.04	70	53	0	0	162	6	984.1	922	488	442	133	315	7	772
Yankees	4.05	71	50	0	0	162	6	1001.1	997	489	451	143	273	8	878
White Sox	4.15	60	52	0	0	162	6	980.0	947	469	452	129	324	14	829
Rangers	4.30	72	55	0	0	162	7	984.2	972	514	470	122	309	4	847
Orioles	4.42	61	58	0	0	162	1	937.2	946	504	460	136	307	15	723
Blue Jays	**4.82**	**52**	**69**	**0**	**0**	**162**	**5**	**916.0**	**932**	**521**	**491**	**134**	**368**	**5**	**639**
Royals	5.01	47	69	0	0	162	2	890.0	981	527	495	119	315	12	642
Red Sox	5.19	48	72	0	0	162	6	928.1	979	575	535	135	336	8	701
Indians	5.25	48	76	0	0	162	2	913.2	1026	599	533	121	351	14	621
Twins	5.40	39	75	0	0	162	3	880.0	1015	571	528	141	284	12	541
League Avg.	**4.36**	**58**	**60**	**0**	**0**	**162**	**4**	**953.0**	**966**	**502**	**462**	**124**	**305**	**10**	**740**

AL RELIEF PITCHING

	ERA	W	L	Sv	SvOp	GS	CG	IP	H	R	ER	HR	TBB	IBB	SO
Rays	2.88	20	21	50	58	0	0	466.0	354	162	149	40	149	21	483
Athletics	2.90	30	14	47	64	0	0	512.0	388	180	165	45	209	21	469
Orioles	3.00	32	11	55	73	0	0	545.1	487	201	182	48	174	21	454
Royals	3.17	25	21	44	64	0	0	561.1	523	219	198	44	227	32	535
Rangers	3.33	21	14	43	52	0	0	457.1	406	193	169	53	137	11	439
Mariners	3.37	20	25	43	62	0	0	454.0	384	185	170	44	186	32	448
Yankees	3.39	24	17	51	64	0	0	444.0	404	179	167	47	158	24	440
Tigers	3.73	25	23	40	56	0	0	458.2	428	212	190	47	175	24	433
White Sox	3.75	25	25	37	57	0	0	465.2	418	207	194	57	179	15	417
Twins	3.77	27	21	35	49	0	0	558.2	521	261	234	57	181	31	402
Red Sox	3.83	21	21	35	57	0	0	514.2	470	231	219	55	193	25	475
Angels	3.97	19	20	38	60	0	0	449.0	417	211	198	53	168	13	385
Indians	3.97	20	18	43	56	0	0	528.1	477	246	233	53	192	13	465
Blue Jays	**4.33**	**21**	**20**	**29**	**44**	**0**	**0**	**527.2**	**507**	**263**	**254**	**70**	**206**	**15**	**503**
League Avg.	**3.53**	**23**	**19**	**42**	**58**	**0**	**0**	**495.0**	**441**	**210**	**194**	**50**	**181**	**21**	**453**

AL PITCHING AT HOME

	ERA	W	L	Sv	SvOp	GS	CG	IP	H	R	ER	HR	TBB	IBB	SO
Rays	2.81	46	35	27	31	81	4	753.0	603	265	235	55	223	16	760
Mariners	2.96	40	41	24	33	81	3	743.0	629	260	244	60	210	15	616
Athletics	3.05	50	31	22	29	81	1	763.2	652	282	259	66	221	16	569
Angels	3.44	46	35	17	22	81	4	730.0	638	309	279	79	212	8	632
Tigers	3.47	50	31	18	27	81	5	739.0	711	329	285	67	216	12	684
Yankees	3.67	51	30	26	33	81	4	739.0	668	327	301	94	223	15	672
Indians	4.11	37	44	22	29	81	1	757.0	748	393	346	85	266	13	595
Orioles	4.15	47	34	24	34	81	0	751.0	766	378	346	99	245	17	614
Rangers	4.17	50	31	21	26	81	1	741.0	742	374	343	94	222	9	685
Royals	4.27	37	44	22	35	81	1	749.0	757	382	355	87	268	24	593
White Sox	4.42	45	36	19	28	81	3	737.0	711	379	362	108	275	11	644
Blue Jays	**4.50**	**41**	**40**	**17**	**25**	**81**	**1**	**734.0**	**728**	**385**	**367**	**102**	**256**	**8**	**587**
Twins	4.74	31	50	10	17	81	2	738.0	764	417	389	98	231	17	501
Red Sox	4.75	34	47	12	22	81	2	746.2	782	423	394	97	258	17	599
League Avg.	**3.89**	**46**	**40**	**21**	**30**	**87**	**2**	**801.0**	**761**	**377**	**346**	**91**	**255**	**15**	**673**

AL PITCHING ON THE ROAD

	ERA	W	L	Sv	SvOp	GS	CG	IP	H	R	ER	HR	TBB	IBB	SO
Rays	3.60	44	37	23	27	81	3	706.2	630	312	283	84	246	19	623
White Sox	3.61	40	41	18	29	81	3	708.2	654	297	284	78	228	18	602
Orioles	3.64	46	35	31	39	81	1	732.0	667	327	296	85	236	19	563
Rangers	3.80	43	38	22	26	81	6	701.0	636	333	296	81	224	6	601
Athletics	3.95	44	37	25	35	81	0	706.1	708	332	310	81	241	18	567
Yankees	4.04	44	37	25	31	81	2	706.1	733	341	317	96	208	17	646
Tigers	4.05	38	43	22	29	81	4	691.2	698	341	311	84	222	23	634
Royals	4.33	35	46	22	29	81	1	702.1	747	364	338	76	274	20	584
Mariners	4.59	35	46	19	29	81	5	713.2	730	391	364	106	239	24	550
Angels	4.62	43	38	21	38	81	2	703.1	701	390	361	107	271	12	525
Red Sox	4.65	35	46	23	35	81	4	696.1	667	383	360	93	271	16	577
Twins	4.79	35	46	25	32	81	1	700.2	772	415	373	100	234	26	442
Blue Jays	**4.79**	**32**	**49**	**12**	**19**	**81**	**4**	**709.2**	**711**	**399**	**378**	**102**	**318**	**12**	**555**
Indians	5.52	31	50	21	27	81	1	685.0	755	452	420	89	277	14	491
League Avg.	**4.27**	**41**	**45**	**23**	**32**	**87**	**2**	**758.0**	**754**	**390**	**360**	**97**	**268**	**18**	**612**

AL PITCHING, PRE ALL-STAR BREAK

	ERA	W	L	Sv	SvOp	GS	CG	IP	H	R	ER	HR	TBB	IBB	SO
Athletics	3.40	43	43	22	32	86	1	773.1	686	316	292	67	275	19	555
Angels	3.61	48	38	21	31	86	5	762.1	688	334	306	76	273	13	605
Rangers	3.72	52	34	21	25	86	5	771.0	728	364	319	85	226	5	670
Yankees	3.73	52	33	27	34	85	2	758.0	748	347	314	94	240	19	713
Rays	3.73	45	41	27	32	86	2	766.1	712	359	318	87	274	23	685
White Sox	3.91	47	38	19	31	85	6	764.1	692	346	332	95	239	10	654
Mariners	3.96	36	51	18	28	87	3	779.0	717	365	343	100	251	24	653
Tigers	3.97	44	42	19	28	86	5	760.1	769	381	335	86	240	21	715
Orioles	4.05	45	40	30	41	85	1	776.0	757	387	349	97	253	21	608
Red Sox	4.22	43	43	21	32	86	4	775.2	758	389	364	91	253	15	623
Royals	4.35	37	47	22	31	84	1	748.2	769	385	362	78	303	21	617
Blue Jays	**4.45**	**43**	**43**	**16**	**27**	**86**	**4**	**770.2**	**751**	**408**	**381**	**111**	**307**	**11**	**601**
Indians	4.50	44	41	26	31	85	2	762.0	757	414	381	84	289	12	566
Twins	4.86	36	49	20	26	85	1	755.1	827	441	408	110	238	20	485
League Avg.	**4.04**	**43**	**41**	**22**	**30**	**85**	**3**	**765.0**	**739**	**374**	**343**	**90**	**261**	**16**	**625**

AL PITCHING, POST ALL-STAR BREAK

	ERA	W	L	Sv	SvOp	GS	CG	IP	H	R	ER	HR	TBB	IBB	SO
Rays	2.60	45	31	23	26	76	5	693.1	521	218	200	52	195	12	698
Tigers	3.50	44	32	21	28	76	4	670.1	640	289	261	65	198	14	603
Mariners	3.52	39	36	25	34	75	5	677.2	642	286	265	66	198	15	513
Athletics	3.58	51	25	25	32	76	0	696.2	674	298	277	80	187	15	581
Orioles	3.73	48	29	25	32	77	0	707.0	676	318	293	87	228	15	569
Yankees	3.98	43	34	24	30	77	4	687.1	653	321	304	96	191	13	605
White Sox	4.15	38	39	18	26	77	0	681.1	673	330	314	91	264	19	592
Royals	4.24	35	43	22	33	78	1	702.2	735	361	331	85	239	23	560
Rangers	4.29	41	35	22	27	76	2	671.0	650	343	320	90	220	10	616
Angels	4.48	41	35	17	29	76	1	671.0	651	365	334	110	210	7	552
Twins	4.66	30	47	15	23	77	2	683.1	709	391	354	88	227	23	458
Blue Jays	**4.87**	**30**	**46**	**13**	**17**	**76**	**1**	**673.0**	**688**	**376**	**364**	**93**	**267**	**9**	**541**
Indians	5.10	24	53	17	25	77	0	680.0	746	431	385	90	254	15	520
Red Sox	5.26	26	50	14	25	76	2	667.1	691	417	390	99	276	18	553
League Avg.	**4.12**	**38**	**38**	**20**	**27**	**76**	**1**	**683.0**	**667**	**338**	**313**	**85**	**225**	**14**	**568**

10 CONSECUTIVE HITS

The Toronto Blue Jays tied an American League record September 4, 1992 at SkyDome by collecting 10 consecutive hits in an eight-run second inning against the Minnesota Twins.

The Blue Jays tied the mark set by the Boston Red Sox on June 2, 1901 and equalled by the Detroit Tigers on September 20, 1983.

The Major League record of 12 straight hits was set by the St. Louis Cardinals in 1920 and equalled by the Brooklyn Dodgers in 1930.

With one out in the second, Toronto's Kelly Gruber reached on an infield single against Twins' starter Kevin Tapani. Singles by Pat Borders and Manuel Lee scored Gruber to cut Minnesota's lead to 3-1.

Devon White doubled in a run and Roberto Alomar followed with a two-run single to give the Blue Jays a 4-3 lead. Joe Carter tripled home Alomar and scored on Dave Winfield's single off reliever Tom Edens. Winfield was thrown out at second for the inning's second out, but John Olerud singled and scored on Candy Maldonado's triple to open a 7-3 cushion. Gruber's bloop double to right-center scored Maldonado and ended the string of 10 straight hits.

Borders flied to center to end the inning.

Toronto's previous club record was nine consecutive hits, set against California on July 3, 1992.

TORONTO BLUE JAYS HISTORY

ROBERTO ALOMAR

HISTORY OF THE TORONTO BLUE JAYS™

1977 – First Pitch: *On April 7, 1977, 44,649 fans brave snow and freezing temperatures as the Blue Jays play their first ever regular season game, a 9-5 win over the Chicago White Sox at Exhibition Stadium.*

1970s

The City of Toronto is awarded a franchise in the American League on March 26, 1976 and name Peter Bavasi Executive Vice-President and General Manager on June 18. On August 12, the "Blue Jays" are selected by Directors from over 4,000 names and 30,000 entries in a "Name the Team" contest. Roy Hartsfield becomes the first on-field manager and catcher Phil Roof is purchased from the Chicago White Sox becoming the first player in franchise history.

On March 11, 1977 the Blue Jays play in their first spring training game, defeating the New York Mets in Dunedin, Florida by a 3-1 score. On April 7, 1977, 44,649 fans brave snow and freezing temperatures as the Blue Jays win their first ever regular season game 9-5 over the Chicago White Sox. Doug Ault becomes an instant hero hitting two home runs in the contest. In their inaugural season, highlights include a 19-3 win over the Yankees, with Roy Howell collecting nine RBI, while the home attendance of 1,701,052 sets a record for attendance by a first year expansion club.

Bell/Moseby/Barfied: *George Bell, Lloyd Moseby and Jesse Barfield played together in Toronto's outfield for six straight seasons from 1984-1989*

Over the next two seasons in 1978-79 the Blue Jays see several firsts. Jim Clancy gets the 4-2 victory in front of 44,327 fans, which is marked by the pitcher starting the first Triple Play in franchise history. On June 26, 1978 the Blue Jays explode for a franchise high 24 runs. Bobby Mattick becomes the team's second manager on October 18, 1979. For his performance in 1979, SS Alfredo Griffin is named co-winner of the AL Rookie of the Year Award. From December 2-7 Toronto plays host to the Winter Meetings, the first held outside the United States.

1980s

The decade of the 1980's represented another birth for the franchise, as by the end of the decade the club rose from an expansion team to formidable AL East contender. Still in the early years in 1980 the club set a franchise record with 67 victories while pushing attendance past six million, an expansion record. Field manager Bobby Cox takes over the reins in 1982 and leads the club to new heights in his four years as manager. 1982 saw the club climb out of the basement for the first time in its history, winning 78 games finishing in a tie for 6th with Cleveland.

1983 marks a significant time as the Blue Jays finish over .500 for the first time in franchise history with an 89-73 record, good for 4th place only nine games out of first. Notable performances include the first 100 RBI season by a Blue Jay (Willie Upshaw) and first 100 run scored season (Lloyd Moseby). The Blue Jays become only the second team in league history to win Player of the Week honours in three consecutive weeks, when Luis Leal, Dave Stieb and Lloyd Moseby turned the trick in May. The enthusiasm for the club continues to build as a club record 9,104 season tickets are sold for the 1984 season. They see a club that marches up the standings for a second place finish at 89-73 solidifying their position as AL East contenders. Over the course of the season the Blue Jays would win 19 one-run contests in a row, while Cliff Johnson sets a Major League record mark for pinch hit home runs with his 19th career shot. All of this is witnessed by 2,110,009 fans, which puts the Blue Jays in elite company as just the 18th franchise to top two million fans in a season.

PLAYOFF BOUND:

The ascent to AL East Champions is complete in 1985 as on the second to last day of the regular season the Blue Jays defeat the New York Yankees by a 5-1 score to secure their first post-season berth. During the 1985 season a Blue Jays ticket was a hot commodity. On July 27, the club sees average attendance top 30,000 per game for the first time. 47,686 fans show up for an October 4th contest vs. New York to set a single game mark, while final attendance reaches a new high of 2,468,925. Season ticket sales are capped at 11,500.

The Blue Jays first foray into the playoffs provides lots of drama and some valuable learning experiences that may prove to be valuable in

George Bell MVP: *George Bell cements himself as the AL's best posting a .308 average with 47 home runs and 134 RBI to earn the honour as MVP. Is the only Blue Jay in franchise history to win this award.*

future years. Jumping out to 2-0 and 3-1 series leads vs. the AL West Champion Kansas City Royals it appeared as though the Blue Jays would make their first World Series appearance inevitable. Unfortunately the Kansas City Royals had other ideas as they would come from behind becoming only the 5th club in Major League history to win a series after trailing 3-1. George Brett would lead the way collecting several key hits while Jim Sundberg would deliver the decisive blow off Blue Jays ace Dave Stieb, with a bases clearing wind assisted triple off the top of the right field fence in Game 7.

Heading into 1986 season tickets are capped at 14,000 as the club celebrates its 10th anniversary. On July 10 Damaso Garcia becomes the first Blue Jay to record 1,000 hits in a Blue Jays uniform, while RHP Jim Clancy becomes the first to win 100 games for the franchise. Tony Fernandez becomes the first to punch out 200 hits in a season and RF Jesse Barfield earns the franchise its first Gold Glove award. The Blue Jays drop to 4th place in the East with an 86-76 record as Jimy Williams takes over as team manager.

MVP:

George Bell cements himself as AL's best posting a .308 average with 47 home runs and 134 RBI to earn the honour as AL MVP. In 1987, he beame the first Blue Jay ever selected by fans to appear in an All-Star Game. The Blue Jays set several club marks, including a 10-home run game vs. Baltimore on September 14, with Ernie Whitt belting three. A franchise record 11-game winning streak begins on June 2, while attendance soars to 2,778,429. The attendance mark is an all-time high for any AL East club. On Canada Day a single game record 47,828 pack their way into Exihibition Stadium in a contest vs. the New York Yankees. The season ends in shocking fashion as a 3.5 game lead is lost in the final week with seven consecutive losses. Four of the losses came to eventual champions Detroit, with all of them being one-run losses, including two in extra innings. On the season's final day LHP Jimmy Key loses a 1-0 battle to Frank Tanana with the lone coming from a wall scraping home run to left field by OF Larry Herndon in the 2nd inning. Key injuries to C Ernie Whitt and SS Tony Fernandez down the stretch proved to be too much to overcome.

A 3rd place finish in 1988 (87-75) is highlighted by some individual accomplishments. George Bell begins the season the same way he left off his 1987 MVP campaign. He becomes the first player in Major League history to hit three home runs on Opening day and is the only player over the course of the season to earn two Player of the Week awards. Dave Stieb continues his dominance of AL hitters, flirting with no-hitters on three occasions, with three one-hitters, including back-to-back one-hitters on Sept. 24 and Sept. 30. Incredibly both games see him lose the no-hitter with two outs in the 9th inning.

A SIGNIFICANT CHANGE:

1989 begins with Paul Beeston being named team President on January 10. On May 15 with the team sitting with a 12-24 record manager Jimy Williams is replaced by Cito Gaston on an interim basis. On May 28 the Blue Jays play their final game at Exihibition Stadium defeating the White Sox 7-5. The team moves into the SkyDome and cap season tickets at 26,000. They open the SkyDome on June 5 with a loss to the Milwaukee Brewers. 49,501 watch the Blue Jays on September 16 to set a new record for home attendance. The Blue Jays would go on to post a 77-49 record under Cito Gaston and clinch their second division title. Dave Stieb posts two more one-hitters, and comes within one out of a perfect game vs. New York on August 4, when Roberto Kelly broke up the bid with a double.

BEEN HERE BEFORE:

For the second time in five seasons the Blue Jays were East Division Champions, and for the second time they would succumb in the Divisional Series, this time to the AL West Champ Oakland Athletics. The Blue Jays were no match for Ricky Henderson as he batted .400 in the series with a 1.609 OPS and a LCS record eight stolen bases in the five game series. They were outscored 31-16 with the Blue Jays only victory coming in Game 3 behind Jimmy Key.

1990s

The Toronto Blue Jays entered the 90's as an established contender, looking to build on regular season performance that had yet to yield playoff success. With a State of the Art building in the SkyDome now their home, it was time to see this vision become reality.

In the first full season at SkyDome and the first full season under Cito Gaston the club would come up just short of a post-season berth, finishing two games behind the Red Sox with an 86-76 record. Set a Major League attendance record by passing the Dodgers 1982 mark on Sept. 19. Dave Stewart tosses SkyDome's first no-hitter, pitching for the Oakland A's

AND THEN HE WAS PERFECT:

On September 2, 1990 Dave Stieb would accomplish what had appeared so elusive, by tossing his first and only no-hitter vs. the Cleveland Indians. Jerry Browne would line out to RF Junior Felix to end the contest.

1991 was a big year for the franchise in many ways. Chosen to host their first All-Star Game, 52,382 fans pack the SkyDome to see Jimmy Key pick up the win for the home side. In December of 1990 the Blue Jays cement a deal that would change the fortunes of the club by acquiring future Hall of Famer Roberto Alomar and OF Joe Carter from San Diego in exchange for SS Tony

Stieb No-Hitter: *On Sept. 2, 1990 vs. Cleveland, Dave Stieb tosses the only no-hitter in Blue Jay history.*

Joe Carter – '93: *The Blue Jays win their 2nd consecutive World Series title after Joe Carter hits a walk-off home run in game #6 vs. the Phillies as Toronto captured the series in six games.*

Fernandez and 1B Fred McGriff. Another attendance mark is set and the 4 million fan barrier is broken as 4,001,526 see the Blue Jays return to the post-season by winning the AL East with a 91-71 record. Tom Henke sets a then record for consecutive saves with 25. On May 1 in Texas, Nolan Ryan no-hits the Blue Jays for his 7th and final no-hitter.

THIRD TIME A CHARM:

The AL West Champion Minnesota Twins would await in the AL Championship Series. The Blue Jays would come home to Toronto with a 1-1 series split, primed to make their first World Series appearance. Unfortunately an 11-inning heart-breaker would see the series tide turn as Mike Pagliarulo would homer off Mike Timlin to put the Blue Jays down 2-1. In Game 5 the Twins would finish off the series by scoring three runs in the 8th inning, winning 8-5 and sending the Blue Jays home early once again.

Newly acquired RHP Jack Morris would lead the Blue Jays into the 1992 season by making his Major League record 13th consecutive Opening Day start. He tosses a complete game 4-2 win in Detroit. The Blue Jays would set a Major League attendance record again in 1992 with 4,028,318 fans. The Blue Jays would clinch their 4th playoff berth on October 3. Dave Winfield sets a Blue Jays mark with 23 home runs as a DH while becoming the oldest player to register 100 or more RBI in a season.

TIME TO CELEBRATE:

An old foe would await in the 1992 Championship series in the Oakland Athletics, a team very similar to the club that handled the Blue Jays just two seasons ago in the playoffs. The Blue Jays would split the first two games at home before heading to Oakland for Games 4, 5 and 6. Juan Guzman would give the Blue Jays a 2-1 series lead before the dramatic Game 4 would be the catalyst for the Blue Jays first ever World Series appearance. In Game 4 the Blue Jays found themselves down 5-1 after three and 6-1 heading into the 8th inning. They would come within striking distance with a three-run 8th inning before Dennis Eckersley, the games widely known "best closer" attempted to close out the game in the 9th. With a man on, Roberto Alomar would deliver the biggest hit in franchise history, belting a game-tying two-run home run to right field. They would go on to win in 11 and then the series in six games.

More drama would ensue in the Blue Jays first World Series appearance as perennial playoff club the Atlanta Braves provided the opposition. After dropping the first contest, Game 2 saw backup C/INF Ed Sprague propel the Blue Jays to their first ever World Series win with a pinch-hit two-run home run off Jeff Reardon in a 5-4 win. Game 3, the first World Series game played outside of the US, was noteworthy for 'the catch" made by Devon White in the 4th inning. Resulting in a near triple play it was key in keeping the score tied at 2-2 in the 9th inning. Candy Maldonado would drive in Roberto Alomar for the game-winner and a 3-1 series lead. Unable to close the series out in Game 5 the Blue Jays would need one more dramatic at-bat to bring the World Series to Canada. Tied in the 11th inning, Dave Winfield would double down the left field line to drive in two and when Mike Timlin tossed an Otis Nixon bunt to Joe Crater the long journey to World Series Champions had concluded.

In 1993 a record tying seven Blue Jays are selected to the All-Star team (Alomar, Carter, Hentgen, Molitor, Olerud, Ward, White). John Olerud would flirt with .400 average, going as late as August 2 at the .400 mark and eventually becoming the first Blue Jay to win a batting title. In fact the top three spots at seasons end belonged to Blue Jays (Olerud - .363/ Molitor - .332/Alomar - .326), the first time in 100 years this had occurred. The Blue Jays would win the AL East again and on July 31 they would acquire OF Ricky Henderson to propel them into another post-season run.

In the 1993 AL Championship Series the Blue Jays and Chicago White Sox would both win two games on opposition soil before the Blue Jays reversed the trend and won Game 5 at SkyDome. In all six games the team that scored first won the contest. Roberto Alomar once again led the way with a .316 average, including reaching base in all five plate appearances in Game 5. Dave Stewart would close out the series moving to 8-0 in ALCS play with a 6-3 victory.

In a highly entertaining series the Blue Jays would bring back-to-back championships back to Canada, defeating the Philadelphia Phillies in six games. The series was highlighted by a classic Game 4 contest in Philadelphia on October 20, that saw the Blue Jays overcome 12-7 and 14-9 deficits with a six-run 8th inning. 10 men would come to the plate in the 8th, with Devon White tying the contest with a 2-out RBI triple. Ricky Henderson provided the game-winning hit in a contests that took four hours and 14 minutes to play. In Game 6 in Toronto, the Blue Jays would trail the Phillies 6-5 entering the bottom of the 9th. Phillies closer LHP Mitch Williams allowed a walk to Henderson and a one-out single to Molitor before Joe Carter ended the series with a three-run home run to left field. The "You'll never hit a bigger home run in your life" quote was made famous by longtime Blue Jays announcer Tom Cheek.

1994 sees the season end prematurely on August 12 as a player strike begins. It does not end until late April of 1995. The Blue Jays would not return to the post-season during the balance of the 90's, finishing as high as 3rd place in 1998 and 1999. Paul Beeston is named Canada's Baseball Man of the Year in 1994, while Howard Starkman picks up the Robert O. Fishel award for Public Relations Excellence in 1996. The Blue Jays would open their 20th season in Las Vegas vs., Oakland, a season where RHP Pat Hentgen would begin a string of three successive Blue Jays winning a CY Young award with Roger Clemens winning in 1997 and 1998.

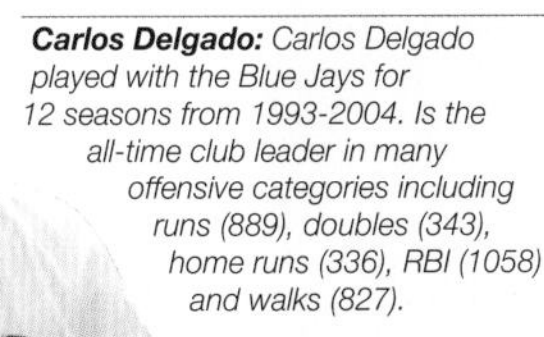

Carlos Delgado: *Carlos Delgado played with the Blue Jays for 12 seasons from 1993-2004. Is the all-time club leader in many offensive categories including runs (889), doubles (343), home runs (336), RBI (1058) and walks (827).*

EXCELLENCE IS MEASURED:

The Blue Jays honour OF George Bell and RHP Dave Stieb by unveiling their names as the first, on the Level of Excellence. Over the years only the most prominent Blue Jays will see their names on the outfield facade. Joe Carter and Cito Gaston would be added in 1999.

Cito Gaston would end a glorious run with the club after being relieved of his duties on September 24, 1997. During his tenure the club would win three divisional titles and two World Series. Interleague play begins in 1997 and the Blue Jays play the Montreal Expos in regular season play for the first time. The decade closes out with some significant accomplishments after Gord Ash assumes the role of General Manager in 1998. The same year Tony Fernandez becomes the all-time hits leader and Roger Clemens becomes just the 11th pitcher in MLB history to record 3,000 strikeouts. Shawn Green becomes the first Blue Jay to post 30 home runs and 30 stolen bases in 1998. Pat Hentgen is the 4th Blue Jay to win 100 games and Billy Koch posts his 31st save in 1999 to set a then AL Rookie record.

2000s:

The Blue Jays field many competitive teams over the course of the next decade, winning 80 or more games in eight of the 10 seasons. Rogers Communications assumes control of the franchise in September of 2000. During the summer of the same year the Blue Jays put on a power display becoming the first Major League team to have four players with 20 or more home runs at the All-Star break (Delgado, Batista, Mondesi, Cruz).

Ted Rogers: *In September of 2000, local ownership returned to the Toronto Blue Jays as Rogers Communications Inc. purchased 80% control of the franchise.*

Along the way they set a franchise record with home runs in 23 straight contests. The 134 home runs at home set a new AL mark and the 244 home runs set a new franchise record. Carlos Delgado is named Sporting News Player of the Year.

2001 sees the club open the season with one game vs. the Texas Rangers in Puerto Rico. Raul Mondesi pulls off the first straight steal of home in franchise history, while on April 19 the club plays the longest game in franchise history. A 6-5, 17-inning loss to the Yankees, in a game that took 5:57 minutes. Carlos Delgado assumes the franchise lead in home runs passing Joe Carter. Jeff Frye hits for the cycle on August 17, joining Kelly Gruber as the only Blue Jays to accomplish the feat.

Carlos Tosca takes over as Blue Jays manager, replacing Jim Fregosi during the 2002 season. Carlos Delgado's team record streak of 432 consecutive games comes to an end on August 4, 2002. Pat Gillick is enshrined on the Level of Excellence on August 7, 2002. The 2002 campaign came to a close with 3B Eric Hinske named as the Rookie of the Year.

Halladay 2003 Cy Young: *Roy Halladay wins the Cy Young Award in 2003 becoming the 3rd Blue Jay to do so as he joined Pat Hentgen (1996) and Rogers Clemens (1997-1998). Halladay is the all-time club leader in winning % (.661) while ranking 2nd in wins (148), shutouts (15) and strikeouts (1495).*

Through 2005 although the Blue Jays would not finish higher than 3rd place, fans would see many exciting moments. They would complete their first four game sweep of the Yankees in NY during the 2003 season. On June 15, 2003 Reed Johnson becomes only the fourth player in MLB history to hit a leadoff and walk-off home run in the same game. Roy Halladay wins 15 straight decisions in 2003 on his way to a club record 22 wins and a Cy Young award. On September 2, 2003 Carlos Delgado bangs out four home runs to become the 15th player in MLB history to accomplish the feat. Legendary broadcaster Tom Cheek sees his streak of 4,306 consecutive games come to an end after the sudden passing of his father on June 3, 2004. Later in the season he is enshrined on the Level of Excellence. John Gibbons relieves Carlos Tosca of his duties on August 8, 2004. The final day of the season is overshadowed by the sudden passing of longtime Blue Jay and current broadcaster John Cerutti. Vernon Wells picks up a Gold Glove Award in 2004 and 2005, while Orlando Hudson earns the distinction in 2005. On April 4, Tom Cheek calls back-to-back home runs by Orlando Hudson and Vernon Wells in his last game as a Blue Jays broadcaster. He would later pass away on October 9, 2005.

After key signings of RHP A.J. Burnett and LHP B.J. Ryan in 2006, the team would go on to post its best finish of the decade, finishing in 2nd place with an 87-75 record. It marked the first time they would place higher than 3rd place since the World Series winning clubs in 1992 and 1993. They would see five players go to the All-Star Game (Halladay, Ryan, Wells, Glaus, Rios).

The Blue Jays would sign free agent Frank Thomas to a two-year contract in 2007 as he would pursue his run at 500 career home runs. On June 28 in Minnesota, he would become just the 21st player in MLB history to accomplish the feat hitting a 1st inning home run off Carlos Silva. Completed 2007 with the highest home attendance (2,454,283) since 1998.

Robert Alomar would take center stage once again on April 4, 2008 as he would see his name honoured with many Blue Jay greats on the Level of Excellence. Cito Gaston makes his return to the dugout as he replaces John Gibbons as manager with the team sitting with a 35-39 record. Gaston would lead the team to a 10-game winning streak in September and finish with a 51-37 record the rest of the way in 2008. He would be rewarded with two-year contract following the season.

Home Run Record: *Jose Bautista broke the Blue Jays home run record in 2010, leading the Majors with 54 home runs. Is the only Toronto player to ever hit at least 50 home runs in a season.*

Cito Gaston: *Cito Gaston waves goodbye as he is honoured at Rogers Centre in the final game of 2010. Gaston has the most wins as a manager in club history with 913 in 1764 games (1989-1997; 2008-2010).*

The decade concludes with a 75 win, 4th place finish, which would see General Manager JP Ricciardi replaced following the season by assistant Alex Anthopoulos on October 3. Aaron Hill and Adam Lind have stellar offensive seasons earning both a Silver Slugger Award. Hill also is named Comeback Player of the Year, while Lind is recognized as the AL's best Designated Hitter, picking up the Edgar Martinez Award.

2010s:

2010 begins the decade with plenty of promise under the guidance of Alex Anthopoulos, as the team posts an 85-77 record. The club makes a concerted effort to beef up the Player Development staff and strengthen the organizations farm system. Jose Bautista wins the Hank Aaron award and a Silver Slugger Award, after setting a club mark with 54 home runs. Bautista would become just the 16th player in MLB history to record 54 home runs and just the 7th player to post 50 home runs, 30 doubles and 100 walks in the same season. Overall the team would hit 257 home runs tying them for the 3rd highest total in MLB history. For the first time since 2002, someone other than Roy Halladay took to the mound on Opening Day as Shaun Marcum got the nod. Brandon Morrow would turn in one of the most impressive performances in franchise history on August 8 vs. Tampa Bay. Morrow would see his no-hitter lost with two outs in the 9th inning, however he would finish with a one-hitter and 17 strikeouts. Cito Gaston is honoured in the final home game with a pre-game ceremony on September 29, 2010.

THE HALL IS CALLING:

Roberto Alomar, a 12-time All-Star and 10-time Gold Glove winning second baseman was inducted into the National Baseball Hall of Fame by the Baseball Writers' Association of America on July 24, 2011 at the Clark Sports Center in Cooperstown, NY. Alomar, the two-time World Series Champion donned the Toronto Blue Jays cap in the Hall, marking the first ever Blue Jay player to be elected into the Hall of Fame. Alomar, who was in his 2nd year on the ballot, received 523 votes which represented the 3rd highest total in history, for a 90% majority.

John Farrell is appointed as the 12th manager in franchise history and leads the club to an 81-81 record in his first season. Jose Bautitsa is once again the offensive leader, earning a second consecutive Hank Aaron award as the league's best hitter. He once again led the AL in home runs with 47, while also posting league leading numbers in walks (132), slugging % (.608) and OPS (1.056). Becomes the first player to lead the Majors in the above categories since Barry Bonds in 2001, and the first AL player since Ted Williams in 1942. The fans also recognize his dominance by registering 7,454,753 All-Star votes, the most in MLB history. In the minors, four of the Blue Jays affiliates make the playoffs, with two clubs (New Hampshire/Vancouver) winning league championships. Baseball America has the Blue Jays minor league system rated 4th up from 19th just one year prior. On November 18, 2011, the Blue Jays unveil a new logo that brings the "blue" back to the Blue Jays, by updating the original logo and recognizing the classic Blue Jays look.

On March 30, 2012, building off of the agreement with Little League Baseball Canada and continuing with its commitment to amateur baseball in Canada, the Toronto Blue Jays have partnered with Baseball Canada on a sponsorship package for all National Programs. For the 3rd consecutive season, OF Jose Bautista was named to the American League All-Star team. Was voted in as a starter for the 2nd straight year. Ranked 3rd in voting among OF at 4,971,155 votes. Is the 3rd Blue Jay to be voted in as a starter in back to back seasons (Roberto Alomar & Joe Carter being the oth-

ers). Started in RF, batted 4th (0-1, BB, K). Represented the AL in the 2012 State Farm Home Run Derby. Lost in the finals to Prince Fielder. In June of 2012, Jose Bautista batted .271 with four doubles, 14 home runs, 30 RBI, 22 walks & 24 runs scored in 27 games to capture his 5th career monthly award. Finished tops in homers, RBI and slugging percentage (.750), T-1st in walks & extra-base hits (18). His 14 homers established a new Club record for the most hits in any single month & it marked the most hits in a calendar month by any player since Colorado's Troy Tulowitzki hit 15 round trippers in September 2010. It also was the most for an A.L. player since New York's Alex Rodriguez hit 14 home runs in April 2007. In a breakout season for Edwin Encarnacion, slamming 42 home runs while driving in 110 runs, signed a three year contract extension to remain with the club thru the 2015 season. On Sept. 18, 2012 the club announces that they have entered into a Player Development Contract with the Buffalo Bisons of the International League (AAA) for the 2013 and 2014 seasons. On Oct. 21, 2012 the Blue Jays released Manager John Farrell from his contract as he was hired by the Red Sox to take over that same position with them, an agreement reached by both teams. On Nov. 19, 2012 the Blue Jays and Marlins complete the biggest trade in baseball history, measured in number of players changing hands as Toronto acquires RHP Josh Johnson, LHP Mark Buehrle, SS Jose Reyes, IF/OF Emilio Bonifacio and C John Buck in exchange for C Jeff Mathis, SS Yunel Escobar, SS Adeiny Hechavarria, RHP Henderson Alvarez, LHP Justin Nicolino, OF Jake Marisnick and RHP Anthony Desclafani. On Nov. 20, the Blue Jays hire John Gibbons as Manager to take over for John Farrell. Gibbons becomes the second person to have two tenures as Blue Jays manager along with Cito Gaston. Gibbons served as Blue Jays manager from August 9, 2004 through to June 20, 2008 posting a record of 305-305 in 610 games and is the 3rd winningest manager in franchise history.

Tom Cheek: *Tom Cheek, who called the first 4,306 regular-season and 41 postseason games in Toronto Blue Jays history has been selected as the 2013 recipient of the Ford C. Frick Award, presented annually for excellence in broadcasting by the National Baseball Hall of Fame and Museum. Cheek, who passed away on Oct. 9, 2005, will be honored as part of Hall of Fame Weekend 2013 in Cooperstown, N.Y.*

Alomar – Gillick HOF: *Roberto Alomar was inducted into the National Baseball Hall of Fame in July of 2011, becoming the first and only member of the Blue Jays to have accomplished that feat. Alomar is joined by former Blue Jays General Manager, Pat Gillick, who was inducted in to the Hall of Fame on the same day. Gillick was instrumental in building the Blue Jays from an expansion team in 1977 to World Series Champions. Gillick was also responsible for bringing Alomar to Toronto, acquiring him in a trade with San Diego.*

HISTORY OF THE LOGO

PRIMARY LOGO (1977 - 1996)

A Blue Jay head with a maple leaf on a baseball surrounded by team name

Designed by Savage Sloan, Ltd.

Unveiled on October 8, 1976
First worn on April 7, 1977
Last worn on September 29, 1996
Championships won with this logo 1992, 1993
World Series Champions 1992, 1993
American League Champions

PRIMARY LOGO (1997 - 2002)

A Blue Jay head on a baseball over a maple leaf above team name

Designed by MLB Properties

Unveiled on November 19, 1996
First worn on April 1, 1997
Last worn on September 29, 2002

PRIMARY LOGO (2003)

A Blue Jay holding a bat and tossing a ball behind red and blue T

Unveiled on February 1, 2000
Last worn on September 28, 2003

PRIMARY LOGO (2004 - 2011)

A Blue Jay head inside Jays in white with silver and graphite beveling and black and blue outlines

Designed by Brandid

Unveiled on September 2, 2003
First worn on April 5, 2004
Last worn on September 28, 2011

PRIMARY LOGO (2012-)

Blue and navy blue blue jay head with red maple leaf to the right on a baseball with split-lettered team script surrounding it within a blue double-outline

Unveiled on November 18, 2011

First Worn on April 5, 2012

HISTORY OF THE UNIFORM

HOME UNIFORMS

(1977 - 1979)

Blue Jays arched in blue and white on a white pullover uniform with blue and light blue sleeve and neck trim, primary logo below team name

Unveiled on February 17, 1977

First worn on April 7, 1977

(1980 - 1988)

Blue Jays arched in blue and white on a white pullover uniform with blue and light blue sleeve and neck trim, primary logo below team name

(1989 - 1993)

Blue Jays arched in blue and white on a white uniform with blue and light blue sleeve trim, primary logo below team name

First worn on April 14, 1989

Last worn on July 5, 1993

Championships won in this uniform

1992, 1993 World Series Champions

1992, 1993 American League Champions

(1993 - 1996)

Blue Jays arched in blue and white on a white uniform with blue and light blue sleeve trim, primary logo below team name

First worn on July 6, 1993

Last worn on September 29, 1996

Championships won in this uniform

1993 World Series Champions

1993 American League Champions

(1997 - 1999)

Blue Jays arched in blue and light blue on a white uniform with red, light blue, and blue sleeve ends, maple leaf patch on left sleeve

(2000)

Blue Jays arched in blue and light blue on a white uniform with red, light blue, and blue sleeve ends, maple leaf patch on left sleeve (uniform structure change and MLB batter logo added in 2000)

(2001)

Blue Jays arched in blue and light blue on a white uniform with blue piping, American League 100th Anniversary patch on right sleeve, Blue Jays 25th Anniversary patch on left sleeve

(2002)

Blue Jays arched in blue and light blue on a white uniform with blue piping, maple leaf patch on left sleeve

(2003)

Blue Jays arched in blue and light blue on a white uniform with blue piping, T-Jay patch on left sleeve

(2004)

Primary logo slanted up on a white uniform

(2005)

Primary logo slanted up on a white uniform, Cerutti/Ault/Mattick memorial patch on right sleeve

(2006)

Primary logo slanted up on a white uniform, Tom Cheek memorial patch on left sleeve, Blue Jays' 30th Anniversary patch on right sleeve

(2007 - 2008)

Primary logo slanted up on a white uniform

(2009)

Primary logo slanted up on a white uniform, Ted Rogers memorial patch on left sleeve, maple leaf patch on right sleeve

(2010 - 2011)

Primary logo slanted up on a white uniform, maple leaf patch on right sleeve

Last worn on September 22, 2011

(2012 -)

Unveiled on November 18, 2011

CURRENT BLUE JAYS UNIFORMS

Home

Road

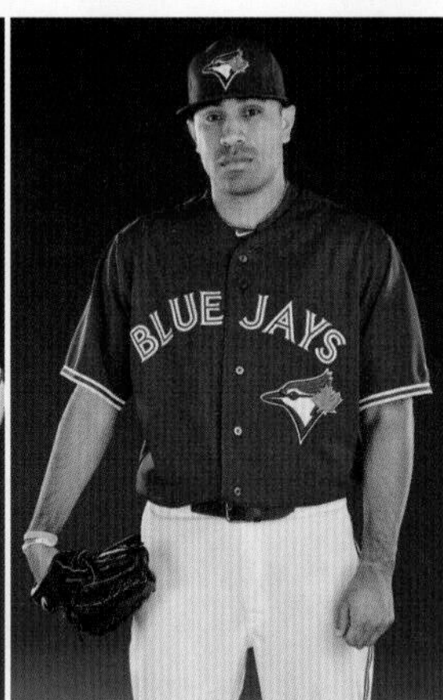

Alternate

ALL TIME ROSTER

MANAGERS, COACHES AND PLAYERS 1977 THRU 2012

TOTAL NUMBER OF PLAYERS — 611 + INTERIM MANAGER
INCLUDES ALL PLAYERS WHO HAVE PLAYED IN ONE OR MORE OFFICIAL MAJOR LEAGUE GAMES

MANAGERS (12)
Cox, Bobby ('82-'85)..........6
Farrell, John ('11-'12)..........42*,52
Fregosi, Jim ('99-'00)..........11
Gaston, Cito ('89-'97; '08-'10....42*,43
Gibbons, John ('04-'08)..........5
Hartsfield, Roy ('77-'79)..........7
Johnson, Tim ('98)..........17
Martinez, Buck ('01-'02)..........13
Mattick, Bobby ('80-'81)..........3
Queen, Mel ('97)..........34
Tosca, Carlos ('02-'04)..........14
Williams, Jimy ('86-'89)..........3

COACHES (61)
Arnsberg, Brad ('05-'09)..........38, 42*
Bailor, Bob ('92-'95)..........3
Barnett, Mike ('02-'05)..........56
Bevington, Terry ('99-'01)..........35
Brantley, Mickey ('05-'07)..........14, 42*
Breeden, Joe ('04)..........53
Butera, Sal ('98)..........11, 22
+Butterfield, Brian ('02-'12)..........42*,55
Cisco, Galen ('88; '90-'95)..........42
Connor, Mark ('01-'02)..........53
de Armas, Roly ('00)..........56
Denbo, Gary ('08)..........47
Doerr, Bobby ('77-'81)..........31
Elia, Lee ('00)..........3
Felske, John ('80-'81)..........28
Gaston, Cito ('82-'89; '00-'01)....41, 43
+Gibbons, John ('02-'04)..........58
Griffin, Alfredo ('96-'97)..........4
Guerrero, Epy ('81)..........53
Hacker, Rich ('91-'94)..........7
Hentgen, Pat ('11)..........41,42*
Hisle, Larry ('92-'95)..........39
Holmberg, Dennis ('94-'95)..........46
Hubbard, Jack ('98)..........16
Iorg, Garth ('96; '01-'02)..........16
Knoop, Bobby ('00)..........29
Langford, Rick ('00; '06, '10)....22, 42*
Leppert, Don ('77-'79)..........43
Lett, Jim ('97-'99)..........10
Leyva, Nick ('93-'97; '08-'10)...16, 42*
Llenas, Winston ('88)..........57
Lovullo, Torey ('11-'12)..........7,42*
Malave, Omar ('10)..........52, 42*
Matthews, Gary ('98-'99)..........36
McLaren, John ('86-'90)..........7, 24
Menke, Denis ('80-'81)..........14
Miller, Bob ('77-'79)..........15
Moore, Jackie ('77-'79)..........42
Moseby, Lloyd ('99)..........16
Murphy, Dwayne ('08-)..........21,41,42*
Patterson, Gil ('01-'04)..........47
Pevey, Marty ('99; '05-'08)...30, 45, 58
Queen, Mel ('96-'99)..........34
Rivera, Luis ('11-)..........63
Rodriguez, Eddie ('98)..........7
+Rojas, Cookie ('01-'02)..........1, 4
Smith, Billy ('84-'88)..........42
Squires, Mike ('89-'91)..........25
Stewart, Dave ('00)..........34,45
Sullivan, John ('82-'93)..........8
+Tenace, Gene
('90-'97;'08-'09)...... 15, 16, 18, 42*
Torres, Hector ('90-'91)..........56
Tosca, Carlos ('02)..........14
Upshaw, Willie ('96-'97)..........26, 28
+Wakamatsu, Don ('11-'12)..........22,42*
Walker, Pete ('12-)..........40,42*
Walton, Bruce ('02-'12)........ 42*,52, 53
+Warner, Harry ('77-'80)..........41
+Whitt, Ernie ('05-'08)..........12
Widmar, Al ('80-'89)..........41
Williams, Jimy ('80-'85)..........3, 24

PLAYERS
A (21)
Accardo, Jeremy (rhp) ('06-'10)..........49
Acevedo, Juan (rhp) ('03)..........57
Acker, Jim (rhp)
('83-'86; '89-'91)..........24, 31, 34
Adams, Glenn (dh) ('82)..........55
Adams, Russ (if) ('04-'09)..........8
Adams, Terry (rhp) ('04)..........51
Aikens, Willie (dh-1b) ('84-'85)..........24
Ainge, Danny (if-of) ('79-'81)..........2
Alberts, Butch (dh) ('78)..........14
Alexander, Doyle (rhp) ('83-'86)...33, 47
Alfonso, Edgardo (if) ('06)..........13
Allenson, Gary (c) ('85)..........38
Almanzar, Carlos (rhp) ('97-'98)..........40
Alomar, Roberto (if) ('91-'95)..........12
Alvarez, Henderson ('rhp) ('11-'12)....37
Andrews, Clayton (lhp) ('00)..........36
Andujar, Luis (rhp) ('96-'98)..........49
Aquino, Luis (rhp) ('86)..........32
Arencibia, J.P. (c) ('10-)..........9, 42*
Ashby, Alan (c) ('77-'78)..........8
Ault, Doug (1b-of) ('77-'78; '80)..........25

B (60)
Bailor, Bob (if-of-p) ('77-'80)..........1
Bair, Doug (rhp) ('88)..........40
Baker, Dave (if) ('82)..........31
Bale, John (lhp) ('99-'00)..........49
Banks, Josh (rhp) ('07)..........58
Barajas, Rod (c) ('08-'09)..........20
Barfield, Jesse (of) ('81-'89)..........29
Barker, Kevin (if) ('06)..........43
Barlow, Mike (rhp) ('80-'81)..........46
Barrett, Michael (c) ('09)..........5, 42*
Batista, Miguel (rhp) ('04-'05)..........43
Batista, Tony (if) ('99-'01)..........7
Batiste, Kevin (of) ('89)..........34
Battle, Howard (3b) ('95)..........14
Bautista, Jose (of) ('08-)...... 19, 23, 42*
Beamon, Charlie (1b-dh) ('81)..........32
Beck, Chad (rhp) ('11-)..........58
Beirne, Kevin (rhp) ('01)..........40
Bell, Derek (of) ('91-'92)..........14
Bell, George (of) ('81; '83-'90)..........11
Benitez, Armando (rhp) ('08)..........48
Beniquez, Juan (of-dh) ('87-'88)....7, 21
Berenguer, Juan (rhp) ('81)..........30
Berg, Dave (if) ('02-'04)..........2
Berroa, Geronimo (of) ('99)..........29
Black, Bud (lhp) ('90)..........35
Blair, Willie (rhp) ('90)..........27
Blake, Casey (if) ('99)..........28
Bohanon, Brian (lhp) ('96)..........32, 60
Bomback, Mark (rhp) ('81-'82)....17, 45
Bonnell, Barry (of) ('80-'83)..........9
Borbon, Pedro (lhp) ('00-'02)..........34, 51
Borders, Pat (c) ('88-'94; '99)......10, 29
Bordick, Mike (if) ('03)..........16
Bosetti, Rick (of) ('78-'81)..........22
Boucher, Denis (lhp) ('91)..........35
Bowles, Brian (rhp) ('01-'03)..........26, 37
Bowling, Steve (of) ('77)..........3
Braun, Steve (if-dh) ('80)..........11
Brenly, Bob (c) ('89)..........9
Brito, Tilson (if) ('96-'97)..........12, 14
Brow, Scott (rhp) ('93-'94; '96)....27, 44
Brown, Bobby (of) ('79)..........5
Brown, Kevin (c) ('98-'99)..........14
Brumfield, Jacob (of) ('96-97; 99).....2,5
Bruno, Tom (rhp) ('77)..........21
Buchholz, Taylor (rhp) ('10)..........30
Buck, John (c) ('10)..........14, 42*
Buice, DeWayne (rhp) ('89)..........38
Bullington, Bryan (rhp) ('09)..........36
Burnett, A.J. (rhp) ('06-'08)..........34
Burres, Brian (lhp) ('09)..........14
Burroughs, Jeff (dh) ('85)..........44
Bush, Dave (rhp) ('04-'05)..........49
Bush, Homer (if) ('99-'02)..........18
Buskey, Tom (rhp) ('78-'80)..........44
Butera, Sal (c) ('88)..........26
Butler, Rich (of) ('97)..........12
Butler, Rob (of) ('93-'94; '99)........2, 20
Byrd, Jeff (rhp) ('77)..........27

C (63)
Cabrera, Francisco (c) ('89)..........21
Cadaret, Greg (rhp) ('94)..........23
Cairo, Miguel (if) ('96)..........3
Camp, Shawn (rhp) ('08-'11)...... 42*,57
Campusano, Sil (of) ('88)..........6
Canate, Willie (of) ('93)..........21
Candelaria, John (lhp) ('90)..........48
Candiotti, Tom (rhp) ('91)..........49
Cannon, J.J. (Joe) (of) ('79-'80)..........30
Canseco, Jose (of-dh) ('98)..........33, 44
Carlson, Jesse (lhp) ('08-'11) 39, 43, 48
Carpenter, Chris (rhp) ('97-'02)....26, 50
Carpenter, David (rhp) ('12)..........39
Carpenter, Drew (rhp) ('12)..........39
Carrara, Giovanni (rhp) ('95-'96)........38
Carreno, Joel (rhp) ('11-)..........34
Carter, Joe (of) ('91-'97)..........29, 43
Carty, Rico (dh) ('78-'79)..........21
Cash, Kevin (c) ('02-'04)..........29
Cassidy, Scott (rhp) ('02)..........40
Castillo, Alberto (c) ('00-'01)..........30
Castillo, Frank (rhp) ('00)..........37
Castillo, Tony (lhp) ('88-'89;
'93-'96)..........27, 49
Catalanotto, Frank (of) ('03-'06)..........27
Caudill, Bill (rhp) ('85-'86)..........36
Cecil, Brett (lhp) ('09-)..........27, 42*
Cedeno, Domingo (if) ('93-'96)....20, 70
Cerone, Rick (c) ('77-'79)..........9
Cerutti, John (lhp) ('85-'90)..........55
Chacin, Gustavo (lhp) ('04-'07)..........39
Chavez, Jesse (rhp) ('12)..........20
Chavez, Raul (c) ('09)..........13
Chulk, Vinnie (rhp) ('03-'06)..........50
Clancy, Jim (rhp) ('77-'88)..........18
Clark, Bryan (lhp) ('84)..........35
Clark, Howie (if) ('03-'04; '07)..........4, 6
Clarke, Stan (lhp) ('83;'85-'86)..........34
Clayton, Royce (if) ('07)..........11, 42*
Clemens, Roger (rhp) ('97-'98)..........21
Coats, Buck (of) ('08)..........21
Coco, Pasqual (rhp) ('00-'02)..........38, 54
Coello, Robert (rhp) ('12)..........56
Coleman, Joe (rhp) ('78)..........16, 40
Coles, Darnell (of) ('93-'94)..........11
Collins, Dave (of) ('83-'84)..........10
Cone, David (rhp) ('92; '95)..........11
Cooper, Brian (rhp) ('02)..........50
Cooper, David (if) ('11-)..........30,40
Cooper, Don (rhp) ('83)..........36
Cordero, Francisco (rhp) ('12)..........48
Cordova, Marty (of) ('00)..........15
Cornett, Brad (rhp) ('94-'95)..........22, 58
Cox, Danny (rhp) ('93-'95)..........50
Cox, Ted (if) ('81)..........34
Crabtree, Tim (rhp) ('95-'97)..........37
Crawford, Evan (lhp) ('12-)..........42*,46
Creek, Doug (lhp) ('03)..........39
Crespo, Felipe (if) ('96-'98)..........3, 6
Crozier, Eric (if) ('04)..........17
Cruz Jr., Jose (of) ('97-'02)..........23
Cruz, Victor (rhp) ('78)..........47
Cubillan, Darwin (rhp) ('00)..........34
Cummings, Steve (rhp) ('89-'90)..........32

D (29)
Daal, Omar (lhp) ('97)..........54
Dalesandro, Mark (c) ('98-'99)..........5, 59
Darr, Mike (rhp) ('77)..........28
Darwin, Danny (rhp) ('95)..........44
Davey, Tom (rhp) ('99)..........43
Davis, Bob (c) ('79-'80)..........8
Davis, Dick (of) ('82)..........35
Davis, Doug (lhp) ('03)..........48
Davis, Rajai (of) ('11-)..........11,42*
Davis, Steve (lhp) ('85-'86)..........25
Dayley, Ken (lhp) ('91; '93)..........46
DeBarr, Dennis (lhp) ('77)..........22
Delgado, Carlos (1b) ('93-'04) .6, 21, 25
De Jong, Jordan, (rhp) ('07)..........57
Delabar, Stevel (rhp) ('12-)..........50
Dellucci, David (of) ('09)..........17
de los Santos, Valerio (lhp) ('04)..........26
DeWillis, Jeff (c) ('87)..........27
DeWitt, Matt (rhp) ('00; '01)..........40, 49
Diaz, Carlos (c) ('90)..........59
Diaz, Robinzon (c) ('08)..........14
Dominique, Andy (c) ('05)..........56
Dotel, Octavio (rhp) ('11)..........29
Douglass, Sean (rhp) ('04)..........24
Downs, Scott (lhp) ('05-'10)..........37
Drabek, Kyle (rhp) ('10-)..........4,42*
Ducey, Rob (of)
('87-'92; '00)..........20, 22 40
Duncan, Mariano (if) ('97)..........24
Dyson, Sam (rhp) ('12-)..........35

E (14)
Eckstein, David (if) ('08)..........11
Edge, Butch (rhp) ('79)..........16
Eichhorn, Mark (rhp) ('82;
'86-'88; '92-'93)..........28, 38, 48
Encarnacion, Edwin (if)
('09-)..........7,10,12,42*
Eppard, Jim (ph) ('90)..........26
Escobar, Kelvim (rhp) ('97-'03)....45, 47
Escobar, Yunel (if) ('10-'12)..........5, 42*
Espinosa, Nino (rhp) ('81)..........38
Estalella, Bobby (c) ('04)..........20
Estrella, Leo (rhp) ('00)..........53
Evans, Tom (if) ('97-'98)..........2, 28
Eveland, Dana (lhp) ('10)..........30, 42*
Ewing, Sam (if-of-dh) ('77-'78)..........5
Eyre, Scott (lhp) ('01-'02)..........29

F (22)
Fairly, Ron (if-of) ('77)..........6
Farquhar, Danny (rhp) ('11-'12)..........49
Fasano, Sal (c) ('07)..........13
Felix, Junior (of) ('89-'90)..........47, 54
Fernandez, Tony (if) ('83-'90;
'93; '98-'99; '01)..........1
Fielder, Cecil (dh-1b) ('85-'88)..........23
Figueroa, Luis (if) ('06)..........46
File, Bob (rhp) ('01-'02; '04)..........36
Filer, Tom (rhp) ('85)..........49
Flanagan, Mike (lhp) ('87-'90)..........46
Flener, Huck (lhp) ('93; '96-'97)...32, 38
Fletcher, Darrin (c) ('98-'02)..........9
Francisco, Ben (of) ('12)..........8,42*
Francisco, Frank (rhp) ('11)..........50
Frascatore, John (rhp) ('99-'01)..........52
Fraser, Willie (rhp) ('91)..........27
Frasor, Jason (rhp)
('04-'11; '12)..........54, 42*
Frederick, Kevin (rhp) ('04)..........48
Freel, Ryan (if) ('01)..........11
Freisleben, Dave (rhp) ('79)..........25

Stottlemyre, Todd (rhp) ('88-'94)..16, 30
Sturtze, Tanyon (rhp) ('03)................31
Swann, Pedro (of) ('02)........................8

T (17)
Tabler, Pat (if) ('91-'92)......................15
Tallet, Brian (lhp) ('06-'10; '11)..........56
Tam, Jeff (rhp) ('03)..........................33
Taubenheim, Ty (rhp) ('06-'07)..........48
Teahen, Mark (if) ('11).......................20
Thames, Eric (of) ('11-'12)............14,46
Thigpen, Curtis (c) ('07-'08)..........7, 59
Thomas, Frank (dh) ('07-'08)..... 35, 42*
Thompson, Andy (of) ('00).................16
Thornton, Lou (of) ('85; '87-'88)........28
Thurman, Corey (rhp) ('02-'03)..........35
Timlin, Mike (rhp) ('91-'97)...............40
Todd, Jackson (rhp) ('79-'81)......32, 40
Torres, Hector (if) ('77).....................29
Towers, Josh (rhp) ('03-'07)................7
Trachsel, Steve (rhp) ('00).................46
Trlicek, Rick (rhp) ('92).....................35

U (2)
Underwood, Tom (lhp) ('78-'79).........24
Upshaw, Willie (if-of)
('78; '80-'87)..............................26

V (10)
Valdez, Merkin (rhp) ('10)..................47
Van Ryn, Ben (lhp) ('98)....................50
Velandia, Jorge (if) ('08)......................4
Velez, Otto (if-of-dh) ('77-'82)...........19
Vermilyea, Jamie (rhp) ('07)...............36
Villanueva, Carlos (rhp) ('11-'12)........33
Viola, Frank (lhp) ('96).......................19
Virgil, Ozzie (c) ('89-'90).............21, 26
Vizquel, Omar (if) ('12).......... 13,17,42*
Vuckovich, Pete (rhp) ('77)................30

W (39)
Walker, Pete (rhp) ('02-03; '05-06)....41
Wallace, Dave (rhp) ('78)..................46
Walters, P.J. (rhp) ('11).....................40
Ward, Duane (rhp) ('86-'95)..............31
Ward, Turner (of) ('91-'93).........16, 24
Ware, Jeff (rhp) ('95-'96)..................52
Wasdin, John (rhp) ('03)....................38
Weathers, David (rhp) ('91-'92).........53
Webster, Mitch (of) ('83-'85).............23
Wells, David (lhp)
('87-'92; '99-'00)..................33, 36
Wells, Greg (1b-dh) ('81)...................43
Wells, Randy (rhp) ('08)....................59
Wells, Vernon (of)
('99-'10).......................... 3, 10, 42*
Werth, Jayson (of) ('02-'03).........13, 54
Weston, Mickey (rhp) ('91).................26
White, Devon (of) ('91-'95)...............25
Whiteside, Matt (rhp) ('05)................48
Whiten, Mark (of) ('90-'91).........23, 40
Whitmer, Dan (c) ('81)........................6
Whitt, Ernie (c) ('77-'78;'80-'89).......12
Wiggins, Scott (lhp) ('02)...................57
Wilborn, Ted (of) ('79).......................35
Wiley, Mark (rhp) ('78).......................21
Wilkerson, Brad (of) ('08)...................35
Williams, Kenny (of) ('90-'91)......12, 13
Williams, Matt (rhp) ('83)...................45
Williams, Woody (rhp)
('93-'98)..............................30, 54
Willis, Mike (lhp) ('77-'81)..........23, 33
Wills, Frank (rhp) ('88-'91)................44
Wilson, Mookie (of) ('89-'91)...............3
Wilson, Tom (c) ('02-'03)..............9, 15
Winfield, Dave (of) ('92).....................32
Wise, Dewayne (of)
('00; '02; '10; '11).........1, 3, 16, 55
Withem, Shannon (rhp) ('98).............58
Witt, Kevin (1b) ('98-'99).....................6
Wolfe, Brian (rhp) ('07-'09)................40
Woods, Al (of) ('77-'82).....................20
Woods, Gary (of) ('77-'78).................35
Woodward, Chris (if)
('99-'04; '11-'12)..............5, 25, 31

Z (3)
Zambrano, Victor (rhp) ('07)...............31
Zaun, Gregg (c) ('04-'08).....................9
Zosky, Eddie (if) ('91-'92)....................1

#12 Retired on July 31, 2011
#42* In honour of Jackie Robinson Day

THE ORIGINAL BLUE JAYS

AMERICAN LEAGUE EXPANSION DRAFT SELECTIONS NOVEMBER 5, 1976

1. Bob Bailor, if-of, Baltimore
2. Jerry Garvin, lhp, Minnesota
3. Jim Clancy, rhp, Texas
4. Gary Woods, of, Oakland
5. Rico Carty, if-dh, Cleveland
6. Butch Edge, rhp, Milwaukee
7. Al Fitzmorris, rhp, Kansas City
8. Al Woods, of, Minnesota
9. Mike Darr, rhp, Baltimore
10. Pete Vuckovich, rhp, Chicago
11. Jeff Byrd, rhp, Texas
12. Steve Bowling, of, Milwaukee
13. Dennis DeBarr, lhp, Detroit
14. Bill Singer, rhp, Minnesota
15. Jim Mason, if, New York
16. Doug Ault, if, Texas
17. Ernie Whitt, c, Boston
18. Mike Weathers, if, Oakland
19. Steve Staggs, if, Kansas City
20. Steve Hargan, rhp, Texas
21. Garth Iorg, if, New York
22. Dave Lemanczyk, rhp, Detroit
23. Larry Anderson, rhp, Milwaukee
24. Jesse Jefferson, rhp, Chicago
25. Dave McKay, if, Minnesota
26. Tom Bruno, rhp, Kansas City
27. Otto Velez, of, New York
28. Mike Willis, lhp, Baltimore
29. Sam Ewing, of, Chicago
30. Leon Hooten, rhp, Oakland

ALL-TIME UNIFORM NUMBERS 1977-2012

MANAGERS

3
Bobby Mattick, Jimy Williams

5
John Gibbons

6
Bobby Cox

7
Roy Hartsfield

11
Jim Fregosi

13
Buck Martinez

14
Carlos Tosca

17
Tim Johnson

34
Mel Queen

42
In honour of Jackie Robinson Day

Cito Gaston ('09-'10), John Farrell ('11-'12)

43
Cito Gaston

52
John Farrell

COACHES

1
Cookie Rojas

3
Bob Bailor, Lee Elia, Jimy Williams

4
Alfredo Griffin, Cookie Rojas

7
Rich Hacker, Torey Lovullo, John McLaren, Eddie Rodriguez

8
John Sullivan

10
Jim Lett

11
Sal Butera

12
Ernie Whitt

14
Mickey Brantley, Denis Menke, Carlos Tosca

15
Bob Miller, Gene Tenace

16
Jack Hubbard, Garth Lorg, Nick Leyva, Lloyd Moseby, Gene Tenace

18
Gene Tenace

21
Dwayne Murphy

22
Sal Butera, Rick Langford, Don Wakamatsu

24
John McLaren, Jimy Williams

25
Mike Squires

26
Willie Upshaw

28
John Felske, Willie Upshaw

29
Bobby Knoop

30
Marty Pevey

31
Bobby Doerr

34
Mel Queen, Dave Stewart

35
Terry Bevington

36
Gary Matthews

38
Brad Arnsberg

39
Larry Hisle

40
Pete Walker

41
Cito Gaston, Pat Hentgen, Dwayne Murphy, Harry Warner, Al Widmar

42
Galen Cisco, Jackie Moore, Billy Smith

In honour of Jackie Robinson Day

Brad Arnsberg ('09), Mickey Brantley ('07), Brian Butterfield ('09-'12), Pat Hentgen ('11), Rick Langford ('10), Nick Leyva ('09-'10), Torey Lovullo ('11-'12), Omar Malave ('10), Dwayne Murphy ('09-'12), Gene Tenace ('09), Don Wakamatsu ('11-'12), Pete Walker ('12), Bruce Walton ('09-'12)

43
Cito Gaston, Don Leppert

45
Marty Pevey

46
Dennis Holmberg

47
Gary Denbo, Gil Patterson

52
Omar Malave, Bruce Walton

53
Joe Breedon, Mark Connor, Epy Guerrero, Bruce Walton

55
Brian Butterfield

56
Mike Barnett, Roly de Armas, Hector Torres

57
Winston Llenas

58
John Gibbons, Marty Pevey

63
Luis Rivera

PLAYERS

0
Al Oliver

00
Cliff Johnson

1
Bob Bailor, Tony Fernandez, Orlando Hudson, Joe Inglett, Darin Mastroianni, Bengie Molina, Mickey Morandini, Ray Olmedo, Tomas Perez, Dewayne Wise, Eddie Zosky

2
Danny Ainge, Dave Berg, Jacob Brumfield, Rob Butler, Tom Evans, Aaron Hill, Cesar Izturis, Kelly Johnson, Manny Lee, Nelson Liriano, Fred Manrique, Otis Nixon, Luis Sojo, Steve Staggs

3
Steve Bowling, Miguel Cairo, Felipe Crespo, Jeff Frye, Chris Gomez, Adeiny Hechavarria, Jarrett Hoffpauir, Orlando Hudson, Reed Johnson, Norberto Martin, Brian Milner, Wayne Nordhagen, Leon Roberts, Randy Ruiz, Vernon Wells, Mookie Wilson, Dewayne Wise

4
Howie Clark, Kyle Drabek, Craig Grebeck, Alfredo Griffin, Joe Inglett, Manny Lee, Frank Menechino, Ryan Roberts, Phil Roof, Dick Schofield, Jason Smith, Jorge Velandia

5
Michael Barrett, Bobby Brown, Jacob Brumfield, Mark Dalesandro, Yunel Escobar, Sam Ewing, Jarrett Hoffpauir, Craig Kusick, Domingo Martinez, Rance Mulliniks, Bob Robertson, Chris Woodward

6
Sil Campusano, Howie Clark, Felipe Crespo, Carlos Delgado, Ron Fairly, Pat D. Kelly, Joe Lawrence, Jeff Mathis, John McDonald, Orlando Merced, Luis Sojo, Dan Whitmer, Kevin Witt

7
Tony Batista, Juan Beniquez, Edwin Encarnacion, Damaso Garcia, Pat F. Kelly, Felipe Lopez, Jeremy Reed, Shannon Stewart, Curtis Thigpen, Josh Towers

8
Russ Adams, Alan Ashby, Bob Davis, Ben Francisco, Alex S. Gonzalez, Ken Macha, Jose Molina, Pedro Swann

9
J. P. Arencibia, Barry Bonnell, Bob Brenly, Rick Cerone, Darrin Fletcher, Rick Leach, John Olerud, Tom Wilson, Gregg Zaun

10
Pat Borders, Dave Collins, Edwin Encarnacion, Jim Mason, John Mayberry, Doug Rader, Dave Revering, Mark Sharperson, Vernon Wells

11
George Bell, Steve Braun, Royce Clayton, Darnell Coles, David Cone, Rajai Davis, David Eckstein, Ryan Freel, Luis Gomez, Alex Gonzalez, John-Ford Griffin, Eric Hinske, Jeff Kent, Mike Macha, Mike Matheny, Juan Samuel, John Scott

12 (NUMBER RETIRED-7/31/11)
Roberto Alomar, Tilson Brito, Rich Butler, Edwin Encarnacion, Willie Greene, Luis Lopez, Tony Phillips, Ernie Whitt, Kenny Williams

13
Edgardo Alfonzo, Raul Chavez, Sal Fasano, Carlos Garcia, Roy Howell, Brett Lawrie, Buck Martinez, Lee Mazzilli, Peter Munro, Jeff Musselman, Lance Parrish, Tomas Perez, Luis Sojo, Omar Vizquel, Jayson Werth, Kenny Williams

14
Butch Alberts, Howard Battle, Derek Bell, Tilson Brito, Kevin Brown, John Buck, Brian Burres, Robinzon Diaz, Rickey Henderson, Tommy Hutton, Alex Infante, Darrin Jackson, Dave Martinez, Geno Petralli, Moises Sierra, Ruben Sierra, Eric Thames

15
Marty Cordova, Shawn Green, Fred Lewis, Kevin Millar, Lloyd Moseby, Alex Rios, Pat Tabler, Tom Wilson

16
Mike Bordick, Joe Coleman, Butch Edge, Garth Iorg, Tim Johnson, Greg Myers, Tim Nordbrook, Corey Patterson, Tom Quinlan, Guillermo Quiroz, Todd Stottlemyre, Andy Thompson, Turner Ward, Dewayne Wise

17
Mark Bomback, Eric Crozier, David Dellucci, Curtis Goodwin, Kelly Gruber, Dave Hollins, Tim Johnson, Brett Lawrie, Chris Michalak, Randy Moffitt, Lyle Overbay, Robert Perez, Josh Phelps, Domingo Ramos, Josh Roenicke, Omar Vizquel

18
Homer Bush, Jim Clancy, Gabe Gross, Tom Lawless, Hector Luna, Mike McCoy, Tomo Ohka, Simon Pond, Benito Santiago

19
Jose Bautista, Ray Giannelli, Domingo Martinez, Fred McGriff, Paul Molitor, Dan Plesac, Cliff Politte, Marco Scutaro, David Segui, Otto Velez, Frank Viola

20
Rod Barajas, Rob Butler, Domingo Cedeno, Jesse Chavez, Rob Ducey, Bobby Estalella, Brad Fullmer, Ken Huckaby, Patrick Lennon, Juan Rivera, Ryan Roberts, Mike Stanley, Mark Teahen, Al Woods

21
Juan Beniquez, Tom Bruno, Francisco Cabrera, Willie Canate, Rico Carty, Roger Clemens, Buck Coats, Carlos Delgado, Nick Green, Charlie Greene, Gabe Gross, Cory Lidle, Esteban Loaiza, Mike Maksudian, Charlie Moore, Chad Mottola, Greg Myers, Willis Otanez, Mark Ross, Randy Ruiz, Sergio Santos, Ken Schrom, Ron Shepherd, Ozzie Virgil, Mark Wiley

22
Rick Bosetti, Brad Cornett, Dennis DeBarr, Rob Ducey, Jimmy Key, Brandon League, Mike Matheny, Chad Mottola, Charlie O'Brien, Hosken Powell, Dick Schofield, Brian Simmons

23
Jose Bautista, Greg Cadaret, Jose Cruz Jr., Cecil Fielder, John Hattig, Jason Kershner, Dave Lemanczyk, Candy Maldonado, Brandon Morrow, Shannon Stewart, Mitch Webster, Mark Whiten, Mike Willis

24
Jim Acker, Willie Aikens, Sean Douglass, Mariano Duncan, John-Ford Griffin, Chuck Hartenstein, Rickey Henderson, Glenallen Hill, Bobby Kielty, Dave Righetti, Ricky Romero, Paul Spoljaric, Matt Stairs, Shannon Stewart, Tom Underwood, Turner Ward

25
Doug Ault, Steve Davis, Carlos Delgado, Dave Freisleben, Troy Glaus, Roy Lee Jackson, Len Matuszek, David Purcey, Devon White, Chris Woodward

26
Brian Bowles, Sal Butera, Chris Carpenter, Valerio de los Santos, Jim Eppard, Steve Hargan, Vince Horsman, Michael Huff, Adam Lind, Doug Linton, Willie Upshaw, Ozzie Virgil, Mickey Weston

27
Willie Blair, Scott Brow, Jeff Byrd, Tony Castillo, Frank Catalanotto, Brett Cecil, Jeff DeWillis, Willie Fraser, Todd Greene, Jimmy Key, Mickey Klutts, Randy Knorr, Chris Latham, Anthony Sanders, Cory Snyder, Tony Solaita

28
Casey Blake, Mike Darr, Mark Eichhorn, Tom Evans, Al Leiter, Brandon Lyon, Shaun Marcum, Greg Myers, Randy Myers, Jayson Nix, Lance Painter, Colby Rasmus, Lou Thornton

29
Jesse Barfield, Geronimo Berroa, Pat Borders, Joe Carter, Kevin Cash, Octavio Dotel, Scott Eyre, Pedro Hernandez, Glenallen Hill, Shea Hillenbrand, Garth Iorg, Dustin McGowan, Hector Torres

30
Juan Berenguer, Taylor Buchholz, Joe (J.J.) Cannon, Alberto Castillo, David Cooper, Dana Eveland, Doug Linton, Kevin Millar, Mike Morgan, Ron Musselman, Wayne Nordhagen, Justin Speier, Todd Stottlemyre, Pete Vuckovich, Woody Williams

31
Jim Acker, Dave Baker, Shawn Hill, Brian Lesher, Ted Lilly, Brandon Lyon, John Parrish, Robert Person, Kyle Phillips, Ken Schrom, Tanyon Sturtze, Duane Ward, Chris Woodward, Victor Zambrano

32
Luis Aquino, Charlie Beamon, Brian Bohanon, Steve Cummings, Huck Flener, Roy Halladay, Edwin Hurtado, Don Kirkwood, Jack Kucek, Aaron Laffey, Jeff Musselman, Jackson Todd, Dave Winfield

33
Doyle Alexander, Jose Canseco, Chad Hermansen, Joey Johnson, Dale Murray, Jorge Orta, Josh Roenicke, Scott Rolen, Alex Sanchez, Ed Sprague, Jeff Tam, Carlos Villanueva, David Wells, Mike Willis

34
Jim Acker, Kevin Batiste, Pedro Borbon, A.J. Burnett, Joel Carreno, Stan Clarke, Ted Cox, Darwin Cubillan, Jesse Jefferson, Justin Miller, Mark Rzepczynski, Steve Senteney, Dave Stewart

35
Bud Black, Denis Boucher, Bryan Clark, Dick Davis, Sam Dyson, Chad Gaudin, Dave Geisel, Brandon League, Rommie Lewis, Sandy Martinez, Jeff Musselman, Steve Nicosia, Phil Niekro, Lyle Overbay, Frank Thomas, Corey Thurman, Rick Trlicek, Ted Wilborn, Brad Wilkerson, Gary Woods

36
Clayton Andrews, Brian Bullington, Bill Caudill, Don Cooper, Bob File, Jerry Garvin, Darren Hall, Drew Hutchison, Marty Janzen, Kevin Mench, Francisco Rosario, Jamie Vermilyea, David Wells

37
Henderson Alvarez, Brian Bowles, Frank Castillo, Tim Crabtree, Scott Downs, Reed Johnson, Graeme Lloyd, Jo-Jo Reyes, Randy St. Claire, Dave Stieb

38
Gary Allenson, DeWayne Buice, Giovanni Carrara, Pasqual Coco, Mark Eichhorn, Nino Espinosa, Huck Flener, Pedro Garcia, Jim Gott, Mark Guthrie, Rick Luecken, Norberto Martin, Balor Moore, Darren Oliver, Aaron Small, John Wasdin

39
Jesse Carlson, David Carpenter, Drew Carpenter, Gustavo Chacin, Doug Creek, Don Gordon, Eric Gunderson, Erik Hanson, Pedro Hernandez, Paul Kilgus, Adam Loewen, Dave McKay, Dave Parker, Steve Parris, Nerio Rodriguez

40
Carlos Almanzar, Doug Bair, Kevin Beirne, Scott Cassidy, Joe Coleman, David Cooper, Matt DeWitt, Rob Ducey, Mark Lemongello, Eric Ludwick, Mickey Mahler, Dustin McGowan, Lance Painter, Paul Spoljaric, Mike Timlin, Jackson Todd, P.J. Walters, Mark Whiten, Brian Wolfe

41
Pat Hentgen, Pete Walker

42
Xavier Hernandez, Paul Mirabella

43
Kevin Barker, Miguel Batista, Jesse Carlson, Joe Carter, Tom Davey, Anthony Gose, Mark Hendrickson, John Hudek, Trever Miller, Raul Mondesi, Greg Wells

BIOGRAPHIES LAST SEASON HISTORY RECORDS OPPONENTS PLAYER DEV. MEDIA & MISC.

44
Scott Brow, Jeff Burroughs, Tom Buskey, Jose Canseco, Danny Darwin, Casey Janssen, Cliff Johnson, Jerry Johnson, Billy Koch, Aquilino Lopez, Luke Prokopec, Kenny Robinson, Frank Wills

45
Mark Bomback, Kelvim Escobar, Steve Grilli, Tony Johnson, Bob MacDonald, Tom Murphy, Jose Nunez, Jose Silva, Travis Snider, Paul Spoljaric, Matt Williams

46
Mike Barlow, Evan Crawford, Ken Dayley, Luis Figueroa, Mike Flanagan, Tom Gilles, Joe Kennedy, Jason Kershner, Gary Lavelle, Kerry Ligtenberg, Steve Luebber, Dyar Miller, Julio Mosquera, Mike Romano, Steve Sinclair, Eric Thames, Steve Trachsel, Dave Wallace

47
Doyle Alexander, Victor Cruz, Kelvim Escobar, Junior Felix, Mauro Gozzo, Phil Huffman, Corey Koskie, Jack Morris, Luis Perez, Jason Phillips, Jimmy Rogers, Matt Stark, Merkin Valdez

48
Armando Benitez, John Candelaria, Jesse Carlson, Francisco Cordero, Doug Davis, Mark Eichhorn, Kevin Frederick, J.A. Happ, Willie Horton, Luis Leal, Paul Quantrill, Scott Richmond, Bill Singer, Ty Taubenheim, Matt Whiteside

49
Jeremy Accardo, Luis Andujar, John Bale, Dave Bush, Tom Candiotti, Tony Castillo, Matt DeWitt, Danny Farquhar, Tom Filer, Felix Heredia, Paul Hodgson, Ricardo Jordan, Brad Lincoln, David Pauley

50
Chris Carpenter, Vinnie Chulk, Brian Cooper, Danny Cox, Steve Delabar, Frank Francisco, Joey Hamilton, Tom Henke, Dane Johnson, Rommie Lewis, Joey McLaughlin, Davis Romero, Ben Van Ryn

51
Terry Adams, Pedro Borbon, Gary Glover, Ryan Glynn, Jesse Litsch, David Maurer, Trever Miller

52
John Frascatore, Roy Halladay, Greg Myers, Kenny Robinson, B.J. Ryan, Jeff Ware

53
Leo Estrella, Dennis Lamp, Sandy Martinez, Michael Nakamura, Scott Service, Steve Sinclair, Mike Smith, David Weathers

54
Pasqual Coco, Omar Daal, Junior Felix, Jason Frasor, Jeff Hearron, Toby Hernandez, Randy Knorr, Dan Reichert, Jayson Werth, Woody Williams

55
Glenn Adams, John Cerutti, Paul Menhart, Bill Risley, Dewayne Wise

56
Robert Coello, Andy Dominique, Ryota Igarashi, Brian McRae, Zach Stewart, Brian Tallet

57
Juan Acevedo, Shawn Camp, Jordan De Jong, Juan Guzman, Scott Richmond, Scott Wiggins

58
Josh Banks, Chad Beck, Brad Cornett, Dirk Hayhurst, Wilfredo Ledezma, Shannon Withem

59
Mark Dalesandro, Carlos Diaz, Brad Mills, Adam Peterson, Curtis Thigpen, Randy Wells

60
Brian Bohanon, Jon Rauch, Robert Ray, Scott Schoeneweis

62
Lee Gronkiewicz, Aaron Loup, Bill Murphy

63
Kevin Gregg

64
Chad Jenkins

66
Juan Guzman

68
Yan Gomes

69
Peter Munro

70
Domingo Cedeno

88
Rene Gonzales

Players wearing #42 in honour of Jackie Robinson Day:

April 15, 2007 (60th anniversary):
Royce Clayton, Frank Thomas, Vernon Wells

April 15, 2008:
Shannon Stewart, Frank Thomas, Vernon Wells

April 15, 2009:
Michael Barrett, Jose Bautista, Shawn Camp, Aaron Hill, Adam Lind, Brandon League, John McDonald, Bill Murphy, Lyle Overbay, Scott Richmond, Alex Rios, Scott Rolen, Marco Scutaro, Travis Snider, Vernon Wells

April 15, 2010:
Jose Bautista, John Buck, Shawn Camp, Dana Eveland, Jason Frasor, Alex Gonzalez, Casey Janssen, Adam Lind, Mike McCoy, Lyle Overbay, Jeremy Reed, Travis Snider, Vernon Wells

April 15, 2011:
J.P. Arencibia, Jose Bautista, Brett Cecil, Yunel Escobar, Jason Frasor, Aaron Hill, Casey Janssen, Adam Lind, Jayson Nix, Corey Patterson, Jon Rauch, Juan Rivera, Marc Rzepczynski, Travis Snider

April 15, 2012:
Jose Bautista, Evan Crawford, Rajai Davis, Kyle Drabek, Edwin Encarnacion, Yunel Escobar, Ben Francisco, Kelly Johnson, Brett Lawrie, Jeff Mathis, Luis Perez, Colby Rasmus, Omar Vizquel

PLAYER TRANSACTIONS

BLUE JAYS TRADES

DATE	CLUB	OBTAINED	FOR
PAT GILLICK			
11-5-76	Cleveland	Alan Ashby, c Doug Howard, 1b-of	Al Fitzmorris, rhp
12-6-76	Cleveland	Rick Cerone, c John Lowenstein, of	Rico Carty, 1b-of
02-17-77	San Diego	Jerry Johnson, rhp	Dave Roberts, c-if
02-24-77	Oakland	Ron Fairly, 1b-of	Mike Weathers, if
03-29-77	Cleveland	Hector Torres, if	John Lowenstein, of
05-9-77	Texas	Roy Howell, if	Steve Hargan, rhp Jim Mason, if
12-6-77	St. Louis	Tom Underwood, lhp Victor Cruz, rhp	Peter Vuckovich, rhp John Scott, of
12-8-77	California	Pat Kelly, c Butch Alberts, 1b-of	Ron Fairly, 1b-of
03-3-78	St. Louis	Rick Bosetti, of	Tom Bruno, rhp
03-3-78	Cleveland	Rico Carty, dh	Dennis DeBarr, lhp
04-28-78	Milwaukee	Tim Johnson, if	Tim Nordbrook, inf
08-15-78	Oakland	Willie Horton, dh Phil Huffman, rhp	Rico Carty, dh
09-12-78	San Diego	Mark Wiley, rhp	Andrew Dyes, of
11-27-78	Houston	Mark Lemongello, rhp Joe Cannon, of Pedro Hernandez, if	Alan Ashby, c
12-5-78	Houston	Don Pisker, of	Gary Woods, of
12-6-78	Cleveland	Alfredo Griffin, if Phil Lansford, 3b	Victor Cruz, rhp
11-1-79	New York (AL)	Chris Chambliss, 1b Paul Mirabella, lhp Damaso Garcia, if	Tom Underwood, lhp Rick Cerone, c Ted Wilborn, of
12-5-79	Atlanta	Barry Bonnell, of Joey McLaughlin, rhp Pat Rockett, inf	Chris Chambliss, 1b Luis Gomez, ss
12-12-80	New York (NL)	Roy Lee Jackson, rhp	Bob Bailor, if-of
04-6-81	New York (NL)	Mark Bomback, rhp	Charlie Puleo, rhp
05-11-81	Milwaukee	Buck Martinez, c	Gil Kubski, of
06-10-81	Oakland	Future considerations	Rick Bosetti, of
11-18-81	New York (AL)	Aurelio Rodriguez, if	Mike Lebo, c
12-28-81	Minnesota	Hosken Powell, of	Greg Wells, 1b
12-28-81	Chicago (NL)	Dave Geisel, lhp	Paul Mirabella, lhp
03-25-82	Kansas City	Rance Mulliniks, if	Phil Huffman, rhp
04-2-82	Chicago (AL)	Wayne Nordhagen, of-dh	Aurelio Rodriguez, 3b
05-5-82	New York (AL)	Dave Revering, 1b-dh Jeff Reynolds, 3b	John Mayberry, 1b
06-15-82	Philadelphia	Dick Davis, of	Wayne Nordhagen, of (to Pittsburgh)
10-27-82	New York (AL)	Tucker Ashford, 3b	'conditional'
11-5-82	Oakland	Cliff Johnson, dh	Al Woods, of
12-9-82	New York (AL)	Dave Collins, of Mike Morgan, rhp Fred McGriff, 1b	Dale Murray, rhp Tom Dodd, of-c
02-4-83	Kansas City	Cecil Fielder, 1b	Leon Roberts, of
02-4-83	New York (NL)	Jorge Orta, dh-of	Steve Senteney, rhp
12-9-83	Seattle	Bryan Clark, lhp	Barry Bonnell, of
12-19-83	Kansas City	Willie Aikens, if-dh	Jorge Orta, dh-of
12-8-84	Oakland	Bill Caudill, rhp	Dave Collins, of Alfredo Griffin, ss
01-26-85	San Francisco	Gary Lavelle, lhp	Jim Gott, rhp Jack McKnight, rhp Augie Schmidt, if
04-1-85	Philadelphia	Len Matuszek, 1b-dh	Dave Shipanoff, rhp Jose Escobar, if Ken Kinnard, of
07-9-85	Los Angeles	Al Oliver, dh	Len Matuszek, 1b-dh
08-29-85	Texas	Cliff Johnson, dh	Matt Williams, rhp Greg Ferlenda, rhp Jeff Mays, rhp
07-5-86	Atlanta	Duane Ward, rhp	Doyle Alexander, rhp
07-6-86	Atlanta	Joe Johnson, rhp	Jim Acker, rhp

DATE	CLUB	OBTAINED	FOR
02-2-87	Atlanta	Craig McMurtry, rhp	Damaso Garcia, if
			Luis Leal, rhp
07-14-87	Kansas City	Juan Beniquez, of-dh	Luis Aquino, rhp
08-31-87	Baltimore	Mike Flanagan, lhp	Oswald Peraza, rhp
			Jose Mesa, rhp
04-30-89	New York (AL)	Al Leiter, lhp	Jesse Barfield, of
07-31-89	New York (NL)	Mookie Wilson, of	Jeff Musselman, lhp
			Mike Brady, rhp
08-24-89	Atlanta	Jim Acker, rhp	Tony Castillo, lhp
			Francisco Cabrera, c
12-17-89	Atlanta	Ricky Trlicek, rhp	Ernie Whitt, c
			Kevin Batiste, of
07-27-90	Minnesota	John Candelaria, lhp	Nelson Liriano, if
			Pedro Munoz, of
09-17-90	Cleveland	Bud Black, lhp	Mauro Gozzo, rhp
			Alex Sanchez, rhp
			Steve Cummings, rhp
11-6-90	Atlanta	Nate Cromwell, lhp	Earl Sanders, rhp
12-2-90	California	Devon White, of	Junior Felix, of
		Willie Fraser, rhp	Luis Sojo, if
		Marcus Moore, rhp	Ken Rivers, c
12-5-90	San Diego	Joe Carter, of	Tony Fernandez, ss
		Roberto Alomar, if	Fred McGriff, 1b
01-15-91	Baltimore	Rene Gonzales, if	Rob Blumberg, lhp
06-27-91	Cleveland	Tom Candiotti, rhp	Glenallen Hill, of
		Turner Ward, of	Mark Whiten, of
			Denis Boucher, lhp
07-14-91	Chicago (AL)	Cory Snyder, of	Shawn Jeter, of
			Steve Wapnick, rhp
08-9-91	Milwaukee	Candy Maldonado, of	Rob Wishnevski, rhp
			William Suero, 2b
07-30-92	California	Mark Eichhorn, rhp	Rob Ducey, of
			Greg Myers, C
08-28-92	New York (NL)	David Cone, rhp	Jeff Kent, if
			Ryan Thompson, of
12-8-92	California	Luis Sojo, if	Kelly Gruber, 3b
03-30-93	San Diego	Darrin Jackson, of	Derek Bell, of
			Stoney Briggs, of
06-11-93	New York (NL)	Tony Fernandez, ss	Darrin Jackson, of
07-31-93	Oakland	Rickey Henderson, of	Steve Karsay, rhp
			Jose Herrera, of
03-29-94	Chicago (AL)	Mike Huff, of	Domingo Martinez, if
GORD ASH			
11-18-94	Florida	Scott Pace, lhp	Eddie Zosky, if
12-5-94	Philadelphia	Monetary compensation	Rob Butler, of
04-6-95	Kansas City	David Cone, rhp	David Sinnes, rhp
			Anthony Medrano, if
			Chris Stynes, if
07-28-95	New York (AL)	Marty Janzen, rhp	David Cone, rhp
		Jason Jarvis, rhp	
		Mike Gordon, rhp	
08-31-95	Texas	Player to be named later	Candy Maldonado, of
12-7-95	Philadelphia	Paul Quantrill, rhp	Howard Battle, if
			Ricardo Jordan, lhp
12-18-95	Seattle	Bill Risley, rhp	Paul Menhart, rhp
		Miguel Cairo, if	Edwin Hurtado, rhp
05-15-96	Pittsburgh	Jacob Brumfield, of	D.J.Boston, 1b
08-22-96	Chicago (AL)	Luis Andujar, rhp	Domingo Cedeno, if
		Allen Halley, rhp	Tony Castillo, lhp
11-14-96	Pittsburgh	Carlos Garcia, if	Jose Silva, rhp
		Orlando Merced, of	Jose Pett, rhp
		Dan Plesac, lhp	Mike Halperin, lhp
			Abraham Nunez, if
			Craig Wilson, c
			Brandon Cromer, if
11-20-96	Texas	Player to be named later	Lonell Roberts, of
11-20-96	Chicago (NL)	Jason Stevenson, rhp	Miguel Cairo, if
12-11-96	Detroit	Anton French, of	Roberto Duran, lhp
12-20-96	New York (NL)	Robert Person, rhp	John Olerud, 1b
03-17-97	Texas	Lonell Roberts, of	Player to be named from
			11-20-96 trade
07-31-97	Seattle	Jose Cruz Jr., of	Mike Timlin, rhp
			Paul Spoljaric, lhp
08-12-97	Los Angeles	Bobby Cripps, c	Otis Nixon, of

DATE	CLUB	OBTAINED	FOR
03-14-98	Texas	Kevin Brown, c	Tim Crabtree, rhp
07-30-98	Boston	Peter Munro, rhp Jay Yanneco, rhp	Mike Stanley, dh
07-31-98	Baltimore	Nerio Rodriguez, rhp Shannon Carter, of	Juan Guzman, rhp
07-31-98	New York (NL)	Leoncio Estrella, rhp	Tony Phillips, of
08-6-98	San Diego	Brian Loyd, c	Randy Myers, lhp
12-13-98	San Diego	Joey Hamilton, rhp	Woody Williams, rhp Carlos Almanzar, rhp Peter Tucci, of
12-14-98	Detroit	Eric Ludwick, rhp	Beiker Graterol, rhp
02-18-99	New York (AL)	Homer Bush, if Graeme Lloyd, lhp David Wells, lhp	Roger Clemens, rhp
03-30-99	Anaheim	Dave Hollins, if	Tomas Perez, if
05-05-99	Philadelphia	Paul Spoljaric, lhp	Robert Person, rhp
06-12-99	Arizona	Tony Batista, if John Frascatore, rhp	Dan Plesac, lhp
07-28-99	Seattle	David Segui, if	Tom Davey, rhp Steve Sinclair, lhp
08-09-99	Colorado	Brian McRae, of	Player to be named later (Pat Lynch, rhp, 08-25-99)
09-03-99	Cincinnati	Player to be named later (Jamie Goudie, if, 09-13-99)	Juan Melo, if
11-08-99	Los Angeles	Pedro Borbon, lhp Raul Mondesi, of	Shawn Green, of Jorge Nunez, if
11-11-99	St. Louis	Alberto Castillo, c Matt Dewitt, rhp Lance Painter, lhp	Pat Hentgen, rhp Paul Spoljaric, lhp
03-16-00	Montreal/Texas	Brad Fullmer, if	David Segui, if (Texas) Lee Stevens, if (Montreal)
03-22-00	New York (NL)	Jersen Perez, if	Jim Mann, rhp
07-19-00	Texas	Esteban Loaiza, rhp	Mike Young, if Darwin Cubillan, rhp
07-26-00	Philadelphia	Rob Ducey, of	Player to be named later (John Sneed, rhp, 07-31-00)
07-31-00	Tampa Bay	Steve Trachsel, rhp Mark Guthrie, lhp	Brent Abernathy, if
08-04-00	Texas	Dave Martinez, of	Player to be named later (Pete Munro, rhp, 08-08-00)
08-06-00	Philadelphia	Mickey Morandini, if	Player to be named later (Rob Ducey, of, 08-07-00)
11-07-00	Chicago (AL)	Scott Eyre, lhp	Gary Glover, rhp
11-22-00	Cincinnati	Steve Parris, rhp	Clayton Andrew, lhp Leo Estrella, rhp
12-11-00	Baltimore	Jayson Werth, c	John Bale, lhp
12-11-00	Chicago (NL)	Cole Liniak, if	Player to be named later
01-14-01	Chicago (AL)	Mike Sirotka, lhp Kevin Beirne, rhp Mike Williams, rhp Brian Simmons, of	David Wells, lhp Matt DeWitt, rhp
01-16-01	Florida	Player to be named later (Cash considerations)	Chad Mottola, of
03-22-01	Chicago (AL)	Matt DeWitt, rhp	Mike Williams, rhp
J.P. RICCIARDI			
12-07-01	Oakland	Eric Hinske, if Justin Miller, rhp	Billy Koch, rhp
12-10-01	Chicago (NL)	Felix Heredia, lhp Player to be named later (James Deschaine, if, 12-13-01)	Alex Gonzalez, if
12-13-01	Los Angeles	Luke Prokopec, rhp Chad Ricketts, rhp	Cesar Izturis, if Paul Quantrill, rhp
01-02-02	Oakland	Tom Wilson, c	Mike Kremblas, c
01-17-02	Anaheim	Brian Cooper, rhp	Brad Fullmer, if
05-15-02	Houston	Player to be named later (cash considerations)	Pedro Borbon, lhp
05-26-02	Philadelphia	Cliff Politte, rhp	Dan Plesac, lhp
07-01-02	New York (AL)	Scott Wiggins, lhp	Raul Mondesi, of
11-16-02	Oakland	Cory Lidle, rhp	Mike Rouse, if Chris Mowday, rhp
12-15-02	Oakland/Arizona/Cincinnati	Player to be named later (Jason Arnold, rhp, 12-16-02)	Felipe Lopez, if
01-07-03	Oakland	John-Ford Griffin, of	Player to be named later
07-16-03	Minnesota	Bobby Kielty, OF	Shannon Stewart, OF Player to be named later (David Gassner, lhp, 12-17-03)

DATE	CLUB	OBTAINED	FOR
11-18-03	Oakland	Ted Lilly, lhp	Bobby Kielty, of Player to be named later
12-14-03	Colorado/Tampa Bay	Justin Speier, rhp	Mark Hendrickson, lhp (Tampa Bay) Player to be named later (Colorado) (Sandy Nin, rhp, 12-15-03) Joe Kennedy, lhp (Colorado)
03-29-04	Los Angeles	Jason Frasor, rhp	Jayson Werth, of
05-12-04	Oakland	Frank Menechino, if	Future Considerations
07-24-04	Boston	John Hattig, if	Terry Adams, rhp
08-06-04	Cleveland	Eric Crozier, if	Josh Phelps, if
12-02-04	Cleveland	John McDonald, if	Thomas Mastny, rhp
12-12-04	Tampa Bay	Chad Gaudin, rhp	Kevin Cash, c
01-12-05	Arizona	Shea Hillenbrand, if	Adam Peterson, rhp
07-22-05	Detroit	Player to be named later (cash considerations)	John McDonald, if
11-10-05	Detroit	John McDonald, if	Cash Considerations
12-05-05	Oakland	Player to be named later (Dustin Majewski, of)	Chad Gaudin, rhp
12-07-05	Milwaukee	Lyle Overbay, if Player to be named later (Ty Taubenheim, rhp)	Dave Bush, rhp Gabe Gross, of Player to be named later (Zach Jackson, lhp)
12-27-05	Arizona	Troy Glaus, if Sergio Santos, if	Orlando Hudson, 2B Miguel Batista, rhp
01-06-06	Milwaukee	Brian Wolfe, rhp	Corey Koskie, if
01-17-06	Cleveland	Brian Tallet, rhp	Bubbie Buzachero, rhp
07-22-06	San Francisco	Jeremy Accardo, rhp	Shea Hillenbrand, if Vinnie Chulk, rhp
08-16-06	Cincinnati	Player to be named later (Trevor Lawhorn, if)	Scott Schoeneweis, lhp
08-17-06	Boston	Player to be named later	Eric Hinske, if-of
11-18-07	Oakland	Marco Scutaro, if	Graham Godfrey, if Kristian Bell, rhp
12-05-07	Cincinnati	Buck Coats, of	Player to be named later (RHP Justin James)
01-14-08	St. Louis	Scott Rolen, if	Troy Glaus, if
05-09-08	Texas	Kevin Mench, of	Cash considerations
06-05-09	Oakland	Kevin Melillo, if	Cash considerations
08-21-08	Pittsburgh	Jose Bautista, if	Player to be named later (Robinzon Diaz, c)
08-30-08	Philadelphia	Player to be named later (Fabio Castro, lhp)	Matt Stairs, of
08-31-08	Arizona	Chad Beck, rhp	David Eckstein, if
02-10-09	San Diego	Matt Bush, rhp	Player to be named later or cash considerations
03-27-09	Oakland	Player to be named later	Curtis Thigpen, c
07-31-09	Cincinnati	Edwin Encarnacion, if Josh Roenicke, rhp Zach Stewart, rhp	Scott Rolen, if
ALEX ANTHOPOULOS			
12-16-09	Philadelphia	Kyle Drabek, rhp Michael Taylor, of Travis D'Arnaud, c	Roy Halladay, rhp Cash Considerations
12-16-09	Oakland	Brett Wallace, if	Michael Taylor, of
12-23-09	Seattle	Brandon Morrow, rhp	Brandon League, rhp Johermyn Chavez, of
01-9-10	Cleveland	Zach Jackson, lhp	Cash considerations
01-20-10	San Francisco	Merkin Valdez, rhp	Cash considerations
02-06-10	Oakland	Dana Eveland, lhp	Cash considerations
04-15-10	San Francisco	Fred Lewis, of	Cash considerations
06-01-10	Pittsburgh	Ronald Uviedo, rhp	Dana Eveland, lhp
07-14-10	Atlanta	Yunel Escobar, if Jo-Jo Reyes, lhp	Alex Gonzalez, if Tyler Pastornicky, if Tim Collins, lhp
07-29-10	Houston	Anthony Gose, of	Brett Wallace, if
11-04-10	Colorado	Miguel Olivo, c	Player to be named later or cash considerations
11-17-10	Oakland	Rajai Davis, of	Trystan Magnuson, rhp Daniel Farquhar, rhp
12-03-10	Milwaukee	Carlos Villanueva, rhp	cash considerations
12-06-10	Milwaukee	Brett Lawrie, if	Shaun Marcum, rhp
01-21-11	Los Angeles (AL)	Mike Napoli, c Juan Rivera, of	Vernon Wells, of
01-25-11	Texas	Frank Francisco, rhp	Mike Napoli, c

DATE	CLUB	OBTAINED	FOR
03-29-11	Cleveland	Jayson Nix, if	Cash considerations
04-18-11	Oakland	Daniel Farquhar, rhp	David Purcey, lhp
07-12-11	Los Angeles (NL)	Cash considerations	Juan Rivera, of
07-27-11	Chicago (AL)	Edwin Jackson, rhp Mark Teahen, if/of	Jason Frasor, rhp Zach Stewart, rhp
07-27-11	St. Louis	Colby Rasmus, of Brian Tallet, lhp Tever Miller, lhp P.J. Walter, rhp	Edwin Jackson, rhp Octavio Dotel, rhp Marc Rzepczynski, lhp Corey Patterson, of
08-23-11	Arizona	Kelly Johnson, if	Aaron Hill, if John McDonald, if
11-04-11	Oakland	Trystan Magnuson, rhp	Cash considerations
11-26-11	Cleveland	Luis Valbuena, if	Cash considerations
12-03-11	Los Angeles (AL)	Jeff Mathis, c	Brad Mills, lhp
12-06-11	Chicago (AL)	Sergio Santos, rhp	Nestor Molina, rhp
12-12-11	Philadelphia	Ben Francisco, of	Frank Gailey, lhp
01-01-12	Chicago (AL)	Jason Frasor, rhp	Daniel Webb, rhp Myles Jaye, rhp
07-20-12	Houston	J.A. Happ, lhp Brandon Lyon, rhp David Carpenter, rhp	Francisco Cordero, rhp Ben Francisco, of Carlos Perez, c Asher Wojciechowski, rhp David Rollins, lhp Joe Musgrove, rhp Player to be named later (Kevin Comer, rhp)
07-30-12	Pittsburgh	Brad Lincoln, rhp	Travis Snider, of
07-30-12	Seattle	Steve Delabar, rhp	Eric Thames, of
08-24-12	Oakland	Cash considerations	Jesse Chavez, rhp
09-21-12	Milwaukee	Cash considerations	Yorvit Torrealba, c
10-21-12	Boston	Mike Aviles, if	David Carpenter, rho
11-03-12	Cleveland	Esmil Rogers, rhp	Mike Aviles, if Yan Gomes, c/if
11-08-12	Kansas City	Jeremy Jeffress, rhp	Cash considerations
11-19-12	Miami	Josh Johnson, rhp Mark Buehrle, lhp Jose Reyes, if Emilio Bonifacio, if/of John Buck, c	Yunel Escobar, if Jeff Mathis, c Adeiny Hechavarria, if Henderson Alvarez, rhp Jake Marisnick, of Justin Nicolino, lhp Anthony Desclafani, rhp
12-17-12	New York (NL)	R.A. Dickey, rhp Josh Thole, c Mike Nickeas, c	Noah Syndergaard, rhp Travis d'Arnaud, c John Buck, c Wuilmer Beccera, of

FREE AGENCY FOR PLAYERS ON THE 40-MAN ROSTER

Free agency came about in 1976 when 244 players refused to sign contracts and opted for, at season's end, the right to participate in a re-entry draft.

That draft took place in New York on November 4. Clubs were permitted to select players with whom they could negotiate. There was no compensation for clubs who lost players in this draft. In later years, the draft was abolished and compensation was required.

Other than signing their own players who had opted for free agency and free agent players signed after being released, the Blue Jays' involvement in the free agent market has been:

Signed for:

1978	Luis Gomez	from ATLANTA BRAVES
1984	Dennis Lamp	from CHICAGO WHITE SOX
1985	Gary Allenson	from BOSTON RED SOX
1989	Bob Brenly	from SAN FRANCISCO GIANTS
	Tom Lawless	from ST. LOUIS CARDINALS
1991	Ken Dayley	from ST. LOUIS CARDINALS
1991	Pat Tabler	from NEW YORK METS
1992	Jack Morris	from MINNESOTA TWINS
	Dave Winfield	from CALIFORNIA ANGELS
	Alfredo Griffin	from LOS ANGELES DODGERS
	Kent Anderson	from CALIFORNIA ANGELS
	Eric Plunk	from NEW YORK YANKEES
1993	Dick Schofield	from CALIFORNIA ANGELS
	Dave Stewart	from OAKLAND ATHLETICS
	Paul Molitor	from MILWAUKEE BREWERS
	Darnell Coles	from CINCINNATI REDS
	Danny Cox	from PITTSBURGH PIRATES
	Tony Castillo	from NEW YORK METS
1994	Greg Cadaret	from KANSAS CITY ROYALS
1995	Danny Darwin	from BOSTON RED SOX
	Candy Maldonado	from TEXAS RANGERS
1996	Erik Hanson	from BOSTON RED SOX
	Otis Nixon	from TEXAS RANGERS
	Charlie O'Brien	from ATLANTA BRAVES
	Ruben Amaro	from CLEVELAND INDIANS
	Brian Bohanon	from DETROIT TIGERS
	Rich Rowland	from BOSTON RED SOX
	Juan Samuel	from KANSAS CITY ROYALS
	Frank Viola	from CINCINNATI REDS
1997	Benito Santiago	from PHILADELPHIA PHILLIES
	Roger Clemens	from BOSTON RED SOX
	Darrell Whitmore	from CHIBA LOTTE MARINES
	Mike Aldrete	from NEW YORK YANKEES
1998	Darrin Fletcher	from MONTREAL EXPOS
	Randy Myers	from BALTIMORE ORIOLES
	Pat Kelly	from NEW YORK YANKEES
	Craig Grebeck	from ANAHEIM ANGELS
	Mike Stanley	from NEW YORK YANKEES
	Tony Fernandez	from CLEVELAND INDIANS
	Phil Plantier	from ST. LOUIS CARDINALS
	Jose Canseco	from OAKLAND ATHLETICS
1999	Joey Cora	from CLEVELAND INDIANS
	Mike Matheny	from MILWAUKEE BREWERS
	Willie Greene	from BALTIMORE ORIOLES
	Cecil Fielder	from CLEVELAND INDIANS
	Mark Dalesandro	from CHICAGO CUBS
	Geronimo Berroa	from DETROIT TIGERS
2000	Frank Castillo	from PITTSBURGH PIRATES
2001	Jason Dickson	from ANAHEIM ANGELS
	Jeff Frye	from COLORADO ROCKIES
	Trenidad Hubbard	from BALTIMORE ORIOLES
	Dan Plesac	from ARIZONA DIAMONDBACKS
	Ryan Thompson	from NEW YORK YANKEES
	Marty Cordova	from BOSTON RED SOX
2002	Dave Berg	from FLORIDA MARLINS
2003	Mike Bordick	from BALTIMORE ORIOLES
	Frank Catalanotto	from TEXAS RANGERS
	Doug Creek	from SEATTLE MARINERS
	Greg Myers	from OAKLAND ATHLETICS
	Tanyon Sturtze	from TAMPA BAY DEVIL RAYS
	Jeff Tam	from OAKLAND ATHLETICS
2004	Miguel Batista	from ARIZONA DIAMONDBACKS
	V. DeLosSantos	from PHILADELPHIA PHILLIES
	Pat Hentgen	from BALTIMORE ORIOLES
	Kerry Ligtenberg	from BALTIMORE ORIOLES
	Chris Gomez	from MINNESOTA TWINS
	Terry Adams	from PHILADELPHIA PHILLIES
	Corey Koskie	from MINNESOTA TWINS
2005	Billy Koch	from FLORIDA MARLINS
	Scott Schoeneweis	from CHICAGO WHITE SOX
	B.J. Ryan	from BALTIMORE ORIOLES
	A.J. Burnett	from FLORIDA MARLINS
	Bengie Molina	from LOS ANGELES ANGELS
2006	Jean Machi	from TAMPA BAY DEVIL RAYS
	Matt Roney	from OAKLAND ATHLETICS
	Frank Thomas	from OAKLAND ATHLETICS
	Royce Clayton	from WASHINGTON NATIONALS
	John Thomson	from ATLANTA BRAVES
	Tomo Ohka	from MILWAUKEE BREWERS
2007	David Eckstein	from ST. LOUIS CARDINALS
	Rod Barajas	from PHILADELPHIA PHILLIES
2009	Alex Gonzalez	from BOSTON RED SOX
	John Buck	from KANSAS CITY ROYALS
	Kevin Gregg	from CHICAGO CUBS
2010	Jose Molina	from NEW YORK YANKEES
	Nick Green	from LOS ANGELES DODGERS
2011	Octavio Dotel	from COLORADO ROCKIES
	Jon Rauch	from MINNESOTA TWINS
2012	Darren Oliver	from TEXAS RANGERS
	Francisco Cordero	from CINCINNATI REDS
	Rick Vandenurk	from BALTIMORE ORIOLES
2013	Maicer Izturis	from LOS ANGELES ANGELS
	Melky Cabrera	from SAN FRANCISCO GIANTS
	Henry Blanco	from ARIZONA DIAMONDBACKS
	Mark DeRosa	from WASHINGTON NATIONALS

MAJOR LEAGUE RULE 5 DRAFT, 1977-2012

Toronto has selected 30 players in the Major League Baseball Draft, since their inaugural season in 1977. Players with at least three years of professional service who are not protected on a team's major league roster are eligible for selection by another club for $50,000 (prior to 1985 the draft price was $25,000). The drafted player must remain with his new club for the full season or be offered back to his original club for $25,000. The drafting is in reverse order of previous season records and alternating between leagues. Following this major league draft, a separate selection is held by National Association clubs from class AAA to A levels. An "AAA" selection price is $12,000. An "AA" selection is $4,000.

TORONTO SELECTIONS:

Year	Player	Original Club	Status with Toronto
1977	Willie Upshaw (1B)	AAA-Syracuse, (NYY)	Played nine seasons in Toronto
	Andy Dyes (OF)	AAA-Denver, (MTL)	Spent one season in Toronto organization
1978	Ted Wilborn (OF)	AAA-Tacoma, (NYY)	Spent one season in Toronto organization
	Bob Davis (C)	AAA-Hawaii, (SD)	Played two seasons in Toronto
1979	Mike Macha (IF)	AAA-Richmond, (ATL)	Played one season in Toronto
1980	George Bell (OF)	AAA-Okl.City, (PHI)	Played nine seasons in Toronto
	Dan Whitmer (C)	AAA-Salt Lake, (CAL)	Played one season in Toronto
1981	Jim Gott (RHP)	AAA-Springfield, (STL)	Played three seasons in Toronto
	Anthony Johnson (OF)	AAA-Denver, (MTL)	Played one season in Toronto
1982	Jim Acker (RHP)	AAA-Richmond, (ATL)	In 2 stints,played 7 seasons for Toronto
	Mercedes Esquer (LHP)	AAA-Portland, (PIT)	Remained in the Toronto organization
1983	Kelly Gruber (IF)	AAA-Charleston, (CLE)	Played nine seasons in Toronto
	Terry Cormack (C)	AAA-Richmond, (ATL)	Returned to Atlanta March 25, 1984
1984	Manuel Lee (IF)	AAA-Tuscon, (HOU)	Played eight seasons in Toronto
	Louis Thornton (OF)	AAA-Tidewater, (NYM)	Played three seasons in Toronto
1985	Jose DeJesus (RHP)	AAA-Omaha, (KC)	Returned to Kansas City April 3, 1986
1986	Jose Nunez (RHP)	AAA-Omaha, (KC)	Played three seasons in Toronto
1990	Ricky Rhodes (RHP)	AAA-Columbus, (NYY)	Returned to New York March 29, 1991
1992	Billy Taylor (RHP)	AAA-Richmond, (ATL)	Returned to Atlanta April 1, 1993
1995	Carey Paige (RHP)	AA-Greenville, (ATL)	Remained in Toronto organization for two seasons
1997	Luis Saturria (OF)	A-Peoria, (STL)	Returned to St. Louis March 20, 1998
1999	Dewayne Wise (OF)	A-Rockford, (CIN)	Played three seasons in Toronto
2001	Corey Thurman (RHP)	AAA-Omaha, (KAN)	Played two seasons in Toronto
2002	Jason Dubois (OF)	A-Daytona, (CHI-NL)	Returned to Chicago March 15, 2003
	Aquilino Lopez (RHP)	AAA-Tacoma, (SEA)	Played two seasons in Toronto
	Gary Majewski (RHP)	AA-Birmingham, (CHI-AL)	Returned to Chicago March 17, 2003
2003	Talley Haines (RHP)	AAA-Durham (TB)	Remained in Toronto organization, played for one season
2006	Jason Smith (IF)	AAA-Iowa (CHI-NL)	Remained with the Club until May 15, 2007
2007	Randy Wells (RHP)	AAA-Iowa (CH-NL)	Returned to the Cubs on April 16, 2008
2009	Zech Zinicola (RHP)	AAA-Syracuse (WSH-NL)	Returned to the Nationals on March 18, 2010

Kelly Gruber was selected by Toronto in the 1983 Rule 5 Major League Draft... Gruber played with Toronto from 1984-1992 and is the all-time club leader among third basemen in games (830), runs (386), hits (745), HR (107) and RBI (403)

SELECTED FROM TORONTO:

Year	Player	Team	Status after draft
1981	Ramon Lora (C)	by Los Angeles	Returned to Toronto March 31, 1982
	Domingo Ramos (IF)	by Seattle	Played five seasons with Seattle
1983	Dave Geisel (LHP)	by Seattle	Played two seasons with Seattle
1984	Mike Morgan (RHP)	by Seattle	Played two seasons with Seattle
1986	Cliff Young (LHP)	by Oakland	Returned to Toronto April 6, 1987
	Stan Clarke (LHP)	by Seattle	Played one season with Seattle
1987	Joe Johnson (RHP)	by California	Played in California farm system
	Santiago Garcia (IF)	by Chicago (AL)	Played in Chicago farm system
1988	Colin McLaughlin (RHP)	by Seattle	Played in Seattle farm system
	Chris Jones (RHP)	by Los Angeles	Returned to Toronto March 31, 1989
	Geronimo Berroa (OF)	by Atlanta	Played two seasons with Atlanta
	Matt Stark (C)	by Atlanta	Returned to Toronto March 27, 1989
	Eric Yelding (IF)	by Chicago (NL)	Claimed on waivers by Houston April 3,1989
1989	Steve Wapnick (RHP)	by Detroit	Returned to Toronto May 1, 1990
	Sil Campusano (OF)	by Philadelphia	Played one season with Philadelphia
	Xavier Hernandez (RHP)	by Houston	Played four seasons with Houston
1991	Jesse Cross (RHP)	by Minnesota	Returned to Toronto April 3, 1992
1992	Graeme Lloyd (LHP)	by Philadelphia	Acquired by Milwaukee for P John Trisler
1993	Tim Hyers (1B)	by San Diego	Played two seasons with San Diego
1994	Todd Steverson (OF)	by Detroit	Played with Detroit in 1995
	Freddy Garcia (3B)	by Pittsburgh	Played with Pittsburgh in 1995
1996	Mike Johnson (RHP)	by San Francisco	Traded to Baltimore
	Tom Davey (RHP)	by Baltimore	Returned to Toronto
1999	Brian Smith (RHP)	by Pittsburgh	Non-tendered, signed by Pittsburgh
	Jim Mann (RHP)	by New York (NL)	Spent one season in New York organization
2000	Jay Gibbons (1B)	by Baltimore	Played seven years in Baltimore
	Rendy Espina (LHP)	by Anaheim	Returned to Toronto
2002	Matt Ford (LHP)	by Milwaukee	Played one season in Milwaukee
2004	Tyrell Godwin (OF)	By Washington	Played one season in Washington
2005	Jamie Vermilyea (RHP)	By Boston	Returned to Toronto
	Steve Andrade (RHP)	By Tampa Bay	Played one season with both San Diego and Kansas City
2006	Francisco Mateo (LHP)	By Cincinnati	Released by the Reds on Aug. 9, 2007
2008	Ryan Klosterman (SS)	By Florida	Played full season in Florida organization
	Anthony Hatch (IF)	By Los Angeles (NL)	Played full season in Los Angeles Dodgers organization
2010	Brad Emaus (IF)	By New York (NL)	Played with New York Mets then returned to Toronto in 2011
2012	Mark Sobolewski (IF)	By Minnesota	--

MLB HALL OF FAME

Roberto Alomar

SECOND BASEMAN

On July 24, 2011, thousands of Blue Jays fans were on hand in the village of Cooperstown, New York, to officially welcome Roberto Alomar to the Baseball Hall of Fame. It was a proud moment for the star second basemen, who was just the third Puerto Rican inductee, and the first Hall of Famer to be inducted as a member of the Toronto Blue Jays.

> **"My time in Toronto was the best of my career. It was with Toronto that we won two World Series together. You guys embraced me from day one. You were with me through ups and downs and I am so proud to represent you here in Cooperstown as the first Toronto Blue Jay inducted into the Baseball Hall of Fame."**
>
> **ROBERTO ALOMAR**

In five seasons with the Blue Jays from 1991 through 1995, Alomar displayed sparkling defense while winning five straight Gold Gloves. He never hit less than .295 and finished third in the American League behind teammates John Olerud and Paul Molitor with a .326 average in 1993 His five-year mark of .307 gives him the highest lifetime average of any player in Blue Jays history. Over the course of his 17-year career, Roberto Alomar hit .300 with a .371 on-base percentage. He totaled 2,724 hits, 1,508 runs, 504 doubles, 80 triples, 210 home runs, 474 stolen bases, and 1,134 RBI.

TORONTO BLUE JAYS

RETIRED NUMBERS

Roberto Alomar

SECOND BASEMAN

Hall of Fame second baseman Roberto Alomar was given the Toronto Blue Jays highest honour on July 31, 2011 when his uniform number was retired in a pregame ceremony at Rogers Centre. Alomar's number 12 is the first number retired by the Blue Jays in their 35 year history. Jackie Robinson's number 42 was retired by Major League Baseball on April 15, 1997.

"Roberto is a very special part of the Toronto Blue Jays organization and arguably the greatest second baseman of all-time. His number deserves to be retired so that his contributions and excellence can stand as a model for all those who have the honour of wearing a Blue Jays uniform."

**PAUL BEESTON
(President & CEO,
Toronto Blue Jays)**

"This is an honour that I was not expecting. I knew my numbers were worthy of consideration for the Hall of Fame but for the Blue Jays to select my number 12 to be the first number they retire is a great honour."

ROBERTO ALOMAR

TORONTO BLUE JAYS

LEVEL OF EXCELLENCE

The Level of Excellence is an award bestowed by the Toronto Blue Jays Baseball Club, recognizing tremendous individual achievement. The names and, in some cases, uniform numbers of each of the honourees are displayed on large banners hanging in Rogers Centre's 500 Level. The recipients of this prestigious award are as follows: **ROBERTO ALOMAR** (April 4, 2008), **PAUL BEESTON** (April 4, 2008), **GEORGE BELL** (April 9, 1996), **JOE CARTER** (July 30, 1999), **TOM CHEEK** (August 29, 2004), **TONY FERNANDEZ** (September 23, 2001), **CITO GASTON** (July 30, 1999), **PAT GILLICK** (August 7, 2002) & **DAVE STIEB** (April 9, 1996). The Blue Jays will honour **1B CARLOS DELGADO** on July 21, 2013 as the 10th member inducted on the Level of Excellence.

Roberto Alomar

SECOND BASEMAN

ROBERTO ALOMAR was elected into the National Baseball Hall of Fame on January 5, 2011 - first player in franchise history to achieve that honour. On July 24, 2011 was inducted in the National Baseball Hall of Fame in Cooperstown along with the person who brought him over to Toronto from San Diego back in 1990, former Blue Jays GM Pat Gillick & RHP Bert Blylevin. Was selected on 90 percent of the ballots. Was acquired by Toronto along with OF Joe Carter in exchange for SS Tony Fernandez & 1B Fred McGriff from the San Diego Padres on December 5, 1990. Played five seasons in Toronto from 1990-1995, batted .307 with 55 HR, 342 RBI & 206 SB. In his time with the Blue Jays won two World Series Championships ('92 & '93), named the ALCS MVP in '92 vs. Oakland, appeared in five all-star games ('91-'95), won five gold gloves ('91-'95) and awarded a Silver Slugger in 1992. Appeared in 29 post-season games with the Blue Jays & batted .373 (44-118) with 18 runs, nine XBH, 18 RBI & 18 SB. Among the all-time Blue Jays second basemen ranks 1st in runs (447), 3B (35), RBI (338), AVG (.308), XBH (241) & SB (206). In 17 major league seasons with San Diego, Toronto, Baltimore, Cleveland, New York Mets, Chicago White Sox & Arizona, batted .300 with 2724 hits, 210 HR, 1134 RBI & 474 SB. In 58 post season contests, batted .313 with four HR and 33 RBI.

Paul Beeston

CHIEF EXECUTIVE OFFICER

PAUL BEESTON a Welland, ON native, is one of the Toronto Blue Jays founding fathers. Was the first employee of the Toronto Blue Jays, joining the Club on May 10, 1976 only a month and a half after the granting of the Franchise. He became Vice-President of Business Operations in 1977, Executive Vice-President, Business in 1984, President and Chief Operating Officer in 1989 & Chief Executive Officer in 1991. His hard work and dedication have been recognized by many & in 1988, was named a Member of the Order of Canada. He was elected to the Board of Directors of the Baseball Hall of Fame in 1998 & then in 2002 was inducted into the Canadian Baseball Hall of Fame. From 1997 until 2002, Paul was President & COO of Major League Baseball in New York City. He then returned to Toronto in 2002 & serves on the board of a number of philanthropic endeavours. On October 14, 2008, was appointed CEO of the Toronto Blue Jays on an interim basis, responsible for the day-to-day operations of the baseball club & Rogers Centre. On October 27, 2009 had the interim tag lifted and was appointed CEO of the Toronto Blue Jays and Rogers Centre.

George Bell

OUTFIELDER

GEORGE BELL spent nine seasons with Toronto and ranks 3rd in Club history in total bases (2201), RBI (740) and extra base hits (471). Is one of four players in the Clubs history to have hit at least 200 home runs as a Blue Jay, ranking 4th with 202. In 1987, he was named the American League MVP, only Blue Jay in Club history to achieve the honour. That season he batted .308 with 47 home runs & 134 RBI. Made his first of two All Star appearances in 1987 when he became the first Blue Jay ever voted to the starting line-up. During his nine seasons was a four-time Club MVP, the Sporting News AL and Major League Player of the year in 1987, a three-time Sporting News Silver Slugger, a two-time Sporting News All Star team selection and the American League Player of the Week eight times. He also set a Major League record hitting three home runs on Opening Day, April 4, 1988 at Kansas City.

Joe Carter

OUTFIELDER

JOE CARTER ranks 3rd in Club history in HR with 203 but will forever be remembered for just one, the 9th inning blast on October 23 to win the 1993 World Series. In 1,039 games from 1991 to 1997 with Toronto, hit .257 with 578 runs scored, 218 2B, 28 3B, 203 HR with 736 RBI and 78 SB. In his seven seasons he represented Toronto in five All-Star games including 1991 in Toronto, his first season with the Blue Jays after he was acquired from San Diego along with Roberto Alomar on December 5, 1990 in exchange for Tony Fernandez and Fred McGriff. Along with his tremendous on-field accomplishments Joe and his wife were active off the field as the Diana & Joe Carter Foundation operated the "Jumpin' with Joe" program which provided needy children throughout the Toronto area with a day at Teen-Ranch, Christian Youth Camp and tickets for a Toronto Blue Jay game where Joe would speak to all of the children. He worked with many other charities including Ronald McDonald House and also hosted an annual charity golf tournament. In his 16 year major league career, hit .259 with 432 2B, 396 HR and 1,445 RBI while playing for the Chicago Cubs (1983), Cleveland Indians (1984-1989), San Diego Padres (1990), Toronto Blue Jays (1991-1997), Baltimore Orioles (1998) and the San Francisco Giants (1998).

Photo credit: Chuck Kotchman

Tom Cheek

BROADCASTER

TOM CHEEK who called the first 4,306 regular-season and 41 postseason games in Toronto Blue Jays history was selected as the 2013 recipient of the Ford C. Frick Award, presented annually for excellence in broadcasting by the National Baseball Hall of Fame and Museum. Cheek, who passed away after a lengthy and brave battle with brain cancer on Oct. 9, 2005, will be honored as part of Hall of Fame Weekend 2013 July 26-29 in Cooperstown, N.Y. He stood as the radio voice of the Blue Jays and, as one fan wrote, the "soundtrack of summer in Toronto" since the Club's inception through 2004. He broadcast 4,306 consecutive regular season games (including 41 postseason contests) from 1977 through the midway point of the 2004 season when he was called away from the booth first by the sudden and ultimately passing of his father and later by his own personal health problems. The banner in the Level of Excellence bearing his name, first unveiled in formal ceremonies held on August 29, 2004, is adorned with the number 4,306. That pays tribute to his longevity as the iron-man of baseball broadcasting. A veteran of the radio industry, he first joined the Blue Jays prior to the Club's inaugural season after spending three seasons working on Montreal Expos broadcasts. Tom had been calling the balls, strikes and home runs starting with Doug Ault's big blasts on Opening Day in 1977. His call of Joe Carter's dramatic home run to win the 1993 World Series-"Touch 'em all Joe, you'll never hit a bigger home run in your life"- stands as one of the most memorable and famous moments in Canadian sports broadcasting history.

Tony Fernandez

SHORTSTOP

TONY FERNANDEZ is the franchise leader in games (1,450), hits (1,583), 3B (72), 3rd in 2B (291), AVG (.297), 4th in runs (704), TB (2,198), BB (439) and SB (172). Had four separate stints with the Blue Jays resulting in 12 seasons and was a member of the 1993 World Series Champions where he led the team with nine RBI and batted .333 in the six WS games. Was selected to play on five All-Star Teams, including four with Toronto, and won four straight AL Gold Glove Awards at shortstop from 1986-1989 with the Blue Jays. Ranks 6th on the all-time hits list for a Dominican born player (2276 total).

Cito Gaston

MANAGER

CITO GASTON led the Blue Jays to two World Championships, two American League Championships, four American League East titles in nine seasons as the Manager from 1989 to 1997. Began as the Blue Jays hitting coach in 1981 where he groomed many young players including George Bell, Lloyd Moseby, Cecil Fielder, Jesse Barfield and Fred McGriff. In 1989 he served as the interim manager of the Club before he was named the 5th manager in Club history on May 31, 1989. Had the honour of managing in two All-Star games, 1993 and 1994. During his years as manager Cito gave much of his time to charity events throughout Toronto including the annual Cito Gaston Golf Classic. Gaston returned to the Blue Jays for two seasons as hitting coach in 2000 and 2001. Was named Club Ambassador and Special Assistant to the President and CEO, along with former Blue Jay right-hander Pat Hentgen, in early 2007. On June 20, 2008 was named Manager of the Toronto Blue Jays, his 2nd stint as the Clubs skipper. In 2010, Cito's last season as the Clubs manager, led the Blue Jays to an 85-77 record. Has a Club high 913 victories as the Blue Jays manager (913-851 overall). Is currently a consultant for the organization.

Pat Gillick

GENERAL MANAGER

PAT GILLICK, who was instrumental in building the organization from an expansion team in 1977 to World Series Champions in 1992 and 1993, was inducted into the National Baseball Hall of Fame in Cooperstown on July 24, 2011 along with the player he brought over from San Diego to Toronto, Roberto Alomar. Was then the 6th man to be honoured by the Toronto Blue Jays to the Level of Excellence in August of 2002. Began his career with the Blue Jays in 1976 as the VP of Player Personnel. Was responsible for the development of players like Dave Stieb, Jesse Barfield and Jimmy Key through the draft and utilized the Major League Rule 5 draft to secure talents such as Willie Upshaw, George Bell, Jim Gott and Kelly Gruber. Was known for completing shrewd trades to acquire the likes of Alfredo Griffin, Damaso Garcia, Fred McGriff, Roberto Alomar, Joe Carter and assembling talent like Tom Henke, Devon White, Dave Winfield, Jack Morris and Paul Molitor. During his tenure, the Blue Jays produced 11 consecutive winning seasons from 1983 to 1993 and in that span, brought five American League East Division titles to Toronto, two American League Championships and World Series victories in 1992 and 1993.

Dave Stieb

PITCHER

DAVE STIEB is the franchise leader in wins (175), IP (2873.0), SO (1658), GS (408), ShO (30) and CG (103). Spent 15 seasons with Toronto, longer than any player in franchise history. Appeared in an AL record seven All Star games and was the starting pitcher in both 1983 and 1984. Recorded the only no-hitter in Blue Jays history on September 2 1990 vs. the Indians in Cleveland. In 1982, was named the Sporting News Pitcher of the Year after a 17-14 season with a 3.25 ERA and led the league in IP (288.0) and CG (20). Was the Blue Jays Pitcher of the Year six times, a three-time winner of the AL Pitcher of the Month and a three-time winner of the AL Player of the Week.

STIEB'S NO-HITTER

SEPTEMBER 2, 1990 AT CLEVELAND — TORONTO 3, CLEVELAND 0

DAVE STIEB chalked up his first no-hitter and the first in BLUE JAYS history as he stopped the Cleveland Indians on a sunny Sunday afternoon at Cleveland Stadium before a crowd of 23,640.

The game ended as Cleveland's Jerry Browne whacked a fly to right field where JUNIOR FELIX put the squeeze on it.

Stieb had a season high nine strikeouts and walked four over his 122-pitch afternoon.

There were no tough plays and only a couple of well hit balls. Closest the Tribe came to a hit was KEN PHELPS pulling a liner about three feet foul to open the eighth inning.

The BLUE JAYS and STIEB got their offensive support from FRED McGRIFF who hit two solo home runs and from MANNY LEE who doubled home KENNY WILLIAMS in the fifth inning.

Stieb had previously gone 8.2 innings, three times, protecting no-hitters. He had back-to-back attempts in September 1988; on September 24, 1988 at Cleveland Stadium, JULIO FRANCO had a bad hop single over second baseman MANNY LEE's head. In his next start, against Baltimore at Exhibition Stadium, JIM TRABER looped a single over his first baseman FRED McGRIFF's outstretched glove hand. Both no-hit bids were lost on 2-2 pitches. STIEB also had a perfect game for 8.2 innings on August 4, 1989 vs the Yankees at SkyDome. ROBERTO KELLY doubled to left to break it up.

TORONTO	0	0	0	1	1	0	0	0	1	—	3	8	0
CLEVELAND	0	0	0	0	0	0	0	0	0	—	0	0	1

STIEB and BORDERS

BLACK, OROSCO (8), OLIN (9) and SKINNER

WP–STIEB (17-5) LP–BLACK (10-9)

STIEB PITCHING LINE: 9 IP 0 H 0 R 0 ER 4 BB 9 SO

LEAGUE AWARDS

BASEBALL WRITERS ASSOCIATION OF AMERICA AWARDS

MOST VALUABLE PLAYER (AL)
1987 — George Bell

ROOKIE OF THE YEAR (AL)
1979 — Alfredo Griffin
2002 — Eric Hinske

CY YOUNG AWARD (AL)
1996 — Pat Hentgen
1997 — Roger Clemens
1998 — Roger Clemens
2003 — Roy Halladay

MANAGER OF THE YEAR (AL)
1985 — Bobby Cox

HANK AARON AWARD

2000 — Carlos Delgado
2010 — Jose Bautista
2011 — Jose Bautista

EDGAR MARTINEZ AWARD

2009 — Adam Lind

SILVER SLUGGER AWARD

1982 — Damaso Garcia, 2B
1983 — Lloyd Moseby, OF
1985 — George Bell, OF
1986 — George Bell, OF
1986 — Jesse Barfield, OF
1987 — George Bell, OF
1989 — Fred McGriff, 1B
1990 — Kelly Gruber, 3B
1991 — Joe Carter, OF
1992 — Roberto Alomar, 2B
1992 — Joe Carter, OF
1992 — Dave Winfield, DH
1993 — Paul Molitor, DH
1998 — Jose Canseco, DH
1999 — Shawn Green, OF
Carlos Delgado, 1B
2000 — Carlos Delgado, 1B
2003 — Carlos Delgado, IB
Vernon Wells, OF
2009 — Aaron Hill, 2B
Adam Lind, DH
2010 — Jose Bautista, OF
2011 — Jose Bautista, OF

LELAND S. MACPHAIL JR. AWARD (MVP OF ALCS)

1992 — Roberto Alomar
1993 — Dave Stewart

WORLD SERIES MOST VALUABLE PLAYER

1992—Pat Borders
1993—Paul Molitor

HITTING FOR THE CYCLE

FOR TORONTO:

PLAYER	OPP	DATE & SITE
Kelly Gruber	(vs. KC)	April 16, 1989 Exhibition Stadium
Jeff Frye	(vs. TEX)	August 17, 2001 SkyDome

FOR OPPONENTS:

PLAYER	OPP	DATE & SITE
Mike Cubbage	(Twins)	July 27, 1978 Metropolitan Stadium
Rich Gedman	(Boston)	September 18, 1985 Fenway Park
George Brett	(Royals)	July 25, 1990 SkyDome

What Gruber Did: Went 4-4 with a career high 6 RBI... Homered in the first inning against Floyd Bannister, had a 2-run double in the second inning also against Bannister... In the seventh inning, he notched a two-run triple versus Tom Gordon... In the ninth, Gruber had an RBI single off Jerry Don Gleaton to complete the cycle.

What Frye Did: Went 4-4 with three RBI to tie his career high... Tripled in the second inning off Darren Oliver and then doubled in the fifth inning, again off Oliver... In the sixth hit a two run home run off Pat Mahomes... In the seventh inning facing Kevin Foster, hit an RBI single to right center to complete the cycle... Is just the second ninth hitter to hit for the cycle since 1978, the last was Charlie Moore for Milwaukee at California on October 1, 1980.

TORONTO BLUE JAYS ALL-STAR GAME SELECTIONS

ALL-STAR PLAYERS

YEAR	PLAYER	PERFORMANCE	VOTES
1977	Ron Fairly-PH	0-1	
1978	Roy Howell-PH	0-1	
1979	Dave Lemanczyk-P	DID NOT PLAY	
1980	Dave Stieb-P	1.0 IP, H, BB	
1981	Dave Stieb-P	1.2 IP, H, BB, K	
1982	Jim Clancy-P	1.0 IP	
1983	**Dave Stieb-P**	3.0 IP, H, BB, 4K	--
1984	**Dave Stieb-P**	2.0 IP, 2H, ER, 2K	--
	Damaso Garcia-2B	0-1	
	Alfredo Griffin-SS	--	
1985	Dave Stieb-P	1.0 IP, BB, K	
	Jimmy Key-P	0.1 IP	
	Damaso Garcia-2B	1-2	
	Ernie Whitt-C	--	
1986	Jesse Barfield-PH/LF	0-3	
	Lloyd Moseby-LF	0-0	
	Tony Fernandez-PR/SS	0-0	
1987	**George Bell-LF**	0-3	1,144,575
	Tony Fernandez-SS	0-2	
	Tom Henke-P	2.2 IP, 2H	
1988	Dave Stieb-P	1.0 IP, H	
1989	Kelly Gruber-3B	DID NOT PLAY	
	Tony Fernandez-PR/SS	0-1	
1990	George Bell-PH/LF	0-2	
	Kelly Gruber-PR/3B	0-1, 2 SB	
	Dave Stieb-P	2.0 IP, BB, K	
1991	**Roberto Alomar-2B**	0-4	1,868,247
	Joe Carter-PH/LF	1-1, BB, R	
	Jimmy Key-P	**Won** (1.0 IP, H, K)	
1992	**Roberto Alomar-2B**	1-3, R, 2 SB	1,868,247
	Joe Carter-RF	2-3, RBI (Replaced J. Canseco)	--
	Juan Guzman-P	1.0 IP, 2H, BB, 2K	
1993	**Roberto Alomar-2B**	1-3, HR, RBI	1,852,280
	Joe Carter-RF	1-3, K	1,407,179
	Pat Hentgen-P	DID NOT PLAY	
	Paul Molitor-DH	0-1, BB	
	John Olerud-1B	0-2	1,285,280
	Duane Ward-P	SV, 1.0 IP, 2K	
	Devon White-CF	1-2, 2B, RBI, R, SB	
1994	**Roberto Alomar-2B**	1-3, R	3,675,730
	Joe Carter-LF	0-3, R	3,683,682
	Pat Hentgen-P	1.0 IP, H	
	Paul Molitor-PH	0-1	
1995	Roberto Alomar-2B	0-1, SB	
1996	Joe Carter-CF	1-1	
1997	Roger Clemens-P	1.0 IP, H	
	Pat Hentgen-P	1.0 IP	
1998	Roger Clemens-P	1.0 IP, 2H, 2R, 2ER, BB, K	
1999	Tony Fernandez-3B	0-1	
	Shawn Green-RF	1-2	
2000	Carlos Delgado-1B	1-1, 2B	
	Tony Batista-3B	0-1, K	
	David Wells-P	2.0 IP, 2H, 2K	--
2001	Paul Quantrill-P	0.1 IP, 2H, ER	
2002	Roy Halladay-P	1.0 IP, 3H, 3ER, K	
2003	**Carlos Delgado-IB**	1-3, RBI, K	862,610
	Vernon Wells PR-CF	1-2, 2B, RBI, R	
	Roy Halladay-P	DID NOT PLAY	
2004	Ted Lilly-P	1.0 IP, 2H, K	
2005	Roy Halladay-P	DID NOT PLAY (Injury)	
	Shea Hillenbrand-3B	--	
2006	Roy Halladay-P	2.0 IP, 3H, ER, K	
	B.J. Ryan-P	**Won** (1.0 IP, K)	
	Troy Glaus-3B	1-2, 2B, R	
	Vernon Wells-CF	1-2 (Replaced M. Ramirez)	--
	Alex Rios-OF	DID NOT PLAY (Injury)	
2007	Alex Rios-RF	--	
2008	Roy Halladay-P	1.0 IP, H, K	
2009	**Roy Halladay-P**	2.0, 4H, 2ER	--
	Aaron Hill-2B	0-3 (Replaced D. Pedroia)	--
2010	Jose Bautista-PR/RF	0-1	
	John Buck-C	1-2, 2B	
	Vernon Wells-LF	0-1	
2011	**Jose Bautista-RF**	1-2	**7,454,753
	Ricky Romero	DID NOT PLAY	
2012	**Jose Bautista-RF**	0-1, BB, K	4,971,155

NOTE: **Bold** indicates this player was as a starter

NOTE: ** indicates a Major League record

ALL-STAR MANAGERS, COACHES, AND TRAINERS

1979	Roy Hartsfield, Coach
1980	Ken Carson, Trainer
1985	Bobby Cox, Coach
1991	Cito Gaston, Coach
1991	Tommy Craig, Trainer
1993	Cito Gaston, Manager
1993	Gene Tenace, Coach
1993	John Sullivan, Coach
1993	Galen Cisco, Coach
1994	Cito Gaston, Manager
1994	Galen Cisco, Coach
1994	Bob Bailor, Coach
1994	Gene Tenace, Coach
2004	Carlos Tosca, Coach
2006	John Gibbons, Coach
2011	John Farrell, Coach

RAWLINGS GOLD GLOVE

Since 1957, the Rawlings Gold Glove Award has been presented annually to 18 of baseball's best fielders- one from each position in both the National and American Leagues. The winners are selected by Major League coaches and managers. Below are listed the Toronto Blue Jays players that have won Gold Gloves.

PLAYER	POSITION	YEAR
Tony Fernandez	SS	1986
Jesse Barfield	OF	1986
Tony Fernandez	SS	1987
Jesse Barfield	OF	1987
Tony Fernandez	SS	1988
Tony Fernandez	SS	1989
Kelly Gruber	3B	1990
Devon White	OF	1991
Roberto Alomar	2B	1991
Devon White	OF	1992
Roberto Alomar	2B	1992
Devon White	OF	1993

PLAYER	POSITION	YEAR
Roberto Alomar	2B	1993
Devon White	OF	1994
Roberto Alomar	2B	1994
Roberto Alomar	2B	1995
Devon White	OF	1995
Shawn Green	OF	1999
Vernon Wells	OF	2004
Orlando Hudson	2B	2005
Vernon Wells	OF	2005
Vernon Wells	OF	2006

AMERICAN LEAGUE PLAYER AND PITCHER HONOURS

PLAYER OF THE WEEK

1979

- Otto Velez, July 23-29 (.500, 9 RBI, 5 R, 1.050 SLG)

1980

- Dave Stieb, April 21-27 (2 CG, 0.50 ERA)

1982

- Jim Clancy, June 14-20 (1-0, 19.0 IP, 1 ER)
- Jim Clancy, Sept. 27-Oct. 3 (2 wins including 1-hitter vs Twins, Sept. 28)

1983

- Luis Leal, May 9-15 (2-0, 0.64 ERA)
- Dave Stieb, May 16-22 (2-0, 0.50 ERA)
- Lloyd Moseby, May 23-29 (.556, 3 HR, 2 2B)
- Cliff Johnson, June 20-26 (.500, 2 2B, HR in consecutive at-bats)
- Jesse Barfield, Aug. 29-Sept. 4 (.424, 7 HR, 39 TB)

1985

- Willie Upshaw, April 21-28 (.409, 3 HR, 2 2B, 20 TB, .909 SLG)
- Lloyd Moseby, Sept. 2-8 (.435, 5 HR, 1.174 SLG)

1986

- Lloyd Moseby, Aug. 18-24 (.435, 3 HR, 8 RBI, .870 SLG)
- George Bell, Sept. 1-7 (.433, 3 HR, 10 RBI, 9 R)

1987

- Jim Clancy, May 19-24 (2 CG, 1 ShO, 0.50 ERA, 18.0 IP, 18 K)
- George Bell, June 8-14 (.407, 5 HR, 15 RBI, 1.037 SLG)
- George Bell, July 27-Aug. 3 (.500, 3 HR, 7 RBI)

1988

- George Bell, April 4-10 (.455, 4 HR, 7 XBH, 1.136 SLG)
- George Bell, Aug. 29-Sept. 4 (.379, 3 HR, 12 RBI)

1989

- Nelson Liriano, May 15-21 (.600, 3 2B, 23 TB, 7 RBI)
- Junior Felix, May 29-June 4 (.435, 2 HR, 11 RBI, 6 R)
- George Bell, Aug. 14-20 (.467, 3 HR, 3 2B, 12 RBI)
- Lloyd Moseby, Sept. 4-10 (.440, 7 R, 3 2B, 4 SB, .548 OBP)

1990

- Kelly Gruber, April 23-29 (.414, 4 HR, 9 RBI, 5 R, .897 SLG)
- George Bell, June 4-10 (.464, 3 HR, 11 RBI, 2 2B, 7R)
- George Bell, June 18-24 (.500, 5 HR, 11 RBI, 9 R)
- Dave Stieb, Aug. 27-Sept. 2 (pitched no-hitter at Cleveland Sept. 2)
- Kelly Gruber, Sept. 9-16 (.464, 2 HR, 3 2B, 14 RBI)

1991

- Joe Carter, June 17-23 (5 HR, 7 RBI, 7 R, 26 TB)

1992

- Robert Alomar, April 20-26 (.600, 15 H, 9 RBI, 7 consecutive hits)
- Joe Carter, Aug. 10-16 (.407, 11 H, 3 HR, 4 2B, 24 TB)

1993

- John Olerud, June 1-6 (.445, 5 HR, 11 RBI, 29 TB)

1994

- Joe Carter, April 4-10 (.333, 4 HR, 12 RBI, 7 R)
- Joe Carter, April 18-24 (9 H, 4 HR, 4 2B, 12 RBI)
- Pat Hentgen, May 1-7 (2-0, 0.51 ERA, 17.2 IP, 8 H, 23 K)
- Paul Molitor, July 12-18 (.500 BA, 13 H, 4 HR, 10 RBI, 10 R)

1995

- John Olerud, July 12-16 (.500, 4 R, 2 2B, 18 TB, .588 OBP, 1.286 SLG)

1997

- Roger Clemens, May 6-11 (2-0, 2.81 ERA, 2 GS, 16.0 IP, 24 K)

1998

- Carlos Delgado, June 1-7 (.407, 4 HR, 9 RBI)
- Carlos Delgado, Aug. 17-23 (.370, 4 HR, 10 RBI)
- Roger Clemens, Aug. 24-30 (2-0, 0.00 ERA, 18.0 IP, 5 H, 25 K, 2 CG-SHO)

1999

- Shannon Stewart, April 26-May 2 (.471, 16 H, 5 R, 3 2B, 5 RBI)
- Tony Fernandez, June 14-20 (.411, 10 H, 15 TB, 2 2B, .789 SLG)
- Homer Bush, Sept. 30-Oct. 3 (.452, 14 H, 6 R, 2 2B, 2 RBI)

2000

- Carlos Delgado, April 17-23 (.480, 12 H, 4 HR, 8 RBI, 11 R, 1.080 SLG)
- Jose Cruz, May 1-7 (.387, 4 HR, 9 RBI, 3 2B, 9 R, 5 BB)
- Carlos Delgado, June 5-11 (.556, 10 H, 4 HR, 13 RBI, 25 TB, 9 BB, 1.389 SLG)

2001

- Carlos Delgado, April 1-8 (.348, 5 HR, 11 RBI, 1.043 SLG, 8 BB, 8 R, 24 TB).
- Raul Mondesi, April 30-May 6 (.464, 13 H, 4 HR, 11 RBI, 1.071 SLG, 5 2B, 8 R, 30 TB).
- Kelvim Escobar, Aug. 20-26 (2-0, 1.04 ERA, 17.1 IP, 10 H, 3 BB, 15 K, 1 CG).
- Jose Cruz Jr., Oct. 1-7 (.423, 4 HR, 11 RBI, 7 R, 2 2B, 4 SB).

2002

- Carlos Delgado, Sept. 23-29 (.450, 4 HR, 11 RBI, 1.150 SLG)

2003

- Vernon Wells, June 15-22 (.476, 10 H, 5 HR, 10 RBI, 9 R, 1.286 SLG)
- Roy Halladay, Sept. 1-7 (2-0, 0.46 ERA, 19.0 IP, 7 H, 15 K, 10.0 inning shutout vs. DET on Sept. 6)
- Carlos Delgado, Sept. 22-28 (.318, 6 HR, 11 RBI, 26 TB, 1.182 SLG, 4 HR game vs. TB on Sept. 25)

2004

- Carlos Delgado, Aug. 30-Sept. 5 (.381, 3 HR, 7 RBI, 6 R)

2005

- Frank Catalanotto, July 18-24 (.565, 1 HR, 9 RBI, 5 multi-hit games)
- Frank Catalanotto, Sept. 26 - Oct. 2 (.500, 15 H, 15 RBI, 29 TB)

2006

- Roy Halladay, May 7-14 (2-0, 2 CG, 1.00 ERA, 9 K)
- Vernon Wells, July 16-23 (.448, 3 2B, 4 HR, 10 RBI, .966 SLG)
- Lyle Overbay, June 27-July 2 (.423, 4 HR, 9 RBI, 1.077 SLG)

2007

- Troy Glaus, May 1-7 (.400, 4 HR, 7 RBI, 8 R)

2008

- Alex Rios, Sept. 1-7 (.414, 3 HR, 966 SLG)

2009

- Roy Halladay, May 11-17 (2-0, 1.13, CG, 2 ER, 16.0 IP, 13 K)
- Lyle Overbay, June 1-7 (.533, 4 2B, 2 HR, 8 RBI)
- Adam Lind, Aug. 31-Sept. 6 (.321, 4 2B, 3 HR, 12 RBI)

2010

- Jose Bautista, May 10-16 (.444, 4 HR, 8 RBI, 5 BB)
- Jose Bautista, July 26-Aug. 1 (.545, 3 2B, 5 HR, 13 RBI, 8 R)
- Jose Bautista, Aug. 23-29 (.500, 3 2B, 4 HR, 7 RBI, 9 BB)
- Edwin Encarnacion, Sept. 27-Oct. 3 (.400, 5 HR, 11 RBI, 6 R)

2011

- Jose Bautista, June 27-July 3 (.391, 3 2B, 4 HR, 8 RBI)

2012

- J.P. Arencibia, May 14-20 (.360, 4 HR, 10 RBI)

PLAYER OF THE MONTH

1977

- Otto Velez, April (5 HR, 11 RBI, 11 R, .865 SLG, .422 BA)

1979

- Alred Griffin, Sept. (.407 BA, 4-3B, 62 TB)

1983

- Lloyd Moseby, Aug. (.351 BA, 25 RBI, 15 XBH)

1989

- Fred McGriff, April (7 HR, 17 RBI, 28 H, 21 R)
- George Bell, Aug. (22 game hit streak, .370 BA)

1990

- Kelly Gruber, Sept. (.352 BA, 20 R, 30 RBI)

1991

- Joe Carter, June (11 HR, 36 H, .352 BA, 11-2B, 29 RBI, 21 R)

BIOGRAPHIES LAST SEASON HISTORY RECORDS OPPONENTS PLAYER DEV. MEDIA & MISC.

1992

- Roberto Alomar, April (.382 BA, 34 H, 19 R, 3 HR, 19 RBI, 8 SB, .439 OBA)

1993

- John Olerud, April (.450 BA, 36 H, .650 SLG, .527 OBP, 18 RBI, 15 R, 7-2B, 3 HR)
- Paul Molitor, May (.374 BA, 43 H, 5 HR, 22 RBI, 25 R)
- John Olerud, June (.427 BA, 41 H, 17-2B, 5 HR, 30 RBI, 17 R, 73 TB, .525 OBP)

1994

- Joe Carter, April (.312 BA, ML 31 RBI, 9 HR, 8-2B, 64 TB)

2010

- Jose Bautista, July (.418, 11 HR, 8 2B, 29 RBI, 12 BB, 75 TB, .765 SLG)
- Jose Bautista, Aug. (.299, 12 HR, 24 RBI, 23 R, 23 BB, .742 SLG)

2011

- Jose Bautista, April (.366, 9 HR, 5 2B, 15 RBI, 28 BB, .780 SLG)
- Jose Bautista, May (.360, 11 HR, 4 2B, 23 RBI, 18 BB, .791)

2012

- Jose Bautista, June (.271, 14 HR, 30 RBI, 22 BB, .750 SLG)

ROOKIE OF THE MONTH

2002

- Eric Hinske, June (.338 BA, 27 H, 7-2B, 6 HR, 15 RBI, 19 R)
- Josh Phelps, Aug. (.310 BA, 31 H, 5-2B, 7 HR, 30 RBI, 18 R)
- Josh Phelps, Sept. (.338 BA, 26 H, 10-2B, 6 HR, 19 RBI, 15 R)

2003

- Reed Johnson, Sept. (.363 BA, 33 H, 5-2B, 3 HR, 16 RBI, 18 R)

2005

- Gustavo Chacin, April (4-1, 2.41 ERA in 6 GS)
- Gustavo Chacin, July (5-0, 2.97 ERA in 6 GS)

2009

- Scott Richmond, April (3-0, 2.70 ERA in 4 GS)

PITCHER OF THE MONTH

1980

- Dave Stieb, April (3-0, 15 K, 1 ShO, 1.09 ERA)

1983

- Dave Stieb, May (5 W, 2 ShO, 43 K)

1984

- Doyle Alexander, Sept. (2.23 ERA, 5-1, 6 CG)

1985

- Dave Stieb, May (4-1, 34 K, 1.69 ERA)

1987

- Jim Clancy, May (5-1, 1.71 ERA, 40 K in 47.1 IP)

1996

- Juan Guzman, April (3-1, 1.88 ERA, 39 K in 43.0 IP)
- Pat Hentgen, July (5-1, 2.72 ERA, 28 K in 46.1 IP)
- Pat Hentgen, Aug. (5-1, 2.60 ERA, 33 K in 52.0 IP)

1997

- Roger Clemens, May (6-0, 1.96 ERA, 46.0 IP, 51 K)
- Roger Clemens, Aug. (4-0, 2.47 ERA, 2 CG, 47.1 IP, 54 K)

1998

- Roger Clemens, Aug. (4-0, 0.90 ERA, 3 CG, 50.0 IP, 68 K)

2003

- Roy Halladay, May (6-0, 3.22 ERA, CG, 44.2 IP, 35 K)
- Roy Halladay, Sept. (5-1, 1.41 ERA, 5 CG, 51.0 IP, 42 K)

2007

- Roy Halladay, April (4-0, 2.28 ERA, 2 CG, 47.1 IP, 33 K)

2011

- Ricky Romero, Aug. (5-0, 2.05 ERA, 1 ShO, 44.0 IP, 26 K)

MEDIA AWARDS

TORONTO CHAPTER BBWAA AWARD WINNERS

Each year, the members of the Toronto chapter of the BBWAA select the Blue Jays top player, pitcher and rookie as well as the team's most improved player. The player of the year receives the Neil MacCarl Award, named for the longtime baseball writer from the Toronto Star... The John Cerutti Award is given annually, as voted by the Toronto Chapter of the BBWAA, to a person associated with the day-to-day workings of Blue Jays' baseball who displays goodwill, cooperation and character, as exemplified by the late John Cerutti.

YEAR	PLAYER OF THE YEAR	PITCHER OF THE YEAR	ROOKIE OF THE YEAR	GOOD GUY AWARD	MOST IMPROVED
1977	Bob Bailor	Dave Lemanczyk	Bob Bailor	Roy Hartsfield	—
1978	Bob Bailor	Jim Clancy Victor Cruz	Victor Cruz	Mike Cannon	Alan Ashby
1979	Alfredo Griffin	Tom Underwood	Alfredo Griffin	John Silverman	Rick Cerone
1980	John Mayberry	Jim Clancy	Damaso Garcia	Howard Starkman	Al Woods
1981	Dave Stieb	Dave Stieb	—	Bob Mattick	Joey McLaughlin
1982	Damaso Garcia	Dave Stieb	Jesse Barfield	Buck Martinez	Jim Clancy
1983	Lloyd Moseby	Dave Stieb	Jim Acker	Ernie Whitt	Lloyd Moseby
1984	Dave Collins	Doyle Alexander	Tony Fernandez	Dave Collins	Dave Collins
1985	Jesse Barfield	Dennis Lamp	—	Rance Mulliniks	Dennis Lamp
1986	Jesse Barfield	Mark Eichhorn	Mark Eichhorn	Garth Iorg	Rick Leach
1987	George Bell	Jimmy Key	Jeff Musselman	Garth Iorg	Lloyd Moseby
1988	Fred McGriff	Dave Stieb	Pat Borders	John Cerutti	Kelly Gruber
1989	George Bell	Tom Henke	Junior Felix	Kelly Gruber	Todd Stottlemyre
1990	Kelly Gruber	Dave Steib	John Olerud	Jeff Ross Tommy Craig	Pat Borders
1991	Roberto Alomar	Duane Ward	Juan Guzman	Joe Carter	Devon White
1992	Roberto Alomar	Jack Morris	Jeff Kent	John Brioux	Pat Borders
1993	Paul Molitor	Duane Ward	Randy Knorr	Bob Bailor	John Olerud
1994	Joe Carter	Pat Hentgen	Darren Hall	Rich Hacker	Randy Knorr
1995	Roberto Alomar	Al Leiter	Shawn Green	Galen Cisco Larry Hisle	Ed Sprague
1996	Ed Sprague	Pat Hentgen	Paul Spoljaric	Howard Starkman	Juan Guzman
1997	Carlos Delgado	Roger Clemens	Jose Cruz Jr.	Brent Andrews	Paul Quantrill
1998	Carlos Delgado	Roger Clemens	Kevin Brown	Dan Plesac	Shawn Green
1999	Shawn Green	Billy Koch	Billy Koch	Pat Hentgen	Homer Bush
2000	Carlos Delgado	David Wells	—	Andy Stewart	Brad Fullmer
2001	Jose Cruz Jr.	Paul Quantrill	Bob File	Gord Ash	Roy Halladay
2002	Vernon Wells	Roy Halladay	Eric Hinske	Darrin Fletcher	Chris Woodward
2003	Carlos Delgado	Roy Halladay	Aquilino Lopez	Vernon Wells	Orlando Hudson
2004	Carlos Delgado	Ted Lilly	Alex Rios	John Cerutti	Gregg Zaun
				JOHN CERUTTI AWARD	
2005	Vernon Wells	Roy Halladay	Russ Adams	Shirley Cheek	Josh Towers
2006	Vernon Wells	Roy Halladay	Casey Janssen	Larry Millson	Alex Rios
2007	Alex Rios	Roy Halladay	Jesse Litsch	John McDonald	Dustin McGowan
2008	Vernon Wells	Roy Halladay	Jesse Carlson	Paul Godfrey	Adam Lind
2009	Aaron Hill	Roy Halladay	Ricky Romero	Aaron Hill	Adam Lind
2010	Jose Bautista	Ricky Romero	—	Jose Bautista	Jose Bautista
2011	Jose Bautista	Ricky Romero	J.P. Arencibia	Dustin McGowan	Casey Janssen
2012	Edwin Encarnacion	Casey Janssen	Aaron Loup	Brian Butterfield	Edwin Encarnacion

Casey Janssen recorded a team high 22 saves in 2012

THE SPORTING NEWS AWARDS

PITCHER OF THE YEAR (AL)

1982 — Dave Stieb
1987 — Jimmy Key
1996 — Pat Hentgen
1997 — Roger Clemens
1998 — Roger Clemens
2003 — Roy Halladay

ROOKIE PITCHER OF THE YEAR (AL)

1986 — Mark Eichhorn
1991 — Juan Guzman

MANAGER OF THE YEAR (ML)

1985 — Bobby Cox

MLB PLAYER OF THE YEAR

1987 — George Bell
2000 — Carlos Delgado

AL PLAYER OF THE YEAR

1987 — George Bell

AL COMEBACK PLAYER

2009 — Aaron Hill

SPORTSMEN OF THE YEAR

1993 — Pat Gillick/Cito Gaston

ALL-STAR TEAM (AL)

1982 — Damaso Garcia, 2B
1982 — Dave Stieb, P
1983 — Lloyd Moseby, OF
1985 — Damaso Garcia, 2B
1986 — Tony Fernandez, SS
1986 — George Bell, OF
1987 — George Bell, OF
1987 — Jimmy Key, LHP
1988 — Ernie Whitt, C
1989 — Fred McGriff, 1B
1990 — Kelly Gruber, 3B
1991 — Joe Carter, OF
1992 — Roberto Alomar, 2B
1992 — Joe Carter, OF
1992 — Dave Winfield, DH
1993 — Paul Molitor, DH
1996 — Pat Hentgen, RHP
1997 — Roger Clemens, RHP
1998 — Roger Clemens, RHP
1999 — Shawn Green, OF
2000 — Carlos Delgado, 1B
2000 — David Wells, LHP
2003 — Carlos Delgado, 1B
2009 — Aaron Hill, 2B
2010 — Jose Bautista, 3B
2011 — Jose Bautista, OF

BASEBALL MAN OF THE YEAR IN CANADA

(TORONTO—MONTREAL BBWAA)

Peter Bavasi, 1977
Pat Gillick, 1983
Jesse Barfield, 1986
Cito Gaston, 1989
Pat Gillick, 1991
Paul Beeston, 1993

BASEBALL AMERICA

ALL-STAR TEAM (AL)

1983 — Dave Stieb, P
1983 — Lloyd Moseby, OF
1984 — Dave Stieb, P
1986 — Tony Fernandez, SS
1986 — Jesse Barfield, OF
1987 — George Bell, OF
1987 — Jimmy Key, SP
1987 — Tom Henke, RP
1989 — George Bell, OF
1989 — Dave Stieb, P
1990 — Kelly Gruber, 3B
1992 — Roberto Alomar, 2B
1992 — Dave Winfield, 2B
1993 — Roberto Alomar, 2B
1993 — John Olerud, 1B
1993 — Duane Ward, P
1996 — Pat Hentgen, P
1997 — Roger Clemens, P
1998 — Roger Clemens, P

PLAYER OF THE YEAR (AL)

1987 — George Bell

MAJOR LEAGUE PITCHER OF THE YEAR

1998 — Roger Clemens

LATIN AMERICAN ALL-STAR TEAM-TSN

1985 — Damaso Garcia, 2B
1985 — George Bell, OF

ALL-ROOKIE TEAM — TOPPS

1977 — Bob Bailor, SS; Doug Ault, 1B; Jerry Garvin, LHP
1978 — Rick Bosetti, OF
1979 — Alfredo Griffin, SS; Dan Ainge, 2B
1980 — Damaso Garcia, 2B
1987 — Jeff Musselman, LHP
1995 — Shawn Green, OF
1997 — Jose Cruz, Jr., OF
1999 — Billy Koch, RHP
2002 — Eric Hinske, 3B
2005 — Russ Adams, SS
2005 — Gustavo Chacin, LHP

ALL-ROOKIE TEAM — BASEBALL DIGEST

1977 — Bob Bailor, CF; Jerry Garvin, LHP
1978 — Rick Bosetti, CF
1979 — Alfredo Griffin, SS; Dan Ainge, 2B
1980 — Damaso Garcia, 2B

ROLAIDS RELIEF AWARDS

1985, April — Bill Caudill
1987, July — Tom Henke
1987, Aug. — Tom Henke
1989, July — Tom Henke
1993, April — Duane Ward
1993, Aug. — Duane Ward
1999, July — Billy Koch
2002, Sept. — Kelvim Escobar

PLAYER AND PITCHER OF THE MONTH

Each month throughout the season, the Toronto Chapter of the Baseball Writers Association of America votes for the player and pitcher based on their appraisal of that player's or pitcher's performance during that particular month.

PLAYER OF THE MONTH

Year	April	May	June	July	August	Sept./Oct.	Most Valuable Player
1977	Velez	Fairly	Fairly	Rader	Bailor	Bowling	Bailor
1978	Howell	Bosetti	Howell	Mayberry	Bailor	Bailor & Bosetti	Howell
1979	Mayberry	Griffin	Underwood	Velez	Griffin	Griffin	Griffin
1980	Stieb	Woods	Mayberry	Woods	Garcia	Mayberry	Mayberry
1981	Todd	Bonnell	—	—	Moseby	Stieb	Stieb
1982	Barfield	Bonnell	Upshaw	Garcia	Garcia	Clancy	Garcia
1983	Barfield	Upshaw	Johnson	Moseby	Moseby	Upshaw	Moseby & Upshaw
1984	Upshaw	Collins	Upshaw	Mulliniks	Bell	Collins	Bell
1985	Upshaw	Garcia	Bell	Mulliniks	Barfield	Moseby	Barfield
1986	Bell	Barfield	Fernandez	Bell	Moseby	Barfield	Bell
1987	Bell	Bell	Moseby	Fernandez	Bell	Moseby	Bell
1988	Gruber	McGriff	Gruber	McGriff	Whitt	Fernandez	McGriff
1989	McGriff	Liriano	Gruber	McGriff	Bell	Bell	Bell
1990	Gruber	Gruber	Bell	McGriff	McGriff	Gruber	Gruber
1991	Carter	Alomar	Carter	Alomar	White	Alomar	Alomar
1992	Alomar	Alomar	Carter	Maldonado	Winfield	White	Alomar
1993	Olerud	Molitor	Olerud	Olerud	Molitor/ Alomar	Alomar	Molitor
1994	Carter	Carter	Alomar	Molitor			Carter
1995		Alomar	Maldonado	Olerud	Molitor	Green	Alomar
1996	Carter	Olerud	Sprague	Carter	Brumfield	Sprague	Sprague
1997	Sprague	Carter	Merced	Green	Cruz Jr.	Stewart	Delgado
1998	Canseco	Delgado	Delgado	Stewart	Green	Fernandez	Delgado
1999	Green	Green	Fletcher	Green	Delgado	Bush	Green
2000	Fullmer	Delgado	Delgado	Delgado	Delgado	Fletcher	Delgado
2001	Delgado	Mondesi	Stewart	Cruz Jr.	Delgado	Cruz Jr.	Cruz Jr.
2002	Delgado	Wilson	Hinske	Wells	Phelps	Delgado	Wells
2003	Delgado	Wells	Delgado	Wells	Wells	Delgado	Delgado
2004	Delgado	Wells	Hudson	Phelps	Delgado	Delgado	Delgado
2005	Hillenbrand	Wells	Wells	Wells	Hudson	Catalanotto	Wells
2006	Wells	Glaus	Overbay	Wells	Overbay	Rios	Wells
2007	Hill	Rios	Thomas	Rios	Thomas	Hill	Rios
2008	Rios	Barajas	Rolen	Lind	Wells	Rios	Rios
2009	Hill	Scutaro	Lind	Scutaro	Lind	Lind	Lind
2010	Wells	Bautista	Lewis	Bautista	Bautista	Wells	Bautista
2011	Bautista	Bautista	Lind	Escobar	Lawrie	Bautista	Bautista
2012	Encarnacion	Bautista	Bautista	Villanueva	Encarnacion	Encarnacion	Encarnacion

J.P. Arencibia became the first Blue Jays catcher to win AL Player-of-the-Week honours (May 14-20, 2012) batting .360 with four home runs and 10 RBI.

PITCHER OF THE MONTH

Year	April	May	June	July	August	Sept./Oct.	Most Valuable Pitcher
1983	Stieb	Stieb	Gott	Clancy	Stieb	Alexander	Stieb
1984	Stieb	Alexander	Stieb	Stieb	Stieb & Clancy	Alexander	Stieb
1985	Caudill	Stieb	Stieb	Stieb	Henke	Alexander	Stieb
1986	Alexander	Eichhorn	Key	Clancy	Eichhorn	Stieb	Key
1987	Key	Key	Clancy	Key	Cerutti	Flanagan	Key
1988	Cerutti	Stieb	Ward	Key	Clancy	Stieb	Stieb
1989	Key	Key	Cerutti	Henke	Stieb	Stieb	Stieb
1990	Ward	Stieb	Henke	Stieb	Key	Key	Stieb
1991	Key	Wells	Key	Henke	Candiotti	Guzman	Ward
1992	Guzman	Guzman	Guzman	Ward	Morris	Key	Morris
1993	Hentgen	Cox	Hentgen	Ward	Ward	Stewart	Ward
1994	Castillo	Hentgen	Hentgen	Castillo	--	--	Hentgen
1995	--	Cone	Leiter	Castillo	Leiter	Timlin	Leiter
1996	Guzman	Timlin	Guzman	Hentgen	Hentgen	Hentgen	Hentgen
1997	Clemens	Clemens	Clemens	Clemens	Clemens	Clemens	Clemens
1998	Williams	Williams	Clemens	Clemens	Clemens	Escobar	Clemens
1999	Wells	Halladay	Wells	Koch	Hentgen	Wells	Koch
2000	Wells	Wells	Wells	Koch	Wells	Loaiza	Wells
2001	Quantrill	Michalak	Koch	Escobar	Escobar	Halladay	Quantrill
2002	Halladay	Loaiza	Halladay	Carpenter	Politte	Escobar	Halladay
2003	Lidle	Halladay	Halladay	Halladay	Escobar	Halladay	Halladay
2004	Halladay	Frasor	Batista	Towers	Lilly	Bush	Lilly
2005	Halladay	Halladay	Halladay	Chacin	Towers	Towers	Halladay
2006	Halladay	Halladay	Ryan	Halladay	Ryan	Burnett	Halladay
2007	Halladay	Burnett	Marcum	McGowan	Halladay	McGowan	Halladay
2008	Carlson	Litsch	Halladay	Halladay	Halladay	Litsch	Halladay
2009	Downs	Halladay	Romero	League	Frasor	Halladay	Halladay
2010	Romero	Marcum	Morrow	Cecil	Morrow	Frasor	Romero
2011	Villanueva	Romero	Romero	Cecil	Romero	Francisco	Romero
2012	Romero	Morrow	Villanueva	Villanueva	Janssen	Morrow	Janssen

Most Valuable Pitcher: 1978 - Clancy & Underwood; 1979 - Underwood; 1980 - Clancy; 1981 - Stieb; 1982 - Stieb

BLUE JAYS & CY YOUNG VOTING

YEAR	WINNER	PTS	BLUE JAYS	RANK	PTS
1982	Pete Vuckovich	87	Dave Stieb	4th	36
1984	Willie Hernandez	88	Dave Stieb	8th	1
1985	Bret Saberhagen	127	Doyle Alexander	6th	5
			Dave Stieb	9th	2
1986	Roger Clemens	140	Mark Eichhorn	6th	2
1987	Roger Clemens	124	Jimmy Key	2nd	64
1990	Bob Welch	107	Dave Stieb	6th	2
1991	Roger Clemens	119	Duane Ward	10th	3
1992	Dennis Eckersley	107	Jack Morris	5th	10
1993	Jack McDowell	124	Duane Ward	5th	5
			Pat Hentgen	6th	3
			Juan Guzman	7th	1
1995	Randy Johnson	136	David Cone	4th	18
1996	**PAT HENTGEN**	**110**	**PAT HENTGEN**	**1st**	**110**
1997	**ROGER CLEMENS**	**134**	**ROGER CLEMENS**	**1st**	**134**
1998	**ROGER CLEMENS**	**140**	**ROGER CLEMENS**	**1st**	**140**
2000	Pedro Martinez	140	David Wells	3rd	46
2003	**ROY HALLADAY**	136	**ROY HALLADAY**	**1st**	**136**
2006	Johan Santana	140	Roy Halladay	3rd	48
2007	C.C. Sabathia	119	Roy Halladay	5th	1
2008	Cliff Lee	132	Roy Halladay	2nd	71
2009	Zach Greinke	134	Roy Halladay	5th	11
2011	Justin Verlander	196	Ricky Romero	10th	2

BLUE JAYS AND THE AL MANAGER OF THE YEAR VOTING

YEAR	WINNER	PTS	1ST PLACE VOTES	BLUE JAYS	RANK	PTS	1ST PLACE VOTES
1984	Sparky Anderson-DET	96	13	Bobby Cox	4	9	0
1985	**BOBBY COX-TOR**	104	14	–	–	–	–
1989	Frank Robinson-BAL	125	23	Cito Gaston	2	62	3
1990	Jeff Torborg-CWS	128	23	Cito Gaston	5	6	0
1991	Tom Kelly-MIN	138	27	Cito Gaston	3	17	0
1992	Tony LaRussa-OAK	132	25	Cito Gaston	4	13	1
1993	Gene Lamont-CWS	72	8	Cito Gaston	3	49	3
1998	Joe Torre-NYY	128	23	Tim Johnson	T6	4	0
2003	Tony Péna-KC	130	24	Carlos Tosca	7	3	0
2005	Ozzie Guillen-CWS	105	17	John Gibbons	7	1	0
2008	Joe Maddon-TB	138	27	Cito Gaston	6	2	0
2010	Ron Gardenhire-MIN	108	16	Cito Gaston	5	5	1

ROOKIE-OF-THE-YEAR

18 Toronto Blue Jays have received votes in Rookie-of-the-Year balloting by the Baseball Writers Association of America.

YEAR	PLAYER	FINISHED	WINNER
1979	**Alfredo Griffin**	Tied 1st	**Alfredo Griffin** & John Castino
1980	Damaso Garcia	4th	Joe Charboneau
1981	George Bell	8th	Dave Righetti
1982	Jesse Barfield	8th	Cal Ripken
1985	Tom Henke	7th	Ozzie Guillen
1986	Mark Eichhorn	3rd	Jose Canseco
1987	Nelson Liriano	7th	Mark McGwire
1990	John Olerud	4th	Sandy Alomar
1991	Juan Guzman	2nd	Chuck Knoblauch
	Mike Timlin	6th	—
1994	Darren Hall	4th	Bob Hamelin
1995	Shawn Green	5th	Marty Cordova
1996	Tim Crabtree	Tied 7th	Derek Jeter
1997	Jose Cruz	2nd	Nomar Garciaparra
1999	Billy Koch	Tied 7th	Carlos Beltran
2002	**Eric Hinske**	1st	**Eric Hinske**
	Josh Phelps	6th	—
2005	Gustavo Chacin	5th	Huston Street

YOUNGEST BLUE JAYS TO RECORD FIRST MULTI-HOMER GAME

Player	Date	Age
Travis Snider	4/13/2009	21 years, 70 days
Felipe Lopez	9/04/2001	21 years, 115 days
Carlos Delgado	4/11/1994	21 years, 290 days
John Olerud	6/21/1990	21 years, 320 days
Alex Gonzalez	5/23/1995	22 years, 45 days

BLUE JAYS AND THE MVP VOTING

YEAR	WINNER	PTS	BLUE JAYS	RANK	PTS
1981	Rollie Fingers	319	Dave Stieb	T27	1
1982	Robin Yount	385	Damaso Garcia	T26	5
1983	Cal Ripken	322	Willie Upshaw	11	41.5
			Lloyd Moseby	14	21
1984	Willie Hernandez	306	Willie Upshaw	T16	8
			George Bell	T16	5
			Dave Stieb	T23	4
			Lloyd Moseby	T23	4
			Doyle Alexander	T27	1
1985	Don Mattingly	367	Jesse Barfield	7	88
			George Bell	8	84
			Tom Henke	20	5
			Dennis Lamp	T21	3
			Doyle Alexander	T21	3
			Damaso Garcia	24	2
1986	Roger Clemens	339	George Bell	4	125
			Jesse Barfield	5	107
			Tony Fernandez	14	17
1987	**GEORGE BELL**	332	George Bell	1	332
			Tony Fernandez	8	79
			Tom Henke	T13	14
1988	Jose Canseco	392	Fred McGriff	17	9
			Tony Fernandez	26	1
1989	Robin Yount	205	George Bell	4	205
			Fred McGriff	6	96
			Tony Fernandez	19	9
			Mookie Wilson	T25	1
1990	Rickey Henderson	317	Kelly Gruber	4	175
			Fred McGriff	10	30
			Dave Stieb	T25	1
1991	Cal Ripken	318	Joe Carter	5	136
			Roberto Alomar	6	128
			Devon White	16	15
1992	Dennis Eckersley	306	Joe Carter	3	201
			Dave Winfield	5	141
			Roberto Alomar	6	118
			Jack Morris	13	18
1993	Frank Thomas	392	Paul Molitor	2	209
			John Olerud	3	198
			Roberto Alomar	6	102
			Joe Carter	12	25
			Duane Ward	22	3
1994	Frank Thomas	372	Joe Carter	10	35
			Paul Molitor	T18	9
1997	Ken Griffey Jr.	392	Roger Clemens	10	56
1998	Juan Gonzalez	357	Roger Clemens	11	49
1999	Ivan Rodriguez	252	Shawn Green	9	44
			Carlos Delgado	12	16
2000	Jason Giambi	317	Carlos Delgado	4	206
			David Wells	18	2
2001	Ichiro Suzuki	289	Shannon Stewart	T25	1
2003	Alex Rodriguez	242	Carlos Delgado	2	213
2006	Justin Morneau	320	Vernon Wells	T22	3
			Troy Glaus	T31	1
2009	Joe Mauer	387	Aaron Hill	T12	23
			Adam Lind	15	14
2010	Josh Hamilton	358	Jose Bautista	4	165
2011	Justin Verlander	280	Jose Bautista	3	231
2012	Miguel Cabrera	362	Edwin Encarnacion	11	33

BOBBY MATTICK AND AL LAMACCHIA AWARDS

In 1996 the Blue Jays organization established two awards: the **Bobby Mattick Player Development Award** and the **Al LaMacchia Scouting Award**. The awards were created to acknowledge the dedication, success and work ethics of Blue Jays baseball operations personnel, attributes so aptly displayed by the awards' namesakes.The Bobby Mattick Award was named after the longtime baseball executive who had spent 25 years of his career with the Blue Jays. The late Bobby Mattick was responsible for the development of many of the young players who have gone through the Blue Jays system. As well as being Director of Player Development for many years he also managed the Major League Blue Jays for two seasons in 1980 and 1981.The Al LaMacchia Award was named after the veteran scout who spent 20 seasons with the Blue Jays. The late Al LaMacchia's scouting talents have been deeply etched in the Blue Jays short history.

	BOBBY MATTICK AWARD	AL LaMACCHIA AWARD
1996	Rockett Wheeler	Duane Larson
1997	Omar Malave	Jim Hughes
1998	Rolando Pino	Tom Hinkle
1999	Bruce Walton	Ellis Dungan
2000	Marty Pevey	Tim Wilken
2001	Dan Rajkowski	David Blume
2002	Dane Johnson	Charles Aliano
2003	Mike Basso	Ty Nichols
2004	Ken Joyce	Andy Beene
2005	Rick Langford	Demerius Pittman
2006	Dennis Holmberg	Tom Burns
2007	Gary Cathcart	Marc Tramuta
2008	Clayton McCullough	Aaron Jersild
2009	Charlie Wilson	Matt Briggs
2010	Dane Johnson	Tim Rooney
2011	Dennis Holmberg	John Hendricks
2012	Chad Mottola	Blake Crosby

CANADIANS IN THE BLUE JAYS SYSTEM

17 Canadian born players have worn the Blue Jays uniform in the 35 year history of the franchise.

PLAYERS WHO HAVE PLAYED AT THE MAJOR LEAGUE LEVEL (17)

NAME	POS.	HOMETOWN	YEAR(S)
Dave McKay	INF	Vancouver, BC	1977-1979
Paul Hodgson	OF	Fredericton, NB	1980
Rob Ducey	OF	Cambridge, ON	1987-1992; 2000
Denis Boucher	LHP	Lachine, PQ	1991
Vince Horsman	LHP	Dartmouth, NS	1991
Rob Butler	OF	Toronto, ON	1993-1994; 1999
Paul Spoljaric	LHP	Kelowna, BC	1994; 1996-1997; 1999
Paul Quantrill	RHP	Cobourg, ON	1996-2001
Rich Butler	OF	Toronto, ON	1997
Steve Sinclair	LHP	Victoria, BC	1998-1999
Simon Pond	OF	North Vancouver, BC	2004
Corey Koskie	INF	Anola, MB	2005
Matt Stairs	INF/OF	St. John, NB	2007-2008
Scott Richmond	RHP	North Vancouver, BC	2008-2009; 2011-2012
Shawn Hill	RHP	Mississauga, ON	2010; 2012
Brett Lawrie	INF	Langley, BC	2011-
Adam Loewen	OF	Vancouver, BC	2011

OTHER CANADIAN BORN PLAYERS ON THE 40-MAN ROSTER (6)

NAME	POS.	HOMETOWN	YEAR(S)
Dave Shipanoff	RHP	Edmonton, AB	1982-1984
Nigel Wilson	OF	Ajax, ON	1991
Greg O'Halloran	C	Mississauga, ON	1992
Joe Young	RHP	Ft. McMurray, BC	1996-98
Chad Ricketts	RHP	Waterloo, ON	2002
Vince Perkins	RHP	Victoria, BC	2004, 2005

R. HOWARD WEBSTER AWARDS

In 1982 the Blue Jays established a set of awards to be bestowed annually upon the 'Most Valuable Player' on each Blue Jay farm club. The awards are named in honor of R. HOWARD WEBSTER, who was the first Chairman of the Board for the Toronto Blue Jays.

	AAA	**AA**	**A**	**A**	**A**	**Rookie**	**Rookie**
Year	**Syracuse**	**Knoxville**	**Kinston**	**Florence**		**Medicine Hat**	**Bradenton**
1982	T. Fernandez	T. Thompson	D. Shipanoff	K. Kinnard		C. Johnston	E. Bolivar
1983	T. Fernandez	D. Shipanoff	J. Escobar	C. Fielder		R. Robbbins	S. Escobar
1984	F. Manrique	M. Sharpeson	L. Aquino	P. Borders		R. Ducey	S. Garcia
1985	R. Leach	S. Davis	E. Yelding	S. Campusano		G. Berroa	D. Martinez
			Ventura		**St. Catharines**		
1986	M. Sharpeson	G. Hill	G. Myers	P. Munoz	W. Blair	M. Whiten	
			Dunedin	**Myrtle Beach**			
1987	T. Stottlemyre	G. Berroa	S. Cummings	D. Linton	D. Bell	A. Dziadkoweic	
1988	A. Infante	A. Sanchez	P. Munoz	L. Sojo	W. Williams	E. Mendez	W. Rojas
1989	G. Hill	D. Bell	N. Cromwell	R. Gianelli	G. O'Halloran	S. Holtzclaw	
1990	M. Whiten	T. Quinlan	J. Kent	M. Ogliaruso	C. Delgado	B. Bowers	
							Gulf Coast
1991	D. Bell	J. Kent	N. Wilson	H. Battle	R. Butler	F. Crespo	C. Stynes
1992	B. Davis	J. De La Rosa	C. Delgado	A. Gonzalez	T. Crabtree	J. Hererra	T. Brito
				Hagerstown			
1993	R. Perez	C. Delgado	C. Weinke	D.J. Boston	A. Beltran	L. De La Cruz	A. Hightowerr
1994	S. Green	C. Stynes	K. Harmes	D. Sinnes	J. Ladd	J. Mosquera	K. Escobar
1995	R. Perez	S. Stewart	J. Patzke	J. Ladd	J. Young	M. Peeples	M. Whitlock
1996	S. Stewart	R. Jones	R. Halladay	M. Whitlock	W. Skett	R. Stromsberg	
1997	R. Butler	K Witt	W. Skett	L. Lopez	S. Langaigne	G. Morrison	
1998	P. Lennon	L. Lopez	B. Abernathy	J. Sneed	J. Kingery	J. Gibbons	
1999	L. Lopez	T. Giles	C. Izturis	J. Nunez	B. Jackson	G. Chacin	
		Tennessee			**Queens**		
2000	C. Mottola	J. Gibbons	J. Lawrence	R. Johnson	M. Malpica	J. Johnson	
				Charleston	**Auburn**		
2001	L. Lopez	J. Phelps	R. Thompson	A. McCullock	M. Mayorson	N. Tempesta	
2002	G. Burnham	V. Chulk	D. Rich	M. Snyder	J. Owens	J. DeJong	
		New Haven				**Pulaski**	
2003	S. Pond	A. Rios	J. Harper	R. Medina	V. Chiaravalloti	R. Diaz	
		New Hampshire					
2004	G. Williams	A. Hill	I. Ramirez	C. Johnston	A. Lind	Y. Rodriguez	
				Lansing			
2005	J. Griffin	J. Banks	A. Lind	C. Snavely	R. Patterson	J. Butler	
2006	K. Barker	A. Lind	R. Pattterson	C. Cheng	J. Campbell	T. Snider	
2007	J. Banks	D. Smith	J. Kreuzer	T. Snider	B. Cecil	**(Ended)**	J. Chavez
2008	D. Purcey	S. Campbell	B. Dopriak	M. Rzepczynski	R. Bell	--	B. Fuenmayer
	Las Vegas					--	
2009	R. Ruiz	B. Dopirak	M. Sierra	J. Chavez	S. Ochinko	--	C. Perez
2010	J. Arencibia	E. Thames	M. McDade	S. Ochinko	C. Perez	--	J. Marisnick
					Vancouver	**Bluefield**	
2011	D. Cooper	T. d'Arnaud	A. Jimenez	J. Marisnik	J. Nicolino	C. Hawkins	J. Rosado
2012	A. Hechavarria	R. Goins	D. Barnes	J. Nicolino	J. Avendano	C. Lopes	A. Tirado

The 2012 R. Howard Webster Award winners

BLUE JAYS IN THE POST-SEASON

1985

AMERICAN LEAGUE CHAMPIONSHIP SERIES

TORONTO VS KANSAS CITY (L, 3-4)

As the Blue Jays entered post season play for the first time, they would face the Kansas City Royals in the first ever best-of-seven American League Championship Series. The Blue Jays, who finished nine games ahead of the Royals in the loss column, were the favourites and would enjoy the extra home game.

GAME #1: Dave Stieb lived up to superstar billing, shutting out the Royals on three hits through eight innings with no base runner advancing past second base. The Blue Jays struck quickly with two runs in the second, three in the third and one in the fourth. The Blue Jays offense was sparked by 2 RBI performances by Ernie Whitt and Tony Fernandez.

GAME #2: A much more even affair with the Blue Jays eeking out a 6-5, 10-inning win. The Royals jumped into a quick 3-0 lead after 3 innings primarily on the strength of a 2 run HR by Willie Wilson in the 3rd inning. The Blue Jays rallied and took the lead on a George Bell sacrifice fly in the 8th. The Royals rallied, however, in the 9th on a pinch hit HR by Pat Sheridan with the go ahead run being delivered in the 10th on a Frank White single. The Blue Jays won it in the bottom of the 10th on a two-out 2 run single by Al Oliver. On to Kansas City, the Blue Jays were up 2 games to none.

GAME #3: George Brett put on a baseball clinic going 4-4, 2 HR's, 3 RBI with 4 runs scored enroute to a 6-5 Royals win. Leading 5-2 after 4 innings the Blue Jays squandered the lead for good in the 8th when Brett led off the inning with a single and eventually scored.

GAME #4: The Blue Jays came within one win of a World Series berth with a 3-1 come-from-behind victory. The Blue Jays won the game dramatically with 3 runs in the top of the ninth inning, the big blow being a 2 run pinch hit double by Al Oliver.

GAME #5: LHP Danny Jackson went the distance checking Toronto on 8 hits and scoring a run in each of the first two innings. Blue Jays still led the series 3 games to 2.

GAME #6: The Blue Jays and Royals returned to Exhibition Stadium. Entering the 5th inning tied at 2-2 George Brett once again delivered the decisive blow with a solo HR. And, with 3.2 shutout innings of relief from Buddy Black and Dan Quisenberry, the Royals pulled even in the series for the first time at three games apiece.

GAME #7: Dave Stieb, the ace of the Toronto staff vs eventual Cy Young Award winner Bret Saberhagen. The Royals came out on top 6-2 shellacking Dave Stieb for six runs in 5.2 innings. The big blow being a wind-assisted bases clearing triple by Jim Sundberg to cap a four run 6th inning.

The Kansas City Royals became only the 5th club in major league history to trail a series 3 games to one and come back to win the series. The Blue Jays? They slumped immediately after scoring five runs in the 5th inning of Game 3 scoring only eight runs in the last 40 innings.

1989

AMERICAN LEAGUE CHAMPIONSHIP SERIES

TORONTO VS OAKLAND (L, 1-4)

For the second time in five seasons, the Blue Jays were American League East Division Champions. The Blue Jays would face the Oakland Athletics who had the best record in the Major Leagues in 1989.

GAME #1: The Blue Jays surrendered 2-0 and 3-1 leads as the Athletics scored three times in the sixth and twice in the eighth to win 7-3. In the sixth inning Mark McGwire cracked a lead off HR to tie the game and two runs scored when Carney Lansford's double play ball was botched. Dave Stewart allowed five hits over eight innings for the win.

GAME #2: The Athletics tallied twice in the fourth inning and three in the sixth en route to a 6-3 win. As outfielder Rickey Henderson was a one-man wrecking crew going 2-for-2 with two runs scored and four stolen bases. Athletics' righthander Mike Moore allowed just three hits and an unearned run in seven innings.

GAME #3: The Blue Jays snapped a five game post season losing streak dating back to 1985 with a convincing 7-3 win. The Blue Jays jumped on Athletics' starter Storm Davis for four runs on four hits in the fourth inning and salted the game away with another three runs in the seventh inning. The win ran the Blue Jays' record to 11-0 at SkyDome with the roof closed. Overcoming a 3-0 Athletics' lead Mookie Wilson and Tony Fernandez paced the Blue Jays with two hits apiece, the latter with two doubles.

GAME #4: The Athletics took a commanding 3-1 lead in games with a 6-6 win over the Blue Jays. Rickey Henderson was again a major catalyst with two HR's which accounted for four RBI. The Blue Jays collected 13 hits, 11 of which were singles and attempted to overcome a 5-2 deficit with one run in the sixth and seventh innings and two in the eighth.

GAME #5: The Blue Jays spotted the Athletics a 4-0 lead into the seventh inning before eventually losing the game 4-3 and the best-of-seven series in five games. Trailing 4-1 after eight innings the Blue Jays scored twice in the ninth inning on a leadoff HR by Geroge Bell and a sacrifice fly by Kelly Gruber.

Epilogue: In essence it was Rickey Henderson defeating the Blue Jays four games to one. Henderson batted .400, slugged 1.000, had a .609 on-base percentage and swiped a LCS record eight stolen bases. The Blue Jays hit .242 as a team (com-

pared to Oakland's .272) with only eight of their hits being for extra bases. They were outscored 8-3 in the first three innings and 12-7 in the middle three before outscoring the Athletics 11-6 in the final three innings. Unfortunately it is virtually impossible to consistently battle back from an early inning deficit. Although anything can happen in a "short series" the best team of the regular season continued that charted course into post-season, winning eight of nine contests.

1991

AMERICAN LEAGUE CHAMPIONSHIP SERIES

TORONTO VS MINNESOTA (L, 1-4)

In 1991, the Toronto Blue Jays won the American League East for the third time in the history of the organization. The Blue Jays faced the Western Division Champion Minnesota Twins in a series that would decide the American League Champion. The Minnesota Twins emerged victorious as they won the best of seven games series by a 4 games to 1 count. Below is a summary of the series.

GAME #1: Toronto starter Tom Candiotti lasted just 2.2 innings and allowed five earned runs before being lifted in favour of David Wells. The Twins would not need to score another run. The Blue Jays rallied for a run in the fourth and three runs in the sixth on five consecutive hits off Twins starter Jack Morris. Those four runs would be all Toronto could muster as they lost 5-4 at the Metrodome.

GAME #2: Toronto took an early lead as they jumped on Twins starter Kevin Tapani, scoring three times in the first three innings. Rookie Toronto starter Juan Guzman lasted 5.2 innings allowing four hits and just two earned runs before the ball was handed to the bullpen. Tom Henke and Duane Ward combined for 2.1 innings of shutout relief and six strikeouts. Devon White scored three of the five Toronto runs as the Blue Jays won their only 1991 ALCS game 5-2 in Minneapolis.

GAME #3: Joe Carter's first inning home run and a Candy Maldonado double put the Blue Jays ahead 2-0 until the sixth inning when the Twins were able to put their second run across the plate and tie the game at two apiece. Toronto starter Jimmy Key scattered five hits over six innings and allowed two earned runs. The game went into extra-innings and ended in dramatic fashion as Mike Pagliarulo, pinch hitting for Scott Leius, homered to right off of Blue Jays reliever Mike Timlin. Toronto was retired 1-2-3 in their half of the tenth as the Twins defeated Toronto 3-2 at SkyDome.

GAME #4: Blue Jays starter Todd Stottlemyre allowed seven hits in 3.2 innings before exiting with Toronto trailing 4-1. The Twins' Kirby Puckett hit his first home run of the series and Dan Gladden collected three RBI on three hits to pace Minnesota to a 9-3 win at SkyDome. It was Jack Morris' second win of the ALCS as he pitched eight innings allowing just two runs.

GAME #5: Kirby Puckett displayed his power once again as he homered in the first inning off Tom Candiotti to put the Twins ahead 1-0. Toronto put together three runs in the third and a pair in the fourth to go ahead 5-2. Minnesota was able to post three runs in their half of the sixth inning and tie the game at five. Duane Ward was handed the loss for Toronto as he allowed three runs in the eighth. Toronto was shutdown by five shutout innings of relief. Devon White, Roberto Alomar and Manuel Lee each collected a pair of hits in the losing effort as Minnesota took the American League crown with an 8-5 win.

1992

AMERICAN LEAGUE CHAMPIONSHIP SERIES

TORONTO VS OAKLAND (W, 4-2)

GAME #1: Home runs were the story of the game as Oakland used three of them to beat the Blue Jays 4-3. The A's scored three runs in the second inning off Toronto starter Jack Morris on back-to-back homers by Mark McGwire and Terry Steinbach. The 3-0 lead stood until Pat Borders homered off Dave Stewart in the Blue Jays' fifth followed by a Dave Winfield homer in the sixth making the score 3-2. John Olerud tied the score at 3 in the bottom of the eighth with a two out single off reliever Jeff Russell scoring Winfield who had doubled in the previous at-bat. Harold Baines broke the tie with a solo shot to lead off the ninth and Dennis Eckersley shut down the Blue Jays in the home half of the ninth to seal the 4-3 Oakland victory.

GAME #2: The Blue Jays were able to rebound from a Game #1 loss as David Cone held the A's to just one run over 8.0 innings en route to a 3-1 win. Cone, the Major League's strikeout leader in 1992, fanned six as he collected his second career post-season victory. Mike Moore lasted seven innings in the losing effort for Oakland. Kelly Gruber doubled and hit a 2-run homer in the fifth which would prove to be the winning runs. Closer Tom Henke came on for the save in the ninth, his first ever post-season save.

GAME #3: For the first time since 1985 vs Kansas City, the Blue Jays put together a pair of wins in the post-season as they got past the A's 7-5. Toronto starter Juan Guzman notched his second career LCS win in as many starts (1991 vs Twins) lasting six inning before being lifted in favour of Duane Ward. Tom Henke earned his second save in as many games. Despite being out-hit 13-9 by the A's, 4 of Toronto's hits went for extra-bases including homers from Alomar (solo) and Maldonado (solo). The A's collected just 1 extra-base hit.

GAME #4: In what appeared at first to be a certain Oakland victory, the Toronto Blue Jays fought back to erase a five run deficit late in the game sending the game into extra-innings. Oakland batted around earning five runs in the third inning as they jumped on Toronto starter Jack Morris. The A's added another run in the sixth making the score 6-1. Toronto began their comeback in the top of the eighth as they strung together five consecutive hits. By the end of the inning, the score was 6-4. The A's were held of the board in the bottom of the eighth but in the top of the ninth, Devon White started off the inning with a single that was misplayed allowing White to get to third base. Roberto Alomar then homered off Dennis Eckersley to tie the game at 6-6. Toronto eventually won the game in the eleventh as they scored a run off Kelly Downs to win 7-6.

GAME #5: Oakland starter Dave Stewart held the Blue Jays in check for nine innings scattering seven hits, allowing just 2 runs as Oakland sent the series back to SkyDome. The complete game win was Stewart's first win of the 1992 post-season.

The 6-2 loss for the Blue Jays ended their three game win streak. David Cone took the loss for Toronto. He lasted just 4.0 innings before Jimmy Key made his first appearance of the 1992 playoffs. Ruben Sierra homered and drove in 3 runs for the A's. Devon White notched 3 hits on the day including a double in the losing effort.

GAME #6: Toronto scored a pair of runs in the first on a Joe Carter homer off A's starter Mike Moore. The Blue Jays then added four more runs in the third including a Candy Maldonado 3-run homer to put Toronto ahead 6-0. Blue Jays' starter Juan Guzman went seven innings allowing just five hits and striking out eight before the ball was handed to Duane Ward in the eighth with the score Toronto 7, Oakland 1. The A's managed a run in the top of the eighth but the home town Blue Jays secured the win as Tom Henke tossed a perfect ninth sending Toronto to its first ever World Series with a 9-2 win over Oakland.

WORLD SERIES

TORONTO VS ATLANTA (W, 4-2)

GAME #1: In the first game of the 89th World Series, the Blue Jays suffered a 3-1 loss to the Atlanta Braves. Home runs were the story of the game as Toronto took an early 1-0 lead in the fourth on a Joe Carter solo homer off starter Tom Glavine. It would be the only run Toronto would score. Jack Morris continued his shutout innings streak vs the Braves extending it to 18.0 innings until a 3-run homer by catcher Damon Berryhill in the sixth inning ended the streak. Glavine went the distance for the Braves becoming the first pitcher to toss a complete game in a World Series opener since Jack Morris accomplished the feat in 1984 vs San Diego.

GAME #2: Reserve catcher Ed Sprague proved to be the hero for the Blue Jays on this night at Fulton County Stadium. David Cone lasted just 4.1 innings allowing 4 runs over that span before exiting in favour of David Wells. Cone also contributed at the plate with a pair of hits and an RBI. His two hits marked the first two hit game by an AL pitcher in the World Series since Mickey Lolitch went 2-4 on October 3, 1968. Heading into the eighth inning, the Blue Jays trailed 4-2. After a run in the top of the eighth Toronto entered the ninth inning trailing by 1. After a Pat Borders fly out, rookie Derek Bell (pinch hitting for Lee) walked. Ed Sprague then pinch hitting for the pitcher Duane Ward knocked a first pitch offering from Jeff Reardon over the left field fence to put the Blue Jays ahead 5-4. Tom Henke was able to retire the Braves in the bottom of the ninth for the save.

GAME #3: The game marked the first time the World Series had been played outside of the United States as the series moved to SkyDome. In another pitching duel, Steve Avery and Juan Guzman both went 8.0 innings. Atlanta was kept off the board in the fourth with a splendid defensive effort by Devon White. White ran down a deep drive off the bat of Dave Justice that sent Devon into the wall to make the catch. White returned the ball to the infield where Pendleton was doubled-up off first. The Blue Jays drew first blood in the fourth inning as Joe Carter connected for his second homer of the series, a solo shot putting Toronto ahead 1-0. In the sixth inning, the Braves rallied to tie things at 1-1. Each team traded runs in the eighth keeping the game knotted at 2-2. The Braves attempted a rally as Duane Ward came on to pitch the ninth. But after a key double play and a strikeout the inning was over. In the home half of the ninth, Roberto Alomar started the inning off with a leadoff single. After stealing second and a Dave Winfield sacrifice, Alomar stood at third with one out. Jeff Reardon came in to try to halt the Blue Jays' advance but Candy Maldonado with the bases loaded, hit a 2-strike pitch to right centre for a base hit allowing Alomar to score the winning run.

GAME #4: In what was the third consecutive 1-run game of the 1992 World Series, the Blue Jays posted a 2-1 win behind a strong pitching effort from starter Jimmy Key. Key went 7.2 innings allowing just 5 hits and 1 earned run while striking out six Braves batters. Toronto earned their first run in the third inning as catcher Pat Borders continued on his post season hit streak with a solo homer to left. Toronto made the score 2-0 in the seventh when Devon White drove in Kelly Gruber from second base. Atlanta managed to score a run in their half of the eighth as Ron Gant led off with a double and eventually scored on a Mark Lemke groundout. Tom Henke came in to pitch the ninth for Toronto and tacked up a 1-2-3 inning for his second save of the series.

GAME #5: The game began in similar fashion as the previous four. Entering the fifth inning, the game was tied at 2-2. The Braves had collected a run in the first and fourth inning while the Blue Jays captured runs in the second and fourth. The fifth inning proved to be Atlanta's inning as they crossed the plate five times to seal the victory and send the series back to Atlanta for at least one more game. The fifth inning began for the Braves with 2 consecutive routine outs. An Otis Nixon single started the ball rolling and the Braves eventually loaded the bases on Toronto starter Jack Morris. Lonnie Smith stepped up to the plate and sent Morris' 1-2 offering over the right field wall for a grand slam making the score 7-2. The score remained the same over the final four innings making a winner out of John Smoltz.

GAME #6: The Toronto Blue Jays make history as they capture their first ever World Series and bring the Commissioner's Trophy outside of the United States for the first time. The 11-inning game began with the Blue Jays scoring in their first inning of the game. Devon White led off the game with a single off starter Steve Avery. After a stolen base and a ground out by Alomar, White stood on third. Carter then drove in White with a sacrifice fly. Atlanta answered the call in their half of the third as Deon Sanders scored his fourth run of the series. Toronto returned the favour immediately as they regained the lead with a run in the top of the fourth on a Maldonado lead off homer. The score remained that way until the bottom of the ninth when Atlanta shortstop Jeff Blauser tied the game sending it into extra-innings. The tenth inning proved to be uneventful. In the eleventh, the Blue Jays led off with Jimmy Key popping out for out number 1. Devon White was hit by a Charlie Leibrandt offering. Alomar then singled to centre allowing White to move up to second. With two out, Dave Winfield stepped up to the plate and doubled down the left-field line allowing White and Alomar to score making it 4-2 Toronto. In the Braves eleventh, Atlanta was able to score once with Jimmy Key on the mound. Mike Timlin then came in to pitch for the Blue Jays with pinch runner Smoltz on third and two out... Otis Nixon attempted a drag bunt up the first base line, that was fielded by Timlin who threw to Carter at first in time for the final out.

1993

AMERICAN LEAGUE CHAMPIONSHIP SERIES

TORONTO VS CHICAGO (W, 4-2)

GAME #1: The Blue Jays took a 2-0 lead in the fourth inning when third baseman Ed Sprague tripled to right field with Olerud and Molitor on base. Chicago then used their half of the fourth inning to produce three runs on two hits as they sent nine men to the plate. Toronto starting pitcher Juan Guzman managed to hold the White Sox in check for six innings but walked 8 batters and stranded 11 Chicago runners before exiting with a 5-3 lead. Jack McDowell lasted 6.2 innings allowing thirteen hits and all seven Toronto runs before the White Sox relief corps came on to hold Toronto for the remainder of the game. Danny Cox worked a shutout seventh and eighth allowing a single by Ozzie Guillen. Duane Ward came out for the ninth and walked the first two batters before striking out the side to end the Chicago threat.

GAME #2: Both clubs scored once in the first inning but it was the Blue Jays that would prevail as their two-run fourth inning provided the edge. The 3-1 win saw Toronto take a two games to none lead in the best of seven games series. The fourth inning started with a pair of outs by Carter and Olerud. Paul Molitor then doubled off starter and loser Alex Fernandez. Next, Tony Fernandez singled to score Molitor and moved to second on the throw home. After an intentional walk to Ed Sprague, Pat Borders singled to second base but Joey Cora threw the ball away allowing the third Toronto run to score. Dave Stewart worked six strong innings surrendering just four hits (all singles) and one run for his seventh career ALCS win against no losses. Al Leiter was credited with a hold as he pitched the seventh and eighth innings before closer Duane Ward came in to save the game in the ninth.

GAME #3: Nineteen game winner, Pat Hentgen started for Toronto but could not collect a win on this day as Toronto suffered their worst defeat of the series losing 6-1. The Blue Jays were able to hold off the White Sox attack until the third inning when they sent 10 players to the plate and combined for five runs on five singles. Hentgen lasted just three innings plus 2 batters before he was removed in favour of Danny Cox. Toronto scored their lone run in the bottom of the third as Rickey Henderson scored from third on a Devon White single. Wilson Alvarez, the Chicago starter pitched a complete game for his first career ALCS victory. He permitted just seven hits while issuing two walks and striking out six. Tim Raines provided most of the offensive support for Chicago going 4-5 with a run scored.

GAME #4: A two run home run by centre fielder Lance Johnson in the second inning gave the White Sox a 2-0 lead over Toronto. The light hitting Johnson had not hit a home run since the 1992 regular season. Todd Stottlemyre, making his first start of the 1993 ALCS lasted six innings for the home team but failed to hold onto a 3-2 lead that was handed to him in the third when Toronto batted around on rookie starter Jason Bere. The right hander lasted just 2.1 innings before being pulled in favour of Tim Belcher. Stottlemyre allowed three more Chicago runs in the sixth including a Frank Thomas solo homer and a Lance Johnson triple before departing. Roberto Alomar doubled home Henderson in the bottom of the sixth to cut the Chisox lead to one (5-4) but the visiting White Sox notched a single run off Al Leiter in the seventh and another run off Mike Timlin in the ninth to seal the win by a 7-4 margin.

GAME #5: As was the case with each of the previous four games, the team that scored first emerged victorious. This time, Toronto scored first when Rickey Henderson crossed the plate in the first inning after leading off the game with a double and a stolen base. Starting pitcher Jack McDowell allowed a Toronto run in the second and third before being lifted following just 2.1 innings. Meanwhile, Blue Jays starter Juan Guzman cruised through the first 4.1 innings without allowing a hit or a walk until Ellis Burks went deep to left field for what would be the only blemish on Guzman's slate that afternoon. He lasted seven innings permitting just two hits while walking one and striking out six. Roberto Alomar reached base in all five plate appearances (3 hits, 2 walks) to lead the Toronto attack. Tony Castillo worked a scoreless eighth allowing a single and a base on balls. Duane Ward had some difficulty in the ninth. He struck out Joey Cora and Frank Thomas following a single to lead off the inning by Raines. He then issued a two run homer to Robin Ventura that brought Chicago within two. With the tying run at the plate, Ward struck out Bo Jackson to end the game and preserve the 5-3 Toronto win.

GAME #6: With his 7-0 record in ALCS play on the line, Blue Jays' starter Dave Stewart provided the win which put Toronto into their second consecutive World Series as the Blue Jays won 6-3 over Chicago. Toronto scored first with a pair of runs in the second inning as a 2-out single by catcher Pat Borders off Alex Fernandez cashed in John Olerud and Paul Molitor. The White Sox tied the game in the third inning when a bases loaded walk by Frank Thomas and a fielder's choice by Robin Ventura scored two runs. Stewart managed to restrict the Chisox to just 4 hits and 2 earned runs before handing Duane Ward a 3-2 lead after 7.1 innings. Ward struck out the final two batters to end the eighth. Toronto added to their lead as Devon White homered off reliever Scott Radinsky to make the score 4-2. Toronto added two more runs before the inning was over as Paul Molitor tripled to centre. Duane Ward allowed his second home run of the series as Warren Newson hit a solo shot in the bottom of the ninth but that was all the scoring that the Pale Hose would achieve as the Blue Jays were crowned American League Champions for the second straight season.

WORLD SERIES

TORONTO VS PHILADELPHIA (W, 4-2)

GAME #1: For the first time in baseball annals, the World Series began on Canadian soil. The Blue Jays fell behind 2-0 in the first inning as the Phillies' catcher Darren Daulton singled home a pair of runs off starting pitcher Juan Guzman. After holding Philadelphia in check in the top of the second, Toronto rallied with two runs of their own on four singles off Curt Schilling. Both teams traded solo runs in the third and fifth to keep the score knotted at 4-4. With 1 out in the bottom of the sixth, John Olerud took a first pitch offering from Schilling over the right field fence for a solo home run putting Toronto ahead by one. Toronto scored what would prove to be the winning run in the bottom of the seventh as four consecutive hits by Borders, Henderson, White and Alomar produced an 8-4 lead heading into the eighth. Al Leiter, who would prove to be the winning pitcher, relieved Guzman to start the sixth and held the Phillies scoreless over 2.2 innings before turning the ball over to closer Duane Ward. Ward surrendered a run in the ninth inning as a Jim Eisenreich single scored John Kruk who had led off the frame with a single and moved to second on an error. Ricky Jordan flied out to Joe Carter for the last out to put Toronto ahead 1 game to 0 with the 8-5 win.

GAME #2: The big inning would prove to be the Philly advantage on this night as a Jim Eisenreich three run homer in the top of the third capped a five run inning that saw eight Philadelphia batters step up to the plate. Toronto starter and eventual loser, Dave Stewart lasted six innings with all five earned runs coming in that third frame. Toronto answered the Philly onslaught with a pair of runs in the bottom of the fourth as Joe Carter connected for his first of two World Series home runs. Philadelphia starter Terry Mulholland would allow just three runs over 5.2 innings before handing the ball to the bullpen. Lenny Dykstra led off the seventh inning with a solo homer off reliever Tony Castillo to stretch the Philly lead to 3 as the visitors were now ahead 6-3. Toronto scored one run in the eighth as Molitor led off with a double and eventually scored on an Olerud sac fly. Philly relievers Roger Mason (1.2 innings) and Mitch Williams (1.2 innings) closed out the game to preserve the 6-4 win and even the series.

GAME #3: The venue moved from SkyDome to Veteran's Stadium in Philadelphia for games three, four and five. This game featured solid pitching by the Blue Jays combined with a potent offence. The visiting Blue Jays jumped on Philly starter Danny Jackson in the top of the first as Paul Molitor drove home a pair of runs with a triple. He would also score as Carter lifted a sacrifice fly to right field. Molitor added a solo homer in the third to make it 4-0. Starting pitcher Pat Hentgen pitched six innings allowing just one run- that coming in the sixth as a two-out single by Eisenreich scored John Kruk who had reached base via a walk. Blue Jays added another run in the top of the sixth as Roberto Alomar scored on a sac fly after having reached base on a single and stealing second and third. Toronto continued to add to their lead as they scored three more runs in the seventh off reliever Ben Rivera. Roberto Alomar finished the night with a 4-hit game while Molitor had three hits, three runs and three RBI. Duane Ward surrendered a solo homer to Milt Thompson in the ninth to make the final score Toronto 10, Philadelphia 3.

GAME #4: In a slugfest, the Blue Jays put together one of the wildest comebacks in World Series history to beat the Phillies 15-14 and take a three games to one lead. Toronto opened the scoring with three in the first off Philly starter Tommy Greene. But the home team would take advantage of four first inning walks by starter Todd Stottlemyre as they scored four runs to move ahead 4-3. Philadelphia added two more runs to their tally as Lenny Dykstra connected for his second homer of the series, a 2-run shot in the second. The Blue Jays batted around in the third and collected four runs and sent Tommy Greene to the bench in favour of Roger Mason. Philadelphia then posted a five run fifth that included home runs from Dykstra and Daulton to extend their lead 12-7. Toronto countered with two runs in the top of the sixth as White and Alomar scored on a single and a ground out. The Phillies added a run in the sixth and one in the seventh to make the score 14-9. The Phillies relief corps could not hold Toronto from making a comeback. In the top of the eighth, the Blue Jays sent ten players to the plate. Devon White's triple with two out scored Pat Borders to tie the game and Rickey Henderson to put Toronto ahead 15-14. Mike Timlin, started the eighth and struck out the first two batters he faced before Duane Ward came on to strikeout Dykstra to end the inning. In the ninth Ward hurled a 1-2-3 inning for his second save of the series in a game that took 4 hours and 14 minutes to play and was the highest scoring game in World Series history. Tony Fernandez had five RBI in the game and White had four.

GAME #5: Curt Schilling shutout Toronto 2-0 in what was the second ever shutout of Toronto in the post season. Pitted against Blue Jays ace Juan Guzman, he allowed just five hits (all singles) and struck out six Toronto batters for his first World Series win. The Phillies scored the only run they would need in the first inning when Dykstra, who had walked to lead off the game, scored on a John Kruk groundout. They added a second run in the very next inning as a pair of doubles cashed in Daulton. In the eighth, the Blue Jays threatened with a pair of runners on base but a strikeout by White followed by an Alomar ground out ended their attempt. Guzman was equal to the challenge as he went seven innings allowing both Philly runs while fanning six. The win sent the series back to Toronto with the Blue Jays holding a 3-2 edge.

GAME #6: Toronto started their quest for a second straight World Series Championship early as they notched three runs off Philly starter Terry Mulholland in the bottom of the first. A run in the fourth and a solo home run by Molitor in the fifth put Toronto up 5-1. Dave Stewart, the Toronto starter held the Phillies to just one run over his first six innings. In the seventh he surrendered a three run homer to Lenny Dykstra- his fourth of the series. That led to Stewart being pulled from the game. Reliever Danny Cox came in with none out and surrendered two more runs before the Phillies were halted by Al Leiter. The damage had been done and Philadelphia was now leading 6-5. After leaving the bases loaded in the eighth, Toronto made World Series history by erasing a 1-run lead in the bottom of the ninth. Mitch Williams came in to start the inning and he walked Rickey Henderson who led off. After a Devon White fly out, Molitor singled to centre to put runners at first and second. Right fielder Joe Carter then stepped up to the plate. On a 2-2 offering from Williams, Carter homered over the left field wall for a three run home run and propelled Toronto to its second consecutive World Series Championship with an 8-6 win.

WORLD SERIES RINGS

The Toronto Blue Jays commissioned Tiffany & Co., the world-renowned purveyor of fine jewellery, timepieces, and arts of the table to design rings commemorating both their 1992 and 1993 World Series victories.

To commemorate the 1992 Blue Jays victory, the 14 karat gold ring's design features the team's logo: the head of a Blue Jay with a maple leaf on a baseball backdrop. The eye of the bird is set with a solitaire diamond. Sixteen diamonds representing each year of the club's history surround the bird and the maple leaf is enamelled in red to match the team's official colour. The inscription of World Champions 1992 wraps around the bezel. One side depicts the team's name - Toronto Blue Jays - set in two lines across the top. The 1992 World Series logo is set in a maple leaf with the inscription - Canada's 1st - positioned below the logo denoting the first Canadian World Series victory. The other side depicts the player's name and the jersey number, the American League logo and the team's 1992 season attendance record - 4,028,318 - positioned below the American League logo. Each side of the ring is accented with two rows representing the stitches of a baseball.

The 1993 World Series Championship ring features the symbols of the Toronto Blue Jays and Canada. A field of 45 diamonds in a pave style setting surrounds the Toronto Blue Jays' logo: the head of a Blue Jay enamelled in the team's official colours overlapping another Blue Jay in gold. The eye of the Blue Jay is set with a diamond solitaire stone. Two Maple Leafs, enamelled in red, symbolize Canada's back-to-back World Series victories. Two baseballs overlay each other in the background. Each ring is personalized with each player's name and jersey number, and incorporating the American League logo and the World Series logo with the inscription "Back to Back" and the years 92-93.

OPENING DAY

SEASON OPENER

DATE	OPPONENT	W/L	SCORE	WP	LP	ATT
April 7, 1977	Chicago	W	9-5	Johnson	Brett	44,649
April 7, 1978	at Detroit	L	6-2	Fidrych	Lemanczyk	52,528
April 5, 1979	at Kansas City	L	11-2	Leonard	Underwood	37,754
April 9, 1980	at Seattle	L	8-6	Parrott	Lemanczyk	22,588
April 9, 1981	at Detroit	L	6-2	Morris	McLaughlin	51,452
April 9, 1982	Milwaukee	L	15-4	Vuckovich	Bomback	30,216
April 5, 1983	at Boston	W	7-1	Stieb	Eckersley	33,842
April 4, 1984	at Seattle	L	3-2 (10)	Stanton	Lamp	43,200
April 8, 1985	at Kansas City	L	2-1	Black	Stieb	41,086
April 8, 1986	at Texas	L	6-3	Guzman	Stieb	40,602
April 6, 1987	Cleveland	W	7-3	Key	Candiotti	40,404
April 4, 1988	at Kansas City	W	5-3	Key	Saberhagen	40,648
April 3, 1989	at Kansas City	W	4-3	Key	Gubicza	38,595
April 9, 1990	at Texas	L	4-2	Ryan	Stottlemyre	40,907
April 8, 1991	Boston	L	6-2	Clemens	Stieb	50,114
April 6, 1992	at Detroit	W	4-2	Morris	Gullickson	51,068
April 6, 1993	at Seattle	L	8-1	Johnson	Morris	56,120
April 4, 1994	Chicago	W	7-3	Guzman	McDowell	50,484
April 26, 1995	Oakland	W	13-1	Cone	Stewart	50,426
April 1, 1996	at Oakland (Las Vegas)	W	9-6	Hanson	Reyes	7,294
April 1, 1997	Chicago	L	6-5 (10)	Castillo	Plesac	40,299
April 1, 1998	Minnesota	W	3-2	Clemens	Tewksbury	41,387
April 6, 1999	at Minnesota	L	6-1	Radke	Hentgen	45,601
April 3, 2000	Kansas City	W	5-4	Koch	Spradlin	40,898
April 1, 2001	Texas (Puerto Rico)	W	8-1	Loaiza	Helling	19,891
April 1, 2002	at Boston	W	12-11	Escobar	Urbina	33,520
March 31, 2003	New York (AL)	L	8-4	Clemens	Halladay	50,119
April 5, 2004	Detroit	L	7-0	Johnson	Halladay	47,817
April 4, 2005	at Tampa Bay	W	5-2	Halladay	Brazelton	26,018
April 4, 2006	Minnesota	W	6-3	Halladay	Santana	50,449
April 2, 2007	at Detroit	W	5-3 (10)	Frasor	Rodney	44,297
April 1, 2008	at New York (AL)	L	2-3	Wang	Halladay	55,112
April 6, 2009	Detroit	W	12-5	Halladay	Verlander	48,027
April 5, 2010	at Texas	L	4-5	Francisco	Frasor	50,299
April 1, 2011	Minnesota	W	13-3	Romero	Pavano	47,984
April 5, 2012	at Cleveland	W	7-4 (16)	Perez	Asencio	43,190

OPENING UP

Toronto's 16-inning contest at Cleveland to begin the 2012 season was the of longest opening day game in Major League history…The Jays won 7-4 in 16 innings after J.P. Arencibia broke the tie with a three-run home run.

In fact, the Blue Jays started the 2012 season with consecutive extra-inning games for the first time in franchise history…It marked the 5th time in MLB history that a team started 2-0 with two extra innings wins on the road - others were the 1908 St. Louis Browns, 1910 Cleveland Naps, 1935 Indians and 2007 Braves.

HOME OPENER

DATE	OPPONENT	W/L	SCORE	WP	LP	ATT
April 7, 1977	Chicago	W	9-5	Johnson	Brett	44,649
April 14, 1978	Detroit	W	10-8	Kirkwood	Wilcox	35,761
April 13, 1979	Kansas City	W	4-1	Clancy	Splittorf	40,035
April 16, 1980	Milwaukee	W	11-2	Stieb	Slaton	12,688
April 13, 1981	New York	W	5-1	Clancy	John	25,112
April 9, 1982	Milwaukee	L	15-4	Vuckovich	Bomback	30,216
April 9, 1983	New York	W	7-4	Jackson	Gossage	36,459
April 17, 1984	Baltimore	W	3-2	Key	T.Martinez	35,602
April 16, 1985	Texas	L	9-4	Mason	Leal	41,284
April 14, 1986	Baltimore	L	2-1	Boddicker	Alexander	43,587
April 6, 1987	Cleveland	W	7-3	Key	Candiotti	40,404
April 11, 1988	New York	W	17-9	Wells	Rhoden	45,185
April 14, 1989	Kansas City	W	3-0	Key	Leibrandt	46,028
April 10, 1990	Texas	W	2-1	Stieb	Hough	49,673
April 8, 1991	Boston	L	6-2	Clemens	Stieb	50,114
April 10, 1992	Baltimore	W	4-3	Hentgen	Olson	50,424
April 9, 1993	Cleveland	W	13-10	Eichhorn	Power	50,533
April 4, 1994	Chicago	W	7-3	Guzman	McDowell	50,484
April 26, 1995	Oakland	W	13-1	Cone	Stewart	50,426
April 9, 1996	California	W	5-0	Hentgen	Langston	36,316
April 1, 1997	Chicago	L	6-5(10)	Castillo	Plesac	40,299
April 1, 1998	Minnesota	W	3-2	Clemens	Tewksbury	41,387
April 12, 1999	Tampa Bay	W	7-1	Wells	Saunders	37,160
April 3, 2000	Kansas City	W	5-4	Koch	Spradlin	40,898
April 9, 2001	Tampa Bay	W	8-1	Hamilton	Wilson	48,115
April 4, 2002	Minnesota	W	7-2	Halladay	Mays	47,469
March 31, 2003	New York (AL)	L	8-4	Clemens	Halladay	50,119
April 5, 2004	Detroit	L	7-0	Johnson	Halladay	47,817
April 8, 2005	Boston	L	6-5	Arroyo	Bush	50,560
April 4, 2006	Minnesota	W	6-3	Halladay	Santana	50,449
April 9, 2007	Kansas City	W	9-1	Burnett	Perez	50,125
April 4, 2008	Boston	W	6-3	Marcum	Aardsma	50,171
April 6, 2009	Detroit	W	12-5	Halladay	Verlander	48,027
April 12, 2010	Chicago (AL)	L	7-8	Thornton	Accardo	46,321
April 1, 2011	Minnesota	W	13-3	Romero	Pavano	47,984
April 9, 2012	Boston	L	2-4	Atchison	Santos	48,473

SEASON OPENING DAY

RECORDS

OVERALL RECORD:	19-17
HOME OPENERS:	26-10
EXTRA INNINGS:	3-1
MOST RUNS:	13, 2x, last April 1, 2011 vs. Minnesota
MOST HITS:	16 vs Chicago, April 7, 1977
FEWEST HITS:	3 at Texas, April 9, 1990
MOST RUNS, OPPONENT:	15 vs Milwaukee, April 9, 1982
MOST HITS, OPPONENT:	16 vs Milwaukee, April 9, 1982
FEWEST HITS, OPPONENT:	3 at Boston, April 5, 1983
EARLIEST OPENING DAY:	vs New York (AL), March 31, 2003
LATEST OPENING DAY:	vs Oakland April 26, 1995
RECORD VS OPPONENTS:	Boston, 3-1; Chicago, 2-1; Cleveland, 2-0; Detroit, 3-3; Kansas City, 3-2; Milwaukee, 0-1; Minnesota, 3-1; Seattle, 0-3; Tampa Bay, 1-0; Texas, 1-2; Oakland, 2-0; New York, 0-1
MOST STARTS:	Roy Halladay (7)
MOST WINS:	Roy Halladay (3), Jimmy Key (3)
MOST LOSSES:	Dave Stieb (3), Roy Halladay (3)
LARGEST OPENING DAY CROWD:	50,560, April 8, 2005 vs. Boston
SMALLEST OPENING DAY CROWD:	12,688, April 16, 1980 vs Milwaukee

LINEUPS

1977
vs CHICAGO

John Scott	-LF
Hector Torres	-SS
Doug Ault	-1B
Otto Velez	-DH
Gary Woods	-CF
Steve Bowling	-RF
Pedro Garcia	-2B
Dave McKay	-3B
Rick Cerone	-C
Bill Singer	-P
Roy Hartsfield	-MGR

1978
at DETROIT

Rick Bosetti	-CF
Al Woods	-LF
Roy Howell	-3B
Rico Carty	-DH
John Mayberry	-1B
Tommy Hutton	-RF
Dave McKay	-2B
Luis Gomez	-SS
Alan Ashby	-C
Dave Lemanczyk	-P
Roy Hartsfield	-MGR

1979
at KANSAS CITY

Alfredo Griffin	-SS
Bob Bailor	-RF
Roy Howell	-3B
Rico Carty	-DH
John Mayberry	-1B
Rick Bosetti	-CF
Bobby Brown	-LF
Dave McKay	-2B
Rick Cerone	-C
Tom Underwood	-P
Roy Hartsfield	-MGR

1980
at SEATTLE

Alfredo Griffin	-SS
Bob Bailor	-RF
John Mayberry	-1B
Otto Velez	-DH
Roy Howell	-3B
Barry Bonnell	-LF
Rick Bosetti	-CF
Damaso Garcia	-2B
Ernie Whitt	-C
Dave Lemanczyk	-P
Bob Mattick	-MGR

1981
at DETROIT

Alfredo Griffin	-SS
Lloyd Moseby	-CF
Otto Velez	-DH
John Mayberry	-1B
Willie Upshaw	-LF
Damaso Garcia	-2B
Barry Bonnell	-RF
Danny Ainge	-3B
Ernie Whitt	-C
Jim Clancy	-P
Bob Mattick	-MGR

1982
vs MILWAUKEE

Alfredo Griffin	-SS
Al Woods	-LF
Lloyd Moseby	-CF
Willie Upshaw	-1B
John Mayberry	-DH
Jesse Barfield	-RF
Ernie Whitt	-C
Damaso Garcia	-2B
Rance Mulliniks	-3B
Mark Bomback	-P
Bobby Cox	-MGR

1983
at BOSTON

Damaso Garcia	-2B
Dave Collins	-LF
Willie Upshaw	-1B
Cliff Johnson	-DH
Jesse Barfield	-RF
Ernie Whitt	-C
Lloyd Moseby	-CF
Rance Mulliniks	-3B
Alfredo Griffin	-SS
Dave Stieb	-P
Bobby Cox	-MGR

1984
at SEATTLE

Damaso Garcia	-2B
Rance Mulliniks	-3B
Lloyd Moseby	-CF
Willie Upshaw	-1B
Cliff Johnson	-DH
George Bell	-LF
Jesse Barfield	-RF
Ernie Whitt	-C
Alfredo Griffin	-SS
Jim Clancy	-P
Bobby Cox	-MGR

1985
at KANSAS CITY

Damaso Garcia	-2B
Lloyd Moseby	-CF
George Bell	-LF
Jesse Barfield	-RF
Jeff Burroughs	-DH
Willie Upshaw	-1B
Buck Martinez	-C
Garth Iorg	-3B
Tony Fernandez	-SS
Dave Stieb	-P
Bobby Cox	-MGR

1986
at TEXAS

Lloyd Moseby	-CF
Tony Fernandez	-SS
Rance Mulliniks	-3B
Willie Upshaw	-1B
George Bell	-LF
Jesse Barfield	-RF
Ernie Whitt	-C
Cecil Fielder	-DH
Damaso Garcia	-2B
Dave Stieb	-P
Jimy Williams	-MGR

1987
vs CLEVELAND

Tony Fernandez	-SS
Rance Mulliniks	-3B
Lloyd Moseby	-CF
George Bell	-LF
Jesse Barfield	-RF
Willie Upshaw	-1B
Ernie Whitt	-C
Fred McGriff	-DH
Mike Sharperson	-2B
Jimmy Key	-P
Jimy Williams	-MGR

1988
at KANSAS CITY

Nelson Liriano	-2B
Lloyd Moseby	-LF
Tony Fernandez	-SS
George Bell	-DH
Rance Mulliniks	-3B
Ernie Whitt	-C
Jesse Barfield	-RF
Fred McGriff	-1B
Sil Campusano	-CF
Jimmy Key	-P
Jimy Williams	-MGR

1989
at KANSAS CITY

Lloyd Moseby	-CF
Rance Mulliniks	-3B
Tony Fernandez	-SS
George Bell	-LF
Fred McGriff	-1B
Jesse Barfield	-RF
Ernie Whitt	-C
Nelson Liriano	-DH
Manny Lee	2B
Jimmy Key	-P
Jimy Williams	-MGR

1990
at TEXAS

Tony Fernandez	-SS
Mookie Wilson	-CF
Kelly Gruber	-3B
George Bell	-LF
Fred McGriff	-1B
John Olerud	-DH
Greg Myers	-C
Nelson Liriano	-2B
Junior Felix	-RF
Todd Stottlemyre	-P
Cito Gaston	-MGR

1991
vs BOSTON

Devon White	-CF
Roberto Alomar	-2B
Kelly Gruber	-3B
Joe Carter	-RF
John Olerud	-1B
Rance Mulliniks	-DH
Greg Myers	-C
Manuel Lee	-SS
Mookie Wilson	-LF
Dave Stieb	-P
Cito Gaston	-MGR

1992
at DETROIT

Devon White	-CF
Roberto Alomar	-2B
Joe Carter	-RF
Dave Winfield	-DH
Kelly Gruber	-3B
John Olerud	-1B
Derek Bell	-LF
Pat Borders	-C
Manuel Lee	-SS
Jack Morris	-P
Cito Gaston	-MGR

1993
at SEATTLE

Devon White	-CF
Roberto Alomar	-2B
Paul Molitor	-DH
Joe Carter	-LF
Darrin Jackson	-RF
Domingo Martinez	-1B
Ed Sprague	-3B
Pat Borders	-C
Dick Schofield	-SS
Jack Morris	-P
Cito Gaston	-MGR

1994
vs CHICAGO

Devon White	-CF
Roberto Alomar	-2B
Paul Molitor	-DH
Joe Carter	-RF
John Olerud	-1B
Carlos Delgado	-LF
Ed Sprague	-3B
Pat Borders	-C
Alex Gonzalez	-SS
Juan Guzman	-P
Cito Gaston	-MGR

1995
vs OAKLAND

Devon White	-CF
Alex Gonzalez	-SS
Paul Molitor	-DH
Joe Carter	-LF
John Olerud	-1B
Roberto Alomar	-2B
Shawn Green	-RF
Ed Sprague	-3B
Lance Parrish	-C
David Cone	-P
Cito Gaston	-MGR

1996
at OAKLAND (Las Vegas)

Otis Nixon	-CF
Domingo Cedeno	-2B
Joe Carter	-LF
John Olerud	-DH
Ed Sprague	-3B
Carlos Delgado	-1B
Shawn Green	-RF
Sandy Martinez	-C
Alex Gonzalez	-SS
Erik Hanson	-P
Cito Gaston	-MGR

1997
vs Chicago
- Otis Nixon -CF
- Carlos Garcia -2B
- Orlando Merced -RF
- Joe Carter -1B
- Ed Sprague -3B
- Carlos Delgado -DH
- Benito Santiago -C
- Shawn Green -LF
- Alex Gonzalez -SS
- Pat Hentgen -P
- Cito Gaston -MGR

1998
vs Minnesota
- Shannon Stewart -LF
- Tony Fernandez -2B
- Shawn Green -RF
- Jose Canseco -DH
- Mike Stanley -1B
- Darrin Fletcher -C
- Ed Sprague -3B
- Jose Cruz Jr. -CF
- Alex Gonzalez -SS
- Roger Clemens -P
- Tim Johnson -MGR

1999
at Minnesota
- Shannon Stewart -LF
- Homer Bush -2B
- Shawn Green -RF
- Dave Hollins -DH
- Carlos Delgado -1B
- Tony Fernandez -3B
- Jose Cruz Jr. -CF
- Darrin Fletcher -C
- Alex Gonzalez -SS
- Pat Hentgen -P
- Jim Fregosi -MGR

2000
vs Kansas City
- Shannon Stewart -LF
- Homer Bush -2B
- Raul Mondesi -RF
- Carlos Delgado -1B
- Brad Fullmer -DH
- Tony Batista -3B
- Darrin Fletcher -C
- Jose Cruz Jr. -CF
- Alex Gonzalez -SS
- David Wells -P
- Jim Fregosi -MGR

2001
vs Texas (Puerto Rico)
- Shannon Stewart -LF
- Alex Gonzalez -SS
- Raul Mondesi -RF
- Carlos Delgado -1B
- Brad Fullmer -DH
- Tony Batista -3B
- Darrin Fletcher -C
- Jose Cruz Jr. -CF
- Homer Bush -2B
- Esteban Loaiza -P
- Buck Martinez -MGR

2002
at Boston
- Shannon Stewart -DH
- Eric Hinske -3B
- Raul Mondesi -RF
- Carlos Delgado -1B
- Jose Cruz Jr. -LF
- Darrin Fletcher -C
- Vernon Wells -CF
- Homer Bush -2B
- Felipe Lopez -SS
- Chris Carpenter -P
- Buck Martinez -MGR

2003
vs New York
- Shannon Stewart -LF
- Frank Catalanotto -RF
- Vernon Wells -CF
- Carlos Delgado -1B
- Josh Phelps -DH
- Eric Hinske -3B
- Orlando Hudson -2B
- Chris Woodward -SS
- Ken Huckaby -C
- Roy Halladay -P
- Carlos Tosca -MGR

2004
vs Detroit
- Reed Johnson -RF
- Frank Catalanotto -LF
- Vernon Wells -CF
- Carlos Delgado -1B
- Josh Phelps -DH
- Eric Hinske -3B
- Orlando Hudson -2B
- Chris Woodward -SS
- Kevin Cash -C
- Roy Halladay -P
- Carlos Tosca -MGR

2005
at Tampa Bay
- Frank Catalanotto -LF
- Orlando Hudson -2B
- Vernon Wells -CF
- Corey Koskie -3B
- She Hillenbrand -DH
- Eric Hinske -1B
- Gregg Zaun -C
- Gabe Gross -RF
- Russ Adams -SS
- Roy Halladay -P
- John Gibbons -MGR

2006
at Minnesota
- Reed Johnson -LF
- Alex Rios -RF
- Vernon Wells -CF
- Troy Glaus -3B
- Lyle Overbay -1B
- Shea Hillenbrand -DH
- Bengie Molina -C
- Aaron Hill -2B
- Russ Adams -SS
- Roy Halladay -P
- John Gibbons -MGR

2007
at Detroit
- Reed Johnson -LF
- Lyle Overbay -1B
- Vernon Wells -CF
- Frank Thomas -DH
- Troy Glaus -3B
- Alex Rios- -RF
- Aaron Hill -2B
- Gregg Zaun -C
- Royce Clayton -SS
- Roy Halladay -P
- John Gibbons -MGR

2008
at New York
- David Eckstein -SS
- Shannon Stewart -LF
- Alex Rios- -RF
- Vernon Wells -CF
- Frank Thomas -DH
- Lyle Overbay -1B
- Aaron Hill -2B
- Marco Scutaro -3B
- Gregg Zaun -C
- Roy Halladay -P
- John Gibbons -MGR

2009
vs. Detroit
- Marco Scutaro -SS
- Aaron Hill -2B
- Alex Rios- -RF
- Vernon Wells -CF
- Adam Lind -DH
- Scott Rolen -3B
- Lyle Overbay -1B
- Rod Barajas -C
- Travis Snider -LF
- Roy Halladay -P
- Cito Gaston -MGR

2010
at Texas
- Jose Bautista -RF
- Aaron Hill -2B
- Adam Lind -DH
- Vernon Wells -CF
- Lyle Overbay -1B
- John Buck -C
- Edwin Encarnacion-3B
- Alex Gonzalez -SS
- Travis Snider -LF
- Shaun Marcum -P
- Cito Gaston -MGR

2011
vs. Minnesota
- Rajai Davis -CF
- Yunel Escobar -SS
- Jose Bautista -RF
- Adam Lind -1B
- Aaron Hill -2B
- Edwin Encarnacion-3B
- Travis Snider -LF
- Juan Rivera -DH
- J.P. Arencibia -C
- Ricky Romero -P
- John Farrell -MGR

2012
at Indians
- Yunel Escobar -SS
- Kelly Johnson -2B
- Jose Bautista -RF
- Adam Lind -1B
- Edwin Encarnacion-DH
- Brett Lawrie -3B
- Eric Thames -LF
- J.P. Arencibia -C
- Colby Rasmus -CF
- Ricky Romero -P
- John Farrell -MGR

Home Opener vs. Boston, 2012

HISTORICAL STATISTICS

SEASON SUMMARY

2011

BATTER	Pos	AVG	G	AB	R	H	HR	RBI
ARENCIBIA,JP		.219	129	443	47	97	23	78
BAUTISTA,Jose		.302	149	513	105	155	43	103
COOPER,David		.211	27	71	9	15	2	12
DAVIS,Rajai		.238	95	320	44	76	1	29
ENCARNACION,Edwin		.272	134	481	70	131	17	55
ESCOBAR,Yunel		.290	133	513	77	149	11	48
HILL,Aaron		.225	104	396	38	89	6	45
JOHNSON,Kelly		.270	33	115	16	31	3	9
LAWRIE,Brett		.293	43	150	26	44	9	25
LIND,Adam		.251	125	499	56	125	26	87
LOEWEN,Adam		.188	14	32	4	6	1	4
MASTROIANNI,Darin		.000	1	2	0	0	0	0
MCCOY,Mike		.198	80	197	26	39	2	10
MCDONALD,John		.250	65	168	19	42	2	20
MOLINA,Jose		.281	55	171	19	48	3	15
MORROW,Brandon		.000	30	6	0	0	0	0
NIX,Jayson		.169	46	136	15	23	4	16
PATTERSON,Corey		.252	89	317	44	80	6	33
RASMUS,Colby		.173	35	133	14	23	3	13
REYES,Jo-Jo		.250	20	4	0	1	0	0
RIVERA,Juan		.243	70	247	22	60	6	28
ROMERO,Ricky		.167	32	6	0	1	0	2
SNIDER,Travis		.225	49	187	23	42	3	30
STEWART,Zach		.000	3	2	0	0	0	0
TEAHEN,Mark		.190	27	42	3	8	1	3
THAMES,Eric		.262	95	362	58	95	12	37
VILLANUEVA,Carlos		.000	33	4	1	0	0	0
WISE,Dewayne		.125	20	32	4	4	2	2
WOODWARD,Chris		.000	11	10	3	0	0	0
2011 Totals		**.249**	**162**	**5559**	**743**	**1384**	**186**	**704**

PITCHER	W	L	ERA	SV	IP	H	ER	BB	SO
ALVAREZ,Henderson	1	3	3.53	0	63.2	64	25	8	40
BECK,Chad	0	0	0.00	0	2.1	1	0	0	3
CAMP,Shawn	6	3	4.21	1	66.1	79	31	22	32
CARRENO,Joel	1	0	1.15	0	15.2	11	2	4	14
CECIL,Brett	4	11	4.73	0	123.2	122	65	42	87
DOTEL,Octavio	2	1	3.68	1	29.1	20	12	12	30
DRABEK,Kyle	4	5	6.06	0	78.2	87	53	55	51
FARQUHAR,Daniel	0	0	13.50	0	2.0	4	3	2	1
FRANCISCO,Francisco	1	4	3.55	17	50.2	49	20	18	53
FRASOR,Jason	2	1	2.98	0	42.1	38	14	15	37
JANSSEN,Casey	6	0	2.26	2	55.2	47	14	14	53
LEDEZMA,Wil	0	0	15.00	0	6.0	11	10	7	6
LEWIS JR.,Rommie	0	0	9.00	0	5.0	12	5	2	5
LITSCH,Jesse	6	3	4.44	1	75.0	69	37	28	66
MCCOY,Mike	0	0	0.00	0	1.0	0	0	0	0
MCGOWAN,Dustin	0	2	6.43	0	21.0	20	15	13	20
MILLER,Trever	0	0	4.91	0	3.2	6	2	2	2
MILLS,Brad	1	2	9.82	0	18.1	23	20	12	18
MORROW,Brandon	11	11	4.72	0	179.1	162	94	69	203
PEREZ,Luis	3	3	5.12	0	65.0	74	37	27	54
PURCEY,David	0	0	11.57	0	2.1	3	3	4	3
RAUCH,Jon	5	4	4.85	11	52.0	56	28	14	36
REYES,Jo-Jo	5	8	5.40	0	110.0	140	66	35	64
RICHMOND,Scott	0	0	0.00	0	0.1	0	0	0	0
ROMERO,Ricky	15	11	2.92	0	225.0	176	73	80	178
RZEPCZYNSKI,Marc	2	3	2.97	0	39.1	28	13	15	33
STEWART,Zach	0	1	4.86	0	16.2	26	9	5	10
TALLET,Brian	0	1	54.00	0	0.1	2	2	2	1
VILLANUEVA,Carlos	6	4	4.04	0	107.0	103	48	32	68
WALTERS,PJ	0	0	0.00	0	1.0	0	0	1	1
2011 Totals	**81**	**81**	**4.32**	**33**	**1458.2**	**1433**	**700**	**540**	**1169**

2010

BATTER	Pos	AVG	G	AB	R	H	HR	RBI
ARENCIBIA,J.P	C-DH	.143	11	35	3	5	2	4
BAUTISTA,Jose	IF-OF-DH	.260	161	569	109	148	54	124
BUCK,John	C-DH	.281	118	409	53	115	20	66
CAMP,Shawn	P	1.000	70	1	0	1	0	0
CECIL,Brett	P	.000	28	2	0	0	0	0
ENCARNACION,Edwin	IF-DH	.244	96	332	47	81	21	51
ESCOBAR,Yunel	IF	.275	60	236	32	65	4	16
GONZALEZ,Alex	IF	.259	85	328	47	85	17	50
GREEN,Nick	IF-DH	.154	9	13	2	2	0	1
HILL,Aaron	IF-DH	.205	138	528	70	108	26	68
HOFFPAUIR,Jarrett	IF	.206	13	34	1	7	0	0
JANSSEN,Casey	P	.000	56	1	0	0	0	0
LEWIS,Fred	OF-DH	.262	110	428	70	112	8	36
LIND,Adam	IF-OF	.237	150	569	57	135	23	72
LITSCH,Jesse	P	.000	9	1	0	0	0	0
MARCUM,Shaun	P	.250	31	4	1	1	0	1
MCCOY,Mike	IF-OF	.195	46	82	9	16	0	3
McDONALD,John	IF-OF	.250	63	152	27	38	6	23
MOLINA,Jose	C-DH	.246	57	167	13	41	6	12
MORROW,Brandon	P	.000	26	3	0	0	0	0
OVERBAY,Lyle	IF	.243	154	534	75	130	20	67
REED,Jeremy	OF	.143	14	21	1	3	1	3
ROMERO,Ricky	P	.000	32	4	0	0	0	0
RUIZ,Randy	IF-OF-DH	.150	13	40	3	6	1	1
SNIDER,Travis	OF	.255	82	298	36	76	14	32
TALLET,Brian	P	.000	34	1	0	0	0	0
WELLS,Vernon	OF-DH	.273	157	590	79	161	31	88
WISE,Dewayne	OF-DH	.250	52	112	20	28	3	14
2010 Totals		**.248**	**162**	**5495**	**755**	**1364**	**257**	**732**

PITCHER	W	L	ERA	SV	IP	H	ER	BB	SO
ACCARDO,Jeremy	0	1	8.10	0	6.2	12	6	3	3
BUCHHOLZ,Taylor	0	0	0.00	0	2.0	0	0	0	0
CAMP,Shawn	4	3	2.99	2	72.1	71	24	18	46
CARLSON,Jesse	0	0	4.61	1	13.2	13	7	5	8
CECIL,Brett	15	7	4.22	0	172.2	175	81	54	117
DOWNS,Scott	5	5	2.64	0	61.1	47	18	14	48
DRABEK,Kyle	0	3	4.76	0	17.0	18	9	5	12
EVELAND,Dana	3	4	6.45	0	44.2	57	32	27	21
FRASOR,Jason	3	4	3.68	4	63.2	61	26	27	65
GREGG,Kevin	2	6	3.51	37	59.0	52	23	30	58
HILL,Shawn	1	2	2.61	0	20.2	24	6	4	14
JANSSEN,Casey	5	2	3.67	0	68.2	74	28	21	63
LEWIS,Rommie	0	0	6.75	0	18.2	20	14	8	15
LITSCH,Jesse	1	5	5.79	0	46.2	53	30	15	16
MARCUM,Shaun	13	8	3.64	0	195.1	181	79	43	165
MILLS,Brad	1	0	5.64	0	22.1	20	14	13	18
MORROW,Brandon	10	7	4.49	0	146.1	136	73	66	178
PURCEY,David	1	1	3.71	1	34.0	26	14	15	32
RAY,Robert	0	0	2.45	0	3.2	2	1	5	3
ROENICKE,Josh	1	0	5.68	0	19.0	18	12	13	18
ROMERO,Ricky	14	9	3.73	0	210.0	189	87	82	174
RZEPCZYNSKI,Marc	4	4	4.95	0	63.2	72	35	30	57
TALLET,Brian	2	6	6.40	0	77.1	84	55	38	53
VALDEZ,Merkin	0	0	20.25	0	1.1	2	3	3	0
2010 Totals	**85**	**77**	**4.22**	**45**	**1440.2**	**1407**	**676**	**539**	**1184**

2009

BATTER	Pos	AVG	G	AB	R	H	HR	RBI
ADAMS,Russ	IF-OF	.200	8	20	2	4	0	0
BARAJAS,Rod	C	.226	125	429	43	97	19	71
BARRETT,Michael	C	.167	7	18	3	3	1	2
BAUTISTA,Jose	IF-OF	.235	113	336	54	79	13	40
CECIL,Brett	P	.000	18	2	0	0	0	0
CHAVEZ,Raul	C	.258	51	159	10	41	2	15
DELLUCCI,David	OF	.040	8	25	2	1	0	2
DOWNS,Scott	P	.000	48	1	0	0	0	0
ENCARNACION,Edwin	IF	.240	42	154	25	37	8	23
HALLADAY,Roy	P	.000	32	1	0	0	0	0
HILL,Aaron	IF	.286	158	682	103	195	36	108
INGLETT,Joe	IF-OF	.281	36	89	11	25	0	6
JANSSEN,Casey	P	.000	21	1	0	0	0	0
LIND,Adam	OF-DH	.305	151	587	93	179	35	114
McDONALD,John	IF	.258	73	151	18	39	4	13
MILLAR,Kevin	IF-DH	.223	78	251	29	56	7	29
MILLS,Brad	P	.000	2	1	0	0	0	0
OVERBAY,Lyle	IF	.265	132	423	57	112	16	64
PHILLIPS,Kyle	C	.278	5	18	1	5	0	2
RICHMOND,Scott	P	.000	27	6	0	0	0	0
RIOS,Alex	OF	.264	108	436	52	115	14	62
ROLEN,Scott	IF	.320	88	338	52	108	8	43
ROMERO,Ricky	P	.000	29	6	0	0	0	0
RUIZ,Randy	IF-DH	.313	33	115	25	36	10	17
SCUTARO,Marco	IF	.282	144	574	100	162	12	60
SNIDER,Travis	OF	.241	77	241	34	58	9	29
TALLET,Brian	P	.000	37	2	0	0	0	0
WELLS,Vernon	OF	.260	158	630	84	164	15	66
2009 Totals		**.266**	**162**	**5696**	**798**	**1516**	**209**	**766**

PITCHER	W	L	ERA	SV	IP	H	ER	BB	SO
ACCARDO,Jeremy	0	0	2.55	1	24.2	23	7	17	18
BILLINGTON,Brian	0	0	3.00	0	6.0	7	2	6	5
BURRES,Brian	0	2	14.21	0	6.1	12	10	5	4
CAMP,Shawn	2	6	3.50	1	79.2	73	31	29	58
CARLSON,Jesse	1	6	4.66	0	67.2	67	35	21	51
CECIL,Brett	7	4	5.30	0	93.1	116	55	38	69
DOWNS,Scott	1	3	3.09	9	46.2	46	16	13	43
FRASOR,Jason	7	3	2.50	11	57.2	43	16	16	56
HALLADAY,Roy	17	10	2.79	0	239.0	234	74	35	208
HAYHURST,Dirk	0	0	2.78	0	22.2	23	7	9	13
JANSSEN,Casey	2	4	5.85	1	40.0	59	26	14	24
LEAGUE,Brandon	3	6	4.58	0	74.2	72	38	21	76
LITSCH,Jesse	0	1	9.00	0	9.0	14	9	1	8
MILLS,Brad	0	1	14.09	0	7.2	14	12	6	9
MURPHY,Bill	0	0	3.18	0	11.1	4	4	8	6
PURCEY,David	1	3	6.19	0	48.0	54	33	30	39
RAY,Robert	1	2	4.44	0	24.1	23	12	6	13
RICHMOND,Scott	8	11	5.52	0	138.2	147	85	59	117
ROENICKE,Josh	0	0	7.13	0	17.2	19	14	12	19
ROMERO,Ricky	13	9	4.30	0	178.0	192	85	79	141
RYAN,B.J.	1	1	6.53	2	20.2	22	15	17	13
RZEPCZYNSKI,Marc	2	4	3.67	0	61.1	51	25	30	60
TALLET,Brian	7	9	5.32	0	160.2	169	95	72	120
WOLFE,Brian	2	2	8.22	0	15.1	25	14	7	11
2009 Totals	**75**	**87**	**4.47**	**25**	**1451.0**	**1509**	**720**	**551**	**1181**

2008

BATTER	Pos	AVG	G	AB	R	H	HR	RBI
BARAJAS, Rod	C	.249	104	349	44	87	11	49
BAUTISTA,Jose	IF-OF	.214	21	56	7	12	3	10
BURNETT, A.J.	P	.000	35	3	0	0	0	0
HALLADAY, Roy	P	.000	34	4	0	0	0	0
HILL, Aaaron	IF	.263	55	205	19	54	2	20
INGLETT, Joe	IF-OF	.297	109	344	45	102	3	39
LIND, Adam	OF-DH	.282	88	326	48	92	9	40
LITSCH, Jesse	P	.000	29	3	0	0	0	0
MARCUM, Shaun	P	.000	25	2	0	0	0	0
McDONALD, John	IF	.210	84	186	21	39	1	18
McGOWAN, Dustin	P	.000	19	3	0	0	0	0
MENCH, Kevin	OF	.243	51	115	18	28	0	10
OVERBAY, Lyle	IF	.270	158	544	74	147	15	69
PURCEY, David	P	.000	12	1	0	0	0	0
RIOS, Alex	OF	.291	155	635	91	185	15	79
ROLEN, Scott	IF	.262	115	408	58	107	11	50
SCUTARO, Marco	IF	.267	145	517	76	138	7	60
SNIDER, Travis	OF	.301	24	73	9	22	2	13
THIGPEN, Curtis	C	.176	10	17	2	3	1	1
WELLS, Vernon	OF	.300	108	427	63	128	20	78
WILKERSON, Brad	OF	.216	85	208	20	45	4	23
ZAUN, Gregg	C	.237	86	245	29	58	6	30
2008 Totals		**.264**	**162**	**5503**	**714**	**1453**	**126**	**681**

PITCHER	W	L	ERA	SV	IP	H	ER	BB	SO
ACCARDO, Jeremy	0	3	6.57	4	12.1	15	9	4	5
BENITEZ, Armando	0	1	5.68	0	6.1	4	4	2	9
BURNETT, A.J.	18	10	4.07	0	221.1	211	100	86	231
CAMP, Shawn	3	1	4.12	0	39.1	40	18	11	31
CARLSON, Jesse	7	2	2.25	2	60.0	41	15	21	55
DOWNS, Scott	0	3	1.78	5	70.2	54	14	27	57
FRASOR, Jason	1	2	4.18	0	47.1	36	22	32	42
HALLADAY, Roy	20	11	2.78	0	246.0	220	76	39	206
LEAGUE, Brandon	1	2	2.18	1	33.0	28	8	15	23
LITSCH, Jesse	13	9	3.58	0	176.0	178	70	39	99
MARCUM, Shaun	9	7	3.39	0	151.1	126	57	50	123
McGOWAN, Dustin	6	7	4.37	0	111.1	115	54	38	85
PARRISH, John	1	1	4.04	0	42.1	47	19	15	21
PURCEY, David	3	6	5.54	0	65.0	67	40	29	58
RICHMOND, Scott	1	3	4.00	0	27.0	32	12	2	20
RYAN, B.J.	2	4	2.95	32	58.0	46	19	28	58
TALLET, Brian	1	2	2.88	0	56.1	52	18	22	47
WELLS, Randy	0	0	0.00	0	1.0	0	0	1	0
WOLFE, Brian	0	2	2.45	0	22.0	18	6	6	14
2008 Totals	**86**	**76**	**3.49**	**44**	**1446.2**	**1330**	**561**	**467**	**1184**

2007

BATTER	Pos	AVG	G	AB	R	H	HR	RBI
ADAMS,Russ	IF	.233	27	60	14	14	2	12
BURNETT,A.J.	P	.000	25	2	0	0	0	0
CLARK,Howie	IF-OF	.204	31	49	6	10	0	2
CLAYTON, Royce	IF	.254	69	189	23	48	1	12
FASANO, Sal	C	.178	16	45	5	8	1	4
GLAUS, Troy	IF	.262	115	385	60	101	20	62
GRIFFIN, John-Ford	OF	.300	6	10	4	3	1	3
HALLADAY, Roy	P	.500	31	4	0	2	0	1
HILL, Aaron	IF	.291	160	608	87	177	17	78
INGLETT, Joe	IF-OF	.600	2	5	0	3	0	2
JOHNSON, Reed	OF	.236	79	275	31	65	2	14
LIND, Adam	OF-DH	.238	89	290	34	69	11	46
LITSCH, Jesse	P	.000	20	1	0	0	0	0
LUNA, Hector	IF	.167	22	42	5	7	1	4
MARCUM, Shaun	P	.000	38	4	0	0	0	0
MCDOANLD, John	IF	.251	123	327	32	82	1	31
MCGOWAN, Dustin	P	.286	28	7	1	2	0	0
OLEMDO, Ray	IF	.216	27	51	6	11	0	1
OVERBAY, Lyle	IF	.240	122	425	49	102	10	44
PHILLIPS, Jason	C	.208	55	144	11	30	1	12
RIOS, Alex	OF	.297	161	643	114	191	24	85
ROBERTS, Ryan	IF-OF	.077	8	13	2	1	0	0
SMITH, Jason	IF	.212	27	52	7	11	0	4
STAIRS, Matt	IF-OF-DH	.289	125	357	58	103	21	64
THIGPEN, Curtis	C	.238	47	101	13	24	0	11
THOMAS, Frank	DH	.277	155	531	63	147	26	95
TOWERS, Josh	P	.000	25	1	0	0	0	0
WELLS, Vernon	OF	.245	149	584	85	143	16	80
ZAUN, Gregg	C	.242	110	331	43	80	10	52
2007 Totals		**.259**	**162**	**5536**	**753**	**1434**	**165**	**719**

PITCHER	W	L	ERA	SV	IP	H	ER	BB	SO
ACCARDO, Jeremy	4	4	2.14	30	67.1	51	16	24	57
BANKS, Josh	0	0	7.36	0	7.1	11	6	2	2
BURNETT, A.J.	10	8	3.75	0	165.2	131	69	66	176
CHACIN, Gustavo	2	1	5.60	0	27.1	29	17	7	11
DE JONG, Jordan	0	0	8.00	0	9	11	8	5	7
DOWNS, Scott	4	2	2.17	1	58	47	14	24	57
FRASOR, Jason	1	5	4.58	3	57	47	29	23	59
GRONKEWEICZ, Lee	0	0	2.25	0	4	2	1	2	2
HALLADAY, Roy	16	7	3.71	0	225.1	232	93	48	139
JANSSEN, Casey	2	3	2.35	6	72.2	67	19	20	39
KENNEDY, Joe	1	0	5.14	0	7	6	4	5	8
LEAGUE, Brandon	0	0	6.17	0	11.2	19	8	7	7
LITSCH, Jesse	7	9	3.81	0	111	116	47	36	50
MARCUM, Shaun	12	6	4.13	1	159	149	73	49	122
MCGOWAN, Dustin	12	10	4.08	0	169.2	146	77	61	144
OHKA, Tomo	2	5	5.79	0	56	68	36	22	21
RYAN, B.J.	0	2	12.46	3	4.1	7	6	4	3
TALLET, Brian	2	4	3.47	0	62.1	49	24	28	54
TAUBENHEIM, Ty	0	0	9.00	0	5	5	5	4	4
TOWERS, Josh	5	10	5.38	0	107	129	64	22	76
VERMILYEA, Jamie	0	0	0.00	0	6	5	0	0	2
WOLFE, Brian	3	1	2.98	0	45.1	36	15	9	22
ZAMBRANO, Victor	0	3	10.17	0	23	32	26	22	16
2007 Totals	**83**	**79**	**4.00**	**44**	**1448.2**	**1383**	**644**	**479**	**1067**

2006

BATTER	Pos	AVG	G	AB	R	H	HR	RBI
ADAMS, Russ	IF	.219	90	251	31	55	3	28
BARKER, Kevin	IF-OF	.235	12	17	3	4	1	1
BURNETT, A.J.	P	.000	21	3	0	0	0	0
CATALANOTTO, Frank	OF-DH	.300	128	437	56	131	7	56
GLAUS, Troy	3B	.252	153	540	105	136	38	104
HALLADAY, Roy	P	.000	32	3	0	0	0	0
HATTIG, John	IF-DH	.333	13	24	2	8	0	3
HILL, Aaron	IF	.291	155	546	70	159	6	50
JOHNSON, Reed	OF	.319	134	461	86	147	12	49
LILLY, Ted	P	.000	32	3	0	0	0	0
LIND, Adam	OF	.367	18	60	8	22	2	8
MCDONALD, John	IF	.223	104	260	35	58	3	23
MOLINA, Bengie	C	.284	117	433	44	123	19	57
OVERBAY, Lyle	1B	.312	157	581	82	181	22	92
PHILLIPS, Jason	C-1B	.250	25	48	4	12	0	6
RIOS, Alex	OF	.302	128	450	68	136	17	82
ROSARIO, Francisco	P	.000	17	1	0	0	0	0
TOWERS, Josh	P	.200	15	5	1	1	0	0
WELLS, Vernon	OF	.303	154	611	91	185	32	106
ZAUN, Gregg	C	.272	99	290	39	79	12	40
2006 Totals		**.284**	**162**	**5596**	**809**	**1591**	**199**	**778**

PITCHER	W	L	ERA	SV	IP	H	ER	BB	SO
ACCARDO, Jeremy	1	1	5.97	0	28.2	38	19	0	2
BURNETT, A.J.	10	8	3.98	0	135.2	138	60	39	118
CHACIN, Gustavo	9	4	5.05	0	87.1	90	49	38	47
DOWNS, Scott	6	2	4.09	1	77.0	73	35	30	61
FRASOR, Jason	3	2	4.32	0	50.0	47	24	17	51
HALLADAY, Roy	16	5	3.19	0	220.0	208	78	34	132
LEAGUE, Brandon	1	2	2.53	1	42.2	34	12	9	29
LILLY, Ted	15	13	4.31	0	181.2	179	87	81	160
MARCUM, Shaun	3	4	5.06	0	78.1	87	44	38	65
MCGOWAN, Dustin	1	2	7.24	0	27.1	35	22	25	22
ROMERO, Davis	1	0	3.86	0	16.1	19	7	6	10
ROSARIO, Francisco	1	2	6.65	0	23.0	24	17	16	21
RYAN, B.J.	2	2	1.37	38	72.1	42	11	20	86
SPEIER, Justin	2	0	2.98	0	51.1	47	17	21	55
TALLET, Brian	3	0	3.81	0	54.1	45	23	31	37
TOWERS, Josh	2	10	8.42	0	62.0	93	58	17	35
WALKER, Pete	1	1	5.40	1	30.0	37	18	13	27
2006 Totals	**87**	**75**	**4.37**	**42**	**1428.1**	**1447**	**694**	**504**	**1076**

2005

BATTER	Pos	AVG	G	AB	R	H	HR	RBI
ADAMS, Russ	SS	.256	139	481	68	123	8	63
CATALANOTTO, Frank	OF	.301	130	419	56	126	8	59
GRIFFIN, John-Ford	OF	.308	7	13	3	4	1	6
GROSS, Gabe	OF	.250	40	92	11	23	1	7
HILL, Aaron	IF	.274	105	361	49	99	3	40
HILLENBRAND, Shea	DH-IF	.291	152	594	91	173	18	82
HINSKE, Eric	1B	.262	147	477	79	125	15	68
HUCKABY, Ken	C	.207	35	87	8	18	0	6
HUDSON, Orlando	2B	.271	131	461	62	125	10	63
JOHNSON, Reed	OF	.269	142	398	55	107	8	58
KOSKIE, Corey	3B	.249	97	354	49	88	11	36
MENECHINO, Frank	IF	.216	70	148	22	32	4	13
QUIROZ, Guillermo	C	.194	12	36	3	7	0	4
RIOS, Alex	OF	.262	146	481	71	126	10	59
WELLS, Vernon	OF	.269	156	620	78	167	28	97
ZAUN, Gregg	C	.251	133	434	61	109	11	61
CHACIN, Gustavo	P	.000	34	7	1	0	0	0
HALLADAY, Roy	P	.000	19	2	0	0	0	0
LILLY, Ted	P	.000	25	3	0	0	0	0
TOWERS, Josh	P	.000	33	6	0	0	0	0
2005 Totals		**.265**	**162**	**5581**	**775**	**1480**	**136**	**735**

PITCHER	W	L	ERA	SV	IP	H	ER	BB	SO
BATISTA, Miguel	5	8	4.10	31	74.2	80	34	27	54
BUSH, Dave	5	11	4.49	0	136.1	142	68	29	75
CHACIN, Gustavo	13	9	3.72	0	203.0	213	84	70	121
CHULK, Vinnie	0	1	3.88	0	72.0	68	31	26	39
DOWNS, Scott	4	3	4.31	0	94.0	93	45	34	75
FRASOR, Jason	3	5	3.25	1	74.2	67	27	28	62
HALLADAY, Roy	12	4	2.41	0	141.2	118	38	18	108
LEAGUE, Brandon	1	0	6.56	0	35.2	42	26	20	17
LILLY, Ted	10	11	5.56	0	126.1	135	78	58	96
MARCUM, Shaun	0	0	0.00	0	8.0	6	0	4	4
MCGOWAN, Dustin	1	3	6.35	0	45.1	49	32	17	34
SCHOENEWEIS, Scott	3	4	3.32	1	57.0	54	21	25	43
SPEIER, Justin	3	2	2.57	0	66.2	48	19	15	56
TOWERS, Josh	13	12	3.71	0	208.2	237	86	29	112
WALKER, Pete	6	6	3.54	2	84.0	81	33	33	43
2005 Totals	**80**	**82**	**4.06**	**35**	**1447.0**	**1475**	**653**	**444**	**958**

2004

BATTER	Pos	AVG	G	AB	R	H	HR	RBI
ADAMS, Russ	SS	.306	22	72	10	22	4	10
BATISTA, Miguel	P	.000	38	5	0	0	0	0
BERG, Dave	IF-OF	.253	58	154	13	39	3	23
BUSH, Dave	P	.000	16	2	0	0	0	0
CASH, Kevin	C	.193	60	181	18	35	4	21
CATALANOTTO, Frank	OF	.293	75	249	27	73	1	26
CLARK, Howie	IF-OF	.217	40	115	17	25	3	12
CROZIER, Eric	1B	.152	14	33	5	5	2	4
DELGADO, Carlos	1B	.269	128	458	74	123	32	99
ESTALELLA, Bobby	C	.231	5	13	1	3	0	0
FILE, Bob	P	.000	24	1	0	0	0	0
GOMEZ, Chris	IF	.282	109	341	41	96	3	37
GROSS, Gabe	OF	.209	44	129	18	27	3	16
HALLADAY, Roy	P	.000	21	6	0	0	0	0
HENTGEN, Pat	P	.000	18	1	0	0	0	0
HERMANSEN, Chad	OF	.000	4	7	0	0	0	0
HINSKE, Eric	IF	.246	155	570	66	140	15	69
HUDSON, Orlando	2B	.270	135	489	73	132	12	58
JOHNSON, Reed	OF	.270	141	537	68	145	10	61
LILLY, Ted	P	.000	32	3	0	0	0	0
MENECHINO, Frank	IF	.301	72	236	40	71	9	25
MYERS, Greg	C	.222	8	18	0	4	0	1
PHELPS, Josh	1B-DH	.237	79	295	38	70	12	51
POND, Simon	IF-OF	.163	16	49	4	8	1	6
QUIROZ, Guillermo	C	.212	17	52	2	11	0	6
RIOS, Alex	OF	.286	111	426	55	122	1	28
SPEIER, Justin	P	.000	62	1	0	0	0	0
TOWERS, Josh	P	.000	21	1	0	0	0	0
WELLS, Vernon	OF	.272	134	536	82	146	23	67
WOODWARD, Chris	IF	.235	69	213	21	50	1	24
ZAUN, Gregg	C	.269	107	338	46	91	6	36
2004 Totals		**.260**	**161**	**5531**	**719**	**1438**	**145**	**680**

PITCHER	W	L	ERA	SV	IP	H	ER	BB	SO
ADAMS, Terry	4	4	3.98	3	43.0	49	19	22	35
BATISTA, Miguel	10	13	4.8	5	198.2	206	106	96	104
BUSH, Dave	5	4	3.69	0	97.2	95	40	25	64
CHACIN, Gustavo	1	1	2.57	0	14.0	8	4	3	6
CHULK, Vinnie	1	3	4.66	2	56.0	59	29	27	44
DE LOS SANTOS, Valerio	0	0	6.17	0	11.2	11	8	10	10
DOUGLASS, Sean	0	2	6.28	0	38.2	37	27	28	36
FILE, Bob	1	0	4.81	0	33.2	45	18	12	15
FRASOR, Jason	4	6	4.08	17	68.1	64	31	36	54
FREDERICK, Kevin	0	2	6.59	0	28.2	32	21	16	22
GLYNN, Ryan	1	0	4.05	0	20.0	19	9	8	14
HALLADAY, Roy	8	8	4.2	0	133.0	140	62	39	95
HENTGEN, Pat	2	9	6.95	0	80.1	90	62	42	33
KERSHNER, Jason	0	1	6.04	0	22.1	30	15	8	15
LEAGUE, Brandon	1	0	0	0	4.2	3	0	1	2
LIGTENBERG, Kerry	1	6	6.38	3	55.0	73	39	25	49
LILLY, Ted	12	10	4.06	0	197.1	171	89	89	168
LOPEZ, Aquilino	1	1	6	0	21.0	21	14	13	13
MAUER, Dave	0	0	54	0	1.1	6	8	5	1
MENECHINO, Frank	0	0	0	0	0.1	2	0	0	0
MILLER, Justin	3	4	6.06	0	81.2	101	55	42	47
NAKAMURA, Micheal	0	3	7.36	0	25.2	27	21	7	24
PETERSON, Adam	0	0	16.88	0	2.2	7	5	3	2
SPEIER, Justin	3	8	3.91	7	69.0	61	30	25	52
TOWERS, Josh	9	9	5.11	0	116.1	148	66	26	51
2004 Totals	**67**	**94**	**4.91**	**37**	**1421.0**	**1505**	**775**	**608**	**956**

2003

BATTER	Pos.	Avg.	G	AB	R	H	HR	RBI
BERG, Dave	IF-OF-DH	.255	61	161	26	41	4	18
BORDICK, Mike	SS-3B-2B	.274	102	343	39	94	5	54
CASH, Kevin	C	.142	34	106	10	15	1	8
CATALANOTTO, Frank	OF-DH-1B	.299	133	489	83	146	13	59
CLARK, Howie	IF-OF-DH	.357	38	70	9	25	0	7
DAVIS, Doug	P	.000	12	1	0	0	0	0
DELGADO, Carlos	1B-DH	.302	161	570	117	172	42	145
ESCOBAR, Kelvim	P	.167	41	6	1	1	0	1
HALLADAY, Roy	P	.111	36	9	2	1	0	0
HENDRICKSON, Mark	P	.250	30	4	1	1	1	1
HINSKE, Eric	3B	.243	124	449	74	109	12	63
HUCKABY, Ken	C	.182	5	11	1	2	0	2
HUDSON, Orlando	2B	.268	142	474	54	127	9	57
JOHNSON, Reed	OF	.294	114	412	79	121	10	52
KIELTY, Bobby	OF-1B	.233	62	189	31	44	4	25
LIDLE, Cory	P	.333	31	6	1	2	0	0
MYERS, Greg	C-DH	.307	121	329	51	101	15	52
PHELPS, Josh	DH-1B	.268	119	396	57	106	20	66
STEWART, Shannon	OF-DH	.294	71	303	47	89	7	35
TAM, Jeff	P	1.000	44	1	0	1	0	1
TOWERS, Josh	P	.000	14	1	0	0	0	0
WELLS, Vernon	OF	.317	161	678	118	215	33	117
WERTH, Jayson	OF	.208	26	48	7	10	2	10
WILSON, Tom	C-1B-OF-DH	.258	96	256	37	66	5	35
WOODWARD, Chris	SS	.261	104	349	49	91	7	45
2003 Totals		**.279**	**162**	**5661**	**894**	**1580**	**190**	**853**

PITCHER	ERA	W-L	SV	G	IP	H	ER	BB	SO
ACEVEDO, Juan	4 .26	1-2	0	14	12.2	18	6	8	9
BOWLES, Brian	2.57	0-0	0	5	7.0	8	2	2	2
CHULK, Vinnie	5.06	0-0	0	3	5.1	6	3	3	2
CREEK, Doug	3.29	0-0	0	21	13.2	14	5	12	11
DAVIS, Doug	5.00	4-6	0	12	54.0	70	30	26	25
ESCOBAR, Kelvim	4.29	13-9	4	41	180.1	189	86	78	159
HALLADAY, Roy	3.25	22-7	0	36	266.0	253	96	32	204
HENDRICKSON, Mark	5.51	9-9	0	30	158.1	207	97	40	76
KERSHNER, Jason	3.17	3-3	0	40	54.0	43	19	15	32
LIDLE, Cory	5.75	12-15	0	31	192.2	216	123	60	112
LINTON, Doug	3.00	0-0	0	7	9.0	7	3	4	7
LOPEZ, Aquilino	3.42	1-3	14	72	73.2	58	28	34	64
MILLER, Trever	4.61	2-2	4	79	52.2	46	27	28	44
POLITTE, Cliff	5.66	1-5	12	54	49.1	52	31	17	40
REICHERT, Dan	6.06	0-0	0	15	16.1	28	11	8	13
SERVICE, Scott	4.50	0-0	0	15	16.0	17	8	6	17
STURTZE, Tanyon	5.94	7-6	0	40	89.1	107	59	43	54
TAM, Jeff	5.64	0-4	1	44	44.2	58	28	25	26
THURMAN, Corey	6.46	1-1	0	6	15.1	21	11	9	11
TOWERS, Josh	4.48	8-1	1	14	64.1	67	32	7	42
WALKER, Pete	4.88	2-2	0	23	55.1	59	30	24	29
WASDIN, John	23.40	0-1	0	3	5.0	16	13	4	5
2003 Totals	**4.69**	**86-76**	**36**	**162**	**1435.0**	**1560**	**748**	**485**	**984**

2002

BATTER	Pos.	Avg.	G	AB	R	H	HR	RBI
BERG, David	IF-OF	.270	109	374	42	101	4	39
BUSH, Homer	2B	.231	23	78	9	18	1	2
CARPENTER, Chris	P	1.000	13	1	1	1	0	0
CASH, Kevin	C	.143	7	14	1	2	0	0
CRUZ Jr., Jose	OF	.245	124	466	64	114	18	70
DELGADO, Carlos	1B	.277	143	505	103	140	33	108
FLETCHER, Darrin	C	.220	45	127	8	28	3	22
HALLADAY, Roy	P	.000	34	6	0	0	0	0
HINSKE, Eric	3B	.279	151	566	99	158	24	84
HUCKABY, Ken	C	.245	88	273	29	67	3	22
HUDSON, Orlando	2B	.276	54	192	20	53	4	23
LAWRENCE, Joe	2B	.180	55	150	16	27	2	15
LESHER, Brian	1B-OF	.132	24	38	2	5	0	2
LOAIZA, Esteban	P	.167	25	6	0	1	0	0
LOPEZ, Felipe	SS	.227	85	282	35	64	8	34
MILLER, Justin	P	.000	25	2	0	0	0	0
MONDESI, Raul	OF-DH	.224	75	299	51	67	15	45
PARRIS, Steve	P	.000	14	4	0	0	0	0
PHELPS, Josh	DH	.309	74	265	41	82	15	58
STEWART, Shannon	OF-DH	.303	141	577	103	175	10	45
SWANN, Pedro	OF	.083	13	12	3	1	0	1
THURMAN, Corey	P	.000	43	1	0	0	0	0
WELLS, Vernon	OF	.275	159	608	87	167	23	100
WERTH, Jayson	OF	.261	15	46	4	12	0	6
WILSON, Tom	C-DH	.257	96	265	33	68	8	37
WISE, Dewayne	OF	.179	42	112	14	20	3	13
WOODWARD, Chris	SS	.276	90	312	48	86	13	45
2002 Totals		**.261**	**162**	**5581**	**813**	**1457**	**187**	**771**

PITCHER	ERA	W-L	SV	G	IP	H	ER	BB	SO
BORBON, Pedro	4.97	1-2	0	16	12.2	12	7	6	11
BOWLES, Brian	4.05	2-1	0	17	20.0	13	9	14	19
CARPENTER, Chris	5.28	4-5	0	13	73.1	89	43	27	45
CASSIDY, Scott	5.73	1-4	0	58	66.0	52	42	32	48
COCO, Pasqual	18.00	0-1	0	2	1.0	4	2	3	0
COOPER, Brian	14.04	0-1	0	2	8.1	14	13	4	3
ESCOBAR, Kelvim	4.27	5-7	38	76	78.0	75	37	44	85
EYRE, Scott	4.97	2-4	0	49	63.1	69	35	29	51
FILE, Bob	18.90	0-1	0	5	3.1	8	7	2	2
HALLADAY, Roy	2.93	19-7	0	34	239.1	223	78	62	168
HENDRICKSON, Mark	2.45	3-0	0	16	36.2	25	10	12	21
HEREDIA, Felix	3.61	1-2	0	53	52.1	51	21	26	31
KERSHNER, Jason	1.69	0-0	1	10	5.1	5	1	4	7
LOAIZA, Esteban	5.71	9-10	0	25	151.1	192	96	38	87
LYON, Brandon	6.53	1-4	0	15	62.0	78	45	19	30
MILLER, Justin	5.54	9-5	0	25	102.1	103	63	66	68
PARRIS, Steve	5.97	5-5	0	14	75.1	96	50	35	48
PLESAC, Dan	3.38	1-2	0	19	13.1	11	5	6	14
POLITTE, Cliff	3.61	1-3	1	55	57.1	38	23	19	57
PROKOPEC, Luke	6.78	2-9	0	22	71.2	90	54	25	41
SMITH, Mike	6.62	0-3	0	14	35.1	43	26	20	16
THURMAN, Corey	4.37	2-3	0	43	68.0	65	33	45	56
WALKER, Pete	4.33	10-5	1	37	139.1	143	67	51	80
WIGGINS, Scott	3.38	0-0	0	3	2.2	5	1	1	3
2002 Totals	**4.80**	**78-84**	**41**	**162**	**1438.2**	**1504**	**767**	**590**	**991**

2001

BATTER	Pos.	Avg.	G	AB	R	H	HR	RBI
BATISTA, Tony	3B	.207	72	271	29	56	13	45
BUSH, Homer	2B	.306	78	271	32	83	3	27
CARPENTER, Chris	P	.167	34	6	0	1	0	0
CASTILLO, Alberto	C	.198	66	131	9	26	1	4
CRUZ Jr., Jose	OF	.274	146	577	92	158	34	88
DELGADO, Carlos	1B	.279	162	574	102	160	39	102
FERNANDEZ, Tony	DH	.305	48	59	5	18	1	12
FLETCHER, Darrin	C	.226	134	416	36	94	11	56
FREEL, Ryan	2B	.273	9	22	1	6	0	3
FRYE, Jeff	2B-3B	.246	74	175	24	43	2	15
FULLMER, Brad	DH	.274	146	522	71	143	18	83
GONZALEZ, Alex	SS	.253	154	636	79	161	17	76
HALLADAY, Roy	P	.000	17	1	0	0	0	0
HAMILTON, Joey	P	.333	22	3	0	1	0	1
IZTURIS, Cesar	2B-SS	.269	46	134	19	36	2	9
LATHAM, Chris	OF	.274	43	73	12	20	2	10
LOAIZA, Esteban	P	.000	36	2	0	0	0	0
LOPEZ, Felipe	3B	.260	49	177	21	46	5	23
LOPEZ, Luis	3B	.244	41	119	10	29	3	10
MICHALIK, Chris	P	.333	24	3	0	1	0	0
MONDESI, Raul	OF	.252	149	572	88	144	27	84
PARRIS, Steve	P	.000	19	1	0	0	0	0
PHELPS, Josh	C	.000	8	12	3	0	0	1
SIMMONS, Brian	OF	.178	60	107	8	19	2	8
STEWART, Shannon	OF	.316	155	640	103	202	12	60
WELLS, Vernon	OF	.313	30	96	14	30	1	6
WOODWARD, Chris	IF	.190	37	63	9	12	2	5
2001 Totals		**.263**	**162**	**5663**	**767**	**1489**	**195**	**728**

PITCHER	ERA	W-L	SV	G	IP	H	ER	BB	SO
BEIRNE, Kevin	12.86	0-0	0	5	7.0	13	10	6	5
BORBON, Pedro	3.71	2-4	0	71	53.1	48	22	12	45
BOWLES, Brian	0.00	0-0	0	2	3.2	4	0	1	4
CARPENTER, Chris	4.09	11-11	0	34	215.2	229	98	75	157
COCO, Pasqual	4.40	1-0	0	7	14.1	12	7	6	9
DEWITT, Matt	3.79	0-2	0	16	19.0	22	8	10	13
ESCOBAR, Kelvim	3.50	6-8	0	59	126.0	93	49	52	121
EYRE, Scott	3.45	1-2	2	17	15.2	15	6	7	16
FILE, Bob	3.27	5-3	0	60	74.1	57	28	29	38
FRASCATORE, John	2.20	1-0	0	12	16.1	16	4	4	9
HALLADAY, Roy	3.16	5-3	0	17	105.1	97	37	25	96
HAMILTON, Joey	5.89	5-8	0	22	122.1	170	80	38	82
KOCH, Billy	4.80	2-5	36	69	69.1	69	37	33	55
LOAIZA, Esteban	5.02	11-11	0	36	190.0	239	106	40	110
LYON, Brandon	4.29	5-4	0	11	63.0	63	30	15	35
MICHALAK, Chris	4.62	6-7	0	24	115.0	133	59	49	57
PAINTER, Lance	7.85	0-1	0	10	18.1	27	16	11	14
PARRIS, Steve	4.60	4-6	0	19	105.2	126	54	41	49
PLESAC, Dan	3.57	4-5	1	62	45.1	34	18	24	68
QUANTRILL, Paul	3.04	11-2	2	80	83.0	86	28	12	58
2001 Totals	**4.28**	**80-82**	**41**	**162**	**1462.2**	**1553**	**696**	**490**	**1041**

2000

BATTER	Pos.	Avg.	G	AB	R	H	HR	RBI
ANDREWS, Clayton	P	.000	8	3	0	0	0	0
BATISTA, Tony	3B	.263	154	620	96	163	41	114
BUSH, Homer	2B	.215	76	297	38	64	1	18
CARPENTER, Chris	P	.000	34	2	0	0	0	0
CASTILLO, Alberto	C	.211	66	185	14	39	1	16
CASTILLO, Frank	P	.143	25	7	0	1	0	0
CORDOVA, Marty	OF-DH	.245	62	200	23	49	4	18
CRUZ Jr., Jose	OF	.242	162	603	91	146	31	76
CUBILLAN, Darwin	P	.000	7	1	0	0	0	0
DELGADO, Carlos	1B	.344	162	569	115	196	41	137
DUCEY, Rob	OF	.154	5	13	2	2	0	1
ESCOBAR, Kelvim	P	.000	43	7	0	0	0	0
FLETCHER, Darrin	C	.320	122	416	43	133	20	58
FULLMER, Brad	DH	.295	133	482	76	142	32	104
GONZALEZ, Alex	SS	.252	141	527	68	133	15	69
GREBECK, Craig	2B-SS	.295	66	241	38	71	3	23
GREENE, Charlie	C	.111	3	9	0	1	0	0
GREENE, Todd	DH	.235	34	85	11	20	5	10
KOCH, Billy	P	.000	68	1	0	0	0	0
MARTINEZ, Dave	OF	.311	47	180	29	56	2	22
MONDESI, Raul	OF	.271	96	388	78	105	24	67
MORANDINI, Mickey	2B	.271	35	107	10	29	0	7
MOTTOLA, Chad	OF	.222	3	9	1	2	0	2
MUNRO, Pete	P	.000	9	1	0	0	0	0
PHELPS, Josh	C	.000	1	1	0	0	0	0
QUANTRILL, Paul	P	--	68	0	0	0	0	0
STEWART, Shannon	OF	.319	136	583	107	186	21	69
THOMPSON, Andy	OF	.167	2	6	2	1	0	1
WELLS, David	P	.167	35	6	0	1	0	0
WELLS, Vernon	OF	.000	3	2	0	0	0	0
WISE, Dewayne	OF	.136	28	22	3	3	0	0
WOODWARD, Chris	IF	.183	37	104	16	19	3	14
2000 Totals		**.275**	**162**	**5677**	**861**	**1562**	**244**	**826**

PITCHER	ERA	W-L	SV	G	IP	H	ER	BB	SO
ANDREWS, Clayton	10.02	1-2	0	8	20.2	34	23	9	12
BALE, John	14.73	0-0	0	2	3.2	5	6	3	6
BORBON, Pedro	6.48	1-1	1	59	41.2	45	30	38	29
CARPENTER, Chris	6.26	10-12	0	34	175.1	204	122	83	113
CASTILLO, Frank	3.59	10-5	0	25	138.0	112	55	56	104
COCO, Pasqual	9.00	0-0	0	1	4.0	5	4	5	2
CUBILLAN, Darwin	8.04	1-0	0	7	15.2	20	14	11	14
DeWITT, Matt	8.56	1-0	0	8	13.2	20	13	9	6
ESCOBAR, Kelvim	5.35	10-15	2	43	180.0	186	107	85	142
ESTRELLA, Leoncio	5.79	0-0	0	2	4.2	9	3	0	3
FRASCATORE, John	5.42	2-4	0	60	73.0	87	44	33	30
GUNDERSON, Eric	7.11	0-1	0	6	6.1	15	5	2	2
GUTHRIE, Mark	4.79	0-2	0	23	20.2	20	11	9	20
HALLADAY, Roy	10.64	4-7	0	19	67.2	107	80	42	44
HAMILTON, Joey	3.55	2-1	0	6	33.0	28	13	12	15
KOCH, Billy	2.63	9-3	33	68	78.2	78	23	18	60
LOAIZA, Esteban	3.62	5-7	0	14	92.0	95	37	26	62
MUNRO, Pete	5.96	1-1	0	9	25.2	38	17	16	16
PAINTER, Lance	4.73	2-0	0	42	66.2	69	35	22	53
QUANTRILL, Paul	4.52	2-5	1	68	83.2	100	42	25	47
TRACHSEL, Steve	5.29	2-5	0	11	63.0	72	37	25	32
WELLS, David	4.11	20-8	0	35	229.2	266	105	31	166
2000 Totals	**5.14**	**83-79**	**37**	**162**	**1437.1**	**1615**	**821**	**560**	**978**

1999

BATTER	Pos.	Avg.	G	AB	R	H	HR	RBI
BATISTA, Tony	SS	.285	98	375	61	107	26	79
BERROA, Geronimo	DH	.194	22	62	11	12	1	6
BLAKE, Casey	3B	.256	14	39	6	10	1	1
BORDERS, Pat	C-DH	.214	6	14	1	3	1	3
BROWN, Kevin	C	.444	2	9	1	4	0	1
BRUMFIELD, Jacob	OF	.235	62	170	25	40	2	19
BUSH, Homer	2B-SS	.320	128	485	69	155	5	55
BUTLER, Rich	DH-OF	.143	8	7	1	1	0	1
CARPENTER, Chris	P	.000	24	1	0	0	0	0
CRUZ Jr., Jose	OF	.241	106	349	63	84	14	45
DALESANDRO, Mark	C-DH-3B	.185	16	27	3	5	0	1
DELGADO, Carlos	1B	.272	152	573	113	156	44	134
ESCOBAR, Kelvim	P	.000	33	1	0	0	0	0
FERNANDEZ, Tony	3B	.328	142	485	73	159	6	75
FLETCHER, Darrin	C	.291	115	412	48	120	18	80
GONZALEZ, Alex	SS	.292	38	154	22	45	2	12
GOODWIN, Curtis	OF	.000	2	8	0	0	0	0
GREBECK, Craig	IF-DH	.363	34	113	18	41	0	10
GREEN, Shawn	OF	.309	153	614	134	190	42	123
GREENE, Willie	DH-3B-OF	.204	81	226	22	46	12	41
HALLADAY, Roy	P	.000	36	2	0	0	0	0
HAMILTON, Joey	P	.000	22	2	0	0	0	0
HENTGEN, Pat	P	.167	34	6	0	1	0	0
HOLLINS, Dave	DH	.222	27	99	12	22	2	6
KELLY, Pat	2B	.267	37	116	17	31	6	20
KOCH, Billy	P	.000	56	1	0	0	0	0
LENNON, Patrick	OF	.207	9	29	3	6	1	6
MARTIN, Noberto	2B	.222	9	27	3	6	0	0
MATHENY, Mike	C	.215	57	163	16	35	3	17
McRAE, Brian	DH-OF	.195	31	82	11	16	3	11
OTANEZ, Willis	3B-1B	.252	42	127	21	32	5	13
SANDERS, Anthony	DH-OF	.286	3	7	1	2	0	2
SEGUI, David	DH-1B	.316	31	95	14	30	5	13
STEWART, Shannon	OF	.304	145	608	102	185	11	67
WELLS, David	P	.000	34	6	0	0	0	0
WELLS, Vernon	OF	.261	24	88	8	23	1	8
WITT, Kevin	DH	.206	15	34	3	7	1	5
WOODWARD, Chris	SS	.231	14	26	1	6	0	2
1999 Totals		**.280**	**162**	**5642**	**883**	**1580**	**212**	**856**

PITCHER	ERA	W-L	SV	G	IP	H	ER	BB	SO
BALE, John	13.50	0-0	0	1	2.0	2	3	2	4
CARPENTER, Chris	4.38	9-8	0	24	150.0	177	73	48	106
DAVEY, Tom	4.70	1-1	1	29	44.0	40	23	26	42
ESCOBAR, Kelvim	5.69	14-11	0	33	174.0	203	110	81	129
FRASCATORE, John	3.41	7-1	1	33	37.0	42	14	9	22
GLOVER, Gary	0.00	0-0	0	1	0.0	0	0	1	0
HALLADAY, Roy	3.92	8-7	1	36	149.1	156	65	79	82
HAMILTON, Joey	6.52	7-8	0	22	98.0	118	71	39	56
HENTGEN, Pat	4.79	11-12	0	34	199.0	225	106	65	118
HUDEK, John	12.27	0-0	0	3	3.2	8	5	1	2
KOCH, Billy	3.39	0-5	31	56	63.2	55	24	30	57
LLOYD, Graeme	3.63	5-3	3	74	72.0	68	29	23	47
LUDWICK, Eric	27.00	0-0	0	1	1.0	3	3	2	0
MUNRO, Peter	6.02	0-2	0	31	55.1	70	37	23	38
PERSON, Robert	9.82	0-2	2	11	11.0	9	12	15	12
PLESAC, Dan	8.34	0-3	0	30	22.2	28	21	9	26
QUANTRILL, Paul	3.33	3-2	0	41	48.2	53	18	17	28
RODRIGUEZ, Nerio	13.50	0-1	0	2	2.0	2	3	2	2
ROMANO, Mike	11.81	0-0	0	3	5.1	8	7	5	3
SINCLAIR, Steve	12.71	0-0	0	3	5.2	7	8	4	3
SPOLJARIC, Paul	4.65	2-2	0	37	62.0	62	32	32	63
WELLS, David	4.82	17-10	0	34	231.2	246	124	62	169
1999 Totals	**4.93**	**84-78**	**39**	**162**	**1439.0**	**1582**	**788**	**575**	**1009**

1998

BATTER	Pos.	Avg.	G	AB	R	H	HR	RBI
BROWN, Kevin	C	.264	52	110	17	29	2	15
CANSECO, Jose	DH-OF	.237	151	583	98	138	46	107
CARPENTER, Chris	P	.000	33	1	0	0	0	0
CLEMENS, Rogers	P	.000	33	4	0	0	0	0
CRESPO, Felipe	OF-IF	.262	66	130	11	34	1	15
CRUZ Jr., Jose	OF	.253	105	352	55	89	11	42
DALESANDRO, Mark	C-3B-1B	.299	32	67	8	20	2	14
DELGADO, Carlos	1B	.292	142	530	94	155	38	115
EVANS, Tom	3B	.000	7	10	0	0	0	0
FERNANDEZ, Tony	2B-3B	.321	138	486	71	156	9	72
FLETCHER, Darrin	C	.283	124	407	37	115	9	52
GONZALEZ, Alex	SS	.239	158	568	70	136	13	51
GREBECK, Craig	IF	.256	102	301	33	77	2	27
GREEN, Shawn	OF	.278	158	630	106	175	35	100
GUZMAN, Juan	P	.000	22	2	0	0	0	0
HENTGEN, Pat	P	.000	29	5	0	0	0	0
LENNON, Patrick	OF	.500	2	4	1	2	0	0
MYERS, Randy	P	.000	41	1	0	0	0	0
PEREZ, Tomas	SS-2B	.111	6	9	1	1	0	0
PHILLIPS, Tony	OF	.354	13	48	9	17	1	7
SAMUEL, Juan	DH-OF	.180	43	50	14	9	1	2
SANTIAGO, Benito	C	.310	15	29	3	9	0	4
SPRAGUE, Ed	3B	.238	105	382	49	91	17	51
STANLEY, Mike	DH-1B	.240	98	341	49	82	22	47
STEWART, Shannon	OF	.279	144	516	90	144	12	55
STIEB, Dave	P	.000	19	1	0	0	0	0
WILLIAMS, Woody	P	.333	32	6	0	2	0	0
WITT, Kevin	1B	.143	5	7	0	1	0	0
1998 Totals		**.266**	**163**	**5580**	**816**	**1482**	**221**	**776**

PITCHER	ERA	W-L	SV	G	IP	H	ER	BB	SO
ALMANZAR, Carlos	5.34	2-2	0	25	28.2	34	17	8	20
ANDUJAR, Luis	9.53	0-0	0	5	5.2	12	6	2	1
CARPENTER, Chris	4.37	12-7	0	33	175	177	85	61	136
CLEMENS, Roger	2.65	20-6	0	33	234.2	169	69	88	271
ESCOBAR, Kelvim	3.73	7-3	0	22	79.2	72	33	35	72
GUZMAN, Juan	4.41	6-12	0	22	145.0	133	71	65	113
HALLADAY, Roy	1.93	1-0	0	2	14.0	9	3	2	13
HANSON, Eric	6.24	0-3	0	11	49.0	73	34	29	21
HENTGEN, Pat	5.17	12-11	0	29	177.0	208	102	69	94
MYERS, Randy	4.46	3-4	28	41	42.1	44	21	19	32
PERSON, Robert	7.04	3-1	6	27	38.1	45	30	22	31
PLESAC, Dan	3.78	4-3	4	78	50.0	41	21	16	55
QUANTRILL, Paul	2.59	3-4	7	82	80.0	88	23	22	59
RISLEY, Bill	5.27	3-4	0	44	54.2	52	32	34	42
RODRIGUEZ, Nerio	9.72	1-0	0	7	8.1	10	9	8	3
SINCLAIR, Steve	3.60	0-2	0	24	15.0	13	6	5	8
STIEB, Dave	4.83	1-2	2	19	50.1	58	27	17	27
Van RYN, Ben	9.00	0-1	0	10	4.0	6	4	2	3
WILLIAMS, Woody	4.46	10-9	0	32	209.2	196	104	81	151
WITHEM, Shannon	3.00	0-0	0	1	3.0	3	1	2	2
1998 Totals	**4.28**	**88-74**	**47**	**163**	**1465.0**	**1443**	**697**	**587**	**1154**

1997

BATTER	Pos.	Avg.	G	AB	R	H	HR	RBI
BRITO, Tilson	IF	.222	49	126	9	28	0	8
BRUMFIELD, Jacob	OF	.207	58	174	22	36	2	20
BUTLER, Rob	OF-DH	.286	7	14	3	4	0	2
CARTER, Joe	DH-OF-1B	.234	157	612	76	143	21	102
CLEMENS, Roger	P	.500	34	2	1	1	0	0
CRESPO, Felipe	3B-DH-2B	.286	12	28	3	8	1	5
CRUZ Jr., Jose	OF	.231	55	212	31	49	14	34
DELGADO, Carlos	1B-DH	.262	153	519	79	136	30	91
DUNCAN, Mariano	2B	.228	39	167	20	38	0	12
EVANS, Tom	3B	.289	12	38	7	11	1	2
GARCIA, Carlos	2B	.220	103	350	29	77	3	23
GONZALEZ, Alex	SS	.239	126	426	46	102	12	35
GREEN, Shawn	OF-DH	.287	135	429	57	123	16	53
HENTGEN, Pat	P	.000	35	7	0	0	0	0
MARTINEZ, Sandy	C	.000	3	2	1	0	0	0
MERCED, Orlando	OF	.266	98	368	45	98	9	40
MOSQUERA, Julio	C	.250	3	8	0	2	0	0
NIXON, Otis	OF	.262	103	401	54	105	1	26
O'BRIEN, Charlie	C	.218	69	225	22	49	4	27
PEREZ, Robert	OF-DH	.192	37	78	4	15	2	6
PEREZ, Tomas	SS-2B	.195	40	123	9	24	0	9
PERSON, Robert	P	.000	23	4	0	0	0	0
QUANTRILL, Paul	P	.000	77	1	0	0	0	0
SAMUEL, Juan	DH-1B-OF	.284	45	95	13	27	3	15
SANTIAGO, Benito	C	.243	97	341	31	83	13	42
SIERRA, Ruben	OF-DH	.208	14	48	4	10	1	5
SPOLJARIC, Paul	P	.000	37	1	0	0	0	0
SPRAGUE, Ed	3B	.228	138	504	63	115	14	48
STEWART, Shannon	OF	.286	44	168	25	48	0	22
WILLIAMS, Woody	P	.500	31	2	0	1	0	0
1997 Totals		**.244**	**162**	**5473**	**654**	**1333**	**147**	**627**

PITCHER	ERA	W-L	SV	G	IP	H	ER	BB	SO
ALMANZAR, Carlos	2.70	0-1	0	4	3.1	1	1	1	4
ANDUJAR, Luis	6.48	0-6	0	17	50.0	76	36	21	28
CARPENTER, Chris	5.09	3-7	0	14	81.1	108	46	37	55
CLEMENS, Roger	2.05	21-7	0	34	264.0	204	60	68	292
CRABTREE, Tim	7.08	3-3	2	37	40.2	65	32	17	26
DAAL, Omar	4.00	1-1	0	9	27.0	34	12	6	28
ESCOBAR, Kelvim	2.90	3-2	14	27	31.0	28	10	19	36
FLENER, Huck	9.87	0-1	0	8	17.1	40	19	6	9
GUZMAN, Juan	4.95	3-6	0	13	60.0	48	33	31	52
HANSON, Eric	7.80	0-0	0	3	15.0	15	13	6	18
HENTGEN, Pat	3.68	15-10	0	35	264.0	253	108	71	160
JANZEN, Marty	3.60	2-1	0	12	25.0	23	10	13	17
PERSON, Robert	5.61	5-10	0	23	128.1	125	80	60	99
PLESAC, Dan	3.58	2-4	1	73	50.1	47	20	19	61
QUANTRILL, Paul	1.94	6-7	5	77	88.0	103	19	17	56
RISLEY, Bill	8.31	0-1	0	3	4.1	3	4	2	2
ROBINSON, Ken	2.70	0-0	0	3	3.1	1	1	1	4
SPOLJARIC, Paul	3.19	0-3	3	37	48.0	37	17	36	70
TIMLIN, Mike	2.87	3-2	9	38	47.0	41	15	15	36
WILLIAMS, Woody	4.35	9-14	0	31	194.2	201	94	66	124
1997 Totals	**3.92**	**76-86**	**34**	**162**	**1442.2**	**1453**	**628**	**497**	**1150**

1996

BATTER	Pos.	Avg.	G	AB	R	H	HR	RBI
BRITO, Tilson	2B-SS	.238	26	80	10	19	1	7
BRUMFIELD, Jacob	OF-DH	.256	90	308	52	79	12	52
CAIRO, Miguel	2B	.222	9	27	5	6	0	1
CARTER, Joe	OF-1B-DH	.253	157	625	84	158	30	107
CEDENO, Domingo	2B-SS	.280	77	282	44	79	2	17
CRESPO, Felipe	IF	.184	22	49	6	9	0	4
DELGADO, Carlos	1B-DH	.270	138	488	68	132	25	92
GONZALEZ, Alex	SS	.235	147	527	64	124	14	64
GREEN, Shawn	OF	.280	132	422	52	118	11	45
HUFF, Mike	OF-3B	.172	11	29	5	5	0	0
MARTINEZ, Sandy	C	.227	76	229	17	52	3	18
MOSQUERA, Julio	C	.227	8	22	2	5	0	2
NIXON, Otis	OF	.286	125	496	87	142	1	29
O'BRIEN, Charlie	C	.238	109	324	33	77	13	44
OLERUD, John	1B-DH	.274	125	398	59	109	18	61
PEREZ, Robert	OF-DH	.327	86	202	30	66	2	21
PEREZ, Tomas	IF	.251	91	295	24	74	1	19
SAMUEL, Juan	DH-OF-1B	.255	69	188	34	48	8	26
SPRAGUE, Ed	3B-DH	.247	159	591	88	146	36	101
STEWART, Shannon	OF	.176	7	17	2	3	0	2
1996 Totals		**.259**	**162**	**5599**	**766**	**1451**	**177**	**712**

PITCHER	ERA	W-L	SV	G	IP	H	ER	BB	SO
ANDUJAR, Luis	5.02	1-1	0	3	14.1	14	8	1	5
BOHANON, Brian	7.77	0-1	1	20	22.0	27	19	19	17
BROW, Scott	5.59	1-0	0	18	38.2	45	24	25	23
CARRARA, Giovanni	11.40	0-1	0	11	15.0	23	19	12	10
CASTILLO, Tony	4.23	2-3	1	40	72.1	72	34	20	48
CRABTREE, Tim	2.54	5-3	1	53	67.1	59	19	22	57
FLENER, Huck	4.58	3-2	0	15	70.2	68	36	33	44
GUZMAN, Juan	2.93	11-8	0	27	187.2	158	61	53	165
HANSON, Eric	5.41	13-17	0	35	214.2	243	129	102	156
HENTGEN, Pat	3.22	20-10	0	35	265.2	238	95	94	177
JANZEN, Marty	7.33	4-6	0	15	73.2	95	60	38	47
JOHNSON, Dane	3.00	0-0	0	10	9.0	5	3	5	7
QUANTRILL, Paul	5.43	5-14	0	38	134.1	172	81	51	86
RISLEY, Bill	3.89	0-1	0	25	41.2	33	18	25	29
SILVA, Jose	13.50	0-0	0	2	2.0	5	3	0	0
SPOLJARIC, Paul	3.08	2-2	1	28	38.0	30	13	19	38
TIMLIN, Mike	3.65	1-6	31	59	56.2	47	23	18	52
VIOLA, Frank	7.71	1-3	0	6	30.1	43	26	21	18
WARE, Jeff	9.09	1-5	0	13	32.2	35	33	31	11
WILLIAMS, Woody	4.73	4-5	0	12	59.0	64	31	21	43
1996 Totals	**4.57**	**74-88**	**35**	**162**	**1445.2**	**1476**	**734**	**610**	**1033**

1995

BATTER	Pos.	Avg.	G	AB	R	H	HR	RBI
ALOMAR, Roberto	2B	.300	130	517	71	155	13	66
BATTLE, Howard	3B	.200	9	15	3	3	0	0
CARTER, Joe	OF	.253	139	558	70	141	25	76
CEDENO, Domingo	SS-2B	.236	51	161	18	38	4	14
DELGADO, Carlos	OF-DH-1B	.165	37	91	7	15	3	11
GONZALEZ, Alex	SS	.243	111	367	51	89	10	42
GREEN, Shawn	OF	.288	121	379	52	109	15	54
HUFF, Michael	OF	.232	61	138	14	32	1	9
KNORR, Randy	C	.212	45	132	18	28	3	16
MALDONADO, Candy	OF	.269	61	160	22	43	7	25
MARTINEZ, Sandy	C	.241	62	191	12	46	2	25
MOLITOR, Paul	DH	.270	130	525	63	142	15	60
OLERUD, John	1B	.291	135	492	72	143	8	54
PARRISH, Lance	C	.202	70	178	15	36	4	22
PEREZ, Robert	OF	.188	17	48	2	9	1	3
PEREZ, Tomas	SS-2B	.245	41	98	12	24	1	8
SPRAGUE, Ed	3B	.244	144	521	77	127	18	74
STEWART, Shannon	OF	.211	12	38	2	8	0	1
WHITE, Devon	OF	.283	101	427	61	121	10	53
1995 Totals		**.260**	**144**	**5036**	**642**	**1309**	**140**	**613**

PITCHER	ERA	W-L	SV	G	IP	H	ER	BB	SO
CARRARA, Giovanni	7.21	2-4	0	12	48.2	64	39	25	27
CASTILLO, Tony	3.22	1-5	13	55	72.2	64	26	24	38
CONE, David	3.38	9-6	0	17	130.1	113	49	41	102
CORNETT, Brad	9.00	0-0	0	5	5.0	9	5	3	4
COX, Danny	7.40	1-3	0	24	45.0	57	37	33	38
CRABTREE, Tim	3.09	0-2	0	31	32.0	30	11	13	21
DARWIN, Danny	7.62	1-8	0	13	65.0	91	55	24	36
GUZMAN, Juan	6.32	4-14	0	24	135.1	151	95	73	94
HALL, Darren	4.41	0-2	3	17	16.1	21	8	9	11
HENTGEN, Pat	5.11	10-14	0	30	200.2	236	114	90	135
HURTADO, Edwin	5.45	5-2	0	14	77.2	81	47	40	33
JORDAN, Ricardo	6.60	1-0	1	15	15.0	18	11	13	10
LEITER, Al	3.64	11-11	0	28	183.0	162	74	108	153
MENHART, Paul	4.92	1-4	0	21	78.2	72	43	47	50
ROBINSON, Ken	3.69	1-2	0	21	39.0	25	16	22	31
ROGERS, Jimmy	5.70	2-4	0	19	23.2	21	15	18	13
TIMLIN, Mike	2.14	4-3	5	31	42.0	38	10	17	36
WARD, Duane	27.00	0-1	0	4	2.2	11	8	5	3
WARE, Jeff	5.47	2-1	0	5	26.1	28	16	21	18
WILLIAMS, Woody	3.69	1-2	0	23	53.2	44	22	28	41
1995 Totals	**4.88**	**56-88**	**22**	**144**	**1292.2**	**1336**	**701**	**654**	**894**

1994

BATTER	Pos.	Avg.	G	AB	R	H	HR	RBI
ALOMAR, Roberto	2B	.306	107	392	78	120	8	38
BORDERS, Pat	C	.247	85	295	24	73	3	26
BUTLER, Rob	OF	.176	41	74	13	13	0	5
CARTER, Joe	OF	.271	111	435	70	118	27	103
CEDENO, Domingo	2B-SS	.196	47	97	14	19	0	10
COLES, Darnell	OF-1B	.210	48	143	15	30	4	15
DELGADO, Carlos	OF	.215	43	130	17	28	9	24
GONZALEZ, Alex	SS	.151	15	53	7	8	0	1
GREEN, Shawn	OF	.091	14	33	1	3	0	1
HUFF, Mike	OF	.304	80	207	31	63	3	25
KNORR, Randy	C	.242	40	124	20	30	7	19
MOLITOR, Paul	DH	.341	115	454	86	155	14	75
OLERUD, John	1B	.297	108	384	47	114	12	67
PEREZ, Robert	OF	.125	4	8	0	1	0	0
SCHOFIELD, Dick	SS	.255	95	325	38	83	4	32
SPRAGUE, Ed	3B	.240	109	405	38	97	11	44
WHITE, Devon	OF	.270	100	403	67	109	13	49
1994 Totals		**.269**	**115**	**3962**	**566**	**1064**	**115**	**534**

PITCHER	ERA	W-L	SV	G	IP	H	ER	BB	SO
BROW, Scott	5.90	0-3	2	18	29.0	34	19	19	15
CADARET, Greg	5.85	0-1	0	21	20.0	24	13	17	15
CASTILLO, Tony	2.51	5-2	1	41	68.0	66	19	28	43
CORNETT, Brad	6.68	1-3	0	9	31.0	40	23	11	22
COX, Danny	1.45	1-1	3	10	18.2	7	3	7	14
GUZMAN, Juan	5.68	12-11	0	25	147.1	165	93	76	124
HALL, Darren	3.41	2-3	17	30	31.2	26	12	14	28
HENTGEN, Pat	3.40	13-8	0	24	174.2	158	66	59	147
LEITER, Al	5.08	6-7	0	20	111.2	125	63	65	100
RIGHETTI, Dave	6.75	0-1	0	13	13.1	9	10	10	10
St. CLAIRE, Randy	9.00	0-0	0	2	2.0	4	2	2	2
SMALL, Aaron	9.00	0-0	0	1	2.0	5	2	2	0
SPOLJARIC, Paul	38.57	0-1	0	2	2.1	5	10	9	2
STEWART, Dave	5.87	7-8	0	22	133.1	151	87	62	111
STOTTLEMYRE, Todd	4.22	7-7	1	26	140.2	149	66	48	105
TIMLIN, Mike	5.18	0-1	2	34	40.0	41	23	20	38
WILLIAMS, Woody	3.64	1-3	0	38	59.1	44	24	33	56
1994 Totals	**4.70**	**55-60**	**26**	**115**	**1025.0**	**1053**	**535**	**482**	**832**

1993

BATTER	Pos.	Avg.	G	AB	R	H	HR	RBI
ALOMAR, Roberto	2B	.326	153	589	109	192	17	93
BORDERS, Pat	C	.254	138	488	38	124	9	55
BUTLER, Rob	OF	.271	17	48	8	13	0	2
CANATE, Willie	OF	.213	38	47	12	10	1	3
CARTER, Joe	OF	.254	155	603	92	153	33	121
CEDENO, Domingo	SS-2B	.174	15	46	5	8	0	7
COLES, Darnell	OF-3B	.253	64	194	26	49	4	26
DELGADO, Carlos	C	.000	2	1	0	0	0	0
FERNANDEZ, Tony	SS	.306	94	353	45	108	4	50
GREEN, Shawn	OF	.000	3	6	0	0	0	0
GRIFFIN, Alfredo	IF	.211	46	95	15	20	0	3
HENDERSON, Rickey	OF	.215	44	163	37	35	4	12
JACKSON, Darrin	OF	.216	46	176	15	38	5	19
KNORR, Randy	C	.248	39	101	11	25	4	20
MARTINEZ, Domingo	1B	.286	8	14	2	4	1	3
MOLITOR, Paul	DH-1B	.332	160	636	121	211	22	111
OLERUD, John	1B-DH	.363	158	551	109	200	24	107
SCHOFIELD, Dick	SS	.191	36	110	11	21	0	5
SOJO, Luis	IF	.170	19	47	5	8	0	6
SPRAGUE, Ed	3B	.260	150	546	50	142	12	73
WARD, Turner	OF	.192	72	167	20	32	4	28
WHITE, Devon	OF	.273	146	598	116	163	15	52
1993 Totals		**.279**	**162**	**5579**	**847**	**1556**	**159**	**796**

PITCHER	ERA	W-L	SV	G	IP	H	ER	BB	SO
BROW, Scott	6.00	1-1	0	6	18.0	19	12	10	7
CASTILLO, Tony	3.38	3-2	0	51	50.2	44	19	22	28
COX, Danny	3.12	7-6	2	44	83.2	73	29	29	84
DAYLEY, Ken	0.00	0-0	0	2	0.2	1	0	4	2
EICHHORN, Mark	2.72	3-1	0	54	72.2	76	22	22	47
FLENER, Huck	4.05	0-0	0	6	6.2	7	3	4	2
GUZMAN, Juan	3.99	14-3	0	33	221.0	211	98	110	194
HENTGEN, Pat	3.87	19-9	0	34	216.1	215	93	74	122
LEITER, Al	4.11	9-6	2	34	105.0	93	48	56	66
LINTON, Doug	6.55	0-1	0	4	11.0	11	8	9	4
MORRIS, Jack	6.19	7-12	0	27	152.2	189	105	65	103
STEWART, Dave	4.44	12-8	0	26	162.0	146	80	72	96
STOTTLEMYRE, Todd	4.84	11-12	0	30	176.2	204	95	69	98
TIMLIN, Mike	4.69	4-2	1	54	55.2	63	29	27	49
WARD, Duane	2.13	2-3	45	71	71.2	49	17	25	97
WILLIAMS, Woody	4.38	3-1	0	30	37.0	40	18	22	24
1993 Totals	**4.21**	**95-67**	**50**	**162**	**1441.1**	**1441**	**674**	**620**	**1023**

1992

BATTER	Pos.	Avg.	G	AB	R	H	HR	RBI
ALOMAR, Roberto	2B	.310	152	571	105	177	8	76
BELL, Derek	OF	.242	61	161	23	39	2	15
BORDERS, Pat	C	.242	138	480	47	116	13	53
CARTER, Joe	OF-DH	.264	158	622	97	164	34	119
DUCEY, Rob	OF-DH	.048	23	21	3	1	0	0
GRIFFIN, Alfredo	SS-2B	.233	63	150	21	35	0	10
GRUBER, Kelly	3B	.229	120	446	42	102	11	43
KENT, Jeff	IF	.240	65	192	36	46	8	35
KNORR, Randy	C	.263	8	19	1	5	1	2
LEE, Manuel	SS	.263	128	396	49	104	3	39
MAKSUDIAN, Mike	PH	.000	3	3	0	0	0	0
MALDONADO, Candy	OF	.272	137	489	64	133	20	66
MARTINEZ, Domingo	1B	.625	7	8	2	5	1	3
MULLINIKS, Rance	PH	.500	3	2	1	1	0	0
MYERS, Greg	C	.230	22	61	4	14	1	13
OLERUD, John	1B	.284	138	458	68	130	16	66
QUINLAN, Tom	3B	.067	13	15	2	1	0	2
SPRAGUE, Ed	C-IF	.234	22	47	6	11	1	7
TABLER, Pat	1B-OF	.252	49	135	11	34	0	16
WARD, Turner	OF	.345	18	29	7	10	1	3
WHITE, Devon	OF	.248	153	641	98	159	17	60
WINFIELD, Dave	DH-OF	.290	156	583	92	169	26	108
ZOSKY, Eddie	SS	.286	8	7	1	2	0	1
1992 Totals		**.263**	**162**	**5536**	**780**	**1458**	**163**	**737**

PITCHER	ERA	W-L	SV	G	IP	H	ER	BB	SO
CONE, David	2.55	4-3	0	8	53.0	39	15	29	47
EICHHORN, Mark	4.35	2-0	0	23	31.0	35	15	7	19
GUZMAN, Juan	2.64	16-5	0	28	180.2	135	53	72	165
HENKE, Tom	2.26	3-2	34	57	55.2	40	14	22	46
HENGTEN, Pat	5.36	5-2	0	28	50.1	49	30	32	39
KEY, Jimmy	3.53	13-13	0	33	216.2	205	85	59	117
LEITER, Al	9.00	0-0	0	1	1.0	1	1	2	0
LINTON, Doug	8.63	1-3	0	8	24.0	31	23	17	16
MacDONALD, Bob	4.37	1-0	0	27	47.1	50	23	16	26
MORRIS, Jack	4.04	21-6	0	34	240.2	222	108	80	132
STIEB, Dave	5.04	4-6	0	21	96.1	98	54	43	45
STOTTLEMYRE, Todd	4.50	12-11	0	28	174.0	175	87	63	98
TIMLIN, Mike	4.12	0-2	1	26	43.2	45	20	20	35
TRLICEK, Ricky	10.80	0-0	0	2	1.2	2	2	2	1
WARD, Duane	1.95	7-4	12	79	101.1	76	22	39	103
WEATHERS, David	8.10	0-0	0	2	3.1	5	3	2	3
WELLS, David	5.40	7-9	2	41	120.0	138	72	36	62
1992 Totals	**3.91**	**96-66**	**49**	**162**	**1440.2**	**1346**	**626**	**541**	**954**

1991

BATTER	Pos.	Avg.	G	AB	R	H	HR	RBI
ALOMAR, Roberto	2B	.295	161	637	88	188	9	69
BELL, Derek	OF	.143	18	28	5	4	0	1
BORDERS, Pat	C	.244	105	291	22	71	5	36
CARTER, Joe	OF	.273	162	638	89	174	33	108
DUCEY, Rob	OF	.235	39	68	8	16	1	4
GIANNELLI, Ray	3B	.167	9	24	2	4	0	0
GONZALES, Rene	IF	.195	71	118	16	23	1	6
GRUBER, Kely	3B	.252	113	429	58	108	20	65
HILL, Glenallen	DH-OF	.253	35	99	14	25	3	11
KNORR, Randy	C	.000	3	1	0	0	0	0
LEE, Manny	SS	.234	138	445	41	104	0	29
MALDONADO, Candy	OF	.277	52	177	26	49	7	28
MULLINIKS, Rance	DH	.250	97	240	27	60	2	24
MYERS, Greg	C	.262	107	309	25	81	8	36
OLERUD, John	1B	.256	139	454	64	116	17	68
PARKER, Dave	DH	.333	13	36	2	12	0	3
SNYDER, Cory	OF-1B	.143	21	49	4	7	0	6
SPRAGUE, Ed	3B-1B	.275	61	160	17	44	4	20
TABLER, Pat	DH-1B	.216	82	185	20	40	1	21
WARD, Turner	OF	.308	8	13	1	4	0	2
WHITE, Devon	OF	.282	156	642	110	181	17	60
WHITEN, Mark	OF	.221	46	149	12	33	2	19
WILLIAMS, Kenny	OF	.207	13	29	5	6	1	3
WILSON, Mookie	OF-DH	.241	86	241	26	58	2	28
ZOSKY, Eddie	SS	.148	18	27	2	4	0	2
1991 Totals		**.257**	**162**	**5489**	**684**	**1412**	**133**	**649**

PITCHER	ERA	W-L	SV	G	IP	H	ER	BB	SO
ACKER, Jim	5.20	3-5	1	54	88.1	77	51	36	44
BOUCHER, Denis	4.58	0-3	0	7	35.1	39	18	16	16
CANDIOTTI, Tom	2.98	6-7	0	19	129.2	114	43	45	81
DAYLEY, Ken	6.23	0-0	0	8	4.1	7	3	5	3
FRASER, Willie	6.15	0-2	0	13	26.1	33	18	11	12
GUZMAN, Juan	2.99	10-3	0	23	138.2	98	46	66	123
HENKE, Tom	2.32	0-2	32	49	50.1	33	13	11	53
HENGTEN, Pat	2.45	0-0	0	3	7.1	5	2	3	3
HORSMAN, Vince	0.00	0-0	0	4	4.0	2	0	3	2
KEY, Jimmy	3.05	16-12	0	33	209.1	207	71	44	125
LEITER, Al	27.00	0-0	0	3	1.2	3	5	5	1
MacDONALD, Bob	2.85	3-3	0	45	53.2	51	17	25	24
STIEB, Dave	3.17	4-3	0	9	59.2	52	21	23	29
STOTTLEMYRE, Todd	3.78	15-8	0	34	219.0	194	92	75	116
TIMLIN, Mike	3.16	11-6	3	63	108.1	94	38	50	85
WARD, Duane	2.77	7-6	23	81	107.1	80	33	33	132
WEATHERS, David	4.91	1-0	0	15	14.2	15	8	17	13
WELLS, David	3.72	15-10	1	40	198.1	188	82	49	106
WESTON, Mickey	0.00	0-0	0	2	2.0	1	0	1	1
WILLS, Frank	16.62	0-1	0	4	4.1	8	8	5	2
1991 Totals	**3.50**	**91-71**	**60**	**162**	**1462.2**	**1301**	**569**	**523**	**971**

1990

BATTER	Pos.	Avg.	G	AB	R	H	HR	RBI
BELL, George	OF-DH	.265	142	562	67	149	21	86
BORDERS, Pat	C	.286	125	346	36	99	15	49
DIAZ, Carlos	C	.333	9	3	1	1	0	0
DUCEY, Rob	OF	.302	19	53	7	16	0	7
EPPARD, Jim	OF	.200	6	5	0	1	0	0
FELIX, Junior	OF	.263	127	463	73	122	15	65
FERNANDEZ, Tony	SS	.276	161	635	84	175	4	66
GRUBER, Kelly	3B	.274	150	592	92	162	31	118
HILL, Glenallen	OF-DH	.231	84	260	47	60	12	32
LAWLESS, Tom	IF-OF	.083	15	12	1	1	0	1
LEE, Manny	2B	.243	117	391	45	95	6	41
LIRIANO, Nelson	2B	.212	50	170	16	36	1	15
McGRIFF, Fred	1B	.300	153	557	91	167	35	88
MULLINIKS, Rance	3B-DH	.289	57	97	11	28	2	16
MYERS, Greg	C	.236	87	250	33	59	5	22
OLERUD, John	DH-1B	.265	111	358	43	95	14	48
QUINLAN, Tom	3B	.500	1	2	0	1	0	0
SOJO, Luis	IF	.225	33	80	14	18	1	9
VIRGIL, Ozzie	C-DH	.000	3	5	0	0	0	0
WHITEN, Mark	OF	.273	33	88	12	24	2	7
WILLIAMS, Kenny	OF-DH	.194	49	72	13	14	0	8
WILSON, Mookie	OF	.265	147	588	81	156	3	51
1990 Totals		**.265**	**162**	**5589**	**767**	**1479**	**167**	**729**

PITCHER	ERA	W-L	SV	G	IP	H	ER	BB	SO
ACKER, Jim	3.83	4-4	1	59	91.2	103	39	30	54
BLACK, Bud	4.02	2-1	0	3	15.2	10	7	3	3
BLAIR, Willie	4.06	3-5	0	27	68.2	66	31	28	43
CANDELARIA, John	5.48	0-3	1	13	21.1	32	13	11	19
CERUTTI, John	4.76	9-9	0	30	140.0	162	74	49	49
CUMMINGS. Steve	5.11	0-0	0	6	12.1	22	7	5	4
FLANAGAN, Mike	5.31	2-2	0	5	20.1	28	12	8	5
GILLES, Tom	6.75	1-0	0	2	1.1	2	1	0	1
HENKE, Tom	2.17	2-4	32	61	74.2	58	18	19	75
KEY, Jimmy	4.25	13-7	0	27	154.2	169	73	22	88
KILGUS, Paul	6.06	0-0	0	11	16.1	19	11	7	7
LEITER, Al	0.00	0-0	0	4	6.1	1	0	2	5
LUECKEN, Rick	9.00	0-0	0	1	1.0	2	1	1	0
MacDONALD, Bob	0.00	0-0	0	4	2.1	0	0	2	0
STIEB, Dave	2.93	18-6	0	33	208.2	179	68	64	125
STOTTLEMYRE, Todd	4.34	13-17	0	33	203.0	214	98	69	115
WARD, Duane	3.45	2-8	11	73	127.2	101	49	42	112
WELLS, David	3.14	11-6	3	43	189.0	165	66	45	115
WILLS, Frank	4.73	6-4	0	44	99.0	101	52	38	72
1990 Totals	**3.84**	**86-76**	**48**	**162**	**1454.0**	**1434**	**620**	**445**	**892**

1989

BATTER	Pos.	Avg.	G	AB	R	H	HR	RBI
BARFIELD, Jesse	OF	.200	21	80	8	16	5	11
BATISTE, Kevin	OF	.250	6	8	1	2	0	0
BELL, George	OF	.297	153	613	88	182	18	104
BORDERS, Pat	C-DH	.257	94	241	22	62	3	29
BRENLY, Bob	DH-C	.170	48	88	9	15	1	6
CABRERA, Francisco	DH	.167	3	12	1	2	0	0
DUCEY, Rob	OF	.211	41	76	5	16	0	7
FELIX, Junior	OF	.258	110	415	62	107	9	46
FERNANDEZ, Tony	SS	.257	140	573	64	147	11	64
GRUBER, Kelly	3B	.290	135	545	83	158	18	73
HILL, Glenallen	OF	.288	19	52	4	15	1	7
INFANTE, Alexis	IF	.167	20	12	1	2	0	0
LAWLESS, Tom	OF-IF	.229	59	70	20	16	0	3
LEE, Manny	IF	.260	99	300	27	78	3	34
LIRIANO, Nelson	2B	.263	132	418	51	110	5	53
MAZZILLI, Lee	DH-1B	.227	28	66	12	15	4	11
McGRIFF, Fred	1B	.269	161	551	98	148	36	92
MOSEBY, Lloyd	OF	.221	135	502	72	111	11	43
MULLINIKS, Rance	DH-3B	.238	103	273	25	65	3	29
MYERS, Greg	C-DH	.114	17	44	0	5	0	1
OLERUD, John	1B	.375	6	8	2	3	0	0
VIRGIL, Ozzie	DH-C	.182	9	11	2	2	1	2
WHITT, Ernie	C	.262	129	385	42	101	11	53
WILSON, Mookie	OF	.298	54	238	32	71	2	17
1989 Totals		**.260**	**162**	**5581**	**731**	**1449**	**142**	**685**

PITCHER	ERA	W-L	SV	G	IP	H	ER	BB	SO
ACKER, Jim	1.59	2-1	0	14	28.1	24	5	12	24
BUICE, DeWayne	5.82	1-0	0	7	17.0	13	11	13	10
CASTILLO, Tony	6.11	1-1	1	17	17.2	23	12	10	10
CERUTTI, John	3.07	11-11	0	33	205.1	214	70	53	69
CUMMINGS, Steve	3.00	2-0	0	5	21.0	18	7	11	8
FLANAGAN, Mike	3.93	8-10	0	30	171.2	186	75	47	47
GOZZO, Mauro	4.83	4-1	0	9	31.2	35	17	9	10
HENKE, Tom	1.92	8-3	20	64	89.0	66	19	25	116
HERNANDEZ, Xavier	4.76	1-0	0	7	22.2	25	12	8	7
KEY, Jimmy	3.88	13-14	0	33	216.0	226	93	27	118
LEITER, Al	4.05	0-0	0	1	6.2	9	3	2	4
MUSSELMAN, Jeff	10.64	0-1	0	5	11.0	19	13	9	3
NUNEZ, Jose	2.53	0-0	0	6	10.2	8	3	2	14
SANCHEZ, Alex	10.03	0-1	0	4	11.2	16	13	14	4
STIEB, Dave	3.35	17-8	0	33	206.2	164	77	76	101
STOTTLEMYRE, Todd	3.88	7-7	0	27	127.2	137	55	44	63
WARD, Duane	3.77	4-10	15	66	114.2	94	48	58	122
WELLS, David	2.40	7-4	2	54	86.1	66	23	28	78
WILLS, Frank	3.66	3-1	0	24	71.1	65	29	30	41
1989 Totals	**3.58**	**89-73**	**38**	**162**	**1467.0**	**1408**	**584**	**478**	**849**

1988

BATTER	Pos.	Avg.	G	AB	R	H	HR	RBI
BARFIELD, Jesse	OF	.244	137	468	62	114	18	56
BELL, George	OF	.269	156	614	78	165	24	97
BENIQUEZ, Juan	DH	.293	27	58	9	17	1	8
BORDERS, Pat	C	.273	56	154	15	42	5	21
BUTERA, Sal	C	.233	23	60	3	14	1	6
CAMPUSANO, Sil	OF	.218	73	142	14	31	2	12
DUCEY, Rob	OF	.315	27	54	15	17	0	6
FERNANDEZ, Tony	SS	.287	154	648	76	186	5	70
FIELDER, Cecil	DH-1B	.230	74	174	24	40	9	23
GRUBER, Kelly	3B	.278	158	569	75	158	16	81
INFANTE, Alexis	IF	.200	19	15	7	3	0	0
LEACH, Rick	OF	.276	87	199	21	55	0	23
LEE, Manny	2B-SS	.291	116	381	38	111	2	38
LIRIANO, Nelson	2B	.264	99	276	36	73	3	23
McGRIFF, Fred	1B	.282	154	536	100	151	34	82
MOSEBY, Lloyd	OF	.239	128	472	77	113	10	42
MULLINIKS, Rance	DH	.300	119	337	49	101	12	48
THORNTON, Lou	OF	.000	11	2	1	0	0	0
WHITT, Ernie	C	.251	127	398	63	100	16	70
1988 Totals		**.268**	**162**	**5557**	**763**	**1491**	**158**	**706**

PITCHER	ERA	W-L	SV	G	IP	H	ER	BB	SO
BAIR, Doug	4.05	0-0	0	10	13.1	14	6	3	8
CASTILLO, Tony	3.00	1-0	0	14	15.0	10	5	2	14
CERUTTI, John	3.13	6-7	1	46	123.2	120	43	42	65
CLANCY, Jim	4.49	11-13	1	36	196.1	207	98	47	118
EICHHORN, Mark	4.19	0-3	1	37	66.2	79	31	27	28
FLANAGAN, Mike	4.18	13-13	0	34	211.0	220	98	80	99
HENKE, Tom	2.91	4-4	25	52	68.0	60	22	24	66
KEY, Jimmy	3.29	12-5	0	21	131.1	127	48	30	65
MUSSELMAN, Jeff	3.18	8-5	0	15	85.0	80	30	30	39
NUNEZ, Jose	3.07	0-1	0	13	29.1	28	10	17	18
ROSS, Mark	4.91	0-0	0	3	7.1	5	4	4	4
STIEB, Dave	3.04	16-8	0	32	207.1	157	70	79	147
STOTTLEMYRE, Todd	5.69	4-8	0	28	98.0	109	62	46	67
WARD, Duane	3.30	9-3	15	64	111.2	101	41	60	91
WELLS, David	4.62	3-5	4	41	64.1	65	33	31	56
WILLS, Frank	5.23	0-0	0	10	20.2	22	12	6	19
1988 Totals	**3.80**	**87-75**	**47**	**162**	**1449.0**	**1404**	**611**	**528**	**904**

1987

BATTER	Pos.	Avg.	G	AB	R	H	HR	RBI
BARFIELD, Jesse	OF	.263	159	590	89	155	28	84
BELL, George	OF	.308	156	610	111	188	47	134
BENIQUEZ, Juan	DH-OF	.284	39	81	6	23	5	21
DEWILLIS, Jeff	C	.120	13	25	2	3	1	2
DUCEY, Rob	OF	.188	34	48	12	9	1	6
FERNANDEZ, Tony	SS	.322	146	578	90	186	5	67
FIELDER, Cecil	DH-1B	.269	82	175	30	47	14	32
GRUBER, Kelly	3B-SS	.235	138	341	50	80	12	36
INFANTE, Alexis	PR	.000	1	0	0	0	0	0
IORG, Garth	2B-3B	.210	122	310	35	65	4	30
LEACH, Rick	OF-DH	.282	98	195	26	55	3	25
LEE, Manny	2B-SS	.256	56	121	14	31	1	11
LIRIANO, Nelson	2B	.241	37	158	29	38	2	10
McGRIFF, Fred	DH-1B	.247	107	295	58	73	20	43
MOORE, Charlie	C	.215	51	107	15	23	1	7
MOSEBY, Lloyd	OF	.282	155	592	106	167	26	96
MULLINIKS, Rance	3B-DH	.310	124	332	37	103	11	44
MYERS, Greg	C	.111	7	9	1	1	0	0
SHARPERSON, Mike	2B	.208	32	96	4	20	0	9
STARK, Matt	C	.083	5	12	0	1	0	0
THORNTON, Lou	DH-OF	.500	12	2	5	1	0	0
UPSHAW, Willie	1B	.244	150	512	68	125	15	58
WHITT, Ernie	C	.269	135	446	57	120	19	75
1987 Totals		**.269**	**162**	**5635**	**845**	**1514**	**215**	**790**

PITCHER	ERA	W-L	SV	G	IP	H	ER	BB	SO
CERUTTI, John	4.40	11-4	0	44	151.1	144	74	59	92
CLANCY, Jim	3.54	15-11	0	37	241.1	234	95	80	180
EICHHORN, Mark	3.17	10-6	4	89	127.2	110	45	52	96
FLANAGAN, Mike	2.37	3-2	0	7	49.1	46	13	15	43
GORDON, Don	4.09	0-0	0	5	11.0	8	5	3	3
HENKE, Tom	2.49	0-6	34	72	94.0	62	26	25	128
JOHNSON, Joey	5.13	3-5	0	14	66.2	77	38	18	27
KEY, Jimmy	2.76	17-8	0	36	261.0	210	80	66	161
LAVELLE, Gary	5.53	2-3	1	23	27.2	36	17	19	17
MUSSELMAN, Jeff	4.15	12-5	3	68	89.0	75	41	54	54
NIEKRO, Phil	8.25	0-2	0	3	12.0	15	11	7	7
NUNEZ, Jose	5.01	5-2	0	37	97.0	91	54	58	99
STIEB, Dave	4.09	13-9	0	33	185.0	164	84	87	115
WARD, Duane	6.94	1-0	0	12	11.2	14	9	12	10
WELLS, David	3.99	4-3	1	18	29.1	37	13	12	32
1987 Totals	**3.74**	**96-66**	**43**	**162**	**1454.0**	**1323**	**605**	**567**	**1064**

1986

BATTER	Pos.	Avg.	G	AB	R	H	HR	RBI
BARFIELD, Jesse	OF	.289	158	589	107	170	40	108
BELL, George	OF	.309	159	641	101	198	31	108
FERNANDEZ, Tony	SS	.310	163	687	91	213	10	65
FIELDER, Cecil	DH-1B	.157	34	83	7	13	4	13
GARCIA, Damaso	2B	.281	122	424	57	119	6	46
GRUBER, Kelly	IF	.196	87	143	20	28	5	15
HEARRON, Jeff	C	.217	12	23	2	5	0	4
IORG, Garth	3B-2B	.260	137	327	30	85	3	44
JOHNSON, Cliff	DH	.250	107	336	48	84	15	55
LEACH, Rick	DH-OF	.309	110	246	35	76	5	39
LEE, Manny	2B-SS	.205	35	78	8	16	1	7
MARTINEZ, Buck	C	.181	81	160	13	29	2	12
McGRIFF, Fred	1B-DH	.200	3	5	1	1	0	0
MOSEBY, Lloyd	OF	.253	152	589	89	149	21	86
MULLINIKS, Rance	3B	.259	117	348	50	90	11	45
SHEPHERD, Ron	OF	.203	65	69	16	14	2	4
UPSHAW, Willie	1B	.251	155	573	85	144	9	60
WHITT, Ernie	C	.268	131	395	48	106	16	56
1986 Totals		**.269**	**163**	**5716**	**809**	**1540**	**181**	**767**

PITCHER	ERA	W-L	SV	G	IP	H	ER	BB	SO
ACKER, Jim	4.35	2-4	0	23	60.0	63	29	22	32
ALEXANDER, Doyle	4.46	5-4	0	17	111.0	120	55	20	65
AQUINO, Luis	6.35	1-1	0	7	11.1	14	8	3	5
CAUDILL, Bill	6.19	2-4	2	40	36.1	36	25	17	32
CERUTTI, John	4.15	9-4	1	34	145.1	150	67	47	89
CLANCY, Jim	3.94	14-14	0	34	219.1	202	96	63	126
CLARKE, Stan	9.24	0-1	0	10	12.2	18	13	10	9
DAVIS, Steve	17.18	0-0	0	3	3.2	8	7	5	5
EICHHORN, Mark	1.72	14-6	10	69	157.0	105	30	45	166
GORDON, Don	7.06	0-1	1	14	21.2	28	17	8	13
HENKE, Tom	3.35	9-5	27	63	91.1	63	34	32	118
JOHNSON, Joe	3.89	7-2	0	16	88.0	94	38	22	39
KEY, Jimmy	3.57	14-11	0	36	232.0	222	92	74	141
LAMP, Dennis	5.05	2-6	2	40	73.0	93	41	23	30
MAHLER, Mickey	0.00	0-0	0	2	1.0	1	0	0	0
MUSSELMAN, Jeff	10.13	0-0	0	6	5.1	8	6	5	4
STIEB, Dave	4.74	7-12	1	37	205.0	239	108	87	127
WARD, Duane	13.50	0-1	0	2	2.0	3	3	4	1
1986 Totals	**4.08**	**86-76**	**44**	**163**	**1476.0**	**1467**	**669**	**487**	**1002**

1985

BATTER	Pos.	Avg.	G	AB	R	H	HR	RBI
AIKENS, Willie	DH	.200	12	20	2	4	1	5
ALLENSON, Gary	C	.118	14	34	2	4	0	3
BARFIELD, Jesse	OF	.289	155	539	94	156	27	84
BELL, George	OF	.275	157	607	87	167	28	95
BURROUGHS, Jeff	DH	.257	86	191	19	49	6	28
FERNANDEZ, Tony	SS	.289	161	564	71	163	2	51
FIELDER, Cecil	1B	.311	30	74	6	23	4	16
GARCIA, Damaso	2B	.282	146	600	70	169	8	65
GRUBER, Kelly	3B	.231	5	13	0	3	0	1
HEARRON, Jeff	C	.143	4	7	0	1	0	0
IORG, Garth	3B-2B	.313	131	288	33	90	7	37
JOHNSON, Cliff	DH-1B	.274	24	73	4	20	1	10
LEACH, Rick	1B-OF	.200	16	35	2	7	0	1
LEE, Manny	IF	.200	64	40	9	8	0	0
MARTINEZ, Buck	C	.162	42	99	11	16	4	14
MATUSZEK, Len	DH-1B	.212	62	151	23	32	2	15
MOSEBY, Lloyd	OF	.259	152	584	92	151	18	70
MULLINIKS, Rance	3B	.295	129	366	55	108	10	57
NICOSIA, Steve	C	.267	6	15	0	4	0	1
OLIVER, Al	DH	.251	61	187	20	47	5	23
SHEPHERD, Ron	OF-DH	.114	38	35	7	4	0	1
THORNTON, Lou	OF-DH	.236	56	72	18	17	1	8
UPSHAW, Willie	1B	.275	148	501	79	138	15	65
WEBSTER, Mitch	OF-DH	.000	4	1	0	0	0	0
WHITT, Ernie	C	.245	139	412	55	101	19	64
1985 Totals		**.269**	**161**	**5508**	**759**	**1482**	**158**	**714**

PITCHER	ERA	W-L	SV	G	IP	H	ER	BB	SO
ACKER, Jim	3.23	7-2	10	61	86.1	86	31	43	42
ALEXANDER, Doyle	3.45	17-10	0	36	260.2	268	100	67	142
CAUDILL, Bill	2.99	4-6	14	67	69.1	53	23	35	46
CERUTTI, John	5.40	0-2	0	4	6.2	10	4	4	5
CLANCY, Jim	3.78	9-6	0	23	128.2	117	54	37	66
CLARKE, Stan	4.50	0-0	0	4	4.0	3	2	2	2
DAVIS, Steve	3.54	2-1	0	10	28.0	23	11	13	22
FILER, Tom	3.88	7-0	0	11	48.2	38	21	18	24
HENKE, Tom	2.03	3-3	13	28	40.0	29	9	8	42
KEY, Jimmy	3.00	14-6	0	35	212.2	188	71	50	85
LAMP, Dennis	3.32	11-0	2	53	105.2	96	39	27	68
LAVELLE, Gary	3.10	5-7	8	69	72.2	54	25	36	50
LEAL, Luis	5.75	3-6	0	15	67.1	82	43	24	33
MUSSELMAN, Ron	4.47	3-0	0	25	52.1	59	26	24	29
STIEB, Dave	2.48	14-13	0	36	265.0	206	73	96	167
1985 Totals	**3.29**	**99-62**	**47**	**161**	**1448.0**	**1312**	**529**	**484**	**823**

1984

BATTER	Pos.	Avg.	G	AB	R	H	HR	RBI
AIKENS, Willie	DH	.205	93	234	21	48	11	26
BARFIELD, Jesse	OF	.284	110	320	51	91	14	49
BELL, George	OF	.292	159	606	85	177	26	87
COLLINS, Dave	OF	.308	128	441	59	136	2	44
FERNANDEZ, Tony	SS	.270	88	233	29	63	3	19
GARCIA, Damaso	2B	.284	152	633	79	180	5	46
GRIFFIN, Alfredo	SS-2B	.241	140	419	53	101	4	30
GRUBER, Kelly	3B	.063	15	16	1	1	1	2
HERNANDEZ, Toby	C	.500	3	2	1	1	0	0
IORG, Garth	3B	.227	121	247	24	56	1	25
JOHNSON, Cliff	DH	.304	127	359	51	109	16	61
LEACH, Rick	OF-1B	.261	65	88	11	23	0	7
MANRIQUE, Fred	2B	.333	10	9	0	3	0	1
MARTINEZ, Buck	C	.220	102	232	24	51	5	37
MOSEBY, Lloyd	OF	.280	158	592	97	166	18	92
MULLINIKS, Rance	IF	.324	125	343	41	111	3	42
PETRALLI, Geno	C	.000	3	3	0	0	0	0
SHEPHERD, Ron	OF	.000	12	4	0	0	0	0
UPSHAW, Willie	1B	.278	152	569	79	158	19	84
WEBSTER, Mitch	OF	.227	26	22	9	5	0	4
WHITT, Ernie	C	.238	124	315	35	75	15	46
1984 Totals		**.273**	**163**	**5687**	**750**	**1555**	**143**	**702**

PITCHER	ERA	W-L	SV	G	IP	H	ER	BB	SO
ACKER, Jim	4.38	3-5	1	32	72.0	79	35	25	33
ALEXANDER, Doyle	3.13	17-6	0	36	261.2	238	91	59	139
CLANCY, Jim	5.12	13-15	0	36	219.2	249	125	88	118
CLARK, Bryan	5.91	1-2	0	20	45.2	66	30	22	21
GOTT, Jim	4.02	7-6	2	35	109.2	93	49	49	73
JACKSON, Roy Lee	3.56	7-8	10	54	86.0	73	34	31	58
KEY, Jimmy	4.65	4-5	10	63	62.0	70	32	32	44
LAMP, Dennis	4.55	8-8	9	56	85.0	97	43	38	45
LEACH, Rick	27.00	0-0	0	1	1.0	2	3	2	0
LEAL, Luis	3.89	13-8	0	35	222.1	221	96	77	134
McLAUGHLIN, Joey	2.53	0-0	0	6	10.2	12	3	7	3
MUSSELMAN, Ron	2.11	0-2	1	11	21.1	18	5	10	9
STIEB, Dave	2.83	16-8	0	35	267.0	215	84	88	198
1984 Totals	**3.86**	**89-73**	**33**	**162**	**1464.0**	**1433**	**628**	**528**	**875**

1983

BATTER	Pos.	Avg.	G	AB	R	H	HR	RBI
BARFIELD, Jesse	OF	.253	128	388	58	98	27	68
BELL, George	OF	.268	39	112	5	30	2	17
BONNELL, Barry	OF	.318	121	377	49	120	10	54
COLLINS, Dave	OF	.271	118	402	55	109	1	34
FERNANDEZ, Tony	SS	.265	15	34	5	9	0	2
GARCIA, Damaso	2B	.307	131	525	84	161	3	38
GRIFFIN, Alfredo	SS	.250	162	528	62	132	4	47
IORG, Garth	3B-2B	.275	122	375	40	103	2	39
JOHNSON, Cliff	DH	.265	142	407	59	108	22	76
KLUTTS, Mickey	3B	.256	22	43	3	11	3	5
MARTINEZ, Buck	C	.253	88	221	27	56	10	33
MOSEBY, Lloyd	OF	.315	151	539	104	170	18	81
MULLINIKS, Rance	3B-SS	.275	129	364	54	100	10	49
ORTA, Jorge	DH-OF	.237	103	245	30	58	10	38
PETRALLI, Geno	C	.000	6	4	0	0	0	0
POWELL, Hosken	OF	.169	40	83	6	14	1	7
UPSHAW, Willie	1B	.306	160	579	99	177	27	104
WEBSTER, Mitch	OF	.182	11	11	2	2	0	0
WHITT, Ernie	C	.256	123	344	53	88	17	56
1983 Totals		**.277**	**162**	**5581**	**795**	**1546**	**167**	**748**

PITCHER	ERA	W-L	SV	G	IP	H	ER	BB	SO
ACKER, Jim	4.33	5-1	1	38	97.2	103	47	38	44
ALEXANDER, Doyle	3.93	7-6	0	17	116.2	126	51	26	46
CLANCY, Jim	3.91	15-11	0	34	223.0	238	97	61	99
CLARKE, Stan	3.27	1-1	0	10	11.0	10	4	5	7
COOPER, Don	6.75	0-0	0	4	5.1	8	4	0	5
GEISEL, Dave	4.64	0-3	5	47	52.1	47	27	31	50
GOTT, Jim	4.74	9-14	0	34	176.2	195	93	68	121
JACKSON, Roy Lee	4.50	8-3	7	49	92.0	92	46	41	48
LEAL, Luis	4.31	13-12	0	35	217.1	216	104	65	116
McLAUGHLIN, Joey	4.45	7-4	9	50	64.2	63	32	37	47
MOFFITT, Randy	3.77	6-2	10	45	57.1	52	24	24	38
MORGAN, Mike	5.16	0-3	0	16	45.1	48	26	21	22
STIEB, Dave	3.04	17-12	0	36	278.0	223	94	93	187
WILLIAMS, Matt	14.63	1-1	0	4	8.0	13	13	7	5
1983 Totals	**4.12**	**89-73**	**32**	**162**	**1445.1**	**1434**	**662**	**517**	**835**

1982

BATTER	Pos.	Avg.	G	AB	R	H	HR	RBI
ADAMS, Glenn	DH	.258	30	66	2	17	1	11
BAKER, Dave	3B	.250	9	20	3	5	0	2
BARFIELD, Jesse	OF	.246	139	394	54	97	18	58
BONNELL, Barry	OF	.293	140	437	59	128	6	49
DAVIS, Dick	OF-DH	.286	3	7	0	2	0	2
GARCIA, Damaso	2B	.310	147	597	89	185	5	42
GRIFFIN, Alfredo	SS	.241	162	539	57	130	1	48
HERNANDEZ, Pedro	3B	.000	8	9	1	0	0	0
IORG, Garth	3B-2B	.285	129	417	45	119	1	36
JOHNSON, Anthony	OF-DH	.235	70	98	17	23	3	14
MARTINEZ, Buck	C	.242	96	260	26	63	10	37
MAYBERRY, John	DH-1B	.273	17	33	7	9	2	3
MOSEBY, Lloyd	OF	.236	147	487	51	115	9	52
MULLINIKS, Rance	3B-SS	.244	112	311	32	76	4	35
NORDHAGEN, Wayne	DH-OF	.270	72	185	12	50	1	20
PETRALLI, Geno	C	.364	16	44	3	16	0	1
POWELL, Hosken	OF-DH	.275	112	265	43	73	3	26
REVERING, Dave	DH	.215	55	135	15	29	5	18
ROBERTS, Leon	OF-DH	.229	40	105	6	24	1	5
UPSHAW, Willie	1B	.267	160	580	77	155	21	75
VELEZ, Otto	DH	.192	28	52	4	10	1	5
WHITT, Ernie	C	.261	105	284	28	74	11	42
WOODS, Al	OF	.234	85	201	20	47	3	24
1982 Totals		**.262**	**162**	**5526**	**651**	**1447**	**106**	**605**

PITCHER	ERA	W-L	SV	G	IP	H	ER	BB	SO
BOMBACK, Mark	6.03	1-5	0	16	59.2	87	40	25	22
CLANCY, Jim	3.71	16-14	0	40	266.2	251	110	77	139
EICHHORN, Mark	5.45	0-3	0	7	38.0	40	23	14	16
GARVIN, Jerry	7.25	1-1	0	32	58.1	81	47	26	35
GEISEL, Dave	3.98	1-1	0	16	31.2	32	14	17	22
GOTT, Jim	4.43	5-10	0	30	136.0	134	67	66	82
JACKSON, Roy Lee	3.06	8-8	6	48	97.0	77	33	31	71
LEAL, Luis	3.93	12-15	0	38	249.2	250	109	79	111
McLAUGHLIN, Joey	3.21	8-6	8	44	70.0	54	25	30	49
MURRAY, Dale	3.16	8-7	11	56	111.0	115	39	32	60
SCHROM, Ken	5.87	1-0	0	6	15.1	13	10	15	8
SENTENEY, Steve	4.91	0-0	0	11	22.0	23	12	6	20
STIEB, Dave	3.25	17-14	0	38	288.1	271	104	75	141
1982 Totals	**3.95**	**78-84**	**25**	**162**	**1443.2**	**1428**	**633**	**493**	**776**

1981

BATTER	Pos.	Avg.	G	AB	R	H	HR	RBI
AINGE, Danny	3B	.187	86	246	20	46	0	14
BARFIELD, Jesse	OF	.232	25	95	7	22	2	9
BEAMON, Charlie	DH-1B	.200	8	15	1	3	0	0
BELL, George	OF	.233	60	163	19	38	5	12
BONNELL, Barry	OF	.220	66	227	21	50	4	28
BOSETTI, Rick	OF	.234	25	47	5	11	0	4
COX, Ted	3B	.300	16	50	6	15	2	9
GARCIA, Damaso	2B	.252	64	250	24	63	1	13
GRIFFIN, Alfredo	SS	.209	101	388	30	81	0	21
IORG, Garth	2B-3B	.242	70	215	17	52	0	10
MACHA, Ken	3B-1B	.200	37	85	4	17	0	6
MANRIQUE, Fred	IF	.143	14	28	1	4	0	1
MARTINEZ, Buck	C	.227	45	128	13	29	4	21
MAYBERRY, John	1B	.248	94	290	34	72	17	43
MOSEBY, Lloyd	OF	.233	100	378	36	88	9	43
STIEB, Dave	PR	.000	1	0	1	0	0	0
UPSHAW, Willie	DH-1B-OF	.171	61	111	15	19	4	10
VELEZ, Otto	DH	.213	80	240	32	51	11	28
WELLS, Greg	1B-DH	.247	32	73	7	18	0	5
WHITMER, Dan	C	.111	7	9	0	1	0	0
WHITT, Ernie	C	.236	74	195	16	46	1	16
WOODS, Al	OF	.247	85	288	20	71	1	21
1981 Totals		**.226**	**106**	**3521**	**329**	**797**	**61**	**314**

PITCHER	ERA	W-L	SV	G	IP	H	ER	BB	SO
BARLOW, Mike	4.20	0-0	0	12	15.0	22	7	6	5
BERENGUER, Juan	4.31	2-9	0	12	71.0	62	34	35	29
BOMBACK, Mark	3.89	5-5	0	20	90.1	84	39	35	33
CLANCY, Jim	4.90	6-12	0	22	125.0	126	68	64	56
ESPINOSA, Nino	9.00	0-0	0	1	1.0	4	1	0	0
GARVIN, Jerry	3.40	1-2	0	35	53.0	46	20	23	25
JACKSON, Roy Lee	2.61	1-2	7	39	62.0	65	18	25	27
LEAL, Luis	3.68	7-13	1	29	129.2	127	53	44	71
McLAUGHLIN, Joey	2.85	1-5	10	40	60.0	55	19	21	38
MIRABELLA, Paul	7.36	0-0	0	8	14.2	20	12	7	9
MURRAY, Dale	1.17	1-0	0	11	15.1	12	2	5	12
STIEB, Dave	3.19	11-10	0	25	183.2	148	65	61	89
TODD, Jackson	3.96	2-7	0	21	97.2	94	43	31	41
WILLIS, Mike	5.91	0-4	0	20	35.0	43	23	20	16
1981 Totals	**3.81**	**37-69**	**18**	**106**	**953.1**	**908**	**404**	**377**	**451**

1980

BATTER	Pos.	Avg.	G	AB	R	H	HR	RBI
AINGE, Danny	OF-IF	.243	38	111	11	27	0	4
AULT, Doug	1B-DH	.194	64	144	12	28	3	15
BAILOR, Bob	OF-IF	.236	117	347	44	82	1	16
BONNELL, Barry	OF	.268	130	463	55	124	13	56
BOSETTI, Rick	OF	.213	53	188	24	40	4	18
BRAUN, Steve	PH-DH	.273	37	55	4	15	1	9
CANNON, J.J.	PR-OF	.080	70	50	16	4	0	4
DAVIS, Bob	C	.216	91	218	18	47	4	19
GARCIA, Damaso	2B	.278	140	543	50	151	4	46
GRIFFIN, Alfredo	SS	.254	155	653	63	166	2	41
HODGSON, Paul	OF	.220	20	41	5	9	1	5
HOWELL, Roy	3B	.269	142	528	51	142	10	57
IORG, Garth	IF	.248	80	222	24	55	2	14
KELLY, Pat	C	.286	3	7	0	2	0	0
MACHA, Mike	3B-C	.000	5	8	0	0	0	0
MAYBERRY, John	1B	.248	149	501	62	124	30	82
MOSEBY, Lloyd	OF	.229	114	389	44	89	9	46
RAMOS, Domingo	IF	.125	5	16	0	2	0	0
STIEB, Dave	P-OF	.000	1	1	0	0	0	0
UPSHAW, Willie	1B-DH	.213	34	61	10	13	1	5
VELEZ, Otto	DH	.269	104	357	54	96	20	62
WHITT, Ernie	C	.237	106	295	23	70	6	34
WOODS, Al	OF	.300	109	373	54	112	15	47
1980 Totals		**.251**	**162**	**5571**	**624**	**1398**	**126**	**580**

PITCHER	ERA	W-L	SV	G	IP	H	ER	BB	SO
BAILOR, Bob	7.71	0-0	0	3	2.1	4	2	1	0
BARLOW, Mike	4.09	3-1	5	40	55.0	57	25	21	19
BUSKEY, Tom	4.46	3-1	0	33	66.2	68	33	26	34
CLANCY, Jim	3.30	13-16	0	34	250.2	217	92	128	152
GARVIN, Jerry	2.29	4-7	8	61	82.2	70	21	27	52
JEFFERSON, Jesse	5.47	4-13	0	29	121.2	130	74	52	53
KUCEK, Jack	6.75	3-8	1	23	68.0	83	51	41	35
LEAL, Luis	4.53	3-4	0	13	59.2	72	30	31	26
LEMANCZYK, Dave	5.40	2-5	0	10	43.1	57	26	15	10
McLAUGHLIN, Joey	4.51	6-9	4	55	135.2	159	68	53	70
MIRABELLA, Paul	4.34	5-12	0	33	130.2	151	63	66	53
MOORE, Balor	5.29	1-1	1	31	64.2	76	38	31	22
SCHROM, Ken	5.23	1-0	1	17	31.0	32	18	19	13
STIEB, Dave	3.71	12-15	0	34	242.2	232	100	83	108
TODD, Jackson	4.02	5-2	0	12	85.0	90	38	30	44
WILLIS, Mike	1.71	2-1	3	20	26.1	25	5	11	14
1980 Totals	**4.19**	**67-95**	**23**	**162**	**1466.1**	**1523**	**683**	**635**	**705**

1979

BATTER	Pos.	Avg.	G	AB	R	H	HR	RBI
AINGE, Danny	2B	.237	87	308	26	73	2	19
BAILOR, Bob	OF-3B	.229	130	414	50	95	1	38
BOSETTI, Rick	OF	.260	162	619	59	161	8	65
BROWN, Bobby	OF	.000	4	10	1	0	0	0
CANNON, J.J.	OF	.211	61	142	14	30	1	5
CARTY, Rico	DH	.256	132	461	48	118	12	55
CERONE, Rick	C	.239	136	469	47	112	7	61
DAVIS, Bob	C	.124	32	89	6	11	1	8
GOMEZ, Luis	IF	.239	59	163	11	39	0	11
GRIFFIN, Alfredo	SS	.287	153	624	81	179	2	31
HERNANDEZ, Pedro	PR	.000	3	0	1	0	0	0
HOWELL, Roy	3B	.247	138	511	60	126	15	72
JOHNSON, Tim	IF	.186	43	86	6	16	0	6
KUSICK, Craig	1B	.204	24	54	3	11	2	7
MAYBERRY, John	1B	.274	137	464	61	127	21	74
McKAY, Dave	2B	.218	47	156	19	34	0	12
ROBERTSON, Bob	1B	.103	15	29	1	3	1	1
SOLAITA, Tony	DH-1B	.265	36	102	14	27	2	13
VELEZ, Otto	OF	.288	99	274	45	79	15	48
WILBORN, Ted	OF	.000	22	12	3	0	0	0
WOODS, Al	OF	.278	132	436	57	121	5	36
1979 Totals		**.251**	**162**	**5423**	**613**	**1362**	**95**	**562**

PITCHER	ERA	W-L	SV	G	IP	H	ER	BB	SO
BUSKEY, Tom	3.43	6-10	7	44	78.2	74	30	25	44
CLANCY, Jim	5.51	2-7	0	12	63.2	65	39	31	33
EDGE, Butch	5.23	3-4	0	9	51.2	60	30	24	19
FREISLEBEN, Dave	4.95	2-3	3	42	91.0	101	50	53	35
GARVIN, Jerry	2.78	0-1	0	8	22.2	15	7	10	14
GRILLI, Steve	0.00	0-0	0	1	2.1	1	0	0	1
HUFFMAN, Phil	5.77	6-18	0	31	173.0	220	111	68	56
JEFFERSON, Jesse	5.51	2-10	1	34	116.0	150	71	45	43
KUSICK, Craig	4.91	0-0	0	1	3.2	3	2	0	0
LEMANCZYK, Dave	3.71	8-10	0	22	143.0	137	59	45	63
LEMONGELLO, Mark	6.29	1-9	0	18	83.0	97	58	34	40
LUEBBER, Steve	0.00	0-0	0	1	0.0	2	1	1	0
MILLER, Dyar	10.57	0-0	0	10	15.1	27	18	5	7
MOORE, Balor	4.84	5-7	0	34	139.1	135	75	79	51
MURPHY, Tom	5.40	1-2	0	10	18.1	23	11	8	6
STIEB, Dave	4.31	8-8	0	18	129.1	139	62	48	52
TODD, Jackson	5.85	0-1	0	12	32.1	40	21	7	14
UNDERWOOD, Tom	3.69	9-16	0	33	227.0	213	93	95	127
WILLIS, Mike	8.44	0-3	0	17	26.2	35	25	16	8
1979 Totals	**4.81**	**53-109**	**11**	**162**	**1417.0**	**1537**	**758**	**594**	**613**

1978

BATTER	Pos.	Avg.	G	AB	R	H	HR	RBI
ALBERTS, Butch	DH	.278	6	18	1	5	0	0
ASHBY, Alan	C	.261	81	264	27	69	9	29
AULT, Doug	1B	.240	54	104	10	25	3	7
BAILOR, Bob	OF-IF	.264	154	621	74	164	1	52
BOSETTI, Rick	OF	.259	136	568	61	147	5	42
CARTY, Rico	DH	.284	104	387	51	110	20	68
CERONE, Rick	C	.223	88	282	25	63	3	20
EWING, Sam	DH-OF	.179	40	56	3	10	2	9
GOMEZ, Luis	SS	.223	153	413	39	92	0	32
HORTON, Willie	DH	.205	33	122	12	25	3	19
HOWELL, Roy	IF	.270	140	551	67	149	8	61
HUTTON, Tommy	OF-1B	.254	64	173	19	44	2	9
IORG, Garth	2B	.163	19	49	3	8	0	3
JOHNSON, Tim	SS-2B	.241	68	79	9	19	0	3
MAYBERRY, John	1B	.250	152	515	51	129	22	70
McKAY, Dave	2B	.238	145	504	59	120	7	45
MILNER, Brian	C	.444	2	9	3	4	0	2
NORDBROOK, Tim	SS	.000	7	0	1	0	0	0
UPSHAW, Willie	OF-DH	.237	95	224	26	53	1	17
VELEZ, Otto	OF	.266	91	248	29	66	9	38
WHITT, Ernie	C	.000	2	4	0	0	0	0
WOODS, Al	OF	.241	62	220	19	53	3	25
WOODS, Gary	OF	.158	8	19	1	3	0	0
1978 Totals		**.250**	**161**	**5430**	**590**	**1358**	**98**	**551**

PITCHER	ERA	W-L	SV	G	IP	H	ER	BB	SO
BUSKEY, Tom	3.38	0-1	0	8	13.1	14	5	5	7
CLANCY, Jim	4.09	10-12	0	31	193.2	199	88	91	106
COLEMAN, Joe	4.60	2-0	0	31	60.2	67	31	30	28
CRUZ, Victor	1.71	7-3	9	32	47.1	28	9	35	51
GARVIN, Jerry	5.54	4-12	0	26	144.2	189	89	48	67
JEFFERSON, Jesse	4.38	7-16	0	31	211.2	214	103	86	97
KIRKWOOD, Don	4.24	4-5	0	16	68.0	76	32	25	29
LEMANCZYK, Dave	6.26	4-14	0	29	136.2	170	95	65	62
MOORE, Balor	4.93	6-9	0	37	144.1	165	79	54	75
MURPHY, Tom	3.93	6-9	7	50	94.0	87	41	37	36
UNDERWOOD, Tom	4.10	6-14	0	31	197.2	201	90	87	139
WALLACE, Dave	3.86	0-0	0	6	14.0	12	6	11	7
WILEY, Mark	6.75	0-0	0	2	2.2	3	2	1	2
WILLIS, Mike	4.56	3-7	7	44	100.2	104	51	39	52
1978 Totals	**4.54**	**59-102**	**23**	**161**	**1429.1**	**1529**	**723**	**614**	**758**

1977

BATTER	Pos.	Avg.	G	AB	R	H	HR	RBI
ASHBY, Alan	C	.210	124	396	25	83	2	29
AULT, Doug	1B-DH	.245	129	445	44	109	11	64
BAILOR, Bob	IF-OF	.310	122	496	62	154	5	32
BOWLING, Steve	OF	.206	89	194	19	40	1	13
CERONE, Rick	C	.200	31	100	7	20	1	10
EWING, Sam	OF-DH	.287	97	244	24	70	4	34
FAIRLY, Ron	DH-1B-OF	.279	132	458	60	128	19	64
GARCIA, Pedro	2B	.208	41	130	10	27	0	9
HOWELL, Roy	3B	.316	96	364	41	115	10	44
MASON, Jim	SS	.165	22	79	10	13	0	2
McKAY, Dave	IF	.197	95	274	18	54	3	22
NORDBROOK, Tim	SS	.175	24	63	9	11	0	1
RADER, Doug	3B-DH	.240	96	313	47	75	13	40
ROOF, Phil	C	.000	3	5	0	0	0	0
SCOTT, John	OF	.240	79	233	26	56	2	15
STAGGS, Steve	2B	.259	72	290	37	75	2	28
TORRES, Hector	IF	.241	91	266	33	64	5	26
VELEZ, Otto	OF-DH	.256	120	360	50	92	16	62
WHITT, Ernie	C	.171	23	41	4	7	0	6
WOODS, Al	OF	.284	122	440	58	125	6	35
WOODS, Gary	OF	.216	60	227	21	49	0	17
1977 Totals		**.252**	**161**	**5418**	**605**	**1367**	**100**	**553**

PITCHER	ERA	W-L	SV	G	IP	H	ER	BB	SO
BRUNO, Tom	7.85	0-1	0	12	18.1	30	16	13	9
BYRD, Jeff	6.18	2-13	0	17	87.1	98	60	68	40
CLANCY, Jim	5.05	4-9	0	13	76.2	80	43	47	44
DARR, Mike	33.75	0-1	0	1	1.1	3	5	4	1
DeBARR, Dennis	5.91	0-1	0	14	21.1	29	14	8	10
GARVIN, Jerry	4.19	10-18	0	34	244.2	247	114	85	127
HARGAN, Steve	5.22	1-3	0	6	29.1	36	17	14	11
HARTENSTEIN, Chuck	6.59	0-2	0	13	27.1	40	20	6	15
JEFFERSON, Jesse	4.31	9-17	0	33	217.0	224	104	83	114
JOHNSON, Jerry	4.60	2-4	5	43	86.0	91	44	54	54
LEMANCZYK, Dave	4.25	13-16	0	34	252.0	278	119	87	105
MURPHY, Tom	3.63	2-1	2	19	52.0	63	21	18	26
SINGER, Bill	6.79	2-8	0	13	59.2	71	45	39	33
VUKOVICH, Pete	3.47	7-7	8	53	148.0	143	57	59	123
WILLIS, Mike	3.94	2-6	5	43	107.1	105	47	38	59
1977 Totals	**4.57**	**54-107**	**20**	**161**	**1428.1**	**1538**	**726**	**623**	**771**

CLUB STATISTICS

YEAR-BY-YEAR RECORD

YEAR	WON-LOST	PCT		HOME	PCT	ROAD	PCT	POS	GB	MANAGER
1977	54-107	.335		25-55	.313	29-52	.358	7th	45.5	Roy Hartsfield
1978	59-102	.366		37-44	.457	22-58	.275	7th	50.0	Roy Hartsfield
1979	53-109	.327		32-49	.395	21-60	.259	7th	50.5	Roy Hartsfield
1980	67-95	.414		35-46	.432	32-49	.395	7th	36.0	Bob Mattick
1981	16-42	.276	(1st half)	17-36	.320	20-33	.377	7th	19.0	Bob Mattick
	21-27	.438	(2nd half)					7th	7.5	Bob Mattick
1982	78-84	.481		44-37	.543	34-47	.420	T6th	17.0	Bobby Cox
1983	89-73	.549		48-33	.593	41-40	.506	4th	9.0	Bobby Cox
1984	89-73	.549		49-32	.605	40-41	.494	2nd	15.0	Bobby Cox
1985	99-62	.615		54-26	.675	45-36	.556	1st	+2.0	Bobby Cox
1986	86-76	.531		42-39	.519	44-37	.543	4th	9.5	Jimy Williams
1987	96-66	.593		52-29	.642	44-37	.543	2nd	2.0	Jimy Williams
1988	87-75	.537		45-36	.556	42-39	.519	T3rd	2.0	Jimy Williams
1989	89-73	.549		46-35	.568	43-38	.531	1st	+2.0	Williams/Gaston
1990	86-76	.531		44-37	.543	42-39	.519	2nd	2.0	Cito Gaston
1991	91-71	.562		46-35	.568	45-36	.556	1st	+7.0	Gaston/Tenace
1992	96-66	.593		53-28	.654	43-38	.531	1st	+4.0	Cito Gaston
1993	95-67	.586		48-33	.593	47-34	.580	1st	+7.0	Cito Gaston
1994	55-60	.478		33-26	.559	22-34	.393	3rd	16.0	Cito Gaston
1995	56-88	.389		29-43	.403	27-45	.375	5th	31.0	Cito Gaston
1996	74-88	.457		35-46	.432	39-42	.481	4th	18.0	Cito Gaston
1997	76-86	.469		42-39	.519	34-47	.420	5th	22.0	Gaston/Queen
1998	88-74	.543		51-30	.630	37-44	.457	3rd	26.0	Tim Johnson
1999	84-78	.519		40-41	.494	44-37	.543	3rd	14.0	Jim Fregosi
2000	83-79	.512		45-36	.556	38-43	.469	3rd	4.5	Jim Fregosi
2001	80-82	.493		40-42	.488	40-40	.500	3rd	16.0	Buck Martinez
2002	78-84	.481		42-39	.519	36-45	.444	3rd	25.5	Martinez/Tosca
2003	86-76	.530		41-40	.506	45-36	.556	3rd	15.0	Carlos Tosca
2004	67-94	.416		40-41	.494	27-53	.338	5th	33.5	Tosca/Gibbons
2005	80-82	.494		43-38	.531	37-44	.457	3rd	15.0	John Gibbons
2006	87-75	.537		50-31	.617	37-44	.457	2nd	10.0	John Gibbons
2007	83-79	.512		49-32	.605	34-47	.420	3rd	13.0	John Gibbons
2008	86-76	.531		47-34	.580	39-42	.481	4th	11.0	Gibbons/Gaston
2009	75-87	.463		44-37	.543	31-50	.383	4th	28.0	Cito Gaston
2010	85-77	.525		45-33	.577	40-44	.476	4th	11.0	Cito Gaston
2011	81-81	.500		42-39	.519	39-42	.481	4th	16.0	John Farrell
2012	73-89	.451		41-40	.506	32-49	.395	4th	22.0	John Farrell
TOTAL	**2828-2879**	**.496**		**1516-1337**	**.531**	**1312-1542**	**.460**			

WORLD SERIES/LCS SHARES:

Here are the individual share/total of all shares that Blue Jays players have received when reaching the post season.

1985	$26,697.41/$975.671.41	(1st place-East)
1989	$37,927.84/$1,513,851.10	(1st place-East)
1991	$35,163.53/$1,541,918.45	(1st place-East)
1992	$114,962.16/$4,871,020.61	(1st place-East/AL/World Series)
1993	$127,920.77/$5,327,335.76	(1st place-East/AL/World Series)

CLINCHING/ELIMINATION DATES (DIVISION WINNER)

YEAR	DATE	GP		ELIMINATED BY	H/A	TOR-OPP	WINNER	GBL
1977	Aug. 30	129	a	Did not play	–	–	New York	33.0
1978	Aug. 29	133	b	Texas	A	4-1	New York	30.5
1979	Aug. 19	123		California	A	2-4	Baltimore	41.0
1980	Sept. 7	137	c	Chicago	H	7-6	New York	27.0
+1981	May 17	34	d	Cleveland	A	0-1	New York	10.0
	Sept. 22	39		Oakland	H	2-4	Milwaukee	5.5
1982	Sept. 14	143	e	Did not play	–	–	Milwaukee	19.0
1983	Sept. 21	153		Seattle	H	4-3	Baltimore	11.0
1984	Sept. 18	151		Boston	H	10-3	Detroit	13.0
1985	Oct. 5	160		New York	H	5-1	Toronto	+2.0
1986	Sept. 28	156		Boston	A	3-12	Boston	9.0
1987	Oct. 4	162		Detroit	A	0-1	Detroit	2.0
1988	Sept. 25	156		Cleveland	A	3-4	Boston	7.5
1989	Sept. 30	161		Baltimore	H	4-3	Toronto	+2.0
1990	Oct. 3	162		Baltimore	A	2-3	Boston	2.0
1991	Oct. 2	159		California	H	6-5	Toronto	+7.0
1992	Oct. 3	161		Detroit	H	3-1	Toronto	+3.0
1993	Sept. 27	156		Milwaukee	A	2-0	Toronto	+6.5
1994	SEASON ENDED DUE TO PLAYER STRIKE							
1995	Sept. 3	118		Chicago	A	5-6	Boston	24.5
1996	Sept. 13	147		New York	H	1-4	New York	16.5
1997	Sept. 9	144	f	Anaheim	H	2-0	Baltimore	20.0
1998	Aug. 28	136	g	New York	H	7-6	New York	29.0
1999	Sept. 19	150		Chicago	H	2-3	New York	13.5
2000	Sept. 28	159		Baltimore	A	1-23	New York	4.5
2001	Sept. 21	147		Tampa Bay	H	4-7	New York	16.0
2002	Sept. 3	138		Chicago	H	4-5	New York	25.5
2003	Sept. 13	148	h	Baltimore	H	6-1	New York	16.0
2004	Sept. 4	136		Oakland	H	5-9	New York	27.5
2005	Sept. 20	150	i	Baltimore	H	6-4	New York	15.0
2006	Sept. 19	151		New York	H	3-6	New York	13.0
2007	Sept. 14	147	j	Baltimore	H	2-6	Boston	13.0
2008	Sept. 19	154		Boston	H	3-4	Tampa Bay	11.0
2009	Sept. 7	137		Minnesota	H	3-6	New York	28.0
2010	Sept. 18	148	k	Baltimore	A	4-3	Tampa Bay	11.0
2011	Sept. 13	148		Boston	A	6-18	New York	16.0
2012	Sept. 19	146		New York	A	2-4 (GM 1)	New York	22.0

a New York defeated Seattle, 6-5, to eliminate Blue Jays
b Boston (leader on Aug. 29) defeated Seattle, 10-5, to eliminate Blue Jays
c New York defeated California, 4-1, to eliminate Blue Jays, 2nd game of DH
d 1st game of DH
\+ Split-Season
e Milwaukee defeated Detroit, 6-3, to eliminate Blue Jays
f Baltimore defeated Detroit, 16-6, to eliminate Blue Jays
g Baltimore defeated Cleveland, 9-3, to eliminate Blue Jays
h New York defeated Tampa Bay in Gm #1 of double header, 6-5, to eliminate Blue Jays.
i Yankees defeated Orioles 12-9, to eliminate Blue Jays
j Yankees defeated Orioles 2-1, to eliminate Blue Jays
k Yankees defeated Orioles 11-3, to eliminate Blue Jays

ALL-TIME WON-LOST BREAKDOWN

Year	Home	Road	Day	Night	vs East	vs Cent	vs West	vs NL	1-Run	Extra Inn's	DH's W-L-S
1977	25-55	29-52	27-39	27-68	31-58	–	23-49	–	17-27	4-11	1-7-8
1978	37-44	22-58	20-42	39-60	28-61	–	31-41	–	23-30	7-8	3-8-6
1979	32-49	21-60	21-44	32-65	22-56	–	31-53	–	19-28	2-10	0-3-7
1980	35-46	32-49	29-27	38-68	28-50	–	39-45	–	23-21	10-8	5-1-4
1981	17-36	20-33	16-27	21-42	15-27	–	22-42	–	10-17	1-8	0-5-0
1982	44-37	34-47	30-28	48-56	33-45	–	45-39	–	28-30	10-5	3-3-2
1983	48-33	41-40	35-23	54-50	39-39	–	50-34	–	25-20	11-6	1-1-4
1984	49-32	40-41	32-27	57-46	37-41	–	52-32	–	34-25	6-12	2-4-1
1985	54-26	45-36	34-24	65-38	44-33	–	55-29	–	26-21	12-5	2-0-1
1986	42-39	44-37	30-30	56-46	42-36	–	44-40	–	22-25	10-13	1-2-1
1987	52-29	44-37	29-28	67-38	44-34	–	52-32	–	27-24	10-7	0-1-0
1988	45-36	42-39	24-30	63-45	47-31	–	40-44	–	21-17	6-6	0-0-0
1989	46-35	43-38	22-29	67-44	46-32	–	43-41	–	25-22	13-4	1-0-0
1990	44-37	42-39	26-24	60-52	42-36	–	44-40	–	24-27	4-8	0-0-0
1991	46-35	45-36	28-24	63-47	46-32	–	45-39	–	28-20	8-10	0-0-0
1992	53-28	43-38	32-22	64-44	45-33	–	51-33	–	28-20	7-2	0-0-2
1993	48-33	47-34	38-16	57-51	50-28	–	45-39	–	23-22	6-3	0-0-0
1994	33-26	22-34	21-15	34-45	13-22	24-25	18-13	–	13-15	3-6	0-0-1
1995	29-43	27-45	23-27	33-61	18-34	22-31	16-23	–	16-23	5-13	0-0-2
1996	35-46	39-42	25-31	49-57	22-30	30-32	22-26	–	19-22	7-10	0-0-0
1997	42-39	34-47	23-34	53-52	23-25	29-26	20-24	4-11	29-30	5-9	0-1-1
1998	51-30	37-44	35-14	53-60	27-21	28-26	24-20	9-7	28-17	8-8	0-1-0
1999	40-41	44-37	26-26	58-52	24-25	34-20	17-24	9-9	26-18	6-3	0-0-0
2000	45-36	38-43	28-28	55-51	28-21	28-25	18-24	9-9	21-19	2-6	0-0-0
2001	40-42	40-40	25-32	55-50	37-39	19-13	16-20	8-10	28-21	10-6	1-0-0
2002	42-39	36-45	33-25	45-59	41-35	16-16	12-24	9-9	23-21	4-8	0-0-0
2003	41-40	45-36	30-23	56-53	37-39	22-14	17-15	10-8	14-23	4-4	0-0-0
2004	40-41	27-53	25-31	42-63	29-46	13-19	17-19	8-10	17-22	4-7	0-1-1
2005	43-38	37-44	22-35	58-47	38-36	15-19	19-17	8-10	16-31	4-6	0-0-0
2006	50-31	37-44	30-26	57-49	43-31	18-17	17-18	9-9	20-10	7-1	0-0-0
2007	49-32	34-47	28-25	55-54	36-36	19-18	18-17	10-8	29-25	8-9	0-0-0
2008	47-34	39-42	32-18	54-58	37-35	24-12	17-19	8-10	24-32	6-9	0-0-0
2009	44-37	31-50	31-29	44-58	22-46	23-15	19-15	7-11	21-28	7-13	0-1-0
2010	45-33	40-44	33-29	52-48	39-33	22-19	17-14	7-11	24-28	4-6	0-0-1
2011	42-39	39-42	26-34	55-47	33-39	18-15	22-17	8-10	29-28	13-4	0-0-0
2012	41-40	32-49	29-30	44-59	29-43	21-16	14-21	9-9	15-25	7-6	0-0-1

TORONTO BLUE JAYS OWNERSHIP

On March 26, 1976, the American League granted an expansion franchise to a group consisting of Labatt Breweries, Imperial Trust Limited and The Canadian Imperial Bank of Commerce. Both Labatt Breweries and Imperial Trust each controlled 45% of the team. The C.I.B.C. had the other 10% of the club. Imperial Trust was a holding company set up by the late R. Howard Webster, who was instrumental in the granting of the franchise in 1976. The Webster family still maintained their share of the ownership until selling their 45% to Labatt in November, 1991. The ownership then consisted of John Labatt Limited, 90% and Canadian Imperial Bank of Commerce, 10%. In June of 1995 John Labatt Limited was purchased by Interbrew S.A., Belgium's leading brewer.

In September of 2000, local ownership returned to the Toronto Blue Jays as Rogers Communications Inc. purchased 80% control of the franchise. John Labatt Limited (Interbrew) maintains a 20% interest while The Canadian Imperial Bank of Commerce relinquished their stake. In January of 2004 Rogers Communications Inc. acquired the remaining 20% of the Club. Rogers Communications Inc. now owns 100% of the Toronto Blue Jays Baseball Club.

On November 29, 2004, the Toronto Blue Jays reached an agreement with Sportsco International to acquire the former SkyDome. The purchase price for the stadium, now known as Rogers Centre, was approximately $25 million (CDN).

STANDING BY MONTH

Year	May 1st (GB)	June 1st (GB)	July 1st (GB)	Aug. 1st (GB)	Sept. 1st (GB)
1977	5 (–3.0)	7 (–9.0)	7 (–13.5)	7 (–23.0)	7 (–32.5)
1978	7 (–6.5)	7 (–16.0)	7 (–25.5)	7 (–27.0)	7 (–30.5)
1979	6 (–7.0)	7 (–19.0)	7 (–30.5)	7 (–39.5)	7 (–45.0)
1980	1 (+1.0)	3 (–5.5)	7 (–14.0)	7 (–18.5)	7 (–24.0)
*1981	7 (–5.0)	7 (–14.0)	—	—	6 (–3.0)
1982	5 (–5.0)	7 (–9.0)	7 (–11.0)	7 (–10.0)	7 (–17.5)
1983	6 (–2.0)	1 (+0.5)	1 (+2.0)	4 (–2.5)	5 (–7.5)
1984	2 (–6.0)	2 (–5.5)	2 (–10.0)	2 (–12.0)	2 (–9.5)
1985	1 (+0.5)	1 (+4.0)	1 (+3.5)	1 (+7.5)	1 (+5.0)
1986	7 (–5.0)	7 (–10.0)	5 (–10.5)	4 (–5.5)	2 (–3.5)
1987	3 (5.5)	2 (–2.0)	2 (–2.0)	2 (–2.5)	2 (–1.0)
1988	6 (–7.0)	6 (–12.0)	T5 (–9.0)	6 (–11.5)	5 (–10.5)
1989	7 (–3.5)	7 (–7.5)	4 (–7.0)	2 (–3.0)	T1
1990	3 (–1.5)	1 (+0.5)	2 (–3.5)	T1	2 (–6.5)
1991	2 (–0.5)	T1	1 (+4.5)	1 (+6.0)	1 (+3.5)
1992	1 (+2.0)	1 (+1.0)	1 (+1.0)	1 (+4.5)	1 (+1.5)
1993	4 (–2.5)	T2 (–2.5)	1 (+2.0)	T1	1 (+1.5)
1994	4 (–3.0)	4 (–10.0)	5 (–15.5)	4 (–15.5)	—
1995	3 (–0.5)	3 (–6.5)	5 (–10.0)	5 (–10.0)	4 (–21.5)
1996	3 (–3.0)	3 (–6.5)	3 (–11.5)	3 (–15.0)	4 (–13.5)
1997	4 (–5.0)	3 (–10.0)	3 (–13.5)	3 (–17.0)	4 (–21.0)
1998	5 (–8.5)	3 (–11.5)	3 (–17.5)	4 (–25.5)	3 (–28.0)
1999	2 (–2.5)	3 (–8.0)	3 (–9.5)	2 (–6.0)	3 (–12.5)
2000	4 (–4.5)	3 (–4.0)	1 (+3.0)	3 (–4.5)	3 (–5.5)
2001	T1	3 (–4.0)	T4 (–8.5)	3 (–15.5)	3 (–14.0)
2002	5 (–8.5)	4 (–18.0)	4 (–15.5)	4 (–20.5)	4 (–25.5)
2003	4 (–11.5)	3 (–2.0)	3 (–6.5)	3 (–13.0)	3 (–16.5)
2004	4 (–8.5)	4 (–9.0)	4 (–16.5)	5 (–21.0)	5 (–27.5)
2005	3 (–4.0)	3 (–3.5)	3 (–6.0)	3 (–6.0)	3 (–11.5)
2006	T2 (–1.0)	3 (–2.5)	3 (–4.0)	3 (–6.5)	3 (–11.5)
2007	2 (–3.5)	3 (–11.5)	2 (–10.5)	3 (–11.0)	3 (–11.5)
2008	5 (–5.5)	3 (–4.0)	5 (–10.0)	4 (–9.5)	4 (–14.5)
2009	1 (+1.0)	3 (–2.0)	4 (–7.0)	4 (–12.0)	4 (–24.5)
2010	3 (-5.5)	3 (-3.5)	4 (-8.0)	4 (-12.5)	4 (-13.0)
2011	3 (-3.5)	4 (-3.0)	4 (-9.5)	4 (-12.0)	4 (-15.5)
2012	4 (-3.0)	T4 (-3.0)	5 (-8.5)	5 (-10.0)	5th (-16.0)

* Split-Season

2-0 in WORLD SERIES PLAY

In 1993 the Toronto Blue Jays won the World Series and became just the 4th team in history to go undefeated in their first two trips to the Fall Classic. In 2003 the Florida Marlins became the 5th to do so.

1903, 1912 Boston Red Sox
1906, 1917 Chicago White Sox
1920, 1948 Cleveland Indians
1992, 1993 Toronto Blue Jays
1997, 2003 Florida Marlins

PLAYING STATISTICS

BATTING

YEAR	AVG	G	AB	R	H	TB	2B	3B	HR T- H -A	RBI	BB	SO	SH-SF	HP	SB-CS	LOB	SLG	OBP
1977	.252	161	5418	605	1367	2099	230	41	100- 45 -55	553	499	819	81-34	23	65-55	1094	.365	.316
1978	.250	161	5430	590	1358	1947	217	39	98- 50 -48	551	448	645	77-37	23	28-52	1075	.359	.308
1979	.251	162	5423	613	1362	1968	253	34	95- 50 -45	562	448	663	65-38	36	75-56	1064	.363	.311
1980	.251	162	5571	624	1398	2131	249	53	126- 56 -70	580	448	813	63-34	33	67-72	1083	.383	.309
1981	.226	106	3521	329	797	1163	137	23	61- 34 -27	314	284	556	44-18	20	66-57	658	.330	.286
1982	.262	162	5526	651	1447	2117	262	45	106- 62 -44	605	415	749	48-50	28	118-81	1071	.383	.314
1983	.277	162	5581	795	1546	2431	268	58	167-101-66	748	510	810	36-54	32	131-72	1106	.436	.338
1984	.273	163	5687	750	1555	2395	275	68	143- 59 -84	702	460	816	35-49	52	193-67	1177	.421	.331
1985	.269	161	5508	759	1482	2343	281	53	158- 75 -83	714	503	807	21-44	30	143-77	1067	.425	.331
1986	.269	163	5716	809	1540	2438	285	35	181- 87 -94	767	496	848	24-49	33	110-59	1099	.427	.329
1987	.269	162	5635	845	1514	2512	277	38	215-101-114	790	555	970	30-35	38	126-50	1126	.446	.336
1988	.268	162	5557	763	1491	2330	271	47	158- 78 -80	706	521	935	34-50	31	107-36	1105	.419	.332
1989	.260	162	5581	731	1449	2220	265	40	142- 64 -78	685	521	923	30-53	31	144-58	1102	.398	.323
1990	.265	162	5589	767	1479	2343	263	50	167- 93 -74	729	526	970	18-62	28	111-52	1113	.419	.328
1991	.257	162	5489	684	1412	2196	295	45	133- 75 -58	649	499	1043	56-65	58	148-53	1134	.400	.322
1992	.263	162	5536	780	1458	2292	265	40	163- 79 -84	737	561	933	26-54	47	129-39	1159	.414	.333
1993	.279	162	5579	847	1556	2434	317	42	159- 90 -69	796	588	861	46-54	52	170-49	1187	.436	.350
1994	.269	115	3962	566	1064	1679	210	30	115- 63 -52	534	387	691	30-44	38	79-26	820	.424	.336
1995	.260	144	5036	642	1309	2058	275	27	140- 67 -73	613	492	906	33-45	44	75-16	1079	.409	.328
1996	.259	162	5599	766	1451	2354	302	35	177- 87 -90	712	529	1105	38-37	92	116-38	1169	.420	.331
1997	.244	162	5473	654	1333	2131	275	41	147- 68 -79	627	487	1138	38-52	59	134-50	1113	.389	.310
1998	.266	163	5580	816	1482	2499	316	19	221-112-109	776	564	1132	43-49	87	184-81	1133	.448	.340
1999	.280	162	5642	883	1580	2581	337	14	212- 96 -116	856	578	1077	28-45	76	119-48	1177	.457	.352
2000	.275	162	5677	861	1562	2664	328	21	244-134-110	826	526	1026	29-34	60	89-34	1152	.469	.341
2001	.263	162	5663	767	1489	2433	287	36	195- 94 -101	728	470	1094	34-43	74	156-55	1124	.430	.325
2002	.261	162	5581	813	1457	2399	305	38	187-102-85	771	522	1142	17-57	53	71-18	1104	.430	.327
2003	.279	162	5661	894	1580	2573	357	33	190- 94 -96	853	546	1081	11-56	90	37-25	1175	.455	.349
2004	.260	161	5531	719	1438	2231	290	34	145- 80 -65	680	513	1083	20-42	71	58-31	1164	.403	.328
2005	.265	162	5581	775	1480	2273	307	39	136- 76 -60	735	486	955	21-56	89	72-35	1118	.407	.331
2006	.284	162	5596	809	1591	2590	348	27	199-121-78	778	514	906	16-52	63	65-33	1162	.463	.348
2007	.259	162	5536	753	1434	2321	344	24	165- 90 -75	719	533	1044	33-48	47	57-22	1112	.419	.327
2008	.264	162	5503	714	1453	2198	303	32	126- 69 -57	681	521	938	48-56	59	80-27	1155	.399	.331
2009	.266	162	5696	798	1516	2508	339	13	209-104-105	766	548	1028	24-49	45	73-23	1195	.440	.333
2010	.248	162	5495	755	1364	2496	319	21	257-146-111	732	471	1164	16-34	55	58-20	1017	.454	.312
2011	.249	162	5559	743	1384	2295	285	34	186-103-83	704	525	1184	31-47	48	131-52	1090	.413	.317
2012	.245	162	5487	716	1346	2231	247	22	198-102-96	677	473	1251	33-45	55	123-41	1026	.407	.309

10 HOME RUN GAME

The BLUE JAYS etched a page in the record book with a 10 HR performance against the Baltimore Orioles on September 14th, 1987. Following is a list of highlights from that game:

In the 18-3 victory the BLUE JAYS received HR's from ERNIE WHITT (3), GEORGE BELL (2), RANCE MULLINIKS (2), FRED McGRIFF (1), ROB DUCEY (1) and LLOYD MOSEBY (1)... WHITT became the second BLUE JAYS player since Otto Velez on May 10, 1980 to hit three HR's in one game... The clubs combined to hit 11 HR's in the game, to tie the Major League mark... RANCE MULLINIKS hit his 10th and 11th of the season, enabling the BLUE JAYS to become the 12th team in major league history to have at least nine players with at least 10 HR's... A club mark with 53 total bases in the game was set... The club hit three HR's in the second inning, marking the third time in 1987 and seventh time in franchise history that the club had a three HR inning... ROB DUCEY hit his first Major League HR... Most players with two or more home runs, club, game was tied as three BLUE JAYS, Bell, Mulliniks and Whitt had multiple home run games. The 10 home runs surpassed the previous record of eight.

PITCHING

YEAR	W-L	ERA	G	RE	CG	SHO	SV	IP	H	R	ER	HR	HB	BB	SO	WP
1977	54-107	4.57	161	187	40	3	20	1428	1538	822	726	152	20	623	771	62
1978	59-102	4.54	161	213	35	5	23	1429	1529	775	721	149	22	614	758	47
1979	53-109	4.82	162	195	44	7	11	1417	1537	862	759	165	40	594	613	64
1980	67-95	4.19	162	286	39	9	23	1466	1523	762	683	135	28	635	705	41
1981	37-69	3.81	106	189	20	4	18	953	908	466	404	72	36	377	451	41
1982	78-84	3.95	162	220	41	13	25	1444	1428	701	633	147	25	493	776	38
1983	89-73	4.12	162	257	43	8	32	1445	1434	726	662	145	42	517	835	25
1984	89-73	3.86	163	257	34	10	33	1464	1433	696	628	140	34	528	875	42
1985	99-62	3.31	161	316	18	9	47	1448	1312	588	529	147	26	484	823	36
1986	86-76	4.08	163	290	16	12	44	1476	1467	733	669	164	45	487	1002	38
1987	96-66	3.74	162	336	18	8	43	1454	1323	655	605	158	22	567	1064	56
1988	87-75	3.80	162	293	16	17	47	1449	1404	680	611	143	59	528	904	48
1989	89-73	3.58	162	293	12	12	38	1467	1408	651	584	99	45	478	849	58
1990	86-76	3.84	162	317	6	9	48	1454	1434	661	620	143	37	445	892	43
1991	91-71	3.50	162	346	10	16	60	1462	1301	622	569	121	43	523	971	55
1992	96-66	3.91	162	284	18	14	49	1441	1346	682	626	124	45	541	954	66
1993	95-67	4.21	162	344	11	11	50	1441	1441	742	674	134	32	620	1023	83
1994	55-60	4.70	115	221	13	4	26	1025	1053	579	535	127	32	482	832	54
1995	56-88	4.88	144	265	16	8	22	1293	1336	777	701	145	51	654	894	73
1996	74-88	4.57	162	303	19	7	35	1446	1476	809	734	187	36	610	1033	61
1997	76-86	3.92	162	336	19	16	34	1443	1453	694	628	167	39	497	1150	54
1998	88-74	4.28	163	384	10	11	47	1465	1443	768	697	169	45	587	1154	34
1999	84-78	4.92	162	377	14	9	39	1439	1582	862	787	191	53	575	1009	55
2000	83-79	5.14	162	388	15	4	37	1437	1615	908	821	195	64	560	978	37
2001	80-82	4.28	162	471	7	10	41	1463	1553	753	696	165	76	490	1041	33
2002	78-84	4.80	162	461	6	6	41	1438	1504	828	767	177	71	590	991	57
2003	86-76	4.69	162	443	14	6	36	1435	1560	826	748	184	57	485	984	56
2004	67-94	4.91	161	431	6	11	37	1421	1505	823	775	181	58	608	956	60
2005	80-82	4.06	162	432	9	8	35	1447	1475	705	653	185	68	444	958	39
2006	87-75	4.37	162	482	6	6	42	1428	1447	754	694	185	59	504	1076	53
2007	83-79	4.00	162	421	11	9	44	1448	1383	699	644	157	55	479	1067	42
2008	86-76	3.49	162	421	15	13	44	1446	1330	610	561	134	67	467	1184	51
2009	75-87	4.47	162	445	10	10	25	1451	1509	771	720	181	58	551	1181	43
2010	85-77	4.22	162	455	5	11	45	1441	1407	728	676	150	60	539	1184	69
2011	81-81	4.32	162	474	7	10	33	1458	1433	761	700	179	77	540	1169	73
2012	73-89	4.64	162	495	5	11	29	1443	1439	784	745	204	55	574	1142	56

THE LAST TIME

BLUE JAYS PITCHING – TEAM

NO-HITTER: Sept. 2, 1990 at CLE

ONE-HITTER: Aug. 21, 2011 at OAK

SHUTOUT: Sept. 27, 2012 vs. NYY

BACK-TO-BACK COMPLETE GAMES: May 3, 2012 at LAA and May 4, 2012 at LAA

BACK-TO-BACK COMPLETE GAME WINS: May 3, 2012 at LAA and May 4, 2012 at LAA

BACK-TO-BACK-TO-BACK COMPLETE GAMES: Aug. 21,1996 at KC, Aug. 22, 1996 at CWS and Aug. 23, 1996 at CWS

BACK-TO-BACK-TO-BACK COMPLETE GAME WINS: Aug. 21,1996 at KC, Aug. 22, 1996 at CWS and Aug. 23, 1996 at CWS

FOUR CONSECUTIVE COMPLETE GAMES: Sept. 20, 1983 vs. SEA, Sept. 21, 1983 vs. SEA, Sept. 23, 1983 at OAK and Sept. 24, 1983 at OAK

BACK-TO-BACK SHUTOUTS: May 3, 2012 at LAA and May 4, 2012 at LAA

BACK-TO-BACK 1-0 SHUTOUTS: June 12, 1991 at CLE and June 13, 1991 at CLE

1-0 GAME, WIN: Sept. 5, 2011 vs. BOS

1-0 GAME, LOSS: July 13, 2012 vs. CLE

BLUE JAYS PITCHING – INDIVIDUAL

NO-HITTER: Dave Stieb, Sept. 2, 1990 at CLE

ONE-HITTER: Shaun Marcum, Aug. 16, 2010 at OAK

TEN OR MORE STRIKEOUTS: Brandon Morrow (11), Oct. 3, 2012 vs. MIN

SHUTOUT: Brandon Morrow, June 6, 2012 at CWS

BACK-TO-BACK COMPLETE GAMES: Roy Halladay, Sept. 25, 2009 vs. SEA and Sept. 30, 2009 at BOS

BACK-TO-BACK COMPLETE GAME WINS: Roy Halladay, Sept. 25, 2009 vs. SEA and Sept. 30, 2009 at BOS

FOUR CONSECUTIVE COMPLETE GAMES: Roy Halladay, April 12, 2008 at TEX, April 17, 2008 vs. TEX, April 23, 2008 at TB and April 29, 2008 at BOS

BACK-TO-BACK SHUTOUTS: Roy Halladay, Sept. 25, 2009 vs. SEA and Sept. 30, 2009 at BOS

10+ INNINGS PITCHED: Roy Halladay, April 13, 2007 vs. DET

4 STRIKEOUTS TO START A GAME: Josh Towers, April 27, 2007 vs. TEX

POSITION PLAYER PITCHING: Jeff Mathis, July 25, 2012 vs. OAK

PITCHER PLAYING POSITION: Dave Stieb, Aug. 29, 1980 vs. MIN (left field)

BLUE JAYS HITTING – TEAM

BACK-TO-BACK HOME RUNS: J.P. Arencibia and Rajai Davis, July 22, 2012 at BOS

BACK-TO-BACK-TO-BACK HOME RUNS: Colby Rasmus, Jose Bautista and Edwin Encarnacion, June 19, 2012 at MIL

THREE HOME RUNS, ONE INNING: Colby Rasmus, Jose Bautista and Edwin Encarnacion, June 19, 2012 at MIL

FOUR HOME RUNS, ONE INNING: Aug. 17, 2001 vs. TEX (6th inning), Jeff Frye (2R), Jose Cruz Jr. (1R), Shannon Stewart (1R), Carlos Delgado (1R)

SIX HOME RUNS, ONE GAME: June 19, 2012 at MIL

TWO GRAND SLAMS, ONE GAME: None

HOME RUNS BY FIRST TWO BATTERS OF A GAME: Alex Rios & Frank Catalanotto, June 14, 2006 vs. BAL

20 or MORE HITS ONE GAME: 20, Aug. 31, 2011 at BAL

THREE CONSECUTIVE 10 RUN GAMES: May 30–June 1, 2003

5 or MORE STOLEN BASES: 5, July 19, 2001 at BOS

NO STRIKEOUTS, BATTING: May 1, 2008 vs. BOS

10 OR MORE RUNS, ONE INNING: 10 runs, Aug. 31, 2010 at TB

HOME RUN BY PITCHER: Mark Hendrickson, June 21, 2003 at MTL

BLUE JAYS HITTING – INDIVIDUAL

LEADOFF HOME RUN: Rajai Davis, July 31, 2012 at SEA

INSIDE-THE-PARK HOME RUN: Jose Bautista, July 7, 2010 vs. MIN

GRAND SLAM HOME RUN: J.P. Arencibia, Sept. 24, 2012 at BAL (GM 2)

PINCH HIT HOME RUN: Yan Gomes, June 11, 2012 vs. WSH

PINCH HIT GRAND SLAM: Reed Johnson, July 1, 2005 at BOS

WALK OFF HOME RUN: Brett Lawrie, May 1, 2012 vs. TEX

TWO HOME RUNS, ONE GAME: Edwin Encarnacion, July 14, 2012 vs. CLE

THREE HOME RUNS, ONE GAME: Jose Bautista, May 15, 2011 at MIN

FOUR HOME RUNS, ONE GAME: Carlos Delgado, Sept. 25, 2003 vs. TB

TWO PLAYERS, MULTI-HR GAME, SAME GAME: Jose Bautista and Colby Rasmus, June 19, 2012 at MIL

TWO HOME RUNS, SAME INNING: Joe Carter, Oct. 3, 1993 at BAL, 2nd inning
HOME RUNS FROM BOTH SIDES OF THE PLATE, ONE GAME: Gregg Zaun, Sept. 13, 2006 at SEA
HOME RUN, FIRST MAJOR LEAGUE AT-BAT: J.P. Arencibia, Aug. 7, 2010 vs. TB
HOME RUN, FIRST MAJOR LEAGUE HIT: J.P. Arencibia, Aug. 7, 2010 vs. TB
MULTI-HR GAME, MLB DEBUT: J.P. Arencibia, Aug. 7, 2010 vs. TB (2-HR)
HIT, FIRST MAJOR LEAGUE PLATE APPEARANCE: Moises Sierra, July 31, 2012 at SEA (single)
HOME RUN INTO ROGERS CENTRE FIFTH DECK: Vernon Wells, Sept. 16, 2004 vs. BAL (445 feet)
FIVE HITS, ONE GAME: Colby Ramus, June 5, 2012 at CWS
SIX HITS, ONE GAME: Frank Catalanotto, May 1, 2004 at CWS (GM #2)
TWO HITS, SAME INNING: Brett Lawrie, July 3, 2012 vs. KC (2-1B)
TWO HITS, SAME INNING (2 or more players): Alex Rios & Vernon Wells, July 9, 2008 vs. BAL (4th inning)
HOME RUN IN FIRST TWO INNINGS: Lyle Overbay, June 30, 2006 vs. PHI
THREE TRIPLES (ONE INNING, TEAM): Eric Thames, Rajai Davis and Jayson Nix, June 1, 2011 vs. CLE
FOUR OR MORE STEALS, ONE GAME: Otis Nixon, Aug. 14, 1996 vs. BOS (4)
STEAL OF HOME: Brett Lawrie, April 22, 2012 at KC
STRAIGHT STEAL OF HOME: Aaron Hill, May 29, 2007 vs. NYY
MULTI-HIT GAME BY PITCHER: Roy Halladay (2), June 10, 2007 at LAD
BATTING FOR THE CYCLE: Jeff Frye, Aug. 17, 2001 vs. TEX

BLUE JAYS MISCELLANEOUS – TEAM

TRIPLE PLAY: April 20, 2012 at KC
TURNED FIVE OR MORE DP'S: April 9, 2011 at LAA (13.2 innings)
FOUR GAME SWEEP: April 20-23, 2012 at KC
TIE GAME: April 26, 1998 at CWS (5-5)
THREE CONSECUTIVE EXTRA INNING GAMES: April 19-21, 1998
SUSPENDED GAME: July 23, 2008 at BAL (7th inning due to rain), completed July 24, 2008 (won 5-1)
RAIN SHORTENED GAME: July 18, 2012 at NYY (7.0 inn, lost 0-6)
GAME POSTPONED: Aug. 26, 2012 at BAL (due to rain, made up as part of DH on Sept. 24)
DOUBLEHEADER: Sept. 24, 2012 at BAL (split)
DOUBLEHEADER SWEEP: Oct. 5, 2001 vs. CLE
SPLIT DOUBLEHEADER: Sept. 19, 2012 at NYY (lost both)
SELLOUT AT HOME: Aug. 11, 2012 vs. NYY
PLAYER EJECTION: Yunel Escobar, Aug. 18, 2012 vs. TEX
MANAGER EJECTION: John Farrell, Oct. 1, 2012 vs. MIN

OPPONENTS PITCHING – TEAM

PERFECT GAME: May 7, 2011 vs. DET
NO-HITTER: May 7, 2011 vs. DET
ONE-HITTER: June 14, 2005 vs. STL
SHUTOUT: Sept. 23, 2012 at TB
BACK-TO-BACK SHUTOUTS: Sept. 3, 2012 at BAL and Sept. 4, 2012 at BAL
BACK-TO-BACK 1-0 SHUTOUTS: Aug. 25, 1990 vs. BOS and Aug. 26, 1990 vs. BOS

OPPONENTS PITCHING – INDIVIDUAL

PERFECT GAME: Justin Verlander, May 7, 2011 vs. DET
NO-HITTER: Justin Verlander, May 7, 2011 vs. DET
ONE-HITTER: Chris Carpenter (9.0), June 14, 2005 vs. STL
TEN OR MORE STRIKEOUTS: Justin Verlander (13), Aug. 23, 2012 at DET
SHUTOUT: Hiroki Kuroda, July 18, 2012 at NYY (7.0)
BACK-TO-BACK SHUTOUTS: Mike Mussina, Sept. 26, 1995 vs. BAL and Scott Erickson, Sept. 27, 1995 vs. BAL
HOME RUN BY PITCHER: Tim Hudson, June 20, 2011 at ATL

OPPONENTS HITTING – TEAM

BACK-TO-BACK HOME RUNS: Dayan Viciedo and Tyler Flowers, Aug. 16, 2012 vs. CWS
BACK-TO-BACK-TO-BACK HOME RUNS: Nelson Cruz, Yorvit Torrealba and Mitch Moreland, April 26, 2012 at TEX
THREE HOME RUNS, ONE INNING: Jim Thome, Manny Machado and Chris Davis, Sept. 26, 2012 at BAL
FOUR HOME RUNS, ONE INNING: Jason Varitek, David Ortiz, Jason Bay and Mike Lowell, May 20, 2009 at BOS
SIX or MORE HOME RUNS, ONE GAME: Sept. 26, 2012 at BAL (7)
TWO GRAND SLAMS, ONE GAME: Ramon Hernandez and Miguel Tejada, Aug. 24, 2003 vs. OAK
HOME RUNS BY FIRST TWO BATTERS OF A GAME: Derek Jeter, Robinson Cano, Sept. 23, 2005 at NYY
20 or MORE HITS, ONE GAME: Sept. 6, 2011 vs. BOS (20)
THREE CONSECUTIVE 10 RUN GAMES: April 14-16, 2000

OPPONENTS HITTING – INDIVIDUAL

LEAD OFF HOME RUN: Dustin Ackley, July 31, 2012 at SEA
INSIDE-THE-PARK HOME RUN: Ben Zobrist, Sept. 25, 2011 at TB
GRAND SLAM HOME RUN: Nick Swisher, Sept. 20, 2012 at NYY
PINCH HIT HOME RUN: Rick Ankiel, June 11, 2012 vs. WSH
PINCH HIT GRAND SLAM: Gregg Zaun, Aug. 16, 2009 at TB
WALK OFF HOME RUN: Josh Hamilton, May 26, 2012 at TEX
TWO HOME RUNS, ONE GAME: Chris Davis and Manny Machado, Sept. 26, 2012 at BAL
THREE HOME RUNS, ONE GAME: Chris Davis, Aug. 24, 2012 at BAL
HOME RUNS FROM BOTH SIDES OF THE PLATE, ONE GAME: Tony Clark, Aug. 28, 2004 vs. NYY
HOME RUN INTO ROGERS CENTRE FIFTH DECK: Shelly Duncan, May 30, 2011 vs. CLE
FIVE HITS, ONE GAME: Carl Crawford, May 24, 2006 vs. TB
FOUR OR MORE STEALS, ONE GAME: Carl Crawford, May 24, 2006 vs. TB (4)
STRAIGHT STEAL OF HOME: Eric Aybar, Sept. 20, 2011 vs. LAA
STEAL OF HOME: B.J. Upton, July 8, 2009 at TB (part of a double steal)
BATTING FOR THE CYCLE: George Brett, vs. KC, July 25, 1990

OPPONENTS MISCELLANEOUS – TEAM

TRIPLE PLAY: May 12, 2008 at CLE (GM 2)—unassisted
TURNED FIVE OR MORE DP'S: April 2, 2008 at NYY
FOUR GAME SWEEP: June 28-July 1, 2010 at CLE
FIVE GAME SWEEP: July 1-4, 2002 at BOS

MOST HOME RUNS HIT IN 3 GAME SERIES

The Blue Jays hit 13 home runs in a three-game series sweep in Boston on Sept. 28-30, 2009. That's a Toronto record for home runs in a three-game series against any team.

NON-PITCHERS WHO PITCHED FOR THE BLUE JAYS

Player	Position	Pitched	W-L	ERA	G	IP	H	ER	BB	SO
Bailor, Bob	IF/OF	1980	0-0	7.71	3	2.1	4	**2**	1	0
Kusick, Craig	1B	1979	0-0	4.91	1	3.2	3	**2**	0	0
Leach, Rick	1B/OF	1984	0-0	27.00	1	1.0	2	**3**	2	0
Mathis, Jeff	C	2012	0-0	9.00	2	2.0	4	**2**	1	0
McCoy, Mike	IF/OF	2011	0-0	0.00	1	1.0	0	**0**	0	0
Menechino, Frank	IF	2004	0-0	0.00	1	0.1	2	**0**	0	0

TORONTO BLUE JAYS RECORDS

CARLOS DELGADO

ATTENDANCE RECORDS

2012 ATTENDANCE

BLUE JAYS

AMERICAN LEAGUE	AT ROGERS CENTRE			ON THE ROAD		
CLUB	DATES	TOTAL	AVERAGE	DATES	TOTAL	AVERAGE
BALTIMORE	9	167,510	18,612	8	173,767	21,721
BOSTON	9	286,013	31,779	9	338,196	37,577
NEW YORK (AL)	9	307,699	34,189	9	385,591	42,843
TAMPA BAY	9	162,951	18,106	9	134,219	14,913
CHICAGO (AL)	4	75,721	18,930	6	154,240	25,707
CLEVELAND	3	91,232	30,411	3	72,550	24,183
DETROIT	3	111,769	37,256	3	116,634	38,878
KANSAS CITY	4	71,072	17,768	4	91,027	22,757
MINNESOTA	3	46.058	15,353	4	140,534	35,134
LOS ANGELES (AL)	4	113,346	28,337	4	138,085	34,521
OAKLAND	3	88,637	29,546	6	102,020	17,003
SEATTLE	6	117,598	19,560	3	66,414	22,138
TEXAS	6	158,392	26,399	3	140,856	46,952
AL TOTALS	**72**	**1,797,998**	**24,972**	**71**	**2,054,133**	**28,931**

NATIONAL LEAGUE	AT ROGERS CENTRE			ON THE ROAD		
CLUB	DATES	TOTAL	AVERAGE	DATES	TOTAL	AVERAGE
ATLANTA	-	-	-	3	95,529	31,843
MIAMI	-	-	-	3	74,723	24,908
MILWAUKEE	-	-	-	3	101,634	33,878
NEW YORK (NL)	3	103,541	34,514	-	-	-
PHILADELPHIA	3	115,396	38,465	-	-	-
WASHINGTON	3	82,728	27,576	-	-	-
NL TOTALS	**9**	**301,665**	**33,518**	**9**	**271,886**	**30,210**
TOTALS	**81**	**2,099,663**	**25,922**	**80**	**2,326,019**	**29,075**

AMERICAN LEAGUE

	HOME			ROAD		
CLUB	TOTAL	AVERAGE	DATES	TOTAL	AVERAGE	DATES
NEW YORK	3,542,406	43,733	81	2,766,502	34,154	81
TEXAS	3,460,280	42,720	81	2,256,784	28,210	80
LOS ANGELES	3,061,770	37,800	81	2,497,339	30,831	81
BOSTON	3,043,003	37,568	81	2,514,090	31,038	81
DETROIT	3,028,033	37,383	81	2,473,687	30,539	81
MINNESOTA	2,776,354	34,276	81	2,264,492	28,306	80
BALTIMORE	2,102,240	26,611	79	2,393,520	29,550	81
TORONTO	2,099,663	25,922	81	2,326,019	29,075	80
CHICAGO	1,965,955	24,271	81	2,428,679	29,984	81
KANSAS CITY	1,739,859	21,748	80	2,223,264	27,448	81
SEATTLE	1,721,920	21,258	81	2,289,275	28,263	81
OAKLAND	1,679,013	20,729	81	2,428,269	29,979	81
CLEVELAND	1,603,596	19,797	81	2,291,136	28,286	81
TAMPA BAY	1,559,681	19,255	81	2,462,698	30,404	81
TOTALS	**33,383,773**	**29,517**	**1131**	**33,615,754**	**29,722**	**1131**

ALL-TIME ATTENDANCE

RECORDS

(REGULAR SEASON)

Largest Home	50,560	Fri., April 8/05	Boston
Smallest Home	10,074	Tues., April 17/79	Chicago
Smallest Rogers Centre	10,314	Mon, April 19/10	Kansas City
Largest Opening Day	50,533	Fri., April 8/05	Boston
Largest Day	50,533	Fri., April 9/93	Cleveland
Smallest Day	746	Wed., April 9/97	Chicago
Largest Night	61,340	Fri., May 23/86	Cleveland
Smallest Night	8,193	Mon., Aug., 4/03	Tampa Bay
Doubleheader (Day)	48,641	Mon., July 17/89	California
Doubleheader (TN)	45,102	Tues., Aug. 2/83	New York (AL)
Series, Four Dates (Home)	202,093	July 29-Aug. 1/93 (4 Games)	Detroit
Series, Four Dates (Road)	214,510	Sept. 12-15/85 (4 Games)	New York (AL)
Series, Three Dates (Home)	151,584	Sept. 21-23/93 (3 Games)	Boston
Series, Three Dates (Road)	161,793	Sept. 29, 30, Oct. 1/06 (3 Games)	New York (AL)
Series, Two Dates (Home)	101,036	July 27,28/93 (2 Games)	Baltimore
Series, Two Dates (Road)	91,522	July 16, 17/97 (2 Games)	Texas
Largest Road	61,340	Fri., May 23/86	Cleveland
Smallest Road	746	Wed., April 9/97	Chicago
Season, Home	4,057,947	1993	
Season, Road	2,549,438	1993	
Season, Home & Road	6,607,385	1993	

OPPONENTS IN TORONTO

	LARGEST		SMALLEST	
BALTIMORE	50,528	June 25/94	11,080	Sept. 13/79
BOSTON	50,560	April 8/05	10,428	April 23/82
CHICAGO (AL)	40,738	June 15/08	10,074	April 17/79
CLEVELAND	50,533	April 9/93	10,173	April 20/83
DETROIT	50,532	July 31/93	10,087	April 13/82
KANSAS CITY	50,531	July 16/93	10,169	April 17/78
LOS ANGELES (AL)	50,529	Sept. 11/93 & May 29/94	11,295	May 15/78
MILWAUKEE (AL)	50,517	Aug. 6/93	10,127	April 14/83
MINNESOTA	50,530	Aug. 10/93	10,155	May 1/79
NEW YORK (AL)	50,530	June 11/94	13,306	April 19/78
OAKLAND	50,529	Sept. 8/93	11,339	May 9/78
SEATTLE	50,527	Aug. 20/93	10,213	June 11/79
TAMPA BAY	48,115	April 9/01	13,002	June 3/02
TEXAS	50,529	July 23/94	10,101	April 27/82
ARIZONA	30,349	June 12/04	14,259	June 11/04
ATLANTA	34,409	June 16/97	16,885	June 11/01
CHICAGO (NL)	40,738	June 15/08	23,018	June 13/03
CINCINNATI	30,351	June 23/09	25,129	June 26/08
COLORADO	33,910	June 24/07	20,032	June 7/02
FLORIDA	35,229	Aug. 30/97	17,922	June 12/09
HOUSTON	21,494	May 21/11	15,478	May 20/11
LOS ANGELES (NL)	25,265	June 21/07	22,763	June 19/07
MILWAUKEE (NL)	30,480	June 19/05	17,615	June 17/05
MONTREAL	50,436	July 1/97	20,074	July 6/01
NEW YORK (NL)	37,252	July 1/98	23,129	July 17/00
PHILADELPHIA	45,512	July 1/11	17,311	June 30/06
PITTSBURGH	32,036	June 11/03	14,090	June 10/03
SAN FRANCISCO	21,106	June 12/02	18,081	June 10/02
ST. LOUIS	37,536	June 14/05	20,032	June 13/05
WASHINGTON	41,677	June 13/12	17,067	June 28/06

BLUE JAYS ON THE ROAD

AT	LARGEST		SMALLEST	
BALTIMORE	47,900	June 27/97	7,053	Sept. 6/79
BOSTON	38,347	May 21/09	7,542	April 16/82
CHICAGO (AL)	42,796	July 25/91	746	April 9/97
CLEVELAND	61,340	May 23/86	2,724	April 28/77
DETROIT	52,528	April 7/78	6,210	Sept. 22/80
KANSAS CITY	41,086	April 8/85	9,593	April 27/09
LOS ANGELES (AL)	61,292	July 4/95	10,239	June 7/77
MILWAUKEE (AL)	53,852	May 6/79	5,298	April 21/82
MINNESOTA	53,067	April 8/88	2,830	Sept. 20/82
NEW YORK (AL)	55,367	May 27/78	8,848	Sept. 8/03
OAKLAND	46,770	July 4/85	1,289	Aug. 14/79
SEATTLE	56,120	April 6/93	4,113	June 1/79
TAMPA BAY	41,546	April 3/01	8,193	Aug. 4/03
TEXAS	48,336	May 19/01	6,819	May 13/82
ARIZONA	39,062	June 22/02	34,288	June 21/02
ATLANTA	48,338	June 27/98	21,533	May 22/09
CHICAGO (NL)	39,159	June 7/05	38,086	June 8/05
CINCINNATI	32,618	June 19/11	28,277	June 6/03
COLORADO	30,293	May 21/06	26,011	May 19/06
MIAMI	27,888	June 24/12	10,242	June 16/06
HOUSTON	34,925	June 11/05	28,607	June 10/05
LOS ANGELES (NL)	52,173	June 8/07	24,977	June 20/02
MILWAUKEE	37,065	June 17/08	32,223	June 18/12
MONTREAL	22,489	July 9/00	7,015	June 17/01
NEW YORK (NL)	34,203	July 16/01	14,513	Sept. 3/97
PHILADELPHIA	44,958	June 16/09	18,279	July 13/01
PITTSBURGH	28,962	June 20/08	22,983	June 22/08
SAN DIEGO	40,511	June 18/04	40,307	June 19/04
SAN FRANCISCO	40,086	June 13/07	37,574	June 12/07
ST. LOUIS	40,289	June 25/11	28,840	June 4/03
WASHINGTON	39,859	June 25/05	20,860	June 19/09

TWENTY LARGEST HOME CROWDS

ATTENDANCE	DATE	OPPONENT
50,560*	Friday, April 8, 2005	Boston
50,533*	Friday, April 9, 1993	Cleveland
50,532	Saturday, July 31, 1993	Detroit
50,532	Wednesday, Sept. 22, 1993	Boston
50,531	Friday, July 16, 1993	Kansas City
50,530	Tuesday, Aug. 10, 1993	Minnesota
50,530	Saturday, June 11, 1994	New York (AL)
50,529	Thursday, Sept. 8, 1993	Oakland
50,529	Saturday, Sept. 10, 1993	California
50,529	Sunday, May 29, 1994	California
50,529	Saturday, July 23, 1994	Texas
50,528	Thursday, June 17, 1993	Boston
50,528	Thursday, July 29, 1993	Detroit
50,5[illegible]	Thursday, July 23, 1993	Boston
50,528	Saturday, June 25, 1994	Baltimore
50,527	Thursday, Aug. 12, 1993	Minnesota
50,527	Friday, Aug. 20, 1993	Seattle
50,527	Saturday, Sept. 25, 1993	New York (AL)
50,527	Tuesday, Aug. 9, 1994	Cleveland
50,525	Thursday, July 8, 1993	Texas
50,525	Wednesday, Aug. 11, 1993	Minnesota
50,525	Wednesday, Aug. 25, 1993	Cleveland

* Home Opener

HOW THEY HAVE DRAWN

ATTENDANCE RECAP 1977–2012

AMERICAN LEAGUE

RANK	CLUB	DATES	ATTENDANCE	AVERAGE
1	NEW YORK	252	8,719,312	34,600
2	BOSTON	257	7,989,788	31,087
3	BALTIMORE	255	7,165,438	28,100
4	DETROIT	192	6,164,766	32,108
5	OAKLAND	185	5,388,046	29,125
6	CLEVELAND	178	5,241,186	29,445
7	KANSAS CITY	179	5,206,986	29,089
8	CHICAGO	180	5,232,291	29,068
9	SEATTLE	185	5,229,529	28,268
10	LOS ANGELES	185	5,263,183	28,450
11	TEXAS*	185	5,240,146	28,325
12	MINNESOTA	172	5,065,577	29,273
13	MILWAUKEE**	132	4,287,402	32,480
14	TAMPA BAY	130	2,913,460	22,411
AL TOTALS		**2,667**	**79,107,110**	**29,661**

* Does not include game in Puerto Rico to start 2001 season

** Milwaukee moved over to the NL in 1998

NATIONAL LEAGUE

RANK	CLUB	DATES	ATTENDANCE	AVERAGE
1	MONTREAL	23	653,451	28,411
2	PHILADELPHIA*	21	671,400	31,971
3	ATLANTA	12	328,597	27,383
4	MIAMI	12	289,363	24,114
5	NEW YORK	12	368,452	30,704
6	WASHINGTON	12	284,900	23,742
7	CHICAGO	6	192,995	32,166
8	COLORADO	6	155,419	25,903
9	CINCINNATI	6	139,808	20,363
10	ST. LOUIS	6	123,774	20,629
11	LOS ANGELES	6	123,210	20,535
12	SAN FRANCISCO	6	120,179	20,030
15	PITTSBURGH	6	108,797	18,133
13	MILWAUKEE	3	73,359	24,453
14	ARIZONA	3	67,374	22,458
16	HOUSTON	3	56,459	18,820
NL TOTALS		**143**	**3,757,537**	**26,276**
GRAND TOTALS		**2,810**	**82,864,647**	**29,489**

*Three home games with the Phillies on June 25-27, 2010 were played in Philadelphia due to G20 Summit in Toronto

TOP ALL-TIME ATTENDANCE MARKS

FOUR MILLION CLUB

1.	Colorado Rockies	4,483,350	1993
2.	New York Yankees	4,287,132	2008
3.	New York Yankees	4,271,083	2007
4.	New York Yankees	4,248,067	2006
5.	New York Yankees	4,090,696	2005
6.	**Toronto Blue Jays**	**4,057,947**	**1993**
7.	New York Mets	4,042,045	2008
8.	**Toronto Blue Jays**	**4,028,318**	**1992**
9.	**Toronto Blue Jays**	**4,001,526**	**1991**

ATTENDANCE YEAR-BY-YEAR

	HOME	DATES	AVG.	AWAY	DATES	AVG.	TOTAL
1977	1,701,052	72	23,626	1,035,344	73	14,183	2,736,396
1978	1,562,585	73	21,405	1,264,940	71	17,816	2,827,525
1979	1,431,651	77	18,593	1,261,000	75	16,813	2,692,651
1980	1,400,327	75	18,671	1,285,409	77	16,694	2,685,736
1981	755,083	51	14,806	814,365	50	16,287	1,569,448
1982	1,275,978	77	16,571	1,392,301	77	18,082	2,668,279
1983	1,930,415	77	25,070	1,713,302	81	21,152	3,643,717
1984	2,110,009	79	26,709	1,709,172	77	22,197	3,819,181
1985	2,468,925	78	31,653	1,842,278	81	22,744	4,311,203
1986	2,455,477	78	31,480	1,716,243	81	21,188	4,171,720
1987	2,778,429	81	34,302	1,959,280	81	24,189	4,737,709
1988	2,595,175	81	32,039	1,972,865	81	24,356	4,568,040
1989	3,375,883	80	42,199	1,970,711	81	24,330	5,346,594
1990	3,885,284	81	47,966	2,039,772	81	25,182	5,925,056
1991	4,001,527	81	49,402	2,243,335	81	27,695	6,244,862
1992	4,028,318	81	49,732	2,301,012	81	28,408	6,329,330
1993	4,057,947	81	50,098	2,549,898	81	31,480	6,607,845
1994	2,907,933	59	49,287	1,775,829	55	32,288	4,683,762
1995	2,826,483	72	39,257	1,770,541	70	25,293	4,597,024
1996	2,559,573	81	31,600	1,980,397	81	24,449	4,539,970
1997	2,589,297	81	31,967	2,118,030	81	26,149	4,707,327
1998	2,454,283	81	30,300	2,164,254	81	26,719	4,618,537
1999	2,163,464	81	26,709	2,161,286	81	26,683	4,324,750
2000	1,819,886	81	22,468	2,207,931	81	27,258	4,027,817
2001*	1,895,547	80	23,694	2,219,908	80	27,749	4,115,455
2002	1,636,904	81	20,209	2,086,535	81	25,760	3,723,439
2003	1,799,458	81	22,216	2,120,472	81	26,179	3,919,930
2004	1,900,041	81	23,457	2,127,243	78	27,272	4,027,284
2005	2,014,987	81	24,876	2,421,950	81	29,901	4,436,937
2006	2,302,212	81	28,422	2,313,400	81	28,560	4,615,612
2007	2,360,648	81	29,144	2,529,543	81	31,229	4,890,191
2008	2,400,416	81	29,635	2,409,512	80	30,119	4,809,928
2009	1,876,129	81	23,162	2,198,842	80	27,486	4,074,971
2010	1,625,555	81	20,069	2,249,636	81	27,773	3,875,191
2011	1,818,103	81	22,446	2,240,354	81	27,659	4,058,457
2012	2,099,663	81	25,922	2,326,019	80	29,075	4,425,682
TOTAL	**82,864,647**	**2,810**	**29,489**	**70,490,634**	**2,798**	**25,193**	**153,355,281**

* Does not include game played in Puerto Rico, April 1, 2001 (19,891) vs. Texas

HOME SELLOUT STREAKS — REGULAR SEASON

DATES

60 — May 18, 1990 to April 8, 1991 (Opening Day)
50 — June 9, 1993 to April 4, 1994 (Opening Day)
46 — May 27, 1992 to September 15, 1992
39 — July 4, 1991 to April 11, 1992 (2nd game)
38 — July 13, 1989 to April 10, 1990 (Opening Day)

INDIVIDUAL RECORDS

BLUE JAYS CAREER GAMES BY POSITION

GAMES BY POSITION (TOP 5)

CATCHERS	(63)
ERINE WHITT	1159
PAT BORDERS	691
DARRIN FLETCHER	516
GREGG ZAUN	483
BUCK MARTINEZ	441

FIRST BASEMEN	(89)
CARLOS DELGADO	1168
WILLIE UPSHAW	950
JOHN OLERUD	766
LYLE OVERBAY	703
JOHN MAYBERRY	494

SECOND BASEMEN	(70)
DAMASO GARCIA	869
AARON HILL	746
ROBERTO ALOMAR	695
ORLANDO HUDSON	454
MANUEL LEE	344

SHORTSTOPS	(59)
TONY FERNANDEZ	1104
ALFREDO GRIFFIN	907
ALEX GONZALEZ	874
MANUEL LEE	365
JOHN McDONALD	361

THIRD BASEMEN	(91)
KELLY GRUBER	829
ED SPRAGUE	814
RANCE MULLINIKS	725
GARTH IORG	556
ROY HOWELL	489

OUTFIELDERS	(149)
VERNON WELLS	1367
LLOYD MOSEBY	1349
GEORGE BELL	1066
JESSE BARFIELD	996
JOE CARTER	835

PITCHERS	(306)
JASON FRASOR	505
DUANE WARD	452
TOM HENKE	446
DAVE STIEB	439
PAUL QUANTRILL	386

In the Blue Jays 36 year history, the following number of players have been utilized at each position:

Catcher	63
First Base	89
Second Base	70
Third Base	91
Shortstop	59
Outfielders	149
Pitchers	306

Tony Fernandez is the all-time club leader in games played by a shortstop at 1,104

BATTING LEADERS

* League Leader Bold = Club Record

Year	AVG (350 AB)		AB		R		H		2B	
1977	R. Howell	.316	B. Bailor	496	B. Bailor	62	B. Bailor	154	R. Fairly	24
1978	R. Carty	.284	B. Bailor	621	B. Bailor	74	B. Bailor	164	B. Bailor	29
1979	A. Griffin	.287	A. Griffin	624	A. Griffin	81	A. Griffin	179	R. Bosetti	35
1980	Al Woods	.300	A. Griffin	653	A. Griffin	63	A. Griffin	166	D. Garcia	30
1981	L. Moseby	.233	A. Griffin	388	L. Moseby	36	L. Moseby	88	A. Griffin	19
1982	D. Garcia	.310	D. Garcia	597	D. Garcia	89	D. Garcia	185	D. Garcia	32
1983	B. Bonnell	.318	W. Upshaw	579	L. Moseby	104	W. Upshaw	177	R. Mulliniks	34
1984	D. Collins	.308	D. Garcia	633	L. Moseby	97	D. Garcia	180	G. Bell	39
1985	R. Mulliniks	.295	G. Bell	607	J. Barfield	94	D. Garcia	169	J. Barfield	34
1986	T. Fernandez	.310	**T. Fernandez**	**687**	J. Barfield	107	T. Fernandez	213	G. Bell	38
1987	T. Fernandez	.322	G. Bell	610	G. Bell	111	G. Bell	188	G. Bell	32
1988	M. Lee	.291	T. Fernandez	648	F. McGriff	100	T. Fernandez	186	T. Fernandez	41
1989	G. Bell	.297	G. Bell	613	F. McGriff	98	G. Bell	182	G. Bell	41
1990	F. McGriff	.300	T. Fernandez	635	K. Gruber	92	T. Fernandez	175	K. Gruber	36
									M. Wilson	36
1991	R. Alomar	.295	D. White	642	D. White	110	R. Alomar	188	J. Carter	42
1992	R. Alomar	.310	D. White	641	R. Alomar	105	R. Alomar	177	D. Winfield	32
1993	**J. Olerud**	**.363***	P. Molitor	636	P. Molitor	121	P. Molitor	211*	J. Olerud	54*
1994	P. Molitor	.341	P. Molitor	454	P. Molitor	86	P. Molitor	155	P. Molitor	30
1995	R. Alomar	.300	J. Carter	558	E. Sprague	77	R. Alomar	155	J. Olerud	32
1996	O. Nixon	.286	J. Carter	625	E. Sprague	88	J. Carter	158	J. Carter	35
									E. Sprague	35
1997	S. Green	.287	J. Carter	612	C. Delgado	79	J. Carter	143	C. Delgado	42
1998	T. Fernandez	.321	S. Green	630	S. Green	106	S. Green	175	C. Delgado	43
1999	T. Fernandez	.328	S. Green	614	**S. Green**	**134**	S. Green	190	S. Green	45*
2000	C. Delgado	.344	T. Batista	620	C. Delgado	115	C. Delgado	196	**C. Delgado**	**57***
2001	S. Stewart	.316	S. Stewart	640	S. Stewart	103	S. Stewart	202	S. Stewart	44
2002	S. Stewart	.303	V. Wells	608	C. Delgado	103	S. Stewart	175	E. Hinske	38
					S. Stewart	103			S. Stewart	38
2003	V. Wells	.317	V. Wells	678	V. Wells	118	**V. Wells**	**215***	V. Wells	49*
2004	A. Rios	.286	E. Hinske	570	V. Wells	82	V. Wells	146	V. Wells	34
2005	F. Catalanotto	.301	V. Wells	620	S. Hillenbrand	91	S. Hillenbrand	173	S. Hillenbrand	36
2006	R. Jonhson	.319	V. Wells	611	T. Glaus	105	V. Wells	185	L. Overbay	46
2007	A. Rios	.297	A. Rios	643	A. Rios	114	A. Rios	191	A. Hill	47
2008	V. Wells	.300	A. Rios	635	A. Rios	91	A. Rios	185	A. Rios	47
2009	A. Lind	.305	A. Hill	682	A. Hill	103	A. Hill	195	A. Lind	46
2010	J. Buck	.281	V. Wells	590	J. Bautista	109	V. Wells	161	V. Wells	44
2011	J. Bautista	.302	J. Bautista	513	J. Bautista	105	J. Bautista	155	E. Encarnacion	36
			Y. Escobar	513						
2012	E. Encarnacion	.280	C. Rasmus	565	E. Encarnacion	93	E. Encarnacion	152	B. Lawrie	26

Roberto Alomar was enshrined into the National Baseball Hall of Fame in 2011, becoming the 1st player to go in to Cooperstown in a Toronto Blue Jays uniform

Year	3B		HR		RBI		BB		SO	
1977	S. Staggs	6	R. Fairly	19	R. Fairly	64	O. Velez	65	O. Velez	87
					D. Ault	64				
1978	D. McKay	8	J. Mayberry	22	J. Mayberry	70	J. Mayberry	61	D. McKay	90
1979	A. Griffin	10	J. Mayberry	21	J. Mayberry	74	J. Mayberry	69	R. Howell	91
1980	A. Griffin	15*	J. Mayberry	30	J. Mayberry	82	J. Mayberry	77	R. Howell	92
1981	A. Griffin	6	J. Mayberry	17	J. Mayberry	43	O. Velez	55	L. Moseby	86
					L. Moseby	43				
1982	L. Moseby	9	W. Upshaw	21	W. Upshaw	75	W. Upshaw	52	L. Moseby	106
1983	A. Griffin	9	J. Barfield	27	W. Upshaw	104	C. Johnson	67	J. Barfield	110
			W. Upshaw	27						
1984	D. Collins	15*	G. Bell	26	L. Moseby	92	L. Moseby	78	L. Moseby	122
	L. Moseby	15*								
1985	T. Fernandez	10	G. Bell	28	G. Bell	95	L. Moseby	76	J. Barfield	143
1986	T. Feranadez	9	J. Barfield	40*	J. Barfield	108	W. Upshaw	78	J. Barfield	146
					G. Bell	108				
1987	T. Fernandez	8	G. Bell	47	G. Bell	134*	L. Moseby	70	J. Barfield	141
1988	L. Moseby	7	F. McGriff	34	G. Bell	97	F. McGriff	79	F. McGriff	149
1989	T. Fernandez	9	F. McGriff	36*	G. Bell	104	F. McGriff	119	F. McGriff	132
1990	**T. Fernandez**	**17***	F. McGriff	35	K. Gruber	118	F. McGriff	94	F. McGriff	108
1991	R. Alomar	11	J. Carter	33	J. Carter	108	J. Olerud	68	D. White	135
1992	R. Alomar	8	J. Carter	34	J. Carter	119	R. Alomar	87	D. White	133
1993	T. Fernandez	9	J. Carter	33	J. Carter	121	J. Olerud	114	D. White	127
1994	D. White	6	J. Carter	27	J. Carter	103	J. Olerud	61	D. White	95
1995	R. Alomar	7	J. Carter	25	J. Carter	76	J. Olerud	84	A. Gonzalez	114
1996	J. Carter	7	E. Sprague	36	J. Carter	107	O. Nixon	71	E. Sprague	146
1997	S. Stewart	7	C. Delgado	30	J. Carter	102	C. Delgado	64	C. Delgado	133
1998	S. Green	4	J. Canseco	46	C. Delgado	115	C. Delgado	73	**J. Canseco**	**159***
1999	H. Bush	4	C. Delgado	44	C. Delgado	134	C. Delgado	86	C. Delgado	141
2000	J. Cruz	5	T. Batista	41	C. Delgado	137	C. Delgado	123	J. Cruz	129
	S. Stewart	5	C. Delgado	41						
2001	S. Stewart	7	C. Delgado	39	C. Delgado	102	C. Delgado	111	A. Gonzalez	149
2002	S. Stewart	6	C. Delgado	33	C. Delgado	108	C. Delgado	102	E. Hinske	138
2003	F. Catalanotto	6	C. Delgado	42	**C. Delgado**	**145***	C. Delgado	109	C. Delgado	137
	O. Hudson	6								
2004	O. Hudson	7	C. Delgado	32	C. Delgado	99	C. Delgado	69	C. Delgado	115
	A. Rios	7								
2005	R. Johnson	6	V. Wells	28	V. Wells	97	G. Zaun	73	E. Hinske	121
	A. Rios	6								
2006	A. Rios	6	T. Glaus	38	V. Wells	106	T. Glaus	86	T. Glaus	134
2007	A. Rios	7	F. Thomas	26	F. Thomas	95	F. Thomas	81	A. Rios	103
2008	A. Rios	8	V. Wells	20	A. Rios	79	L. Overbay	74	L. Overbay	116
2009	J. Bautista	3	A. Hill	36	A. Lind	114	M. Scutaro	90	A. Lind	110
	V. Wells	3								
2010	F .lewis	5	**J. Bautista**	**54***	J. Bautista	124	J. Bautista	100	A. Lind	144
2011	R. Davis	6	J. Bautista	43*	J. Bautista	103	**J. Bautista**	**132***	J. Arencibia	133
2012	C. Rasmus	5	E. Encarnacion	42	E. Encarnacion	110	E. Encarnacion	84	K. Johnson	159

Year	SLG %		OBP %		SB		SH		SF	
1977	R. Fairly	.465	R. Howell	.386	B. Bailor	15	A. Ashby	10	O. Velez	6
1978	R. Carty	.481	R. Carty	.340	R. Bosetti	6	**L. Gomez**	**19**	J. Mayberry	7
1979	J. Mayberry	.461	J. Mayberry	.372	A. Griffin	21	A. Griffin	16	R. Bosetti	7
1980	O. Velez	.487	O. Velez	.365	A. Griffin	18	A. Griffin	10	A. Griffin	5
							L. Moseby	10	R. Howell	5
1981	L. Moseby	.357	L. Moseby	.278	D. Garcia	13	A. Woods	8	L. Moseby	4
1982	W. Upshaw	.443	B. Bonnell	.345	D. Garcia	54	A. Griffin	11	G. Iorg	7
1983	W. Upshaw	.515	L. Moseby	.376	D. Collins	31	A. Griffin	11	W. Upshaw	7
					D. Garcia	31				
1984	C. Johnson	.507	C. Johnson	.390	**D. Collins**	**60**	A. Griffin	13	B. Martinez	9
1985	J. Barfield	.536	R. Mulliniks	.383	L. Moseby	37	T. Fernandez	7	G. Bell	8
1986	J. Barfield	.559	J. Barfield	.368	L. Moseby	32	T. Fernandez	5	R. Leach	7
									L. Moseby	7
1987	G. Bell	.605	T. Fernandez	.379	L. Moseby	39	G. Iorg	6	G. Bell	9
1988	F. McGriff	.552	F. McGriff	.376	L. Moseby	31	K. Gruber	5	G. Bell	8
							N. Liriano	5		
1989	F. McGriff	.525	F. McGriff	.399	L. Moseby	24	N. Liriano	10	**G. Bell**	**14**
1990	F. McGriff	.530	F. McGriff	.400	T. Fernandez	26	M. Wilson	6	K. Gruber	13
1991	J. Carter	.503	R. Alomar	.354	R. Alomar	53	R. Alomar	16	J. Olerud	10
1992	J. Carter	.498	R. Alomar	.405	R. Alomar	49	M. Lee	8	J. Carter	13
1993	J. Olerud	.599	**J. Olerud**	**.473***	R. Alomar	55	P. Borders	7	J. Carter	10
1994	J. Carter	.524	P. Molitor	.410	P. Molitor	20	D. Schofield	8	J. Carter	13
1995	S. Green	.509	J. Olerud	.398	R. Alomar	30	A. Gonzalez	9	R. Alomar	7
									E. Sprague	7
1996	E. Sprague	.496	J. Olerud	.382	O. Nixon	54	D. Cedeno	7	C. Delgado	8
							A. Gonzalez	7		
							O. Nixon	7		
1997	C. Delgado	.528	O. Merced	.352	O. Nixon	47	A. Gonzalez	11	J. Carter	9
1998	C. Delgado	.592	T. Fernandez	.387	S. Stewart	51	A. Gonzalez	13	D. Fletcher	7
1999	S. Green	.588	T. Fernandez	.427	S. Stewart	37	H. Bush	8	C. Delgado	7
2000	**C. Delgado**	**.664**	C. Delgado	.470	R. Mondesi	22	A. Gonzalez	16*	B. Fullmer	6
2001	C. Delgado	.540	C. Delgado	.408	J. Cruz Jr.	32	A. Gonzalez	7	A. Gonzalez	10
2002	C. Delgado	.549	C. Delgado	.406	S. Stewart	14	D. Berg	4	C. Delgado	8
									V. Wells	8
									C. Woodward	8
2003	C. Delgado	.593	C. Delgado	.426	E. Hinske	12	K. Cash	5	S. Stewart	8
									V. Wells	8
2004	C. Delgado	.535	C. Delgado	.372	A. Rios	15	H. Clark	3	C. Delgado	11
							C. Gomez	3		
							D. Hudson	3		
							R. Johnson	3		
2005	V. Wells	.463	F. Catalanotto	.367	A. Rios	14	F. Catalannoto	4	R. Adams	8
							K. Huckaby	4	V. Wells	8
2006	V. Wells	.542	R. Johnson	.390	V. Wells	17	J. McDonald	6	A. Rios	10
2007	M. Stairs	.549	F. Thomas	.377	A. Rios	17	J. McDonald	12	A. Rios	7
2008	V. Wells	.496	L. Overbay	.358	A. Rios	32	D. Eckstein	9	M. Scutaro	7
2009	A. Lind	.562	M. Scutaro	.379	A. Rios	19	J. Bautista	6	R. Barajas	7
									M. Scutaro	7
									V. Wells	7
2010	J. Bautista	.617	J. Bautista	.378	F. Lewis	17	Y. Escobar	7	J. Buck	6
2011	J. Bautista	.608*	J. Bautista	.447	R. Davis	34	C. Patterson	6	A. Lind	8
2012	E. Encarnacion	.557	E. Encarnacion	.384	R. Davis	46	Y. Escobar	7	E. Encarnacion	7

Year	IBB		Pinch-Hits		Hitting Streaks	
1977	R. Fairly	11	Sam Ewing	10	Roy Howell (May 10-25)	15
1978	R. Carty	5	Otto Velez	8	Dave McKay (May 19-June 2)	16
1979	J. Mayberry	7	Otto Velez	5	Alfredo Griffin (Aug. 28-Sept. 12)	14
1980	J. Mayberry	9	Steve Braun	9	Alfredo Griffin (Aug. 13-Sept. 1)	19
					John Mayberry (May 31-June 18)	11
1981	A. Woods	5	Willie Upshaw	4	Damaso Garcia (May 29-June 9)	11
1982	W. Upshaw	8	Wayne Nordhagen	11	Damaso Garcia (Aug. 4-21)	20
1983	C. Johnson	8	Rance Mulliniks	10	Damaso Garcia (June 21-July 16)	21*
	W. Upshaw	8			Lloyd Moseby (July 27-Aug. 16)	21*
1984	W. Upshaw	14	Cliff Johnson	11	Damaso Garcia (April 15-May 1)	14
1985	E. Whitt	9	Rance Mulliniks	9	Jesse Barfield (May 8-26)	16
					Damaso Garcia (July 23-Aug. 10)	16
1986	J. Barfield	5	Garth Iorg	10	Damaso Garcia (June 15-July 8)	8
			Rick Leach	10		
1987	G. Bell	7	Rance Mulliniks	8	Tony Fernandez (Aug. 23-Sept. 18)	18
1988	J. Barfield	6	Rance Mulliniks	6	Kelly Gruber (June 22-July 4)	12
	L. Moseby	6				
1989	F. McGriff	12	Bob Brenly	6	George Bell (Aug. 8-31)	22*
1990	F. McGriff	12	Rance Mulliniks	8	Tony Fernandez (April 10-25)	15
					Kelly Gruber (Sept. 10-25)	15
1991	J. Carter	12	Pat Tabler	9	Roberto Alomar (May 24-June 9)	15
1992	J. Olerud	11	John Olerud	4	Dave Winfield (April 22-May 9)	17
1993	**J. Olerud**	**33**	Turner Ward	2	John Olerud (May 26-June 22)	26*
1994	J. Olerud	12	Michael Huff	3	Joe Carter (April 12-28)	15
1995	J. Olerud	10	Michael Huff	4	Roberto Alomar (Aug. 5-21)	19
1996	J. Olerud	6	Robert Perez	5	Otis Nixon (June 4-July 6)	13
1997	C. Delgado	9	Carlos Delgado	4	Carlos Delgado (Sept. 11-28)	16
1998	C. Delgado	13	Felipe Crespo	2	Carlos Delgado (May 21-June 9)	19
			Darrin Fletcher	2		
			Juan Samuel	2		
1999	T. Fernandez	11	Willie Greene	6	**Shawn Green (June 29-July 31)**	**28***
2000	C. Delgado	18	Darrin Fletcher	4	Carlos Delgado (June 4-29)	22
			Todd Greene	4		
2001	C. Delgado	22	**Tony Fernandez**	**16**	Jose Cruz Jr. (April 4-27)	19
2002	C. Delgado	18	Darrin Fletcher	4	Vernon Wells (June 7-26)	13
					Shannon Stewart (May 24-June 6)	13
2003	C. Delgado	23	Tom Wilson	7	Mike Bordick (July 18-Aug. 13)	20
					Reed Johnson (Aug. 30-Sept. 23)	20
					Vernon Wells (June 6-28)	20
2004	C. Delgado	12	Chris Gomez	4	Vernon Wells (May 8-26)	17
2005	E. Hinske	4	Russ Adams	5	Aaron Hill (June 27-July 15)	13
			Orlando Hudson	5		
2006	L. Overbay	7	Frank Catalanotto	5	Benjie Molina (May 23-June 20)	17
2007	G. Zaun	8	Matt Stairs	7	Aaron Hill (Sept. 14-end of season)	15
					Frank Thomas (Aug. 20-Sept. 5)	15
2008	M. Stairs	9	Matt Stairs	5	Alex Rios (Aug. 30-Sept. 11)	12
2009	A. Lind	7	Rod Barajas	3	Scott Rolen (June 8-July 8)	25
2010	L. Overbay	7	4 Players tied	1	Adam Lind (July 1-22)	14
					Vernon Wells (May 21-June 6)	14
2011	J. Bautista	24*	10 Players tied	1	Edwin Encarnacion (July 31-Aug. 14)	13
2012	E. Encarnacion	12	D. Cooper	4	3 players tied	10

BIOGRAPHIES LAST SEASON HISTORY RECORDS OPPONENTS PLAYER DEV. MEDIA & MISC.

PITCHING LEADERS

*** League Leader** **Bold = Club Record**

Year	W		L		ERA (MIN 162 INN)		G	
1977	D. Lemanczyk	13	**J. Garvin**	**18**	J. Garvin	4.19	P. Vuckovich	53
1978	J. Clancy	10	J. Jefferson	16	J. Clancy	4.09	T. Murphy	50
1979	T. Underwood	9	**P. Huffman**	**18**	T. Underwood	3.69	T. Buskey	44
1980	J. Clancy	13	J. Clancy	16	J. Clancy	3.30	J. Garvin	61
1981	D. Stieb	11	L. Leal	13	D. Stieb	3.19	J. McLaughlin	40
1982	D. Stieb	17	L. Leal	15	D. Stieb	3.25	D. Murray	56
1983	D. Stieb	17	J. Gott	14	D. Stieb	3.04	J. McLaughlin	50
1984	D. Alexander	17	J. Clancy	15	D. Stieb	2.83	J. Key	63
1985	D. Alexander	17	D. Stieb	13	D. Stieb	2.48*	G. Lavelle	69
1986	J. Clancy	14	J. Clancy	14	J. Key	3.57	M. Eichhorn	69
	J. Key	14						
	M. Eichhorn	14						
1987	J. Key	17	J. Clancy	11	J. Key	2.76*	**M. Eichhorn**	**89**
1988	D. Stieb	16	J. Clancy	13	D. Stieb	3.04	D. Ward	64
			M. Flanagan	13				
1989	D. Stieb	17	J. Key	14	J. Cerutti	3.07	D. Ward	66
1990	D. Stieb	18	T. Stottlemyre	17	D. Stieb	2.93	D. Ward	73
1991	J. Key	17	J. Key	12	J. Key	3.05	D. Ward	81
1992	J. Morris	21	J. Key	13	J. Guzman	2.64	D. Ward	79
1993	P. Hentgen	19	T. Stottlemyre	12	P. Hentgen	3.87	D. Ward	71
			J. Morris	12				
1994	P. Hentgen	13	J. Guzman	11	P. Hentgen	3.40	T. Castillo	41
1995	A. Leiter	11	J. Guzman	14	A. Leiter	3.64	T. Castillo	55
			P. Hentgen	14				
1996	P. Hentgen	20	E. Hanson	17	J. Guzman	2.93*	M. Timlin	59
1997	R. Clemens	21*	W. Williams	14	**R. Clemens**	**2.05***	P. Quantrill	77
1998	R. Clemens	20*	J. Guzman	12	R. Clemens	2.65*	P. Quantrill	82
1999	D. Wells	17	P. Hentgen	12	P. Hentgen	4.74	G. Lloyd	74
2000	D. Wells	20*	K. Escobar	15	D. Wells	4.11	B. Koch	68
							P. Quantrill	68
2001	C. Carpenter	11	C. Carpenter	11	C. Carpenter	4.09	P. Quantrill	80*
	E. Loaiza	11	E. Loaiza	11				
	P. Quantrill	11						
2002	R. Halladay	19	E. Loaiza	10	R. Halladay	2.93	K. Escobar	76
2003	**R. Halladay**	**22***	C. Lidle	15	R. Halladay	3.25	T. Miller	79*
2004	T. Lilly	12	M. Batista	13	T. Lilly	4.06	J. Frasor	63
2005	G. Chacin	13	J. Towers	12	R. Halladay	2.41	S. Schoeneweis	80
	J. Towers	13						
2006	R. Halladay	16	T. Lilly	13	R. Halladay	3.19	B.J. Ryan	65
2007	R. Halladay	16	D. McGowan	10	R. Halladay	3.71	S. Downs	81*
			J. Towers	10				
2008	R. Halladay	20	R. Halladay	11	R. Halladay	2.78	J. Carlson	69
2009	R. Halladay	17	S. Richmond	11	R. Halladay	2.79	J. Carlson	73
2010	B. Cecil	15	R. Romero	9	S. Marcum	3.64	S. Camp	70
2011	R. Romero	15	3 players	11	R. Romero	2.92	S. Camp	67
2012	B. Morrow	10	H. Alvarez	14	H. Alvarez	4.85	C. Janssen	62
			R. Romero	14			D. Oliver	62

Year	GS		CG		SV		ShO	
1977	J. Garvin	34	J. Garvin	12	P. Vuckovich	8	3 pitchers	1
	D. Lemanczyk	34						
1978	J. Clancy	30	J. Jefferson	9	V. Cruz	9	J. Jefferson	2
	J. Jefferson	30						
	T. Underwood	30						
1979	T. Underwood	32	T. Underwood	12	T. Buskey	7	D. Lemanczyk	3
1980	J. Clancy	34	J. Clancy	15	J. Garvin	8	D. Steib	4
1981	D. Stieb	25	D. Stieb	11	J. McLaughlin	10	D. Steib	2
1982	**J. Clancy**	**40***	**D. Stieb**	**19**	D. Murray	11	**D. Steib**	**5**
1983	D. Stieb	36	D. Stieb	14	R. Moffitt	10	D. Steib	4
1984	J. Clancy	36*	D. Alexander	11	R.L. Jackson	10	3 tied at	2
			D. Stieb	11	J. Key	10		
1985	D. Alexander	36	D. Stieb	8	B. Caudill	14	D. Steib	2
	D. Stieb	36						
1986	J. Key	35	J. Clancy	6	T. Henke	27	J. Clancy	3
1987	J. Clancy	37	J. Key	8	T. Henke	34*	3 pitchers	1
1988	M. Flanagan	34	D. Stieb	8	T. Henke	25	D. Steib	4
1989	D. Stieb	33	J. Key	5	T. Henke	20	D. Steib	2
	J. Key	33						
1990	D. Stieb	33	T. Stottlemyre	4	T. Henke	32	D. Steib	2
	T. Stottlemyre	33						
1991	T. Stottlemyre	34	T. Candiotti	3	T. Henke	32	J. Key	2
1992	J. Morris	34	J. Morris	6	T. Henke	34	J. Key	2
			T. Stottlemyre	6			T. Stottlemyre	2
1993	J. Guzman	33	J. Morris	4	**D. Ward**	**45**	4 pitchers	1
1994	J. Guzman	25	P. Hentgen	6	D. Hall	17	P. Hentgen	3
1995	P. Hentgen	30	D. Cone	5	T. Castillo	13	D. Cone	2
1996	E. Hanson	35	P. Hentgen	10	M. Timlin	31	P. Hentgen	3
	P. Hentgen	35						
1997	P. Hentgen	35	R. Clemens	9*	K. Escobar	14	R. Clemens	3*
			P. Hentgen	9*			P. Hentgen	3*
1998	R. Clemens	33	R. Clemens	5	R. Myers	28	R. Clemens	3
1999	P. Hentgen	34	D. Wells	7*	B. Koch	31	3 pitchers	1
	D. Wells	34						
2000	D. Wells	35*	D. Wells	9*	B. Koch	33	3 pitchers	1
2001	C. Carpenter	34	C. Carpenter	3	B. Koch	36	C. Carpenter	2
2002	R. Halladay	34	E. Loaiza	3	K. Escobar	38	R. Halladay	1
							E. Loaiza	1
2003	R. Halladay	36*	R. Halladay	9*	A. Lopez	14	R. Halladay	2*
2004	T. Lilly	32	T. Lilly	2	J. Frasor	17	4 pitchers	1
			M. Batista	2				
2005	G. Chacin	34	R. Halladay	5	M. Batista	31	R. Halladay	2
2006	R. Halladay	32	R. Halladay	4	B.J. Ryan	38	A.J. Burnett	1
	T. Lilly							
2007	R. Halladay	31	R. Halladay	7*	J. Accardo	30	R. Halladay	1
							D. McGowan	1
2008	A. Burnett	34	R. Halladay	9*	B.J. Ryan	32	R. Halladay	2
							J. Listch	2
2009	R. Halladay	32	R. Halladay	9*	J. Frasor	11	R. Halladay	4*
2010	R. Romero	32	R. Romero	3	K. Gregg	37	B. Morrow	1
							R. Romero	1
2011	R. Romero	32	R. Romero	4	F. Francisco	17	R. Romero	2
2012	R. Romero	32	B. Morrow	3	C. Janssen	22	B. Morrow	3

Year	IP		SO		BB	
1977	D. Lemanczyk	252.0	J. Garvin	127	D. Lemanczyk	87
1978	J. Jefferson	211.2	T. Underwood	139	J. Clancy	91
1979	T. Underwood	227.0	T. Underwood	127	T. Underwood	95
1980	J. Clancy	250.2	J. Clancy	152	**J. Clancy**	**128**
1981	D. Steib	183.2	D. Steib	89	J. Clancy	64
1982	**D. Steib**	**288.1**	D. Steib	141	L. Leal	79
1983	D. Steib	278.0	D. Steib	187	D. Stieb	83
1984	D. Steib	267.0	D. Steib	198	Clancy/Stieb	88
1985	D. Steib	265.0	D. Steib	167	D. Stieb	96
1986	J. Key	232.0	M. Eichhorn		D. Stieb	87
1987	J. Key	261.0	J. Clancy	180	D. Stieb	87
1988	M. Flanagan	211.0	D. Steib	147	M. Flanagan	80
1989	J. Key	216.0	D. Ward	122	D. Stieb	76
1990	D. Steib	208.2	D. Steib	125	T. Stottlemyre	69
1991	T. Stottlemyre	219.0	D. Ward	132	T. Stottlemyre	75
1992	J. Morris	240.2	J. Guzman	165	J. Morris	80
1993	J. Guzman	221.0	J. Guzman	194	J. Guzman	110
1994	P. Hentgen	174.2	P. Hentgen	147	J. Guzman	76
1995	P. Hentgen	202.2	A. Leiter	153	A. Leiter	108
1996	P. Hentgen	265.2	P. Hentgen	177	E. Hanson	102
1997	R. Clemens	264.0	**R. Clemens**	**292***	P. Hentgen	71
	P. Hentgen	264.0				
1998	R. Clemens	234.2	R. Clemens	271*	R. Clemens	88
1999	D. Wells	231.2	D. Wells	169	K. Escobar	81
2000	D. Wells	229.2	D. Wells	166	K. Escobar	85
2001	C. Carpenter	215.2	C. Carpenter	157	C. Carpenter	75
2002	R. Halladay	239.1	R. Halladay	168	J. Miller	66
2003	R. Halladay	266.0*	R. Halladay	204	K. Escobar	78
2004	M. Batista	198.2	T. Lilly	168	M. Batista	96
2005	J. Towers	208.2	G. Chacin	121	G. Chacin	70
2006	R. Halladay	220.0	T. Lilly	160	T. Lilly	81
2007	R. Halladay	225.1	A. Burnett	176	A. Burnett	66
2008	R. Halladay	246.0*	A. Burnett	231*	A. Burnett	86
2009	R. Halladay	239.0	R. Halladay	208	R. Romero	79
2010	R. Romero	210.0	B. Morrow	178	R. Romero	82
2011	R. Romero	225	B. Morrow	203	R. Romero	80
2012	H. Alvarez	187.1	R. Romero	124	R. Romero	105*

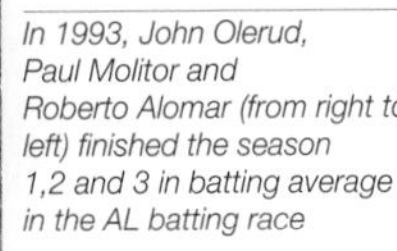

In 1993, John Olerud, Paul Molitor and Roberto Alomar (from right to left) finished the season 1,2 and 3 in batting average in the AL batting race

TOP TEN

SINGLE SEASON

BATTING DEPARTMENTS

BATTING AVERAGE (450PA)

	Player	Year	Avg
1.	John Olerud	1993	.363
2.	Carlos Delgado	2000	.344
3.	Paul Molitor	1994	.341
4.	Paul Molitor	1993	.332
5.	Tony Fernandez	1999	.328
6.	Roberto Alomar	1993	.326
7.	Tony Fernandez	1987	.322
8.	Tony Fernandez	1998	.321
9.	Homer Bush	1999	.320
10.	Shannon Stewart	2000	.319
	Reed Johnson	2006	.319

GAMES

	Player	Year	G
1.	Tony Fernandez	1986	163
2.	Carlos Delgado	2001	162
	Carlos Delgado	2000	162
	Jose Cruz	2000	162
	Joe Carter	1991	162
	Alfredo Griffin	1983	162
	Alfredo Griffin	1982	162
	Rick Bosetti	1979	162
9.	8 players tied		161

HITS

	Player	Year	H
1.	Vernon Wells	2003	215
2.	Tony Fernandez	1986	213
3.	Paul Molitor	1993	211
4.	Shannon Stewart	2001	202
5.	John Olerud	1993	200
6.	George Bell	1986	198
7.	Carlos Delgado	2000	196
8.	Aaron Hill	2009	195
9.	Roberto Alomar	1993	192
10.	Alex Rios	2007	191

AT BATS

	Player	Year	AB
1.	Tony Fernandez	1986	687
2.	Aaron Hill	2009	682
3.	Vernon Wells	2003	678
4.	Alfredo Griffin	1980	653
5.	Tony Fernandez	1988	648
6.	Alex Rios	2007	643
7.	Devon White	1991	642
8.	Devon White	1992	641
	George Bell	1986	641
10.	Shannon Stewart	2001	640

RUNS

	Player	Year	R
1.	Shawn Green	1999	134
2.	Paul Molitor	1993	121
3.	Vernon Wells	2003	118
4.	Carlos Delgado	2003	117
5.	Devon White	1993	116
6.	Carlos Delgado	2000	115
7.	Alex Rios	2007	114
8.	Carlos Delgado	1999	113
9.	George Bell	1987	111
10.	Devon White	1991	110

DOUBLES

	Player	Year	2B
1.	Carlos Delgado	2000	57
2.	John Olerud	1993	54
3.	Vernon Wells	2003	49
4.	Aaron Hill	2007	47
	Alex Rios	2008	47
6.	Lyle Overbay	2006	46
	Adam Lind	2009	46
8.	Eric Hinske	2003	45
	Shawn Green	1999	45
10.	Shannon Stewart	2001	44
	Vernon Wells	2010	44

TRIPLES

	Player	Year	3B
1.	Tony Fernandez	1990	17
2.	Dave Collins	1984	15
	Lloyd Moseby	1984	15
	Alfredo Griffin	1980	15
5.	Roberto Alomar	1991	11
6.	Devon White	1991	10
	Tony Fernandez	1985	10
	Alfredo Griffin	1979	10
9.	8 players tied		9

HOME RUNS

	Player	Year	HR
1.	Jose Bautista	2010	54
2.	George Bell	1987	47
3.	Jose Canseco	1998	46
4.	Carlos Delgado	1999	44
5.	Jose Bautista	2011	43
6.	Carlos Delgado	2003	42
	Shawn Green	1999	42
	Edwin Encarnacion	2012	42
9.	Carlos Delgado	2000	41
	Tony Batista	2000	41

TOTAL BASES

	Player	Year	TB
1.	Carlos Delgado	2000	378
2.	Vernon Wells	2003	373
3.	George Bell	1987	369
4.	Shawn Green	1999	361
5.	Jose Bautista	2010	351
6.	George Bell	1986	341
7.	Aaron Hill	2009	340
8.	Carlos Delgado	2003	338
9.	John Olerud	1993	330
	Adam Lind	2009	330

RUNS BATTED IN

	Player	Year	RBI
1.	Carlos Delgado	2003	145
2.	Carlos Delgado	2000	137
3.	Carlos Delgado	1999	134
	George Bell	1987	134
5.	Jose Bautista	2010	124
6.	Shawn Green	1999	123
7.	Joe Carter	1993	121
8.	Joe Carter	1992	119
9.	Kelly Gruber	1990	118
10.	Vernon Wells	2003	117

SH

	Player	Year	SH
1.	Luis Gomez	1978	19
2.	Alex Gonzalez	2000	16
	Roberto Alomar	1991	16
	Alfredo Griffin	1979	16
5.	Alex Gonzalez	1998	13
	Alfredo Griffin	1984	13
7.	John McDonald	2007	12
8.	Alex Gonzalez	1997	11
	Alfredo Griffin	1983	11
	Alfredo Griffin	1982	11

SF

	Player	Year	SF
1.	George Bell	1989	14
2.	Joe Carter	1994	13
	Joe Carter	1992	13
	Kelly Gruber	1990	13
5.	Carlos Delgado	2004	11
	George Bell	1990	11
7.	Alex Rios	2006	10
	Alex Gonzalez	2001	10
	Joe Carter	1993	10
	John Olerud	1991	10
	Tony Fernandez	1989	10

STOLEN BASES

	Player	Year	SB
1.	Dave Collins	1984	60
2.	Roberto Alomar	1993	55
3.	Otis Nixon	1996	54
	Damaso Garcia	1982	54
5.	Roberto Alomar	1991	53
6.	Shannon Stewart	1998	51
7.	Roberto Alomar	1992	49
8.	Otis Nixon	1997	47
9.	Damaso Garcia	1984	46
	Rajai Davis	2012	46

BASE ON BALLS

	Player	Year	BB
1.	Jose Bautista	2011	132
2.	Carlos Delgado	2000	123
3.	Fred McGriff	1989	119
4.	John Olerud	1993	114
5.	Carlos Delgado	2001	111
6.	Carlos Delgado	2003	109
7.	Carlos Delgado	2002	102
8.	Jose Bautista	2010	100
9.	Fred McGriff	1990	94
10.	Marco Scutaro	2009	90

IBB

	Player	Year	IBB
1.	John Olerud	1993	33
2.	Jose Bautista	2011	24
3.	Carlos Delgado	2003	23
4.	Carlos Delgado	2001	22
5.	Carlos Delgado	2002	18
	Carlos Delgado	2000	18
7.	Willie Upshaw	1984	14
8.	Carlos Delgado	1998	13
9.	5 players tied		12

HBP

	Player	Year	HBP
1.	Shea Hillenbrand	2005	22
2.	Reed Johnson	2006	21
3.	Reed Johnson	2003	20
4.	Carlos Delgado	2003	19
5.	Josh Phelps	2003	17
	Charlie O'Brien	1996	17
7.	Carlos Delgado	2001	16
	Reed Johnson	2005	16
9.	Carlos Delgado	2000	15
	Carlos Delgado	1999	15
	Shannon Stewart	1998	15
	Ed Sprague	1995	15

SLUGGING PCT (450PA)

	Player	Year	SLG
1.	Carlos Delgado	2000	.664
2.	Jose Bautista	2010	.617
3.	Jose Bautista	2011	.608
4.	George Bell	1987	.605
5.	John Olerud	1993	.599
6.	Carlos Delgado	2003	.593
7.	Carlos Delgado	1998	.592
8.	Shawn Green	1999	.588
9.	Carlos Delgado	1999	.571
10.	Adam Lind	2009	.562

ON BASE PCT (450PA)

	Player	Year	OBP
1.	John Olerud	1993	.473
2.	Carlos Delgado	2000	.470
3.	Jose Bautista	2011	.447
4.	Tony Fernandez	1999	.427
5.	Carlos Delgado	2003	.426
6.	Paul Molitor	1994	.410
7.	Roberto Alomar	1993	.408
	Carlos Delgado	2001	.408
9.	Carlos Delgado	2002	.406
10.	Roberto Alomar	1992	.405

OPS (450PA)

	Player	Year	OPS
1.	Carlos Delgado	2000	1.134
2.	John Olerud	1993	1.072
3.	Jose Bautista	2011	1.056
4.	Carlos Delgado	2003	1.019
5.	Jose Bautista	2010	.995
6.	Carlos Delgado	1998	.978
7.	Shawn Green	1999	.972
8.	George Bell	1987	.957
9.	Carlos Delgado	2002	.955
10.	Carlos Delgado	1999	.948

HITTING STREAKS

	Player	Year	G
1.	Shawn Green	1999	28
2.	John Olerud	1993	26
	Shannon Stewart	1999	26
4.	Scott Rolen	2009	25
5.	George Bell	1989	22
	Carlos Delgado	2000	22
7.	Damaso Garcia	1983	21
	Lloyd Moseby	1983	21
	Dave Martinez	2000	21
10.	Damaso Garcia	1982	20
	Mike Bordick	2003	20
	Reed Johnson	2003	20
	Vernon Wells	2003	20

PITCHING DEPARTMENTS

ERA (Min. 162IP)

	Player	Year	ERA
1.	Roger Clemens	1997	2.05
2.	Dave Stieb	1985	2.48
3.	Juan Guzman	1992	2.64
4.	Roger Clemens	1998	2.65
5.	Jimmy Key	1987	2.76
6.	Roy Halladay	2008	2.78
7.	Roy Halladay	2009	2.79
8.	Dave Stieb	1984	2.83
9.	Ricky Romero	2011	2.92
10.	Juan Guzman	1996	2.93
	Dave Stieb	1990	2.93
	Roy Halladay	2002	2.93

WINS

	Player	Year	W
1.	Roy Halladay	2003	22
2.	Roger Clemens	1997	21
	Jack Morris	1992	21
4.	David Wells	2000	20
	Roger Clemens	1998	20
	Pat Hentgen	1996	20
	Roy Halladay	2008	20
8.	Roy Halladay	2002	19
	Pat Hentgen	1993	19
10.	Dave Stieb	1990	18
	A.J. Burnett	2008	18

LOSSES

	Player	Year	L
1.	Phil Huffman	1979	18
	Jerry Garvin	1977	18
3.	Erik Hanson	1996	17
	Todd Stottlemyre	1990	17
	Jesse Jefferson	1977	17
6.	Jim Clancy	1980	16
	Tom Underwood	1979	16
	Jesse Jefferson	1978	16
	Dave Lemanczyk	1977	16
10.	5 players tied		15

GAMES PITCHED

	Player	Year	G
1.	Mark Eichhorn	1987	89
2.	Paul Quantrill	1998	82
3.	Duane Ward	1991	81
	Scott Downs	2007	81
5.	Paul Quantrill	2001	80
	S. Schoeneweis	2005	80
7.	Trever Miller	2003	79
	Duane Ward	1992	79
9.	Dan Plesac	1998	78
10.	Paul Quantrill	1997	77

GAMES STARTED

	Player	Year	GS
1.	Jim Clancy	1982	40
2.	Luis Leal	1982	38
	Dave Stieb	1982	38
4.	Jim Clancy	1987	37
5.	Roy Halladay	2003	36
	Jimmy Key	1987	36
	Doyle Alexander	1985	36
	Dave Stieb	1985	36
	Jim Clancy	1984	36
	Dave Stieb	1983	36

COMPLETE GAMES

	Player	Year	CG
1.	Dave Stieb	1982	19
2.	Jim Clancy	1980	15
3.	Dave Stieb	1983	14
	Dave Stieb	1980	14
5.	Tom Underwood	1979	12
	Jerry Garvin	1977	12
7.	Doyle Alexander	1984	11
	Dave Stieb	1984	11
	Jim Clancy	1983	11
	Jim Clancy	1982	11
	Dave Stieb	1981	11
	Dave Lemanczyk	1979	11
	Dave Lemanczyk	1977	11

SHUTOUTS

	Player	Year	SHO
1.	Dave Stieb	1982	5
2.	Dave Stieb	1988	4
	Dave Stieb	1983	4
	Dave Stieb	1980	4
	Roy Halladay	2009	4
5.	Brandon Morrow	2012	3
	Roger Clemens	1998	3
	Roger Clemens	1997	3
	Pat Hentgen	1997	3
	Pat Hentgen	1996	3
	Pat Hentgen	1994	3
	Jim Clancy	1986	3
	Jim Clancy	1982	3
	Dave Lemanczyk	1979	3

SAVES

	Player	Year	SV
1.	Duane Ward	1993	45
2.	B.J. Ryan	2006	38
	Kelvim Escobar	2002	38
4.	Kevin Gregg	2010	37
5.	Billy Koch	2001	36
6.	Tom Henke	1992	34
	Tom Henke	1987	34
8.	Billy Koch	2000	33
9.	Tom Henke	1991	32
	Tom Henke	1990	32
	B.J. Ryan	2008	32

GAMES FINISHED

	Player	Year	GF
1.	Duane Ward	1993	70
2.	Kelvim Escobar	2002	68
3.	Billy Koch	2000	62
	Tom Henke	1987	62
	Miguel Batista	2005	62
6.	Tom Henke	1990	58
7.	B.J. Ryan	2006	57
8.	Billy Koch	2001	56
	Mike Timlin	1996	56
	Tom Henke	1989	56
	Kevin Gregg	2010	56

INNINGS PITCHED

	Player	Year	IP
1.	Dave Stieb	1982	288.1
2.	Dave Stieb	1983	278.0
3.	Dave Stieb	1984	267.0
4.	Jim Clancy	1982	266.2
5.	Roy Halladay	2003	266.0
6.	Pat Hentgen	1996	265.2
7.	Dave Stieb	1985	265.0
8.	Roger Clemens	1997	264.0
	Pat Hentgen	1997	264.0
10.	Doyle Alexander	1984	261.2

BATTERS FACED

	Player	Year	BF
1.	Dave Stieb	1982	1187
2.	Dave Stieb	1983	1141
3.	Pat Hentgen	1996	1100
	Jim Clancy	1982	1100
5.	Dave Lemanczyk	1977	1092
6.	Doyle Alexander	1985	1090
7.	Dave Stieb	1985	1087
8.	Pat Hentgen	1997	1085
	Dave Stieb	1984	1085
10.	Jim Clancy	1980	1075

BASE ON BALLS

	Player	Year	BB
1.	Jim Clancy	1980	128
2.	Juan Guzman	1993	110
3.	Al Leiter	1995	108
4.	Erik Hanson	1996	102
5.	Miguel Batista	2005	96
	Dave Stieb	1985	96
7.	Tom Underwood	1979	95
8.	Pat Hentgen	1996	94
9.	Dave Stieb	1983	93
10.	Jim Clancy	1978	91

STRIKEOUTS

	Player	Year	SO
1.	Roger Clemens	1997	292
2.	Roger Clemens	1998	271
3.	A.J. Burnett	2008	231
4.	Roy Halladay	2008	206
5.	Roy Halladay	2003	204
6.	Brandon Morrow	2011	203
7.	Dave Stieb	1984	198
8.	Juan Guzman	1993	194
9.	Dave Stieb	1983	187
10.	Jim Clancy	1987	180

W-L PCT (Min. 15 decisions)

	Player	Year	PCT
1.	Juan Guzman	1993	.824
2.	Jack Morris	1992	.778
3.	Roger Clemens	1998	.769
4.	Roy Halladay	2006	.762
	Juan Guzman	1992	.762
6.	Roy Halladay	2003	.759
7.	Roger Clemens	1997	.750
	Dave Stieb	1990	.750
	Roy Halladay	2005	.750
10.	Doyle Alexander	1984	.739

BATTING DEPARTMENTS

GAMES
1. Tony Fernandez 1450
2. Carlos Delgado 1423
3. Vernon Wells 1393
4. Lloyd Moseby 1392
5. Ernie Whitt 1218
6. George Bell 1181
7. Rance Mulliniks 1115
   Willie Upshaw 1115
9. Joe Carter 1039
10. Jesse Barfield 1032

AT BATS
1. Vernon Wells 5470
2. Tony Fernandez 5335
3. Lloyd Moseby 5124
4. Carlos Delgado 5008
5. George Bell 4528
6. Joe Carter 4093
7. Willie Upshaw 3710
8. Shannon Stewart 3625
9. Damaso Garcia 3572
10. Ernie Whitt 3514

RUNS
1. Carlos Delgado 889
2. Vernon Wells 789
3. Lloyd Moseby 768
4. Tony Fernandez 704
5. George Bell 641
6. Shannon Stewart 595
7. Joe Carter 578
8. Willie Upshaw 538
9. Jesse Barfield 530
10. John Olerud 464

HITS
1. Tony Fernandez 1583
2. Vernon Wells 1529
3. Carlos Delgado 1413
4. Lloyd Moseby 1319
5. George Bell 1294
6. Shannon Stewart 1082
7. Joe Carter 1051
8. Damaso Garcia 1028
9. Willie Upshaw 982
10. Jesse Barfield 919

DOUBLES
1. Carlos Delgado 343
2. Vernon Wells 339
3. Tony Fernandez 291
4. Lloyd Moseby 242
5. George Bell 237
6. Shannon Stewart 222
7. Joe Carter 218
8. John Olerud 213
9. Rance Mulliniks 204
10. Alex Rios 195

TRIPLES
1. Tony Fernandez 72
2. Lloyd Moseby 60
3. Alfredo Griffin 50
4. Willie Upshaw 42
5. Roberto Alomar 36
   Alex Rios 36
7. Devon White 34
   Shannon Stewart 34
9. George Bell 32
10. Vernon Wells 30

HOME RUNS
1. Carlos Delgado 336
2. Vernon Wells 223
3. Joe Carter 203
4. George Bell 202
5. Jesse Barfield 179
6. Lloyd Moseby 149
7. Jose Bautista 140
8. Ernie Whitt 131
9. Fred McGriff 125
10. Jose Cruz 122

EXTRA BASE HITS
1. Carlos Delgado 690
2. Vernon Wells 592
3. George Bell 471
4. Lloyd Moseby 451
5. Joe Carter 449
6. Tony Fernandez 423
7. Jesse Barfield 368
8. Willie Upshaw 331
9. Shannon Stewart 330
10. John Olerud 328

RUNS BATTED IN
1. Carlos Delgado 1058
2. Vernon Wells 813
3. George Bell 740
4. Joe Carter 736
5. Lloyd Moseby 651
6. Tony Fernandez 613
7. Jesse Barfield 527
8. Ernie Whitt 518
9. Willie Upshaw 478
10. John Olerud 471

SACRIFICE HITS
1. Alfredo Griffin 74
2. Alex Gonzalez 64
3. Roberto Alomar 39
4. Lloyd Moseby 38
5. Tony Fernandez 34
   John McDonald 34
7. Al Woods 31
8. Manuel Lee 28
9. Damaso Garcia 27
   Willie Upshaw 27

SACRIFICE FLIES
1. Joe Carter 65
2. Carlos Delgado 61
3. George Bell 59
4. Vernon Wells 56
5. Tony Fernandez 44
6. Lloyd Moseby 40
7. Ernie Whitt 36
8. Kelly Gruber 35
   John Olerud 35
10. Alex Rios 33

STOLEN BASES
1. Lloyd Moseby 255
2. Roberto Alomar 206
3. Damaso Garcia 194
4. Tony Fernandez 172
5. Shannon Stewart 166
6. Devon White 126
7. Alex Rios 112
8. Otis Nixon 101
9. Dave Collins 91
10. Vernon Wells 90

WALKS
1. Carlos Delgado 827
2. Lloyd Moseby 547
3. John Olerud 514
4. Tony Fernandez 439
5. Rance Mulliniks 416
6. Vernon Wells 406
7. Ernie Whitt 403
8. Willie Upshaw 390
9. Fred McGriff 352
10. Jose Bautista 349

INTENTIONAL WALKS
1. Carlos Delgado 128
2. John Olerud 87
3. Willie Upshaw 46
4. Ernie Whitt 42
5. Lloyd Moseby 41
6. Joe Carter 39
7. George Bell 37
8. Tony Fernandez 32
9. Jesse Barfield 31
   Fred McGriff 31

HIT BY PITCH
1. Carlos Delgado 122
2. Reed Johnson 80
3. Ed Sprague 68
4. Shannon Stewart 57
5. Lloyd Moseby 50
6. Joe Carter 49
7. Tony Fernandez 48
8. George Bell 35
   Kelly Gruber 35
10. Aaron Hill 34

TOTAL BASES
1. Carlos Delgado 2786
2. Vernon Wells 2597
3. George Bell 2201
4. Tony Fernandez 2198
5. Lloyd Moseby 2128
6. Joe Carter 1934
7. Jesse Barfield 1672
8. Shannon Stewart 1594
9. Willie Upshaw 1579
10. Ernie Whitt 1475

BATTING AVERAGE
(Min. 3000 PA)
1. Roberto Alomar .307
2. Shannon Stewart .298
3. Tony Fernandez .297
4. John Olerud .293
5. Damaso Garcia .288
6. George Bell .286
7. Alex Rios .285
8. Carlos Delgado .282
9. Rance Mulliniks .280
10. Vernon Wells .280

ON BASE PERCENTAGE
(Min. 3000 PA)
1. John Olerud .395
2. Carlos Delgado .392
3. Roberto Alomar .382
4. Rance Mulliniks .365
   Shannon Stewart .365
6. Tony Fernandez .353
7. Willie Upshaw .336
8. Alex Rios .335
9. Jesse Barfield .334
10. Lloyd Moseby .333

SLUGGING PERCENTAGE
(Min. 3000 PA)
1. Carlos Delgado .556
2. George Bell .486
3. Jesse Barfield .483
4. Vernon Wells .475
5. Joe Carter .473
6. John Olerud .471
7. Roberto Alomar .451
8. Alex Rios .451
9. Shannon Stewart .440
10. Kelly Gruber .431

OPS
(Min. 3000 PA)
1. Carlos Delgado .949
2. John Olerud .866
3. Roberto Alomar .833
4. Jesse Barfield .817
5. George Bell .811
6. Shannon Stewart .805
7. Vernon Wells .804
8. Rance Mulliniks .790
9. Alex Rios .786
10. Joe Carter .781

PITCHING DEPARTMENTS

ERA (Min. 1500IP)

	Player	ERA
1.	Dave Stieb	3.42
2.	Jimmy Key	3.42
3.	Roy Halladay	3.43
4.	Jim Clancy	4.10
5.	Pat Hentgen	4.28

WINS

1.	Dave Stieb	175
2.	Roy Halladay	148
3.	Jim Clancy	128
4.	Jimmy Key	116
5.	Pat Hentgen	107
6.	David Wells	84
7.	Juan Guzman	76
8.	Todd Stottlemyre	69
9.	Kelvim Escobar	58
10.	Ricky Romero	51
	Luis Leal	51

LOSSES

1.	Jim Clancy	140
2.	Dave Stieb	134
3.	Pat Hentgen	85
4.	Jimmy Key	81
5.	Roy Halladay	76
6.	Todd Stottlemyre	70
7.	Juan Guzman	62
8.	Luis Leal	58
9.	Jesse Jefferson	56
10.	Kelvim Escobar	55
	David Wells	55

GAMES

1.	Jason Frasor	505
2.	Duane Ward	452
3.	Tom Henke	446
4.	Dave Stieb	439
5.	Paul Quantrill	386
6.	Jim Clancy	352
7.	Scott Downs	347
8.	Jimmy Key	317
9.	Roy Halladay	313
10.	David Wells	306

GAMES STARTED

1.	Dave Stieb	408
2.	Jim Clancy	345
3.	Roy Halladay	287
4.	Jimmy Key	250
5.	Pat Hentgen	238
6.	Juan Guzman	195
7.	Todd Stottlemyre	175
8.	Luis Leal	151
9.	David Wells	138
10.	Chris Carpenter	135

COMPLETE GAMES

1.	Dave Stieb	103
2.	Jim Clancy	73
3.	Roy Halladay	49
4.	Pat Hentgen	31
5.	Jimmy Key	28
6.	Luis Leal	27
7.	Doyle Alexander	25
	Dave Lemanczyk	25
9.	Jesse Jefferson	21
10.	Tom Underwood	19

SHUTOUTS

1.	Dave Stieb	30
2.	Roy Halladay	15
3.	Jim Clancy	11
4.	Jimmy Key	10
5.	Pat Hentgen	9
6.	Roger Clemens	6
7.	Chris Carpenter	5
8.	Jesse Jefferson	4
	Todd Stottlemyre	4
	Brandon Morrow	4

SAVES

1.	Tom Henke	217
2.	Duane Ward	121
3.	Billy Koch	100
4.	B.J. Ryan	75
5.	Kelvim Escobar	58
6.	Mike Timlin	52
7.	Kevin Gregg	37
8.	Miguel Batista	36
	Jason Frasor	36
10.	Jeremy Accardo	35

GAMES FINISHED

1.	Tom Henke	386
2.	Duane Ward	266
3.	Mike Timlin	175
4.	Jason Frasor	169
5.	Billy Koch	166
6.	Kelvim Escobar	130
7.	Paul Quantrill	125
8.	Joey McLaughlin	123
9.	B.J. Ryan	118
10.	Mark Eichhorn	105

INNINGS PITCHED

1.	Dave Stieb	2873.0
2.	Jim Clancy	2204.2
3.	Roy Halladay	2046.2
4.	Jimmy Key	1695.2
5.	Pat Hentgen	1636.0
6.	Juan Guzman	1215.2
7.	David Wells	1148.2
8.	T. Stottlemyre	1139.0
9.	Luis Leal	946.0
10.	Chris Carpenter	870.2

BATTERS FACED

1.	Dave Stieb	11965
2.	Jim Clancy	9397
3.	Roy Halladay	8433
4.	Pat Hentgen	7041
5.	Jimmy Key	6983
6.	Juan Guzman	5209
7.	Todd Stottlemyre	4921
8.	David Wells	4821
9.	Luis Leal	4057
10.	Chris Carpenter	3831

BASE ON BALLS

1.	Dave Stieb	1020
2.	Jim Clancy	814
3.	Pat Hentgen	599
4.	Juan Guzman	546
5.	Roy Halladay	455
6.	Todd Stottlemyre	414
7.	Jimmy Key	404
8.	Kelvim Escobar	394
9.	Ricky Romero	346
10.	Chris Carpenter	331

STRIKEOUTS

1.	Dave Stieb	1658
2.	Roy Halladay	1495
3.	Jim Clancy	1237
4.	Juan Guzman	1030
5.	Pat Hentgen	1028
6.	Jimmy Key	944
7.	David Wells	784
8.	Kelvim Escobar	744
9.	Duane Ward	671
10.	Todd Stottlemyre	662

WIN-LOSS PCT
(Min. 140 DEC.)

	Player	PCT
1.	Roy Halladay	.661
2.	Jimmy Key	.589
3.	Dave Stieb	.566
4.	Pat Hentgen	.557
5.	Jim Clancy	.478

Pat Hentgen, was the first ever Blue Jays pitcher to win the Cy Young Award accomplishing the feat in 1996

MISCELLANEOUS STATISTICS

PITCHING

15-GAME WINNERS

YEAR	PITCHER	W	L
1982	Dave Stieb	17	14
	Jim Clancy	16	14
1983	Dave Stieb	17	12
	Jim Clancy	15	11
1984	Doyle Alexander	17	6
	Dave Stieb	16	8
1985	Doyle Alexander	17	10
1987	Jimmy Key	17	8
	Jim Clancy	15	11

YEAR	PITCHER	W	L
1988	Dave Stieb	16	8
1989	Dave Stieb	17	8
1990	Dave Stieb	18	6
1991	Jimmy Key	16	12
	Todd Stottlemyre	15	8
	David Wells	15	10
1992	Juan Guzman	16	5
	Jack Morris	21	6
1993	Pat Hentgen	19	9

YEAR	PITCHER	W	L
1996	Pat Hentgen	20	10
1997	Roger Clemens	21	7
	Pat Hentgen	15	10
1998	Roger Clemens	20	6
1999	David Wells	17	10
2000	David Wells	20	8
2002	Roy Halladay	19	7
2003	Roy Halladay	22	7

YEAR	PITCHER	W	L
2006	Roy Halladay	16	5
	Ted Lilly	15	13
2007	Roy Halladay	16	7
2008	Roy Halladay	20	11
	A.J. Burnett	18	10
2009	Roy Halladay	17	10
2010	Brett Cecil	15	7
2011	Ricky Romero	15	11

PITCHERS WITH OVER 9 INNINGS IN ONE GAME

PITCHER	DATE	OPPONENT	INNINGS	W-L	SCORE
Jerry Garvin	May 25/77	OAK	9.2	L	L5-6 (10)
Dave Lemanczyk	July 13/77	at CWS (2nd)	11.0	W	W5-3 (11)
Dave Lemanczyk	July 17/77	at DET (2nd)	10.1	L	L6-7 (11)
Dave Lemanczyk	Oct. 2/77	CLE (1st)	11.0	W	W2-1 (11)
Jesse Jefferson	May 23/78	BOS	12.0	W	W2-1 (12)
Tom Underwood	Sept.3/79	at BAL (1st)	10.0	ND	L1-2 (11)
Jesse Jefferson	May 16/80	OAK	11.0	W	W1-0 (11)
Dave Stieb	May 17/80	OAK	12.0	ND	L2-4 (14)
Dave Stieb	Aug. 9/80	KC	10.0	ND	W4-3 (14)
Jim Clancy	June 19/82	at OAK	10.0	W	W2-1(12)
Jim Gott	July 31/82	at DET	10.0	W	W1-0 (10)
Dave Stieb	Sept. 16/82	CAL	11.0	ND	W2-1 (12)
Jim Clancy	Sept. 22/82	at MIN	10.0	W	W3-2 (10)
Dave Stieb	May 11/83	at CWS	10.0	W	W3-1 (10)
Dave Stieb	May 16/83	at MIL	10.0	W	W2-1 (11)
Jim Gott	Aug. 26/83	at DET	9.2	L	L3-4 (10)
Dave Stieb	Sept. 4/83	DET	10.0	W	W6-3 (10)
Jim Clancy	Sept. 24/83	at OAK	9.1	L	L1-2 (10)
Dave Stieb	May 4/84	KC	10.0	W	W4-3 (10)
Jimmy Key	June 6/85	DET	10.0	ND	W2-0 (12)
Jimmy Key	June 17/86	at MIL	10.0	ND	W2-1 (12)
Jimmy Key	July 27/86	at OAK	10.0	ND	L0-1 (15)
Mike Flanagan	Oct. 3/87	at DET	11.0	ND	L2-3 (12)
John Cerutti	April 30/89	at CAL	10.0	ND	L0-1 (11)
Tom Candiotti	July 16/91	at KC	9.1	L	L1-2 (10)
Roy Halladay	Sept. 6/03	DET	10.0	W	W1-0 (10)
Roy Halladay	April 13/07	DET	10.0	W	W2-1 (10)

BLUE JAYS—10 WINS

AT HOME

PITCHER	HOME WINS	YEAR
Doyle Alexander	12	1984
Dave Stieb	12	1988
Roger Clemens	12	1998
Roy Halladay	11	2007
Dave Stieb	11	1983
Doyle Alexander	11	1985
Jack Morris	11	1992
Jimmy Key	10	1985
Jimmy Key	10	1987
Jeff Musselman	10	1987
Roger Clemens	10	1997
Roy Halladay	10	2002
Roy Halladay	10	2003
Roy Halladay	10	2008
A.J. Burnett	10	2008
Roy Halladay	10	2009

ON ROAD

PITCHER	ROAD WINS	YEAR
Pat Hentgen	12	1993
Roy Halladay	12	2003
Pat Hentgen	11	1996
Pat Hentgen	11	1996
Roger Clemens	11	1997
David Wells	11	2000
Dave Stieb	10	1989
Roy Halladay	10	2008
Roy Halladay	10	2008
Jack Morris	10	1992

BLUE JAYS WITH 10 OR MORE STRIKEOUTS IN A GAME

18 STRIKEOUTS	LAST	AGAINST
Roger Clemens	08/25/98	KC
17 STRIKEOUTS		
Brandon Morrow	08/08/10	TB
16 STRIKEOUTS		
Roger Clemens	07/12/97	@BOS
15 STRIKEOUTS		
Roger Clemens **x2**	09/21/98	BAL
14 STRIKEOUTS		
Roger Clemens **x3**	08/02/98	@MIN
Pat Hentgen	05/03/94	KC
Roy Halladay	06/02/09	LAA
13 STRIKEOUTS		
A.J. Burnett **x2**	08/19/08	NYY
Roger Clemens	08/12/97	MIN
Ted Lilly	08/23/04	BOS
12 STRIKEOUTS		
Ricky Romero **x3**	06/15/11	BAL
Brandon Morrow **x2**	08/17/11	@SEA
Roger Clemens **x2**	06/16/97	ATL
Pete Vuckovich	06/26/77	@BAL
Jim Clancy	04/19/88	KC
Dave Stieb	08/22/88	CWS
Tom Candiotti	09/09/91	DET
Chris Carpenter	09/04/01	NYY
Ted Lilly	06/10/06	DET
A.J. Burnett	06/01/07	CWS
Dustin McGowan	09/07/07	@TB
11 STRIKEOUTS		
Roger Clemens **x6**	09/26/98	DET
Juan Guzman **x4**	05/10/98	@SEA
A.J. Burnett **x4**	09/24/08	NYY
Brandon Morrow **x2**	10/03/12	MIN
Jim Clancy **x2**	07/12/87	KC
Dave Stieb **x2**	08/04/89	NYY
David Wells **x2**	07/26/00	CLE
Doyle Alexander	07/23/85	SEA
Jose Nunez	07/09/87	KC
Al Leiter	07/23/94	TEX
David Cone	06/28/95	@BOS
Kelvim Escobar	08/22/98	@ANA
Esteban Loaiza	09/08/00	DET
Chris Carpenter	04/05/01	@TB
Roy Halladay	09/19/01	BAL
Dave Bush	10/01/04	NYY
Scott Downs	09/02/05	TB
David Purcey	08/27/08	@TB
Scott Richmond	06/17/09	@PHI

10 STRIKEOUTS	LAST	AGAINST
Roger Clemens **x9**	07/17/98	NYY
Juan Guzman **x6**	07/30/95	@OAK
A.J. Burnett **x6**	07/28/08	TB
Pat Hentgen **x5**	05/04/97	MIN
Roy Halladay **x5**	07/24/09	TB
Dave Stieb **x4**	08/31/84	MIN
Kelvim Escobar **x4**	09/24/03	TB
Brandon Morrow **x3**	05/09/12	@OAK
Jim Clancy **x3**	09/09/87	@MIL
Ted Lilly **x3**	04/13/06	@BOS
Jimmy Key **x2**	04/24/89	@OAK
Shaun Marcum **x2**	07/30/10	CLE
Jerry Garvin	04/13/77	DET
Jesse Jefferson	05/16/80	OAK
Luis Leal	08/24/84	@MIN
Todd Stottlemyre	09/21/93	BOS
Dave Stewart	04/25/94	@KC
David Cone	07/08/95	@OAK
Al Leiter	09/17/95	@MIL
Chris Carpenter	07/16/98	CWS
David Wells	04/19/00	ANA
Cory Lidle	09/26/03	CLE
David Purcey	04/12/09	@CLE
Scott Richmond	08/22/09	LAA
Brett Cecil	05/03/10	@CLE
Ricky Romero	04/24/11	TB

LOW HIT GAMES BY BLUE JAYS

NO-HITTER (1)

Sept. 2/90 – Dave Stieb, Toronto-3 at Cleveland-0

ONE HIT GAMES (23)

April 24/79 – Dave Lemanczyk (9.0 IP), Toronto-2 at Texas-0, Putnam single in the 3rd inn
Aug. 27/79 – Phil Huffman (9.0 IP), Oakland-0 at Toronto-7, Essian single in the 6th inn
May 30/82 – Jim Gott (6.0 IP), Roy Lee Jackson (3.0 IP) Toronto-6 at Baltimore-0, Dempsey single in the 5th inn
Sept. 28/82 – Jim Clancy (9.0 IP), Minnesota-0 at Toronto-3, Bush bloop single in 9th inn to break up perfect game
May 14/83 – Luis Leal (5.0 IP), Roy Lee Jackson (4.0 IP) Toronto-8 at Cleveland-1, Bando single in the 8th inn
May 22/86 – Jimmy Key (9.0 IP), Toronto-5 at Chicago (AL)-0, Guillen single in the 5th inn
May 31/88 – Dave Stieb (9.0 IP), Milwaukee-0 at Toronto-9, Surhoff single in the 4th inn
Sept. 24/88 – Dave Stieb (9.0 IP), Toronto-1 at Cleveland-0, Franco single in the 9th inn with two out
Sept. 30/88 – Dave Stieb (9.0 IP), Baltimore-0 at Toronto-4, Traber single in the 9th inn with two out
April 10/89 – Dave Stieb (9.0 IP), Toronto-8 at New York (AL)-0, Quirk single in 5th inn
Aug. 26/89 – Dave Stieb (9.0 IP), Milwaukee-0 at Toronto-7, Yount single in 6th inn
Aug. 26/92 – Todd Stottlemyre (9.0 IP), Toronto-9 at Chicago (AL)-0, Pasqua double with one out in the 8th inn
Aug. 2/95 – Paul Menhart (8.0 IP), Toronto-0 at Baltimore-1, Baines home run in the 2nd inn
May 2/98 – Roger Clemens (7.0 IP), Paul Quantrill (2.0 IP), Toronto-7 at Oakland-0, Grieve single in the 7th inn
Sept. 27/98 – Roy Halladay (9.0 IP), Detroit-1 at Toronto-2, Higginson homerun with two out in the 9th inn
May 21/00 – Frank Castillo (7.0 IP), Pedro Borbon (1.0 IP), Billy Koch (1.0 IP), Toronto-1 vs. Chicago (AL)-2, Johnson single in the 3rd inn
June 24/07 – Dustin McGowan (9.0 IP), Colorado-0 at Toronto-5, Baker leadoff single in the 9th inn
Sept. 4/09 – Roy Halladay (9.0 IP), New York (AL)-0 at Toronto-6, Pena doubled in the 6th inn with one out
April 13/10 – Ricky Romero (8.0 IP), Kevin Gregg (1.0 IP), Chicago (AL)-2 at Toronto-4, Rios home run with one out in the 8th inn
Aug. 8/10 – Brandon Morrow (9.0 IP), Tampa Bay-0 at Toronto-1, Longoria single with two outs in the 9th inn
Aug. 16/10 – Shaun Marcum (9.0 IP), Toronto-3 at Oakland-1, Jackson home run with none out in the 7th inn
April 2/11 – Kyle Drabek (7.0 IP), Shawn Camp (1.0 IP), Marc Rzepczynski (1.0 IP), Minnesota-1 at Toronto-6, Span singled in the 6th inning
Aug. 21/11 – Luis Perez (6.0 IP), Casey Janssen (3.0 IP), Toronto-1 at Oakland-0, Weeks singled in the 6th inning

Dave Stieb is the only Blue Jay pitcher to ever throw a no-hitter, accomplished the feat on Sept. 2, 1990 at Cleveland (W, 3-0)

BATTING

.300 HITTERS (502 OR MORE PA)

YEAR	PLAYER	AVG
1977	Bob Bailor	.310
1980	Al Woods	.300
1982	Damaso Garcia	.310
1983	Damaso Garcia	.307
	Lloyd Moseby	.315
	Willie Upshaw	.306
1986	George Bell	.309
1987	Tony Fernandez	.322
	George Bell	.308
1990	Fred McGriff	.300
1992	Roberto Alomar	.310
1993	John Olerud	.363
	Paul Molitor	.332
	Roberto Alomar	.326
1994	Paul Molitor	.341
	Roberto Alomar	.306
1995	Roberto Alomar	.300
1998	Tony Fernandez	.321
1999	Tony Fernandez	.328
	Shawn Green	.309
	Shannon Stewart	.304
2000	Carlos Delgado	.344
	Shannon Stewart	.319
2001	Shannon Stewart	.316
2002	Shannon Stewart	.303
2003	Carlos Delgado	.302
	Vernon Wells	.317
2006	Reed Johnson	.319
	Lyle Overbay	.312
	Vernon Wells	.303
2009	Adam Lind	.305
2011	Jose Bautista	.302

100 RBI

YEAR	PLAYER	RBI
1983	Willie Upshaw	104
1986	Jesse Barfield	108
	George Bell	108
1987	George Bell	134
1989	George Bell	104
1990	Kelly Gruber	118
1991	Joe Carter	108
1992	Joe Carter	119
	Dave Winfield	108
1993	Joe Carter	121
	Paul Molitor	111
	John Olerud	107
1994	Joe Carter	103
1996	Joe Carter	107
	Ed Sprague	101
1997	Joe Carter	102
1998	Carlos Delgado	115
	Jose Canseco	107
	Shawn Green	100
1999	Carlos Delgado	134
	Shawn Green	123
2000	Carlos Delgado	137
	Tony Batista	114
	Brad Fullmer	104
2001	Carlos Delgado	102
2002	Carlos Delgado	108
	Vernon Wells	100
2003	Carlos Delgado	145
	Vernon Wells	117
2006	Vernon Wells	106
	Troy Glaus	104
2009	Adam Lind	114
	Aaron Hill	108
2010	Jose Bautista	124
2011	Jose Bautista	103
2012	Edwin Encarnacion	110

30 HOME RUNS

YEAR	PLAYER	HR's
1980	John Mayberry	30
1986	Jesse Barfield	40
	George Bell	31
1987	George Bell	47
1988	Fred McGriff	34
1989	Fred McGriff	36
1990	Kelly Gruber	31
	Fred McGriff	35
1991	Joe Carter	33
1992	Joe Carter	34
1993	Joe Carter	33
1996	Ed Sprague	36
	Joe Carter	30
1997	Carlos Delgado	30
1998	Jose Canseco	46
	Carlos Delgado	38
	Shawn Green	35
1999	Carlos Delgado	44
	Shawn Green	42
2000	Tony Batista	41
	Carlos Delgado	41
	Brad Fullmer	32
	Jose Cruz Jr.	31
2001	Carlos Delgado	39
	Jose Cruz Jr.	34
2002	Carlos Delgado	33
2003	Carlos Delgado	42
	Vernon Wells	33
2004	Carlos Delgado	32
2006	Troy Glaus	38
	Vernon Wells	32
2009	Aaron Hill	36
	Adam Lind	35
2010	Jose Bautista	54
	Vernon Wells	31
2011	Jose Bautista	43
2012	Edwin Encarnacion	42

30 STOLEN BASES

YEAR	PLAYER	SB
1982	Damaso Garcia	54
1983	Dave Collins	31
	Damaso Garcia	31
1984	Dave Collins	60
	Damaso Garcia	46
	Lloyd Moseby	39
1985	Lloyd Moseby	37
1986	Lloyd Moseby	32
1987	Lloyd Moseby	39
	Tony Fernandez	32
1988	Lloyd Moseby	31
1991	Roberto Alomar	53
	Devon White	33
1992	Roberto Alomar	49
	Devon White	37
1993	Roberto Alomar	55
	Devon White	34
1995	Roberto Alomar	30
1996	Otis Nixon	54
1997	Otis Nixon	47
1998	Shannon Stewart	51
	Shawn Green	35
1999	Shannon Stewart	37
	Homer Bush	32
2001	Jose Cruz Jr.	32
	Raul Mondesi	30
2008	Alex Rios	32
2011	Rajai Davis	34
2012	Rajai Davis	46

HOME/ROAD RBI LEADERS

YEAR	HOME	ROAD
1977	33 Ron Fairly	33 Otto Velez
1978	40 John Mayberry	31 Roy Howell
1979	41 Rick Bosetti	38 John Mayberry
1980	40 Otto Velez	45 John Mayberry
1981	22 John Mayberry	28 Lloyd Moseby
1982	46 Willie Upshaw	29 Willie Upshaw
1983	55 Willie Upshaw	49 Willie Upshaw
1984	52 Lloyd Moseby	42 Willie Upshaw
1985	49 Jesse Barfield	47 George Bell
1986	57 George Bell	57 Jesse Barfield
1987	57 George Bell	78 George Bell
1988	47 George Bell	50 George Bell
1989	48 Fred McGriff	57 George Bell
1990	62 Kelly Gruber	56 Kelly Gruber
1991	64 Joe Carter	44 Joe Carter
1992	65 Joe Carter	61 Dave Winfield
1993	68 Paul Molitor	59 John Olerud
1994	70 Joe Carter	39 John Olerud
1995	39 Ed Sprague	42 Joe Carter
1996	52 Joe Carter	59 Ed Sprague
1997	59 Joe Carter	43 Joe Carter
1998	61 Carlos Delgado	54 Carlos Delgado
1999	60 Shawn Green	76 Carlos Delgado
2000	75 Carlos Delgado	62 Carlos Delgado
2001	47 Jose Cruz Jr.	60 Carlos Delgado
2002	51 Carlos Delgado	58 Vernon Wells
2003	83 Carlos Delgado	62 Carlos Delgado
2004	55 Carlos Delgado	44 Carlos Delgado
2005	49 Shea Hillenbrand	50 Vernon Wells
2006	69 Vernon Wells	42 Troy Glaus
2007	58 Frank Thomas	47 Matt Stairs
2008	42 Alex Rios	38 Lyle Overbay
2009	54 Adam Lind	60 Adam Lind
2010	69 Jose Bautista	55 Jose Bautista
2011	49 Jose Bautista	54 Jose Bautista
2012	57 E. Encarnacion	53 E. Encarnacion

SEASON RECORDS — INDIVIDUAL

*** - League Leader**

BATTING

Highest Average (502 PA)	*.363	John Olerud-'93
Most Games	*163	Tony Fernandez-'86
Most at Bats	687	Tony Fernandez-'86
Most Runs	134	Shawn Green-'99
Most Hits	*215	Vernon Wells-'03
Most Total Bases	*378	Carlos Delgado-'00
Highest SLG %	.664	Carlos Delgado-'00
Highest OBP %	.473	John Olerud-'93
Most Extra Base Hits	*99	Carlos Delgado-'00
Most Doubles	*57	Carlos Delgado-'00
Most Triples	17	Tony Fernandez-'90
Most Home Runs	*54	Jose Bautista-'10
Most Home Runs-Home	*33	Jose Bautista-'10
Most Home Runs-Road	28	George Bell-'87
Most Grand Slam Home Runs	3	Carlos Delgado-'97
	3	Darrin Fletcher-'00
Most Runs Batted In	*145	Carlos Delgado-'03
Most Base On Balls	132	Jose Bautista-'11
Most Intentional Base on Balls	33	John Olerud-'93
Most Times Striking Out	159	Jose Canseco-'98
	159	Kelly Johnson-'12
Most Sacrifice Bunts	19	Luis Gomez-'78
Most Sacrifice Flies	14	George Bell-'89
Most Times Hit by Pitch	22	Shea Hillenbrand-'05

PITCHING

Most Wins	*22	Roy Halladay-'03
Most Home Wins	12	Doyle Alexander-'84
	12	Dave Stieb-'88
	12	Roger Clemens-'98
Most Road Wins	12	Pat Hentgen-'93
	*12	Roy Halladay-'03
Most Losses	18	Phil Huffman-'79
	18	Jerry Garvin-'77/Jimmy Key-'86
Most Home Losses	10	Jesse Jefferson-'77
	10	Dave Stieb-'80
Most Road Losses	12	Luis Leal-'82
Most Decisions	31	Dave Stieb-'82,
	31	Roy Halladay-'08
Highest Winning Pct (15 decisions)	.824	Juan Guzman (14-3)-'93
Lowest ERA (162 IP)	*2.05	Roger Clemens-'97
Most Appearances	89	Mark Eichhorn-'87
Most Games Started	40	Jim Clancy-'82
Most Complete Games	19	Dave Stieb-'82
Most Shutouts	5	Dave Stieb-'82
Most Innings Pitched	288.1	Dave Stieb-'82
Most Hits Allowed	278	Dave Lemanczyk-'77
Most Earned Runs Allowed	129	Erik Hanson-'96
Most Home Runs Allowed	36	Woody Williams-'98
Most Bases on Balls	128	Jim Clancy-'80
Most Strikeouts	*292	Roger Clemens-'97
Most Hit Batsmen	16	Chris Carpenter-'01
Most Balks	6	Mark Eichhorn-'88
Most Wild Pitches	*26	Juan Guzman-'93
Most Relief Wins	14	Mark Eichhorn-'86
Most Relief Losses	10	Tom Buskey-'79
	10	Duane Ward-'89
Most Saves	*45	Duane Ward-'93
Most Decisions in Relief	20	Mark Eichhorn-'86
Innings Pitched In Relief	157.0	Mark Eichhorn-'86
Most Games Finished	70	Duane Ward-'93

MISCELLANEOUS

Most Consecutive Wins	15	Roger Clemens	June 3-Sept. 21/98
	15	Roy Halladay	May 1-July 27/03
Most Consecutive Wins (Starter)	15	Roger Clemens	June 3-Sept. 21/98
	15	Roy Halladay	May 1-July 27/03
Most Consecutive Wins (Reliever)	11	Dennis Lamp	April 6-Oct. 6/85
Most Consecutive Losses (Season)	13	Ricky Romero	June 27-Sept. 12/12
Most Consecutive Losses	13	Tom Underwood	Aug. 28/78 - June 10/79
Most Consecutive Shutouts	3	Dave Stieb	Sept. 18-24-30/88
	3	Roger Clemens	Aug. 20-30/98
Most Consecutive Complete Games	7	Dave Stieb	June 18-July 21/80
Most Consecutive Scoreless Innings	33	Roger Clemens	Aug. 20-Sept. 5/98
Most Consecutive Games, one or more RBI's	8	Willie Upshaw	Sept. 11-20/83
	8	Carlos Delgado	April 16-23/00
	8	Matt Stairs	Aug. 28-Sept. 3/07
Most Consecutive Games, Extra-base Hit	11	Jesse Barfield	Aug. 17-27/85
Most Consecutive Hits	8	Rance Mulliniks	Aug. 24-27/84
	8	Paul Molitor	Aug. 26-27/95
	8	Tony Fernandez	May 6-11/99
	8	Adam Lind	June 3-4/09
Most Consecutive Times Reached Base	12	Lyle Overbay	May 22-25/08
Most Consecutive Games Reached Base Safely	37	Joe Carter	April 8-May 23/94
Most Consecutive Hits, Team	10	vs. Minnesota	Sept. 4/92 (2nd inning)
Most Consecutive Innings, No Earned Runs	41.0	Roy Halladay	Sept. 1-Sept. 22/03
Most Saves, Consecutive Opportunities	25	Tom Henke	April 9-Aug. 7/91
Most Saves, Consecutive Appearances	10	Dwane Ward	April 25-May 13/91
		Darren Hall	July 15-Aug. 5/94
		Billy Koch	July 18-Aug. 8/99
Most Home Runs, One Inning	4	vs. Texas (6th inning)	Aug. 17/01
	4	at Boston (5th inning)	May 20/09
Home Runs in Consecutive AB's	4	Carlos Delgado	Sept. 25/03
Most Consecutive Stolen Bases	23	Joe Carter	1993-1995
Most Runs, One Inning	11	vs. Seattle (A) (9th inning)	July 20/84
	11	vs. Oakland (H) (2nd inning)	April 26/95
	11	vs. Minnesota (H) (6th inning)	July 25/07
Most Hits, One Inning	11	vs. Seattle (A) (9th inning)	July 20/84
	11	vs. Oakland (H) (2nd inning)	April 26/96
Most Batters, One Inning	16	vs. Seattle (A) (9th inning)	July 20/84
Most Consecutive Errorless Games	15		2008
Most Errors, Game	6	Texas	May 13/82
Most Double Plays, Game	6	Detroit	April 16/96
Most Innings, Home	18	vs. Los Angeles (AL)	July 28/05
Most Innings, Road	17	at Boston	Oct. 4/80 (GM 1)
	17	at Florida	June 8/98
Longest Game, Time, Home (9.0 inning)	4:15	vs. New York (AL)	April 11/88
Longest Game, Time, Road (9.0 inning)	4:12	at Detroit	Sept. 15/93
	4:12	at Boston	April 1/02
Longest Game, Time, Home	5:57	vs New York (AL)	April 19/01 (17.0)
Longest Game, Time, Road	5:49	at Baltimore	June 19/98 (15.0)
Shortest Game, Time, Home	1:33	vs Minnesota	Sept. 28/82
Shortest Game, Time, Road	1:39	at Detroit	June 16/77
Hitting Streak	28	Shawn Green	June 29-July 31, 1999
Most Consecutive Times Shutout	3		May 13-15/81
Most Consecutive Scoreless Innings	33.0		May 12-16/81
Most Consecutive Complete Games	4		Sept. 20, 21, 23, 24/83
Most Consecutive Shutout Games	3		May 21, 22, 23/83
Most Consecutive Shutout Innings-Pitchers	28		June 4, 5, 6, 7/85
Most Consecutive Games Played	432	Carlos Delgado	April 3/00-Aug. 4/02
Most Years, Pitcher	15	Dave Stieb	1979-92, 1998
Most Years, Non-Pitcher	12	Ernie Whitt	1977-78, 1980-89
	12	Tony Fernandez	1983-90, 1993, 1998-99, 2001
	12	Vernon Wells	1999-2010
Longest Road Trip	15	Games	1978, 1984, 1995

FIELDING SEASON RECORDS

Based on 108 games

PITCHERS

Category	Record	Player, Year
Games, Most	89	Mark Eichhorn, 1987
Putouts, Most	34	Dave Stieb, 1985; Jim Clancy, 1986
Assists, Most	66	Jerry Garvin, 1977
Errors, Most	8	Jesse Jefferson, 1977
Total Chances, Most	92	Dave Stieb, 1985
Double Plays, Most	8	Dave Stieb, 1980
Best Percentage (35 or more chances)	1.000	Done 20x

CATCHERS

Category	Record	Player, Year
Games, Most	138	Pat Borders, 1993
Putouts, Most	869	Pat Borders, 1993
Assists, Most	88	Pat Borders, 1992
Errors, Most	13	Rick Cerone, 1979; Pat Borders, 1993
Passed Balls, Most	14	Sandy Martinez, 1995
Total Chances, Most	962	Pat Borders, 1993
Double Plays, Most	12	Pat Borders, 1993
Best Percentage	.997	Darrin Fletcher, 1999; Benito Santiago, 1997; Bengie Molina, 2006

FIRST BASEMEN

Category	Record	Player, Year
Games, Most	162	Carlos Delgado, 2000
Putouts, Most	1518	Carlos Delgado, 2001
Assists, Most	155	Lyle Overbay, 2008
Errors, Most	21	Willie Upshaw, 1983
Total Chances, Most	1630	Carlos Delgado, 2001
Double Plays, Most	166	Carlos Delgado, 2001
Best Percentage	.998	Lyle Overbay, 2009 (130 games)

SECOND BASEMEN

Category	Record	Player, Year
Games, Most	160	Roberto Alomar, 1991; Aaron Hill, 2007
Putouts, Most	333	Roberto Alomar, 1991
Assists, Most	560	Aaron Hill, 2007
Errors, Most	16	Damaso Garcia, 1980
Total Chances, Most	818	Aaron Hill, 2007
Double Plays, Most	129	Aaron Hill, 2009
Best Percentage	.994	Roberto Alomar, 1995

THIRD BASEMEN

Category	Record	Player, Year
Games, Most	156	Kelly Gruber, 1988
Putouts, Most	133	Ed Sprague, 1995
Assists, Most	349	Kelly Gruber, 1988
Errors, Most	22	Roy Howell, 1978; Kelly Gruber, 1989; Eric Hinske, 2003
Total Chances, Most	477	Kelly Gruber, 1988
Double Plays, Most	37	Troy Glaus, 2006
Best Percentage	.978	Eric Hinske, 2004

SHORTSTOP

Category	Record	Player, Year
Games, Most	163	Tony Fernandez, 1986
Putouts, Most	319	Alfredo Griffin, 1982
Assists Most	509	Alex Gonzalez, 2001
Errors, Most	37	Alfredo Griffin, 1980
Total Chances, Most	824	Alfredo Griffin, 1982
Double Plays, Most	126	Alfredo Griffin, 1980
Best Percentage	.992	Tony Fernandez, 1989

OUTFIELDERS

Category	Record	Player, Year
Games, Most	162	Rick Bosetti, 1979; Jose Cruz, 2000
Putouts, Most	473	Lloyd Moseby, 1984
Assists, Most	22	Jesse Barfield, 1985
Errors, Most	15	George Bell, 1988
Total Chances, Most	497	Rick Bosetti, 1979
Double Plays, Most	8	Jesse Barfield, 1985 & 1986
Best Percentage	1.000	Vernon Wells, 2005 & 2010; Frank Catalanotto, 2005

GAME RECORDS — INDIVIDUAL

BATTING

Category	Record	Player	Opponent	Date
At Bats	9	Alfredo Griffin (17 inn.)	Boston (A), 1st g	Oct. 4/80
Runs	5	Carlos Delgado	Seattle (A)	May 3/99
	5	Shannon Stewart	Tampa Bay (A)	June 25/02
	5	Orlando Hudson	Boston (H)	May 13/04
Hits	6	Frank Catalanotto	Chicago-AL (A) 2nd g	May 1/04
Doubles	4	Damaso Garcia	New York-AL (A)	June. 27/86
		Shannon Stewart	New York-NL (H)	July 18/00
		Alex Rios	Boston (A)	Aug. 17/08
Triples	2	12x, 10 players, last: Alex Rios	Tampa Bay (H)	April 27/05
Home Runs	4	Carlos Delgado	Tampa Bay (H)	Sept. 25/03
Extra-Base Hits	4	11x, 10 players, last: Yunel Escobar	New York-AL (A)	Aug. 29/12
RBI's	9	Roy Howell	New York-AL (A)	Sept. 10/77
Sacrifice Bunts	2	31x	Last: Chicago-AL (A)	Sept. 9/08
Sacrifice Flies	3	George Bell	Chicago-AL (A)	Aug. 14/90
Strikeouts	6	Alex Gonzalez (13 inn.)	Cleveland (H)	Sept. 9/98
	5	Alex Rios	Oakland (A)	July 29/06
	5	Alex Rios	Los Angeles-AL (H)	June 4/09
Walks	4	15x, 11 players, last: Jose Bautista	New York-AL (H)	Sept. 16/11
Stolen Bases	4	Damaso Garcia	Oakland (H)	April 25/84
		Dave Collins	Baltimore (A)	Aug. 5/84
		Roberto Alomar	Baltimore (A)	June 8/91
		Otis Nixon	Boston (H)	Aug. 14/96
Hit By Pitch	3	Reed Johnson	Texas (A)	April 16/05
		Reed Johnson	Tampa Bay (H)	April 7/06
		Reed Johnson	New York-AL (A)	April 29/06

PITCHING

Category	Record	Player	Opponent	Date
Innings	12	Jesse Jefferson	Boston (H)	May 23/78
		Dave Stieb	Oakland (H)	May 17/80
Most Innings, Reliever	7.1	Mike Willis	Boston (H), 1st g	Sept. 27/77
Hits	14	Josh Towers	Minnesota (H)	May 27/05
Runs	13	David Wells	Milwaukee (A)	Aug. 20/92
Earned Runs	13	David Wells	Milwaukee (A)	Aug. 20/92
Home Runs	5	Pat Hentgen	Cleveland (H)	May 26/95
		Pat Hentgen	Boston (H)	June 25/97
		Brett Cecil	Boston (A)	May 20/10
Strikeouts	18	Roger Clemens	Kansas City (H)	Aug. 25/98
Walks	9	Jesse Jefferson	Baltimore (H)	June 18/77
		Jim Clancy	Chicago-AL (A)	Aug. 30/84
		Pat Hentgen	Seattle (A)	July 15/95
		Chris Carpenter	Seattle (H)	Aug. 16/99
Hit Batsmen	3	6x, last: Brett Cecil	Cleveland (H)	May 5/09
Wild Pitches	4	John Cerutti	Boston (A)	July 3/86
		Edwin Hurtado	Cleveland (A)	Aug. 31/95
		Al Leiter	Boston (A)	Sept. 23/95
		Kyle Drabek	Kansas City (A)	June 7/11

FIELDING

PITCHERS

Category	Record	Player	Opponent	Date
Most Putouts	5	Roy Halladay	Detroit (A)	June 2/02
Most Assists	8	Jim Clancy	Seattle (A)	April 4/84
Most Errors	3	Juan Guzman	Anaheim (H)	May 23/97
Most Double Plays	3	Dave Lemanczyk	Boston (H)	Sept. 7/77
Most Total Chances	8	Jim Clancy	Seattle (A)	April 4/84

CATCHERS

Category	Record	Player	Opponent	Date
Most Putouts	18	Darrin Fletcher	Kansas City (H)	Aug. 25/98
Most Assists	5	Jose Molina	Tampa Bay (A)	April 25/10
Most Errors	2	12x, last: Rod Barajas	Los Angeles-AL (A)	May 7/09
Most Double Plays	2	14x, last: John Buck	Detroit (H)	July 22/10
Most Passed Balls	2	11x, last: J.P. Arencibia	Chicago-AL (H)	May 27/11
Most Total Chances	18	6x, last: Jeff Mathis	Chicago-AL (H)	Aug. 13/12

FIRST BASEMEN

Category	Record	Player	Opponent	Date
Most Putouts	21	Rick Leach (14 inn.)	Milwaukee (H)	Sept. 21/85
	21	Lyle Overbay (14 inn.)	Seattle (H)	July 15/06
	20	5x, last: Juan Rivera	Chicago-AL (H)	May 28/11
Most Assists	4	28x, last: Adam Lind	New York-AL (H)	Aug. 29/12
Most Errors	3	Willie Upshaw (11 inn.)	Boston (A)	July 1/86
		Fred McGriff	Boston (A)	June 4/89
		John Olerud	Texas (A)	May 5/93
Most Double Plays	6	Lyle Overbay	Minnesota (A)	Aug. 12/06
Most Total Chances	24	Carlos Delgado (17 inn.)	New York-AL (H)	April 19/01
	23	Lyle Overbay	Seattle (H)	July 15/06

SECOND BASEMEN

Category	Record	Player	Opponent	Date
Most Putouts	12	Tomas Perez (14 inn.)	Kansas City (A)	Aug. 20/96
	8	6x, last: Carlos Garcia	Boston (H)	July 10/97
Most Assists	10	4x, last: John McDonald	Texas (H)	April 25/11
Most Errors	3	Garth Iorg	California (A)	April 28/78
		Hector Torres	Baltimore (A)	June 24/77
Most Double Plays	5	Roberto Alomar (11 inn.)	New York-AL (H)	May 10/95
		Tilson Brito	Detroit (H)	April 16/96
		Aaron Hill	Minnesota (A)	Aug. 12/06
Most Total Chances	15	Damaso Garcia	Kansas City (H)	May 7/82
		Tomas Perez (14 inn.)	Kansas City (A)	Aug. 20/96

THIRD BASEMEN

Category	Record	Player	Opponent	Date
Most Putouts	6	Kelly Gruber	Milwaukee (H)	Aug. 27/92
		Ed Sprague	Cleveland (A)	June 15/94
Most Assists	9	Roy Howell	Milwaukee (H), 2nd g	June 14/78
Most Errors	3	Dave Baker	Oakland (H), 2nd g	Sept. 15/82
		Kelly Gruber	Baltimore (A)	June 27/89
		Kelly Gruber	Chicago-AL (A)	May 23/92
Most Double Plays	3	4x, last: Eric Hinske	Texas (H)	Aug. 8/03
Most Total Chances	11	Roy Howell	Milwaukee (H)	April 17/80
		Ed Sprague	Seattle (H)	July 1/91

SHORTSTOPS

Category	Record	Player	Opponent	Date
Most Putouts	8	Alfredo Griffin	Texas (A)	Sept. 2/81
		Alex Gonzalez	Cleveland (H)	May 16/97
			Minnesota (H)	Aug. 2/01
Most Assists	13	Alex Gonzalez	Cleveland (H)	April 26/96
Most Errors	3	Hector Torres	Baltimore (A)	June 24/77
		Alfredo Griffin	Texas (A)	May 13/82
		Luis Sojo	Cleveland (A)	Aug. 31/90
Most Double Plays	5	Alfredo Griffin	California (A)	May 7/80
		Alex Gonzalez	Chicago-AL (A)	April 24/98
		Marco Scutaro	Tampa Bay (H)	Sept. 6/08
		John McDonald (13.2 inn.)	Los Angeles-AL (A)	April 9/11
Most Total Chances	16	Alex Gonzalez	Cleveland (H)	April 26/96
		Marco Scutaro (13 inn)	Tampa Bay (H)	Sept. 6/08

OUTFIELDERS

Category	Record	Player	Opponent	Date
Most Putouts	10	Lloyd Moseby (10 inn.)	New York-AL (H) 1st g	Aug. 2/83
		Shannon Stewart (11 inn.)	Boston (H)	Sept. 3/98
		Jose Cruz Jr.	Cleveland (A)	Oct. 1/99
		Raul Mondesi	Montreal (A)	July 8/00
Most Assists	3	Steve Bowling	Oakland (H)	Aug. 27/77
		Rick Bosetti	Detroit (H)	May 28/79
Most Errors	2	19x, last: Jose Bautista	Los Angeles-AL (H)	Aug. 12/11
Most Double Plays	2	4x, last: Dewayne Wise	Chicago-AL (A)	Aug. 6/02
Most Total Chances	10	Lloyd Moseby (10 inn.)	New York-AL (H) 1st g	Aug. 2/83
		Shannon Stewart (11 inn.)	Boston (H)	Sept. 3/98
		Jose Cruz Jr.	Cleveland (A)	Oct. 1/99
		Raul Mondesi	Montreal (A)	July 8/00

MONTHLY RECORDS — INDIVIDUAL

PITCHING

Category	Record	Player	Date
Games	18	Mark Eichhorn	June'87
Wins	6	4x, 4 players, last: Roy Halladay	May '03
Losses	7	Jesse Jefferson	Aug. '80
SO	68	Roger Clemens	Aug. '98
IP	60.2	Doyle Alexander	Sept. '84
Saves	11	Billy Koch	July '99
		Kelvim Escobar	Sept. '02
ERA (Starters)	0.89	Roger Clemens	July '97
CG	5	Tom Underwood	June '79
		Pat Hentgen	Aug. '96
		Roy Halladay	Sept. '03
Starts	8	Luis Leal	Aug. '82
SHO	3	Dave Stieb	Sept. '88
		Roger Clemens	Aug. '98

BATTING

Category	Record	Player	Date
AB	134	Lloyd Moseby	Aug. '83
H	47	Lloyd Moseby	Aug. '83
R	31	Shawn Green	Aug. '98
2B	19	Carlos Delgado	July '00
3B	5	Alfredo Griffin	May '79
	5	Lloyd Moseby	June '84
	5	Orlando Hudson	Aug. '02
HR	14	Jose Bautista	June '12
RBI	34	Carlos Delgado	June '03
XBH	24	Carlos Delgado	July '00
BB	30	Fred McGriff	Aug.'89
SB	18	Dave Collins	Aug. '84
AVG	.450	John Olerud	April '93
SLG %	.865	Otto Velez	April '77
OBP %	.550	Frank Catalanotto	April '06

TORONTO'S BEST WON/LOST RECORDS

G	BEST W-L	YR	WORST W-L	YR
1	1-0	19 times	0-1	17 times
2	2-0	12 times	0-2	79/81/03/04
3	3-0	92/96	0-3	79/03/04
4	4-0	92	1-3	78/79/80/03/04
5	5-0	92	1-4	78/04
6	6-0	92	1-5	04
7	6-1	92/94	2-5	78/81/02/04
8	7-1	92	2-6	78/81/04
9	8-1	92	2-7	78
10	9-1	92	2-8	78
11	9-2	92	3-8	78/81/04
12	10-2	92	3-9	78/81/04
13	10-3	92	3-10	81/04
14	11-3	92	3-11	04
15	12-3	92	4-11	04
16	12-4	92/99	4-12	04
17	13-4	92	5-12	04
18	14-4	92	6-12	79/03/04
19	15-4	92	6-13	79/03
20	15-5	92	6-14	79
21	15-6	92	7-14	79/81/03/04
22	16-6	92	7-15	79/03/04
23	16-7	92	7-16	79/04
24	16-8	92/01	7-17	79
25	16-9	92/01/09	7-18	79
26	17-9	92/01/09	8-18	78/79/04
27	18-9	92/09	8-19	79
28	19-9	92	8-20	79
29	20-9	92	8-21	79
30	21-9	92	8-22	79
31	21-10	92	8-23	79
32	21-11	87/92	8-24	79
33	22-11	92	9-24	79
34	23-11	92	9-25	79
35	24-11	92	9-26	79
36	25-11	92	9-27	79
37	25-12	92	10-27	79
38	25-13	92	10-28	79
39	25-14	84/85/92/09	10-29	79
40	26-14	84/85/09	10-30	79
41	27-14	84/85/09	10-31	79
42	28-14	84/85	11-31	79
43	29-14	84/85	11-32	79
44	30-14	84/85	11-33	79
45	31-14	84/85	12-33	79
46	31-15	84/85	12-34	79
47	32-15	84	12-35	79
48	33-15	84	12-36	79
49	34-15	84	12-37	79
50	34-16	84/85	12-38	79
51	35-16	85	12-39	79
52	36-16	85	13-39	79

G	BEST W-L	YR	WORST W-L	YR
53	36-17	84/85	13-40	79
54	36-18	84/85	13-41	79
55	36-19	84/85	13-42	79
56	37-19	85	14-42	79
57	38-19	85	15-42	79
58	38-20	85/87	16-42	79/81
59	39-20	87	16-43	79
60	39-21	87	17-43	79
61	39-22	84/85/87	17-44	79
62	40-22	84	18-44	79
63	41-22	84/87	18-45	79
64	41-23	84/87	18-46	79
65	41-24	84/87	19-46	79
66	42-24	84	20-46	79
67	42-25	84/87	21-46	78/79
68	43-25	84	22-46	78/79
69	43-26	84/85/87	22-47	78/79
70	44-26	87	23-47	78/79
71	44-27	85/87	23-48	79
72	45-27	85/87	23-49	79
73	45-28	85/87	23-50	79
74	46-28	85	23-51	79
75	46-29	85	24-51	79
76	46-30	85/93	24-52	79
77	47-30	85/93	24-53	79
78	48-30	93	24-54	79
79	48-31	85/92/93	24-55	79
80	49-31	92	24-56	79
81	50-31	92	24-57	79
82	51-31	92	25-57	79
83	52-31	92	26-57	79
84	53-31	92	26-58	79
85	53-32	85/92	27-58	79
86	53-33	85/92	27-59	79
87	53-34	85/92	27-60	79
88	54-34	92	28-60	79
89	54-35	92	28-61	79
90	55-35	92	28-62	79
91	56-35	92	28-63	79
92	56-36	92	29-63	79
93	57-36	92	29-64	79
94	57-37	85/92	29-65	79
95	58-37	85/92	29-66	79
96	59-37	85	29-67	79
97	60-37	85	29-68	79
98	61-37	85	29-69	79
99	62-37	85	29-70	79
100	63-37	85	30-70	79
101	63-38	85	31-70	79
102	64-38	85	31-71	79
103	65-38	85	32-71	79
104	66-38	85	32-72	79
105	67-38	85	32-73	79
106	67-39	85	32-74	79
107	68-39	85	32-75	79
108	69-39	85	32-76	79

G	BEST W-L	YR	WORST W-L	YR
109	69-40	85	33-76	79
110	69-41	85	33-77	79
111	70-41	85	33-78	79
112	70-42	85	34-78	79
113	71-42	85	34-79	79
114	72-42	85	34-80	79
115	72-43	85	35-80	79
116	72-44	85	35-81	79
117	73-44	85	36-81	79
118	73-45	85	37-81	79
119	74-45	85	38-81	79
120	74-46	85	38-82	79
121	75-46	85	39-82	79
122	76-46	85	39-83	79
123	77-46	85	39-84	79
124	77-47	85	39-85	79
125	78-47	85	39-86	79
126	79-47	85	39-87	79
127	79-48	85	40-87	79
128	80-48	85	40-88	79
129	81-48	85	41-88	79
130	81-49	85	42-88	79
131	82-49	85	42-89	79
132	82-50	85	42-90	79
133	83-50	85	42-91	79
134	84-50	85	43-91	79
135	84-51	85	43-92	79
136	85-51	85	44-92	79
137	86-51	85	44-93	79
138	87-51	85	44-94	79
139	88-51	85	44-95	79
140	88-52	85	44-96	79
141	89-52	85	44-97	79
142	90-52	85	44-98	79
143	91-52	85	45-98	79
144	91-53	85	46-98	79
145	91-54	85	46-99	79
146	92-54	85	47-99	79
147	93-54	85	48-99	79
148	93-55	85	49-99	79
149	94-55	85	50-99	79
150	95-55	85	50-100	79
151	95-56	85	50-101	79
152	95-57	85	50-102	79
153	96-57	85	51-102	79
154	97-57	85	52-102	77/79
155	98-57	85	52-103	77/79
156	98-58	85	52-104	77/79
157	98-59	85	52-105	77
158	98-60	85	53-105	77/79
159	98-61	85	53-106	77/79
160	99-61	85	53-107	79
161	99-62	85	53-108	79
162	96-66	87/92	53-109	79

BLUE JAYS MONTHLY RECORDS

		APR. W-L	MAY W-L	JUNE W-L	JULY W-L	AUG. W-L	SEPT./ OCT. W-L	AT ALL-STAR W-L	POST ALL-STAR W-L	TOTAL W-L
1977	H	6-4	5-10	3-9	5-10	3-8	3-14	18-27	7-28	25-55
	A	4-7	3-7	7-8	2-11	7-10	6-9	16-31	13-21	29-52
	T	10-11	8-17	10-17	7-21	10-18	9-23	34-58	20-49	54-107
1978	H	4-7	7-7	6-8	7-7	10-3	3-12	19-23	18-21	37-44
	A	4-6	2-11	3-9	6-11	6-11	1-10	13-30	9-28	22-58
	T	8-13	9-18	9-17	13-18	16-14	4-22	32-53	27-49	59-102
1979	H	3-8	3-15	6-5	5-6	6-8	9-7	14-32	18-17	32-49
	A	4-7	2-8	6-14	3-11	5-9	1-11	15-32	6-28	21-60
	T	7-15	5-23	12-19	8-17	11-17	10-18	29-64	24-45	53-109
1980	H	3-1	8-9	7-7	5-10	6-8	6-11	18-19	17-27	35-46
	A	6-6	5-5	3-10	6-7	5-12	7-9	15-24	17-25	32-49
	T	9-7	13-14	10-17	11-17	11-20	13-20	33-43	34-52	67-95
1981	H	2-7	5-10	0-5	—	4-8	6-6	7-22	10-14	17-36
	A	5-5	4-10	0-5	—	5-2	6-11	9-20	11-13	20-33
	T	7-12	9-20	0-10	—	9-10	12-17	16-42	21-27	37-69
1982	H	5-6	6-5	7-10	9-4	7-8	10-4	19-24	25-13	44-37
	A	3-6	7-9	5-4	6-8	6-12	7-8	18-23	16-24	34-47
	T	8-12	13-14	12-14	15-12	13-20	17-12	37-47	41-37	78-84
1983	H	4-4	12-6	6-3	8-8	7-6	11-6	23-15	25-18	48-33
	A	4-6	6-3	10-9	7-4	8-13	6-5	20-18	21-22	41-40
	T	8-10	18-9	16-12	15-12	15-19	17-11	43-33	46-40	89-73
1984	H	5-5	15-2	9-5	7-6	6-5	7-9	34-15	15-17	49-32
	A	8-4	4-4	4-11	7-8	12-7	5-7	16-19	24-22	40-41
	T	13-9	19-6	13-16	14-14	18-12	12-16	50-34	39-39	89-73
1985	H	5-4	9-2	11-5	10-4	5-3	12-8	26-13	28-13	54-26
	A	8-3	8-6	5-8	8-6	12-7	6-6	27-22	18-24	45-36
	T	13-7	17-8	16-13	18-10	17-10	18-14	53-35	46-37	99-62
1986	H	4-7	7-5	10-8	5-5	11-5	5-9	26-25	16-14	42-39
	A	5-4	7-10	7-3	10-6	7-5	8-9	21-18	23-19	44-37
	T	9-11	14-15	17-11	15-11	18-10	13-18	47-43	39-33	86-76
1987	H	7-4	7-3	8-7	12-4	5-6	13-5	28-16	24-13	52-29
	A	5-4	9-8	9-4	3-8	12-6	6-7	23-20	21-17	44-37
	T	12-8	16-11	17-11	15-12	17-12	19-12	51-36	45-30	96-66
1988	H	4-9	6-5	10-4	4-8	7-7	14-3	23-24	22-12	45-36
	A	5-4	7-11	7-7	8-6	7-7	8-4	19-22	23-17	42-39
	T	9-13	13-16	17-11	12-14	14-14	22-7	42-46	45-29	87-75
1989	H	4-5	8-9	6-5	6-8	14-4	8-5	20-23	26-12	46-35
	A	5-11	3-6	11-5	9-4	6-5	9-6	22-22	21-16	43-38
	T	9-16	11-15	17-10	15-12	20-9	17-11	42-45	47-28	89-73
1990	H	9-4	5-9	6-8	9-5	5-8	10-3	26-23	18-14	44-37
	A	3-5	9-5	9-5	5-7	8-8	8-9	21-15	21-24	42-39
	T	12-9	14-14	15-13	14-12	13-16	18-12	47-38	39-38	86-76
1991	H	8-3	8-5	8-7	8-6	6-8	8-6	27-16	19-19	46-35
	A	4-6	7-7	8-5	7-5	9-6	10-7	22-18	23-18	45-36
	T	12-9	15-12	16-12	15-11	15-14	18-13	49-34	42-37	91-71
1992	H	11-4	8-6	4-5	11-4	7-4	12-5	31-18	22-10	53-28
	A	5-3	7-6	10-7	5-6	7-12	9-4	22-16	21-22	43-38
	T	16-7	15-12	14-12	16-10	14-16	21-9	53-34	43-32	96-66
1993	H	9-4	8-6	10-3	7-9	7-6	7-5	28-19	20-14	48-33
	A	4-6	8-6	9-6	5-5	10-6	11-5	21-21	26-13	47-34
	T	13-10	16-12	19-9	12-14	17-12	18-10	49-40	46-27	95-67
1994	H	9-2	10-8	3-8	9-4	2-4	—	24-19	9-7	33-26
	A	5-8	0-8	5-10	8-6	4-2	—	14-29	8-5	22-34
	T	14-10	10-16	8-18	17-10	6-6	—	38-48	17-12	55-60
1995	H	3-2	7-8	6-5	5-8	5-8	3-12	16-17	13-26	29-43
	A	—	4-8	3-11	10-6	6-10	4-10	11-23	16-22	27-45
	T	3-2	11-16	9-16	15-14	11-18	7-22	27-40	29-48	56-88
1996	H	5-9	8-5	5-6	7-7	5-9	5-10	19-22	16-24	35-46
	A	6-5	5-10	7-9	6-7	9-6	6-5	19-27	20-15	39-42
	T	11-14	13-15	12-15	13-14	14-15	11-15	38-49	36-39	74-88
1997	H	5-7	7-8	5-11	8-4	8-6	9-3	20-29	22-10	42-39
	A	6-5	8-5	6-4	5-11	7-9	2-13	20-14	14-33	34-47
	T	11-12	15-13	11-15	13-15	15-15	11-16	40-43	36-43	76-86
1998	H	5-8	8-6	8-5	9-4	11-5	10-2	25-20	26-10	51-30
	A	5-8	10-5	6-9	3-11	6-5	7-6	21-22	16-22	37-44
	T	10-16	18-11	14-14	12-15	17-10	17-8	46-42	42-32	88-74
1999	H	9-1	4-12	13-5	9-5	2-10	3-8	29-19	11-22	40-41
	A	4-10	7-5	2-8	10-2	10-6	11-6	18-24	26-13	44-37
	T	13-11	11-17	15-13	19-7	12-16	14-14	47-43	37-35	84-78
2000	H	7-7	8-8	7-3	6-7	8-3	9-8	22-18	23-18	45-36
	A	5-7	8-4	9-7	5-9	7-8	4-8	26-23	12-20	38-43
	T	12-14	16-12	16-10	11-16	15-11	13-16	48-41	35-38	83-79

		APR. W-L	MAY W-L	JUNE W-L	JULY W-L	AUG. W-L	SEPT./ OCT. W-L	AT ALL-STAR W-L	POST ALL-STAR W-L	TOTAL W-L
	H	11-5	2-8	7-11	4-7	7-5	9-6	22-27	18-15	40-42
2001	A	5-4	8-10	5-4	7-9	9-7	6-6	20-19	20-21	40-40
	T	16-9	10-18	12-15	11-16	16-12	15-12	42-46	38-36	80-82
	H	3-8	5-12	9-4	8-3	7-9	10-3	17-24	25-15	42-39
2002	A	5-8	5-5	6-8	5-11	6-8	9-5	17-28	19-17	36-45
	T	8-16	10-17	15-12	13-14	13-17	19-8	34-52	44-32	78-84
	H	4-10	9-4	9-1	3-11	4-6	12-4	23-24	18-16	41-40
2003	A	6-8	12-4	6-10	5-6	9-9	7-3	26-22	19-14	45-36
	T	10-18	21-8	15-11	8-17	13-15	19-7	49-46	37-30	86-76
	H	1-8	13-6	6-6	7-5	5-10	8-6	23-23	17-18	40-41
2004	A	6-7	2-8	6-9	4-9	4-10	5-10	16-26	11-27	27-53
	T	7-15	15-14	12-15	11-14	9-20	13-16	39-49	28-45	67-94
	H	5-6	9-6	6-4	10-6	6-6	7-10	22-17	21-21	43-38
2005	A	8-6	6-6	6-11	3-6	7-9	7-6	22-27	15-17	37-44
	T	13-12	15-12	12-15	13-12	13-15	14-16	44-44	36-38	80-82
	H	8-6	11-5	9-5	7-5	6-6	9-4	29-17	21-14	50-31
2006	A	4-5	6-7	7-6	5-9	6-11	9-6	20-22	17-22	37-44
	T	12-11	17-12	16-11	12-14	12-17	18-10	49-39	38-36	87-75
	H	7-7	8-5	9-6	7-2	9-7	9-5	26-19	23-13	49-32
2007	A	6-5	4-11	5-7	7-10	6-6	6-8	17-25	17-22	34-47
	T	13-12	12-16	14-13	14-12	15-13	15-13	43-44	40-35	83-79
	H	5-7	10-4	8-7	9-4	7-6	10-5	27-20	20-14	47-34
2008	A	6-10	10-6	2-9	4-7	9-6	6-5	20-28	19-14	39-42
	T	11-17	20-10	10-16	13-11	16-12	16-10	47-48	39-28	86-76
	H	7-3	11-4	6-11	5-5	5-9	10-5	25-18	19-19	44-37
2009	A	8-6	3-11	6-3	3-11	5-7	6-12	19-28	12-22	31-50
	T	15-9	14-15	12-14	8-16	10-16	16-17	44-46	31-41	75-87
	H	6-9	9-2	5-6	7-4	8-6	10-6	23-20	22-13	45-33
2010	A	6-3	10-8	4-11	7-7	7-7	6-8	21-25	19-19	40-44
	T	12-12	19-10	9-17	14-11	15-13	16-14	44-45	41-32	85-77
	H	6-5	9-8	3-7	10-6	5-8	9-5	19-22	23-17	42-39
2011	A	7-9	6-5	9-8	5-5	8-7	4-8	26-25	13-17	39-42
	T	13-14	15-13	12-15	15-11	13-15	13-13	45-47	36-34	81-81
	H	6-7	9-3	6-6	7-7	5-7	8-10	23-19	18-21	41-40
2012	A	6-4	6-10	7-8	4-7	4-12	5-8	20-24	12-25	32-49
	T	12-11	15-13	13-14	11-14	9-19	13-18	43-43	30-46	73-89

Blue Jays win their 1st ever World Series title in 1992 at Atlanta in six games

MISCELLANEOUS STATISTICS

BEST/WORST HOMESTANDS AND ROADTRIPS

(MINIMUM 6 GAMES)

PCT.	W-L	DATES	OPPONENTS
BEST HOMESTANDS			
1.000	6-0	Sept. 24-29, 2002	Baltimore, Detroit
1.000	6-0	Sept. 2-7, 2008	Minnesota, Tampa Bay
.909	10-1	May 9-16, 1978	Oakland Seattle, California
.900	9-1	April 12-22, 1999	Tampa Bay, Baltimore, Anaheim
.857	6-1	Sept. 21-27, 2009	Baltimore, Seattle
.857	6-1	April 10-16, 1992	Baltimore, New York (AL)
.857	6-1	Aug. 7-13, 1978	Baltimore, Chicago (AL), Kansas City
.857	6-1	Sept. 28-Oct. 3, 1982	Minnesota, Seattle
.857	6-1	July 6-12, 1987	Texas, Kansas City
.846	11-2	Aug. 22-Sept. 3, 1989	Detroit, Milwaukee, Chicago (AL), Minnesota
.833	5-1	July 8-13, 2008	Baltimore, New York (AL)
.833	5-1	May 9-16, 1978	Oakland, Seattle, California
.833	5-1	July 22-27, 1997	Milwaukee, Kansas City
.833	5-1	Sept. 4-9, 1997	Texas, Anaheim
.833	5-1	June 29-July 5, 1998	New York (NL), Tampa Bay
.833	5-1	Sept. 3-9, 1998	Boston, Cleveland
.833	5-1	Sept. 21-27, 1998	Baltimore, Detroit
.833	5-1	June 29-July 4, 1999	Baltimore, Tampa Bay
.833	5-1	June 20-25, 2000	Detroit, Boston
.833	5-1	June 10-15, 2003	Pittsburgh, Chicago (NL)
.833	5-1	Sept. 1-7, 2003	New York (AL), Detroit
.833	5-1	May 3-9, 2004	Kansas City Chicago (AL)
.833	5-1	May 24-30, 2004	Anaheim, Texas
.833	5-1	July 20-25, 2007	Seattle, Minnesota
.818	9-2	July 18-28, 1985	Oakland, Seattle, California
BEST ROADTRIPS			
.900	9-1	June 8-17, 1990	Milwaukee, Minnesota, New York (AL)
.857	6-1	June 8-14, 1987	New York (AL), Baltimore
.857	6-1	June 17-24, 1993	Boston, New York (AL)
.857	6-1	Aug. 26-Sept. 1, 1991	Baltimore, New York (AL)
.833	5-1	May 23-29, 1985	Cleveland, Chicago (AL)
.833	5-1	May 28-June 2, 1993	Oakland, California
.833	5-1	Aug. 13-18, 1993	Boston, Cleveland
.833	5-1	Sept. 23-28, 1988	Cleveland, Boston
.833	5-1	July 6-11, 1999	Baltimore, Montreal
.833	5-1	July 21-26, 1999	Cleveland, Chicago
.833	5-1	Sept. 28-Oct. 3, 1999	Tampa Bay, Cleveland
.833	5-1	Sept. 16-21, 2003	Detroit, Baltimore
.833	5-1	Aug. 11-17, 2008	Detroit, Boston
.833	5-1	April 5-11, 2010	Texas, Baltimore
.800	8-2	May 16-25, 2003	Kansas City, Chicago (AL), New York (AL)

WORST HOMESTANDS

.000	0-6	Sept. 26-Oct. 1, 1980	Boston, Detroit
.000	0-6	June 20-26, 1994	Boston, Baltimore
.000	0-6	Aug. 13-18, 1999	Oakland, Seattle
.000	0-6	May 8-13, 2001	Oakland, Seattle
.000	0-6	May 24-29, 2002	Cleveland, Boston
.111	1-8	Sept. 1-9, 1978	California,Cleveland, Milwaukee, Baltimore
.125	1-7	Sept. 2-8, 1977	Seattle, Boston
.125	1-7	May 15-22, 1990	Seattle, California, Oakland
.143	1-6	May 23-June 1, 1977	Oakland, California, Kansas City
.167	2-10	May 18-31, 1979	Baltimore, Cleveland, Boston, Detroit
.167	1-5	Aug. 30-Sept. 4, 1996	Chicago (AL), Kansas City
.167	1-5	May 4-9, 1999	Oakland, Texas
.167	1-5	Sept. 13-19, 1999	New York (AL), Chicago (AL)
.167	1-5	April 30-May 5, 2002	Texas, Anaheim
.167	1-5	July 8-13, 2003	Boston, New York (AL)
.167	1-5	April 14-22, 2004	Baltimore, Boston

WORST ROADTRIPS

.000	0-6	Sept. 3-9, 1979	Baltimore, Cleveland
.000	0-6	May 1-6, 2007	Cleveland, Texas
.000	0-9	May 19-27, 2009	Boston, Atlanta, Baltimore
.125	1-7	July 1-7, 2002	Boston, New York (AL)
.143	1-6	Aug. 20-26, 1982	New York (AL), Baltimore
.143	1-6	April 24-30, 1989	Oakland, Seattle, California
.143	1-6	July 27-Aug. 2, 2000	Seattle, Oakland
.143	1-6	Aug. 28-Sept. 2, 2009	Boston, Texas
.167	1-6	June 16-22, 2004	Texas, Oakland, New York (AL)
.167	1-6	Aug. 6-12, 2004	New York (AL), Cleveland
.167	1-5	June 23-28, 1995	New York (AL), Boston
.167	1-5	June 4-9, 1996	New York (AL), Texas
.167	1-5	June 17-22, 2008	Milwaukee, Pittsburgh
.167	2-10	Sept. 10-22, 1997	Oakland, Seattle, Boston, New York (AL)
.167	1-5	June 7-13, 1999	New York (NL), Philadelphia
.167	1-5	Sept. 26-Oct. 1, 2000	Baltimore, Cleveland
.167	1-5	Aug. 12-18, 2002	Oakland, Texas
.167	1-5	May 21-27, 2012	Tampa Bay, Texas
.182	2-9	Aug. 28-Sept.6, 1995	Cleveland, Chicago (AL), Kansas City

TORONTO GROUND RULES—ROGERS CENTRE

1. Ball hitting any portion of fence or screen in back of home plate—in play.
2. Ball going into camera booth behind home plate: thrown by pitcher from rubber—one base; any other thrown ball—two bases.
3. Ball hitting padding and bouncing over fence—two bases.
4. A fairly batted or thrown ball lodged in the padding—two bases.
5. A fairly batted or thrown ball that goes into the dugout or strikes equipment on the dugout steps is considered in the dugout.
6. Ball hitting padding on outfield fence to foul or seating side of foul line—dead ball.

LONGEST WINNING STREAKS

11	1987	June 2-13	Sea 2, Bal 3, NYY 3, Bal 3
11	1998	Aug. 27-Sept. 7	KC 1, Min 3, KC 2, Bos 4, Cle 1
10	2008	Aug. 30-Sept. 9	NYY 2, Min 3, TB 3, CWS 2
9	1993	Sept. 10-21	Cal 3, Det 2, Min 3, Bos 1
9	1986	Aug. 23-Sept. 1	Min, Cle 3, Min 3, Cle 1
9	1985	July 21-29	Oak 1, Sea 3, Cal 4, Bal 1
8	1985	May 20-28	CWS 3, Cle 4, CWS 1
8	1992	July 1-9	Tex 1, Cal 4, Sea 2, Oak 1
8	1994	July 17-24	Tex 1, Min 3, Tex 4
8	1999	April 14-22	TB 2, Bal 3, Ana 3

LONGEST LOSING STREAKS

12	1981	May 31-Aug. 10	Oak 1, Cal 3, Tex 3, CWS 2, KC 2, Det 1
11	1977	Aug. 26-Sept. 6	Oak 3, Min 2, Sea 3, Bos 3
10	1994	June 18-28	Det 2, Bos 3, Bal 3, Mil 2
9	1977	July 17-30	Det 1, CWS 2, Det 2, Tex 2, Mil 2
9	1978	June 4-14	Tex 1, Mil 4, Min 2, Mil 2
9	2002	April 24-May 3	Tex 2, Ana 3, Tex 3, Ana1
9	2007	May 1-10	Cle 3, Tex 3, Bos 3
9	2009	May 19-27	Bos 3, Atl 3, Bal 3

LONGEST HOME WINNING STREAKS

10	1985	July 21-Aug. 3	Oak 1, Sea 3, Cal 4, Tex 2
9	1984	May 21-June 2	Min 3, Cle 4, NYY 2
9	1994	July 9-24	KC 2, Min 3, Tex 4
9	1998	Aug. 27-Sept. 7	KC 1, Min 3, Bos 4, Cle 1
8	1992	July 1-9	Tex 1, Cal 4, Sea 2, Oak 1
8	1999	April 14-22	TB 2, Bal 3, Ana 3
8	2007	July 21-Aug. 5	Sea 2, Min 3, Tex 3

LONGEST ROAD WINNING STREAKS

9	1993	Sept. 14-30	Det 2, Min 3, Mil 3, Bal 1
7	1985	April 14-May 1	Bal 1, Tex 3, Oak 2, Cal 1
7	1987	May 25-June 13	Sea 1, NYY 3, Bal 3
7	1996	Aug. 18-24	Min 1, KC 3, CWS 3

LONGEST HOME LOSING STREAKS

11	1977	Aug. 15-Sept. 6	Cal 2, Oak 3, Sea 3, Bos 3
9	1999	Aug. 13-29	Oak 3, Sea 3, Tex 3
8	2004	April 15-21	Det 3, Bal 3, Bos 2
7	1977	July 17-30	Det 1, CWS 2, Tex 2, Mil 2
7	1978	June 4-21	Tex 1, Min 2, Mil 2, Det 2
7	1978	Aug. 27-Sept. 6	Min 1, Cal 3, Cle 2, Mil 1
7	1979	April 15-29	KC 1, CWS 3, Mil 3
7	1994	June 20-July 8	Bos 3, Bal 3, KC 1
7	1995	Sept. 9-15	Det 3, Tex 3, Mil 1
7	1997	June 21-July 1	Bal 2, Bos 3, Mon 2

LONGEST ROAD LOSING STREAKS

12	1979	July 7-Aug. 11	Tex 2, Mil 2, Min 4, KC 3, CWS 1
11	1979	Aug. 18-Sept. 9	Cal 1, Sea 3, Bal 3, Cle 3
9	1978	Sept. 15-Oct. 1	Bal 3, NYY 3, Bos 3
9	2009	May 19-27	Bos 3, Atl 3, Bal 3

LONGEST WINNING & LOSING STREAKS

YEAR	WON	LOST	YEAR	WON	LOST	YEAR	WON	LOST	YEAR	WON	LOST
1977	3	11	1986	9	5	1995	4	8	2004	6	6
1978	5	9	1987	11	7	1996	7	6	2005	4	5
1979	4	7	1988	6	6	1997	5	7	2006	5	7
1980	6	8	1989	6	4	1998	11	4	2007	5	9
1981	4	12	1990	6	6	1999	8	7	2008	10	7
1982	6	6	1991	6	7	2000	5	6	2009	6	9
1983	5	6	1992	8	5	2001	4	6	2010	6	5
1984	7	6	1993	9	6	2002	7	9	2011	6	4
1985	9	6	1994	8	10	2003	6	6	2012	4	7

BIGGEST INNINGS

BLUE JAYS

INN.	RUNS	H/A	DATE	OPP.	SCORE	WINNER	LOSER
1st	8	H	July 14, 2011	NYY	16-7	Reyes	Colon
2nd	11	H	April 26, 1995	OAK	13-1	Cone	Stewart
3rd	8	H	July 23, 2006	NYY	13-5	Marcum	Ponson
	8	H	July 14, 2012	CLE	11-9	Laffey	Jimenez
4th	10	A	June 10, 1990	MIL	13-5	Wells	Navarro
5th	9	A	Aug. 24, 2005	NYY	9-5	Bush	Mussina
6th	11	H	July 25, 2007	MIN	13-1	Litsch	Silva
7th	10	A	May 24, 1999	DET	12-6	Wells	Moehler
8th	8	A	May 28, 1986	MIN	14-8	Clancy	Blyleven
	8	H	July 1, 1998	NYM	15-10	Plesac	Rojas
	8	H	June 9, 2006	DET	10-5	Frasor	Jones
9th	11	A	July 20, 1984	SEA	12-7	Acker	Mirabella
10th	6	A	Aug. 3, 1995	BAL	8-2	Jordan	Clark
11th	6	A	May 14, 2011	MIN	9-3	Rauch	Perkins
12th	4	A	Aug. 27, 2007	OAK	6-2	Accardo	Embree
13th	5	A	July 9, 1985	SEA	9-4	Musselman	Vande Berg
14th	5	A	April 29, 1981	MIL	5-0	Leal	Easterly
	5	A	June 21, 1989	CAL	6-1	Henke	Minton
15th	3	A	June 12, 1983	CAL	6-5	Clarke	Brown
16th	3	A	April 5, 2012	CLE	7-4	Perez	Ascencio
17th	1	A	Oct. 4, 1980	BOS	7-6	Leal	Stanley
18th	1	H	July 28, 2005	ANA	2-1	Walker	Shields

OPPONENTS

INN.	RUNS	H/A	DATE	OPP.	SCORE	WINNER	LOSER
1st	10	H	June 21, 1994	BOS	1-13	Sele	Cornett
2nd	9	H	April 5, 1979	KC	2-11	Leonard	Underwood
3rd	10	A	July 3, 2010	NYY	3-11	Pettitte	Romero
4th	10	A	Sept. 28, 2000	BAL	1-23	Rapp	Carpenter
5th	8	H	Sept. 17, 1988	CLE	3-12	Swindell	Key
6th	9	H	April 6, 2000	KC	3-9	Durbin	Escobar
7th	11	H	Aug. 6, 1979	KC	12-16	Mingori	Stieb
8th	8	H	June 30, 1977	NYY	5-11	Hunter	Garvin
	8	A	July 4, 2003	BAL	5-8	Driskill	Lopez
9th	9	H	Aug. 28, 2004	NYY	6-18	Brown	Lilly
10th	4	A	Sept. 17, 1980	NYY	8-7	T. Underwood	Kucek
	4	H	May 10, 1981	BOS	5-9	Burgmeier	Jackson
	4	A	Aug. 24, 1982	BAL	3-7	D. Martinez	McLaughlin
	4	A	Aug. 24, 1983	BAL	4-7	T. Martinez	McLaughlin
11th	5	H	Sept. 7, 1993	OAK	7-11	Honeycutt	Castillo
12th	5	H	July 1, 1987	NYY	1-6	Clements	Musselman
13th	6	H	June 2, 1982	NYY	6-12	Rawley	McLaughlin
14th	4	H	Aug. 8, 1991	DET	0-4	Gibson	Henke
15th	4	H	Sept. 15, 1995	MIL	1-5	Kiefer	Robinson
17th	1	A	June 8, 1998	FLA	3-4	Edmondson	Hanson
	1	H	April 19, 2001	NYY	5-6	Choate	File

HIGHEST SCORING GAMES

BY BLUE JAYS (15 OR MORE RUNS SCORED)

DATE	OPPONENT		SCORE	BLUE JAYS PITCHER OF RECORD
June 26, 1978	vs	Baltimore	24-10	Tom Underwood
June 25, 2002	at	Tampa Bay	20-11	Pete Walker
Sept. 10, 1977	at	New York	19-3	Jim Clancy
June 26, 1983	at	Seattle	19-7	Jim Acker
Aug. 9, 1999	at	Texas	19-4	Joey Hamilton
Sept. 14, 1987	vs	Baltimore	18-3	Jim Clancy
July 29, 1995	vs	Oakland	18-11	Giovanni Carrara
May 16, 2003	at	Kansas City	18-1	Mark Hendrickson
Aug. 31, 2009	at	Texas	18-10	Brett Cecil
April 11, 1988	vs	New York	17-9	David Wells
April 20, 1990	vs	Kansas City	17-6	Todd Stottlemyre
Aug. 7, 2010	vs	Tampa Bay	17-11	Brian Tallet
Sept. 11, 1983	vs	Oakland	16-6	Jim Gott
May 14, 1987	at	Minnesota	16-4	Dave Stieb
June 8, 1992	at	New York	16-3	Todd Stottlemyre
June 22, 1992	at	Texas	16-7	Jack Morris
Sept. 4, 1992	vs	Minnesota	16-5	David Cone
April 22, 1996	at	Seattle	16-7	Tony Castillo
Aug. 19, 1998	at	Seattle	16-2	Pat Hentgen
May 3, 1999	at	Seattle	16-10	David Wells
Sept. 19, 2000	vs	New York	16-3	Steve Trachsel
May 14, 2010	vs	Texas	16-10	Josh Roenicke
Aug. 20, 2010	at	Boston	16-2	Brett Cecil
July 14, 2011	vs.	New York	16-7	Jo-Jo Reyes
June 22, 1986	vs	New York	15-1	Jimmy Key
May 9, 1987	at	Texas	15-4	Dave Stieb
June 19, 1987	vs	Milwaukee	15-6	Jeff Musselman
Aug. 7, 1987	at	Cleveland	15-1	Dave Stieb
June 15, 1988	vs	Cleveland	15-3	Dave Stieb
Sept. 27, 1988	at	Boston	15-9	Mike Flanagan
April 16, 1989	vs	Kansas City	15-8	David Wells
Aug. 6, 1992	at	Detroit	15-11	Jack Morris
July 19, 1993	at	Chicago	15-7	Dave Stewart
June 30, 1996	vs	Milwaukee	15-2	Erik Hanson
July 6, 1996	at	Detroit	15-0	Pat Hentgen
July 13, 1996	at	Milwaukee	15-7	Pat Hentgen
July 1, 1998	vs	New York (N)	15-10	Dan Plesac
Sept. 7, 1998	vs	Cleveland	15-1	Kelvim Escobar
Aug. 10, 2000	at	Kansas City	15-7	Chris Carpenter
May 6, 2003	vs	Texas	15-5	Roy Halladay
April 25, 2004	at	Baltimore	15-3	Roy Halladay
June 12, 2004	vs	Arizona	15-4	Roy Halladay
July 1, 2005	at	Boston	15-2	Ted Lilly
Aug. 8, 2007	at	New York	15-4	Roy Halladay
Aug. 17, 2008	at	Boston	15-4	Shaun Marcum
July 22, 2012	at	Boston	15-7	Henderson Alvarez

BY OPPONENTS (15 OR MORE RUNS SCORED)

DATE	OPPONENT		SCORE	BLUE JAYS PITCHER OF RECORD
Aug. 25, 1979	vs	California	2-24	Balor Moore
Sept. 28, 2000	at	Baltimore	1-23	Chris Carpenter
Aug. 28, 1992	vs	Milwaukee	2-22	Jimmy Key
April 16, 2000	vs	Seattle	7-19	Chris Carpenter
June 24, 2004	vs	Tampa Bay	13-19	Ted Lilly
Sept. 24, 1999	vs	Cleveland	4-18	Peter Munro
June 20, 2000	vs	Detroit	6-18	Chris Carpenter
Aug. 28, 2004	vs	New York	6-18	Ted Lilly
Sept. 13, 2011	at	Boston	6-18	Brandon Morrow
June 3, 1981	vs	California	6-17	Jim Clancy
July 11, 1982	vs	Chicago	7-16	Jim Clancy
May 6, 1986	vs	Oakland	3-17	Jimmy Key
April 28, 1996	vs	Cleveland	3-17	Frank Viola
April 17, 1999	at	Anaheim	1-17	Roy Halladay
April 15, 2000	vs	Seattle	6-17	Roy Halladay
Aug. 24, 2003	vs	Oakland	2-17	Kelvim Escobar
Aug. 21, 2005	at	Detroit	6-17	Dustin McGowan
April 29, 2006	at	New York	6-17	Josh Towers
May 8, 1979	at	Minnesota	6-16	Mike Willis
Aug. 6, 1979	vs	Kansas City	12-16	Dave Stieb
July 31, 1983	vs	Cleveland	11-16	Jim Acker
Aug. 15, 1984 (GM 1)	at	Cleveland	1-16	Luis Leal
June 27, 1989	at	Baltimore	6-16	Mike Flanagan
June 30, 1992	vs	Texas	13-16	David Wells
Aug. 20, 1992	at	Milwaukee	3-16	David Wells
April 18, 2000	vs	Anaheim	10-16	Frank Castillo
June 13, 2000	at	Detroit	3-16	Clayton Andrews
April 8, 2001	at	New York	5-16	Steve Parris
July 2, 2001	vs	Boston	4-16	Esteban Loaiza
April 8, 2002	vs	New York	3-16	Luke Prokopec
April 29, 2003	vs	Texas	11-16	Mark Hendrickson
June 11, 2011	vs	Boston	4-16	Brandon Morrow
July 25, 2012	vs	Oakland	0-16	Ricky Romero
Sept. 25, 1977 (GM 1)	vs	New York	0-15	Jerry Garvin
April 9, 1982	vs	Milwaukee	4-15	Mark Bomback
June 3, 1984	vs	New York	2-15	Jim Clancy
June 29, 1987	vs	New York	14-15	Tom Henke
May 27, 1997	vs	Texas	5-15	Robert Person
July 5, 2000	at	Cleveland	7-15	Paul Quantrill
May 16, 2002	vs	Seattle	2-15	Luke Prokopec
Aug. 19, 2006	at	Baltimore	0-15	Shaun Marcum

MARATHONS IN BLUE JAYS HISTORY

(13 OR MORE INNINGS)

Date	Opponent	H/A	Inn	Score	Winner	Loser
July 28/05	LAA	H	18	2-1	Walker	Shields
Oct. 4/80	Boston (G1)	A	17	7-6	Leal	Stanley
June 8/98	Florida	A	17	3-4	Edmondson	Hanson
April 19/01	New York	H	17	5-6	Choate	File
July 3/88	Oakland	H	16	8-9	Burns	Cerutti
Sept. 9/89	Cleveland	A	16	7-5	Wills	Kaiser
+April 5/12	Cleveland	A	16	7-4	Perez	Ascencio
*Aug. 28/80	Minnesota	H	15	5-7	Verhoeven	Jefferson
May 23/81	Oakland	A	15	2-3	Jones	Leal
June 12/83	California	A	15	6-5	Clarke	Brown
July 27/86	Oakland	A	15	0-1	Leiper	Clarke
June 22/90	New York	H	15	7-8	Cadaret	Blair
Sept. 15/95	Milwaukee	H	15	1-5	Kiefer	Robinson
June 19/98	Baltimore	A	15	4-7	Charlton	Risley
May 3/01	Oakland	A	15	2-3	Bradford	Borbon
Aug. 3/12	Oakland	H	15	4-5	Blackley	Loup
July 19/11	Seattle	H	14	6-5	Janssen	Wright
May 28/11	Chicago	H	14	9-8	Perez	Floyd
April 16/08	Texas	H	14	5-7	Nippert	Burnett
May 17/80	Oakland	H	14	2-4	Keough	McLaughlin
Aug. 9/80	Kansas City	H	14	4-3	Willis	Eastwick
July 31/78	Detroit	H	14	8-7	Coleman	Sykes
Sept. 24/78	Boston	H	14	6-7	Drago	Buskey
April 29/81	Milwaukee	A	14	5-0	Leal	Easterley
Sept. 21/85	Milwaukee	H	14	2-1	Lamp	Darwin
May 17/88	Texas	H	14	6-7	Mohorcic	Eichhorn
June 21/89	California	A	14	6-1	Henke	Minton
Aug. 22/89	Detroit	H	14	3-2	Gozzo	E. Nunez
Aug. 8/91	Detroit	H	14	0-4	Gibson	Henke
Aug. 30/95	Cleveland	A	14	3-4	Assenmacher	Castillo
Aug. 20/96	Kansas City	A	14	6-5	Timlin	Huisman
June 9/99	New York (N)	A	14	3-4	Mahones	Davey
Aug. 7/01	Seattle	A	14	4-5	Halana	DeWitt
April 28/02	Anaheim	A	14	5-8	Lukasiewicz	Borbon
July 20/04	Oakland	A	14	0-1	Lehr	Speier
July 15/06	Seattle	H	14	7-6	Downs	Fruto
Sept. 21/07	New York	H	14	5-4	Kennedy	Braun
June 5/10	New York	H	14	3-2	Janssen	Gaudin
May 8/08	Tampa Bay	H	13	3-8	Howell	Camp
Sept. 6/08	Tampa Bay	H	13	7-4	Tallet	Percival
June 8/77	California	A	13	1-2	LaRoche	Bruno
July 15/77	Detroit	H	13	8-6	Vuckovich	Crawford
May 28/78	New York	A	13	5-6	Gossage	Murphy
June 20/78	Detroit	H	13	3-4	Hiller	Willis
June 8/80	Minnesota (G2)	A	13	6-4	McLaughlin	Arroyo
Sept. 14/80	Baltimore	H	13	4-3	Barlow	D. Martinez
#Sept. 17/80	New York	A	13	7-8	T. Underwood	Kucek
Sept. 22/81	Oakland (G1)	H	13	2-3	Beard	Leal
June 2/82	New York	H	13	6-12	Rawley	McLaughlin
July 30/83	Cleveland	H	13	6-5	McLaughlin	Anderson
April 20/84	California	H	13	6-10	Sanchez	Acker
July 25/84	Kansas City	A	13	4-5	Quisenberry	Clark
Aug. 15/84	Cleveland (G2)	A	13	3-4	Jeffcoat	Key
July 9/85	Seattle	A	13	9-4	R. Musselman	Vande Berg
Sept. 25/85	Boston	H	13	2-4	Crawford	Cerutti
Aug. 13/86	Baltimore	A	13	6-7	Aase	Aquino
April 14/87	Chicago	H	13	4-3	Eichhorn	McKeon
Sept. 27/87	Detroit	H	13	2-3	Henneman	Nunez
June 22/89	Oakland	A	13	4-2	Hernandez	Corsi
Sept. 19/89	Boston	H	13	6-5	Henke	Harris
July 24/90	Kansas City	H	13	3-5	Farr	Ward
July 28/90	Texas	H	13	2-3	Arnsberg	Wills
Sept. 21/90	Cleveland	H	13	1-2	Valdez	Wills
April 20/92	Boston	A	13	6-4	MacDonald	Bolton
June 2/92	Minnesota	A	13	7-5	Hentgen	Wayne
June 15/94	Cleveland	A	13	3-4	Mesa	Brow
Aug. 11/94	New York	A	13	8-7	Hall	Ausanio
Aug. 19/95	Kansas City	H	13	5-4	Rogers	Montgomery
April 21/97	Anaheim	A	13	4-5	DeLucia	Spoljaric
July 2/97	Montreal	H	13	7-6	Timlin	Telford
Aug. 24/97	Kansas City	A	13	11-8	Crabtree	Casian
Sept. 9/98	Cleveland	H	13	3-6	Jones	Almanzar
Sept. 26/98	Detroit	H	13	5-4	Risley	Sager
June 25/00	Boston	H	13	6-5	DeWitt	Florie
July 29/00	Seattle	A	13	5-6	Tomko	Halladay
April 21/01	Kansas City	A	13	4-5	Henry	Plesac
July 24/03	Chicago	H	13	3-4	Gordon	Sturtze
Aug. 20/05	Detroit	A	13	2-3	German	Batista
May 26/07	Minnesota	A	13	9-8	Tallet	Guierrer
May 26/12	Texas	A	13	7-8	Tateyama	Frasor

* Suspended game, due to CNE curfew — completed on August 29
# Suspended game, due to rain — completed on September 18
+ Longest Opening Day game - MLB history (measured by innings)

MILESTONE VICTORIES

VICTORY #	DATE	OPPONENT	SCORE	WINNER	LOSER
1	April 7/77	vs Chicago	9-5	Jerry Johnson	Ken Brett
500	Aug. 5/84	at Baltimore	4-3	Jimmy Key	Tippy Martinez
625	*Oct. 5/85	vs New York	5-1	Doyle Alexander	Joe Cowley
983	*Sept. 30/89	vs Baltimore	4-3	Frank Wills	Mark Williamson
1000	May 9/90	vs Chicago	4-3	Frank Wills	Wayne Edwards
1158	*Oct. 2/91	vs California	6-5	Mike Timlin	Bryan Harvey
1255	*Oct. 3/92	vs Detroit	3-1	Juan Guzman	David Haas
ALCS	**Oct. 14/92	vs Oakland	9-2	Juan Guzman	Mike Moore
WS	#Oct. 24/92	vs Atlanta	4-3	Jimmy Key	Charlie Leibrandt
1347	*Sept. 27/93	at Milwaukee	2-0	Pat Hentgen	Cal Eldred
ALCS	**Oct. 12/93	at Chicago	6-3	Dave Stewart	Alex Fernandez
WS	#Oct. 23/93	vs Philadelphia	8-6	Duane Ward	Mitch Williams
1500	July 6/96	at Detroit	15-0	Pat Hentgen	Omar Olivares
2000	Aug. 19/02	vs Kansas City	2-0	Pete Walker	Paul Byrd
2500	Sept. 3/08	vs Minnesota	5-4	Jesse Carlson	Eddie Guardado

* AL East Pennant Clincher ** AL Pennant Clincher # World Series Clincher

SEASON RECORDS — CLUB

GENERAL

Category	Record	Year
Doubleheaders, Most Played	17	1978
Doubleheaders, Best Record	5-1-4	1980
Doubleheaders, Most Wins	5	1980
Doubleheaders, Most Losses	8	1978
Doubleheaders, Most Split	8	1977
Extra Innings, Most Wins	13	1989, 2011
Extra Innings, Most Losses	13	1986, 2009
Extra Innings, Most Played	23	1986
Extra Innings, Fewest Played	8	2000, 2003, 2006
Games	163	1984, 1986, 1998
Games Won	99	1985
Games Lost	109	1979
Games Won, Consecutively	11	June 2-13, 1987,
	11	Aug. 26-Sept. 7, 1998
Games Lost, Consecutively	12	May 31-June 11 & Aug. 10, 1981
Home Wins, Consecutive	10	July 21-28, Aug. 2-3, 1985
Home Losses, Consecutive	11	Aug. 15-16, 26-28, Sept. 2-6 1977
Road Wins, Consecutive	9	Sept. 14-30, 1993
Road Losses, Consecutive	12	July 7-9, 19-23, 31-Aug. 1
	12	Aug. 11, 1979
Games Won, Highest Percentage	.615	(99-62) 1985
Home Record, Best	54-26	(.675) 1985
Road Record, Best	47-34	(.580) 1993
Homestand, Best	10-1	May 17-27, 1984
Homestand, Worst	0-6	5x, last May 24-29, 2002
Home Wins, Fewest	25	1977
Road Wins, Fewest	21	1979
Home Losses, Most	55	1977
Road Losses, Most	60	1979
Road Trip, Best	9-1	June 8-17, 1990
Road Trip, Worst	0-9	May 19-27, 2009
One Club, Most Wins vs	15	Baltimore, 2002
Consecutive Wins vs One Club	13	Cleveland, 1991-1992
	13	Baltimore, 1999-2000
One Club, Most Losses vs	14	Boston, 2004 and Tampa Bay, 2009/2012
One Club, Most Home Wins	9	Baltimore, 2010
One Club Home Losses	8	Boston, 2001
One Club, Most Road Wins	8	Baltimore, 2002
One Club, Most Road Losses	8	Milwaukee, 1978, Boston, 2004, Tampa Bay, 2009/2012 and Baltimore, 2009
One Run Games, Most	59	1984, 1997
One Run Games, Most Wins	34	1984
One Run Games, Most Losses	31	1978, 1982, 1997, 2005
One Run Games, Fewest Wins	14	2003
One Run Games, Fewest Losses	10	2006
Day Games, Most Played	65	1979
Day Games, Most Won	38	1993
Day Games, Most Lost	44	1979
Night Games, Most Played	113	1998
Night Games, Most Won	67	1987, 1989
Night Games, Most Lost	68	1977, 1980
InterLeague, Most Wins	10	2003, 2007
InterLeague, Most Losses	11	1997, 2009
Players Used, Most	55	2012
Players Used, Fewest	33	1983, 1984
Pitchers Used, Most	34	2012
Pitchers Used, Fewest	13	1982, 1984
Righthanders, Most Wins vs	75	1985
Lefthanders, Most Wins vs	37	1990
Righthanders, Most Losses vs	75	1979
Lefthanders, Most Losses vs	44	1982
Shutouts, Both Teams, Most	27	1997
Shutouts, Most Wins	16	1991, 1997
Shutouts, Most Losses	20	1981
Shutouts, Fewest Won	3	1977
Shutouts, Fewest Lost	2	1993

Category	Record	Year
Shutouts, Most vs One Team	4	vs Detroit, 1989
	4	vs New York (AL), 1997
Shutouts, Most By Opponent	4	vs Milwaukee, 1978, vs Boston, 1990
Winning Margin, Highest	17	at Kansas City, May 16, 2003
Winning Margin, Highest by Opponent	22	vs California, Aug. 25, 1979
	22	at Baltimore, Sept. 28, 2000
Artificial Turf, Most Won	64	1985, 1992
Artificial Turf, Most Lost	60	1977 & 1978
Natural Turf, Most Won	39	1993
Natural Turf, Most Lost	52	1978

BATTING

Category	Record	Year (Not including strike-shortened seasons '81, '94, '95)
At Bats, Most	5716	1986
Batting Average, Highest	.284	2006
Batting Average, Lowest	.244	1997
Grounded Into Double Plays, Most	166	2006
Grounded Into Double Plays, Fewest	91	1984
Hit By Pitch, Most	92	1996
Hit By Pitch, Fewest	23	1977 & 1978
Hits, Most	1591	2006
Hits, Fewest	1333	1997
Home Runs, Most	257	2010
Home Runs, Fewest	95	1979
Home Runs, Home Most	146	2010
Home Runs, Home Fewest	45	1977
Home Runs, Road Most	116	1999
Home Runs, Road Fewest	44	1982
Home Runs vs One Club, Most	34	vs. Baltimore, 2010
Grand Slams, Most	9	2000
Inside The Park, Most	4	1983
Left On Base, Most	1195	2009
Left On Base, Fewest	1026	2012
Doubles, Most	357	2003
Doubles, Fewest	217	1978
Triples, Most	68	1984
Triples, Fewest	13	2009
Most Extra-Base Hits	597	2010
Pinch Hits, Most	72	1982
Pinch Hits, Fewest	4	2010
Pinch Hit Home Runs, Most	6	1984
Runs Batted In, Most	856	1999
Runs Batted In, Fewest	551	1978
Runs Scored, Most	894	2003
Runs Scored, Fewest	590	1978
Sacrifices, Most	81	1977
Sacrifices, Fewest	11	2003
Sacrifice Flies, Most	65	1991
Slugging Percentage, Highest	.469	2000
Slugging Percentage, Lowest	.358	1978
Stolen Bases, Most Stolen	193	1984
Stolen Bases, Times Caught	81	1982, 1998
Stolen Bases, Fewest Stolen	28	1978
Strikeouts, Most	1251	2012
Strikeouts, Fewest	645	1978
Total Bases, Most	2664	2000
Total Bases, Fewest	1947	1978
Walks, Most	588	1993
Walks, Fewest	415	1982
On-Base Percentage, Highest	.352	1999
On-Base Percentage, Lowest	.308	1978

FIELDING

Category	Record	Year
Assists, Most	1939	1980
Assists, Fewest	1532	1998
Chances Total, Most	6470	1980
Chances Total, Fewest	5958	1997
Double Plays, Most	205	1980
Double Plays, Fewest	107	1992
Errors, Most	164	1977
Errors, Fewest	84	2008
Fielding Percentage, Highest	.988	2009
Fielding Percentage, Lowest	.974	1977
Passed Balls, Most	31	1995
Passed Balls, Fewest	3	1985
Putouts, Most	4428	1986
Putouts, Fewest	4251	1979
Triple Plays	2	1979
Most Errorless Games	110	2008
Most Consecutive Errorless Games	15	2008

PITCHING

Category	Record	Year
Complete Games, Most	44	1979
Complete Games, Fewest	5	2010
Earned Run Average, Lowest	3.31	1985
Earned Run Average, Highest	5.14	2000
Hit Batsmen, Most	77	2011
Hit Batsmen, Fewest	20	1977
Hits, Most	1615	2000
Hits, Fewest	1301	1991
Home Runs, Most	204	2012
Home Runs, Fewest	99	1989
Home Runs, Home Most	107	2003
Home Runs, Home Fewest	50	1989
Home Runs, Road Most	103	2000
Home Runs, Road Fewest	49	1989, 1991
One Hit Games	3	1988, 2010
Runs, Most	908	2000
Runs, Fewest	588	1985
Earned Runs, Most	821	2000
Earned Runs, Fewest	532	1985
Relief Appearances, Most	495	2012
Relief Appearances, Fewest	187	1977
Saves, Most	60	1991
Saves, Fewest	11	1979
Strikeouts, Most	1184	2008, 2010
Strikeouts, Fewest	613	1979
Walks, Most	654	1995
Walks, Fewest	444	2005
Wild Pitches, Most	83	1993
Wild Pitches, Fewest	25	1983
Shutouts, Most	17	1988
Shutouts, Fewest	3	1977
1-0 Games, Won, Most	5	1980
1-0 Games, Lost, Most	3	1979, 1992, 2005, 2008

GAME RECORDS — CLUB

BATTING

Category	Record	Opponent	Date
Runs	24	Baltimore (H)	June 26/78
Hits	25	Texas (A)	Aug. 9/99
Doubles	10	Boston (A)	Aug. 17/08
Triples	4	4x: Last--Seattle (H)	July 5/84
Home Runs	10	Baltimore (H)	Sept. 14/87
Total Bases	53	Baltimore (H)	Sept. 14/87
Runs Batted in	24	Baltimore (H)	June 26/78
Extra Base Hits	12	4x: Last--Tampa Bay (H)	Aug. 7/10
Left On Base	17	Seattle (A)	July 17/92
	20	Cleveland (A) (13 Inn) (GM 2)	Aug. 15/84
Strikeouts	19	California (A) (13 Inn)	June 8/77
	19	New York-AL (H) (17 Inn)	April 19/01
	18	California (A)	June 8/77
	18	Texas (A)	July 25/89
Base On Balls	13	Chicago-AL (H)	April 16/79
	13	Texas (A)	June 29/92
	13	Milwaukee (A)	May 13/95
Stolen Bases	7	Baltimore (A)	Aug. 5/84
Sacrifice Hits	4	Cleveland (A)	Sept. 17/77
	4	Cleveland (A)	Oct. 2/77
Sacrifice Flies	4	Chicago-AL (A)	Aug. 14/90
Hit by Pitch	4	Boston (A)	April 1/02
	4	Baltimore (A)	June 19/03
GIDP	6	Minnesota (A) (10 Inn)	Aug. 29/77 (1st g)
	6	Kansas City	April 30/09
Best Shutout Victory	15-0	Detroit (A)	July 6/96
Worst Shutout Defeat	0-16	Oakland (H)	July 25/12
Best Winning Margin	17	Kansas City (A) (Tor 18, KC 1)	May 16/03
Worst Losing Margin	22	California (H) (Tor-2, Cal-24)	Aug. 25/79
	22	Baltimore (A) (Tor-1, Bal-23)	Sept. 28/00
Most Consecutive Games, one or more HRs	23	(44 home runs)	May 31-June 25/00
Most Consecutive Games, No HRs	10	3x, last:	Sept 20-Oct. 1/95
Most Consecutive Strikeouts, Batters	7	Boston (A) (Nomo)	May 25/01
Most Consecutive Strikeouts, Batters to Start a Game	6	Cleveland (H) (Colon)	July 26/00
Most Consecutive Strikeouts, Outs	7	California (A) (Ryan)	June 8/77
	7	Boston (A) (Nomo)	May 25/01

PITCHING

Category	Record	Opponent	Date
Most Runs	24	California (H)	Aug. 25/79
Most Earned Runs	22	Milwaukee (H)	Aug. 28/92
Most Unearned Runs	13	Baltimore (A)	Sept. 28/00
Most Hits	31	Milwaukee (H)	Aug. 28/92
Most Home Runs	8	Boston (A)	July 4/77
	8	Detroit (H)	June 20/00
Most Strikeouts	21	Detroit (H) (14 inn.)	Aug. 8/91
	18	Kansas City (H)	Aug. 25/98
Most Walks	16	Seattle (A) 9 (11 inn.)	May 9/02
	15	Baltimore (A)	June 27/89
Most Wild Pitches	5	Texas (A)	April 8/10
Most Hit Batsmen	5	Boston (H)	July 10/10
Longest 1-0 game, won	12 inn	Boston (A)	Sept. 26/86
Longest 1-0 game, lost	15 inn	Oakland (A)	July 27/86

FIELDING

Category	Record	Opponent	Date
Most Errors	6	Texas (A)	May 13/82
Most Double Plays	6	Detroit (H)	April 16/96
	6	Minnesota (A)	Aug. 12/06
Stolen Bases Allowed	8	Milwaukee (H)	Aug. 29/92

MONTHLY RECORDS — CLUB

Category	Record	Year
Wins	21	May '03
Losses	23	May '79
AVG	.314	Aug. '00
SLG %	.513	Aug. '00/June '03
OBP %	.376	April '99
Runs	193	May '03
Hits	324	Aug. '83
2B	78	April '03
3B	16	June '84/July '84
HR	54	May '10
RBI	185	May '03
SB	47	Aug. '84
CG	11	June '79
ShO	6	Sept '88
HR—Opponents	45	Aug. '99/Aug. '02
ERA (Low)	2.62	Sept. '92
ERA (High)	6.69	April '02
Best Record (winning %)	.760 (19-6)	May '84
Worst Record (winning %)	.160 (4-21)	Sept. '78

HOME RUNS AT ROGERS CENTRE

Club	1989	1990	1991	1992	1993	1994	1995	1996	1997	1998	1999	2000	2001	2002	2003	2004	2005	2006	2007	2008	2009	2010	2011	2012	Total
Arizona	–	–	–	–	–	–	–	–	–	–	–	–	–	–	–	3	–	–	–	–	–	**-**	**-**	**-**	**3**
Atlanta	–	–	–	–	–	–	–	–	2	–	1	–	2	–	–	–	–	–	–	2	–	**-**	**-**	**-**	**7**
Baltimore	4	8	9	3	6	6	7	13	3	4	9	4	7	6	12	6	19	7	7	10	5	**4**	**9**	**13**	**177**
Boston	5	2	6	6	6	1	8	9	11	9	7	3	14	9	11	12	10	16	16	**11**	16	**14**	**17**	**6**	**211**
Chicago (NL)	–	–	–	–	–	–	–	–	–	–	–	–	–	–	1	–	–	–	–	2	–	**-**	**-**	**-**	**3**
Chicago (AL)	0	4	9	3	1	7	4	10	3	6	5	3	5	5	5	2	8	5	2	2	3	**8**	**3**	**10**	**105**
Cincinnati	–	–	–	–	–	–	–	–	–	–	–	–	–	–	–	–	–	–	–	1	2	**-**	**-**	**-**	**3**
Cleveland	3	8	1	9	10	9	12	7	6	10	8	4	4	2	1	7	6	3	5	–	2	**2**	**2**	**4**	**123**
Colorado	–	–	–	–	–	–	–	–	–	–	–	–	–	0	–	–	–	–	3	–	–	**-**	**-**	**-**	**3**
Detroit	4	11	9	3	11	7	8	9	3	8	6	9	1	1	1	6	4	4	3	2	7	**7**	**4**	**4**	**125**
Florida	–	–	–	–	–	–	–	–	2	–	2	–	1	–	–	–	–	–	–	–	5	**-**	**-**	**-**	**10**
Houston	-	-	-	-	-	-	-	-	-	-	-	-	-	-	-	-	-	-	-	-	-	**-**	**2**	**-**	**2**
Kansas City	0	6	4	4	6	8	7	6	4	6	2	5	4	3	7	2	5	3	3	–	3	**2**	**4**	**3**	**95**
Los Angeles (AL)	1	6	5	3	7	0	5	4	7	3	5	9	1	6	2	5	1	1	1	2	5	**3**	**10**	**7**	**96**
Los Angeles (NL)	–	–	–	–	–	–	–	–	–	–	–	–	–	–	–	3	–	–	3	–	–	**-**	**-**	**-**	**6**
Milwaukee[1]	5	6	7	5	10	3	8	8	6	–	–	–	–	–	–	–	3	–	–	–	–	**-**	**-**	**-**	**61**
Minnesota	3	6	1	3	3	5	3	4	1	2	3	4	2	7	4	4	4	5	3	–	3	**9**	**2**	**2**	**74**
New York (AL)	3	10	5	6	2	4	7	7	3	4	6	7	9	20	13	18	10	12	9	7	13	**10**	**8**	**7**	**190**
New York (NL)	–	–	–	–	–	–	–	–	–	6	–	6	–	–	–	–	–	5	–	–	–	**-**	**-**	**1**	**18**
Oakland	7	5	7	6	6	2	4	7	6	3	15	9	9	0	8	3	5	12	4	4	0	**1**	**5**	**6**	**133**
Philadelphia	–	–	–	–	–	–	–	–	–	4	–	4	–	–	–	–	–	3	–	–	3	**-**	**1**	**3**	**18**
Pittsburgh	–	–	–	–	–	–	–	–	–	–	–	–	–	–	5	–	–	–	–	–	–	**-**	**3**	**-**	**8**
San Francisco	–	–	–	–	–	–	–	–	–	–	–	–	–	7	–	–	–	–	–	–	–	**3**	**-**	**-**	**7**
Seattle	2	6	6	7	4	7	4	9	9	10	5	13	3	9	3	5	10	9	3	4	5	**4**	**5**	**8**	**146**
St. Louis	–	–	–	–	–	–	–	–	–	–	–	–	–	–	–	–	5	–	–	–	–	**4**	**-**	**-**	**5**
Tampa Bay	–	–	–	–	–	–	–	–	–	0	7	7	7	5	15	12	10	11	10	7	13	**6**	**16**	**14**	**134**
Texas	2	4	3	2	9	5	2	9	2	1	10	3	10	5	17	2	2	1	8	2	5	**4**	**4**	**6**	**114**
Montreal/ Washington	–	–	–	–	–	–	–	–	4	1	2	2	5	4	2	3	1	2	4	–	–	**-**	**-**	**8**	**38**
Toronto	**45**	**93**	**75**	**79**	**90**	**63**	**73**	**87**	**68**	**112**	**96**	**134**	**92**	**102**	**94**	**80**	**76**	**121**	**90**	**69**	**104**	**146**	**95**	**102**	**2186**
Opponents	**39**	**82**	**72**	**60**	**81**	**64**	**79**	**102**	**72**	**77**	**93**	**92**	**84**	**89**	**107**	**93**	**103**	**94**	**83**	**56**	**90**	**81**	**179**	**102**	**2074**

[1] Milwaukee moved to the National League in 1998

BLUE JAYS ROOKIES

HIGHS & LOWS

TEAM

Category	Record	Year
Rookies on 25-man roster, opening day	9	1977
Rookies on opening day starting lineup	4	1977
Rookies to appear during season	18	2002
Major league debuts	12	1995
Youngest rookie	Brian Milner	18 yrs, 6 days
Oldest rookie	Pete Walker	33 yrs, 28 days
Total number of at bats by rookies	2,477	1977
Total number of hits by rookies	649	1977
Total number of innings pitched by rookies	557	1977
Games started by rookies	68	1977
Games won by rookies	31	1986, 2009

BATTING

Category	Record	Year
Greatest number of rookies in starting lineup, game	7	(many times) 1977
Highest average (502 plate appearances)	.310	Bob Bailor, 1977
Most games	153	Alfredo Griffin, 1979
Most at bats	624	Alfredo Griffin, 1979
Most hits	179	Alfredo Griffin, 1979
Most runs	99	Eric Hinske, 2002
Most total bases	272	Eric Hinske, 2002
Most extra-base hits	64	Eric Hinske, 2002
Most doubles	38	Eric Hinske, 2002
Most triples	10	Alfredo Griffin, 1979
Most home runs	24	Eric Hinske, 2002
Most runs batted in	84	Eric Hinske, 2002
Most bases on balls	77	Eric Hinske, 2002
Most times striking out	138	Eric Hinske, 2002
Highest slugging percentage	.481	Eric Hinske, 2002
Highest on-base percentage	.365	Eric Hinske, 2002
Most stolen bases	21	Alfredo Griffin, 1979
Most stolen base attempts	37	Alfredo Griffin, 1979
Longest hitting streak	20	Reed Johnson, 2003
Longest hitting streak, start of career	8	Jesse Barfield, 1981

PITCHING

Category	Record	Year
Most wins	14	Mark Eichhorn, 1986
Most losses	18	Jerry Garvin, 1977
		Phil Huffman, 1979
Most decisions	28	Jerry Garvin, 1977
Most games	72	Aquilino Lopez, 2003
Most games started	34	Jerry Garvin, 1977
		Gustavo Chacin, 2005
Most relief appearances	72	Aquilino Lopez, 2003
Most saves	31	Billy Koch, 1999
Lowest era (162 IP)	3.72	Gustavo Chacin, 2005
Most innings pitched	244.2	Jerry Garvin, 1977
Most ER allowed	114	Jerry Garvin, 1977
Most home runs allowed	33	Jerry Garvin, 1977
Most bases on balls	85	Jerry Garvin, 1977
Most strikeouts	166	Mark Eichhorn, 1986
Most hit batsmen	12	Chris Michalak, 2001
Most wild pitches	11	Edwin Hurtado, 1995
Most balks	5	Chris Michalak, 2001
Most pickoffs	8	Chris, Michalak, 1995

ROOKIES YEAR BY YEAR

1977 (16): Doug Ault, Bob Bailor, Steve Bowling, Tom Bruno, *Jeff Byrd, Rick Cerone, *Jim Clancy, *Mike Darr, *Dennis DeBarr, Sam Ewing, *Jerry Garvin, *Steve Staggs, Ernie Whitt, *Mike Willis, *Al Woods, Gary Woods, *Major League debut (8).

1978 (7): *Butch Alberts, Rick Bosetti, *Victor Cruz, *Garth Iorg, *Brian Milner, *Willie Upshaw, Dave Wallace, *Major League debut (5).

1979 (9): *Dan Ainge, *Bobby Brown, J.J. Cannon, *Butch Edge, Alfredo Griffin, *Pedro Hernandez, *Phil Huffman, *Dave Stieb, *Ted Wilborn, *Major League debut (7).

1980 (8): Damaso Garcia, *Paul Hodgson, *Pat Kelly, *Luis Leal, Mike Macha, *Lloyd Moseby, Domingo Ramos, *Ken Schrom, *Major League debut (5).

1981 (5): *Jesse Barfield, *George Bell, *Fred Manrique, *Greg Wells, Dan Whitmer, *Major League debut (4).

1982 (9): *Dave Baker, Jesse Barfield, *Mark Eichhorn, *Jim Gott, Pedro Hernandez, Anthony Johnson, *Geno Petralli, Ken Schrom, *Steve Senteney, *Major League debut (5).

1983 (6): *Jim Acker, *Stan Clarke, *Tony Fernandez, Geno Petralli, *Mitch Webster, *Matt Williams, *Major League debut (5).

1984 (7): Tony Fernandez, *Kelly Gruber, *Toby Hernandez, *Jimmy Key, Fred Manrique, *Ron Shepherd, Mitch Webster, *Major League debut (4).

1985 (10): *John Cerutti, Stan Clarke, *Steve Davis, *Cecil Fielder, Kelly Gruber, *Jeff Hearron, *Manny Lee, Ron Shepherd, *Lou Thorton, Mitch Webster, *Major League debut (6).

1986 (13): *Luis Aquino, John Cerutti, Stan Clarke, Steve Davis, Mark Eichhorn, Cecil Fielder, *Don Gordon, Kelly Gruber, Jeff Hearron, Joe Johnson, *Fred McGriff, *Jeff Musselman, Duane Ward, *Major League debut (4).

1987 (12): *Jeff DeWillis, *Rob Ducey, *Alexis Infante, *Nelson Liriano, Fred McGriff, Jeff Musselman, *Greg Myers, *Jose Nunez, *Mike Sharperson, *Matt Stark, Duane Ward, *David Wells, *Major League debut (9).

1988 (7): *Tony Castillo, David Wells, *Todd Stottlemyre, *Pat Borders, Alexis Infante, *Silvestre Campusano, Rob Ducey, *Major League debut (4).

1989 (12): *Kevin Batiste, *Francisco Cabrera, Tony Castillo, *Steve Cummings, *Junior Felix, *Mauro Gozzo, *Xavier Hernandez, *Glenallen Hill, Alexis Infante, Greg Myers, *John Olerud, *Alex Sanchez, *Major League debut (9).

1990 (11): *Willie Blair, Steve Cummings, *Carlos Diaz, Glenallen Hill, Rick Luecken, *Bob MacDonald, Greg Myers, John Olerud, *Tom Quinlan, *Luis Sojo, *Mark Whiten, *Major League debut (6).

1991 (15): *Derek Bell, *Denis Boucher, *Ray Giannelli, *Juan Guzman, *Pat Hentgen, *Vince Horsman, *Randy Knorr, Bob MacDonald, *Ed Sprague, *Mike Timlin, Turner Ward, *David Weathers, Mickey Weston, Mark Whiten, *Eddie Zosky, *Major League debut (11).

1992 (11): Derek Bell, Pat Hentgen, *Jeff Kent, Randy Knorr, *Doug Linton, *Mike Maksudian, Domingo Martinez, Tom Quinlan, *Rick Trlicek, David Weathers, Eddie Zosky, *Major League debut (5).

1993 (11): *Scott Brow, *Rob Butler, *Willie Canate, *Domingo Cedeno, *Carlos Delgado, *Huck Flener, *Shawn Green, Randy Knorr, Doug Linton, Domingo Martinez, *Woody Williams, *Major League debut (8).

1994 (11): Scott Brow, Rob Butler, Domingo Cedeno, *Brad Cornett, Carlos Delgado, *Alex Gonzalez, Shawn Green, *Darren Hall, *Robert Perez, *Aaron Small, *Paul Spoljaric, *Major League debut (6).

1995 (15): *Howard Battle, Alex Gonzalez, Shawn Green, *Sandy Martinez, Robert Perez, *Tomas Perez, *Shannon Stewart, *Giovanni Carrara, *Tim Crabtree, *Edwin Hurtado, *Ricardo Jordan, *Paul Menhart, *Ken Robinson, *Jimmy Rogers, *Jeff Ware, *Major League debut (12).

1996 (13): Luis Andujar, *Tilson Brito, *Miguel Cairo, Giovanni Carrara, *Felipe Crespo, Huck Flener, *Marty Janzen, *Julio Mosquera, Robert Perez, *Jose Silva, Paul Spoljaric, Shannon Stewart, Jeff Ware, *Major League debut (6).

1997 (10): *Carlos Almanzar, *Rich Butler, *Chris Carpenter, Felipe Crespo, Jose Cruz, Jr., *Kelvim Escobar, *Tom Evans, Julio Mosquera, Ken Robinson, Shannon Stewart, *Major League debut (5).

1998 (9): Carlos Almanzar, Kevin Brown, Tom Evans, *Roy Halladay, Nerio Rodriguez, *Steve Sinclair, Ben Van Ryn, *Shannon Withem, *Kevin Witt, *Major League debut (4).

1999 (14): *John Bale, *Casey Blake, *Tom Davey, *Gary Glover, Roy Halladay, *Billy Koch, *Pete Munro, Willis Otanez, *Mike Romano, *Anthony Sanders, Steve Sinclair, *Vernon Wells, Kevin Witt, *Chris Woodward, *Major League debut (10).

2000 (13): *Clayton Andrews, John Bale, *Pasqual Coco, *Darwin Cubillan, *Matt DeWitt, *Leo Estrella, Charlie Greene, Chad Mottola, *Josh Phelps, *Andy Thompson, Vernon Wells, *Dewayne Wise, Chris Woodward, *Major League debut (8).

2001 (12): *Brian Bowles, Pasqual Coco, Matt DeWitt, *Bob File, *Ryan Freel, *Cesar Izturis, *Felipe Lopez, *Luis Lopez, *Brandon Lyon, Chris Michalak, Josh Phelps, Vernon Wells, *Major League debut (7).

2002 (18): Brian Bowles, *Kevin Cash, *Scott Cassidy, Pasqual Coco, *Mark Hendrickson, *Eric Hinske, Ken Huckaby, *Orlando Hudson, Jason Kershner, *Joe Lawrence, *Justin Miller, Josh Phelps, *Mike Smith, Pedro Swann, *Corey Thurman, Pete Walker, *Jayson Werth, *Scott Wiggins, *Major League debut (11).

2003 (8): Brian Bowles, Kevin Cash, *Vinnie Chulk, Howie Clark, Mark Hendrickson, *Reed Johnson, *Aquilino Lopez, Jayson Werth, *Major League debut (3)

2004 (16): *Russ Adams, *Dave Bush, Kevin Cash, *Gustavo Chacin, Vinnie Chulk, *Eric Crozier, *Jason Frasor, Kevin Frederick, *Gabe Gross, *Brandon League, Dave Maurer, Michael Nakamura, *Adam Peterson, *Simon Pond, *Guillermo Quirioz, *Alex Rios, *Major League debut (11).

2005 (9): Russ Adams, Gustavo Chacin, *John-Ford Griffin, Gabe Gross, *Aaron Hill, Guillermo Quiroz, Brandon League, *Shaun Marcum, *Dustin McGowan, *Major League debut (4).

2006 (10): Luis Figueroa, *John Hattig, *Casey Janssen, *Adam Lind, Shaun Marcum, Dustin McGowan, *Ryan Roberts, *Davis Romero, *Francisco Rosario, Brian Tallet, *Major League debut (6).

2007 (11): *Josh Banks, *Jordan De Jong, John-Ford Griffin, *Lee Gronkiewicz, Adam Lind, *Jesse Litsch, Ryan Roberts, *Curtis Thigpen, *Jamie Vermilyea, *Brian Wolfe, *Major League debut (7).

2008 (7): *Jesse Carlson, Buck Coats, *David Purcey, *Scott Richmond, *Travis Snider, *Randy Wells, *Robinzon Diaz (6).

2009 (13): Bryan Bullington, *Brett Cecil, Dirk Hayhurst, *Brad Mills, Bill Murphy, *Kyle Phillips, *Robert Ray, Scott Richmond, Josh Roenicke, *Ricky Romero, Randy Ruiz, *Mark Rzepczynski, Travis Snider (6).

2010 (7): *J.P. Arencibia, *Kyle Drabek, Jarrett Hoffpauir, *Rommie Lewis Jr., Mike McCoy, Brad Mills, Robert Ray (3)

2011 (13): *Henderson Alvarez, J.P. Arencibia, *Chad Beck, *Joel Carreno, *David Cooper, Kyle Drabek, *Daniel Farquhar, *Brett Lawrie, *Darin Mastroianni, Brad Mills, *Luis Perez, *Zach Stewart, *Eric Thames (10).

2012 (15): Chad Beck, Drew Carpenter, Joel Carreno, Robert Coello, David Cooper, *Evan Crawford, Steve Delabar, *Sam Dyson, *Yan Gomes, *Anthony Gose, *Adeiny Hechavarria, *Drew Hutchison, *Chad Jenkins, *Aaron Loup, *Moises Sierra

* Major League Debut

TOP FIVE ROOKIES — THRU 2012

BATTING AVERAGE (502 plate appearnaces)

1	Bob Bailor	.310	1977
2	Alfredo Griffin	.287	1979
3	Eric Hinske	.279	2002
4	Damaso Garcia	.278	1980
5	Rick Bosetti	.259	1978

GAMES

1	Alfredo Griffin	153	1979
2	Eric Hinske	151	2002
3	Damaso Garcia	140	1980
4	Jesse Barfield	139	1982
	Russ Adams	139	2005

AT-BATS

1	Alfredo Griffin	624	1979
2	Rick Bosetti	568	1978
3	Eric Hinske	566	2002
4	Damaso Garcia	543	1980
5	Bob Bailor	496	1977

MOST RUNS

1	Eric Hinske	99	2002
2	Alfredo Griffin	81	1979
3	Reed Johnson	79	2003
4	Russ Adams	68	2005
5	Bob Bailor	62	1977
	Junior Felix	62	1989

MOST HITS

1	Alfredo Griffin	179	1979
2	Eric Hinske	158	2002
3	Bob Bailor	154	1977
4	Damaso Garcia	151	1980
5	Rick Bosetti	147	1978

DOUBLES

1	Eric Hinske	38	2002
2	Shawn Green	31	1995
3	Damaso Garcia	30	1980
4	Russ Adams	27	2005
5	Rick Bosetti	25	1978
	Aaron Hill	25	2005

TRIPLES

1	Alfredo Griffin	10	1979
2	Junior Felix	8	1989
3	Damaso Garcia	7	1980
	Shannon Stewart	7	1997
	Alex Rios	7	2004

HOME RUNS

1	Eric Hinske	24	2002
2	J.P. Arencibia	23	2011
3	Fred McGriff	20	1987
4	Jesse Barfield	18	1982
5	Shawn Green	15	1995
	Josh Phelps	15	2002

RUNS BATTED IN

1	Eric Hinske	84	2002
2	J.P. Arencibia	78	2011
3	Doug Ault	64	1977
4	Russ Adams	63	2005
5	Jesse Barfield	58	1982
	Josh Phelps	58	2002

EXTRA BASE HITS

1	Eric Hinske	64	2002
2	Shawn Green	50	1995
3	J.P. Arencibia	47	2011
4	Damaso Garcia	41	1980
	Eric Thames	41	2011

TOTAL BASES

1	Eric Hinske	272	2002
2	Alfredo Griffin	227	1979
3	Damaso Garcia	207	1980
4	Bob Bailor	200	1977
5	Rick Bosetti	197	1995

STOLEN BASES

1	Alfredo Griffin	21	1979
2	Junior Felix	18	1989
3	Bob Bailor	15	1977
	Alex Rios	15	2004
	Anthony Gose	15	2012

SACRIFICE HITS

1	Alfredo Griffin	16	1979
2	Lloyd Moseby	10	1980
3	Alex Gonzalez	9	1995
4	Dan Ainge	7	1979
5	4 tied at 6		

SACRIFICE FLIES

1	Russ Adams	8	2005
2	Eric Hinske	5	2002
3	11 tied at 4		

HIT BY PITCH

1	Reed Johnson	20	2003
2	Jeff Kent	6	1992
3	4 tied at 5		

BASE ON BALLS

1	Eric Hinske	77	2002
2	Fred McGriff	60	1987
3	John Olerud	57	1990
4	Russ Adams	50	2005
5	Alex Gonzalez	44	1995

STRIKEOUTS

1	Eric Hinske	138	2002
2	Eric Thames	133	2011
3	Alex Gonzalez	114	1995
4	Fred McGriff	104	1987
5	Junior Felix	101	1989

WINS

1	Mark Eichhorn	14	1986
2	Gustavo Chacin	13	2005
	Ricky Romero	13	2009
4	Jeff Musselman	12	1987
5	Mike Timlin	11	1991

LOSSES

1	Jerry Garvin	18	1977
	Phil Huffman	18	1978
3	Jeff Byrd	13	1977
4	Scott Richmond	11	2009
5	Jim Gott	10	1982
	Casey Janssen	10	2006
	Jesse Litsch	10	2007

SAVES

1	Billy Koch	31	1999
2	Darren Hall	17	1994
	Jason Frasor	17	2004
4	Kelvim Escobar	14	1997
	Aquilino Lopez	14	2003

ERA (162 IP)

1	Gustavo Chacin	3.72	2005
2	Jerry Garvin	4.19	1977
3	Ricky Romero	4.30	2009
4	Phil Huffman	5.77	1979

GAMES

1	Aquilino Lopez	72	2003
2	Mark Eichhorn	69	1986
	Jesse Carlson	69	2008
4	Jeff Musselman	68	1987
5	Jim Key	63	1984
	Mike Timlin	63	1991
	Jason Frasor	63	2004

STARTS

1	Jerry Garvin	34	1977
	Gustavo Chacin	34	2005
3	Phil Huffman	31	1978
4	Mark Hendrickson	30	2003
5	Ricky Romero	29	2009

INNINGS

1	Jerry Garvin	244.2	1977
2	Gustavo Chacin	203.0	2005
3	Ricky Romero	178.0	2009
4	Phil Huffman	173.0	1978
5	Mark Hendrickson	158.1	2003

STRIKEOUTS

1	Mark Eichhorn	166	1986
2	Ricky Romero	141	2009
3	Jerry Garvin	127	1977
4	Juan Guzman	123	1991
5	Gustavo Chacin	121	2005

HOME RUNS

CLUB RECORDS

HITTERS

				Consec			1-inn			One-game						Batters					Totals					vs	
Y	Tot	H	A	2	3	4	3	4	5	5	6	7	8	9	10	PH	LO	XN	IP	P	1	10	20	30	40	RHP	LHP
77	100	45	55	3	0	0	1	0	0	0	0	0	0	0	0	5	1	2	1	0	15	5	0	0	0	65	35
78	98	50	48	2	0	0	0	0	0	0	0	0	0	0	0	2	2	2	0	0	15	2	2	0	0	59	39
79	95	50	45	2	0	0	0	0	0	0	0	0	0	0	0	4	1	2	2	0	15	4	1	0	0	67	28
80	126	56	70	3	0	0	0	0	0	0	0	0	0	0	0	3	0	3	1	0	17	5	2	1	0	82	44
81	61	34	27	2	0	0	0	0	0	0	0	0	0	0	0	1	1	0	1	0	12	2	0	0	0	31	30
82	106	62	44	3	0	0	1	0	0	0	0	0	0	0	0	4	1	1	1	0	19	4	1	0	0	56	50
83	167	101	66	10	0	0	2	0	0	1	0	0	0	0	0	5	2	4	4	0	16	9	3	0	0	106	60
84	143	59	84	5	1	0	3	0	0	0	0	0	0	0	0	6	1	1	2	0	15	7	1	0	0	105	38
85	158	75	83	6	0	0	0	0	0	1	0	0	0	0	0	4	2	8	0	0	16	6	2	0	0	102	56
86	181	87	94	5	0	0	0	0	0	0	0	0	0	0	0	4	4	6	1	0	16	7	3	2	1	126	55
87	215	101	114	8	1	0	3	0	0	3	0	0	0	0	1	3	0	4	0	0	18	9	4	1	1	152	63
88	158	78	80	6	0	0	0	0	0	1	0	0	0	0	0	2	1	2	1	0	15	7	2	1	0	105	53
89	142	64	78	4	0	0	0	0	0	0	0	0	0	0	0	3	4	3	1	0	17	6	1	1	0	106	36
90	167	93	74	6	0	0	2	0	0	2	0	0	0	0	0	0	1	3	0	0	15	7	3	2	0	109	58
91	133	75	58	1	0	0	0	0	0	0	0	0	0	0	0	1	6	5	1	0	17	4	2	1	0	86	47
92	163	79	84	4	0	0	0	0	0	0	0	0	0	0	0	0	5	2	1	0	13	7	3	1	0	122	41
93	159	90	69	7	0	0	0	0	0	2	0	0	0	0	0	1	6	0	1	0	15	6	3	1	0	121	38
94	115	63	52	2	0	0	0	0	0	0	1	0	0	0	0	1	4	2	1	0	12	5	1	0	0	74	41
95	140	73	67	5	0	0	1	0	0	0	0	0	0	0	0	1	3	1	1	0	16	7	1	0	0	104	36
96	177	87	90	3	0	0	0	0	0	1	1	0	0	0	0	2	1	3	0	0	15	8	3	2	0	130	47
97	147	68	79	5	0	0	0	0	0	0	0	0	0	0	0	1	0	1	0	0	15	7	2	1	0	109	38
98	221	112	109	6	0	0	0	0	0	0	0	1	0	0	0	1	2	3	3	0	16	8	4	3	1	167	54
99	212	96	116	11	0	0	3	0	0	3	1	0	0	0	0	4	3	3	0	0	23	7	3	2	2	170	42
00	244	134	110	5	1	0	2	0	0	2	0	0	0	0	0	0	8	1	0	0	15	8	7	4	2	205	39
01	195	94	101	8	1	0	2	1	0	4	0	0	0	0	0	2	4	5	1	0	19	8	3	2	0	150	45
02	187	102	85	6	0	0	1	0	0	1	0	0	0	0	0	4	3	3	2	0	17	8	3	1	0	150	37
03	190	94	96	6	0	0	0	0	0	1	0	0	0	0	0	0	6	3	1	1	18	7	3	2	1	150	40
04	145	80	65	2	0	0	0	0	0	0	0	0	0	0	0	4	7	1	0	0	19	6	2	1	0	93	52
05	136	76	60	3	1	0	1	0	0	0	0	0	0	0	0	3	1	0	0	0	14	7	1	0	0	94	42
06	199	121	78	10	0	0	2	0	0	2	0	0	0	0	0	2	6	3	0	0	16	9	3	2	0	146	53
07	165	90	75	6	0	0	2	0	0	0	0	0	0	0	0	4	5	3	0	0	17	9	4	0	0	121	44
08	126	69	57	2	0	0	0	0	0	0	0	0	0	0	0	2	2	1	0	0	19	6	1	0	0	100	26
09	209	104	105	5	0	0	1	0	0	2	1	0	0	0	0	2	3	4	0	0	16	9	2	2	0	156	53
10	257	146	111	10	0	0	1	0	0	2	2	0	1	0	0	1	5	2	1	0	17	9	7	2	1	211	46
11	186	103	83	7	0	0	2	0	0	0	0	0	0	0	0	0	1	7	0	0	22	6	3	1	1	137	49
12	198	102	96	4	1	0	1	0	0	1	1	0	0	0	0	1	3	2	0	0	19	7	3	1	1	141	57

200 HOME RUNS

The Blue Jays have had six seasons in which they hit at least 200 home runs…Toronto hit a Club record 257 home runs in 2010 which led the Majors.

Season	Home Runs
2010	257
2000	244
1998	221
1987	215
1999	212
2009	209

PITCHERS

				Consec			1-inn			One-game						Batters					Totals					vs	
Y	Tot	H	A	2	3	4	3	4	5	5	6	7	8	9	10	PH	LO	XN	IP	P	1	10	20	30	40	RHB	LHB
77	152	94	58	4	1	0	0	2	0	2	0	0	1	0	0	6	0	4	3	0	15	5	3	1	0	93	59
78	149	75	74	2	0	0	0	0	0	0	0	0	0	0	0	2	3	1	0	0	12	8	3	0	0	106	43
79	165	74	91	6	0	0	1	0	0	2	0	0	0	0	0	1	2	3	3	0	17	8	2	0	0	103	62
80	135	75	60	1	0	0	0	0	0	2	0	0	0	0	0	5	1	4	2	0	15	7	0	0	0	63	72
81	72	41	31	1	0	0	0	0	0	0	0	0	0	0	0	2	2	2	1	0	12	3	0	0	0	42	30
82	147	70	77	5	0	0	2	0	0	0	0	0	0	0	0	1	1	2	2	0	13	6	3	0	0	88	59
83	145	84	61	5	0	0	1	0	0	1	0	0	0	0	0	2	3	3	2	0	14	6	3	0	0	85	60
84	140	78	62	2	1	0	2	0	0	1	0	0	0	0	0	3	0	4	1	0	12	5	3	0	0	70	70
85	147	78	69	5	1	0	1	0	0	0	0	0	0	0	0	4	1	2	1	0	15	5	3	0	0	78	69
86	164	89	75	7	0	0	4	0	0	2	0	0	0	0	0	9	4	5	0	0	16	5	4	0	0	96	68
87	158	83	75	2	0	0	0	0	0	1	0	0	0	0	0	4	4	3	1	0	13	8	3	1	0	101	57
88	143	73	70	4	0	0	0	0	0	0	0	0	0	0	0	1	5	5	3	0	15	7	2	0	0	102	41
89	99	50	49	1	0	0	0	0	0	0	0	0	0	0	0	2	2	1	0	0	17	5	0	0	0	70	29
90	143	82	61	4	1	0	2	0	0	1	1	0	0	0	0	3	3	3	0	0	16	6	2	0	0	100	43
91	121	72	49	2	0	0	0	0	0	0	0	0	0	0	0	5	2	5	0	0	16	4	2	0	0	80	41
92	124	60	64	6	0	0	0	0	0	0	0	0	0	0	0	2	2	0	0	0	14	4	2	0	0	86	38
93	134	81	53	4	0	0	0	0	0	1	0	0	0	0	0	1	1	1	1	0	13	5	2	0	0	75	59
94	127	64	63	4	0	0	0	0	0	1	0	0	0	0	0	3	4	2	1	0	15	4	3	0	0	75	52
95	145	79	66	2	0	0	1	0	0	1	0	0	0	0	0	1	2	8	0	0	19	7	1	0	0	74	71
96	187	102	85	6	0	0	0	0	0	1	0	0	0	0	0	6	5	2	0	0	19	5	4	0	0	105	82
97	167	72	95	7	0	0	4	0	0	3	0	0	0	0	0	4	4	3	1	0	20	4	2	2	0	91	76
98	169	77	92	6	0	0	2	0	0	0	1	0	0	0	0	2	4	2	1	0	16	6	2	1	0	82	87
99	191	93	98	4	0	0	0	0	0	1	0	0	0	0	0	2	4	1	0	0	20	7	2	2	0	111	80
00	195	92	103	7	1	0	0	1	0	3	0	0	1	0	0	1	2	3	0	1	21	7	3	1	0	109	86
01	165	84	81	5	0	0	0	0	0	5	0	0	0	0	0	5	0	1	0	0	18	5	2	0	0	89	76
02	177	89	88	3	0	0	1	0	0	2	0	0	0	0	0	1	3	4	0	0	21	11	0	0	0	78	99
03	184	107	77	6	0	0	1	0	0	0	1	0	0	0	0	2	1	0	2	0	21	8	3	0	0	108	76
04	181	93	88	4	2	0	3	0	0	0	1	0	0	0	0	3	2	2	0	0	21	7	2	0	0	80	101
05	185	103	82	9	0	0	0	0	0	3	0	0	0	0	0	2	6	1	2	0	17	8	4	0	0	119	66
06	185	94	91	6	0	0	1	0	0	0	0	0	0	0	0	1	2	0	0	0	21	7	1	0	0	119	66
07	157	83	74	6	0	0	1	0	0	0	0	0	0	0	0	3	3	3	0	0	20	7	2	0	0	75	82
08	134	56	78	2	0	0	1	0	0	1	0	0	0	0	0	3	2	3	1	0	18	4	2	0	0	68	66
09	181	90	91	7	0	0	1	1	0	1	0	0	0	0	0	3	6	4	0	0	21	5	3	0	0	95	86
10	150	81	69	7	0	0	2	0	0	1	0	0	0	0	0	1	2	2	1	0	20	5	2	0	0	99	51
11	179	95	84	5	0	0	0	0	0	0	0	0	0	0	0	2	1	1	1	1	24	8	3	0	0	115	64
12	204	102	102	3	2	0	3	0	0	1	0	1	0	0	0	1	1	2	0	0	29	7	3	0	0	112	92

MULTIPLE 20-PLUS HOME RUN SEASONS

(4 OR MORE SEASONS)

9 – Carlos Delgado
1996 (25), 1997 (30), 1998 (38), 1999 (44), 2000 (41), 2001 (39), 2002 (33), 2003 (42), 2004 (32)

7 – Joe Carter
1991 (33), 1992 (34), 1993 (33), 1994 (27), 1995 (25), 1996 (30), 1997 (21)

7 – Vernon Wells
2002 (23), 2003 (33), 2004 (23), 2005 (28), 2006 (32), 2008 (20), 2010 (31)

6 – George Bell
1984 (26), 1985 (28), 1986 (31), 1987 (47), 1988 (24), 1990 (21)

4 – Jesse Barfield
1983 (27), 1985 (27), 1986 (40), 1987 (28)

4 – Fred McGriff
1987 (20), 1988 (34), 1989 (36), 1990 (35)

HOME RUN SUMMARY (1977-2012)

TOTAL	**5821** (not including Post-Season)
HOME	2911 (Exhibition Stadium-817, Rogers Centre-2194, Puerto Rico-2, Philadelphia-4)
AWAY	2808
3 in inning	31
4 in inning	1
5 in game	27
6 in game	7
7 in game	1 (Aug. 19, 1998 at Seattle)
8 in game	1 (Aug. 7, 2010 vs. Tampa Bay)
10 in game	1 (Sept. 14, 1987 vs Baltimore)
Bases Loaded	123
Inside-the-Park	28
Leadoff	105
Pinch-hit	83
Extra Innings	92
Off RH Pitcher	4209
Off LH Pitcher	1612
Post-Season	**30**
Home	16
Away	14

HOME RUNS AT ROGERS CENTRE

REGULAR SEASON

TEAM TOTALS	
Blue Jays	2194
Opponents	1990
Red Sox	225
Yankees	200
Orioles	181
Mariners	145
Rays	140
Athletics	133
Tigers	132
Indians	125
Rangers	118
White Sox	113
Angels	99
Royals	97
Twins	83
Brewers	61
Expos/Nationals	39
Mets	17
Phillies	18
Giants	10
Marlins	10
Cardinals	9
Pirates	8
Braves	7
Dodgers	6
Diamondbacks	3
Rockies	3
Cubs	3
Reds	3
Astros	2
TOTAL	**4184**

LEADING BLUE JAYS

1.	Carlos Delgado	175
2.	Vernon Wells	124
3.	Joe Carter	121
4.	Jose Bautista	71
5.	Shawn Green	63
6.	Adam Lind	59
7.	Ed Sprague	58
8.	Jose Cruz Jr.	57
9.	Aaron Hill	55
10.	Alex Rios	51

MOST ONE SEASON

	#	BLUE JAYS
Club	146	2010
Individual	33	Bautista, 2010

	#	OPPONENT
Club	102	1996 & 2012
Individual	6	Soriano A, 2002
	6	Giambi J, 2003

POST SEASON AT ROGERS CENTRE

BLUE JAYS

Carter	5
Borders	2
Gruber	2
Bell	1
Maldonado	1
Molitor	1
Moseby	1
Olerud	1
White	1
Winfield	1

BLUE JAYS FIVE OR MORE HOME RUN GAMES (40)

DATE	OPP.	NO.	DATE	OPP.	NO.
9/17/1983	MIN	5	4/04/2001	@TB	5
7/10/1985	@SEA	5	4/20/2001	@KC	5
5/22/1987	@SEA	5	5/06/2001	@SEA	5
8/30/1987	OAK	5	9/18/2001	BAL	5
9/12/1987	NYY	5	6/25/2002	@TB	5
9/14/1987	BAL	10	5/06/2003	@TEX	5
5/23/1988	@MIL	5	9/25/2003	TB	5
4/20/1990	KC	5	5/30/2006	BOS	5
5/06/1990	DET	5	7/23/2006	NYY	5
5/16/1993	@NYY	5	7/22/2009	CLE	5
5/31/1993	@CAL	5	9/15/2009	@NYY	5
7/05/1994	@MIN	6	9/29/2009	@BOS	6
7/06/1996	@DET	6	5/14/2010	TEX	5
7/13/1996	@MIL	5	5/21/2010	@ARI	6
8/19/1998	@SEA	7	7/08/2010	MIN	5
4/30/1999	@SEA	5	8/07/2010	TB	8
6/21/1999	KC	5	9/30/2010	@MIN	6
7/08/1999	@BAL	6	5/18/2012	NYM	5
8/10/1999	@MIN	5	6/19/2012	@MIL	6
5/05/2000	CLE	5			
8/27/2000	@TEX	5			

FOUR HOME RUNS IN ONE INNING

BLUE JAYS (1)

DATE	OPPONENT	INNING	HITTERS	PITCHER(S)
Aug. 17, 2001	vs TEX	6th	FRYE	MAHOMES
			CRUZ JR.	MAHOMES
			STEWART	MAHOMES
			DELAGDO	MAHOMES

OPPONENTS (4)

DATE	OPPONENT	INNING	HITTERS	PITCHER(S)
June 30, 1977	vs NYY	8th	C. JOHNSON	GARVIN
			PINELLA	GARVIN
			MUNSON	J. JOHNSON
			C. JOHNSON	J. JOHNSON
July 4, 1977	at BOS	8th	LYNN	HARTENSTEIN
			RICE	HARTENSTEIN
			YAZSTREMSKI	WILLIS
			SCOTT	WILLIS
May 3, 2000	at CWS	6th	JOHNSON	ESCOBAR
			VALENTIN	ESCOBAR
			THOMAS	FRASCATORE
			KONERKO	FRASCATORE
May 20, 2009	at BOS	5th	ORTIZ	CECIL
			BAY	CECIL
			LOWELL	CECIL
			VARITEK	CECIL

OF Jose Bautista receiving the 2011 Silver Slugger Award among outfielders prior to the Home Opener vs. Boston in 2012

THREE HOME RUNS IN ONE INNING

BLUE JAYS (31)

DATE	OPPONENT	INNING
6/17/1977	BAL	4
6/23/1982	@SEA	9
5/23/1983	DET	4
7/12/1983	@KC	4
4/26/1984	OAK	6
6/5/1984	@DET	4
7/15/1984	@OAK	4
8/30/1987	OAK	7
9/12/1987	NYY	8
9/14/1987	BAL	2
5/6/1990	DET	4
5/22/1990	OAK	6
5/17/1995	@TEX	2
4/30/1999	@SEA	3
6/21/1999	KC	3
10/2/1999	@CLE	3
4/18/2000	ANA	6
4/23/2000	NYY	6
8/11/2001	@ANA	2
8/21/2001	@MIN	6
6/25/2002	@TB	8
4/9/2005	BOS	3
4/21/2006	BOS	8
7/23/2006	NYY	3
5/1/2007	@CLE	1
5/20/2007	@PHI	8
6/24/2009	CIN	1
8/07/2010	TB	3
4/25/2011	@TEX	5
7/3/2011	PHI	8
6/19/2012	@MIL	6

OPPONENTS (34)

DATE	OPP	INN
5/8/1979	@MIN	7
5/5/1982	@CWS	7
6/22/1982	@SEA	4
8/2/1983	NYY	3
6/3/1984	NYY	4
9/18/1984	BOS	6
8/24/1985	@CWS	9
5/6/1986	OAK	3
5/10/1986	@SEA	4
5/14/1986	@OAK	7
6/4/1986	MIN	7
7/14/1990	@CAL	7
8/7/1990	DET	9
6/22/1995	MIL	2
4/25/1997	SEA	8
6/3/1997	@SEA	6
6/23/1997	BOS	7
9/15/1997	@SEA	5
7/14/1998	@BAL	7
9/25/1998	DET	3
6/11/2002	SF	5
8/8/2003	TEX	1
5/24/2004	ANA	3
8/25/2004	@BOS	4
8/28/2004	NYY	9
6/4/2006	@TB	3
4/24/2007	TEX	3
6/6/2008	BAL	8
9/27/2009	SEA	5
7/9/2010	BOS	4
8/24/2010	NYY	3
5/26/2012	@TEX	6
6/20/2012	@MIL	2
9/26/2012	@BAL	5

CONSECUTIVE GAMES WITH AT LEAST ONE HOME RUN

(MINIMUM 10 GAMES)

GAMES	DATE	HOME RUNS
23	May 31-June 25, 2000	44
19	Aug. 29-Sept. 18, 2010	34
15	July 6-23, 2000	28
14	April 18-May 4, 1996	28
14	Sept. 11-26, 2002	23
13	May 19-June 2, 1985	17
13	Sept. 1-15, 1999	22
13	May 6-19, 2003	24
13	July 3-10, 2010	28
13	June 22-July 5, 2011	21
12	June 2-14, 1987	25
12	April 11-23, 2000	29
12	May 1-13, 2000	29
12	July 25-Aug. 6, 2004	19
11	June 19-30, 1986	21
11	May 6-17, 1993	22
11	May 2-14, 1995	20
11	Sept. 16-27, 1998	19

GAMES	DATE	HOME RUNS
11	April 11-22, 1999	17
11	May 3-15, 2001	25
11	Aug. 5-7, 2001	24
11	July 14-26, 2002	19
11	Aug. 28-Sept. 9, 2007	18
11	Aug. 5-18, 2009	20
10	July 31-Aug. 11, 1984	12
10	May 29-June 8, 1993	22
10	June 9-19, 1996	14
10	Sept. 27-Oct. 6, 2001	12
10	April 9-20, 2002	17
10	May 29-June 8, 2002	15
10	Aug. 25-Sept. 5, 2003	12
10	April 6-17, 2004	10
10	April 4-14, 2007	13
10	July 25-Aug. 3, 2010	23

INDIVIDUAL RECORDS

YEARLY HOME RUN LEADERS

AT HOME

YEAR	PLAYER	HR
1977	Ron Fairly	10
1978	John Mayberry	12
1979	John Mayberry	13
1980	Otto Velez	12
1981	John Mayberry	10
1982	Jesse Barfield	11
	Willie Upshaw	11
1983	Jesse Barfield	22
1984	George Bell	12
1985	Jesse Barfield	15
1986	Jesse Barfield	16
1987	George Bell	19
1988	Fred McGriff	18
1989	Fred McGriff	18
1990	Kelly Gruber	23
1991	Joe Carter	23
1992	Joe Carter	21
1993	Joe Carter	21
1994	Joe Carter	18
1995	Joe Carter	13
1996	Ed Sprague	17
1997	Carlos Delgado	17
1998	Jose Canseco	25
1999	Shawn Green	20
2000	Carlos Delgado	30
2001	Jose Cruz Jr.	15
2002	Carlos Delgado	17
2003	Carlos Delgado	24
2004	Carlos Delgado	18
2005	Vernon Wells	28
2006	Troy Glaus	25
2007	Frank Thomas	19
2008	Vernon Wells	11
2009	Aaron Hill	21
2010	Jose Bautista	33
2011	Jose Bautista	20
2012	Edwin Encarnacion	23

ON THE ROAD

YEAR	PLAYER	HR
1977	3 players tied	9
1978	Rico Carty	10
	John Mayberry	10
1979	John Mayberry	8
	Otto Velez	8
1980	John Mayberry	20
1981	John Mayberry	7
1982	Willie Upshaw	10
1983	Cliff Johnson	12
1984	George Bell	14
1985	George Bell	18
1986	Jesse Barfield	24
1987	George Bell	28
1988	Fred McGriff	16
1989	Fred McGriff	18
1990	Fred McGriff	21
1991	Kelly Gruber	12
1992	Joe Carter	13
	Dave Winfield	13
1993	John Olerud	15
1994	Joe Carter	9
1995	Joe Carter	12
1996	Ed Sprague	19
1997	Carlos Delgado	13
1998	Jose Canseco	21
1999	Carlos Delgado	27
2000	3 players tied	16
2001	Carlos Delgado	26
2002	Carlos Delgado	16
2003	Vernon Wells	20
2004	Carlos Delgado	14
2005	Vernon Wells	14
2006	Troy Glaus	13
2007	Matt Stairs	14
2008	Vernon Wells	9
2009	Adam Lind	21
2010	Jose Bautista	21
2011	Jose Bautista	23
2012	Edwin Encarnacion	19

MOST HOME RUNS, ONE MONTH

MONTH	TEAM HIGH	INDIVIDUAL HIGH
March/April	43-2000	Carlos Delgado, 10—2001
April	43-2000	Carlos Delgado, 10—2001
May	54-2010	Jose Bautista, 12—2010
June	48-2000	George Bell, 11—1987/Joe Carter, 11—1991
July	44-2000	Shawn Green, 11—1999/Jose Bautista, 11--2010
August	45-2001	Carlos Delgado, 12—1999/Jose Cruz Jr., 12—2001/Jose Bautista, 12—2010
September	52-2010	Carlos Delgado, 11--1998/Jose Bautista, 11—2010
Sept./Oct.	56-2010	Carlos Delgado, 11—1998/Jose Bautista, 11--2010

HOME RUN TRIOS, ONE SEASON

TOTAL	YEAR	PLAYERS
119	1998	Canseco - 46, Delgado - 38, Green - 35
114	2000	Batista - 41, Delgado - 41, Fullmer - 32
112	1999	Delgado - 44, Green - 42, Batista - 26
111	2010	Bautista - 54, Wells - 31, Hill - 26
101	1987	Bell - 47, Barfield - 28, Moseby - 26
100	2001	Delgado - 39, Cruz Jr. - 34, Mondesi - 27
95	2003	Delgado - 42, Wells - 33, Phelps - 20
92	2012	Encarnacion - 42, Bautista - 27, Rasmus - 23
92	2011	Bautista - 43, Lind - 26, Arencibia - 23
92	1986	Barfield - 40, Bell - 31, Moseby - 21
92	2006	Glaus - 38, Wells - 32, Overbay - 22

HOME RUN DUOS, ONE SEASON

TOTAL	YEAR	PLAYERS
86	1999	Delgado-44, Green-42
85	2010	Bautista-54, Wells-31
84	1998	Canseco-46, Delgado-38
82	2000	Batista-41, Delgado-41
75	1987	Bell-47, Barfield-28
75	2003	Delgado-42, Wells-33
73	2001	Delgado-39, Cruz Jr.-34
71	1986	Barfield-40, Bell-31
71	2009	Hill-36, Lind-35
70	2006	Glaus-38, Wells-32

MOST PLAYERS 10 OR MORE HOME RUNS

9—	1983-	Barfield, Bonnell, Johnson, Martinez, Moseby, Mulliniks, Orta, Upshaw, Whitt
	1987-	Barfield, Bell, Fielder, Gruber, McGriff, Moseby, Mulliniks, Upshaw, Whitt
	2006-	Glaus, Hillenbrand, Hinske, Johnson, Molina, Overbay, Rios, Wells, Zaun
	2007-	Thomas, Rios, Glaus, Wells, Stairs, Hill, Lind, Zaun, Overbay
	2009-	Hill, Lind, Barajas, Overbay, Wells, Rios, Bautista, Scutaro, Ruiz
	2010-	Bautista, Wells, Hill, Lind, Encarnacion, Buck, Overbay, Gonzalez, Snider
8—	1996-	Brumfield, Carter, Delgado, Gonzalez, Green, O'Brien, Olerud, Sprague
	1998-	Canseco, Cruz Jr., Delgado, Gonzalez, Green, Sprague, Stanley, Stewart
	2000-	Batista, Cruz Jr., Delgado, Fletcher, Fullmer, Gonzalez, Mondesi, Stewart
	2001-	Batista, Cruz Jr., Delgado, Fletcher, Fullmer, Gonzalez, Stewart, Mondesi
	2002-	Cruz Jr., Delgado, Hinske, Mondesi, Phelps, Stewart, Wells, Woodward
7—	Done 10x	1984, 1985, 1986, 1988, 1990, 1992, 1995, 1999, 2003, 2005

FOUR HOME RUN GAMES

BLUE JAYS (1)

PLAYER	DATE	H/A	OPPONENT	PITCHERS
CARLOS DELGADO	Sept. 25, 2003	H	Tampa Bay	Jorge Sosa (2), Joe Kennedy, Lance Carter

OPPONENTS (0)

No opponent has ever hit four home runs in a game vs. the Blue Jays

THREE HOME RUN GAMES

BLUE JAYS (17)

PLAYER	DATE	H/A	OPPONENT	PITCHERS
Otto Velez	May 4, 1980	H	Cleveland (G#1)	Dan Spillner, Wayne Garland, Sid Monge
Ernie Whitt	Sept. 14, 1987	H	Baltimore	Ken Dixon (2), Tony Arnold
George Bell	April 4, 1988	A	Kansas City	Bret Saberhagen
Joe Carter	Aug. 23, 1993	H	Cleveland	Albie Lopez (2), Jose Hernandez
Darnell Coles	July 5, 1994	A	Minnesota	Pat Mahomes, Larry Casian (2)
Carlos Delgado	Aug. 4, 1998	A	Texas	Stottlemyre, Gunderson, Patterson
Carlos Delgado	Aug. 6, 1999	A	Texas	Helling (2), Zimmerman
Darrin Fletcher	Aug. 27, 2000	A	Texas	Helling (3)
Carlos Delgado	April 4, 2001	A	Tampa Bay	Wilson, Creek, Hill
Carlos Delgado	April 20, 2001	A	Kansas City	Suzuki, Cogan, Hernandez
Chris Woodward	Aug. 7, 2002	H	Seattle	Piniero (2), Sasaki
Vernon Wells	May 30, 2006	H	Boston	Beckett (2), Riske
Frank Thomas	Sept. 17, 2007	H	Boston	Wakefield (2), Snyder
Adam Lind	Sept. 29, 2009	A	Boston	Buchholz (2), Saito
John Buck	April 29, 2010	H	Oakland	Duchscherer, Blevins, Breslow
Edwin Encarnacion	May 21, 2010	A	Arizona	Haren (2), Gutierrez
Jose Bautista	May 15, 2011	A	Minnesota	Duensing, Slowey (2)

OPPONENTS (16)

PLAYER	DATE	H/A	OPPONENT	PITCHERS
John Mayberry	June 1, 1977	H	Kansas City	Johnson, Willis, Bruno
Cliff Johnson	June 30, 1977	H	New York (AL)	Jerry Garvin
Eddie Murray	Sept. 14, 1980	H	Baltimore	Jackson Todd (2),Barlow
Jim Rice	Aug. 29, 1983 (2nd g)	H	Boston	Acker (2), Moffitt
Jose Canseco	July 3, 1988	H	Oakland	Stottlemyre (2), Henke
Cecil Fielder	May 6, 1990	H	Detroit	Key (2), Wells
Tom Brunansky	Sept. 29, 1990	A	Boston	Stottlemyre, Ward, Leucken
Cecil Fielder	April 16, 1996	H	Detroit	Hanson, Carrara, Risley
Ken Griffey, Jr.	April 25, 1997	H	Seattle	Clemens (2), Timlin
Manny Ramirez	Sept. 15, 1998	A	Cleveland	Stieb (2), Quantrill
Alex Rodriguez	April 16, 2000	H	Seattle	Carpenter (2), Borbon
Alex Rodriguez	Aug. 17, 2002	A	Texas	Parris (2), Thurman
Tony Clark	Aug. 28, 2004	H	New York (AL)	Lilly, Frasor, Ligtenberg
Jayson Werth	May 16, 2008	A	Philadelphia	Purcey (2), Listch
Jose Lopez	Sept. 22, 2010	H	Seattle	Drabek, Tallet, Camp
Chris Davis	Aug. 24, 2012	A	Baltimore	Villabueva (2), Delabar

CONSECUTIVE GAME HOME RUNS

In 2001 **JOSE CRUZ Jr.** set a franchise record, homering in **SIX CONSECUTIVE GAMES**, from Sept. 29 - Oct. 5 (G1), six total home runs... Below is a list of players who have homered in four consecutive games.

FOUR STRAIGHT GAMES

George Bell — Aug. 23-26, 1985 (4 home runs)
Joe Carter — June 20-23, 1991 (5 home runs)
— June 14-18, 1996 (4 home runs)
Carlos Delgado — June 3, 5-7, 1997 (4 home runs)
— Aug. 8-11, 2001 (5 home runs)
Shawn Green — April 5, 7-9, 2001 (4 home runs)
Jose Canseco — Sept. 4-7, 2001 (4 home runs)
Vernon Wells — June 19-22, 2003 (5 home runs)
Jose Bautista — Sept. 28-Oct. 2, 2009 (4 home runs)
Edwin Encarnacion — Sept. 30-Oct. 3, 2010 (5 home runs)
Adam Lind — June 14-17, 2011 (4 home runs)
Edwin Encarnacion — April 27-30, 2012 (4 home runs)

MOST HOME RUNS IN A SEASON SERIES

(EIGHT OR MORE)

YEAR	NAME	OPPONENT	HR
1980	John Mayberry	New York (A)	8
2000	Tony Batista	Baltimore	9
2001	Jose Cruz Jr.	New York (A)	9
2001	Jose Bautista	Boston	8
2001	Vernon Wells	Texas	8
2002	Carlos Delgado	Tampa Bay	8
2003	Carlos Delgado	Tampa Bay	8
2006	Vernon Wells	Boston	8
2010	Jose Bautista	Boston	8
2010	Jose Bautista	Baltimore	9
2010	Vernon Wells	Texas	8

ROGERS CENTRE 500 LEVEL HOME RUNS

Player	Date	Visiting Team	Pitcher	
Jose Canseco	October 7, 1989*	Oakland	Mike Flanagan	480 (LF)
Mark McGwire	July 25, 1996	Oakland	Huck Flener	488 (LF)
Joe Carter	July 27, 1996	Oakland	John Wasdin	483 (LF)
Carlos Delgado	July 19, 1998	New York (A)	Andy Pettitte	467 (RF)
Jose Canseco	Sept. 5, 1998	Boston	Bret Saberhagen	451 (LF)
Jose Canseco	April 12, 1999	Tampa Bay	Graeme Lloyd	459 (LF)
Shawn Green	April 22, 1999	Anaheim	Tim Belcher	449 (RF)
Manny Ramirez	June 3, 2001	Boston	Chris Carpenter	491 (LF)
Raul Mondesi	April 17, 2002	Boston	Darren Oliver	456 (LF)
Josh Phelps	August 29, 2002	New York (A)	Roger Clemens	455 (LF)
Josh Phelps	July 7, 2004	Seattle	Ruben Mateo	435 (LF)
Gary Sheffield	July 28, 2004	New York (A)	Miguel Batista	440 (LF)
Vernon Wells	September 16, 2004	Baltimore	Rodrigo Lopez	445 (LF)
Jayson Werth	June 27, 2009	Philadelphia	Brad Mills	448 (LF)
Shelly Duncan	May 31, 2011	Cleveland	Jo-Jo Reyes	446 (LF)

* Game 4 of the ALCS

LEAD OFF HOME RUNS

BLUE JAYS (105)

PLAYER	TIMES	LAST DATE	LAST TEAM
Devon White	22	6/20/1995	@MIL
Shannon Stewart	15	11/7/2003	NYY
Alex Rios	9	5/15/2007	BAL
Damaso Garcia	7	5/25/1986	@CLE
Jose Cruz Jr.	7	4/9/2001	NYY
Reed Johnson	7	7/23/2007	MIN
Lloyd Mosbey	5	7/9/1989	@MIL
Tony Fernandez	5	5/5/1990	DET
Frank Menechino	4	5/8/2004	CLE
Fred Lewis	4	7/17/2010	@ BAL
Marco Scutaro	3	4/30/2009	@KC
Rick Bosetti	2	9/21/1978	NYY
Frank Catalanotto	2	7/9/2003	DET
Brett Lawrie	2	7/22/2012	@BOS
Rajai Davis	1	7/30/2012	SEA
Yunel Escobar	1	6/15/2011	BAL
Russ Adams	1	9/22/2004	@NYY
Brad Wilkerson	1	5/20/2008	LAA
Jose Bautista	1	9/29/2009	@BOS
Travis Snider	1	9/29/2010	NYY
Bob Bailor	1	4/27/1977	@CLE
Alfredo Griffin	1	8/29/1979	OAK
Rickey Henderson	1	1/9/1993	@OAK
Alex Gonzalez	1	9/19/1995	@NYY
Jacob Brumfield	1	6/13/1996	@CAL

OPPONENTS (92)

	Date	Batter	Tm	Pitcher	Cty
1	April 14/78	Ron LeFlore	DET	Jerry Garvin	TOR
2	May 30/78	Rick Burleson	BOS	Jerry Garvin	BOS
3	Aug. 19/78	Willie Norwood	MIN	Jerry Garvin	MIN
4	Aug. 3/79	Jim Morrison	CWS	Balor Moore	TOR
5	Aug. 12/79	Jim Morrison	CWS	Tom Underwood	CWS
6	May 23/80	Willie Randolph	NYA	Paul Mirabella	TOR
7	May 10/81	Dwight Evans	BOS	Jerry Garvin	TOR
8	Sept. 19/81	Brian Downing	CAL	Jim Clancy	TOR
9	May 1/82	Cesar Geronimo	KC	Mark Bomback	KC
10	Aug. 3/83	Don Mattingly	NYA	Jim Clancy	TOR
11	Aug. 9/83	Rickey Henderson	OAK	Jim Clancy	TOR
12	Sept. 16/83	Tim Teufel	MIN	Jim Gott	MIN
13	July 2/85	Rickey Henderson	NYA	Jimmy Key	TOR
14	July 13/86	Tony Phillips	OAK	John Cerutti	TOR
15	July 17/86	Rick Burleson	CAL	Jimmy Key	CAL
16	July 19/86	Ruppert Jones	CAL	Dave Stieb	CAL
17	Sept. 30/86	Rickey Henderson	NYA	Dave Stieb	NYA
18	May 28/87	Luis Polonia	OAK	Jim Clancy	TOR
19	May 29/87	Ruppert Jones	CAL	Dave Stieb	TOR
20	June 17/87	Lou Whitaker	DET	Jim Clancy	TOR
21	Sept. 19/87	Rickey Henderson	NYA	Mike Flanagan	NYA
22	April 8/88	Dan Gladden	MIN	Dave Stieb	MIN
23	May 15/88	Daryl Boston	CWS	Jim Clancy	CWS
24	June 22/88	Pete Stanicek	BAL	John Cerutti	TOR
25	June 23/88	Ken Gerhart	BAL	Jim Clancy	TOR
26	Sept. 9/88	Joe Orsulak	BAL	Jim Clancy	BAL
27	Aug. 17/89	Phil Bradley	BAL	John Cerutti	BAL
28	Sept. 29/89	Phil Bradley	BAL	Todd Stottlemyre	TOR
29	April 28/90	Sammy Sosa	CWS	Mike Flanagan	CWS
30	June 28/90	Wade Boggs	BOS	Todd Stottlemyre	BOS
31	Sept. 26/90	Paul Molitor	MIL	David Wells	MIL
32	April 19/91	Paul Molitor	MIL	Dave Stieb	MIL
33	May 30/91	Rickey Henderson	OAK	Todd Stottlemyre	TOR
34	May 4/92	Rickey Henderson	OAK	Todd Stottlemyre	OAK
35	July 22/92	Chad Curtis	CAL	Jimmy Key	CAL
36	Aug. 7/93	Pat Listach	MIL	Todd Stottlemyre	TOR
37	April 23/94	Chuck Knoblauch	MIN	Al Leiter	TOR
38	April 24/94	Alex Cole	MIN	Juan Guzman	TOR
39	June 4/94	Luis Sojo	SEA	Todd Stottlemyre	SEA
40	Aug. 7/94	Tony Phillips	DET	Dave Stewart	TOR
41	June 27/95	Lee Tinsley	BOS	Danny Darwin	BOS
42	Sept. 9/95	Chad Curtis	DET	Juan Guzman	TOR
43	May 28/96	Tony Phillips	CWS	Frank Viola	TOR
44	June 28/96	Fernando Vina	MIL	Juan Guzman	TOR
45	Aug. 8/96	Darren Bragg	BOS	Woody Williams	BOS
46	Sept. 26/96	Brady Anderson	BAL	Woody Williams	TOR
47	Sept. 29/96	Brady Anderson	BAL	Pat Hentgen	TOR
48	June 25/97	Nomar Garciaparra	BOS	Pat Hentgen	TOR
49	July 10/97	Nomar Garciaparra	BOS	Juan Guzman	BOS
50	July 15/97	Brady Anderson	BAL	Juan Guzman	BAL
51	Sept. 27/97	Nomar Garciaparra	BOS	Pat Hentgen	TOR
52	June 13/98	Jesus Tavarez	BAL	Chris Carpenter	TOR
53	June 15/98	Quinton McCracken	TBA	Woody Williams	TBA
54	June 19/98	Brady Anderson	BAL	Roger Clemens	BAL
55	July 15/98	Ray Durham	CWS	Pat Hentgen	CWS
56	April 16/99	Brady Anderson	BAL	Pat Hentgen	TOR
57	May 7/99	Tom Goodwin	TEX	Pat Hentgen	TOR
58	Aug. 4/99	Chuck Knoblauch	NYA	Kelvim Escobar	NYA
59	Sept. 11/99	Luis Polonia	DET	Chris Carpenter	DET
60	Sept. 28/00	Brady Anderson	BAL	Chris Carpenter	BAL
61	April 21/02	Alfonso Soriano	NYY	Chris Carpenter	NY
62	June 16/02	Brad Wilkerson	MON	Steve Parris	MON
63	Aug. 5/02	Melvin Mora	BAL	Steve Parris	TOR
64	June 7/03	Adam Dunn	CIN	Roy Halladay	CIN
65	June 6/04	Eric Byrnes	OAK	Jason Kershner	OAK
66	Aug. 17/04	Johnny Damon	BOS	Ted Lilly	BOS
67	April 23/05	Brian Roberts	BAL	Dave Bush	TOR
68	June 5/05	Marco Scutaro	OAK	Chad Gaudin	OAK
69	June 10/05	Willie Tavarez	HOU	Ted Lilly	HOU
70	July 29/05	Gary Matthews	TEX	Scott Downs	TOR
71	Aug. 30/05	Brian Roberts	BAL	Dave Bush	BAL
72	Sept. 23/05	Derek Jeter	NYY	Ted Lilly	NYY
73	June 25/06	Jose Reyes	NYM	Josh Towers	TOR
74	Sept. 23/06	Dustin Pedroia	BOS	A.J. Burnett	TOR
75	April 7/07	Carl Crawford	TB	Tomo Ohka	TB
76	May 30/07	Johnny Damon	NYY	Jesse Litsch	TOR
77	Aug. 5/07	Frank Catalanotto	TEX	Dustin McGowan	TOR
78	May 10/08	Grady Sizemore	CLE	Dustin McGowan	CLE
79	July 12/08	Derek Jeter	NYY	Jesse Listch	TOR
80	May 24/09	Kelly Johnson	ATL	Scott Richmond	ATL
81	June 30/09	B.J. Upton	TB	Scott Richmond	TOR
82	Aug. 10/09	Derek Jeter	NYY	Mark Rzepczynski	TOR
83	Sept. 1/09	Ian Kinsler	TEX	Mark Rzepczynski	TEX
84	Sept. 11/09	Curtis Granderson	DET	Scott Richmond	DET
85	Sept. 14/09	Ryan Raburn	DET	David Purcey	DET
86	Sept. 8/10	Ian Kinsler	TEX	Mark Rzepczynski	TOR
87	Sept. 13/10	Brian Roberts	BAL	Mark Rzepczynski	BAL
88	July 6/11	Jacoby Ellsbury	BOS	Ricky Romero	BOS
89	July 28/11	J.J. Hardy	BAL	Carlos Villanueva	TOR
90	Aug. 28/11	Desmond Jennings	TB	Brandon Morrow	TOR
91	April 29/12	Chone Figgins	SEA	Henderson Alvarez	TOR
92	July 31/12	Dustin Ackley	SEA	Aaron Laffey	TOR

SWITCH HIT HOME RUNS — BLUE JAYS (1 GAME)

	Date	Batter	Pitcher	OPP	Cty	In	On
1	May 10/91	Roberto Alomar	Bobby Thigpen	CWS	TOR	9	0
		Roberto Alomar	Scott Radinsky	CWS	TOR	11	0
2	June 1/92	Devon White	John Smiley	MIN	MIN	1	0
		Devon White	Carl Willis	MIN	MIN	10	0
3	May 3/95	Roberto Alomar	Jim Abbott	CHA	TOR	3	0
		Roberto Alomar	Roberto Hernandez	CHA	TOR	9	0
4	Aug. 24/97	Jose Cruz Jr.	Ricky Bones	KCA	KCA	1	0
		Jose Cruz Jr.	Larry Casian	KCA	KCA	13	1
5	Sept. 13/06	Gregg Zaun	Cha Seung Baek	SEA	SEA	2	0
		Gregg Zaun	Jose Jiminez	SEA	SEA	4	3

PINCH HIT HOME RUNS

BLUE JAYS (83)

Player	Number	Last Date	Last Team
Jesse Barfield	4	7/3/1988	OAK
Ernie Whitt	4	8/1/1984	KC
Willie Greene	3	9/5/1999	@KC
Cliff Johnson	3	6/13/1986	DET
Otto Velez	3	7/4/1979	@DET
Adam Lind	2	5/21/2010	@ARI
Rod Barajas	2	8/26/2009	TB
Alex Rios	2	4/14/2008	@BAL
Matt Stairs	2	8/29/2007	@OAK
Eric Hinske	2	8/19/2005	@DET
Chris Gomez	2	9/11/2004	@TEX
Jose Cruz Jr	2	9/15/2002	TB
Kelly Gruber	2	6/13/1989	@MIL
Fred McGriff	2	5/23/1988	@MIL
Buck Martinez	2	6/14/1986	DET
Jeff Burroughs	2	9/25/1985	BOS
Rance Mulliniks	2	6/12/1985	@NYY
Willie Aikens	2	4/27/1985	@TEX
Doug Ault	2	8/7/1980	@CLE
Rico Carty	2	9/22/1979	NYY
Al Woods	2	4/21/1977	@NYY
Yan Gomes	1	6/11/2012	WSH
Lyle Overbay	1	5/18/2008	@PHI
Gregg Zaun	1	4/10/2007	KC
Shea Hillenbrand	1	6/9/2006	DET
Reed Johnson	1	7/1/2005	@BOS
Orlando Hudson	1	5/30/2005	@SEA
Russ Adams	1	9/29/2004	@BAL
Darrin Fletcher	1	6/23/2002	@ARI
Tom Wilson	1	5/24/2002	CLE
Dave Burg	1	4/5/2002	MIN
Tony Fernandez	1	9/4/2001	NYY
Jacob Brumfield	1	6/8/1999	@NYM
Juan Samuel	1	6/22/1998	MON
Robert Perez	1	6/13/1997	@PHI
John Olerud	1	6/1/1996	KC
Charlie O'Brien	1	5/12/1996	BOS
Carlos Delgado	1	5/23/1995	KC
Michael Huff	1	5/30/1994	OAK
Darnell Coles	1	5/21/1993	MIN
Pat Borders	1	9/20/1991	@OAK
Lee Mazzilli	1	9/9/1989	@CLE
Nelson Liriano	1	5/5/1989	CAL
Cecil Fielder	1	9/4/1987	SEA
Juan Beniquez	1	7/24/1987	MIN
Garth Iorg	1	6/15/1986	DET
Rick Leach	1	6/14/1986	DET
George Bell	1	8/14/1984	@CLE
Mickey Klutts	1	4/29/1983	CWS
Willie Upshaw	1	4/24/1981	@NYY
Bob Davis	1	6/14/1980	@CLE
Roy Howell	1	5/6/1980	@CAL
Sam Ewing	1	7/1/1978	CLE
John Mayberry	1	6/26/1978	BAL
Doug Rader	1	8/24/1977	@SEA

PH HOME RUN LEADERS

The Blue Jays franchise has connected 83 times for pinch-hit home runs during regular season games... Jesse Barfield on April 24, 1982 vs Boston at Exhibition Stadium hit the Blue Jays first pinch-slam... Tony Fernandez hit the second pinch-slam in franchise history on September 4, 2001 vs the Yankees at SkyDome... Alvis Woods in the Blue Jays first ever game, April 7, 1977 vs the Chicago White Sox hit the first pitch of his first Major League career at bat for the Blue Jays first pinch-hit home run... Ed Sprague has the only pinch-hit home run in post-season for the Blue Jays which came on October 18, 1992, Game #2 of the World Series vs Atlanta... On June 30, 1999 vs the Baltimore Orioles Willie Greene became the 16th player in AL history to hit home runs in consecutive pinch-hit at bats.

CAREER	NO
Jesse Barfield	4
Ernie Whitt	4
Otto Velez	3
Cliff Johnson	3
Willie Greene	3

SEASON	NO	YEAR
Willie Greene	3	1999
Alvis Woods	2	1977
Otto Velez	2	1979
Rico Carty	2	1979
Ernie Whitt	2	1982
Jeff Burroughs	2	1985
Chris Gomez	2	2004
Matt Stairs	2	2007
Rod Barajas	2	2009

CLUB	SEASON
6	1984
5	1977
5	1983

OPPONENTS (99)

	Date	Batter	Tm	Pitcher	Cty	In	On
1	May 25/77	Rich McKinney	OAK	Jerry Garvin	TOR	8	0
2	June 24/77	Andres Mora	BAL	Dave Lemanczyk	BAL	7	1
3	July 4/77	Bernie Carbo	BOS	Chuck Hartenstein	BOS	7	0
4	July 9/77	Andre Thornton	CLE	Jerry Garvin	CLE	9	1
5	July 17/77	Milt May	DET	Dave Lemanczyk	TOR	11	0
6	Aug. 22/77	Willie Crawford	OAK	Dave Lemanczyk	OAK	7	2
7	May 13/78	Leon Roberts	SEA	Balor Moore	TOR	4	0
8	May 26/78	Jim Spencer	NYA	Tom Murphy	NYA	7	3
9	July 27/79	John Wockenfuss	DET	Balor Moore	TOR	6	0
10	May 4/80	Cliff Johnson	CLE	Jerry Garvin	TOR	9	0
11	May 23/80	Joe Lefebvre	NYA	Dave Lemanczyk	TOR	6	0
12	June 1/80	Graig Nettles	NYA	Tom Buskey	NYA	6	1
13	Aug. 28/80	Jose Morales	MIN	Jerry Garvin	TOR	8	2
14	Sept. 23/80	John Wockenfuss	DET	Mike Willis	DET	8	2
15	April 12/81	Lynn Jones	DET	Luis Leal	DET	8	1
16	Aug. 23/81	Bob Molinaro	CWS	Roy Lee Jackson	TOR	9	1
17	May 29/82	Benny Ayala	BAL	Jerry Garvin	BAL	7	3
18	May 20/83	Jim Dwyer	BAL	Randy Moffitt	TOR	9	0
19	June 10/83	Reggie Jackson	CAL	Luis Leal	CAL	8	2
20	April 18/84	Joe Nolan	BAL	Dave Stieb	TOR	8	0
21	Aug. 19/84	Rudy Law	CWS	Jim Gott	CWS	7	1
22	Aug. 29/84	Greg Luzinski	CWS	Bryan Clark	TOR	8	0
23	April 19/85	Larry Sheets	BAL	Bill Caudill	TOR	9	0
24	May 15/85	Jerry Narron	CAL	Bill Caudill	TOR	9	3
25	June 4/85	Mark Salas	MIN	Jim Clancy	TOR	8	0
26	Oct. 6/85	Mike Pagliarulo	NYA	Jim Acker	TOR	5	1
27	June 1/86	Greg Walker	CWS	Jim Acker	TOR	8	1
28	June 20/86	Ron Hassey	NYA	Jim Acker	TOR	8	2
29	July 6/86	Bobby Grich	CAL	Stan Clarke	TOR	9	2
30	July 17/86	Ruppert Jones	CAL	Mark Eichhorn	CAL	7	1
31	July 30/86	Jim Sundberg	KCA	John Cerutti	KCA	9	0
32	Aug. 4/86	John Shelby	BAL	Stan Clarke	TOR	4	0
33	Aug. 21/86	Carlton Fisk	CWS	Jimmy Key	TOR	7	2
34	Sept. 17/86	Larry Herndon	DET	Jeff Musselman	TOR	7	2
35	Sept. 23/86	Darrell Evans	DET	Mark Eichhorn	DET	7	0
36	May 8/87	Gene Petralli	TEX	Jim Clancy	TEX	7	2
37	June 14/87	Jim Dwyer	BAL	Tom Henke	BAL	8	2
38	Aug. 6/87	Casey Parsons	CLE	Mark Eichhorn	CLE	6	3
39	Sept. 2/87	George Hendrick	CAL	Tom Henke	TOR	8	1
40	April 26/88	Mark McGwire	OAK	David Wells	TOR	8	2
41	July 2/89	Danny Heep	BOS	Tom Henke	TOR	11	2
42	Aug. 5/89	Ken Phelps	NYA	Duane Ward	TOR	8	1
43	June 21/90	Matt Nokes	NYA	Duane Ward	TOR	8	2
44	Sept. 14/90	Sam Horn	BAL	Duane Ward	TOR	6	3
45	Oct. 1/90	Sam Horn	BAL	Duane Ward	BAL	8	0
46	April 17/91	Lou Whitaker	DET	Duane Ward	DET	9	2
47	June 8/91	Sam Horn	BAL	Tom Henke	BAL	9	1
48	June 16/91	Joe Orsulak	BAL	Duane Ward	TOR	7	3
49	July 21/91	Kevin Reimer	TEX	Mike Timlin	TEX	7	1
50	Aug. 8/91	Mark Salas	DET	Tom Henke	TOR	14	2
51	June 28/92	Paul Sorrento	CLE	Duane Ward	CLE	8	1
52	Sept. 15/92	Wayne Kirby	CLE	Duane Ward	TOR	8	0
53	June 5/93	Dale Sveum	OAK	Mark Eichhorn	TOR	8	0
54	April 6/94	Darrin Jackson	CWS	Paul Spoljaric	TOR	7	0
55	May 21/94	Wayne Kirby	CLE	Mike Timlin	TOR	9	0
56	Aug. 9/94	Ruben Amaro	CLE	Todd Stottlemyre	TOR	6	0
57	June 30/95	Chris Hoiles	BAL	Tony Castillo	TOR	8	0
58	April 10/96	Mike Aldrete	CAL	Juan Guzman	TOR	8	0
59	May 26/96	Ron Coomer	MIN	Brian Bohanon	TOR	9	1
60	May 28/96	Robin Ventura	CWS	Jeff Ware	TOR	7	0
61	July 1/96	Mark Smith	BAL	Paul Spoljaric	TOR	8	0
62	July 26/96	Mark McGwire	OAK	Paul Quantrill	TOR	8	0
63	Sept. 16/96	Ruben Rivera	NYA	Huck Flener	TOR	7	0
64	April 1/97	Norberto Martin	CWS	Mike Timlin	TOR	9	0
65	April 16/97	Mark McGwire	OAK	Tim Crabtree	TOR	8	0
66	April 25/97	Russ Davis	SEA	Dan Plesac	TOR	8	1
67	Aug. 4/97	Greg Colbrunn	MIN	Omar Daal	MIN	5	3
68	Sept. 19/98	Bubba Trammell	TBA	Carlos Almanzar	TBA	8	2
69	Sept. 27/98	Bobby Higginson	DET	Roy Halladay	TOR	9	0
70	May 15/99	Mike Stanley	BOS	Dan Plesac	TOR	7	1
71	May 29/99	Shane Spencer	NYA	Dan Plesac	TOR	9	0
72	July 6/00	Richie Sexson	CLE	John Frascatore	CLE	7	0
73	April 27/01	Shawn Wooten	ANA	Pedro Borbon	TOR	8	1
74	May 5/01	Dan Wilson	SEA	Pedro Borbon	SEA	7	0
75	Aug. 12/01	Ben Molina	ANA	Dan Plesac	ANA	8	0
76	Aug. 14/01	Olmedo Saenz	OAK	Pedro Borbon	TOR	7	1
77	Sept. 20/01	Tony Batista	BAL	Pedro Borbon	TOR	7	2
78	June 15/02	Andres Galarraga	MON	Scott Cassidy	MON	7	0
79	May 18/03	Carlos Beltran	KC	Cliff Politte	KC	9	0
80	June 12/03	Matt Stairs	PIT	Cliff Politte	TOR	9	0
81	May 19/04	Matt Lecroy	MIN	Terry Adams	TOR	9	3
82	Aug. 28/04	Ruben Sierra	NYY	Kerry Ligtenberg	TOR	9	3
83	Aug. 29/04	Jorge Poscala	NYY	Jason Frasor	TOR	9	0
84	Aug. 24/05	Bernie Williams	NYY	Vinnie Chulk	NYY	9	2
85	July 20/05	Scott Spiezio	SEA	Chad Gaudin	TOR	8	0
86	April 5/06	Luis Rodriguez	MIN	Justin Speier	TOR	9	1
87	June 8/07	Olmedo Saenz	LAD	Jeremy Accardo	LAD	10	1
88	Aug. 4/07	Brad Wilkerson	TEX	Brandon League	TOR	9	1
89	Sept. 8/07	B.J. Upton	TB	Jeremy Accardo	TB	9	1
90	May 13/08	Jason Kubel	MIN	Armando Benitez	MIN	8	0
91	June 5/08	Jason Giambi	NYY	B.J. Ryan	NYY	9	1
92	Sept. 6/08	Rocco Baldelli	TB	B.J. Ryan	TOR	9	1
93	June 18/09	Greg Dobbs	PHI	Brandon League	PHI	8	0
94	Aug. 16/09	Gregg Zaun	TB	Brandon League	TB	8	3
95	Sept. 14/09	Aubrey Huff	DET	Jason Frasor	DET	9	2
96	June 22/10	Colby Rasmus	STL	Jason Frasor	TOR	8	1
97	June 22/11	Brooks Conrad	ATL	Jon Rauch	ATL	7	0
98	Aug. 20/11	Josh Willingham	OAK	Rommie Lewis	OAK	8	1
99	June 11/12	Rick Ankiel	WSH	Francisco Cordero	TOR	8	0

INSIDE-THE-PARK HOME RUNS

BLUE JAYS (28)

HR#	DATE	D/N	BATTER	POS	BAT ORD	PITCHER	OPP	H/A	IN	ON	OUT
1	Aug. 21/77	D	Doug Rader	DH	5	Frank Tanana	CAL	A	5	0	2
2	July 9/79	N	Al Woods	LF	6	Lary Sorensen	MIL	H	2	0	0
3	Aug. 28/79	D	Alfredo Griffin	SS	1	Rick Langford	OAK	H	5	1	2
4	Sept. 17/80	N	Roy Howell	3B	3	Tim Lollar	NYY	A	10	1	2
5	April 25/81	D	Lloyd Moseby	CF	1	Bill Castro	NYY	A	9	1	2
6	June 7/82	N	Willie Upshaw	1B	3	John Denny	CLE	H	3	1	2
7	April 14/83	D	Willie Upshaw	1B	7	Jerry Augustine	MIL	H	2	0	2
8	May 25/83	N	Jorge Orta	DH	4	Dan Petry	DET	H	4	0	0
9	May 30/83	N	Lloyd Moseby	CF	7	Dan Petry	DET	A	9	1	2
10	Sept. 14/83	N	Barry Bonnell	CF	5	Matt Young	SEA	A	2	0	0
11	June 6/84	N	George Bell	RF	6	Aurelio Lopez	DET	A	8	0	1
12	Aug. 10/84	N	Tony Fernandez	SS	9	Dennis Martinez	BAL	H	3	0	2
13	June 12/86	N	Kelly Gruber	2B	7	Bill Scherrer	DET	H	7	2	2
14	May 16/88	N	Kelly Gruber	3B	6	Jeff Bittiger	CWS	A	8	0	2
15	June 2/89	N	Junior Felix	RF	1	Bob Stanley	BOS	A	9	3	2
16	July 11/91	N	Rance Mulliniks	DH	5	Kevin Brown	TEX	H	8	0	2
17	June 1/92	N	Devon White	CF	1	Carl Willis	MIN	A	10	0	1
18	June 18/93	N	Roberto Alomar	2B	2	Tony Fossas	BOS	A	8	0	0
19	April 25/94	N	Paul Molitor	DH	3	David Cone	KC	A	1	0	2
20	June 17/95	D	Paul Molitor	DH	2	Kenny Rogers	TEX	H	5	0	2
21	July 28/98	N	Shannon Stewart	CF	3	Eric Gunderson	TEX	H	8	1	1
22	Sept. 7/98	D	Shannon Stewart	LF	1	Steve Karsay	CLE	H	3	2	2
23	Sept. 22/98	N	Tony Fernandez	3B	6	Mike Mussina	BAL	H	4	0	1
24	July 7/01	D	Cesar Izturis	2B	9	Guillermo Mota	MON	H	6	1	1
25	May 11/02	D	Raul Mondesi	RF	5	Barry Zito	OAK	A	6	0	2
26	July 17/02	N	Ken Huckaby	C	8	Jason Johnson	BAL	H	2	1	1
27	Sept. 13/03	D	Greg Myers	DH	5	Pat Hentgen	BAL	H	4	1	2
28	July 7/10	N	Jose Bautista	RF	3	Kevin Slowey	MIN	H	5	1	2

OPPONENTS (30)

	DATE	BATTER	TEAM	PITCHER	CITY	IN	ON
1	May 5/77	Cecil Cooper	MIL	Jerry Garvin	TOR	5	1
2	July 23/77	Alan Bannister	CWS	Dave Lemanczyk	TOR	3	0
3	July 25/77	Ron LeFlore	DET	Mike Willis	DET	6	0
4	April 7/79	Amos Otis	KC	Jim Clancy	KC	1	1
5	May 8/79	Ken Landreaux	MIN	Balor Moore	MIN	7	0
6	June 10/79	Jim Essian	OAK	Mike Willis	OAK	5	3
7	Aug. 15/80	George Brett	KC	Jesse Jefferson	KC	1	2
8	Aug. 20/80	Mike Cubbage	MIN	Jackson Todd	MIN	6	1
9	June 9/81	Wayne Nordhagen	CWS	Luis Leal	CWS	4	1
10	July 21/82	Willie Wilson	KC	Dale Murray	TOR	8	1
11	Sept. 30/82	Kent Hrbek	MIN	Luis Leal	TOR	1	1
12	May 25/83	Kirk Gibson	DET	Jim Gott	TOR	1	1
13	Sept. 27/83	Gary Pettis	CAL	Luis Leal	CAL	2	0
14	July 4/84	Rob Picciolo	CAL	Dave Stieb	TOR	3	0
15	Oct. 2/85	Kirk Gibson	DET	Dave Stieb	DET	6	0
16	June 29/87	Ron Kittle	NYA	John Cerutti	TOR	1	1
17	April 7/88	Kurt Stillwell	KC	Jim Clancy	KC	6	1
18	May 27/88	Ivan Calderon	CWS	Mike Flanagan	TOR	7	0
19	Sept. 4/88	Jim Sundberg	TEX	Frank Wills	TOR	4	0
20	July 17/93	Brian McRae	KC	Danny Cox	TOR	9	1
21	July 21/94	Rusty Greer	TEX	Pat Hentgen	TOR	2	0
22	May 24/97	Darin Erstad	ANA	Woody Williams	TOR	3	0
23	July 26/98	Nomar Garciaparra	BOS	Pat Hentgen	BOS	7	2
24	June 20/03	Endy Chavez	MON	Jeff Tam	MON	8	0
25	Aug. 26/03	Kevin Millar	BOS	Aquilino Lopez	BOS	9	0
26	April 6/05	Carl Crawford	TB	Josh Towers	TB	3	0
27	July 5/05	Bobby Crosby	OAK	Pete Walker	TOR	6	1
28	June 19/08	Prince Fielder	MIL	A.J. Burnett	MIL	5	0
29	July 4/10	Brett Gardner	NYY	Brandon Morrow	NYY	6	1
30	Sept. 25/11	Ben Zobrist	TB	Brett Cecil	TB	1	0

EXTRA-INNING HOME RUNS

BLUE JAYS (96)

PLAYER	TIMES	LAST DATE	LAST TEAM
George Bell	6	6/22/90	NYY
Ernie Whitt	5	9/5/88	@DET
Jesse Barfield	4	6/6/87	BAL
Jose Cruz Jr.	4	8/11/01	@ANA
Otto Valez	3	5/4/80	CLE
Fred McGriff	3	5/25/90	@SEA
Alex S. Gonzalez	3	7/25/01	@BOS
Vernon Wells	3	7/20/06	NYY
Aaron Hill	3	5/27/09	@BAL
Cliff Johnson	2	6/21/86	NYY
John Olerud	2	9/17/92	CLE
Ed Sprague	2	8/3/95	@BAL
Joe Carter	2	6/1/96	KC
Jose Canseco	2	6/10/98	@FLA
Tony Batista	2	7/26/99	@CWS
Darrin Fletcher	2	6/1/02	@DET
Eric Hinske	2	6/29/02	@MTL
Alex Rios	2	5/26/07	@MIN
Gregg Zaun	2	9/6/08	TB
Lyle Overbay	2	9/25/10	BAL
Jose Bautista	2	7/9/11	@CLE
Adam Lind	2	6/14/11	BAL
Brett Lawrie	2	5/1/12	TEX
Doug Rader	1	7/13/77	@CWS
Bob Bailor	1	7/15/77	DET
Dave McKay	1	8/26/78	MIN
Craig Kusick	1	8/31/79	SEA
Roy Howell*	1	9/17/80	@NYY
Steve Braun	1	9/19/80	@BAL
John Mayberry	1	4/25/82	BOS
Barry Bonnell	1	8/25/83	@BAL
Willie Upshaw	1	5/10/84	@BAL
Buck Martinez	1	6/6/85	DET
Rance Mulliniks	1	6/12/85	@NYY
Damaso Garcia	1	7/29/85	@BAL
Garth Iorg	1	8/11/85	@KC
Al Oliver	1	8/11/85	@KC
Lloyd Moseby	1	5/10/86	@SEA
Cecil Fielder	1	8/4/87	SEA
Tony Fernandez	1	7/3/88	OAK
Junior Felix	1	6/4/89	@BOS
Mark Whitten	1	4/12/91	MIL
Roberto Alomar	1	5/10/91	CWS
Pat Boarders	1	9/24/91	@CAL
Rob Ducey	1	10/6/91	@MIN
Devon White*	1	6/1/92	@MIN
Carlos Delgado	1	8/20/96	@KC
Kevin Brown	1	8/15/98	ANA
Raul Mondesi	1	9/24/01	@CLE
Josh Phelps	1	4/5/03	@MIN
Reed Johnson	1	6/15/03	CHC
Shea Hillenbrand	1	5/27/06	CWS
Alex Gonzalez	1	5/7/10	@CWS
Yunel Escobar	1	4/4/11	OAK
John McDonald	1	4/22/11	TB
Corey Patterson	1	5/28/11	CWS
J.P. Arencibia	1	4/5/12	@CLE

INNING	# HIT	
10	49	5/1/12
11	24	9/5/11
12	9	5/7/10
13	8	9/6/08
14	4	5/28/11
15	1	6/22/90
16	1	4/5/12

OPPONENTS (91)

	DATE	BATTER	TEAM	PITCHER	CITY	IN	ON
1	June 8/77	Bobby Grich	CAL	Tom Bruno	CAL	13	0
2	July 3/77	Bump Wills	TEX	Mike Willis	TOR	10	1
3	July 15/77	Milt May	DET	Pete Vuckovich	TOR	10	0
4	July 17/77	Milt May	DET	Dave Lemanczyk	TOR	11	0
5	July 31/78	Lance Parrish	DET	Jerry Garvin	TOR	10	0
6	June 23/79	Bob Watson	BOS	Tom Buskey	BOS	11	0
7	July 4/79	Rusty Staub	DET	Tom Buskey	DET	11	1
8	July 19/79	Sixto Lezcano	MIL	Tom Buskey	MIL	11	0
9	April 12/80	Leon Roberts	SEA	Jerry Garvin	SEA	10	0
10	May 31/80	Reggie Jackson	NYA	Joey McLaughlin	NYA	11	1
11	Sept. 14/80	Eddie Murray	BAL	Mike Barlow	TOR	11	0
12	Sept. 19/80	Doug DeCinces	BAL	Mike Willis	BAL	12	1
13	May 10/81	Joe Rudi	BOS	Roy Lee Jackson	TOR	10	2
14	May 24/81	Tony Armas	OAK	Roy Lee Jackson	OAK	11	0
15	June 2/82	Bobby Murcer	NYA	Mark Bomback	TOR	13	3
16	Aug. 24/82	Joe Nolan	BAL	Joey McLaughlin	BAL	10	3
17	Aug. 24/83	Cal Ripken	BAL	Joey McLaughlin	BAL	10	0
18	Aug. 24/83	Lenn Sakata	BAL	Randy Moffitt	BAL	10	2
19	Aug. 26/83	Alan Trammell	DET	Jim Gott	DET	10	0
20	June 4/84	Dave Bergman	DET	Roy Lee Jackson	DET	10	2
21	June 24/84	Tony Armas	BOS	Dennis Lamp	BOS	10	1
22	Sept. 5/84	Don Baylor	NYA	Roy Lee Jackson	NYA	10	0
23	Sept. 7/84	Dave Bergman	DET	Ron Musselman	TOR	10	2
24	Aug. 10/85	Jim Sundberg	KCA	Bill Caudill	KCA	10	0
25	Sept. 25/85	Mike Greenwell	BOS	John Cerutti	TOR	13	1
26	May 13/86	Dave Kingman	OAK	Dennis Lamp	OAK	10	2
27	June 17/86	Rob Deer	MIL	Jimmy Key	MIL	10	0
28	July 25/86	Carney Lansford	OAK	Bill Caudill	OAK	10	0
29	Aug. 9/86	Pete O'Brien	TEX	Bill Caudill	TEX	10	0
30	Aug. 13/86	Larry Sheets	BAL	Luis Aquino	BAL	13	0
31	May 20/87	Wally Joyner	CAL	Tom Henke	CAL	10	0
32	Aug. 29/87	Mark McGwire	OAK	Mark Eichhorn	TOR	10	0
33	Sept. 27/87	Darrell Evans	DET	Jeff Musselman	TOR	11	0
34	April 22/88	Don Slaught	NYA	Tom Henke	NYA	12	0
35	May 15/88	Dave Gallagher	CHA	Mark Eichhorn	CHA	11	0
36	July 3/88	Jose Canseco	OAK	Tom Henke	TOR	12	1
37	July 3/88	Mark McGwire	OAK	John Cerutti	TOR	16	0
38	July 6/88	Chili Davis	CAL	David Wells	TOR	10	0
39	July 2/89	Danny Heep	BOS	Tom Henke	TOR	11	2
40	July 24/90	George Brett	KCA	Duane Ward	TOR	13	1
41	July 28/90	Harold Baines	TEX	Frank Wills	TOR	13	0
42	Sept. 21/90	Sandy Alomar	CLE	Frank Wills	TOR	13	0

	DATE	BATTER	TEAM	PITCHER	CITY	IN	ON
43	April 21/91	Robin Yount	MIL	Frank Wills	MIL	10	2
44	May 10/91	Sammy Sosa	CHA	Willie Fraser	TOR	12	1
45	Aug. 8/91	Mark Salas	DET	Tom Henke	TOR	14	2
46	Aug. 8/91	Mickey Tettleton	DET	Tom Henke	TOR	14	0
47	Sept. 16/91	Pete O'Brien	SEA	Rob Macdonald	SEA	11	0
48	Sept. 22/93	Rob Deer	BOS	Mike Timlin	TOR	10	1
49	May 4/94	Felix Jose	KCA	Darren Hall	TOR	10	1
50	June 15/94	Jim Thome	CLE	Scott Brow	CLE	13	0
51	April 28/95	Tim Salmon	CAL	Tony Castillo	TOR	10	0
52	May 10/95	Bernie Williams	NYA	Woody Williams	TOR	11	1
53	June 27/95	Bill Haselman	BOS	Woody Williams	BOS	11	0
54	Aug. 30/95	Albert Belle	CLE	Tony Castillo	CLE	14	0
55	Aug. 31/95	Albert Belle	CLE	Jimmy Rogers	CLE	10	1
56	Sept. 5/95	Bob Hamelin	KCA	Ken Robinson	KCA	10	0
57	Sept. 11/95	Travis Fryman	DET	Jimmy Rogers	TOR	10	0
58	Sept. 15/95	John Jaha	MIL	Ken Robinson	TOR	15	2
59	May 10/96	Troy O'Leary	BOS	Giovanni Carrara	TOR	11	0
60	Sept. 28/96	Roberto Alomar	BAL	Paul Spoljaric	TOR	10	0
61	April 23/97	Jim Edmonds	ANA	Paul Spoljaric	ANA	10	0
62	April 29/97	Chili Davis	KCA	Paul Quantrill	KCA	10	0
63	Sept. 21/97	Tino Martinez	NYA	Carlos Almanzar	NYA	10	0
64	June 19/98	Rafael Palmeiro	BAL	Bill Risley	BAL	15	2
65	Sept. 9/98	Travis Fryman	CLE	Carlos Almanzar	TOR	13	2
66	April 26/99	Darin Erstad	ANA	Nerio Rodriguez	ANA	11	0
67	May 24/00	Brian Daubach	BOS	John Frascatore	BOS	11	2
68	Aug. 1/00	Randy Velarde	OAK	Billy Koch	OAK	10	1
69	Sept. 14/00	Ryan Thompson	NYA	Kelvim Escobar	NYA	11	0
70	Sept. 24/01	Jolbert Cabrera	CLE	Bob File	CLE	11	0
71	April 28/02	David Eckstein	ANA	Pedro Borbon	ANA	14	3
72	Aug. 7/02	Dan Wilson	SEA	Luke Prokopec	TOR	10	0
73	Aug. 20/02	Raul Ibanez	KC	Scott Cassidy	TOR	12	2
74	Aug. 27/02	Joe Crede	CHI	Felex Heredia	CHI	10	3
75	April 11/04	David Ortiz	BOS	Aquilino Lopez	BOS	12	1
76	May 3/04	Aaron Guiel	KC	Terry Adams	TOR	10	0
77	Sept. 12/05	David Ortiz	BOS	Pete Walker	TOR	11	0
78	June 8/07	Olmedo Saenz	LAD	Jermey Accardo	LAD	10	1
79	June 22/07	Troy Tulowitzki	COL	Jeremy Accardo	COL	10	1
80	May 8/08	Dioner Navarro	TB	Shawn Camp	TOR	13	3
81	Aug. 24/08	Jed Lowrie	BOS	Brandon League	TOR	11	0
82	Sept. 24/08	Bobby Abreu	NYY	Jesse Carlson	TOR	10	1
83	May 27/09	Nolan Reimold	BAL	Brian Wolfe	BAL	11	2
84	June 20/09	Willie Harris	WSH	Scott Richmond	WSH	12	1
85	July 7/09	Pat Burrell	TB	Brandon League	TB	11	0
86	July 11/09	Melvin Mora	BAL	Jesse Carlson	BAL	12	0
87	April 21/10	Alex Gordon	KC	Scott Downs	TOR	10	0
88	Aug. 21/10	Jed Lowrie	BOS	Casey Janssen	BOS	11	0
89	Aug. 4/11	Desmond Jennings	TB	Jon Rauch	TB	10	0
90	April 27/12	Michael Saunders	SEA	Luis Perez	TOR	10	3
91	May 26/12	Josh Hamilton	TEX	Jason Frasor	TEX	10	1

BIOGRAPHIES LAST SEASON HISTORY RECORDS OPPONENTS PLAYER DEV. MEDIA & MISC.

GRAND SLAM HOME RUNS

LEADERS

CAREER RECORD

Carlos Delgado	9
George Bell	7
Vernon Wells	5
Joe Carter	4
Darrin Fletcher	4

SEASON RECORD

Carlos Delgado	3	1997
Darrin Fletcher	3	2000
Joe Carter	2	1997
Roy Howell	2	1979
George Bell	2	1985
George Bell	2	1987
Jesse Barfield	2	1988
Ed Sprague	2	1995
Carlos Delgado	2	1998
Tony Batista	2	2000
Carlos Delgado	2	2000
Brad Fullmer	2	2001
Raul Mondesi	2	2001
Carlos Delgado	2	2003
Vernon Wells	2	2003
Josh Phelps	2	2004
Vernon Wells	2	2006
Frank Thomas	2	2007
Jose Bautista	2	2010
Adam Lind	2	2011

CLUB RECORD

9	2000
8	1989
7	1997
7	2006
7	2008

BLUE JAYS, FIRST HR WITH TEAM IS GRAND SLAM

Rick Bosetti	May 7, 1978 vs. SEA
Glenallen Hill	Sept. 1, 1989 vs. MIN
Dick Schofield	May 28, 1994 vs. CAL
Chris Gomez	Apr. 22, 2004 vs. BOS
Frank Thomas	Apr. 7, 2007 vs. TB
Joe Inglett	June 19, 2008 vs. MIL
Kevin Millar	Apr. 16, 2009 vs. MIN
Yunel Escobar	July 18, 2010 vs. BAL

BACK-TO-BACK-TO-BACK HOME RUNS

The Blue Jays have hit three consecutive home runs **six** times in their history:

- April 26, 1984 vs. Oakland A's (6th inning): Willie Upshaw (1R), George Bell, Jesse Barfield
- September 12, 1987 vs. New York Yankees (8th inning): Ernie Whitt (3R), Jesse Barfield, Kelly Gruber
- April 18, 2000 vs. Los Angeles Angels (6th inning): Craig Grebek (2R), Raul Mondesi, Carlos Delgado
- August 21, 2001 at Minnesota Twins (6th inning): Shannon Stewart (1R), Raul Mondesi, Carlos Delgado
- April 9, 2005 vs. Boston Red Sox (3rd inning): Vernon Wells (1R), Corey Koskie, Shea Hillenbrand
- June 19, 2012 at Milwaukee (6th inning): Colby Rasmus (1R), Jose Bautista, Edwin Encarnacion

HOME RUN RECORDS BY POSITION (SEASON)

POSITION	PLAYER	HR	YEAR
1B	Carlos Delgado	41	2000
2B	Aaron Hill	36	2009
3B	Tony Batista	41	2000
SS	Tony Batista	26	1999
LF	George Bell	45	1987
CF	Vernon Wells	33	2003
RF	Shawn Green	42	1999
C	John Buck	23	2011
DH	Brad Fullmer	32	2000

GRAND SLAM RECORD

BLUE JAYS (123)

PLAYER	TIMES	LAST	TEAM
Carlos Delgado	9	9/28/2003	CLE
George Bell	7	4/11/1990	TEX
Vernon Wells	5	8/13/2008	@DET
Darrin Fletcher	4	5/26/2000	@DET
Joe Carter	4	7/23/1997	MIL
Adam Lind	3	8/13/2011	LAA
Gregg Zaun	3	9/6/2008	TB
Frank Thomas	3	4/6/2008	BOS
Tony Fernandez	3	9/9/2001	NYY
Brad Fullmer	3	7/6/2001	MTL
Tony Batista	3	7/3/2000	@BAL
Ed Sprague	3	7/3/1996	BAL
Lloyd Moseby	3	7/22/1989	@SEA
Ernie Whitt	3	6/4/1989	@BOS
Jesse Barfield	3	9/13/1988	DET
J.P. Arencibia	2	9/14/2012	@BAL
Jose Bautista	2	9/30/2010	@MIN
Rod Barajas	2	8/24/2009	TB
Matt Stairs	2	5/14/2008	MIN
Josh Phelps	2	7/7/2004	SEA
Raul Mondesi	2	6/29/2001	BOS
Shawn Green	2	7/19/1999	ATL
John Olerud	2	5/27/1996	CWS
Kelly Gruber	2	9/1/1992	CWS
Glenallen Hill	2	8/14/1990	@CWS
Willie Upshaw	2	6/23/1987	@DET
Barry Bonnell	2	5/1/1983	CWS
Rico Carty	2	9/7/1979	@CLE
Roy Howell	2	8/27/1979	OAK
Edwin Encarnacion	1	4/28/12	SEA
Colby Rasmus	1	6/23/2012	@MIA
Aaron Hill	1	5/29/2011	CWS
Brett Lawrie	1	8/10/2011	OAK
Yunel Escobar	1	7/18/2010	@BAL

PLAYER	TIMES	LAST	Team
Kevin Millar	1	4/16/2009	@MIN
Joe Inglett	1	6/19/2008	@MIN
Brad Wilkerson	1	5/24/2008	KC
Russ Adams	1	9/19/2007	BOS
Bengie Molina	1	8/27/2006	@KC
Troy Glaus	1	7/29/2006	OAK
John McDonald	1	7/25/2006	@SEA
Lyle Overbay	1	5/10/2006	OAK
Reed Johnson	1	7/1/2005	@BOS
Gabe Gross	1	9/5/2004	OAK
Chris Woodward	1	8/20/2004	@BAL
Chris Gomez	1	4/22/2004	BOS
Eric Hinske	1	7/4/2003	@BAL
Jose Cruz Jr.	1	10/5/2001	CLE
Marty Cordova	1	7/16/2000	NYM
Jose Canseco	1	7/19/1998	NYY
Benito Santiago	1	8/11/1997	DET
Charlie O'Brien	1	5/14/1997	@DET
Devon White	1	8/25/1995	CWS
Paul Molitor	1	7/5/1994	@MIN
Dick Schofield	1	5/28/1994	CAL
Roberto Alomar	1	8/29/1993	@SEA
Dave Winfield	1	5/7/1992	@SEA
Fred McGriff	1	7/21/1989	@SEA
Pat Borders	1	7/7/1989	@DET
Junior Felix	1	6/2/1989	@BOS
Rance Mulliniks	1	5/2/1989	OAK
Buck Martinez	1	6/5/1983	@BAL
Otto Velez	1	5/4/1980	CLE
Rick Bosetti	1	5/7/1978	@SEA
Hector Torres	1	6/27/1977	NYY

OPPONENTS (132)

DATE	PLAYER/CLUB	H/A	PITCHER
Sept. 6/77	Carlton Fisk, Boston	H	Mike Darr (1st inning)
April 18/78	Amos Otis, Kansas City	H	Dave Lemanczyk (1st inning)
April 25/78	Paul Dade, Cleveland	H	Jerry Garvin (4th inning)
May 26/78	Jim Spencer, New York – PH	A	Tom Murphy (7th inning)
June 24/78	Gary Alexander, Cleveland	A	Mike Willis (4th inning)
Aug. 6/78	Al Cowens, Kansas City	A	Balor Moore (1st inning)
May 22/79	Andre Thornton, Cleveland	H	Mark Lemongello (3rd inning)
June 3/79	Dan Meyer, Seattle	A	Mark Lemongello (3rd inning)
June 10/79	Jim Essian, Oakland – IP	A	Mike Willis (5th inning)
June 13/79 (1st)	Willie Aikens, California	H	Dyar Miller (3rd inning)
June 14/79	Willie Aikens, California	H	Phil Huffman (1st inning)
July 15/79	Dave Edwards, Minnesota	H	Jim Clancy (3rd inning)
Aug. 25/79	Don Baylor, California	H	Balor Moore (1st inning)
Sept. 9/79	Bobby Bonds, Cleveland	A	Tom Buskey (9th inning)
April 22/81	Paul Molitor, Milwaukee	H	Joey McLaughlin (5th inning)
June 7/81	Buddy Bell, Texas	A	Roy Lee Jackson (8th inning)
May 29/82 (2nd)	Benny Ayala, Baltimore – PH	A	Jerry Garvin (7th inning)
June 2/82	Bobby Murcer, New York	H	Mark Bomback (13th inning)
July 11/82	Harold Baines, Chicago	H	Jerry Garvin (2nd inning)
July 30/82	Alan Trammell, Detroit	H	Jim Clancy (4th inning)
Aug. 24/82	Joe Nolan, Baltimore	A	Joey McLaughlin (10th inning)
Aug. 26/82	Eddie Murray, Baltimore	A	Ken Schrom (3rd inning)
June 15/83	Dave Lopes, Oakland	H	Dave Geisel (5th inning)
Aug. 8/83 (2nd)	Ken Griffey, New York	A	Matt Williams (1st inning)
Aug. 20/83	Jim Rice, Boston	A	Dave Stieb (3rd inning)
July 20/84	Alvin Davis, Seattle	A	Roy Lee Jackson (7th inning)
April 19/85	Fritz Connally, Baltimore	H	Doyle Alexander (5th inning)
May 15/85	Jerry Narron, California – PH	H	Bill Caudill (9th inning)
May 8/86	Wally Joyner, California	A	Jim Acker (3rd inning)
May 9/86	Alvin Davis, Seattle	A	Don Gordon (7th inning)
April 9/87	Cory Snyder, Cleveland	H	Joe Johnson (1st inning)

DATE	PLAYER/CLUB	H/A	PITCHER
June 29/87	Don Mattingly, New York	H	John Cerutti (2nd inning)
June 29/87	Dave Winfield, New York	H	Tom Henke (8th inning)
Aug. 6/87	Casey Parsons, Cleveland – PH	A	Mark Eichhorn (6th inning)
Aug. 10/87	Sam Horn, Boston	A	Jose Nunez (8th inning)
Sept. 26/87	Matt Nokes, Detroit	H	John Cerutti (3rd inning)
July 2/88	Terry Steinbach, Oakland	H	Mike Flanagan (3rd inning)
May 2/89	Mark McGwire, Oakland	H	Tom Henke (9th inning)
July 16/89	Terry Steinbach, Oakland	H	Duane Ward (7th inning)
Sept. 12/89	Kent Hrbek, Minnesota	A	Duane Ward (7th inning)
May 17/90	Brian Giles, Seattle	H	Frank Wills (5th inning)
May 22/90	Jose Canseco, Oakland	H	Frank Wills (6th inning)
July 17/90	Alvin Davis, Seattle	A	David Wells (6th inning)
Aug. 3/90	Steve Buechele, Texas	A	Jim Acker (7th inning)
Sept. 14/90	Sam Horn, Baltimore – PH	H	Duane Ward (6th inning)
April 8/91	Jack Clark, Boston	H	Dave Stieb (3rd Inning)
June 1/91	Dave Winfield, California	H	Willie Fraser (2nd Inning)
June 16/91	Joe Orsulak, Baltimore – PH	H	Duane Ward (7th Inning)
Sept. 15/91	Jose Canseco, Oakland	H	Jim Acker (9th Inning)
June 3/92	Kirby Puckett, Minnesota	A	Juan Guzman (3rd Inning)
June 12/92	Wade Boggs, Boston	H	Dave Stieb (5th Inning)
April 13/93	Omar Vizquel, Seattle	H	Danny Cox (6th inning)
April 30/93	Frank Thomas, Chicago	R	Todd Stottlemyre (3rd inning)
April 6/94	Robin Ventura, Chicago	R	Paul Spoljaric (7th inning)
May 5/94	Brent Mayne, Kansas City	R	Juan Guzman (3rd inning)
June 7/94	Darrin Jackson, Chicago	H	Pat Hentgen (1st inning)
Aug. 2/94	Wes Chamberlin, Boston	H	Dave Stewart (4th inning)
June 21/95	Jose Valentin, Milwaukee	H	Mike Timlin (9th inning)
Aug. 1/95	Harold Baines, Baltimore	A	Edwin Hurtado (1st inning)
Aug. 18/95	Wally Joyner, Kansas City	H	Giovanni Carrara (3rd inning)
Aug. 25/95	Ray Durham, Chicago	H	Pat Hentgen (6th inning)
July 7/96	Cecil Fielder, Detroit	A	Jeff Ware (1st inning)
July 31/96	Albert Belle, Cleveland	A	Bill Risley (9th inning)
Sept. 21/96	Eddie Murray, Baltimore	A	Scott Brow (6th inning)
April 20/97	Dean Palmer, Texas	A	Juan Guzman (3rd inning)
May 17/97	Jim Thome, Cleveland	H	Woody Williams (3rd inning)
Aug. 4/97	Greg Colbrunn, Minnesota – PH	A	Omar Daal (5th inning)
July 19/98	Chris Hoiles, Baltimore	A	Woody Williams (1st inning)
July 18/98	Tim Raines, New York (AL)	H	Robert Person (8th inning)
July 23/98	Damon Buford, Boston	A	Dan Plesac (8th inning)
April 29/99	Andy Sheets, Anaheim	A	Roy Halladay (1st inning)
April 30/99	Ken Griffey, Seattle	A	Graeme Lloyd (8th inning)
May 22/99	John Valentin, Boston	A	Chris Carpenter (3rd inning)
July 28/99	Butch Huskey, Boston	H	Joey Hamilton (6th inning)
Aug. 13/99	Matt Stairs, Oakland	H	Paul Spoljaric (5th inning)
Aug. 14/99	A.J. Hinch, Oakland	H	Joey Hamilton (1st inning)
Sept. 14/99	Bernie Williams, New York (AL)	H	Billy Koch (8th inning)
Sept. 14/99	Paul O'Neill, New York (AL)	H	Paul Spoljaric (9th inning)
Sept. 24/99	Manny Ramirez, Cleveland	H	Mike Romano (5th inning)
Sept. 24/99	Dave Roberts, Cleveland	H	John Hudek (8th inning)
April 15/00	Edgar Martinez, Seattle	H	Pedro Borbon (6th inning)
April 16/00	Alex Rodriguez, Seattle	H	Pedro Borbon (8th inning)
April 18/00	Adam Kennedy, Anaheim	H	Frank Castillo (4th inning)
June 27/00	Steve Cox, Tampa Bay	A	Kelvim Escobar (4th inning)
July 18/00	Mike Piazza, New York (NL)	H	Chris Carpenter (5th inning)
April 8/01	Jorge Posada, New York (AL)	A	Steve Parris (1st inning)
Aug. 18/01	Ivan Rodriguez, Texas	H	Billy Koch (9th inning)
April 27/02	David Eckstein, Anaheim	A	Scott Cassidy (5th inning)
April 28/02	David Eckstein, Anaheim	A	Pedro Borbon (14th inning)
May 11/02	Eric Chavez, Oakland	A	Justin Miller (2nd inning)
Aug. 27/02	Joe Crede, Chicago	A	Felix Heredia (10th inning)
May 16/02	Mike Cameron, Seattle	H	Pete Walker (7th inning)
March 31/03	Alfonso Soriano, New York (AL)	H	Roy Halladay (6th inning)
June 15/03	Troy O'Leary, Chicago (NL)	H	Cory Lidle (6th inning)
Aug. 24/03	Ramon Hernandez, Oakland	H	Kelvim Escobar (1st inning)
Aug. 24/03	Miguel Tejada, Oakland	H	Josh Towers (6th inning)
May 19/04	Matt Lecroy, Minnesota	H	Terry Adams (9th inning)
July 10/04	Benji Molina, Anaheim	H	Kerry Ligtenberg (7th inning)
July 18/04	Mark Teixeira, Texas	A	Vinnie Chulk (8th inning)
July 26/04	Jorge Posada, New York	H	Sean Douglass (1st inning)
Aug. 8/04	Bernie Williams, New York	A	Miguel Batista (1st inning)
Aug. 12/04	Ben Broussard, Cleveland	A	Vinnie Chulk (7th inning)
Aug. 28/04	Ruben Sierra, New York	H	Kerry Ligtenberg (9th inning)

June 2/05	Eric Chavez, Oakland	A	Josh Towers (5th inning)
DATE	**PLAYER/CLUB**	**H/A**	**PITCHER**
Sept. 19/05	Richie Sexson, Seattle	H	Miguel Batista (9th inning)
April 5/06	Torii Hunter, Minnesota	H	Jason Frasor (8th inning)
Sept. 5/06	Andy Marte, Cleveland	H	Jeremy Accardo (8th inning)
April 4/07	Curtis Granderson, Detroit	A	Shaun Marcum (3rd inning)
Sept. 11/07	Jason Giambi, New York (AL)	H	Shaun Marcum (5th inning)
May 8/08	Dioner Navarro, Tampa Bay	H	Shaun Camp (13th inning)
May 16/08	Jayson Werth, Philadelphia	A	David Purcey (3rd inning)
July 19/08	Evan Longoria, Tampa Bay	A	Roy Halladay (6th inning)
Sept. 24/08	Bobby Abreu, New York (AL)	H	Jesse Carlson (10th inning)
April 25/09	Alexi Ramirez, Chicago (AL)	A	Shawn Camp (5th inning)
June 12/09	Cody Ross, Florida	H	Brandon League (8th inning)
Aug. 16/09	Gregg Zaun, Tampa Bay	A	Brandon League (8th inning)
April 4/10	Carlos Quentin, Chicago (AL)	H	Brandon Morrow (5th inning)
June 2/10	Carl Crawford, Tampa Bay	H	Scott Downs (9th inning)
June 5/10	Carlos Pena, Tampa Bay	A	Rommie Lewis, Jr. (5th inning)
June 15/10	Aaron Cunningham, San Diego	A	Brett Cecil (2nd inning)
July 3/10	Brett Gardner, New York (AL)	A	Ricky Romero (3rd inning)
Sept. 11/10	Brad Hawpe, Tampa Bay	H	Ricky Romero (4th inning)
June 4/11	Mark Reynolds, Baltimore	A	Ricky Romero (6th inning)
July 7/11	Travis Hafner, Cleveland	A	Luis Perez (9th inning)
July 21/11	Miguel Olivo, Seattle	H	Casey Janssen (8th inning)
April 18/12	Luke Scott, Tampa Bay	H	Carlos Villanueva (9th inning)
April 27/12	Michael Saunders, Seattle	H	Luis Perez (10th inning)
May 8/12	Brandon Inge, Oakland	A	Francisco Cordero (9th inning)
May 25/12	Nelson Cruz, Texas	A	Jason Frasor (7th inning)
June 19/12	Aramis Ramierz, Milwuakee	A	Jason Frasor (6th inning)
July 16/12	Raul Ibanez, New York (AL)	A	Jason Frasor (8th inning)
Sept. 20/12	Nick Swisher, New York (AL)	A	Brad Lincoln (4th inning)

1B Carlos Delgado is the all-time club leader in many offensive categories and will be enshrined into the Blue Jays Level of Excellence on July 21, 2013

POST-SEASON AND ALL-STAR HOMERS

BLUE JAYS

WORLD SERIES

	DATE	BATTER	PITCHER	OPP	CITY	IN	ON
1	Oct. 17/92	Joe Carter	Tom Glavine	ATL	ATL	4	0
2	Oct. 18/92	Ed Sprague	Jeff Reardon	ATL	ATL	9	1
3	Oct. 20/92	Joe Carter	Steve Avery	ATL	TOR	4	0
4	Oct. 20/92	Kelly Gruber	Steve Avery	ATL	TOR	8	0
5	Oct. 21/92	Pat Borders	Tom Glavine	ATL	TOR	3	0
6	Oct. 24/92	Candy Maldonado	Steve Avery	ATL	ATL	4	0
7	Oct. 16/93	Devon White	Curt Schilling	PHI	TOR	5	0
8	Oct. 16/93	John Olerud	Curt Schilling	PHI	TOR	6	0
9	Oct. 17/93	Joe Carter	Terry Mulholland	PHI	TOR	4	1
10	Oct. 19/93	Paul Molitor	Danny Jackson	PHI	PHI	3	0
11	Oct. 23/93	Paul Molitor	Terry Mulholland	PHI	TOR	5	0
12	Oct. 23/93	Joe Carter	Mitch Williams	PHI	TOR	9	2

LEAGUE CHAMPIONSHIP SERIES

	DATE	BATTER	PITCHER	OPP	CITY	IN	ON
1	Oct. 11/85	Rance Mulliniks	Bret Saberhagen	KCA	KCA	5	1
2	Oct. 11/85	Jesse Barfield	Bret Saberhagen	KCA	KCA	5	1
3	Oct. 03/89	Ernie Whitt	Dave Stewart	OAK	OAK	4	0
4	Oct. 08/89	Lloyd Moseby	Dave Stewart	OAK	TOR	8	0
5	Oct. 08/89	George Bell	Dave Stewart	OAK	TOR	9	0
6	Oct. 11/91	Joe Carter	Scott Erickson	MIN	TOR	1	0
7	Oct. 07/92	Pat Borders	Dave Stewart	OAK	TOR	5	0
8	Oct. 07/92	Dave Winfield	Dave Stewart	OAK	TOR	6	0
9	Oct. 08/92	Kelly Gruber	Mike Moore	OAK	TOR	5	1
10	Oct. 10/92	Roberto Alomar	Ron Darling	OAK	OAK	4	0
11	Oct. 10/92	Candy Maldonado	Ron Darling	OAK	OAK	5	0
12	Oct. 11/92	John Olerud	Bob Welch	OAK	OAK	2	0
13	Oct. 11/92	Roberto Alomar	Dennis Eckersley	OAK	OAK	9	1
14	Oct. 12/92	Dave Winfield	Dave Stewart	OAK	OAK	4	0
15	Oct. 14/92	Joe Carter	Mike Moore	OAK	TOR	1	1
16	Oct. 14/92	Candy Maldonado	Mike Moore	OAK	TOR	3	2
17	Oct. 05/93	Paul Molitor	Jack McDowell	CHA	CHA	7	1
18	Oct. 12/93	Devon White	Scott Radinsky	CHA	CHA	9	0

LEAGUE DIVISION SERIES

DATE	BATTER	PITCHER	PTM	CITY	IN	ON
NA						

ALL STAR GAME

	DATE	BATTER	PITCHER	PTM	CITY	IN	ON
1	July 13/93	Roberto Alomar	Andy Benes	SDN	BAL	3	0

OPPONENTS

WORLD SERIES

	DATE	BATTER	TM	PITCHER	CITY	IN	ON
1	Oct. 17/92	Damon Berryhill	ATL	Jack Morris	ATL	6	2
2	Oct. 22/92	David Justice	ATL	Jack Morris	TOR	4	0
3	Oct. 22/92	Lonnie Smith	ATL	Jack Morris	TOR	5	3
4	Oct. 17/93	Jim Eisenreich	PHI	Dave Stewart	TOR	3	2
5	Oct. 17/93	Lenny Dykstra	PHI	Tony Castillo	TOR	7	0
6	Oct. 19/93	Milt Thompson	PHI	Duane Ward	PHI	9	0
7	Oct. 20/93	Lenny Dykstra	PHI	Todd Stottlemyre	PHI	2	1
8	Oct. 20/93	Lenny Dykstra	PHI	Al Leiter	PHI	5	1
9	Oct. 20/93	Darren Daulton	PHI	Al Leiter	PHI	5	1
10	Oct. 23/93	Lenny Dykstra	PHI	Dave Stewart	TOR	7	2

LEAGUE CHAMPIONSHIP SERIES

	DATE	BATTER	TM	PITCHER	CITY	IN	ON
1	Oct. 09/85	Willie Wilson	KCA	Jimmy Key	TOR	3	1
2	Oct. 09/85	Pat Sheridan	KCA	Tom Henke	TOR	9	0
3	Oct. 11/85	George Brett	KCA	Doyle Alexander	KCA	1	0
4	Oct. 11/85	Jim Sundberg	KCA	Doyle Alexander	KCA	5	0
5	Oct. 11/85	George Brett	KCA	Doyle Alexander	KCA	6	1
6	Oct. 15/85	George Brett	KCA	Doyle Alexander	TOR	5	0
7	Oct. 16/85	Pat Sheridan	KCA	Dave Stieb	TOR	4	0
8	Oct. 03/89	Dave Henderson	OAK	Dave Stieb	OAK	2	0
9	Oct. 03/89	Mark McGwire	OAK	Dave Stieb	OAK	6	0
10	Oct. 04/89	Dave Parker	OAK	Todd Stottlemyre	OAK	6	0
11	Oct. 06/89	Dave Parker	OAK	Jimmy Key	TOR	4	0
12	Oct. 07/89	Rickey Henderson	OAK	Mike Flanagan	TOR	3	1
13	Oct. 07/89	Jose Canseco	OAK	Mike Flanagan	TOR	3	0
14	Oct. 07/89	Rickey Henderson	OAK	Mike Flanagan	TOR	5	1
15	Oct. 11/91	Mike Pagliarulo	MIN	Mike Timlin	TOR	10	0
16	Oct. 12/91	Kirby Puckett	MIN	Todd Stottlemyre	TOR	4	0
17	Oct. 13/91	Kirby Puckett	MIN	Tom Candiotti	TOR	1	0
18	Oct. 07/92	Mark McGwire	OAK	Jack Morris	TOR	2	1
19	Oct. 07/92	Terry Steinbach	OAK	Jack Morris	TOR	2	0
20	Oct. 07/92	Harold Baines	OAK	Jack Morris	TOR	9	0
21	Oct. 12/92	Ruben Sierra	OAK	David Cone	OAK	1	1
22	Oct. 09/93	Lance Johnson	CHA	Todd Stottlemyre	TOR	2	1
23	Oct. 09/93	Frank Thomas	CHA	Todd Stottlemyre	TOR	6	0
24	Oct. 10/93	Ellis Burks	CHA	Juan Guzman	TOR	5	0
25	Oct. 10/93	Robin Ventura	CHA	Duane Ward	TOR	9	1
26	Oct. 12/93	Warren Newson	CHA	Duane Ward	CHA	9	0

LEAGUE DIVISION SERIES

DATE	BATTER	TM	PITCHER	CITY	IN	ON
NA						

ALL STAR GAME

	DATE	BATTER	TM	PITCHER	CITY	IN	ON
1	July 10/84	Gary Carter	MON	Dave Stieb	SFN	2	0

OPPONENTS

BRETT LAWRIE

OPPONENTS

LEADING OPPONENTS VS BLUE JAYS

	2012		Record	
Batting Aveage (30 AB's)	.469	Kyle Seager, SEA	.541	Vladimir Guerrero, TEX-2010
Most at Bats	71	J.J. Hardy, BAL	89	Alfonso Soriano, NYY-2002
Most Runs	15	Desmond Jennings, TB	22	Jacoby Ellsbury, BOS-2011
Most Hits	29	Adam Jones, BAL	34	Jacoby Ellsbury, BOS-2011
Most Doubles	9	Robinson Cano, NYY	11	Mike Lowell, BOS-2006
Most Triples	2	Jemile Weeks, OAK	3	14 players, last-2011
Most Home Runs	9	Chris Davis, BAL	9	Manny Ramirez, BOS-2001 Chris Davis, BAL-2012
Most Runs Batted In	17	Chris Davis, BAL	24	David Ortiz, BOS-2005
Most Times Striking Out	21	Mark Reynolds, BAL Nick Swisher, NYY	31	Carlos Pena, TB-2008
Most Walks	15	Ben Zobrist, TB	19	Mickey Tettleton, DET-1992 Jason Giambi, NYY-2003 Alex Rodriguez, NYY-2005
Most Times Hit By Pitch	3	Matt Joyce, TB	6	Melvin Mora, BAL-2002
Most Stolen Bases	5	Pedro Ciriaco, BOS Ichiro Suzuki, SEA-NYY	13	Rickey Henderson, NYY-1988
Most Times Caught Stealing	3	Elliott Johnson, TB	5	Mike Caruso, CWS-1999
Most Wins	3	David Price, TB	4	13 players, last-2010
Most Losses	3	Jon Lester, BOS	4	4 players, last-1993
Most Appearances	10	Cody Eppley, NYY David Robertson, NYY	20	Keith Atherton, OAK-MIN-1988
Most Complete Games	1	Hiroki Kuroda, NYY Jon Lester, BOS	4	Mike Flanagan, BAL-1978 Mike Norris, OAK-1980
Most Saves	6	Fernando Rodney, TB Rafael Soriano, NYY	6	6 players, last 2012
Most Innings Pitched	33.0	Phil Hughes, NYY	41.2	Pedro Martinez, BOS-2004
Most Hits Allowed	36	Phil Hughes, NYY	43	Mike Flanagan, BAL-1978
Most Earned Runs Allowed	21	Phil Hughes, NYY Jon Lester, BOS	22	Tanyon Sturtze, TB-2002 Sergio Mitre, NYY-2009 John Lackey, BOS-2011
Most Home Runs Allowed	7	Tommy Hunter, BAL Jon Lester, BOS	8	Jason Johnson, BAL-2002 Josh Beckett, BOS-2006 James Shields, TB-2010
Most Strikeouts	31	Phil Hughes, NYY	46	Hideo Nomo, DET-2001
Most Base on Balls	14	Phil Hughes, NYY	20	Nolan Ryan, CAL-1977 Tanyon Sturtze, TB-2002

WINNING AND LOSING STREAKS — HOME and ROAD

	HOME		ROAD			HOME		ROAD	
	WIN	LOSS	WIN	LOSS		WIN	LOSS	WIN	LOSS
1977	3	11	6	5	1994	9	7	2	5
1978	5	7	3	9	1995	4	7	5	7
1979	4	7	3	12	1996	3	5	7	4
1980	3	6	6	6	1997	6	7	6	7
1981	3	6	4	7	1998	9	5	4	4
1982	6	4	4	7	1999	8	9	5	5
1983	5	3	4	6	2000	6	5	3	7
1984	9	4	3	6	2001	5	7	4	4
1985	10	3	7	6	2002	6	6	5	8
1986	7	4	5	4	2003	7	6	6	4
1987	7	4	7	5	2004	6	8	3	6
1988	4	5	5	5	2005	6	5	3	6
1989	6	5	4	6	2006	5	3	3	5
1990	6	6	6	4	2007	8	4	3	7
1991	5	5	6	3	2008	6	6	4	7
1992	8	5	5	5	2009	6	4	3	9
1993	5	5	9	4	2010	5	4	6	5
					2011	4	5	5	4
					2012	4	4	4	8

LOW HIT GAMES VS BLUE JAYS

NO HIT GAMES

May 15/81 – Len Barker, Toronto 0 at Cleveland 3, Perfect Game
June 29/90 – Dave Stewart, Oakland 5 at Toronto 0
May 1/91 – Nolan Ryan, Toronto 0 at Texas 3
May 7/11 – Justin Verlander, Detroit 9 at Toronto 0

ONE HIT GAMES

Sept. 3/78 – Chris Knapp, California 3 at Toronto 1, Horton homer in 2nd
July 7/79 – Doc Medich (6.2 IP), Jim Kern (2.1 IP), Toronto 0 at Texas 2, Mayberry single in 2nd
April 30/80 – Larry Gura, Kansas City 3 at Toronto 0, Garcia single in 6th
June 6/80 – Geoff Zahn, Toronto 0 at Minnesota 5, Mayberry single in 7th
Sept. 26/80 – Dennis Eckersley, Boston 3 at Toronto 1, Mayberry home run in 5th
May 27/83 – John Tudor, Boston 2 at Toronto 0, Collins single in 4th
Aug. 13/84 – Mike Boddicker, Baltimore 2 at Toronto 1, Mulliniks double in 3rd
April 23/89 – Nolan Ryan, Texas 4 at Toronto 1, Liriano triple in 9th
April 28/89 – Kirk McCaskill, Toronto 0 at California 9, Liriano double in 9th
Sept. 30/92 – Frank Viola, Boston 1 at Toronto 0, White single in 9th
July 28/97 – Steve Woodard (8.0 IP), Mike Fetters (1.0 IP), Toronto 0 at Milwaukee 1 (G1), Otis Nixon single in 1st
May 25/01 – Hideo Nomo, Toronto 0 at Boston 4, Shannon Stewart double in 4th
June 15/05 – Chris Carpenter, Toronto 0 vs St. Louis 7, Alex Rios single in 2nd

Edwin Encarnacion was one of six players in the Major Leagues to have hit 40+ HR in 2012

OPPONENTS ALL-TIME LEADERS VS. TORONTO

RUNS

1.	Derek Jeter	179
2.	Rickey Henderson	164
3.	Alex Rodriguez	150
4.	Johnny Damon	146
5.	Wade Boggs	132

HITS

1.	Derek Jeter	315
2.	Robin Yount	263
3.	Johnny Damon.	250
4.	Cal Ripken	247
5.	Wade Boggs	235

HOME RUNS

1.	Manny Ramirez	54
	Alex Rodriguez	54
3.	David Ortiz	46
4.	Jose Canseco	41
5.	Rafael Palmiero	38
	Harold Baines.	38

RBI

1.	Alex Rodriguez	169
2.	David Ortiz	143
3.	Manny Ramirez	140
4.	Harold Baines	131
5.	Robin Yount	129
	Cal Ripken	129

BASE ON BALLS

1.	Rickey Henderson	149
2.	Wade Boggs	131
3.	Manny Ramirez	112
4.	Frank Thomas	110
5.	Tony Phillips	107

EXTRA BASE HITS

1.	David Ortiz	102
2.	Alex Rodriguez	98
3.	George Brett	89
4.	Many Ramirez	85
5.	Rafael Palmeiro	84

STOLEN BASES

1.	Rickey Henderson	110
2.	Carl Crawford	53
3.	Willie Wilson	48
4.	Kenny Lofton	42
5.	Paul Molitor	40

BATTING AVERAGE (MIN. 100 GAMES)

1.	Wally Joyner	.345
2.	Ichiro Suzuki	.340
3.	Valdimir Guerrero	.333
4.	Robin Yount	.330
5.	Wade Boggs	.327

ON BASE PERCENTAGE (MIN. 100 GAMES)

1.	Wade Boggs	.431
2.	Wally Joyner	.417
3.	Frank Thomas	.415
4.	Rickey Henderson	.412
5.	Mark McLemore	.406

SLUGGING PERCENTAGE (MIN. 100 GAMES)

1.	Ken Griffey Jr.	.600
2.	Mark Teixeira	.599
3.	Jose Canseco	.595
4.	Albert Belle	.593
5.	Vladimir Guerrero	.569

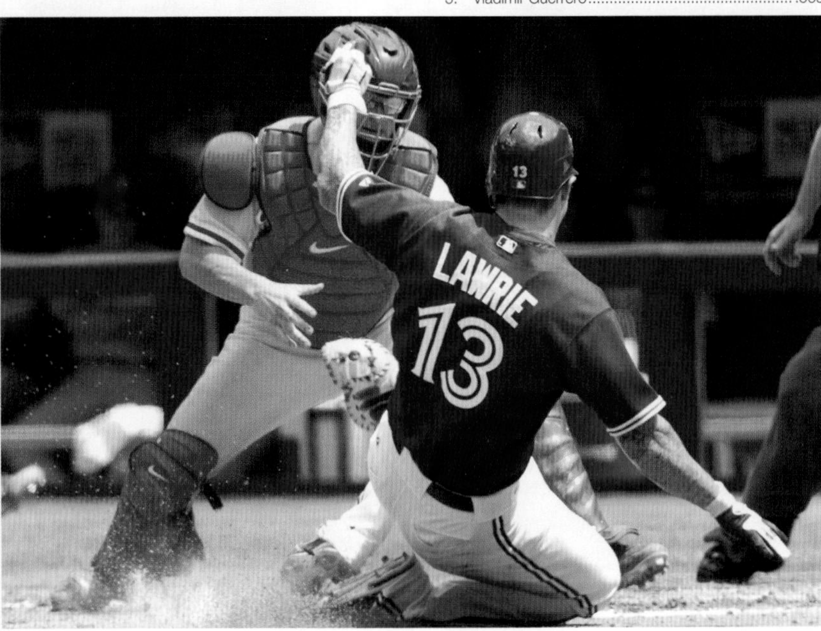

Brett Lawrie hit .319 vs. left-handed pitchers with a .813 OPS in 2012... That .319 average was the highest on the club and ranked 13th in the AL

BALTIMORE ORIOLES

Oriole Park at Camden Yards
333 West Camden St. Baltimore, MD 21201

Capacity: 45,971 **Dimensions:** 330 LF, 400 CF, 318 RF

Executive Vice President, Baseball Operations: Dan Duquette
Field Manager: Buck Showalter

2012 Record, Finish: 93-60, 2nd in AL East (-2.0 games)

Blue Jays vs. Baltimore

2012 vs. BAL 7-11
2012 at TOR 5-4
2012 at BAL 2-7

All-Time vs. BAL 282-242
All-Time at TOR 155-105
All-Time at BAL 127-137

at Exhibition Stadium 41-35
at Rogers Centre 114-70
at Camden Yards 88-79
at Memorial Stadium 39-58

Longest Winning Streaks

by Toronto .... 13 games
(April 11, 1999-May 10, 2000)

by Baltimore .... 15 games
(Sept. 8, 1978-Sept. 6, 1979)

Series Sweeps at Toronto

Last by Toronto

3-game .... May 28-30, 2012
4-game .... June 26-28, 1978

Last by Baltimore

3-game .... April 22-24, 2005
4-game .... None

Series Sweeps at Baltimore

Last by Toronto

3-game .... July 16-18, 2010
4-game .... June 26-29, 1997

Last by Baltimore

3-game .... April 24-26, 2012
4-game .... June 29-July 1, 1979

Series Results, Last 10 Years

Year	Home	Road	Total
2012	5-4	2-7	7-11
2011	6-3	6-3	12-6
2010	9-0	6-3	15-3
2009	8-1	1-8	9-9
2008	6-3	6-3	12-6
2007	6-3	4-5	10-8
2006	7-3	4-5	11-8
2005	4-6	6-3	10-9
2004	2-7	6-4	8-11
2003	6-4	5-4	11-8

2013 Schedule

at Toronto

May 23-26, June 21-23 & Sept. 13-15

at Baltimore

April 22-24, July 12-14 & Sept. 24-26

BOSTON RED SOX

Fenway Park
4 Yawkey Way, Boston, MA 02215

Capacity: 37,495 **Dimensions:** 310 LF, 420 CF, 380 RF

Executive Vice President, General Manager: Ben Cherrington
Field Manager: John Farrell

2012 Record, Finish: 69-93, 5th in AL East (-26.0 games)

Blue Jays vs. Boston

2012 vs. BOS 11-7
2012 at TOR 4-5
2012 at BOS 7-2

All-Time vs. BOS 233-288
All-Time at TOR 116-145
All-Time at BOS 117-143

at Exhibition Stadium 33-44
at Rogers Centre 83-101
at Fenway Park 117-143

Longest Winning Streaks

by Toronto .... 8 games
(Aug. 11, 1987-June 11, 1988)

by Boston .... 11 games
(April 16-July 11, 2002)

Series Sweeps at Toronto

Last by Toronto

3-game .... April 4-6, 2008
4-game .... Sept. 3-6, 1998

Last by Boston

3-game .... June 10-12, 2011
4-game .... May 31-June 3, 2001

Series Sweeps at Boston

Last by Toronto

3-game .... Sept. 7-9, 2012
4-game .... None

Last by Boston

3-game .... Aug. 28-30, 2009
4-game .... July 1-4, 2002 (5-games)

Series Results, Last 10 Years

Year	Home	Road	Total
2012	4-5	7-2	11-7
2011	5-4	3-6	8-10
2010	2-7	4-5	6-12
2009	4-5	3-6	7-11
2008	5-4	4-5	9-9
2007	4-5	5-4	9-9
2006	7-3	5-4	12-7
2005	6-3	5-4	11-7
2004	4-6	1-8	5-14
2003	5-4	4-6	9-10

2013 Schedule

at Toronto

April 5-7, April 30-May 2 & Aug. 13-15

at Boston

May 10-12, June 27-30 & Sept. 20-22

CHICAGO WHITE SOX

U.S. Cellular Field
333 West 35th St. Chicago, IL 60616

Capacity: 40,615 **Dimensions:** 330 LF, 400 CF, 335 RF

Senior Vice President, General Manager: Rick Hahn
Field Manager: Robin Ventura

2012 Record, Finish: 85-77, 2nd in AL Central (-3.0 games)

Blue Jays vs. Chicago

2012 vs. CWS 4-6
2012 at TOR 1-3
2012 at CWS 3-3

All-Time vs. CWS 191-169-1
All-Time at TOR 104-78
All-Time at CWS 87-91-1

at Exhibition Stadium 40-33
at Rogers Centre 64-45
at U.S. Cellular Field 44-51
at Comiskey Park 43-40

Longest Winning Streaks

by Toronto .... 7 games
(2x, last July 29-Sept. 9, 2008)

by Chicago .... 6 games
(July 14, 1977-April 21, 1978)

Series Sweeps at Toronto

Last by Toronto

3-game .... May 7-9, 2004
4-game .... May 15-18, 2009

Last by Chicago

3-game .... May 6-8, 2005
4-game .... None

Series Sweeps at Chicago

Last by Toronto

3-game .... Aug. 22-24, 1996
4-game .... None

Last by Chicago

3-game .... Sept. 1-3, 1995
4-game .... None

Series Results, Last 10 Years

Year	Home	Road	Total
2012	1-3	3-3	4-6
2011	3-1	1-2	4-3
2010	2-2	3-1	5-3
2009	4-0	2-1	6-1
2008	4-0	3-1	7-1
2007	3-1	1-2	4-3
2006	3-3	1-2	4-5
2005	0-3	2-1	2-4
2004	3-0	1-3	4-3
2003	2-4	1-2	3-6

2013 Schedule

at Toronto

April 15-18

at Chicago

June 10-12

CLEVELAND INDIANS

Progressive Field
2401 Ontario St., Cleveland, OH 44115

Capacity: 43,429 **Dimensions:** 330 LF, 400 CF, 335 RF

Executive Vice President, General Manager: Chris Antonetti
Field Manager: Terry Francona

2012 Record, Finish: 68-94, 4th in AL Central (-20.0 games)

Blue Jays vs. Cleveland

2012 vs. CLE 4-2
2012 at TOR 2-1
2012 at CLE 2-1

All-Time vs. CLE 190-188-2
All-Time at TOR 101-88
All-Time at CLE 89-100-2

at Exhibition Stadium 44-34
at Rogers Centre 57-54
at Progressive Field 32-48
at Cleveland Stadium 57-52

Longest Winning Streaks

by Toronto .... 13 games
(June 12, 1991-April 21, 1992)

by Cleveland .... 7 games
(2x, last Aug. 4, 2004-May 14, 2005)

Series Sweeps at Toronto

Last by Toronto

3-game .... Sept. 15-17, 1989
4-game .... June 21-24, 1991

Last by Cleveland

3-game .... Aug. 8-10, 2008
4-game .... June 20-23, 1977

Series Sweeps at Cleveland

Last by Toronto

3-game .... May 3-5, 2010
4-game .... Sept. 5-8, 1991

Last by Cleveland

3-game .... May 1-3, 2007
4-game .... June 28-July 1, 2010

Series Results, Last 10 Years

Year	Home	Road	Total
2012	2-1	2-1	4-2
2011	1-2	3-1	4-3
2010	1-2	3-4	4-6
2009	2-3	2-1	4-4
2008	0-3	1-3	1-6
2007	2-1	0-3	2-4
2006	2-1	0-3	2-4
2005	1-2	1-2	2-4
2004	2-2	0-3	2-5
2003	2-1	2-1	4-2

2013 Schedule

at Toronto

April 2-4

at Cleveland

July 9-11

DETROIT TIGERS

Comerica Park
2100 Woodward Ave., Detroit, MI 48201

Capacity: 41,255 **Dimensions:** 345 LF, 420 CF, 330 RF

President, CEO, General Manager: Dave Dombrowski
Field Manager: Jim Leyland

2012 Record, Finish: 88-74, 1st in AL Central (+3.0 games)

Blue Jays vs. Detroit

2012 vs. DET 2-4
2012 at TOR 2-1
2012 at DET 0-3

All-Time vs. DET 208-179
All-Time at TOR 111-83
All-Time at DET 97-96

at Exhibition Stadium 37-40
at Rogers Centre 74-43
at Tiger Stadium 71-75
at Comerica Park 26-18

Longest Winning Streaks

by Toronto .... 9 games (June 11-Sept. 25, 1989)

by Detroit .... 6 games (Sept. 24, 1980 - April 11, 1981)

Series Sweeps at Toronto

Last by Toronto

3-game .... Sept. 5-7, 2003
4-game .... None

Last by Detroit

3-game .... April 5-7, 2004
4-game .... May 28-31, 1979

Series Sweeps at Detroit

Last by Toronto

3-game .... Sept. 16-18, 2003
4-game .... None

Last by Detroit

3-game .... Aug. 21-23, 2012
4-game .... None

Series Results, Last 10 Years

Year	Home	Road	Total
2012	2-1	0-3	2-4
2011	1-3	1-1	2-4
2010	2-2	2-2	4-4
2009	3-1	2-2	5-3
2008	2-2	3-1	5-3
2007	2-2	1-2	3-4
2006	1-2	2-1	3-3
2005	3-1	0-3	3-4
2004	0-3	2-1	2-4
2003	3-0	4-2	7-2

2013 Schedule

at Toronto

July 1-4

at Detroit

April 9-11

HOUSTON ASTROS

Minute Maid Park
501 Crawford St., Houston, TX 77002

Capacity: 40,981 **Dimensions:** 315 LF, 435 CF, 326 RF

General Manager: Jeff Luhnow
Field Manager: Bo Porter

2012 Record, Finish: 55-107, 6th in NL Central (-42.0 games)

Blue Jays vs. Houston

2012 vs. HOU 0-0
2012 at TOR 0-0
2012 at HOU 0-0

All-Time vs. HOU 1-5
All-Time at TOR 1-2
All-Time at HOU 0-3

at Rogers Centre 1-2
at Minute Maid Park 0-3

Longest Winning Streaks

by Toronto .... 1 game (May 21, 2011)

by Houston .... 4 games (June 10, 2005 - May 20, 2011)

Series Sweeps at Toronto

Last by Toronto

3-game .... None
4-game .... None

Last by Houston

3-game .... None
4-game .... None

Series Sweeps at Houston

Last by Toronto

3-game .... None
4-game .... None

Last by Houston

3-game .... June 10-12, 2005
4-game .... None

Series Results, Last 10 Years

Year	Home	Road	Total
2012	0-0	0-0	0-0
2011	1-2	0-0	1-2
2010	0-0	0-0	0-0
2009	0-0	0-0	0-0
2008	0-0	0-0	0-0
2007	0-0	0-0	0-0
2006	0-0	0-0	0-0
2005	0-0	0-3	0-3
2004	0-0	0-0	0-0
2003	0-0	0-0	0-0

2013 Schedule

at Toronto

July 25-28

at Houston

Aug. 23-25

KANSAS CITY ROYALS

Kauffman Stadium
One Royal Way, Kansas City, MO 64129

Capacity: 37,840 **Dimensions:** 330 LF, 400 CF, 330 RF

Senior Vice President, General Manager: Dayton Moore
Field Manager: Ned Yost

2012 Record, Finish: 72-90, 3rd in AL Central (-16.0 games)

Blue Jays vs. Kansas City

2012 vs. KC 6-2
2012 at TOR 2-2
2012 at KC 4-0

All-Time vs. KC 183-176
All-Time at TOR 98-82
All-Time at KC 85-94

at Exhibition Stadium 37-35
at Rogers Centre 61-47
at Kauffman Stadium 85-94

Longest Winning Streaks

by Toronto .... 5 games
(4x, last April 27-May 6, 2008)

by Kansas City .... 7 games
(2x, last Aug. 10, 1980-Aug. 17, 1981)

Series Sweeps at Toronto

Last by Toronto

3-game .... May 9-11, 2005
4-game .... May 23-26, 2008

Last by Kansas City

3-game .... None
4-game .... None

Series Sweeps at Kansas City

Last by Toronto

3-game .... May 16-18, 2003
4-game .... April 20-23, 2012

Last by Kansas City

3-game .... July 2-4, 1993
4-game .... July 23-25, 1984

Series Results, Last 10 Years

Year	Home	Road	Total
2012	2-2	4-0	6-2
2011	1-2	2-2	3-4
2010	2-1	1-2	3-3
2009	2-1	1-3	3-4
2008	4-0	1-2	5-2
2007	2-1	2-2	4-3
2006	2-1	2-2	4-3
2005	5-1	1-2	6-3
2004	2-1	1-2	3-3
2003	2-1	3-0	5-1

2013 Schedule

at Toronto

Aug. 30-Sept. 1

at Kansas City

April 12-14

LOS ANGELES ANGELS OF ANAHEIM

Angel Stadium of Anaheim
2000 Gene Autry Way, Anaheim, CA 92806

Capacity: 45,285 **Dimensions:** 365 LF, 400 CF, 365 RF

General Manager: Jerry Dipoto
Field Manager: Mike Scioscia

2012 Record, Finish: 89-73, 3rd in AL West (-5.0 games)

Blue Jays vs. Los Angeles

2012 vs. LAA 4-4
2012 at TOR 2-2
2012 at LAA 2-2

All-Time vs. LAA 192-186
All-Time at TOR 107-82
All-Time at LAA 85-104

at Exhibition Stadium 36-37
at Rogers Centre 71-45
at Angel Stadium 85-104

Longest Winning Streaks

by Toronto .... 7 games
(Sept. 8, 1997-Aug. 13, 1998)

by Los Angeles .... 7 games
(2x, last July 20, 1988-May 6, 1989)

Series Sweeps at Toronto

Last by Toronto

3-game .... July 26-28, 2005
4-game .... July 3-6, 1992

Last by Los Angeles

3-game .... July 9-11, 2004
4-game .... None

Series Sweeps at Los Angeles

Last by Toronto

3-game .... May 31-June 2, 1993
4-game .... None

Last by Los Angeles

3-game .... April 26-28, 2002
4-game .... None

Series Results, Last 10 Years

Year	Home	Road	Total
2012	2-2	2-2	4-4
2011	4-3	1-2	5-5
2010	0-3	3-3	3-6
2009	3-3	1-1	4-4
2008	1-2	2-4	3-6
2007	2-1	2-2	4-3
2006	3-1	3-3	6-4
2005	3-0	2-1	5-1
2004	3-3	2-1	5-4
2003	3-0	4-2	7-2

2013 Schedule

at Toronto

Sept. 10-12

at Los Angeles

Aug. 1-4

MINNESOTA TWINS

Target Field
1 Twins Way, Minneapolis, MN 55415

Capacity: 39,800 **Dimensions:** 339 LF, 404 CF, 328 RF

Senior Vice President, General Manager: Terry Ryan
Field Manager: Ron Gardenhire

2012 Record, Finish: 66-96, 5th in AL Central (-22.0 games)

Blue Jays vs. Minnesota

2012 vs. MIN.................................. 5-2
2012 at TOR.................................. 3-0
2012 at MIN.................................. 2-2

All-Time vs. MIN 197-153
All-Time at TOR 105-68
All-Time at MIN.......................... 92-85

at Exhibition Stadium.................. 40-30
at Rogers Centre........................ 65-38
at Target Field 8-3
at Metrodome............................ 79-62
at Metropolitan Stadium 5-20

Longest Winning Streaks

by Toronto.............................10 games
(2x, last July 23, 2007-April 13, 2009)

by Minnesota...........................8 games
(July 15, 1979-June 8, 1980)

Series Sweeps at Toronto

Last by Toronto

3-game........................ Oct. 1-3, 2012
4-game....................................... None

Last by Minnesota

3-game....................April 11-13, 2003
4-game....................................... None

Series Sweeps at Minnesota

Last by Toronto

3-game.................... May 13-15, 2011
4-game....................................... None

Last by Minnesota

3-game.................... July 26-28, 2002
4-game.................... July 21-23, 1979

Series Results, Last 10 Years

Year	Home	Road	Total
2012	3-0	2-2	5-2
2011	2-1	3-0	5-1
2010	3-2	3-1	6-3
2009	2-2	3-1	5-3
2008	3-0	3-0	6-0
2007	3-0	3-4	6-4
2006	2-1	3-1	5-2
2005	1-2	1-2	2-4
2004	1-2	1-2	2-4
2003	0-3	3-0	3-3

2013 Schedule

at Toronto

July 5-7

at Minnesota

Sept. 6-8

NEW YORK YANKEES

Yankee Stadium
1 East 161st St., Bronx, NY 10451

Capacity: 50,291 **Dimensions:** 318 LF, 408 CF, 314 RF

Senior Vice President, General Manager: Brian Cashman
Field Manager: Joe Girardi

2012 Record, Finish: 95-67, 1st in AL East (+2.0 games)

Blue Jays vs. New York

2012 vs. NYY 7-11
2012 at TOR.................................. 5-4
2012 at NYY.................................. 2-7

All-Time vs. NYY 229-289
All-Time at TOR 118-140
All-Time at NYY....................... 111-149

at Exhibition Stadium.................. 31-48
at Rogers Centre........................ 87-92
at Yankee Stadium...................... 11-25
at Original Yankee Stadium...... 100-124

Longest Winning Streaks

by Toronto.............................10 games
(April 14-Sept. 25, 1992)

by New York..........................13 games
(May 10, 1995-June 4, 1996)

Series Sweeps at Toronto

Last by Toronto

3-game....................Sept. 19-21, 2000
4-game....................................... None

Last by New York

3-game........... March 31-April 2, 2003
4-game....................................... None

Series Sweeps at New York

Last by Toronto

3-game...................... June 8-10, 1992
4-game..................... May 22-25, 2003

Last by New York

3-game....................Sept. 19-20, 2012
4-game....................Sept. 18-21, 1995

Series Results, Last 10 Years

Year	Home	Road	Total
2012	5-4	2-7	7-11
2011	5-4	2-7	7-11
2010	6-3	4-5	10-8
2009	3-6	3-6	6-12
2008	5-4	4-5	9-9
2007	4-5	4-5	8-10
2006	5-4	3-6	8-10
2005	2-6	4-6	6-12
2004	4-6	3-6	7-12
2003	3-6	6-4	9-10

2013 Schedule

at Toronto

April 19-21, Aug. 26-28 & Sept. 17-19

at New York

April 25-28, May 17-19 & Aug. 20-22

OAKLAND ATHLETICS

Alameda County Coliseum
7000 Coliseum Way, Oakland, CA 94621

Capacity: 34,077 **Dimensions:** 330 LF, 400 CF, 330 RF

Vice President, General Manager: Billy Beane
Field Manager: Bob Melvin

2012 Record, Finish: 94-68, 1st in AL West (+1.0 games)

Blue Jays vs. Oakland

2012 vs. OAK.......... 4-5
2012 at TOR.......... 1-2
2012 at OAK.......... 3-3

All-Time vs. OAK.......... 176-203
All-Time at TOR.......... 83-104
All-Time at OAK.......... 93-99

at Exhibition Stadium.......... 32-41
at Rogers Centre.......... 51-63
at Oakland Coliseum.......... 91-99

Longest Winning Streaks

by Toronto.......... 8 games
(June 18-Sept. 15, 1982)

by Oakland.......... 9 games
(July 22, 1980-May 24, 1981)

Series Sweeps at Toronto

Last by Toronto

3-game.......... May 17-19, 2003
4-game.......... Aug. 4-7, 2008

Last by Oakland

3-game.......... April 8-10, 2008
4-game.......... None

Series Sweeps at Oakland

Last by Toronto

3-game.......... Aug. 29-31, 1993
4-game.......... None

Last by Oakland

3-game.......... July 31-Aug. 2, 2000
4-game.......... May 22-24, 1981

Series Results, Last 10 Years

Year	Home	Road	Total
2012	1-2	3-3	4-5
2011	3-3	2-2	5-5
2010	3-1	1-2	4-3
2009	2-1	4-2	6-3
2008	4-3	2-1	6-4
2007	0-3	4-2	4-5
2006	3-3	1-3	4-6
2005	2-1	3-4	5-5
2004	1-2	2-4	3-6
2003	1-3	1-2	2-5

2013 Schedule

at Toronto

Aug. 9-12

at Oakland

July 29-31

SEATTLE MARINERS

Safeco Field
1250 First Ave. South, Seattle, WA 98134

Capacity: 47,447 **Dimensions:** 331 LF, 405 CF, 326 RF

Executive Vice President, General Manager: Jack Zduriencik
Field Manager: Eric Wedge

2012 Record, Finish: 75-87, 4th in AL West (-19.0 games)

Blue Jays vs. Seattle

2012 vs. SEA.......... 3-6
2012 at TOR.......... 3-3
2012 at SEA.......... 0-3

All-Time vs. SEA.......... 190-171
All-Time at TOR.......... 101-83
All-Time at SEA.......... 89-88

at Exhibition Stadium.......... 41-29
at Rogers Centre.......... 60-54
at Safeco Field.......... 19-32
at Kingdome.......... 70-56

Longest Winning Streaks

by Toronto.......... 9 games
(May 10-July 24, 1985)

by Seattle.......... 8 games
(Aug. 16, 1999-April 16, 2000)

Series Sweeps at Toronto

Last by Toronto

3-game.......... July 19-21, 2011
4-game.......... None

Last by Seattle

3-game.......... May 11-13, 2001
4-game.......... None

Series Sweeps at Seattle

Last by Toronto

3-game.......... July 5-7, 1991
4-game.......... None

Last by Seattle

3-game.......... July 30-Aug. 1, 2012
4-game.......... None

Series Results, Last 10 Years

Year	Home	Road	Total
2012	3-3	0-3	3-6
2011	3-0	3-3	6-3
2010	2-1	1-1	3-2
2009	3-1	1-2	4-3
2008	3-3	1-2	4-5
2007	5-1	0-3	5-4
2006	2-1	3-3	5-4
2005	5-2	1-2	6-4
2004	5-1	2-1	7-2
2003	2-1	2-2	4-3

2013 Schedule

at Toronto

May 3-5

at Seattle

Aug. 5-7

TAMPA BAY RAYS

Tropicana Field
One Tropicana Drive, St. Petersburg, FL 33705

Capacity: 34,078 **Dimensions:** 315 LF, 404 CF, 322 RF

Executive Vice President, Baseball Operations: Andrew Friedman
Field Manager: Joe Maddon

2012 Record, Finish: 90-72, 3rd in AL East (-5.0 games)

Blue Jays vs. Tampa Bay

2012 vs. TB ... 4-14
2012 at TOR ... 3-6
2012 at TB ... 1-8

All-Time vs. TB ... 121-136
All-Time at TOR ... 71-59
All-Time at TB ... 50-77

at Rogers Centre ... 71-59
at Tropicana Field ... 50-74
at Ballpark at Disney ... 0-3

Longest Winning Streaks

by Toronto ... 5 games (July 1-30, 2004)

by Tampa Bay ... 6 games (May 15-Aug. 5, 2003)

Series Sweeps at Toronto

Last by Toronto

3-game ... Aug. 6-8, 2010
4-game ... None

Last by Tampa Bay

3-game ... July 29-31, 2003
4-game ... None

Series Sweeps at Tampa Bay

Last by Toronto

3-game ... None
4-game ... None

Last by Tampa Bay

3-game ... Sept. 21-23, 2012
4-game ... None

Series Results, Last 10 Years

Year	Home	Road	Total
2012	3-6	1-8	4-14
2011	3-6	3-6	6-12
2010	5-4	3-6	8-10
2009	3-6	1-8	4-14
2008	5-4	2-7	7-11
2007	5-4	4-5	9-9
2006	6-3	6-3	12-6
2005	5-5	6-3	11-8
2004	6-3	3-6	9-9
2003	4-6	4-5	8-11

2013 Schedule

at Toronto

May 20-22, July 19-21 & Sept. 27-29

at Tampa Bay

May 6-9, June 24-26 & Aug. 16-18

TEXAS RANGERS

Rangers Ballpark
1000 Ballpark Way, Arlington, TX 76011

Capacity: 48,194 **Dimensions:** 332 LF, 400 CF, 325 RF

General Manager: Jon Daniels
Field Manager: Ron Washington

2012 Record, Finish: 93-69, 2nd in AL West (-1.0 games)

Blue Jays vs. Texas

2012 vs. TEX ... 3-6
2012 at TOR ... 3-3
2012 at TEX ... 0-3

All-Time vs. TEX ... 190-195
All-Time at TOR ... 109-80
All-Time at TEX ... 81-115

at Exhibition Stadium ... 46-24
at Rogers Centre ... 62-56
at Rangers Ballpark ... 35-40
at Arlington Stadium ... 46-55

Longest Winning Streaks

by Toronto ... 9 games (Aug. 10-1986-May 9, 1987)

by Texas ... 10 games (April 24, 2002-April 30, 2003)

Series Sweeps at Toronto

Last by Toronto

3-game ... May 14-16, 2010
4-game ... July 21-24, 1994

Last by Texas

3-game ... April 30-May 2, 2002
4-game ... July 8-11, 1993

Series Sweeps at Texas

Last by Toronto

3-game ... April 11-13, 2008
4-game ... None

Last by Texas

3-game ... May 25-27, 2012
4-game ... None

Series Results, Last 10 Years

Year	Home	Road	Total
2012	3-3	0-3	3-6
2011	2-1	4-3	6-4
2010	5-2	2-1	7-3
2009	2-1	3-4	5-5
2008	0-2	4-2	4-4
2007	5-2	0-3	5-5
2006	1-2	1-2	2-4
2005	1-2	2-5	3-7
2004	2-1	0-6	2-7
2003	2-4	2-1	4-5

2013 Schedule

at Toronto

June 7-9

at Texas

June 13-16

INTER-LEAGUE OPPONENT

ARIZONA DIAMONDBACKS

Chase Field
401 East Jefferson St., Phoenix, AZ 85004

Capacity: 48,635 **Dimensions:** 330 LF, 407 CF, 335 RF

Executive Vice President, General Manager: Kevin Towers
Field Manager: Kirk Gibson

2012 Record, Finish: 81-81, 3rd in NL West (-13.0 games)

Blue Jays vs. Arizona

2012 vs. ARZ 0-0
2012 at TOR 0-0
2012 at ARZ 0-0

All-Time vs. ARZ 4-5
All-Time at TOR 1-2
All-Time at ARZ 3-3

at Rogers Centre 1-2
at Chase Field 3-3

Longest Winning Streaks

by Toronto .... 2 games
(June 22-23, 2002)

by Arizona .... 3 games
(June 13, 2004-May 22, 2010)

Series Sweeps at Toronto

Last by Toronto

3-game .... None
4-game .... None

Last by Arizona

3-game .... None
4-game .... None

Series Sweeps at Arizona

Last by Toronto

3-game .... None
4-game .... None

Last by Arizona

3-game .... None
4-game .... None

Series Results, Last 10 Years

Year	Home	Road	Total
2012	0-0	0-0	0-0
2011	0-0	0-0	0-0
2010	0-0	1-2	1-2
2009	0-0	0-0	0-0
2008	0-0	0-0	0-0
2007	0-0	0-0	0-0
2006	0-0	0-0	0-0
2005	0-0	0-0	0-0
2004	1-2	0-0	1-2
2003	0-0	0-0	0-0

2013 Schedule

at Toronto

No games

at Arizona

Sept. 2-4

INTER-LEAGUE OPPONENT

ATLANTA BRAVES

Turner Field
755 Hank Aaron Drive, Atlanta, GA 30315

Capacity: 49,586 **Dimensions:** 335 LF, 400 CF, 330 RF

Executive Vice President, General Manager: Frank Wren
Field Manager: Fredi Gonzalez

2012 Record, Finish: 94-68, 2nd in AL East (-4.0 games)

Blue Jays vs. Atlanta

2012 vs. ATL 1-2
2012 at TOR 0-0
2012 at ATL 1-2

All-Time vs. ATL 15-15
All-Time at TOR 8-4
All-Time at ATL 7-11

at Rogers Centre 8-4
at Turner Field 7-11

Longest Winning Streaks

by Toronto .... 4 games
(2x, last June 13, 2001-June 22, 2006)

by Atlanta .... 8 games
(May 22, 2009-June 9, 2012)

Series Sweeps at Toronto

Last by Toronto

3-game .... July 18-20, 1999
4-game .... None

Last by Atlanta

3-game .... None
4-game .... None

Series Sweeps at Atlanta

Last by Toronto

3-game .... June 20-22, 2006
4-game .... None

Last by Atlanta

3-game .... June 20-22, 2011
4-game .... None

Series Results, Last 10 Years

Year	Home	Road	Total
2012	0-0	1-2	1-2
2011	0-0	0-3	0-3
2010	0-0	0-0	0-0
2009	0-0	0-3	0-3
2008	2-1	0-0	2-1
2007	0-0	0-0	0-0
2006	0-0	3-0	3-0
2005	0-0	0-0	0-0
2004	0-0	0-0	0-0
2003	0-0	0-0	0-0

2013 Schedule

at Toronto

May 27-28

at Atlanta

May 29-30

INTER-LEAGUE OPPONENT

COLORADO ROCKIES

Coors Field
2001 Blake Street, Denver, CO 80205

Capacity: 50,398 **Dimensions:** 347 LF, 415 CF, 350 RF

Executive Vice President, General Manager: Dan O'Dowd
Field Manager: Walt Weiss

2012 Record, Finish: 64-98, 5th in NL West (-30.0 games)

Blue Jays vs. Colorado

2012 vs. COL 0-0
2012 at TOR 0-0
2012 at COL 0-0

All-Time vs. COL 6-6
All-Time at TOR 6-0
All-Time at COL 0-6

at Rogers Centre 6-0
at Coors Field 0-6

Longest Winning Streaks

by Toronto .... 3 games
(2x, last June 22-24, 2007)

by Colorado .... 3 games
(2x, last June 11-13, 2010)

Series Sweeps at Toronto

Last by Toronto

3-game .... June 22-24, 2007
4-game .... None

Last by Colorado

3-game .... None
4-game .... None

Series Sweeps at Colorado

Last by Toronto

3-game .... None
4-game .... None

Last by Boston

3-game .... June 11-13, 2010
4-game .... None

Series Results, Last 10 Years

Year	Home	Road	Total
2012	0-0	0-0	0-0
2011	0-0	0-0	0-0
2010	0-0	0-3	0-3
2009	0-0	0-0	0-0
2008	0-0	0-0	0-0
2007	3-0	0-0	3-0
2006	0-0	0-3	0-3
2005	0-0	0-0	0-0
2004	0-0	0-0	0-0
2003	0-0	0-0	0-0

2013 Schedule

at Toronto

June 17-19

at Colorado

No games

INTER-LEAGUE OPPONENT

LOS ANGELES DODGERS

Dodger Stadium
1000 Elysian Park Ave., Los Angeles, CA 90090

Capacity: 56,000 **Dimensions:** 330 LF, 395 CF, 330 RF

General Manager: Ned Colletti
Field Manager: Don Mattingly

2012 Record, Finish: 86-76, 2nd in NL West (-8.0 games)

Blue Jays vs. Los Angeles

2012 vs. LAD 0-0
2012 at TOR 0-0
2012 at LAD 0-0

All-Time vs. LAD 6-6
All-Time at TOR 3-3
All-Time at LAD 3-3

at Rogers Centre 3-3
at Dodger Stadium 3-3

Longest Winning Streaks

by Toronto .... 2 games
(2x, last June 9-10, 2007)

by Los Angeles .... 2 games
(2x, last June 10, 2004-June 8, 2007)

Series Sweeps at Toronto

Last by Toronto

3-game .... None
4-game .... None

Last by Los Angeles

3-game .... None
4-game .... None

Series Sweeps at Los Angeles

Last by Toronto

3-game .... None
4-game .... None

Last by Los Angeles

3-game .... None
4-game .... None

Series Results, Last 10 Years

Year	Home	Road	Total
2012	0-0	0-0	0-0
2011	0-0	0-0	0-0
2010	0-0	0-0	0-0
2009	0-0	0-0	0-0
2008	0-0	0-0	0-0
2007	1-2	2-1	3-3
2006	0-0	0-0	0-0
2005	0-0	0-0	0-0
2004	2-1	0-0	2-1
2003	0-0	0-0	0-0

2013 Schedule

at Toronto

July 22-24

at Los Angeles

No games

INTER-LEAGUE OPPONENT

SAN DIEGO PADRES

PETCO Park
100 Park Blvd., San Diego, CA 92101

Capacity: 42,691 **Dimensions:** 357 LF, 396 CF, 382 RF

Executive Vice President, General Manager: Josh Byrnes
Field Manager: Bud Black

2012 Record, Finish: 76-86, 4th in NL West (-18.0 games)

Blue Jays vs. San Diego

2012 vs. SD 0-0
2012 at TOR 0-0
2012 at SD 0-0

All-Time vs. SD 4-2
All-Time at TOR 0-0
All-Time at SD 4-2

at Rogers Centre 0-0
at PETCO Park 4-2

Longest Winning Streaks

by Toronto .... 2 games
(June 20, 2004-June 14, 2010)

by San Diego .... 1 game
(2x, last June 15, 2010)

Series Sweeps at Toronto

Last by Toronto

3-game .... None
4-game .... None

Last by San Diego

3-game .... None
4-game .... None

Series Sweeps at San Diego

Last by Toronto

3-game .... None
4-game .... None

Last by San Diego

3-game .... None
4-game .... None

Series Results, Last 10 Years

Year	Home	Road	Total
2012	0-0	0-0	0-0
2011	0-0	0-0	0-0
2010	0-0	2-1	2-1
2009	0-0	0-0	0-0
2008	0-0	0-0	0-0
2007	0-0	0-0	0-0
2006	0-0	0-0	0-0
2005	0-0	0-0	0-0
2004	0-0	2-1	2-1
2003	0-0	0-0	0-0

2013 Schedule

at Toronto

No games

at San Diego

May 31-June 2

INTER-LEAGUE OPPONENT

SAN FRANCISCO GIANTS

AT&T Park
24 Willie Mays Plaza, San Francisco, CA 94107

Capacity: 41,888 **Dimensions:** 339 LF, 399 CF, 309 RF

Senior Vice President, General Manager: Brian Sabean
Field Manager: Bruce Bochy

2012 Record, Finish: 94-68, 1st in NL West (94-68, +8.0 games)

Blue Jays vs. San Francisco

2012 vs. SF 0-0
2012 at TOR 0-0
2012 at SF 0-0

All-Time vs. SF 4-8
All-Time at TOR 3-3
All-Time at SF 1-5

at Rogers Centre 3-3
at AT&T Park 1-5

Longest Winning Streaks

by Toronto .... 3 games
(June 13, 2007-June 19, 2010)

by San Francisco .... 7 games
(June 11, 2002-June 12, 2007)

Series Sweeps at Toronto

Last by Toronto

3-game .... None
4-game .... None

Last by San Francisco

3-game .... None
4-game .... None

Series Sweeps at San Francisco

Last by Toronto

3-game .... None
4-game .... None

Last by San Francisco

3-game .... June 15-17, 2004
4-game .... None

Series Results, Last 10 Years

Year	Home	Road	Total
2012	0-0	0-0	0-0
2011	0-0	0-0	0-0
2010	2-1	0-0	2-1
2009	0-0	0-0	0-0
2008	0-0	0-0	0-0
2007	0-0	1-2	1-2
2006	0-0	0-0	0-0
2005	0-0	0-0	0-0
2004	0-0	0-3	0-3
2003	0-0	0-0	0-0

2013 Schedule

at Toronto

May 14-15

at San Francisco

June 4-5

CONSECUTIVE WINS AND LOSSES VS AMERICAN LEAGUE OPPONENTS

vs Baltimore		
Most Consecutive Home Wins:	16	Aug. 8, 2009 - June 15, 2011
Most Consecutive Home Losses:	6	July 1, 1995 - July 2, 1996
Most Consecutive Road Wins:	6	April 24 - Sept. 27, 2004
		April 9-July 18, 2010
Most Consecutive Road Losses:	19	Sept. 15, 1978 - May 2, 1981

vs Boston		
Most Consecutive Home Wins:	6	Sept. 17, 2007-April 6, 2008
Most Consecutive Home Losses:	12	May 20, 1980 - April 25, 1982
Most Consecutive Road Wins:	15	Aug. 11, 1987 - Aug. 16, 1989
Most Consecutive Road Losses:	9	April 10, 2004 - April 18, 2005

vs Chicago		
Most Consecutive Home Wins:	10	June 2, 2007-May 18, 2009
Most Consecutive Home Losses:	7	June 3, 1999 - May 21, 2000
Most Consecutive Road Wins:	6	May 19 - Sept. 6, 1989
Most Consecutive Road Losses:	5	Sept. 1, 1995 - May 22, 1996

vs Cleveland		
Most Consecutive Home Wins:	8	Sept. 23, 1990 - April 21, 1992
Most Consecutive Home Losses:	5	Oct. 7, 2001 - Sept. 26, 2003
Most Consecutive Road Wins:	7	June 12, 1991 - June 26, 1992
Most Consecutive Road Losses:	9	Aug. 28, 2006-May 12, 2008

vs Detroit		
Most Consecutive Home Wins:	8	Sept. 1, 2001 - Sept. 7, 2003
Most Consecutive Home Losses:	6	Aug. 1, 1978 - July 27, 1979
	6	Sept. 29, 1980 - April 18, 1981
Most Consecutive Road Wins:	6	Aug. 17, 1991 - Aug. 6, 1992
Most Consecutive Road Losses:	8	June 14, 1977 - April 7, 1978

vs Kansas City		
Most Consecutive Home Wins:	6	May 4, 2004 - Sept. 30, 2005
	6	April 11, 2007 - June 5, 2009
Most Consecutive Home Losses:	4	3x, last July 27, 1997 - Aug. 24, 1998
Most Consecutive Road Wins:	7	July 30, 2002 - May 10, 2004
Most Consecutive Road Losses:	8	Aug. 5 , 1978 - Aug. 1, 1979

vs Los Angeles Angels		
Most Consecutive Home Wins:	8	Aug. 16, 1998 - April 17, 2000
Most Consecutive Home Losses:	5	Sept. 7, 1983 - July 2, 1984
Most Consecutive Road Wins:	3	7x, last May 5 - Aug. 21, 1998
Most Consecutive Road Losses:	6	June 16, 1982 - June 10, 1983
	6	July 6, 1995 - June 15, 1996

vs Minnesota		
Most Consecutive Home Wins:	10	May 21, 1984 - Sept. 6, 1985
Most Consecutive Home Losses:	7	April 5, 2002 - May 17, 2004
Most Consecutive Road Wins:	6	June 12 - Aug. 19, 1990
	6	June 15, 1993 - April 29, 1994
Most Consecutive Road Losses:	9	May 7, 1979 - June 8, 1980

vs New York		
Most Consecutive Home Wins:	7	April 14, 1992 - June 22, 1993
Most Consecutive Home Losses:	7	May 10, 1995 - June 11, 1996
Most Consecutive Road Wins:	6	Sept. 13, 1985 - June 29, 1986
Most Consecutive Road Losses:	9	June 21, 1979 - Sept. 17, 1980

vs Oakland		
Most Consecutive Home Wins:	4	6x, last April 18-30, 2010
Most Consecutive Home Losses:	7	3x, last Aug. 23, 2006 - April 10, 2008
Most Consecutive Road Wins:	6	May 29, 1993 - April 11, 1994
	6	June 18 - Sept. 8, 1982
Most Consecutive Road Losses:	8	July 22, 1980 - Sept. 30, 1981

vs Seattle

Most Consecutive Home Wins:	6	May 10 - July 24, 1985
Most Consecutive Home Losses:	7	Aug. 16, 1999 - Sept. 5, 2000
Most Consecutive Road Wins:	4	May 25 - July 16, 1990
	4	Sept. 18, 1991 - July 16, 1992
Most Consecutive Road Losses:	5	June 3, 1979 - April 9, 1980

vs Tampa Bay

Most Consecutive Home Wins:	7	May 19, 1998 - April 12, 1999
Most Consecutive Home Losses:	5	May 15 - Sept. 22, 2003
Most Consecutive Road Wins:	4	June 28 - Sept. 10, 2005
	4	May 13 - June 3, 2006
Most Consecutive Road Losses:	8	May 22, 2012 - current

vs Texas

Most Consecutive Home Wins:	9	Aug. 15, 1986 - July 8, 1987
Most Consecutive Home Losses:	8	Sept. 12, 1995 - Sept. 10, 1996
Most Consecutive Road Wins:	4	3x, last April 7, 2010 - April 26, 2011
Most Consecutive Road Losses:	6	July 16 - Sept. 12, 2004

Among AL-CF in 2012, Colby Rasmus ranked 5th in RBI (72), HR (22) and 6th in BB (46).

PLAYER DEVELOPMENT

AARON SANCHEZ

PLAYER DEVELOPMENT & SCOUTING

PLAYER DEVELOPMENT

Director, Minor League Operations .... Charlie Wilson
Minor League Field Coordinator .... Doug Davis
Senior Advisor, Player Development ....Tim Leiper
Senior Roving Instructor .... Rich Miller
Roving Pitching Instructor..............................Dane Johnson
Roving Hitting Instructor .... Mike Barnett
Roving Infield Instructor .... Mike Mordecai
Roving Outfield/Baserunning Instructor ....Tim Raines
Roving Catching Instructor ....Sal Fasano
Rehab Pitching Coach.................................. Rick Langford
Latin Affairs Coordinator .... Omar Malave
Minor League Rehab Coordinator................. Jeff Stevenson
Minor League Strength and
Conditioning Coordinator .... Donovan Santas
Assistant, Strength and
Conditioning Coordinator ....Chris Joyner
Consultant...Sandy Alomar Sr.
Minor League Equipment Coordinator .... Billy Wardlow
Baseball Assistant .... Megan Evans
Assistant, Latin American Administration .... Blake Bentley
Assistant, Player Development......................... Mike Nielsen
Administrative Assistant...................................... Kim Marsh

SCOUTING

Director, Professional Scouting...................... Perry Minasian
Director, Amateur Scouting...............................Brian Parker
Special Assistant, Latin American Operations .....Ismael Cruz
Director, Dominican Republic ....Jose Rosario
Director, Venezuela.. Luis Marquez
Special Assistant, Amateur Scouting .... Chuck LaMar
Coordinator, Professional Scouting .... Pete Holmes
Coordinator, Amateur Scouting .... Harry Einbinder
Coordinator, Amateur Scouting ....Matt Bishoff

MAJOR LEAGUE SCOUTS

Special Assignment Scout................................. Russ Bove
Major League Scout ....Jim Beattie
Major League Scout ....Sal Butera
Major League Scout ....Ed Lynch
Major League Scout .... Jim Skaalen

PROFESSIONAL SCOUTING

Senior Advisor/Professional Scout ....Mel Didier
Professional Crosschecker ....Kevin Briand
Professional Crosschecker ....Jon Lalonde
Professional Scout...Mike Alberts
Professional Scout...................................... Matt Anderson
Professional Scout ....Jon Bunnell
Professional Scout.................................... Steve Connelly
Professional Scout...................................Kimball Crossley
Professional Scout.. C.J. Ebarb
Professional Scout... Bob Fontaine
Professional Scout...Kevin Fox
Professional Scout .... Bryan Lambe
Professional Scout ....Ted Lekas
Professional Scout.. Nick Manno
Professional Scout...................................... Brad Matthews
Professional Scout...David May Jr.
Professional Scout/Performance Coach .... Steve Springer
Professional Scout..Doug Witt

AMATEUR CROSSCHECKERS

National Crosschecker...................................... Blake Davis
National Crosschecker..................................... Dean Decillis
National Crosschecker.................................... Mike Mangan
Regional Crosschecker.......................................Tom Burns
Regional Crosschecker...................................... Steve Miller
Regional Crosschecker......................................Tim Rooney
Regional Crosschecker.................................. Rob St. Julien

AREA SCOUTS

Joey Aversa.. Fountain Valley, CA
Coulson Barbiche.. Columbus, OH
Darold Brown .... Elk Grove, CA
Mike Burns ....Houston, TX
Dan Cox .... Santa Ana, CA
Blake Crosby...Gilbert, AZ
Ryan Fox .... Yakima, WA
Bobby Gandolfo ....Lansdale, PA
Joel Grampietro... Tampa, FL
John Hendricks ....Mocksville, NC
Jeff Johnson ....Denver, CO
Brian Johnston .... Baton Rough, LA
Randy Kramer .... Aptos, CA
Jim Lentine... San Clemente, CA
Mike Medici .... Naperville, IL
Nate Murrie...Bowling Green, KY
Matt O'Brien .... Clermont, FL
Cliff Pastornicky... Birmingham, AL
Wes Penick ....Clive, IA
Michael Pesce .... New Hyde Park, NY
Jorge Rivera .... Puerto Nuevo, PR
Mike Tidick .... Statesboro, GA
Darin Vaughan ....Tulsa, OK
Michael Wagner... Addison, TX

SCOUTS – CANADA

Jamie Lehman... Brampton, ON
Don Cowan .... Delta, BC

SCOUTS – INTERNATIONAL

Jairo Castillo .... East, DR
Jose Contreras...Oriente, VZ
Ruban Contreras .... Santo Domingo, DR
Martin Crespo ....Panama City, PA
Luciano del Rosario ....San Pedro, DR
Juan Garcia ....Oriente, VZ
Rafael Moncada .... San Diego Valencia, VZ
Lorenzo Perez .... Manoguayabo, DR
Daniel Sotelo .... Managua, Nicaragua
Marino Tejada....................................... Santo Domingo, DR
Carlos Villalobos .... Costa Atlantica, CO

VIDEO COORDINATORS

Joe Barbera...Houston, TX
Alan Hull .... Los Angeles, CA

PLAYER DEVELOPMENT

CHARLIE WILSON
DIRECTOR, MINOR LEAGUE OPERATIONS

Born on November 6, 1972 in Toronto and raised in the city... Graduated from Trinity College School in Port Hope, Ontario in 1992... Was a member of the school's football, rugby and downhill skiing teams... Played amateur baseball in Toronto in the summers... Attended Bishops University in Lennoxville Quebec...First joined the organization working the summer seasons in the Public Relations Department between 1993-1996, while continuing his post-secondary studies at Bishops University... Shortly after his graduation from Bishops joined the Club's Baseball Operations Department as a Baseball Assistant, working specifically in player development and scouting... Promoted to the position of Scouting Coordinator in December 2000...Worked in that capacity until August 20, 2003 when he was elevated to the position of Manager, Minor League Operations... On October 9, 2009 was appointed to his current position, Director Minor League Operations... In his current role he oversees the day-to-day operations of the Blue Jays farm system... Resides in Toronto, Ontario... Married with four children.

DOUG DAVIS
MINOR LEAGUE FIELD COORDINATOR

Has been with the Blue Jays since the 2006 season, managing New Hampshire (AA) and Syracuse (AAA) prior to serving as Minor League Catching Coordinator in 2009... Was promoted to his current position as Minor League Field Coordinator on October 9, 2009... Former catcher played professionally for 11 seasons between 1984 and 1994 in the minor league systems of California, Kansas City and Texas... Made it to the Major Leagues on two separate occasions, scoring one run in six games with the Angels in 1988 and collecting a hit in his only at bat with the Rangers in 1992... Has been coaching since 1995, serving as a minor league manager for eight seasons, posting a 515-484 record, winning a NYP League championship in 1997 with Pittsfield, and a 1998 SAL championship with Columbia... Was the Bench Coach for the 2003 and 2004 Florida Marlins, winning a World Series in the 2003 season.

TIM LEIPER
SENIOR ADVISOR, PLAYER DEVELOPMENT

Enters his first season with the Blue Jays as Senior Advisor, Player Development and 18th at the minor league level... Spent the past two seasons as the Miami Marlins Infield Coordinator... Has managed 12 seasons most recently leading the Jacksonvile Suns (AA to it's second consecutive Southern League Championship... Leiper has coached in the Mets sytem (1996-97), Expos (1998-2002), Red Sox (2003), Orioles (2004-05), Pirates (2006-08) and Marlins (2009-12)... Was a coach with the Canadian National Team from 2003-06, a string of fours years that included two Olympic qualifiers, the 2004 Olympic Games in Athens, Greece and the inaugural Winter Classic in 2006... Is a member of the coaching staff for the 2013 WBC Canada team... Had an 11-year minor league career, spending time with in the Tigers, Mets, Royals and Pirates, posting a .273 average with 40 home runs and 460 RBI... Has one son and daughter and resides in Viera, Florida.

The Vancouver Canadians celebrating after winning their 2nd consecutive Northwest League Championship

SCOUTING

PERRY MINASIAN
DIRECTOR, PROFESSIONAL SCOUTING

In his third season in his current role after joining the organization as a Major League Scout on January 30, 2009... Was promoted to his current position on October 9, 2009... Will create the strategy and oversee the direction of all Professional Scouts in the organization... Brings 24 years of baseball experience to the organization, having served as a batboy for the Texas Rangers from 1988-96, then serving as a clubhouse attendant from 1997-2002, before moving into a scouting role in 2003 as a Staff Assistant... Prior to his arrival in Toronto spent two seasons as an Advance Major League Scout for the Rangers... Served as staff assistant to Buck Showalter and Major League coaching staff from 2003 - 2006... Perry comes from a deep rooted baseball family, with his father (Zack) having served over 30 years in professional baseball... Younger brother Calvin is the Minor League Clubhouse Manager Washington Nationals and younger brother Zack serves as the Professional Scouting Director for the Milwaukee Brewers.... Born in Chicago, Illinois and raised in Arlington, Texas... Studied Business at the University of Texas-Arlington... Married with two children.

BRIAN PARKER
DIRECTOR AMATEUR SCOUTING

Joined the Blue Jays in 2009 as a Professional Scout after serving as the Director of Baseball Operations for the Washington Nationals... Was promoted to Professional Crosschecker for the Blue Jays in January of 2012... On June 21, 2012 named to the position of Director, Amatuer Scouting... Began his baseball career with the Colorado Rockies in 1997 and has worked for the Arizona Fall League, the Montreal Expos and Washington Nationals where he worked for five years in the positions of Assistant Director, Scouting and Director of Baseball Operations... Graduated from Indiana State University with a Business Management Degree.

ISMAEL CRUZ
SPECIAL ASSISTANT, LATIN AMERICA OPERATIONS

Born in Santo Domingo, Dominican Republic... Graduated from Santo Cura de Ars High School in 1986 and was chosen for an LAEF scholarship, which he used to attend Eckerd College in St. Petersburg, FL... Was selected for the All-State team and participated in the Jay Hawk and Cape Cod summer leagues while at Eckerd... Drafted in the 20th round by the Philadelphia Phillies... Played professionally for two years (1989-1990), then completed his Bachelor's degree in International Business at Eckerd... Scouted Columbia for Pittsburgh and Cincinnati before relocating to south Florida in 1998 where he worked for Athletes Career Management (later merged with Reich, Katz, & Landis), representing several Major League players... In 2000, managed in the San Diego Padres minor league system... Signed by the Montreal Expos in 2001 as the Director of International Scouting and Development, where he served until 2006... Served as the Director of International Scouting for the New York Mets from 2007-2011... Joined the Toronto Blue Jays as Special Assistant, Latin American Operations in November of 2011.

JOSE ROSARIO
DIRECTOR, DOMINICAN REPUBLIC

Jose Sandy Rosario Valdez, born in Santo Domingo, Dominican Republic on August 11, 1973... Married with three children... Played as an amateur in the Parallel League... Was a bullpen catcher for the DSL Pirates in 1994... Studied engineering in the University Autonoma of Santo Domingo, completing the degree in 2000... Worked with the Montreal Expos from February 2002 until October 2006 as Director of Scouting and Development in the Dominican... Then signed with the Mets as an Area Scout in November 2006 until October 2011... Joined the Toronto Blue Jays as Director of Scouting Dominican Republic on November 2011... Participated in the signings of players such as: Atahualpa Severino, Michael Martinez, Henry Mejia, Juerys Familia, Armando Rodriguez, and Juan Jaime.

LUIS MARQUEZ
DIRECTOR, VENEZUELA

Born June 24, 1980 in Caracas, Venezuela... Graduated from Dodge City Community College in 2000 where he played baseball, also played one year in Georgia State Community College... Spent two seasons as an Assistant Coach and Recruiter at Scottsbluff Community College in Nebraska... In 2008, joined the New York Mets as an area scout in Venezuela... In 2011, was promoted as the Venezuelan Scouting Supervisor for the New York Mets... Joined the Blue Jays in 2012 as their Scouting Director for Venezuela... Has two children... Resides in Caracas, Venezuela.

MAJOR LEAGUE SCOUTS

Russ Bove
Special Assignment Scout

Jim Beattie
Major League Scout

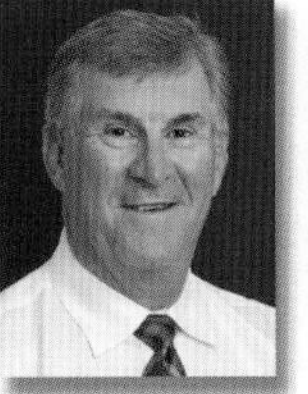

Sal Butera
Major League Scout

Ed Lynch
Major League Scout

Jim Skaalen
Major League Scout

PRO SCOUTS

Mel Didier
Senior Advisor/ Professional Scout

Kevin Briand
Professional Crosschecker

Jon Lalonde
Professional Crosschecker

Mike Alberts
Professional Scout

Matt Anderson
Professional Scout

Jon Bunnell
Professional Scout

Steve Connelly
Professional Scout

Kimball Crossley
Professional Scout

C.J. Ebarb
Professional Scout

Bob Fontaine
Professional Scout

Kevin Fox
Professional Scout

Bryan Lambe
Professional Scout

Ted Lekas
Professional Scout

Nick Manno
Professional Scout

David May Jr.
Professional Scout

Brad Mathews
Professional Scout

Steve Springer
Professional Scout/ Performance Coach

Doug Witt
Professional Scout

AMATEUR CROSSCHECKERS

Blake Davis
National Crosschecker

Dean Decillis
National Crosschecker

Mike Mangan
National Crosschecker

Tom Burns
Regional Crosschecker

Steve Miller
Regional Crosschecker

Tim Rooney
Regional Crosschecker

Rob St. Julien
Regional Crosschecker

C A.J. Jimenez has played in 300 games over five seasons in Toronto's minor league system

Joey Aversa
Fountain Valley, CA

Coulson Barbiche
Columbus, OH

Darold Brown
Elk Grove, CA

Mike Burns
Houston, TX

Dan Cox
Santa Ana, CA

Blake Crosby
Gilbert, AZ

Ryan Fox
Yakima, WA

Bobby Gandolfo
Lansdale, PA

Joel Grampietro
Tampa, FL

John Hendricks
Mocksville, NC

Jeff Johnson
Denber, CO

Brian Johnston
Baton Rough, LA

Randy Kramer
Aptos, CA

Jamie Lehman
Brampton, ON

Jim Lentine
San Clemente, CA

Mike Medici
Napierville, IL

Nate Murrie
Bowling Green, KY

Matt O'Brien
Clermont, FL

Cliff Pastornicky
Birmingham, AL

Wes Penick
Clive, IA

Michael Pesce
New Hyde Park, NY

Jorge Rivera
Puerto Nuevo, PR

Mike Tidick
Statesboro, GA

Darin Vaughan
Tulsa, OK

Michael Wagner
Addison, TX

2013 MINOR LEAGUE INSTRUCTORS

MILLER, Rich — *Senior Roving Instructor*

- Has an extensive background in coaching that began as a Player-Coach for the Jackson Mets in the Texas League in 1979... Has managed six seasons in the minor leagues, posting a 343-292 (.540) record, earning a South Atlantic League Manager-of-the-Year award in 1984... Was in various capacities as on field player or off field personel for 31 consecutive seasons.
- Joined the Twins organization as a Hitting Coach with Rochester (AAA) of the International League for four seasons beginning in 2004... Served as interim manager of Rochester in 2005, beginning April 21, after Phil Roof took a leave of absence to be with his wife who was battling cancer... The Red Wings went 69-62 under Miller, finishing in a second place tie in their division... Began the 2009 season as the hitting coach with the Twins' Single-A Midwest League affiliate, the Beloit Snappers, and was promoted to the same job with Rochester in July 2009.
- Assumed the role of Minor League Outfield and Baserunning Coach in 2010... Returns for a fourth season with Toronto serving now as the Senior Roving Instructor.
- Was the Mets' 6th pick in the 1973 draft... Reached the highest level of the New York Mets farm system, spending 2+ seasons with the Tidewater Tides (AAA) of the International League from 1976-78... In 1977 Miller led the team in hitting with a .284 batting average... During his eight-year minor league career, Miller batted .258 with 28 home runs.

RECORD AS MANAGER

Year	Club & League	W-L	PCT
CAREER TOTALS		343-292	.540

MANAGERIAL/COACHING CAREER

1979-80	Player/Coach, Jackson, Texas League (Mets)
1981	Manager, Little Falls, New York Penn League
1982	Manager, Shelby, South Atlantic League (Mets)
1984-85	Manager, Columbia, South Atlantic League (Mets)
1986-87	Manager, Little Falls, New York Penn League
1988-89	Third Base and Hitting Coach, Tidewater, International League (Mets)
1991-2003	Roving Minor League Outfield and Baserunning Coach (Mets)
2000-03	Assistant Field Coordinator (Mets)
2004-07	Hitting Coach, Rochester, International League (Twins)
2008-09	Roving Minor League Outfield and Baserunning Coach (Twins)
2010-12	Roving Minor League Outfield and Baserunning Coach (Blue Jays)
2013-	Senior Roving Instructor

BARNETT, Mike — *Roving Hitting Instructor*

- Returns the club after serving as the Blue Jays Major League Hitting Coach (2002-05)...Also served as Hitting Coach for the Kansas City Royals (2006-08) and Houston Astros (2011-12)... Served as hitting coach at all levels of the White Sox system from 1990-97 before moving to the Dimaondbacks where he was hitting coach at the AAA level from 1998-2001... During the 1994 season was the hitting coach in Birmingham and Michael Jordan... A graduate of Ohio University with a degree in sports administration, Barnett was also an Assistant Administrator of Baseball Operations in the Yankees organization (1982-87) and a coach at the University of Tennessee (1988-89)
- Played at Ohio University as a catcher.

MANAGERIAL/COACHING CAREER

1990-92	Hitting Coach, Sarasota, Florida State League (White Sox)
1993-95	Hitting Coach, Birmingham, Southern League (White Sox)
1996	Hitting Coach, Hickory, South Atlantic League (White Sox)
1997	Hitting Coach, White Sox, Gulf Coast League (White Sox)
1998-2001	Hitting Coach, Tucson, Pacific Coast League (Diamondbacks)
2002-05	Hitting Coach, Toronto Blue Jays
2006-08	Hitting Coach, Jupiter, Kansas City Royals
2009-10	Minor League Hitting Coordinator, (Astros)
2011-12	Hitting Coach, Houston Astros
2013-	Minor League Roving Hitting Coach, (Blue Jays)

FASANO, Sal

Roving Catching Instructor

- Has managed the past three seasons in the Blue Jays organization beginning with Lansing (A) in 2010, then with New Hampshire in 2011-12 (AA)... Was named Manager of the Year in 2011 with the Fisher Cats after leading the club to an Eastern League championship... 2013 will see him move into the role of Roving Catching Instructor.
- Had an 11-year big league career as a catcher, playing for nine different teams... Played in 427 games, batting .221 with 47 home runs and 140 RBI... When with the Phillies his distinctive Fu Manchu mustache earned him the cult admiration of Phillies fans, which began a Phan Phavorites fan club called Sal's Pals... In 2007 appeared in 16 games for the Blue Jays.

RECORD AS MANAGER

Year	Club & League	W-L	PCT
CAREER TOTALS		208-215	.492

MANAGERIAL/COACHING CAREER

2010	Manager, Lansing, Midwest League (Blue Jays)
2011-12	Manager, New Hampshire, Eastern League (Blue Jays)
2013-	Roving Catching Instructor (Blue Jays)

JOHNSON, Dane Edward

Roving Pitching Instructor

- Began his coaching career as the pitching coach for Medicine Hat (Rookie) of the Pioneer League in 2000... Then moved on to the role of pitching coach for Auburn of the New York-Penn League... Worked as the pitching instructor with the New Haven Ravens of the Eastern League (AA). Under his direction, Dave Gassner and Cameron Reimers finished first and third respectively in the league in ERA... Was appointed to serve as a roving pitching instructor in the Blue Jays' minor league system (2004)... Enters his 10th season as the Blue Jays roving minor league pitching instructor.
- Graduated from Southwest Miami (Fla.) H.S. in 1981 where he played basketball and ran track and cross country... Was sixth in the National Junior Olympic Decathlon... Attended Biscayne College in Miami where he played baseball and basketball... Was an All-Conference selection in basketball. Played two years in the Chinese Professional Baseball League 1990-91 and spent two seasons in Taipei, Taiwan... Returned to the United States as an assistant coach at Lamar University in 1992... Blue Jays' second round selection (No. 48 overall) in 1984 June draft.
- Spent parts of three season in the Majors, compiling a 6-2 record with a 4.70 ERA in 63 relief appearances for the White Sox, Blue Jays and Athletics... Made Major League debut on May 30 at New York and earned his first Major League victory June 8 vs. Toronto... Placed second in the American Association with 24 saves in 1994, and also posted 22 saves in 1996 for the Blue Jays AAA affilate in Syracuse... Overall pitched in 13 seasons in the minor leagues, including six at the AAA level.

MANAGERIAL/COACHING CAREER

2000	Pitching Coach, Medicine Hat, Pioneer League
2001-02	Pitching Coach, Auburn, New York-Penn League
2003	Pitching Coach, New Haven, Eastern League
2004-	Roving Pitching Instructor (Blue Jays)

MORDECAI, Mike

Roving Infield Instructor

- Spent four seasons as Houston Academy High School Head Coach from 2006-09, before joining the Blue Jays in his current role of Minor League Roving Hitting Coach in 2010.
- Graduated from Hewitt-Trussville High School, Trussville, Alabama in 1986 where he played baseball, basketball and football... During his time at South Alabama, he was a two-time All-American and named to the All-Sun Belt Conference team each year... In 1987, he helped the Jaguars to the conference title... Majored in criminal justice and minored in sociology... Drafted by Atlanta in the 6th round of the 1989 draft.
- Had a 12 year career with Atlanta, Montreal and Florida... Was part of the 1995 Atlanta Braves World Champions and the 2005 Florida Marlins World Champion squad... His first hit was a game tying three-run home run in the ninth inning against the Philadelphia Phillies in 1994... Went 5-18 in post season play with two doubles and five RBI... Very versatile, appeared at every position on the diamond except pitcher, including two games at catcher... Batted .244 with 24 home runs and 132 RBI in 793 games.

MANAGERIAL/COACHING CAREER

2010-	Minor League Roving Infield Coach, (Blue Jays)

RAINES, Tim *Roving Outfield/Baserunning Instructor*

- Was with the Marlins serving as minor league baserunning instructor in 2003... Made his Managerial debut with Brevard County (A) in the Expos organization posting a 53-72 record in 2004... Spent three seasons in the White Sox organization, two with the Major League club from 2005-07... In 2005 was the First Base Coach on the World Series Championship team and was Bench Coach in 2006... 2007 served as hitting coach in Harrisburg... Managed in Newark in Independent from 2009-11 before filling the role of Director of Player Development in 2012... 2013 marks his first season with the Blue Jays
- Has four children and resides just outside of Phoenix, Arizona.
- Spent 23 seasons in the Major Leagues with Montreal (1980-90, 2001), Chicago White Sox (1991-95), New York Yankees (1996-98), Oakland (1999), Baltimore (2001) and Florida (2002)... Hit .294 (2605 hits) with 170 home runs, 980 RBI, 806 stolen bases and a .385 OBP... Ranks among the all-time leaders in stolen bases (5th), walks (36th), and hits (76th).... Was successful on 84.7% (806-952) of his stolen base attempts, 3rd best in Major League history... Led the National League in each of his first four seasons... Stole 70+ bases in each of his first six seasons and a career best 90 in 1983... Was named NL Rookie of the Year by the Sporting News in 1981... Hit .300 or better six times and led the NL with a career best .334 mark in 1986... Stole three or more bases 29 times, including four in a game on five occasions... Was named to seven All-Star teams and was the All-Star Game MVP in 1987... Reached the post-season on five occasions, winning World Series titles in 1996 with the Yankees and 1996 and 1998... Is the Expos all-time leader in stolen bases (635), triples (82), walks (793) and is second in hits (1,622) to Tim Wallach... Tied the ALCS record for a six game series with 12 hits vs. Toronto in 1993... Was successful in an AL record 40 consecutive stolen base attempts from July 23, 1993 - Aug. 4, 1995... Had more walks than strikeouts in 19 straight seasons from 1993-2002... Sat out the 2000 season recovering from lupus... Played in four games with son Tim Jr. in Baltimore during 2001 season joining Ken Griffey Jr. and Sr. as the only father/son teammates in Major League history... His uniform #30 was retired by the Expos on June 19, 2004.

RECORD AS MANAGER

Year	Club & League	W-L	PCT
CAREER TOTALS		53-72	.424

MANAGERIAL/COACHING CAREER

2003	Baserunning Instructor (Marlins)
2004	Manager, Brevard County, Florida State League (Expos)
2005	First Base Coach, Chicago White Sox
2006	Bench Coach, Chicago White Sox
2007	Hitting Coach, Harrisburg, (Nationals)
2013-	Minor League Roving Infield Coach, (Blue Jays)

LANGFORD, Rick *Minor League Rehab and Pitching Coach*

- Has been a coach within the Blue Jays organization since the 1996 season... Named pitching coach for Knoxville (AA) in 1996 and 1997... Joined the Dunedin staff (A) in 1998 before moving up to Syracuse (AAA) in 1999... Made his ML debut as a pitching coach during the 2000 season, spending one season in that role... Returned to Syracuse for 2001-02... From 2003-05 returned to Dunedin where in 1995 he earned a Bobby Mattick award for excellence in player development... In each of his seasons in Dunedin the club qualified for the playoffs, while seeing one of his pitchers rank either first or second in league wins... Returned to Syracuse for the 2006-08 seasons... Was appointed Roving Minor League Rehab and Pitching Coach for 2009 before returning the Major Leagues as a Bullpen Coach in 2010... Returns to the role of Pitching and Rehab Coordinator for a third consecutive year in 2013.

- Posted a 73-106 record over 11 Major League seasons (10 with Oakland) with a 4.01 ERA... Completed 85 games in his career, including 28 in 1980... Over a four stretch from 1979-82 completed 75 games... Had his best year in 1980 going 19-12 with a 3.26 ERA in 291.0 innings... In that season he led the AL in CG(28), innings pitched (291.0), while setting an AL record for most consecutive chances accepted by a pitcher without an error from 1977-1980 (230 chances).

MANAGERIAL/COACHING CAREER

1987	Roving Pitching Instructor (Pirates)
1996-97	Pitching Coach, Knoxville, Southern League (Blue Jays)
1998	Pitching Coach, Dunedin, Florida State League (Blue Jays)
1999	Pitching Coach, Syracuse, International League (Blue Jays)
2000	Pitching Coach, Toronto Blue Jays
2001-02	Pitching Coach, Syracuse, International League (Blue Jays)
2003-05	Pitching Coach, Dunedin, Florida State League (Blue Jays)
2006-08	Pitching Coach, Syracuse, International League (Blue Jays)
2009	Minor League Rehab and Pitching Coach (Blue Jays)
2010	Bullpen Coach, Toronto Blue Jays
2011-	Minor League Rehab and Pitching Coach (Blue Jays)

MINOR LEAGUE AFFILIATES

BUFFALO BISONS

AAA - INTERNATIONAL

Coca Cola Field
One James D. Griffin Plaza, Buffalo, NY 14203

Phone .... (716) 846-2000
Fax .... (716) 852-6530
Website .... www.buffalobisons.com
Email .... info@bisons.com
Owner/President .... Robert E. Rich Jr.
President, Rich Baseball Operations ...... Jonathan A. Dandes
Vice President, Finance .... Joseph W. Segarra
Vice President, Secretary .... William G. Gisel Jr.
Controller .... Kevin Parkinson
Corporate Counsel .... William E. Grieshober Jr.
Corporate Counsel .... Jill K. Bond
Executive Assistant .... Tina Lesher
Director, Entertainment and Promotions .... Matt La Sota
Director, Food Services Operations .... Robert Free
Director, Public Relations .... Brad Bisbing
Director, Sales .... Anthony Sprague
Director, Stadium Operations .... Tom Sciarrino
Director, Ticket Operations .... Mike Poreda
Manager, Concessions .... Roger Buczek
Manager, Merchandising .... Sara Burkas
Supervisor, Food Service Operations .... Curt Anderson
Community Relations/Receptionist .... Gail Hodges
Senior Accountant .... Rita Clark
Accountant .... Amy Delaney
Payroll Administrator .... Kate Mancini
Purchasing/Office Manager .... Margaret Russo
Account Executive .... Lindsay Carucci
Account Executive .... Jeffrey Erbes
Account Executive .... Mark Gordon
Account Executive .... Jim Harrington
Account Executive .... Robert Kates
Account Executive .... Geoff Lundquist
Account Executive .... Burt Mirti
Account Executive .... Frank Mooney
Sales Coordinators .... Mike Simoncell, Rachel Szymanski
Chief Engineer .... Pat Chella
Engineers .... Mark Becht, David Wheeler
Chief of Security .... Joe Petronella
Head Groundskeeper .... Chad Laurie
Home Clubhouse/Baseball Operations .... Scott Lesher
Play-by-Play Announcer .... Ben Wagner
High School Baseball Coordinator .... Paul Smaldone
Team Photographer .... James P. McCoy
Pitch-by-Pitch Stringer .... Jon Dare, Nick Iacona
Manager .... Marty Brown
Hitting Coach .... Jon Nunnally
Pitching Coach .... Bob Stanley
Trainer .... Voon Chong
Strength and Conditioning Coach .... Armando Gutierrez
Stadium .... Coca Cola Field
Seating Capacity 18,025
Outfield Distances
.... LF 325, CF 404, RF 325, LCF 371, RCF 367

NEW HAMPSHIRE FISHER CATS

AA - EASTERN

Northeast Delta Dental Stadium
One Line Drive, Manchester, NH 03101

Phone .... (603) 641-2005
Fax .... (603) 641-2055
Website .... www.nhfishercats.com
Email .... info@nhfishercats.com
Ownership .... Operated by DSF Sports
Owner .... Arthur P. Solomon
President and General Manager .... Rick Brenner
Vice President, Business Operations .... Steve Pratt
Vice President, Sales .... Mike Ramshaw
Corporate Controller .... Karl Stone
Director, Box Office Operations .... Tim Hough
Director, Broadcast & Media Relations .... Tom Gauthier
Director, Facilities & Turf .... Shaun Meredith
Director, Marketing and Public Affairs .... Jenna Raizes
Manager, Community Relations .... Megan Shea
Manager, Corporate Sales .... Jason Corbeil
Manager, Merchandise .... Justin Stecz
Manager, Production and Graphic Design .... Sean Hladick
Manager, Stadium Operations .... DJ White
Ticket Sales Account Executive and
Special Events Coordinator .... Stephanie Fournier
Ticket Sales Account Executive .... Chris Aubertin
Ticket Sales Account Executive .... Matt Labossiere
Ticket Sales Account Executive .... Kirby Wade
Ticket Sales Account Executive .... Chris Wall
Ticket Sales Executive and On-Field Promotions .. Jeff Martin
Executive Assistant and Office Manager .... Kayla Hines
Head Groundskeeper .... Dan Boyle
Radio Broadcasters
. Tom Gauthier, Bob Lipman, Dick Lutsk, Charlie Sherman
Manager .... Gary Allenson
Hitting Coach .... Richie Hebner
Pitching Coach .... Tom Signore
Trainer .... Bob Tarpey
Strength and Conditioning Coach .... Brian Pike
Home Clubhouse Manager .... Evan Stokowski
Visiting Clubhouse Manager .... Alex Zapora
Stadium .... Northeast Delta Dental Stadium
Capacity 6,500
Outfield Distances LF-326, CF-400, RF-306

BIOGRAPHIES LAST SEASON HISTORY RECORDS OPPONENTS PLAYER DEV. MEDIA & MISC.

DUNEDIN BLUE JAYS

A - FLORIDA STATE (ADVANCED)

Florida Auto Exchange Stadium
373 Douglas Ave., Dunedin, FL 34698

Phone .... (727) 733-9302
Fax .... (727) 734-7661
Website .... www.dunedinbluejays.com
Email .... dunedin@bluejays.com
Director and General Manager,
Florida Operations .... Shelby Nelson
Assistant General Manager .... Janette Donoghue
Accounting Manager .... Gayle Gentry
Manager, Community Relations,
Group and Retail Sales .... Kathi Beckman
Manager, Sales .... Mike Liberatore
Supervisor, Ticket Sales & Operations .... Jonathan Valdez
Community Relations and Game Day Operations
Coordinator .... Kyra Hallett
Media Coordinator .... Patrick Kurish
Ticket Operations Coordinator .... Dan Hilbert
Administrative Assistant/ Receptionist .... Michelle Smith
Stadium Operations Supervisor .... Leon Harrell
Stadium Operations Supervisor .... Zac Phelps
Senior Advisor .... Ken Carson
FSL Radio Broadcaster .... Tyler Murray
Intern .... Geoffrey Gottlieb
Home Clubhouse Attendant .... Nate Barker
Head Superintendent, Sports Turf .... Patrick Skunda
Assistant Superintendent, Sports Turf .... Matt Johnson
Manager .... Bob Meacham
Hitting Coach .... Stubby Clapp
Pitching Coach .... Darold Knowles
Trainer .... Shawn McDermott
Strength and Conditioning Coach .... Scott Weberg
Stadium .... Florida Auto Exchange Stadium
Capacity 5,509
Outfield Distances LF-335, CF-400, RF-327

LANSING LUGNUTS

A - MIDWEST

Cooley Law School Stadium
505 E. Michigan Avenue, Lansing, MI 48912

Phone .... (517) 485-4500
Fax .... (517) 485-4518
Website .... www.lansinglugnuts.com
Email .... info@lansinglugnuts.com
Principal Owner/President .... Tom Dickson
Co-Owner .... Sherrie Myers
General Manager .... Nick Grueser
Assistant General Manager .... Nick Brzezinski
Senior Director, Food Services .... Brett Telder
Director, Business Operations .... Heather Viele
Director, Marketing .... Jeremy Smoker
Manager, Box Office .... Josh Calver
Manager, Concessions .... Andrew Creswell
Manager, Retail .... Matt Hicks
Manager, Stadium Operations .... Dennis Busse
Administrative Assistant .... Angela Sees
Business Assistant .... Stephanie Hart
Marketing Assistant .... Ben Own
Corporate Account Executive .... Adam Barber
Corporate Account Executive .... Kohl Tyrrell
Group Sales Representative .... Bill Adler
Group Sales Representative .... Faith Brooks
Senior Sponsorship Service
Representative .... Michaela Vryhof
Sponsorship Service Representative .... Ashley Moore
Radio Broadcaster .... Jesse Goldberg-Strassler
Season Ticket Concierge .... David Link
Head Groundskeeper .... Mike Kacsor
Manager .... John Tamargo Jr.
Hitting Coach .... Kenny Graham
Pitching Coach .... Vince Horsman
Trainer .... Drew MacDonald
Strength and Conditioning Coach .... Jason Dowse
Stadium .... Cooley Law School Stadium
Capacity 11,000
Outfield Distances LF-305, CF-412, RF-305

VANCOUVER CANADIANS

A - NORTHWEST LEAGUE (SHORT)

Scotiabank Field at Nat Bailey Stadium
4601 Ontario Street, Vancouver, BC V5V 3H4

Phone .... (604) 872-5232
Fax .... (604) 872-1714
Website .... www.canadiansbaseball.com
Email .... staff@canadiansbaseball.com
Operated By .... Vancouver Professional Baseball LLP
Principal Owner and Managing General Partner ..... Jake Kerr
Co-Owners and Partners .... Jeff Mooney & Andy Dunn
President .... Andy Dunn
General Manager .... Jason Takefman
Assistant General Manager, Ballpark Operations ... JC Fraser
Assistant General Manager,
Broadcast & Media Services .... Rob Fai
Assistant General Manager, Ticket Operations ..... Allan Bailey
Controller .... Eric Gounder
Vice President, Sales and Marketing .... Graham Wall
Manager, Concessions .... Alex Kozak
Manager, Group Sales &
Community Relations .... Jeff Holloway
Manager, Merchandise .... Rich Patterson
Manager, Sales and Marketing Services ..... Angela de Ruiter
Manager, Sales and Promotions .... Grace Kim
Coordinator, Sales and Community Relations ..... Alex Dachis
Coordinator, Sales and
Community Relations .... Vanessa Williams
Head Groundskeeper .... Tom Archibald
Assistant Head Groundskeeper .... Trevor Sheffield
Manager .... Clayton McCullough
Hitting Coach .... Dave Pano
Pitching Coach .... Jim Czajkowski
Trainer .... Reggie Mungrue
Strength and Conditioning Coach .... TBA
Clubhouse Manager .... Glenn Hall
Stadium .... Scotiabank Field at Nat Bailey Stadium
Capacity 5,157
Outfield Distances LF-335, CF-385, RF-335

BLUEFIELD BLUE JAYS

ROOKIE ADVANCED – APPALACHIAN LEAGUE

Bowen Field
Stadium Drive, Bluefield, WV 24701

Phone .... (276) 326-1326
Fax .... (276) 326-1318
Website .... www.minorleaguebaseball.com
Email .... babybirds1@comcast.net
Operated By .... Bluefield Baseball Club Inc.
President .... George McGonagle
General Manager .... Jeff Gray
Director, Field Operations & Grounds .... Mike White
Manager .... Dennis Holmberg
Hitting Coach .... Ken Huckaby
Pitching Coach .... Antonio Caceres
Trainer .... Julian Varela

GULF COAST BLUE JAYS

ROOKIE – GULF COAST LEAGUE

Toronto Blue Jays
Bobby Mattick Training Center at Englebert Complex
1700 Solon Avenue, Dunedin, FL 34698

Phone .... (727) 734-8007
Fax .... (727) 734-8162
General Manager .... Mike Nielsen
Manager .... John Schneider
Hitting Coach .... Paul Elliott
Pitching Coach .... Dave Williams
Coach .... Guillermo Martinez
Trainer .... Jon Woodworth
Home Field .... Bobby Mattick Training Center

DSL BLUE JAYS

ROOKIE - DOMINICAN SUMMER LEAGUE

Phone .... (809) 307-1777
Academy Administrator .... Aldo Reyes
Academy Baseball Operations .... Rocio Jimenez
Field Coordinator .... Pablo Cruz
Administrative Assistant .... Pamela Jacobo
Manager .... Cesar Martin
Hitting Coach .... Luis Hurtado
Pitching Coach .... Rafael Lazo/Oswald Peraza
Pitching Coach/Scout .... Rafael Lazo
Workout Coach .... Julio Germosen
Infield Coach .... Rene Garcia
Outfield/Baserunning Instructor .... Jose Mateo
Head Trainer .... Bob Grimes
Assistant Trainer .... Ysidro Reyes
Strength and Conditioning Coach .... Edwin de la Rosa

OF Kevin Pillar had a breakout season in 2012, splitting time between both Lansing and Dunedin, combined to hit .323 with 40-XBH and 51-SB over 128 games

BUFFALO BISONS

INTERNATIONAL LEAGUE (AAA)

Playoffs: Did not qualify as Las Vegas in 2012

R. HOWARD WEBSTER AWARD WINNER

SS ADEINY HECHAVARRIA – Signed in April of 2010 out of Cuba... Was the only 51s position player to make both the mid-season and postseason PCL All-Star Teams... 43 of his 102 games for Las Vegas were multi-hit games... Finished tied with Moises Sierra for the team lead in RBI (63)... Batted .312 in 102 games, with 20 doubles, six triples, six home runs, 138 hits, 63 RBI and 78 runs scored.

BROWN, Marty — Manager

- Began his managing career in the Pittsburgh Pirates system in 1997... From 2001 to 2002, he managed the Nashville Sounds and then managed of the Buffalo Bisons from 2003 to 2005 with an overall record of 238–193 (.552)... Led the team to the International League title in 2004, being named Manager of the Year and a first place finish in their division in 2005... Was also named Minor League Manager of the Year by Baseball America in that same season... Spent five seasons managing in Japan before returning to join the Blue Jays organization... Now in his third season as manager at the AAA level for the Blue Jays, returning to Buffalo for the first time since 2005.
- The third baseman reached the Major Leagues in 1988 and appeared in 35 games over two seasons with the Reds and one with the Baltimore Orioles, batting .180... Also played in Japan for several years... Was a 12th round selection of the Cincinnati Reds in the 1985 June draft.

RECORD AS MANAGER

	W-L	PCT
CAREER TOTALS	783-719	.521

NUNNALLY, Jon — Hitting Coach

- Began his coaching career in the Cleveland Indians organization in 2007 where he would serve as the hitting coach at Kinston for two seasons... In his first season in Kinston, led the club to a league leading batting average... In 2009 with Columbus (AAA) also led the Clippers to a league leading .275 average... Named to Cleveland's Major League coaching staff for the 2010 season and returned in 2011... Made his debut in the Blue Jays organization in 2012 with New Hampshire (AA) and moves to Buffalo (AAA) for the 2013 season.
- Played professionally for 15 seasons as an outfielder from 1992-2006 with seven different organizations... Spent part of six seasons at the Major League level, posting a .246 average with 42 home runs and 125 RBI... Originally a 3rd round pick by the Indians in 1992 after being named the Junior College Player of the Year

STANLEY, Bob — Pitching Coach

- Made his coaching debut in 2012 as the pitching coach with Las Vegas (AAA) and remains at the AAA level moving to Buffalo for 2013.
- Was the first round pick of the Red Sox in 1974... Played for the only the Red Sox in his 13 year career... Was the Red Sox all-time saves leader with 132 until Jonathan Papelbon passed him on July 1, 2009... He is also the all-time leader in appearances with 637 and is a member of the Red Sox Hall of Fame since 2000... His best season came in 1983 when he led the Sox with 33 saves and posted a 2.45 ERA... Compiled a 115-97 career-record with 693 strikeouts, a 3.64 ERA, 21 complete games, seven shutouts, 132 saves, and 1707 innings in 637 games (85 as a starter).

BUFFALO BISONS — continued

2012 CLUB STATISTICS (LAS VEGAS 51S)

BATTING

PLAYER	AVG	G	AB	R	H	2B	3B	HR	RBI	BB	IBB	SO	SB	CS	OBP	SLG	OPS	SF	SAC	HBP
Bailli, Kenen	.323	12	31	5	10	1	0	1	3	4	0	6	0	0	.400	.452	.852	0	1	0
Bocock, Brian	.211	20	76	9	16	5	1	0	9	5	0	13	1	0	.259	.303	.562	0	0	0
Cooper, David	.314	68	261	45	82	27	1	10	52	37	4	34	0	1	.395	.540	.935	5	0	1
Cust, Jack	.200	16	50	7	10	1	0	0	6	16	0	21	3	0	.397	.220	.617	1	0	1
d'Arnaud, Travis	.333	67	279	45	93	21	2	16	52	19	1	59	1	1	.380	.595	.975	2	0	3
Diaz, Jonathan	.240	95	312	58	75	11	2	3	31	62	0	56	12	4	.374	.317	.691	4	15	7
Eigsti, Ryan	.154	10	26	0	4	1	0	0	3	2	0	7	0	0	.214	.192	.407	0	0	0
Galarraga, Joel	.320	9	25	3	8	1	1	0	3	4	0	5	1	0	.414	.440	.854	0	0	0
Gomes, Yan	.328	79	305	44	100	29	1	13	59	25	0	72	4	0	.380	.557	.938	2	0	2
Gose, Anthony	.286	102	420	87	120	21	10	5	43	49	1	101	34	12	.366	.419	.785	1	4	5
Gosewisch, Tuffy	.277	24	83	9	23	8	1	1	8	9	0	17	0	1	.365	.434	.798	1	1	3
Gotay, Ruben	.346	22	78	14	27	3	0	0	14	13	1	19	3	0	.435	.385	.819	1	0	0
Guerrero, Vladimir	.303	8	33	5	10	2	1	0	4	0	0	1	0	0	.314	.424	.739	1	0	1
Hechavarria, A.	.312	102	443	78	138	20	6	6	63	38	0	86	8	2	.363	.424	.788	5	3	1
Howard, Kevin	.311	35	119	14	37	6	1	4	16	12	1	19	3	1	.374	.479	.853	0	0	0
Hughes, Luke	.314	28	105	20	33	9	3	3	13	13	0	32	1	0	.392	.543	.935	1	1	1
Hurtado, Luis	.167	4	12	0	2	0	0	0	0	0	0	2	0	0	.167	.167	.333	0	0	0
Lind, Adam	.392	32	125	24	49	10	0	8	29	15	0	26	1	0	.448	.664	1.112	3	0	0
McCoy, Mike	.263	85	278	46	73	13	1	3	31	58	0	51	21	10	.386	.349	.735	5	7	1
McDade, Mike	.338	18	71	9	24	3	1	2	18	7	1	11	0	0	.392	.493	.885	1	0	0
Nanita, Ricardo	.306	93	333	49	102	17	0	12	62	23	2	39	3	3	.353	.465	.819	5	1	4
Perales, Danny	.279	72	262	39	73	18	2	6	39	15	0	41	4	2	.319	.431	.750	1	1	1
Phillips, Paul	.333	17	54	5	18	2	0	0	4	5	0	5	0	1	.400	.370	.770	0	3	1
Sierra, Moises	.289	100	377	62	109	16	1	17	63	39	2	86	7	6	.360	.472	.832	2	0	4
Snider, Travis	.335	56	209	49	70	16	0	13	56	34	2	42	2	4	.423	.598	1.021	3	0	0
Sobolewski, Mark	.188	23	80	12	15	4	0	2	8	6	0	12	1	0	.244	.313	.557	0	0	0
Thames, Eric	.330	54	197	31	65	15	3	6	32	26	1	42	1	1	.407	.528	.935	5	0	3
Woodward, Chris	.285	88	309	39	88	25	1	2	34	21	0	58	4	2	.338	.392	.730	2	4	5
Team Total	**.298**	**143**	**4954**	**808**	**1474**	**305**	**39**	**133**	**755**	**557**	**16**	**964**	**115**	**51**	**.370**	**.455**	**.826**	**51**	**41**	**44**

PITCHING

PLAYER	W	L	ERA	G	GS	CG	SHO	SV	IP	H	R	ER	HR	HB	BB	IBB	SO	BK	WP	AVG
Abreu, Juan	0	0	2.70	4	0	0	0	0	3.1	4	1	1	1	0	2	0	5	0	0	.286
Beck, Chad	2	0	1.31	43	0	0	0	18	48.0	39	7	7	2	1	13	1	24	0	2	.218
Carpenter, Andrew	6	3	3.38	21	12	0	0	0	74.2	83	31	28	10	2	19	0	56	1	2	.284
Carpenter, David	0	1	3.57	16	0	0	0	1	17.2	15	8	7	1	1	7	0	19	0	1	.221
Carreno, Joel	2	5	8.92	10	8	0	0	0	36.1	50	41	36	7	2	27	0	30	0	2	.336
Cecil, Brett	1	2	2.50	6	6	0	0	0	39.2	36	11	11	1	1	7	0	33	0	2	.248
Chavez, Jesse	8	5	3.98	19	17	1	0	1	95.0	90	45	42	10	1	20	0	86	1	5	.246
Coello, Robert	4	1	3.00	19	3	0	0	0	42.0	31	16	14	4	0	18	0	43	0	1	.208
Crawford, Evan	1	4	6.83	26	0	0	0	0	27.2	38	22	21	2	2	12	0	20	0	5	.328
Everts, Clint	3	2	3.10	37	0	0	0	2	61.0	53	23	21	2	0	32	0	53	0	6	.236
Gil, Jerry	7	1	4.92	58	0	0	0	9	64.0	68	36	35	8	2	20	1	51	1	6	.268
Hill, Shawn	9	2	4.52	15	15	0	0	0	89.2	115	49	45	10	7	22	0	52	0	2	.312
Hoey, Jim	0	3	4.60	46	0	0	0	1	60.2	59	36	31	5	0	42	0	45	0	22	.261
Hughes, Luke	0	0	0.00	1	0	0	0	0	0.1	0	0	0	0	0	0	0	0	0	0	.000
Igarashi, Ryota	1	1	1.29	19	0	0	0	4	21.0	10	3	3	0	0	3	0	28	0	2	.139
Jakubauskas, Chris	0	0	13.50	3	0	0	0	0	2.2	4	4	4	0	0	2	0	0	0	0	.400
Korecky, Bobby	3	4	3.44	46	2	0	0	0	86.1	89	40	33	10	6	19	0	47	0	3	.266
Laffey, Aaron	3	5	4.52	11	11	1	0	0	63.2	77	41	32	6	3	20	0	38	0	3	.298
Moyer, Jamie	1	1	8.18	2	2	0	0	0	11.0	17	10	10	3	0	3	0	9	0	0	.340
Murphy, Bill	8	5	4.38	28	15	0	0	0	100.2	109	56	49	7	4	47	1	59	1	11	.276
O'Sullivan, Sean	9	3	2.72	14	14	0	0	0	89.1	77	39	27	5	5	23	0	44	0	2	.239
Pino, Yohan	0	2	22.18	3	3	0	0	0	9.1	29	23	23	1	0	3	0	8	0	0	.518
Redding, Tim	0	5	8.66	23	7	0	0	1	62.1	94	64	60	15	5	25	1	38	0	2	.364
Richmond, Scott	11	7	5.61	27	25	0	0	0	134.2	163	93	84	21	4	43	0	112	0	9	.302
Robertson, Nate	0	1	8.00	9	2	0	0	0	9.0	13	9	8	2	0	4	0	5	0	1	.351
Schwinden, Chris	0	1	21.00	1	1	0	0	0	3.0	8	8	7	1	0	1	0	2	0	1	.471
Uviedo, Ronald	0	0	3.00	3	0	0	0	0	6.0	5	3	2	0	0	2	0	5	1	0	.227
Woodward, Chris	0	0	9.00	2	0	0	0	0	2.0	3	2	2	1	0	1	0	0	0	0	.375
Team Total	**79**	**64**	**4.59**	**143**	**143**	**2**	**7**	**37**	**1260.2**	**1379**	**721**	**643**	**135**	**46**	**437**	**4**	**912**	**5**	**90**	**.280**

NEW HAMPSHIRE FISHER CATS

EASTERN LEAGUE (AA)

Playoffs: Did not qualify

R. HOWARD WEBSTER AWARD WINNER

SS RYAN GOINS – Led the Eastern League with 158 base hits en route to a midseason all-star selection... Also led the Fisher Cats with 33 doubles (6th in League), 220 total bases (4th in league), 66 runs scored, and a .289 batting average.

ALLENSON, Gary — Manager

- Has 18 years of managerial experience, highlighted by leading the Oneonta Yankees to a New York-Penn League championship in 1988... Was in the Orioles organization from 2006-12 managing in Norfolk since 2007... Spent part of 2010 as the Orioles Third Base Coach after Juan Samuel took over as manager in June... Managed Ottawa to a playoff spot in 2003 as the Orioles AAA affilaite... Has also managed in the Boston, Milwaukee and Cincinnati organizations... Has served as Bullpen Coach (1992-93) and Third Base Coach (1994) for the Red Sox, First and Third Base Coach for the Brewers (2000-02)... Led Lynchburg to the playoffs in 1989 and Louisville in 1998.
- Spent seven seasons (1978-85) as a catcher in the Major Leagues with the Red Sox and Blue Jays... Was named MVP of the International League in 1978... Backed up Carlton Fisk in his first two years... Played 14 games for the Blue Jays in 1985.

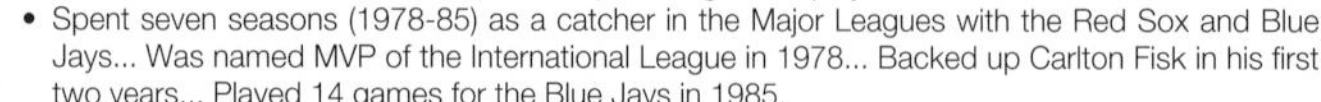

RECORD AS MANAGER

	W-L	PCT
CAREER TOTALS	1032-1148	.473

HEBNER, Richie — Hitting Coach

- Had two previous stints with Toronto serving as both a minor league manager and a roving hitting instructor... He was in voted Manager of the Year in the South Atlantic League in 1988 after leading the Blue Jays' minor league affiliate, Myrtle Beach to a record of 83-56... Has been a hitting coach in the Red Sox, Phillies, Rays and Orioles system as well as stints as a Manger in the Blue Jays, Pirates and Orioles organizations... Was a hitting coach at the Major League level with Boston in from 1989-91 and with the Phillies in 2001.
- Played 18 Major League seasons, posting a .276 career batting average with 1,694 hits and participated in eight National League championship series and won a World Series with Pittsburgh in 1971... Hit 10+ home runs in 11 seasons with a career high 25 in 1973.

RECORD AS MANAGER

	W-L	PCT
CAREER TOTALS	283-300	.485

SIGNORE, Tom — Pitching Coach

- Began his coaching career at Onondaga Community College… In subsequent years, he coached at the collegiate level at Flagler College, his alma mater Quinnipac College and Western Connecticut State University... Jumped to the pro ranks in 1997, joining the Montreal Expos organization… Served as the pitching coach for one season with Vermont in the NY Penn League... Between 1998 and 2000, coached with Cape Fear of the South Atlantic League... Worked as the pitching coach with Harrisburg (AA) of the Eastern League in 2001... Moved to the Florida Marlins' organization in 2002, working as the pitching coach for Portland of the Eastern League... Joined the Blue Jays organization on January 1, 2005, being appointed as the pitching coach for Auburn of the New York-Penn League... Spent three seasons in the role of pithcing coach at Lansing (A)... Returns in 2013 for his 9th season in the Blue Jays organization... Will be his 3rd season in New Hampshire.
- Drafted by the Milwaukee Brewers, he spent one season, 1985, with the club's Pioneer League affiliate in Helena, Montana… Included on the coaching staff of that year's team was former Blue Jays general manager J.P. Ricciardi… Pitched to a 4-4 record in nine games, eight starts, with a 7.02 ERA… Spent one season overseas pitching for a team in Rotterdam, the Netherlands, before beginning his coaching career.

NEW HAMPSHIRE FISHER CATS — continued

2012 CLUB STATISTICS

BATTING

PLAYER	AVG	G	AB	R	H	2B	3B	HR	RBI	BB	IBB	SO	SB	CS	OBP	SLG	OPS	SF	SAC	HBP
Bailli, Kenen	.310	36	129	14	40	7	2	1	13	4	0	23	5	2	.336	.419	.754	0	0	1
Bautista, Jose	.500	1	4	2	2	0	0	2	5	1	0	1	0	0	.600	2.000	2.600	0	0	0
Bocock, Brian	.244	73	270	30	66	17	1	2	25	23	0	42	17	3	.305	.337	.642	3	4	2
Clemens, Koby	.218	41	124	17	27	9	1	5	17	17	0	46	5	4	.324	.427	.752	1	0	3
Diaz, Jonathan	.179	39	145	18	26	2	0	1	9	13	0	28	6	2	.255	.214	.468	1	2	2
Francisco, Ben	.222	9	36	2	8	3	0	0	2	3	0	4	0	0	.282	.306	.588	0	0	0
Galarraga, Joel	.351	16	37	6	13	2	0	0	5	5	0	9	2	1	.455	.405	.860	0	0	2
Glenn, Brad	.239	112	423	50	101	28	0	19	63	29	0	122	8	4	.291	.440	.730	5	0	4
Goins, Ryan	.289	136	546	66	158	33	4	7	61	47	3	78	15	9	.342	.403	.745	6	19	0
Howard, Kevin	.283	65	247	25	70	11	1	6	37	13	1	30	7	2	.318	.409	.727	1	1	0
Jackson, Justin	.225	66	204	24	46	7	3	0	15	23	0	61	11	4	.310	.289	.599	0	2	2
Jacobo, Gabe	.330	25	91	13	30	8	0	2	9	6	0	17	1	0	.371	.484	.855	0	0	0
Jeroloman, Brian	.195	37	113	7	22	0	0	0	9	15	1	25	3	2	.308	.195	.503	1	4	4
Jimenez, A.J.	.257	27	105	14	27	4	1	2	10	5	0	14	2	3	.295	.371	.666	1	1	1
Lind, Adam	.545	3	11	2	6	0	0	1	1	2	1	4	0	0	.615	.818	1.434	0	0	0
Marisnick, Jake	.233	55	223	25	52	11	3	2	15	11	0	45	14	4	.286	.336	.622	4	2	7
McDade, Mike	.275	100	378	44	104	16	0	15	49	43	8	85	1	0	.354	.437	.791	3	0	5
McElroy, Brad	.196	56	148	11	29	2	0	1	7	9	0	36	10	4	.256	.230	.486	0	5	3
Murphy, Jack	.333	8	24	5	8	1	0	2	4	3	0	7	0	0	.393	.625	1.018	1	0	0
Ochinko, Sean	.264	59	216	26	57	11	1	8	29	8	1	40	0	0	.304	.435	.740	1	1	5
Rankin, Pierce	.000	1	4	0	0	0	0	0	0	0	0	4	0	0	.000	.000	.000	0	0	0
Schimpf, Ryan	.279	33	111	21	31	8	0	8	15	23	2	32	3	1	.412	.568	.979	0	1	2
Sobolewski, Mark	.262	94	374	57	98	17	1	18	51	17	0	86	2	2	.295	.457	.752	1	0	1
Tolisano, John	.250	116	436	62	109	27	3	12	42	53	0	82	20	13	.332	.408	.740	1	6	1
Torrealba, Yorvit	.417	4	12	1	5	0	0	0	1	3	0	1	1	0	.533	.417	.950	0	0	0
Van Kirk, Brian	.273	115	399	46	109	28	0	7	44	42	2	70	12	6	.349	.396	.745	3	0	6
Team Total	**.259**	**142**	**4810**	**588**	**1244**	**252**	**21**	**121**	**538**	**418**	**19**	**992**	**145**	**66**	**.322**	**.395**	**.718**	**33**	**48**	**51**

PITCHING

PLAYER	W	L	ERA	G	GS	CG	SHO	SV	IP	H	R	ER	HR	HB	BB	IBB	SO	BK	WP	AVG
Barnes, Danny	0	1	16.20	1	0	0	0	0	1.2	2	3	3	1	0	2	0	2	0	0	.333
Boone, Randy	0	2	10.24	3	3	0	0	0	9.2	19	13	11	5	1	1	0	4	0	0	.413
Carreno, Joel	2	4	3.86	17	7	0	0	0	53.2	43	25	23	4	1	19	0	58	0	3	.218
Cecil, Brett	3	2	3.38	9	9	0	0	0	42.2	44	18	16	2	2	14	0	34	0	1	.267
Crawford, Evan	0	0	0.00	3	0	0	0	0	4.0	3	1	0	0	0	2	0	5	0	0	.200
Daly, Matt	2	4	4.52	47	0	0	0	0	69.2	70	35	35	8	1	35	3	51	0	5	.264
Dubee, Michael	2	1	3.68	16	0	0	0	0	22.0	19	10	9	3	1	7	0	26	0	1	.229
Dyson, Sam	2	2	2.38	33	0	0	9	10	45.1	38	20	12	2	4	15	0	22	0	3	.233
Englebrook, Evan	1	0	6.52	7	0	0	2	3	9.2	11	7	7	0	1	8	0	9	0	2	.282
Everts, Clint	2	1	4.19	12	1	0	1	2	19.1	21	9	9	0	0	12	0	23	0	4	.276
Farquhar, Danny	0	1	2.97	20	0	0	1	3	30.1	28	14	10	2	3	10	0	33	0	1	.237
Gracey, Scott	0	0	3.81	12	0	0	0	1	26.0	26	11	11	1	1	14	2	18	0	3	.265
Hernandez, Fernando	5	8	4.34	36	13	0	0	2	105.2	129	58	51	8	0	29	2	85	0	5	.302
Hutchison, Drew	2	1	2.16	3	3	0	0	0	16.2	16	4	4	1	0	3	0	12	0	0	.262
Jakubauskas, Chris	0	2	2.53	6	1	0	0	0	10.2	8	4	3	1	1	6	0	8	0	0	.200
Jenkins, Chad	5	9	4.96	20	20	0	0	0	114.1	145	67	63	17	5	31	0	57	0	5	.310
Lawrence, Casey	0	1	6.39	3	2	0	0	0	12.2	20	9	9	1	1	5	1	6	0	0	.392
Loup, Aaron	0	3	2.78	37	0	0	3	4	45.1	46	19	14	4	5	14	1	43	1	3	.263
Magnuson, Trystan	0	1	1.95	25	0	0	5	5	32.1	26	10	7	1	2	7	1	24	0	0	.215
Marek, Stephen	1	1	6.94	9	0	0	0	1	11.2	9	9	9	1	1	7	0	13	0	1	.205
McGuire, Deck	5	15	5.88	28	28	0	0	0	144.0	162	103	94	22	6	62	0	97	0	7	.286
Morrow, Brandon	1	0	2.51	3	3	0	0	0	14.1	10	4	4	2	0	3	0	12	0	1	.200
Nolin, Sean	1	0	1.20	3	3	0	0	0	15.0	9	3	2	0	1	6	0	18	0	0	.170
Pino, Yohan	10	8	3.56	25	22	2	0	0	134.0	122	58	53	17	7	29	1	111	0	4	.238
Spoone, Chorye	0	2	3.18	16	1	0	0	1	22.2	14	9	8	1	1	15	0	15	0	0	.182
Stilson, John	2	4	5.04	17	9	0	1	1	50.0	54	33	28	6	3	23	0	44	0	6	.277
Stroman, Marcus	2	0	3.38	8	0	0	0	0	8.0	8	3	3	1	0	6	0	8	0	1	.258
Tepera, Ryan	7	3	4.84	16	15	0	0	0	74.1	82	44	40	4	7	37	0	57	0	6	.280
Uviedo, Ronald	5	3	2.97	43	0	0	7	12	57.2	51	23	19	4	3	25	0	57	1	8	.231
Walrond, Les	0	0	2.25	3	0	0	0	0	4.0	3	4	1	0	0	4	0	3	0	2	.200
Wright, Matt	1	2	3.96	27	2	0	2	3	52.1	39	24	23	9	2	18	0	58	0	2	.204
Team Total	**61**	**81**	**4.14**	**142**	**142**	**2**	**31**	**48**	**1259.2**	**1277**	**654**	**579**	**128**	**60**	**469**	**11**	**1013**	**2**	**74**	**.263**

DUNEDIN BLUE JAYS

FLORIDA STATE LEAGUE (A)

Playoffs: Lost North Division Final 3-0 to Lakeland

R. HOWARD WEBSTER AWARD WINNER

RHP DANIEL BARNES – Led all of Minor League Baseball with 34 saves this season in 36 attempts, setting a new franchise record for saves in a single season... Also named as a mid-season and post-season FSL All-Star.

MEACHAM, Bobby — Manager

- Began coaching career in the Kansas City organization in 1991 at Eugene and managed the club in his 2nd season there... Spent 1993 as a coach with Colorado Springs (AAA) in the Rockies system and returned to the Rockies organization in 2005 as their minor league roving infield instructor... Spent 1994-2001 in the Pirates system, managing in 1994 (Championship Finals), 1995 and 2002... Received his first Major League coaching job in 2006, when new Florida Marlins manager Joe Girardi named him third base coach in 2006... Was the Padres first base coach for the 2007 season and rejoined Girardi as the Yankees' third base coach for 2008... Spent 2009 with the Phillies organization, as the batting coach for the Williamsport... On October 30, 2009, he was hired as the first base coach for the Houston Astros under new manager Brad Mills... Was released in August of 2012 when Mills was relievd of his duties.
- Spent parts of six seasons (1983-88) with the Yankees as a shortstop... In 456 career games posted a .236 average with eight home runs, 114 RBI and 58 stolen bases... Was selected in the first round by the Cardinals in the 1981 draft.

RECORD AS MANAGER

	W-L	PCT
CAREER TOTALS	363-414	.467

CLAPP, Stubby — Hitting Coach

- Began coaching career in 2008 in the Astros organization and remained with them through 2012... Was hitting coach with Lexington (A) and moved to AA Corpus Christi in 2010... In 2011-12 managed the Astros A-affiliate in Tri City, leading the club to a division title in 2012 and an appearance in the finals... Will spend his first season in the Blue Jays system as hitting coach with Dunedin.
- Played 23 games in 2001 for the St. Louis Cardinals, collecting 5 hits in 25 at bats, including 2 doubles and 1 RBI... In 911 minor league games, had a .270 batting average, 48 home runs, 50 triples, 196 doubles, 365 RBI, and 83 steals... Was part of the Canadian team at the Pan American Games in Winnipeg hitting a game-winning, bases-loaded single against the U.S. team on the way to a Bronze medal... Was part of Team Canada in the 2004 Summer Olympics who finished in fourth place... Also played for Canada in the 2006 World Baseball Classic... Clapp's jersey #10 was the first number ever retired by the Memphis Redbirds.

RECORD AS MANAGER

	W-L	PCT
CAREER TOTALS	84-67	.556

KNOWLES, Darold — Pitching Coach

- Entered the coaching ranks with the St. Louis organization after retiring as a Cardinal following the 1980 season… Worked as a minor league instructor for the Cardinals between 1981 and 1988... Joined the Philadelphia Phillies to serve as the pitching coach at the Major League level for the 1989-90 seasons... Coached in the Phillies minor league system with Clearwater in the Florida State League between 1991-99 and then with the Phillies Gulf Coast entry in 2000... Joined the Pittsburgh Pirates organization spending four seasons as the club's Class AAA pitching coach in Nashville and Indianapolis.... Joined the Blue Jays organization on December 13, 2005, being appointed as the pitching coach for the Dunedin Blue Jays of the Florida State League... Returns as Pitching Coach with Dunedin for his 8th consecutive season.
- Pitched professionally for 20 years, spending 15 seasons in the Major Leagues between 1965 and 1980… Went 66-74 with 143 saves and a 3.12 ERA in 765 games at the Major League level... Spent five seasons with the Washington Senators (1967-71), highlighted by a 27 save season in 1970… Selected as an All-Star in 1969 with the Senators when he went 9-2 with a 2.25 ERA and 13 saves… Established a World Series record pitching in all seven games of the 1973 Fall Classic, recording saves in Games 1 and 7 for the Oakland Athletics.

DUNEDIN BLUE JAYS — continued

2012 CLUB STATISTICS

BATTING

PLAYER	AVG	G	AB	R	H	2B	3B	HR	RBI	BB	IBB	SO	SB	CS	OBP	SLG	OPS	SF	SAC	HBP
Ahrens, Kevin	.240	120	409	59	98	17	1	8	53	60	0	87	1	1	.338	.345	.682	5	0	3
Arencibia, J.P.	.200	1	5	0	1	1	0	0	0	1	0	0	0	0	.333	.400	.733	0	0	0
Bailli, Kenen	.267	26	86	15	23	8	1	1	18	6	0	19	0	1	.319	.419	.738	1	0	1
Berti, Jon	.190	50	174	28	33	7	5	0	13	26	0	49	8	3	.301	.287	.588	3	0	3
Clemens, Koby	.299	23	67	7	20	4	0	3	7	11	0	22	0	0	.397	.493	.890	0	0	0
Contreras, Ivan	.056	7	18	2	1	0	0	0	0	0	0	3	2	1	.056	.056	.111	0	1	0
Crouse, Michael	.203	59	202	42	41	9	1	6	26	26	0	73	9	5	.299	.347	.645	1	0	2
Dominguez, Oliver	.253	82	265	40	67	19	2	4	34	30	0	73	4	1	.334	.385	.719	1	5	3
Francisco, Ben	.000	2	6	0	0	0	0	0	0	1	0	1	0	0	.143	.000	.143	0	0	0
Guerrero, Vladimir	.450	4	20	7	9	1	0	4	8	0	0	1	0	0	.450	1.100	1.550	0	0	0
Jackson, Justin	.212	44	137	15	29	6	1	0	8	15	0	43	5	3	.286	.270	.556	2	1	0
Jacobo, Gabe	.338	31	130	28	44	14	0	6	27	12	0	20	2	0	.397	.585	.982	2	0	2
Jeroloman, Brian	.000	3	11	0	0	0	0	0	0	0	0	6	0	0	.000	.000	.000	0	0	0
Jones, Jonathan	.266	90	320	50	85	16	1	0	28	34	1	54	25	4	.356	.322	.678	0	7	11
Knecht, Marcus	.210	126	452	63	95	32	5	13	59	50	1	146	5	1	.302	.389	.692	3	0	11
Lawrie, Brett	.000	1	3	0	0	0	0	0	0	0	0	1	0	0	.000	.000	.000	0	0	0
Marisnick, Jake	.263	65	266	41	70	18	7	6	35	26	0	55	10	5	.349	.451	.800	2	2	10
Murphy, Jack	.223	86	278	31	62	13	1	10	51	35	2	67	0	0	.312	.385	.696	5	2	3
Nolan, Kevin	.316	78	310	54	98	23	5	5	40	34	0	43	12	4	.384	.471	.855	3	0	2
Ochinko, Sean	.306	28	108	21	33	12	0	1	13	10	0	16	0	0	.370	.444	.814	0	0	1
Pillar, Kevin	.323	42	164	16	53	8	2	1	34	5	0	17	16	3	.339	.415	.754	6	1	2
Rankin, Pierce	.292	17	48	7	14	4	0	1	7	6	0	18	0	1	.382	.438	.819	0	0	1
Rodriguez, Alexys	.000	3	5	0	0	0	0	0	0	0	0	3	0	0	.000	.000	.000	0	0	0
Schimpf, Ryan	.266	96	361	59	96	29	3	14	61	48	2	89	4	2	.353	.479	.832	6	0	4
Snider, Travis	.227	5	22	3	5	1	0	0	1	1	0	5	2	0	.261	.273	.534	0	0	0
Talley, Jon	.259	111	410	55	106	27	1	9	68	48	2	105	2	1	.340	.395	.735	5	0	5
Wilson, Kenny	.282	29	117	24	33	6	0	1	13	14	0	22	14	4	.368	.359	.727	0	2	2
Zazueta, Amadeo	.429	6	21	2	9	2	1	1	5	0	0	3	0	0	.391	.762	1.153	2	0	0
Team Total	**.255**	**133**	**4415**	**669**	**1125**	**277**	**37**	**94**	**609**	**499**	**8**	**1041**	**121**	**40**	**.336**	**.398**	**.734**	**47**	**21**	**66**

BATTING

PITCHERS	W	L	ERA	G	GS	CG	SHO	SV	IP	H	R	ER	HR	HB	BB	IBB	SO	BK	WP	AVG
Antolin, Dustin	7	3	4.58	48	0	0	0	1	59.0	72	31	30	3	1	25	0	47	1	5	.305
Barnes, Danny	1	2	1.40	50	0	0	0	34	51.1	37	8	8	3	0	16	1	63	1	1	.198
Boone, Randy	2	1	4.08	18	3	0	0	1	35.1	35	21	16	2	0	7	1	27	0	2	.246
Collazo, Willie	0	0	2.25	2	0	0	0	0	4.0	4	1	1	0	0	0	0	4	0	0	.250
Copeland, Scott	4	1	2.70	7	6	1	0	0	36.2	35	15	11	1	1	14	0	32	0	4	.246
Dyson, Sam	2	0	4.08	6	6	0	0	0	28.2	35	16	13	1	1	5	0	16	0	1	.297
Englebrook, Evan	0	1	2.08	17	0	0	0	0	17.1	13	6	4	0	0	7	0	14	0	0	.197
Escalante, Aleson	0	0	5.40	4	0	0	0	1	8.1	14	6	5	0	0	2	0	1	0	0	.368
Evans, Cody	1	2	6.91	10	2	0	0	0	14.1	18	12	11	2	0	4	0	13	0	0	.310
Farina, Alan	1	2	5.18	24	0	0	0	1	24.1	28	18	14	1	0	14	0	24	0	0	.289
Frasor, Jason	0	0	0.00	2	0	0	0	0	2.0	0	0	0	0	0	0	0	4	0	0	.000
Gailey, Frank	3	0	1.04	8	3	0	0	0	26.0	19	3	3	0	1	5	1	27	0	1	.204
Ghysels, Chuck	0	0	0.00	2	0	0	0	0	3.0	2	0	0	0	0	0	0	6	0	1	.182
Gracey, Scott	2	3	3.81	17	0	0	0	1	28.1	27	14	12	3	0	11	2	42	0	2	.248
Griffith, Shawn	4	3	6.31	27	2	0	0	0	41.1	41	33	29	3	3	26	0	42	0	2	.263
Hernandez, Jesse	1	5	6.61	12	7	0	0	0	47.2	55	37	35	7	4	12	0	38	0	2	.293
Jensen, Tucker	0	1	14.54	1	1	0	0	0	4.1	9	7	7	0	0	2	0	1	1	1	.450
Kaye, Brandon	0	1	2.16	4	0	0	0	0	8.1	4	2	2	0	1	1	0	3	0	0	.143
Lawrence, Casey	9	6	3.63	24	23	1	0	0	138.2	149	60	56	9	1	21	0	90	1	1	.277
Longpre, Bryan	1	0	1.04	7	0	0	0	0	8.2	5	1	1	0	1	2	0	7	0	0	.167
Magnuson, Trystan	0	4	5.40	13	0	0	0	0	18.1	25	14	11	4	2	3	1	26	0	2	.305
Marek, Stephen	1	0	3.60	7	0	0	0	0	10.0	7	4	4	1	1	1	0	11	0	1	.189
Marze, Dayton	2	4	2.82	46	0	0	0	1	70.1	66	26	22	4	5	25	2	37	0	2	.256
Morrow, Brandon	0	0	1.50	2	2	0	0	0	6.0	8	2	1	0	0	3	0	6	0	0	.348
Nolin, Sean	9	0	2.19	17	15	0	0	0	86.1	72	26	21	7	4	21	0	90	0	0	.226
Permison, Drew	0	0	0.00	1	0	0	0	0	1.0	1	0	0	0	0	0	0	0	0	0	.250
Potts, Boomer	0	1	3.34	36	0	0	0	1	32.1	21	12	12	3	2	23	3	35	0	2	.186
Smith, Egan	8	7	3.49	23	15	0	0	1	98.0	94	42	38	4	2	34	2	70	0	6	.247
Stilson, John	3	0	2.82	13	13	0	0	0	54.1	56	22	17	2	1	19	0	47	2	0	.265
Tepera, Ryan	1	3	7.71	5	5	1	0	0	21.0	27	19	18	3	2	12	0	14	1	1	.310
Walden, Marcus	9	2	2.85	13	12	0	0	0	72.2	58	26	23	0	3	18	0	42	0	1	.216
Wojciechowski, A.	7	3	3.57	18	18	0	0	0	93.1	91	40	37	3	5	22	0	76	0	3	.261
Wright, Matt	0	0	0.00	7	0	0	0	0	6.1	7	0	0	0	0	1	1	7	0	1	.292
Team Total	**78**	**55**	**3.59**	**133**	**133**	**3**	**7**	**42**	**1157.2**	**1135**	**524**	**462**	**66**	**41**	**356**	**14**	**962**	**7**	**42**	**.256**

LANSING LUGNUTS

MIDWEST LEAGUE (A)

Playoffs: Lost Eastern Divison Semi-Final 3-0 to Fort Wayne

R. HOWARD WEBSTER AWARD WINNER

LHP JUSTIN NICOLINO – Went 10-4 with a Midwest League best 2.46 ERA and 1.07 WHIP... Pitched 124.1 innings, with 119 strikeouts, 34 earned runs and just 21 walks, while holding opponents to a .241 AVG... It marked his 2nd consecutive Webster award after winning in 2011 with Vancouver (A)... Named top left-hander in the Midwest League.

TAMARGO Jr., John — Manager

- Began his coaching career with the Salem Avalanche in the Carolina League as part pf the Houston Astros organization in 2004... Served as Hitting Coach for Astros affiliate Corpus Christi (AA) in the Texas League between 2005-08... Spent 2010-11 as the Hitting Coach for the Lansing Lugnuts.... Led the Lugnuts in 2012 to a division title and a playoff berth... Will return to Lansing Lugnuts in 2013, for a second season as manager
- The middle infielder played eight seasons of minor league baseball with the first seven in the New York Mets organization… Batted .237 in 704 games with 222 runs batted in and 54 stolen bases… Was a Freshman All-American in 1994 and helped the Gators to the College World Series in 1996, when he was an honorable-mention All-American and named to the NCAA Regional All-Tournament Team… Following his freshman season in Gainesville, competed for Team USA during the World Championships in Nicaragua before earning All-Southeastern Conference honours as a sophomore in 1995.

RECORD AS MANAGER

	W-L	PCT
CAREER TOTALS	82-55	.599

GRAHAM, Kenny — Hitting Coach

HT: 5-9… **WT:** 180… **B/T:** S-R… **BORN:** May 3, 1975 in Tampa, Florida.

- Spent several seasons as a college coach, including at the University of Indianapolis... Was with Independent League Club, Gary SouthShore Railcats, as Hitting Coach for two seasons... The Railcats set 24 individual and team records, including a new Northern League record for hits in a single season (1,057)... The club led the league in batting (.307) for the first time ever and had eight different players hit at least .300... Returns for a fourth season in the Blue Jays organization and third as Hitting Coach for the Lansing Lugnuts.

HORSMAN, Vince — Pitching Coach

- Began his post-playing career as a Batting Practice Pitcher with the Baltimore Orioles from 1998-2004... Spent the 2006 season as Pitching Coach for the Pulaski Blue Jays (Rookie) in the Appalachian League… Stayed with the Rookie League entry, serving as pitching coach for the Gulf Coast Blue Jays... Enters his eighth season with the Blue Jays organization and third as pitching coach with the Lansing Lugnuts.
- Played five seasons in the Major Leagues with Toronto, Oakland and Minnesota... Had his best season in 1992 with Oakland, posting a 2-1 record with a 2.49 ERA in 58 relief appearances.. Signed as a free agent in 1984 by the Blue Jays, he spent seven seasons in the Blue Jays system prior to moving on to the Athletics... With Oakland he played in his only full Major League season, going 2-1 with 1 save and a 2.49 ERA in 58 games.

2012 CLUB STATISTICS

BATTING

PLAYER	AVG	G	AB	R	H	2B	3B	HR	RBI	BB	IBB	SO	SB	CS	OBP	SLG	OPS	SF	SAC	HBP
Baligod, Nick	.291	29	117	20	34	8	0	3	7	16	1	20	1	0	.378	.436	.814	1	0	1
Berti, Jon	.281	60	224	35	63	8	2	2	27	34	0	41	26	8	.391	.362	.753	1	1	7
Brisker, Markus	.192	48	156	23	30	6	2	1	14	19	0	46	18	3	.298	.276	.574	1	2	5
Burns, Andy	.248	78	278	57	69	25	4	9	37	38	0	75	15	2	.351	.464	.815	2	0	7
Crouse, Michael	.194	36	124	18	24	3	0	4	15	15	0	44	6	2	.284	.315	.598	1	0	1
Fermin, Andy	.258	55	178	31	46	7	3	1	17	28	1	28	0	1	.362	.348	.711	0	1	1
Hawkins, Chris	.269	123	491	67	132	17	4	2	43	46	4	78	11	0	.331	.332	.663	1	3	0
Hobson, K.C.	.276	128	490	57	135	43	2	10	86	56	3	85	2	1	.345	.433	.778	9	0	1
Leblebijian, Jason	.222	12	45	7	10	1	0	0	1	7	0	13	1	1	.352	.244	.596	0	0	2
Munoz, Aaron	.223	34	112	11	25	4	0	0	7	11	0	31	1	0	.304	.259	.563	0	3	2
Namba, Bryson	.667	1	3	1	2	0	0	0	1	1	0	0	0	0	.750	.667	1.417	0	0	0
Opitz, Shane	.225	90	315	42	71	19	2	2	37	25	0	65	3	1	.282	.317	.599	3	10	1
Patterson, Kevin	.245	108	387	48	95	22	3	19	79	52	4	124	2	0	.340	.465	.805	5	0	6
Perez, Carlos	.275	71	273	48	75	22	5	5	40	35	1	38	3	2	.358	.447	.804	5	3	3
Peters, Chris	.274	28	95	13	26	7	1	0	9	15	1	21	2	0	.372	.368	.740	2	1	1
Pierre, Gustavo	.252	76	278	35	70	14	8	5	28	16	1	79	8	7	.302	.414	.716	0	5	4
Pillar, Kevin	.322	86	335	49	108	20	4	5	57	35	1	53	35	6	.390	.451	.841	1	1	3
Pompey, Dalton	.227	5	22	1	5	1	1	0	3	1	0	5	1	1	.261	.364	.625	0	1	0
Rankin, Pierce	.162	10	37	6	6	1	0	1	3	1	0	12	0	0	.205	.270	.475	0	0	1
Schaeffer, Chris	.209	28	86	14	18	6	0	2	19	9	0	17	0	0	.317	.349	.666	1	2	5
Schutz, Kipp	.227	19	66	7	15	4	1	0	6	4	0	22	0	0	.292	.318	.610	0	0	2
Sweeney, Kellen	.179	43	140	13	25	2	1	0	12	23	2	30	1	2	.297	.207	.504	1	0	1
Vega-Rosado, J.	.091	6	22	1	2	0	0	0	0	1	0	12	1	0	.130	.091	.221	0	0	0
Wilson, Kenny	.252	94	349	68	88	13	6	4	40	44	0	75	41	8	.360	.358	.718	4	7	17
Team Total	**.254**	**137**	**4623**	**672**	**1174**	**253**	**49**	**75**	**588**	**532**	**19**	**1014**	**178**	**45**	**.338**	**.379**	**.716**	**38**	**40**	**71**

PITCHING

PLAYER	W	L	ERA	G	GS	CG	SHO	SV	IP	H	R	ER	HR	HB	BB	IBB	SO	BK	WP	AVG
Avendano, Javier	2	3	1.48	19	0	0	0	2	30.1	20	8	5	0	2	18	1	39	0	2	.182
Beck, Casey	0	1	0.00	2	0	0	0	0	2.0	2	1	0	0	0	2	0	2	0	1	.286
Berl, Brandon	4	7	3.02	46	0	0	0	1	62.2	67	29	21	2	4	15	4	46	0	2	.275
Brechbuehler, Tim	0	0	19.80	3	0	0	0	0	5.0	11	11	11	1	0	3	0	2	0	2	.423
Brown, Eric	2	0	3.52	8	0	0	0	0	15.1	13	6	6	0	1	4	1	17	0	4	.224
Brua, Philip	3	1	5.36	24	0	0	0	1	40.1	61	26	24	3	2	13	3	27	0	2	.365
Champlin, Kramer	4	1	4.09	29	3	0	0	1	70.1	75	38	32	7	5	19	3	77	0	9	.266
DeSclafani, Anthony	11	3	3.37	28	21	0	0	0	123.0	145	55	46	3	3	25	0	92	2	6	.307
Escalante, Aleson	1	2	6.16	32	0	0	0	0	57.0	79	45	39	11	2	19	2	43	2	3	.320
Griffith, Shawn	2	1	3.16	11	0	0	0	0	25.2	19	10	9	5	2	13	1	23	0	1	.202
Hernandez, Jesse	4	5	2.26	16	15	2	0	0	95.2	82	30	24	2	4	19	0	61	0	3	.234
Kadish, Ian	1	1	4.00	15	0	0	0	2	18.0	14	9	8	0	0	9	1	21	0	0	.209
Longpre, Bryan	0	2	7.08	11	0	0	0	0	20.1	30	25	16	2	4	9	0	10	0	3	.349
McFarland, Blake	5	6	5.68	36	7	0	0	2	90.1	116	58	57	5	5	27	0	73	2	5	.320
Meyer, Ajay	3	3	3.67	54	0	0	0	33	56.1	47	28	23	7	0	13	1	57	1	3	.224
Nicolino, Justin	10	4	2.46	28	22	0	0	0	124.1	112	41	34	6	5	21	1	119	1	4	.241
Rollins, David	6	1	2.78	18	18	0	0	0	77.2	64	29	24	2	2	36	0	75	0	3	.227
Sanchez, Aaron	8	5	2.49	25	18	0	0	0	90.1	64	33	25	3	7	51	0	97	2	6	.204
Syndergaard, Noah	8	5	2.60	27	19	0	0	1	103.2	81	41	30	3	3	31	0	122	0	1	.212
Walden, Marcus	5	2	3.11	14	14	0	0	0	66.2	54	24	23	4	2	30	1	40	3	5	.229
Ybarra, Tyler	3	2	2.27	26	0	0	0	2	43.2	38	16	11	2	2	26	1	57	2	10	.229
Team Total	**82**	**55**	**3.45**	**137**	**137**	**2**	**16**	**45**	**1218.2**	**1194**	**563**	**467**	**68**	**55**	**403**	**20**	**1100**	**15**	**75**	**.258**

VANCOUVER CANADIANS
CHAMPIONS

NORTHWEST LEAGUE (A)
Playoffs: Won Northwest League Final 2-1 over Boise

R. HOWARD WEBSTER AWARD WINNER

RHP JAVIER AVENDANO – Went 8-1 with a 1.27 ERA in 16 games (14 starts)... Pitched 78 innings and gave up 53 hits and 25 walks, while striking out a league best 91 batters (2nd place had 69)... Held opponents to a .193 AVG... Began the season in Lansing, where he pitched 30.1 innings of relief with a 1.48 ERA and 39 strikeouts.

McCULLOUGH, Clayton — Manager

- Spent 2005 as hitting coach for Pulaski of the Appalachian League in his coaching debut... Managed Gulf Coast in 2007 before moving to Lansing from 2008-2009, where he would lead the club to a playoff berth in 2008… In 2010 and 2011 led Dunedin back to the playoffs in each season... Earned **Manager of the Year** honours in 2011... Led the Candians to a second consecutive championship in 2012 and has now reached the post-season in four of his six seasons... Will manage the Vancoouver Canadians in 2013 for a second consecutive season marking his 7th season in the organization.
- A 47th round pick of the Seattle Mariners in the 1998 draft (did not sign)… Was selected by the Cleveland Indians in the 22nd round of the 2002 draft… Spent four seasons catching in the Indians farm system.

RECORD AS MANAGER

	W-L	PCT
CAREER TOTALS	291-263	.525

PANO, Dave — Hitting Coach

- Led St. Petersburg Junior College to the Sun Coast Conference title in both the 2001 and 2002 seasons... Made his professional debut, joining the Blue Jays organization as a coach with Auburn (A) of the New York-Penn League in 2002 and remained through 2004… Managed Pulaski (R) in 2005-06, then spent 2007 as hitting coach with the Gulf Coast Blue Jays... In 2008 managed the Gulf Coast entry... Served as the hitting coach of the Gulf Coast Blue Jays from 2009-2010... In 2013 will represent his 12th season with the Blue Jays and his 3rd with Vancouver.

RECORD AS MANAGER

	W-L	PCT
CAREER TOTALS	95-98	.492

CZAJKOWSKI, Jim — Pitching Coach

- Spent 15 seasons in the Braves organization... During his 11 seasons as a pitching coach in the system, did so with only two clubs, Danville and Rome... Joined the Blue Jays in 2011 and will serve as Pitching Coach at Vancouver in the Appalachian League (A) for a 3rd straight season.
- In his only season in the Major Leagues appeared in five games for Colorado in their inaugural season... Was a three-time All-Star in the minors in 12 seasons... Was a member of six organizations, including Atlanta, Pittsburgh, Milwaukee, Cubs, Colorado and Toronto.

2012 CLUB STATISTICS

BATTING

PLAYER	AVG	G	AB	R	H	2B	3B	HR	RBI	BB	IBB	SO	SB	CS	OBP	SLG	OPS	SF	SAC	HBP
Arcila, Daniel	.176	43	148	17	26	6	1	3	13	11	0	50	4	2	.242	.291	.533	0	1	2
Baligod, Nick	.259	42	158	24	41	8	2	1	25	26	2	19	2	0	.374	.354	.729	0	0	3
Charles, Art	.236	33	127	19	30	10	1	7	18	13	1	41	0	1	.310	.496	.806	1	0	1
Chung, Derrick	.241	34	108	12	26	7	1	0	12	13	0	25	0	1	.341	.324	.665	3	3	5
Davis, D.J.	.167	5	18	3	3	0	0	0	0	5	0	6	1	1	.348	.167	.514	0	0	0
Flores, Jorge	.265	60	215	31	57	14	1	3	19	19	0	45	11	9	.355	.381	.736	0	6	11
Frawley, Tucker	.185	26	81	8	15	0	0	0	8	8	2	20	2	0	.280	.185	.465	1	1	3
Fuenmayor, B.	.282	67	259	35	73	20	1	9	52	14	0	82	1	0	.325	.471	.796	5	0	5
Hernandez, Leo	.104	16	48	3	5	0	0	0	3	1	0	13	1	0	.122	.104	.227	0	1	0
Klein, Daniel	.207	37	116	16	24	5	0	4	15	17	2	40	1	2	.319	.353	.672	2	0	3
Leblebijian, Jason	.291	37	148	24	43	9	1	2	20	10	1	44	6	1	.331	.405	.737	2	0	0
Leyland, Jordan	.235	23	81	11	19	4	1	1	13	13	0	18	0	0	.337	.346	.683	1	0	0
Lopes, Christian	.270	10	37	4	10	1	1	0	4	2	0	6	0	0	.317	.351	.668	1	0	1
Melendez, Ronald	.000	1	1	0	0	0	0	0	0	0	0	0	0	0	.000	.000	.000	0	0	0
Nessy, Santiago	.091	6	22	4	2	1	0	1	3	3	0	7	0	0	.200	.273	.473	0	0	0
Newman, Matt	.262	61	221	34	58	16	5	6	41	30	1	61	6	2	.352	.462	.813	3	0	2
Parmley, Ian	.201	58	209	42	42	9	1	0	12	52	0	44	12	5	.359	.254	.612	1	2	0
Phillips, Eric	.182	8	22	3	4	0	0	0	2	2	0	6	0	1	.280	.182	.462	0	0	1
Pompey, Dalton	.294	11	34	11	10	3	1	0	4	9	0	7	3	0	.442	.441	.883	0	1	0
Ramirez, Carlos	.245	42	159	17	39	5	6	2	19	4	0	45	7	2	.264	.390	.654	0	1	0
Smith, Jr., Dwight	.175	18	63	5	11	3	1	0	8	6	0	11	0	0	.254	.254	.507	1	0	1
Sweeney, Kellen	.229	67	245	35	56	15	2	5	29	35	0	47	5	0	.330	.367	.697	4	0	4
Team Total	**.236**	**76**	**2536**	**360**	**599**	**136**	**26**	**44**	**322**	**299**	**9**	**643**	**67**	**27**	**.324**	**.362**	**.687**	**25**	**16**	**44**

PITCHING

PLAYER	W	L	ERA	G	GS	CG	SHO	SV	IP	H	R	ER	HR	HB	BB	IBB	SO	BK	WP	AVG
Anderson, Kyle	4	2	4.81	13	8	0	0	0	48.2	56	27	26	4	2	12	0	25	0	6	.296
Avendano, Javier	8	1	1.27	16	14	0	0	0	78.0	53	13	11	3	1	25	0	91	0	8	.193
Breault, Zack	2	2	3.93	18	2	0	0	0	34.1	28	15	15	1	2	18	0	21	0	8	.222
Brosnahan, Bobby	2	2	4.50	10	4	0	0	0	32.0	34	17	16	2	4	8	0	16	0	3	.279
Brown, Eric	2	5	7.09	19	9	0	0	1	45.2	62	40	36	9	0	17	0	43	0	7	.310
Browning, Wil	0	0	1.50	5	0	0	0	0	6.0	7	1	1	0	0	0	0	5	0	0	.304
Brua, Philip	2	0	1.23	5	0	0	0	0	7.1	2	1	1	0	0	2	0	3	0	1	.087
Cole, Taylor	6	0	0.81	12	11	0	0	0	66.1	36	6	6	0	6	17	0	57	0	6	.161
Delatte, Brad	0	0	27.00	1	0	0	0	0	0.1	2	1	1	0	1	0	0	0	0	0	.667
Donahue, Tucker	3	2	5.26	22	0	0	0	1	25.2	29	16	15	2	7	14	0	21	0	5	.282
Johnson, Matt	1	1	3.45	14	0	0	0	0	15.2	17	12	6	0	1	5	0	17	0	1	.283
Kadish, Ian	1	1	1.59	15	0	0	0	5	22.2	10	5	4	1	1	11	0	36	2	3	.130
Longpre, Bryan	0	1	8.00	7	0	0	0	0	9.0	14	8	8	1	0	3	0	8	0	0	.341
Lucas, Jonathan	1	1	3.35	27	0	0	0	1	40.1	46	17	15	0	1	20	5	27	0	1	.299
Murphy, Griffin	0	0	3.86	2	0	0	0	0	2.1	2	1	1	0	0	0	0	2	0	0	.222
Norris, Daniel	0	1	10.57	2	2	0	0	0	7.2	14	9	9	0	0	5	0	5	0	1	.400
Osuna, Roberto	1	0	3.20	5	5	0	0	0	19.2	14	9	7	1	1	9	0	25	0	2	.192
Permison, Drew	0	0	0.79	12	0	0	0	5	11.1	9	1	1	0	1	2	0	10	0	3	.220
Purdy, Nicholas	2	3	3.96	19	2	0	0	0	38.2	40	19	17	3	4	22	1	33	0	6	.263
Sikula, Andrew	2	1	2.45	29	0	0	0	10	36.2	25	10	10	3	3	10	0	31	0	4	.189
Stroman, Marcus	1	0	3.18	7	0	0	0	0	11.1	8	5	4	0	0	3	0	15	0	0	.190
Turner, Colton	4	0	1.57	14	4	0	0	0	34.1	23	6	6	0	1	17	0	29	0	2	.200
White, Ben	4	7	5.73	15	15	0	0	0	77.0	76	52	49	7	11	31	1	50	0	7	.255
Team Total	**46**	**30**	**3.54**	**76**	**76**	**0**	**8**	**23**	**671.0**	**607**	**291**	**264**	**37**	**47**	**251**	**7**	**570**	**2**	**74**	**.241**

GULF COAST BLUE JAYS

GULF COAST LEAGUE (RK)
Playoffs: Did not qualify

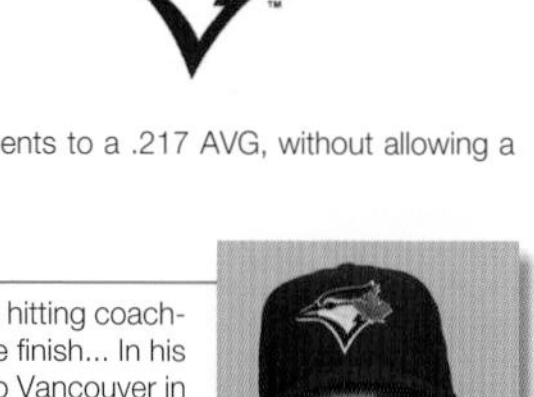

R. HOWARD WEBSTER AWARD WINNER

RHP ALBERT TIRADO – Posted a 2.68 ERA in 11 starts (37 innings)... Held opponents to a .217 AVG, without allowing a home run... Also struck out 34 batters, while walking just 12.

SCHNEIDER, John — Manager

- Made his coaching debut with the Gulf Coast Blue Jays (Rookie) as one of the team hitting coaches in 2008... In his managerial debut led the club to a 30-28 record and a 3rd place finish... In his second season at Gulf Coast finished with a nearly identical 31-28 mark... Moved to Vancouver in 2011 where he managed the Candians for half a season, leaving on August 10 to tend to a family matter... Club was 29-23 at the time and went on to win the Northwest League championship... Returns as manager with the Gulf Coast entry in 2013.
- Was selected by the Blue Jays in the 13th round of the 2002 draft... Played six seasons in the minor leagues advancing as as far as AAA with Syracuse.

RECORD AS MANAGER

	W-L	PCT
CAREER TOTALS	90-79	.533

ELLIOTT, Paul — Hitting Coach

- Was a coach for the Australia National Team in the 2004 Olympics, 2006 World Baseball Classic, 2006 Intercontinental Cup, 2007 Baseball World Cup and 2009 World Baseball Classic... Joined the Blue Jays organization in 1996 as a coach for the Medicine Hat Blue Jays... Has coached in the Blue Jays system since that time including Dunedin, New Hampshire, Gulf Coast and Bluefield.
- Played wiith the Austrailian Senior baseball team in Korea, Japan, the Phillipines, Taiwan and Holland from 1984 to 1987.

RECORD AS MANAGER

	W-L	PCT
CAREER TOTALS	200-233	.462

WILLIAMS, Dave — Pitching Coach

- Made his coaching debut in 2012 as the Pitching Coach of the Gulf Coast club and returns for a second season in the same capacity.
- Had a six-year Major League career with Pittsburgh, Cincinatti and New York Mets... Posted a 22-31 record in 82 games, 72 starts with a 4.83 ERA... Made a career high 25 starts collecting 10 wins in 2005 with the Pirates... Played one season in Japan in 2008.

2012 CLUB STATISTICS

BATTING

PLAYER	AVG	G	AB	R	H	2B	3B	HR	RBI	BB	IBB	SO	SB	CS	OBP	SLG	OPS	SF	SAC	HBP
Alford, Anthony	.167	5	18	1	3	0	0	1	1	2	0	4	4	0	.250	.333	.583	0	0	0
Almonte, Josh	.159	20	69	5	11	1	1	0	2	2	0	30	0	1	.183	.203	.386	0	0	0
Atkinson, Justin	.259	52	185	14	48	1	0	1	23	13	0	29	1	2	.322	.281	.603	0	1	4
Bartlett, Cody	.130	14	46	5	6	2	0	0	2	3	0	7	0	0	.184	.174	.358	0	0	0
Bautista, Jose	.000	1	3	0	0	0	0	0	0	1	0	1	0	0	.250	.000	.250	0	0	0
Becerra, Wuilmer	.250	11	32	5	8	4	0	0	4	4	0	7	0	1	.359	.375	.734	1	0	2
Carroll, George	.182	26	77	9	14	5	0	0	4	7	0	21	1	1	.267	.247	.514	0	1	2
Cenas, Gabriel	.192	49	172	15	33	7	0	2	15	13	0	46	3	1	.271	.267	.538	1	0	6
Conner, Seth	.250	5	16	2	4	1	0	0	2	2	0	3	0	0	.350	.313	.663	1	0	1
Davis, D.J.	.233	43	163	30	38	7	2	4	12	18	0	54	18	7	.339	.374	.713	0	1	8
DeSouza, Nathan	.241	9	29	7	7	0	1	1	3	3	0	6	0	0	.313	.414	.726	0	0	0
Devonshire, Daniel	.148	11	27	4	4	0	0	0	1	5	0	12	0	0	.324	.148	.472	0	0	2
Dupont, Will	.214	15	42	9	9	1	1	0	3	8	0	15	4	1	.365	.286	.651	0	0	2
Gonzalez, Jesus	.206	51	194	16	40	8	1	3	19	14	0	58	3	2	.263	.304	.567	0	0	1
Guerrero, Emilio	.244	24	82	14	20	7	1	2	9	12	0	20	3	3	.347	.427	.774	0	0	1
Jacobo, Gabe	.333	5	18	0	6	3	0	0	4	1	0	2	0	0	.350	.500	.850	1	0	0
Jeroloman, Brian	.286	3	7	1	2	0	0	0	1	0	0	0	0	0	.286	.286	.571	0	0	0
Jones, Dennis	.192	24	73	8	14	3	0	0	4	5	0	29	5	6	.314	.233	.547	0	3	8
Lawrie, Brett	.000	1	1	0	0	0	0	0	0	0	0	0	0	0	.000	.000	.000	0	0	0
Loveless, Derrick	.165	37	115	15	19	5	4	1	11	16	0	38	2	0	.278	.304	.583	0	0	2
Lugo, Dawel	.224	47	170	20	38	2	5	2	20	7	0	25	5	1	.275	.329	.604	0	1	5
Pascazi, Trey	.161	14	31	3	5	1	0	0	4	5	0	19	0	0	.278	.194	.471	0	0	0
Rodriguez, Alexys	.056	7	18	1	1	0	0	0	0	5	0	4	0	1	.261	.056	.316	0	0	0
Saez, Jorge	.200	36	110	19	22	5	0	3	21	23	0	19	4	1	.336	.327	.663	1	0	0
Schaeffer, Chris	.000	3	7	2	0	0	0	0	0	2	0	1	0	0	.222	.000	.222	0	0	0
Silviano, John	.164	39	116	11	19	4	2	2	17	22	0	21	0	3	.298	.284	.582	2	0	1
Valeriote, Shaun	.227	27	88	17	20	4	0	2	12	12	0	25	0	1	.327	.341	.668	0	0	1
Vega-Rosado, J.	.143	9	21	3	3	2	0	0	2	4	0	3	4	1	.308	.238	.546	0	0	1
Team Total	**.204**	**60**	**1930**	**236**	**394**	**73**	**18**	**24**	**196**	**209**	**0**	**499**	**57**	**33**	**.296**	**.298**	**.594**	**7**	**7**	**47**

PITCHING

PLAYER	W	L	ERA	G	GS	CG	SHO	SV	IP	H	R	ER	HR	HB	BB	IBB	SO	BK	WP	AVG
Adams, Zak	1	1	13.06	6	1	0	0	0	10.1	21	18	15	2	3	11	0	8	0	3	.412
Anderson, John	0	1	9.00	2	2	0	0	0	4.0	3	4	4	0	1	1	0	4	0	1	.214
Anderson, Kyle	0	0	1.80	2	0	0	0	0	5.0	6	1	1	0	0	1	0	2	0	0	.286
Beck, Casey	1	0	0.00	3	0	0	0	0	4.0	0	0	0	0	0	1	0	6	0	0	.000
Biggs, Mark	1	4	5.93	11	4	0	0	0	27.1	32	20	18	4	6	9	0	20	0	5	.291
Borucki, Ryan	1	0	3.00	4	0	0	0	0	6.0	4	2	2	1	0	0	0	10	0	0	.182
Brechbuehler, Tim	1	0	3.71	21	0	0	0	2	26.2	28	13	11	0	3	18	0	29	1	7	.269
Browning, Wil	0	0	1.35	7	0	0	0	0	6.2	2	1	1	0	0	1	0	12	0	1	.087
Cabrera, Oscar	0	1	5.40	2	1	0	0	0	5.0	6	3	3	0	0	2	0	5	0	2	.286
Cardona, Adonys	0	1	6.32	8	2	0	0	0	15.2	15	11	11	1	1	10	0	20	1	3	.246
Collazo, Willie	0	0	4.50	2	0	0	0	0	2.0	2	1	1	0	0	1	0	3	0	0	.250
D'Alessandro, Justin	1	0	3.07	14	0	0	0	0	14.2	16	6	5	0	1	8	0	12	0	1	.281
Dawson, Shane	2	1	2.35	10	3	0	0	0	30.2	33	13	8	2	1	10	0	35	1	3	.282
DeJong, Chase	1	0	1.50	6	0	0	0	0	12.0	7	2	2	0	0	1	0	15	0	0	.171
Del Rosario, Yeyfry	1	5	3.63	13	12	0	0	0	44.2	37	18	18	1	4	12	0	52	3	5	.222
Dragmire, Brady	0	3	1.14	15	0	0	0	1	23.2	17	10	3	0	3	5	0	14	0	2	.215
Ghysels, Chuck	0	3	3.86	25	0	0	0	7	25.2	22	11	11	4	2	8	0	41	0	1	.232
Gonzales, Tyler	1	1	8.40	9	3	0	0	0	15.0	20	14	14	1	2	4	0	7	0	3	.328
Gonzalez, Alonzo	3	3	5.15	10	7	0	0	0	36.2	37	26	21	3	1	12	0	22	1	1	.272
Gracesqui, Francisco	3	2	2.88	22	0	0	0	0	34.1	24	14	11	1	3	26	0	46	1	4	.195
Kaye, Brandon	0	2	3.55	13	0	0	0	0	25.1	24	10	10	0	2	4	0	28	0	0	.258
Kelly, Adaric	2	0	1.48	14	0	0	0	1	24.1	20	8	4	2	1	7	0	22	0	1	.220
Labourt, Jairo	0	3	3.79	12	12	0	0	0	38.0	38	20	16	2	0	23	0	39	0	9	.253
Lara, Wilmin	0	0	6.23	3	0	0	0	0	4.1	4	3	3	0	2	5	0	2	0	5	.235
Mendez, Luis	1	1	8.38	9	0	0	0	0	9.2	19	10	9	0	0	3	0	3	0	0	.413
Ramirez, Alex	0	0	13.50	1	0	0	0	0	0.2	2	1	1	0	0	2	0	0	0	0	.667
Tinoco, Jesus	1	1	6.00	2	0	0	0	0	6.0	7	4	4	0	1	1	0	8	1	0	.280
Tirado, Alberto	1	2	2.68	11	11	0	0	0	37.0	28	12	11	0	1	12	0	34	0	2	.217
Wasilewski, Zakery	0	3	7.89	10	2	0	0	0	21.2	30	21	19	1	2	19	0	21	0	5	.333
Team Total	**22**	**38**	**4.13**	**60**	**60**	**0**	**3**	**11**	**517.0**	**504**	**277**	**237**	**25**	**40**	**217**	**0**	**520**	**9**	**64**	**.256**

BLUEFIELD BLUE JAYS

APPALACHIAN LEAGUE (RK)

Playoffs: Did not qualify

R. HOWARD WEBSTER AWARD WINNER

SS CHRISTIAN LOPES – Hit .280 with an .827 OPS in 49 games for Bluefield... Finished the season with 25 XBH (16-2B, 5-3B, 4-HR), 29 RBI, 33 runs scored, and a .484 SLG... Was promoted to Vancouver, where he hit .270 in 10 games to complete his season.

HOLMBERG, Dennis — Manager

- Has been with the Blue Jays for all but one of his 36 seasons as a coach or manager... Has led his teams to a post-season birth on 10 occasions, including six of the nine at Auburn... Culminated with a championship at Auburn in 2007, his first... Led Dunedin towards FSL record 53-14 in the first half of 1990 season (.791 winning percentage was also league record for a half season)... Made his **Major League debut** as coach with Toronto in 1994... Was Toronto's bullpen coach in 1994 and 1995... In 2003, Auburn posted a record of 56-18 which fell just two wins short of the best mark in the history of the New York Penn League... Managed the Blue Jays new entry at Bluefield in the Appalachian League in 2011 to a playoff berth with a 40-28 mark... Picked up his first **Manager of the Year** award for his efforts... Returns to Bluefield for a 3rd consecutive season.
- Was drafted by the Brewers in the 5th round in 1970... Played eight seasons in the minors.. Played every position except first base, also pitching in three games... Brewers' fifth pick in 1970 January draft.

RECORD AS MANAGER

	W-L	PCT
CAREER TOTALS	1308-1219	.518

HUCKABY, Ken — Hitting Coach

- Makes his coaching debut in 2013 as the hitting coach with the Gulf Coast entry.
- Had a six year career with Arizona, Toronto, Texas, Baltimore and Boston... In 161 career games batted .222 with three home runs and 31 RBI... Appeared in a career high 88 games for the Blue Jays in 2002.

CACERES, Antonio Gonzalez — Pitching Coach

- Began his coaching career as the Pitching Coach with the Blue Jays of the Dominican Summer League... Led an Auburn clubto a league lead in strikeouts and finished second in ERA in 2006... Returns for his 14th year coaching in the Blue Jays organization... Will be his 3rd with Bluefield.
- Signed as a non-drafted free agent by the Blue Jays on February 2, 1995... Played four seasons in the minor leagues (1995-1998), all within the Blue Jays organization.

2012 CLUB STATISTICS

BATTING

PLAYER	AVG	G	AB	R	H	2B	3B	HR	RBI	BB	IBB	SO	SB	CS	OBP	SLG	OPS	SF	SAC	HBP
Alvarez, Hector	.083	20	48	1	4	0	0	0	2	2	0	12	0	0	.135	.083	.218	1	2	1
Anderson, Jacob	.194	57	191	25	37	10	1	3	13	11	0	72	3	3	.271	.304	.575	2	1	10
Arce, Eric	.236	47	127	26	30	5	1	8	27	27	0	55	0	0	.384	.480	.864	1	0	4
Atkinson, Justin	.300	3	10	2	3	1	0	0	1	0	0	1	0	1	.364	.400	.764	0	0	1
Azor, Alex	.250	14	40	5	10	1	0	0	1	3	0	5	0	1	.302	.275	.577	0	2	0
Charles, Art	.235	31	85	18	20	5	3	6	16	33	0	33	2	0	.463	.576	1.040	1	0	4
Conner, Seth	.296	49	142	23	42	8	2	2	28	24	1	33	0	0	.421	.423	.844	3	1	9
Davis, D.J.	.340	12	47	9	16	3	1	1	6	4	0	10	6	2	.415	.511	.926	0	0	2
Dean, Matthew	.222	49	167	22	37	8	4	2	24	12	0	60	3	2	.282	.353	.635	0	1	2
Frias, Christian	.229	18	48	7	11	1	1	0	3	6	0	12	0	0	.315	.292	.606	0	1	0
Guerrero, Emilio	.185	16	54	8	10	1	1	0	8	2	0	17	1	0	.207	.241	.448	2	2	0
Jones, Dennis	.192	18	52	6	10	2	0	0	6	1	0	17	7	0	.222	.231	.453	0	2	1
Leblebijian, Jason	.194	9	31	3	6	3	0	0	3	5	0	8	1	0	.333	.290	.624	1	0	2
Leyland, Jordan	.235	16	51	3	12	3	0	1	4	1	0	12	0	1	.264	.353	.617	0	0	1
Lopes, Christian	.280	49	186	33	52	16	5	4	29	15	0	34	6	1	.343	.484	.827	0	1	3
Nessy, Santiago	.256	45	160	26	41	8	0	8	23	13	0	47	0	0	.320	.456	.776	2	0	3
Peters, Chris	.267	11	15	5	4	2	0	0	4	4	0	2	1	0	.421	.400	.821	0	2	0
Pompey, Dalton	.357	4	14	2	5	1	1	0	1	0	0	2	1	0	.357	.571	.929	0	0	0
Ramirez, Carlos	.273	10	33	4	9	2	0	1	6	2	0	6	0	1	.333	.424	.758	0	0	1
Smith, Jr., Dwight	.226	41	159	20	36	6	0	4	21	11	0	22	1	1	.289	.340	.629	0	0	3
Taylor, Nico	.268	49	164	21	44	9	1	1	14	13	0	49	5	3	.324	.354	.678	1	1	1
Thon, Dickie	.221	48	149	18	33	5	1	2	14	19	0	34	7	3	.331	.309	.640	1	1	6
Vega-Rosado, J.	.275	41	149	20	41	6	1	2	12	16	1	40	7	4	.355	.369	.724	1	2	3
Team Total	**.242**	**66**	**2122**	**307**	**513**	**106**	**23**	**45**	**266**	**224**	**2**	**583**	**51**	**23**	**.328**	**.377**	**.705**	**16**	**19**	**57**

PITCHING

PITCHERS	W	L	ERA	G	GS	CG	SHO	SV	IP	H	R	ER	HR	HB	BB	IBB	SO	BK	WP	AVG
Broussard, Colby	0	4	7.04	17	0	0	0	3	23.0	28	22	18	3	4	16	0	27	0	7	.295
Browning, Wil	0	1	0.82	10	0	0	0	4	11.0	6	3	1	0	3	3	1	16	1	1	.146
Carmona, Julio	0	4	2.83	17	0	0	0	2	28.2	22	13	9	0	1	15	0	34	0	11	.208
Comer, Kevin	3	3	3.95	10	7	0	0	0	43.1	43	25	19	4	3	8	0	29	0	3	.249
Davis, Shane	0	2	4.84	13	0	0	0	0	22.1	24	17	12	1	1	12	0	20	0	2	.279
Dorsett, Brandon	3	2	1.71	18	0	0	0	4	31.2	26	16	6	0	5	6	0	19	0	3	.211
Estrada, Deivy	3	6	4.29	13	12	0	0	0	56.2	62	48	27	7	3	15	0	49	3	4	.267
Gabryszwski, Jeremy	3	0	2.35	11	9	0	0	0	46.0	44	13	12	5	1	4	0	22	0	1	.253
Gonzalez, Alonzo	2	0	0.00	2	2	0	0	0	12.0	3	0	0	0	0	3	0	9	0	0	.077
James, Justin	2	4	7.36	12	5	0	0	0	25.2	37	27	21	2	0	11	0	24	0	2	.339
Jensen, Tucker	3	1	3.83	12	8	0	0	1	49.1	45	29	21	5	7	10	0	42	0	3	.230
Kaye, Brandon	0	0	0.00	3	0	0	0	0	5.0	3	0	0	0	0	0	0	3	0	0	.167
Murphy, Griffin	1	2	1.70	15	2	0	0	1	37.0	24	13	7	1	3	13	0	42	1	2	.180
Musgrove, Joseph	0	0	1.13	2	1	0	0	0	8.0	5	1	1	0	1	0	0	9	0	0	.179
Norris, Daniel	2	3	7.97	11	10	0	0	0	35.0	44	35	31	4	2	13	0	38	0	3	.301
Osuna, Roberto	1	0	1.50	7	4	0	0	0	24.0	18	5	4	1	2	6	0	24	1	1	.209
Robson, Tom	0	2	4.09	3	3	0	0	0	11.0	10	6	5	2	1	0	0	7	0	1	.238
Spano, Joe	1	1	5.00	17	0	0	0	1	27.0	29	16	15	0	0	20	1	33	0	8	.282
Tirado, Alberto	2	0	2.45	3	3	0	0	0	11.0	4	3	3	0	3	5	0	5	0	3	.121
Valdez, Denny	1	1	5.03	16	0	0	0	0	19.2	14	14	11	3	4	18	0	20	1	4	.192
Williams, Les	2	1	5.40	13	0	0	0	0	23.1	22	15	14	3	0	6	0	17	0	3	.239
Team Total	**29**	**37**	**3.87**	**66**	**66**	**0**	**6**	**16**	**550.2**	**513**	**321**	**237**	**41**	**44**	**184**	**2**	**489**	**7**	**62**	**.241**

2013 MINOR LEAGUE PLAYERS

Adams, Zak — PITCHER

HT: 6-3... **WT:** 210... **B-T:** L-L... **BORN:** 19 Mar 92, Flower Mound, TX... **RESIDES:** Flower Mound, TX... **EDUCATION:** Flower Mound High School... **TRANSACTIONS:** Selected by the Toronto Blue Jays in the 15th round of the 2010 June draft... Signed on August 30, 2010... **SIGNED BY:** Steve Miller

YR	Club & League	W-L	ERA	G	GS	CG	SHO	SV	IP	H	R	ER	HR	HB	BB-IB	SO	WP	BK	OBA
2011	Blue Jays (GCL)	0-1	9.00	7	3	0	0	0	21.0	19	21	21	3	3	19-0	28	5	0	.232
2012	Blue Jays (GCL)	1-1	13.06	6	1	0	0	0	10.1	21	18	15	2	3	11-0	8	3	0	.412
Minor Totals		1-2	10.34	13	4	0	0	0	31.1	40	39	36	5	6	30-0	36	8	0	.301

Ahrens, Kevin — INFIELDER

HT: 6-2... **WT:** 200... **B-T:** S-R... **BORN:** 26 Apr 89, Houston, TX... **RESIDES:** Houston, TX... **EDUCATION:** Memorial High School... **TRANSACTIONS:** Selected by the Toronto Blue Jays in the 1st round (16th overall) of the 2007 June draft... Signed on June 14, 2008... **SIGNED BY:** Andy Beene

YR	Club & League	AVG	G	AB	R	H	2B	3B	HR	RBI	SH-SF	HB	BB-IB	SO	SB-CS	SLG	OBP	OPS
2007	Blue Jays (GCL)	.230	48	165	19	38	6	0	3	21	0-0	2	25-1	47	3-0	.321	.339	.660
2008	Lansing (MID)	.259	122	460	54	119	25	5	5	42	0-4	5	45-2	135	5-1	.367	.329	.696
2009	Dunedin (FSL)	.215	105	377	35	81	17	2	4	36	1-7	1	37-1	76	1-1	.302	.282	.584
2010	Lansing (MID)	.265	66	253	30	67	12	2	8	35	0-2	0	21-0	51	2-4	.423	.319	.742
	Dunedin (FSL)	.187	28	107	12	20	6	1	1	8	2-1	1	7-0	20	1-0	.290	.241	.531
2011	Dunedin (FSL)	.242	121	429	59	104	24	0	13	54	0-6	6	56-2	99	0-2	.389	.334	.723
2012	Dunedin (FSL)	.240	120	409	59	98	17	1	8	53	0-5	3	60-0	87	1-1	.345	.338	.683
Minor Totals		.240	610	2200	268	527	107	11	42	249	3-25	18	251-6	515	13-9	.355	.319	.675

Aleton, Wilfri — PITCHER

HT: 6-3... **WT:** 165... **B-T:** L-L... **BORN:** 18 Nov 95, Santo Domingo, DR... **RESIDES:** La Romana, DR... **EDUCATION:** NA... **TRANSACTIONS:** Signed by the Toronto Blue Jays on November 30, 2012... **SIGNED BY:** Ismael Cruz, Sandy Rosario & Marino Tejada

Alford, Anthony — OUTFIELDER

HT: 6-1... **WT:** 193... **B-T:** R-R... **BORN:** 20 Jul 94, Columbia, MS... **RESIDES:** Petal, MS... **EDUCATION:** Petal High School... **TRANSACTIONS:** Selected by the Toronto Blue Jays in the 3rd round of the 2012 June draft... Signed on June 14, 2012... **SIGNED BY:** Brian Johnston

YR	Club & League	AVG	G	AB	R	H	2B	3B	HR	RBI	SH-SF	HB	BB-IB	SO	SB-CS	SLG	OBP	OPS
2012	Blue Jays (GCL)	.167	5	18	1	3	0	0	1	1	0-0	0	2-0	4	4-0	.333	.250	.583

Almonte, Josh — OUTFIELDER

HT: 6-3... **WT:** 193... **B-T:** R-R... **BORN:** 28 Jan 94, Corona, NY... **RESIDES:** Queens, NY... **EDUCATION:** Long Island City High School... **TRANSACTIONS:** Selected by the Toronto Blue Jays in the 22nd round of the 2012 June draft... Signed on July 7, 2012... **SIGNED BY:** Michael Pesce

YR	Club & League	AVG	G	AB	R	H	2B	3B	HR	RBI	SH-SF	HB	BB-IB	SO	SB-CS	SLG	OBP	OPS
2012	Blue Jays (GCL)	.159	20	69	5	11	1	1	0	2	0-0	0	2-0	30	0-1	.203	.183	.386

Anderson, Jacob — OUTFIELDER

HT: 6-4... **WT:** 190... **B-T:** R-R... **BORN:** 22 Nov 92, Chino, CA... **RESIDES:** Chino, CA... **EDUCATION:** Chino High School... **TRANSACTIONS:** Selected by the Toronto Blue Jays in the 1st round (supplemental, 35th overall) of the 2011 June draft... Signed on August 3, 2011... **SIGNED BY:** Joe Aversa

YR	Club & League	AVG	G	AB	R	H	2B	3B	HR	RBI	SH-SF	HB	BB-IB	SO	SB-CS	SLG	OBP	OPS
2011	Blue Jays (GCL)	.405	9	37	9	15	2	0	2	7	0-0	1	4-0	8	2-0	.622	.476	1.098
2012	Bluefield (APP)	.194	57	191	25	37	10	1	3	13	1-2	10	11-0	72	3-3	.304	.271	.575
Minor Totals		.228	66	228	34	52	12	1	5	20	1-2	11	15-0	80	5-3	.355	.305	.660

Anderson, John — PITCHER

HT: 6-1... **WT:** 198... **B-T:** L-L... **BORN:** 11 Sep 88, Pleasanton, CA... **RESIDES:** Pleasanton, CA... **EDUCATION:** Chabot College... **TRANSACTIONS:** Selected by the Toronto Blue Jays in the 28th round of the 2008 June draft... Signed on June 10, 2008... **SIGNED BY:** Chris Becerra

YR	Club & League	W-L	ERA	G	GS	CG	SHO	SV	IP	H	R	ER	HR	HB	BB-IB	SO	WP	BK	OBA
2008	Auburn (NYP)	0-0	0.00	1	0	0	0	0	1.1	1	0	0	0	0	1-0	0	0	0	.200
	Blue Jays (GCL)	1-3	4.32	16	0	0	0	2	25.0	29	15	12	1	0	8-1	22	6	0	.293
2009	Dunedin (FSL)	0-0	0.00	1	0	0	0	0	3.0	0	0	0	0	0	0-0	5	0	0	.000
	Lansing (MID)	3-6	4.52	21	21	0	0	0	99.2	130	64	50	6	3	30-0	76	6	3	.316
2010		Injured – Did Not Play																	
2011	Lansing (MID)	1-1	3.52	5	5	0	0	0	15.1	13	8	6	0	2	6-0	14	2	0	.217
2012	Blue Jays (GCL)	0-1	9.00	2	2	0	0	0	4.0	3	4	4	0	1	1-0	4	1	0	.214
Minor Totals		5-11	4.37	46	28	0	0	2	148.1	176	91	72	7	6	46-1	121	15	3	.294

Anderson, Kyle — PITCHER

HT: 6-2... **WT:** 205... **B-T:** R-L... **BORN:** 24 May 90, Woodenville, WA... **RESIDES:** Aptos, CA... **EDUCATION:** Cal Poly San Luis Obispo College... **TRANSACTIONS:** Signed by the Toronto Blue Jays on June 13, 2012... **SIGNED BY:** Randy Kramer

YR	Club & League	W-L	ERA	G	GS	CG	SHO	SV	IP	H	R	ER	HR	HB	BB-IB	SO	WP	BK	OBA
2012	Blue Jays (GCL)	0-0	1.80	2	0	0	0	0	5.0	6	1	1	0	0	1-0	2	0	0	.286
	Vancouver (NOR)	4-2	4.81	13	8	0	0	0	48.2	56	27	26	4	2	12-0	25	6	0	.296
Minor Totals		4-2	4.53	15	8	0	0	0	53.2	62	28	27	4	2	13-0	27	6	0	.295

Antolin, Dustin — PITCHER

HT: 6-2... **WT:** 180... **B-T:** R-R... **BORN:** 09 Aug 89, Mililani, HI... **RESIDES:** Mililani, HI... **EDUCATION:** Mililani High School... **TRANSACTIONS:** Selected by the Toronto Blue Jays in the 11th round of the 2008 June draft... Signed on June 11, 2008... **SIGNED BY:** Demerius Pittman

YR	Club & League	W-L	ERA	G	GS	CG	SHO	SV	IP	H	R	ER	HR	HB	BB-IB	SO	WP	BK	OBA
2008	Blue Jays (GCL)	2-2	4.64	12	0	0	0	0	21.1	26	12	11	1	1	10-0	14	1	0	.302
2009	Lansing (MID)	2-5	4.47	28	0	0	0	1	48.1	48	28	24	1	3	20-0	40	8	0	.261
2010	Lansing (MID)	2-2	2.93	18	0	0	0	0	27.2	21	10	9	0	2	9-0	24	1	0	.206
2011	Dunedin (FSL)	1-0	0.00	1	0	0	0	0	1.2	0	0	0	0	0	1-0	3	0	0	.000
	Lansing (MID)	3-2	4.26	23	0	0	0	0	31.2	31	19	15	1	1	16-0	35	3	0	.263
2012	Dunedin (FSL)	7-3	4.58	48	0	0	0	1	59.0	72	31	30	3	1	25-0	47	5	1	.305
Minor Totals		17-14	4.22	130	0	0	0	2	189.2	198	100	89	6	8	81-0	163	18	1	.271

Arce, Eric — OUTFIELDER

HT: 5-10... **WT:** 199... **B-T:** L-R... **BORN:** 29 Nov 91, Tampa, FL... **RESIDES:** Tampa, FL... **EDUCATION:** NA... **TRANSACTIONS:** Selected by the Toronto Blue Jays in the 25th round of the 2011 June draft... Signed on June 10, 2011... **SIGNED BY:** Joel Grampietro

YR	Club & League	AVG	G	AB	R	H	2B	3B	HR	RBI	SH-SF	HB	BB-IB	SO	SB-CS	SLG	OBP	OPS
2011	Blue Jays (GCL)	.268	49	153	34	41	6	3	14	40	0-4	11	38-2	48	1-1	.621	.437	1.058
	Bluefield (APP)	.263	6	19	1	5	1	0	0	1	0-0	0	2-0	4	0-0	.316	.333	.649
2012	Bluefield (APP)	.236	47	127	26	30	5	1	8	27	0-1	4	27-0	55	0-0	.480	.384	.864
Minor Totals		.254	102	299	61	76	12	4	22	68	0-5	15	67-2	107	1-1	.542	.409	.951

Arcila, Daniel — INFIELDER

HT: 6-1... **WT:** 170... **B-T:** L-R... **BORN:** 04 Jul 90, Barcelona-Anzoategui, VZ... **RESIDES:** Barcelona-Anzoategui, VZ... **EDUCATION:** NA... **TRANSACTIONS:** Signed by the Toronto Blue Jays on March 22, 2007... **SIGNED BY:** Juan Salabarria

YR	Club & League	AVG	G	AB	R	H	2B	3B	HR	RBI	SH-SF	HB	BB-IB	SO	SB-CS	SLG	OBP	OPS
2007	DSL Blue Jays1 (DSL)	.167	54	162	12	27	5	2	0	11	4-1	0	21-0	56	2-2	.222	.261	.483
2008	DSL Blue Jays2 (DSL)	.224	56	170	25	38	3	2	0	16	5-1	2	49-1	56	18-4	.265	.401	.666
2009	DSL (DSL)	.209	50	187	29	39	11	2	1	19	6-0	4	19-0	61	16-3	.305	.295	.600
2010	Blue Jays (GCL)	.181	29	94	7	17	2	2	3	9	2-0	1	5-0	21	1-0	.340	.230	.570
2011	Bluefield (APP)	.243	54	210	43	51	10	5	10	37	5-0	3	24-0	50	3-3	.481	.329	.810
2012	Vancouver (NOR)	.176	43	148	17	26	6	1	3	13	1-0	2	11-0	50	4-2	.291	.242	.533
Minor Totals		.204	286	971	133	198	37	14	17	105	23-2	12	129-1	294	44-14	.323	.304	.628

Atkinson, Justin — INFIELDER

HT: 6-1... **WT:** 211... **B-T:** R-R... **BORN:** 24 Jul 93, Surrey, BC... **RESIDES:** Surrey, BC... **EDUCATION:** North Surrey High School... **TRANSACTIONS:** Selected by the Toronto Blue Jays in the 26th round of the 2011 June draft... Signed on July 6, 2011... **SIGNED BY:** Jamie Lehman

YR	Club & League	AVG	G	AB	R	H	2B	3B	HR	RBI	SH-SF	HB	BB-IB	SO	SB-CS	SLG	OBP	OPS
2011	Blue Jays (GCL)	.279	12	43	6	12	3	1	0	6	1-2	0	2-0	3	0-0	.395	.298	.693
2012	Blue Jays (GCL)	.259	52	185	14	48	1	0	1	23	1-0	4	13-0	29	1-2	.281	.322	.603
	Bluefield (APP)	.300	3	10	2	3	1	0	0	1	0-0	1	0-0	1	0-1	.400	.364	.764
Minor Totals		.265	67	238	22	63	5	1	1	30	2-2	5	15-0	33	1-3	.307	.319	.626

Avendano, Javier — PITCHER

HT: 6-3... **WT:** 168... **B-T:** R-R... **BORN:** 06 Sep 90, Maracaibo, VZ... **RESIDES:** Maracaibo, VZ... **EDUCATION:** NA... **TRANSACTIONS:** Signed by the St. Louis Cardinals on July 2, 2007... Selected by the Toronto Blue Jays in the minor league phase of the Rule 5 Draft on December 8, 2011... **SIGNED BY:** Marco Diaz

YR	Club & League	W-L	ERA	G	GS	CG	SHO	SV	IP	H	R	ER	HR	HB	BB-IB	SO	WP	BK	OBA
2008	VSL (VSL)	1-1	2.34	12	10	0	0	1	42.1	35	12	11	1	2	18-0	33	5	3	.232
2009	VSL (VSL)	6-3	1.79	13	13	0	0	0	65.1	59	24	13	0	3	21-0	60	7	0	.238
	Cardinals (GCL)	1-0	2.08	5	1	0	0	0	13.0	10	4	3	2	2	6-0	14	1	0	.208
2010	Cardinals (GCL)	0-0	1.35	10	8	0	0	0	40.0	26	8	6	1	3	14-0	52	6	0	.179
	Batavia (NYP)	0-0	4.50	1	1	0	0	0	4.0	3	2	2	0	0	4-0	4	3	0	.187
2011	Batavia (NYP)	1-2	3.14	9	1	0	0	2	14.1	11	5	5	1	0	8-0	19	0	0	.216
2012	Lansing (MID)	2-3	1.48	19	0	0	0	2	30.1	20	8	5	0	2	18-1	39	2	0	.182
	Vancouver (NOR)	8-1	1.27	16	14	0	0	0	78.0	53	13	11	3	1	25-0	91	8	0	.193
Minor Totals		19-10	1.75	85	48	0	0	5	287.1	217	76	56	8	13	114-1	312	32	3	.208

Bailli, Kenen
OUTFIELDER

HT: 6-0... **WT:** 190... **B-T:** L-L... **BORN:** 25 Jan 85, Guantanamo, Cuba... **RESIDES:** Cancun, Mexico... **EDUCATION:** NA... **TRANSACTIONS:** Signed by the Toronto Blue Jays on July 22, 2011... **SIGNED BY:** Marco Paddy & Rafael Moncada

YR	Club & League	AVG	G	AB	R	H	2B	3B	HR	RBI	SH-SF	HB	BB-IB	SO	SB-CS	SLG	OBP	OPS
2011	Blue Jays (GCL)	.364	4	11	0	4	0	0	0	1	0-0	0	0-0	2	0-1	.364	.364	.728
	Dunedin (FSL)	.294	7	17	5	5	1	0	1	3	0-0	0	1-0	4	0-0	.529	.333	.862
2012	Dunedin (FSL)	.267	26	86	15	23	8	1	1	18	0-1	1	6-0	19	0-1	.419	.319	.738
	New Hampshire (EAS)	.310	36	129	14	40	7	2	1	13	0-0	1	4-0	23	5-2	.419	.336	.755
	Las Vegas (PCL)	.323	12	31	5	10	1	0	1	3	1-0	0	4-0	6	0-0	.452	.400	.852
Minor Totals		.299	85	274	39	82	17	3	4	38	1-1	2	15-0	54	5-4	.427	.339	.766

Baligod, Nick
OUTFIELDER

HT: 5-10... **WT:** 190... **B-T:** L-R... **BORN:** 28 Sep 87, Fairfield, CA... **RESIDES:** Fairfield, CA... **EDUCATION:** Oral Roberts University... **TRANSACTIONS:** Selected by the Toronto Blue Jays in the 40th round of the 2011 June draft... Signed on June 12, 2011... **SIGNED BY:** Darin Vaughan

YR	Club & League	AVG	G	AB	R	H	2B	3B	HR	RBI	SH-SF	HB	BB-IB	SO	SB-CS	SLG	OBP	OPS
2011	Vancouver (NOR)	.248	70	238	28	59	13	1	2	32	1-2	2	38-0	38	2-1	.336	.354	.690
2012	Vancouver (NOR)	.259	42	158	24	41	8	2	1	25	0-0	3	26-2	19	2-0	.354	.374	.728
	Lansing (MID)	.291	29	117	20	34	8	0	3	7	0-1	1	16-1	20	1-0	.436	.378	.814
Minor Totals		.261	141	513	72	134	29	3	6	64	1-3	6	80-3	77	5-1	.365	.365	.730

Barnes, Daniel
PITCHER

HT: 6-1... **WT:** 195... **B-T:** L-R... **BORN:** 21 Oct 89, Manhasset, NY... **RESIDES:** Manhasset, NY... **EDUCATION:** Princeton University... **TRANSACTIONS:** Selected by the Toronto Blue Jays in the 35th round of the 2010 June draft... Signed on June 13, 2010... **SIGNED BY:** Bobby Gandolfo

YR	Club & League	W-L	ERA	G	GS	CG	SHO	SV	IP	H	R	ER	HR	HB	BB-IB	SO	WP	BK	OBA
2010	Blue Jays (GCL)	1-1	0.67	14	0	0	0	1	27.0	17	2	2	1	0	5-0	37	0	0	.173
	Lansing (MID)	0-0	5.91	8	0	0	0	0	10.2	17	8	7	0	1	8-1	16	2	0	.354
2011	Lansing (MID)	5-1	2.32	44	2	0	0	13	66.0	44	20	17	3	2	20-2	99	3	0	.184
2012	New Hampshire (EAS)	0-1	16.20	1	0	0	0	0	1.2	2	3	3	1	0	2-0	2	0	0	.333
	Dunedin (FSL)	1-2	1.40	50	0	0	0	34	51.1	37	8	8	3	0	16-1	63	1	1	.198
Minor Totals		7-5	2.13	117	2	0	0	48	156.2	117	41	37	8	3	51-4	217	6	1	.202

Barreto, Deiferson
INFIELDER

HT: 5-10... **WT:** 165... **B-T:** R-R... **BORN:** 19 May 95, Turmero, VZ... **RESIDES:** Turmero, VZ... **EDUCATION:** NA... **TRANSACTIONS:** Signed by the Toronto Blue Jays on September 23, 2011... **SIGNED BY:** Ismael Cruz, Luis Marquez & Rafael Moncada

YR	Club & League	AVG	G	AB	R	H	2B	3B	HR	RBI	SH-SF	HB	BB-IB	SO	SB-CS	SLG	OBP	OPS
2012	DSL (DSL)	.292	46	171	18	50	7	1	0	9	3-1	5	12-0	23	4-3	.345	.354	.699

Barreto, Franklin
INFIELDER

HT: 5-9... **WT:** 174... **B-T:** R-R... **BORN:** 27 Feb 96, Caracas, VZ... **RESIDES:** Caracas, VZ... **EDUCATION:** NA... **TRANSACTIONS:** Signed by the Toronto Blue Jays on July 2, 2012... **SIGNED BY:** Ismael Cruz, Luis Marquez & Rafael Moncada

Bartlett, Cody
INFIELDER

HT: 6-5... **WT:** 180... **B-T:** R-R... **BORN:** 22 Jul 88, Kent, WA... **RESIDES:** Kent, WA... **EDUCATION:** Washington State University... **TRANSACTIONS:** Selected by the Toronto Blue Jays in the 41st round of the 2011 June draft... Signed on June 12, 2011... **SIGNED BY:** Ryan Fox

YR	Club & League	AVG	G	AB	R	H	2B	3B	HR	RBI	SH-SF	HB	BB-IB	SO	SB-CS	SLG	OBP	OPS
2011	Bluefield (APP)	.198	27	91	9	18	7	0	1	17	2-0	0	11-0	22	2-1	.308	.284	.592
2012	Blue Jays (GCL)	.130	14	46	5	6	2	0	0	2	0-0	0	3-0	7	0-0	.174	.184	.358
Minor Totals		.175	41	137	14	24	9	0	1	19	2-0	0	14-0	29	2-1	.263	.252	.514

Beck, Casey
PITCHER

HT: 6-1... **WT:** 215... **B-T:** R-R... **BORN:** 28 Mar 87, Woodville, TX... **RESIDES:** Woodville, TX... **EDUCATION:** San Jacinto North Junior College... **TRANSACTIONS:** Selected by the Atlanta Braves in the 8th round of the 2006 June draft... Signed on June 11, 2006... Signed by the Toronto Blue Jays on April 8, 2009... **SIGNED BY:** John Barron & Ralph Garr

YR	Club & League	W-L	ERA	G	GS	CG	SHO	SV	IP	H	R	ER	HR	HB	BB-IB	SO	WP	BK	OBA
2006	Braves (GULF)	0-0	1.69	8	0	0	0	1	10.2	7	3	2	0	0	6-0	8	1	0	.194
2007	Danville (APPY)	1-2	7.71	13	0	0	0	1	16.1	15	15	14	1	1	19-1	22	3	0	.242
2008	Rome (SAL)	1-4	4.75	30	0	0	0	0	41.2	41	26	22	2	8	27-0	38	7	0	.255
2009	Auburn (NYP)	1-3	2.84	29	0	0	0	10	31.2	22	12	10	0	1	17-2	43	1	0	.190
2010	Lansing (MID)	1-3	3.74	38	0	0	0	6	43.1	31	19	18	4	1	23-1	54	4	0	.199
2011	Dunedin (FSL)	0-0	3.00	9	0	0	0	0	9.0	10	6	3	1	1	4-0	5	1	0	.278
2012	Blue Jays (GCL)	1-0	0.00	3	0	0	0	0	4.0	0	0	0	0	0	1-0	6	0	0	.000
	Lansing (MID)	0-1	0.00	2	0	0	0	0	2.0	2	1	0	0	0	2-0	2	1	0	.286
Minor Totals		5-13	3.91	132	0	0	0	18	158.2	128	82	69	8	12	99-5	178	18	0	.218

Bell, Dean — INFIELDER

HT: 5-9... **WT:** 172... **B-T:** R-R... **BORN:** 14 Oct 92, Manhattan, NY... **RESIDES:** La Romana, DR... **EDUCATION:** NA... **TRANSACTIONS:** Signed by the Toronto Blue Jays on October 14, 2012... **SIGNED BY:** Blue Jays

Benacka, Michael — PITCHER

HT: 6-2... **WT:** 210... **B-T:** R-R... **BORN:** 02 Aug 82, Chicago, IL... **RESIDES:** University City, MO... **EDUCATION:** NA... **TRANSACTIONS:** Signed by the Oakland Athletics on July 23, 2008... Signed by the Toronto Blue Jays on January 4, 2013... **SIGNED BY:** Armann Brown

YR	Club & League	W-L	ERA	G	GS	CG	SHO	SV	IP	H	R	ER	HR	HB	BB-IB	SO	WP	BK	OBA
2007	River City (FRN)	2-5	5.01	36	2	0	0	20	41.1	32	25	23	3	5	35-2	60	3	0	.213
2008	River City (FRN)	3-0	0.35	22	0	0	0	13	26.0	10	1	1	0	4	17-2	51	2	2	.127
	Stockton (CAL)	4-2	2.39	15	0	0	0	0	26.1	18	8	7	4	3	11-1	37	4	0	.200
2009	Midland (TEX)	3-0	2.74	45	0	0	0	4	65.2	52	21	20	0	2	32-2	72	8	0	.218
	Sacramento River (PCL)	0-1	1.98	10	0	0	0	0	13.2	6	3	3	0	3	6-0	18	4	0	.133
2010	Sacramento River (PCL)	6-2	4.08	40	0	0	0	5	46.1	30	22	21	5	2	39-3	61	9	0	.189
2011	Sacramento River (PCL)	0-1	6.35	4	0	0	0	0	5.2	7	6	4	3	0	6-0	4	2	0	.333
	Stockton (CAL)	1-0	2.84	22	0	0	0	1	31.2	25	11	10	3	1	15-0	30	7	0	.214
2012									Did Not Play										
Minor Totals		14-6	3.09	136	0	0	0	10	189.1	138	71	65	15	11	109-6	222	34	0	.206

Berl, Brandon — PITCHER

HT: 6-0... **WT:** 185... **B-T:** R-R... **BORN:** 09 Apr 88, Moreno Valley, CA... **RESIDES:** Moreno Valley, CA... **EDUCATION:** St. Marys College... **TRANSACTIONS:** Selected by the Toronto Blue Jays in the 40th round of the 2010 June draft... Signed on June 13, 2010... **SIGNED BY:** Randy Kramer

YR	Club & League	W-L	ERA	G	GS	CG	SHO	SV	IP	H	R	ER	HR	HB	BB-IB	SO	WP	BK	OBA
2010	Blue Jays (GCL)	0-0	0.00	3	0	0	0	0	3.0	2	0	0	0	0	0-0	3	0	0	.200
	Auburn (NYP)	1-1	4.41	19	0	0	0	0	34.2	40	23	17	3	1	10-0	34	2	0	.284
2011	Lansing (MID)	3-5	2.28	30	0	0	0	3	51.1	53	22	13	3	3	9-1	42	3	0	.256
2012	Lansing (MID)	4-7	3.02	46	0	0	0	1	62.2	67	29	21	2	4	15-4	46	2	0	.275
Minor Totals		8-13	3.03	98	0	0	0	4	151.2	162	74	51	8	8	34-5	125	7	0	.269

Berti, Jonathan — INFIELDER

HT: 5-10... **WT:** 175... **B-T:** R-R... **BORN:** 22 Jan 90, Troy, MI... **RESIDES:** Troy, MI... **EDUCATION:** Bowling Green State University... **TRANSACTIONS:** Selected by the Toronto Blue Jays in the 18th round of the 2011 June draft... Signed on June 12, 2011... **SIGNED BY:** Nick Manno

YR	Club & League	AVG	G	AB	R	H	2B	3B	HR	RBI	SH-SF	HB	BB-IB	SO	SB-CS	SLG	OBP	OPS
2011	Vancouver (NOR)	.291	60	213	37	62	5	5	1	21	1-1	12	22-0	44	23-5	.376	.387	.763
2012	Lansing (MID)	.281	60	224	35	63	8	2	2	27	1-1	7	34-0	41	26-8	.362	.391	.753
	Dunedin (FSL)	.190	50	174	28	33	7	5	0	13	0-3	3	26-0	49	8-3	.287	.301	.588
Minor Totals		.259	170	611	100	158	20	12	3	61	2-5	22	82-0	134	57-16	.345	.364	.709

Bibens-Dirkx, Austin — PITCHER

HT: 6-1... **WT:** 210... **B-T:** R-R... **BORN:** 29 Apr 85, Salem, OR... **RESIDES:** Keizer, OR... **EDUCATION:** University of Portland... **TRANSACTIONS:** Selected by the Seattle Mariners in the 16th round of the 2006 June draft... Signed on June 8, 2006... Signed by the Chicago Cubs on July 5, 2009... Signed by the Washington Nationals on January 10, 2012... Signed by the Colorado Rockies on August 15, 2012... Signed by the Toronto Blue Jays on January 15, 2013... **SIGNED BY:** Phil Geisler

YR	Club & League	W-L	ERA	G	GS	CG	SHO	SV	IP	H	R	ER	HR	HB	BB-IB	SO	WP	BK	OBA
2006	Tacoma (PCL)	0-0	0.00	1	0	0	0	0	2.0	2	0	0	0	0	1-0	5	0	0	.250
	Everett (NOR)	0-0	0.00	3	0	0	0	1	4.0	1	0	0	0	0	1-0	6	1	0	.083
	Wisconsin Timber (MID)	2-2	1.95	25	0	0	0	4	32.1	24	7	7	0	0	7-1	38	0	0	.200
2007	High Desert (CAL)	3-1	4.42	31	0	0	0	8	38.2	40	25	19	2	5	20-1	26	6	0	.258
2008	AZL (AZL)	0-0	2.25	6	6	0	0	0	8.0	5	2	2	0	0	0-0	10	0	0	.179
	High Desert (CAL)	1-1	7.95	32	0	0	0	1	43.0	58	39	38	9	3	16-1	31	5	0	.324
2009	Peoria (MID)	7-2	2.04	12	8	1	0	1	70.2	55	19	16	4	0	9-0	50	1	0	.215
2010	Tennessee (SOU)	5-3	3.27	16	16	0	0	0	85.1	59	34	31	6	2	27-1	68	2	0	.196
	Iowa (PCL)	5-4	4.61	13	8	0	0	0	52.2	55	34	27	9	1	21-0	34	2	0	.264
2011	Tennessee (SOU)	2-2	5.40	5	5	0	0	0	25.0	26	15	15	3	1	9-0	16	2	0	.265
	Iowa (PCL)	4-5	6.07	24	17	0	0	0	105.1	125	75	71	18	10	31-1	75	3	0	.298
2012	Harrisburg (EAS)	1-0	2.25	3	2	0	0	0	12.0	9	3	3	1	0	2-0	12	1	0	.209
	Syracuse (INT)	0-3	5.59	29	2	0	0	1	46.2	57	31	29	4	3	16-1	41	2	0	.298
	Colorado Springs (PCL)	1-1	13.89	7	0	0	0	0	11.2	20	18	18	2	0	12-1	10	1	0	.392
Minor Totals		31-24	4.62	207	64	1	0	16	537.1	536	302	276	58	25	172-7	422	26	0	.259

Biggs, Mark — PITCHER

HT: 6-3... **WT:** 205... **B-T:** R-R... **BORN:** 10 May 93, Bowling Green, KY... **RESIDES:** Bowling Green, KY... **EDUCATION:** Warren East High School... **TRANSACTIONS:** Selected by the Toronto Blue Jays in the 8th round of the 2011 June draft... Signed on August 14, 2011... **SIGNED BY:** Nate Murrie

YR	Club & League	W-L	ERA	G	GS	CG	SHO	SV	IP	H	R	ER	HR	HB	BB-IB	SO	WP	BK	OBA
2012	Blue Jays (GCL)	1-4	5.93	11	4	0	0	0	27.1	32	20	18	4	6	9-0	20	5	0	.291

Boone, Randy — PITCHER

HT: 6-3... **WT:** 215... **B-T:** R-R... **BORN:** 06 Aug 84, Yoakum, TX... **RESIDES:** Austin, TX... **EDUCATION:** Texas Austin University... **TRANSACTIONS:** Selected by the Toronto Blue Jays in the 7th round of the 2007 June draft... Signed on August 27, 2007... **SIGNED BY:** Andy Beene

YR	Club & League	W-L	ERA	G	GS	CG	SHO	SV	IP	H	R	ER	HR	HB	BB-IB	SO	WP	BK	OBA
2008	Lansing (MID)	6-2	2.50	15	10	1	1	0	75.2	75	26	21	3	3	20-0	53	0	0	.264
	Dunedin (FSL)	5-4	4.68	12	11	0	0	0	67.1	76	36	35	7	3	20-0	44	3	0	.291
2009	New Hampshire (EAS)	9-8	3.70	25	23	0	0	0	129.0	127	63	53	4	8	42-1	90	7	1	.261
	Las Vegas (PCL)	0-2	15.75	2	2	0	0	0	8.0	15	15	14	3	0	4-0	7	0	0	.395
2010	New Hampshire (EAS)	5-10	3.98	24	22	2	0	0	133.1	128	68	59	8	6	39-0	96	10	0	.252
2011	Las Vegas (PCL)	1-0	1.00	2	2	0	0	0	9.0	6	3	1	0	2	1-0	7	0	0	.182
2012	New Hampshire (EAS)	0-2	10.24	3	3	0	0	0	9.2	19	13	11	5	1	1-0	4	0	0	.413
	Dunedin (FSL)	2-1	4.08	18	3	0	0	1	35.1	35	21	16	2	0	7-1	27	2	0	.246
Minor Totals		28-29	4.04	101	76	3	1	1	467.1	481	245	210	32	23	134-2	328	22	1	.268

Borucki, Ryan — PITCHER

HT: 6-4... **WT:** 175... **B-T:** L-L... **BORN:** 31 Mar 94, Mundelein, IL... **RESIDES:** Mundelein, IL... **EDUCATION:** Mundelein High School... **TRANSACTIONS:** Selected by the Toronto Blue Jays in the 15th round of the 2012 June draft... **SIGNED BY:** Mike Medici

YR	Club & League	W-L	ERA	G	GS	CG	SHO	SV	IP	H	R	ER	HR	HB	BB-IB	SO	WP	BK	OBA
2012	Blue Jays (GCL)	1-0	3.00	4	0	0	0	0	6.0	4	2	2	1	0	0-0	10	0	0	.182

Breault, Zachary — PITCHER

HT: 6-4... **WT:** 210... **B-T:** L-R... **BORN:** 06 Dec 88, Amherstburg, ON... **RESIDES:** Amherstburg, ON... **EDUCATION:** St. Thomas of Villanova High School... **TRANSACTIONS:** Signed by the Toronto Blue Jays on August 30, 2010... **SIGNED BY:** Jamie Lehman

YR	Club & League	W-L	ERA	G	GS	CG	SHO	SV	IP	H	R	ER	HR	HB	BB-IB	SO	WP	BK	OBA
2011	Vancouver (NOR)	2-2	6.32	15	15	0	0	0	68.1	82	52	48	5	9	33-0	42	7	1	.301
2012	Vancouver (NOR)	2-2	3.93	18	2	0	0	0	34.1	28	15	15	1	2	18-0	21	8	0	.222
Minor Totals		4-4	5.52	33	17	0	0	0	102.2	110	67	63	6	11	51-0	63	15	1	.276

Brechbuehler, Tim — PITCHER

HT: 6-8... **WT:** 205... **B-T:** R-R... **BORN:** 21 Oct 89, Gillette, NJ... **RESIDES:** Gillette, NJ... **EDUCATION:** Louisburg College... **TRANSACTIONS:** Signed by the Toronto Blue Jays on June 10, 2012... **SIGNED BY:** John Hendricks

YR	Club & League	W-L	ERA	G	GS	CG	SHO	SV	IP	H	R	ER	HR	HB	BB-IB	SO	WP	BK	OBA
2012	Blue Jays (GCL)	1-0	3.71	21	0	0	0	2	26.2	28	13	11	0	3	18-0	29	7	1	.269
	Lansing (MID)	0-0	19.80	3	0	0	0	0	5.0	11	11	11	1	0	3-0	2	2	0	.423
Minor Totals		1-0	6.25	24	0	0	0	2	31.2	39	24	22	1	3	21-0	31	9	1	.300

Brisker, Markus — OUTFIELDER

HT: 6-4... **WT:** 192... **B-T:** R-R... **BORN:** 21 Aug 90, Winter Haven, FL... **RESIDES:** Winter Haven, FL... **EDUCATION:** Daytona Beach Community College... **TRANSACTIONS:** Selected by the Toronto Blue Jays in the 6th round of the 2008 June draft... Signed on June 9, 2008... **SIGNED BY:** Joel Grampietro

YR	Club & League	AVG	G	AB	R	H	2B	3B	HR	RBI	SH-SF	HB	BB-IB	SO	SB-CS	SLG	OBP	OPS
2008	Blue Jays (GCL)	.306	32	108	16	33	4	0	0	6	1-0	0	11-0	22	13-4	.343	.370	.713
2009	Lansing (MID)	.114	40	105	7	12	1	0	0	2	0-1	0	10-0	35	12-4	.124	.190	.314
	Auburn (NYP)	.200	59	200	27	40	4	0	1	23	2-1	2	19-0	59	11-4	.235	.275	.510
2010	Lansing (MID)	.167	6	18	0	3	0	0	0	0	0-0	0	3-0	5	0-1	.167	.286	.453
	Auburn (NYP)	.184	56	185	26	34	9	1	1	17	2-0	3	17-0	66	7-2	.259	.263	.522
2011	Lansing (MID)	.233	97	348	72	81	18	4	5	33	0-1	9	55-1	112	24-8	.351	.351	.702
2012	Lansing (MID)	.192	48	156	23	30	6	2	1	14	2-1	5	19-0	46	18-3	.276	.298	.574
Minor Totals		.208	338	1120	171	233	42	7	8	95	7-4	19	134-1	345	85-26	.279	.302	.582

Brito, Jose — PITCHER

HT: 6-2... **WT:** 185... **B-T:** R-R... **BORN:** 19 Dec 94, Rio San Juan, DR... **RESIDES:** Rio San Juan, DR... **EDUCATION:** NA... **TRANSACTIONS:** Signed by the Toronto Blue Jays on April 11, 2012... **SIGNED BY:** Ismael Cruz, Sandy Rosario, Jean Carlos Alvarez & Marino Tejada

YR	Club & League	W-L	ERA	G	GS	CG	SHO	SV	IP	H	R	ER	HR	HB	BB-IB	SO	WP	BK	OBA
2012	DSL (DSL)	0-1	5.23	4	2	0	0	0	10.1	10	7	6	0	1	3-0	8	1	1	.244

Brosnahan, Bobby — PITCHER

HT: 6-0... **WT:** 155... **B-T:** L-L... **BORN:** 02 Jun 89, Ann Arbor, MI... **RESIDES:** Ann Arbor, MI... **EDUCATION:** University of Michigan... **TRANSACTIONS:** Signed by the Toronto Blue Jays on June 10, 2012... **SIGNED BY:** Coulson Barbiche

YR	Club & League	W-L	ERA	G	GS	CG	SHO	SV	IP	H	R	ER	HR	HB	BB-IB	SO	WP	BK	OBA
2012	Vancouver (NOR)	2-2	4.50	10	4	0	0	0	32.0	34	17	16	2	4	8-0	16	3	0	.279

Brown, Eric — *PITCHER*

HT: 6-1... **WT:** 185... **B-T:** L-R... **BORN:** 23 Feb 89, Thunder Bay, ON... **RESIDES:** Thunder Bay, ON... **EDUCATION:** University of British Columbia... **TRANSACTIONS:** Selected by the Toronto Blue Jays in the 50th round of the 2011 June draft... Signed on June 16, 2011... **SIGNED BY:** Jamie Lehman

YR	Club & League	W-L	ERA	G	GS	CG	SHO	SV	IP	H	R	ER	HR	HB	BB-IB	SO	WP	BK	OBA
2011	Vancouver (NOR)	0-1	3.62	18	0	0	0	0	27.1	25	19	11	3	0	7-0	30	5	1	.238
	Lansing (MID)	0-0	2.25	2	0	0	0	0	4.0	4	1	1	0	0	2-0	4	0	0	.308
2012	Lansing (MID)	2-0	3.52	8	0	0	0	0	15.1	13	6	6	0	1	4-1	17	4	0	.224
2012	Vancouver (NOR)	2-5	7.09	19	9	0	0	1	45.2	62	40	36	9	0	17-0	43	7	0	.310
Minor Totals		4-6	5.26	47	9	0	0	1	92.1	104	66	54	12	1	30-1	94	16	1	.277

Browning, Wil — *PITCHER*

HT: 6-3... **WT:** 175... **B-T:** R-R... **BORN:** 08 Sep 88, Sallis, MS... **RESIDES:** Sallis, MS... **EDUCATION:** Louisiana-Monroe College... **TRANSACTIONS:** Signed by the Toronto Blue Jays on June 11, 2012... **SIGNED BY:** Brian Johnston

YR	Club & League	W-L	ERA	G	GS	CG	SHO	SV	IP	H	R	ER	HR	HB	BB-IB	SO	WP	BK	OBA
2012	Blue Jays (GCL)	0-0	1.35	7	0	0	0	0	6.2	2	1	1	0	0	1-0	12	1	0	.087
	Bluefield (APP)	0-1	0.82	10	0	0	0	4	11.0	6	3	1	0	3	3-1	16	1	1	.146
	Vancouver (NOR)	0-0	1.50	5	0	0	0	0	6.0	7	1	1	0	0	0-0	5	0	0	.304
Minor Totals		0-1	1.14	22	0	0	0	4	23.2	15	5	3	0	3	4-1	33	2	1	.172

Brummett, Tyson — *PITCHER*

HT: 6-0... **WT:** 185... **B-T:** R-R... **BORN:** 15 Aug 84, Columbus, MS... **RESIDES:** Salt Lake City, UT... **EDUCATION:** UCLA... **TRANSACTIONS:** Selected by the Philadelphia Phillies in the 7th round of the 2007 June draft... Signed June 15, 2007... Claimed off waivers by the Toronto Blue Jays on October 18, 2012... **SIGNED BY:** Mike Smith

YR	Club & League	W-L	ERA	G	GS	CG	SHO	SV	IP	H	R	ER	HR	HB	BB-IB	SO	WP	BK	OBA
2007	Williamsport (NYP)	5-5	3.40	15	12	1	0	0	76.2	71	34	29	2	4	14-0	55	1	0	.240
2008	Lakewood (SAL)	3-0	1.95	6	6	0	0	0	37.0	28	12	8	1	1	10-0	36	0	0	.214
	Clearwater (FSL)	2-3	3.59	8	8	0	0	0	52.2	52	24	21	8	1	13-1	39	1	0	.252
	Reading (EAS)	2-9	7.28	14	14	0	0	0	80.1	105	68	65	10	3	46-2	47	7	0	.319
2009	Lehigh Valley (INT)	0-1	11.25	1	1	0	0	0	4.0	7	6	5	1	0	1-0	3	0	1	.412
	Reading (EAS)	3-9	5.22	26	15	0	0	2	98.1	119	63	57	12	4	27-0	70	5	0	.303
	Clearwater (FSL)	0-0	9.00	4	0	0	0	0	5.0	5	7	5	0	0	4-0	3	2	0	.263
2010	Clearwater (FSL)	0-0	0.59	11	0	0	0	2	15.1	7	1	1	0	0	4-0	11	1	0	.130
	Reading (EAS)	1-2	5.01	28	2	0	0	1	55.2	66	34	31	2	2	15-1	34	2	0	.292
2011	Lehigh Valley (INT)	1-4	5.82	7	6	0	0	0	34.0	41	22	22	6	0	11-0	20	1	0	.306
	Reading (EAS)	4-8	4.52	30	11	0	0	0	91.2	103	53	46	11	2	28-0	72	5	0	.282
2012	Reading (EAS)	1-0	1.50	10	1	0	0	1	18.0	7	3	3	2	1	2-0	18	1	0	.117
	Lehigh Valley (INT)	4-6	3.63	34	7	0	0	1	72.0	67	33	29	2	3	27-1	65	4	1	.251
	PHILADELPHIA (NL)	0-0	0.00	1	0	0	0	0	0.2	2	0	0	0	0	0-0	2	0	0	.500
Minor Totals		26-47	4.52	194	83	1	0	7	640.2	678	360	322	57	21	202-5	473	30	2	.272

Burgos, Miguel — *PITCHER*

HT: 5-9... **WT:** 155... **B-T:** L-L... **BORN:** 16 Jun 95, Valencia, VZ... **RESIDES:** Valencia, VZ... **EDUCATION:** NA... **TRANSACTIONS:** Signed by the Toronto Blue Jays on January 12, 2012... **SIGNED BY:** Ismael Cruz & Luis Marquez

YR	Club & League	W-L	ERA	G	GS	CG	SHO	SV	IP	H	R	ER	HR	HB	BB-IB	SO	WP	BK	OBA
2012	DSL (DSL)	2-1	5.34	15	0	0	0	0	30.1	34	25	18	1	1	12-0	27	4	0	.274

Burns, Andrew — *INFIELDER*

HT: 6-2... **WT:** 190... **B-T:** R-R... **BORN:** 07 Aug 90, Fort Collins, CO... **RESIDES:** Fort Collins, CO... **EDUCATION:** University of Arizona... **TRANSACTIONS:** Selected by the Toronto Blue Jays in the 11th round of the 2011 draft... Signed on July 25, 2011... **SIGNED BY:** Blake Crosby

YR	Club & League	AVG	G	AB	R	H	2B	3B	HR	RBI	SH-SF	HB	BB-IB	SO	SB-CS	SLG	OBP	OPS
2011	Blue Jays (GCL)	.625	5	16	5	10	0	0	1	7	0-1	1	2-0	0	0-1	.813	.650	1.463
	Vancouver (NOR)	.179	23	84	10	15	4	0	2	7	0-0	0	6-0	14	2-1	.298	.233	.531
2012	Lansing (MID)	.248	78	278	57	69	25	4	9	37	0-2	7	38-0	75	15-2	.464	.351	.815
Minor Totals		.249	106	378	72	94	29	4	12	51	0-3	8	46-0	89	17-4	.442	.340	.782

Cabrera, Juan — *PITCHER*

HT: 6-2... **WT:** 204... **B-T:** R-R... **BORN:** 21 Sep 91, Santiago, DR... **RESIDES:** Puerto Plata, DR... **EDUCATION:** NA... **TRANSACTIONS:** Signed by the Toronto Blue Jays on March 7, 2011... **SIGNED BY:** Marco Paddy & Domingo Toribio

YR	Club & League	W-L	ERA	G	GS	CG	SHO	SV	IP	H	R	ER	HR	HB	BB-IB	SO	WP	BK	OBA
2011	DSL (DSL)	0-2	3.19	15	3	0	0	1	36.2	34	18	13	2	2	14-0	34	3	1	.246
2012									Injured – Did Not Play										
Minor Totals		0-2	3.19	15	3	0	0	1	36.2	34	18	13	2	2	14-0	34	3	1	.246

Cabrera, Oscar — PITCHER

HT: 6-2... **WT:** 215... **B-T:** L-L... **BORN:** 22 May 94, Villa Mella, DR... **RESIDES:** Villa Mella, DR... **EDUCATION:** NA... **TRANSACTIONS:** Signed by the Los Angeles Angels of Anaheim on November 15, 2010... Signed by the Toronto Blue Jays on January 1, 2012... **SIGNED BY:** Denny Suarez

YR	Club & League	W-L	ERA	G	GS	CG	SHO	SV	IP	H	R	ER	HR	HB	BB-IB	SO	WP	BK	OBA
2012	DSL (DSL)	0-2	2.12	9	7	0	0	0	34.0	26	8	8	0	3	15-0	40	4	1	.224
	Blue Jays (GCL)	0-1	5.40	2	1	0	0	0	5.0	6	3	3	0	0	2-0	5	2	0	.286
Minor Totals		0-3	2.54	11	8	0	0	0	39.0	32	11	11	0	3	17-0	45	6	1	.234

Cardona, Adonys — PITCHER

HT: 6-1... **WT:** 170... **B-T:** R-R... **BORN:** 16 Jan 94, La Sabana, Vargas, VZ... **RESIDES:** Caracas, VZ... **EDUCATION:** NA... **TRANSACTIONS:** Signed by the Toronto Blue Jays on July 5, 2010... **SIGNED BY:** Rafael Moncada

YR	Club & League	W-L	ERA	G	GS	CG	SHO	SV	IP	H	R	ER	HR	HB	BB-IB	SO	WP	BK	OBA
2011	Blue Jays (GCL)	1-3	4.55	10	7	0	0	0	31.2	31	17	16	2	2	12-0	35	2	0	.256
2012	Blue Jays (GCL)	0-1	6.32	8	2	0	0	0	15.2	15	11	11	1	1	10-0	20	3	1	.246
Minor Totals		1-4	5.13	18	9	0	0	0	47.1	46	28	27	3	3	22-0	55	5	1	.253

Carlyle, Buddy — PITCHER

HT: 6-3... **WT:** 210... **B-T:** L-R... **BORN:** 21 Dec 77, Omaha, NE... **RESIDES:** Tyrone, GA... **EDUCATION: Bellevue East High School**... **TRANSACTIONS:** Selected by the Cincinnati Reds in the 2nd round of the 1996 June draft... Signed on June 21, 1996... Traded by the Cincinnati Reds to the San Diego Padres for RHP Marc Kroon on April 8, 1998... Purchased by Hanshin Tigers (Japan Central) from the San Diego Padres November 3, 2000... Signed by the Kansas City Royals December 18, 2002... Signed by the New York Yankees on December 23, 2003... Signed by the Los Angeles Dodgers on November 18, 2004... Signed by the Florida Marlins on December 15, 2005... Signed by the Atlanta Braves on December 4, 2006... Signed by the New York Yankees on December 2, 2010... Signed by the Atlanta Braves on January 30, 2012... Signed by the Toronto Blue Jays on December 11, 2012... **SIGNED BY:** Bobby Szymkowski

YR	Club & League	W-L	ERA	G	GS	CG	SHO	SV	IP	H	R	ER	HR	HB	BB-IB	SO	WP	BK	OBA
1996	Princeton (APP)	2-4	4.66	10	9	1	0	0	46.1	47	33	24	4	1	16-0	42	8	0	.255
1997	Charleston (WV) (SAL)	14-5	2.77	23	23	4	1	0	143.0	130	51	44	9	3	27-0	111	5	1	.240
1998	Chattanooga (SOU)	0-1	5.40	1	1	0	0	0	5.0	6	3	3	0	0	0-0	3	0	0	.300
	Mobile (SOU)	14-6	3.38	27	27	2	1	0	183.2	179	77	69	13	7	46-0	97	4	1	.256
1999	Las Vegas (PCL)	11-8	4.89	25	25	0	0	0	160.0	180	99	87	25	6	42-1	138	6	0	.286
	SAN DIEGO (NL)	1-3	5.97	7	7	0	0	0	37.2	36	28	25	7	2	17-0	29	1	0	.257
2000	Las Vegas (PCL)	8-6	4.29	27	27	1	0	0	151.0	165	93	72	25	2	44-0	127	3	0	.273
	SAN DIEGO (NL)	0-0	21.00	4	0	0	0	0	3.0	6	7	7	0	0	3-0	2	0	0	.400
2001	Hanshin (CNT)	7-10	3.87	28	26	0	0	0	153.1	151	73	66	22	1	64-0	111	1	0	.000
2002	Hanshin (CNT)	0-2	7.53	3	3	0	0	0	14.1	17	12	12	1	1	5-0	13	1	0	.000
2003	Omaha (PCL)	0-1	5.40	2	0	0	0	0	5.0	5	3	3	2	0	1-0	4	0	0	.263
	Wichita (TEX)	3-2	1.98	15	0	0	0	3	27.1	19	6	6	0	0	7-0	41	1	0	.192
2004	Trenton (EAS)	4-0	0.72	8	5	0	0	0	37.1	23	4	3	0	0	4-0	48	0	0	.178
	Columbus (INT)	8-5	4.05	19	18	0	0	0	106.2	113	51	48	14	7	21-0	92	1	0	.274
2005	LOS ANGELES (NL)	0-0	8.36	10	0	0	0	0	14.0	16	13	13	4	1	4-0	13	0	0	.291
	Dodgers (GCL)	0-0	3.00	1	1	0	0	0	3.0	3	1	1	0	0	0-0	1	0	0	.273
	Las Vegas (PCL)	1-2	4.88	20	6	0	0	2	48.0	51	28	26	7	5	21-0	53	0	0	.280
2006	Albuquerque (PCL)	3-1	1.93	13	2	0	0	0	28.0	17	6	6	3	1	7-1	22	0	0	.177
2007	Gwinnett (INT)	5-2	2.59	9	9	1	1	0	48.2	40	15	14	5	2	9-1	56	1	0	.225
	ATLANTA (NL)	8-7	5.21	22	20	0	0	0	107.0	117	67	62	19	2	32-8	74	3	0	.284
2008	Gwinnett (INT)	0-0	7.04	2	2	0	0	0	7.2	11	7	6	0	0	3-0	7	2	1	.355
	ATLANTA (NL)	2-0	3.59	45	0	0	0	0	62.2	52	26	25	5	1	26-6	59	4	1	.228
2009	Rome (SAL)	0-0	0.00	1	1	0	0	0	2.0	1	0	0	0	1	0-0	1	0	0	.200
	Gwinnett (INT)	3-1	1.76	12	1	0	0	0	15.1	13	3	3	0	1	1-0	23	0	2	.228
	ATLANTA (NL)	0-1	8.86	16	0	0	0	0	21.1	35	23	21	5	0	12-4	12	2	0	.380
2010	Nippon Ham (PAC)	0-3	4.88	7	0	-	-	0	27.2	35	18	15	2	1	11-0	14	1	1	.000
2011	NEW YORK (AL)	0-1	4.70	8	0	0	0	0	7.2	5	4	4	1	0	7-1	9	2	0	.185
	Scranton/W.-Barre (INT)	2-2	3.98	27	2	0	0	1	43.0	35	19	19	5	1	16-0	31	4	0	.223
2012	Gwinnett (INT)	5-4	3.43	33	1	0	0	0	76.0	81	33	29	5	1	14-1	73	2	1	.279
Minor Totals		83-50	3.67	275	160	9	3	6	1137.0	1119	532	463	117	38	279-4	970	37	6	.258
MAJOR TOTALS		11-12	5.58	112	27	0	0	0	253.1	267	168	157	41	6	101-19	198	12	1	.276

Carmona, Julio — PITCHER

HT: 6-1... **WT:** 205... **B-T:** R-R... **BORN:** 10 Oct 90, Bani, DR... **RESIDES:** Bani, DR... **EDUCATION:** NA... **TRANSACTIONS:** Signed by the Toronto Blue Jays on April 12, 2010... **SIGNED BY:** Hilario Soriano

YR	Club & League	W-L	ERA	G	GS	CG	SHO	SV	IP	H	R	ER	HR	HB	BB-IB	SO	WP	BK	OBA
2010	DSL (DSL)	1-3	3.26	16	14	0	0	0	58.0	38	28	21	0	14	33-0	67	20	1	.189
2011	Blue Jays (GCL)	3-2	6.41	23	0	0	0	2	26.2	20	21	19	1	4	22-0	30	9	0	.208
2012	Bluefield (APP)	0-4	2.83	17	0	0	0	2	28.2	22	13	9	0	1	15-0	34	11	0	.208
Minor Totals		4-9	3.89	56	14	0	0	4	113.1	80	62	49	1	19	70-0	131	40	1	.199

Carreno, Joel — *PITCHER*

HT: 6-0... **WT:** 218... **B-T:** R-R... **BORN:** 07 Mar 87, San Cristobal, DR... **RESIDES:** San Cristobal, DR... **EDUCATION:** NA... **TRANSACTIONS:** Signed by the Toronto Blue Jays on October 11, 2004... **SIGNED BY:** Hilario Soriano

YR	Club & League	W-L	ERA	G	GS	CG	SHO	SV	IP	H	R	ER	HR	HB	BB-IB	SO	WP	BK	OBA
2005	DSL (DSL)	2-1	4.15	8	4	0	0	1	30.1	29	17	14	0	4	12-0	29	2	0	.236
2006	DSL (DSL)	8-3	1.53	15	15	0	0	0	82.1	48	26	14	2	5	28-0	86	3	0	.168
2007	Blue Jays (GCL)	6-4	2.62	12	12	0	0	0	65.1	60	27	19	4	9	13-0	64	3	0	.243
2008	Auburn (NYP)	5-5	3.42	15	13	0	0	0	76.1	74	32	29	6	5	19-0	85	4	0	.255
2009	Auburn (NYP)	1-0	0.82	2	2	0	0	0	11.0	6	2	1	0	1	3-0	12	0	0	.158
	Lansing (MID)	2-4	3.62	14	14	0	0	0	79.2	76	36	32	5	1	29-0	62	3	1	.255
2010	Dunedin (FSL)	9-6	3.73	27	25	1	0	0	137.2	147	65	57	8	12	30-0	173	6	3	.275
2011	New Hampshire (EAS)	7-9	3.41	24	23	0	0	0	134.2	100	56	51	12	12	68-0	152	16	3	.208
	TORONTO (AL)	1-0	1.15	11	0	0	0	0	15.2	11	2	2	1	0	4-0	14	0	0	.200
2012	Las Vegas (PCL)	2-5	8.92	10	8	0	0	0	36.1	50	41	36	7	2	27-0	30	2	0	.336
	New Hampshire (EAS)	2-4	3.86	17	7	0	0	0	53.2	43	25	23	4	1	19-0	58	3	0	.218
	TORONTO (AL)	0-2	6.14	11	2	0	0	0	22.0	22	15	15	7	0	14-0	16	0	0	.265
Minor Totals		44-41	3.51	144	123	1	0	1	707.1	633	327	276	48	52	248-0	751	42	7	.240
MAJOR TOTALS		1-2	4.06	22	2	0	0	0	37.2	33	17	17	8	0	18-0	30	0	0	.239

Castillo, Rauly — *PITCHER*

HT: 6-2... **WT:** 195... **B-T:** R-R... **BORN:** 08 Jun 93, Caja Seca, VZ... **RESIDES:** Santa Maria, VZ... **EDUCATION:** NA... **TRANSACTIONS:** Signed by the Toronto Blue Jays on November 21, 2012... **SIGNED BY:** Ismael Cruz, Luis Marquez, Sandy Rosario & Rafael Moncada

Castro, Miguel — *PITCHER*

HT: 6-5... **WT:** 190... **B-T:** R-R... **BORN:** 24 Dec 94, La Romana, DR... **RESIDES:** La Romana, DR... **EDUCATION:** NA... **TRANSACTIONS:** Signed by the Toronto Blue Jays on January 5, 2012... **SIGNED BY:** Ismael Cruz, Jose Rosario & Jean Alvarez

YR	Club & League	W-L	ERA	G	GS	CG	SHO	SV	IP	H	R	ER	HR	HB	BB-IB	SO	WP	BK	OBA
2012	DSL (DSL)	3-2	4.87	8	3	0	0	0	20.1	16	13	11	1	3	11-0	20	2	2	.232

Cenas, Gabriel — *INFIELDER*

HT: 6-1... **WT:** 155... **B-T:** R-R... **BORN:** 16 Oct 93, Maracaibo, VZ... **RESIDES:** Estado Zulia, VZ... **EDUCATION:** NA... **TRANSACTIONS:** Signed by the Toronto Blue Jays on July 6, 2010... **SIGNED BY:** Robinson Garces

YR	Club & League	AVG	G	AB	R	H	2B	3B	HR	RBI	SH-SF	HB	BB-IB	SO	SB-CS	SLG	OBP	OPS
2011	DSL (DSL)	.208	19	53	6	11	1	0	0	3	0-1	5	9-0	11	1-0	.226	.368	.594
2012	Blue Jays (GCL)	.192	49	172	15	33	7	0	2	15	0-1	6	13-0	46	3-1	.267	.271	.538
Minor Totals		.196	68	225	21	44	8	0	2	18	0-2	11	22-0	57	4-1	.258	.296	.554

Champlin, Kramer — *PITCHER*

HT: 6-6... **WT:** 200... **B-T:** R-R... **BORN:** 08 Mar 90, Olympia, WA... **RESIDES:** Olympia, WA... **EDUCATION:** Arizona State University... **TRANSACTIONS:** Selected by the Toronto Blue Jays in the 33rd round of the 2011 June draft... Signed on June 22, 2011... **SIGNED BY:** Blake Crosby

YR	Club & League	W-L	ERA	G	GS	CG	SHO	SV	IP	H	R	ER	HR	HB	BB-IB	SO	WP	BK	OBA
2011	Blue Jays (GCL)	0-0	20.25	1	0	0	0	0	1.1	6	3	3	1	0	1-0	0	0	0	.600
	Vancouver (NOR)	0-2	4.91	7	3	0	0	0	14.2	20	8	8	1	0	3-0	11	0	0	.339
2012	Lansing (MID)	4-1	4.09	29	3	0	0	1	70.1	75	38	32	7	5	19-3	77	9	0	.266
Minor Totals		4-3	4.48	37	6	0	0	1	86.1	101	49	43	9	5	23-3	88	9	0	.288

Charles, Art — *INFIELDER*

HT: 6-6... **WT:** 221... **B-T:** L-L... **BORN:** 10 Nov 90, Bakersfield, CA... **RESIDES:** Bakersfield, CA... **EDUCATION:** Bakersfield College... **TRANSACTIONS:** Selected by the Toronto Blue Jays in the 20th round of the 2010 June draft... Signed on June 21, 2010... **SIGNED BY:** Blake Crosby

YR	Club & League	AVG	G	AB	R	H	2B	3B	HR	RBI	SH-SF	HB	BB-IB	SO	SB-CS	SLG	OBP	OPS
2010	Blue Jays (GCL)	.244	37	123	17	30	11	0	4	13	0-2	1	16-0	48	5-0	.431	.331	.762
2011	Bluefield (APP)	.240	68	250	46	60	18	3	11	61	0-4	6	39-0	89	1-1	.468	.351	.819
2012	Bluefield (APP)	.235	31	85	18	20	5	3	6	16	0-1	4	33-0	33	2-0	.576	.463	1.039
	Vancouver (NOR)	.236	33	127	19	30	10	1	7	18	0-1	1	13-1	41	0-1	.496	.310	.806
Minor Totals		.239	169	585	100	140	44	7	28	108	0-8	12	101-1	211	8-2	.482	.358	.840

Chung, Byung Jo — *INFIELDER*

HT: 5-11... **WT:** 180... **B-T:** R-R... **BORN:** 23 Feb 88, Garden Grove, CA... **RESIDES:** Sacramento, CA... **EDUCATION:** Sacramento State University... **TRANSACTIONS:** Selected by the Toronto Blue Jays in the 31st round of the 2012 draft... Signed on June 10, 2012... **SIGNED BY:** Donald Brown

YR	Club & League	AVG	G	AB	R	H	2B	3B	HR	RBI	SH-SF	HB	BB-IB	SO	SB-CS	SLG	OBP	OPS
2012	Vancouver (NOR)	.241	34	108	12	26	7	1	0	12	3-3	5	13-0	25	0-1	.324	.341	.665

Cole, Taylor — PITCHER

HT: 6-1... **WT:** 180... **B-T:** R-R... **BORN:** 20 Aug 89, Las Vegas, NV... **RESIDES:** Las Vegas, NV... **EDUCATION:** Brigham Young University... **TRANSACTIONS:** Selected by the Toronto Blue Jays in the 29th round of the 2011 June draft... Signed on June 8, 2011... **SIGNED BY:** Blake Crosby

YR	Club & League	W-L	ERA	G	GS	CG	SHO	SV	IP	H	R	ER	HR	HB	BB-IB	SO	WP	BK	OBA
2011	Vancouver (NOR)	1-3	5.88	11	8	0	0	0	33.2	35	23	22	3	4	17-1	25	5	0	.276
2012	Vancouver (NOR)	6-0	0.81	12	11	0	0	0	66.1	36	6	6	0	6	17-0	57	6	0	.161
Minor Totals		7-3	2.52	23	19	0	0	0	100.0	71	29	28	3	10	34-1	82	11	0	.202

Collazo, Willie — PITCHER

HT: 5-8... **WT:** 180... **B-T:** L-L... **BORN:** 07 Nov 79, Carolina, PR... **RESIDES:** Miami, FL... **EDUCATION:** NA... **TRANSACTIONS:** Signed by the Atlanta Braves on June 8, 2001... Selected by the Anaheim Angels in the Rule 5 Draft on December 15, 2003... Signed by the New York Mets on March 1, 2006... Signed by the Florida Marlins on November 25, 2008... Signed by the Toronto Blue Jays on January 10, 2010... **SIGNED BY:** Marco Paddy

YR	Club & League	W-L	ERA	G	GS	CG	SHO	SV	IP	H	R	ER	HR	HB	BB-IB	SO	WP	BK	OBA
2001	Jamestown (NYP)	3-1	0.60	9	0	0	0	1	15.0	9	2	1	0	1	0-0	13	2	0	.170
	Macon (SAL)	3-2	2.70	12	0	0	0	1	23.1	13	9	7	3	2	4-0	23	2	0	.171
2002	Greenville (SOU)	4-2	3.47	51	0	0	0	4	72.2	70	34	28	7	2	27-2	74	4	1	.253
2003	Myrtle Beach (CAR)	0-1	3.07	11	0	0	0	1	14.2	12	5	5	1	1	4-0	15	0	0	.222
	Greenville (SOU)	6-2	3.66	39	0	0	0	0	46.2	41	22	19	3	1	21-1	34	3	2	.241
2004	Arkansas (TEX)	6-10	4.56	32	20	3	2	0	148.0	156	88	75	11	12	38-0	100	8	0	.268
2005	Salt Lake (PCL)	0-1	7.71	11	1	0	0	0	23.1	29	20	20	7	4	9-0	12	2	0	.337
	Arkansas (TEX)	1-5	6.78	26	10	0	0	0	71.2	85	60	54	16	4	29-1	58	1	0	.293
2006	Norfolk (INT)	3-3	4.79	7	5	0	0	0	41.1	45	24	22	4	1	13-0	26	1	2	.280
	Binghamton (EAS)	7-6	3.11	18	18	1	1	0	118.2	104	44	41	7	8	16-0	79	2	1	.239
2007	New Orleans (PCL)	6-5	2.46	53	4	0	0	4	98.2	91	33	27	5	7	19-1	69	2	0	.252
	NEW YORK (NL)	0-0	6.35	6	0	0	0	0	5.2	7	4	4	0	0	5-1	0	0	0	.318
2008	New Orleans (PCL)	4-9	4.05	37	16	0	0	2	135.2	134	66	61	18	6	35-2	71	4	2	.266
2009	New Orleans (PCL)	9-5	3.70	34	16	0	0	0	126.1	125	57	52	14	9	35-0	74	4	0	.264
2010	Las Vegas (PCL)	0-0	4.70	4	0	0	0	0	7.2	11	7	4	0	0	1-0	6	2	0	.324
2011	Las Vegas (PCL)	1-2	4.98	14	6	0	0	0	47.0	52	28	26	5	2	14-0	26	0	0	.289
	Dunedin (FSL)	0-0	6.00	1	1	0	0	0	3.0	5	2	2	1	0	0-0	4	0	0	.385
	New Hampshire (EAS)	2-0	2.95	5	3	0	0	0	18.1	15	6	6	2	1	1-0	11	0	0	.224
2012	Blue Jays (GCL)	0-0	4.50	2	0	0	0	0	2.0	2	1	1	0	0	1-0	3	0	0	.250
	Dunedin (FSL)	0-0	2.25	2	0	0	0	0	4.0	4	1	1	0	0	0-0	4	0	0	.250
Minor Totals		55-54	4.00	368	100	4	3	13	1018.0	1003	509	452	104	61	267-7	702	37	8	.261

Conde, Greylor — PITCHER

HT: 6-4... **WT:** 195... **B-T:** R-R... **BORN:** 25 Jun 95, Caracus, VZ... **RESIDES:** Isla de Margairita, VZ... **EDUCATION:** NA... **TRANSACTIONS:** Signed by the Toronto Blue Jays on December 6, 2011... **SIGNED BY:** Ismael Cruz & Luis Marquez

YR	Club & League	W-L	ERA	G	GS	CG	SHO	SV	IP	H	R	ER	HR	HB	BB-IB	SO	WP	BK	OBA
2012	DSL (DSL)	1-3	3.57	12	2	0	0	0	35.1	43	17	14	1	5	12-0	13	3	0	.323

Conner, Seth — INFIELDER

HT: 6-2... **WT:** 205... **B-T:** R-R... **BORN:** 29 Jan 92, Rogersville, MO... **RESIDES:** Rogersville, MO... **EDUCATION:** Logan-Rogersville High School... **TRANSACTIONS:** Selected by the Toronto Blue Jays in the 41st round of the 2010 June draft... Signed on August 16, 2010... **SIGNED BY:** Darin Vaughan

YR	Club & League	AVG	G	AB	R	H	2B	3B	HR	RBI	SH-SF	HB	BB-IB	SO	SB-CS	SLG	OBP	OPS
2011	Blue Jays (GCL)	.276	50	174	29	48	9	2	4	23	2-1	5	30-1	37	4-2	.420	.395	.815
2012	Blue Jays (GCL)	.250	5	16	2	4	1	0	0	2	0-1	1	2-0	3	0-0	.313	.350	.663
	Bluefield (APP)	.296	49	142	23	42	8	2	2	28	1-3	9	24-1	33	0-0	.423	.421	.844
Minor Totals		.283	104	332	54	94	18	4	6	53	3-5	15	56-2	73	4-2	.416	.404	.820

Contreras, Jorge — PITCHER

HT: 6-2... **WT:** 190... **B-T:** R-R... **BORN:** 07 Oct 92, Bayaguana, DR... **RESIDES:** Bayaguana, DR... **EDUCATION:** NA... **TRANSACTIONS:** Signed by the Toronto Blue Jays on March 7, 2011... **SIGNED BY:** Marco Paddy & Domingo Toribio

YR	Club & League	W-L	ERA	G	GS	CG	SHO	SV	IP	H	R	ER	HR	HB	BB-IB	SO	WP	BK	OBA
2012	DSL (DSL)	3-3	2.55	13	13	1	1	0	60.0	51	22	17	1	2	24-0	44	9	2	.238

Copeland, Scott — PITCHER

HT: 6-3... **WT:** 210... **B-T:** R-R... **BORN:** 15 Dec 87, White Oak, TX... **RESIDES:** White Oak, TX... **EDUCATION:** University of Southern Mississippi... **TRANSACTIONS:** Selected by the Baltimore Orioles in the 21st round of the 2010 June draft... Signed on June 15, 2010... **SIGNED BY:** Mike Tullier

YR	Club & League	W-L	ERA	G	GS	CG	SHO	SV	IP	H	R	ER	HR	HB	BB-IB	SO	WP	BK	OBA
2010	Aberdeen (NYP)	2-5	2.91	12	12	0	0	0	65.0	45	22	21	1	7	23-0	49	7	0	.197
	Delmarva (SAL)	1-0	0.00	1	1	0	0	0	6.0	5	0	0	0	0	2-0	4	0	0	.238
2011	Delmarva (SAL)	5-9	6.58	20	20	0	0	0	108.0	136	88	79	10	7	46-0	55	14	0	.308
	Frederick (CAR)	3-2	2.14	6	6	0	0	0	33.2	25	8	8	0	3	15-1	22	2	0	.216
2012	Frederick (CAR)	3-8	6.88	18	18	1	0	0	86.1	118	79	66	11	12	38-1	64	8	1	.330
	Dunedin (FSL)	4-1	2.70	7	6	1	0	0	36.2	35	15	11	1	1	14-0	32	4	0	.246
Minor Totals		18-25	4.96	64	63	2	0	0	335.2	364	212	185	23	30	138-2	226	35	1	.278

Cordero, Jimmy — PITCHER

HT: 6-3... **WT:** 195... **B-T:** R-R... **BORN:** 19 Oct 91, San Cristobal, DR... **RESIDES:** San Cristobal, DR... **EDUCATION:** NA... **TRANSACTIONS:** Signed by the Toronto Blue Jays on January 6, 2012... **SIGNED BY:** Ismael Cruz & Jose Rosario

YR	Club & League	W-L	ERA	G	GS	CG	SHO	SV	IP	H	R	ER	HR	HB	BB-IB	SO	WP	BK	OBA
2012	DSL (DSL)	1-3	5.60	7	3	0	0	0	17.2	13	14	11	3	1	11-0	18	3	0	.203

Cordova, Manuel — PITCHER

HT: 6-4... **WT:** 180... **B-T:** R-R... **BORN:** 17 Jan 95, Margarita, VZ... **RESIDES:** Margarita, VZ... **EDUCATION:** NA... **TRANSACTIONS:** Signed by the Toronto Blue Jays on July 6, 2011... **SIGNED BY:** Marco Paddy & Pablo Leal

YR	Club & League	W-L	ERA	G	GS	CG	SHO	SV	IP	H	R	ER	HR	HB	BB-IB	SO	WP	BK	OBA
2012									Did Not Play										

Crouse, Michael — OUTFIELDER

HT: 6-4... **WT:** 205... **B-T:** R-R... **BORN:** 11 Nov 90, Port Moody, BC... **RESIDES:** Port Moody, BC... **EDUCATION:** Centennial SS... **TRANSACTIONS:** Selected by the Toronto Blue Jays in the 16th round of the 2008 June draft... Signed on June 9, 2008... **SIGNED BY:** Don Cowan & Kevin Briand

YR	Club & League	AVG	G	AB	R	H	2B	3B	HR	RBI	SH-SF	HB	BB-IB	SO	SB-CS	SLG	OBP	OPS
2008	Blue Jays (GCL)	.133	7	15	2	2	0	1	0	0	1-0	1	3-0	7	1-1	.267	.316	.583
2009	Blue Jays (GCL)	.218	55	188	28	41	9	4	2	17	0-1	2	23-1	53	25-5	.340	.308	.648
2010	Blue Jays (GCL)	.333	28	96	17	32	7	3	4	20	0-0	2	9-0	32	9-6	.594	.402	.996
	Lansing (MID)	.216	28	88	11	19	5	2	2	9	1-1	1	14-0	35	5-2	.386	.327	.713
2011	Lansing (MID)	.261	101	364	73	95	26	5	14	55	0-4	9	44-2	113	38-8	.475	.352	.827
2012	Dunedin (FSL)	.203	59	202	42	41	9	1	6	26	0-1	2	26-0	73	9-5	.347	.299	.646
	Lansing (MID)	.194	36	124	18	24	3	0	4	15	0-1	1	15-0	44	6-2	.315	.284	.599
Minor Totals		.236	314	1077	191	254	59	16	32	142	2-8	18	134-3	357	93-29	.409	.328	.738

D'Alessandro, Justin — PITCHER

HT: 6-4... **WT:** 190... **B-T:** R-R... **BORN:** 27 Sep 89, Pittsburgh, PA... **RESIDES:** Pittsburgh, PA... **EDUCATION:** Catholic University of America... **TRANSACTIONS:** Signed by the Toronto Blue Jays on June 10, 2012... **SIGNED BY:** Bobby Gandolfo

YR	Club & League	W-L	ERA	G	GS	CG	SHO	SV	IP	H	R	ER	HR	HB	BB-IB	SO	WP	BK	OBA
2012	Blue Jays (GCL)	1-0	3.07	14	0	0	0	0	14.2	16	6	5	0	1	8-0	12	1	0	.281

Daly, Matthew — PITCHER

HT: 5-11... **WT:** 185... **B-T:** R-R... **BORN:** 14 Aug 86, Yorba Linda, CA... **RESIDES:** Honolulu, HI... **EDUCATION:** University of Hawaii... **TRANSACTIONS:** Selected by the Toronto Blue Jays in the 13th round of the 2008 June draft... Signed on June 9, 2008... **SIGNED BY:** Demerius Pittman

YR	Club & League	W-L	ERA	G	GS	CG	SHO	SV	IP	H	R	ER	HR	HB	BB-IB	SO	WP	BK	OBA
2008	Auburn (NYP)	2-2	1.46	23	0	0	0	5	24.2	19	6	4	0	3	10-1	28	4	0	.204
2009	Lansing (MID)	1-5	1.95	44	0	0	0	19	50.2	35	13	11	0	1	20-2	54	9	0	.188
	Dunedin (FSL)	0-0	0.00	8	0	0	0	1	9.1	4	0	0	0	0	4-1	11	1	0	.129
2010	Dunedin (FSL)	2-2	2.50	56	0	0	0	31	57.2	45	19	16	2	1	23-1	63	4	0	.214
2011	New Hampshire (EAS)	4-0	6.25	29	0	0	0	0	36.0	39	26	25	2	3	28-1	29	5	0	.275
	Dunedin (FSL)	0-1	8.59	11	0	0	0	4	14.2	18	14	14	4	0	9-0	13	3	0	.321
2012	New Hampshire (EAS)	2-4	4.52	47	0	0	0	0	69.2	70	35	35	8	1	35-3	51	5	0	.264
Minor Totals		11-14	3.60	218	0	0	0	60	262.2	230	113	105	16	9	129-9	249	31	0	.234

Davis, D.J. — OUTFIELDER

HT: 6-1... **WT:** 180... **B-T:** L-L... **BORN:** 25 Jul 94, Wiggins, MS... **RESIDES:** Wiggins, MS... **EDUCATION:** Stone County High School... **TRANSACTIONS:** Selected by the Toronto Blue Jays in the 1st round (17th overall) of the 2012 June Draft... Signed on June 10, 2012... **SIGNED BY:** Brian Johnston

YR	Club & League	AVG	G	AB	R	H	2B	3B	HR	RBI	SH-SF	HB	BB-IB	SO	SB-CS	SLG	OBP	OPS
2012	Blue Jays (GCL)	.233	43	163	30	38	7	2	4	12	1-0	8	18-0	54	18-7	.374	.339	.713
	Bluefield (APP)	.340	12	47	9	16	3	1	1	6	0-0	2	4-0	10	6-2	.511	.415	.926
	Vancouver (NOR)	.167	5	18	3	3	0	0	0	0	0-0	0	5-0	6	1-1	.167	.348	.515
Minor Totals		.250	60	228	42	57	10	3	5	18	1-0	10	27-0	70	25-10	.386	.355	.741

BIOGRAPHIES LAST SEASON HISTORY RECORDS OPPONENTS PLAYER DEV. MEDIA & MISC.

Davis, Tony — PITCHER

HT: 5-11... **WT:** 185... **B-T:** S-L... **BORN:** 16 Jan 88, Newberry, FL... **RESIDES:** Lake Worth, FL... **EDUCATION:** **University of Florida**... **TRANSACTIONS:** Selected by the Minnesota Twins in the 12th round of the 2009 June draft... Signed on June 17, 2009...Signed by the Toronto Blue Jays on December 18, 2012... **SIGNED BY:** Billy Corigan

YR	Club & League	W-L	ERA	G	GS	CG	SHO	SV	IP	H	R	ER	HR	HB	BB-IB	SO	WP	BK	OBA
2009	Elizabethton (APP)	2-3	5.35	21	0	0	0	6	35.1	43	23	21	2	1	21-4	47	2	0	.312
	New Britain Rock (EAS)	0-0	0.00	2	0	0	0	0	3.0	1	0	0	0	0	0-0	1	0	0	.111
2010	Fort Myers (FSL)	0-0	2.87	17	0	0	0	1	31.1	32	13	10	1	2	18-0	19	0	0	.267
	New Britain Rock (EAS)	1-2	2.68	25	0	0	0	1	37.0	26	16	11	0	2	28-1	26	2	0	.203
2011	New Britain Rock (EAS)	2-2	2.57	17	0	0	0	0	28.0	23	9	8	1	3	12-2	24	2	0	.225
2012	Fort Myers (FSL)	2-0	15.19	5	0	0	0	0	5.1	10	9	9	1	0	3-0	4	1	0	.357
Minor Totals		7-7	3.79	87	0	0	0	8	140.0	135	70	59	5	8	82-7	121	7	0	.257

Dawson, Shane — PITCHER

HT: 6-1... **WT:** 180... **B-T:** R-L... **BORN:** 09 Sep 93, Drayton Valley, AB... **RESIDES:** Drayton Valley, AB... **EDUCATION:** Lethbridge Community College... **TRANSACTIONS:** Selected by the Toronto Blue Jays in the 17th round of the 2012 June draft... Signed on June 10, 2012... **SIGNED BY:** Jamie Lehman

YR	Club & League	W-L	ERA	G	GS	CG	SHO	SV	IP	H	R	ER	HR	HB	BB-IB	SO	WP	BK	OBA
2012	Blue Jays (GCL)	2-1	2.35	10	3	0	0	0	30.2	33	13	8	2	1	10-0	35	3	1	.282

De Aza, Andres — OUTFIELDER

HT: 6-4... **WT:** 200... **B-T:** R-R... **BORN:** 17 Nov 94, San Isidro, DR... **RESIDES:** San Luis, DR... **EDUCATION:** NA... **TRANSACTIONS:** Signed by the Toronto Blue Jays on February 29, 2012... **SIGNED BY:** Ismael Cruz, Sandy Rosario & Marino Tejada

YR	Club & League	AVG	G	AB	R	H	2B	3B	HR	RBI	SH-SF	HB	BB-IB	SO	SB-CS	SLG	OBP	OPS
2012	DSL (DSL)	.227	28	97	11	22	3	1	3	17	0-2	4	6-0	26	0-0	.371	.294	.665

De La Cruz, Michael — CATCHER

HT: 5-10... **WT:** 175... **B-T:** L-R... **BORN:** 15 May 93, Tamboril, DR... **RESIDES:** Tamboril, DR... **EDUCATION:** NA... **TRANSACTIONS:** Signed by the Toronto Blue Jays on November 19, 2012... **SIGNED BY:** Ismael Cruz, Sandy Rosario & Lorenzo Perez

De La Rosa, Luis — PITCHER

HT: 6-2... **WT:** 170... **B-T:** R-R... **BORN:** 11 Aug 93, Santo Domingo, DR... **RESIDES:** Santo Domingo, DR... **EDUCTAION:** NA... **TRANSACTIONS:** Signed by the Toronto Blue Jays on November 18, 2011... **SIGNED BY:** Ismael Cruz, Jose Rosario & Luis Marquez

YR	Club & League	W-L	ERA	G	GS	CG	SHO	SV	IP	H	R	ER	HR	HB	BB-IB	SO	WP	BK	OBA
2012	DSL (DSL)	2-1	8.38	10	4	0	0	0	19.1	22	21	18	2	6	14-0	11	5	1	.286

DeJong, Chase — PITCHER

HT: 6-4... **WT:** 185... **B-T:** R-L... **BORN:** 29 Dec 93, Long Beach, CA... **RESIDES:** Long Beach, CA... **EDUCATION:** Woodrow Wilson High School... **TRANSACTIONS:** Selected by the Toronto Blue Jays in the 2nd round of the 2012 June draft... Signed on July 1, 2012... **SIGNED BY:** Joey Aversa

YR	Club & League	W-L	ERA	G	GS	CG	SHO	SV	IP	H	R	ER	HR	HB	BB-IB	SO	WP	BK	OBA
2012	Blue Jays (GCL)	1-0	1.50	6	0	0	0	0	12.0	7	2	2	0	0	1-0	15	0	0	.171

DeSouza, Nathan — OUTFIELDER

HT: 6-0... **WT:** 185... **B-T:** L-R... **BORN:** 13 Jul 94, Milton, ON... **RESIDES:** Milton, ON... **EDUCATION:** Drury High School... **TRANSACTIONS:** Selected by the Toronto Blue Jays in the 26th round of the 2012 June Draft... Signed on July 3, 2012... **SIGNED BY:** Jamie Lehman

YR	Club & League	AVG	G	AB	R	H	2B	3B	HR	RBI	SH-SF	HB	BB-IB	SO	SB-CS	SLG	OBP	OPS
2012	Blue Jays (GCL)	.241	9	29	7	7	0	1	1	3	0-0	0	3-0	6	0-0	.414	.313	.727

Dean, Matt — INFIELDER

HT: 6-3... **WT:** 190... **B-T:** R-R... **BORN:** 22 Dec 92, Highland Village, TX... **RESIDES:** Highland Village, TX... **EDUCATION:** The Colony High School... **TRANSACTIONS:** Selected by the Toronto Blue Jays in the 13th round of the 2011 June Draft... Signed on August 15, 2011... **SIGNED BY:** Michael Wagner

YR	Club & League	AVG	G	AB	R	H	2B	3B	HR	RBI	SH-SF	HB	BB-IB	SO	SB-CS	SLG	OBP	OPS
2012	Bluefield (APP)	.222	49	167	22	37	8	4	2	24	1-0	2	12-0	60	3-2	.353	.282	.635

Del Rosario, Yeyfry — PITCHER

HT: 6-2... **WT:** 182... **B-T:** R-R... **BORN:** 27 Apr 94, Sosua, DR... **RESIDES:** Puerto Plata, DR... **EDUCATION:** NA... **TRANSACTIONS:** Signed by the Toronto Blue Jays on March 7, 2011... **SIGNED BY:** Marco Paddy & Domingo Toribio

YR	Club & League	W-L	ERA	G	GS	CG	SHO	SV	IP	H	R	ER	HR	HB	BB-IB	SO	WP	BK	OBA
2011	DSL (DSL)	1-8	2.78	14	13	0	0	0	45.1	33	24	14	2	4	10-0	31	3	0	.195
2012	Blue Jays (GCL)	1-5	3.63	13	12	0	0	0	44.2	37	18	18	1	4	12-0	52	5	3	.222
Minor Totals		2-13	3.20	27	25	0	0	0	90.0	70	42	32	3	8	22-0	83	8	3	.208

Delatte, Brad — PITCHER

HT: 6-0... **WT:** 175... **B-T:** L-L... **BORN:** 13 Jan 90, Baton Rouge, LA... **RESIDES:** Baton Rouge, LA... **EDUCATION:** **Nicholls State University**... **TRANSACTIONS:** Selected by the Toronto Blue Jays in the 5th round of the 2012 June draft... Signed on July 10, 2012... **SIGNED BY:** Brian Johnston

YR	Club & League	W-L	ERA	G	GS	CG	SHO	SV	IP	H	R	ER	HR	HB	BB-IB	SO	WP	BK	OBA
2012	Vancouver (NOR)	0-0	27.00	1	0	0	0	0	0.1	2	1	1	0	1	0-0	0	0	0	.667

Demorizi, Ronniel — INFIELDER

HT: 6-0... **WT:** 170... **B-T:** S-R... **BORN:** 19 Jul 95, San Francisco De Macoris, DR... **RESIDES:** San Francisco De Macoris, DR... **EDUCATION:** NA... **TRANSACTIONS:** Signed by the Toronto Blue Jays on January 17, 2012... **SIGNED BY:** Ismael Cruz & Sandy Rosario

YR	Club & League	AVG	G	AB	R	H	2B	3B	HR	RBI	SH-SF	HB	BB-IB	SO	SB-CS	SLG	OBP	OPS
2012	DSL (DSL)	.178	43	129	16	23	1	0	2	12	3-1	2	17-0	38	4-4	.233	.282	.515

Devonshire, Daniel — INFIELDER

HT: 6-1... **WT:** 220... **B-T:** L-R... **BORN:** 30 Mar 92, Colby, KS... **RESIDES:** Colby, KS... **EDUCATION:** Colby Community College... **TRANSACTIONS:** Selected by the Toronto Blue Jays in the 37th round of the 2012 June Draft... Signed on July 2, 2012... **SIGNED BY:** Joe Bunnell

YR	Club & League	AVG	G	AB	R	H	2B	3B	HR	RBI	SH-SF	HB	BB-IB	SO	SB-CS	SLG	OBP	OPS
2012	Blue Jays (GCL)	.148	11	27	4	4	0	0	0	1	0-0	2	5-0	12	0-0	.148	.324	.472

Diaz, Misaul — PITCHER

HT: 6-3... **WT:** 172 ... **B-T:** R-R... **BORN:** 20 Dec 89, Villa Tapia, DR... **RESIDES:** Santo Domingo, DR... **EDUCATION:** NA... **TRANSACTIONS:** Signed by the Toronto Blue Jays on March 7, 2008... **SIGNED BY:** Hilario Soriano & Lorenzo Perez

YR	Club & League	W-L	ERA	G	GS	CG	SHO	SV	IP	H	R	ER	HR	HB	BB-IB	SO	WP	BK	OBA
2008	Toronto 2 (DSL)	1-5	6.21	13	4	0	0	1	37.2	44	33	26	1	4	16-0	32	2	0	.284
2009	Toronto (DSL)	5-3	2.11	14	0	0	0	1	42.2	35	16	10	1	12	12-0	50	5	1	.217
2010	Blue Jays (GCL)	0-4	2.52	8	8	0	0	0	35.2	27	11	10	0	0	7-0	33	1	1	.208
	Auburn (NYP)	1-1	2.78	5	5	0	0	0	22.2	20	8	7	0	1	4-0	23	1	0	.227
2011	Lansing (MID)	1-3	5.63	12	7	0	0	0	38.1	41	33	24	5	3	24-0	33	6	1	.266
	Blue Jays (GCL)	1-0	3.86	3	1	0	0	0	7.0	6	3	3	1	0	1-0	9	1	0	.231
	Bluefield (APP)	1-0	4.35	6	0	0	0	1	10.1	6	5	5	2	0	5-1	15	1	0	.167
2012		Did Not Play																	
Minor Totals		10-16	3.94	61	25	0	0	3	194.1	179	109	85	10	20	69-1	195	17	3	.239

Dominguez, Luis — CATCHER

HT: 6-2... **WT:** 190... **B-T:** R-R... **BORN:** 26 Dec 95, San Miguelito, PAN... **RESIDES:** San Miguelito, PAN... **EDUCATION:** NA... **TRANSACTIONS:** Signed by the Toronto Blue Jays on September 11, 2012... **SIGNED BY:** Ismael Cruz & Sandy Rosario

Dominguez, Oliver — INFIELDER

HT: 5-10... **WT:** 150... **B-T:** S-R... **BORN:** 23 Apr 89, Santo Domingo, DR... **RESIDES:** Higuey, DR... **EDUCATION:** NA... **TRANSACTIONS:** Signed by the Toronto Blue Jays on April 27, 2006... **SIGNED BY:** Hilario Soriano

YR	Club & League	AVG	G	AB	R	H	2B	3B	HR	RBI	SH-SF	HB	BB-IB	SO	SB-CS	SLG	OBP	OPS
2006	DSL (DSL)	.154	49	136	15	21	4	0	0	13	2-1	5	19-0	36	6-3	.184	.280	.464
2007		Injured – Did Not Play																
2008	DSL Blue Jays2 (DSL)	.305	69	266	49	81	22	3	5	39	0-5	3	45-1	57	9-3	.466	.404	.870
2009	Blue Jays (GCL)	.225	49	142	17	32	6	0	3	16	2-1	0	15-0	32	13-0	.331	.297	.628
2010	New Hampshire (EAS)	.000	2	2	0	0	0	0	0	0	0-0	0	0-0	2	0-0	.000	.000	.000
	Auburn (NYP)	.241	57	199	39	48	12	1	3	21	5-1	2	32-0	48	14-2	.357	.350	.707
	Lansing (MID)	.264	41	110	22	29	6	0	3	14	2-1	1	21-0	19	11-4	.400	.383	.783
2011	Las Vegas (PCL)	.200	2	5	1	1	1	0	0	1	0-0	0	0-0	1	0-0	.400	.200	.600
	New Hampshire (EAS)	.000	2	4	0	0	0	0	0	0	0-0	0	0-0	1	0-0	.000	.000	.000
	Lansing (MID)	.217	97	322	56	70	11	6	4	39	2-2	2	55-0	76	15-6	.326	.333	.659
2012	Dunedin (FSL)	.253	82	265	40	67	19	2	4	34	5-1	3	30-0	73	4-1	.385	.334	.719
Minor Totals		.241	450	1451	239	349	81	12	22	177	18-12	16	217-1	345	72-19	.358	.343	.702

Donahue, Tucker — PITCHER

HT: 6-2... **WT:** 200... **B-T:** R-R... **BORN:** 27 Aug 90, Coral Springs, FL... **RESIDES:** Coral Springs, FL... **EDUCATION:** Stetson University... **TRANSACTIONS:** Selected by the Toronto Blue Jays in the 4th round of the 2012 June draft... Signed on June 10, 2012... **SIGNED BY:** Joel Grampietro

YR	Club & League	W-L	ERA	G	GS	CG	SHO	SV	IP	H	R	ER	HR	HB	BB-IB	SO	WP	BK	OBA
2012	Vancouver (NOR)	3-2	5.26	22	0	0	0	1	25.2	29	16	15	2	7	14-0	21	5	0	.282

Dorsett, Brandon — *PITCHER*

HT: 6-3... **WT:** 200... **B-T:** R-R... **BORN:** 01 Nov 89, Terre Haute, IN... **RESIDES:** Terre Haute, IN... **EDUCATION:** Indiana State University... **TRANSACTIONS:** Signed by the Toronto Blue Jay on June 12, 2012... **SIGNED BY:** Mike Medici

YR	Club & League	W-L	ERA	G	GS	CG	SHO	SV	IP	H	R	ER	HR	HB	BB-IB	SO	WP	BK	OBA
2012	Bluefield (APP)	3-2	1.71	18	0	0	0	4	31.2	26	16	6	0	5	6-0	19	3	0	.211

Dragmire, Brady — *PITCHER*

HT: 6-1... **WT:** 180... **B-T:** R-R... **BORN:** 05 Feb 93, Sacramento, CA... **RESIDES:** Elk Grove, CA... **EDUCATION:** Bradshaw Christian High School... **TRANSACTIONS:** Selected by the Toronto Blue Jays in the 17th round of the 2011 June draft... Signed on August 5, 2011... **SIGNED BY:** Darold Brown

YR	Club & League	W-L	ERA	G	GS	CG	SHO	SV	IP	H	R	ER	HR	HB	BB-IB	SO	WP	BK	OBA
2011	Blue Jays (GCL)	0-0	27.00	1	0	0	0	0	1.0	2	3	3	1	0	1-0	1	0	0	.400
2012	Blue Jays (GCL)	0-3	1.14	15	0	0	0	1	23.2	17	10	3	0	3	5-0	14	2	0	.215
Minor Totals		0-3	2.19	16	0	0	0	1	24.2	19	13	6	1	3	6-0	15	2	0	.226

Dupont, William — *INFIELDER*

HT: 6-0... **WT:** 170... **B-T:** L-R... **BORN:** 01 Dec 93, Ellisville, MO... **RESIDES:** Ellisville, MO... **EDUCATION:** Lafayette High School... **TRANSACTIONS:** Selected by the Toronto Blue Jays in the 16th round of the 2012 June Draft... Signed on July 9, 2012... **SIGNED BY:** Darin Vaughan

YR	Club & League	AVG	G	AB	R	H	2B	3B	HR	RBI	SH-SF	HB	BB-IB	SO	SB-CS	SLG	OBP	OPS
2012	Blue Jays (GCL)	.214	15	42	9	9	1	1	0	3	0-0	2	8-0	15	4-1	.286	.365	.651

Duvall, Myles — *PITCHER*

HT: 6-5... **WT:** 220... **B-T:** R-R... **BORN:** 23 Apr 89, Houston, TX... **RESIDES:** Sugarland, TX... **EDUCATION:** NA... **TRANSACTIONS:** Signed by the Toronto Blue Jays on June 16, 2011... **SIGNED BY:** Michael Wagner

YR	Club & League	W-L	ERA	G	GS	CG	SHO	SV	IP	H	R	ER	HR	HB	BB-IB	SO	WP	BK	OBA
2011	Bluefield (APP)	2-1	5.40	14	0	0	0	1	25.0	33	19	15	3	2	9-0	25	4	0	.311
2012	Did Not Play																		
Minor Totals		2-1	5.40	14	0	0	0	1	25.0	33	19	15	3	2	9-0	25	4	0	.311

Eduado, Francis — *PITCHER*

HT: 6-2... **WT:** 190... **B-T:** R-R... **BORN:** 24 May 94, Consuelo, DR... **RESIDES:** Consuelo, DR... **EDUCATION:** NA... **TRANSACTIONS:** Signed by the Toronto Blue Jays on November 18, 2011... **SIGNED BY:** Ismael Cruz, Jean Alvarez & Lorenzo Perez

YR	Club & League	W-L	ERA	G	GS	CG	SHO	SV	IP	H	R	ER	HR	HB	BB-IB	SO	WP	BK	OBA
2012	DSL (DSL)	3-2	6.39	12	3	0	0	0	31.0	26	25	22	2	3	17-0	33	5	5	.243

Etsrada, Deivy — *PITCHER*

HT: 6-1... **WT:** 170... **B-T:** L-L... **BORN:** 22 Aug 92, Valencia, Carabobo, VZ... **RESIDES:** Valencia, Carabobo, VZ... **EDUCATION:** NA... **TRANSACTIONS:** Signed by the Toronto Blue Jays on November 9, 2008... **SIGNED BY:** Rafael Moncada

YR	Club & League	W-L	ERA	G	GS	CG	SHO	SV	IP	H	R	ER	HR	HB	BB-IB	SO	WP	BK	OBA
2009	Toronto (DSL)	1-0	2.66	13	10	0	0	0	44.0	40	13	13	1	4	13-0	48	1	2	.244
2010	Blue Jays (GCL)	4-3	3.02	12	8	0	0	0	53.2	55	23	18	4	2	21-0	42	0	2	.259
2011	Blue Jays (GCL)	0-1	2.25	3	3	1	0	0	16.0	14	4	4	1	1	3-0	18	2	0	.233
	Bluefield (APP)	3-4	6.94	9	9	0	0	0	36.1	46	29	28	5	3	16-0	27	0	1	.311
2012	Bluefield (APP)	3-6	4.29	13	12	0	0	0	56.2	62	48	27	7	3	15-0	49	4	3	.267
Minor Totals		11-14	3.92	50	42	1	0	0	206.2	217	117	90	18	13	68-0	184	7	8	.266

Everts, Clint
PITCHER

HT: 6-2... **WT:** 195... **B-T:** S-R... **BORN:** 10 Aug 84, Houston, TX... **RESIDES:** Cypress, TX... **EDUCATION:** Cypress Falls High School... **TRANSACTIONS:** Selected by the Montreal Expos in the 1st round (5th overall) of the 2002 June Draft... Signed on August 24, 2002... Signed by the New York Mets on March 3, 2010... Traded to the Toronto Blue Jays on June 26, 2010... **SIGNED BY:** Ray Corbett

YR	Club & League	W-L	ERA	G	GS	CG	SHO	SV	IP	H	R	ER	HR	HB	BB-IB	SO	WP	BK	OBA
2003	Vermont Lake (NYP)	2-4	4.17	10	10	0	0	0	54.0	49	26	25	4	4	35-0	50	7	0	.247
	Savannah Sand (SAL)	0-3	3.46	5	5	0	0	0	26.0	23	13	10	1	2	10-0	21	2	0	.230
2004	Savannah Sand (SAL)	7-3	2.49	17	17	1	1	0	90.1	67	29	25	3	6	21-0	103	6	0	.208
	Brevard County (FSL)	2-2	2.25	4	4	0	0	0	20.0	16	5	5	2	0	10-0	19	0	0	.239
2005	Nationals (GCL)	0-1	3.38	7	7	0	0	0	16.0	18	9	6	0	2	8-0	15	1	0	.269
	Vermont Lake (NYP)	0-1	3.79	8	1	0	0	0	19.0	21	12	8	0	2	12-0	21	4	0	.266
2006	Potomac (CAR)	5-10	6.00	20	19	0	0	0	90.0	96	69	60	11	2	53-0	92	10	0	.264
2007	Potomac (CAR)	4-10	4.81	38	12	0	0	2	97.1	102	62	52	8	5	56-0	78	5	0	.272
2008	Hagerstown (SAL)	0-2	4.63	8	0	0	0	2	11.2	7	7	6	0	1	9-0	10	2	0	.163
	Potomac (CAR)	4-2	4.80	30	1	0	0	3	69.1	74	41	37	7	9	30-1	75	3	0	.269
2009	Potomac (CAR)	3-0	0.90	13	0	0	0	2	20.0	14	4	2	2	3	5-1	26	1	0	.194
	Harrisburg (EAS)	3-1	1.53	20	0	0	0	4	29.1	21	7	5	0	3	11-4	31	1	0	.206
	Syracuse (INT)	2-0	3.38	11	0	0	0	0	10.2	14	4	4	1	0	10-0	11	2	0	.341
2010	Binghamton (EAS)	3-1	6.94	26	0	0	0	2	35.0	46	28	27	3	5	21-3	37	4	0	.317
	New Hampshire (EAS)	1-0	4.38	15	3	0	0	0	39.0	36	19	19	3	3	27-1	30	4	0	.254
2011	Las Vegas (PCL)	0-0	6.00	9	0	0	0	0	15.0	21	11	10	3	0	8-1	12	3	0	.344
	New Hampshire (EAS)	0-1	2.59	40	0	0	0	5	48.2	32	18	14	2	1	20-0	56	9	0	.186
2012	New Hampshire (EAS)	2-1	4.19	12	1	0	0	1	19.1	21	9	9	0	0	12-0	23	4	0	.276
	Las Vegas (PCL)	3-2	3.10	37	0	0	0	2	61.0	53	23	21	2	0	32-0	53	6	0	.236
Minor Totals		41-44	4.02	330	80	1	1	23	771.2	731	396	345	52	48	390-11	763	74	0	.250

Farina, Alan
PITCHER

HT: 5-11... **WT:** 190... **B-T:** R-R... **BORN:** 09 Aug 86, Winter Park, FL... **RESIDES:** Chuluota, FL... **EDUCATION:** Clemson University... **TRANSACTIONS:** Selected by the Toronto Blue Jays in the 3rd round of the 2007 June Draft... Signed on July 2, 2007... **SIGNED BY:** Marc Tramuta

YR	Club & League	W-L	ERA	G	GS	CG	SHO	SV	IP	H	R	ER	HR	HB	BB-IB	SO	WP	BK	OBA
2007	Auburn (NYP)	0-2	4.91	6	3	0	0	0	11.0	10	7	6	1	1	10-0	14	1	0	.233
2008	Lansing (MID)	3-1	3.07	15	0	0	0	1	29.1	19	11	10	2	1	14-0	37	1	0	.179
2009	Dunedin (FSL)	1-3	6.51	27	2	0	0	5	37.1	47	32	27	4	1	24-0	34	4	1	.307
2010	Dunedin (FSL)	2-1	1.24	32	0	0	0	2	36.1	19	7	5	0	0	11-0	46	4	0	.156
	New Hampshire (EAS)	1-0	1.40	17	0	0	0	4	19.1	6	3	3	0	1	9-0	28	1	0	.092
2011	New Hampshire (EAS)	2-1	1.56	17	0	0	0	6	17.1	15	3	3	2	0	7-0	16	2	0	.224
2012	Dunedin (FSL)	1-2	5.18	24	0	0	0	1	24.1	28	18	14	1	0	14-0	24	0	0	.289
Minor Totals		10-10	3.50	138	5	0	0	19	175.0	144	81	68	10	4	89-0	199	13	1	.221

Fermin, Andy
INFIELDER

HT: 6-0... **WT:** 180... **B-T:** L-R... **BORN:** 27 Jul 89, Marianna, FL... **RESIDES:** Santiago, DR... **EDUCATION:** Chipola Junior College... **TRANSACTIONS:** Selected by the Toronto Blue Jays in the 32nd round of the 2010 June Draft... Signed on June 15, 2010... **SIGNED BY:** Cliff Pastornicky

YR	Club & League	AVG	G	AB	R	H	2B	3B	HR	RBI	SH-SF	HB	BB-IB	SO	SB-CS	SLG	OBP	OPS
2010	Blue Jays (GCL)	.462	7	26	4	12	3	0	0	5	0-0	1	4-0	2	0-0	.577	.548	1.125
	Auburn (NYP)	.273	45	150	13	41	9	0	1	20	1-1	2	15-0	28	0-0	.353	.345	.698
2011	Bluefield (APP)	.261	59	218	41	57	15	0	5	33	1-6	2	35-0	37	2-1	.399	.360	.759
2012	Lansing (MID)	.258	55	178	31	46	7	3	1	17	1-0	1	28-1	28	0-1	.348	.362	.710
Minor Totals		.273	166	572	89	156	34	3	7	75	3-7	6	82-1	95	2-2	.379	.366	.745

Fernandez, Jose
PITCHER

HT: 6-3... **WT:** 170... **B-T:** L-L... **BORN:** 13 Feb 93, Mao, DR... **RESIDES:** Mao, DR... **EDUCATION:** NA... **TRANSACTIONS:** Signed by the Toronto Blue Jays on January 5, 2012... **SIGNED BY:** Ismael Cruz, Lorenzo Perez & Marino Tejada

YR	Club & League	W-L	ERA	G	GS	CG	SHO	SV	IP	H	R	ER	HR	HB	BB-IB	SO	WP	BK	OBA
2012	DSL (DSL)	2-0	1.52	9	4	0	0	0	29.2	25	7	5	1	2	2-0	34	1	1	.234

Flores, Jorge
INFIELDER

HT: 5-5... **WT:** 160... **B-T:** R-R... **BORN:** 25 Nov 91, Chandler, AZ... **RESIDES:** Chandler, AZ... **EDUCATION:** Central Arizona College... **TRANSACTIONS:** Selected by the Toronto Blue Jays in the 19th round of the 2012 June draft... Signed on June 10, 2012... **SIGNED BY:** Blake Crosby

YR	Club & League	AVG	G	AB	R	H	2B	3B	HR	RBI	SH-SF	HB	BB-IB	SO	SB-CS	SLG	OBP	OPS
2012	Vancouver (NOR)	.265	60	215	31	57	14	1	3	19	6-0	11	19-0	45	11-9	.381	.355	.736

Frawley, Tucker — CATCHER

HT: 6-0... **WT:** 185... **B-T:** R-R... **BORN:** 01 Jun 89, Lexington, SC... **RESIDES:** Lexington, SC... **EDUCATION:** Coastal Carolina University... **TRANSACTIONS:** Selected by the Toronto Blue Jays in the 8th round of the 2012 June draft... Signed on June 10, 2012... **SIGNED BY:** John Hendricks

YR	Club & League	AVG	G	AB	R	H	2B	3B	HR	RBI	SH-SF	HB	BB-IB	SO	SB-CS	SLG	OBP	OPS
2012	Vancouver (NOR)	.185	26	81	8	15	0	0	0	8	1-1	3	8-2	20	2-0	.185	.280	.465

Fuenmayor, Balbino — INFIELDER

HT: 6-2... **WT:** 195... **B-T:** R-R... **BORN:** 26 Nov 89, Valencia Edo Carabobo, VZ... **RESIDES:** Guigue, Carabobo, VZ... **EDUCATION:** NA... **TRANSACTIONS:** Signed by the Toronto Blue Jays on August 23, 2006... **SIGNED BY:** Rafael Moncada

YR	Club & League	AVG	G	AB	R	H	2B	3B	HR	RBI	SH-SF	HB	BB-IB	SO	SB-CS	SLG	OBP	OPS
2007	Blue Jays (GCL)	.174	48	178	13	31	5	2	1	12	0-2	5	12-0	68	0-0	.242	.244	.486
2008	Blue Jays (GCL)	.307	50	179	25	55	14	2	3	26	0-2	5	11-2	48	0-3	.458	.360	.818
2009	Lansing (MID)	.263	113	419	43	110	21	3	8	54	1-4	2	9-0	119	1-3	.384	.279	.663
2010	Lansing (MID)	.220	100	346	32	76	20	3	9	46	0-3	3	20-0	123	0-0	.373	.266	.639
2011	Lansing (MID)	.287	29	94	10	27	5	1	0	11	0-1	1	8-0	19	0-1	.362	.346	.708
	Vancouver (NOR)	.234	61	231	24	54	13	0	6	29	0-1	4	14-0	56	1-0	.368	.288	.656
2012	Vancouver (NOR)	.282	67	259	35	73	20	1	9	52	0-5	5	14-0	82	1-0	.471	.325	.796
Minor Totals		.250	468	1706	182	426	98	12	36	230	1-18	25	88-2	515	3-7	.385	.293	.678

Fuentes, Edwin — INFIELDER

HT: 6-0... **WT:** 172... **B-T:** R-R... **BORN:** 14 Aug 94, Cartagena, COL... **RESIDES:** Cartagena, COL... **EDUCATION:** None... **TRANSACTIONS:** Signed by the Toronto Blue Jays on November 19, 2011... **SIGNED BY:** Ismael Cruz & Erick Medina

YR	Club & League	AVG	G	AB	R	H	2B	3B	HR	RBI	SH-SF	HB	BB-IB	SO	SB-CS	SLG	OBP	OPS
2012	DSL (DSL)	.260	54	181	21	47	5	2	0	20	5-4	4	36-0	34	11-5	.309	.387	.696

Gabryszwski, Jeremy — PITCHER

HT: 6-4... **WT:** 195... **B-T:** R-R... **BORN:** 16 Mar 93, Crosby, TX... **RESIDES:** Crosby, TX... **EDUCATION:** Crosby High School... **TRANSACTIONS:** Selected by the Toronto Blue Jays in the 2nd round of the 2011 June draft... Signed on July 21, 2011... **SIGNED BY:** C.J. Ebarb

YR	Club & League	W-L	ERA	G	GS	CG	SHO	SV	IP	H	R	ER	HR	HB	BB-IB	SO	WP	BK	OBA
2011	Blue Jays (GCL)	0-0	0.00	3	1	0	0	0	4.1	3	0	0	0	1	1-0	5	0	0	.187
	Bluefield (APP)	0-0	0.00	1	0	0	0	0	1.0	1	0	0	0	0	0-0	1	0	0	.250
2012	Bluefield (APP)	3-0	2.35	11	9	0	0	0	46.0	44	13	12	5	1	4-0	22	1	0	.253
Minor Totals		3-0	2.10	15	10	0	0	0	51.1	48	13	12	5	2	5-0	28	1	0	.247

Galarraga, Joel — CATCHER

HT: 5-11... **WT:** 185... **B-T:** R-R... **BORN:** 20 Mar 82, Havana, Cuba... **RESIDES:** Phoeniz, AZ... **EDUCATION:** NA... **TRANSACTIONS:** Signed by the Oakland Athletics on March 13, 2009... Traded to the Toronto Blue Jays on June 15, 2012... **SIGNED BY:** Luis Ruiz

YR	Club & League	AVG	G	AB	R	H	2B	3B	HR	RBI	SH-SF	HB	BB-IB	SO	SB-CS	SLG	OBP	OPS
2009	Sacramento (PCL)	.357	13	42	9	15	3	1	0	6	1-0	1	6-0	10	0-1	.476	.449	.925
2010	AZL (AZL)	.197	19	61	8	12	2	0	0	5	0-1	1	7-0	18	3-0	.230	.286	.516
	Stockton (CAL)	.235	5	17	2	4	0	0	0	0	0-0	0	1-0	3	0-0	.235	.278	.513
2011	Sacramento (PCL)	.406	8	32	8	13	2	0	0	3	1-0	0	1-0	3	0-0	.469	.424	.893
2012	Sacramento (PCL)	.273	3	11	1	3	0	0	0	0	0-0	0	0-0	3	0-0	.273	.273	.546
	Las Vegas (PCL)	.320	9	25	3	8	1	1	0	3	0-0	0	4-0	5	1-0	.440	.414	.854
	New Hampshire (EAS)	.351	16	37	6	13	2	0	0	5	0-0	2	5-0	9	2-1	.405	.455	.860
Minor Totals		.302	73	225	37	68	10	2	0	22	2-1	4	24-0	51	6-2	.364	.378	.742

Garcia, Leudy — OUTFIELDER

HT: 6-4... **WT:** 195... **B-T:** R-R... **BORN:** 18 Apr 95, Bajabonica Arriba, DR... **RESIDES:** Bajabonica Arriba, DR **EDUCATION:** NA... **TRANSACTIONS:** Signed by the Toronto Blue Jays on February 10, 2012... **SIGNED BY:** Ismael Cruz, Sandy Rosario & Jean Carlos Alvarez

YR	Club & League	AVG	G	AB	R	H	2B	3B	HR	RBI	SH-SF	HB	BB-IB	SO	SB-CS	SLG	OBP	OPS
2012	DSL (DSL)	.277	36	137	15	38	6	1	0	12	0-0	2	14-0	39	2-2	.336	.353	.689

Garcia, Melvin — OUTFIELDER

HT: 6-0... **WT:** 175... **B-T:** R-R... **BORN:** 17 Sep 91, Bronx, NY... **RESIDES:** Bronx, NY... **EDUCATION:** James Monroe High School... **TRANSACTIONS:** Selected by the Toronto Blue Jays in the 33rd round of the 2010 June draft... Signed on June 15, 2010... **SIGNED BY:** Michael Pesce

YR	Club & League	AVG	G	AB	R	H	2B	3B	HR	RBI	SH-SF	HB	BB-IB	SO	SB-CS	SLG	OBP	OPS
2010	Blue Jays (GCL)	.209	19	43	5	9	3	1	0	5	0-0	1	5-0	17	0-1	.326	.306	.632
2011	Bluefield (APP)	.167	26	78	9	13	2	0	0	5	0-1	1	7-0	26	2-1	.192	.241	.433
	Blue Jays (GCL)	.238	11	42	7	10	1	0	2	7	0-0	1	3-0	14	0-0	.405	.304	.709
2012	Did Not Play																	
Minor Totals		.196	56	163	21	32	6	1	2	17	0-1	3	15-0	57	2-2	.282	.275	.557

Garrett, Travis

PITCHER

HT: 5-11... **WT:** 205... **B-T:** R-R... **BORN:** 27 Oct 89, Long Beach, CA... **RESIDES:** Long Beach, CA... **EDUCATION:** Cypress Junior College... **TRANSACTIONS:** Selected by the Toronto Blue Jays in the 19th round of the 2010 June draft... Signed on June 15, 2010... **SIGNED BY:** Chris Becerra

YR	Club & League	W-L	ERA	G	GS	CG	SHO	SV	IP	H	R	ER	HR	HB	BB-IB	SO	WP	BK	OBA
2010	Auburn (NYP)	4-3	4.05	20	0	0	0	0	26.2	29	17	12	0	3	13-2	31	4	0	.279
2011	Vancouver (NOR)	4-4	4.28	20	0	0	0	0	33.2	31	19	16	3	5	20-4	32	7	1	.263
2012		Injured – Did Not Play																	
Minor Totals		8-7	4.18	40	0	0	0	0	60.1	60	36	28	3	8	33-6	63	11	1	.270

Ghysels, Chuck

PITCHER

HT: 5-11... **WT:** 200... **B-T:** R-R... **BORN:** 28 Nov 89, Springboro, OH... **RESIDES:** Springboro, OH... **EDUCATION:** University of Maryland College Park... **TRANSACTIONS:** Signed by the Toronto Blue Jays on June 10, 2012... **SIGNED BY:** Eric McQueen

YR	Club & League	W-L	ERA	G	GS	CG	SHO	SV	IP	H	R	ER	HR	HB	BB-IB	SO	WP	BK	OBA
2012	Blue Jays (GCL)	0-3	3.86	25	0	0	0	7	25.2	22	11	11	4	2	8-0	41	1	0	.232
2012	Dunedin (FSL)	0-0	0.00	2	0	0	0	0	3.0	2	0	0	0	0	0-0	6	1	0	.182
Minor Totals		0-3	3.45	27	0	0	0	7	28.2	24	11	11	4	2	8-0	47	2	0	.226

Glenn, Brad

OUTFIELDER

HT: 6-2... **WT:** 220... **B-T:** R-R... **BORN:** 02 Apr 87, Tuscan, AZ... **RESIDES:** Tuscon AZ... **EDUCATION:** Arizona University... **TRANSACTIONS:** Selected by the Toronto Blue Jays in the 23rd round of the 2009 June draft... Signed on June 14, 2009... **SIGNED BY:** Dan Cholowsky

YR	Club & League	AVG	G	AB	R	H	2B	3B	HR	RBI	SH-SF	HB	BB-IB	SO	SB-CS	SLG	OBP	OPS
2009	Auburn (NYP)	.221	64	213	27	47	14	0	8	38	0-2	4	18-0	68	4-2	.399	.291	.690
2010	Lansing (MID)	.271	109	398	63	108	21	5	17	69	0-4	4	41-0	100	14-5	.477	.342	.819
2011	Dunedin (FSL)	.263	111	418	59	110	25	1	26	80	0-4	6	30-1	123	0-0	.514	.319	.833
2012	New Hampshire (EAS)	.239	112	423	50	101	28	0	19	63	0-5	4	29-0	122	8-4	.440	.291	.731
Minor Totals		.252	396	1452	199	366	88	6	70	250	0-15	18	118-1	413	26-11	.466	.313	.779

Gomez, Angel

OUTFIELDER

HT: 6-2... **WT:** 182... **B-T:** S-R... **BORN:** 12 Jan 92, San Lorenzo, PR... **RESIDES:** San Lorenzo, PR... **EDUCATION:** Maria Cruz Buitrago High School... **TRANSACTIONS:** Selected by the Toronto Blue Jays in the 23rd round of the 2010 June draft... Signed on June 14, 2010... **SIGNED BY:** Jorge Rivera

YR	Club & League	AVG	G	AB	R	H	2B	3B	HR	RBI	SH-SF	HB	BB-IB	SO	SB-CS	SLG	OBP	OPS
2010	Blue Jays (GCL)	.074	15	27	1	2	0	0	0	1	0-0	2	1-0	7	0-1	.074	.167	.241
2011	Blue Jays (GCL)	.228	36	114	11	26	3	1	0	6	1-2	2	7-0	24	5-3	.272	.280	.552
2012		Injured – Did Not Play																
Minor Totals		.199	51	141	12	28	3	1	0	7	1-2	4	8-0	31	5-4	.234	.258	.492

Gonzales, Tyler

PITCHER

HT: 6-2... **WT:** 175... **B-T:** R-R... **BORN:** 22 Jan 93, San Antonio, TX... **RESIDES:** San Antonio, TX... **EDUCATION:** James Madison High School... **TRANSACTIONS:** Selected by the Toronto Blue Jays in the 1st round (supplemental – 60th overall) of the 2012 June draft... Signed on June 10, 2012... **SIGNED BY:** Mike Burns

YR	Club & League	W-L	ERA	G	GS	CG	SHO	SV	IP	H	R	ER	HR	HB	BB-IB	SO	WP	BK	OBA
2012	Blue Jays (GCL)	1-1	8.40	9	3	0	0	0	15.0	20	14	14	1	2	4-0	7	3	0	.328

Gonzalez, Estevan

PITCHER

HT: 6-5... **WT:** 205... **B-T:** L-L... **BORN:** 15 Jan 92, Santa Monica, CA... **RESIDES:** Santa Monica, CA... **EDUCATION:** Glendale, College... **TRANSACTIONS:** Selected by the Toronto Blue Jays in the 18th round of the 2012 June draft... Signed on June 17, 2012... **SIGNED BY:** Kevin Fox

YR	Club & League	W-L	ERA	G	GS	CG	SHO	SV	IP	H	R	ER	HR	HB	BB-IB	SO	WP	BK	OBA
2012	Blue Jays (GCL)	3-3	5.15	10	7	0	0	0	36.2	37	26	21	3	1	12-0	22	1	1	.272
	Bluefield (APP)	2-0	0.00	2	2	0	0	0	12.0	3	0	0	0	0	3-0	9	0	0	.077
Minor Totals		5-3	3.88	12	9	0	0	0	48.2	40	26	21	3	1	15-0	31	1	1	.229

Gonzalez, Jesus

OUTFIELDER

HT: 6-0... **WT:** 178... **B-T:** R-R... **BORN:** 11 Jan 95, Cumana, VZ... **RESIDES:** Cumana, VZ... **EDUCATION:** NA... **TRANSACTIONS:** Signed by the Toronto Blue Jays on July 3, 2011... **SIGNED BY:** Marco Paddy & Rafael Moncada

YR	Club & League	AVG	G	AB	R	H	2B	3B	HR	RBI	SH-SF	HB	BB-IB	SO	SB-CS	SLG	OBP	OPS
2012	Blue Jays (GCL)	.206	51	194	16	40	8	1	3	19	0-0	1	14-0	58	3-2	.304	.263	.567

Gracesqui, Francisco — *PITCHER*

HT: 6-0... **WT:** 175... **B-T:** L-L... **BORN:** 26 Nov 91, Bronx, NY... **RESIDES:** Bronx, NY... **EDUCATION:** Sullivan County Community College... **TRANSACTIONS:** Signed by the Toronto Blue Jays on August 24, 2011... **SIGNED BY:** Mike Pesce

YR	Club & League	W-L	ERA	G	GS	CG	SHO	SV	IP	H	R	ER	HR	HB	BB-IB	SO	WP	BK	OBA
2012	Blue Jays (GCL)	3-2	2.88	22	0	0	0	0	34.1	24	14	11	1	3	26-0	46	4	1	.195

Gracey, Scott — *PITCHER*

HT: 6-2... **WT:** 190... **B-T:** R-R... **BORN:** 15 Oct 86, Albuquerque, NM... **RESIDES:** Albuquerque, NM... **EDUCATION:** University of New Mexico... **TRANSACTIONS:** Selected by the Toronto Blue Jays in the 15th round of the 2008 June draft... Signed on June 10, 2008... **SIGNED BY:** Dan Cholowsky

YR	Club & League	W-L	ERA	G	GS	CG	SHO	SV	IP	H	R	ER	HR	HB	BB-IB	SO	WP	BK	OBA
2008	Blue Jays (GULF)	0-1	3.00	10	6	0	0	0	24.0	19	9	8	0	4	15-0	22	7	0	.216
2009	Dunedin (FSL)	0-0	6.75	2	1	0	0	0	6.2	11	5	5	0	0	3-0	1	1	0	.393
	Auburn (NYP)	2-8	5.30	15	15	0	0	0	73.0	85	53	43	8	1	22-0	58	3	1	.283
2010	Auburn (NYP)	1-0	0.00	2	0	0	0	0	5.0	1	0	0	0	0	1-0	6	0	0	.059
	Lansing (MID)	0-0	5.28	31	1	0	0	0	59.2	75	42	35	2	2	21-1	41	6	0	.307
2011	Lansing (MID)	4-1	1.44	15	0	0	0	0	25.0	13	4	4	1	0	5-0	27	1	0	.148
	Dunedin (FSL)	1-3	3.86	32	3	0	0	1	51.1	50	27	22	5	2	15-2	41	2	0	.255
2012	Dunedin (FSL)	2-3	3.81	17	0	0	0	1	28.1	27	14	12	3	0	11-2	42	2	0	.248
	New Hampshire (EAS)	0-0	3.81	12	0	0	0	0	26.0	26	11	11	1	1	14-2	18	3	0	.265
Minor Totals		10-16	4.21	136	26	0	0	2	299.0	307	165	140	20	10	107-7	256	25	1	.263

Griffith, Shawn — *PITCHER*

HT: 5-10... **WT:** 180... **B-T:** R-R... **BORN:** 24 May 87, St. Petersburg, FL... **RESIDES:** St. Petersburg, FL... **EDUCATION:** George Mason University... **TRANSACTIONS:** Selected by the Toronto Blue Jays in the 37th round of the 2009 June draft... Signed on June 14, 2009... **SIGNED BY:** Tom Burns

YR	Club & League	W-L	ERA	G	GS	CG	SHO	SV	IP	H	R	ER	HR	HB	BB-IB	SO	WP	BK	OBA
2009	Blue Jays (GULF)	2-2	0.66	22	0	0	0	9	27.1	9	3	2	0	1	6-0	43	4	0	.102
	Auburn (NYP)	0-0	0.00	3	0	0	0	0	6.1	4	0	0	0	0	4-0	9	0	0	.182
2010	Dunedin (FSL)	0-0	2.25	4	0	0	0	0	4.0	3	1	1	1	0	1-0	4	0	0	.231
	Auburn (NYP)	2-4	4.91	20	1	0	0	1	36.2	25	22	20	4	4	23-1	47	4	0	.195
2011	Dunedin (FSL)	0-0	0.00	3	0	0	0	0	5.1	3	0	0	0	0	2-0	3	0	0	.167
	Lansing (MID)	5-0	4.82	24	1	0	0	0	37.1	30	22	20	2	1	30-1	41	11	0	.221
2012	Dunedin (FSL)	4-3	6.31	27	2	0	0	0	41.1	41	33	29	3	3	26-0	42	2	0	.263
	Lansing (MID)	2-1	3.16	11	0	0	0	0	25.2	19	10	9	5	2	13-1	23	1	0	.202
Minor Totals		15-10	3.96	114	4	0	0	10	184.0	134	91	81	15	11	105-3	212	22	0	.205

Guerrero, Emilio — *INFIELDER*

HT: 6-4... **WT:** 170... **B-T:** R-R... **BORN:** 21 Aug 92, San Pedro de Macoris, DR... **RESIDES:** San Pedro de Macoris, DR... **EDUCATION:** NA... **TRANSACTIONS:** Signed by the Toronto Blue Jays on May 23, 2011... **SIGNED BY:** Marco Paddy & Domingo Toribio

YR	Club & League	AVG	G	AB	R	H	2B	3B	HR	RBI	SH-SF	HB	BB-IB	SO	SB-CS	SLG	OBP	OPS
2011	DSL (DSL)	.239	53	180	16	43	11	1	0	22	2-0	4	11-0	47	4-1	.311	.297	.608
2012	Blue Jays (GCL)	.244	24	82	14	20	7	1	2	9	0-0	1	12-0	20	3-3	.427	.347	.774
	Bluefield (APP)	.185	16	54	8	10	1	1	0	8	2-2	0	2-0	17	1-0	.241	.207	.448
Minor Totals		.231	93	316	38	73	19	3	2	39	4-2	5	25-0	84	8-4	.329	.296	.625

Guillen, Patrico — *PITCHER*

HT: 6-4... **WT:** 195... **B-T:** R-R... **BORN:** 17 Mar 95, San Cristobal, DR... **RESIDES:** San Cristobal, DR... **EDUCATION:** NA... **TRANSACTIONS:** Signed by the Toronto Blue Jays on September 6, 2012... **SIGNED BY:** Isamel Cruz & Sandy Rosario

Gutierrez, Osman — *PITCHER*

HT: 6-4... **WT:** 185... **B-T:** R-R... **BORN:** 15 Dec 94, Leo, NIC... **RESIDES:** Leon, NIC... **EDUCATION:** NA... **TRANSACTIONS:** Signed by the Toronto Blue Jays on July 4, 2011... **SIGNED BY:** Marco Paddy & Daniel Sotelo

YR	Club & League	W-L	ERA	G	GS	CG	SHO	SV	IP	H	R	ER	HR	HB	BB-IB	SO	WP	BK	OBA
2012	DSL (DSL)	1-0	4.50	7	2	0	0	0	14.0	17	9	7	0	2	9-0	10	2	0	.309

Guzman, Alberto — *PITCHER*

HT: 6-1... **WT:** 180... **B-T:** R-R... **BORN:** 07 Dec 92, Sanchez, DR... **RESIDES:** Santo Domingo, DR... **EDUCATION:** NA... **TRANSACTIONS:** Signed by the Toronto Blue Jays on November 30, 2012... **SIGNED BY:** Ismael Cruz, Sandy Rosario & Ruben Contreras

Hawkins, Chris

INFIELDER

HT: 6-2... **WT:** 195... **B-T:** L-R... **BORN:** 17 Aug 91, Sugar Hill, GA... **RESIDES:** Sugar Hill, GA... **EDUCATION:** North Gwinnett High School... **TRANSACTIONS:** Selected by the Toronto Blue Jays in the 3rd round of the June 2010 Draft... Signed on June 9, 2010... **SIGNED BY:** Eric McQueen

YR	Club & League	AVG	G	AB	R	H	2B	3B	HR	RBI	SH-SF	HB	BB-IB	SO	SB-CS	SLG	OBP	OPS
2010	Blue Jays (GCL)	.255	46	157	29	40	9	3	0	15	1-0	1	15-0	37	8-3	.350	.324	.674
2011	Dunedin (FSL)	.000	2	4	0	0	0	0	0	0	0-0	0	0-0	2	0-0	.000	.000	.000
	Bluefield (APP)	.318	68	242	49	77	15	6	5	52	2-2	1	22-1	46	14-4	.492	.375	.867
2012	Lansing (MID)	.269	123	491	67	132	17	4	2	43	3-1	0	46-4	78	11-0	.332	.331	.663
Minor Totals		.279	239	894	145	249	41	13	7	110	6-3	2	83-5	163	33-7	.377	.340	.717

Herdenez, Yonardo

PITCHER

HT: 6-1... **WT:** 168... **B-T:** R-R... **BORN:** 20 Sep 95, Maracay, VZ... **RESIDES:** Maracay, VZ... **EDUCATION:** NA... **TRANSACTIONS:** Signed by the Toronto Blue Jays on December 4, 2012... **SIGNED BY:** Ismael Cruz & Luis Marquez

Hernandez, Javier

CATCHER

HT: 6-1... **WT:** 180... **B-T:** R-R... **BORN:** 21 Jul 96, Maracay, VZ... **RESIDES:** Maracay, VZ... **EDUCATION:** NA... **TRANSACTIONS:** Signed by the Toronto Blue Jays on August 12, 2012... **SIGNED BY:** Ismael Cruz, Luis Marquez & Jose Contreras

Hernandez, Jesse

PITCHER

HT: 6-1... **WT:** 200... **B-T:** R-R... **BORN:** 23 Aug 88, Grand Rapids, MI... **RESIDES:** Kentwood, MI... **EDUCATION:** Central Michigan University... **TRANSACTIONS:** Signed by the Toronto Blue Jays on June 15, 2010... **SIGNED BY:** Nick Manno

YR	Club & League	W-L	ERA	G	GS	CG	SHO	SV	IP	H	R	ER	HR	HB	BB-IB	SO	WP	BK	OBA
2010	Blue Jays (GCL)	0-1	27.00	1	0	0	0	0	1.0	4	3	3	0	0	0-0	1	0	0	.571
	Auburn (NYP)	3-4	3.73	14	11	0	0	0	50.2	60	37	21	2	1	16-1	60	2	0	.287
2011	Vancouver (NOR)	4-4	4.28	15	15	0	0	0	75.2	86	42	36	1	4	25-0	52	3	0	.286
2012	Lansing (MID)	4-5	2.26	16	15	2	0	0	95.2	82	30	24	2	4	19-0	61	3	0	.234
	Dunedin (FSL)	1-5	6.61	12	7	0	0	0	47.2	55	37	35	7	4	12-0	38	2	0	.293
Minor Totals		12-19	3.96	58	48	2	0	0	270.2	287	149	119	12	13	72-1	212	10	0	.272

Hernandez, Fernando, Jr.

PITCHER

HT: 5-11... **WT:** 215... **B-T:** R-R... **BORN:** 31 Jul 84, Miami, FL... **RESIDES:** Miami, FL... **EDUCATION:** Broward College... **TRANSACTIONS:** Signed by the Chicago White Sox on May 26, 2003... Selected by the Oakland Athletics in the Rule 5 draft on December 6, 2007... Returned to the Chicago White Sox on April 16, 2008... Signed by the Oakland Athletics on March 19, 2009... Signed by the New York Yankees on February 9, 2011... Signed by the Toronto Blue Jays on March 4, 2012... **SIGNED BY:** Jose Ortega

YR	Club & League	W-L	ERA	G	GS	CG	SHO	SV	IP	H	R	ER	HR	HB	BB-IB	SO	WP	BK	OBA
2003	Great Falls White (PIO)	1-3	2.70	24	0	0	0	7	23.1	23	10	7	0	1	10-0	14	7	0	.261
2004	Kannapolis (SAL)	3-3	2.98	28	0	0	0	4	45.1	43	20	15	2	3	16-1	59	3	0	.240
	Winston-Salem (CAR)	0-0	0.00	2	0	0	0	0	2.0	1	0	0	0	0	1-0	1	0	0	.143
2005	Winston-Salem (CAR)	4-1	5.14	45	0	0	0	1	70.0	83	44	40	6	4	30-0	59	3	0	.303
2006	Winston-Salem (CAR)	7-5	1.93	57	0	0	0	13	65.1	50	24	14	4	4	32-3	81	4	0	.207
2007	Birmingham (SOU)	1-3	3.06	60	0	0	0	9	85.1	73	30	29	4	2	23-0	84	4	0	.230
2008	OAKLAND (AL)	1-0	18.00	3	0	0	0	0	3.0	4	6	6	0	1	5-0	2	0	0	.308
	Birmingham (SOU)	6-5	4.66	41	0	0	0	0	58.0	60	32	30	2	4	29-1	47	1	0	.274
2009	Birmingham (SOU)	2-3	1.71	44	0	0	0	20	52.2	34	12	10	2	3	18-0	53	1	0	.181
	Charlotte (INT)	1-1	1.59	13	0	0	0	0	17.0	11	4	3	0	0	8-1	17	0	0	.180
2010	Sacramento River (PCL)	5-6	4.77	45	4	0	0	4	77.1	82	52	41	8	6	26-1	65	4	0	.266
2011	Trenton (EAS)	6-4	5.91	33	0	0	0	7	35.0	55	24	23	6	0	15-2	39	2	0	.353
	Scranton/W. Barre (INT)	0-0	9.00	1	0	0	0	0	2.0	4	2	2	0	0	2-0	5	0	0	.400
2012	New Hampshire (EAS)	5-8	4.34	36	13	0	0	0	105.2	129	58	51	8	0	29-2	85	5	0	.302
Minor Totals		41-42	3.73	429	17	0	0	65	639.0	648	312	265	42	27	239-11	609	34	0	.262

Hernandez, Leo

CATCHER

HT: 5-11... **WT:** 180... **B-T:** R-R... **BORN:** 22 Feb 90, La Guaira, Vargas, VZ... **RESIDES:** Catia La Mar, Vargas, VZ... **EDUCATION:** NA... **TRANSACTIONS:** Signed by the Toronto Blue Jays on April 10, 2007... **SIGNED BY:** Rafael Moncada

YR	Club & League	AVG	G	AB	R	H	2B	3B	HR	RBI	SH-SF	HB	BB-IB	SO	SB-CS	SLG	OBP	OPS
2007	DSL Blue Jays1 (DSL)	.261	46	176	16	46	4	0	0	18	2-0	3	14-0	34	1-1	.284	.326	.610
2008	DSL Blue Jays2 (DSL)	.256	44	164	15	42	4	1	0	26	1-1	0	12-0	13	2-1	.293	.305	.598
2009	DSL (DSL)	.292	38	120	16	35	9	0	1	15	1-1	8	13-0	13	2-2	.392	.394	.786
2010	DSL (DSL)	.207	41	121	5	25	5	0	0	14	0-2	1	8-0	17	0-0	.248	.258	.506
2011	Bluefield (APP)	.333	29	93	10	31	4	1	1	12	0-3	0	2-0	9	0-0	.430	.337	.767
2012	Vancouver (NOR)	.104	16	48	3	5	0	0	0	3	1-0	0	1-0	13	1-0	.104	.122	.226
Minor Totals		.255	214	722	65	184	26	2	2	88	5-7	12	50-0	99	6-4	.305	.311	.616

Higuera, Juliandry
PITCHER

HT: 6-1... **WT:** 180... **B-T:** L-L... **BORN:** 06 Sep 94, Bella Vista, VZ... **RESIDES:** Bella Vista... **EDUCATION:** NA... **TRANSACTIONS:** Signed by the Toronto Blue Jays on September 15, 2012... **SIGNED BY:** Ismael Cruz, Sandy Rosario & Lorenzo Perez

Hobson, KC
INFIELDER

HT: 6-2... **WT:** 205... **B-T:** L-L... **BORN:** 22 Aug 90, Bakersfield, CA... **RESIDES:** Bakersfield, CA... **EDUCATION:** Stockdale High School... **TRANSACTIONS:** Selected by the Toronto Blue Jays in the 6th round of the 2009 June draft... Signed on August 17, 2009... **SIGNED BY:** Tim Rooney

YR	Club & League	AVG	G	AB	R	H	2B	3B	HR	RBI	SH-SF	HB	BB-IB	SO	SB-CS	SLG	OBP	OPS
2010	Blue Jays (GCL)	.279	35	129	17	36	5	0	4	17	0-0	0	7-0	17	1-5	.411	.316	.727
	Lansing (MID)	.261	23	92	14	24	4	1	2	9	0-2	0	4-0	17	0-0	.391	.286	.677
2011	Lansing (MID)	.250	128	480	65	120	24	2	4	53	0-3	3	61-1	73	1-0	.333	.336	.669
2012	Lansing (MID)	.276	128	490	57	135	43	2	10	86	0-9	1	56-3	85	2-1	.433	.345	.778
Minor Totals		.264	314	1191	153	315	76	5	20	165	0-14	4	128-4	192	4-6	.387	.334	.721

Hoffpauir, Jarrett
INFIELDER

HT: 5-9... **WT:** 190... **B-T:** R-R... **BORN:** 18 Jun 83, Natchez, MS... **RESIDES: Vidalia, LA**... **EDUCATION:** University of Southern Mississippi... **TRANSACTIONS:** Selected by the St. Louis Cardinals in the 6th round of the 2004 June draft... Signed on June 15, 2004... Claimed off waivers by the Toronto Blue Jays on November 3, 2009... Claimed off waivers by the San Diego Padres on October 6, 2010... Signed by the Washington Nationals on December 9, 2011... Signed by the Toronto Blue Jays on January 15, 2013... **SIGNED BY:** Aaron Lane

YR	Club & League	AVG	G	AB	R	H	2B	3B	HR	RBI	SH-SF	HB	BB-IB	SO	SB-CS	SLG	OBP	OPS
2004	New Jersey (NYP)	.361	9	36	8	13	3	0	3	6	0-0	0	3-0	2	1-0	.694	.410	1.104
	Peoria (MID)	.268	62	231	34	62	20	1	5	30	0-1	6	29-2	21	2-4	.429	.363	.792
2005	Quad (MID)	.313	61	227	27	71	15	1	2	28	1-3	4	21-1	14	5-1	.414	.376	.790
	Palm Beach (FSL)	.257	63	226	23	58	10	1	0	19	5-2	0	32-0	26	11-5	.310	.346	.656
2006	Springfield (TEX)	.249	119	393	55	98	20	1	7	46	5-3	5	54-4	41	8-6	.359	.345	.704
2007	Springfield (TEX)	.345	61	203	23	70	16	0	7	33	5-1	1	26-2	18	3-1	.527	.420	.947
	Memphis (PCL)	.300	55	190	27	57	10	0	4	24	4-1	1	29-0	21	2-3	.416	.394	.810
2008	Memphis (PCL)	.273	121	410	48	112	31	1	4	45	6-6	4	49-3	45	2-4	.383	.352	.735
2009	ST. LOUIS (NL)	.250	8	12	1	3	2	0	0	2	0-0	0	4-0	2	0-0	.417	.438	.855
	Memphis (PCL)	.291	108	358	53	104	22	3	14	53	4-2	3	35-1	28	4-1	.486	.357	.843
2010	Las Vegas (PCL)	.295	107	431	73	127	26	6	16	73	3-6	2	58-1	34	8-3	.494	.376	.870
	TORONTO (AL)	.206	13	34	1	7	1	0	0	0	1-0	0	2-0	5	0-0	.235	.250	.485
2011	Tucson (PCL)	.281	91	306	49	86	26	2	5	34	2-8	5	35-1	36	2-3	.428	.356	.784
2012	Syracuse (INT)	.280	106	336	45	94	16	2	3	44	2-6	2	32-0	41	4-0	.366	.340	.706
Minor Totals		.284	963	3347	465	952	215	18	70	435	37-39	33	403-15	327	52-31	.422	.363	.785
MAJOR TOTALS		.217	21	46	2	10	3	0	0	2	1-0	0	6-0	7	0-0	.283	.308	.590

Izturis, Julio
INFIELDER

HT: 5-11... **WT:** 165... **B-T:** S-L... **BORN:** 29 Aug 89, Cabudare Lara, VZ... **RESIDES:** Cabudare Lara, VZ... **EDUCATION:** NA... **TRANSACTIONS:** Signed by the San Francisco Giants on February 23, 2006... Signed by the Toronto Blue Jays on November 19, 2012... **SIGNED BY:** Luis Marquez

YR	Club & League	AVG	G	AB	R	H	2B	3B	HR	RBI	SH-SF	HB	BB-IB	SO	SB-CS	SLG	OBP	OPS
2006	DSL (DSL)	.214	44	98	17	21	1	1	0	7	8-1	6	16-0	21	10-6	.245	.355	.600
2007	DSL (DSL)	.246	67	232	43	57	5	0	0	30	2-2	12	30-0	30	36-7	.267	.359	.626
2008	DSL (DSL)	.284	47	155	49	44	4	2	1	23	1-0	9	46-0	21	24-5	.355	.471	.826
2009	AZL (AZL)	.313	25	99	22	31	5	0	1	11	1-1	4	12-1	20	10-1	.394	.405	.799
2010	Salem-Keizer (NOR)	.281	51	185	32	52	4	1	0	16	4-0	1	10-0	29	7-4	.314	.321	.635
2011	Salem-Keizer (NOR)	.209	22	67	10	14	0	1	0	2	1-1	3	5-0	14	6-2	.239	.289	.528
2012		Did Not Play																
Minor Totals		.262	256	836	173	219	19	5	2	89	17-5	35	119-1	135	93-25	.304	.375	.679

Jackson, Justin
OUTFIELDER

HT: 6-2... **WT:** 190... **B-T:** R-R... **BORN:** 11 Dec 88, Asheville, NC... **RESIDES:** Tampa, FL... **EDUCATION:** TC Roberson High School... **TRANSACTIONS:** Selected by the Toronto Blue Jays in the 1st round (supplemental, 48th overall) of the 2007 June draft... Signed on June 26, 2007... **SIGNED BY:** Marc Tramuta

YR	Club & League	AVG	G	AB	R	H	2B	3B	HR	RBI	SH-SF	HB	BB-IB	SO	SB-CS	SLG	OBP	OPS
2007	Blue Jays (GCL)	.187	42	166	20	31	1	1	2	13	2-0	0	20-0	44	7-4	.241	.274	.515
2008	Lansing (MID)	.238	121	454	74	108	26	6	7	47	4-0	8	62-0	154	17-8	.368	.340	.708
2009	Dunedin (FSL)	.213	78	249	44	53	12	1	0	17	1-3	2	39-0	87	17-4	.269	.321	.590
2010	Lansing (MID)	.249	61	229	27	57	3	3	1	17	1-0	1	26-0	67	13-4	.301	.328	.329
	Dunedin (FSL)	.200	10	30	2	6	1	0	0	0	0-0	0	5-0	8	1-0	.233	.314	.547
2011	New Hampshire (EAS)	.212	28	85	11	18	6	1	1	6	2-0	0	8-0	26	2-0	.341	.280	.621
	Dunedin (FSL)	.259	92	316	67	82	16	2	4	24	5-1	2	38-0	89	8-5	.361	.342	.703
2012	New Hampshire (EAS)	.225	66	204	24	46	7	3	0	15	2-0	2	23-0	61	11-4	.289	.310	.599
	Dunedin (FSL)	.212	44	137	15	29	6	1	0	8	1-2	0	15-0	43	5-3	.270	.286	.556
Minor Totals		.230	542	1870	284	430	78	18	15	147	18-6	15	236-0	579	81-32	.315	.320	.635

Jacobo, Gabe — INFIELDER

HT: 6-2... **WT:** 190... **B-T:** R-R... **BORN:** 14 Apr 87, Visalia, CA... **RESIDES:** Tulare, CA... **EDUCATION:** Cal St. Sacramento... **TRANSACTIONS:** Selected by the Los Angeles Angels in the 10th round of the 2008 June draft... Signed on June 12, 2008... Selected by the Toronto Blue Jays in the minor league phase of the Rule 5 Draft on December 8, 2011... **SIGNED BY:** Scott Richardson

YR	Club & League	AVG	G	AB	R	H	2B	3B	HR	RBI	SH-SF	HB	BB-IB	SO	SB-CS	SLG	OBP	OPS
2008	Orem (PIO)	.327	36	150	27	49	16	2	7	32	1-2	3	9-0	23	2-1	.600	.372	.972
	Cedar Rapids (MID)	.320	34	125	15	40	12	1	3	24	0-3	3	2-0	25	5-0	.504	.338	.842
2009	Cedar Rapids (MID)	.257	118	440	59	113	27	9	10	72	0-7	11	31-0	84	6-8	.427	.317	.744
2010	R. Cucamonga (CAL)	.296	133	541	82	160	26	7	22	107	3-6	9	24-1	94	6-9	.492	.333	.825
2011	Arkansas (TEX)	.270	86	341	40	92	13	4	10	49	1-4	4	17-1	72	2-1	.419	.309	.728
2012	Dunedin (FSL)	.338	31	130	28	44	14	0	6	27	0-2	2	12-0	20	2-0	.585	.397	.982
	Blue Jays (GCL)	.333	5	18	0	6	3	0	0	4	0-1	0	1-0	2	0-0	.500	.350	.850
	New Hampshire (EAS)	.330	25	91	13	30	8	0	2	9	0-0	0	6-0	17	1-0	.484	.371	.855
Minor Totals		.291	468	1836	264	534	119	23	60	324	5-25	32	102-2	337	24-19	.479	.335	.814

James, Justin — PITCHER

HT: 6-1... **WT:** 195... **B-T:** R-R... **BORN:** 17 Mar 90, Ponte Vedra Beach, FL... **RESIDES: Ponte Vedra Beach**, FL... **EDUCATION:** Ave Maria University... **TRANSACTIONS:** Signed by the Toronto Blue Jays on June 10, 2012... **SIGNED BY:** Matt O'Brien

YR	Club & League	W-L	ERA	G	GS	CG	SHO	SV	IP	H	R	ER	HR	HB	BB-IB	SO	WP	BK	OBA
2012	Bluefield (APP)	2-4	7.36	12	5	0	0	0	25.2	37	27	21	2	0	11-0	24	2	0	.339

Jensen, Tucker — PITCHER

HT: 6-2... **WT:** 205... **B-T:** R-R... **BORN:** 03 Aug 89, Woodward, PA... **RESIDES:** Ormond Beach, FL... **EDUCATION:** NA... **TRANSACTIONS:** Signed by the Toronto Blue Jays on June 12, 2011... **SIGNED BY:** Matt O'Brien

YR	Club & League	W-L	ERA	G	GS	CG	SHO	SV	IP	H	R	ER	HR	HB	BB-IB	SO	WP	BK	OBA
2011	Lansing (MID)	0-0	5.40	1	1	0	0	0	5.0	4	3	3	0	1	1-0	3	0	0	.222
	Blue Jays (GCL)	2-2	1.77	8	8	0	0	0	40.2	31	10	8	1	1	6-0	40	5	0	.208
	Bluefield (APP)	0-2	11.12	4	4	0	0	0	11.1	26	23	14	2	2	8-0	13	0	1	.441
2012	Bluefield (APP)	3-1	3.83	12	8	0	0	1	49.1	45	29	21	5	7	10-0	42	3	0	.230
	Dunedin (FSL)	0-1	14.54	1	1	0	0	0	4.1	9	7	7	0	0	2-0	1	1	1	.450
Minor Totals		5-6	4.31	26	22	0	0	1	110.2	115	72	53	8	11	27-0	99	9	2	.260

Jimenez, Alvido — PITCHER

HT: 6-1... **WT:** 160... **B-T:** R-R... **BORN:** 22 Nov 91, La Romana, DR... **RESIDES:** La Romana, DR... **EDUCATION:** NA... **TRANSACTIONS:** Signed by the Chicago Cubs on July 23, 2008... Selected in the minor league phase of the Rule 5 draft on December 6, 2012... **SIGNED BY:** Jose Serra

YR	Club & League	W-L	ERA	G	GS	CG	SHO	SV	IP	H	R	ER	HR	HB	BB-IB	SO	WP	BK	OBA
2009	DSL Cubs2 (DSL)	1-1	3.91	8	3	0	0	0	25.1	28	17	11	0	2	10-0	24	2	2	.275
	DSL Cubs1 (DSL)	0-0	2.20	7	4	0	0	0	28.2	31	14	7	1	4	6-0	28	4	0	.258
2010	AZL (AZL)	0-2	4.40	14	0	0	0	1	28.2	34	20	14	3	2	9-0	33	3	0	.286
2011	AZL (AZL)	3-1	2.50	13	0	0	0	2	36.0	34	14	10	1	5	13-0	22	3	0	.262
2012	AZL (AZL)	3-4	2.64	15	1	0	0	1	30.2	19	13	9	2	1	7-1	30	6	1	.174
Minor Totals		7-8	3.07	57	8	0	0	4	149.1	146	78	51	7	14	45-1	137	18	3	.252

Johnson, Matt — INFIELDER

HT: 6-3... **WT:** 210... **B-T:** R-R... **BORN:** 26 May 88, Orrville, OH... **RESIDES:** Orrville, OH... **EDUCATION:** Wooster College... **TRANSACTIONS:** Signed by the Toronto Blue Jays on June 15, 2010... **SIGNED BY:** Nick Manno

YR	Club & League	AVG	G	AB	R	H	2B	3B	HR	RBI	SH-SF	HB	BB-IB	SO	SB-CS	SLG	OBP	OPS
2010	Auburn (NYP)	.205	29	78	11	16	1	1	1	7	2-0	2	8-0	23	4-1	.282	.295	.577
2011	Vancouver (NOR)	.233	13	43	7	10	4	1	0	6	0-1	2	1-0	16	0-0	.372	.277	.649
	Bluefield (APP)	.203	20	74	10	15	2	0	1	7	0-0	3	2-0	16	3-2	.270	.253	.523
2012	Vancouver (NOR)	.313	9	16	2	5	0	0	0	2	0-0	2	6-0	6	5-0	.313	.542	.855
Minor Totals		.218	71	211	30	46	7	2	2	22	2-1	9	17-0	61	12-3	.299	.303	.601

Jones, D.J. — OUTFIELDER

HT: 6-3... **WT:** 185... **B-T:** R-R... **BORN:** 04 Sep 92, Montgomery, AL... **RESIDES:** Pike Road, AL... **EDUCATION:** Hillsborough Community College... **TRANSACTIONS:** Selected by the Toronto Blue Jays in the 20th round of the 2012 June draft... Signed on June 10, 2012... **SIGNED BY:** Joel Grampietro

YR	Club & League	AVG	G	AB	R	H	2B	3B	HR	RBI	SH-SF	HB	BB-IB	SO	SB-CS	SLG	OBP	OPS
2012	Bluefield (APP)	.192	18	52	6	10	2	0	0	6	2-0	1	1-0	17	7-0	.231	.222	.453
	Blue Jays (GCL)	.192	24	73	8	14	3	0	0	4	3-0	8	5-0	29	5-6	.233	.314	.547
Minor Totals		.192	42	125	14	24	5	0	0	10	5-0	9	6-0	46	12-6	.232	.279	.511

Jones, Jonathan — *OUTFIELDER*

HT: 6-0... **WT:** 190... **B-T:** R-R... **BORN:** 02 Aug 89, Vacaville, CA... **RESIDES:** Vacaville, CA... **EDUCATION:** Cal St. Long Beach... **TRANSACTIONS:** Selected by the Toronto Blue Jays in the 29th round of the 2010 June draft... Signed on June 18, 2010... **SIGNED BY:** Chris Becerra

YR	Club & League	AVG	G	AB	R	H	2B	3B	HR	RBI	SH-SF	HB	BB-IB	SO	SB-CS	SLG	OBP	OPS
2010	Blue Jays (GCL)	.000	4	6	0	0	0	0	0	2	0-0	0	1-0	0	0-0	.000	.143	.143
	Auburn (NYP)	.237	52	194	35	46	9	2	0	16	3-0	9	29-0	25	10-4	.304	.362	.366
2011	Vancouver (NOR)	.283	64	254	32	72	13	1	1	26	3-4	3	28-1	43	18-3	.354	.356	.710
	Lansing (MID)	.298	35	124	20	37	4	1	1	15	0-1	3	15-0	23	10-5	.371	.385	.756
2012	Dunedin (FSL)	.266	90	320	50	85	16	1	0	28	7-0	11	34-1	54	25-4	.322	.356	.678
Minor Totals		.267	245	898	137	240	42	5	2	87	13-5	26	107-2	145	63-16	.332	.360	.692

Kadish, Ian — *PITCHER*

HT: 6-0... **WT:** 205... **B-T:** L-R... **BORN:** 29 Aug 88, Cincinnati, OH... **RESIDES:** Cincinnati, OH... **EDUCATION:** Marshall University... **TRANSACTIONS:** Signed by the Toronto Blue Jays on June 12, 2011... **SIGNED BY:** Nick Manno

YR	Club & League	W-L	ERA	G	GS	CG	SHO	SV	IP	H	R	ER	HR	HB	BB-IB	SO	WP	BK	OBA
2011	Bluefield (APP)	2-3	2.67	23	0	0	0	7	30.1	24	11	9	0	4	11-1	35	5	0	.209
2012	Vancouver (NOR)	1-1	1.59	15	0	0	0	5	22.2	10	5	4	1	1	11-0	36	3	2	.130
	Lansing (MID)	1-1	4.00	15	0	0	0	2	18.0	14	9	8	0	0	9-1	21	0	0	.209
Minor Totals		4-5	2.66	53	0	0	0	14	71.0	48	25	21	1	5	31-2	92	8	2	.185

Kelly, Adaric — *PITCHER*

HT: 5-10... **WT:** 180... **B-T:** R-R... **BORN:** 01 Dec 92, San Nicholas, Aruba... **RESIDES:** San Nicholas, Aruba... **EDUCATION:** Trinity Christian Academy High School... **TRANSACTIONS:** Selected by the Toronto Blue Jays in the 28th round of the 2010 June draft... Signed on August 16, 2010... **SIGNED BY:** Carlos Rodriguez

YR	Club & League	W-L	ERA	G	GS	CG	SHO	SV	IP	H	R	ER	HR	HB	BB-IB	SO	WP	BK	OBA
2011	Blue Jays (GCL)	2-2	7.13	15	1	0	0	0	24.0	37	22	19	0	0	14-0	18	7	0	.359
2012	Blue Jays (GCL)	2-0	1.48	14	0	0	0	1	24.1	20	8	4	2	1	7-0	22	1	0	.220
Minor Totals		4-2	4.28	29	1	0	0	1	48.1	57	30	23	2	1	21-0	40	8	0	.294

Kelly, Juan — *CATCHER*

HT: 5-10... **WT:** 155... **B-T:** L-R... **BORN:** 16 Jul 94, Santo Domingo, DR... **RESIDES:** Santo Domingo, DR... **EDUCATION:** NA... **TRANSACTIONS:** Signed by the Toronto Blue Jays on January 11, 2012... **SIGNED BY:** Ismael Cruz, Jose Rosario & Jean Alvarez

YR	Club & League	AVG	G	AB	R	H	2B	3B	HR	RBI	SH-SF	HB	BB-IB	SO	SB-CS	SLG	OBP	OPS
2012	DSL (DSL)	.170	37	100	10	17	3	0	0	8	1-1	1	14-0	19	2-1	.200	.276	.476

Kervin, Bryan — *INFIELDER*

HT: 5-11... **WT:** 180... **B-T:** L-R... **BORN:** 23 Mar 85, Grapevine, TX... **RESIDES:** Grapevine, TX... **EDUCATION:** Texas Christian University... **TRANSACTIONS:** Selected by the Toronto Blue Jays in the 27th round of the 2008 June draft... Signed on June 10, 2008... **SIGNED BY:** Aaron Jersild

YR	Club & League	AVG	G	AB	R	H	2B	3B	HR	RBI	SH-SF	HB	BB-IB	SO	SB-CS	SLG	OBP	OPS
2008	Auburn (NYP)	.224	69	223	21	50	7	0	0	22	4-1	1	29-1	55	2-5	.256	.315	.571
2009	Lansing (MID)	.130	8	23	2	3	0	0	0	2	0-0	1	3-0	6	1-0	.130	.259	.389
	New Hampshire (EAS)	.161	54	143	10	23	2	1	1	11	1-1	1	6-1	38	0-3	.210	.199	.409
2010	Injured – Did Not Play																	
2011	Vancouver (NOR)	.198	34	111	7	22	6	0	0	7	4-1	0	5-0	28	2-3	.252	.231	.483
2012	Injured – Did Not Play																	
Minor Totals		.196	165	500	40	98	15	1	1	42	9-3	3	43-2	127	5-11	.236	.262	.498

Klein, Daniel — *CATCHER*

HT: 5-10... **WT:** 185... **B-T:** R-R... **BORN:** 29 Aug 90, Olathe, KS... **RESIDES:** Olathe, KS... **EDUCATION:** Kansas State University... **TRANSACTIONS:** Selected by the Toronto Blue Jays in the 28th round of the 2012 June draft... Signed on June 10, 2012... **SIGNED BY:** Jon Brunnell

YR	Club & League	AVG	G	AB	R	H	2B	3B	HR	RBI	SH-SF	HB	BB-IB	SO	SB-CS	SLG	OBP	OPS
2012	Vancouver (NOR)	.207	37	116	16	24	5	0	4	15	0-2	3	17-2	40	1-2	.353	.319	.672

Knecht, Marcus — *OUTFIELDER*

HT: 6-1... **WT:** 200... **B-T:** R-R... **BORN:** 21 Jun 90, Toronto, ON... **RESIDES:** Toronto, ON... **EDUCATION:** Connors St. Junior College... **TRANSACTIONS:** Selected by the Toronto Blue Jays in the 2nd round of the 2010 June draft... Signed on June 9, 2010... **SIGNED BY:** Darin Vaughan

YR	Club & League	AVG	G	AB	R	H	2B	3B	HR	RBI	SH-SF	HB	BB-IB	SO	SB-CS	SLG	OBP	OPS
2010	Auburn (NYP)	.268	61	231	32	62	18	3	5	34	0-0	1	26-0	48	7-1	.437	.345	.782
2011	Lansing (MID)	.273	121	439	77	120	34	3	16	86	0-10	12	67-3	124	4-3	.474	.377	.851
2012	Dunedin (FSL)	.210	126	452	63	95	32	5	13	59	0-3	11	50-1	146	5-1	.389	.302	.691
Minor Totals		.247	308	1122	172	277	84	11	34	179	0-13	24	143-4	318	16-5	.432	.341	.773

Korecky, Bobby — PITCHER

HT: 5-11... **WT:** 185... **B-T:** R-R... **BORN:** 16 Sep 79, Hillside, NJ... **RESIDES:** Estero, FL... **EDUCATION:** University of Michigan... **TRANSACTIONS:** Selected by the Philadelphia Phillies in the 19th round of the 2002 June Draft... Signed June 8, 2002... Traded to the Minnesota Twins on December 17, 2003... Claimed off waivers by the Arizona Diamondbacks on February 18, 2009... Signed by the Toronto Blue Jays on March 6, 2011... **SIGNED BY:** John Livingstone

YR	Club & League	W-L	ERA	G	GS	CG	SHO	SV	IP	H	R	ER	HR	HB	BB-IB	SO	WP	BK	OBA
2002	Batavia (NYP)	2-2	2.31	7	5	0	0	0	35.0	30	12	9	2	0	6-0	25	2	0	.242
	Lakewood (SAL)	2-2	3.00	8	4	2	0	1	27.0	25	10	9	0	0	3-0	15	1	0	.245
2003	Clearwater (FSL)	5-4	2.26	49	0	0	0	25	59.2	52	19	15	3	2	9-1	46	2	0	.236
2004	New Britain Rock (EAS)	3-4	3.36	55	0	0	0	31	67.0	52	29	25	5	3	20-2	58	3	0	.207
2005	New Britain Rock (EAS)	0-0	6.75	2	0	0	0	0	1.1	2	1	1	0	0	1-0	1	0	0	.333
2006	New Britain Rock (EAS)	1-2	3.24	16	0	0	0	5	25.0	30	15	9	1	1	13-5	14	1	0	.297
	Rochester Red (INT)	5-3	3.33	34	0	0	0	8	51.1	52	25	19	4	0	16-7	28	5	0	.260
2007	Rochester Red (INT)	5-6	3.71	66	0	0	0	35	85.0	80	42	35	5	0	34-9	71	3	0	.252
2008	Rochester Red (INT)	6-5	2.91	53	0	0	0	26	74.1	66	26	24	3	1	22-3	71	3	0	.237
	MINNESOTA (AL)	2-0	4.58	16	0	0	0	0	17.2	19	9	9	2	0	8-0	6	0	0	.288
2009	ARIZONA (NL)	0-0	13.50	5	0	0	0	0	6.0	11	9	9	0	0	4-0	3	3	0	.423
	Reno (PCL)	2-1	2.10	27	0	0	0	13	30.0	26	9	7	1	0	3-0	25	2	0	.232
2010	Winnipeg (NRT)	0-2	5.32	23	0	-	-	10	22.0	20	15	13	2	2	4-0	21	2	0	.000
2011	Las Vegas (PCL)	1-0	0.68	9	0	0	0	1	13.1	4	1	1	0	0	6-0	11	1	0	.095
	New Hampshire (EAS)	3-3	2.50	35	0	0	0	12	39.2	28	11	11	3	2	10-1	40	0	0	.194
2012	Las Vegas (PCL)	3-4	3.44	46	2	0	0	0	86.1	89	40	33	10	6	19-0	47	3	0	.266
	TORONTO (AL)	0-0	18.00	1	0	0	0	0	1.0	1	2	2	1	0	1-0	0	0	0	.250
Minor Totals		38-36	3.00	407	11	2	0	157	595.0	536	240	198	37	15	162-28	452	26	0	.240
MAJOR TOTALS		2-0	7.30	22	0	0	0	0	24.2	31	20	20	3	0	13-0	9	3	0	.323

Labourt, Jairo — PITCHER

HT: 6-4... **WT:** 204... **B-T:** L-L... **BORN:** 07 Mar 94, Azua, DR... **RESIDES:** Azua, DR... **EDUCATION:** NA... **TRANSACTIONS:** Signed by the Toronto Blue Jays on March 7, 2011... **SIGNED BY:** Marco Paddy & Hilario Soriano

YR	Club & League	W-L	ERA	G	GS	CG	SHO	SV	IP	H	R	ER	HR	HB	BB-IB	SO	WP	BK	OBA
2011	DSL (DSL)	0-4	2.23	12	12	0	0	0	36.1	29	18	9	0	5	14-0	29	0	0	.220
2012	Blue Jays (GCL)	0-3	3.79	12	12	0	0	0	38.0	38	20	16	2	0	23-0	39	9	0	.253
Minor Totals		0-7	3.03	24	24	0	0	0	74.1	67	38	25	2	5	37-0	68	9	0	.238

Lara, Wilmin — PITCHER

HT: 6-2... **WT:** 173... **B-T:** R-R... **BORN:** 05 Jun 94, Bani, DR... **RESIDES:** Bani, DR... **EDUCATION:** NA... **TRANSACTIONS:** Signed by the Toronto Blue Jays on January 1, 2012... **SIGNED BY:** Ismael Cruz & Jose Rosario

YR	Club & League	W-L	ERA	G	GS	CG	SHO	SV	IP	H	R	ER	HR	HB	BB-IB	SO	WP	BK	OBA
2012	DSL (DSL)	0-3	5.13	13	1	0	0	0	26.1	23	19	15	1	4	22-4	22	7	0	.264
	Blue Jays (GCL)	0-0	6.23	3	0	0	0	0	4.1	4	3	3	0	2	5-0	2	5	0	.235
Minor Totals		0-3	5.28	16	1	0	0	0	30.2	27	22	18	1	6	27-4	24	12	0	.260

Lawrence, Casey — PITCHER

HT: 6-2... **WT:** 170... **B-T:** R-R... **BORN:** 28 Oct 87, McSherrystown , PA... **RESIDES:** McSherrystown, PA... **EDUCATION:** Albright College... **TRANSACTIONS:** Signed by the Toronto Blue Jays on June 15, 2010... **SIGNED BY:** Bobby Gandolfo

YR	Club & League	W-L	ERA	G	GS	CG	SHO	SV	IP	H	R	ER	HR	HB	BB-IB	SO	WP	BK	OBA
2010	Auburn (NYP)	6-1	1.74	12	10	0	0	0	57.0	41	13	11	2	2	9-0	48	0	1	.202
	Lansing (MID)	1-1	3.98	4	3	0	0	1	20.1	21	9	9	1	3	3-0	13	1	0	.273
2011	Lansing (MID)	11-8	3.08	22	21	2	0	0	125.2	123	57	43	9	1	22-0	97	1	2	.252
	Dunedin (FSL)	3-1	2.84	4	4	1	0	0	25.1	26	8	8	3	0	2-0	14	1	0	.268
2012	New Hampshire (EAS)	0-1	6.39	3	2	0	0	0	12.2	20	9	9	1	1	5-1	6	0	0	.392
	Dunedin (FSL)	9-6	3.63	24	23	1	0	0	138.2	149	60	56	9	1	21-0	90	1	1	.277
Minor Totals		30-18	3.22	69	63	4	0	1	379.2	380	156	136	25	8	62-1	268	4	4	.262

Leblebijian, Jason — INFIELDER

HT: 6-1... **WT:** 190... **B-T:** R-R... **BORN:** 13 May 91, Arlington Heights, IL... **RESIDES:** Arlington Heights, IL... **EDUCATION:** Bradley University... **TRANSACTIONS:** Selected by the Toronto Blue Jays in the 25th round of the 2012 June draft... Signed on June 10, 2012... **SIGNED BY:** Mike Medici

YR	Club & League	AVG	G	AB	R	H	2B	3B	HR	RBI	SH-SF	HB	BB-IB	SO	SB-CS	SLG	OBP	OPS
2012	Bluefield (APP)	.194	9	31	3	6	3	0	0	3	0-1	2	5-0	8	1-0	.290	.333	.623
	Vancouver (NOR)	.291	37	148	24	43	9	1	2	20	0-2	0	10-1	44	6-1	.405	.331	.736
	Lansing (MID)	.222	12	45	7	10	1	0	0	1	0-0	2	7-0	13	1-1	.244	.352	.596
Minor Totals		.263	58	224	34	59	13	1	2	24	0-3	4	22-1	65	8-2	.357	.336	.693

Leyland, Jordan — INFIELDER

HT: 6-4... **WT:** 205... **B-T:** R-R... **BORN:** 06 Sep 89, San Dimas, CA... **RESIDES:** San Dimas, CA... **EDUCATION:** Azusa Pacific University... **TRANSACTIONS:** Selected by the Toronto Blue Jays in the 9th round of the 2012 June draft... Signed on June 10, 2012... **SIGNED BY:** Joey Aversa

YR	Club & League	AVG	G	AB	R	H	2B	3B	HR	RBI	SH-SF	HB	BB-IB	SO	SB-CS	SLG	OBP	OPS
2012	Vancouver (NOR)	.235	23	81	11	19	4	1	1	13	0-1	0	13-0	18	0-0	.346	.337	.683
	Bluefield (APP)	.235	16	51	3	12	3	0	1	4	0-0	1	1-0	12	0-1	.353	.264	.617
Minor Totals		.235	39	132	14	31	7	1	2	17	0-1	1	14-0	30	0-1	.348	.311	.659

Lopes, Christian — INFIELDER

HT: 6-0... **WT:** 185... **B-T:** R-R... **BORN:** 01 Oct 82, Valencia, CA... **RESIDES:** Huntington Beach, CA... **EDUCATION:** Edison High School... **TRANSACTIONS:** Selected by the Toronto Blue Jays in the 7th round of the 2011 June Draft... Signed on August 15, 2011... **SIGNED BY:** Joe Aversa

YR	Club & League	AVG	G	AB	R	H	2B	3B	HR	RBI	SH-SF	HB	BB-IB	SO	SB-CS	SLG	OBP	OPS
2012	Bluefield (APP)	.280	49	186	33	52	16	5	4	29	1-0	3	15-0	34	6-1	.484	.343	.827
	Vancouver (NOR)	.270	10	37	4	10	1	1	0	4	0-1	1	2-0	6	0-0	.351	.317	.668
Minor Totals		.278	59	223	37	62	17	6	4	33	1-1	4	17-0	40	6-1	.462	.339	.801

Loveless, Derrick — OUTFIELDER

HT: 6-1... **WT:** 200... **B-T:** L-R... **BORN:** 07 Mar 93, Solon, IA... **RESIDES:** Solon, IA... **EDUCATION:** Solon High School... **TRANSACTIONS:** Selected by the Toronto Blue Jays in the 27th round of the 2011 June Draft... Signed on August 2, 2011... **SIGNED BY:** Wes Penick

YR	Club & League	AVG	G	AB	R	H	2B	3B	HR	RBI	SH-SF	HB	BB-IB	SO	SB-CS	SLG	OBP	OPS
2011	Blue Jays (GCL)	.059	5	17	2	1	0	0	0	1	1-0	0	3-0	7	0-0	.059	.200	.259
2012	Blue Jays (GCL)	.165	37	115	15	19	5	4	1	11	0-0	2	16-0	38	2-0	.304	.278	.582
Minor Totals		.152	42	132	17	20	5	4	1	12	1-0	2	19-0	45	2-0	.273	.268	.541

Lucas, Jonathan — PITCHER

HT: 5-10... **WT:** 205... **B-T:** L-R... **BORN:** 12 Dec 87, Mendham, NJ... **RESIDES:** Hackettstown, NJ... **EDUCATION:** Wagner College... **TRANSACTIONS:** Signed by the Toronto Blue Jays on June 12, 2011... **SIGNED BY:** Michael Pesce

YR	Club & League	W-L	ERA	G	GS	CG	SHO	SV	IP	H	R	ER	HR	HB	BB-IB	SO	WP	BK	OBA
2011	Bluefield (APP)	3-3	3.93	21	0	0	0	0	36.2	31	16	16	2	2	9-1	24	4	0	.231
2012	Vancouver (NOR)	1-1	3.35	27	0	0	0	1	40.1	46	17	15	0	1	20-5	27	1	0	.299
Minor Totals		4-4	3.62	48	0	0	0	1	77.0	77	33	31	2	3	29-6	51	5	0	.267

Lugo, Dawel — INFIELDER

HT: 6-0... **WT:** 188... **B-T:** R-R... **BORN:** 31 Dec 94, Bani, DR... **RESIDES:** Bani, DR... **EDUCATION:** NA... **TRANSACTIONS:** Signed by the Toronto Blue Jays on July 3, 2011... **SIGNED BY:** Marco Paddy & Hilario Soriano

YR	Club & League	AVG	G	AB	R	H	2B	3B	HR	RBI	SH-SF	HB	BB-IB	SO	SB-CS	SLG	OBP	OPS
2012	Blue Jays (GCL)	.224	47	170	20	38	2	5	2	20	1-0	5	7-0	25	5-1	.329	.275	.604

Magnuson, Trystan — PITCHER

HT: 6-7... **WT:** 220... **B-T:** L-R... **BORN:** 06 Jun 85, Vancouver, BC... **RESIDES:** Louisville, KY... **EDUCATION:** Louisville University... **TRANSACTIONS:** Selected by the Toronto Blue Jays in the 1st round (supplemental – 56th overall) of the 2007 June draft... Signed on July 11, 2007... Traded to the Oakland Athletics along with RHP Daniel Farquhar in exchange for OF Rajai Davis on November 17, 2010... Traded to the Toronto Blue Jays in exchange for cash considerations on November 4, 2011... **SIGNED BY:** Steve Miller

YR	Club & League	W-L	ERA	G	GS	CG	SHO	SV	IP	H	R	ER	HR	HB	BB-IB	SO	WP	BK	OBA
2008	Lansing (MID)	0-9	5.40	24	24	0	0	0	81.2	91	57	49	6	7	35-0	49	8	0	.282
2009	Dunedin (FSL)	4-1	2.77	38	0	0	0	1	61.2	56	23	19	2	4	27-1	45	3	0	.248
	New Hampshire (EAS)	1-0	0.00	5	0	0	0	0	10.0	4	0	0	0	0	1-0	7	0	0	.118
2010	New Hampshire (EAS)	3-0	2.58	46	0	0	0	5	73.1	70	22	21	1	2	10-0	63	2	1	.256
2011	Sacramento River (PCL)	4-2	2.98	30	0	0	0	5	45.1	34	20	15	4	2	19-3	46	3	0	.210
	OAKLAND (AL)	0-0	6.14	9	0	0	0	0	14.2	15	11	10	3	0	5-0	11	3	0	.250
2012	Dunedin (FSL)	0-4	5.40	13	0	0	0	0	18.1	25	14	11	4	2	3-1	26	2	0	.305
	New Hampshire (EAS)	0-1	1.95	25	0	0	0	5	32.1	26	10	7	1	2	7-1	24	0	0	.215
Minor Totals		12-17	3.40	181	24	0	0	16	322.2	306	146	122	18	19	102-6	260	18	1	.251

Martin, Luis — OUTFIELDER

HT: 6-4... **WT:** 210... **B-T:** R-R... **BORN:** 12 Feb 94, San Pedro de Macoris, DR... **RESIDES:** San Pedro de Macoris, DR... **EDUCATION:** NA... **TRANSACTIONS:** Signed by the Toronto Blue Jays on November 25, 2010... **SIGNED BY:** Marco Paddy & Blake Bentley

YR	Club & League	AVG	G	AB	R	H	2B	3B	HR	RBI	SH-SF	HB	BB-IB	SO	SB-CS	SLG	OBP	OPS
2011	DSL (DSL)	.183	54	180	15	33	7	2	1	14	1-0	2	18-0	92	5-3	.261	.265	.526
2012	DSL (DSL)	.214	51	154	21	33	5	0	2	20	1-5	5	13-0	65	5-1	.286	.288	.574
Minor Totals		.198	105	334	36	66	12	2	3	34	2-5	7	31-0	157	10-4	.272	.276	.548

Marze, Dayton
PITCHER

HT: 6-2... **WT:** 185... **B-T:** R-R... **BORN:** 01 Jan 89, Lafayette, LA... **RESIDES:** Lafayette, LA... **EDUCATION:** University of Louisiana Lafayette... **TRANSACTIONS:** Selected by the Toronto Blue Jays in the 14th round of the 2010 June draft... Signed on June 16, 2010... **SIGNED BY:** Rob St. Julien

YR	Club & League	W-L	ERA	G	GS	CG	SHO	SV	IP	H	R	ER	HR	HB	BB-IB	SO	WP	BK	OBA
2010	Auburn (NYP)	2-1	2.73	21	0	0	0	8	26.1	25	14	8	0	5	6-0	20	0	1	.250
2011	Lansing (MID)	6-5	4.10	44	0	0	0	7	85.2	86	41	39	6	5	31-0	71	4	3	.263
2012	Dunedin (FSL)	2-4	2.82	46	0	0	0	1	70.1	66	26	22	4	5	25-2	37	2	0	.256
Minor Totals		10-10	3.41	111	0	0	0	16	182.1	177	81	69	10	15	62-2	128	6	4	.258

McFarland, Blake
PITCHER

HT: 6-5... **WT:** 230... **B-T:** R-R... **BORN:** 02 Feb 88, San Jose, CA... **RESIDES:** San Jose, CA... **EDUCATION:** San Jose State University... **TRANSACTIONS:** Signed by the Toronto Blue Jays on June 13, 2011... **SIGNED BY:** Randy Kramer

YR	Club & League	W-L	ERA	G	GS	CG	SHO	SV	IP	H	R	ER	HR	HB	BB-IB	SO	WP	BK	OBA
2011	Vancouver (NOR)	6-7	5.32	14	11	0	0	0	64.1	68	41	38	3	4	23-0	34	6	0	.273
2012	Lansing (MID)	5-6	5.68	36	7	0	0	2	90.1	116	58	57	5	5	27-0	73	5	2	.320
Minor Totals		11-13	5.53	50	18	0	0	2	154.2	184	99	95	8	9	50-0	107	11	2	.301

McGuire, Deck
PITCHER

HT: 6-6... **WT:** 220... **B-T:** R-R... **BORN:** 23 Jun 89, Richmond, VA... **RESIDES:** Clearwater, FL... **EDUCATION:** Georgia Tech University... **TRANSACTIONS:** Selected by the Toronto Blue Jays in the 1st round (11th overall) of the 2010 June draft... Signed on August 16, 2011... **SIGNED BY:** Eric McQueen

YR	Club & League	W-L	ERA	G	GS	CG	SHO	SV	IP	H	R	ER	HR	HB	BB-IB	SO	WP	BK	OBA
2011	Dunedin (FSL)	7-4	2.75	19	18	0	0	0	104.2	89	38	32	9	6	38-0	102	1	0	.228
	New Hampshire (EAS)	2-1	4.35	4	3	1	0	0	20.2	20	10	10	4	1	7-0	22	3	0	.253
2012	New Hampshire (EAS)	5-15	5.88	28	28	0	0	0	144.0	162	103	94	22	6	62-0	97	7	0	.286
Minor Totals		14-20	4.55	51	49	1	0	0	269.1	271	151	136	35	13	107-0	221	11	0	.261

Melendez, Ronnie
OUTFIELDER

HT: 5-10... **WT:** 170... **B-T:** R-R... **BORN:** 29 Sep 89, Jacksonville, FL... **RESIDES:** Jacksonville, FL... **EDUCATION:** Cowley County Junior College... **TRANSACTIONS:** Selected by the Toronto Blue Jays in the 24th round of the 2010 June draft... Signed on June 13, 2010... **SIGNED BY:** Jon Bunnell

YR	Club & League	AVG	G	AB	R	H	2B	3B	HR	RBI	SH-SF	HB	BB-IB	SO	SB-CS	SLG	OBP	OPS
2010	Blue Jays (GCL)	.259	36	112	18	29	8	3	0	5	6-1	2	11-1	23	11-5	.384	.333	.717
2011	Blue Jays (GCL)	.265	10	34	6	9	2	0	0	5	1-0	0	3-0	3	3-0	.324	.324	.648
	Bluefield (APP)	.300	6	10	0	3	2	0	0	4	0-0	0	0-0	2	0-0	.500	.300	.800
2012	Vancouver (NOR)	.000	1	1	0	0	0	0	0	0	0-0	0	0-0	0	0-0	.000	.000	.000
Minor Totals		.261	53	157	24	41	12	3	0	14	7-1	2	14-1	28	14-5	.376	.328	.703

Meyer, Ajay
PITCHER

HT: 6-6... **WT:** 185... **B-T:** L-R... **BORN:** 19 Jul 87, Hamler, OH... **RESIDES:** Hamler, OH... **EDUCATION:** NA... **TRANSACTIONS:** Signed by the Toronto Blue Jays on June 12, 2011... **SIGNED BY:** Nick Manno

YR	Club & League	W-L	ERA	G	GS	CG	SHO	SV	IP	H	R	ER	HR	HB	BB-IB	SO	WP	BK	OBA
2011	Bluefield (APP)	4-2	3.02	13	13	0	0	0	65.2	62	26	22	3	0	13-0	55	3	1	.243
2012	Lansing (MID)	3-3	3.67	54	0	0	0	33	56.1	47	28	23	7	0	13-1	57	3	1	.224
Minor Totals		7-5	3.32	67	13	0	0	33	122.0	109	54	45	10	0	26-1	112	6	2	.234

Mooney, Peter
INFIELDER

HT: 5-6... **WT:** 155... **B-T:** L-R... **BORN:** 19 Aug 90, Loxahatchee, FL... **RESIDES: Loxahatchee**, FL... **EDUCATION:** University of South Carolina Columbia... **TRANSACTIONS:** Selected by the Toronto Blue Jays in the 21st round of the 2011 June draft... Signed on July 18, 2011... **SIGNED BY:** John Hendricks

YR	Club & League	AVG	G	AB	R	H	2B	3B	HR	RBI	SH-SF	HB	BB-IB	SO	SB-CS	SLG	OBP	OPS
2011	Blue Jays (GCL)	.300	3	10	2	3	1	1	0	1	1-1	0	2-0	2	0-0	.600	.385	.985
	Bluefield (APP)	.260	21	77	19	20	7	2	1	11	1-2	0	17-0	13	1-0	.442	.385	.827
	Lansing (MID)	.360	7	25	3	9	2	2	0	1	0-0	0	5-0	5	0-1	.600	.467	1.067
2012	Injured – Did Not Play																	
Minor Totals		.286	31	112	24	32	10	5	1	13	2-3	0	24-0	20	1-1	.491	.403	.894

Munoz, Aaron
CATCHER

HT: 5-9... **WT:** 190... **B-T:** R-R... **BORN:** 24 Dec 88, Laveen, LA... **RESIDES: Laveen**, LA... **EDUCATION:** Northwestern State University... **TRANSACTIONS:** Selected by the Toronto Blue Jays in the 34th round of the 2011 June Draft... Signed on June 12, 2011... **SIGNED BY:** Rob St. Julien

YR	Club & League	AVG	G	AB	R	H	2B	3B	HR	RBI	SH-SF	HB	BB-IB	SO	SB-CS	SLG	OBP	OPS
2011	Bluefield (APP)	.231	45	130	12	30	3	0	0	21	5-2	4	11-0	28	0-0	.254	.306	.560
2012	Lansing (MID)	.223	34	112	11	25	4	0	0	7	3-0	2	11-0	31	1-0	.259	.304	.563
Minor Totals		.227	80	242	23	55	7	0	0	28	8-2	6	22-0	59	1-0	.256	.305	.561

Murphy, Griffin — *PITCHER*

HT: 6-3... **WT:** 200... **B-T:** R-L... **BORN:** 16 Jan 91, Highland, CA... **RESIDES:** Highland, CA... **EDUCATION:** Redlands East Valley High School... **TRANSACTIONS:** Selected by the Toronto Blue Jays in the 2nd round of the 2010 June draft... Signed on August 16, 2010... **SIGNED BY:** Dan Cox

YR	Club & League	W-L	ERA	G	GS	CG	SHO	SV	IP	H	R	ER	HR	HB	BB-IB	SO	WP	BK	OBA
2011	Blue Jays (GCL)	2-2	4.39	11	11	0	0	0	41.0	48	27	20	6	3	16-0	39	5	0	.294
2012	Bluefield (APP)	1-2	1.70	15	2	0	0	1	37.0	24	13	7	1	3	13-0	42	2	1	.180
	Vancouver (NOR)	0-0	3.86	2	0	0	0	0	2.1	2	1	1	0	0	0-0	2	0	0	.222
Minor Totals		3-4	3.14	28	13	0	0	1	80.1	74	41	28	7	6	29-0	83	7	1	.243

Nay, Mitch — *INFIELDER*

HT: 6-3... **WT:** 200... **B-T:** R-R... **BORN:** 20 Sep 93, Tarzana, CA... **RESIDES:** Tarzana, CA... **EDUCATION:** Hamilton High School... **TRANSACTIONS:** Selected by the Toronto Blue Jays in the 1st round (supplemental – 58th overall) of the 2012 June draft... Signed on June 10, 2012... **SIGNED BY:** Blake Crosby

Nessy, Santiago — *CATCHER*

HT: 6-2... **WT:** 230... **B-T:** R-R... **BORN:** 08 Dec 92, Caracas, VZ... **RESIDES:** Caracas, VZ... **EDUCATION:** NA... **TRANSACTIONS:** Signed by the Toronto Blue Jays on July 2, 2009... **SIGNED BY:** Rafael Moncada

YR	Club & League	AVG	G	AB	R	H	2B	3B	HR	RBI	SH-SF	HB	BB-IB	SO	SB-CS	SLG	OBP	OPS
2010	DSL (DSL)	.248	44	141	15	35	12	0	2	17	0-3	4	14-1	44	4-0	.376	.327	.703
2011	Blue Jays (GCL)	.306	35	134	12	41	7	0	3	19	0-1	1	8-0	29	0-2	.425	.347	.772
2012	Bluefield (APP)	.256	45	160	26	41	8	0	8	23	0-2	3	13-0	47	0-0	.456	.320	.776
	Vancouver (NOR)	.091	6	22	4	2	1	0	1	3	0-0	0	3-0	7	0-0	.273	.200	.473
Minor Totals		.260	130	457	57	119	28	0	14	62	0-6	8	38-1	127	4-2	.414	.324	.738

Newman, Matthew — *OUTFIELDER*

HT: 5-10... **WT:** 170... **B-T:** L-L... **BORN:** 20 Sep 88, Phoenix, AZ... **RESIDES:** Glendale, AZ... **EDUCATION:** Arizona State University... **TRANSACTIONS:** Signed by the Toronto Blue Jays on June 17, 2011... **SIGNED BY:** Blake Crosby

YR	Club & League	AVG	G	AB	R	H	2B	3B	HR	RBI	SH-SF	HB	BB-IB	SO	SB-CS	SLG	OBP	OPS
2011	Blue Jays (GCL)	.167	2	6	1	1	0	0	0	0	0-0	0	0-0	2	0-0	.167	.167	.334
	Vancouver (NOR)	.228	49	149	17	34	9	0	3	17	3-4	0	18-0	41	3-5	.349	.304	.653
2012	Vancouver (NOR)	.262	61	221	34	58	16	5	6	41	0-3	2	30-1	61	6-2	.462	.352	.814
Minor Totals		.247	112	376	52	93	25	5	9	58	3-7	2	48-1	104	9-7	.412	.330	.742

Nieves, Efrain — *PITCHER*

HT: 6-0... **WT:** 169... **B-T:** L-L... **BORN:** 15 Nov 89, Caguas, PR... **RESIDES:** Toa Alta, PR... **EDUCATION:** Puerto Rico Baseball Academy... **TRANSACTIONS:** Selected by the Milwaukee Brewers in the 7th round of the 2007 June draft... Signed on June 9, 2007... Signed by the Detroit Tigers on November 1, 2012... Selected by the Toronto Blue Jays in the minor league phase of the Rule 5 draft on December 6, 2012... **SIGNED BY:** Manola Hernandez

YR	Club & League	W-L	ERA	G	GS	CG	SHO	SV	IP	H	R	ER	HR	HB	BB-IB	SO	WP	BK	OBA
2007	AZL (AZL)	2-4	5.31	13	7	0	0	0	40.2	38	29	24	3	2	25-0	45	7	2	.244
	Helena (PIO)	1-0	0.00	2	0	0	0	0	4.2	3	0	0	0	0	1-0	4	0	0	.188
2008	Helena (PIO)	6-3	4.48	16	11	0	0	0	76.1	78	40	38	9	2	10-0	66	5	0	.264
2009	Wisconsin Timber (MID)	5-7	5.70	27	11	0	0	1	94.2	116	62	60	7	8	35-0	86	5	0	.311
2010	Wisconsin Timber (MID)	4-5	5.56	23	7	0	0	1	69.2	83	52	43	4	6	41-0	53	10	0	.295
2011	Brevard County (FSL)	3-0	4.86	41	0	0	0	0	63.0	70	38	34	7	5	27-0	53	6	0	.286
2012	Connecticut (NYP)	4-1	2.79	21	0	0	0	3	42.0	28	13	13	2	4	8-0	42	4	0	.181
Minor Totals		25-20	4.88	143	36	0	0	5	391.0	416	234	212	32	27	147-0	349	37	2	.273

Nolan, Kevin — *INFIELDER*

HT: 6-2... **WT:** 200... **B-T:** R-R... **BORN:** 13 Dec 87, Nashua, NH... **RESIDES:** Nashua, NH... **EDUCATION:** Winthrop University... **TRANSACTIONS:** Selected by the Toronto Blue Jays in the 20th round of the 2009 June draft... Signed on June 14, 2009... **SIGNED BY:** Matt Briggs

YR	Club & League	AVG	G	AB	R	H	2B	3B	HR	RBI	SH-SF	HB	BB-IB	SO	SB-CS	SLG	OBP	OPS
2009	Auburn (NYP)	.191	48	157	10	30	4	0	0	10	4-1	2	7-0	29	2-2	.217	.234	.451
2010	Lansing (MID)	.295	83	285	42	84	25	2	0	30	3-2	5	31-0	34	11-10	.396	.372	.768
2011	Lansing (MID)	.319	24	91	20	29	6	0	3	19	0-2	1	12-0	15	2-1	.484	.396	.880
	Dunedin (FSL)	.281	72	242	32	68	20	0	4	20	0-1	1	36-1	47	2-3	.413	.375	.788
2012	Dunedin (FSL)	.316	78	310	54	98	23	5	5	40	0-3	2	34-0	43	12-4	.471	.384	.855
Minor Totals		.285	305	1085	158	309	78	7	12	119	7-9	11	120-1	168	29-20	.403	.359	.762

Norris, Daniel — *PITCHER*

HT: 6-2... **WT:** 195... **B-T:** L-L... **BORN:** 25 Apr 93, Johnson City, TN... **RESIDES:** Johnson City, TN... **EDUCATION:** Science Hill High School... **TRANSACTIONS:** Selected by the Toronto Blue Jays in the 2nd round of the 2011 June draft... Signed on August 15, 2011... **SIGNED BY:** Nate Murrie

YR Club & League	W-L	ERA	G	GS	CG	SHO	SV	IP	H	R	ER	HR	HB	BB-IB	SO	WP	BK	OBA
2012 Bluefield (APP)	2-3	7.97	11	10	0	0	0	35.0	44	35	31	4	2	13-0	38	3	0	.301
2012 Vancouver (NOR)	0-1	10.57	2	2	0	0	0	7.2	14	9	9	0	0	5-0	5	1	0	.400
Minor Totals	2-4	8.44	13	12	0	0	0	42.2	58	44	40	4	2	18-0	43	4	0	.320

Opitz, Shane — *INFIELDER*

HT: 6-1... **WT:** 180... **B-T:** L-R... **BORN:** 10 Jan 92, Centennial, CO... **RESIDES:** Centennial, CO... **EDUCATION:** Heritage High School... **TRANSACTIONS:** Selected by the Toronto Blue Jays in the 11th round of the 2010 June draft... Signed on July 30, 2010... **SIGNED BY:** Jon Bunnell

YR Club & League	AVG	G	AB	R	H	2B	3B	HR	RBI	SH-SF	HB	BB-IB	SO	SB-CS	SLG	OBP	OPS
2010 Blue Jays (GCL)	.303	10	33	3	10	3	1	0	3	0-0	1	2-0	5	1-0	.455	.361	.816
2011 Vancouver (NOR)	.259	63	239	25	62	6	0	0	25	0-2	0	19-0	34	8-2	.285	.312	.597
2012 Lansing (MID)	.225	90	315	42	71	19	2	2	37	10-3	1	25-0	65	3-1	.317	.282	.599
Minor Totals	.244	163	587	70	143	28	3	2	65	10-5	2	46-0	104	12-3	.312	.298	.610

Orozco, Rodrigo — *INFIELDER*

HT: 5-11... **WT:** 155... **B-T:** S-R... **BORN:** 02 Apr 95, Tocumen, Panama... **RESIDES:** Tocumen, Panama... **EDUCATION:** NA... **TRANSACTIONS:** Signed by the Toronto Blue Jays on July 4, 2012... **SIGNED BY:** Ismael Cruz & Sandy Rosario

Osuna, Roberto — *PITCHER*

HT: 6-2... **WT:** 230... **B-T:** R-R... **BORN:** 07 Feb 95, San Jose Rios, Cuba... **RESIDES:** Los Mochis, MEX... **EDUCATION:** NA... **TRANSACTIONS:** Signed by the Toronto Blue Jays on August 3, 2011... **SIGNED BY:** Marco Paddy

YR Club & League	W-L	ERA	G	GS	CG	SHO	SV	IP	H	R	ER	HR	HB	BB-IB	SO	WP	BK	OBA
2012 Bluefield (APP)	1-0	1.50	7	4	0	0	0	24.0	18	5	4	1	2	6-0	24	1	1	.209
2012 Vancouver (NOR)	1-0	3.20	5	5	0	0	0	19.2	14	9	7	1	1	9-0	25	2	0	.192
Minor Totals	2-0	2.27	12	9	0	0	0	43.2	32	14	11	2	3	15-0	49	3	1	.201

Parmley, Ian — *OUTFIELDER*

HT: 5-11... **WT:** 175... **B-T:** L-L... **BORN:** 19 Dec 89, Snohomish, WA... **RESIDES:** Snohomish, WA... **EDUCATION:** Liberty University... **TRANSACTIONS:** Selected by the Toronto Blue Jays in the 7th round of the 2012 June draft... Signed on June 10, 2012... **SIGNED BY:** Bobby Gandolfo

YR Club & League	AVG	G	AB	R	H	2B	3B	HR	RBI	SH-SF	HB	BB-IB	SO	SB-CS	SLG	OBP	OPS
2012 Vancouver (NOR)	.201	58	209	42	42	9	1	0	12	2-1	0	52-0	44	12-5	.254	.359	.613

Pascazi, Trey — *INFIELDER*

HT: 6-1... **WT:** 175... **B-T:** S-R... **BORN:** 07 Aug 93, East Rochester, NY... **RESIDES:** Rochester, NY... **EDUCATION:** East Rochester High School... **TRANSACTIONS:** Selected by the Toronto Blue Jays in the 23rd round of the 2012 June draft... Signed on June 26, 2012... **SIGNED BY:** Jamie Lehman

YR Club & League	AVG	G	AB	R	H	2B	3B	HR	RBI	SH-SF	HB	BB-IB	SO	SB-CS	SLG	OBP	OPS
2012 Blue Jays (GCL)	.161	14	31	3	5	1	0	0	4	0-0	0	5-0	19	0-0	.194	.278	.472

Patterson, Kevin — *INFIELDER*

HT: 6-4... **WT:** 220... **B-T:** L-R... **BORN:** 28 Sep 88, Atlanta, GA... **RESIDES:** Atlanta, GA... **EDUCATION:** Auburn University... **TRANSACTIONS:** Selected by the Toronto Blue Jays in the 30th round of the 2011 June draft... Signed on June 13, 2011... **SIGNED BY:** Cliff Pastornicky

YR Club & League	AVG	G	AB	R	H	2B	3B	HR	RBI	SH-SF	HB	BB-IB	SO	SB-CS	SLG	OBP	OPS
2011 Blue Jays (GCL)	.370	15	54	11	20	5	0	5	11	0-0	0	5-0	13	2-0	.741	.424	1.165
Vancouver (NOR)	.270	33	115	16	31	6	2	5	21	0-2	2	18-1	40	1-0	.487	.372	.859
2012 Lansing (MID)	.245	108	387	48	95	22	3	19	79	0-5	6	52-4	124	2-0	.465	.340	.805
Minor Totals	.263	156	556	75	146	33	5	29	111	0-7	8	75-5	177	5-0	.496	.354	.851

Perdomo, Angel — *PITCHER*

HT: 6-6... **WT:** 198... **B-T:** L-L... **BORN:** 07 May 94, San Cristobal, DR... **RESIDES:** San Cristobal, DR... **EDUCATION:** NA... **TRANSACTIONS:** Signed by the Toronto Blue Jays on November 28, 2011... **SIGNED BY:** Ismael Cruz, Marino Tejada & Jose Rosario

YR Club & League	W-L	ERA	G	GS	CG	SHO	SV	IP	H	R	ER	HR	HB	BB-IB	SO	WP	BK	OBA
2012 DSL (DSL)	0-0	5.40	7	0	0	0	0	11.2	2	7	7	0	4	13-0	13	6	0	.059

Perinan, Gustavo
INFIELDER

HT: 5-11... **WT:** 185... **B-T:** L-R... **BORN:** 02 Jan 95, Cartagena, Columbia... **RESIDES:** Cartagena, Columbia... **EDUCATION:** NA... **TRANSACTIONS:** Signed by the Toronto Blue Jays on February 9, 2012... **SIGNED BY:** Ismael Cruz & Sandy Rosario

YR	Club & League	AVG	G	AB	R	H	2B	3B	HR	RBI	SH-SF	HB	BB-IB	SO	SB-CS	SLG	OBP	OPS
2012	DSL (DSL)	.287	40	122	20	35	6	1	0	10	0-1	4	20-0	24	3-2	.352	.401	.753

Permison, Drew
PITCHER

HT: 5-10... **WT:** 170... **B-T:** R-R... **BORN:** 24 Feb 84, Columbia, MD... **RESIDES:** Columbia, MD... **EDUCATION:** Towson Unviversity... **TRANSACTIONS:** Selected by the Toronto Blue Jays in the 42nd round of the 2010 June Draft... Signed on June 13, 2010... **SIGNED BY:** Bobby Gandolfo

YR	Club & League	W-L	ERA	G	GS	CG	SHO	SV	IP	H	R	ER	HR	HB	BB-IB	SO	WP	BK	OBA
2010	Auburn (NYP)	1-1	2.31	27	0	0	0	7	39.0	23	15	10	0	0	19-1	59	7	0	.164
2011	Lansing (MID)	0-0	12.00	4	0	0	0	1	6.0	10	8	8	2	0	4-0	4	1	0	.385
	Vancouver (NOR)	1-1	1.69	29	0	0	0	15	32.0	23	8	6	0	2	8-0	27	0	0	.205
2012	Dunedin (FSL)	0-0	0.00	1	0	0	0	0	1.0	1	0	0	0	0	0-0	0	0	0	.250
	Vancouver (NOR)	0-0	0.79	12	0	0	0	5	11.1	9	1	1	0	1	2-0	10	3	0	.220
Minor Totals		2-2	2.52	73	0	0	0	28	89.1	66	32	25	2	3	33-1	100	11	0	.204

Peters, Chris
INFIELDER

HT: 6-0... **WT:** 175... **B-T:** R-R... **BORN:** 29 Dec 88, Dayton, OH... **RESIDES:** Tripp City, OH... **EDUCATION:** NA... **TRANSACTIONS:** Signed by the Toronto Blue Jays on June 12, 2011... **SIGNED BY:** Nick Manno

YR	Club & League	AVG	G	AB	R	H	2B	3B	HR	RBI	SH-SF	HB	BB-IB	SO	SB-CS	SLG	OBP	OPS
2011	Blue Jays (GCL)	.246	42	118	13	29	5	3	1	17	4-2	0	14-0	26	3-0	.364	.321	.685
2012	Bluefield (APP)	.267	11	15	5	4	2	0	0	4	2-0	0	4-0	2	1-0	.400	.421	.821
	Lansing (MID)	.274	28	95	13	26	7	1	0	9	1-2	1	15-1	21	2-0	.368	.372	.740
Minor Totals		.259	81	228	31	59	14	4	1	30	7-4	1	33-1	49	6-0	.368	.350	.718

Phillips, Eric
INFIELDER

HT: 6-2... **WT:** 195... **B-T:** R-R... **BORN:** 16 Jul 90, Carrollton, GA... **RESIDES:** Carrollton, GA... **EDUCATION:** Georgia Southern University... **TRANSACTIONS:** Selected by the Toronto Blue Jays in the 6th round of the 2012 June draft... Signed on June 10, 2012... **SIGNED BY:** Eric McQueen

YR	Club & League	AVG	G	AB	R	H	2B	3B	HR	RBI	SH-SF	HB	BB-IB	SO	SB-CS	SLG	OBP	OPS
2012	Vancouver (NOR)	.182	8	22	3	4	0	0	0	2	0-0	1	2-0	6	0-1	.182	.280	.462

Pierre, Gustavo
INFIELDER

HT: 6-2... **WT:** 183... **B-T:** R-R... **BORN:** 12 Dec 91, La Romana, DR... **RESIDES:** La Romana, DR... **EDUCATION:** NA... **TRANSACTIONS:** Signed by the Toronto Blue Jays on July 2, 2008... **SIGNED BY:** Hilario Soriano & Miguel Bernard

YR	Club & League	AVG	G	AB	R	H	2B	3B	HR	RBI	SH-SF	HB	BB-IB	SO	SB-CS	SLG	OBP	OPS
2009	Blue Jays (GCL)	.259	48	174	22	45	10	4	4	22	2-2	1	3-0	45	8-5	.431	.272	.703
2010	Auburn (NYP)	.236	66	250	29	59	12	3	3	22	3-4	1	17-0	64	8-4	.344	.283	.627
2011	Lansing (MID)	.187	56	187	25	35	4	2	2	18	1-0	1	13-0	52	6-3	.262	.244	.506
	Bluefield (APP)	.252	63	250	47	63	12	3	6	23	0-1	1	26-0	73	9-5	.396	.324	.720
2012	Lansing (MID)	.252	76	278	35	70	14	8	5	28	5-0	4	16-1	79	8-7	.414	.302	.716
Minor Totals		.239	309	1139	158	272	52	20	20	113	11-7	8	75-1	313	39-24	.372	.289	.661

Pillar, Kevin
OUTIELDER

HT: 6-0... **WT:** 200... **B-T:** R-R... **BORN:** 04 Jan 89, West Hills, CA... **RESIDES:** West Hills, CA... **EDUCATION:** California State Dominguez Hills ... **TRANSACTIONS:** Selected by the Toronto Blue Jays in the 32nd round of the 2011 June Draft... Signed on June 12, 2011... **SIGNED BY:** Kevin Fox

YR	Club & League	AVG	G	AB	R	H	2B	3B	HR	RBI	SH-SF	HB	BB-IB	SO	SB-CS	SLG	OBP	OPS
2011	Bluefield (APP)	.347	60	236	44	82	17	3	7	37	4-3	3	10-0	36	8-4	.534	.377	.911
2012	Lansing (MID)	.322	86	335	49	108	20	4	5	57	1-1	3	35-1	53	35-6	.451	.390	.841
	Dunedin (FSL)	.323	42	164	16	53	8	2	1	34	1-6	2	5-0	17	16-3	.415	.339	.754
Minor Totals		.331	188	735	109	243	45	9	13	128	6-10	8	50-1	106	59-13	.469	.375	.844

Pina, Carlos
PITCHER

HT: 5-11... **WT:** 169... **B-T:** L-L... **BORN:** 05 Mar 90, Carabobo, VZ... **RESIDES:** Carabobo, VZ... **EDUCATION:** NA... **TRANSACTIONS:** Signed by the Toronto Blue Jays on January 4, 2008... **SIGNED BY:** Rafael Moncada

YR	Club & League	W-L	ERA	G	GS	CG	SHO	SV	IP	H	R	ER	HR	HB	BB-IB	SO	WP	BK	OBA
2008	DSL Blue Jays2 (DSL)	4-3	3.69	13	13	0	0	0	68.1	68	35	28	3	3	13-0	64	5	0	.253
2009	Blue Jays (GCL)	3-2	1.57	12	10	0	0	0	51.2	46	23	9	2	2	16-0	35	3	0	.231
2010									Injured – Did Not Play										
2011									Injured – Did Not Play										
2012									Injured – Did Not Play										
Minor Totals		7-5	2.77	25	23	0	0	0	120.0	114	58	37	5	5	29-0	99	8	0	.244

Pompey, Dalton — *OUTFIELDER*

HT: 6-1... **WT:** 170... **B-T:** S-R... **BORN:** 11 Dec 92, Mississauga, ON... **RESIDES:** Mississauga, ON... **EDUCATION:** John Fraser High School... **TRANSACTIONS:** Selected by the Toronto Blue Jays in the 16th round of the 2010 June draft... Signed on June 15, 2010... **SIGNED BY:** Jamie Lehman

YR	Club & League	AVG	G	AB	R	H	2B	3B	HR	RBI	SH-SF	HB	BB-IB	SO	SB-CS	SLG	OBP	OPS
2010	Blue Jays (GCL)	.191	11	47	4	9	0	0	2	5	0-0	1	3-0	10	4-1	.319	.255	.574
2011	Blue Jays (GCL)	.259	42	158	34	41	7	2	4	12	1-0	1	24-0	35	19-0	.405	.361	.766
	Bluefield (APP)	.191	18	68	15	13	3	0	1	5	1-0	3	14-0	23	4-1	.279	.353	.632
2012	Vancouver (NOR)	.294	11	34	11	10	3	1	0	4	1-0	0	9-0	7	3-0	.441	.442	.883
	Bluefield (APP)	.357	4	14	2	5	1	1	0	1	0-0	0	0-0	2	1-0	.571	.357	.928
	Lansing (MID)	.227	5	22	1	5	0	1	0	3	1-0	0	1-0	5	1-1	.318	.261	.579
Minor Totals		.242	91	343	67	83	14	5	7	30	4-0	5	51-0	82	32-3	.373	.348	.722

Purdy, Nicholas — *PITCHER*

HT: 6-5... **WT:** 205... **B-T:** R-R... **BORN:** 02 Oct 89, Ajax, ON... **RESIDES:** Grafton, ON... **EDUCATION:** Hillsborough Junior College... **TRANSACTIONS:** Signed by the Toronto Blue Jays on March 20, 2010... **SIGNED BY:** Jamie Lehman

YR	Club & League	W-L	ERA	G	GS	CG	SHO	SV	IP	H	R	ER	HR	HB	BB-IB	SO	WP	BK	OBA
2010	Blue Jays (GCL)	3-4	3.76	12	10	0	0	0	55.0	48	26	23	6	5	16-0	50	2	3	.241
2011	Vancouver (NOR)	0-0	8.62	8	0	0	0	0	15.2	23	16	15	5	2	9-0	16	6	0	.348
	Blue Jays (GCL)	3-0	2.88	6	3	0	0	0	25.0	25	9	8	0	2	7-0	38	5	0	.255
	Bluefield (APP)	1-0	2.70	2	0	0	0	0	6.2	4	2	2	0	0	6-0	6	1	0	.167
2012	Vancouver (NOR)	2-3	3.96	19	2	0	0	0	38.2	40	19	17	3	4	22-1	33	6	0	.263
Minor Totals		9-7	4.15	47	15	0	0	0	141.0	140	72	65	14	13	60-1	143	20	3	.260

Ramirez, Carlos — *OUTFIELDER*

HT: 6-3... **WT:** 170... **B-T:** L-L... **BORN:** 24 Apr 91, Santo Domingo, DR... **RESIDES:** Santo Domingo, DR... **EDUCATION:** NA... **TRANSACTIONS:** Signed by the Toronto Blue Jays on March 5, 2009... **SIGNED BY:** Hilario Soriano

YR	Club & League	AVG	G	AB	R	H	2B	3B	HR	RBI	SH-SF	HB	BB-IB	SO	SB-CS	SLG	OBP	OPS
2009	DSL (DSL)	.229	52	179	29	41	5	1	3	14	1-0	5	15-1	56	4-3	.318	.307	.625
2010	Blue Jays (GCL)	.205	47	151	14	31	4	1	2	12	0-1	5	16-0	48	2-1	.285	.301	.586
2011	Bluefield (APP)	.232	40	112	18	26	7	2	2	9	0-0	1	10-0	39	2-1	.384	.301	.685
2012	Bluefield (APP)	.273	10	33	4	9	2	0	1	6	0-0	1	2-0	6	0-1	.424	.333	.757
	Vancouver (NOR)	.245	42	159	17	39	5	6	2	19	1-0	0	4-0	45	7-2	.390	.264	.654
Minor Totals		.230	191	634	82	146	23	10	10	60	2-1	12	47-1	194	15-8	.345	.295	.641

Rankin, Pierce — *CATCHER*

HT: 6-1... **WT:** 200... **B-T:** R-R... **BORN:** 26 Apr 89, Seattle, WA... **RESIDES:** Seattle, WA... **EDUCATION:** University of Wahington... **TRANSACTIONS:** Selected by the Toronto Blue Jays in the 38th round of the 2010 June Draft... Signed on June 16, 2010... **SIGNED BY:** Ryan Fox

YR	Club & League	AVG	G	AB	R	H	2B	3B	HR	RBI	SH-SF	HB	BB-IB	SO	SB-CS	SLG	OBP	OPS
2010	Blue Jays (GCL)	.265	41	136	17	36	11	1	4	22	1-1	7	15-0	33	2-1	.449	.365	.814
2011	Vancouver (NOR)	.230	38	126	25	29	4	0	3	8	0-1	5	20-0	35	2-4	.333	.355	.688
2012	Lansing (MID)	.162	10	37	6	6	1	0	1	3	0-0	1	1-0	12	0-0	.270	.205	.475
	New Hampshire (EAS)	.000	1	4	0	0	0	0	0	0	0-0	0	0-0	4	0-0	.000	.000	.000
	Dunedin (FSL)	.292	17	48	7	14	4	0	1	7	0-0	1	6-0	18	0-1	.438	.382	.820
Minor Totals		.242	107	351	55	85	20	1	9	40	1-2	14	42-0	102	4-6	.382	.345	.727

Rios, Francisco — *PITCHER*

HT: 6-1... **WT:** 180... **B-T:** R-R... **BORN:** 06 May 95, Monciova, MEX... **RESIDES:** Monciova, MEX... **EDUCATION:** NA... **TRANSACTIONS:** Signed by the Toronto Blue Jays on July 20, 2012... **SIGNED BY:** Ismael Cruz & Sandy Rosario

Robson, Thomas  — *PITCHER*

HT: 6-4... **WT:** 210... **B-T:** R-R... **BORN:** 27 Jun 93, Delta, BC... **RESIDES:** Delta, BC... **EDUCATION:** Delta High School... **TRANSACTIONS:** Selected by the Toronto Blue Jays in the 4th round of the 2011 June Draft... Signed on August 11, 2011... **SIGNED BY:** Jamie Lehman

YR	Club & League	W-L	ERA	G	GS	CG	SHO	SV	IP	H	R	ER	HR	HB	BB-IB	SO	WP	BK	OBA
2012	Bluefield (APP)	0-2	4.09	3	3	0	0	0	11.0	10	6	5	2	1	0-0	7	1	0	.238

Rodriguez, Carlos
PITCHER

HT: 6-0... **WT:** 185... **B-T:** L-L... **BORN:** 29 Jan 95, Valencia, VZ... **RESIDES:** Valencia, VZ... **EDUCATION:** NA... **TRANSACTIONS:** Signed by the Toronto Blue Jays on March 1, 2012... **SIGNED BY:** Ismael Cruz, Luis Marquez & Rafael Moncada

YR	Club & League	W-L	ERA	G	GS	CG	SHO	SV	IP	H	R	ER	HR	HB	BB-IB	SO	WP	BK	OBA
2012	DSL (DSL)	3-2	4.19	13	4	0	0	0	34.1	29	19	16	0	3	12-0	33	7	2	.232

Rodriguez, Dalton
PITCHER

HT: 6-1... **WT:** 180... **B-T:** R-R... **BORN:** 20 Aug 96, Mexicali, MEX... **RESIDES:** Mexicali, MEX... **EDUCATION:** NA... **TRANSACTIONS:** Signed by the Toronto Blue Jays on August 28, 2012... **SIGNED BY:** Ismael Cruz & Sandy Rosario

Rojas, Angel
INFIELDER

HT: 5-11... **WT:** 160... **B-T:** R-R... **BORN:** 07 Apr 93, Maracay, VZ... RESIDES: Turmero, VZ... **EDUCATION:** NA... **TRANSACTIONS:** Signed by the Toronto Blue Jays on December 18, 2009... **SIGNED BY:** Rafael Moncada

YR	Club & League	AVG	G	AB	R	H	2B	3B	HR	RBI	SH-SF	HB	BB-IB	SO	SB-CS	SLG	OBP	OPS
2010	DSL (DSL)	.169	43	130	11	22	3	0	0	3	2-0	1	6-0	38	7-3	.192	.212	.404
2011	DSL (DSL)	.199	62	211	27	42	4	2	0	10	6-1	4	24-0	62	15-5	.237	.292	.529
2012	DSL (DSL)	.271	63	218	32	59	7	3	0	21	8-3	6	28-0	50	11-6	.330	.365	.695
Minor Totals		.220	168	559	70	123	14	5	0	34	16-4	11	58-0	150	33-14	.263	.304	.567

Saez, Jorge
CATCHER

HT: 5-10... **WT:** 185... **B-T:** R-R... **BORN:** 28 Aug 90, Miami, FL... **RESIDES:** Miami, FL... **EDUCATION:** Lee University... **TRANSACTIONS:** Selected by the Toronto Blue Jays in the 32nd round of the 2012 June draft... Signed on June 10, 2012... **SIGNED BY:** Nate Murrie

YR	Club & League	AVG	G	AB	R	H	2B	3B	HR	RBI	SH-SF	HB	BB-IB	SO	SB-CS	SLG	OBP	OPS
2012	Blue Jays (GCL)	.200	36	110	19	22	5	0	3	21	0-1	0	23-0	19	4-1	.327	.336	.663

Salas, Roan
INFIELDER

HT: 5-11... **WT:** 175... **B-T:** R-R... **BORN:** 09 Jun 90, Coro, VZ... **RESIDES:** Coro, VZ... **EDUCATION:** NA... **TRANSACTIONS:** Signed by the Texas Rangers on August 21, 2006... Signed by the Tampa Bay Rays on December 16, 2008... Selected by the Toronto Blue Jays in the minor league phase of the Rule 5 Draft on December 9, 2010... **SIGNED BY:** Ronnie Blanco

YR	Club & League	AVG	G	AB	R	H	2B	3B	HR	RBI	SH-SF	HB	BB-IB	SO	SB-CS	SLG	OBP	OPS
2007	DSL (DSL)	.290	44	124	15	36	6	0	0	23	2-2	2	10-0	13	3-3	.339	.348	.687
2008	DSL Rangers1 (DSL)	.281	33	114	18	32	8	0	2	16	0-2	2	11-1	16	4-2	.404	.349	.753
2009	VSL (VSL)	.338	61	222	49	75	19	3	15	59	0-3	4	25-2	31	1-0	.653	.409	1.062
2010	VSL (VSL)	.345	60	220	35	76	16	2	5	42	1-4	6	23-0	24	3-1	.505	.415	.920
2011	Vancouver (NOR)	.259	39	139	19	36	10	1	4	14	0-0	4	5-0	31	1-0	.432	.304	.736
2012	Injured – Did Not Play																	
Minor Totals		.311	237	819	136	255	59	6	26	154	3-11	18	74-3	115	12-6	.493	.376	.869

Sanchez, Aaron
PITCHER

HT: 6-4... **WT:** 190... **B-T:** R-R... **BORN:** 01 Jul 92, Barstow, CA... **RESIDES:** Barstow, CA... **EDUCATION:** Barstow High School... **TRANSACTIONS:** Selected by the Toronto Blue Jays in the 1st round (supplemental - 34th overall) of the 2010 June Draft... Signed on June 8, 2010... **SIGNED BY:** Blake Crosby

YR	Club & League	W-L	ERA	G	GS	CG	SHO	SV	IP	H	R	ER	HR	HB	BB-IB	SO	WP	BK	OBA
2010	Blue Jays (GCL)	0-2	1.42	8	8	0	0	0	19.0	19	10	3	1	4	12-0	28	3	0	.271
	Auburn (NYP)	0-1	4.50	2	2	0	0	0	6.0	4	5	3	0	0	5-0	9	1	0	.182
2011	Bluefield (APP)	3-2	5.48	11	6	0	0	1	42.2	45	27	26	4	1	18-0	43	2	0	.269
	Vancouver (NOR)	0-1	4.63	3	3	0	0	0	11.2	8	6	6	0	1	8-0	13	1	0	.195
2012	Lansing (MID)	8-5	2.49	25	18	0	0	0	90.1	64	33	25	3	7	51-0	97	6	2	.204
Minor Totals		11-11	3.34	49	37	0	0	1	169.2	140	81	63	8	13	94-0	190	13	2	.228

Sanchez, Cesar
PITCHER

HT: 6-3... **WT:** 193... **B-T:** R-R... **BORN:** 29 Aug 91, Santo Domingo, DR... **RESIDES:** Santo Domingo, DR... **EDUCATION:** NA... **TRANSACTIONS:** Signed by the Toronto Blue Jays on June 30, 2009... **SIGNED BY:** Hilario Soriano

YR	Club & League	W-L	ERA	G	GS	CG	SHO	SV	IP	H	R	ER	HR	HB	BB-IB	SO	WP	BK	OBA
2009	DSL (DSL)	0-2	4.13	8	8	0	0	0	24.0	23	13	11	0	7	13-0	25	5	1	.256
2010	DSL (DSL)	2-5	3.69	14	7	0	0	0	53.2	42	28	22	0	12	20-1	35	5	0	.219
2011	DSL (DSL)	4-7	3.66	16	11	0	0	0	64.0	47	39	26	0	11	25-0	63	12	0	.200
Minor Totals		6-14	3.75	38	26	0	0	0	141.2	112	80	59	0	30	58-1	123	22	1	.217

Schaeffer, Chris

CATCHER

HT: 5-10... **WT:** 195... **B-T:** R-R... **BORN:** 19 Nov 87, Port St. Lucie, FL... **RESIDES:** Port St. Lucie, FL... **EDUCATION:** North Carolina State University... **TRANSACTIONS:** Signed by the Toronto Blue Jays on June 12, 2011... **SIGNED BY:** John Hendricks

YR	Club & League	AVG	G	AB	R	H	2B	3B	HR	RBI	SH-SF	HB	BB-IB	SO	SB-CS	SLG	OBP	OPS
2011	Bluefield (APP)	.378	10	37	6	14	4	0	1	7	1-1	0	1-0	5	0-0	.568	.385	.953
	Vancouver (NOR)	.210	26	81	6	17	3	0	0	8	0-0	2	9-0	21	0-0	.247	.304	.551
2012	Blue Jays (GCL)	.000	3	7	2	0	0	0	0	0	0-0	0	2-0	1	0-0	.000	.222	.222
	Lansing (MID)	.209	28	86	14	18	6	0	2	19	2-1	5	9-0	17	0-0	.349	.317	.666
Minor Totals		.232	67	211	28	49	13	0	3	34	3-2	7	21-0	44	0-0	.336	.320	.656

Segovia, Rolando

INFIELDER

HT: 5-11... **WT:** 165... **B-T:** S-R... **BORN:** 26 Oct 94, Barquisimeto, VZ... **RESIDES:** Barquisimeto, VZ... **EDUCATION:** NA... **TRANSACTIONS:** Signed by the Toronto Blue Jays on December 20, 2011... **SIGNED BY:** Ismael Cruz & Luis Marquez

YR	Club & League	AVG	G	AB	R	H	2B	3B	HR	RBI	SH-SF	HB	BB-IB	SO	SB-CS	SLG	OBP	OPS
2012	DSL (DSL)	.299	44	164	33	49	12	2	1	18	3-0	5	22-0	33	18-6	.415	.398	.813

Sikula, Arik

PITCHER

HT: 6-0... **WT:** 193... **B-T:** R-R... **BORN:** 21 Dec 88, South Charlestown, WV... **RESIDES:** South Charlestown, WV... **EDUCATION:** Marshall University... **TRANSACTIONS:** Selected by the Toronto Blue Jays in the 36th round of the 2011 June Draft... Signed on June 12, 2011... **SIGNED BY:** Nick Manno

YR	Club & League	W-L	ERA	G	GS	CG	SHO	SV	IP	H	R	ER	HR	HB	BB-IB	SO	WP	BK	OBA
2011	Bluefield (APP)	1-1	2.97	18	0	0	0	1	30.1	38	12	10	2	1	9-0	35	3	0	.309
2012	Vancouver (NOR)	2-1	2.45	29	0	0	0	10	36.2	25	10	10	3	3	10-0	31	4	0	.189
Minor Totals		3-2	2.69	47	0	0	0	11	67.0	63	22	20	5	4	19-0	66	7	0	.247

Silviano, John

CATCHER

HT: 5-11... **WT:** 190... **B-T:** L-R... **BORN:** 11 Jul 94, Hypoluxo, FL... **RESIDES:** Hypoluxo, FL... **EDUCATION:** Summit Christian School... **TRANSACTIONS:** Selected by the Toronto Blue Jays in the 13th round of the 2012 June draft... Signed on June 10, 2012... **SIGNED BY:** Matt O'Brien

YR	Club & League	AVG	G	AB	R	H	2B	3B	HR	RBI	SH-SF	HB	BB-IB	SO	SB-CS	SLG	OBP	OPS
2012	Blue Jays (GCL)	.164	39	116	11	19	4	2	2	17	0-2	1	22-0	21	0-3	.284	.298	.582

Smith Jr., Gregory

PITCHER

HT: 6-2... **WT:** 190... **B-T:** L-L... **BORN:** 22 Dec 83, Alexandria, LA... **RESIDES:** Sulphur, LA... **EDUCATION:** Louisiana State University... **TRANSACTIONS:** Selected by the Arizona Diamondbacks in the 6th round of the 2005 June Draft... Signed on June 9, 2005... Traded to the Oakland Athletics on December 14, 2007... Traded to the Colorado Rockies on November 8, 2008... Signed by the New York Yankees on June 13, 2011... Signed by the Boston Red Sox on August 18, 2011... Signed by the Los Angeles Angels of Anaheim on January 23, 2012... Signed by the Toronto Blue Jays on December 11, 2012... **SIGNED BY:** Mike Valarezzo

YR	Club & League	W-L	ERA	G	GS	CG	SHO	SV	IP	H	R	ER	HR	HB	BB-IB	SO	WP	BK	OBA
2005	Missoula (PIO)	8-5	4.15	16	14	0	0	0	82.1	69	40	38	8	5	18-2	100	6	0	.231
2006	Lancaster (CAL)	9-0	1.63	13	13	2	2	0	88.1	57	21	16	3	4	31-0	71	2	1	.190
	Tennessee (SOU)	5-4	3.90	11	11	0	0	0	60.0	65	32	26	4	4	23-0	38	2	4	.284
2007	Mobile (SOU)	5-3	3.36	12	12	2	0	0	69.2	64	30	26	7	2	14-0	62	2	1	.251
	Tucson (PCL)	4-2	3.78	10	10	1	0	0	52.1	61	27	22	4	0	18-0	34	3	1	.296
2008	Sacramento River (PCL)	0-1	3.00	1	1	0	0	0	6.0	6	2	2	0	0	1-0	4	0	0	.261
	OAKLAND (AL)	7-16	4.16	32	32	2	0	0	190.1	169	92	88	21	3	87-5	111	5	1	.243
2009	Modesto (CAL)	1-0	3.86	2	2	0	0	0	11.2	11	6	5	1	0	4-0	7	1	0	.250
	Tulsa (TEX)	0-1	7.88	2	2	0	0	0	8.0	12	7	7	3	0	1-0	5	0	0	.353
	Colorado Springs Sky (PCL)	1-2	7.28	7	7	0	0	0	29.2	34	24	24	5	1	11-0	15	2	0	.309
2010	COLORADO (NL)	1-2	6.23	8	8	0	0	0	39.0	49	28	27	8	1	24-2	31	1	0	.322
	Colorado Springs Sky (PCL)	2-5	6.12	15	15	0	0	0	75.0	88	59	51	14	1	30-1	49	5	1	.288
2011	Scranton/Wilkes-Barre (INT)	3-3	4.84	13	10	0	0	0	57.2	68	34	31	9	1	27-0	36	2	0	.304
	Pawtucket Red (INT)	2-1	3.75	4	4	0	0	0	24.0	19	10	10	2	1	7-0	15	0	0	.213
2012	Arkansas (TEX)	2-1	4.37	6	6	1	0	0	35.0	44	19	17	5	1	7-0	23	1	1	.310
	Salt Lake (PCL)	9-10	3.97	22	21	0	0	0	138.1	136	67	61	18	3	38-0	83	5	2	.257
Minor Totals		51-38	4.10	134	128	6	2	0	738.0	734	378	336	83	23	230-3	542	31	11	.263
MAJOR TOTALS		8-18	4.51	40	40	2	0	0	229.1	218	120	115	29	4	111-7	142	6	1	.257

Smith, Dwight

OUTFIELDER

HT: 5-11... **WT:** 185... **B-T:** L-R... **BORN:** 26 Oct 92, Peachtree City, FL... **RESIDES:** Peachtree City, FL... **EDUCATION:** McIntosh High School... **TRANSACTIONS:** Selected by the Toronto Blue Jays in the 1st round (supplemental – 53rd overall) of the 2011 June draft... Signed on August 14, 2011... **SIGNED BY:** Eric McQueen

YR	Club & League	AVG	G	AB	R	H	2B	3B	HR	RBI	SH-SF	HB	BB-IB	SO	SB-CS	SLG	OBP	OPS
2012	Bluefield (APP)	.226	41	159	20	36	6	0	4	21	0-0	3	11-0	22	1-1	.340	.289	.629
	Vancouver (NOR)	.175	18	63	5	11	3	1	0	8	0-1	1	6-0	11	0-0	.254	.254	.507
Minor Totals		.212	59	222	25	47	9	1	4	29	0-1	4	17-0	33	1-1	.315	.279	.594

Smith, Egan — PITCHER

HT: 6-5... **WT:** 200... **B-T:** L-L... **BORN:** 16 Mar 89, American Fork, UT... **RESIDES:** Pleasant Grove, UT... **EDUCATION:** Southern Navada College... **TRANSACTIONS:** Selected by the Toronto Blue Jays in the 7th round of the 2009 June Draft... Signed on June 14, 2009... **SIGNED BY:** Dan Cholowsky

YR	Club & League	W-L	ERA	G	GS	CG	SHO	SV	IP	H	R	ER	HR	HB	BB-IB	SO	WP	BK	OBA
2009	Auburn (NYP)	2-1	2.56	9	9	0	0	0	38.2	37	14	11	2	0	11-0	36	0	1	.239
2010	Auburn (NYP)	2-0	0.00	2	2	0	0	0	11.0	9	3	0	0	0	2-0	11	1	0	.205
	Lansing (MID)	7-4	4.54	15	14	0	0	0	81.1	100	47	41	4	2	22-0	65	5	1	.303
2011	Lansing (MID)	7-7	3.84	24	24	1	0	0	117.1	141	67	50	10	2	24-0	95	4	0	.298
2012	Dunedin (FSL)	8-7	3.49	23	15	0	0	1	98.0	94	42	38	4	2	34-2	70	6	0	.247
Minor Totals		26-19	3.64	73	64	1	0	1	346.1	381	173	140	20	6	93-2	277	16	2	.276

Smoral, Matt — PITCHER

HT: 6-8... **WT:** 220... **B-T:** L-L... **BORN:** 18 Mar 94, Solon, OH... **RESIDES: Key Biscayne, FL**... **EDUCATION:** Solon High School... **TRANSACTIONS:** Selected by the Toronto Blue Jays in the 1st round (supplemental – 50th overall) of the 2012 June Draft... Signed on June 18, 2012... **SIGNED BY:** Coulson Barbiche

Solarte, Alejandro — PITCHER

HT: 6-4... **WT:** 180... **B-T:** L-L... **BORN:** 22 Sep 94, Sucre, VZ... **RESIDES:** Sucre, VZ... **EDUCATION:** NA... **TRANSACTIONS:** Signed by the Blue Jays on September 9, 2011... **SIGNED BY:** Marco Paddy & Robinson Garces

YR	Club & League	W-L	ERA	G	GS	CG	SHO	SV	IP	H	R	ER	HR	HB	BB-IB	SO	WP	BK	OBA
2012	DSL (DSL)	3-0	1.53	9	2	0	0	0	29.1	10	6	5	0	0	10-0	25	2	1	.104

Sotillo, Andres — CATCHER

HT: 5-11... **WT:** 180... **B-T:** R-R... **BORN:** 28 Dec 93, Tucupita, VZ... **RESIDES:** Tucupita, VZ... **EDUCATION:** NA... **TRANSACTIONS:** Signed by the Toronto Blue Jays on January 16, 2012... **SIGNED BY:** Ismael Cruz & Luis Marquez

YR	Club & League	AVG	G	AB	R	H	2B	3B	HR	RBI	SH-SF	HB	BB-IB	SO	SB-CS	SLG	OBP	OPS
2012	DSL (DSL)	.305	43	105	17	32	5	0	1	14	0-0	9	10-0	23	8-4	.381	.411	.792

Spano, Joe — PITCHER

HT: 5-10... **WT:** 175... **B-T:** L-L... **BORN:** 27 Oct 89, Verona, NJ... **RESIDES:** Verona, NJ... **EDUCATION:** University of Notre Dame... **TRANSACTIONS:** Signed by Toronto Blue Jays on June 10, 2012... **SIGNED BY:** Mike Medici

YR	Club & League	W-L	ERA	G	GS	CG	SHO	SV	IP	H	R	ER	HR	HB	BB-IB	SO	WP	BK	OBA
2012	Bluefield (APP)	1-1	5.00	17	0	0	0	1	27.0	29	16	15	0	0	20-1	33	8	0	.282

Spoone, Chorye — PITCHER

HT: 6-1... **WT:** 215... **B-T:** R-R... **BORN:** 16 Sep 85, Baltimore, MD... **RESIDES:** Pasadena, MD... **EDUCATION:** Catonsville Community College... **TRANSACTIONS:** Selected by the Baltimore Orioles in the 8th round of the 2005 June Draft... Signed on June 14, 2005... Signed by the Boston Red Sox on November 21, 2011... Signed by the Toronto Blue Jays on July 19, 2012... **SIGNED BY:** Dave Holland

YR	Club & League	W-L	ERA	G	GS	CG	SHO	SV	IP	H	R	ER	HR	HB	BB-IB	SO	WP	BK	OBA
2005	Bluefield (APP)	2-5	8.03	15	3	0	0	0	24.2	27	25	22	3	2	13-0	27	11	1	.273
2006	Delmarva (SAL)	7-9	3.56	26	25	0	0	0	129.0	118	72	51	5	14	80-0	90	14	0	.241
2007	Frederick (CAR)	10-9	3.26	26	25	3	0	0	152.0	108	65	55	8	13	67-0	133	5	1	.200
2008	Bowie (EAS)	3-3	4.57	9	9	0	0	0	41.1	40	23	21	4	1	27-0	32	4	1	.252
2009	Orioles (GCL)	0-1	4.38	5	5	0	0	0	12.1	9	6	6	1	0	2-0	11	0	0	.220
	Aberdeen (NYP)	0-0	0.00	1	1	0	0	0	3.0	1	0	0	0	0	3-0	3	0	0	.100
	Frederick (CAR)	0-2	9.42	4	4	0	0	0	14.1	17	16	15	3	0	14-0	12	4	0	.298
2010	Bowie (EAS)	7-6	4.02	24	24	0	0	0	132.0	132	71	59	12	14	79-1	88	10	1	.267
2011	Norfolk (INT)	2-1	5.50	8	8	0	0	0	34.1	41	26	21	1	2	26-2	16	6	0	.293
	Bowie (EAS)	5-5	4.11	23	11	1	0	1	87.2	83	46	40	5	11	41-0	64	3	0	.250
2012	Pawtucket Red (INT)	1-1	2.79	14	0	0	0	0	19.1	18	8	6	2	1	20-0	10	2	0	.254
	Portland Sea (EAS)	2-1	4.15	12	0	0	0	0	21.2	19	12	10	1	2	14-0	17	2	0	.237
	New Hampshire (EAS)	0-2	3.18	16	1	0	0	0	22.2	14	9	8	1	1	15-0	15	0	0	.182
Minor Totals		39-45	4.07	183	116	4	0	1	694.1	627	379	314	46	61	401-3	518	61	4	.242

Stroman, Marcus — PITCHER

HT: 5-9... **WT:** 185... **B-T:** R-R... **BORN:** 01 May 91, Medford, NY... **RESIDES: Medford, NY**... **EDUCATION:** Duke University... **TRANSACTIONS:** Selected by the Toronto Blue Jays in the 1st round (22nd overall) of the 2012 June Draft... Signed on July 3, 2012... **SIGNED BY:** John Hendricks

YR	Club & League	W-L	ERA	G	GS	CG	SHO	SV	IP	H	R	ER	HR	HB	BB-IB	SO	WP	BK	OBA
2012	Vancouver (NOR)	1-0	3.18	7	0	0	0	0	11.1	8	5	4	0	0	3-0	15	0	0	.190
	New Hampshire (EAS)	2-0	3.38	8	0	0	0	0	8.0	8	3	3	1	0	6-0	8	1	0	.258
Minor Totals		3-0	3.26	15	0	0	0	0	19.1	16	8	7	1	0	9-0	23	1	0	.219

Suero, Hamly — *PITCHER*

HT: 6-3... **WT:** 195... **B-T:** R-R... **BORN:** 17 Oct 94, Pimentel, DR... **RESIDES: Pimentel, DR**... **EDUCATION:** NA... **TRANSACTIONS:** Signed by the Toronto Blue Jays on July 3, 2012... **SIGNED BY:** Ismael Cruz, Sandy Rosario & Jean Carlos Alvarez

Sweeney, Kellen — *INFIELDER*

HT: 6-0... **WT:** 180... **B-T:** L-R... **BORN:** 14 Sep 91, Cedar Rapids, IA... **RESIDES:** Tampa, FL... **EDUCATION:** Jefferson, High School... **TRANSACTIONS:** Selected by the Toronto Blue Jays in the 2nd round of the 2010 June draft... Signed on July 26, 2010... **SIGNED BY:** Wes Penick

YR	Club & League	AVG	G	AB	R	H	2B	3B	HR	RBI	SH-SF	HB	BB-IB	SO	SB-CS	SLG	OBP	OPS
2010	Blue Jays (GCL)	.267	16	45	7	12	3	1	1	7	1-0	0	15-0	12	0-1	.444	.450	.894
2011	Bluefield (APP)	.114	9	35	4	4	1	0	0	1	0-0	0	9-0	17	1-0	.143	.295	.438
2012	Lansing (MID)	.179	43	140	13	25	2	1	0	12	0-1	1	23-2	30	1-2	.207	.297	.504
	Vancouver (NOR)	.229	67	245	35	56	15	2	5	29	0-4	4	35-0	47	5-0	.367	.330	.697
Minor Totals		.209	135	465	59	97	21	4	6	49	1-5	5	82-2	106	7-3	.310	.330	.640

Talley, Jon — *CATCHER*

HT: 6-4... **WT:** 220... **B-T:** L-R... **BORN:** 18 Feb 89, Oceanside, CA... **RESIDES:** Oceanside, CA... **EDUCATION:** Carlsbad High School... **TRANSACTIONS:** Selected by the Toronto Blue Jays in the 13th round of the 2007 June draft... Signed on June 10, 2007... **SIGNED BY:** Demerius Pittman

YR	Club & League	AVG	G	AB	R	H	2B	3B	HR	RBI	SH-SF	HB	BB-IB	SO	SB-CS	SLG	OBP	OPS
2007	Blue Jays (GCL)	.227	25	75	3	17	3	0	1	10	0-0	1	4-0	21	0-1	.307	.275	.582
2008	Blue Jays (GCL)	.300	42	140	18	42	7	1	6	29	0-3	3	9-1	48	1-0	.493	.348	.841
	Lansing (MID)	.500	1	2	0	1	0	0	0	0	0-0	0	1-0	0	0-0	.500	.667	1.167
2009	Lansing (MID)	.228	76	241	23	55	10	1	3	25	2-1	5	28-0	71	0-0	.315	.320	.635
2010	Lansing (MID)	.273	7	22	2	6	2	0	0	3	0-0	0	3-0	5	0-1	.364	.360	.724
	Dunedin (FSL)	.231	72	242	34	56	19	0	6	36	0-0	3	19-1	87	0-1	.384	.295	.679
2011	Dunedin (FSL)	.241	102	378	58	91	21	1	20	63	0-4	3	37-0	99	0-1	.460	.310	.770
2012	Dunedin (FSL)	.259	111	410	55	106	27	1	9	68	0-5	5	48-2	105	2-1	.395	.340	.735
Minor Totals		.248	436	1510	193	374	89	4	45	234	2-13	20	149-4	436	3-5	.401	.321	.722

Taylor, Nico — *OUTFIELDER*

HT: 6-4... **WT:** 215... **B-T:** R-R... **BORN:** 09 Feb 92, McKinney, TX... **RESIDES:** McKinney, TX... **EDUCATION:** Northwood University... **TRANSACTIONS:** Selected by the Toronto Blue Jays in the 38th round of the 2011 June draft... Signed on June 12, 2011... **SIGNED BY:** Michael Wagner

YR	Club & League	AVG	G	AB	R	H	2B	3B	HR	RBI	SH-SF	HB	BB-IB	SO	SB-CS	SLG	OBP	OPS
2011	Blue Jays (GCL)	.319	30	91	17	29	8	0	3	13	1-0	1	15-0	24	2-2	.505	.421	.926
2012	Bluefield (APP)	.268	49	164	21	44	9	1	1	14	1-1	1	13-0	49	5-3	.354	.324	.678
Minor Totals		.286	79	255	38	73	17	1	4	27	2-1	2	28-0	73	7-5	.408	.360	.768

Tejada, Juan — *OUTFIELDER*

HT: 6-3... **WT:** 181... **B-T:** R-R... **BORN:** 12 Feb 94, Bani, DR... **RESIDES:** Bani, DR... **EDUCATION:** NA... **TRANSACTIONS:** Signed by the Toronto Blue Jays on March 22, 2011... **SIGNED BY:** Marco Paddy & Lorenzo Perez

YR	Club & League	AVG	G	AB	R	H	2B	3B	HR	RBI	SH-SF	HB	BB-IB	SO	SB-CS	SLG	OBP	OPS
2012	DSL (DSL)	.236	58	182	25	43	8	0	1	12	0-2	4	20-0	66	16-12	.297	.322	.619

Tepera, Ryan — *PITCHER*

HT: 6-1... **WT:** 180... **B-T:** R-R... **BORN:** 03 Nov 87, Lake Jackson, TX... **RESIDES:** Lake Jackson, TX... **EDUCATION:** Sam Houston University... **TRANSACTIONS:** Selected by the Toronto Blue Jays in the 19th round of the 2009 June Draft... Signed on July 1, 2009... **SIGNED BY:** Aaron Jersild

YR	Club & League	W-L	ERA	G	GS	CG	SHO	SV	IP	H	R	ER	HR	HB	BB-IB	SO	WP	BK	OBA
2009	Blue Jays (GCL)	3-1	1.72	11	5	1	1	0	36.2	19	11	7	4	3	4-0	42	2	0	.150
2010	Lansing (MID)	9-6	3.98	24	22	0	0	0	120.0	113	61	53	7	4	44-1	79	11	0	.251
2011	Dunedin (FSL)	11-6	4.43	27	23	0	0	0	146.1	156	75	72	13	5	38-1	93	11	0	.276
2012	Dunedin (FSL)	1-3	7.71	5	5	1	0	0	21.0	27	19	18	3	2	12-0	14	1	1	.310
	New Hampshire (EAS)	7-3	4.84	16	15	0	0	0	74.1	82	44	40	4	7	37-0	57	6	0	.280
Minor Totals		31-19	4.29	83	70	2	1	0	398.1	397	210	190	31	21	135-2	285	31	1	.261

Thon, Dickie — *INFIELDER*

HT: 6-2... **WT:** 190... **B-T:** R-R... **BORN:** 16 Nov 91, Houston, TX... **RESIDES:** Dorado, PR... **EDUCATION:** Academia Perpetuo Socorro High School... **TRANSACTIONS:** Selected by the Toronto Blue Jays in the 5th round of the 2010 June draft... Signed on August 16, 2010... **SIGNED BY:** Jorge Rivera

YR	Club & League	AVG	G	AB	R	H	2B	3B	HR	RBI	SH-SF	HB	BB-IB	SO	SB-CS	SLG	OBP	OPS
2011	Blue Jays (GCL)	.223	45	121	23	27	3	0	3	15	2-0	5	23-0	44	6-2	.322	.369	.691
2012	Bluefield (APP)	.221	48	149	18	33	5	1	2	14	1-1	6	19-0	34	7-3	.309	.331	.640
Minor Totals		.222	93	270	41	60	8	1	5	29	3-1	11	42-0	78	13-5	.315	.349	.664

Tinoco, Jesus — *PITCHER*

HT: 6-4... **WT:** 190... **B-T:** R-R... **BORN:** 30 Apr 95, Piar, VZ... **RESIDES:** Pair, VZ... **EDUCATION:** NA... **TRANSACTIONS:** Signed by the Toronto Blue Jays on September 22, 2011... **SIGNED BY:** Marco Paddy & Rafael Moncada

YR	Club & League	W-L	ERA	G	GS	CG	SHO	SV	IP	H	R	ER	HR	HB	BB-IB	SO	WP	BK	OBA
2012	DSL (DSL)	0-4	4.14	12	7	0	0	0	37.0	37	24	17	0	3	12-0	26	6	0	.266
	Blue Jays (GCL)	1-1	6.00	2	0	0	0	0	6.0	7	4	4	0	1	1-0	8	0	1	.280
Minor Totals		1-5	4.40	14	7	0	0	0	43.0	44	28	21	0	4	13-0	34	6	1	.268

Tirado, Alberto — *PITCHER*

HT: 6-0... **WT:** 180... **B-T:** R-R... **BORN:** 10 Dec 94, Nagua, DR... **RESIDES:** Nagua, DR... **EDUCATION:** NA... **TRANSACTIONS:** Signed by the Toronto Blue Jays on July 7, 2011... **SIGNED BY:** Marco Paddy & Domingo Toribio

YR	Club & League	W-L	ERA	G	GS	CG	SHO	SV	IP	H	R	ER	HR	HB	BB-IB	SO	WP	BK	OBA
2012	Blue Jays (GCL)	1-2	2.68	11	11	0	0	0	37.0	28	12	11	0	1	12-0	34	2	0	.217
	Bluefield (APP)	2-0	2.45	3	3	0	0	0	11.0	4	3	3	0	3	5-0	5	3	0	.121
Minor Totals		3-2	2.63	14	14	0	0	0	48.0	32	15	14	0	4	17-0	39	5	0	.198

Tolentino, Nelson — *PITCHER*

HT: 6-2... **WT:** 190... **B-T:** R-R... **BORN:** 02 Oct 93, La Vega, DR... **RESIDES:** La Vega, DR... **EDUCATION:** NA... **TRANSACTIONS:** Signed by the Toronto Blue Jays on July 3, 2012... **SIGNED BY:** Ismael Cruz, Sandy Rosario & Lorenzo Perez

Tolisano, John — *OUTFIELDER*

HT: 5-11... **WT:** 190... **B-T:** S-R... **BORN:** 07 Oct 88, Sanibel, FL... **RESIDES:** Sanibel, FL... **EDUCATION:** Estero High School... **TRANSACTIONS:** Selected by the Toronto Blue Jays in the 2nd round of the 2007 June draft... Signed on June 14, 2007... **SIGNED BY:** Joel Grampietro

YR	Club & League	AVG	G	AB	R	H	2B	3B	HR	RBI	SH-SF	HB	BB-IB	SO	SB-CS	SLG	OBP	OPS
2007	Blue Jays (GCL)	.246	49	183	35	45	5	0	10	33	0-2	0	26-0	40	7-1	.437	.336	.773
2008	Lansing (MID)	.229	120	432	64	99	20	8	6	47	1-6	1	56-0	110	5-2	.354	.315	.669
2009	Dunedin (FSL)	.232	106	401	53	93	19	2	12	58	1-6	1	44-0	78	5-4	.379	.305	.384
2010	Dunedin (FSL)	.252	61	218	39	55	12	3	5	21	1-2	0	29-1	65	4-3	.404	.337	.741
2011	New Hampshire (EAS)	.221	111	339	46	75	22	1	14	53	0-3	2	47-0	101	7-4	.416	.317	.733
2012	New Hampshire (EAS)	.250	116	436	62	109	27	3	12	42	6-1	1	53-0	82	20-13	.408	.332	.740
Minor Totals		.237	563	2009	299	476	105	17	59	254	9-20	5	255-1	476	48-27	.394	.322	.716

Torres, Jonathan — *PITCHER*

HT: 6-4... **WT:** 190... **B-T:** L-L... **BORN:** 31 Dec 94, Puerto Ayacucho, VZ... **RESIDES:** La Asuncion, VZ... **EDUCATION:** NA... **TRANSACTIONS:** Signed by the Toronto Blue Jays on March 1, 2012... **SIGNED BY:** Ismael Cruz, Luis Marquez & Rafael Moncada

YR	Club & League	W-L	ERA	G	GS	CG	SHO	SV	IP	H	R	ER	HR	HB	BB-IB	SO	WP	BK	OBA
2012	DSL (DSL)	0-1	4.29	11	4	0	0	0	21.0	17	11	10	0	6	21-0	24	3	1	.243

Turner, Colton — *PITCHER*

HT: 6-3... **WT:** 185... **B-T:** L-L... **BORN:** 17 Jan 91, Cleburne, TX... **RESIDES:** Cleburne, TX... **EDUCATION:** Texas State University... **TRANSACTIONS:** Selected by the Toronto Blue Jays in the 21st round of the 2012 June draft... Signed on June 10, 2012... **SIGNED BY:** Mike Burns

YR	Club & League	W-L	ERA	G	GS	CG	SHO	SV	IP	H	R	ER	HR	HB	BB-IB	SO	WP	BK	OBA
2012	Vancouver (NOR)	4-0	1.57	14	4	0	0	0	34.1	23	6	6	0	1	17-0	29	2	0	.200

Urena, Richard — *INFIELDER*

HT: 6-1... **WT:** 170... **B-T:** L-R... **BORN:** 26 Feb 96, San Francisco De Maci... **RESIDES:** San Francisco De Maci... **EDUCATION:** NA... **TRANSACTIONS:** Signed by the Toronto Blue Jays on July 3, 2012... **SIGNED BY:** Ismael Cruz, Sandy Rosario & Luciano Del Rosario

Uviedo, Ronald — PITCHER

HT: 6-1... **WT:** 160... **B-T:** R-R... **BORN:** 07 Oct 86, Guarico, VZ... **RESIDES:** Guarico, VZ... **EDUCATION:** NA... **TRANSACTIONS:** Signed by the Seattle Mariners on July 2, 2003... Signed by the Pittsburgh Pirates on May 5, 2006... Traded to the Toronto Blue Jays on June 1, 2010... **SIGNED BY:** Luis Martinez

YR	Club & League	W-L	ERA	G	GS	CG	SHO	SV	IP	H	R	ER	HR	HB	BB-IB	SO	WP	BK	OBA
2004	VSL (VSL)	2-1	5.81	11	2	0	0	0	31.0	44	23	20	2	3	13-1	20	3	0	.333
2005	VSL (VSL)	4-3	2.76	12	10	1	0	0	62.0	42	22	19	2	5	17-1	52	5	0	.193
2006	VSL (VSL)	2-0	2.02	25	0	0	0	11	35.2	31	13	8	1	1	10-1	44	5	1	.233
2007	Lynchburg (CAR)	0-0	4.09	4	0	0	0	0	11.0	9	5	5	2	1	3-0	7	0	0	.225
	State College (NYP)	2-0	3.92	21	0	0	0	12	20.2	16	9	9	4	1	3-0	26	1	0	.216
	Hickory (SAL)	0-0	9.00	3	0	0	0	0	3.0	3	3	3	1	0	2-0	7	0	0	.250
2008	Hickory (SAL)	3-1	3.01	33	0	0	0	5	71.2	70	31	24	8	3	15-0	76	7	0	.248
	Lynchburg (CAR)	0-0	2.25	7	0	0	0	0	16.0	5	4	4	1	0	5-0	12	0	0	.094
2009	Pirates (GCL)	0-1	3.24	3	3	0	0	0	8.1	8	4	3	0	0	2-0	10	0	0	.229
	Lynchburg (CAR)	5-5	3.36	23	18	0	0	3	101.2	98	42	38	12	3	28-1	79	0	3	.254
2010	Altoona (EAS)	0-2	3.22	16	0	0	0	0	22.1	13	8	8	3	0	12-0	28	3	0	.165
	New Hampshire (EAS)	5-3	5.31	25	5	0	0	1	57.2	56	41	34	12	3	27-2	65	3	0	.241
2011	Las Vegas (PCL)	1-0	4.74	24	0	0	0	0	38.0	36	23	20	5	2	15-0	43	4	0	.245
	New Hampshire (EAS)	3-1	4.29	26	0	0	0	1	35.2	37	17	17	3	0	13-0	39	3	1	.266
2012	Las Vegas (PCL)	0-0	3.00	3	0	0	0	0	6.0	5	3	2	0	0	2-0	5	0	1	.227
	New Hampshire (EAS)	5-3	2.97	43	0	0	0	7	57.2	51	23	19	4	3	25-0	57	8	1	.231
Minor Totals		32-20	3.63	279	38	1	0	40	578.1	524	271	233	60	25	192-6	570	42	7	.238

Valeriote, Shaun — INFIELDER

HT: 6-1... **WT:** 200... **B-T:** R-R... **BORN:** 22 Jan 90, Guelph, ON... **RESIDES:** Guelph, ON... **EDUCATION:** Brock University... **TRANSACTIONS:** Selected by the Toronto Blue Jays in the 39th round of the 2012 June draft... Signed on June 10, 2012... **SIGNED BY:** Jamie Lehman

YR	Club & League	AVG	G	AB	R	H	2B	3B	HR	RBI	SH-SF	HB	BB-IB	SO	SB-CS	SLG	OBP	OPS
2012	Blue Jays (GCL)	.227	27	88	17	20	4	0	2	12	0-0	1	12-0	25	0-1	.341	.327	.668

Van Kirk, Brian — OUTFIELDER

HT: 6-1... **WT:** 195... **B-T:** R-R... **BORN:** 10 Aug 85, Southwest Ranches, FL... **RESIDES:** Southwest Ranches, FL... **EDUCATION:** Oral Roberts University... **TRANSACTIONS:** Selected by the Toronto Blue Jays in the 21st round of the 2008 June draft... Signed on June 14, 2007... **SIGNED BY:** Ty Nichols

YR	Club & League	AVG	G	AB	R	H	2B	3B	HR	RBI	SH-SF	HB	BB-IB	SO	SB-CS	SLG	OBP	OPS
2008	Auburn (NYP)	.282	59	181	24	51	12	1	4	37	0-2	1	34-0	54	1-0	.425	.394	.819
2009	Lansing (MID)	.278	105	370	54	103	21	2	13	63	0-2	8	60-1	95	5-0	.451	.389	.840
	New Hampshire (EAS)	.111	10	36	3	4	2	0	0	0	0-0	0	1-0	17	0-0	.167	.135	.302
	Dunedin (FSL)	.300	6	20	5	6	0	0	2	8	0-1	0	6-0	8	0-0	.600	.444	1.044
2010	Dunedin (FSL)	.241	117	399	48	96	14	2	10	47	0-5	5	44-1	97	1-0	.361	.320	.681
2011	Dunedin (FSL)	.292	103	359	54	105	21	1	17	66	0-2	2	50-1	89	1-0	.499	.380	.879
2012	New Hampshire (EAS)	.273	115	399	46	109	28	0	7	44	0-3	6	42-2	70	12-6	.396	.349	.745
Minor Totals		.269	515	1764	234	474	98	6	53	265	0-15	22	237-5	430	20-6	.421	.360	.781

Vega-Rosado, Jorge — INFIELDER

HT: 5-8... **WT:** 175... **B-T:** R-R... **BORN:** 05 Dec 91, Rio Piedras, PR... **RESIDES:** Deltona, FL... **EDUCATION:** Miami Dade Community College South... **TRANSACTIONS:** Selected by the Toronto Blue Jays in the 28th round of the 2011 June draft... Signed on June 12, 2011... **SIGNED BY:** Matt O'Brien

YR	Club & League	AVG	G	AB	R	H	2B	3B	HR	RBI	SH-SF	HB	BB-IB	SO	SB-CS	SLG	OBP	OPS
2011	Blue Jays (GCL)	.317	51	183	39	58	12	2	4	30	2-4	2	19-0	40	22-4	.470	.380	.850
2012	Lansing (MID)	.091	6	22	1	2	0	0	0	0	0-0	0	1-0	12	1-0	.091	.130	.221
	Blue Jays (GCL)	.143	9	21	3	3	2	0	0	2	0-0	1	4-0	3	4-1	.238	.308	.546
	Bluefield (APP)	.275	41	149	20	41	6	1	2	12	2-1	3	16-1	40	7-4	.369	.355	.724
Minor Totals		.277	107	375	63	104	20	3	6	44	4-5	6	40-1	95	34-9	.395	.352	.747

Walden, Marcus — PITCHER

HT: 6-0... **WT:** 195... **B-T:** R-R... **BORN:** 13 Sep 88, Fresno, CA... **RESIDES:** Fresno, CA... **EDUCATION:** Fresno City College... **TRANSACTIONS:** Selected by the Toronto Blue Jays in the 9th round of the 2007 June draft... Signed on June 12, 2007... **SIGNED BY:** Tim Rooney

YR	Club & League	W-L	ERA	G	GS	CG	SHO	SV	IP	H	R	ER	HR	HB	BB-IB	SO	WP	BK	OBA
2007	Blue Jays (GCL)	2-4	3.05	12	10	0	0	0	44.1	45	21	15	3	0	12-0	32	2	0	.265
2008	Auburn (NYP)	2-3	4.80	14	11	0	0	0	60.0	70	38	32	4	3	20-0	51	1	0	.288
2009	Dunedin (FSL)	2-1	8.64	4	4	0	0	0	16.2	30	20	16	1	2	10-0	8	1	0	.385
2010	Injured – Did Not Play																		
2011	Lansing (MID)	6-6	3.24	28	13	0	0	0	100.0	90	48	36	1	6	28-0	54	4	3	.239
2012	Lansing (MID)	5-2	3.11	14	14	0	0	0	66.2	54	24	23	4	2	30-1	40	5	3	.229
	Dunedin (FSL)	9-2	2.85	13	12	0	0	0	72.2	58	26	23	0	3	18-0	42	1	0	.216
Minor Totals		26-18	3.62	85	64	0	0	0	360.1	347	177	145	13	16	118-1	227	14	6	.253

Wasilewski, Zak — *PITCHER*

HT: 6-1... **WT:** 190... **B-T:** L-L... **BORN:** 16 Jun 93, Tazewell, VA... **RESIDES:** Tazewell, VA... **EDUCATION:** Tazewell High School... **TRANSACTIONS:** Selected by the Toronto Blue Jays in the 14th round of the 2012 June draft... Signed on June 10, 2012... **SIGNED BY:** Bobby Gandolfo

YR	Club & League	W-L	ERA	G	GS	CG	SHO	SV	IP	H	R	ER	HR	HB	BB-IB	SO	WP	BK	OBA
2012	Blue Jays (GCL)	0-3	7.89	10	2	0	0	0	21.2	30	21	19	1	2	19-0	21	5	0	.333

White, Ben — *PITCHER*

HT: 6-2... **WT:** 185... **B-T:** R-R... **BORN:** 10 May 89, Parkesburg, PA... **RESIDES:** Parkesburg, PA... **EDUCATION:** Temple University... **TRANSACTIONS:** Signed by the Toronto Blue Jays on June 12, 2011... **SIGNED BY:** Bobby Gandolfo

YR	Club & League	W-L	ERA	G	GS	CG	SHO	SV	IP	H	R	ER	HR	HB	BB-IB	SO	WP	BK	OBA
2011	Vancouver (NOR)	1-1	7.00	8	5	0	0	0	27.0	36	23	21	3	4	10-0	10	6	0	.319
2012	Vancouver (NOR)	4-7	5.73	15	15	0	0	0	77.0	76	52	49	7	11	31-1	50	7	0	.255
Minor Totals		5-8	6.06	23	20	0	0	0	104.0	112	75	70	10	15	41-1	60	13	0	.273

Wilson, Kenny — *OUTFIELDER*

HT: 6-0... **WT:** 165... **B-T:** R-R... **BORN:** 30 Jan 90, Tampa, FL... **RESIDES:** Tampa, FL... **EDUCATION:** Sickles High School... **TRANSACTIONS:** Selected by the Toronto Blue Jays in the 2nd round of the 2008 June draft... Signed on June 9, 2008... **SIGNED BY:** Joel Grampietro

YR	Club & League	AVG	G	AB	R	H	2B	3B	HR	RBI	SH-SF	HB	BB-IB	SO	SB-CS	SLG	OBP	OPS
2008	Blue Jays (GCL)	.210	51	162	25	34	6	2	0	12	1-2	7	20-0	60	25-3	.272	.319	.591
2009	Blue Jays (GCL)	.200	8	25	6	5	2	1	0	0	0-0	1	3-0	8	3-1	.360	.310	.670
	Lansing (MID)	.212	87	321	51	68	12	3	4	27	1-5	11	35-0	99	37-12	.305	.306	.611
2010	Lansing (MID)	.216	95	361	54	78	10	4	0	22	6-0	8	51-0	112	35-11	.266	.326	.592
	Dunedin (FSL)	.138	18	58	5	8	1	0	0	4	2-0	0	8-0	15	5-0	.155	.242	.397
2011	Dunedin (FSL)	.201	48	164	21	33	8	2	0	10	2-0	6	16-0	52	17-4	.274	.296	.570
2012	Lansing (MID)	.252	94	349	68	88	13	6	4	40	7-4	17	44-0	75	41-8	.358	.360	.718
	Dunedin (FSL)	.282	29	117	24	33	6	0	1	13	2-0	2	14-0	22	14-4	.359	.368	.727
Minor Totals		.223	430	1557	254	347	58	18	9	128	21-11	52	191-0	443	177-43	.301	.326	.626

Wright, Matt — *PITCHER*

HT: 5-10... **WT:** 170... **B-T:** L-L... **BORN:** 07 May 87, McClure, PA... **RESIDES:** Shippensburg, PA... **EDUCATION:** Shippensburg University... **TRANSACTIONS:** Selected by the Toronto Blue Jays in 12th round of 2008 June draft... Signed on June 10, 2008... **SIGNED BY:** Tom Burns

YR	Club & League	W-L	ERA	G	GS	CG	SHO	SV	IP	H	R	ER	HR	HB	BB-IB	SO	WP	BK	OBA
2008	Auburn (NYP)	0-3	3.58	15	15	0	0	0	50.1	53	27	20	0	2	22-0	54	5	0	.270
2009	Auburn (NYP)	2-2	3.77	16	12	0	0	0	59.2	55	34	25	2	1	23-0	73	5	1	.240
2010	Lansing (MID)	5-2	2.53	38	0	0	0	1	67.2	50	25	19	2	2	22-1	82	4	1	.201
2011	Dunedin (FSL)	4-2	3.27	50	0	0	0	1	77.0	70	30	28	4	3	18-1	88	7	0	.237
2012	New Hampshire (EAS)	1-2	3.96	27	2	0	0	2	52.1	39	24	23	9	2	18-0	58	2	0	.204
	Dunedin (FSL)	0-0	0.00	7	0	0	0	0	6.1	7	0	0	0	0	1-1	7	1	0	.292
Minor Totals		12-11	3.30	153	29	0	0	4	313.1	274	140	115	17	10	104-3	362	24	2	.231

Ybarra, Tyler — *PITCHER*

HT: 6-2... **WT:** 170... **B-T:** L-L... **BORN:** 11 Dec 89, Wellington, KS... **RESIDES:** Wellington, KS... **EDUCATION:** Wellington High School... **TRANSACTIONS:** Selected by the Toronto Blue Jays in 43rd round of 2008 June draft... Signed on July 26, 2008... **SIGNED BY:** Ty Nichols

YR	Club & League	W-L	ERA	G	GS	CG	SHO	SV	IP	H	R	ER	HR	HB	BB-IB	SO	WP	BK	OBA
2009	Blue Jays (GCL)	2-4	6.64	16	0	0	0	0	20.1	29	20	15	1	2	10-0	11	7	0	.333
2010								Did Not Play											
2011	Bluefield (APP)	2-0	2.15	14	5	0	0	0	46.0	34	12	11	2	1	16-0	54	6	2	.200
2012	Lansing (MID)	3-2	2.27	26	0	0	0	2	43.2	38	16	11	2	2	26-1	57	10	2	.229
Minor Totals		7-6	3.03	56	5	0	0	2	110.0	101	48	37	5	5	52-1	122	23	4	.239

Zazueta, Amadeo — *INFIELDER*

HT: 5-10... **WT:** 160... **B-T:** R-R... **BORN:** 31 Jan 86, Culican, MEX... **RESIDES:** Culican, MEX... **EDUCATION:** NA... **TRANSACTIONS:** Signed by the Houston Astros on July 2, 2003... Signed by the Atlanta Braves on November 11, 2009... Signed by the San Diego Padres on August 10, 2011... Signed by the Toronto Blue Jays on August 28, 2012... **SIGNED BY:** Andres Reiner

YR	Club & League	AVG	G	AB	R	H	2B	3B	HR	RBI	SH-SF	HB	BB-IB	SO	SB-CS	SLG	OBP	OPS
2005	VSL (VSL)	.313	57	198	31	62	19	2	7	36	0-3	2	19-1	28	2-5	.535	.374	.909
2006	Greeneville (APP)	.170	28	53	4	9	2	0	1	5	1-0	0	3-0	9	0-0	.264	.214	.478
2007									Did Not Play									
2008	Lincoln (AAA)	.250	6	8	0	2	0	0	0	0	0-0	0	0-0	1	0-0	.250	.250	.500
2008	Harlingen (UNT)	.291	56	227	29	66	14	1	5	43	1-1	3	10-0	26	6-3	.427	.328	.755
2009									Did Not Play									
2010	Mississippi (SOU)	.000	2	4	0	0	0	0	0	0	1-0	0	0-0	1	0-0	.000	.000	.000
	Myrtle Beach (CAR)	.163	23	92	7	15	4	0	2	7	2-0	1	2-0	11	2-0	.272	.189	.461
2011	San Antonio (TEX)	.283	15	53	4	15	1	1	1	5	0-1	0	0-0	9	1-0	.396	.278	.674
2012	Tucson (PCL)	.183	46	115	8	21	4	1	0	5	3-1	1	1-0	19	0-0	.235	.195	.430
	Dunedin (FSL)	.429	6	21	2	9	2	1	1	5	0-2	0	0-0	3	0-0	.762	.391	1.153
Minor Totals		.244	177	536	56	131	32	5	12	63	7-7	4	25-1	80	5-5	.390	.280	.670

RHP Deck McGuire was selected in the 1st round (11th overall) in the 2010 First Year Player Draft

2013 ORGANIZATIONAL COMPOSITE SCHEDULE

APRIL 2013

	SUN	MON 1	TUE 2	WED 3	THU 4	FRI 5	SAT 6
TOR			CLE	CLE	CLE	BOS	BOS
BUF					ROC	ROC	@ ROC
NH					REA	REA	REA
DUN					CLR	@ CLR	@ DUN
LAN					@ LC	@ LC	@ LC
VAN							
BLU							
GC							

	SUN 7	MON 8	TUE 9	WED 10	THU 11	FRI 12	SAT 13
TOR	BOS	OFF DAY	@ DET	@ DET	@ DET	@ KC	@ KC
BUF	@ ROC	SYR	SYR	SYR	SWB	SWB	SWB
NH	REA	TRN	TRN	TRN	@ BIN	@ BIN	@ BIN
DUN	@ CLR	OFF DAY	TAM	TAM	TAM	LAK	LAK
LAN	@ LC	@ BG	@ BG	@ BG	MSU	SB	SB
VAN							
BLU							
GC							

	SUN 14	MON 15	TUE 16	WED 17	THU 18	FRI 19	SAT 20
TOR	@ KC	CWS	CWS	CWS	CWS	NYY	NYY
BUF	SWB	@ SYR	@ SYR	@ SYR	@ SYR	@ LHV	@ LHV
NH	@ BIN	@ NBR	@ NBR	@ NBR	BIN	BIN	BIN
DUN	LAK	@ TAM	@ TAM	@ TAM	@ LAK	@ LAK	@ LAK
LAN	SB	OFF DAY	WM	WM	WM	@ FTW	@ FTW
VAN							
BLU							
GC							

	SUN 21	MON 22	TUE 23	WED 24	THU 25	FRI 26	SAT 27
TOR	NYY	@ BAL	@ BAL	@ BAL	@ NYY	@ NYY	@ NYY
BUF	@ LHV	@ LHV	PAW	PAW	PAW	PAW	@ ROC
NH	BIN	OFF DAY	NBR	NBR	NBR	@ REA	@ REA
DUN	DAY	DAY	DAY	OFF DAY	@ BRE	@ BRE	@ BRE
LAN	@ FTW	DAY	DAY	DAY	@ QC	@ QC	@ QC
VAN							
BLU							
GC							

	SUN 28	MON 29	TUE 30
TOR	@ NYY	OFF DAY	BOS
BUF	@ ROC	@ ROC	@ ROC
NH	@ REA	@ TRN	@ TRN
DUN	@ JUP	@ JUP	@ JUP
LAN	@ CR	@ CR	@ CR
VAN			
BLU			
GC			

MAY 2013

	SUN	MON	TUE	WED 1	THU 2	FRI 3	SAT 4
TOR				BOS	BOS	SEA	SEA
BUF				OFF DAY	LOU	LOU	LOU
NH				@ TRN	@ TRN	REA	REA
DUN				@ JUP	BRE	BRE	BRE
LAN				WIS	WIS	WIS	BEL
VAN							
BLU							
GC							

	SUN 5	MON 6	TUE 7	WED 8	THU 9	FRI 10	SAT 11
TOR	SEA	@ TAM	@ TAM	@ TAM	@ TAM	@ BOS	@ BOS
BUF	LOU	NOR	NOR	NOR	NOR	@ LOU	@ LOU
NH	REA	NBR	NBR	NBR	@ TRN	@ TRN	@ TRN
DUN	BRD	BRD	BRD	BRD	@ DAY	@ DAY	@ DAY
LAN	BEL	BEL	OFF DAY	@ DAY	@ DAY	@ DAY	GL
VAN							
BLU							
GC							

	SUN 12	MON 13	TUE 14	WED 15	THU 16	FRI 17	SAT 18
TOR	@ BOS	OFF DAY	SF	SF	OFF DAY	@ NYY	@ NYY
BUF	@ LOU	@ LOU	@ IND	@ IND	@ IND	@ IND	CHA
NH	@ TRN	OFF DAY	POR	POR	POR	@ NBR	@ NBR
DUN	OFF DAY	@ FTM	@ FTM	@ FTM	@ FTM	BRE	BRE
LAN	GL	GL	@ LC	@ LC	@ LC	GL	GL
VAN							
BLU							
GC							

	SUN 19	MON 20	TUE 21	WED 22	THU 23	FRI 24	SAT 25
TOR	@ NYY	TAM	TAM	TAM	BAL	BAL	BAL
BUF	CHA	CHA	CHA	OFF DAY	IND	IND	IND
NH	@ NBR	@ POR	@ POR	@ POR	@ POR	NBR	NBR
DUN	BRE	STL	STL	STL	STL	@ TAM	TAM
LAN	GL	GL	LC	LC	LC	OFF DAY	@ SB
VAN							
BLU							
GC							

	SUN 26	MON 27	TUE 28	WED 29	THU 30	FRI 31
TOR	BAL	ATL	ATL	@ ATL	@ ATL	@ SD
BUF	IND	@ DUR	@ DUR	@ DUR	@ DUR	@ NOR
NH	NBR	NBR	@ POR	@ POR	@ POR	BIN
DUN	@ TAM	OFF DAY	@ LAK	@ LAK	@ LAK	CLR
LAN	@ SB	@ SB	@ FTW	@ FTW	@ FTW	@ GL
VAN						
BLU						
GC						

JUNE 2013

	SUN	MON	TUE	WED	THU	FRI	SAT 1
TOR							@ SD
BUF							@ NOR
NH							BIN
DUN							@ CLR
LAN							@ GL
VAN							
BLU							
GC							

	SUN 2	MON 3	TUE 4	WED 5	THU 6	FRI 7	SAT 8
TOR	@ SD	OFF DAY	@ SF	@ SF	OFF DAY	TEX	TEX
BUF	@ NOR	@ NOR	LHV	LHV	LHV	LHV	@ SWB
NH	BIN	OFF DAY	@ AKR	@ AKR	@ AKR	@ ERI	@ ERI
DUN	CLR	CHA	CHA	CHA	CHA	CLR	@ CLR
LAN	@ GL	@ GL	OFF DAY	FTW	FTW	FTW	@ WM
VAN							
BLU							
GC							

	SUN 9	MON 10	TUE 11	WED 12	THU 13	FRI 14	SAT 15
TOR	TEX	@ CWS	@ CWS	@ CWS	@ TEX	@ TEX	@ TEX
BUF	@ SWB	@ SWB	@ SWB	OFF DAY	@ PAW	@ PAW	@ PAW
NH	@ ERI	OFF DAY	AKR	AKR	AKR	ERI	ERI
DUN	@ CLR	@ PMB	@ PMB	@ PMB	@ PMB	A.S. Break	A.S. Game
LAN	@ WM	@ WM	SB	SB	SB	BG	BG
VAN						@ TRI	@ TRI
BLU							
GC							

	SUN 16	MON 17	TUE 18	WED 19	THU 20	FRI 21	SAT 22
TOR	@ TEX	COL	COL	COL	OFF DAY	BAL	BAL
BUF	@ PAW	GWN	GWN	GWN	GWN	DUR	DUR
NH	ERI	OFF DAY	@ ALT	@ ALT	@ ALT	@ HAR	@ HAR
DUN	A.S. Break	TAM	@ TAM	TAM	@ DAY	@ DAY	@ DAY
LAN	BG	A.S. Break	A.S. Break	A.S. Break	@ BG	@ BG	@ BG
VAN	@ TRI	SPO	SPO	SPO	@ SK	@ SK	@ SK
BLU					GRN	GRN	GRN
GC						TOR	PHI

	SUN 23	MON 24	TUE 25	WED 26	THU 27	FRI 28	SAT 29
TOR	BAL	@ TAM	@ TAM	@ TAM	@ BOS	@ BOS	@ BOS
BUF	DUR	DUR	@ GWN	@ GWN	@ GWN	@ GWN	@ CHA
NH	@ HAR	REA	REA	REA	POR	POR	POR
DUN	@ BRE	@ BRE	@ BRE	LAK	LAK	LAK	TAM
LAN	@ DAY	@ DAY	@ DAY	FTW	FTW	FTW	GL
VAN	@ SK	@ SK	@ SPO	@ SPO	@ SPO	TRI	TRI
BLU	@ PUL	@ PUL	@ PUL	BUR	BUR	BUR	@ DAN
GC	OFF DAY	PIT	@ PIT	@ NYY	NYY	ATL	@ ATL

JULY 2013

	SUN 30	MON 1	TUE 2	WED 3	THU 4	FRI 5	SAT 6
TOR	@ BOS	DET	DET	DET	DET	MIN	MIN
BUF	@ CHA	@ CHA	BUF	ROC	@ SWB	@ SWB	SYR
NH	POR	@ NBR	@ NBR	@ NBR	BIN	BIN	BIN
DUN	TAM	TAM	OFF DAY	@ CLR	CLR	@ CLR	DAY
LAN	GL	GL	@ LC	@ LC	LC	LC	@ BG
VAN	TRI	EVE	EVE	EVE	@ HIL	@ HIL	@ HIL
BLU	@ DAN	@ DAN	OFF DAY	@ PRN	ELZ	ELZ	ELZ
GC	OFF DAY	DET	@ DET	@ NYY	NYY	@ HOU	HOU

	SUN 7	MON 8	TUE 9	WED 10	THU 11	FRI 12	SAT 13
TOR	MIN	OFF DAY	@ CLE	@ CLE	@ CLE	@ BAL	@ BAL
BUF	SYR	OFF DAY	@ SYR	@ SYR	@ LHV	@ LHV	SWB
NH	BIN	BIN	A.S. Break	A.S. Break	@ REA	@ REA	@ REA
DUN	DAY	DAY	@ TAM	@ TAM	@ TAM	@ STL	@ STL
LAN	@ BG	@ BG	OFF DAY	PEO	PEO	PEO	BUR
VAN	@ HIL	@ HIL	OFF DAY	BOI	BOI	BOI	BOI
BLU	JC	JC	JC	@ BUR	@ BUR	@ BUR	@ PUL
GC	OFF DAY	PHI	@ PHI	@ PIT	PIT	NYY	@ NYY

	SUN 14	MON 15	TUE 16	WED 17	THU 18	FRI 19	SAT 20
TOR	@ BAL	A.S. Break	A.S. Game	A.S. Break	A.S. Break	TB	TB
BUF	SWB	A.S. Break	A.S. Break	A.S. Game	TOL	TOL	TOL
NH	@ REA	POR	POR	POR	@ TRN	@ TRN	@ TRN
DUN	@ STL	@ STL	OFF DAY	FTM	FTM	FTM	FTM
LAN	BUR	BUR	OFF DAY	@ CLI	@ CLI	@ CLI	@ KC
VAN	BOI	@ EVE	@ EVE	@ EVE	EUG	EUG	EUG
BLU	@ PUL	@ PUL	OFF DAY	BUR	BUR	BUR	BRS
GC	OFF DAY	@ ATL	ATL	@ DET	DET	NYY	TOR

	SUN 21	MON 22	TUE 23	WED 24	THU 25	FRI 26	SAT 27
TOR	TB	LAD	LAD	LAD	HOU	HOU	HOU
BUF	TOL	COL	COL	COL	COL	@ TOL	@ TOL
NH	@ TRN	HAR	HAR	HAR	ALT	ALT	ALT
DUN	@ CHA	@ CHA	@ CHA	@ CHA	JUP	JUP	JUP
LAN	@ KC	@ KC	OFF DAY	DAY	DAY	@ LAN	BG
VAN	EUG	EUG	@ SPO	@ SPO	@ SPO	@ EUG	@ EUG
BLU	BRS	BRS	@ DAN	@ DAN	@ DAN	PRN	PRN
GC	OFF DAY	@ HOU	HOU	PHI	@ PHI	PIT	@ PIT

	SUN 28	MON 29	TUE 30	WED 31
TOR	HOU	@ OAK	@ OAK	@ OAK
BUF	@ TOL	@ TOL	@ COL	@ COL
NH	ALT	OFF DAY	@ BOW	@ BOW
DUN	JUP	@ BRD	@ BRD	@ BRD
LAN	BG	BG	SB	SB
VAN	@ EUG	@ EUG	@ EUG	HIL
BLU	PRN	DAN	DAN	DAN
GC	OFF DAY	@ NYY	NYY	ATL

AUGUST 2013

	SUN	MON	TUE	WED	THU 1	FRI 2	SAT 3
TOR					@ LAA	@ LAA	@ LAA
BUF					@ COL	@ COL	PAW
NH					@ BOW	@ RIC	@ RIC
DUN					@ BRD	PMB	PMB
LAN					@ SB	@ SB	@ FTW
VAN					HIL	HIL	HIL
BLU					@ ELZ	@ ELZ	@ ELZ
GC					@ ATL	DET	@ DET

	4	5	6	7	8	9	10
TOR	@ LAA	@ SEA	@ SEA	@ SEA	OFF DAY	OAK	OAK
BUF	PAW	PAW	PAW	OFF DAY	SWB	SWB	@ SWB
NH	@ RIC	OFF DAY	BOW	BOW	BOW	RIC	RIC
DUN	PMB	PMB	OFF DAY	@ LAK	@ LAK	@ LAK	BRE
LAN	@ FTW	@ FTW	@ FTW	WM	WM	WM	@ GL
VAN	HIL	OFF DAY	A.S. Game	A.S. Break	@ BOI	@ BOI	@ BOI
BLU	PRN	OFF DAY	@ PRN	@ PRN	@ PRN	@ JC	@ JC
GC	OFF DAY	@ NYY	NYY	HOU	@ HOU	@ PHI	PHI

	11	12	13	14	15	16	17
TOR	OAK	OAK	BOS	BOS	BOS	@ TAM	@ TAM
BUF	@ SWB	SYR	SYR	ROC	ROC	ROC	@ PAW
NH	RIC	OFF DAY	NBR	@ NBR	@ NBR	TRN	TRN
DUN	BRE	BRE	LAK	LAK	LAK	@ CLR	@ CLR
LAN	@ GL	@ GL	OFF DAY	@ WM	@ WM	@ WM	LC
VAN	@ BOI	OFF DAY	EVE	EVE	EVE	SK	SK
BLU	JC	@ BRS	@ BRS	@ BRS	PRN	PRN	PRN
GC	OFF DAY	@ PIT	@ TOR	NYY	@ NYY	@ ATL	ATL

	18	19	20	21	22	23	24
TOR	@ TAM	OFF DAY	@ NYY	@ NYY	@ NYY	@ HOU	@ HOU
BUF	@ PAW	@ PAW	@ PAW	OFF DAY	LHV	LHV	LHV
NH	TRN	@ POR	@ POR	@ POR	@ REA	@ REA	@ REA
DUN	CLR	OFF DAY	DAY	DAY	DAY	@ BRE	@ BRE
LAN	LC	LC	LC	@ GL	@ GL	@ GL	DAY
VAN	SK	SK	SK	@ EVE	@ EVE	@ EVE	SPO
BLU	PUL	PUL	PUL	OFF DAY	KNG	KNG	KNG
GC	OFF DAY	@ DET	DET	NYY	@ NYY	@ PHI	PHI

	25	26	27	28	29	30	31
TOR	@ HOU	NYY	NYY	NYY	OFF DAY	KC	KC
BUF	LHV	@ LHV	@ LHV	ROC	ROC	@ ROC	@ ROC
NH	@ REA	POR	POR	POR	POR	@ BIN	@ BIN
DUN	@ BRE	@ DAY	@ DAY	@ DAY	CLR	CLR	@ CLR
LAN	DAY	DAY	OFF DAY	@ LC	@ LC	@ LC	WM
VAN	SPO	SPO	OFF DAY	TRI	TRI	TRI	@ TRI
BLU	@ GRN	@ GRN	@ GRN	@ KNG	@ KNG	@ KNG	
GC	OFF DAY	PIT	@ PIT	@ NYY	NYY		

SEPTEMBER 2013

	SUN 1	MON 2	TUE 3	WED 4	THU 5	FRI 6	SAT 7
TOR	KC	@ ARZ	@ ARZ	@ ARZ	OFF DAY	@ MIN	@ MIN
BUF	@ SYR	@ SYR					
NH	@ BIN	@ BIN					
DUN	CLR						
LAN	WM	WM					
VAN	@ TRI	@ TRI					
BLU							
GC							

	8	9	10	11	12	13	14
TOR	@ MIN	OFF DAY	LAA	LAA	LAA	BAL	BAL
BUF							
NH							
DUN							
LAN							
VAN							
BLU							
GC							

	15	16	17	18	19	20	21
TOR	BAL	OFF DAY	NYY	NYY	NYY	@ BOS	@ BOS
BUF							
NH							
DUN							
LAN							
VAN							
BLU							
GC							

	22	23	24	25	26	27	28
TOR	@ BOS	OFF DAY	@ BAL	@ BAL	@ BAL	TAM	TAM
BUF							
NH							
DUN							
LAN							
VAN							
BLU							
GC							

	29	30
TOR	TAM	
BUF		
NH		
DUN		
LAN		
VAN		
BLU		
GC		

KEY TO ABBREVIATIONS

BUFFALO

CHA CHARLOTTE KNIGHTS
COL COLUMBUS CLIPPERS
DUR DURHAM BULLS
GWN GWINNETT BRAVES
IND INDIANAPOLIS INDIANS
LHV LEHIGH VALLEY IRONPIGS
LOU LOUISVILLE BATS
NOR NORFOLK TIDES
PAW PAWTUCKET RED SOX
ROC ROCHESTER RED WINGS
SWB SCRANTON/WILKES–BARRE YANKEES
SYR SYRACUSE CHIEFS
TOL TOLEDO MUD HENS

NEW HAMPSHIRE

AKR AKRON AEROS
ALT ALTOONA CURVE
BIN BINGHAMTON METS
BOW BOWIE BAYSOX
ERI ERIE SEAWOLVES
HAR HARRISBURG SENATORS
NBR NEW BRITAIN ROCK CATS
NH NEW HAMPSHIRE FISHER CATS
POR PORTLAND SEA DOGS
REA READING PHILLIES
RIC RICHMOND FLYING SQUIRRELS
TRN TRENTON THUNDER

DUNEDIN

BRD BRADENTON MARAUDERS
BRE BREVARD COUNTY MANATEES
CHA CHARLOTTE STONE CRABS
CLR CLEARWATER THRESHERS
DAY DAYTONA CUBS
DUN DUNEDIN BLUE JAYS
FTM FORT MYERS MIRACLE
JUP JUPITER HAMMERHEADS
LAK LAKELAND FLYING TIGERS
PMB PALM BEACH CARDINALS
STL ST LUCIE METS
TAM TAMPA YANKEES

*Palm Beach Cardinals play out of Jupiter Stadium.

LANSING

BEL BELOIT SNAPPERS
BG BOWLING GREEN HOT RODS
BUR BURLINGTON BEES
CR CEDAR RAPIDS KERNELS
CLI CLINTON LUMBERKINGS
DAY DAYTON DRAGONS
FTW FORT WAYNE TIN CAPS
GL GREAT LAKES LOONS
KC KANE COUNTY COUGARS
LAN LANSING LUGNUTS
LC LAKE COUNTY CAPTAINS
PEO PEORIA CHIEFS
QC QUAD CITY RIVER BANDITS
SB SOUTH BEND SILVERHAWKS
WIS WISCONSIN TIMBER RATTLERS
WM WEST MICHIGAN WHITECAPS

VANCOUVER

BOI BOISE HAWKS
EUG EUGENE EMERALDS
EVE EVERETT AQUASOX
SK SALEM-KEIZER VOLCANOES
SPO SPOKANE INDIANS
TRI TRI CITY DUST DEVILS
VAN VANCOUVER CANADIANS
HIL HILLSBORO HOPS

BLUEFIELD

BLU BLUEFIELD BLUE JAYS
BRS BRISTOL WHITE SOX
BUR BURLINGTON ROYALS
DAN DANVILLE BRAVES
ELZ ELIZABETHTON TWINS
GRN GREENVILLE ASTROS
JC JOHNSON CITY CARDINALS
KNG KINGSPORT METS
PRN PRINCETON RAYS
PUL PULASKI MARINERS

GULF COAST

ATL ATLANTA BRAVES
DET DETROIT TIGERS
NYY NEW YORK YANKEES
PIT PITTSBURGH PIRATES
PHI PHILADELPHIA PHILLIES
TOR TORONTO BLUE JAYS

2012 TOPS IN THE ORGANIZATION

BATTING TOP 10
(MINIMUM 2.7 PA/TEAM GAME)

BATTER	CLUB	AVG	G	AB	R	H	HR	RBI
Pillar, Kevin	DUN	.323	128	499	65	161	6	91
Hechavarria, Adeiny	LAS	.312	102	443	78	138	6	63
Howard, Kevin	LAS	.292	100	366	39	107	10	53
Conner, Seth	BLU	.291	54	158	25	46	2	30
Goins, Ryan	NH	.289	136	546	66	158	7	61
Sierra, Moises	LAS	.289	100	377	62	109	17	63
Gose, Anthony	LAS	.286	102	420	87	120	5	43
McDade, Mike	LAS	.285	118	449	53	128	17	67
Fuenmayor, Balbino	VAN	.282	67	259	35	73	9	52
Lopes, Christian	VAN	.278	59	223	37	62	4	33

PITCHING TOP 10
(MINIMUM 0.8 IP/TEAM GAME)

PITCHER	CLUB	W-L	ERA	IP	H	BB	SO
Cole, Taylor	VAN	6 -0	0.81	66.1	36	17	57
Avendano, Javier	VAN	10 -4	1.33	108.1	73	43	130
Nicolino, Justin	LAN	10 -4	2.46	124.1	112	21	119
Walden, Marcus	DUN	14 -4	2.97	139.1	112	48	82
DeSclafani, Anthony	LAN	11 -3	3.37	123.0	145	25	92
Hernandez, Jesse	DUN	5 -10	3.70	143.1	137	31	99
Lawrence, Casey	DUN	9 -7	3.87	151.1	169	26	96
Estrada, Deivy	BLU	3 -6	4.29	56.2	62	15	49
Jensen, Tucker	BLU	3 -2	4.70	53.2	54	12	43
Pino, Yohan	NH	10 -10	4.77	143.1	151	32	119

HOME RUNS

Schimpf, Ryan	NH	22
Sobolewski, Mark	NH	20
Glenn, Brad	NH	19
Patterson, Kevin	LAN	19

2 others tied at 17.

RBI

Pillar, Kevin	DUN	91
Hobson, K.C.	LAN	86
Patterson, Kevin	LAN	79
Schimpf, Ryan	NH	76
Talley, Jon	DUN	68

STOLEN BASES

Wilson, Kenny	DUN	55
Pillar, Kevin	DUN	51
Berti, Jon	DUN	34
Gose, Anthony	LAS	34

2 others tied at 25.

WINS

Walden, Marcus	DUN	14
DeSclafani, Anthony	LAN	11
Richmond, Scott	LAS	11

4 others tied at 10.

SAVES

Barnes, Danny	DUN	34
Meyer, Ajay	LAN	33
Beck, Chad	LAS	18
Sikula, Andrew	VAN	10

2 others tied at 9.

STRIKEOUTS

Avendano, Javier	VAN	130
Syndergaard, Noah	LAN	122
Nicolino, Justin	LAN	119
Pino, Yohan	NH	119
Richmond, Scott	LAS	112

TEAM BATTING

	AVG	AB	R	H	HR	BB	SO	SB	CS
Las Vegas	.298	4954	808	1474	133	557	964	115	51
New Hampshire	.259	4810	588	1244	121	418	992	145	66
Dunedin	.255	4415	669	1125	94	499	1041	121	40
Lansing	.254	4623	672	1174	75	532	1014	178	45
Bluefield	.242	2122	307	513	45	224	583	51	23
Vancouver	.236	2536	360	599	44	299	643	67	27
GCL Blue Jays	.204	1930	236	394	24	209	499	57	33

TEAM PITCHING

	W-L	ERA	H	CG	SHO	SV	HR	BB	SO
Lansing	82 -55	3.45	1194	2	16	45	68	403	1100
Vancouver	46 -30	3.54	607	0	8	23	37	251	570
Dunedin	78 -55	3.59	1135	3	7	42	66	356	962
Bluefield	29 -37	3.87	513	0	6	16	41	184	489
GCL Blue Jays	22 -38	4.13	504	0	3	11	25	217	520
New Hampshire	61-81	4.14	1277	2	8	31	128	469	1013
Las Vegas	79-64	4.59	1379	2	7	37	135	437	912

BLUE JAYS FIRST-YEAR PLAYER DRAFT PICKS

1977-2011 DRAFT (Still in Blue Jays Organization)

Player	Pos.	Year Drafted	Round Phase	#
Dustin McGowan	RHP	2000-June	REG	1
Adam Lind	OF	2004-June	REG	3
Casey Janssen	RHP	2004-June	REG	4
Ricky Romero	LHP	2005-June	REG	1
Kevin Ahrens	IF	2007-June	REG	1
J.P. Arencibia	C	2007-June	REG	1
Brett Cecil	LHP	2007-June	COMP	1
Justin Jackson	IF	2007-June	COMP	1
John Tolisano	IF	2007-June	REG	2
Alan Farina	RHP	2007-June	REG	3
Randy Boone	RHP	2007-June	REG	7
Marcus Walden	RHP	2007-June	REG	9
Jon Talley	C	2007-June	REG	13
David Cooper	IF	2008-June	REG	1
Kenny Wilson	OF	2008-June	REG	2
Andrew Liebel	RHP	2008-June	REG	3
Markus Brisker	OF	2008-June	REG	6
Evan Crawford	LHP	2008-June	REG	8
A.J. Jimenez	C	2008-June	REG	9
Dustin Antolin	RHP	2008-June	REG	11
Matt Wright	LHP	2008-June	REG	12
Matthew Daly	RHP	2008-June	REG	13
Scott Gracey	RHP	2008-June	REG	15
Michael Crouse	OF	2008-June	REG	16
Brian Van Kirk	OF	2008-June	REG	21
Bryan Kervin	IF	2008-June	REG	27
John Anderson	LHP	2008-June	REG	28
Tyler Ybarra	LHP	2008-June	REG	43
Chad Jenkins	RHP	2009-June	REG	1
Ryan Goins	IF	2009-June	REG	4
Ryan Schimpf	IF	2009-June	REG	5
K.C. Hobson	OF	2009-June	REG	6
Egan Smith	LHP	2009-June	REG	7
Aaron Loup	LHP	2009-June	REG	9
Sean Ochinko	C	2009-June	REG	11
Drew Hutchison	RHP	2009-June	REG	15
Ryan Tepera	RHP	2009-June	REG	19
Kevin Nolan	IF	2009-June	REG	20
Brad Glenn	OF	2009-June	REG	23
John Murphy	C	2009-June	REG	31
Shawn Griffith	RHP	2009-June	REG	37
Deck McGuire	RHP	2010-June	REG	1
Aaron Sanchez	RHP	2010-June	COMP	1
Griffin Murphy	LHP	2010-June	REG	2
Kellen Sweeney	IF	2010-June	REG	2
Chris Hawkins	IF	2010-June	REG	2
Marcus Knecht	OF	2010-June	COMP	3
Dickie Thon	IF	2010-June	REG	5
Sean Nolin	LHP	2010-June	REG	6
Shane Opitz	IF	2010-June	REG	11
Dayton Marze	RHP	2010-June	REG	14
Zak Adams	LHP	2010-June	REG	15
Dalton Pompey	OF	2010-June	REG	16
Travis Garrett	RHP	2010-June	REG	19
Art Charles	LHP	2010-June	REG	20
Angel Gomez	OF	2010-June	REG	23
Ronnie Melendez	OF	2010-June	REG	24
Jonathan Jones	OF	2010-June	REG	29
Andy Fermin	IF	2010-June	REG	32
Melvin Garcia	OF	2010-June	REG	33
Tyler Powell	RHP	2010-June	REG	34
Daniel Barnes	RHP	2010-June	REG	35
Pierce Rankin	C	2010-June	REG	38
Brandon Berl	RHP	2010-June	REG	40
Drew Permison	RHP	2010-June	REG	42
Jacob Anderson	OF	2011-June	COMP	1
Dwight Smith	OF	2011-June	COMP	1
Daniel Norris	LHP	2011-June	REG	2
Jeremy Garbyszwski	RHP	2011-June	REG	2
John Stilson	RHP	2011-June	REG	3
Thomas Robson	RHP	2011-June	REG	4
Christian Lopes	IF	2011-June	REG	7
Mark Biggs	RHP	2011-June	REG	8
Andrew Burns	IF	2011-June	REG	11
Matthew Dean	IF	2011-June	REG	13
Brady Dragmire	RHP	2011-June	REG	17
Jonathan Berti	IF	2011-June	REG	18
Peter Mooney	IF	2011-June	REG	21
Eric Arce	IF	2011-June	REG	25
Justin Atkinson	IF	2011-June	REG	26
Derrick Loveless	OF	2011-June	REG	27
Jorge Vega-Rosado	IF	2011-June	REG	28
Taylor Cole	RHP	2011-June	REG	29
Kevin Patterson	IF	2011-June	REG	30
Kevin Pillar	OF	2011-June	REG	32
Kramer Champlin	RHP	2011-June	REG	33
Aaron Munoz	C	2011-June	REG	34
Andrew Sikula	RHP	2011-June	REG	36
Nico Taylor	OF	2011-June	REG	38
Nicholas Baligod	OF	2011-June	REG	40
Cody Bartlett	IF	2011-June	REG	41
Shane Davis	RHP	2011-June	REG	42
Eric Brown	RHP	2011-June	REG	50

RHP Javier Avendano went 8-1 with a 1.27 ERA in 16 games (14 starts) while holding opponents to a .193 batting average with Vancouver (A) in 2012

TORONTO BLUE JAYS
JUNE 2012 FIRST YEAR PLAYER DRAFT

RD	Pick	Player	School	Hometown	Pos	B/T	Ht	Wt	DOB	Cl.	Scout
1	17	**Dylan (DJ) Davis**	Stone County High School, MS	Wiggins, MS	CF	L/R	6'0	170	6/27/1993	HS	Brian Johnston
1	22	**Marcus Stroman**	Duke University, NC	Medford, NY	RHP	R/R	5'9	185	5/1/1991	JR	John Hendricks
1A	50	**Matthew Smoral**	Solon High School, OH	Solon, OH	LHP	L/L	6'8	230	3/18/1994	HS	Coulson Barbiche
1A	58	**Mitchell Nay**	Hamilton High School, AZ	Chandler, AZ	RF	R/R	6'3	195	9/20/1993	HS	Blake Crosby
1A	60	**Tyler Gonzales**	James Madison H.S., TX	San Antonio, TX	RHP	R/R	6'2	170	1/22/1993	HS	Mike Burns
2	81	**Chase DeJong**	Woodrow Wilson H.S., CA	Long Beach, CA	RHP	L/R	6'5	190	12/29/1993	HS	Joey Aversa
3	112	**Anthony Alford**	Petal High School, MS	Columbia, MS	CF	R/R	6'1	205	7/20/1994	HS	Brian Johnston
4	145	**Tucker Donahue**	Stetson University, FL	Coral Springs, FL	RHP	R/R	6'2	214	8/27/1990	SR	Joel Grampietro
5	175	**Brad Delatte**	Nicholls State University, LA	Baton Rouge, LA	LHP	L/L	5'11	180	1/13/1990	SR	Brian Johnston
6	205	**Eric Phillips**	Georgia Southern U., GA	Carrollton, GA	UTL	R/R	6'2	200	7/16/1990	SR	Eric McQueen
7	235	**Ian Parmley**	Liberty University, VA	Snohomish, WA	OF	L/L	6'0	175	12/19/1989	SR	Bobby Gandolfo
8	265	**Harrison Frawley**	Coastal Carolina U., SC	Lexington, SC	C	R/R	6'1	195	6/1/1989	5S	John Hendricks
9	295	**Jordan Leyland**	Azusa Pacific University, CA	San Dimas, CA	1B	R/R	6'4	235	9/6/1989	SR	Joey Aversa
10	325	**Alex Azor**	US Naval Academy, MD	Miami, FL	OF	L/L	5'11	190	11/21/1988	SR	Harry Einbinder
11	355	Grant Heyman	Pittsford Sutherland H.S., NY	Pittsford, NY	CF	L/R	6'4	185	11/7/1993	HS	Jamie Lehman
12	385	Ryan Kellogg**	Henry Street High School, ON	Whitby, ON	LHS	R/L	6'5	215	2/4/1994	HS	Jamie Lehman
13	415	**John Silviano**	Summit Christian School, FL	Hypoluxo, FL	C	L/R	5'10	195	7/11/1994	HS	Matt O'Brien
14	445	**Zakery Wasilewski**	Tazewell High School, VA	Tazewell, VA	LHP	L/L	6'2	200	6/16/1993	HS	Bobby Gandolfo
15	475	**Ryan Borucki**	Mundelein High School, IL	Mundelein, IL	LHP	L/L	6'4	180	3/31/1994	HS	Mike Medici
16	505	**Will Dupont**	Lafeyette High School, MO	Ellisville, MO	2B	L/R	6'0	170	12/1/1993	HS	Darin Vaughan
17	535	**Shane Dawson****	Lethbridge Comm. Col., AB	Drayton Valley, AB	LHP	R/L	6'1	180	9/9/1993	J1	Jamie Lehman
18	565	**Alonzo Gonzalez**	Glendale College, CA	Santa Monica, CA	LHP	L/L	6'5	190	1/15/1992	J1	Kevin Fox
19	595	**Jorge Flores**	Central Arizona College, AZ	Chandler, AZ	SS	R/R	5'7	160	11/25/1991	J2	Blake Crosby
20	625	**Dennis Jones**	Hillsborough Comm. Col., FL	Montgomery, AL	CF	S/R	6'3	180	9/4/1992	J1	Joel Grampietro
21	655	**Colton Turner**	Texas State University, TX	Cleburne, TX	LHP	L/L	6'2	185	1/17/1991	JR	Mike Burns
22	685	**Joshua Almonte**	Long Island City H.S., NY	Corona, NY	RF	R/R	6'3	195	1/28/1994	HS	Michael Pesce
23	715	**Trey Pascazi**	East Rochester H.S., NY	East Rochester, NY	SS	S/R	6'0	175	8/7/1993	HS	Jamie Lehman
24	745	Matt Rose	Palm Bay High School, FL	Palm Bay, FL	RHP	R/R	6'4	195	8/12/1994	HS	Matt O'Brien
25	775	**Jason Leblenijian**	Bradley University, IL	Arlington Heights, IL	SS	R/R	6'1	185	5/13/1991	JR	Mike Medici
26	805	**Nathan Desouza****	Drury HS, ON	Milton, ON	LF	L/R	5'11	175	7/13/1994	HS	Jamie Lehman
27	835	Daniel Zamora	Bishop Amat High School, CA	La Puente, CA	LHP	L/L	6'3	185	4/15/1993	HS	Joey Aversa
28	865	**Daniel Klein**	Kansas State University, KS	Anaheim, CA	C	R/R	5'10	185	8/29/1990	SR	Jon Brunnell
29	895	Cole Irvin	Servite High School, CA	Yorba Linda, CA	LHP	L/L	6'4	175	1/31/1994	HS	Joey Aversa
30	925	Devin Pearson	Carmel High School, CA	Carmel, CA	CF	R/R	6'0	190	1/10/1994	HS	Randy Kramer
31	955	**Derrick Chung**	Sacramento State U., CA	Garden Grove, CA	2B	R/R	5'9	175	2/23/1988	5S	Donald Brown
32	985	**Jorge Saez**	Lee University, TN	Miami, FL	C	R/R	5'10	185	8/28/1990	JR	Nate Murrie
33	1015	Jonathan Harris	Hazelwood Central H.S., MO	Florissant, MO	RHP	R/R	6'4	170	10/16/1991	HS	Darin Vaughan
34	1045	Brandon Lopez	American Heritage H.S., FL	Miramar, FL	SS	R/R	6'2	175	9/9/1993	HS	Matt O'Brien
35	1075	**Devyn Rivera**	California Baptist U., CA	Higley, AZ	RHP	R/R	6'3	195	6/13/1990	SR	Jim Lentine
36	1105	Brian Cruz	Galveston College, TX	Miami, FL	SS	R/R	5'11	178	10/12/1991	J1	Mike Burns
37	1135	**Daniel Devonshire**	Colby Community College, KS	Colby, KS	1B	L/R	6'1	220	3/30/1992	J1	Joe Bunnell
38	1165	Nicholas Lovullo	Newbury Park High School, CA	Thousand Oaks, CA	SS	R/R	6'0	175	12/1/1993	HS	Joey Aversa
39	1195	**Shaun Valeriote****	Brock University, ON	Guelph, ON	3B	R/R	6'1	200	1/22/1990	JR	Jamie Lehman
40	1225	Jose Cuas	Grand Street Campus, NY	Brooklyn, NY	SS	R/R	6'2	170	6/28/1994	HS	Michael Pesce

Players in bold were signed by the Club
****Indicates player is Canadian**

MEDIA & MISCELLANEOUS

JOSE REYES

TORONTO BLUE JAYS™
MEDIA SERVICES

TORONTO BLUE JAYS COMMUNICATIONS
ROGERS CENTRE
ONE BLUE JAYS WAY, SUITE 3200
TORONTO, ONTARIO M5V 1J1
OFFICE: (416) 341-1301/1302/1303 **FAX: (416) 341-1250 E-MAIL: firstname.lastname@bluejays.com**

JAY STENHOUSE
Vice President,
Communications

MAL ROMANIN
Manager,
Baseball Information

SUE MALLABON
Coordinator,
Communications

ERIK GROSMAN
Coordinator,
Baseball Information

CREDENTIALS: To obtain regular season media credentials to cover Toronto Blue Jays 2013 home games, please log on to http://credentials.mlb.com and fill out the appropriate information to apply. Credential requests for individual games must be submitted at least 48 hours in advance of the requested game date, subject to the discretion of the Toronto Blue Jays. We will respond to your request as soon as possible. If you are not contacted by someone from our office, please call at least one day in advance, to confirm that you have credentials before arriving at the ballpark. Credentials will be issued only to members of the working media 18 years of age and older. No spouses, guests or children of members of the media will be issued passes. Media passes are not transferable. Media passes must be visible at all times. Any violation of these guidelines will result in immediate revocation of the credential and future access. Only credentials issued by the Toronto Blue Jays, Major League Baseball or the BBWAA will be honoured.

SEASON CREDENTIAL APPLICATIONS: The Blue Jays will issue full-season credentials to those media members who cover the club on a regular basis throughout the season. Media will be asked to submit a written request for Blue Jays season media credentials on their official letterhead. All requests for season credentials must be received by Friday February 15, 2013.

CREDENTIAL PICKUP: Members of the media can pick up approved daily credentials inside Gate 9 at Rogers Centre, located on the south side of the building. Using the Gate 9 elevator, the media centre is located on the 300 level and the broadcast booths are located on the 400 level. Press Gate opens 4 hours prior to game time.

PHOTO CREDENTIALS: Credentials will be issued to those photographers on assignment for legitimate newsgathering organizations and those representatives of companies licensed by Major League Baseball. No freelance photographers will be granted credentials and all photographs taken are to be used for newsgathering purposes or official licensed products.

CLUBHOUSE ACCESS: The clubhouse is open to media with proper credentials for working purposes 3 ½ hours prior to each game and then closes 1 hour prior to the start of each game. The clubhouse will re-open no later than 10 minutes following the final out of each game. Access to the visiting clubhouse is subject to the visiting club's guidelines.

FIELD ACCESS: Only credentialed media with field access to the playing field will be allowed onto the field prior to the game. No media will be allowed in fair territory or beyond the first and third base bags. All non-uniformed personnel must clear the field at the conclusion of visitors batting practice unless that individual had credentials expressly for in-game field privileges (photo passes, pre-game ceremonies. etc).

LIVE TRANSMISSIONS: Television and radio stations not holding broadcast rights for Blue Jays games will be allowed to transmit live reports prior to and after Blue Jays games. All live television shots will be done on the field. No live shots will be permitted from the clubhouses. No live transmissions inside the stadium by non-rights holders will be permitted while the rights holders are on the air or the game is in progress. Radio stations will be permitted to provide "scene setters" and score updates between innings but these reports may not continue once an inning is underway. Any violations of these policies will result in revocation of credentials.

AUTOGRAPHS: No member of the media may use their access to solicit autographs or equipment from players or staff of either participating team. Any autograph needs should be directed to the Communications Department. Failure to do so will result in the revocation of credential privileges and forfeiture of any items obtained.

NOTES & STATISTICS: Game information is available in the media centre two hours prior to first pitch. As well, this information is available at www.mlbpressbox.com.

MEDIA GUIDES: Media Guides are available upon request in the media centre. As well, all MLB club media guides are available at www.mlbpressbox.com.

POST GAME PROCEDURES: Manager John Gibbons will be available to the media immediately after the game in the Interview room across from the Blue Jays clubhouse. Postgame interviews with the manager and players, conducted by the media with deadlines should be related to game comments.

INTERNET/MEDIA WEBSITES: Due to the growth of online services and our limited number of press box seats, the Blue Jays will only issue daily credentials to those websites affiliated with a recognized news gathering organization.

FREELANCE: The Toronto Blue Jays do not credential freelance writers or photographers.

An exception can be made if, and only if, the writer or photographer is on assignment with a specific news organization. It is the responsibility of the requesting affiliation to confirm receipt, and subsequent approval/denial of access to the game requested.

LOST CREDENTIALS: Those members of the media who lose their Blue Jays Credential will be asked to make a $50.00 donation to the Jays Care Foundation prior to being issued a replacement credential.

TELEPHONES: As a courtesy, charge-a-call phones are available for media use in the press box. To order a dedicated phone line at a specific press box location, please contact Katrina LaCavalier at (416) 341-3037 or by email at katrina.lacavalier@rci.rogers.com.

INTERNET CONNECTION: We are pleased to offer both wireless and hard wire internet connections in the media centre and wireless connection in the photo dugouts. Please contact a member of the Communications Department for assistance.

MEDIA DINING: Located on the 300 Level of the Media Centre, there is a $12.00 CDN/US per meal. Media dining is open for service two-and-a-half hours prior to first pitch to accredited members of the media.

MAJOR LEAGUE BASEBALL GUIDELINES: Clothing should be appropriate for a business casual work environment. No flip-flops, no t-shirts bearing offensive, disrespectful or inappropriate messages and no ripped jeans are permitted. Clothing bearing MLB club logos should not be worn in press areas. Sheer or see-through clothing, excessively short skirts, dresses or shorts are not permitted. Tank tops, muscle shirts, one-shouldered or strapless shirts as well as clothing exposing bare midriffs or visible undergarments are not permitted.

2013 REGULAR SEASON CLUB/MEDIA REGULATIONS

The following are Major League Baseball's regulations for Club/Media Relations. They are to be observed by all parties:

1. All accredited press, radio and TV representatives shall have pre-game access to the clubhouse from three hours and 30 minutes prior to game time until one hour prior to game time, except that: (a) the media shall not have access to the clubhouse when the club is on the field for batting practice; and (b) the media may not return to the home clubhouse once the home club has taken batting practice. No Club may provide pre-game access prior to three hours and 30 minutes prior to game time. The media shall have access (outside of the clubhouse) to the home Club's manager, players or coaches after home batting practice to discuss developments (such as lineup changes, injuries, and workouts) that occur after the clubhouse closes.

2. Absent unusual circumstances that require a team meeting immediately following a game, the working media shall have access to both clubhouses no later than 10 minutes following the final out of each game (including doubleheaders and day/night split admission games). When such unusual circumstances exist, and such instances are expected to be rare, the working media shall have access to the clubhouse no later than 20 minutes following the final out of the game. The Commissioner's Office reserves the right to require access to the clubhouse 10 minutes following the final out of all games if the "team meeting" exception is abused.

3. The working media's access following a game shall be for a period no longer than one hour unless reasonable access to players is not provided during that time; provided, however, that card-carrying members of the Baseball Writers Association of America ("BBWAA") will have unlimited access after the post-game opening of the clubhouse. If reasonable access is not provided, the clubhouse must remain open. Members of the media, other than BBWAA members, may make arrangements with the club PR Director for extended access.

4. Media credentials are not transferable.

5. Clubhouses, the dugouts and the field are off-limits except to appropriate club, Commissioner's Office personnel and media bearing appropriate credentials. Club credentials are not to be issued to unauthorized personnel. The Commissioner's Office reserves the right to revoke inappropriately issued credentials.

6. Players will be available to the media before and after games for interviews. These periods should not be limited except for the pre-game period described in #1 above, and the post-game period described in #2 above. Upon request by the media, players who had key roles in the first game of a doubleheader are to be made available for a time between games.

7. The trainer's room and players' lounge may be off-limits to the media, but each club controls these areas, and it is vital these areas not be used as a sanctuary for players seeking to avoid the media. It is very important to our game that ALL players are available to the media for reasonable periods and it is the player's responsibility to cooperate.

8. Ropes or other restraining barriers are not permitted to bar the media.

9. A general code is to be observed by the media so uniformed personnel may do their work unimpeded. Media are to be allowed in foul territory, in an unrestricted manner, in an area that is to be not less than the territory between first and third bases, and which territory includes the area around the batting cage, except the dirt area around the batting cage.

10. Under no circumstances shall any club discriminate in any fashion against an accredited member of the media based upon race, creed, sex or national origin.

11. Physical abuse or threats directed to members of the media (and/or official scorers) by baseball personnel will not be tolerated. Disciplinary action, including fines and suspensions, will be considered in any cases that arise.

12. Visitors in the clubhouse, including accredited media members, should conduct themselves in a professional manner. There shall be no seeking of autographs, no touching or removing of equipment or personal items from lockers, and no sampling of players' food spreads. Clubhouses are work places. Clubhouse business should be conducted as expeditiously as possible with a minimum of disruption of regular game routines. Members of the media should not excessively linger in the clubhouse when not interviewing players. Members of the media who violate the code of conduct set forth in this paragraph shall be subject to sanctions, including the loss of their accreditation as provided for in paragraph 17 below.

While in the clubhouse, members of the media are expected to be doing business. Members of the media are expected to conduct themselves in a professional manner and to respect the privileges and environment of restricted areas and working press areas at all times. Any media member in violation of this conduct policy is subject to revocation of his or her privileges and may be subject to immediate ejection.

13. Live TV and/or radio interviews with uniformed personnel during the course of a game are not authorized or permitted, nor is attaching a microphone to any uniformed personnel permitted without approval from the Commissioner's Office. Microphones may not be placed in or adjacent to dugouts and/or bullpens in a manner that will allow uniformed personnel's remarks or conversations to be overheard during the course of a game without the prior approval of the Commissioner's Office.

14. Live telephone interviews are not allowed from the clubhouse or the field without prior approval of the club. Mobile telephones with digital photography capabilities are prohibited.

15. Telephones from both dugouts to the press box are to be maintained in working order for the purpose of providing information regarding special circumstances to the media during the course of a game. Explanations of injuries should be made as soon as possible (to both the media and fans in the stadium).

16. Any club whose personnel violate these regulations will be disciplined. Any member of the media who violates these regulations will lose his or her accreditation.

17. BBWAA members are not required to sign in for clubhouse or other restricted area access but may be logged in by club personnel, subject to individual club policies. Other accredited media may be required to sign in for clubhouse access, subject to individual club policies

MEDIA MILESTONES

TOM CHEEK NAMED 2013 FORD C. FRICK AWARD WINNER FOR BROADCASTING EXCELLENCE

Tom Cheek, who called the first 4,306 regular-season and 41 postseason games in Toronto Blue Jays history has been selected as the 2013 recipient of the Ford C. Frick Award, presented annually for excellence in broadcasting by the National Baseball Hall of Fame and Museum. Cheek, who passed away on Oct. 9, 2005, will be honoured as part of Hall of Fame Week-end (July 26-29, 2013) in Cooperstown, NY. Cheek becomes the second Frick Award winner whose career came primarily with a Canadian team, following Dave Van Horne's selection as the Frick Award winner in 2011. Van Horne spent parts of four decades broadcasting Montreal Expos games.

The Ford C. Frick Award is voted upon annually and is named in memory of the sportswriter, radio broadcaster, National League president and Baseball commissioner. The complete list of recipients includes:

FORD C. FRICK AWARD RECIPIENTS

1978 Mel Allen
Red Barber
1979 Bob Elson
1980 Russ Hodges
1981 Ernie Harwell
1982 Vin Scully
1983 Jack Brickhouse
1984 Curt Gowdy
1985 Buck Canel
1986 Bob Prince
1987 Jack Buck
1988 Lindsey Nelson
1989 Harry Caray
1990 By Saam
1991 Joe Garagiola
1992 Milo Hamilton
1993 Chuck Thompson
1994 Bob Murphy
1995 Bob Wolff
1996 Herb Carneal
1997 Jimmy Dudley
1998 Jaime Jarrin
1999 Arch McDonald
2000 Marty Brennaman
2001 Felo Ramirez
2002 Harry Kalas
2003 Bob Uecker
2004 Lon Simmons
2005 Jerry Coleman
2006 Gene Elston
2007 Denny Matthews
2008 Dave Niehaus
2009 Tony Kubek
2010 Jon Miller
2011 Dave Van Horne
2012 Tim McCarver
2013 Tom Cheek

HOWARTH TO BE HONOURED WITH CANADIAN BALL HALL'S JACK GRANEY AWARD

Jerry Howarth, the longtime radio voice of the Toronto Blue Jays, has been named the winner of the Canadian Baseball Hall of Fame's 2012 Jack Graney Award. The St. Marys, Ont.-based shrine generally presents this award annually to a member of the media who has made significant contributions to baseball in Canada through their life's work. Born in 1946 in York, Pennsylva-nia, Howarth grew up in San Francisco. He attended Hastings Law School at the University of California where he met his wife, Mary. Now heading into his 33rd season in the Jays' radio booth, Howarth has called more than 5,000 games for the club – the most of any broadcaster in franchise history.

Howarth, who became a Canadian citizen in 1994, resides in Toronto with his wife, Mary. He will be presented with the Jack Graney Award in a pre-game ceremony at Rogers Centre early in the 2013 season.

JACK GRANEY AWARD RECIPIENTS

1987 Neil MacCarl – Toronto Star
1988 Milt Dunnell – Toronto Star
1990 Austin "Dink" Carroll – Montreal Gazette
1991 Joe Crysdale & Hal Kelly – CKEY
1996 Dave Van Horne – TSN & CIQC
2001 Tom Cheek – Toronto Blue Jays
2002 Ernie Harwell – Detroit Tigers
2003 Allan Simpson – Baseball America
2004 Jacques Doucet – Montreal Expos
2005 Len Bramson – TBS Sports
2009 Ian MacDonald – Montreal Gazette
2010 Bob Elliott – Sun Media & canadianbaseballnetwork.com
2011 W. P. Kinsella – "Shoeless Joe" novel adapted to film "Field of Dreams"
2012 Jerry Howarth –Toronto Blue Jays

BOB ELLIOTT WINS SPINK AWARD

Bob Elliott, who has been a positive influence on an entire country for the past 30 years as a writer, columnist and ambassador for baseball and Canada, was elected the 2012 winner of the J.G. Taylor Spink Award in balloting by the Baseball Writers' Association of America. This award is presented annually to a sportswriter "for meritorious contributions to baseball writing." He was honoured with the award this past July during the National Baseball Hall of Fame and Museum's induction weekend in Cooperstown, NY.

Elliott received 205 votes from the 455 ballots cast by BBWAA members with 10 or more consecutive years' service in becoming the 63rd winner of the award since its inception in 1962 and named for the first recipient. Spink was a driving force of The Sporting News, known during his lifetime as the "Baseball Bible."

SPINK AWARD RECIPIENTS

2013 Paul Hagen
2012 Bob Elliott (Columnist, Toronto Sun)
2011 Bill Conlin
2010 Bill Madden
2009 Nick Peters
2008 Larry Whiteside
2006 Rick Hummel
2005 Tracy Ringolsby
2004 Peter Gammons
2003 Murray Chass
2002 Hal McCoy
2001 Joe Falls
2000 Ross Newhan
1999 Hal Lebovitz
1998 Bob Stevens
1997 Sam Lacy
1996 Charley Feeney
1995 Joseph Durso
1993 Wendell Smith
1992 Leonard Koppett & Bus Saidt
1991 Ritter Collett
1990 Phil Collier
1989 Jerome Holtzman
1988 Bob Hunter & Ray Kelly
1987 Jim Murray
1986 Jack Lang
1985 Earl Lawson
1984 Joe McGuff
1983 Ken Smith
1982 Si Burick
1981 Bob Addie & Allen Lewis
1980 Joe Reichler & Milton Richman
1979 Bob Broeg & Tommy Holmes
1978 Tim Murnane & Dick Young
1977 Gordon Cobbledick & Edgar Munzel
1976 Harold Kaese & Red Smith
1975 Tom Meany & Shirley Povich
1974 John Carmichael & James Isaminger
1973 Warren Brown, John Drebinger & John F. Kieran
1972 Dan Daniel, Fred Lieb & J. Roy Stockton
1971 Frank Graham
1970 Heywood C. Broun
1969 Sid Mercer
1968 H.G. Salsinger
1967 Damon Runyon
1966 Grantland Rice
1965 Charles Dryden
1964 Hugh Fullerton
1963 Ring Lardner
1962 J.G. Taylor Spink

BASEBALL WRITER'S ASSOCIATION OF AMERICA

BBWAA TORONTO CHAPTER - 2013

EXECUTIVE

HONORARY CHAIRMAN - Neil MacCarl
CHAIRMAN - Richard Griffin, Toronto Star
VICE-CHAIRMAN - Bob Elliott, Toronto Sun*#
SECRETARY/TREASURER - Shi Davidi

DIRECTORS:

Mark Zwolinski, Toronto Star
Dave Perkins, Toronto Star
Mike Rutsey, Toronto Sun
John Lott, National Post

MEMBERS:

At Large: Shi Davidi

Associated Press: Rob Gillies, Ian Harrison

Canadian Press: Larry Millson, Gregory Strong

Globe & Mail: Tom Maloney, Jeff Blair, Robert MacLeod, Paul Attfield

National Post: John Lott

Toronto Star: Richard Griffin, Dave Perkins, Mark Zwolinski, Doug Smith, Damian Cox, Brandon Kennedy, Cathal Kelly, Rosie DiManno

Toronto Sun: Bob Elliott*#, Ken Fidlin, Steve Simmons, Mike Rutsey, Bill Lankhoff, Steve Buffery

HONORARY MEMBERS:

Milt Dunnell
Trent Frayne
George Gross
Neil MacCarl
Larry Millson

* Named the Jack Graney Award winner in 2010

\# Named the J.G. Taylor Spink Award winner in 2012

NATIONAL BASEBALL HALL OF FAME AND MUSEUM

25 Main Street, Cooperstown, New York 13326
Phone: (607) 547-7200 **Fax:** (607) 547-2044
Public Relations: (607) 547-0215
e-mail address: info@baseballhalloffame.org
Web site: baseballhalloffame.org

Summer Hours: Memorial Day Weekend – Labor Day Weekend: 9 a.m. to 9 p.m.
Regular Hours: 9 a.m. to 5 p.m.
Holiday Closings: Thanksgiving Day, Christmas Day, and New Year's Day.

DIRECTORY: Jane Forbes Clark (Chairman), Joe Morgan (Vice Chairman), Jeff Idelson (President), Bill Haase (Senior Vice President), Sean Gahagan (Vice President, Retail Merchandising & Licensing), Erik Strohl (Senior Director of Exhibitions and Collections), Ken Meifert (Senior Director, Development)

RESEARCH AND LIBRARY CONTACTS: Jim Gates (Librarian), Tim Wiles (Research Director), Pat Kelly (Photo Archivist)

PR CONTACTS: Brad Horn (Senior Director, Communications & Education) and Craig Muder (Communications Director)

HALL OF FAME WEEKEND 2013: July 26 – 29

Inductees: Hank O'Day, Jacob Ruppert and Deacon White
Awards: Sat. July 27, 4:30 p.m. ET, Doubleday Field
Induction: Sun. July 28, 1:30 p.m. ET, Clark Sports Center

HALL OF FAME CLASSIC 2013: May 25-26

Golf tournament & other events all weekend
Game: Sat. May 25, Doubleday Field;
For more information, visit **baseballhall.org**

BLUE JAYS IN THE HALL OF FAME

With the Inductions of Roberto Alomar and Pat Gillick in 2011, a total of five former players and one executive in the Hall of Fame spent some of their professional careers with the Toronto Blue Jays. Alomar spent five seasons (1991-1995) with the Blue Jays and is the first player to enter the Hall of Fame wearing a Blue Jays cap, while Pat Gillick joined the team's front office in 1978 and left the team in 1994. They join Rickey Henderson (1993), Paul Molitor (1993-1995), Phil Niekro (1987) and Dave Winfield (1992). For more information on Blue Jays in the Hall of Fame, visit the "Hall of Famers" team pages at **www.baseballhall.org**.

NOTABLE BLUE JAYS ARTIFACTS IN COOPERSTOWN

- Cap worn by Yan Gomes on May 17, 2012 when he became the first Brazilian to appear in an MLB game.
- Jersey worn by Frank Thomas to hit his 500th HR on June 28, 2007.
- Bat used by Carlos Delgado to hit four home runs in one game on Sept. 25, 2003.
- Cap worn by Tony Batista against the Texas Rangers on Opening Day 2001, Major League Baseball's first Opening Day game in Puerto Rico.
- Bat used by Cliff Johnson to set a record for most career pinch hit home runs (19).
- Ball from Roger Clemens' 200th career win against the New York Yankees on May 21, 1997.
- Bat used by Joe Carter to hit his game-winning home run in Game 6 of the 1993 World Series against the Philadelphia Phillies.
- Cap and spikes worn by Dave Stieb and a ball from his no-hitter on Sept. 2, 1990.

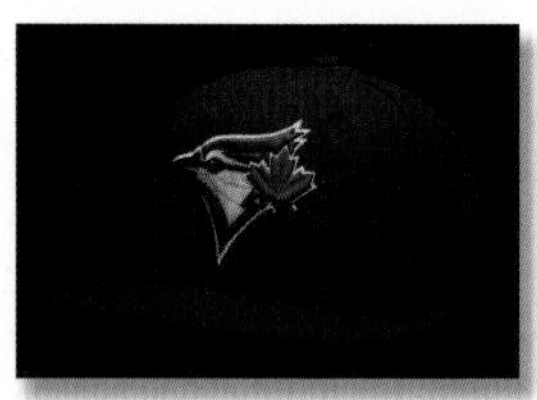

Yan Gomes cap from May 17, 2012 when he became the first native of Brazil to appear in the big leagues.

A LOOK AHEAD TO 2014

Ballots for the 2014 Hall of Fame/BBWAA election will be distributed in early December with results from the voting scheduled to be announced in January 2014. A partial list of first-year candidates for election include: Moises Alou, Eric Gagne, Tom Glavine, Greg Maddux, Mike Mussina, Hideo Nomo, Jeff Kent and Frank Thomas. Historical information on past BBWAA elections and the election process can be accessed at **www.baseballhall.org** or by contacting the Hall of Fame Public Relations department.

CONNECT TO COOPERSTOWN

- For up-to-the-minute news from Cooperstown, visit at **www.baseballhall.org**. Stay up-to-date on all the activity at the Hall of Fame's official site and through social networking on Facebook, LinkedIn, Twitter and YouTube.
- If you would like to receive interesting stories and timely news items direct from the Hall of Fame and get the inside track on the latest happenings in Cooperstown, sign up for Inside Pitch. There's no cost to receive our weekly electronic newsletter in your e-mail box at home or work and it's easy to enroll: Just log on to **www.hofclubhouse.com**.
- If you have an interest in receiving ***Around The Horn***, the Hall's monthly media newsletter, please send an e-mail to **info@baseballhall.org**. Be sure to include your name, name of organization and e-mail address.

RESEARCH ASSISTANCE

The Hall of Fame is pleased to provide assistance in baseball research and members of the media are encouraged to utilize this valuable baseball resource whenever necessary by calling the Public Relations department at (607) 547-0215, or the Library Reference desk at (607) 547-0330.

BROADCASTING

TELEVISION

SPORTSNET™

BUCK MARTINEZ
PLAY-BY-PLAY ANNOUNCER

Buck Martinez returns for a 4th season in the broadcast booth after returning to the Blue Jays for the first time since managing the club in 2002… The 64 year old brings with him 45 years of baseball experience, including 20 years as a player, 25 years in broadcasting, and two as a manager… Beginning in 1967 when he was signed by the Philadelphia Phillies, Martinez spent 20 years as a catcher in professional baseball with the Kansas City Royals, Milwaukee Brewers and his final six seasons with the Blue Jays… He appeared in the postseason with Kansas City in 1976, batting .333 in the 5-game ALCS against the New York Yankees… Wrote two books about his experiences with the Blue Jays, "From Worst to First" (1985) and "The Last Out" (1986)… Among his 12 seasons associated with the Blue Jays, he served as manager for Toronto in 2001 and part of the 2002 season, compiling a 100-115 record… In 2006, he managed the United States team in the inaugural World Baseball Classic… Martinez' first experience with broadcasting came in 1982, when he covered the American League Championship Series, the World Series and the All-Star Game for the Telemedia Radio Network…. His television broadcast career began in 1987 as a color commentator for the Toronto Blue Jays on TSN… Began working with ESPN radio and television in 1992, and in 1995, Martinez was awarded a Sports EMMY Award for his work on ESPN's coverage of Cal Ripken's 2,131st consecutive game… Worked as a television analyst for the Baltimore Orioles from 2003 -2009 and has also served as a co-host of XM Radio's Baseball This Morning show on the MLB Home Plate channel… Martinez also contributed colour commentary for Sunday afternoon games on TBS, as well as for the network's postseason coverage… A California native, Martinez attended Sacramento City College, Sacramento State University, and Central Missouri State University... He and his wife, reside in Clearwater, FL... They have one son, Casey, a 47th round pick by Toronto in the 2000 First Year Player Draft.

PAT TABLER
COLOUR COMMENTATOR

Pat Tabler brings a wealth of experience to Rogers Sportsnet as the network's baseball colour commentator... A former major leaguer, Tabler started as a studio analyst on TSN Baseball Tonight in 1993... In 2001, Tabler became the network's full-time analyst on Blue Jays telecasts... Tabler, a native of Hamilton, OH, began his Major League career with the Chicago Cubs in 1981 before stops in Cleveland, Kansas City, New York and eventually Toronto where he won a World Series in 1992... An All-Star in 1987, Tabler was perhaps best known to baseball fans as one of the game's greatest career clutch hitters, batting nearly .500 in bases loaded situations... Tabler was a first round pick of the New York Yankees in the 1976 free agent draft, and had a career batting average of .282.

JAMIE CAMPBELL
HOST, BLUE JAYS CENTRAL

Jamie Campbell got his start in sports broadcasting in 1993 at CBC Edmonton before moving on to CJOH Ottawa in 1997… In 1998, he became one of Sportsnet's original broadcasters and co-hosted the first edition of Sportscentral (now Sportsnet Connected)… Has hosted coverage of the Grey Cup, Super Bowl, NHL Draft, MLB All-Star Game and MLB post-season... He called play-by-play for the Toronto Phantoms of the Arena Football League from 2002-2003, the CFL on Sportsnet in 2004, and was the play-by-play voice of the Toronto Blue Jays from 2005 to 2009… In 2010 at the Olympic Winter Games in Vancouver, millions of Canadians were watching when Campbell announced the country's historic first gold medal won by Alexandre Bilodeau…He also called the play-by-play for cycling at London 2012… Now serves as host of the popular Blue Jays Central with analyst Gregg Zaun.

GREGG ZAUN
ANALYST, BLUE JAYS CENTRAL

Former Major League Baseball catcher Gregg Zaun's career began in 1989 when he was drafted by the Baltimore Orioles... He was traded to the Florida Marlins in 1996, where one year later he helped the team win the World Series... After playing for the Texas Rangers, the Kansas City Royals and the Colorado Rockies, signed with the Toronto Blue Jays in 2004... He quickly became a fan favourite in Toronto, notably becoming the second Blue Jay of all time to hit a walk-off grand slam and the first to do so in extra innings... His charisma paired with his deep love of the game earned Zaun a gig as post-season MLB analyst for Sportsnet in 2006... He continued to support Sportsnet's post-season coverage until his retirement from the MLB in 2011... Returns in 2013 for his third season as analyst for Blue Jays Central alongside host Jamie Campbell.

DIRK HAYHURST
ANALYST

Joining the Sportsnet broadcast team for a second year, Dirk Hayhurst returns as co-host of Baseball Central @ Noon on Sportsnet 590 The FAN... A former Major League Baseball pitcher, motivational speaker, and a bestselling author, Hayhurst's career in baseball began when he was drafted by the San Diego Padres in the eighth round of the 2003 amateur player draft... His eight-year MLB career included time with the San Diego Padres, Toronto Blue Jays and the Tampa Bay Rays organizations before retiring in 2011... In 2010, he released his first book, The Bullpen Gospels, and was met with a surge of acclaim... His follow-up sequel, Out of My League, about Dirk's 40 days and nights as a rookie in the big leagues, was also a bestseller and earned him the title of "best author to wear a baseball uniform" according The New York Times... In addition to his success as an author, Hayhurst has also contributed to Sportsnet magazine, Sports Illustrated, ESPN, Baseball America and Athletes Quarterly... Holds a degree in communication studies from Kent State University where he is also a member of the athletic hall of fame... He and his wife currently reside in Hudson, Ohio.

The Baseball Media Press Box at Rogers Centre

THE FAN RADIO NETWORK

A Division of Rogers Communications
1 Ted Rogers Way
Toronto, ON M4Y 3B7

Main: (416) 935-0590
Flagship station: Sportsnet Radio FAN 590
www.thefan590.com
Engineer: Tom Young

JERRY HOWARTH
PLAY-BY-PLAY ANNOUNCER

Back for his 33rd season as a member of the BLUE JAYS radio team... On December 13, 2012, was named the winner of the Canadian Baseball Hall of Fame's 2012 Jack Graney Award... 66 years old... Grew up in San Francisco and graduated from the University of Santa Clara in 1968 with a degree in Economics... Served two years as an officer in the U.S. Army, V Corps Headquarters, in Frankfurt, Germany, from 1968 to 1970... On return, attended Hastings Law School in San Francisco where he met his wife, Mary, who is a lawyer... Started broadcasting career in 1974 with play-by-play of the Tacoma Twins AAA baseball team and also for the University of Puget Sound's football and basketball teams... Moved to Salt Lake City, Utah, in 1976 and did the radio play-by-play for the Salt Lake Gulls AAA baseball team for three years... Switched to basketball and was the Assistant General Manager and radio broadcaster for the Utah Pros in the Western Basketball Association and later the Group Sales Director for the NBA's Utah Jazz prior to joining KWMS Radio in 1980... Moved to Toronto in 1981 to become one of the Blue Jays radio broadcasters with Tom Cheek... Jerry is the Junior Varsity Basketball Coach at Etobicoke Collegiate High School in Toronto... He has coached basketball since 1991... He is also active in raising funds for Special Olympics and other charities in Toronto... He and his wife Mary have two grown sons, Ben and Joe, and reside in Toronto all year round.

JACK MORRIS
ANALYST AND BASEBALL CENTRAL

A familiar face is returning to Toronto this 2013 MLB season, as former Toronto Blue Jays pitcher Jack Morris returns to the city where he won two World Series titles as Sportsnet's newest Blue Jays analyst. Morris will provide analysis for Sportsnet 590 The FAN's Blue Jays radio broadcasts, and will also make appearances on Sportsnet's Blue Jays game telecasts, Blue Jays Central, Blue Jays Central at Noon and sportsnet.ca.

Morris was drafted in 1976 by the Detroit Tigers and played in 18 big league seasons with five different teams. Best known for his devastating forkball, the right-handed pitcher won four World Series titles with three different teams ('84 Tigers, '91 Twins, and '92 and '93 Blue Jays) over his big league career.

Among his many accolades, the native of St. Paul, Minnesota amassed 254 wins over his pitching career, threw a no-hitter in 1984 for the Detroit Tigers and was named World Series MVP in 1991 while a member of the Minnesota Twins.

The five-time All-Star however, will forever be known to Blue Jays fans as the first 20-game winner in club history (21-wins) and propelling his team into the playoffs for the first of their back-to-back World Series Championships in 1992 and 1993.

Morris retired in 1995 and has spent time as a colour analyst for the Minnesota Twins and as well as a guest on Detroit Tigers broadcasts.

MIKE WILNER
HOST, JAYS TALK/PLAY-BY-PLAY ANNOUNCER

Enters his 12th season as a member of the Blue Jays' broadcast crew... Is the host of the Blue Jays post-game show which is aired after each game during the season... Born in Toronto, Ontario... Graduated from the University of Toronto in 1994 (B.Sc. Psychology; Ethics, Society and Law)... Began radio career with University of Toronto Radio in 1988, named Sports Director in 1989, and did play-by-play of hockey, football and basketball... Started professional play-by-play career at age 19 with the single-A Welland Pirates, later broadcast for the single-A Watertown Indians and double-A Hardware City (New Britain) Rock Cats... Married with two daughters...Wife hails from Buenos Aires, Argentina... Resides in Mississauga.

LE BASEBALL DES BLUES JAYS

JACQUES DOUCET
PLAY-BY-PLAY ANNOUNCER (FRENCH)

For 33 years on CKAC, Roger Doucet was the voice of the Montreal Expos… Followed suit with the play-by-play calls for the Capitales de Québec of the Can-Am league... Inducted into the Québec (2002) and Canadian (2003) Baseball Hall of Fame, he met again with his long-time friend Rodger Brulotte to put together again the celebrity duo that is so synonymous with the Montreal Expos, but is now the French-speaking voice of the Toronto Blue Jays

RODGER BRULOTTE
PLAY-BY-PLAY ANNOUNCER (FRENCH)

His association with the Expos began in 1969 as a member of the club's scouting department… The following year he was named administrative assistant to the director of scouting and player personnel, Mel Didier… Also has been in public relations and marketing as well as serving as the team's traveling secretary in 1977-78… Spent 17 seasons with Jacques Doucet on the Expos' French radio network… For his work on television, more than 20 years at RDS analyzing Expos games, Major League baseball games, All-Star games and post season games, he and his partner, Denis Casavant, were nominated twice for a Gemeaux Award for sports broadcasting… As of august 2012, he has joined TVA Sports Network, as an analyst on the Blue Jays' French broadcasts… His hobbies are golf, books and movies.

2013 BLUE JAYS RADIO STATION LIST

BRITISH COLUMBIA

CKST/Team 1410	Vancouver	1410 AM

ALBERTA

SPORTSNET 960 THE FAN	Calgary	960 AM
CKER	Edmonton	101.7 FM

SASKATCHEWAN

CJSL	Estevan	1280 AM
CJYM	Rosetown	1330 AM
CFYM	Kindersley	1210 AM
CFSL	Weyburn	1190 AM

MANITOBA

CKMW	Winkler	1570 AM

ONTARIO

CKGL	Kitchener	570 AM
CJBK	London	1290 AM
CKAT	North Bay	600 AM
CIWW	Ottawa	1310 AM
CJMB-FM	Peterborough	90.5 FM
CHOK	Sarnia	1070 AM
CJCS	Stratford	1240 AM
CJCL/Sportsnet 590 The FAN	Toronto	590 AM
CKNX	Wingham	920 AM

QUEBEC

CKGM/TSN RADIO 990	Montreal	990 AM

NEW BRUNSWICK

CKNI-FM	Moncton	91.9 FM
CHNI-FM	Saint John	88.9 FM

NOVA SCOTIA

CJNI-FM	Halifax	95.7 FM

As the only sports and entertainment venue of its size and design in Canada, *Rogers Centre* has hosted some of the greatest music, sport, trade and community events of our time.

Rock stars, entertainers, athletes, religious figures and inspirational leaders have all delighted audiences under the dome.

Rogers Centre is one of the most dynamic and versatile entertainment centres in the world. No other venue has the diversity of events that *Rogers Centre* hosts on an annual basis across over 200 event days. Since its spectacular opening on June 3, 1989, *Rogers Centre* has achieved the highest honours in the stadium entertainment industry and currently is a leader in the fight for corporate environmental responsibility. Formerly known as SkyDome, the venue was renamed *Rogers Centre* on February 2, 2005.

Structurally, *Rogers Centre* remains the same today as it was when it opened in 1989 with the exception of several key cosmetic changes over the last few years. Widened concourses, updated and upgraded suites, new video and broadcast technology were just some of the areas touched during an extensive $20 million rejuvenation project.

One of the unique features of *Rogers Centre* is that it can be transformed to meet the needs of any event by converting between two primary modes; baseball and football. The 100 level seats sit on a railway track system that allows them to rotate between each mode within hours.

In addition, *Rogers Centre*'s **fully retractable roof** allows the venue to be an open-air facility with the ability to close pending weather conditions. This innovative roof function ensures that no event needs to be cancelled due to inclement weather. The roof system features a series of three moveable panels and one stationary panel which takes 25 minutes to open or close fully. The roof weighs 11,000 tons and covers an area of 339,343 square feet. The highest point stands 282 feet above field level.

Architects Rod Robbie and Michael Allen designed the building patenting its retractable roof system. Preparation of the site began in April 1986, with groundbreaking taking place in October of that same year. The last exterior concrete was poured in November 1988 and the first test of the moveable roof panels was performed in January 1989. More than 10,000 person-years of employment were created with the construction of *Rogers Centre*.

Rogers Centre is home to impressive technology including the **video and ribbon boards** located in the north end and around the circumference of the 300 Level. Purchased in 2005 from Daktronics, the screen is one of the industry's leading with PROSTAR® VIDEOPLUS which uses state of the art LED technology. Measuring 110 feet wide by 33 feet high, the video board is capable of projecting 4.3 trillion colours.

The **playing surface** at *Rogers Centre* took on a new look for the 2010 baseball season with the installation of AstroTurf Gameday 3D synthetic turf system. The field is comprised of 97 panels for the baseball configuration. The largest roll is 51 meters (170 feet) long by 4.5 meters (15 feet) wide, weighing 8,925 pounds with a roll diameter of 1.4 meters (4.8 feet). AstroTurf Gameday 3D is a "Rollup System" with each roll panel having crumb rubber and sand in between the fibres to produce similar playing properties as natural grass. In 2009, AstroTurf Gameday 3D was installed at the Jays training facility in Dunedin (infield practice area only).

With a symmetrical layout in baseball mode, the field measures 328' down the foul lines, 375' to the power alleys and 400' to dead centre field. The diamond is centred two degrees off perfect north and the 10' high outfield wall is fully padded for the protection of the players. The pitcher's mound is constructed on a fibreglass dish that is lowered and raised by a hydraulic system.

ARAMARK - In the 6th year of a 10 year deal - provides *Rogers Centre* with club level concessions as well as manages the HSBC Club VIP Restaurant. A world class leader in professional services, Aramark brings tasty treats to fans at *Rogers Centre* which includes everything from traditional baseball fare to Asian delights and Mediterranean treats. In 2009, a new marche designed Muddy York Market (section 108) and the Roundhouse Carvery and Bar (Gate 8 - Level 100) were unveiled.

Conveniently located in the heart of Toronto's vibrant downtown community, at the base of the CN Tower and close to the Entertainment and Financial Districts, the stadium is easily accessible via the TTC or GO Transit. Also located at the stadium is the Renaissance Toronto Hotel, a 348-room hotel with 70 rooms overlooking the field.

ROGERS CENTRE INTERESTING FACTS

- The entire *Rogers Centre* complex spans 12.7 acres (5.14 hectares). The building itself takes up 11.5 acres (4.66 hectares).
- The diameter of the building is 700 feet while the volume inside the stadium with the roof closed is 56.5 million cubic feet (1.6 million cubic meters).
- On average, it takes approximately 40 hours to convert the field from baseball to football mode.
- Seating Capacity: approximately 54,000 (depending on layout of event)
- Baseball Capacity: 49,282
- Suites: 151 suites are conveniently located on the 300 and 400 levels of the venue.
- The Toronto Blue Jays 1993 World Series Title was won on home turf at *Rogers Centre* (Saturday, October 23 vs. Philadelphia; 8-6)
- On March 17, 2002 *Rogers Centre* set a venue attendance record when it hosted 68,237 fans for WrestleMania X8.
- The names of workers who helped build *Rogers Centre* can be found in a permanent tribute located in the north end of the 100L concourse.

ROGERS CENTRE MARQUEE DATES

- Official Groundbreaking: October 3, 1986
- Opening Ceremony: June 3, 1989
- Firsts: Baseball: June 5, 1989
  Concert: Rod Stewart - June 8, 1989
  Football: June 29, 1989 (pre-season)
  July 12, 1989 (regular season)

SKYDOME/ROGERS CENTRE FIRSTS

GAME — Monday June 5, 1989 (Blue Jays-3, Milwaukee Brewers-5)

WIN — Wednesday, June 7, 1989 (Blue Jays-4, Milwaukee-2)

ATTENDANCE — 48,378

TIME/TEMP — 2:43/18°C

PITCHER — Jimmy Key, Toronto

BATTER — Paul Molitor, Milwaukee (doubled)

PLATE UMPIRE — Rocky Roe

PITCH — Fastball, called strike

HIT — Double by Molitor in 1st inning

RUN — Molitor in 1st inning

SINGLE — Kelly Gruber, Toronto, 1st inning

DOUBLE — Paul Molitor, 1st inning

HOME RUN — Fred McGriff, Toronto, 2nd inning

RBI — Gary Sheffield, Milwaukee, 1st inning

WINNING PITCHER — Don August, Milwaukee

BLUE JAYS WINNING PITCHER — John Cerutti

LOSING PITCHER — Jimmy Key, Toronto

SAVE — Dan Plesac, Milwaukee

PUTOUT — Nelson Liriano, Toronto

ASSIST — Kelly Gruber, Toronto

STOLEN BASE — Fred McGriff, 6th inning

WALK — George Bell, Toronto, 2nd inning

FIRST GAME PLAYED AT EXHIBITION STADIUM

The Blue Jays slugged their way to a 9-5 triumph over the Chicago White Sox in their April 7, 1977, debut.

Despite snow flurries before the game and near-freezing temperatures, 44,649 fans witnessed the exciting contest, which featured 16 hits by the Blue Jays and 15 by Chicago.

Doug Ault smacked two homers and a single and rookie Al Woods hit a pinch-homer in his first big-league at bat for Toronto. Richie Zisk had four hits for the visitors.

The Blue Jays played 968-games from April 7, 1977-May 28, 1989 at Exhibition Stadium posting a record of 492-476 with 23,213,567 fans passing through the turnstiles.

EXHIBITION STADIUM FIRSTS

GAME — Thurs. April 7, 1977 (Blue Jays 9, Chicago White Sox 5)

ATTENDANCE — 44,649

TIME/TEMP. — 3:22/0°C. (32°F)

PITCHER — Bill Singer, Toronto

BATTER — Ralph Garr, Chicago (walked)

PLATE UMPIRE — Nestor Chylak

PITCH — Called strike

HIT — Home run by Richie Zisk, first inning, none on

RUN — Ralph Garr (scored on sacrifice fly by Jorge Orta)

SINGLE — Jim Spencer, Chicago, April 7, 1977, first inning

DOUBLE — Richie Zisk, Chicago, April 7, 1977, second inning

TRIPLE — Ron LeFlore, Detroit, April 12, 1977, fifth inning

HOME RUN — Richie Zisk, April 7, 1977, first inning

FIRST RBI — Jorge Orta, Chicago, April 7, 1977, 1st inning

INSIDE-THE-PARK HOME RUN — Cecil Cooper, Milwaukee, May 5, 1977 (fifth inning)

GRAND SLAM HOME RUN — Hector Torres vs. New York, June 27, 1977 (fifth inning, off Ron Guidry)

TWO HOME-RUN GAME — Doug Ault, Toronto, April 7, 1977

THREE HOME-RUN GAME — John Mayberry, K.C., June 1, 1977

PINCH-HIT HOME RUN — Al Woods, Toronto, April 7, 1977 (fifth inning)

WINNING PITCHER — Jerry Johnson, Toronto (in relief), April 7, 1977

LOSING PITCHER — Ken Brett, Chicago (starter), April 7, 1977

SAVE — Pete Vuckovich, Toronto, April 7, 1977

PUTOUT — Steve Bowling, Toronto (fly ball to right field) April 7, 1977

ASSIST — Hector Torres, Toronto (ground ball to shortstop) April 7, 1977

ERROR — Rick Cerone, Toronto, April 7, 1977

SHUTOUT — Ferguson Jenkins, Boston, Sun. April 24, 1977 (9-0)

COMPLETE GAME — Dave Lemanczyk, Toronto vs. Chicago, April 9, 1977

WALK — Ralph Garr by Bill Singer, April 7, 1977 (first inning)

STRIKEOUT — John Scott by Ken Brett, April 7, 1977 (first inning)

FORFEIT — Baltimore, Thurs. September 15, 1977 (Blue Jays 9, Baltimore 0)

NIGHT GAME — Mon., May 2, 1977 vs. Milwaukee (Brewers 3, Blue Jays 1)

STOLEN BASE — Ralph Garr, Chicago, April 7, 1977 (first inning)

TRIPLE PLAY — Clancy to Mayberry to Gomez, April 22, 1978 (sixth inning)

BALK — Balor Moore, Toronto vs. Seattle, May 13, 1978

ONE-HITTER — Chris Knapp, California, September 3, 1978 (Angels 3, Blue Jays 1)

NO-HITTER — Never happened

EXHIBITION STADIUM LASTS

GAME — May 28, 1989 (Blue Jays 7, Chicago White Sox 5), 10 innings

ATTENDANCE — 46,120

TIME/TEMP. — 3:19/20°C. (68°F)

PITCHER — Bobby Thigpen, Chicago

BATTER — George Bell, Toronto, home run

PLATE UMPIRE — Dan Morrison

PITCH — fastball, home run

HIT — Home Run by George Bell, 10th inning

RUN — George Bell on home run

SINGLE — Steve Lyons, Chicago, 10th inning

DOUBLE — Kelly Gruber, Toronto 10th inning

HOME RUN — George Bell, 10th inning

RBI — George Bell, 10th inning

WINNING PITCHER — Tom Henke

LOSING PITCHER — Bobby Thigpen

PUTOUT — Fred McGriff, Toronto, 10th inning

ASSIST — Nelson Liriano, Toronto, 10th inning

ERROR — Matt Merullo, Chicago, 4th inning

STOLEN BASE — Steve Lyons, Chicago, 10th inning

BLUE JAYS AT ROGERS CENTRE AND EXHIBITION STADIUM

	AT EXHIBITION W-L	AT ROGERS CENTRE W-L	OPEN W-L	CLOSED W-L	CLOSED DURING GAME W-L
1977	25-55				
1978	37-44				
1979	32-49				
1980	35-46				
1981	17-36				
1982	44-37				
1983	48-33				
1984	49-32				
1985	54-26				
1985 ALCS	2-2				
1986	42-39				
1987	52-29				
1988	45-36				
1989	12-14	34-21	23-21	9-0	2-0
1989 ALCS		1-2	–	1-2	–
1990		44-37	12-18	29-17	3-2
1991		46-35	26-22	19-10	1-3
1991 ALCS		0-3	–	0-3	–
1992		53-28	19-11	31-16	3-1
1992 ALCS		2-1	–	2-1	–
1992 WS		2-1	–	2-1	–
1993		48-33	15-14	30-17	3-2
1993 ALCS		1-2	–	1-2	–
1993 WS		2-1	–	2-1	–
1994		33-26	11-12	16-11	6-3
1995		29-43	17-26	12-16	0-1
1996		35-46	18-25	14-16	3-5
1997		42-39	20-20	18-16	4-3
1998		51-30	33-12	16-13	2-5
1999		40-41	18-34	18-5	4-2
2000		45-36	26-12	16-21	3-3
2001		39-42	20-19	18-22	1-1
2002		42-39	30-22	11-17	1-0
2003		41-40	21-17	19-20	1-4
2004		40-41	28-26	12-14	0-1
2005		43-38	27-24	13-13	3-1
2006		50-31	24-19	24-12	2-0
2007		49-32	32-19	15-13	2-0
2008		47-34	26-20	19-10	2-4
2009		44-37	17-20	22-15	5-2
2010		45-33	29-19	10-14	6-0
2011		42-39	29-30	12-9	1-0
2012		41-40	22-24	15-14	4-2
OVERALL	**492-476**	**1024-861**	**543-486**	**418-331**	**62-44**
POST SEASON	**2-2**	**8-10**	**—**	**8-10**	**—**

All-time regular season home wins 1516, All-time post season home wins 10 = 1485
All-time regular season home losses 1337, All-time post season home losses 12 = 1309
* Included is 1 win in Puerto Rico in 2001 (Jays were home team)
* Games played against Philadelphia in June 2010 are considered away games in W-L records but home games in attendance records.

ROGERS CENTRE ROOF OPENINGS

FIRST OPENING DATE OF EACH SEASON

YEAR	DATE OPENED	OPPONENT	FINAL SCORE	W-L	TEMPERATURE & WIND
1989	Monday June 5	Milwaukee Brewers	Blue Jays 3 - Brewers 5	0-1	18' C/64'F, 6K
1990	Thursday April 26	Cleveland Indians	Blue Jays 3 - Indians 4	0-2	29'C/84'F, 20K
1991	Saturday April 27	Detroit Tigers	Blue Jays 2 - Tigers 4	0-3	20'C/68'F, 9K
1992	Saturday May 16	Seattle Mariners	Blue Jays 6 - Mariners 7	0-4	21'C/70'F, 17K
1993	Thursday May 6	Baltimore Orioles	Blue Jays 10 - Orioles 8	1-4	19'C/66'F, 30K
1994	Saturday May 7**	Milwaukee Brewers	Blue Jays 3 - Brewers 2	2-4	11'C/52'F, 15K
1995	Friday May 26	Cleveland Indians	Blue Jays 4 - Indians 7	2-5	20'C/68'F, 20K
1996	Saturday May 25	Minnesota Twins	Blue Jays 4 - Twins 6	2-6	15'C/59'F, 18K
1997	Saturday April 26	Seattle Mariners	Blue Jays 4 - Mariners 3	3-6	15'C/59'F, 17K
1998	Wednesday May 13	Oakland Athletics	Blue Jays 2 - Athletics 4	3-7	20'C/68'F, 10K
1999	Tuesday May 4	Oakland Athletics	Blue Jays 4 - Athletics 13	3-8	21'C/70'F, 15K
2000	Friday May 5	Cleveland Indians	Blue Jays 11 - Indians 10	4-8	26'C/79'F, 30K
2001	Wednesday June 6	Tampa Bay Rays	Blue Jays 2 - Rays 6	4-9	22'C/72'F, 20K
2002	Wednesday April 16	Boston Red Sox	Blue Jays 3 - Red Sox 14	4-10	27'C/81'F, 29K
2003	Monday May 26	Chicago White Sox	Blue Jays 11 - White Sox 5	5-10	17'C/63'F, 15K
2004	Thursday May 13	Boston Red Sox	Blue Jays 12 - Red Sox 6	6-10	17'C/63'F, 10K
2005	Friday May 6	Chicago White Sox	Blue Jays 3 - White Sox 5	6-11	17'C/63'F, 17K
2006	Wednesday April 19	New York Yankees	Blue Jays 1 - Yankees 3	6-12	17'C/63'F, 11K
2007	Sunday April 29	Texas Rangers	Blue Jays 7 - Rangers 3	7-12	17'C/63'F. 10K
2008	Thursday April 17	Texas Rangers	Blue Jays 1 - Rangers 4	7-13	21'C/70'F, 19K
2009	Thursday May 14	New York Yankees	Blue Jays 2 - Yankees 3	7-14	21'C/70'F, 35K
2010	Wednesday April 21	Kansas City Royals	Blue Jays 3 - Royals 4	7-15	14'C/57'F, 15K
2011	Saturday May 7	Detroit Tigers	Blue Jays 0 - Tigers 9	7-16	13'C/55'F, 13K
2012	Thursday April 19	Tamap Bay Rays	Blue Jays 4 - Rays 9	7-17	16' C/61'F,11K

** - indicates roof was closed during game

BLUE JAYS SPRING TRAINING DIRECTORY

SITE

MINOR LEAGUE COMPLEX
Bobby Mattick Training Center at Englebert Complex
1700 Solon Ave.
Dunedin, Florida 34698

FLORIDA AUTO EXCHANGE STADIUM
373 Douglas Avenue
Dunedin, Florida 34698

All home games will be played at Florida Auto Exchange Stadium

MINOR LEAGUE DATES:
March 2nd Pitchers & Catchers Report, March 5th Position Players Report

MAILING ADDRESS:
TORONTO BLUE JAYS
373 Douglas Avenue
Dunedin, Florida 34698

HOTEL HEADQUARTERS:
MINOR LEAGUE
BAYMONT INN & SUITES
26508 U.S. 19 North
Clearwater, Florida 33761

TELEPHONES:
BAYMONT INN & SUITES ....(727) 796-1234
FLORIDA AUTO EXCHANGE STADIUM OFFICE ....(727) 733-9302
FLORIDA AUTO EXCHANGE STADIUM TICKETS ....(727) 733-0429
MEDIA RELATIONS OFFICE ....(727) 733-9302
FAX - DUNEDIN STADIUM ....(727) 734-7661
PRESS BOX ....(727) 738-7040

TICKET DATA:
Ticket Office at FLORIDA AUTO EXCHANGE STADIUM, 373 Douglas Avenue, Dunedin
Monday to Friday: 8:00 a.m. to 6:00 p.m. for Phone Orders 1-888-525-JAYS
In Person: Starting on January 7 (Monday-Friday; 9:00 am - 5:00 pm and Saturday; 10:00 am - 2:00 pm)
Saturday: 10:00 a.m. to 2:00 p.m.

TICKET PRICES: Reserved $30.00–$15.00 US

Media Phones: Three phones are located in the press box.

Media Parking: Limited available.

Trainer's Room: Trainer's room is not accessible to media at any time.

FLORIDA AUTO EXCHANGE STADIUM

Located at the corner of Douglas Avenue and Beltrees Street in Dunedin, Florida. Florida Auto Exchange Stadium (re-named in 2011) has been the training home for the Toronto Blue Jays since the Club's first season in 1977 and home of the Dunedin Blue Jays of the Florida State League (A).

From 1977 to 1989 the Blue Jays played at Grant Field in Dunedin, which had a seating capacity of 3,417. In 1990 the City of Dunedin, at a cost of approximately 2.4 million, built a new stadium for the Blue Jays, Dunedin Stadium at Grant Field. The stadium was designed by the architect firm of Johnston Dana Associates and was built by Case Contracting Company of Plant City, Florida. With the construction the stadium saw an increase in the seating capacity from 3,417 to 6,106.

On September 8, 2000 the City of Dunedin and the Toronto Blue Jays reached an agreement to keep the Blue Jays in Dunedin for a minimum of 15 years pending approvals. Under the agreement major renovations would be made to Dunedin Stadium and a new minor league facility would be constructed. The $12.5 million renovation was shared between the State of Florida, Pinellas County, the City of Dunedin and the Toronto Blue Jays.

The renovations to Dunedin Stadium in February 2002 were designed by the architectural firm HOK Sports + Venue + Event and were built by J.A. Jones Construction. The changes to Dunedin Stadium included a new two-story building beyond the right field wall, which holds the Blue Jays clubhouse, training room and weight room on the ground floor with office space for the major league club on the second floor. The visiting clubhouse is now located on the third-base line. As well, the bleacher seats along the right-field foul line were removed and permanent seating installed. The dimensions of the Stadium increased from 315 feet to 327 feet. The capacity of the Stadium is 5,509.

DIMENSIONS

Left-field line	335 ft/102.1 m
Left-centre	375 ft/114.3 m
Centre field	400 ft/121.9 m
Right-centre	375 ft/114.3 m
Right-field line	327 ft/ 99.7 m

Fence – 16 feet high
Warning track – 20 ft/6.1 m
Capacity – 5,509

Construction on the minor league facility was completed for the 2003 season. The Bobby Mattick Training Center is located on the same grounds of the Englebert Complex. The facility features new clubhouses, offices, weight room, five full fields and a half field. Four of the fields are arranged in a cloverleaf pattern with an observation tower in the middle.

The largest ever spring exhibition game crowd was 6,218 on Tuesday March 27, 1990 for the game between the Blue Jays and the Kansas City Royals and on Wednesday March 13, 1985 for the Blue Jays and the New York Mets. The first ever Blue Jays game played at Grant Field was on March 11, 1977. The Blue Jays defeated the New York Mets by a score of 3-1.

SPRING TRAINING RECORD

YEAR	HOME W-L-T	ROAD W-L-T	OTHER W-L-T	OVERALL W-L-T	PCT
1977	5-8-0	3-8-0	0-0-0	8-16-0	.333
1978	3-8-0	5-9-0	0-0-0	8-17-0	.320
1979	6-6-0	6-6-0	0-0-0	12-12-0	.500
1980	5-4-0	5-3-0	0-0-0	10-7-0	.588
1981	7-6-0	6-7-1	0-0-0	13-13-1	.500
1982	7-7-0	8-5-1	0-0-0	15-12-1	.556
1983	9-4-0	7-6-0	1-1-0	16-10-0	.615
1984	8-6-0	5-10-0	2-2-0	13-16-0	.448
1985	11-4-0	8-5-1	1-2-0	19-9-1	.679
1986	10-3-0	5-9-0	0-0-0	15-12-0	.556
1987	5-5-1	4-6-1	0-0-1	9-11-2	.450
1988	9-5-0	9-5-2	1-1-0	18-10-2	.643
1989	12-4-0	9-6-0	0-0-0	21-10-0	.677
1990	1-5-0	3-5-0	0-0-0	4-10-0	.286
1991	6-10-0	3-9-2	1-2-0	9-19-2	.321
1992	12-4-0	1-14-0	1-3-0	13-18-0	.419
1993	8-8-0	3-11-0	2-2-0	11-19-0	.367
1994	7-10-0	5-8-1	0-4-0	12-18-1	.400
1995	4-2-1	1-3-1	0-1-0	5-5-2	.500
1996	6-8-1	3-14-0	0-3-0	9-22-1	.290
1997	12-4-0	5-10-1	0-0-0	17-14-1	.548
1998	7-10-0	9-6-0	2-0-0	16-16-0	.500
1999	8-9-0	4-11-0	0-0-0	12-20-0	.375
2000	12-5-1	6-7-0	2-2-1	18-12-1	.600
2001	8-5-0	4-11-0	0-1-0	12-16-0	.429
2002	7-5-2	6-8-1	0-0-0	13-13-3	.500
2003	8-4-2	5-6-2	0-0-0	13-10-4	.565
2004	7-8-1	6-7-1	0-0-0	13-15-2	.464
2005	9-6-0	7-4-2	0-2-0	16-10-2	.615
2006	5-10-0	7-8-0	0-0-0	12-18-0	.400
2007	6-7-2	6-7-2	0-0-0	12-14-4	.462
2008	7-7-0	6-9-0	2-0-0	13-16-0	.448
2009	7-8-1	6-9-2	1-0-1	13-17-3	.433
2010	4-6-1	8-8-0	1-1-0	12-14-1	.462
2011	8-7-0	8-7-1	0-0-0	16-14-1	.533
2012	13-3-1	11-4-0	0-0-0	24-7-1	.774
Total	**269-221-14**	**203-271-22**	**17-27-3**	**472-492-36**	**.489**

* Other venues are included in home and road.

Newly acquired pitcher, R.A. Dickey, warming up for the first time at Spring Training in Dunedin, FL

BIOGRAPHIES LAST SEASON HISTORY RECORDS OPPONENTS PLAYER DEV. MEDIA & MISC.

SPRING TRAINING ATTENDANCE

YEAR	HOME	ROAD	OTHER	TOTAL
1977	21,728	22,093	—	43,821
1978	20,009	36,334	—	56,343
1979	21,420	26,496	—	47,916
1980	15,377	18,499	—	33,876
1981	24,180	33,391	—	57,571
1982	26,442	37,237	—	63,679
1983	27,662	31,590	28,871	88,123
1984	32,869	53,900	110,990	197,759
1985	39,022	45,268	67,007	151,297
1986	43,263	62,936	—	106,199
1987	35,101	38,383	16,620	90,104
1988	42,673	73,234	39,570	155,477
1989	54,270	77,284	—	131,554
1990	21,410	27,695	—	49,105
1991	80,461	96,300	70,471	247,232
1992	84,356	102,651	103,952	290,959
1993	73,195	89,701	172,919	335,815
1994	80,310	83,782	141,465	305,557
1995	17,059	17,775	22,533	57,367
1996	54,158	83,311	18,232	155,701
1997	61,827	89,998	—	151,825
1998	48,313	78,940	31,523	158,776
1999	54,485	79,371	—	133,856
2000	48,450	77,416	35,198	161,064
2001	52,080	75,978	15,870	143,928
2002	46,530	80,262	—	126,792
2003	48,291	68,132	—	116,423
2004	58,840	82,037	—	140,877
2005	53,620	72,979	20,007	146,606
2006	53,930	82,153	—	136,083
2007	62,591	94,742	—	157,333
2008	64,444	84,835	56,257	205,536
2009	68,674	100,606	—	169,280
2010	52,550	93,019	45,257	190,826
2011	68,195	115,359	—	183,554
2012	77,108	111,493	—	188,601
TOTALS	**1,734,893**	**2,445,180**	**996,742**	**5,176,815**

Florida Auto Exchange Stadium in Dunedin, FL...Home of the Toronto Blue Jays Spring Training site and the Dunedin Blue Jays (A) of the Florida State League

2012 SPRING TRAINING STATISTICS

BATTING

																									Pinch Hit			
NAME	**BA**	**SLG**	**OBP**	**G**	**AB**	**R**	**H**	**TB**	**2B**	**3B**	**HR**	**RBI**	**SH**	**SF**	**HBP**	**BB**	**IBB**	**SO**	**SB**	**CS**	**GDP**	**E**		**AB**	**H**	**HR**	**RBI**
Ahrens	.400	1.000	.400	2	5	2	2	5	0	0	1	3	0	0	0	0	0	1	0	0	0	1		1	1	1	1
Arencibia	.245	.528	.259	18	53	8	13	28	3	0	4	9	0	0	0	1	0	6	1	0	0	1					
Bautista	.288	.635	.345	18	52	6	15	33	6	0	4	10	0	1	2	3	0	6	1	0	1	2					
Berti	---	---	---	1	0	0	0	0	0	0	0	0	0	0	0	0	0	0	0	0	0	0					
Bocock	.462	.846	.650	11	13	7	6	11	0	1	1	5	0	0	0	7	0	1	0	1	0	1					
Burns	.000	.000	.000	2	1	0	0	0	0	0	0	0	0	0	0	0	0	0	0	0	0	1					
Cooper	.275	.375	.375	18	40	8	11	15	4	0	0	11	0	1	1	6	0	6	0	0	2	0		1	0	0	0
Crouse	.286	.429	.444	8	7	2	2	3	1	0	0	0	0	0	0	2	0	4	1	0	0	0					
d'Arnaud	.143	.381	.217	9	21	3	3	8	2	0	1	4	0	0	0	2	0	5	0	0	1	1		2	0	0	0
Davis	.289	.289	.377	21	45	8	13	13	0	0	0	3	0	1	1	6	0	4	7	1	0	1					
Diaz	.405	.486	.439	23	37	9	15	18	1	1	0	7	1	1	0	3	0	8	0	0	0	0					
Encarnacion	.306	.581	.343	22	62	8	19	36	5	0	4	14	0	1	2	2	0	13	0	1	0	1					
Escobar	.237	.305	.308	20	59	7	14	18	4	0	0	5	0	0	0	6	0	10	0	0	1	4					
Francisco	.200	.200	.216	15	35	3	7	7	0	0	0	2	0	1	0	1	0	3	1	0	0	0					
Goins	.333	.333	.429	6	6	1	2	2	0	0	0	1	0	0	0	1	0	1	1	0	0	0					
Gomes	.333	.590	.333	20	39	6	13	23	7	0	1	9	0	0	0	0	0	13	0	0	1	0		1	1	1	1
Gose	.233	.333	.303	19	30	8	7	10	1	1	0	2	1	0	0	3	0	9	7	1	0	0		2	1	0	1
Gotay	.200	.200	.200	6	5	0	1	1	0	0	0	0	0	0	0	0	0	2	0	0	0	0		1	0	0	0
Hawkins	.000	.000	.000	2	2	0	0	0	0	0	0	0	0	0	0	0	0	1	0	0	0	0		1	0	0	0
Hechavarria	.353	.647	.389	7	17	5	6	11	2	0	1	3	0	0	0	1	0	3	0	0	1	0					
Howard	.000	.000	.000	1	1	0	0	0	0	0	0	0	0	0	0	0	0	0	0	0	0	0					
Jeroloman	.250	.375	.250	6	8	1	2	3	1	0	0	3	0	0	0	0	0	1	0	0	0	0		2	0	0	0
Jimenez	.333	.444	.400	9	9	1	3	4	1	0	0	0	0	0	1	0	0	4	0	0	0	1		1	0	0	0
Johnson	.304	.446	.381	20	56	6	17	25	4	2	0	6	0	0	0	7	0	15	3	1	1	2					
Jones	.750	1.250	.750	2	4	1	3	5	0	1	0	2	0	0	0	0	0	1	0	0	0	0		1	0	0	0
Knecht	.500	1.000	.500	4	6	2	3	6	0	0	1	1	0	0	0	0	0	2	0	0	0	0					
Lawrie	.524	.810	.535	16	42	7	22	34	8	2	0	9	0	0	0	1	0	2	5	0	1	4					
Lind	.302	.581	.400	16	43	7	13	25	4	1	2	9	0	0	1	6	0	5	0	0	1	0					
Marisnick	.154	.385	.154	10	13	3	2	5	0	0	1	1	0	0	0	0	0	4	0	0	2	0					
Mathis	.163	.186	.265	17	43	7	7	8	1	0	0	2	0	0	0	6	0	14	0	0	2	0		0	0	0	0
McCoy	.182	.242	.270	19	33	6	6	8	2	0	0	2	0	0	2	2	0	7	2	1	0	3		1	0	0	0
McDade	.143	.143	.333	12	14	2	2	2	0	0	0	0	0	0	1	3	0	5	0	0	0	0		1	0	0	0
Nanita	.286	.286	.267	12	14	2	4	4	0	0	0	2	0	1	0	0	0	1	0	0	0	0		1	0	0	0
Nolan	1.000	1.000	1.000	1	1	1	1	1	0	0	0	0	0	0	0	0	0	0	0	0	0	0		1	1	0	0
Ochinko	.000	.000	.000	1	1	0	0	0	0	0	0	0	0	0	0	0	0	0	0	0	0	0					
Opitz	.000	.000	.000	2	2	0	0	0	0	0	0	1	0	0	0	0	0	0	0	0	0	0		1	0	0	0
Perales	.500	2.000	.500	3	2	1	1	4	0	0	1	1	0	0	0	0	0	1	0	0	0	0					
C. Perez	---	---	---	1	0	0	0	0	0	0	0	0	0	0	0	0	0	0	0	0	0	0					
Pompey	.000	.000	.000	3	4	1	0	0	0	0	0	0	0	0	0	0	0	1	0	0	0	0		1	0	0	0
Rasmus	.185	.241	.274	20	54	7	10	13	3	0	0	8	0	1	0	7	0	17	1	0	0	0					
Schimpf	1.000	4.000	1.000	2	1	2	1	4	0	0	1	4	0	0	1	1	0	0	0	0	0	2		1	1	1	4
Sierra	.316	.421	.350	8	19	2	6	8	2	0	0	0	0	0	0	1	0	6	0	0	0	0		1	0	0	0
Snider	.271	.625	.340	17	48	11	13	30	5	0	4	16	0	0	0	5	0	17	2	1	0	0		1	0	0	0
Sweeney	.250	.250	.250	5	4	0	1	1	0	0	0	0	0	0	0	0	0	2	0	0	0	1					
Talley	.000	.000	.000	2	4	1	0	0	0	0	0	0	0	0	0	0	0	2	0	0	0	0					
Thames	.359	.578	.408	23	64	9	23	37	8	0	2	13	0	1	0	6	0	14	1	1	2	0		1	0	0	0
Tolisano	.500	.625	.600	7	8	2	4	5	1	0	0	0	0	0	0	2	0	2	0	0	0	0					
Valbuena	.163	.349	.196	24	43	8	7	15	2	0	2	5	0	1	0	2	0	6	0	0	0	1					
Vizquel	.395	.526	.410	19	38	6	15	20	2	0	1	5	0	0	1	0	0	4	0	0	1	2		1	0	0	0
Woodward	.111	.167	.238	15	18	4	2	3	1	0	0	1	0	0	1	2	0	6	1	1	0	2					
TEAM	**.282**	**.455**	**.342**	**32**	**1126**	**191**	**317**	**512**	**81**	**9**	**32**	**179**	**2**	**10**	**14**	**95**	**0**	**235**	**34**	**9**	**17**	**33**		**24**	**5**	**3**	**7**
OPPONENTS	**.240**	**.361**	**.295**	**32**	**1073**	**112**	**258**	**387**	**55**	**7**	**20**	**106**	**5**	**9**	**12**	**75**	**0**	**209**	**22**	**9**	**32**	**35**		**31**	**6**	**1**	**5**

PITCHING

NAME	**W**	**L**	**ERA**	**G**	**GS**	**CG**	**GF**	**SHO**	**SV**	**INN**	**H**	**BFP**	**AB**	**R**	**ER**	**HR**	**SH**	**SF**	**HBP**	**BB**	**IBB**	**SO**	**WP**	**BK**	**BA**
Alvarez	3	0	3.00	5	5	0	0	0	0	15.0	14	61	58	5	5	1	0	0	0	3	0	10	0	0	.241
Antolin	0	0	18.00	1	0	0	1	0	0	1.0	3	6	6	2	2	0	0	0	0	0	0	1	0	0	.500
Barnes	0	0	0.00	1	0	0	0	0	0	1.0	1	5	4	0	0	0	0	0	0	1	0	2	0	0	.250
Beck	0	0	6.00	3	0	0	2	0	0	3.0	4	14	12	2	2	1	0	0	0	2	0	3	0	0	.333
Carpenter	1	1	2.89	7	0	0	1	0	0	9.1	6	34	31	3	3	1	0	1	0	2	0	7	0	0	.194
Carreno	0	0	5.40	3	0	0	1	0	0	5.0	6	22	21	4	3	0	0	0	0	1	0	5	0	0	.286
Cecil	3	1	6.48	6	6	0	0	0	0	16.2	21	80	71	14	12	2	0	0	0	9	0	10	1	0	.296
Chavez	0	0	2.57	7	0	0	1	0	1	7.0	9	30	26	2	2	0	0	1	0	3	0	3	1	0	.346
Coello	0	0	2.16	8	0	0	7	0	3	8.1	6	35	32	2	2	1	0	0	1	2	0	13	0	0	.188
Cordero	0	0	2.70	10	0	0	2	0	0	10.0	10	41	40	5	3	1	0	0	0	1	0	8	1	0	.250
Crawford	0	0	0.00	3	0	0	0	0	0	4.0	0	12	11	0	0	0	0	0	0	1	0	5	0	0	.000
Drabek	2	0	3.72	6	3	0	1	0	1	19.1	18	83	71	11	8	2	1	2	0	9	0	14	0	0	.254
Everts	1	0	3.60	4	0	0	2	0	0	5.0	5	20	19	2	2	1	0	0	0	1	0	1	0	0	.263
Farquhar	0	0	9.00	1	0	0	0	0	0	1.0	2	5	4	1	1	0	0	0	1	0	0	0	0	0	.500
Figueroa	0	0	4.50	2	0	0	1	0	0	2.0	2	9	7	1	1	0	0	0	0	2	0	0	1	0	.286
Frasor	0	0	2.70	10	0	0	1	0	1	10.0	10	42	37	3	3	0	0	0	0	5	0	11	0	0	.270
Gil	0	1	4.05	6	0	0	2	0	0	6.2	4	24	21	3	3	1	0	0	1	2	0	5	0	0	.190
Gracey	0	0	40.50	1	0	0	0	0	0	0.2	4	6	5	3	3	0	0	0	0	1	0	0	1	0	.800
Hoey	1	0	1.00	9	0	0	3	0	1	9.0	7	35	34	1	1	1	0	0	0	1	0	7	0	0	.206
Hutchison	1	1	3.00	5	2	0	1	0	0	15.0	13	62	54	6	5	1	1	2	2	3	0	8	1	0	.241
Janssen	0	0	0.00	9	0	0	0	0	0	9.1	6	33	33	0	0	0	0	0	0	0	0	3	1	0	.182
Jenkins	1	0	1.13	3	0	0	0	0	0	8.0	5	29	29	1	1	0	0	0	0	0	0	8	0	0	.172
Korecky	0	1	9.00	3	0	0	2	0	0	2.0	4	12	10	3	2	0	1	0	0	1	0	1	0	0	.400
Laffey	2	1	5.40	5	4	0	0	0	0	20.0	26	86	83	12	12	2	0	1	1	1	0	13	0	0	.313
Loup	0	0	9.00	1	0	0	1	0	1	1.0	1	5	4	2	1	0	0	0	1	0	0	1	1	0	.250
McGowan	1	0	0.00	2	2	0	0	0	0	5.0	3	19	18	1	0	0	0	0	0	1	0	4	1	0	.167
McGuire	1	0	2.57	3	0	0	1	0	1	7.0	8	28	28	2	2	1	0	0	0	0	0	5	0	0	.286
Morrow	2	0	0.52	5	5	0	0	0	0	17.1	10	64	60	1	1	1	1	0	0	3	0	12	0	0	.167
Oliver	1	0	6.43	7	0	0	0	0	0	7.0	10	31	28	5	5	1	0	1	0	2	0	4	1	0	.357
L. Perez	0	0	0.59	9	0	0	0	0	0	15.1	8	56	50	1	1	1	0	0	1	5	0	12	1	0	.160
Richmond	0	0	0.00	2	0	0	0	0	0	3.0	3	12	12	0	0	0	0	0	0	0	0	1	0	0	.250
Romero	2	0	0.00	4	4	0	0	0	0	11.0	2	36	34	0	0	0	0	0	0	2	0	10	0	0	.059
Santos	0	0	0.00	5	0	0	1	0	0	5.0	1	19	16	0	0	0	0	0	0	3	0	4	0	0	.063
Tepera	1	0	3.52	3	1	0	0	0	0	7.2	5	33	28	4	3	1	0	0	3	2	0	4	1	0	.179
Uviedo	0	0	0.00	1	0	0	1	0	1	1.0	2	5	5	0	0	0	0	0	0	0	0	3	0	0	.400
VandenHurk	0	1	9.95	4	0	0	0	0	0	6.1	10	35	27	8	7	0	1	1	0	6	0	3	0	0	.370
Villanueva	1	0	0.79	7	0	0	0	0	0	11.1	9	45	44	2	1	0	0	0	1	0	0	8	2	1	.205
TEAM	**24**	**7**	**3.05**	**32**	**32**	**0**	**32**	**5**	**10**	**286.1**	**258**	**1174**	**1073**	**112**	**97**	**20**	**5**	**9**	**12**	**75**	**0**	**209**	**14**	**1**	**.240**
OPPONENTS	**7**	**24**	**5.65**	**32**	**32**	**0**	**32**	**1**	**3**	**277.0**	**317**	**1247**	**1126**	**191**	**174**	**32**	**2**	**10**	**14**	**95**	**0**	**235**	**19**	**1**	**.282**

2013 SPRING TRAINING SCHEDULE

Date and Times subject to change

DATE	LOCATION	VERSUS	TIME	Radio	TV
Saturday, February 23	Lakeland	Detroit Tigers	1:05	SNET RADIO 590	SNET
Sunday February 24	DUNEDIN	Baltimore Orioles	1:05	SNET RADIO 590	
	Tampa	New York Yankees	1:05		
Monday February 25	DUNEDIN	Boston Red Sox (SS)	1:05	Bluejays.com	
Tuesday February 26	DUNEDIN	Minnesota Twins	1:05	Bluejays.com	
Wednesday February 27	DUNEDIN	Houston Astros	1:05	Bluejays.com	
Thursday February 28	Tampa	New York Yankees (SS)	1:05	Bluejays.com	
Friday March 1	DUNEDIN	Tampa Bay	1:05	Bluejays.com	
Saturday March 2	DUNEDIN	Philadelphia Phillies	1:05	SNET RADIO 590	SNET
Sunday, March 3	Clearwater	Philadelphia Phillies (SS)	1:05	SNET RADIO 590	
Monday, March 4	OFF DAY				
Tuesday, March 5	DUNEDIN	Baltimore Orioles	1:05	Bluejays.com	
Wednesday, March 6	Lakeland	Detroit Tigers	1:05	Bluejays.com	
Thursday, March 7	Sarasota	Baltimore Orioles	1:05	Bluejays.com	
Friday, March 8	Disney World	Atlanta Braves (SS)	1:05	Bluejays.com	
Saturday, March 9	DUNEDIN	Detroit Tigers	1:05	SNET RADIO 590	
Sunday, March 10	DUNEDIN	New York Yankees	1:05	SNET RADIO 590	SNET
Monday, March 11	OFF DAY				
Tuesday, March 12	Fort Myers	Boston Red Sox	1:35	Bluejays.com	
Wednesday, March 13	Bradenton	Pittsburgh Pirates	1:05	Bluejays.com	
Thursday, March 14	DUNEDIN	New York Yankees	1:05	Bluejays.com	
Friday March 15	Lakeland	Detroit Tigers	1:05	Bluejays.com	
Saturday, March 16	DUNEDIN	Baltimore Orioles	1:05	SNET RADIO 590	
Sunday, March 17	Kissimmee	Houston Astros	1:05	SNET RADIO AFL	
Monday, March 18	OFF DAY				
Tuesday, March 19	DUNEDIN	Houston Astros	1:05	Bluejays.com	
Wednesday, March 20	Sarasota	Baltimore Orioles	1:05	Bluejays.com	
Thursday, March 21	Port Charlotte	Tampa Bay Rays	1:05	Bluejays.com	
Friday, March 22	DUNEDIN	Boston Red Sox	1:05	Bluejays.com	
Saturday, March 23	DUNEDIN	Atlanta Braves (SS)	1:05	SNET RADIO 590	SNET
Sunday, March 24	Lee County	Minnesota Twins	1:05	SNET RADIO 590	
Mon March 25	DUNEDIN	Philadelphia Phillies	1:05	Bluejays.com	
Tuesday, March 26	DUNEDIN	Pittsburgh Pirates	1:05	Bluejays.com	
Wednesday, March 27	Port Charlotte	Tampa Bay Rays	1:05	Bluejays.com	
Thursday, March 28	Clearwater	Philadelphia Phillies	1:05	Bluejays.com	
Friday, March 29	Philadelphia	Philadelphia Phillies	7:05	SNET RADIO AFL	SNET
Saturday, March 30	Philadelphia	Philadelphia Phillies	1:05	SNET RADIO 590	SNET

SNET RADIO 590 available to affiliates also
SNET RADIO AFL available to affiliates only

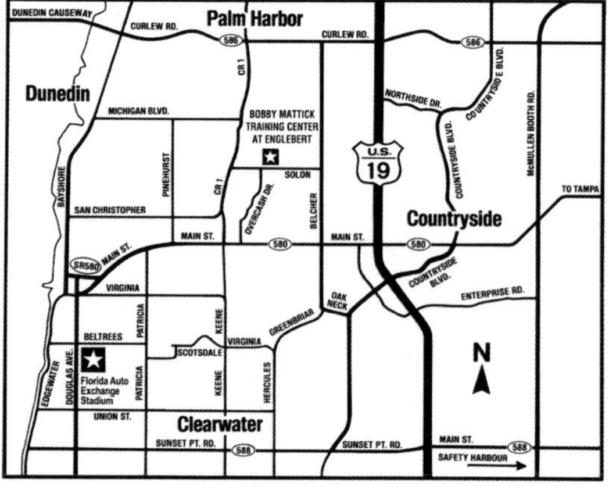

ITEMS OF INTEREST

MLB BASIC AGREEMENT

I. TERM

A. Five-year contract

B. December 1, 2016 termination date

II. SCHEDULING, REALIGNMENT, AND POSTSEASON PLAY

A. Beginning no later than the 2013 Postseason, Postseason play will be expanded for the first time since 1995. A second Wild Card will be awarded to the Club in each league with the second-best overall record among Clubs that do not win a division. The two Wild Card Clubs will play a single Postseason game, the winner of which will advance to the Division Series. A decision on adding two Wild Cards for 2012 will be made no later than March 1, 2012.

B. The Houston Astros will move to the American League West starting in 2013, creating two leagues of 15 Clubs each.

C. Starting in 2013, Interleague games will be played throughout the entire schedule, rather than exclusively in specific Interleague segments.

D. Active Roster limits will be expanded to 26 for certain regular or split doubleheaders.

III. RESERVE SYSTEM INCLUDING AMATEUR PLAYERS

A. Free Agency

1. All eligible Players will become free agents as of the end of the World Series, with no election required, and the "quiet period" will be five days.
2. The tender date will be December 2 beginning in 2012.
3. Article XX(B) free agents signing minor league contracts who are not added to the Opening Day roster or unconditionally released 5 days prior to Opening Day shall receive an additional $100,000 retention bonus and the right to opt out on June 1.

B. Draft Pick Compensation

1. Starting in 2012, "Type A" and "Type B" free agents and the use of the Elias ranking system will be eliminated.
2. The current system of draft pick compensation will be replaced with the following system:
3. Only Players who have been with their Clubs for the entire season will be subject to compensation.
4. A free agent will be subject to compensation if his former Club offers him a guaranteed one-year contract with a salary equal to the average salary of the 125-highest paid Players from the prior season. The offer must be made at the end of the five-day free agent "quiet period," and the Player will have seven days to accept the offer.
5. A Club that signs a player subject to compensation will forfeit its first round selection, unless it selects in the top 10, in which case it will forfeit its second highest selection in the draft.
6. The Player's former Club will receive a selection at the end of the first round beginning after the last regularly scheduled selection in the round. The former Clubs will select based on reverse order of winning percentage from the prior championship season.

C. Salary Arbitration Eligibility

1. The percentage of players with two years of service who will be arbitration eligible will be increased from the top 17% to the top 22% in terms of service.
2. All players tied at the 22% cutoff will be eligible for arbitration.

D. Minimum Salaries

1. Major League will increase from $414,000 in 2011 to: $480,000 in 2012; $490,000 in 2013; and $500,000 in 2014; COLA in 2015 and 2016.
2. Minor League will increase from $67,300 in 2011 to: $78,250 in 2012; $79,900 in 2013; and $81,500 in 2014; COLA in 2015 and 2016.

E. Rule 4 Draft

1. The draft will continue to be conducted in June, but the signing deadline will be moved to a date between July 12 and July 18 depending on the date of the All-Star Game.
2. Drafted players may only sign Minor League contracts.
3. Signing Bonus Pools

A. Each Club will be assigned an aggregate Signing Bonus Pool prior to each draft. For the purpose of calculating the Signing Bonus Pools, each pick in the first 10 rounds of the draft has been assigned a value. (These values will grow each year with the rate of growth of industry revenue.) A Club's Signing Bonus Pool equals the sum of the values of that Club's selections in the first 10 rounds of the draft. Players selected after the 10th round do not count against a Club's Signing Bonus Pool if they receive bonuses up to $100,000. Any amounts paid in excess of $100,000 will count against the Pool.

B. Clubs that exceed their Signing Bonus Pools will be subject to penalties as follows:

Excess of Pool Penalty (Tax on Overage/Draft Picks)

0-5% 75% tax on overage

5-10% 75% tax on overage and loss of 1st round pick

10-15% 100% tax on overage and loss of 1st and 2nd round picks

15%+ 100% tax on overage and loss of 1st round picks in next two drafts

4. Proceeds generated by the tax will be distributed to payee Clubs under the Revenue Sharing Plan that do not exceed their Signing Bonus Pools. Draft picks that are forfeited by Clubs will be awarded to other Clubs through a lottery in which a Club's odds of winning will be based on its prior season's winning percentage and its prior season's revenue. Only Clubs that do not exceed their Signing Bonus Pools are eligible for the lottery.
5. Competitive Balance Lottery

A. For the first time, Clubs with the lowest revenues and in the smallest markets will have an opportunity to obtain additional draft picks through a lottery.

B. The ten Clubs with the lowest revenues, and the ten Clubs in the smallest markets, will be entered into a lottery for the six draft selections immediately following the completion of the first round of the draft. A Club's odds of winning the lottery will be based on its prior season's winning percentage.

C. The eligible Clubs that did not receive one of the six selections after the first round, and all other payee Clubs under the Revenue Sharing Plan, will be entered into a second lottery for the six picks immediately following the completion of the second round of the draft. A Club's odds of winning the lottery will be based on its prior season's winning percentage.

D. Picks awarded in the Competitive Balance Lottery may be assigned by a Club, subject to certain restrictions.

E. Top 200 prospects will be subject to a pre-draft drug test and will participate in a pre-draft medical program.

F. International Talent Acquisition

1. By December 15, 2011, the parties will form an International Talent Committee to discuss the development and acquisition of international players, including the potential inclusion of international amateur players in a draft or in multiple drafts.

2. For the 2012-13 signing season, each Club will be allocated an equal Signing Bonus Pool.

3. For each signing period after 2012-13, Clubs will be allocated different Signing Bonus Pools, based on reverse order of winning percentage the prior championship season (i.e., the Club with the lowest winning percentage the prior season shall receive the largest Pool).

4. Bonus Regulation of International Amateur Players

A. Beginning in the 2013-2014 signing period (July 2, 2013 - June 15, 2014), Clubs may trade a portion of their Signing Bonus Pool, subject to certain restrictions.

B. Clubs that exceed their Signing Bonus Pools will be subject to the following penalties in the 2012-2013 and 2013-2014 signing periods:

Excess of Pool Penalty (Tax on Overage/Draft Picks)

0-5% 75% tax

5-10% 75% tax and loss of right to provide more than one player in the next signing period with a bonus in excess of $500,000.

10-15% 100% tax and loss of right to provide any player in the next signing period with a bonus in excess of $500,0000.

15%+ 100% tax and loss of right to provide any player in the next signing period with a bonus in excess of $250,000.

C. The penalties for exceeding the Signing Bonus Pool will increase beginning with the 2014-2015 signing period if a draft or drafts is not agreed to by July 2014.

5. All international amateur players must register with the Scouting Bureau to be eligible to sign, and the top 100 prospects will be subject to a drug test.

6. The Office of the Commissioner and the Union will form a joint committee to assist international players with their transition to educational/vocational programs after their baseball careers are over

IV. REVENUE SHARING

A. The net transfer value of the Revenue Sharing Plan will be the same as the current plan. Net transfer amounts will continue to grow with revenue and changes in disparity.

B. The fifteen Clubs in the largest markets will be disqualified from receiving revenue sharing by 2016. The revenue sharing funds that would have been distributed to the disqualified Clubs will be refunded to the payor Clubs, except that payor Clubs that have exceeded the CBT threshold two or more consecutive times will forfeit some or all of their refund.

C. The Commissioner's Discretionary Fund will increase from $10 to $15 million per year.

V. COMPETITIVE BALANCE TAX

A. The threshold level of $178 million in 2011 will remain unchanged in 2012 and 2013. The threshold will increase to $189 million for 2014, 2015, and 2016.

B. The tax rate will decrease to 17.5% for Clubs that exceed the threshold for the first time, and the rate will increase to 50% for Clubs that exceed the threshold for the fourth time or more. Rates will remain the same for Clubs that exceed the threshold for the second time (30%) and third time (40%). The CBT rates in 2012 will be subject to a transition rule.

C. The Competitive Balance Tax structure under the 2006 Basic Agreement will be modified so that a team that moves below the threshold will be treated as going over for the first time when it next exceeds the threshold.

VI. DEBT SERVICE RULE

A. The Debt Service Rule will be maintained, but the default EBITDA multiplier has been lowered from ten to eight, and from fifteen to twelve for Clubs incurring stadium-related debt in the first ten years of a new or renovated stadium.

B. Debt of a Club's owner or related party will be covered by the Debt Service Rule if the debt is serviced, in whole or in part, using Club funds or assets.

C. Debt Service Rule certification process for new ownership has been modified.

VII. BENEFIT PLAN

A. Players will continue to receive the maximum allowable pension benefit under IRS rules.

B. Owners will make a $184.5 million annual contribution.

C. Waiting periods for life insurance and disability insurance for active players have been eliminated.

D. Pension benefits and life insurance benefits for certain classes of retired players and widows have been improved.

E. The payments to the former non-vested players that began in 2011 will continue for the term of the Basic Agreement.

F. Access to health coverage has been improved for international players and their families.

G. Health care benefits have been improved while managed care initiatives have been introduced to help with costs.

VIII. HEALTH AND SAFETY

A. Players, managers, and coaches will be prohibited from using smokeless tobacco during televised interviews and Club appearances. In addition, at any time when fans are permitted in the ballpark, players, managers and coaches must conceal tobacco products (including packages and tins), and may not carry tobacco products in their uniforms or on their bodies. Individuals who violate the policy will be subject to discipline. The parties also agreed upon an extensive program of education and public outreach regarding the dangers of smokeless tobacco.

B. The parties agreed on a program of mandatory evaluation by a trained professional for Players who are suspected of an alcohol use problem (including Players who are arrested for DWI or other crimes involving alcohol), and for players who are arrested for crimes involving the use of force or violence.

C. The parties agreed that no new players will be permitted to use a low density maple bat during the term of the agreement.

D. By 2013, all Major League players will wear a new batting helmet developed by Rawlings that protects against pitches thrown at 100 miles per hour. The new version of the helmet is significantly less "bulky" than prior versions of the more protective helmet.

E. The concussion policy that was implemented prior to the 2011 season has been improved and will remain in effect for the duration of the Basic Agreement.

IX. DRUG PROGRAM

Commencing in Spring Training 2012, all players will be subject to hGH blood testing for reasonable cause at all times during the year. In addition, during each year, all players will be tested during Spring Training. Starting with the 2012-2013 off-season, players will be subject to random unannounced testing for hGH. The parties have also agreed on a process to jointly study the possibility of expanding blood testing to include inseason collections.

X. OTHER

A. Participation in the All-Star Game will be required unless the Player is unable to play due to injury or is otherwise excused by the Office of the Commissioner. Players Trust will receive an increased contribution and players will receive additional benefits.

B. All Players will be subject to a policy governing the use of Social Media.

C. Weekend waivers during the regular season will be implemented beginning in 2012.

D. The parties will agree upon a comprehensive international play plan in which Clubs and Player will visit countries in which games have not been staged in the past.

E. Non-discrimination protections based on sexual orientation were added to Article XV.

F. Instant Replay will be expanded to include fair/foul and "trapped" ball plays, subject to the Office of the Commissioner's discussions with the World Umpires Association.

G. Modifications to Fourth Option and Outright Assignment rules.

H. The parties agreed to an improved process for challenging official scorer decisions.

TRANSACTIONS AND CONTRACTS

PLAYER LIMITS: 40 until opening day, when the number must be reduced to 25 until September 1, when it again becomes 40. The minimum number of active players maintained by each club throughout the championship season shall be 24.

TRADING REGULATIONS: The trading deadline is July 31.

Trades may be made with any other major league club in the period from the end of the championship season through July 31 (4:00 p.m. EDT) without waivers. Waivers are required, however:

1. If the assignment is to another major league club: From August 1 and ending at 5 pm EDT the day after the end of the season.
2. If assignment is to a minor league club, with right of recall, at any time after three years from the date the player first reported to a major league club during a championship season.
3. If assigned to a minor league club without right of recall, after acquiring three years service: At any time during the year.
4. If assigned to a minor league club, without right of recall, at any time prior to acquiring three years of service, special waivers are required between September 1 and the opening of the following season. If player is claimed, request may be withdrawn. If no claims are made, club has 7-day period in which to make assignment to minor leagues.

WAIVERS: A permission granted from all 30 clubs to assign a Major League player's contract to another Major League team or a minor league affiliate. Such permission is granted only for a specific period of time. The actual request is filed through the Commissioner's Office and is not disclosed to the public until the contract is rewarded.

PROCEDURES FOR OBTAINING WAIVERS:

- May request 7 players on any given business day.
- The waivers must be requested by 2:00pm ET on any business day.
- Waiver claiming period expires on the second business day after the initial request at 1:00pm ET.
- A Club desiring the assignment of a player on the waiver wire must submit a claim prior to 1:00pm ET on the last day of the claiming period.
- Priority for the waiver claim awards is given to the Club with the lowest winning percentage in the player's league when there are multiple claims submitted for the same player.
- If only one claim is entered, the claiming Club is eligible to be awarded the player contract.
- There is no specific limit on the number of claims that may be submitted on a particular day. However, no Club is permitted to exceed the 40-man or the 25-man roster limit.
- If a Club is awarded a player on a waiver claim which causes them to exceed the 40-man or the 25-man roster limit they must designate a different player for assignment.

FOUR WAIVER PERIODS:

- November 11-February 15
- February 16-April 28
- April 29-July 31
- August 1-November 10

All waivers that have been granted expire at 5:00pm ET on the last day of a particular waiver period.

TYPES OF WAIVERS

- ***OUTRIGHT WAIVERS (OR)*** — this type of irrevocable waiver needs to be secured in order to Outright a player. An outright is to assign a player to a club's minor league affiliate without the right of recall. In other words, to remove a player from the 40-man roster. Also a player who has exhausted his options must clear this type of waiver if the club wishes to assign him to minor league affiliate. An outright waiver secured is good for entire waiver period. These waivers are needed from the 31st day of the season through August 31.
- ***SPECIAL WAIVERS (SPL)*** — also irrevocable, the special waiver is used for the same purpose as an outright waiver. One difference is these waivers are used from September 1 to the 30th day of the following season. A secured special waiver is good for seven days, as opposed to being good for an entire period like the outright waiver.
- ***UNCONDITIONAL RELEASE WAIVER (UR)*** — this irrevocable waiver is used for the purpose of an unconditional release of a player. At the time of the request the player shall be removed from all player limits. A player may be informed of the clubs intention to release him on a weekend, but the actual waiver process won't begin until the following business day. During the time a player is on an unexpired waiver request bulletin he may discuss employment with other clubs but may not contract with another club. If the player has been claimed, he must be informed the end of the two-day period that his contract has been claimed. The player has five days from the time he was notified of the claim to either accept the assignment or terminate his contract. If the player terminates his contract he forfeits termination pay. Termination pay may vary depending on the time of year.
- ***MAJOR LEAGUE WAIVER (ML)*** — this type of revocable waiver is common and it is used to either option a player to a club's minor league affiliate or assign a player outright to another Major league club from August 1st to the end of the regular season. A player claimed on this type of waiver may be pulled back by the requesting club. This is known as a waiver withdrawal. Generally a club needs to secure this type of waiver in order to option a player if the date of the assignment is three or more years after the date the player first reported to a Major League club during a championship season. One year shall be deducted from the above three-year period for each season in which the player may have been charged with an option prior to first reporting to a Major League club during a championship season. A claimed player pulled back by the requesting club may not be assigned and cannot be placed on waivers again (except for UR waivers) for 30 days. When ML waivers are asked for a second time in the same period the request shall state that it is irrevocable.

ASSIGNMENT OF PLAYER CONTRACTS:

- Ten and Five Rule: Players with ten or more years of Major League service (MLS), the last five of which have been with one Club, shall not be assignable to another Major League Club without the Player's written consent.
- When a player with five or more years of MLS is asked by his club to consent to an assignment to the National Association, he has three choices;

1. Accept the assignment, 2. Refuse the assignment, 3. Elect Free Agency

- Any player who has at least three years of MLS and whose contract is assigned outright to a National Association club may elect, in lieu of accepting such assignment, to become a free agent.

- Any player whose contract is assigned outright to a National Association club for second time or any subsequent time in his career may elect, in lieu of accepting such assignment, to become a free agent. Unlike a player with five or more years of MLS, this type of player does not have the option of refusing the assignment.

OPTIONAL ASSIGNMENT: To assign a player from the active 25-man roster to a minor league affiliate with the right of recall. The player remains on the 40-man roster.

RECALL: To add a player from your reserve limit (40-man roster) to the 25-man roster. This player must serve at least 10 days on option in order to be recalled unless he is replacing a player placed on the disabled list.

OUTRIGHT ASSIGENEMENT:

- MAJOR TO MINOR: to assign a player to the Club's minor league affiliate without the right of recall. The player is removed from the 40-man roster.
- MAJOR TO MAJOR: to assign a player from one Club's 40-man roster to another Club's 40-man roster. This transaction is more commonly known as a trade.

DESIGNATED FOR ASSIGNMENT:

- When a club that has reached it 40 and /or 25 man roster limit, either reinstates a player, or acquires a new player (through a selection, a signing, a trade or a waiver claim); they must designate a player for assignment or release. If they are going to assign the player, they must do it within 10 days.

WAIVER WITHDRAWALS:

- Waiver request may only be withdrawn on players who have been claimed on a Major League Waiver wire. If a player is claimed on a Major League Waiver wire, the request must be withdrawn within two business days or the contract will be awarded to the eligible club. During the two-day waiver withdrawal period the requesting Club can try to negotiate a deal with the eligible Club and make a waiver claim award under the terms of that deal.

WAIVER PRICES:

- Major League, Special and Outright Waivers are $20,000 or $25,000, while Unconditional Waivers are $1.00.

FREE AGENCY (RE-ENTRY): The 1985 collective bargaining agreement brought about changes in the free agency process. Following is the appropriate information:

Six years of Major League Service continues to be required to be eligible for free agency.

The Re-Entry Draft has been abolished.

A player has 15 days from the first day following the World Series to file for free agency.

If club and player proceed to arbitration, maximum salary cut rules do not apply.

Player who accepts former club's offer to arbitrate is not subject to repeater rights limitations.

SALARY ARBITRATION: Beginning in 1987, three years Major League Service required for eligibility.

Beginning in 1987, maximum cut rules do not apply if in immediately preceding year player won arbitration increase of over 50%.

Three-man panels heard cases instead of single arbitrators in 50 percent of the cases in 1998, 75 percent in 1999 and 100 percent in 2000 ongoing.

Beginning in 1987, arbitrator is officially instructed to give particular attention for purposes of comparison to salaries of players with Major League Service no more than one annual service group higher than player who is arbitrating.

Beginning in 1991, a player with at least 2 but less than 3 years of Major League Service, shall be eligible for salary arbitration if: a)he has accumulated at least 86 days of service during the immediately preceeding season or b)he ranks in the top 17 percent in total service in the class of players who have at least 2 but less than 3 years of ML service, however accumulated, but with at least 86 days of service accumulated during the immediately preceeding season.

FIRST-YEAR PLAYER DRAFT (AMATEUR DRAFT) — REVISED FOR 1987: One selection meeting shall be conducted each year in June to be known at the "Summer Meeting".

Major League Clubs shall select in reverse order of their league standing at the close of the preceeding season (determined by the percentage of games it won). No club may transfer to another club its right to select.

A club may not transfer its Negotiation Right to any other club.

DISABLED LISTS:

15-Day: The player must remain off the active roster for a minimum of 15 calendar days, starting on the day following the player's last game.

60-Day: Same rules apply, however, this may only be used when the team's 40-man roster is full. Any player placed on the 60-day disabled list after August 1 may not play for the remainder of the season, including any post-season game.

EMERGENCY DISABLED LIST: Maximum number of players on list at one time-no limit. Minimum period of inactivity-sixty (60) calendar days. Players placed on this list after August 1st shall remain there for the balance of the season. This list may only be used when a club is at the maximum limit of 40 players.

TERMINATION PAY: One full season's pay if player released opening day or later. Thirty days pay for player who is released on the 16th day before opening day or earlier. If player is released after that 16th day prior to opening day he receives one additional day's pay (over the 30 days) for each additional day.

SERVICE TIME AND ROOKIES

MAJOR LEAGUE YEAR: 172 days constitute a full year in the major leagues.

MAJOR LEAGUE SERVICE:

- is credited for each day the player appears on an active roster or major league disabled list or suspended list.
- in the case of a player called up from the minor leagues, is credited beginning with the date he physically reports.
- in the case of a major league player who is traded and reports in the normal course, service is not interrupted.
- in the case of a player sent down to the minor leagues, is credited through the date of the assignment.
- in the case of a player who is unconditionally released, is credited through the date waivers were requested.
- in the case of a player designated for release or assignment (MLR 2), is credited after the designation, through the date of the actual assignment or the request for unconditional release waivers.
- for a player who appears on his club's opening day roster, is credited as of the earliest scheduled opener, without regard to the actual opening date of his own club.
- is credited at the rate of 172 days per "year", though the season is actually 182 days long.
- is not credited during any period or periods of optional assignment totalling 20 days or more during a single season.

ROOKIE QUALIFICATION: A player shall be considered a rookie unless, during a previous season or seasons, he has (a) exceeded 130 at bats or 50 innings pitched in the major leagues; or (b) accumulated more than 45 days on the active roster of a major league club or clubs during the period of a 25-man limit (excluding time in military service and time on the disabled list).

THE GAME

REGULATION GAME: A regulation game consists of nine innings unless extended because of a tie score or shortened because (1) the home team needs none of its half of the ninth or only part of it; or (2) because the umpire-in-chief calls the game after five completed innings. A regulation game may be less than five innings if the home team is ahead after the first of the fifth, or takes the lead or ties the score while at bat in the fifth.

TIE GAME: A regulation game that is called by the umpire-in-chief when both teams have the same number of runs is a tie game. Individual player performances are official and are entered in the records, but the game does not count in the league standings and may be re-scheduled at a later date.

NIGHT GAME: In the American League any game scheduled to start after 5:00 p.m. (i.e. 5:01 p.m., or later), will be considered a night game. If a game is scheduled to start at 5:00 p.m., and is delayed by rain or for any other reason, it will be considered a day game.

However, both games of a twi-night doubleheader shall be considered night games. When afternoon and night games are played on the same date and separate admissions are charged, they will be counted as one day and one night game, and will not be included in doubleheader statistics.

SUSPENDED GAME RULE:

Rule 4.12 SUSPENDED GAMES

(a) A league shall adopt the following rules providing for completion at a future date of games terminated for any of the following reasons:

(1) A curfew imposed by law;

(2) A time limit permissible under league rules;

(3) Light failure or malfunction of a mechanical field device under control of the home club. (Mechanical field device shall include automatic tarpaulin or water removal equipment.);

(4) Darkness because of any law, the lights may not be turned on.

(5) Weather, if the game is called while an inning is in progress and before it is completed, and one of the following situations prevails:

(i) The visiting team has scored one or more runs to tie the score, and the home team has not scored.

(ii) The visiting team has scored one or more runs to take the lead, and the home team has not tied the score or retaken the lead.

(b) Such games shall be known as suspended games. No game called because of a curfew, weather, or a time limit shall be a suspended game unless it has progressed far enough to have been a regulation game under the provisions of Rule 4.10. A game called under the provisions of 4.12(a)(3) or (4) shall be a suspended game at any time after it starts.

(c) By amending NOTE to read as follows:

NOTE: Weather and similar conditions—4.12(a) (1 through 5)—shall take precedence in determining whether a called game shall be a suspended game. A game can only be considered a suspended game if stopped for any of the five (5) reasons specified in Section (a). Any legal game called due to weather with the score tied (unless situation outlined in 4.12(a)(5)(i) prevails) is a tie game and must be replayed in its entirety.

(d) A suspended game shall be resumed and completed as follows:

(1) Immediately preceding the next scheduled single game between the two clubs on the same grounds; or

(2) Immediately preceding the next scheduled double-header between the two clubs on the same grounds, if no single game remains on the schedule, or

(3) If suspended on the last scheduled date between the two clubs in the city, transferred and played on the grounds of the opposing club, if possible;

(i) Immediately preceding the next scheduled single game, or

(ii) Immediately preceding the next scheduled double-header, if no single game remains on the schedule.

(4) If a suspended game has not been resumed and completed on the last date scheduled for the two clubs, it shall be a called game.

(e) A suspended game shall be resumed at the exact point of suspension of the original game. The completion of a suspended game is a continuation of the original game. The lineup and batting order of both teams shall be exactly the same as the lineup and batting order at the moment of suspension, subject to the rules governing substitution. Any player may be replaced by a player who had not been in the game prior to the suspension. No player removed before the suspension may be returned to the lineup. A player who was not with the club when the game was suspended may be used as a substitute, even if he has taken the place of a player no longer with the club who would not have been eligible because he had been removed from the lineup before the game was suspended.

SUSPENDED GAME: For the purpose of this rule, all performances in the completion of a suspended game shall be considered as occurring on the original date of the game.

SCHEDULE: The American League schedule for the 2013 season will be the 16th year to incorporate Inter-League Play.

AL EAST

	H	A
BAL	10	9
BOS	9	10
NYY	9	10
TB	9	10
Total	**37**	**39**

AL WEST

	H	A
HOU	4	3
LAA	3	4
OAK	4	3
SEA	3	3
TEX	3	4
Total	**17**	**17**

AL CENTRAL

	H	A
CWS	4	3
CLE	3	3
DET	4	3
KC	3	3
MIN	3	3
Total	**17**	**15**

INTERLEAGUE

	H	A
ATL	2	2
ARZ	0	3
COL	3	0
LAD	3	0
SD	0	3
SF	2	2
Total	**10**	**10**

PLAYING RULES: Spectator Interference—batter, runner and other runner(s) will be placed at the base(s) which the umpires feel they would have reached with no interference.

Time—ball is dead, play suspended. This sign used when ball is foul, umpire then pointing to foul territory.

Batted Balls Fair or Foul—if fair, umpire points to fair territory —if foul he raises arms overhead (as in "Time" above) and then turns and points to foul territory, and vocally calls "foul".

BAT AROUND: When all nine batters in a team's lineup come to bat during an inning.

DESIGNATED HITTER RULE: A hitter may be designated to bat for the pitcher in any spot in the batting order in any game without affecting the status of the pitcher. The designated hitter must be selected and be included on the lineup cards presented to the umpire-in-chief prior to the game. Failure to do so precludes the use of a designated hitter for that game.

The designated hitter is "locked" into the batting order but may be removed for a pinch-hitter or pinch-runner, who in turn becomes the designated hitter. The designated hitter, while still in the game, may be used defensively but the pitcher then assumes the batting order of the replaced defensive player, thus terminating the designated hitter role.

The designated hitter is eligible for all American League batting titles.

The designated hitter named in the starting lineup must come to bat at least one time, unless the opposition changes pitchers.

SCORING RULE ON PINCH-HITTERS: A player shall be considered a pinch-hitter only if he enters the game as a substitute batter and then only on his first time at bat which must be before he becomes a fielder. If the team bats around and a pinch hitter comes up a second time in the inning in which he first appeared he will not be considered a pinch hitter during that second time up.

A substitute hitter for a designated hitter is both a pinch hitter and a designated hitter on his first time at bat. On subsequent trips to the plate he is a designated hitter only.

DOCTORED BAT: A batter is out for illegal action when he uses or attempts to use a bat that, in the umpire's judgment, has been altered or tampered with in such a way to improve the distance factor or cause an unusual reaction on the baseball. This includes bats that are filled, flat-surfaced, nailed, hollowed, grooved or covered with a substance such as paraffin, wax, etc. No advancement on the bases will be allowed and any out or outs made during a play shall stand. In addition to being called out, the player shall be ejected from the game and may be subject to additional penalties as determined by his League President. (Rule 6.06d).

STATISTICS AND STREAKS

BATTING CHAMPION QUALIFICATIONS: A batting champion must have 502 or more actual plate appearances. (The equivalent of 3.1 appearances for each of the 162 scheduled games.). If, however, there is any player with fewer than the required number of plate appearances whose average would be the highest if he were charged with the required number of official at bats, then the player shall be awarded the batting championship.

EARNED-RUN AVERAGE CHAMPION QUALIFICATIONS: To win the earned-run average championship a pitcher must pitch at least as many innings as the number of games scheduled for each club in his league that season and have the lowest earned-run average.

FIELDING CHAMPION QUALIFICATIONS: The individual fielding champions shall be the fielders with the highest fielding average at each position, provided:

(1) A catcher must have participated as a catcher in at least one-half the number of games scheduled for each club in his league that season;

(2) An infielder or outfielder must have participated at his position in at least two-thirds of the number of games scheduled for each club in his league that season;

(3) A pitcher must have pitched at least as many innings as the number of games scheduled for each club in his league that season. **EXCEPTION:** If another pitcher has a fielding average as high or higher, and has handled more total chances in a lesser number of innings, he shall be the fielding champion.

DETERMINING EARNED-RUNS: The determination of earned-run is as follows:

"An earned-run is a run for which the pitcher is held accountable. In determining earned-runs, the inning should be reconstructed without the errors and passed balls; and the benefit of the doubt should always be given to the pitcher in determining which bases would have been reached with errorless play."

Until 1969, the reliever could not be charged with an earned-run if he entered the game after the side could have been retired but for an error, no matter how many runs he subsequently gave up in that inning. Now, runs, scored by batters who reach base off the reliever are charged as earned on that pitcher's record. They are not, however, charged as earned against the team as a whole. Therefore, a discrepancy may occur between the total earned-runs charged against a team and the sum total of the earned-runs charged against the individual pitchers of that team.

DETERMINING THE MAGIC NUMBERS: Determine the number of games yet to be played, add one, then subtract the number of games ahead in the loss column of the standings from the closest opponent.

DETERMINING BATTING AVERAGE: Divide the number of at bats into the number of hits.

DETERMINING EARNED-RUN AVERAGE: Multiply the number of earned runs by nine; take the number and divide it by the number of innings pitched.

DETERMINING SLUGGING PERCENTAGE: Divide the total bases of all safe hits by the total times at bat. (At bats do not include walks, sacrifices, hit by pitcher, or times awarded first base because of interference or obstruction.)

DETERMINING ON-BASE PERCENTAGE: Add the total of hits, walks and hit by pitches and divide by the total of at-bats, walks, hit by pitches and sacrifice flies.

DETERMINING FIELDING AVERAGE: Divide the total putouts and assists by the total of putouts, assists and errors.

DETERMINING WINNING PERCENTAGE: Divide the number of games won by the total games won and lost.

CREDITING A SAVE: A pitcher shall be credited with a save when he meets all three of the following conditions:

(1) He is the finishing pitcher in a game won by his club, and

(2) He is not the winning pitcher, and

(3) He qualifies under one of the following conditions:

(4) (a) He enters the game with a lead of no more than three runs and pitches for at least one inning, or

(b) He enters the game regardless of the count, with the potential tying run either on base, at bat, or on deck (that is, the potential tying run is either already on base or is one of the first two batsmen he faces), or

(c) He pitches effectively for at least three innings.

TOUGH SAVE: The reliever comes into the game with the tying runs on base and saves the game. Example: Reliever comes in with a 5-3 lead, two outs and the bases loaded in the ninth inning.

BLOWN SAVE: When a relief pitcher enters a game in a save situation and departs or the game ends with the save situation no longer in effect because he has given up the lead, he is charged with a "blown save." (If the save opportunity still exists when he leaves the game, he is not charged with a save opportunity. If the pitcher has not given up the lead when he leaves the game, though the save opportunity may no longer exist, he is not charged with a save opportunity.

HITTING STREAKS: A consecutive hitting streak shall not be terminated if the plate appearance results in a base on balls, hit batsman, defensive interference or a sacrifice bunt. A sacrifice fly shall terminate the streak.

CONSECUTIVE-GAME HITTING STREAKS: A consecutive-game hitting streak shall not be terminated if all the player's plate appearances (one or more) result in a base on balls, hit batsman, defensive interference or a sacrifice bunt. The streak shall terminate if the player has a sacrifice fly and no hit. The player's individual consecutive-game hitting streak shall be determined by the consecutive games in which the player appears and is not determined by his club's games.

CONSECUTIVE-GAME PLAYING STREAK: A consecutive-game playing streak shall be extended if the player plays one-half inning on defense, or if he completes a time at bat by reaching base or being put out. A pinch-running appearance only shall not extend the streak. If a player is ejected from a game by an umpire before he can comply with the requirements of this rule, his streak shall continue.

GLOSSARY OF MINOR LEAGUE TRANSACTION TERMS

Minor League players are generally under contract to a Major League Club and are assigned to play for a Minor League Club (1) that the Major League Club owns or (2) that has a Player Development Contract with the Major League Club. Major League Clubs may freely assign their Minor League players among their affiliated Minor League Clubs, subject to certain league age and service requirements.

The following glossary describes some terms used in Minor League transactions. References to "players" in the glossary apply only to Minor League players.

Active List: The roster of players eligible to participate in a game: For Class AAA and AA Clubs, the Active List is 24 players from opening day through the 30th day of the championship season and from August 10 through the end of the championship season, and is 23 players from the 31st day of the championship season until August 10; for Class A Clubs, the Active List is 25 players from opening day through the end of the championship season; for Short-Season A Clubs, the Active List is 30 players, only 25 of whom may be in uniform and eligible to play in a given game, from opening day through the end of the championship season; for Rookie Clubs, the Active List is 35 players, only 30 of whom may be in uniform and eligible to play in a given game, from opening day through the end of the championship season.

Championship Season: The regular season of games, not including any post-season playoffs.

Contract Voided: A player's contract is terminated under provisions described in the contract. A player whose contract is voided becomes a free agent and may sign with any Club.

Disabled List: An injured Minor League Player may be placed on this list during the championship season only. A player on the Disabled List must remain there for a minimum period of seven days before the player can be reinstated to the Active List. A player on the Disabled List does not count against a Club's Active List limits, but does count against a Club's Reserve List limits.

Disqualified List: A player who violates a player contract or reservation may be placed on this list. There is no minimum number of days the player must remain on the Disqualified List before the player can be reinstated to the Active List. A player on the Disqualified List does not count against a Club's Active List limits or its Reserve List limits.

Emergency Disabled List: An injured Minor League Player may be placed on this list during the championship season only. A player on the Emergency Disabled List must remain on the list for a minimum period of 60 days or until the end of the championship season (whichever is earlier) before the player can be reinstated to the Active List. A player on the Emergency Disabled List does not count against a Club's Active List limits or its Reserve List limits.

Free Agent: A Minor League player is a free agent, able to sign with any Club, when the term of the player's Minor League contract has expired. If the player has not re-signed with the same Club, the player becomes a Minor League free agent on October 15 at 5:00 p.m. (ET).

Ineligible List: A player found to have committed misconduct may be placed on this list. There is no minimum number of days the player must remain on the Ineligible List before the player can be reinstated to the Active List. A player on the Ineligible List does not count against a Club's Active List limits or its Reserve List limits.

Loan: A Minor League player's contract may be loaned from one organization to another, so long as the new Club is also under the jurisdiction of the Commissioner of Baseball. The Assignor Club retains contractual rights to the player. The player must be returned to the assignor Club at the end of the championship season. Loans of players are most commonly made to Mexican League Clubs.

Outright Assignment: A player who is traded from one Major League organization to another is assigned outright. The assignor Club transfers all contractual rights regarding the player to the assignee Club.

Rehabilitation Assignment: A Minor League Player on either the Disabled List or Emergency Disabled List may be sent to a Short-Season A or Rookie classification Minor League Club to play on a rehabilitation assignment, while the player remains on the Disabled List or Emergency Disabled List of the player's original Club. A rehabilitation assignment may not exceed 20 days for non-pitchers or 30 days for pitchers. A player on a Minor League rehabilitation assignment does not count against the Active List or Reserve List limits of the Club for which the player is playing on the rehabilitation assignment.

Release: A player's contract is terminated and the player becomes a free agent.

Reserve List: The roster of players eligible for placement on the Active List: For Class MA, the Reserve List limit is 38 players; For Class AA, the Reserve List limit is 37 players; and For Class A, Short-Season and Rookie, the Reserve List limit is 35 players.

Restricted List: A player who fails to report or fails to sign a contract with the Club to which the player is reserved may be placed on the Restricted List. There is no minimum number of days the player must remain on the Restricted List before the player can be reinstated to the Active List. A player on the Restricted List does not count against a Club's Active List limits or its Reserve List limits.

Return: The act of moving a loaned player's contract back to the Minor League Club that loaned the player. All players who have been loaned must be returned no later than September 30.

Selected Rule 5: A player selected in the Class MA or Class AA phase of the Rule 5 draft, which is conducted in December each year, is assigned from one Major League organization to another. The selecting Club pays a set price to the player's former Club for the right to the player's contract.

Suspended List: A player may be placed on the Suspended List for misconduct or rule or contract violations. There is no minimum amount of days the player must be on the Suspended List before the player can be reinstated to the Active List. A player on the Suspended List does not count against a Club's Active List limits, but the player does count against its Reserve List limits.

Temporarily Inactive List: A player with an excused absence to perform personal obligations is placed on this list. The player must be on the Temporarily Inactive List for a minimum of three days before the player can be reinstated to the Active List. A player on the Temporarily Inactive List does not count against a Club's Active List limits, but does count against its Reserve List limits.

Transfer: Minor League Player is moved from one Minor League Club to another within the same Major League organization.

Voluntary Retired: A player who wishes to retire is placed on this list. The player may not be reinstated until the player has missed 60 playing days of the championship season.

MLB, MLBPA AGREE TO RANDOM IN-SEASON TESTING FOR HGH AND LONGITUDINAL PROFILE PROGRAM

BASEBALL TAKES UNPRECEDENTED ANTI-DOPING STEPS IN AMERICAN PROFESSIONAL SPORTS

Major League Baseball and the Major League Baseball Players Association have modified their Joint Drug Prevention and Treatment Program to provide for unannounced, random blood testing for the detection of human growth hormone (hGH) during the regular season, beginning in 2013. It marks another significant step in the progression of Baseball's hGH testing policy, which continues to be the strongest in American professional sports. Since July 2010, Major League Baseball has conducted random blood testing for the detection of hGH among Minor League players. As a part of the 2012- 2016 Basic Agreement, the parties agreed to blood testing for hGH during 2012 Spring Training, during the off-season, and for reasonable cause, making Baseball the first sport to deploy this kind of testing at its highest level.

Under the new agreement, all of those aspects of the Program will continue, and there will be in-season, unannounced, random blood testing. In addition, beginning in the 2013 season, the parties have authorized the World Anti-Doping Agency (WADA)-accredited Montreal Laboratory to establish a longitudinal profile program, in which a Player's baseline Testosterone/Epitestosterone (T/E) ratio and other data will be maintained by the laboratory, with strict protections for confidentiality, in order to enhance its ability to detect the use of Testosterone and other prohibited substances. The laboratory will automatically conduct Carbon Isotope Ratio Mass Spectrometry (IRMS) analysis on all specimens that vary materially from a Player's baseline values. The laboratory also will increase the number of random IRMS analysis it conducts on specimens. The longitudinal program being implemented by the parties will be one of the most significant programs of its kind in the world.

Baseball Commissioner Allan H. (Bud) Selig said: "This agreement addresses critical drug issues and symbolizes Major League Baseball's continued vigilance against synthetic human growth hormone, Testosterone and other performance-enhancing substances. I am proud that our system allows us to adapt to the many evolving issues associated with the science and technology of drug testing. We will continue to do everything we can to maintain a leadership stature in anti-doping efforts in the years ahead." MLBPA Executive Director Michael Weiner said: "The Players are determined to do all they can to continually improve the sport's Joint Drug Agreement. Players want a program that is tough, scientifically accurate, backed by the latest proven scientific methods, and fair; I believe these changes firmly support the Players' desires while protecting their legal rights."

GLOSSARY OF MEDICAL TERMS

ABDUCT – Movement of any extremity away from the midline of the body. This action is achieved by an abductor muscle.

AC JOINT – Acromioclavicular joint; joint of the shoulder where acromion process of the scapula and the distal end of the clavicle meet; most shoulder separations occur at this point.

ADDUCT – Movement of any extremity towards the midline of the body. This action is achieved by an adductor muscle.

ANTERIOR – In front of; the front surface of.

ANTERIOR CRUCIATE LIGAMENT (ACL) – A primary stabilizing ligament within the center of the knee joint that prevents hyperextension and excessive rotation of the joint. A complete tear of the ACL necessitating reconstruction could require up to 12 months of rehabilitation.

ANTI-INFLAMMATORY – Any agent which prevents inflammation, such as aspirin or ibuprofen.

ARTHROGRAM – X-ray technique for joints using air and/or dye injected into the affected area; useful in diagnosing meniscus tears of the knee and rotator cuff tears of the shoulder.

ARTHROSCOPY – A surgical examination of the internal structures of a joint by means of viewing through an arthroscope. An arthroscopic procedure can be used to remove or repair damaged tissue or as a diagnostic procedure in order to inspect the extent of any damage or confirm a diagnosis.

BONE SCAN – An imaging procedure in which a radioactive-labeled substance is injected into the body to determine the status of a bone injury. If the radioactive substance is taken up by the bone at the injury site, the injury will show as a "hot spot" on the scan image. The bone scan is particularly useful in the diagnosis of stress fractures.

CARTILAGE – Smooth, slippery substance preventing two ends of bones from rubbing together.

CAT SCAN – Use of a computer to produce a cross-sectional view of the anatomical part being investigated from x-ray data.

CHARLEY HORSE – A contusion or bruise to any muscle resulting in intramuscular bleeding.

CONCUSSION – Jarring injury of the brain resulting in dysfunction. It can be graded as mild, moderate or severe depending on loss of consciousness, amnesia and loss of equilibrium.

CONTUSION – An injury to muscle and tissues cause by a blow from a blunt object.

DEBRIDEMENT – Removal of non-healthy tissues and foreign material from a wound or burn to prevent infection and permit healing.

DELTOID MUSCLE – Muscles at the top of the arm, just below the shoulder, responsible for shoulder motions to the front, side and back.

DISC – A flat, rounded plate between each vertebrae of the spine. The disc consists of a thick fibering which surrounds a soft gel-like interior. It functions as a cushion for the spinal column.

FEMUR – Thigh bone; largest bone in the body.

FIBULA – Smaller of the two bones in the lower leg; runs from the knee to the ankle along the outside of the lower leg.

FRACTURE – Breach in continuity of a bone. Types of fractures include simple, compound, comminuted, greenstick, incomplete, impacted, longitudinal, oblique, stress or transverse.

GADOLINIUM MRI – The chemical gadolinium is injected into the joint being studied so as to enhance the diagnosis of the structure under investigation.

GLENOID – Cavity of the scapula into which the head of the humerus fits to form the shoulder girdle.

GRADE ONE INJURY – A mild injury in which ligament, tendon, or other musculoskeletal tissue may have been stretched or confused, but not torn or otherwise disrupted.

GRADE TWO INJURY – A moderate injury when musculoskeletal tissue has been partially, but not totally torn which causes appreciable limitation in function of the injured tissue.

GRADE THREE INJURY – A severe injury in which tissue has been significant, and in some cases totally, torn or otherwise disrupted causing a virtual total loss of function.

GROIN – Junction of the thigh and abdomen; location of muscles that rotate, flex and adduct the hip.

HEMATOMA – Tumor-like mass produced by an accumulation of coagulated blood in a cavity.

HYPEREXTENSION – Extreme extension of a limb or body part.

IMPINGEMENT SYNDROME – Pinching together of the supraspinatus muscle and other soft tissue in the shoulder. The most common (throwing) arm injury, which represents many pathologies and generall involves supraspinatus overuse.

INFLAMMATION – The body's natural response to injury in which the injury site might display various degrees of pain, swelling, heat, redness and/or loss of function.

LABRUM (Labrum Glenoidule) – The cartilage of the glenoid cavity in the shoulder. A lip-edge or lip-like structure.

LATERAL – To the outside of the body.

LIGAMENT – Band of fibrous tissue that connects bone to bone, or bone to cartilage and supports and strengthens joints.

MAGNETIC RESONANCE IMAGING (MRI) – Imaging procedure in which a radio frequency pulse causes certain electrical elements of the injured tissue to react to this pulse and through this process a computer display and permanent film establish a visual image. MRI does not require radiation and is very useful in the diagnosis of soft tissue, disc, and meniscus injuries.

MEDIAL – To the inside of the body.

MEDIAL COLLATERAL LIGAMENT (MCL) – Ligament of knee along the medial aspect that connects the femur to the joint.

MENISCUS – Crescent shaped cartilage, usually pertaining to the knee joint; also known as "cartilage." There are two menisci in the knee, medial and lateral. These work to absorb weight within the knee and provide stability.

METACARPALS – Five long bones of the hand running from the wrist to the fingers.

METATARSALS – Five long bones of the foot, running from the ankle to the toes.

POSTERIOR – At the back part, or rear of the body.

POSTERIOR CRUCIATE LIGAMENT (PCL) – A primary stabilizing ligament of the knee that provides significant stability and prevents displacement of the tibia backward within the knee joint. A complete tear of this ligament necessitating reconstruction could require up to 12 months of rehabilitation.

QUADRICEP MUSCLES "QUADS" – A group of four muscles of the front thigh that run from the hip and form a common tendon at the patella; they are responsible for knee extension.

ROTATOR CUFF – Comprised of four muscles in the shoulder area that can be irritated by overuse. The muscles are the supraspinatus (most commonly injured), infraspinatus, teres minor and subscapularis.

ROTATOR CUFF IMPINGEMENT SYNDROME – A microtrauma or overuse injury caused by stress. The four stages are: 1) tendenitis with temporary thickening of the bursa and rotator cuff 2) fiber dissociation in the tendon with permanent thickening of the bursa and scar formation 3) a partial rotator cuff tear of less than 1 cm and 4) a complete tear of 1 cm or more.

SHIN SPLINT – A catch-all syndrome describing pain in the shin that is not a fracture or tumor, and cannot be defined otherwise.

SPRAIN – Injury resulting from the stretch or twist of the joint and causes various degrees of stretch or tear of a ligament or other soft tissue at the joint.

STRAIN – Injury resulting from a pull or torsion to the muscle or tendon that causes various degrees of stretch or tear to the muscle or tendon tissue.

STRESS FRACTURE – A hair-line type of break in a bone caused by overuse.

SYNOVITIS – Inflammation of the synovial lining of a joint.

TENDINITIS – Inflammation of the tendon and/or tendon sheath, caused by chronic overuse or sudden injury.

TENDON – Tissue that connects muscle to bone.

TIBIA – Larger of the two bones of the lower leg and is the weight-bearing bone of the shin.

ULNAR NERVE – Nerve in the elbow commonly irritated from excessive throwing.

ULTRASOUND – An electrical modality that transmits a sound wave through an applicator into the skin to the soft tissue in order to heat the local area for relaxing the injured tissue and/or disperse edema.

NOTE: This list is not meant to be all inclusive, nor should it be used as a substitute for a physician's diagnosis and/or description of an injury or illness.

2013 MAJOR LEAGUE IMPORTANT DATES

Jan. 15 Salary arbitration filing date

Jan. 18 Salary arbitration exchange date

Feb. 4 - 21 Salary arbitration hearings

Feb. 12 Voluntary date all non-WBC pitchers, catchers and injured players may be invited to Spring Training workouts

Mandatory date all Major League players participating in the WBC competition in Asia must report to Spring Training, unless they are reporting directly to their Federation Teams' training camps

Mandatory date all other WBC Major League pitchers and catchers must report to Spring Training

First date players may be placed on the 60-day Disabled List

Feb. 15 Mandatory date Major League position players participating in the WBC but not competing in Asia must report to Spring Training

Voluntary date all remaining non-WBC position players may be invited to Spring Training workouts

All Outright Waivers in effect expire at 5:00 p.m. ET

Feb. 16 New waiver period begins (includes Optional and Outright Waivers)

First date weekend waivers will be processed; continues through end of season (except March 30 & 31)

Feb. 20 Mandatory date all non-WBC players must report to Spring Training

Feb. 23 Anticipated start of Spring Training games among Major League Clubs

Mar. 2 First date to renew Major League contracts

Mar. 6 First date Clubs may ask waivers on selected Rule 5 or draft-excluded players

Mar. 11 First date Clubs may assign selected Rule 5 or draft-excluded players

Last date to renew Major League contracts

Mar. 13 Last date to request UR Waivers to owe 30 days' termination pay (before 2 p.m. ET)

Mar. 14 UR Waivers requested today until 2 p.m. ET on March 27 - Club will owe player 45 days' termination pay

Mar. 15 Last date to assign an injured player to a Minor League club, if permissible

Mar. 21 Last date a XX(B) player signed to a Minor League contract qualifies for a Retention Bonus

Mar. 22 Earliest date that a Club may place a player on the 15-day Disabled List

Mar. 26 Last date to select or release a XX(B) "Retention Bonus" player before bonus obligation

Mar. 27 Last date to request UR Waivers to owe 45 days' termination pay (before 2 p.m. ET)

Mar. 30-31 No waivers processed this weekend

Mar. 31 Official opening of the 2013 season - rosters reduced to 25

First date that assignable draft selections may be traded (through 5 p.m. ET on June 6)

Apr. 6 First date 15-day Disabled List players may be reinstated, if permissible

Apr. 10 First date optioned players may be recalled, if permissible

Apr. 29 Waivers secured on or after February 16th expire at 5:00 p.m. ET

Apr. 30 New waiver period begins

May 1 International player registration deadline

May 15 Earliest date Clubs may re-sign Major League players they released after August 31, 2012

May 30 Start of Closed Period – First-Year Player Draft

June 1 XX(B) "Retention Bonus" player may require release if not added to 25-man roster

June 6-8 2013 First-Year Player Draft

June 15 End of 2012 - 2013 international signing period

June 16 First date Clubs may trade a XX(B) player without his consent

June 21 Release of the 2013-2014 signing period registration list

July 2 Beginning of 2013 - 2014 international signing period

July 12 Signing deadline for Rule 4 drafted players – 5:00 p.m. ET

July 16 All-Star Game at Citi Field, Queens, NY

July 17 Competitive Balance Lottery (and, if necessary, Forfeited Pick Lottery) TENTATIVE

July 18 First date that assignable draft selections may be traded (through September 29, 2013)

July 31 Trade deadline – 4:00 p.m. ET

Waivers secured on or after April 30, 2013 expire at 5:00 p.m. ET

Aug. 1 New waiver period begins – Trade Waivers now required

Aug. 15 Last date to select player to avoid draft-excluded status

Aug. 29 Unconditional Release Waivers must be requested by 2:00 p.m. ET to avoid May 15, 2014 signing restriction

Aug. 31 Post-season eligibility lists are established at midnight ET
Secured Outright Waivers expire at midnight ET

Sept. 1 Active Major League player limit increases from 25 to 40

New Outright Waiver period – secured waivers are good for seven days

Sept. 29 Last day of the 2013 championship season

Last weekend date waivers will be processed until next Spring Training

Last date that assignable draft selections may be traded (until start of 2014 season)

Sept. 30 All players on optional assignment must be recalled (to report or not to report)

All players on the 7-day and the 15-day Disabled Lists must be reinstated

First date players may be traded between Major League Clubs without waivers (unless play-in game necessary)

Injured players now may be assigned to Minor Leagues until November 20, 2013, if permissible

Sept. 30 - Oct. 15
Article XX(D) Free Agency period

Right After World Series
Eligible XX(B) players become free agents

4th Day After World Series
Last date to request waivers on draft-excluded players until next spring

5th Day After World Series
Last date to reinstate players from the 60-day Disabled List

Last date to outright potential Minor League free agent without Major League contract, if permissible

Last date for former Club to tender qualifying offer to XX(B) players

Minor League players become free agents at 5:00 p.m. ET, if applicable

6th Day After World Series
XX(B) and Minor League free agents may sign with all Clubs

12th Day After World Series
Last date for XX(B) players to accept qualifying offer from former Club

Nov. 10 Outright Waivers secured on or after September 1 expire at 5:00 p.m. ET

Nov. 11 New waiver period begins

Nov. 18 Last date to ask Outright Waivers on an injured player, if permissible

Nov. 20 Last date to outright an injured player to the Minor Leagues, if permissible

Reserve lists for all Major and Minor League levels filed

Dec. 2 Tender deadline

Dec. 5 Last date to request Outright Waivers to assign player prior to Rule 5 Draft

Dec. 9 Last date to outright a player prior to the Rule 5 Draft

Dec. 12 Major League Rule 5 Draft - Winter Meetings, Orlando, FL

DETAILED CONTENTS

Printed and bound in Canada by: **General Printers, Oshawa. ON**

Typesetting and Data Management by: **Caledon Data Management, Eden, ON (519) 866-5900**

ISBN 978-1-894801-25-6